CHRISTIAN WRITERS' MARKET GUIDE 2011

2011

Christian Writers' Market Guide

The Essential Reference Tool
for the Christian Writer

Sally E. Stuart

Tyndale House Publishers, Inc.
CAROL STREAM, ILLINOIS

Visit Tyndale's exciting Web site at www.tyndale.com.

Visit Sally Stuart's Web site at www.stuartmarket.com.

TYNDALE and Tyndale's quill logo are registered trademarks of Tyndale House Publishers, Inc.

Christian Writers' Market Guide 2011

Copyright © 2011 by Sally E. Stuart. All rights reserved.

Cover photo of books copyright © by Vitaly Raduntsev/iStockphoto. All rights reserved.

Designed by Ron Kaufmann

Edited by Susan Taylor

Published in association with the literary agency of Books & Such, Janet Kobobel Grant, 52 Mission Circle, Suite 122 PMB 170, Santa Rosa, CA 95409.

ISSN 1080-3955

ISBN 978-1-4143-3426-4

Printed in the United States of America

17	16	15	14	13	12	11
7	6	5	4	3	2	1

CONTENTS

Introduction xiii
How to Use This Book xvii

PART 1: BOOK PUBLISHERS

Chapter 1: Topical/Subject Listings of Book Publishers 3
(Note: * indicates a new category this year.)
African American Markets 3
Apologetics. 3
Archaeology 4
Art, Freelance. 4
Autobiography 5
Bible/Biblical Studies 5
Bible Commentary 6
Biography. 7
Booklets. 8
Canadian/Foreign 8
Celebrity Profiles 8
Charismatic 9
Children's Board Books 9
Children's Devotionals 9
Children's Easy Readers 9
Children's Picture Books (nonfiction) 10
Christ 10
Christian Business 11
Christian Education 11
Christian Homeschooling 12
Christian Living. 12
Christian School Books. 14
Christmas Books. 14
*Church Growth 14
Church History 14
Church Life. 15
Church Management. 16
Church Renewal 16
Church Traditions. 17
Coffee-Table Books. 17
Compilations 18
Controversial Issues 18
Cookbooks. 18
Counseling Aids 19
Creation Science. 19
Cults/Occult 20
Current/Social Issues 20
Curriculum. 21
Dating/Sex 21
Death/Dying 22
Devotional Books 22
Discipleship 23

Divorce. 24
Doctrinal 25
Drama 25
E-books 25
Economics 26
Encouragement 26
Environmental Issues 27
Eschatology 27
Ethics 28
Ethnic/Cultural 28
Evangelism/Witnessing 29
Exegesis 30
Exposés 30
Faith 30
Family Life 31
Fiction: Adult/General. 32
Fiction: Adult/Religious. 33
Fiction: Adventure. 34
Fiction: Allegory 34
Fiction: Biblical 34
Fiction: Chick Lit. 35
Fiction: Contemporary 35
Fiction: Cozy Mysteries 36
Fiction: Ethnic 36
Fiction: Fables/Parables 36
Fiction: Fantasy. 37
Fiction: Frontier 37
Fiction: Frontier/Romance 37
Fiction: Historical. 38
Fiction: Historical/Romance 38
Fiction: Humor. 39
Fiction: Juvenile (ages 8-12) 39
Fiction: Literary 40
Fiction: Mystery/Romance. 40
Fiction: Mystery/Suspense. 41
Fiction: Novellas 41
Fiction: Plays 42
Fiction: Romance 42
Fiction: Science Fiction. 42
Fiction: Short Story Collections 43
Fiction: Speculative. 43
Fiction: Teen/Young Adult. 43
Fiction: Westerns 44
Forgiveness. 44
Games/Crafts 45
Gift Books. 45
*Grandparenting. 45
Grief. 46
Group Study Books. 46
Healing. 46
Health. 47
Hispanic Markets 48
Historical 48
Holiday/Seasonal 49
Holiness 49

Holy Spirit 50
Homeschooling Resources 50
Homiletics 51
How-To 51
Humor 51
Inspirational 52
Lay Counseling 53
Leadership 53
Lifestyle 54
Liturgical Studies 54
Marriage 54
Memoirs 55
Men's Books 56
Minibooks 56
Miracles 56
Missions/Missionary 57
Money Management 57
Music-Related Books 58
Novelty Books for Kids 58
Pamphlets 58
Parenting 59
Pastors' Helps 59
Personal Experience 60
Personal Growth 60
Personal Renewal 61
Philosophy 62
Photographs (for covers) 62
Poetry 63
Politics 63
Popular Culture 64
Postmodernism 64
Prayer 64
Print-on-Demand 65
Prophecy 65
Psychology 66
Racism 66
Recovery 67
Reference 67
Relationships 68
Religion 68
Religious Tolerance 69
Retirement 70
Scholarly 70
Science 71
Self-Help 71
Senior Adult Concerns 72
Sermons 72
Singles' Issues 72
*Small-Group Resources 73
Social Justice Issues 73
Sociology 74
Spiritual Gifts 74
Spirituality 74
Spiritual Life 75
Spiritual Warfare 76

Sports/Recreation 77
Stewardship 77
Theology 78
Time Management 79
Tracts 79
Travel 79
Tween Books 79
Women's Issues 80
World Issues 81
Worship 81
Worship Resources 82
Writing How-To 82
Youth Books (nonfiction) 83
Youth Programs 83

Chapter 2: Alphabetical Listings of Book Publishers 85

Chapter 3: Subsidy Publishers 165

Chapter 4: Distributors 187

Chapter 5: Market Analysis: Books 191
Publishers in Order of Most Books Published per Year .191
Book Topics Most Popular with Publishers 193
Publishers with the Most Books on the Bestseller List 194
Top 50 Bestsellers 195

PART 2: PERIODICAL PUBLISHERS

Chapter 6: Topical Listings of Periodicals 199
*(Note: * indicates a new category this year.)*
Apologetics 199
*Arts/Entertainment 200
*Beauty/Fashion 200
Bible Studies 200
Book Excerpts 201
Book Reviews 201
Canadian/Foreign Markets 202
Celebrity Pieces 203
Christian Business 204
Christian Education 204
Christian Living 205
Church Growth 207
Church History 208
Church Life 209
Church Management 210
Church Outreach 210
Church Traditions 211
Controversial Issues 212
Crafts 213
Creation Science 213
Cults/Occult 214
Current/Social Issues 214
Death/Dying 215
*Depression 216
Devotionals/Meditations 216

Discipleship 217
Divorce 218
Doctrinal 219
DVD Reviews 219
Economics 219
Encouragement 220
Environmental Issues 221
Essays 221
Ethics 222
Ethnic/Cultural Pieces 223
Evangelism/Witnessing 224
Exegesis 225
Faith 225
Family Life 226
Feature Articles 228
Fillers: Anecdotes 228
Fillers: Cartoons 229
Fillers: Facts 230
Fillers: Games 230
Fillers: Ideas 230
Fillers: Jokes 231
Fillers: Kid Quotes 231
Fillers: Newsbreaks 231
Fillers: Party Ideas 231
Fillers: Prayers 232
Fillers: Prose 232
Fillers: Quizzes 232
Fillers: Quotes 233
Fillers: Sermon Illustrations 233
Fillers: Short Humor 233
Fillers: Tips 234
Fillers: Word Puzzles 234
Food/Recipes 235
Grandparenting 235
Healing 235
Health 236
Historical 237
Holiday/Seasonal 237
*Holy Spirit 239
Homeschooling 239
Homiletics 239
How-To 239
How-To Activities (juvenile) 240
Humor 240
Inner Life 241
Inspirational 242
Interviews/Profiles 243
Leadership 245
Lifestyle Articles 245
Liturgical 246
Marriage 246
Men's Issues 247
Miracles 248
Missions 249
Money Management 249

Movie Reviews 250
Music Reviews 250
Nature 251
News Features. 251
Newspapers/Tabloids 252
Nostalgia. 252
Online Publications 253
Opinion Pieces. 254
Parenting 254
*Pastors' Helps. 255
Peace Issues. 256
Personal Experience. 256
Personal Growth. 257
Photo Essays. 258
Photographs. 259
Poetry. 260
Politics 261
*Praise 262
Prayer. 262
Prophecy 263
Psychology 263
Puppet Plays 264
Racism 264
Recovery. 264
Relationships 264
Religious Freedom 266
Religious Tolerance 266
Revival 267
Salvation Testimonies 267
Science. 267
Self-Help. 268
Senior Adult Issues. 268
Sermons. 269
Short Story: Adult/General 269
Short Story: Adult/Religious 269
Short Story: Adventure 270
Short Story: Allegory. 270
Short Story: Biblical 270
Short Story: Contemporary 271
Short Story: Ethnic 272
Short Story: Fantasy 272
Short Story: Frontier. 272
Short Story: Frontier/Romance. 272
Short Story: Historical. 272
Short Story: Historical/Romance. 273
Short Story: Humorous. 273
Short Story: Juvenile. 273
Short Story: Literary 274
Short Story: Mystery/Romance 274
Short Story: Mystery/Suspense 274
Short Story: Parables 274
Short Story: Plays 275
Short Story: Romance. 275
Short Story: Science Fiction 275
Short Story: Senior Adult Fiction. 275

Short Story: Skits 275
Short Story: Speculative 275
Short Story: Teen/Young Adult 276
Short Story: Westerns 276
Singles' Issues 276
Small-Group Helps 277
Social Justice 277
Sociology 277
Spiritual Gifts 278
Spirituality 278
Spiritual Life 280
Spiritual Renewal 281
Spiritual Warfare 281
Sports/Recreation 282
Stewardship 282
Take-Home Papers 283
Theological 283
Think Pieces 284
Time Management 285
Travel 285
True Stories 286
Video Reviews 287
Website Reviews 287
Witnessing (see Evangelism)
Women's Issues 287
Workplace Issues 289
World Issues 289
Worship 290
Writing How-To 291
Young-Writer Markets 291
Youth Issues 292

Chapter 7: Periodicals and E-zines .295
Adult/General Markets 295
Children's Markets 377
Christian Education/Library Markets 386
Daily Devotional Markets 393
Missions Markets 396
Music Markets 400
Pastor/Leadership Markets 401
Teen/Young-Adult Markets 417
Women's Markets 424
Writers' Markets 437

Chapter 8: Market Analysis for Periodicals 445
Periodicals in Order by Circulation 445
Periodical Topics in Order of Popularity 448
Summary of Information in Alphabetical Periodical Listings 449

PART 3: SPECIALTY MARKETS

Chapter 9: Greeting Card/Gift/Specialty Markets 453
Card Publishers 453
Game Markets 457
Gift/Specialty-Item Markets 458

Software Developers...460
Video/CD/DVD Markets 461
Specialty-Products Topical Listings...462

PART 4: HELPS FOR WRITERS

Chapter 10: Christian Writers' Conferences and Workshops......................467

Chapter 11: Area Christian Writers' Clubs/Groups 483

Chapter 12: Editorial Services 499

Chapter 13: Christian Literary Agents..519

Chapter 14: Contests 535
Children/Young-Adult Contests, Writing for.......................................535
Fiction Contests 536
Nonfiction Contests...538
Play/Scriptwriting/Screenwriting Contests..539
Poetry Contests...540
Multiple-Genre Contests 542
Resources for Contests...545
Major Literary Awards 545

Chapter 15: Denominational Listings of Book Publishers and Periodicals.........547

Chapter 16: Book Publishers and Periodicals by Corporate Group...............551

Glossary of Terms 553
General Index 559

INTRODUCTION

As I started this annual edition, it was with a myriad of mixed feelings. I wondered if there would be a large number of publishers or publications reporting they were going out of business or closing their doors to freelance submissions—given the state of the economy. I wondered if there was any way to add anything new to a book I had been perfecting for 25 years. What could I possibly do to make the guide even more helpful to my faithful readers? Well, I'm happy to report that none of those fears were realized.

As I went to work on the new guide, I couldn't ignore the ideas for improvements that kept coming to mind. Although there are a few smaller changes I probably don't need to mention, there are some I am really excited about. Many years ago I started highlighting the phrases that indicated the amount of subsidy publishing each publisher did, or identifying the periodicals that didn't pay. This year, I realized that in most cases that was not as important to the writer for royalty publishers as it was to know what they paid in royalties and advances. Starting with this edition, the phrase indicating such payment is highlighted.

The same is true for the periodical publishers. I am still highlighting those who do not pay, but also highlighting what the pay rate is for those that do pay. Since that is always a prime concern for writers, it will make it helpful in recognizing immediately where they fall on the payment scale—as well as helping to compare publishers in the same genre or section of the guide. Several periodicals have lowered their subscription rates, and most now have a Website.

Over the years I have always gotten a few comments from publishers who say writers who submit to them don't read their guidelines first—some even drop their listings in the guide for that reason. So as I thought about that, I realized that even though most publishers now have their guidelines on their Website, finding them is often a frustrating problem for the interested writer. For that reason, this year most of the listings will include the path you follow on each site to find those guidelines (those that are missing are ones I couldn't find). My hope is that this will make it easier for writers to carefully read the guidelines before submitting—a critical step if you want to sell in today's tighter market. I noticed that more book publishers than periodical publishers have guidelines on their Website. Hopefully, periodical publishers will close that gap in the next year as they recognize it is to their advantage to have them readily available.

I'm also always looking for the industry or marketing changes that affect the writer. This year I've noticed that many more publishers are dropping their fax numbers or even their addresses and depending almost entirely on e-mail or Website contacts. Curious about how many publishers or periodicals we lost over the last year—either going out of business or closing their doors to freelance—I counted and came up with 27 book publishers and 60 periodicals. Not as bad as I had feared. I was even surprised by the number of new markets I was able to add: 25 book publishers and 29 periodicals. So even with those losses, we still have 383 book publishers and 605 periodicals listed.

The "Resources for Writers" section, which continues to be available only on the optional CD, includes 190 new entries, bringing the total number of Website links to nearly 2,200. This wealth of information would make the CD a bargain if that were all it contained. My thanks to Donna Schlachter for the hard work and care she puts into preparing this section each year.

This year I want to remind you again not to rely entirely on the topical listings for potential markets. Many good markets never fill out their list of topics, so you are likely to miss opportunities if you look only at that list. I encourage you to spend time perusing each listing and looking for more opportunities to sell what you write.

Since a number of periodical publishers are now accepting assignments only, it is even more important that you establish a reputation in your areas of interest and expertise. Once you have acquired a number of credits in a given field, write to some of those assignment-only editors, giving your credits, and ask for an assignment. In general, you will be better off striving to get an assignment than hoping to fill one of the few slots left for unsolicited material.

Last year the agent list dropped to 75, but this year it's back up to 80 with 9 new listings. It is still crucial that you carefully check out agents before signing a contract or committing to work with them. See the introduction to the agent section for some tips on how to do that. Because contacting agents has become more important in a writer's quest for publication, I indicate which conferences have agents, as well as editors, on staff. Attending conferences is becoming one of the best ways to make contact with agents as well as publishers.

If you are new to this Guide or only want to find specific markets for your work, you'll want to check out the supplementary lists that appear throughout the book. Read through the glossary and spend a few minutes learning terms you are not familiar with. Review the lists of writers' groups and conferences, and mark those you might be interested in pursuing. The denominational and corporate-family listings will help you start connecting periodicals and book publishers with their different denominations or publishing groups. With so many publishers being bought out or merging, this will help keep you up-to-date on the new members of these growing families.

Also be sure to study the "How to Use This Book" section. It will save you time trying to understand the meanings of the notations in the primary listings, and it's full of helpful hints. Remember to send for a catalog and guidelines or sample copies from any of the publishers or periodicals you are not familiar with. Study those carefully before submitting anything to that publisher or periodical. Also realize that publishers who make their guidelines available on their Websites do sometimes include more or different information online than you get in the usual guidelines sheet.

One of the most common complaints I've received from publishers over the years is that the material they receive is often not appropriate for their needs. Editors tell me repeatedly that they are looking for writers who understand their periodical or publishing house and its unique approach to the marketplace. With a little time and effort, you can meet an editor's expectations, distinguish yourself as a professional, and sell what you write.

Please also note that I have started a marketing blog (see below) where you can find all kinds of information about the industry and keep your market guide up-to-date during the year. I make entries almost every day.

Finally, my special thanks to Patrick Schlachter for developing and overseeing the database I use to produce the guide each year. I couldn't do it without his professional help. He's also open to helping others with their computer needs, so check out his listing in the "Resources for Writers" section on the CD.

As always, I wish you well as you travel this exciting road to publication, whether for the first time or as a longtime veteran. And as I remind you every year, each of you has been given a specific mission in the field of writing. You and I often feel inadequate for the task, but I learned a long time ago that the writing assignments God has given me could not be written quite as well by anyone else.

Sally E. Stuart

1647 S.W. Pheasant Dr.
Aloha OR 97006
(503) 642-9844 (Please call after 9:00 a.m. Pacific time.)
Fax: (503) 848-3658
E-mail: stuartcwmg@aol.com
Website: www.stuartmarket.com
Blog: www.stuartmarket.blogspot.com
Facebook: Sally E. Stuart
Twitter: stuartmarket

- Please contact me for information on how to receive the *Christian Writers' Market Guide* automatically every year and freeze the price at $24.99, plus postage, for future editions (no matter how much the price goes up), or for information on getting the guide at a discounted group rate or getting books on consignment for your next seminar or conference.

- For a list of more than 60 additional books or pamphlets to help you with your specific writing needs, visit the bookstore on my Website.

- For information on editorial services (including book proposals and book contract evaluations), see my listing in the "Editorial Services" section under "Oregon."

- I also have a limited number of dates available to speak at writers' conferences. Contact me for availability.

HOW TO USE THIS BOOK

The purpose of this market guide is to make your marketing job easier and more targeted. It will serve you well, however, only if you use it as a springboard for becoming an expert on those publishers best suited to your writing topics and style. The following explanations and guidelines will help you become an expert on marketing yourself.

1. Spend time getting acquainted with the setup of this resource book. You cannot make the best use of it until you know exactly what it has to offer. Study the table of contents, where you will find comprehensive listings of periodical and book topics.

2. When looking at the topical sections, be sure to check topics related to your primary subject. Some cross-referencing may be helpful. For example, if you have a novel that deals with doctor-assisted suicide, you might look at the list for adult fiction and the list for controversial issues and see which publishers are on both lists. Those would be good potential markets. In the topical sections you will find a letter R following both book and periodical publishers that accept reprints (pieces that have been printed by other publishers/publications but for which you retain the rights). You will find a dollar sign ($) in front of the periodicals that are paying markets. That will help you find those quickly when getting paid is your primary goal for a particular piece. There is an A in front of the names of book publishers that require the use of an agent.

3. In each book-publisher listing you will find the following information (as available) in this format:

(a) Name of publisher
(b) Address, phone and fax numbers, e-mail address, Website
(c) Denomination or affiliation
(d) Name of editor—This may include the senior editor's name, followed by the name of another editor to whom submissions should be sent. In a few cases, several editors are named with the types of books each is responsible for. Address any correspondence to the appropriate editor.
(e) Statement of purpose
(f) List of imprint names
(g) Number of inspirational/religious titles published per year, followed by formats of books published (hardcover, trade paperbacks, mass-market paperbacks, coffee-table books). Note that coffee-table books have a listing in the topical listings for books.
(h) Number of submissions received annually
(i) Percentage of books from first-time authors
(j) (Usually) whether the publisher accepts, prefers, requires, or doesn't accept manuscripts through agents
(k) Percentage of books from freelance authors they subsidy publish (if any). This does not refer to percentage paid by author. If percentage of subsidy is over 50 percent, the publisher will be listed in a separate section under "Subsidy Publishers."
(l) Whether they reprint out-of-print books from other publishers
(m) Preferred manuscript length in words or pages; "pages" refers to double-spaced manuscript pages.
(n) Average amount of royalty, if provided. If royalty is a percentage of wholesale or net, it is based on price paid by bookstores or distributors. If it is on retail price, it is based on cover price of the book.
(o) Average amount paid for advances. Whether publishers pay an advance or not is noted in the listing; if they did not answer the question, there is no mention of it.

(p) Whether they pay flat fees (in these cases the author receives no royalties)

(q) Average first printing (number of books usually printed for a first-time author)

(r) Average length of time between acceptance of a manuscript and publication of the work

(s) Whether they consider simultaneous submissions. This means you can send a query or complete manuscript simultaneously to more than one publisher, as long as you advise everyone involved that you are doing so.

(t) Length of time it should take them to respond to a query/proposal or to a complete manuscript (when two lengths of time are given, the first refers to a query and the latter to a complete manuscript). Give them a one-month grace period beyond that, and then send a polite follow-up letter if you haven't heard from them.

(u) Whether a publisher "accepts," "prefers," or "requires" the submission of an accepted manuscript on disk. (Do not send your unsolicited manuscripts/submissions on disk.) Most publishers now do accept or require that books be sent on a computer disk (usually along with a hard copy) or by e-mail, but since each publisher's needs are different, that information will be supplied to you by the individual publisher when the time comes. This section also indicates whether publishers accept submissions by e-mail and whether they want one sent as an attachment or copied into the message.

(v) Which Bible version the publisher may prefer

(w) Whether they do print-on-demand publishing

(x) Availability and cost of writer's guidelines and book catalogs. If the listing says "Guidelines," it means guidelines are available for a #10 (business size) SASE with a first-class stamp. The cost of the catalog (if any), the size of envelope, and amount of postage are given, if specified (affix stamps to envelope; don't send them loose). Tip: If postage required would be more than $2.38, I suggest you put $2.38 in postage on the envelope and clearly mark it "Media Mail." (That is enough for up to one pound.) If the listing says "free catalog," it means you need only request it; they do not ask for payment or an SASE. Note: If sending for both guidelines and catalog, it is not necessary to send two envelopes; guidelines will be sent with the catalog. The listing will also indicate whether guidelines are available by e-mail or on the Website.

(y) Nonfiction and Fiction sections indicate preference for query letter, book proposal, or complete manuscript, and whether they accept phone, fax, or e-queries. (If it does not say they accept them, assume they do not; this reference applies to fiction as well as nonfiction.) If they want a query letter, send just a letter describing your project. If they want a query letter/proposal, you can add a chapter-by-chapter synopsis and sample chapters. If not specified, send from one to three chapters. This data is often followed by a quote from the publishers about their needs or what they don't want to see.

(z) Special Needs—If a publisher has specific needs, especially those that are not included in the subject listings, they are indicated here.

(aa) Ethnic Books—Usually specifies which ethnic groups they target

(bb) Also Does—Indicates which publishers also publish booklets, pamphlets, tracts, or e-books

(cc) Photos/Artwork—Indicates whether they accept freelance photos for book covers. If interested, contact them for details or photography guidelines. This year I have also added information on whether publishers will accept queries about artwork from freelancers.

(dd) Tips—Specific tips provided by the editor/publisher

Note: At the end of some listings you will find an indication that the publisher receives mailings of book proposals from The Writer's Edge (see "Editorial Services/Illinois" for an explanation of that service) and/or ChristianManuscriptSubmissions.com (see Website or index).

4. In each periodical listing you will find the following information (as available) in this format:

(a) Name of periodical
(b) Address, phone and fax numbers, e-mail address, Website
(c) Denomination or affiliation
(d) Name of senior editor and editor to submit to (if different)
(e) Theme of publication
(f) Format of publication, frequency of publication, number of pages, and size of circulation. Format refers to whether it is a magazine, newsletter, journal, tabloid, newspaper, or take-home paper. Frequency of publication and number of pages are both indicators of how much material the publishers can use. Circulation indicates the amount of exposure your material will receive and often indicates how well the publishers might pay or the probability that they will stay in business.
(g) Subscription rate—Amount given is for a one-year subscription in the country of origin. I suggest you subscribe to at least one of your primary markets every year to become better acquainted with its specific focus.
(h) Date established—Included only if 2007 or later
(i) Openness to freelance work; percentage of freelance written. This indicates the percentage of unsolicited freelance versus assigned articles. Since not all publishers have responded to this question, some will still give the two percentages combined or indicate only the unsolicited number. If they buy only a small percentage, it often means they are open but receive little material that is appropriate. When you have a choice, choose those with the higher percentage of freelance-written work, but only if you have done your homework and know they are an appropriate market for your material.
(j) Preference for query or complete manuscript also tells whether they want a cover letter with complete manuscripts and whether they accept phone, fax, or e-mail queries. If it does not mention cover letters or phone, fax, or e-mail queries, assume they do not accept them.
(k) Payment schedule, payment on acceptance (they pay when the piece is accepted) or on publication (they pay when it is published), and rights purchased. (See glossary for definitions of different rights.)
(l) If a publication does not pay or pays in copies or subscription, that is indicated in bold capital letters.
(m) If a publication is not copyrighted, you should ask for your copyright notice to appear on your published piece so your rights will be protected.
(n) Preferred word lengths and average number of manuscripts purchased per year (in parentheses)
(o) Response time—The time they usually take to respond to your query or manuscript submission. (Add at least two weeks for mail delays.)
(p) Seasonal material (also refers to holiday)—Holiday or seasonal material should reach them by at least the specified length of time in advance.
(q) Acceptance of simultaneous submissions and reprints—If they accept simultaneous submissions, it means they will look at submissions (usually a timely topic or holiday material)sent simultaneously to several publishers. It's best to send to nonoverlapping markets (such as denominational), and be sure to indicate that it is a simultaneous submission. Reprints are pieces you have sold previously but to which you hold the rights (which means you sold only first or onetime rights to the original publisher and the rights reverted to you as soon as they were published).
(r) Whether they accept, prefer, or require submissions on disk or by e-mail. Many now prefer an e-mail submission rather than on disk. Most will want a query or hard copy first. If it

does not say they prefer or require disks, you should wait to see if they ask for them. If they accept an e-mail submission, it will indicate whether they want it as an attached file or copied into the message. If it says they accept e-mail submissions but doesn't indicate a reference, it usually means they will take them either way.

(s) Average kill-fee amount (see glossary for definition), if they pay one

(t) Whether or not they use sidebars (see glossary for definition) and whether they do so regularly or occasionally

(u) Their preferred Bible version—The version most frequently listed is the NIV (New International Version). If no version is indicated, they usually have no preference. See glossary for "Bible Versions" list.

(v) Whether they accept submissions from children or teens. A list of the publishers open to submissions from young writers is in the topical listings under "Young-Writer Markets."

(w) Availability and cost for writer's guidelines, theme lists, and sample copies—If the listing says "Guidelines," it means they are available for a #10 SASE (business size) with a first-class stamp. Many more now have guidelines available by e-mail or Website, and the listing will indicate that. The cost for a sample copy, the size of envelope, and number of stamps required are given, if specified (affix stamps to envelope; don't send them loose). Tips: (1) If postage required is more than $2.38, I suggest you put $2.38 in postage on the envelope and clearly mark it "Media Mail." (That is enough for up to one pound.) If the listing says "free sample copy," it means you need only to request it; they do not ask for payment or an SASE. (2) If you're sending for both guidelines and sample copy, it is not necessary to send two envelopes; guidelines will be sent with sample copy. If a listing doesn't mention guidelines or sample copy, they probably don't have them.

(x) "Not in topical listings" means the publisher has not supplied a list of topics it is interested in. Send for guidelines or study sample copies to determine topics used.

(y) Poetry—Name of poetry editor (if different). Average number of poems bought each year. Types of poetry. Number of lines. Payment rate. Maximum number of poems you may submit at one time.

(z) Fillers—Name of fillers editor (if different). Types of fillers accepted; word length. Payment rate.

(aa) Columns/Departments—Name of column editor (if different). Names of columns in the periodical (information in parentheses gives focus of column); word-length requirements. Payment rate. Be sure to see sample before sending ms or query. Most columns require a query.

(bb) Special Issues or Needs—Indicates topics of special issues they have planned for the year or unique topics not included in regular subject listings

(cc) Ethnic—Any involvement they have in the ethnic market

(dd) Contest—Information on contests they sponsor or how to obtain that information. See "Contest" section at back of book for full list of contests.

(ee) Tips—Tips from the editor on how to break into this market or how to be successful as an author

(ff) At the end of some listings you will find a notation about where that particular periodical placed in the Top 50+ Christian Periodicals list in 2009 and/or its place in previous years. This list is compiled annually to indicate the most writer-friendly publications. To receive a complete listing, plus a prepared analysis sheet and writer's guidelines for the top 50 of those markets, send $25 (includes postage) to Sally Stuart, 1647 S.W. Pheasant Dr., Aloha OR 97006, or order from www.stuartmarket.com.

(gg) Some listings also include EPA winners. These awards are made annually by the Evangelical Press Association (a trade organization for Christian periodicals). This section also indicates the top-ten best-selling magazines in Christian retail stores.

5. It is important that you adhere closely to the guidelines set out in these listings. If a publisher asks for a query only, do not send a complete manuscript. Following these guidelines will mark you as a professional.

6. If your manuscript is completed, select the proper topical listing and target audience, and make up a list of possible publishers. Check first to see which ones will accept a complete manuscript (if you want to send it to those that require a query, you will have to write a query letter or book proposal to send first). Please do not assume that your manuscript will be appropriate for all those on the list. Read the primary listing for each, and if you are not familiar with a publisher, read its writer's guidelines and study one or more sample copies or the book catalog. (The primary listings tell how to get these.) Be sure the slant of your manuscript fits the slant of the publisher.

7. If you have an idea for an article, short story, or book but you have not written it yet, reading the appropriate topical listing will help you decide on a possible slant or approach. Select some publishers to whom you might send a query about your idea. If your idea is for an article, do not overlook the possibility of writing on the same topic for a number of different periodicals listed under that topic, either with the same target audience or another from the list. For example, you could write on money management for a general adult magazine, a teen magazine, a women's publication, or a magazine for pastors. Each would require a different slant, but you would get a lot more mileage from that idea.

8. If you do not have an idea, simply start reading through the topical listings or the primary listings. They are sure to trigger any number of book or magazine article ideas you could go to work on.

9. If you run into words or terms you are not familiar with, check the glossary at the back of the book for definitions.

10. If you need someone to look at your material to evaluate it or to give it a thorough editing, look up the section on "Editorial Services," and find someone to send it to for such help. That often will make the difference between success or failure in publishing.

11. If you are a published author with other books to your credit, you may be interested in finding an agent. Some agents will consider unpublished authors (their listing will indicate that), but many require an author to have a completed manuscript before being considered (see agent list). Christian agents are at a premium, so it can be hard to find an agent unless you have had some success in book writing. The agent list also includes secular agents who handle religious/inspirational material.

12. Check the "Group" list to find a group to join in your area. Go to the "Conference" list to find a conference you might attend this year. Attending a conference every year or two is almost essential to your success as a writer, especially when you get into book writing.

13. Send an SASE with every query or manuscript. If you do not want your manuscript returned, indicate that in your cover letter, and send a #10 SASE for the acceptance or rejection letter.

14. Do not rely solely on the information provided in this guide! It is just that—a guide—and is not intended to be complete by itself. It is important to your success as a freelance writer that you learn how to use writer's guidelines and study book catalogs or sample copies before submitting to any publisher.

PART 1
Book Publishers

1

Topical/Subject Listings of Book Publishers

One of the most difficult aspects of marketing is trying to determine which publishers might be interested in the book you want to write. This topical listing was designed to help you do just that.

First, look up your topic of interest in the following lists. If you don't find the specific topic, check the list of topics in the table of contents, find any related topics, and pursue those. Once you have discovered which publishers are interested in a particular topic, the next step is to secure writer's guidelines and book catalogs from those publishers. Just because a particular publisher is listed under your topic, don't assume that it would automatically be interested in your book. It is your job to determine whether your approach to the subject will fit within the unique scope of that publisher's catalog. It is also helpful to visit a Christian bookstore to actually see some of the books produced by each publisher you are interested in pursuing.

Note, too, that the primary listings for each publisher indicate what the publisher prefers to see in the initial contact—a query, book proposal, or complete manuscript.

An (a) before a listing indicates the publisher accepts submissions only through agents. These appear at the top of each topical list.

An R indicates which publishers reprint out-of-print books from other publishers.

An asterisk (*) following a topic indicates it is a new topic this year.

An (s) before a listing indicates it is a publisher listed in the Subsidy Publishers' section and does at least 50% subsidy publishing or print-on-demand. Please note that some of these publishers do some royalty publishing as well (check their listings), so if you aren't interested in a subsidy deal, you can contact them indicating you are interested only in a royalty contract.

AFRICAN AMERICAN MARKETS
(a)-Abingdon Press
(a)-Doubleday Religious—R
(a)-One World/Ballantine

(s)-American Binding—R
(s)-Booklocker.com—R
Branden Publishing—R
Bridge Logos—R
Cambridge Scholars Pub.
CharismaKids
CLC Publications—R
E.F.S. Online Pub.
Fortress Press
Forward Movement
(s)-House of Ali
(s)-IMD Press—R
InterVarsity Press—R
Judson Press—R
Lift Every Voice—R

Moody Publishers
National Black Theatre
New Hope—R
Pilgrim Press—R
Praeger Publishers
Rill & Associates
St. Anthony Mess. Press—R
(s)-Tate Publishing—R
Third World Press—R
Torch Legacy
UMI Publishing—R
Univ. Press of America—R
Whitaker House

APOLOGETICS
(a)-Bethany House—R
(a)-FaithWords
(a)-Harvest House
(a)-Kregel—R
(a)-Nelson, Thomas
(a)-Regal

Aadeon Publishing—R
Aaron Book—R
Abingdon Press
(s)-ACW Press—R
Ambassador Intl.—R
(s)-American Binding—R
AMG Publishers—R
Baylor Univ. Press
(s)-Bfree Publishing
(s)-Black Forest—R
Blue Dolphin
BMH Books—R
(s)-Booklocker.com—R
(s)-Bookstand Publishing—R
Bridge Logos—R
(s)-Brown Books
Cambridge Scholars
Canticle Books—R
Catholic Answers—R
Chapter Two—R
Christian Family—R

Christian Heritage—R
College Press—R
Continuum Intl.—R
(s)-Creation House—R
Crossway
CSS Publishing—R
(s)-Deo Volente
Discovery House—R
Earthen Vessel—R
Eerdmans Pub., Wm. B.—R
(s)-Elderberry Press
Emmaus Road
(s)-Essence—R
Evangelical Press
Fair Havens—R
(s)-Fairway Press—R
(s)-Faith Books & More—R
Father's Press
(s)-Forever Books—R
Forward Movement
Four Craftsmen—R
(s)-Grace Acres Press—R
GRQ—R
Guardian Angel
Hendrickson—R
Hensley Publishing
Hidden Brook Press—R
(s)-Holy Fire Publishing—R
Hope Publishing—R
Howard Books
(s)-IMD Press—R
(s)-Insight Publishing—R
InterVarsity Press—R
Lighthouse Publishing—R
Lighthouse Trails—R
Lion and Lamb
Lutheran Univ. Press
Magnus Press—R
Master Books
Messianic Jewish—R
Millennium III—R
Monarch Books
New Leaf
Nordskog Publishing—R
(s)-One World—R
Our Sunday Visitor—R
P & R Publishing—R
Parson Place—R
(s)-Pleasant Word—R
Power Publishing—R

(s)-Providence House—R
Randall House
Reformation Heritage—R
Reformation Trust
Rose Publishing
(s)-Salt Works—R
Samaritan Press—R
Scepter Publishers—R
(s)-Star Bible Public.
Strang Book—R
(s)-Tate Publishing—R
Th1nk/NavPress—R
(s)-Trafford Publishing—R
VBC Publishing
Whitaker House
(s)-WinePress—R
(s)-Word Alive
(s)-Zoë Life Publishing

ARCHAEOLOGY
(a)-Baker Academic
(a)-Baker Books
(a)-Doubleday Relig.—R
(a)-HarperOne
(a)-Kregel—R

Aaron Book—R
Abingdon Press
(s)-ACW Press—R
(s)-American Binding—R
(s)-Bfree Publishing
(s)-Black Forest—R
Blue Dolphin
BMH Books—R
(s)-Booklocker.com—R
Boyds Mills Press—R
(s)-Brentwood—R
(s)-Brown Books
Cambridge Scholars
Chapter Two—R
Christian Writer's Ebook—R
Comfort Publishing
Conciliar Press—R
Dover Publications—R
Eerdmans Pub., Wm. B.—R
(s)-Elderberry Press
(s)-Essence—R
Facts On File
(s)-Fairway Press—R
(s)-Faith Books & More—R
FaithWalk

Fordham Univ. Press—R
(s)-Forever Books—R
Hendrickson—R
Hidden Brook Press—R
(s)-Holy Fire Publishing—R
(s)-Insight Publishing—R
Lighthouse Publishing—R
Lion and Lamb
Master Books
Monarch Books
New Leaf
Nordskog Publishing—R
(s)-One World—R
Pacific Press
Palgrave Macmillan—R
(s)-Pleasant Word—R
Power Publishing—R
(s)-Providence House—R
Reformation Heritage—R
Rose Publishing
(s)-Tate Publishing—R
(s)-TEACH Services—R
(s)-Trafford Publishing—R
Univ. Press of America—R
VBC Publishing
(s)-WinePress—R
(s)-Word Alive
Yale Univ. Press

ART, FREELANCE
Aaron Book—R
Abingdon Press
Ambassador Books
Ambassador Intl.—R
AMG Publishers—R
Anglicans United—R
(s)-Bfree Publishing
(s)-Black Forest—R
Blue Dolphin
(s)-Booklocker.com—R
Cambridge Scholars
Carson-Dellosa
Chelsea House—R
Christian Ed. Pub.
CrossLink Publishing
Dawn Publications
Dove Inspirational—R
(s)-E.F.S. Online Pub.
Earthen Vessel—R
Editorial Portavoz

Eerdmans/Yg Readers
(s)-Essence—R
Fair Havens—R
Faith Alive
(s)-Faith Books & More—R
Focus on the Family—R
(s)-Forever Books—R
Four Craftsmen—R
(s)-Grace Acres Press—R
Group Publishing
Guardian Angel
(s)-Halo Publishing Intl.
(s)-Holy Fire Publishing—R
Jebaire
JourneyForth/BJU
Judson Press—R
Knight George Pub.
Legacy Press—R
Lighthouse Publishing—R
Lighthouse Trails—R
Lion and Lamb
Liturgy Training—R
Marcher Lord Press
Master Books
Messianic Jewish—R
Mission City Press
Monarch Books
New Leaf
Nordskog Publishing—R
Parson Place—R
Parsons Publishing—R
Pauline Kids—R
Pelican Publishing—R
Players Press—R
(s)-Pleasant Word—R
Power Publishing—R
(s)-Providence House—R
Quintessential Books—R
Rainbow Publishers—R
Randall House
Ravenhawk Books—R
Reformation Heritage—R
(s)-Rill & Associates
Rose Publishing
(s)-Salt Works—R
Samaritan Press—R
Sheed & Ward
Starik Publishing
Sunpenny Publishing
(s)-TEACH Services—R

Treble Heart—R
Two Fish Publishing—R
VBC Publishing
Warner Press
Wilshire Book—R
(s)-WinePress—R

AUTOBIOGRAPHY
(a)-Baker Books
(a)-Doubleday Relig.—R
(a)-FaithWords
(a)-HarperOne
(a)-Nelson, Thomas
(a)-WaterBrook Press—R

Aaron Book—R
(s)-ACW Press—R
Ambassador Intl.—R
(s)-American Binding—R
Believe Books
(s)-Bfree Publishing
(s)-Black Forest—R
Blue Dolphin
(s)-Booklocker.com—R
(s)-Book Publishers Net.—R
(s)-Bookstand Publishing—R
Boyds Mills Press—R
Branden Publishing—R
(s)-Brentwood—R
Bridge Logos—R
(s)-Brown Books
Carey Library, Wm.—R
Chapter Two—R
Christian Heritage—R
Christian Writer's Ebook—R
CLC Publications—R
Continuum Intl.—R
(s)-Creation House—R
CrossLink Publishing
(s)-Dean Press, Robbie—R
(s)-Deep River Books
Earthen Vessel—R
(s)-E.F.S. Online Pub.
(s)-Elderberry Press
(s)-Essence—R
Evergreen Press
(s)-Fairway Press—R
(s)-Faith Books & More—R
Father's Press
(s)-Forever Books—R

Four Craftsmen—R
Friends United Press
Georgetown Univ. Press
(s)-Grace Acres Press—R
Hidden Brook Press—R
His Work Christian Pub.—R
(s)-Holy Fire Publishing—R
(s)-IMD Press—R
(s)-Insight Publishing—R
Kirk House
Life Changing Media
(s)-LifeVest Publishing
Lighthouse Publishing—R
Lighthouse Trails—R
Lion and Lamb
(s)-McDougal Publishing—R
Monarch Books
Nordskog Publishing—R
(s)-One World—R
Pacific Press
Palgrave Macmillan—R
Parson Place—R
Parsons Publishing—R
(s)-Pleasant Word—R
Power Publishing—R
(s)-Providence House—R
Quiet Waters—R
Reformation Heritage—R
(s)-Selah Publishing—R
(s)-So. Baptist Press—R
Still Waters Revival—R
Strang Book—R
(s)-Tate Publishing—R
(s)-TEACH Services—R
Third World Press—R
(s)-Trafford Publishing—R
Univ. Press of America—R
(s)-WinePress—R
(s)-Word Alive
(s)-Zoë Life Publishing

BIBLE/BIBLICAL STUDIES
(a)-Baker Academic
(a)-Baker Books
(a)-Bethany House—R
(a)-Cook, David C.
(a)-Doubleday Relig.—R
(a)-Kregel—R
(a)-Regal
(a)-WaterBrook Press—R

Aadeon Publishing—R
Aaron Book—R
Abingdon Press
ACTA Publications
(s)-ACW Press—R
Ambassador Books
Ambassador Intl.—R
(s)-American Binding—R
AMG Publishers—R
Anglicans United—R
Baylor Univ. Press
(s)-Bfree Publishing
Blue Dolphin
BMH Books—R
(s)-Booklocker.com—R
(s)-Bookstand Publishing—R
(s)-Brentwood—R
Bridge Logos—R
(s)-Brown Books
Cambridge Scholars
Canticle Books—R
Carey Library, Wm.—R
Catholic Answers—R
Chalice Press—R
Chapter Two—R
Christian Ed. Pub.
Christian Family—R
Christian Focus—R
Christian Liberty Press
Christian Writer's Ebook—R
Church Publishing
Clarke & Co., James—R
College Press—R
Conciliar Press—R
Concordia Academic
Congregational Life
Conquest Publishers
Contemporary Drama
Continuum Intl.—R
CrossLink Publishing
CSS Publishing—R
(s)-DCTS Publishers
(s)-Dean Press, Robbie—R
(s)-Deep River Books
(s)-Deo Volente
Discovery House—R
Earthen Vessel—R
Editorial Portavoz
Eerdmans Pub., Wm. B.—R
(s)-Elderberry Press

Emmaus Road
(s)-Essence—R
Evangelical Press
Evergreen Press
Fair Havens—R
(s)-Fairway Press—R
Faith Alive
(s)-Faith Books & More—R
FaithWalk
Father's Press
First Fruits of Zion
(s)-Forever Books—R
Fortress Press
Four Craftsmen—R
Foursquare Media
Good Book—R
Gospel Publishing
Group Publishing
Grupo Nelson
Hannibal Books
Harrison House
Hendrickson—R
Hensley Publishing
Hidden Brook Press—R
(s)-Holy Fire Publishing—R
(s)-IMD Press—R
Inkling Books—R
(s)-Insight Publishing—R
InterVarsity Press—R
JourneyForth/BJU
Jubilant Press—R
(s)-Kindred Books—R
Leafwood
Libros Liguori
Lift Every Voice—R
Lighthouse Publishing—R
Lion and Lamb
Lutheran Univ. Press
Lutterworth Press—R
Magnus Press—R
(s)-McDougal Publishing—R
Mercer Univ. Press—R
Messianic Jewish—R
Monarch Books
NavPress
New Hope—R
New York Univ. Press
Nordskog Publishing—R
(s)-One World—R
On My Own Now—R

Our Sunday Visitor—R
P & R Publishing—R
Pacific Press
Palgrave Macmillan—R
Paradise Research—R
Parson Place—R
Parsons Publishing—R
Pauline Kids—R
Paulist Press
Pflaum Publishing
Pilgrim Press—R
(s)-Pleasant Word—R
Power Publishing—R
(s)-Providence House—R
Randall House Digital
Reformation Heritage—R
Revival Nation
Rose Publishing
(s)-Salt Works—R
Samaritan Press—R
Sheed & Ward
Smyth & Helwys
(s)-So. Baptist Press—R
(s)-Star Bible Public.
St. Bede's Public.—R
St. Pauls/Alba—R
(s)-Tate Publishing—R
(s)-TEACH Services—R
Th1nk/NavPress—R
(s)-Trafford Publishing—R
UMI Publishing—R
Univ. Press of America—R
VBC Publishing
Wesleyan Publishing
Westminster John Knox
Whitaker House
(s)-WinePress—R
(s)-Word Alive
Yale Univ. Press
Youth Specialties
(s)-Zoë Life Publishing
Zondervan

BIBLE COMMENTARY
(a)-B & H Publishing
(a)-Baker Books
(a)-Cook, David C.
(a)-Doubleday Relig.—R
(a)-Kregel—R
(a)-Tyndale House—R

Aaron Book—R
Abingdon Press
(s)-ACW Press—R
Ambassador Books
Ambassador Intl.—R
(s)-American Binding—R
AMG Publishers—R
Anglicans United—R
(s)-Bfree Publishing
(s)-Black Forest—R
Blue Dolphin
BMH Books—R
(s)-Booklocker.com—R
(s)-Bookstand Publishing—R
Bridge Logos—R
(s)-Brown Books
Cambridge Scholars
Carey Library, Wm.—R
Catholic Answers—R
Chalice Press—R
Chapter Two—R
Christian Family—R
Christian Focus—R
Christian Writer's Ebook—R
Clarke & Co., James—R
College Press—R
Conciliar Press—R
Continuum Intl.—R
CrossLink Publishing
CSS Publishing—R
Discovery House—R
Editorial Portavoz
Eerdmans Pub., Wm. B.—R
(s)-Elderberry Press
Emmaus Road
(s)-Essence—R
Evangelical Press
(s)-Fairway Press—R
(s)-Faith Books & More—R
Father's Press
(s)-Forever Books—R
Grupo Nelson
Harrison House
Hendrickson—R
Hidden Brook Press—R
(s)-Holy Fire Publishing—R
(s)-IMD Press—R
Inkling Books—R
(s)-Insight Publishing—R
InterVarsity Press—R

Intl. Awakening—R
Libros Liguori
Lighthouse Publishing—R
Lutheran Univ. Press
Messianic Jewish—R
Monarch Books
New Canaan—R
Nordskog Publishing—R
(s)-One World—R
Our Sunday Visitor—R
P & R Publishing—R
Paulist Press
(s)-Pleasant Word—R
Power Publishing—R
(s)-Providence House—R
Reformation Heritage—R
Reformation Trust
Rose Publishing
Scepter Publishers—R
Sheed & Ward
(s)-Star Bible Public.
St. Bede's Public.—R
St. Pauls/Alba—R
(s)-Tate Publishing—R
(s)-TEACH Services—R
(s)-Trafford Publishing—R
UMI Publishing—R
VBC Publishing
Westminster John Knox
(s)-WinePress—R
Wipf and Stock
(s)-Word Alive
Yale Univ. Press
(s)-Zoë Life Publishing
Zondervan

BIOGRAPHY

(a)-Baker Books
(a)-Ballantine
(a)-Doubleday Relig.—R
(a)-HarperOne
(a)-Nelson, Thomas
(a)-One World/Ballantine
(a)-WaterBrook Press—R
(a)-W Publishing

Aaron Book—R
(s)-ACW Press—R
Ambassador Intl.—R
(s)-American Binding—R

Believe Books
(s)-Bfree Publishing
(s)-Black Forest—R
Blue Dolphin
(s)-Booklocker.com—R
(s)-Book Publishers Net.—R
Boyds Mills Press—R
Branden Publishing—R
(s)-Brentwood—R
Bridge Logos—R
(s)-Brown Books
Carey Library, Wm.—R
Catholic Answers—R
Chapter Two—R
CharismaKids
Christian Family—R
Christian Focus—R
Christian Heritage—R
Christian Liberty Press
Christian Writer's Ebook—R
Cistercian—R
Clarke & Co., James—R
CLC Publications—R
College Press—R
Comfort Publishing
Conciliar Press—R
Continuum Intl.—R
(s)-Creation House—R
CrossLink Publishing
(s)-Dean Press, Robbie—R
(s)-Deep River Books
Discovery House—R
Eerdmans Pub., Wm. B.—R
(s)-E.F.S. Online Pub.
(s)-Elderberry Press
(s)-Essence—R
Evangelical Press
Facts On File
Fair Havens—R
(s)-Fairway Press—R
(s)-Faith Books & More—R
FaithWalk
Fordham Univ. Press—R
(s)-Forever Books—R
Friends United Press
Gentle Path Press
Georgetown Univ. Press
(s)-Grace Acres Press—R
Guideposts Books
Hannibal Books

Hidden Brook Press—R
His Work Christian Pub.—R
(s)-Holy Fire Publishing—R
Hope Publishing—R
(s)-IMD Press—R
Inkling Books—R
(s)-Insight Publishing—R
Intl. Awakening—R
Kirk House
(s)-LifeVest Publishing
Lighthouse Publishing—R
Lighthouse Trails—R
Lion and Lamb
Lutterworth Press—R
Master Books
(s)-McDougal Publishing—R
Mercer Univ. Press—R
Millennium III—R
Mission City Press
Monarch Books
New Leaf
Nordskog Publishing—R
(s)-One World—R
On My Own Now—R
Pacific Press
Palgrave Macmillan—R
Parson Place—R
Parsons Publishing—R
Pauline Books—R
Pauline Kids—R
(s)-Pleasant Word—R
Power Publishing—R
(s)-Providence House—R
Quintessential Books—R
Ravenhawk Books—R
Reformation Heritage—R
Reformation Trust
Scepter Publishers—R
(s)-Selah Publishing—R
Sheed & Ward
(s)-So. Baptist Press—R
St. Anthony Mess. Press—R
Still Waters Revival—R
Strang Book—R
(s)-Tate Publishing—R
(s)-TEACH Services—R
Third World Press—R
(s)-Trafford Publishing—R
Univ. of AR Press—R
Univ. Press of America—R

Whitaker House
(s)-WinePress—R
(s)-Word Alive
Yale Univ. Press
(s)-Zoë Life Publishing

BOOKLETS
(a)-Harvest House

Aaron Book—R
(s)-American Binding—R
Anglicans United—R
Catholic Answers—R
Chapter Two—R
Christian Writer's Ebook—R
(s)-Creation House—R
(s)-Dean Press, Robbie—R
Doulos Resources—R
Emmaus Road
(s)-Essence—R
Evergreen Press
Fair Havens—R
Forward Movement
Four Craftsmen—R
(s)-Fruitbearer Pub.
Good Book—R
(s)-Holy Fire Publishing—R
(s)-IMD Press—R
(s)-Insight Publishing—R
InterVarsity Press—R
Intl. Awakening—R
Libros Liguori
Life Cycle Books—R
Lighthouse Trails—R
Liguori Public.—R
Liturgy Training—R
(s)-One World—R
Our Sunday Visitor—R
P & R Publishing—R
Pacific Press
Paradise Research—R
Paulist Press
Power Publishing—R
(s)-Providence House—R
Randall House
Reformation Heritage—R
Rose Publishing
(s)-Salt Works—R
(s)-Star Bible Public.
Strang Book—R

(s)-Tate Publishing—R
Trinity Foundation—R
(s)-WinePress—R
(s)-Word Alive

CANADIAN/FOREIGN
Cambridge Scholars
Canadian Inst. for Law—R
Chapter Two—R
Christian Focus—R
Clarke & Co., James—R
Congregational Life
(s)-Essence—R
(s)-Forever Books—R
Guernica Editions—R
Hidden Brook Press—R
(s)-Kindred Books—R
Kingsley Pub., Jessica—R
Lutterworth Press—R
Monarch Books
(s)-One World—R
Ponder Publishing
Revival Nation
Still Waters Revival—R
Sunpenny Publishing
(s)-Trafford Publishing—R
(s)-Word Alive

CELEBRITY PROFILES
(a)-Baker Books
(a)-FaithWords
(a)-Hay House
(a)-Nelson, Thomas

Aaron Book—R
(s)-ACW Press—R
(s)-American Binding—R
Blue Dolphin
(s)-Booklocker.com—R
(s)-Brown Books
Christian Writer's Ebook—R
Comfort Publishing
(s)-Deep River Books
(s)-Elderberry Press
(s)-Essence—R
(s)-Fairway Press—R
(s)-Faith Books & More—R
FaithWalk
(s)-Forever Books—R
(s)-Grace Acres Press—R

Hidden Brook Press—R
(s)-Holy Fire Publishing—R
Howard Books
(s)-Insight Publishing—R
Life Changing Media
Lighthouse Publishing—R
Monarch Books
Nordskog Publishing—R
(s)-One World—R
On My Own Now—R
(s)-Pleasant Word—R
Power Publishing—R
(s)-Providence House—R
Ravenhawk Books—R
(s)-Selah Publishing—R
Strang Book—R
(s)-Tate Publishing—R
Third World Press—R
(s)-Trafford Publishing—R
Whitaker House
(s)-WinePress—R
(s)-Word Alive

CHARISMATIC
(a)-Nelson, Thomas
(a)-Regal

Aaron Book—R
(s)-ACW Press—R
(s)-American Binding—R
Anglicans United—R
(s)-Black Forest—R
Blue Dolphin
(s)-Booklocker.com—R
Bridge Logos—R
Canticle Books—R
CharismaKids
Chosen Books
Comfort Publishing
(s)-Creation House—R
CSS Publishing—R
(s)-Destiny Image (books)—R
Eerdmans Pub., Wm. B.—R
(s)-Elderberry Press
(s)-Essence—R
(s)-Fairway Press—R
(s)-Faith Books & More—R
(s)-Forever Books—R
Four Craftsmen—R
(s)-Fruitbearer Pub.

Gospel Publishing
Harrison House
Hidden Brook Press—R
(s)-Holy Fire Publishing—R
(s)-IMD Press—R
Life Changing Media
Lighthouse Publishing—R
Lutheran Univ. Press
Magnus Press—R
(s)-MileStones Intl.
Monarch Books
(s)-One World—R
Parsons Publishing—R
(s)-Pleasant Word—R
Power Publishing—R
(s)-Providence House—R
Revival Nation
(s)-Rill & Associates
(s)-Salvation Publisher—R
Strang Book—R
(s)-Tate Publishing—R
(s)-Trafford Publishing—R
Whitaker House
(s)-WinePress—R
(s)-Word Alive
(s)-Zoë Life Publishing

CHILDREN'S BOARD BOOKS
Ambassador Books
Candy Cane Press
Eerdmans/Yg Readers
(s)-Elderberry Press
(s)-Faith Books & More—R
(s)-Halo Publishing Intl.
Knight George Pub.
Messianic Jewish—R
(s)-One World—R
Pauline Kids—R
(s)-Seed Faith Books—R
(s)-Tate Publishing—R
(s)-Trafford Publishing—R
(s)-WinePress—R
(s)-Word Alive

CHILDREN'S DEVOTIONALS
(s)-Bfree Publishing
Conquest Publishers
Emmaus Road

(s)-Essence—R
Fair Havens—R
(s)-IMD Press—R
Master Books
(s)-MileStones Intl.
New Leaf
Pauline Books—R
(s)-Seed Faith Books—R
Warner Press
(s)-Zoë Life Publishing

CHILDREN'S EASY READERS
(a)-Baker Books
(a)-Cook, David C.
(a)-Tyndale House—R

Aaron Book—R
Ambassador Books
(s)-Bfree Publishing
(s)-Booklocker.com—R
(s)-Bookstand Publishing—R
Boyds Mills Press—R
(s)-Brown Books
Carson-Dellosa
CharismaKids
Conciliar Press—R
Conquest Publishers
(s)-Creation House—R
Dawn Publications
(s)-Dean Press, Robbie—R
(s)-Deep River Books
(s)-E.F.S. Online Pub.
(s)-Elderberry Press
(s)-Essence—R
Evergreen Press
Fair Havens—R
(s)-Fairway Press—R
(s)-Faith Books & More—R
Father's Press
Guardian Angel
Hidden Brook Press—R
His Work Christian Pub.—R
(s)-Holy Fire Publishing—R
(s)-IMD Press—R
Inkling Books—R
JourneyForth/BJU
JourneyStone—R
Knight George Pub.
Legacy Press—R
Lift Every Voice—R

Lighthouse Publishing—R
Lion and Lamb
McRuffy Press
Nordskog Publishing—R
(s)-One World—R
Our Sunday Visitor—R
Pacific Press
Pauline Books—R
Pauline Kids—R
Paulist Press
Pelican Publishing—R
(s)-Providence House—R
(s)-Salty's Books—R
Samaritan Press—R
Standard Publishing
Strang Book—R
(s)-Tate Publishing—R
(s)-Trafford Publishing—R
VBC Publishing
Warner Press
(s)-Word Alive
(s)-Zoë Life Publishing

CHILDREN'S PICTURE BOOKS (NONFICTION)

(a)-Baker Books
(a)-Bethany House—R
(a)-Cook, David C.
(a)-Tyndale House—R
(a)-WaterBrook Press—R

Aaron Book—R
Abingdon Press
Ambassador Books
(s)-Bfree Publishing
(s)-Black Forest—R
(s)-Book Publishers Net.—R
(s)-Bookstand Publishing—R
Boyds Mills Press—R
Bridge Logos—R
(s)-Brown Books
Candy Cane Press
Christian Focus—R
Conciliar Press—R
Conquest Publishers
(s)-Creation House—R
Dove Inspirational—R
Editorial Portavoz
Eerdmans Pub., Wm. B.—R
Eerdmans/Yg Readers

(s)-Elderberry Press
(s)-Essence—R
Evergreen Press
Extreme Diva
Fair Havens—R
(s)-Faith Books & More—R
Faith Communications
Father's Press
(s)-Fruitbearer Pub.
Gentle Path Press
Grupo Nelson
Guardian Angel
(s)-Halo Publishing Intl.
(s)-Holy Fire Publishing—R
(s)-IMD Press—R
JourneyStone—R
(s)-LifeVest Publishing
Lighthouse Publishing—R
Lighthouse Trails—R
Lion and Lamb
Master Books
Messianic Jewish—R
Monarch Books
New Leaf
Nordskog Publishing—R
(s)-One World—R
Pauline Books—R
Pauline Kids—R
Pelican Publishing—R
(s)-Pleasant Word—R
(s)-Providence House—R
Putnam/Young Readers
Reformation Heritage—R
Revival Nation
(s)-Salty's Books—R
Samaritan Press—R
(s)-Seed Faith Books—R
(s)-Selah Publishing—R
Standard Publishing
(s)-Tate Publishing—R
(s)-TEACH Services—R
Third World Press—R
(s)-Trafford Publishing—R
Warner Press
(s)-WinePress—R
(s)-Zoë Life Publishing

CHRIST

(a)-Bethany House—R

(a)-Cook, David C.
(a)-Doubleday Relig.—R
(a)-Nelson, Thomas

Aaron Book—R
(s)-ACW Press—R
Ambassador Intl.—R
(s)-American Binding—R
Barbour
(s)-Bfree Publishing
(s)-Black Forest—R
Blue Dolphin
BMH Books—R
(s)-Booklocker.com—R
(s)-Bookstand Publishing—R
(s)-Brown Books
Canticle Books—R
Catholic Answers—R
Chalice Press—R
CharismaKids
Christian Family—R
Christian Focus—R
Christian Heritage—R
Christian Writer's Ebook—R
CLC Publications—R
Continuum Intl.—R
(s)-Creation House—R
CrossLink Publishing
CSS Publishing—R
(s)-Deep River Books
Discovery House—R
Earthen Vessel—R
Eerdmans Pub., Wm. B.—R
(s)-E.F.S. Online Pub.
(s)-Elderberry Press
Eldridge Plays
Emmaus Road
(s)-Essence—R
Evangelical Press
(s)-Fairway Press—R
(s)-Faith Books & More—R
Father's Press
(s)-Forever Books—R
(s)-Grace Acres Press—R
GRQ—R
Guardian Angel
Guideposts Books
Hendrickson—R
Hidden Brook Press—R
(s)-Holy Fire Publishing—R

(s)-IMD Press—R
(s)-Insight Publishing—R
JourneyForth/BJU
Lift Every Voice—R
Lighthouse Publishing—R
Lion and Lamb
Lutheran Univ. Press
Magnus Press—R
Master Books
Monarch Books
New Leaf
Nordskog Publishing—R
(s)-One World—R
Our Sunday Visitor—R
P & R Publishing—R
Paradise Research—R
Parson Place—R
Pauline Kids—R
Pilgrim Press—R
(s)-Pleasant Word—R
Power Publishing—R
(s)-Providence House—R
Quintessential Books—R
Reformation Heritage—R
Reformation Trust
Revival Nation
Rose Publishing
(s)-Salt Works—R
(s)-Star Bible Public.
St. Bede's Public.—R
Strang Book—R
(s)-Tate Publishing—R
(s)-TEACH Services—R
Th1nk/NavPress—R
Torch Legacy
(s)-Trafford Publishing—R
VBC Publishing
(s)-WinePress—R
(s)-Word Alive
Yale Univ. Press
(s)-Zoë Life Publishing

CHRISTIAN BUSINESS
(a)-Cook, David C.
(a)-Doubleday Relig.—R
(a)-Nelson, Thomas
(a)-WaterBrook Press—R

Aaron Book—R
(s)-ACW Press—R

Ambassador Intl.—R
(s)-American Binding—R
Anglicans United—R
(s)-Bfree Publishing
(s)-Black Forest—R
Blue Dolphin
BMH Books—R
(s)-Booklocker.com—R
(s)-Bookstand Publishing—R
(s)-Brown Books
Chalice Press—R
Christian Family—R
Christian Writer's Ebook—R
Comfort Publishing
(s)-Creation House—R
CSS Publishing—R
(s)-Deep River Books
Eerdmans Pub., Wm. B.—R
(s)-E.F.S. Online Pub.
(s)-Elderberry Press
(s)-Essence—R
Evergreen Press
(s)-Fairway Press—R
(s)-Faith Books & More—R
Father's Press
(s)-Forever Books—R
Forward Movement
Four Craftsmen—R
(s)-Grace Acres Press—R
Grupo Nelson
Hannibal Books
Hidden Brook Press—R
(s)-Holy Fire Publishing—R
Howard Books
(s)-IMD Press—R
(s)-Insight Publishing—R
InterVarsity Press—R
JourneyForth/BJU
Jubilant Press—R
Kirk House
Lift Every Voice—R
Lighthouse Publishing—R
Lion and Lamb
Lutheran Univ. Press
Master Books
Monarch Books
New Leaf
Nordskog Publishing—R
(s)-One World—R
Pilgrim Press—R

(s)-Pleasant Word—R
Power Publishing—R
PREP Publishing—R
(s)-Providence House—R
Quintessential Books—R
Ravenhawk Books—R
(s)-Rill & Associates
(s)-Salvation Publisher—R
(s)-Star Bible Public.
Starik Publishing
Strang Book—R
(s)-Tate Publishing—R
(s)-TEACH Services—R
(s)-Trafford Publishing—R
Treble Heart—R
Trinity Foundation—R
VBC Publishing
Westminster John Knox
Whitaker House
(s)-WinePress—R
(s)-Word Alive
(s)-Zoë Life Publishing

CHRISTIAN EDUCATION
(a)-Baker Academic
(a)-Baker Books
(a)-Cook, David C.
(a)-Doubleday Relig.—R
(a)-Kregel—R

Aaron Book—R
(s)-ACW Press—R
Ambassador Intl.—R
(s)-American Binding—R
(s)-Bfree Publishing
Blue Dolphin
(s)-Booklocker.com—R
(s)-Bookstand Publishing—R
(s)-Brentwood—R
(s)-Brown Books
Carson-Dellosa
Chalice Press—R
Christian Ed. Pub.
Christian Family—R
Christian Heritage—R
Christian Liberty Press
Christian Writer's Ebook—R
Church Growth Inst.
College Press—R
Congregational Life

Contemporary Drama
CSS Publishing—R
(s)-DCTS Publishers
(s)-Dean Press, Robbie—R
Eerdmans Pub., Wm. B.—R
(s)-E.F.S. Online Pub.
(s)-Elderberry Press
Eldridge Plays
Emmaus Road
(s)-Essence—R
ETC Publications
Evangelical Press
(s)-Fairway Press—R
Faith Alive
(s)-Faith Books & More—R
Father's Press
(s)-Forever Books—R
Gospel Publishing
(s)-Grace Acres Press—R
Group Publishing
(s)-Halo Publishing Intl.
Hensley Publishing
Hidden Brook Press—R
(s)-Holy Fire Publishing—R
(s)-IMD Press—R
(s)-Insight Publishing—R
InterVarsity Press—R
Judson Press—R
Kingsley Pub., Jessica—R
Kirk House
Knight George Pub.
Lift Every Voice—R
Lighthouse Publishing—R
Lion and Lamb
Liturgical Press
Lutheran Univ. Press
Master Books
Meriwether
Millennium III—R
Monarch Books
New Canaan—R
New Leaf
Nordskog Publishing—R
Northwestern
(s)-One World—R
Our Sunday Visitor—R
Pacific Press
Pilgrim Press—R
(s)-Pleasant Word—R
Power Publishing—R

(s)-Providence House—R
Quintessential Books—R
Rainbow Publishers—R
Reference Service
Rose Publishing
(s)-Salvation Publisher—R
Samaritan Press—R
Smyth & Helwys
(s)-So. Baptist Press—R
Standard Publishing
(s)-Star Bible Public.
Starik Publishing
Still Waters Revival—R
(s)-Tate Publishing—R
(s)-TEACH Services—R
Torch Legacy
(s)-Trafford Publishing—R
Treble Heart—R
Trinity Foundation—R
UMI Publishing—R
Univ. Press of America—R
VBC Publishing
(s)-WinePress—R
(s)-Word Alive
(s)-Zoë Life Publishing

CHRISTIAN HOMESCHOOLING
(a)-Baker Books

Aaron Book—R
(s)-ACW Press—R
(s)-American Binding—R
(s)-Bfree Publishing
Blue Dolphin
BMH Books—R
(s)-Booklocker.com—R
(s)-Bookstand Publishing—R
(s)-Brentwood—R
(s)-Brown Books
Carson-Dellosa
Christian Family—R
Christian Focus—R
Christian Writer's Ebook—R
(s)-CrossHouse—R
CSS Publishing—R
(s)-Dean Press, Robbie—R
Eerdmans Pub., Wm. B.—R
(s)-Elderberry Press
Emmaus Road

(s)-Essence—R
ETC Publications
Evangelical Press
(s)-Fairway Press—R
(s)-Faith Books & More—R
Father's Press
(s)-Forever Books—R
(s)-Fruitbearer Pub.
(s)-Grace Acres Press—R
Hannibal Books
Heart of Wisdom
Hidden Brook Press—R
(s)-Holy Fire Publishing—R
(s)-IMD Press—R
Inkling Books—R
(s)-Insight Publishing—R
Jesus Filled Day (books)
Jubilant Press—R
Lift Every Voice—R
Lighthouse Publishing—R
Lion and Lamb
Master Books
(s)-MileStones Intl.
Mission City Press
Monarch Books
New Leaf
Nordskog Publishing—R
(s)-One World—R
Pacific Press
Parsons Publishing—R
(s)-Pleasant Word—R
Power Publishing—R
(s)-Providence House—R
Reformation Heritage—R
Rose Publishing
Standard Publishing
(s)-Star Bible Public.
Starik Publishing
Still Waters Revival—R
(s)-Tate Publishing—R
(s)-TEACH Services—R
(s)-Trafford Publishing—R
(s)-WinePress—R
(s)-Word Alive
(s)-Zoë Life Publishing

CHRISTIAN LIVING
(a)-B & H Publishing
(a)-Baker Books
(a)-Bethany House—R

(a)-Cook, David C.

(a)-Doubleday Relig.—R

(a)-FaithWords

(a)-HarperOne

(a)-Harvest House

(a)-Multnomah

(a)-Nelson, Thomas

(a)-Regal

(a)-Revell

(a)-Tyndale House—R

(a)-WaterBrook Press—R

(a)-W Publishing

Aadeon Publishing—R

Aaron Book—R

Abingdon Press

ACTA Publications

(s)-ACW Press—R

Ambassador Books

Ambassador Intl.—R

(s)-American Binding—R

Barbour

Beacon Hill Press—R

(s)-Bfree Publishing

(s)-Black Forest—R

Blue Dolphin

(s)-Booklocker.com—R

(s)-Bookstand Publishing—R

(s)-Brentwood—R

(s)-Brown Books

Canticle Books—R

Chalice Press—R

Christian Family—R

Christian Focus—R

Christian Writer's Ebook—R

CLC Publications—R

Comfort Publishing

(s)-Creation House—R

CrossLink Publishing

Crossroad Publishing—R

Crossway

CSS Publishing—R

(s)-DCTS Publishers

(s)-Deep River Books

(s)-Destiny Image (books)—R

Dimensions for Living

Discovery House—R

Editorial Portavoz

Eerdmans Pub., Wm. B.—R

(s)-E.F.S. Online Pub.

(s)-Elderberry Press

Elijah Press

Emmaus Road

(s)-Essence—R

Evangelical Press

Evergreen Press

Fair Havens—R

(s)-Fairway Press—R

(s)-Faith Books & More—R

FaithWalk

Father's Press

(s)-Forever Books—R

Forward Movement

Four Craftsmen—R

Fresh Air Books

(s)-Grace Acres Press—R

GRQ—R

Guideposts Books

HeartSpring Pub.—R

Hendrickson—R

Hidden Brook Press—R

His Work Christian Pub.—R

(s)-Holy Fire Publishing—R

Hope Publishing—R

Howard Books

(s)-IMD Press—R

(s)-Impact Christian—R

Inheritance Press

(s)-Insight Publishing—R

InterVarsity Press—R

Jebaire

Jesus Filled Day (books)

JourneyForth/BJU

Judson Press—R

(s)-Kindred Books—R

Kingsley Pub., Jessica—R

Life Changing Media

Life Cycle Books—R

Lift Every Voice—R

Lighthouse Publishing—R

Lighthouse Trails—R

Lion and Lamb

Liturgical Press

Lutheran Univ. Press

Lutheran Voices

Lutterworth Press—R

Magnus Press—R

Master Books

(s)-McDougal Publishing—R

Millennium III—R

Monarch Books

Moody Publishers

NavPress

New Hope—R

New Leaf

Nordskog Publishing—R

On My Own Now—R

(s)-One World—R

Our Sunday Visitor—R

Parsons Publishing—R

Pauline Kids—R

Pilgrim Press—R

(s)-Pleasant Word—R

(s)-Port Hole Public.

Power Publishing—R

(s)-Providence House—R

Quintessential Books—R

Ragged Edge—R

Randall House

Reformation Heritage—R

Reformation Trust

Review and Herald

(s)-Rill & Associates

Rose Publishing

(s)-Salvation Publisher—R

Samaritan Press—R

(s)-Selah Publishing—R

Smyth & Helwys

Standard Publishing

St. Anthony Mess. Press—R

(s)-Star Bible Public.

Starik Publishing

Still Waters Revival—R

Strang Book—R

Sunpenny Publishing

(s)-Tate Publishing—R

Tau-Publishing—R

(s)-TEACH Services—R

Th1nk/NavPress—R

Torch Legacy

(s)-Trafford Publishing—R

Treble Heart—R

UMI Publishing—R

Univ. Press of America—R

VBC Publishing

Wesleyan Publishing

Westminster John Knox

(s)-WinePress—R

(s)-Word Alive

(s)-Zoë Life Publishing

CHRISTIAN SCHOOL BOOKS

(a)-Baker Books
Aaron Book—R
(s)-ACW Press—R
(s)-American Binding—R
(s)-Bfree Publishing
Blue Dolphin
(s)-Booklocker.com—R
(s)-Bookstand Publishing—R
Carson-Dellosa
Christian Liberty Press
Christian Writer's Ebook—R
CrossLink Publishing
CSS Publishing—R
(s)-Dean Press, Robbie—R
Eerdmans Pub., Wm. B.—R
(s)-E.F.S. Online Pub.
(s)-Elderberry Press
(s)-Essence—R
ETC Publications
Facts On File
(s)-Fairway Press—R
(s)-Faith Books & More—R
Father's Press
(s)-Forever Books—R
(s)-Grace Acres Press—R
Heart of Wisdom
Hidden Brook Press—R
(s)-Holy Fire Publishing—R
(s)-IMD Press—R
Inkling Books—R
(s)-Insight Publishing—R
JourneyForth/BJU
Kingsley Pub., Jessica—R
Knight George Pub.
Lighthouse Publishing—R
Lion and Lamb
Mason Crest
McRuffy Press
Monarch Books
New Canaan—R
(s)-One World—R
Our Sunday Visitor—R
Pacific Press
Pauline Kids—R
(s)-Pleasant Word—R
Power Publishing—R
(s)-Providence House—R
Rose Publishing

(s)-So. Baptist Press—R
(s)-Star Bible Public.
Starik Publishing
(s)-Tate Publishing—R
(s)-Trafford Publishing—R
Trinity Foundation—R
(s)-WinePress—R
(s)-Word Alive
(s)-Zoë Life Publishing

CHRISTMAS BOOKS

(s)-Bfree Publishing
Chalice Press—R
(s)-Essence—R
GRQ—R
(s)-IMD Press—R
(s)-MileStones Intl.
(s)-Rill & Associates
Warner Press
(s)-Zoë Life Publishing

CHURCH GROWTH*

(a)-Kregel—R

Aadeon Publishing—R
Aaron Book—R
Ambassador Intl.—R
(s)-Bfree Publishing
(s)-Booklocker.com—R
(s)-Book Publishers Net.—R
(s)-Bookstand Publishing—R
Boyds Mills Press—R
(s)-Brown Books
Chalice Press—R
(s)-CrossHouse—R
Dove Inspirational—R
Eerdmans/Yg Readers
(s)-Essence—R
(s)-Faith Books & More—R
(s)-Forever Books—R
(s)-Grace Acres Press—R
Guardian Angel
His Work Christian Pub.—R
(s)-Holy Fire Publishing—R
(s)-IMD Press—R
Knight George Pub.
Legacy Press—R
(s)-LifeVest Publishing
Master Books
Messianic Jewish—R

New Leaf
P & R Publishing—R
Pauline Kids—R
Pelican Publishing—R
(s)-Providence House—R
Putnam/Young Readers
Randall House
Revival Nation
(s)-Salt Works—R
(s)-Salty's Books—R
Samaritan Press—R
(s)-WinePress—R
(s)-Zoë Life Publishing

CHURCH HISTORY

(a)-B & H Publishing
(a)-Baker Books
(a)-Doubleday Relig.—R
(a)-HarperOne
(a)-Kregel—R

Aaron Book—R
Abingdon Press
ACTA Publications
(s)-ACW Press—R
Ambassador Intl.—R
(s)-American Binding—R
Anglicans United—R
Baylor Univ. Press
(s)-Bfree Publishing
(s)-Black Forest—R
Blue Dolphin
(s)-Booklocker.com—R
(s)-Bookstand Publishing—R
Boyds Mills Press—R
Branden Publishing—R
Carey Library, Wm.—R
Catholic Answers—R
Chapter Two—R
Christian Family—R
Christian Focus—R
Christian Heritage—R
Christian Writer's Ebook—R
Cistercian—R
Clarke & Co., James—R
College Press—R
Continuum Intl.—R
(s)-Creation House—R
(s)-CrossHouse—R
CrossLink Publishing

Crossroad Publishing—R
Crossway
CSS Publishing—R
Earthen Vessel—R
Editorial Portavoz
Eerdmans Pub., Wm. B.—R
(s)-E.F.S. Online Pub.
(s)-Elderberry Press
Elijah Press
Emmaus Road
(s)-Essence—R
Evangelical Press
(s)-Fairway Press—R
(s)-Faith Books & More—R
FaithWalk
Father's Press
(s)-Forever Books—R
Fortress Press
Forward Movement
Founders Press
Hannibal Books
Hendrickson—R
Hidden Brook Press—R
(s)-Holy Fire Publishing—R
(s)-IMD Press—R
(s)-Insight Publishing—R
InterVarsity Press—R
Intl. Awakening—R
Kirk House
Leafwood
Libros Liguori
Lighthouse Publishing—R
Lion and Lamb
Loyola Press
Lutheran Univ. Press
Lutterworth Press—R
Mercer Univ. Press—R
Messianic Jewish—R
Millennium III—R
Monarch Books
New Canaan—R
New York Univ. Press
Nordskog Publishing—R
(s)-One World—R
Our Sunday Visitor—R
Pacific Press
Palgrave Macmillan—R
Pauline Books—R
Paulist Press
(s)-Pleasant Word—R

Power Publishing—R
(s)-Providence House—R
Quintessential Books—R
Randall House
Reformation Heritage—R
Reformation Trust
Revival Nation
Rose Publishing
Scepter Publishers—R
(s)-Selah Publishing—R
Sheed & Ward
Smyth & Helwys
(s)-Star Bible Public.
St. Anthony Mess. Press—R
St. Bede's Public.—R
(s)-Tate Publishing—R
Th1nk/NavPress—R
Third World Press—R
(s)-Trafford Publishing—R
Trinity Foundation—R
Univ. of AR Press—R
Univ. Press of America—R
Westminster John Knox
(s)-WinePress—R
Wipf and Stock
(s)-Word Alive
Yale Univ. Press
(s)-Zoë Life Publishing
Zondervan

CHURCH LIFE
(a)-Baker Books
(a)-Bethany House—R
(a)-Doubleday Relig.—R
(a)-HarperOne
(a)-Kregel—R
(a)-Nelson, Thomas
(a)-W Publishing

Aaron Book—R
Abingdon Press
(s)-ACW Press—R
Ambassador Intl.—R
(s)-American Binding—R
(s)-Bfree Publishing
(s)-Black Forest—R
Blue Dolphin
(s)-Booklocker.com—R
(s)-Brentwood—R
Chalice Press—R

Chapter Two—R
CharismaKids
Christian Writer's Ebook—R
Clarke & Co., James—R
CLC Publications—R
Continuum Intl.—R
(s)-Creation House—R
Crossway
CSS Publishing—R
(s)-DCTS Publishers
(s)-Deep River Books
Destiny Image (gifts)—R
Discovery House—R
Earthen Vessel—R
Editorial Unilit
Eerdmans Pub., Wm. B.—R
(s)-E.F.S. Online Pub.
(s)-Elderberry Press
Emmaus Road
(s)-Essence—R
Evangelical Press
(s)-Fairway Press—R
(s)-Faith Books & More—R
FaithWalk
Father's Press
(s)-Forever Books—R
Forward Movement
(s)-Grace Acres Press—R
Hannibal Books
Harrison House
Hendrickson—R
Hidden Brook Press—R
(s)-Holy Fire Publishing—R
Hope Publishing—R
Howard Books
(s)-IMD Press—R
(s)-Impact Christian—R
(s)-Insight Publishing—R
InterVarsity Press—R
Jubilant Press—R
Judson Press—R
Kirk House
Leafwood
Libros Liguori
Lift Every Voice—R
Lighthouse Publishing—R
Lion and Lamb
Lutheran Univ. Press
Lutterworth Press—R
Monarch Books

NavPress
New Hope—R
Nordskog Publishing—R
(s)-One World—R
P & R Publishing—R
Pacific Press
Palgrave Macmillan—R
Pauline Kids—R
Pilgrim Press—R
(s)-Pleasant Word—R
Power Publishing—R
(s)-Providence House—R
Quintessential Books—R
Randall House
Reformation Heritage—R
Reformation Trust
Resource Public.
Revival Nation
(s)-Selah Publishing—R
Smyth & Helwys
(s)-Star Bible Public.
Strang Book—R
(s)-Tate Publishing—R
(s)-TEACH Services—R
Th1nk/NavPress—R
Torch Legacy
Touch Publications—R
(s)-Trafford Publishing—R
Wesleyan Publishing
Westminster John Knox
(s)-WinePress—R
(s)-Word Alive
Youth Specialties
(s)-Zoë Life Publishing

CHURCH MANAGEMENT
(a)-B & H Publishing
(a)-Doubleday Relig.—R
(a)-Kregel—R

Aaron Book—R
Abingdon Press
(s)-ACW Press—R
Ambassador Intl.—R
(s)-American Binding—R
(s)-Bfree Publishing
(s)-Black Forest—R
Blue Dolphin
BMH Books—R
(s)-Booklocker.com—R

Chalice Press—R
Christian Heritage—R
CLC Publications—R
Conquest Publishers
(s)-Creation House—R
CSS Publishing—R
Eerdmans Pub., Wm. B.—R
(s)-Elderberry Press
(s)-Essence—R
Evangelical Press
(s)-Fairway Press—R
(s)-Faith Books & More—R
Father's Press
(s)-Forever Books—R
(s)-Grace Acres Press—R
Group Publishing
Hannibal Books
Harrison House
Hidden Brook Press—R
(s)-Holy Fire Publishing—R
Hope Publishing—R
(s)-IMD Press—R
(s)-Insight Publishing—R
JourneyForth/BJU
Judson Press—R
Kirk House
Lighthouse Publishing—R
Lion and Lamb
Lutheran Univ. Press
Monarch Books
Nordskog Publishing—R
(s)-One World—R
Our Sunday Visitor—R
(s)-Pleasant Word—R
Power Publishing—R
(s)-Providence House—R
Randall House
(s)-Star Bible Public.
Strang Book—R
(s)-Tate Publishing—R
(s)-TEACH Services—R
(s)-Trafford Publishing—R
Wesleyan Publishing
(s)-WinePress—R
(s)-Word Alive
(s)-Zoë Life Publishing

CHURCH RENEWAL
(a)-Baker Books
(a)-Doubleday Relig.—R

(a)-HarperOne
(a)-Kregel—R

Aaron Book—R
Abingdon Press
(s)-ACW Press—R
Ambassador Intl.—R
(s)-American Binding—R
(s)-Bfree Publishing
Blue Dolphin
BMH Books—R
(s)-Booklocker.com—R
(s)-Brentwood—R
Bridge Logos—R
Canticle Books—R
Carey Library, Wm.—R
CharismaKids
Christian Focus—R
Christian Writer's Ebook—R
Church Growth Inst.
CLC Publications—R
(s)-Creation House—R
CSS Publishing—R
(s)-Deep River Books
Destiny Image (gifts)—R
(s)-Destiny Image (books)—R
Earthen Vessel—R
Eerdmans Pub., Wm. B.—R
(s)-Elderberry Press
Emmaus Road
(s)-Essence—R
Evangelical Press
(s)-Fairway Press—R
(s)-Faith Books & More—R
FaithWalk
Father's Press
(s)-Forever Books—R
Forward Movement
Four Craftsmen—R
(s)-Grace Acres Press—R
Hannibal Books
Hidden Brook Press—R
(s)-Holy Fire Publishing—R
Hope Publishing—R
Howard Books
(s)-IMD Press—R
(s)-Impact Christian—R
(s)-Insight Publishing—R
InterVarsity Press—R
Intl. Awakening—R

Judson Press—R
Libros Liguori
Lighthouse Publishing—R
Lion and Lamb
Lutheran Univ. Press
Lutterworth Press—R
Magnus Press—R
(s)-McDougal Publishing—R
(s)-MileStones Intl.
Monarch Books
Nordskog Publishing—R
(s)-One World—R
Pacific Press
Parson Place—R
Pilgrim Press—R
(s)-Pleasant Word—R
Power Publishing—R
(s)-Providence House—R
Quintessential Books—R
Randall House
Reformation Heritage—R
Resource Public.
Revival Nation
(s)-Salvation Publisher—R
(s)-Selah Publishing—R
(s)-Sermon Select Press
Smyth & Helwys
(s)-So. Baptist Press—R
(s)-Star Bible Public.
(s)-Tate Publishing—R
(s)-TEACH Services—R
Th1nk/NavPress—R
(s)-Trafford Publishing—R
Wesleyan Publishing
Westminster John Knox
(s)-WinePress—R
(s)-Word Alive
(s)-Zoë Life Publishing

CHURCH TRADITIONS
(a)-Baker Books
(a)-Doubleday Relig.—R
(a)-Kregel—R
(a)-Nelson, Thomas

Aaron Book—R
Abingdon Press
(s)-ACW Press—R
Ambassador Intl.—R
(s)-American Binding—R

Anglicans United—R
(s)-Bfree Publishing
(s)-Black Forest—R
Blue Dolphin
(s)-Booklocker.com—R
Boyds Mills Press—R
Carey Library, Wm.—R
Catholic Answers—R
Christian Family—R
Christian Heritage—R
Christian Writer's Ebook—R
Cistercian—R
Clarke & Co., James—R
Conciliar Press—R
Continuum Intl.—R
(s)-Creation House—R
CSS Publishing—R
(s)-Deep River Books
Earthen Vessel—R
Eerdmans Pub., Wm. B.—R
(s)-E.F.S. Online Pub.
(s)-Elderberry Press
Emmaus Road
(s)-Essence—R
(s)-Fairway Press—R
(s)-Faith Books & More—R
FaithWalk
Father's Press
(s)-Forever Books—R
Forward Movement
Founders Press
Hidden Brook Press—R
(s)-Holy Fire Publishing—R
Howard Books
(s)-IMD Press—R
Inkling Books—R
(s)-Insight Publishing—R
InterVarsity Press—R
Libros Liguori
Lighthouse Publishing—R
Lion and Lamb
Lutheran Univ. Press
Lutterworth Press—R
Monarch Books
New York Univ. Press
Nordskog Publishing—R
(s)-One World—R
Our Sunday Visitor—R
Pacific Press
Palgrave Macmillan—R

Pauline Kids—R
(s)-Pleasant Word—R
Power Publishing—R
Praeger Publishers
(s)-Providence House—R
Rose Publishing
St. Anthony Mess. Press—R
(s)-Star Bible Public.
St. Bede's Public.—R
St. Pauls/Alba—R
(s)-Tate Publishing—R
Th1nk/NavPress—R
(s)-Trafford Publishing—R
(s)-WinePress—R
(s)-Word Alive
(s)-Zoë Life Publishing

COFFEE-TABLE BOOKS
(a)-Harvest House

Aaron Book—R
ACTA Publications
(s)-ACW Press—R
Ambassador Intl.—R
(s)-Bfree Publishing
(s)-Black Forest—R
Branden Publishing—R
(s)-Brown Books
Cistercian—R
(s)-Creation House—R
(s)-Deep River Books
(s)-Essence—R
Father's Press
(s)-Forever Books—R
GRQ—R
(s)-Halo Publishing Intl.
Hidden Brook Press—R
Kirk House
Liturgical Press
Liturgy Training—R
Lutheran Univ. Press
(s)-MileStones Intl.
Monarch Books
Nordskog Publishing—R
Players Press—R
(s)-Pleasant Word—R
(s)-Providence House—R
(s)-Salt Works—R
(s)-Salty's Books—R
Samaritan Press—R

(s)-TEACH Services—R
(s)-Trafford Publishing—R
(s)-WinePress—R
(s)-Zoë Life Publishing

COMPILATIONS
(a)-Doubleday Relig.—R
(a)-WaterBrook Press—R

Aaron Book—R
(s)-ACW Press—R
Ambassador Intl.—R
(s)-American Binding—R
Barbour
(s)-Black Forest—R
(s)-Booklocker.com—R
(s)-Bookstand Publishing—R
(s)-Brentwood—R
Chalice Press—R
Christian Heritage—R
Christian Writer's Ebook—R
CLC Publications—R
(s)-Creation House—R
(s)-Deep River Books
Earthen Vessel—R
Eerdmans Pub., Wm. B.—R
(s)-Elderberry Press
(s)-Essence—R
(s)-Fairway Press—R
(s)-Faith Books & More—R
Father's Press
(s)-Forever Books—R
Group Publishing
GRQ—R
Hidden Brook Press—R
(s)-Holy Fire Publishing—R
InterVarsity Press—R
Lighthouse Publishing—R
Monarch Books
Nordskog Publishing—R
(s)-One World—R
Palgrave Macmillan—R
(s)-Pleasant Word—R
(s)-Providence House—R
(s)-Salt Works—R
Strang Book—R
(s)-Tate Publishing—R
(s)-Trafford Publishing—R
Treble Heart—R
Univ. Press of America—R

(s)-WinePress—R
(s)-Word Alive
(s)-Zoë Life Publishing

CONTROVERSIAL ISSUES
(a)-Baker Books
(a)-Doubleday Relig.—R
(a)-FaithWords
(a)-HarperOne
(a)-Harvest House
(a)-Hay House
(a)-Kregel—R

Aadeon Publishing—R
Aaron Book—R
(s)-ACW Press—R
(s)-American Binding—R
AMG Publishers—R
(s)-Bfree Publishing
(s)-Black Forest—R
Blue Dolphin
(s)-Booklocker.com—R
(s)-Bookstand Publishing—R
(s)-Brentwood—R
Bridge Logos—R
Canadian Inst. for Law—R
Canticle Books—R
Catholic Answers—R
Chalice Press—R
Chapter Two—R
Christian Family—R
Christian Writer's Ebook—R
Conciliar Press—R
Continuum Intl.—R
(s)-Creation House—R
(s)-Dean Press, Robbie—R
(s)-Deep River Books
Destiny Image (gifts)—R
(s)-Destiny Image (books)—R
Earthen Vessel—R
Eerdmans Pub., Wm. B.—R
(s)-E.F.S. Online Pub.
(s)-Elderberry Press
(s)-Essence—R
Evangelical Press
(s)-Fairway Press—R
(s)-Faith Books & More—R
FaithWalk
Father's Press
(s)-Forever Books—R

Gentle Path Press
Hannibal Books
Hidden Brook Press—R
(s)-Holy Fire Publishing—R
Hope Publishing—R
Howard Books
Inkling Books—R
(s)-Insight Publishing—R
InterVarsity Press—R
Judson Press—R
Kingsley Pub., Jessica—R
Life Cycle Books—R
Lighthouse Publishing—R
Lighthouse Trails—R
Magnus Press—R
(s)-MileStones Intl.
Millennium III—R
Monarch Books
MountainView
Nordskog Publishing—R
(s)-One World—R
Palgrave Macmillan—R
Pilgrim Press—R
(s)-Pleasant Word—R
Power Publishing—R
(s)-Providence House—R
Ravenhawk Books—R
Resource Public.
Revival Nation
Rose Publishing
(s)-Salt Works—R
(s)-Selah Publishing—R
Still Waters Revival—R
Strang Book—R
(s)-Tate Publishing—R
Th1nk/NavPress—R
(s)-Trafford Publishing—R
(s)-WinePress—R
(s)-Word Alive
(s)-Zoë Life Publishing

COOKBOOKS
(a)-Ballantine
(a)-Countryman, J.
(a)-Harvest House
(a)-Nelson, Thomas
(a)-One World/Ballantine

Aaron Book—R
Adams Media

(s)-American Binding—R
Barbour
(s)-Black Forest—R
(s)-Booklocker.com—R
(s)-Book Publishers Net.—R
(s)-Bookstand Publishing—R
(s)-Brentwood—R
Bridge Logos—R
(s)-Brown Books
Christian Writer's Ebook—R
(s)-CrossHouse—R
DiskUs Publishing
Dove Inspirational—R
Dover Publications—R
(s)-Elderberry Press
(s)-Essence—R
Evergreen Press
Extreme Diva
(s)-Fairway Press—R
(s)-Faith Books & More—R
Guardian Angel
(s)-Halo Publishing Intl.
Hannibal Books
Health Commun.
Hidden Brook Press—R
His Work Christian Pub.—R
(s)-Holy Fire Publishing—R
(s)-IMD Press—R
JourneyStone—R
(s)-LifeVest Publishing
Monarch Books
(s)-One World—R
Pacific Press
Pelican Publishing—R
(s)-Pleasant Word—R
Power Publishing—R
(s)-Providence House—R
(s)-Rill & Associates
Siloam
(s)-So. Baptist Press—R
Strang Book—R
Sunpenny Publishing
(s)-Tate Publishing—R
(s)-TEACH Services—R
Third World Press—R
(s)-Trafford Publishing—R
(s)-WinePress—R
(s)-Word Alive
Xyzzy Press
(s)-Zoë Life Publishing

COUNSELING AIDS

(a)-Baker Books
(a)-Kregel—R
(a)-Nelson, Thomas

Aaron Book—R
(s)-ACW Press—R
Ambassador Intl.—R
(s)-American Binding—R
(s)-Bfree Publishing
(s)-Black Forest—R
Blue Dolphin
(s)-Booklocker.com—R
(s)-Brentwood—R
Bridge Logos—R
(s)-Brown Books
CarePoint Publishing—R
Chalice Press—R
Christian Family—R
Christian Writer's Ebook—R
CSS Publishing—R
(s)-Dean Press, Robbie—R
(s)-Deep River Books
Editorial Portavoz
Eerdmans Pub., Wm. B.—R
(s)-E.F.S. Online Pub.
(s)-Elderberry Press
(s)-Essence—R
Evangelical Press
Evergreen Press
Fair Havens—R
(s)-Fairway Press—R
(s)-Faith Books & More—R
FaithWalk
Father's Press
(s)-Forever Books—R
Four Craftsmen—R
Gentle Path Press
Good Book—R
Hidden Brook Press—R
(s)-Holy Fire Publishing—R
(s)-Insight Publishing—R
InterVarsity Press—R
JourneyForth/BJU
Kingsley Pub., Jessica—R
Langmarc
Leafwood
Life Cycle Books—R
Lighthouse Publishing—R
Lion and Lamb

(s)-McDougal Publishing—R
Millennium III—R
Monarch Books
Nordskog Publishing—R
(s)-One World—R
On My Own Now—R
P & R Publishing—R
Paradise Research—R
Pilgrim Press—R
(s)-Pleasant Word—R
Power Publishing—R
(s)-Providence House—R
Quintessential Books—R
Randall House
Reference Service
(s)-Sermon Select Press
(s)-So. Baptist Press—R
(s)-Star Bible Public.
Strang Book—R
(s)-Tate Publishing—R
(s)-Trafford Publishing—R
Treble Heart—R
(s)-WinePress—R
(s)-Word Alive
Youth Specialties
(s)-Zoë Life Publishing

CREATION SCIENCE

(a)-Harvest House

Aaron Book—R
(s)-ACW Press—R
Ambassador Intl.—R
(s)-American Binding—R
(s)-Bfree Publishing
(s)-Black Forest—R
Blue Dolphin
BMH Books—R
(s)-Booklocker.com—R
(s)-Bookstand Publishing—R
Bridge Logos—R
Cambridge Scholars
Chapter Two—R
Christian Family—R
Christian Writer's Ebook—R
Editorial Portavoz
Eerdmans Pub., Wm. B.—R
(s)-Elderberry Press
(s)-Essence—R
Evangelical Press

Fair Havens—R
(s)-Fairway Press—R
(s)-Faith Books & More—R
(s)-Forever Books—R
Hidden Brook Press—R
(s)-Holy Fire Publishing—R
Hope Publishing—R
Inkling Books—R
(s)-Insight Publishing—R
Lighthouse Publishing—R
Master Books
Millennium III—R
Monarch Books
New Leaf
Nordskog Publishing—R
(s)-One World—R
Pacific Press
Palgrave Macmillan—R
Parson Place—R
(s)-Pleasant Word—R
Power Publishing—R
(s)-Providence House—R
Reformation Heritage—R
(s)-Salt Works—R
(s)-Star Bible Public.
Strang Book—R
(s)-Tate Publishing—R
(s)-TEACH Services—R
Th1nk/NavPress—R
(s)-Trafford Publishing—R
Whitaker House
(s)-WinePress—R
(s)-Word Alive
(s)-Zoë Life Publishing

CULTS/OCCULT
(a)-Baker Books
(a)-HarperOne
(a)-Harvest House
(a)-Kregel—R

Aaron Book—R
(s)-ACW Press—R
(s)-American Binding—R
(s)-Black Forest—R
(s)-Booklocker.com—R
Catholic Answers—R
Chapter Two—R
Christian Writer's Ebook—R
CLC Publications—R
Comfort Publishing

Conciliar Press—R
Editorial Portavoz
Eerdmans Pub., Wm. B.—R
(s)-Elderberry Press
(s)-Essence—R
Evangelical Press
(s)-Fairway Press—R
(s)-Faith Books & More—R
(s)-Forever Books—R
Hidden Brook Press—R
(s)-Holy Fire Publishing—R
(s)-IMD Press—R
(s)-Impact Christian—R
(s)-Insight Publishing—R
Lighthouse Publishing—R
Monarch Books
New York Univ. Press
Nordskog Publishing—R
(s)-One World—R
Palgrave Macmillan—R
(s)-Pleasant Word—R
Power Publishing—R
(s)-Providence House—R
Ravenhawk Books—R
Revival Nation
Rose Publishing
(s)-Selah Publishing—R
(s)-Star Bible Public.
(s)-Tate Publishing—R
(s)-Trafford Publishing—R
Whitaker House
(s)-WinePress—R
(s)-Word Alive

CURRENT/SOCIAL ISSUES
(a)-B & H Publishing
(a)-Baker Academic
(a)-Baker Books
(a)-Bethany House—R
(a)-Doubleday Relig.—R
(a)-FaithWords
(a)-HarperOne
(a)-Harvest House
(a)-Kregel—R
(a)-Nelson, Thomas
(a)-Tyndale House—R
(a)-W Publishing

Aadeon Publishing—R
Aaron Book—R
(s)-ACW Press—R

(s)-American Binding—R
AMG Publishers—R
(s)-Ampelos Press
Beacon Hill Press—R
(s)-Black Forest—R
Blue Dolphin
(s)-Booklocker.com—R
(s)-Bookstand Publishing—R
Boyds Mills Press—R
Branden Publishing—R
(s)-Brentwood—R
Bridge Logos—R
(s)-Brown Books
Canadian Inst. for Law—R
Catholic Answers—R
Chalice Press—R
Christian Family—R
Christian Writer's Ebook—R
Conari Press
Concordia Academic
(s)-Creation House—R
CrossLink Publishing
Crossroad Publishing—R
(s)-DCTS Publishers
(s)-Deep River Books
(s)-Deo Volente
Destiny Image (gifts)—R
Editorial Portavoz
Eerdmans Pub., Wm. B.—R
(s)-E.F.S. Online Pub.
(s)-Elderberry Press
Eldridge Plays
(s)-Essence—R
Evangelical Press
(s)-Fairway Press—R
(s)-Faith Books & More—R
FaithWalk
Father's Press
(s)-Forever Books—R
Forward Movement
Gentle Path Press
Georgetown Univ. Press
Hannibal Books
Health Commun.
Hendrickson—R
Hidden Brook Press—R
(s)-Holy Fire Publishing—R
Howard Books
(s)-IMD Press—R
Inkling Books—R

(s)-Insight Publishing—R
InterVarsity Press—R
JourneyForth/BJU
Judson Press—R
Kingsley Pub., Jessica—R
Leafwood
Life Cycle Books—R
Lighthouse Publishing—R
Liguori Public.—R
Loyola Press
Lutheran Univ. Press
Lutterworth Press—R
Master Books
Mercer Univ. Press—R
(s)-MileStones Intl.
Monarch Books
New Canaan—R
New Hope—R
New Leaf
New York Univ. Press
Nordskog Publishing—R
(s)-One World—R
On My Own Now—R
Palgrave Macmillan—R
Pilgrim Press—R
(s)-Pleasant Word—R
Power Publishing—R
(s)-Providence House—R
Putnam/Young Readers
Ravenhawk Books—R
(s)-Rill & Associates
Rose Publishing
(s)-Salt Works—R
(s)-Selah Publishing—R
Sheed & Ward
Smyth & Helwys
(s)-Star Bible Public.
Still Waters Revival—R
Strang Book—R
(s)-Tate Publishing—R
Th1nk/NavPress—R
(s)-Trafford Publishing—R
Treble Heart—R
VBC Publishing
Whitaker House
(s)-WinePress—R
(s)-Word Alive
Yale Univ. Press
(s)-Zoë Life Publishing

CURRICULUM
(a)-Cook, David C.
(a)-W Publishing

Aaron Book—R
CarePoint Publishing—R
Christian Ed. Pub.
Christian Liberty Press
College Press—R
Congregational Life
CrossLink Publishing
Eerdmans Pub., Wm. B.—R
(s)-E.F.S. Online Pub.
(s)-Elderberry Press
Facts On File
(s)-Fairway Press—R
Faith Alive
(s)-Forever Books—R
Gospel Light
Gospel Publishing
(s)-Grace Acres Press—R
Group Publishing
Hannibal Books
Hidden Brook Press—R
(s)-Holy Fire Publishing—R
(s)-IMD Press—R
Inheritance Press
Knight George Pub.
Lighthouse Publishing—R
Lighthouse Trails—R
Lion and Lamb
Mason Crest
Master Books
Messianic Jewish—R
Monarch Books
New Leaf
Northwestern
(s)-One World—R
Power Publishing—R
Praxis Press
(s)-Providence House—R
Randall House Digital
(s)-Seed Faith Books—R
Smyth & Helwys
Standard Publishing
Starik Publishing
(s)-Tate Publishing—R
(s)-Trafford Publishing—R
UMI Publishing—R
Univ. Press of America—R

(s)-WinePress—R
(s)-Word Alive
Youth Specialties
(s)-Zoë Life Publishing

DATING/SEX
(a)-Ballantine
(a)-Bethany House—R
(a)-Cook, David C.
(a)-Doubleday Relig.—R
(a)-FaithWords
(a)-HarperOne
(a)-Kregel—R
(a)-Nelson, Thomas
(a)-WaterBrook Press—R

Aaron Book—R
(s)-ACW Press—R
(s)-American Binding—R
Barbour
Blue Dolphin
(s)-Booklocker.com—R
Bridge Logos—R
Catholic Answers—R
Chalice Press—R
Chapter Two—R
Christian Writer's Ebook—R
Comfort Publishing
Crossroad Publishing—R
(s)-Deep River Books
(s)-Destiny Image (books)—R
Eerdmans Pub., Wm. B.—R
(s)-E.F.S. Online Pub.
(s)-Elderberry Press
Emmaus Road
(s)-Essence—R
Evangelical Press
Evergreen Press
(s)-Fairway Press—R
(s)-Faith Books & More—R
FaithWalk
Fell, Frederick—R
(s)-Forever Books—R
Forward Movement
Gentle Path Press
GRQ—R
Health Commun.
Hidden Brook Press—R
(s)-Holy Fire Publishing—R
(s)-IMD Press—R

(s)-Insight Publishing—R
Lift Every Voice—R
Lighthouse Publishing—R
Monarch Books
Nordskog Publishing—R
(s)-One World—R
On My Own Now—R
P & R Publishing—R
Palgrave Macmillan—R
Pauline Books—R
(s)-Pleasant Word—R
Power Publishing—R
(s)-Providence House—R
Rose Publishing
Siloam
(s)-Star Bible Public.
Strang Book—R
(s)-Tate Publishing—R
Th1nk/NavPress—R
Third World Press—R
(s)-Trafford Publishing—R
Whitaker House
(s)-WinePress—R
(s)-Word Alive
Youth Specialties
(s)-Zoë Life Publishing

DEATH/DYING

(a)-Baker Books
(a)-Cook, David C.
(a)-Doubleday Relig.—R
(a)-HarperOne
(a)-Kregel—R
(a)-Nelson, Thomas
(a)-WaterBrook Press—R

Aaron Book—R
Abingdon Press
ACTA Publications
(s)-ACW Press—R
(s)-American Binding—R
(s)-Black Forest—R
Blue Dolphin
(s)-Booklocker.com—R
(s)-Book Publishers Net.—R
Bridge Logos—R
(s)-Brown Books
Chalice Press—R
Christian Family—R
Christian Writer's Ebook—R

Comfort Publishing
(s)-Creation House—R
Crossroad Publishing—R
CSS Publishing—R
(s)-Deep River Books
Discovery House—R
Editorial Portavoz
Eerdmans Pub., Wm. B.—R
(s)-E.F.S. Online Pub.
(s)-Elderberry Press
Emmaus Road
(s)-Essence—R
Evangelical Press
Evergreen Press
(s)-Fairway Press—R
(s)-Faith Books & More—R
FaithWalk
Father's Press
(s)-Forever Books—R
Forward Movement
GRQ—R
Guardian Angel
(s)-Halo Publishing Intl.
Health Commun.
Hidden Brook Press—R
(s)-Holy Fire Publishing—R
Hope Publishing—R
(s)-IMD Press—R
(s)-Insight Publishing—R
Kingsley Pub., Jessica—R
Life Cycle Books—R
Lift Every Voice—R
Lighthouse Publishing—R
Lion and Lamb
Loyola Press
Lutheran Univ. Press
Monarch Books
Nordskog Publishing—R
(s)-One World—R
P & R Publishing—R
Pacific Press
Palgrave Macmillan—R
Pauline Books—R
Paulist Press
Pilgrim Press—R
(s)-Pleasant Word—R
Power Publishing—R
(s)-Providence House—R
Reformation Heritage—R
Rose Publishing

Sheed & Ward
Siloam
Smyth & Helwys
(s)-Star Bible Public.
Strang Book—R
(s)-Tate Publishing—R
(s)-TEACH Services—R
Third World Press—R
(s)-Trafford Publishing—R
Whitaker House
(s)-WinePress—R
(s)-Word Alive
(s)-Zoë Life Publishing

DEVOTIONAL BOOKS

(a)-Baker Books
(a)-Bethany House—R
(a)-Cook, David C.
(a)-Countryman, J.
(a)-Doubleday Relig.—R
(a)-FaithWords
(a)-HarperOne
(a)-Harvest House
(a)-Kregel—R
(a)-Nelson, Thomas
(a)-Regal
(a)-Tyndale House—R
(a)-WaterBrook Press—R
(a)-W Publishing

Aaron Book—R
Abingdon Press
(s)-ACW Press—R
Ambassador Books
Ambassador Intl.—R
(s)-American Binding—R
(s)-Ampelos Press
Barbour
(s)-Bfree Publishing
(s)-Black Forest—R
Blue Dolphin
(s)-Booklocker.com—R
(s)-Bookstand Publishing—R
(s)-Brentwood—R
(s)-Brown Books
Chalice Press—R
Chapter Two—R
Christian Family—R
Christian Focus—R
Christian Heritage—R
Christian Writer's Ebook—R

Church Publishing
CLC Publications—R
Congregational Life
Conquest Publishers
Contemporary Drama
Continuum Intl.—R
(s)-Creation House—R
CrossLink Publishing
CSS Publishing—R
(s)-Deep River Books
Dimensions for Living
Discovery House—R
Editorial Portavoz
Eerdmans Pub., Wm. B.—R
(s)-E.ES. Online Pub.
(s)-Elderberry Press
Emmaus Road
(s)-Essence—R
Evangelical Press
Evergreen Press
Extreme Diva
Fair Havens—R
(s)-Fairway Press—R
(s)-Faith Books & More—R
FaithWalk
(s)-Forever Books—R
Forward Movement
Founders Press
Friends United Press
(s)-Fruitbearer Pub.
Group Publishing
GRQ—R
Guideposts Books
Hannibal Books
Harrison House
HeartSpring Pub.—R
Hidden Brook Press—R
(s)-Holy Fire Publishing—R
Howard Books
(s)-IMD Press—R
(s)-Impact Christian—R
Inheritance Press
Inkling Books—R
(s)-Insight Publishing—R
Judson Press—R
Leafwood
Legacy Press—R
Libros Liguori
Lift Every Voice—R
Lighthouse Publishing—R

Liguori Public.—R
Lion and Lamb
Lutterworth Press—R
Master Books
(s)-McDougal Publishing—R
Messianic Jewish—R
Mission City Press
Monarch Books
MOPS Intl.
New Hope—R
New Leaf
Nordskog Publishing—R
(s)-One World—R
On My Own Now—R
P & R Publishing—R
Parson Place—R
Parsons Publishing—R
Pauline Books—R
Pilgrim Press—R
(s)-Pleasant Word—R
Power Publishing—R
Praxis Press
(s)-Providence House—R
Ragged Edge—R
Reformation Heritage—R
Revival Nation
Rose Publishing
(s)-Salt Works—R
(s)-Salvation Publisher—R
Samaritan Press—R
(s)-Selah Publishing—R
Smyth & Helwys
Standard Publishing
St. Anthony Mess. Press—R
(s)-Star Bible Public.
Strang Book—R
(s)-Tate Publishing—R
(s)-Trafford Publishing—R
Treble Heart—R
VBC Publishing
Warner Press
Wesleyan Publishing
(s)-WinePress—R
(s)-Word Alive
Youth Specialties
(s)-Zoë Life Publishing

DISCIPLESHIP
(a)-B & H Publishing
(a)-Baker Books

(a)-Bethany House—R
(a)-Cook, David C.
(a)-Doubleday Relig.—R
(a)-HarperOne
(a)-Kregel—R
(a)-Nelson, Thomas
(a)-Regal
(a)-WaterBrook Press—R
(a)-W Publishing

Aadeon Publishing—R
Aaron Book—R
Abingdon Press
(s)-ACW Press—R
Ambassador Intl.—R
(s)-American Binding—R
Anglicans United—R
Barbour
Beacon Hill Press—R
(s)-Bfree Publishing
(s)-Black Forest—R
Blue Dolphin
BMH Books—R
(s)-Booklocker.com—R
(s)-Bookstand Publishing—R
(s)-Brentwood—R
Bridge Logos—R
(s)-Brown Books
Carey Library, Wm.—R
Chalice Press—R
Chapter Two—R
CharismaKids
Christian Family—R
Christian Focus—R
Christian Heritage—R
Christian Writer's Ebook—R
CLC Publications—R
College Press—R
Conquest Publishers
Continuum Intl.—R
(s)-Creation House—R
Crossway
CSS Publishing—R
(s)-DCTS Publishers
(s)-Deep River Books
(s)-Deo Volente
(s)-Destiny Image (books)—R
Discovery House—R
Editorial Portavoz
Eerdmans Pub., Wm. B.—R

(s)-E.F.S. Online Pub.
(s)-Elderberry Press
(s)-Essence—R
Evangelical Press
Evergreen Press
Fair Havens—R
(s)-Fairway Press—R
(s)-Faith Books & More—R
FaithWalk
Father's Press
(s)-Forever Books—R
Forward Movement
Founders Press
Four Craftsmen—R
Foursquare Media
Gospel Publishing
(s)-Grace Acres Press—R
Group Publishing
Harrison House
Hendrickson—R
Hensley Publishing
Hidden Brook Press—R
(s)-Holy Fire Publishing—R
Howard Books
(s)-IMD Press—R
Inheritance Press
Inkling Books—R
(s)-Insight Publishing—R
InterVarsity Press—R
Jebaire
JourneyForth/BJU
Judson Press—R
Lift Every Voice—R
Lighthouse Publishing—R
Lion and Lamb
Lutheran Univ. Press
Master Books
(s)-McDougal Publishing—R
Messianic Jewish—R
Mission City Press
Monarch Books
Moody Publishers
NavPress
New Hope—R
New Leaf
Nordskog Publishing—R
(s)-One World—R
On My Own Now—R
P & R Publishing—R
Pacific Press

Parson Place—R
Pauline Books—R
Pilgrim Press—R
(s)-Pleasant Word—R
Power Publishing—R
Praxis Press
(s)-Providence House—R
Quintessential Books—R
Randall House
Reformation Trust
Revival Nation
Rose Publishing
(s)-Salt Works—R
(s)-Salvation Publisher—R
Samaritan Press—R
Smyth & Helwys
(s)-So. Baptist Press—R
Standard Publishing
(s)-Star Bible Public.
Strang Book—R
(s)-Tate Publishing—R
(s)-TEACH Services—R
Th1nk/NavPress—R
Touch Publications—R
(s)-Trafford Publishing—R
Whitaker House
(s)-WinePress—R
(s)-Word Alive
Youth Specialties
(s)-Zoë Life Publishing

DIVORCE
(a)-Baker Books
(a)-Bethany House—R
(a)-Cook, David C.
(a)-Kregel—R
(a)-Nelson, Thomas
(a)-WaterBrook Press—R

Aaron Book—R
(s)-ACW Press—R
Ambassador Books
Ambassador Intl.—R
(s)-American Binding—R
(s)-Bfree Publishing
(s)-Black Forest—R
Blue Dolphin
(s)-Booklocker.com—R
(s)-Brentwood—R
Bridge Logos—R

(s)-Brown Books
Christian Writer's Ebook—R
College Press—R
Comfort Publishing
(s)-Creation House—R
CSS Publishing—R
(s)-Dean Press, Robbie—R
(s)-Deep River Books
Earthen Vessel—R
Editorial Portavoz
Eerdmans Pub., Wm. B.—R
(s)-E.F.S. Online Pub.
(s)-Elderberry Press
(s)-Essence—R
Evangelical Press
Fair Havens—R
(s)-Fairway Press—R
(s)-Faith Books & More—R
FaithWalk
(s)-Forever Books—R
Forward Movement
Gentle Path Press
Guideposts Books
(s)-Halo Publishing Intl.
Health Commun.
Hidden Brook Press—R
(s)-Holy Fire Publishing—R
(s)-IMD Press—R
(s)-Insight Publishing—R
InterVarsity Press—R
Lighthouse Publishing—R
Lion and Lamb
Messianic Jewish—R
(s)-MileStones Intl.
Monarch Books
Nordskog Publishing—R
(s)-One World—R
P & R Publishing—R
Pacific Press
Pauline Books—R
(s)-Pleasant Word—R
Power Publishing—R
(s)-Providence House—R
(s)-Rill & Associates
Rose Publishing
Samaritan Press—R
(s)-So. Baptist Press—R
(s)-Star Bible Public.
Strang Book—R
(s)-Tate Publishing—R

Third World Press—R
(s)-Trafford Publishing—R
(s)-WinePress—R
(s)-Word Alive
(s)-Zoë Life Publishing

DOCTRINAL

(a)-Baker Books
(a)-Bethany House—R
(a)-Doubleday Relig.—R
(a)-Kregel—R
(a)-Tyndale House—R

Aaron Book—R
(s)-ACW Press—R
Ambassador Intl.—R
(s)-American Binding—R
Beacon Hill Press—R
(s)-Bfree Publishing
(s)-Black Forest—R
Blue Dolphin
(s)-Booklocker.com—R
(s)-Bookstand Publishing—R
(s)-Brentwood—R
(s)-Brown Books
Canticle Books—R
Catholic Answers—R
Chapter Two—R
Christian Family—R
Christian Focus—R
Christian Heritage—R
Christian Writer's Ebook—R
Cistercian—R
Clarke & Co., James—R
CLC Publications—R
College Press—R
Continuum Intl.—R
(s)-Creation House—R
Crossway
(s)-DCTS Publishers
Earthen Vessel—R
Editorial Portavoz
Eerdmans Pub., Wm. B.—R
(s)-Elderberry Press
(s)-Essence—R
Evangelical Press
Fair Havens—R
(s)-Fairway Press—R
(s)-Faith Books & More—R
(s)-Forever Books—R

Forward Movement
Hidden Brook Press—R
(s)-Holy Fire Publishing—R
(s)-IMD Press—R
(s)-Impact Christian—R
(s)-Insight Publishing—R
InterVarsity Press—R
Libros Liguori
Lighthouse Publishing—R
Liturgical Press
Lutheran Univ. Press
Messianic Jewish—R
Millennium III—R
Monarch Books
Nordskog Publishing—R
(s)-One World—R
Pacific Press
(s)-Pleasant Word—R
Power Publishing—R
(s)-Providence House—R
Randall House
Reformation Heritage—R
Reformation Trust
Review and Herald
Rose Publishing
Scepter Publishers—R
(s)-So. Baptist Press—R
(s)-Star Bible Public.
Still Waters Revival—R
(s)-Tate Publishing—R
(s)-Trafford Publishing—R
Trinity Foundation—R
UMI Publishing—R
VBC Publishing
(s)-WinePress—R
(s)-Word Alive
(s)-Zoë Life Publishing

DRAMA

(a)-Kregel—R

Aaron Book—R
(s)-American Binding—R
Baker's Plays—R
(s)-Bfree Publishing
(s)-Black Forest—R
(s)-Brentwood—R
Contemporary Drama
(s)-E.F.S. Online Pub.
(s)-Elderberry Press

Eldridge Plays
Encore Performance
Fair Havens—R
(s)-Fairway Press—R
(s)-Faith Books & More—R
(s)-Forever Books—R
Guardian Angel
Guernica Editions—R
(s)-Halo Publishing Intl.
Hidden Brook Press—R
(s)-Holy Fire Publishing—R
Lighthouse Publishing—R
Lion and Lamb
Meriwether
(s)-MileStones Intl.
Monarch Books
National Black Theatre
National Drama
Nordskog Publishing—R
(s)-One World—R
Players Press—R
(s)-Pleasant Word—R
Power Publishing—R
(s)-Providence House—R
Ravenhawk Books—R
(s)-Rill & Associates
(s)-Salt Works—R
Samaritan Press—R
(s)-So. Baptist Press—R
(s)-Tate Publishing—R
Third World Press—R
(s)-Trafford Publishing—R
Treble Heart—R
(s)-WinePress—R
(s)-Word Alive
Youth Specialties

E-BOOKS

(a)-Harvest House
(a)-Tyndale House—R

(s)-Advantage Books
Ambassador Intl.—R
(s)-Believers Press
(s)-Bfree Publishing
Blue Dolphin
(s)-Booklocker.com—R
(s)-Bookstand Publishing—R
Chalice Press—R
Christian Writer's Ebook—R

College Press—R
Comfort Publishing
CSS Publishing—R
(s)-Dean Press, Robbie—R
DiskUs Publishing
Doulos Resources—R
Emmaus Road
Evangelical Press
Fair Havens—R
(s)-Faith Books & More—R
Four Craftsmen—R
(s)-Grace Acres Press—R
Guardian Angel
(s)-IMD Press—R
InterVarsity Press—R
Jebaire
Jubilant Press—R
Life Changing Media
Lighthouse Publishing—R
Liturgical Press
Lutterworth Press—R
Master Books
(s)-MileStones Intl.
More Than Novellas
New Leaf
(s)-One World—R
Palgrave Macmillan—R
Paradise Research—R
Power Publishing—R
Randall House Digital
Resource Public.
(s)-Salt Works—R
Samaritan Press—R
(s)-Selah Publishing—R
Smyth & Helwys
Sunpenny Publishing
(s)-Trafford Publishing—R
Treble Heart—R
Univ. Press of America—R
(s)-Westbow Press
White Rose—R
(s)-Word Alive
(s)-Zoë Life Publishing

ECONOMICS

(a)-Baker Books
Aaron Book—R
(s)-ACW Press—R
(s)-American Binding—R

Baylor Univ. Press
Blue Dolphin
(s)-Booklocker.com—R
(s)-Brentwood—R
(s)-Brown Books
Canadian Inst. for Law—R
Chalice Press—R
Christian Writer's Ebook—R
(s)-Creation House—R
(s)-Deep River Books
Eerdmans Pub., Wm. B.—R
(s)-E.F.S. Online Pub.
(s)-Elderberry Press
(s)-Essence—R
Evergreen Press
(s)-Fairway Press—R
(s)-Faith Books & More—R
FaithWalk
Father's Press
(s)-Forever Books—R
Four Craftsmen—R
Hidden Brook Press—R
(s)-Holy Fire Publishing—R
(s)-Insight Publishing—R
Lighthouse Publishing—R
Master Books
Monarch Books
New Hope—R
New Leaf
Nordskog Publishing—R
(s)-One World—R
Pilgrim Press—R
(s)-Pleasant Word—R
Power Publishing—R
Praeger Publishers
(s)-Providence House—R
Quintessential Books—R
(s)-Salvation Publisher—R
Sheed & Ward
(s)-Star Bible Public.
(s)-Tate Publishing—R
(s)-TEACH Services—R
Third World Press—R
(s)-Trafford Publishing—R
Trinity Foundation—R
Univ. Press of America—R
(s)-WinePress—R
(s)-Word Alive
(s)-Zoë Life Publishing

ENCOURAGEMENT

(a)-Doubleday Relig.—R
(a)-WaterBrook Press—R

Aaron Book—R
(s)-ACW Press—R
(s)-American Binding—R
Barbour
(s)-Bfree Publishing
(s)-Black Forest—R
Blue Dolphin
(s)-Booklocker.com—R
(s)-Brown Books
CarePoint Publishing—R
Chalice Press—R
Christian Family—R
Christian Focus—R
CLC Publications—R
Comfort Publishing
(s)-Creation House—R
CSS Publishing—R
Discovery House—R
Earthen Vessel—R
Editorial Portavoz
Eerdmans Pub., Wm. B.—R
(s)-E.F.S. Online Pub.
(s)-Elderberry Press
(s)-Essence—R
Evangelical Press
Fair Havens—R
(s)-Fairway Press—R
Father's Press
(s)-Faith Books & More—R
(s)-Forever Books—R
Four Craftsmen—R
Fresh Air Books
(s)-Grace Acres Press—R
GRQ—R
Guardian Angel
Hidden Brook Press—R
(s)-Holy Fire Publishing—R
Howard Books
(s)-IMD Press—R
(s)-Insight Publishing—R
Jebaire
JourneyForth/BJU
Life Changing Media
Lift Every Voice—R
Lighthouse Publishing—R
Lion and Lamb

Messianic Jewish—R
(s)-MileStones Intl.
Monarch Books
New Hope—R
Nordskog Publishing—R
(s)-One World—R
On My Own Now—R
Parson Place—R
(s)-Pleasant Word—R
(s)-Port Hole Public.
Power Publishing—R
(s)-Providence House—R
Quintessential Books—R
Randall House
Revival Nation
(s)-Salvation Publisher—R
Samaritan Press—R
(s)-Star Bible Public.
Strang Book—R
(s)-Tate Publishing—R
Th1nk/NavPress—R
(s)-Trafford Publishing—R
VBC Publishing
(s)-WinePress—R
(s)-Word Alive
(s)-Zoë Life Publishing

ENVIRONMENTAL ISSUES
(a)-Baker Books
(a)-Doubleday Relig.—R

Aaron Book—R
ACTA Publications
(s)-ACW Press—R
(s)-American Binding—R
(s)-Black Forest—R
Blue Dolphin
(s)-Booklocker.com—R
Boyds Mills Press—R
Chalice Press—R
Christian Writer's Ebook—R
Church Publishing
Cladach Publishing
Crossroad Publishing—R
Dawn Publications
(s)-Deep River Books
Eerdmans Pub., Wm. B.—R
(s)-E.F.S. Online Pub.
(s)-Elderberry Press
(s)-Essence—R

Evangelical Press
Facts On File
(s)-Fairway Press—R
(s)-Faith Books & More—R
FaithWalk
(s)-Forever Books—R
Forward Movement
Georgetown Univ. Press
Grupo Nelson
Hendrickson—R
Hidden Brook Press—R
(s)-Holy Fire Publishing—R
(s)-Insight Publishing—R
InterVarsity Press—R
Judson Press—R
Lighthouse Publishing—R
Master Books
Monarch Books
New Leaf
Nordskog Publishing—R
(s)-One World—R
Palgrave Macmillan—R
Pilgrim Press—R
(s)-Pleasant Word—R
Power Publishing—R
Praeger Publishers
(s)-Providence House—R
Quintessential Books—R
Ravenhawk Books—R
Review and Herald
Sheed & Ward
(s)-So. Baptist Press—R
Sunpenny Publishing
Tarcher, Jeremy P.—R
(s)-Tate Publishing—R
(s)-Trafford Publishing—R
Univ. Press of America—R
(s)-WinePress—R
(s)-Word Alive

ESCHATOLOGY
(a)-Baker Books
(a)-Harvest House
(a)-Kregel—R
(a)-Nelson, Thomas

Aaron Book—R
(s)-ACW Press—R
(s)-American Binding—R
Anglicans United—R

(s)-Bfree Publishing
(s)-Black Forest—R
Blue Dolphin
BMH Books—R
(s)-Booklocker.com—R
(s)-Bookstand Publishing—R
Bridge Logos—R
Chapter Two—R
Christian Family—R
Christian Heritage—R
Christian Writer's Ebook—R
College Press—R
Conquest Publishers
Continuum Intl.—R
(s)-Creation House—R
CSS Publishing—R
(s)-DCTS Publishers
Eerdmans Pub., Wm. B.—R
(s)-Elderberry Press
Emmaus Road
(s)-Essence—R
Evangelical Press
(s)-Fairway Press—R
(s)-Faith Books & More—R
(s)-Forever Books—R
(s)-Grace Acres Press—R
Grupo Nelson
Hidden Brook Press—R
(s)-Holy Fire Publishing—R
(s)-IMD Press—R
(s)-Insight Publishing—R
Kirk House
Lighthouse Publishing—R
Lighthouse Trails—R
Lutheran Univ. Press
Messianic Jewish—R
Millennium III—R
Monarch Books
Nordskog Publishing—R
(s)-One World—R
Pacific Press
Parson Place—R
(s)-Pleasant Word—R
Power Publishing—R
(s)-Providence House—R
Reformation Heritage—R
Revival Nation
Rose Publishing
(s)-Selah Publishing—R
(s)-Star Bible Public.

St. Pauls/Alba—R
Strang Book—R
(s)-Strong Tower—R
(s)-Tate Publishing—R
(s)-TEACH Services—R
(s)-Trafford Publishing—R
VBC Publishing
(s)-WinePress—R
(s)-Word Alive
(s)-Zoë Life Publishing

ETHICS
(a)-Baker Books
(a)-Kregel—R

Aadeon Publishing—R
Aaron Book—R
(s)-ACW Press—R
(s)-American Binding—R
(s)-Bfree Publishing
(s)-Black Forest—R
Blue Dolphin
(s)-Booklocker.com—R
(s)-Bookstand Publishing—R
(s)-Brentwood—R
Cambridge Scholars
Catholic Answers—R
Christian Heritage—R
Christian Writer's Ebook—R
Clarke & Co., James—R
CLC Publications—R
Conciliar Press—R
Continuum Intl.—R
(s)-Creation House—R
Crossroad Publishing—R
Crossway
(s)-Deep River Books
Dover Publications—R
Earthen Vessel—R
Eerdmans Pub., Wm. B.—R
(s)-E.F.S. Online Pub.
(s)-Elderberry Press
(s)-Essence—R
Evangelical Press
(s)-Fairway Press—R
(s)-Faith Books & More—R
FaithWalk
Father's Press
(s)-Forever Books—R
Fortress Press

Forward Movement
Georgetown Univ. Press
(s)-Grace Acres Press—R
Guardian Angel
Hannibal Books
Hendrickson—R
Hidden Brook Press—R
(s)-Holy Fire Publishing—R
Howard Books
(s)-IMD Press—R
Inkling Books—R
(s)-Insight Publishing—R
InterVarsity Press—R
Kingsley Pub., Jessica—R
Kirk House
Leafwood
Libros Liguori
Life Cycle Books—R
Lift Every Voice—R
Lighthouse Publishing—R
Lion and Lamb
Lutheran Univ. Press
Mercer Univ. Press—R
Messianic Jewish—R
Monarch Books
(s)-One World—R
Our Sunday Visitor—R
Pacific Press
Palgrave Macmillan—R
Paragon House—R
Paulist Press
Pilgrim Press—R
(s)-Pleasant Word—R
Power Publishing—R
(s)-Providence House—R
Quintessential Books—R
Randall House
Ravenhawk Books—R
Revival Nation
(s)-Salt Works—R
Sheed & Ward
Smyth & Helwys
St. Anthony Mess. Press—R
(s)-Star Bible Public.
St. Pauls/Alba—R
Still Waters Revival—R
(s)-Tate Publishing—R
(s)-TEACH Services—R
Th1nk/NavPress—R
Third World Press—R

(s)-Trafford Publishing—R
Treble Heart—R
Trinity Foundation—R
Univ. Press of America—R
Westminster John Knox
Whitaker House
(s)-WinePress—R
(s)-Word Alive
Yale Univ. Press
(s)-Zoë Life Publishing

ETHNIC/CULTURAL
(a)-Baker Books
(a)-Doubleday Relig.—R
(a)-HarperOne
(a)-Kregel—R
(a)-One World/Ballantine

Aaron Book—R
(s)-ACW Press—R
(s)-American Binding—R
(s)-Bfree Publishing
(s)-Black Forest—R
Blue Dolphin
(s)-Booklocker.com—R
(s)-Bookstand Publishing—R
Boyds Mills Press—R
Branden Publishing—R
Bridge Logos—R
Cambridge Scholars
Carey Library, Wm.—R
CharismaKids
Christian Writer's Ebook—R
CLC Publications—R
College Press—R
Conquest Publishers
(s)-Creation House—R
(s)-Dean Press, Robbie—R
(s)-Deep River Books
Eerdmans Pub., Wm. B.—R
(s)-E.F.S. Online Pub.
(s)-Elderberry Press
Emmaus Road
(s)-Essence—R
Evangelical Press
Facts On File
(s)-Fairway Press—R
(s)-Faith Books & More—R
FaithWalk
(s)-Forever Books—R

Fortress Press
Forward Movement
Friends United Press
Georgetown Univ. Press
Grupo Nelson
Guardian Angel
Guernica Editions—R
Hidden Brook Press—R
(s)-Holy Fire Publishing—R
(s)-House of Ali
Howard Books
(s)-IMD Press—R
(s)-Insight Publishing—R
InterVarsity Press—R
Judson Press—R
Kirk House
Libros Liguori
Lift Every Voice—R
Lighthouse Publishing—R
Liguori Public.—R
Lutheran Univ. Press
Mercer Univ. Press—R
Messianic Jewish—R
Millennium III—R
Monarch Books
Moody Publishers
New Hope—R
New York Univ. Press
Nordskog Publishing—R
(s)-One World—R
Oregon Catholic
Pacific Press
Palgrave Macmillan—R
Paulist Press
(s)-Pleasant Word—R
Power Publishing—R
Praeger Publishers
(s)-Providence House—R
Standard Publishing
St. Anthony Mess. Press—R
Sunpenny Publishing
(s)-Tate Publishing—R
Th1nk/NavPress—R
Third World Press—R
Torch Legacy
(s)-Trafford Publishing—R
UMI Publishing—R
Univ. of AR Press—R
Univ. Press of America—R
Whitaker House

(s)-WinePress—R
(s)-Word Alive
Yale Univ. Press
(s)-Zoë Life Publishing
Zondervan

EVANGELISM/ WITNESSING
(a)-Baker Books
(a)-Cook, David C.
(a)-Kregel—R
(a)-Nelson, Thomas
(a)-Tyndale House—R
(a)-W Publishing

Aaron Book—R
(s)-ACW Press—R
Ambassador Intl.—R
(s)-American Binding—R
Anglicans United—R
(s)-Bfree Publishing
(s)-Black Forest—R
Blue Dolphin
BMH Books—R
(s)-Booklocker.com—R
(s)-Bookstand Publishing—R
(s)-Brentwood—R
Bridge Logos—R
Carey Library, Wm.—R
Catholic Answers—R
Chalice Press—R
Chapter Two—R
Christian Family—R
Christian Focus—R
Christian Heritage—R
Christian Writer's Ebook—R
Church Growth Inst.
CLC Publications—R
Conquest Publishers
(s)-Creation House—R
(s)-CrossHouse—R
CrossLink Publishing
CSS Publishing—R
(s)-DCTS Publishers
(s)-Deep River Books
(s)-Deo Volente
Discovery House—R
Earthen Vessel—R
Editorial Portavoz
Eerdmans Pub., Wm. B.—R

(s)-E.F.S. Online Pub.
(s)-Elderberry Press
Emmaus Road
(s)-Essence—R
Evangelical Press
Evergreen Press
Fair Havens—R
(s)-Fairway Press—R
Faith Alive
(s)-Faith Books & More—R
FaithWalk
Father's Press
(s)-Forever Books—R
Founders Press
Four Craftsmen—R
Good Book—R
Gospel Publishing
(s)-Grace Acres Press—R
Group Publishing
Hidden Brook Press—R
(s)-Holy Fire Publishing—R
(s)-IMD Press—R
(s)-Impact Christian—R
(s)-Insight Publishing—R
InterVarsity Press—R
Judson Press—R
Lift Every Voice—R
Lighthouse Publishing—R
Lion and Lamb
Lutheran Univ. Press
(s)-McDougal Publishing—R
Messianic Jewish—R
Monarch Books
Moody Publishers
New Hope—R
Nordskog Publishing—R
(s)-One World—R
P & R Publishing—R
Pacific Press
Paradise Research—R
Parson Place—R
Pilgrim Press—R
(s)-Pleasant Word—R
Power Publishing—R
Praxis Press
(s)-Providence House—R
Randall House
Reformation Heritage—R
Review and Herald
Revival Nation

(s)-Rill & Associates
Rose Publishing
(s)-Salt Works—R
Samaritan Press—R
(s)-Seed Faith Books—R
(s)-Selah Publishing—R
(s)-So. Baptist Press—R
(s)-Star Bible Public.
Still Waters Revival—R
Strang Book—R
(s)-Tate Publishing—R
(s)-TEACH Services—R
Th1nk/NavPress—R
(s)-Trafford Publishing—R
VBC Publishing
Wesleyan Publishing
(s)-WinePress—R
(s)-Word Alive
Yale Univ. Press
(s)-Zoë Life Publishing

EXEGESIS
(a)-Baker Books
(a)-Doubleday Relig.—R
(a)-Kregel—R

Aaron Book—R
Abingdon Press
(s)-ACW Press—R
(s)-American Binding—R
(s)-Bfree Publishing
(s)-Black Forest—R
Blue Dolphin
BMH Books—R
(s)-Booklocker.com—R
(s)-Bookstand Publishing—R
Canticle Books—R
Catholic Answers—R
Chalice Press—R
Chapter Two—R
Christian Family—R
Christian Focus—R
Christian Writer's Ebook—R
Cistercian—R
CLC Publications—R
College Press—R
Continuum Intl.—R
CSS Publishing—R
(s)-Deep River Books
Earthen Vessel—R

Eerdmans Pub., Wm. B.—R
(s)-Elderberry Press
(s)-Essence—R
Evangelical Press
(s)-Fairway Press—R
(s)-Faith Books & More—R
(s)-Forever Books—R
(s)-Grace Acres Press—R
Hendrickson—R
Hidden Brook Press—R
(s)-Holy Fire Publishing—R
(s)-IMD Press—R
(s)-Insight Publishing—R
InterVarsity Press—R
Lighthouse Publishing—R
Lutheran Univ. Press
(s)-McDougal Publishing—R
Millennium III—R
Monarch Books
Nordskog Publishing—R
(s)-One World—R
Paradise Research—R
Paulist Press
(s)-Pleasant Word—R
Power Publishing—R
(s)-Providence House—R
Reformation Trust
Rose Publishing
(s)-Salt Works—R
(s)-Star Bible Public.
St. Bede's Public.—R
(s)-Tate Publishing—R
(s)-Trafford Publishing—R
VBC Publishing
Westminster John Knox
(s)-WinePress—R
(s)-Word Alive
Yale Univ. Press
(s)-Zoë Life Publishing

EXPOSÉS
(a)-Baker Books
Aaron Book—R
(s)-ACW Press—R
(s)-American Binding—R
Blue Dolphin
(s)-Booklocker.com—R
(s)-Brentwood—R
Chapter Two—R
Christian Writer's Ebook—R

Eerdmans Pub., Wm. B.—R
(s)-E.F.S. Online Pub.
(s)-Elderberry Press
(s)-Fairway Press—R
(s)-Faith Books & More—R
(s)-Forever Books—R
Hidden Brook Press—R
(s)-Holy Fire Publishing—R
(s)-Insight Publishing—R
Lighthouse Publishing—R
Lighthouse Trails—R
(s)-MileStones Intl.
Nordskog Publishing—R
(s)-One World—R
Power Publishing—R
(s)-Providence House—R
Ravenhawk Books—R
(s)-Salt Works—R
(s)-So. Baptist Press—R
(s)-Star Bible Public.
(s)-Trafford Publishing—R
(s)-WinePress—R
(s)-Word Alive
(s)-Zoë Life Publishing

FAITH
(a)-B & H Publishing
(a)-Baker Books
(a)-Bethany House—R
(a)-Doubleday Relig.—R
(a)-FaithWords
(a)-HarperOne
(a)-Kregel—R
(a)-Nelson, Thomas
(a)-Tyndale House—R
(a)-WaterBrook Press—R
(a)-W Publishing

Aadeon Publishing—R
Aaron Book—R
Abingdon Press
ACTA Publications
(s)-ACW Press—R
Ambassador Books
Ambassador Intl.—R
(s)-American Binding—R
Barbour
(s)-Bfree Publishing
(s)-Black Forest—R
Blue Dolphin

(s)-Booklocker.com—R
(s)-Bookstand Publishing—R
Bridge Logos—R
(s)-Brown Books
Chalice Press—R
Chapter Two—R
Christian Family—R
Christian Focus—R
Christian Heritage—R
Christian Writer's Ebook—R
Church Publishing
CLC Publications—R
Comfort Publishing
Congregational Life
Continuum Intl.—R
(s)-Creation House—R
CrossLink Publishing
(s)-DCTS Publishers
(s)-Deep River Books
Destiny Image (gifts)—R
(s)-Destiny Image (books)—R
Discovery House—R
Earthen Vessel—R
Eerdmans Pub., Wm. B.—R
(s)-E.F.S. Online Pub.
(s)-Elderberry Press
Eldridge Plays
Emmaus Road
(s)-Essence—R
Evangelical Press
Evergreen Press
(s)-Fairway Press—R
(s)-Faith Books & More—R
Faith Communications
FaithWalk
Father's Press
(s)-Forever Books—R
Forward Movement
Fresh Air Books
Friends United Press
(s)-Fruitbearer Pub.
Good Book—R
(s)-Grace Acres Press—R
Group Publishing
GRQ—R
Grupo Nelson
Guardian Angel
Guideposts Books
(s)-Halo Publishing Intl.
Harrison House

Hensley Publishing
Hidden Brook Press—R
(s)-Holy Fire Publishing—R
Howard Books
(s)-IMD Press—R
Inheritance Press
(s)-Insight Publishing—R
InterVarsity Press—R
Jebaire
JourneyForth/BJU
Judson Press—R
Leafwood
Life Changing Media
Lift Every Voice—R
Lighthouse Publishing—R
Liguori Public.—R
Lion and Lamb
Loyola Press
Lutheran Univ. Press
Magnus Press—R
(s)-McDougal Publishing—R
Messianic Jewish—R
(s)-MileStones Intl.
Mission City Press
Monarch Books
New Hope—R
Nordskog Publishing—R
(s)-One World—R
On My Own Now—R
Pacific Press
Palgrave Macmillan—R
Paradise Research—R
Parson Place—R
Parsons Publishing—R
Pauline Books—R
Pflaum Publishing
Pilgrim Press—R
(s)-Pleasant Word—R
Power Publishing—R
Praxis Press
(s)-Providence House—R
Quintessential Books—R
Randall House
Reformation Heritage—R
Revival Nation
(s)-Rill & Associates
Rose Publishing
(s)-Salt Works—R
(s)-Salvation Publisher—R
Samaritan Press—R

Scepter Publishers—R
(s)-Selah Publishing—R
(s)-Star Bible Public.
St. Bede's Public.—R
St. Pauls/Alba—R
Strang Book—R
(s)-Tate Publishing—R
(s)-TEACH Services—R
Th1nk/NavPress—R
(s)-Trafford Publishing—R
Treble Heart—R
UMI Publishing—R
VBC Publishing
Wesleyan Publishing
Whitaker House
(s)-WinePress—R
(s)-Word Alive
Youth Specialties
(s)-Zoë Life Publishing

FAMILY LIFE

(a)-B & H Publishing
(a)-Baker Books
(a)-Bethany House—R
(a)-Cook, David C.
(a)-FaithWords
(a)-HarperOne
(a)-Harvest House
(a)-Kregel—R
(a)-Nelson, Thomas
(a)-Regal
(a)-Tyndale House—R
(a)-WaterBrook Press—R
(a)-W Publishing

Aaron Book—R
Abingdon Press
ACTA Publications
(s)-ACW Press—R
Ambassador Books
Ambassador Intl.—R
(s)-American Binding—R
Barbour
Beacon Hill Press—R
(s)-Bfree Publishing
(s)-Black Forest—R
Blue Dolphin
(s)-Booklocker.com—R
(s)-Bookstand Publishing—R
Boyds Mills Press—R

Branden Publishing—R
(s)-Brentwood—R
Bridge Logos—R
(s)-Brown Books
CarePoint Publishing—R
Chalice Press—R
Chapter Two—R
Christian Family—R
Christian Focus—R
Christian Writer's Ebook—R
Church Publishing
Cladach Publishing
College Press—R
Comfort Publishing
Conari Press
(s)-Creation House—R
CrossLink Publishing
Crossroad Publishing—R
Crossway
(s)-DCTS Publishers
(s)-Deep River Books
Destiny Image (gifts)—R
(s)-Destiny Image (books)—R
Dimensions for Living
Discovery House—R
Dove Inspirational—R
Editorial Portavoz
Eerdmans Pub., Wm. B.—R
(s)-E.F.S. Online Pub.
(s)-Elderberry Press
Eldridge Plays
Emmaus Road
(s)-Essence—R
Evangelical Press
Evergreen Press
Extreme Diva
Fair Havens—R
(s)-Fairway Press—R
(s)-Faith Books & More—R
Faith Communications
FaithWalk
Father's Press
Focus on the Family—R
(s)-Forever Books—R
Forward Movement
Gentle Path Press
(s)-Grace Acres Press—R
Grupo Nelson
Guardian Angel
Guideposts Books

(s)-Halo Publishing Intl.
Hannibal Books
Health Commun.
Heart of Wisdom
Hensley Publishing
Hidden Brook Press—R
(s)-Holy Fire Publishing—R
Hope Publishing—R
Howard Books
(s)-IMD Press—R
(s)-Insight Publishing—R
InterVarsity Press—R
JourneyForth/BJU
Judson Press—R
Langmarc
Legacy Press—R
Life Changing Media
Life Cycle Books—R
LifeSong Publishers
Lift Every Voice—R
Lighthouse Publishing—R
Liguori Public.—R
Lion and Lamb
Loyola Press
Master Books
(s)-McDougal Publishing—R
(s)-MileStones Intl.
Monarch Books
MOPS Intl.
MountainView
New Hope—R
New Leaf
Nordskog Publishing—R
(s)-One World—R
Our Sunday Visitor—R
P & R Publishing—R
Pacific Press
Pauline Books—R
Pelican Publishing—R
Pilgrim Press—R
(s)-Pleasant Word—R
(s)-Port Hole Public.
Power Publishing—R
(s)-Providence House—R
Quiet Waters—R
Quintessential Books—R
Randall House
(s)-Recovery Commun.
Reformation Heritage—R
Review and Herald

Revival Nation
(s)-Rill & Associates
(s)-Salvation Publisher—R
Samaritan Press—R
(s)-Selah Publishing—R
Sheed & Ward
(s)-So. Baptist Press—R
St. Anthony Mess. Press—R
(s)-Star Bible Public.
Starik Publishing
Still Waters Revival—R
Strang Book—R
(s)-Tate Publishing—R
(s)-TEACH Services—R
Third World Press—R
Torch Legacy
(s)-Trafford Publishing—R
VBC Publishing
Vision Forum
Whitaker House
(s)-WinePress—R
(s)-Word Alive
(s)-Zoë Life Publishing

FICTION: ADULT/ GENERAL

(a)-Ballantine
(a)-FaithWords
(a)-HarperOne
(a)-Kregel—R
(a)-Multnomah
(a)-Nelson, Fiction, Thomas
(a)-One World/Ballantine

Aaron Book—R
Ambassador Intl.—R
(s)-American Binding—R
Blue Dolphin
(s)-Book Publishers Net.—R
(s)-Bookstand Publishing—R
(s)-Brown Books
Chalice Press—R
Cladach Publishing
Comfort Publishing
(s)-Creation House—R
(s)-E.F.S. Online Pub.
(s)-Essence—R
Fair Havens—R
Fell, Frederick—R
Guernica Editions—R

(s)-Halo Publishing Intl.
(s)-Holy Fire Publishing—R
Howard Books
(s)-Infinity Publishing
LifeSong Publishers
(s)-LifeVest Publishing
Lighthouse Publishing—R
Lighthouse Trails—R
Master Books
MountainView
New Leaf
Parson Place—R
(s)-Providence House—R
Quintessential Books—R
Ravenhawk Books—R
Revival Nation
Samaritan Press—R
Steeple Hill
Strang Book—R
Third World Press—R
(s)-Trafford Publishing—R
Treble Heart—R
Virtual Tales—R
Whitaker House
Xyzzy Press

FICTION: ADULT/ RELIGIOUS

(a)-B & H Publishing
(a)-Baker Books
(a)-Ballantine
(a)-Bethany House—R
(a)-Doubleday Relig.—R
(a)-FaithWords
(a)-HarperOne
(a)-Harvest House
(a)-Kregel—R
(a)-Multnomah
(a)-Nelson, Fiction, Thomas
(a)-One World/Ballantine
(a)-Revell
(a)-WaterBrook Press—R

Aaron Book—R
(s)-ACW Press—R
Adams Media
Ambassador Books
Ambassador Intl.—R
(s)-American Binding—R
Barbour

(s)-Bfree Publishing
(s)-Black Forest—R
(s)-Booklocker.com—R
(s)-Book Publishers Net.—R
(s)-Bookstand Publishing—R
Branden Publishing—R
Bridge Logos—R
(s)-Brown Books
Chalice Press—R
Christian Focus—R
Christian Liberty Press
Christian Writer's Ebook—R
Cladach Publishing
Comfort Publishing
Conquest Publishers
(s)-Creation House—R
(s)-CrossHouse—R
Dan River Press
(s)-Deep River Books
(s)-Deo Volente
Destiny Image (gifts)—R
(s)-Destiny Image (books)—R
DiskUs Publishing
Earthen Vessel—R
Eerdmans Pub., Wm. B.—R
(s)-E.F.S. Online Pub.
(s)-Elderberry Press
Elijah Press
(s)-Essence—R
Evergreen Press
(s)-Fairway Press—R
(s)-Faith Books & More—R
FaithWalk
Father's Press
Focus on the Family—R
(s)-Forever Books—R
(s)-Fruitbearer Pub.
Guideposts Books
(s)-Halo Publishing Intl.
Hannibal Books
Heartsong Presents
HeartSpring Pub.—R
Hidden Brook Press—R
His Work Christian Pub.—R
(s)-Holy Fire Publishing—R
Howard Books
(s)-Infinity Publishing
(s)-Insight Publishing—R
(s)-LifeVest Publishing
Lift Every Voice—R

Lighthouse Publishing—R
Lighthouse Trails—R
Lion and Lamb
Love Inspired
Love Inspired Historical
Master Books
(s)-McDougal Publishing—R
Mercer Univ. Press—R
Messianic Jewish—R
(s)-MileStones Intl.
Millennium III—R
Moody Publishers
MountainView
NavPress
New Leaf
Nordskog Publishing—R
OakTara—R
(s)-One World—R
Pacific Press
Parson Place—R
Parsons Publishing—R
(s)-Pleasant Word—R
(s)-Port Hole Public.
Power Publishing—R
PREP Publishing—R
(s)-Providence House—R
Quiet Waters—R
Quintessential Books—R
Resource Public.
(s)-Rill & Associates
(s)-Salt Works—R
Samaritan Press—R
Scepter Publishers—R
(s)-Selah Publishing—R
(s)-Self Publish Press—R
(s)-Sonfire Media
(s)-Star Bible Public.
Starik Publishing
Steeple Hill
Strang Book—R
Sunpenny Publishing
(s)-Tate Publishing—R
Third World Press—R
(s)-Trafford Publishing—R
Treble Heart—R
Two Fish Publishing—R
Virtual Tales—R
Vision Forum
Whitaker House
White Rose—R

(s)-WinePress—R
(s)-Word Alive
Xyzzy Press
(s)-Zoë Life Publishing

FICTION: ADVENTURE
(a)-Baker Books
(a)-Multnomah
(a)-One World/Ballantine
(a)-WaterBrook Press—R

Aadeon Publishing—R
Aaron Book—R
(s)-ACW Press—R
Ambassador Books
Ambassador Intl.—R
(s)-American Binding—R
Barbour
(s)-Black Forest—R
(s)-Booklocker.com—R
(s)-Book Publishers Net.—R
(s)-Bookstand Publishing—R
Boyds Mills Press—R
(s)-Brentwood—R
Bridge Logos—R
(s)-Brown Books
Chalice Press—R
Christian Ed. Pub.
Christian Family—R
Christian Writer's Ebook—R
Comfort Publishing
(s)-Creation House—R
(s)-Deep River Books
DiskUs Publishing
Eerdmans/Yg Readers
(s)-E.F.S. Online Pub.
(s)-Elderberry Press
(s)-Essence—R
Evergreen Press
Fair Havens—R
(s)-Fairway Press—R
(s)-Faith Books & More—R
FaithWalk
(s)-Forever Books—R
(s)-Halo Publishing Intl.
Hidden Brook Press—R
(s)-Holy Fire Publishing—R
Howard Books
(s)-Infinity Publishing
(s)-Insight Publishing—R

JourneyForth/BJU
Knight George Pub.
(s)-LifeVest Publishing
Lift Every Voice—R
Lighthouse Publishing—R
Lion and Lamb
Master Books
Messianic Jewish—R
Mission City Press
MountainView
New Leaf
Nordskog Publishing—R
(s)-One World—R
P & R Publishing—R
Parson Place—R
Parsons Publishing—R
Pauline Kids—R
(s)-Pleasant Word—R
(s)-Port Hole Public.
PREP Publishing—R
Quintessential Books—R
Ravenhawk Books—R
(s)-Rill & Associates
(s)-Salt Works—R
Samaritan Press—R
(s)-Selah Publishing—R
(s)-Self Publish Press—R
(s)-So. Baptist Press—R
Starik Publishing
Strang Book—R
Sunpenny Publishing
(s)-Tate Publishing—R
Third World Press—R
(s)-Trafford Publishing—R
Treble Heart—R
(s)-WinePress—R
(s)-Zoë Life Publishing

FICTION: ALLEGORY
(a)-Baker Books
(a)-Multnomah

Aadeon Publishing—R
Aaron Book—R
(s)-ACW Press—R
(s)-American Binding—R
Barbour
(s)-Black Forest—R
(s)-Booklocker.com—R
(s)-Bookstand Publishing—R

Bridge Logos—R
(s)-Brown Books
Christian Family—R
Christian Writer's Ebook—R
(s)-Creation House—R
(s)-Deep River Books
(s)-Destiny Image (books)—R
(s)-E.F.S. Online Pub.
(s)-Elderberry Press
(s)-Essence—R
Evergreen Press
(s)-Fairway Press—R
(s)-Faith Books & More—R
(s)-Forever Books—R
Hidden Brook Press—R
(s)-Holy Fire Publishing—R
Howard Books
(s)-Infinity Publishing
(s)-Insight Publishing—R
(s)-LifeVest Publishing
Lighthouse Publishing—R
Lion and Lamb
(s)-MileStones Intl.
Nordskog Publishing—R
OakTara—R
(s)-One World—R
(s)-Pleasant Word—R
(s)-Port Hole Public.
Realms
Reformation Trust
(s)-Rill & Associates
(s)-Salt Works—R
Samaritan Press—R
(s)-Selah Publishing—R
Strang Book—R
(s)-Tate Publishing—R
(s)-TEACH Services—R
(s)-Trafford Publishing—R
Wilshire Book—R
(s)-WinePress—R
(s)-Zoë Life Publishing

FICTION: BIBLICAL
(a)-Baker Books
(a)-Multnomah
(a)-Nelson, Fiction, Thomas
(a)-WaterBrook Press—R

Aadeon Publishing—R
Aaron Book—R

Abingdon Press
(s)-ACW Press—R
Ambassador Intl.—R
(s)-American Binding—R
(s)-Black Forest—R
(s)-Booklocker.com—R
(s)-Bookstand Publishing—R
(s)-Brentwood—R
Bridge Logos—R
(s)-Brown Books
Chalice Press—R
CharismaKids
Christian Family—R
Christian Writer's Ebook—R
Cladach Publishing
College Press—R
(s)-Creation House—R
(s)-Deep River Books
Destiny Image (gifts)—R
(s)-Destiny Image (books)—R
Earthen Vessel—R
Eerdmans Pub., Wm. B.—R
Eerdmans/Yg Readers
(s)-E.F.S. Online Pub.
(s)-Elderberry Press
(s)-Essence—R
Evergreen Press
Fair Havens—R
(s)-Fairway Press—R
(s)-Faith Books & More—R
Father's Press
(s)-Forever Books—R
Guideposts Books
Hannibal Books
Hidden Brook Press—R
(s)-Holy Fire Publishing—R
Howard Books
(s)-Infinity Publishing
(s)-Insight Publishing—R
(s)-Kindred Books—R
LifeSong Publishers
(s)-LifeVest Publishing
Lift Every Voice—R
Lighthouse Publishing—R
Lighthouse Trails—R
Lion and Lamb
Love Inspired Historical
Messianic Jewish—R
(s)-MileStones Intl.
Mission City Press

Moody Publishers
NavPress
Nordskog Publishing—R
OakTara—R
(s)-One World—R
P & R Publishing—R
Pacific Press
Parsons Publishing—R
(s)-Pleasant Word—R
(s)-Port Hole Public.
Power Publishing—R
(s)-Providence House—R
Quintessential Books—R
Realms
Reformation Trust
(s)-Salt Works—R
Samaritan Press—R
(s)-Self Publish Press—R
(s)-So. Baptist Press—R
Steeple Hill
Strang Book—R
(s)-Tate Publishing—R
Th1nk/NavPress—R
(s)-Trafford Publishing—R
(s)-WinePress—R
(s)-Zoë Life Publishing

FICTION: CHICK LIT
(a)-Multnomah
(a)-Nelson, Fiction, Thomas
(a)-WaterBrook Press—R

Aaron Book—R
(s)-ACW Press—R
Ambassador Books
Ambassador Intl.—R
(s)-American Binding—R
(s)-Booklocker.com—R
(s)-Bookstand Publishing—R
(s)-Brown Books
Chalice Press—R
Christian Writer's Ebook—R
(s)-Creation House—R
(s)-Deep River Books
(s)-Elderberry Press
(s)-Essence—R
(s)-Faith Books & More—R
(s)-Forever Books—R
Hidden Brook Press—R
(s)-Holy Fire Publishing—R

(s)-Infinity Publishing
(s)-Insight Publishing—R
(s)-LifeVest Publishing
Lighthouse Publishing—R
Lion and Lamb
Love Inspired Suspense
Nordskog Publishing—R
(s)-One World—R
(s)-Pleasant Word—R
(s)-Port Hole Public.
Ravenhawk Books—R
Steeple Hill
Strang Book—R
Th1nk/NavPress—R
(s)-Trafford Publishing—R
Whitaker House
(s)-WinePress—R
(s)-Zoë Life Publishing

FICTION: CONTEMPORARY
(a)- Avon Inspire
(a)-B & H Publishing
(a)-Baker Books
(a)-Ballantine
(a)-Bethany House—R
(a)-FaithWords
(a)-Kregel—R
(a)-Multnomah
(a)-Nelson, Fiction, Thomas
(a)-One World/Ballantine
(a)-Revell
(a)-Tyndale House—R
(a)-WaterBrook Press—R

Aadeon Publishing—R
Aaron Book—R
(s)-ACW Press—R
Ambassador Books
(s)-American Binding—R
AMG Publishers—R
Barbour
(s)-Black Forest—R
(s)-Booklocker.com—R
(s)-Bookstand Publishing—R
Branden Publishing—R
(s)-Brentwood—R
(s)-Brown Books
Chalice Press—R
CharismaKids

Christian Ed. Pub.
Christian Writer's Ebook—R
Conquest Publishers
(s)-Creation House—R
(s)-Deep River Books
Desert Breeze Pub.
Destiny Image (gifts)—R
(s)-Destiny Image (books)—R
DiskUs Publishing
Eerdmans/Yg Readers
(s)-E.F.S. Online Pub.
(s)-Elderberry Press
(s)-Essence—R
(s)-Fairway Press—R
(s)-Faith Books & More—R
FaithWalk
Fell, Frederick—R
Focus on the Family—R
(s)-Forever Books—R
Heartsong Presents
Hidden Brook Press—R
(s)-Holy Fire Publishing—R
Howard Books
(s)-Infinity Publishing
(s)-Insight Publishing—R
JourneyForth/BJU
(s)-LifeVest Publishing
Lift Every Voice—R
Lighthouse Publishing—R
Lion and Lamb
Love Inspired
Master Books
(s)-McDougal Publishing—R
Millennium III—R
Mission City Press
Moody Publishers
MountainView
NavPress
New Leaf
Nordskog Publishing—R
OakTara—R
(s)-One World—R
Parson Place—R
Pauline Books—R
Pauline Kids—R
(s)-Pleasant Word—R
(s)-Port Hole Public.
Putnam/Young Readers
Ravenhawk Books—R
(s)-Rill & Associates

(s)-Salt Works—R
Samaritan Press—R
(s)-Self Publish Press—R
(s)-So. Baptist Press—R
Steeple Hill
Strang Book—R
Sunpenny Publishing
(s)-Tate Publishing—R
Th1nk/NavPress—R
Third World Press—R
(s)-Trafford Publishing—R
Whitaker House
(s)-WinePress—R
(s)-Zoë Life Publishing

FICTION: COZY MYSTERIES

Ambassador Intl.—R
Chalice Press—R
Comfort Publishing
(s)-Essence—R
(s)-Rill & Associates
(s)-Zoë Life Publishing

FICTION: ETHNIC

(a)-Baker Books
(a)-Ballantine
(a)-Multnomah
(a)-One World/Ballantine

Aaron Book—R
(s)-ACW Press—R
(s)-American Binding—R
(s)-Black Forest—R
(s)-Booklocker.com—R
(s)-Bookstand Publishing—R
Boyds Mills Press—R
Branden Publishing—R
Christian Writer's Ebook—R
Conquest Publishers
(s)-Deep River Books
Destiny Image (gifts)—R
DiskUs Publishing
(s)-E.F.S. Online Pub.
(s)-Elderberry Press
(s)-Essence—R
Evergreen Press
(s)-Fairway Press—R
(s)-Faith Books & More—R
Focus on the Family—R

(s)-Forever Books—R
Guernica Editions—R
Hidden Brook Press—R
(s)-Holy Fire Publishing—R
(s)-Infinity Publishing
(s)-Insight Publishing—R
(s)-LifeVest Publishing
Lift Every Voice—R
Lighthouse Publishing—R
Nordskog Publishing—R
(s)-One World—R
(s)-Pleasant Word—R
Putnam/Young Readers
(s)-Rill & Associates
Samaritan Press—R
Strang Book—R
Sunpenny Publishing
(s)-Tate Publishing—R
Third World Press—R
(s)-Trafford Publishing—R
(s)-WinePress—R
(s)-Zoë Life Publishing

FICTION: FABLES/ PARABLES

(a)-HarperOne

Aadeon Publishing—R
Aaron Book—R
(s)-ACW Press—R
(s)-American Binding—R
(s)-Black Forest—R
Blue Dolphin
(s)-Booklocker.com—R
(s)-Bookstand Publishing—R
(s)-Brown Books
(s)-Deep River Books
(s)-E.F.S. Online Pub.
(s)-Elderberry Press
(s)-Essence—R
(s)-Faith Books & More—R
(s)-Forever Books—R
Hidden Brook Press—R
(s)-Holy Fire Publishing—R
(s)-Infinity Publishing
(s)-Insight Publishing—R
(s)-LifeVest Publishing
Lighthouse Publishing—R
Nordskog Publishing—R
(s)-One World—R

Parson Place—R
Pauline Books—R
(s)-Pleasant Word—R
Quintessential Books—R
Resource Public.
(s)-Salt Works—R
Samaritan Press—R
(s)-Tate Publishing—R
(s)-Trafford Publishing—R
(s)-WinePress—R
(s)-Zoë Life Publishing

FICTION: FANTASY
(a)-Ballantine
(a)-Multnomah
(a)-WaterBrook Press—R

Aaron Book—R
(s)-ACW Press—R
(s)-American Binding—R
AMG Publishers—R
Barbour
(s)-Booklocker.com—R
(s)-Bookstand Publishing—R
Chalice Press—R
Christian Writer's Ebook—R
Comfort Publishing
(s)-Creation House—R
(s)-Deep River Books
Desert Breeze Pub.
Destiny Image (gifts)—R
(s)-Destiny Image (books)—R
DiskUs Publishing
Dover Publications—R
Eerdmans Pub., Wm. B.—R
(s)-E.F.S. Online Pub.
(s)-Elderberry Press
(s)-Essence—R
Evergreen Press
(s)-Fairway Press—R
(s)-Faith Books & More—R
(s)-Forever Books—R
Hidden Brook Press—R
(s)-Holy Fire Publishing—R
(s)-Infinity Publishing
(s)-Insight Publishing—R
(s)-LifeVest Publishing
Lighthouse Publishing—R
Marcher Lord Press
Mission City Press

MountainView
Nordskog Publishing—R
OakTara—R
(s)-One World—R
P & R Publishing—R
Parsons Publishing—R
(s)-Pleasant Word—R
(s)-Port Hole Public.
Putnam/Young Readers
Ravenhawk Books—R
Realms
Revival Nation
Samaritan Press—R
Starik Publishing
Strang Book—R
(s)-Tate Publishing—R
Th1nk/NavPress—R
(s)-Trafford Publishing—R
Treble Heart—R
Whitaker House
(s)-WinePress—R
(s)-Zoë Life Publishing

FICTION: FRONTIER
(a)-Baker Books
(a)-Bethany House—R
(a)-Harvest House
(a)-Multnomah
(a)-Nelson, Fiction, Thomas

Aaron Book—R
(s)-ACW Press—R
Ambassador Intl.—R
(s)-American Binding—R
AMG Publishers—R
(s)-Black Forest—R
(s)-Booklocker.com—R
(s)-Bookstand Publishing—R
(s)-Brentwood—R
(s)-Brown Books
Chalice Press—R
Christian Writer's Ebook—R
Cladach Publishing
(s)-Deep River Books
(s)-Elderberry Press
(s)-Essence—R
(s)-Fairway Press—R
(s)-Faith Books & More—R
(s)-Forever Books—R
Guardian Angel

Hidden Brook Press—R
(s)-Holy Fire Publishing—R
(s)-Infinity Publishing
(s)-Insight Publishing—R
JourneyForth/BJU
(s)-LifeVest Publishing
Lighthouse Publishing—R
Lion and Lamb
Mission City Press
MountainView
Nordskog Publishing—R
(s)-One World—R
Parson Place—R
(s)-Pleasant Word—R
(s)-Port Hole Public.
Ravenhawk Books—R
Samaritan Press—R
(s)-Self Publish Press—R
(s)-So. Baptist Press—R
Strang Book—R
(s)-Tate Publishing—R
Third World Press—R
(s)-Trafford Publishing—R
Treble Heart—R
Whitaker House
(s)-WinePress—R
(s)-Zoë Life Publishing

FICTION: FRONTIER/ ROMANCE
(a)-Baker Books
(a)-Bethany House—R
(a)-Harvest House
(a)-Multnomah
(a)-Nelson, Fiction, Thomas

Aaron Book—R
(s)-ACW Press—R
Ambassador Intl.—R
(s)-American Binding—R
AMG Publishers—R
Barbour
(s)-Black Forest—R
(s)-Booklocker.com—R
(s)-Bookstand Publishing—R
(s)-Brentwood—R
(s)-Brown Books
Chalice Press—R
Christian Writer's Ebook—R
Conquest Publishers

(s)-Deep River Books
Desert Breeze Pub.
(s)-Elderberry Press
(s)-Essence—R
(s)-Fairway Press—R
(s)-Faith Books & More—R
(s)-Forever Books—R
Heartsong Presents
Hidden Brook Press—R
(s)-Holy Fire Publishing—R
(s)-Infinity Publishing
(s)-Insight Publishing—R
(s)-LifeVest Publishing
Lighthouse Publishing—R
Love Inspired Historical
More Than Novellas
MountainView
Nordskog Publishing—R
(s)-One World—R
Parson Place—R
(s)-Pleasant Word—R
(s)-Port Hole Public.
Ravenhawk Books—R
(s)-Rill & Associates
Samaritan Press—R
(s)-Self Publish Press—R
(s)-So. Baptist Press—R
Steeple Hill
Strang Book—R
(s)-Tate Publishing—R
(s)-Trafford Publishing—R
Treble Heart—R
Whitaker House
White Rose—R
(s)-WinePress—R
(s)-Zoë Life Publishing

FICTION: HISTORICAL

(a)-Avon Inspire
(a)-B & H Publishing
(a)-Baker Books
(a)-Ballantine
(a)-Bethany House—R
(a)-FaithWords
(a)-Kregel—R
(a)-Multnomah
(a)-Nelson, Fiction, Thomas
(a)-One World/Ballantine
(a)-Revell
(a)-WaterBrook Press—R

Aadeon Publishing—R
Aaron Book—R
Abingdon Press
(s)-ACW Press—R
Ambassador Books
Ambassador Intl.—R
(s)-American Binding—R
AMG Publishers—R
(s)-Black Forest—R
Blue Dolphin
(s)-Booklocker.com—R
(s)-Book Publishers Net.—R
(s)-Bookstand Publishing—R
Boyds Mills Press—R
Branden Publishing—R
(s)-Brentwood—R
Bridge Logos—R
(s)-Brown Books
Chalice Press—R
CharismaKids
Christian Family—R
Christian Liberty Press
Christian Writer's Ebook—R
Cladach Publishing
Comfort Publishing
Conquest Publishers
(s)-Deep River Books
(s)-Deo Volente
DiskUs Publishing
Earthen Vessel—R
Eerdmans Pub., Wm. B.—R
Eerdmans/Yg Readers
(s)-Elderberry Press
(s)-Essence—R
Fair Havens—R
(s)-Fairway Press—R
(s)-Faith Books & More—R
Father's Press
Focus on the Family—R
(s)-Forever Books—R
Hannibal Books
Hidden Brook Press—R
(s)-Holy Fire Publishing—R
Howard Books
(s)-Infinity Publishing
(s)-Insight Publishing—R
JourneyForth/BJU
(s)-LifeVest Publishing
Lift Every Voice—R
Lighthouse Publishing—R

Mission City Press
Moody Publishers
MountainView
NavPress
New Canaan—R
Nordskog Publishing—R
OakTara—R
(s)-One World—R
Parson Place—R
Parsons Publishing—R
Pauline Books—R
Pauline Kids—R
(s)-Pleasant Word—R
(s)-Port Hole Public.
(s)-Providence House—R
Putnam/Young Readers
Quintessential Books—R
Ravenhawk Books—R
Realms
Reformation Trust
(s)-Salt Works—R
Samaritan Press—R
(s)-Self Publish Press—R
(s)-So. Baptist Press—R
Strang Book—R
Sunpenny Publishing
(s)-Tate Publishing—R
(s)-TEACH Services—R
Third World Press—R
(s)-Trafford Publishing—R
Treble Heart—R
Vision Forum
Whitaker House
(s)-WinePress—R
(s)-Zoë Life Publishing

FICTION: HISTORICAL/ ROMANCE

(a)-B & H Publishing
(a)-Baker Books
(a)-Bethany House—R
(a)-Harvest House
(a)-Multnomah
(a)-Nelson, Fiction, Thomas
(a)-Tyndale House—R
(a)-WaterBrook Press—R

Aaron Book—R
Abingdon Press
(s)-ACW Press—R

Ambassador Intl.—R
(s)-American Binding—R
AMG Publishers—R
Barbour
(s)-Black Forest—R
(s)-Booklocker.com—R
(s)-Bookstand Publishing—R
(s)-Brentwood—R
(s)-Brown Books
Chalice Press—R
Christian Writer's Ebook—R
Comfort Publishing
Conquest Publishers
(s)-Deep River Books
Desert Breeze Pub.
(s)-Elderberry Press
(s)-Essence—R
(s)-Fairway Press—R
(s)-Faith Books & More—R
(s)-Forever Books—R
Hannibal Books
Heartsong Presents
Hidden Brook Press—R
(s)-Holy Fire Publishing—R
(s)-Infinity Publishing
(s)-Insight Publishing—R
(s)-LifeVest Publishing
Lift Every Voice—R
Lighthouse Publishing—R
Love Inspired Historical
More Than Novellas
MountainView
Nordskog Publishing—R
(s)-One World—R
Parson Place—R
(s)-Pleasant Word—R
(s)-Port Hole Public.
PREP Publishing—R
Ravenhawk Books—R
(s)-Rill & Associates
(s)-Self Publish Press—R
(s)-So. Baptist Press—R
Steeple Hill
Strang Book—R
(s)-Tate Publishing—R
Third World Press—R
(s)-Trafford Publishing—R
Treble Heart—R
Whitaker House
White Rose—R

(s)-WinePress—R
(s)-Zoë Life Publishing

FICTION: HUMOR
(a)-Baker Books
(a)-Ballantine
(a)-FaithWords
(a)-Multnomah
(a)-One World/Ballantine

Aadeon Publishing—R
Aaron Book—R
(s)-ACW Press—R
Ambassador Books
(s)-American Binding—R
(s)-Black Forest—R
(s)-Booklocker.com—R
(s)-Bookstand Publishing—R
Boyds Mills Press—R
Chalice Press—R
Christian Focus—R
Christian Writer's Ebook—R
Conquest Publishers
(s)-Creation House—R
(s)-Deep River Books
DiskUs Publishing
Eerdmans/Yg Readers
(s)-Elderberry Press
Encore Performance
(s)-Essence—R
Evergreen Press
(s)-Fairway Press—R
(s)-Faith Books & More—R
(s)-Forever Books—R
(s)-Halo Publishing Intl.
Hidden Brook Press—R
His Work Christian Pub.—R
(s)-Holy Fire Publishing—R
(s)-Infinity Publishing
(s)-Insight Publishing—R
JourneyForth/BJU
(s)-LifeVest Publishing
Lighthouse Publishing—R
Lion and Lamb
(s)-MileStones Intl.
MountainView
Nordskog Publishing—R
(s)-One World—R
Parson Place—R
Parsons Publishing—R

(s)-Pleasant Word—R
(s)-Port Hole Public.
PREP Publishing—R
Putnam/Young Readers
Quintessential Books—R
Ravenhawk Books—R
(s)-Rill & Associates
(s)-Salt Works—R
Samaritan Press—R
(s)-Selah Publishing—R
Strang Book—R
Sunpenny Publishing
(s)-Tate Publishing—R
Th1nk/NavPress—R
(s)-Trafford Publishing—R
Treble Heart—R
(s)-WinePress—R
(s)-Zoë Life Publishing

FICTION: JUVENILE (AGES 8-12)
(a)-Baker Books
(a)-Kregel—R
(a)-Tyndale House—R

Aadeon Publishing—R
Aaron Book—R
(s)-ACW Press—R
Ambassador Books
(s)-American Binding—R
AMG Publishers—R
Barbour
(s)-Black Forest—R
Blue Dolphin
(s)-Booklocker.com—R
(s)-Book Publishers Net.—R
(s)-Bookstand Publishing—R
Boyds Mills Press—R
(s)-Brown Books
Carson-Dellosa
Christian Ed. Pub.
Christian Focus—R
Comfort Publishing
Conquest Publishers
(s)-Creation House—R
(s)-CrossHouse—R
(s)-Dean Press, Robbie—R
(s)-Deep River Books
DiskUs Publishing
Dover Publications—R

Eerdmans Pub., Wm. B.—R
Eerdmans/Yg Readers
(s)-E.F.S. Online Pub.
(s)-Elderberry Press
(s)-Essence—R
Evergreen Press
Fair Havens—R
(s)-Fairway Press—R
(s)-Faith Books & More—R
(s)-Forever Books—R
(s)-Fruitbearer Pub.
Guardian Angel
(s)-Halo Publishing Intl.
Hidden Brook Press—R
His Work Christian Pub.—R
(s)-Holy Fire Publishing—R
(s)-Infinity Publishing
(s)-Insight Publishing—R
JourneyForth/BJU
(s)-Kindred Books—R
Knight George Pub.
LifeSong Publishers
(s)-LifeVest Publishing
Lift Every Voice—R
Lighthouse Publishing—R
Lion and Lamb
Mission City Press
Moody Publishers
New Canaan—R
Nordskog Publishing—R
(s)-One World—R
P & R Publishing—R
Pacific Press
Parson Place—R
Pauline Books—R
Pauline Kids—R
(s)-Pleasant Word—R
(s)-Port Hole Public.
Power Publishing—R
(s)-Providence House—R
Putnam/Young Readers
Quiet Waters—R
Reformation Trust
Revival Nation
(s)-Salt Works—R
(s)-Salty's Books—R
Samaritan Press—R
(s)-Selah Publishing—R
(s)-Self Publish Press—R
Standard Publishing

Strang Book—R
(s)-Tate Publishing—R
(s)-TEACH Services—R
Third World Press—R
(s)-Trafford Publishing—R
Warner Press
(s)-WinePress—R
(s)-Word Alive
(s)-Zoë Life Publishing

FICTION: LITERARY
(a)-Baker Books
(a)-Ballantine
(a)-Bethany House—R
(a)-FaithWords
(a)-HarperOne
(a)-Multnomah
(a)-Nelson, Fiction, Thomas
(a)-One World/Ballantine
(a)-WaterBrook Press—R

Aadeon Publishing—R
Aaron Book—R
(s)-ACW Press—R
Ambassador Books
(s)-American Binding—R
(s)-Black Forest—R
(s)-Booklocker.com—R
(s)-Bookstand Publishing—R
Boyds Mills Press—R
Branden Publishing—R
(s)-Brown Books
Chalice Press—R
Christian Writer's Ebook—R
(s)-Deep River Books
DiskUs Publishing
Dover Publications—R
Eerdmans Pub., Wm. B.—R
Eerdmans/Yg Readers
(s)-E.F.S. Online Pub.
(s)-Elderberry Press
(s)-Essence—R
(s)-Fairway Press—R
(s)-Faith Books & More—R
FaithWalk
Father's Press
Focus on the Family—R
(s)-Forever Books—R
Guernica Editions—R
Hidden Brook Press—R
(s)-Holy Fire Publishing—R

Hourglass Books—R
(s)-Infinity Publishing
(s)-Insight Publishing—R
JourneyForth/BJU
(s)-LifeVest Publishing
Lighthouse Publishing—R
Mercer Univ. Press—R
Moody Publishers
NavPress
Nordskog Publishing—R
(s)-One World—R
(s)-Pleasant Word—R
(s)-Port Hole Public.
(s)-Providence House—R
Putnam/Young Readers
Quintessential Books—R
Ravenhawk Books—R
(s)-Salt Works—R
(s)-Self Publish Press—R
Strang Book—R
Sunpenny Publishing
(s)-Tate Publishing—R
(s)-Trafford Publishing—R
(s)-WinePress—R
(s)-Zoë Life Publishing

FICTION: MYSTERY/ ROMANCE
(a)-B & H Publishing
(a)-Baker Books
(a)-Ballantine
(a)-Bethany House—R
(a)-Kregel—R
(a)-Multnomah
(a)-Nelson, Fiction, Thomas
(a)-Summerside Press

Aaron Book—R
(s)-ACW Press—R
(s)-American Binding—R
Barbour
(s)-Black Forest—R
(s)-Booklocker.com—R
(s)-Bookstand Publishing—R
(s)-Brentwood—R
(s)-Brown Books
Christian Writer's Ebook—R
Comfort Publishing
Conquest Publishers
Dan River Press
(s)-Deep River Books

Desert Breeze Pub.
Destiny Image (gifts)—R
(s)-Elderberry Press
(s)-Essence—R
(s)-Fairway Press—R
(s)-Faith Books & More—R
(s)-Forever Books—R
Guideposts Books
Heartsong/Mysteries
Hidden Brook Press—R
(s)-Holy Fire Publishing—R
Howard Books
(s)-Infinity Publishing
(s)-Insight Publishing—R
(s)-LifeVest Publishing
Lift Every Voice—R
Lighthouse Publishing—R
Love Inspired Suspense
More Than Novellas
MountainView
Nordskog Publishing—R
(s)-One World—R
Parson Place—R
(s)-Pleasant Word—R
(s)-Port Hole Public.
PREP Publishing—R
(s)-Selah Publishing—R
(s)-Self Publish Press—R
(s)-So. Baptist Press—R
Starik Publishing
Steeple Hill
Strang Book—R
(s)-Tate Publishing—R
Third World Press—R
(s)-Trafford Publishing—R
Treble Heart—R
White Rose—R
(s)-WinePress—R
(s)-Zoë Life Publishing

**FICTION: MYSTERY/
SUSPENSE**
(a)-B & H Publishing
(a)-Baker Books
(a)-Ballantine
(a)-Bethany House—R
(a)-Kregel—R
(a)-Multnomah
(a)-One World/Ballantine
(a)-Revell

(a)-Tyndale House—R

Aadeon Publishing—R
Aaron Book—R
(s)-ACW Press—R
Ambassador Books
(s)-American Binding—R
(s)-Black Forest—R
Blue Dolphin
(s)-Booklocker.com—R
(s)-Bookstand Publishing—R
(s)-Brown Books
Chalice Press—R
Christian Ed. Pub.
Christian Focus—R
Christian Writer's Ebook—R
Comfort Publishing
Conquest Publishers
(s)-Creation House—R
Dan River Press
(s)-Deep River Books
(s)-Deo Volente
Desert Breeze Pub.
DiskUs Publishing
Eerdmans/Yg Readers
(s)-E.F.S. Online Pub.
(s)-Elderberry Press
(s)-Essence—R
(s)-Fairway Press—R
(s)-Faith Books & More—R
Father's Press
Focus on the Family—R
(s)-Forever Books—R
Guideposts Books
Heartsong/Mysteries
Hidden Brook Press—R
His Work Christian Pub.—R
(s)-Holy Fire Publishing—R
Howard Books
(s)-Infinity Publishing
(s)-Insight Publishing—R
JourneyForth/BJU
(s)-LifeVest Publishing
Lift Every Voice—R
Lighthouse Publishing—R
Love Inspired Suspense
Master Books
Mission City Press
Moody Publishers
MountainView

New Leaf
Nordskog Publishing—R
OakTara—R
(s)-One World—R
Parson Place—R
Parsons Publishing—R
Pauline Books—R
Pauline Kids—R
(s)-Pleasant Word—R
(s)-Port Hole Public.
PREP Publishing—R
(s)-Providence House—R
Putnam/Young Readers
Quintessential Books—R
Ravenhawk Books—R
(s)-Salt Works—R
(s)-Selah Publishing—R
(s)-Self Publish Press—R
Starik Publishing
Steeple Hill
Strang Book—R
Sunpenny Publishing
(s)-Tate Publishing—R
Third World Press—R
(s)-Trafford Publishing—R
Treble Heart—R
(s)-WinePress—R
(s)-Zoë Life Publishing

FICTION: NOVELLAS
(a)-Baker Books
Aadeon Publishing—R
Aaron Book—R
(s)-ACW Press—R
(s)-American Binding—R
Barbour
(s)-Booklocker.com—R
(s)-Bookstand Publishing—R
Christian Writer's Ebook—R
(s)-E.F.S. Online Pub.
(s)-Elderberry Press
(s)-Essence—R
(s)-Fairway Press—R
(s)-Faith Books & More—R
(s)-Forever Books—R
Guernica Editions—R
(s)-Halo Publishing Intl.
Hidden Brook Press—R
(s)-Holy Fire Publishing—R
(s)-Infinity Publishing

(s)-Insight Publishing—R
Lighthouse Publishing—R
Mission City Press
More Than Novellas
MountainView
(s)-One World—R
(s)-Pleasant Word—R
Quintessential Books—R
(s)-Salt Works—R
Samaritan Press—R
(s)-Trafford Publishing—R
Treble Heart—R
Two Fish Publishing—R
Virtual Tales—R
(s)-WinePress—R
(s)-Zoë Life Publishing

FICTION: PLAYS

Aadeon Publishing—R
(s)-American Binding—R
Baker's Plays—R
(s)-Bookstand Publishing—R
(s)-Brentwood—R
CSS Publishing—R
Dover Publications—R
(s)-E.F.S. Online Pub.
Eldridge Plays
Encore Performance
(s)-Essence—R
(s)-Fairway Press—R
(s)-Forever Books—R
Guardian Angel
Guernica Editions—R
(s)-Holy Fire Publishing—R
Meriwether
Mission City Press
National Black Theatre
National Drama
(s)-One World—R
Players Press—R
(s)-Pleasant Word—R
(s)-Salt Works—R
(s)-So. Baptist Press—R
Third World Press—R

FICTION: ROMANCE

(a)-Baker Books
(a)-Ballantine
(a)-Bethany House—R
(a)-Harvest House

(a)-Multnomah
(a)-Nelson, Fiction, Thomas
(a)-One World/Ballantine
(a)-Summerside Press
(a)-Tyndale House—R
(a)-WaterBrook Press—R

Aaron Book—R
(s)-ACW Press—R
(s)-American Binding—R
Barbour
(s)-Black Forest—R
(s)-Booklocker.com—R
(s)-Bookstand Publishing—R
(s)-Brown Books
Chalice Press—R
Christian Writer's Ebook—R
Comfort Publishing
Conquest Publishers
(s)-Creation House—R
Dan River Press
(s)-Deep River Books
DiskUs Publishing
(s)-Elderberry Press
(s)-Essence—R
(s)-Fairway Press—R
(s)-Faith Books & More—R
(s)-Forever Books—R
Hannibal Books
Heartsong Presents
Hidden Brook Press—R
(s)-Holy Fire Publishing—R
(s)-Infinity Publishing
(s)-Insight Publishing—R
(s)-LifeVest Publishing
Lift Every Voice—R
Lighthouse Publishing—R
Love Inspired
Love Inspired Suspense
(s)-MileStones Intl.
More Than Novellas
MountainView
Nordskog Publishing—R
OakTara—R
(s)-One World—R
Parson Place—R
(s)-Pleasant Word—R
(s)-Port Hole Public.
(s)-Rill & Associates
(s)-Selah Publishing—R

Steeple Hill
Strang Book—R
Sunpenny Publishing
(s)-Tate Publishing—R
(s)-Trafford Publishing—R
Treble Heart—R
Whitaker House
White Rose—R
(s)-WinePress—R
(s)-Zoë Life Publishing

FICTION: SCIENCE FICTION

(a)-WaterBrook Press—R

Aaron Book—R
(s)-ACW Press—R
(s)-American Binding—R
(s)-Booklocker.com—R
(s)-Bookstand Publishing—R
Christian Focus—R
Christian Writer's Ebook—R
Comfort Publishing
Conquest Publishers
(s)-Creation House—R
(s)-Deep River Books
Desert Breeze Pub.
Destiny Image (gifts)—R
DiskUs Publishing
Dover Publications—R
(s)-Elderberry Press
(s)-Essence—R
Evergreen Press
(s)-Fairway Press—R
(s)-Faith Books & More—R
(s)-Forever Books—R
Hidden Brook Press—R
(s)-Holy Fire Publishing—R
(s)-Infinity Publishing
(s)-Insight Publishing—R
(s)-LifeVest Publishing
Lighthouse Publishing—R
Marcher Lord Press
MountainView
Nordskog Publishing—R
OakTara—R
(s)-One World—R
(s)-Pleasant Word—R
(s)-Port Hole Public.
PREP Publishing—R
Putnam/Young Readers

Quintessential Books—R
Realms
(s)-Rill & Associates
Starik Publishing
Strang Book—R
Sunpenny Publishing
(s)-Tate Publishing—R
(s)-Trafford Publishing—R
Treble Heart—R
(s)-WinePress—R
(s)-Zoë Life Publishing

FICTION: SHORT STORY COLLECTIONS

(a)-Baker Books
(a)-Ballantine

Aadeon Publishing—R
Aaron Book—R
(s)-ACW Press—R
(s)-American Binding—R
(s)-Black Forest—R
(s)-Booklocker.com—R
(s)-Bookstand Publishing—R
Branden Publishing—R
Chalice Press—R
Christian Writer's Ebook—R
Comfort Publishing
(s)-Deep River Books
DiskUs Publishing
Earthen Vessel—R
Eerdmans Pub., Wm. B.—R
(s)-E.F.S. Online Pub.
(s)-Elderberry Press
(s)-Essence—R
(s)-Fairway Press—R
(s)-Faith Books & More—R
(s)-Forever Books—R
Hidden Brook Press—R
His Work Christian Pub.—R
(s)-Holy Fire Publishing—R
Hourglass Books—R
(s)-Insight Publishing—R
Knight George Pub.
MountainView
(s)-One World—R
Parson Place—R
Pauline Books—R
Pauline Kids—R
(s)-Pleasant Word—R

(s)-Port Hole Public.
(s)-Providence House—R
Quintessential Books—R
(s)-Salt Works—R
Samaritan Press—R
(s)-Tate Publishing—R
Third World Press—R
(s)-Trafford Publishing—R
Virtual Tales—R
White Rose—R
(s)-WinePress—R
(s)-Zoë Life Publishing

FICTION: SPECULATIVE

(a)-Baker Books
(a)-Multnomah

Aadeon Publishing—R
Aaron Book—R
(s)-ACW Press—R
(s)-American Binding—R
(s)-Booklocker.com—R
(s)-Bookstand Publishing—R
Christian Writer's Ebook—R
(s)-Deep River Books
(s)-Elderberry Press
(s)-Essence—R
(s)-Faith Books & More—R
(s)-Forever Books—R
Hidden Brook Press—R
(s)-Holy Fire Publishing—R
(s)-Infinity Publishing
(s)-Insight Publishing—R
(s)-LifeVest Publishing
Lighthouse Publishing—R
Marcher Lord Press
MountainView
Nordskog Publishing—R
OakTara—R
(s)-One World—R
(s)-Pleasant Word—R
(s)-Port Hole Public.
Realms
Revival Nation
(s)-Salt Works—R
Strang Book—R
(s)-Tate Publishing—R
(s)-Trafford Publishing—R
(s)-WinePress—R
(s)-Zoë Life Publishing

FICTION: TEEN/YOUNG ADULT

(a)-Baker Books
(a)-FaithWords
(a)-Kregel—R
(a)-Multnomah
(a)-Nelson, Fiction, Thomas
(a)-WaterBrook Press—R

Aaron Book—R
(s)-ACW Press—R
Ambassador Books
(s)-American Binding—R
AMG Publishers—R
Barbour
Blue Dolphin
(s)-Booklocker.com—R
(s)-Book Publishers Net.—R
(s)-Bookstand Publishing—R
Boyds Mills Press—R
Christian Focus—R
Christian Writer's Ebook—R
Comfort Publishing
(s)-Creation House—R
(s)-Deep River Books
DiskUs Publishing
Eerdmans Pub., Wm. B.—R
Eerdmans/Yg Readers
(s)-E.F.S. Online Pub.
(s)-Elderberry Press
(s)-Essence—R
Evergreen Press
(s)-Fairway Press—R
(s)-Faith Books & More—R
Faith Communications
(s)-Forever Books—R
(s)-Fruitbearer Pub.
Hidden Brook Press—R
His Work Christian Pub.—R
(s)-Holy Fire Publishing—R
(s)-Infinity Publishing
(s)-Insight Publishing—R
JourneyForth/BJU
Kirk House
Legacy Press—R
(s)-LifeVest Publishing
Lift Every Voice—R
Lighthouse Publishing—R
Lighthouse Trails—R
Lion and Lamb

Mission City Press
Moody Publishers
MountainView
NavPress
New Canaan—R
Nordskog Publishing—R
(s)-One World—R
P & R Publishing—R
Parson Place—R
Parsons Publishing—R
(s)-Pleasant Word—R
Power Publishing—R
Putnam/Young Readers
Quiet Waters—R
Ravenhawk Books—R
Revival Nation
(s)-Rill & Associates
Samaritan Press—R
(s)-Selah Publishing—R
Starik Publishing
Strang Book—R
(s)-Tate Publishing—R
(s)-TEACH Services—R
Th1nk/NavPress—R
Third World Press—R
(s)-Trafford Publishing—R
Treble Heart—R
Two Fish Publishing—R
Warner Press
(s)-WinePress—R
(s)-Word Alive
(s)-Zoë Life Publishing

FICTION: WESTERNS

(a)-Baker Books
(a)-Multnomah

Aaron Book—R
(s)-ACW Press—R
(s)-American Binding—R
(s)-Black Forest—R
(s)-Booklocker.com—R
(s)-Bookstand Publishing—R
(s)-Brown Books
Christian Writer's Ebook—R
(s)-Deep River Books
(s)-Deo Volente
Desert Breeze Pub.
DiskUs Publishing
(s)-Elderberry Press

(s)-Essence—R
(s)-Fairway Press—R
(s)-Faith Books & More—R
(s)-Forever Books—R
Hidden Brook Press—R
(s)-Holy Fire Publishing—R
(s)-Infinity Publishing
(s)-Insight Publishing—R
JourneyForth/BJU
(s)-LifeVest Publishing
Lighthouse Publishing—R
MountainView
Nordskog Publishing—R
(s)-One World—R
Parson Place—R
(s)-Pleasant Word—R
Quintessential Books—R
Ravenhawk Books—R
(s)-Salt Works—R
Strang Book—R
(s)-Tate Publishing—R
Third World Press—R
(s)-Trafford Publishing—R
Treble Heart—R
Whitaker House
(s)-WinePress—R
(s)-Zoë Life Publishing

FORGIVENESS

(a)-B & H Publishing
(a)-Doubleday Relig.—R
(a)-FaithWords
(a)-HarperOne
(a)-Harvest House
(a)-Kregel—R
(a)-Nelson, Thomas
(a)-Regal

Aaron Book—R
Abingdon Press
ACTA Publications
(s)-ACW Press—R
Ambassador Intl.—R
(s)-American Binding—R
Barbour
(s)-Black Forest—R
Blue Dolphin
(s)-Booklocker.com—R
(s)-Bookstand Publishing—R
Bridge Logos—R

(s)-Brown Books
CarePoint Publishing—R
Chalice Press—R
Chapter Two—R
Christian Family—R
Christian Focus—R
Christian Writer's Ebook—R
CLC Publications—R
Comfort Publishing
(s)-Creation House—R
CrossLink Publishing
CSS Publishing—R
(s)-DCTS Publishers
(s)-Deep River Books
(s)-Destiny Image (books)—R
Discovery House—R
Editorial Portavoz
Eerdmans Pub., Wm. B.—R
(s)-E.F.S. Online Pub.
(s)-Elderberry Press
Eldridge Plays
(s)-Essence—R
Evangelical Press
Evergreen Press
(s)-Fairway Press—R
(s)-Faith Books & More—R
FaithWalk
Father's Press
(s)-Forever Books—R
Forward Movement
Four Craftsmen—R
Gentle Path Press
(s)-Grace Acres Press—R
Guardian Angel
(s)-Halo Publishing Intl.
Health Commun.
Hensley Publishing
Hidden Brook Press—R
(s)-Holy Fire Publishing—R
Howard Books
(s)-IMD Press—R
(s)-Insight Publishing—R
InterVarsity Press—R
JourneyForth/BJU
Judson Press—R
Lift Every Voice—R
Lighthouse Publishing—R
Lion and Lamb
Lutheran Univ. Press
(s)-MileStones Intl.

Monarch Books
NavPress
New Hope—R
Nordskog Publishing—R
(s)-One World—R
On My Own Now—R
Pacific Press
Parson Place—R
Parsons Publishing—R
Pauline Books—R
Pilgrim Press—R
(s)-Pleasant Word—R
Power Publishing—R
PREP Publishing—R
(s)-Providence House—R
Revival Nation
(s)-Rill & Associates
Rose Publishing
(s)-Salt Works—R
(s)-Salvation Publisher—R
Samaritan Press—R
(s)-Star Bible Public.
St. Pauls/Alba—R
Strang Book—R
(s)-Tate Publishing—R
(s)-TEACH Services—R
Th1nk/NavPress—R
Torch Legacy
(s)-Trafford Publishing—R
Treble Heart—R
VBC Publishing
(s)-WinePress—R
(s)-Word Alive
(s)-Zoë Life Publishing

GAMES/CRAFTS
(a)-Baker Books

(s)-Booklocker.com—R
(s)-Bookstand Publishing—R
Chalice Press—R
Church Publishing
Contemporary Drama
(s)-Elderberry Press
(s)-Essence—R
(s)-Fairway Press—R
(s)-Faith Books & More—R
Group Publishing
Guardian Angel
Hidden Brook Press—R

(s)-Holy Fire Publishing—R
Jubilant Press—R
Knight George Pub.
Legacy Press—R
Lighthouse Publishing—R
Lion and Lamb
Mission City Press
Monarch Books
(s)-One World—R
Players Press—R
Praxis Press
Rainbow Publishers—R
Samaritan Press—R
Standard Publishing
(s)-Tate Publishing—R
(s)-Trafford Publishing—R
Warner Press
(s)-Zoë Life Publishing

GIFT BOOKS
(a)-Harvest House

Aaron Book—R
ACTA Publications
(s)-Black Forest—R
Blue Dolphin
(s)-Book Publishers Net.—R
(s)-Bookstand Publishing—R
Bridge Logos—R
(s)-Brown Books
(s)-Creation House—R
Dimensions for Living
Eerdmans Pub., Wm. B.—R
(s)-Essence—R
Evangelical Press
(s)-Faith Books & More—R
(s)-Forever Books—R
(s)-Fruitbearer Pub.
GRQ—R
(s)-Holy Fire Publishing—R
Howard Books
(s)-IMD Press—R
Lighthouse Publishing—R
Lion and Lamb
Nordskog Publishing—R
(s)-Pleasant Word—R
Power Publishing—R
Ravenhawk Books—R
(s)-Salt Works—R
Strang Book—R

(s)-Trafford Publishing—R
(s)-WinePress—R
(s)-Zoë Life Publishing

GRANDPARENTING*
(a)-Bethany House—R
(a)-Nelson, Thomas

Aaron Book—R
Abingdon Press
ACTA Publications
(s)-ACW Press—R
(s)-American Binding—R
Anglicans United—R
(s)-Black Forest—R
Blue Dolphin
(s)-Booklocker.com—R
(s)-Bookstand Publishing—R
Bridge Logos—R
(s)-Brown Books
Cambridge Scholars
CarePoint Publishing—R
CLC Publications—R
(s)-Creation House—R
CrossLink Publishing
Crossroad Publishing—R
Discovery House—R
Eerdmans Pub., Wm. B.—R
(s)-Elderberry Press
(s)-Essence—R
Evangelical Press
(s)-Faith Books & More—R
Father's Press
(s)-Forever Books—R
Gentle Path Press
Health Commun.
(s)-Holy Fire Publishing—R
Howard Books
(s)-IMD Press—R
(s)-Insight Publishing—R
Kingsley Pub., Jessica—R
Lighthouse Publishing—R
Lion and Lamb
Monarch Books
New Hope—R
Nordskog Publishing—R
Parson Place—R
(s)-Pleasant Word—R
Power Publishing—R
(s)-Providence House—R

Rose Publishing
(s)-Salvation Publisher—R
(s)-Star Bible Public.
(s)-TEACH Services—R
Third World Press—R
(s)-Trafford Publishing—R
VBC Publishing
Whitaker House
(s)-WinePress—R
(s)-Zoë Life Publishing

GRIEF
(a)-Bethany House—R
(a)-Harvest House

Aaron Book—R
(s)-ACW Press—R
(s)-American Binding—R
Blue Dolphin
BMH Books—R
(s)-Booklocker.com—R
(s)-Bookstand Publishing—R
Chalice Press—R
Comfort Publishing
(s)-Creation House—R
CrossLink Publishing
Discovery House—R
Eerdmans Pub., Wm. B.—R
(s)-E.F.S. Online Pub.
(s)-Elderberry Press
(s)-Essence—R
Evangelical Press
Fair Havens—R
(s)-Faith Books & More—R
(s)-Forever Books—R
Fresh Air Books
GRQ—R
Health Commun.
Heart of Wisdom
(s)-Holy Fire Publishing—R
Howard Books
(s)-IMD Press—R
(s)-Insight Publishing—R
Lift Every Voice—R
Lighthouse Publishing—R
Lutterworth Press—R
Messianic Jewish—R
(s)-MileStones Intl.
Monarch Books
NavPress
Nordskog Publishing—R

Pauline Books—R
(s)-Pleasant Word—R
(s)-Port Hole Public.
Power Publishing—R
(s)-Providence House—R
Ravenhawk Books—R
(s)-Rill & Associates
(s)-Salvation Publisher—R
Samaritan Press—R
St. Anthony Mess. Press—R
(s)-Star Bible Public.
Strang Book—R
(s)-TEACH Services—R
Th1nk/NavPress—R
(s)-Trafford Publishing—R
(s)-WinePress—R
Xyzzy Press
(s)-Zoë Life Publishing

GROUP STUDY BOOKS
(a)-Baker Books

Aaron Book—R
Abingdon Press
(s)-ACW Press—R
(s)-American Binding—R
AMG Publishers—R
(s)-Bfree Publishing
BMH Books—R
(s)-Booklocker.com—R
(s)-Bookstand Publishing—R
(s)-Brentwood—R
Bridge Logos—R
CarePoint Publishing—R
Carey Library, Wm.—R
Chalice Press—R
Christian Writer's Ebook—R
College Press—R
Congregational Life
(s)-CrossHouse—R
CrossLink Publishing
CSS Publishing—R
(s)-Deep River Books
Eerdmans Pub., Wm. B.—R
(s)-E.F.S. Online Pub.
Emmaus Road
(s)-Essence—R
Evangelical Press
Evergreen Press
Fair Havens—R
(s)-Fairway Press—R

(s)-Forever Books—R
Founders Press
Four Craftsmen—R
Foursquare Media
Good Book—R
Gospel Publishing
(s)-Grace Acres Press—R
Group Publishing
Hannibal Books
Hensley Publishing
Hidden Brook Press—R
(s)-Holy Fire Publishing—R
(s)-IMD Press—R
InterVarsity Press—R
Jesus Filled Day (books)
Jubilant Press—R
Judson Press—R
Lighthouse Publishing—R
Lion and Lamb
Mission City Press
Monarch Books
New Hope—R
Nordskog Publishing—R
(s)-One World—R
Pacific Press
Paradise Research—R
Parson Place—R
Pilgrim Press—R
(s)-Pleasant Word—R
Power Publishing—R
(s)-Providence House—R
Randall House
Revival Nation
Rose Publishing
(s)-Salt Works—R
Smyth & Helwys
(s)-So. Baptist Press—R
(s)-Star Bible Public.
(s)-Tate Publishing—R
Th1nk/NavPress—R
(s)-Trafford Publishing—R
UMI Publishing—R
(s)-WinePress—R
(s)-Word Alive
(s)-Zoë Life Publishing

HEALING
(a)-Baker Books
(a)-Cook, David C.
(a)-FaithWords

(a)-Hay House
(a)-Nelson, Thomas

Aaron Book—R
ACTA Publications
(s)-ACW Press—R
(s)-American Binding—R
(s)-Bfree Publishing
(s)-Black Forest—R
Blue Dolphin
(s)-Book Publishers Net.—R
(s)-Booklocker.com—R
(s)-Bookstand Publishing—R
(s)-Brentwood—R
Bridge Logos—R
(s)-Brown Books
Cambridge Scholars
Canticle Books—R
CarePoint Publishing—R
Christian Heritage—R
Christian Writer's Ebook—R
CLC Publications—R
Comfort Publishing
(s)-Creation House—R
Crossroad Publishing—R
CSS Publishing—R
(s)-Deep River Books
Destiny Image (gifts)—R
(s)-Destiny Image (books)—R
Eerdmans Pub., Wm. B.—R
(s)-E.F.S. Online Pub.
(s)-Elderberry Press
(s)-Essence—R
(s)-Fairway Press—R
(s)-Faith Books & More—R
FaithWalk
Father's Press
(s)-Forever Books—R
Forward Movement
Four Craftsmen—R
Gentle Path Press
Good Book—R
Harrison House
Health Commun.
Hidden Brook Press—R
(s)-Holy Fire Publishing—R
Hope Publishing—R
(s)-IMD Press—R
(s)-Impact Christian—R
(s)-Insight Publishing—R

Kingsley Pub., Jessica—R
Life Changing Media
Lighthouse Publishing—R
Lion and Lamb
Loyola Press
Lutheran Univ. Press
Magnus Press—R
(s)-McDougal Publishing—R
(s)-MileStones Intl.
Monarch Books
Nordskog Publishing—R
(s)-One World—R
Pacific Press
Paradise Research—R
Parson Place—R
Parsons Publishing—R
Pauline Books—R
Pilgrim Press—R
(s)-Pleasant Word—R
Power Publishing—R
(s)-Providence House—R
(s)-Recovery Commun.
Revival Nation
(s)-Rill & Associates
(s)-Salvation Publisher—R
(s)-Selah Publishing—R
Siloam
(s)-So. Baptist Press—R
(s)-Star Bible Public.
Strang Book—R
(s)-Tate Publishing—R
(s)-TEACH Services—R
(s)-Trafford Publishing—R
Whitaker House
(s)-WinePress—R
(s)-Word Alive
(s)-Zoë Life Publishing

HEALTH

(a)-Baker Books
(a)-Ballantine
(a)-FaithWords
(a)-Harvest House
(a)-Hay House
(a)-Nelson, Thomas

Aaron Book—R
(s)-ACW Press—R
Ambassador Books
(s)-American Binding—R
(s)-Bfree Publishing

Blue Dolphin
(s)-Booklocker.com—R
(s)-Book Publishers Net.—R
(s)-Bookstand Publishing—R
(s)-Brentwood—R
(s)-Brown Books
Cambridge Scholars
Canticle Books—R
Christian Writer's Ebook—R
Church Publishing
Cladach Publishing
(s)-Creation House—R
(s)-Deep River Books
(s)-Destiny Image (books)—R
Eerdmans Pub., Wm. B.—R
(s)-E.F.S. Online Pub.
(s)-Elderberry Press
(s)-Essence—R
Evangelical Press
Evergreen Press
Facts On File
Fair Havens—R
(s)-Fairway Press—R
(s)-Faith Books & More—R
(s)-Forever Books—R
Forward Movement
Gentle Path Press
Good Book—R
Grupo Nelson
Guardian Angel
Health Commun.
Hidden Brook Press—R
His Work Christian Pub.—R
(s)-Holy Fire Publishing—R
Hope Publishing—R
(s)-IMD Press—R
(s)-Insight Publishing—R
Kingsley Pub., Jessica—R
Langmarc
Life Changing Media
Life Cycle Books—R
Lighthouse Publishing—R
Lion and Lamb
Loyola Press
Magnus Press—R
Messianic Jewish—R
(s)-MileStones Intl.
Monarch Books
MountainView
New Hope—R

Nordskog Publishing—R
(s)-One World—R
Pacific Press
Paradise Research—R
Parsons Publishing—R
(s)-Pleasant Word—R
Power Publishing—R
(s)-Providence House—R
Quintessential Books—R
(s)-Recovery Commun.
Review and Herald
Revival Nation
(s)-Rill & Associates
(s)-Salvation Publisher—R
Sheed & Ward
Siloam
(s)-So. Baptist Press—R
(s)-Star Bible Public.
Strang Book—R
Sunpenny Publishing
Tarcher, Jeremy P.—R
(s)-Tate Publishing—R
(s)-TEACH Services—R
Third World Press—R
(s)-Trafford Publishing—R
Treble Heart—R
VBC Publishing
(s)-WinePress—R
(s)-Word Alive
Xyzzy Press
(s)-Zoë Life Publishing

HISPANIC MARKETS
(a)-Doubleday Religious—R

Abingdon Press
(s)-American Binding—R
Anglicans United—R
B & H Publishing
(s)-Booklocker.com—R
Bridge Logos—R
Cambridge Scholars Pub.
Chapter Two—R
Editorial Portavoz
Editorial Unilit
Forward Movement
Georgetown Univ. Press
Groupo Nelson (5 Imprints)
InterVarsity Press—R
Judson Press—R

Libros Liguori
Liturgy Training—R
Oregon Catholic
Pacific Press
Parsons Publishing—R
Paulist Press
Pilgrim Press—R
Praeger Publishers
St. Anthony Mess. Press—R
Strang Book Group (2
    imprints)—R
(s)-Tate Publishing—R
Third World Press—R
Tyndale Español
Whitaker House

HISTORICAL
(a)-Baker Academic
(a)-Baker Books
(a)-Doubleday Relig.—R
(a)-HarperOne
(a)-Kregel—R
(a)-Nelson, Thomas
(a)-One World/Ballantine

Aadeon Publishing—R
Aaron Book—R
(s)-ACW Press—R
Ambassador Books
(s)-American Binding—R
AMG Publishers—R
Anglicans United—R
(s)-Bfree Publishing
(s)-Black Forest—R
Blue Dolphin
(s)-Booklocker.com—R
(s)-Bookstand Publishing—R
Boyds Mills Press—R
(s)-Brentwood—R
Bridge Logos—R
(s)-Brown Books
Cambridge Scholars
Canadian Inst. for Law—R
Carey Library, Wm.—R
Catholic Answers—R
Chapter Two—R
Christian Family—R
Christian Heritage—R
Christian Liberty Press
Christian Writer's Ebook—R

Cistercian—R
Clarke & Co., James—R
College Press—R
Comfort Publishing
Conciliar Press—R
Concordia Academic
Continuum Intl.—R
(s)-Creation House—R
CrossLink Publishing
Custom Book
Earthen Vessel—R
Eerdmans Pub., Wm. B.—R
(s)-E.F.S. Online Pub.
(s)-Elderberry Press
Elijah Press
(s)-Essence—R
ETC Publications
Evangelical Press
Facts On File
(s)-Fairway Press—R
(s)-Faith Books & More—R
FaithWalk
Fordham Univ. Press—R
(s)-Forever Books—R
Founders Press
Foursquare Media
Heart of Wisdom
Hidden Brook Press—R
His Work Christian Pub.—R
(s)-Holy Fire Publishing—R
(s)-IMD Press—R
(s)-Impact Christian—R
Inkling Books—R
(s)-Insight Publishing—R
InterVarsity Press—R
Kirk House
(s)-LifeVest Publishing
Lift Every Voice—R
Lighthouse Publishing—R
Lion and Lamb
Loyola Press
Lutheran Univ. Press
Lutterworth Press—R
Mercer Univ. Press—R
Messianic Jewish—R
Monarch Books
New York Univ. Press
Nordskog Publishing—R
(s)-One World—R
Palgrave Macmillan—R

Paradise Research—R
(s)-Pleasant Word—R
Power Publishing—R
(s)-Providence House—R
Quintessential Books—R
Ragged Edge—R
Reformation Heritage—R
Revival Nation
(s)-Salt Works—R
Scepter Publishers—R
Sheed & Ward
(s)-So. Baptist Press—R
(s)-Star Bible Public.
St. Augustine's Press—R
Still Waters Revival—R
Sunpenny Publishing
(s)-Tate Publishing—R
(s)-TEACH Services—R
Third World Press—R
(s)-Trafford Publishing—R
Treble Heart—R
Trinity Foundation—R
Univ. of AR Press—R
Univ. Press of America—R
Vision Forum
(s)-WinePress—R
(s)-Word Alive
Yale Univ. Press
(s)-Zoë Life Publishing

HOLIDAY/SEASONAL
(a)-Cook, David C.
(a)-FaithWords
(a)-HarperOne

Aaron Book—R
Abingdon Press
(s)-ACW Press—R
Ambassador Books
(s)-American Binding—R
Barbour
Blue Dolphin
(s)-Booklocker.com—R
Chalice Press—R
Christian Writer's Ebook—R
CSS Publishing—R
(s)-Deep River Books
Discovery House—R
(s)-E.F.S. Online Pub.
(s)-Elderberry Press

Eldridge Plays
Encore Performance
(s)-Essence—R
Evangelical Press
Evergreen Press
(s)-Fairway Press—R
(s)-Faith Books & More—R
(s)-Forever Books—R
Forward Movement
GRQ—R
Guardian Angel
Guideposts Books
Hidden Brook Press—R
(s)-Holy Fire Publishing—R
Howard Books
(s)-IMD Press—R
(s)-Insight Publishing—R
Judson Press—R
Lighthouse Publishing—R
Lion and Lamb
Meriwether
Messianic Jewish—R
Monarch Books
New Hope—R
Nordskog Publishing—R
(s)-One World—R
Palgrave Macmillan—R
Pauline Books—R
Pflaum Publishing
(s)-Pleasant Word—R
Power Publishing—R
(s)-Providence House—R
Putnam/Young Readers
Ravenhawk Books—R
(s)-Salt Works—R
Standard Publishing
Strang Book—R
(s)-Tate Publishing—R
(s)-Trafford Publishing—R
Warner Press
(s)-WinePress—R
(s)-Word Alive

HOLINESS
(a)-Bethany House—R

Aaron Book—R
(s)-ACW Press—R
Ambassador Intl.—R
(s)-American Binding—R

(s)-Bfree Publishing
(s)-Black Forest—R
Blue Dolphin
(s)-Booklocker.com—R
Bridge Logos—R
(s)-Brown Books
Chapter Two—R
Christian Family—R
Christian Focus—R
Christian Heritage—R
CLC Publications—R
(s)-Creation House—R
Eerdmans Pub., Wm. B.—R
(s)-E.F.S. Online Pub.
(s)-Elderberry Press
Emmaus Road
(s)-Essence—R
Evangelical Press
(s)-Faith Books & More—R
Father's Press
(s)-Forever Books—R
Forward Movement
Four Craftsmen—R
(s)-Grace Acres Press—R
Hidden Brook Press—R
(s)-Holy Fire Publishing—R
Howard Books
(s)-IMD Press—R
(s)-Insight Publishing—R
InterVarsity Press—R
Lighthouse Publishing—R
(s)-MileStones Intl.
Monarch Books
Nordskog Publishing—R
Parson Place—R
Parsons Publishing—R
Pauline Books—R
(s)-Pleasant Word—R
Power Publishing—R
(s)-Providence House—R
Revival Nation
(s)-Rill & Associates
(s)-Salt Works—R
(s)-Salvation Publisher—R
(s)-Star Bible Public.
St. Bede's Public.—R
St. Pauls/Alba—R
Strang Book—R
(s)-Tate Publishing—R
(s)-TEACH Services—R

Th1nk/NavPress—R
(s)-Trafford Publishing—R
Wesleyan Publishing
(s)-WinePress—R

HOLY SPIRIT

(a)-Kregel—R
(a)-Nelson, Thomas
(a)-Regal

Aaron Book—R
(s)-ACW Press—R
(s)-American Binding—R
Baylor Univ. Press
(s)-Bfree Publishing
(s)-Black Forest—R
Blue Dolphin
(s)-Booklocker.com—R
Bridge Logos—R
Canticle Books—R
Chalice Press—R
Chapter Two—R
Christian Family—R
Christian Focus—R
Christian Heritage—R
Christian Writer's Ebook—R
CLC Publications—R
Comfort Publishing
(s)-Creation House—R
CSS Publishing—R
(s)-Deep River Books
Destiny Image (gifts)—R
(s)-Destiny Image (books)—R
Eerdmans Pub., Wm. B.—R
(s)-E.F.S. Online Pub.
(s)-Elderberry Press
(s)-Essence—R
Evangelical Press
(s)-Fairway Press—R
(s)-Faith Books & More—R
Father's Press
(s)-Forever Books—R
Forward Movement
Four Craftsmen—R
Gospel Publishing
Harrison House
Hidden Brook Press—R
(s)-Holy Fire Publishing—R
(s)-IMD Press—R
(s)-Insight Publishing—R
InterVarsity Press—R

Jebaire
Lift Every Voice—R
Lighthouse Publishing—R
Lion and Lamb
Lutheran Univ. Press
Magnus Press—R
(s)-MileStones Intl.
Monarch Books
Nordskog Publishing—R
(s)-One World—R
Pacific Press
Palgrave Macmillan—R
Parson Place—R
Parsons Publishing—R
Pilgrim Press—R
(s)-Pleasant Word—R
Power Publishing—R
(s)-Providence House—R
Reformation Heritage—R
Revival Nation
(s)-Rill & Associates
Rose Publishing
(s)-Salvation Publisher—R
(s)-Star Bible Public.
St. Bede's Public.—R
St. Pauls/Alba—R
Strang Book—R
(s)-Tate Publishing—R
(s)-TEACH Services—R
Th1nk/NavPress—R
(s)-Trafford Publishing—R
VBC Publishing
Westminster John Knox
Whitaker House
(s)-WinePress—R
(s)-Word Alive
(s)-Zoë Life Publishing

HOMESCHOOLING RESOURCES

(a)-Baker Books

Aaron Book—R
(s)-ACW Press—R
(s)-American Binding—R
(s)-Bfree Publishing
(s)-Booklocker.com—R
(s)-Book Publishers Net.—R
(s)-Bookstand Publishing—R
(s)-Brentwood—R
Chapter Two—R

Christian Focus—R
Christian Writer's Ebook—R
(s)-CrossHouse—R
CrossLink Publishing
Eerdmans Pub., Wm. B.—R
(s)-E.F.S. Online Pub.
(s)-Elderberry Press
Eldridge Plays
Emmaus Road
(s)-Essence—R
ETC Publications
Evangelical Press
Fair Havens—R
(s)-Fairway Press—R
(s)-Faith Books & More—R
(s)-Forever Books—R
(s)-Grace Acres Press—R
Guardian Angel
Hannibal Books
Heart of Wisdom
Hidden Brook Press—R
(s)-Holy Fire Publishing—R
(s)-IMD Press—R
JourneyForth/BJU
Lighthouse Publishing—R
Lighthouse Trails—R
Lion and Lamb
Mason Crest
Master Books
McRuffy Press
(s)-MileStones Intl.
Mission City Press
Monarch Books
New Canaan—R
New Leaf
Nordskog Publishing—R
(s)-One World—R
(s)-Pleasant Word—R
Power Publishing—R
(s)-Providence House—R
Rose Publishing
(s)-Salt Works—R
Samaritan Press—R
(s)-Seed Faith Books—R
Starik Publishing
(s)-Tate Publishing—R
(s)-Trafford Publishing—R
(s)-WinePress—R
(s)-Word Alive
(s)-Zoë Life Publishing

HOMILETICS
(a)-Baker Books
(a)-Kregel—R

Aaron Book—R
Abingdon Press
(s)-ACW Press—R
(s)-American Binding—R
(s)-Bfree Publishing
(s)-Black Forest—R
(s)-Booklocker.com—R
Chalice Press—R
Christian Family—R
Christian Focus—R
Christian Writer's Ebook—R
Church Publishing
CSS Publishing—R
(s)-DCTS Publishers
(s)-Deep River Books
Earthen Vessel—R
Eerdmans Pub., Wm. B.—R
(s)-Elderberry Press
Emmaus Road
(s)-Essence—R
Evangelical Press
(s)-Fairway Press—R
(s)-Faith Books & More—R
(s)-Forever Books—R
Hidden Brook Press—R
(s)-Holy Fire Publishing—R
(s)-IMD Press—R
(s)-Insight Publishing—R
Judson Press—R
Lighthouse Publishing—R
Lutheran Univ. Press
Monarch Books
Nordskog Publishing—R
(s)-One World—R
(s)-Pleasant Word—R
Power Publishing—R
(s)-Providence House—R
Resource Public.
Rose Publishing
(s)-Salt Works—R
(s)-Star Bible Public.
St. Pauls/Alba—R
(s)-Tate Publishing—R
(s)-Trafford Publishing—R
VBC Publishing
Westminster John Knox

(s)-WinePress—R
(s)-Word Alive
(s)-Zoë Life Publishing

HOW-TO
(a)-Baker Books
(a)-Ballantine
(a)-Harvest House
(a)-Nelson, Thomas
(a)-One World/Ballantine
(a)-Revell

Aaron Book—R
(s)-ACW Press—R
Adams Media
(s)-American Binding—R
(s)-Bfree Publishing
(s)-Black Forest—R
Blue Dolphin
(s)-Booklocker.com—R
(s)-Bookstand Publishing—R
(s)-Brentwood—R
Bridge Logos—R
Christian Writer's Ebook—R
Church Growth Inst.
(s)-Deep River Books
Destiny Image (gifts)—R
DiskUs Publishing
(s)-E.F.S. Online Pub.
(s)-Elderberry Press
Encore Performance
(s)-Essence—R
Evangelical Press
Evergreen Press
Fair Havens—R
(s)-Fairway Press—R
(s)-Faith Books & More—R
FaithWalk
Fell, Frederick—R
(s)-Forever Books—R
Gospel Light
GRQ—R
Guardian Angel
(s)-Halo Publishing Intl.
Hidden Brook Press—R
His Work Christian Pub.—R
(s)-Holy Fire Publishing—R
Howard Books
(s)-IMD Press—R
Inkling Books—R
(s)-Insight Publishing—R

Kirk House
(s)-LifeVest Publishing
Lighthouse Publishing—R
Lion and Lamb
Meriwether
(s)-MileStones Intl.
Monarch Books
MountainView
Nordskog Publishing—R
(s)-One World—R
Our Sunday Visitor—R
Pacific Press
Parson Place—R
Perigee Books
Players Press—R
(s)-Pleasant Word—R
Power Publishing—R
PREP Publishing—R
(s)-Providence House—R
Quintessential Books—R
(s)-Recovery Commun.
Review and Herald
(s)-Rill & Associates
(s)-Salt Works—R
(s)-Salvation Publisher—R
(s)-So. Baptist Press—R
Standard Publishing
Still Waters Revival—R
Tarcher, Jeremy P.—R
(s)-Tate Publishing—R
Third World Press—R
(s)-Trafford Publishing—R
Treble Heart—R
VBC Publishing
Wilshire Book—R
(s)-WinePress—R
(s)-Word Alive
(s)-Zoë Life Publishing

HUMOR
(a)-Baker Books
(a)-Ballantine
(a)-Cook, David C.
(a)-Countryman, J.
(a)-FaithWords
(a)-Harvest House
(a)-Nelson, Thomas
(a)-One World/Ballantine

Aaron Book—R
ACTA Publications

(s)-ACW Press—R
Ambassador Books
(s)-American Binding—R
Barbour
(s)-Bfree Publishing
(s)-Black Forest—R
Blue Dolphin
(s)-Booklocker.com—R
(s)-Bookstand Publishing—R
Boyds Mills Press—R
(s)-Brentwood—R
Bridge Logos—R
Chalice Press—R
Christian Writer's Ebook—R
Comfort Publishing
(s)-Creation House—R
(s)-Deep River Books
(s)-E.F.S. Online Pub.
(s)-Elderberry Press
Eldridge Plays
(s)-Essence—R
Evergreen Press
(s)-Fairway Press—R
(s)-Faith Books & More—R
(s)-Forever Books—R
Forward Movement
Guideposts Books
Health Commun.
Hidden Brook Press—R
(s)-Holy Fire Publishing—R
(s)-IMD Press—R
(s)-Insight Publishing—R
Jebaire
Kirk House
Lighthouse Publishing—R
Lion and Lamb
Loyola Press
Lutterworth Press—R
Meriwether
(s)-MileStones Intl.
Monarch Books
MOPS Intl.
Nordskog Publishing—R
(s)-One World—R
On My Own Now—R
Pacific Press
Palgrave Macmillan—R
Parson Place—R
(s)-Pleasant Word—R
Power Publishing—R

(s)-Providence House—R
Putnam/Young Readers
Quintessential Books—R
Review and Herald
(s)-Salt Works—R
(s)-Salvation Publisher—R
Samaritan Press—R
(s)-Selah Publishing—R
(s)-So. Baptist Press—R
(s)-Tate Publishing—R
Th1nk/NavPress—R
Third World Press—R
(s)-Trafford Publishing—R
Treble Heart—R
(s)-WinePress—R
(s)-Word Alive
Xyzzy Press
(s)-Zoë Life Publishing

INSPIRATIONAL

(a)-Baker Books
(a)-Bethany House—R
(a)-Countryman, J.
(a)-Doubleday Relig.—R
(a)-FaithWords
(a)-Harvest House
(a)-Hay House
(a)-Nelson, Thomas
(a)-Tyndale House—R
(a)-WaterBrook Press—R
(a)-W Publishing

Aadeon Publishing—R
Aaron Book—R
Abingdon Press
(s)-ACW Press—R
Adams Media
Ambassador Books
(s)-American Binding—R
Barbour
Beacon Hill Press—R
Believe Books
(s)-Bfree Publishing
(s)-Black Forest—R
Blue Dolphin
(s)-Booklocker.com—R
(s)-Bookstand Publishing—R
(s)-Brentwood—R
Bridge Logos—R
(s)-Brown Books
Canticle Books—R

Catholic Book
Chalice Press—R
Chapter Two—R
CharismaKids
Christian Family—R
Christian Focus—R
Christian Writer's Ebook—R
CLC Publications—R
Comfort Publishing
Continuum Intl.—R
(s)-Creation House—R
(s)-CrossHouse—R
CrossLink Publishing
CSS Publishing—R
(s)-DCTS Publishers
(s)-Deep River Books
Destiny Image (gifts)—R
(s)-Destiny Image (books)—R
Dimensions for Living
Discovery House—R
Dove Inspirational—R
Earthen Vessel—R
(s)-E.F.S. Online Pub.
 (s)-Elderberry Press
Eldridge Plays
(s)-Essence—R
Evangelical Press
Evergreen Press
(s)-Fairway Press—R
(s)-Faith Books & More—R
Faith Communications
FaithWalk
(s)-Forever Books—R
Forward Movement
Fresh Air Books
(s)-Fruitbearer Pub.
GRQ—R
Grupo Nelson
Guardian Angel
Harrison House
Health Commun.
HeartSpring Pub.—R
Hidden Brook Press—R
(s)-Holy Fire Publishing—R
Hope Publishing—R
(s)-House of Ali
Howard Books
(s)-IMD Press—R
(s)-Impact Christian—R
(s)-Insight Publishing—R

JourneyForth/BJU
JourneyStone—R
Judson Press—R
Kirk House
Langmarc
Leafwood
Life Changing Media
(s)-LifeVest Publishing
Lighthouse Publishing—R
Lion and Lamb
Loyola Press
Lutheran Univ. Press
Lutheran Voices
Magnus Press—R
Master Books
(s)-McDougal Publishing—R
(s)-MileStones Intl.
Monarch Books
MountainView
New Leaf
Nordskog Publishing—R
(s)-One World—R
On My Own Now—R
Pacific Press
Paradise Research—R
Parson Place—R
Parsons Publishing—R
Pauline Books—R
Paulist Press
Pelican Publishing—R
Perigee Books
Pilgrim Press—R
(s)-Pleasant Word—R
(s)-Port Hole Public.
Power Publishing—R
(s)-Providence House—R
Quintessential Books—R
Ragged Edge—R
Ravenhawk Books—R
Review and Herald
Revival Nation
(s)-Rill & Associates
(s)-Salt Works—R
(s)-Salvation Publisher—R
Samaritan Press—R
(s)-Selah Publishing—R
Smyth & Helwys
(s)-So. Baptist Press—R
St. Anthony Mess. Press—R
(s)-Star Bible Public.

St. Pauls/Alba—R
Strang Book—R
Sunpenny Publishing
(s)-Tate Publishing—R
Tau-Publishing—R
(s)-TEACH Services—R
Th1nk/NavPress—R
Torch Legacy
(s)-Trafford Publishing—R
Treble Heart—R
VBC Publishing
Wesleyan Publishing
Whitaker House
(s)-WinePress—R
(s)-Word Alive
(s)-Zoë Life Publishing

LAY COUNSELING
Four Craftsmen—R
(s)-IMD Press—R
Randall House
(s)-Zoë Life Publishing

LEADERSHIP
(a)-B & H Publishing
(a)-Baker Books
(a)-Bethany House—R
(a)-Cook, David C.
(a)-Kregel—R
(a)-Nelson, Thomas
(a)-Regal
(a)-WaterBrook Press—R

Aaron Book—R
Abingdon Press
(s)-ACW Press—R
Ambassador Intl.—R
(s)-American Binding—R
Beacon Hill Press—R
(s)-Bfree Publishing
(s)-Black Forest—R
Blue Dolphin
BMH Books—R
(s)-Booklocker.com—R
(s)-Bookstand Publishing—R
Bridge Logos—R
Chalice Press—R
Christian Family—R
Christian Focus—R
Christian Writer's Ebook—R
Church Growth Inst.

Church Publishing
CLC Publications—R
College Press—R
(s)-Creation House—R
CrossLink Publishing
Crossroad Publishing—R
Crossway
CSS Publishing—R
(s)-DCTS Publishers
(s)-Deep River Books
Destiny Image (gifts)—R
Doulos Resources—R
Editorial Portavoz
Eerdmans Pub., Wm. B.—R
(s)-E.F.S. Online Pub.
(s)-Elderberry Press
(s)-Essence—R
Evangelical Press
Evergreen Press
(s)-Fairway Press—R
Faith Alive
(s)-Faith Books & More—R
FaithWalk
(s)-Forever Books—R
Gospel Publishing
(s)-Grace Acres Press—R
Group Publishing
Grupo Nelson
Guardian Angel
Harrison House
Hidden Brook Press—R
(s)-Holy Fire Publishing—R
(s)-IMD Press—R
(s)-Insight Publishing—R
InterVarsity Press—R
Jubilant Press—R
Judson Press—R
Kirk House
Lift Every Voice—R
Lighthouse Publishing—R
Lion and Lamb
Lutheran Univ. Press
Master Books
(s)-McDougal Publishing—R
(s)-MileStones Intl.
Monarch Books
NavPress
Neibauer Press—R
New Hope—R
New Leaf

Nordskog Publishing—R
(s)-One World—R
Parson Place—R
Parsons Publishing—R
Pilgrim Press—R
(s)-Pleasant Word—R
Ponder Publishing
Power Publishing—R
Praxis Press
(s)-Providence House—R
Quintessential Books—R
Randall House
Ravenhawk Books—R
Revival Nation
(s)-Rill & Associates
(s)-Salt Works—R
(s)-Salvation Publisher—R
(s)-Selah Publishing—R
Sheed & Ward
Standard Publishing
(s)-Star Bible Public.
Strang Book—R
(s)-Tate Publishing—R
Th1nk/NavPress—R
Third World Press—R
Touch Publications—R
(s)-Trafford Publishing—R
UMI Publishing—R
Univ. Press of America—R
VBC Publishing
Wesleyan Publishing
Whitaker House
(s)-WinePress—R
(s)-Word Alive
(s)-Zoë Life Publishing

LIFESTYLE

(s)-Bfree Publishing
Chalice Press—R
Cladach Publishing
Comfort Publishing
(s)-Halo Publishing Intl.
(s)-IMD Press—R
Master Books
New Leaf
(s)-Zoë Life Publishing

LITURGICAL STUDIES

(a)-Baker Books
(a)-Doubleday Relig.—R

Aaron Book—R
(s)-ACW Press—R
(s)-American Binding—R
American Cath. Press—R
(s)-Booklocker.com—R
(s)-Bookstand Publishing—R
(s)-Brentwood—R
Catholic Answers—R
Catholic Book
Christian Heritage—R
Christian Writer's Ebook—R
Church Publishing
Cistercian—R
Clarke & Co., James—R
Conciliar Press—R
Continuum Intl.—R
CSS Publishing—R
Eerdmans Pub., Wm. B.—R
(s)-E.F.S. Online Pub.
(s)-Elderberry Press
(s)-Fairway Press—R
(s)-Faith Books & More—R
(s)-Forever Books—R
Group Publishing
Hidden Brook Press—R
(s)-Holy Fire Publishing—R
(s)-Insight Publishing—R
InterVarsity Press—R
Lighthouse Publishing—R
Liturgical Press
Liturgy Training—R
Lutheran Univ. Press
Mercer Univ. Press—R
Messianic Jewish—R
Monarch Books
Nordskog Publishing—R
(s)-One World—R
Oregon Catholic
Parson Place—R
Paulist Press
Pilgrim Press—R
(s)-Pleasant Word—R
Power Publishing—R
(s)-Providence House—R
Ravenhawk Books—R
Resource Public.
(s)-Salt Works—R
(s)-So. Baptist Press—R
St. Bede's Public.—R
(s)-Tate Publishing—R

(s)-Trafford Publishing—R
Univ. Press of America—R
(s)-WinePress—R
(s)-Word Alive
(s)-Zoë Life Publishing

MARRIAGE

(a)-B & H Publishing
(a)-Baker Books
(a)-Bethany House—R
(a)-Cook, David C.
(a)-Doubleday Relig.—R
(a)-FaithWords
(a)-HarperOne
(a)-Kregel—R
(a)-Nelson, Thomas
(a)-Regal
(a)-Revell
(a)-Tyndale House—R
(a)-WaterBrook Press—R
(a)-W Publishing

Aaron Book—R
ACTA Publications
(s)-ACW Press—R
Ambassador Books
Ambassador Intl.—R
(s)-American Binding—R
Anglicans United—R
Barbour
Beacon Hill Press—R
(s)-Bfree Publishing
(s)-Black Forest—R
Blue Dolphin
(s)-Booklocker.com—R
(s)-Bookstand Publishing—R
(s)-Brentwood—R
(s)-Brown Books
Catholic Answers—R
Chalice Press—R
Chapter Two—R
Christian Family—R
Christian Writer's Ebook—R
College Press—R
Comfort Publishing
(s)-Creation House—R
(s)-CrossHouse—R
CrossLink Publishing
Crossroad Publishing—R
Crossway
CSS Publishing—R

(s)-Dean Press, Robbie—R
(s)-Deep River Books
Destiny Image (gifts)—R
(s)-Destiny Image (books)—R
Dimensions for Living
Discovery House—R
Earthen Vessel—R
Editorial Portavoz
Eerdmans Pub., Wm. B.—R
(s)-E.F.S. Online Pub.
(s)-Elderberry Press
Emmaus Road
(s)-Essence—R
Evangelical Press
Evergreen Press
Fair Havens—R
(s)-Fairway Press—R
(s)-Faith Books & More—R
FaithWalk
Focus on the Family—R
(s)-Forever Books—R
Forward Movement
Four Craftsmen—R
(s)-Grace Acres Press—R
GRQ—R
Guideposts Books
(s)-Halo Publishing Intl.
Hannibal Books
Health Commun.
Hensley Publishing
Hidden Brook Press—R
(s)-Holy Fire Publishing—R
Hope Publishing—R
Howard Books
(s)-IMD Press—R
(s)-Insight Publishing—R
InterVarsity Press—R
JourneyForth/BJU
Judson Press—R
Life Changing Media
Lift Every Voice—R
Lighthouse Publishing—R
Lion and Lamb
Loyola Press
Master Books
(s)-McDougal Publishing—R
Messianic Jewish—R
(s)-MileStones Intl.
Monarch Books
MOPS Intl.

New Hope—R
New Leaf
Nordskog Publishing—R
(s)-One World—R
Pacific Press
Parson Place—R
Parsons Publishing—R
Paulist Press
Pilgrim Press—R
(s)-Pleasant Word—R
Power Publishing—R
(s)-Providence House—R
Quiet Waters—R
Quintessential Books—R
Randall House
Reformation Heritage—R
Review and Herald
(s)-Rill & Associates
Samaritan Press—R
Scepter Publishers—R
(s)-Selah Publishing—R
(s)-So. Baptist Press—R
Standard Publishing
St. Anthony Mess. Press—R
(s)-Star Bible Public.
Still Waters Revival—R
Strang Book—R
(s)-Tate Publishing—R
(s)-TEACH Services—R
Third World Press—R
(s)-Trafford Publishing—R
VBC Publishing
Whitaker House
(s)-WinePress—R
(s)-Word Alive
(s)-Zoë Life Publishing

MEMOIRS

(a)-Baker Books
(a)-Ballantine
(a)-Doubleday Relig.—R
(a)-FaithWords
(a)-HarperOne
(a)-Nelson, Thomas
(a)-One World/Ballantine

Aaron Book—R
(s)-ACW Press—R
Ambassador Intl.—R
(s)-American Binding—R

(s)-Black Forest—R
(s)-Booklocker.com—R
(s)-Book Publishers Net.—R
(s)-Bookstand Publishing—R
(s)-Brown Books
Chalice Press—R
Christian Heritage—R
Christian Writer's Ebook—R
Cistercian—R
Cladach Publishing
(s)-Creation House—R
(s)-Deep River Books
(s)-E.F.S. Online Pub.
(s)-Elderberry Press
(s)-Essence—R
(s)-Fairway Press—R
(s)-Faith Books & More—R
FaithWalk
(s)-Forever Books—R
Forward Movement
(s)-Fruitbearer Pub.
(s)-Grace Acres Press—R
Guideposts Books
(s)-Halo Publishing Intl.
Health Commun.
Hidden Brook Press—R
His Work Christian Pub.—R
(s)-Holy Fire Publishing—R
(s)-IMD Press—R
Inheritance Press
(s)-Insight Publishing—R
(s)-LifeVest Publishing
Lighthouse Publishing—R
Lighthouse Trails—R
Lutterworth Press—R
Monarch Books
Nordskog Publishing—R
(s)-One World—R
On My Own Now—R
Pacific Press
Palgrave Macmillan—R
(s)-Pleasant Word—R
Power Publishing—R
(s)-Providence House—R
Quintessential Books—R
(s)-Rill & Associates
(s)-Salvation Publisher—R
Samaritan Press—R
St. Anthony Mess. Press—R
Sunpenny Publishing

(s)-Tate Publishing—R
(s)-TEACH Services—R
Th1nk/NavPress—R
(s)-Trafford Publishing—R
Univ. Press of America—R
(s)-WinePress—R
(s)-Word Alive
(s)-Zoë Life Publishing

MEN'S BOOKS

(a)-B & H Publishing
(a)-Baker Books
(a)-Bethany House—R
(a)-Doubleday Relig.—R
(a)-Harvest House
(a)-Kregel—R
(a)-Nelson, Thomas
(a)-Regal
(a)-WaterBrook Press—R
(a)-W Publishing

Aaron Book—R
(s)-ACW Press—R
Ambassador Books
(s)-American Binding—R
AMG Publishers—R
Barbour
Beacon Hill Press—R
(s)-Bfree Publishing
(s)-Black Forest—R
Blue Dolphin
BMH Books—R
(s)-Booklocker.com—R
(s)-Bookstand Publishing—R
Bridge Logos—R
Chalice Press—R
Christian Writer's Ebook—R
College Press—R
Comfort Publishing
(s)-Creation House—R
CrossLink Publishing
Crossroad Publishing—R
Crossway
(s)-Deep River Books
Dimensions for Living
Editorial Portavoz
Eerdmans Pub., Wm. B.—R
(s)-E.F.S. Online Pub.
(s)-Elderberry Press
Emmaus Road
(s)-Essence—R

Evangelical Press
Evergreen Press
Fair Havens—R
(s)-Fairway Press—R
(s)-Faith Books & More—R
Faith Communications
FaithWalk
(s)-Forever Books—R
Gentle Path Press
GRQ—R
(s)-Halo Publishing Intl.
Hensley Publishing
Hidden Brook Press—R
(s)-Holy Fire Publishing—R
Howard Books
(s)-IMD Press—R
Inkling Books—R
(s)-Insight Publishing—R
InterVarsity Press—R
Lift Every Voice—R
Lighthouse Publishing—R
Loyola Press
Master Books
(s)-McDougal Publishing—R
Messianic Jewish—R
(s)-MileStones Intl.
Monarch Books
New Leaf
Nordskog Publishing—R
(s)-One World—R
Pacific Press
Parson Place—R
Pilgrim Press—R
(s)-Pleasant Word—R
Power Publishing—R
(s)-Providence House—R
Quintessential Books—R
Randall House
Ravenhawk Books—R
Revival Nation
Samaritan Press—R
(s)-Selah Publishing—R
St. Anthony Mess. Press—R
(s)-Star Bible Public.
Strang Book—R
(s)-Tate Publishing—R
Th1nk/NavPress—R
Third World Press—R
(s)-Trafford Publishing—R
VBC Publishing

Whitaker House
(s)-WinePress—R
(s)-Word Alive
(s)-Zoë Life Publishing

MINIBOOKS

(s)-American Binding—R
(s)-Black Forest—R
(s)-Bookstand Publishing—R
GRQ—R
Harrison House
(s)-Holy Fire Publishing—R
(s)-IMD Press—R
Legacy Press—R
Lighthouse Publishing—R
Monarch Books
Nordskog Publishing—R
(s)-One World—R
Rose Publishing
(s)-Salt Works—R
Strang Book—R
(s)-Tate Publishing—R
(s)-Trafford Publishing—R
Treble Heart—R

MIRACLES

(a)-Baker Books
(a)-HarperOne

Aaron Book—R
(s)-ACW Press—R
(s)-American Binding—R
(s)-Bfree Publishing
(s)-Black Forest—R
Blue Dolphin
(s)-Booklocker.com—R
(s)-Brentwood—R
Christian Heritage—R
Christian Writer's Ebook—R
Comfort Publishing
(s)-Creation House—R
CrossLink Publishing
CSS Publishing—R
(s)-Deep River Books
(s)-Destiny Image (books)—R
(s)-E.F.S. Online Pub.
(s)-Elderberry Press
(s)-Essence—R
Evangelical Press
Evergreen Press
(s)-Fairway Press—R

(s)-Faith Books & More—R
(s)-Forever Books—R
Four Craftsmen—R
Guideposts Books
Harrison House
Hidden Brook Press—R
(s)-Holy Fire Publishing—R
(s)-IMD Press—R
(s)-Impact Christian—R
(s)-Insight Publishing—R
Lighthouse Publishing—R
Lion and Lamb
Loyola Press
(s)-McDougal Publishing—R
Monarch Books
Nordskog Publishing—R
(s)-One World—R
On My Own Now—R
Pacific Press
Paradise Research—R
Parson Place—R
Parsons Publishing—R
(s)-Pleasant Word—R
Power Publishing—R
(s)-Providence House—R
Revival Nation
(s)-Rill & Associates
(s)-Salvation Publisher—R
Samaritan Press—R
(s)-Selah Publishing—R
(s)-So. Baptist Press—R
(s)-Star Bible Public.
Strang Book—R
(s)-Tate Publishing—R
(s)-TEACH Services—R
(s)-Trafford Publishing—R
Whitaker House
(s)-WinePress—R
(s)-Word Alive
(s)-Zoë Life Publishing

MISSIONS/MISSIONARY
(a)-Baker Books

Aaron Book—R
(s)-ACW Press—R
Ambassador Intl.—R
(s)-American Binding—R
(s)-Ampelos Press
Believe Books
(s)-Bfree Publishing

(s)-Black Forest—R
(s)-Booklocker.com—R
(s)-Brentwood—R
(s)-Brown Books
Carey Library, Wm.—R
Chalice Press—R
Chapter Two—R
Christian Focus—R
Christian Heritage—R
Christian Writer's Ebook—R
CLC Publications—R
Comfort Publishing
(s)-Creation House—R
(s)-CrossHouse—R
CSS Publishing—R
(s)-Deep River Books
Discovery House—R
Earthen Vessel—R
Eerdmans Pub., Wm. B.—R
(s)-E.F.S. Online Pub.
(s)-Elderberry Press
(s)-Essence—R
Evangelical Press
Evergreen Press
Fair Havens—R
(s)-Fairway Press—R
(s)-Faith Books & More—R
FaithWalk
Father's Press
(s)-Forever Books—R
Forward Movement
Four Craftsmen—R
Friends United Press
(s)-Grace Acres Press—R
Hannibal Books
Hidden Brook Press—R
(s)-Holy Fire Publishing—R
Hope Publishing—R
(s)-IMD Press—R
(s)-Insight Publishing—R
InterVarsity Press—R
Lift Every Voice—R
Lighthouse Publishing—R
Lighthouse Trails—R
Lion and Lamb
Lutheran Univ. Press
(s)-McDougal Publishing—R
Monarch Books
Nordskog Publishing—R
(s)-One World—R

P & R Publishing—R
Pacific Press
Parson Place—R
Parsons Publishing—R
(s)-Pleasant Word—R
Power Publishing—R
Praxis Press
(s)-Providence House—R
Quiet Waters—R
Randall House
Reformation Heritage—R
Revival Nation
Rose Publishing
(s)-Salt Works—R
(s)-Seed Faith Books—R
(s)-So. Baptist Press—R
(s)-Star Bible Public.
Strang Book—R
(s)-Tate Publishing—R
(s)-TEACH Services—R
(s)-Trafford Publishing—R
VBC Publishing
(s)-WinePress—R
(s)-Word Alive
Yale Univ. Press
(s)-Zoë Life Publishing

MONEY MANAGEMENT
(a)-Baker Books
(a)-Cook, David C.
(a)-FaithWords
(a)-Harvest House
(a)-Nelson, Thomas
(a)-WaterBrook Press—R

Aaron Book—R
(s)-ACW Press—R
Ambassador Intl.—R
(s)-American Binding—R
Barbour
(s)-Bfree Publishing
Blue Dolphin
BMH Books—R
(s)-Booklocker.com—R
(s)-Brentwood—R
Chalice Press—R
Christian Writer's Ebook—R
Conquest Publishers
(s)-Creation House—R
(s)-Deep River Books

Editorial Portavoz
Eerdmans Pub., Wm. B.—R
(s)-E.F.S. Online Pub.
(s)-Elderberry Press
(s)-Essence—R
Evangelical Press
Evergreen Press
(s)-Fairway Press—R
(s)-Faith Books & More—R
FaithWalk
(s)-Forever Books—R
Forward Movement
Four Craftsmen—R
Grupo Nelson
Hannibal Books
Health Commun.
Hensley Publishing
Hidden Brook Press—R
His Work Christian Pub.—R
(s)-Holy Fire Publishing—R
(s)-IMD Press—R
(s)-Insight Publishing—R
JourneyForth/BJU
Judson Press—R
Lift Every Voice—R
Lighthouse Publishing—R
Lion and Lamb
Master Books
Millennium III—R
Moody Publishers
MountainView
New Hope—R
New Leaf
Nordskog Publishing—R
(s)-One World—R
Pacific Press
Parson Place—R
(s)-Pleasant Word—R
Power Publishing—R
(s)-Providence House—R
Quintessential Books—R
Ravenhawk Books—R
Reference Service
(s)-Salvation Publisher—R
Samaritan Press—R
(s)-So. Baptist Press—R
(s)-Star Bible Public.
Strang Book—R
(s)-Tate Publishing—R
(s)-TEACH Services—R

(s)-Trafford Publishing—R
VBC Publishing
(s)-WinePress—R
(s)-Word Alive
Xyzzy Press
(s)-Zoë Life Publishing

MUSIC-RELATED BOOKS
(a)-Baker Books
(a)-Countryman, J.

Aaron Book—R
American Cath. Press—R
(s)-Bfree Publishing
Blue Dolphin
BMH Books—R
(s)-Booklocker.com—R
Cambridge Scholars
Christian Writer's Ebook—R
Contemporary Drama
(s)-Deep River Books
(s)-Destiny Image (books)—R
Eerdmans Pub., Wm. B.—R
(s)-E.F.S. Online Pub.
Eldridge Plays
(s)-Essence—R
Evangelical Press
(s)-Fairway Press—R
(s)-Faith Books & More—R
FaithWalk
(s)-Forever Books—R
Guardian Angel
Hidden Brook Press—R
His Work Christian Pub.—R
(s)-Holy Fire Publishing—R
(s)-Insight Publishing—R
Lighthouse Publishing—R
Lion and Lamb
Lutheran Univ. Press
Monarch Books
(s)-One World—R
Players Press—R
(s)-Pleasant Word—R
Power Publishing—R
(s)-Providence House—R
Samaritan Press—R
Standard Publishing
(s)-Star Bible Public.
(s)-Tate Publishing—R
(s)-Trafford Publishing—R

(s)-WinePress—R
(s)-Word Alive
(s)-Zoë Life Publishing

NOVELTY BOOKS FOR KIDS
(a)-Baker Books

(s)-Bfree Publishing
(s)-Brown Books
(s)-E.F.S. Online Pub.
(s)-Elderberry Press
(s)-Fairway Press—R
(s)-Forever Books—R
Guardian Angel
(s)-IMD Press—R
JourneyStone—R
Legacy Press—R
Lift Every Voice—R
Lion and Lamb
Monarch Books
(s)-One World—R
(s)-Salt Works—R
Samaritan Press—R
(s)-Seed Faith Books—R
Standard Publishing
(s)-Tate Publishing—R
(s)-Trafford Publishing—R
(s)-Word Alive
(s)-Zoë Life Publishing

PAMPHLETS
(a)-Harvest House

Chalice Press—R
Chapter Two—R
Christian Writer's Ebook—R
Doulos Resources—R
(s)-Essence—R
Evangelical Press
(s)-Forever Books—R
Forward Movement
Founders Press
Four Craftsmen—R
(s)-Fruitbearer Pub.
Good Book—R
Intl. Awakening—R
Libros Liguori
Lift Every Voice—R
Liguori Public.—R
Liturgy Training—R

Neibauer Press—R
(s)-One World—R
Our Sunday Visitor—R
Paradise Research—R
Paulist Press
Rose Publishing
(s)-Salt Works—R
Trinity Foundation—R

PARENTING
(a)-B & H Publishing
(a)-Baker Books
(a)-Ballantine
(a)-Bethany House—R
(a)-Cook, David C.
(a)-FaithWords
(a)-Kregel—R
(a)-Nelson, Thomas
(a)-Regal
(a)-Revell
(a)-Tyndale House—R
(a)-W Publishing
(a)-WaterBrook Press—R

Aaron Book—R
(s)-ACW Press—R
Adams Media
Ambassador Books
Ambassador Intl.—R
(s)-American Binding—R
AMG Publishers—R
Barbour
Beacon Hill Press—R
(s)-Bfree Publishing
(s)-Black Forest—R
Blue Dolphin
(s)-Booklocker.com—R
(s)-Book Publishers Net.—R
(s)-Brentwood—R
(s)-Brown Books
Chalice Press—R
Christian Family—R
Christian Writer's Ebook—R
Church Publishing
College Press—R
Conari Press
Conciliar Press—R
(s)-Creation House—R
CrossLink Publishing
Crossroad Publishing—R

(s)-Dean Press, Robbie—R
(s)-Deep River Books
(s)-Destiny Image (books)—R
Dimensions for Living
Discovery House—R
Editorial Portavoz
Eerdmans Pub., Wm. B.—R
(s)-E.F.S. Online Pub.
(s)-Elderberry Press
(s)-Essence—R
Evangelical Press
Evergreen Press
(s)-Fairway Press—R
(s)-Faith Books & More—R
Focus on the Family—R
(s)-Forever Books—R
Forward Movement
(s)-Grace Acres Press—R
Grupo Nelson
(s)-Halo Publishing Intl.
Harrison House
Health Commun.
Hensley Publishing
Hidden Brook Press—R
His Work Christian Pub.—R
(s)-Holy Fire Publishing—R
Howard Books
(s)-IMD Press—R
(s)-Insight Publishing—R
InterVarsity Press—R
JourneyForth/BJU
Kingsley Pub., Jessica—R
Langmarc
Life Changing Media
Lift Every Voice—R
Lighthouse Publishing—R
Liguori Public.—R
Lion and Lamb
Master Books
(s)-McDougal Publishing—R
Messianic Jewish—R
(s)-MileStones Intl.
Mission City Press
Monarch Books
MOPS Intl.
New Hope—R
New Leaf
Nordskog Publishing—R
(s)-One World—R
Our Sunday Visitor—R

P & R Publishing—R
Pacific Press
Parsons Publishing—R
Pauline Books—R
(s)-Pleasant Word—R
(s)-Port Hole Public.
Power Publishing—R
(s)-Providence House—R
Quintessential Books—R
Randall House
Reformation Heritage—R
(s)-Rill & Associates
Rose Publishing
(s)-Salt Works—R
Scepter Publishers—R
(s)-Selah Publishing—R
Standard Publishing
St. Anthony Mess. Press—R
(s)-Star Bible Public.
Starik Publishing
Still Waters Revival—R
Strang Book—R
Sunpenny Publishing
Tarcher, Jeremy P.—R
(s)-Tate Publishing—R
(s)-TEACH Services—R
Third World Press—R
Torch Legacy
(s)-Trafford Publishing—R
Treble Heart—R
VBC Publishing
Whitaker House
(s)-WinePress—R
(s)-Word Alive
(s)-Zoë Life Publishing

PASTORS' HELPS
(a)-B & H Publishing
(a)-Baker Academic
(a)-Baker Books
(a)-Kregel—R

Aaron Book—R
(s)-ACW Press—R
Ambassador Intl.—R
(s)-American Binding—R
Beacon Hill Press—R
(s)-Bfree Publishing
Blue Dolphin
(s)-Booklocker.com—R

(s)-Bookstand Publishing—R
(s)-Brentwood—R
Bridge Logos—R
Chalice Press—R
Christian Focus—R
Christian Writer's Ebook—R
Church Growth Inst.
Conquest Publishers
(s)-Creation House—R
CrossLink Publishing
CSS Publishing—R
(s)-DCTS Publishers
(s)-Deep River Books
Doulos Resources—R
Earthen Vessel—R
Editorial Portavoz
Eerdmans Pub., Wm. B.—R
(s)-E.F.S. Online Pub.
(s)-Elderberry Press
(s)-Essence—R
Evangelical Press
(s)-Fairway Press—R
(s)-Faith Books & More—R
(s)-Forever Books—R
Fortress Press
Gospel Publishing
Group Publishing
Hidden Brook Press—R
(s)-Holy Fire Publishing—R
(s)-IMD Press—R
(s)-Insight Publishing—R
(s)-Kindred Books—R
Kingsley Pub., Jessica—R
Leafwood
Lighthouse Publishing—R
Lion and Lamb
Liturgical Press
Liturgy Training—R
Lutheran Univ. Press
Monarch Books
Neibauer Press—R
Nordskog Publishing—R
(s)-One World—R
Pilgrim Press—R
(s)-Pleasant Word—R
Power Publishing—R
(s)-Providence House—R
Randall House
Reformation Heritage—R
(s)-Sermon Select Press

(s)-So. Baptist Press—R
Standard Publishing
(s)-Star Bible Public.
(s)-Tate Publishing—R
(s)-TEACH Services—R
Torch Legacy
Touch Publications—R
(s)-Trafford Publishing—R
Treble Heart—R
VBC Publishing
Wesleyan Publishing
(s)-WinePress—R
(s)-Word Alive
(s)-Zoë Life Publishing
Zondervan

PERSONAL EXPERIENCE
(a)-Baker Books
(a)-HarperOne
(a)-Kregel—R
(a)-Nelson, Thomas
(a)-W Publishing

Aaron Book—R
(s)-ACW Press—R
Ambassador Intl.—R
(s)-American Binding—R
(s)-Ampelos Press
(s)-Bfree Publishing
(s)-Black Forest—R
Blue Dolphin
(s)-Booklocker.com—R
(s)-Bookstand Publishing—R
(s)-Brentwood—R
Bridge Logos—R
Canticle Books—R
CarePoint Publishing—R
Chicken Soup
Christian Family—R
Christian Writer's Ebook—R
Comfort Publishing
(s)-Creation House—R
CrossLink Publishing
Crossroad Publishing—R
(s)-DCTS Publishers
(s)-Deep River Books
Destiny Image (gifts)—R
(s)-E.F.S. Online Pub.
(s)-Elderberry Press
(s)-Essence—R
Evangelical Press

Fair Havens—R
(s)-Fairway Press—R
(s)-Faith Books & More—R
FaithWalk
(s)-Forever Books—R
Four Craftsmen—R
Fresh Air Books
(s)-Fruitbearer Pub.
Gentle Path Press
GRQ—R
Guideposts Books
(s)-Halo Publishing Intl.
Hannibal Books
Hidden Brook Press—R
(s)-Holy Fire Publishing—R
(s)-IMD Press—R
(s)-Insight Publishing—R
Jesus Filled Day (books)
Life Changing Media
Lighthouse Publishing—R
Lighthouse Trails—R
Lion and Lamb
(s)-McDougal Publishing—R
(s)-MileStones Intl.
Monarch Books
Nordskog Publishing—R
(s)-One World—R
On My Own Now—R
Pacific Press
(s)-Pleasant Word—R
Power Publishing—R
(s)-Providence House—R
Ravenhawk Books—R
Revival Nation
(s)-Salvation Publisher—R
Samaritan Press—R
(s)-So. Baptist Press—R
(s)-Star Bible Public.
Strang Book—R
(s)-Tate Publishing—R
(s)-TEACH Services—R
Th1nk/NavPress—R
Third World Press—R
(s)-Trafford Publishing—R
(s)-WinePress—R
(s)-Word Alive

PERSONAL GROWTH
(a)-B & H Publishing
(a)-Baker Books

(a)-Bethany House—R
(a)-FaithWords
(a)-HarperOne
(a)-Hay House
(a)-Kregel—R
(a)-Nelson, Thomas
(a)-Regal
(a)-Tyndale House—R
(a)-WaterBrook Press—R
(a)-W Publishing

Aadeon Publishing—R
Aaron Book—R
(s)-ACW Press—R
Ambassador Books
Ambassador Intl.—R
(s)-American Binding—R
AMG Publishers—R
Barbour
(s)-Bfree Publishing
(s)-Black Forest—R
Blue Dolphin
BMH Books—R
(s)-Booklocker.com—R
(s)-Book Publishers Net.—R
(s)-Bookstand Publishing—R
Bridge Logos—R
Canticle Books—R
CarePoint Publishing—R
CharismaKids
Christian Family—R
Christian Writer's Ebook—R
CLC Publications—R
Comfort Publishing
Conari Press
(s)-Creation House—R
CrossLink Publishing
Crossroad Publishing—R
(s)-DCTS Publishers
(s)-Deep River Books
Destiny Image (gifts)—R
(s)-Destiny Image (books)—R
Discovery House—R
(s)-E.F.S. Online Pub.
(s)-Elderberry Press
(s)-Essence—R
Evangelical Press
Evergreen Press
(s)-Fairway Press—R
(s)-Faith Books & More—R

FaithWalk
(s)-Forever Books—R
Forward Movement
Gentle Path Press
GRQ—R
Guideposts Books
(s)-Halo Publishing Intl.
Hannibal Books
Health Commun.
Hensley Publishing
Hidden Brook Press—R
(s)-Holy Fire Publishing—R
(s)-House of Ali
Howard Books
(s)-IMD Press—R
(s)-Insight Publishing—R
InterVarsity Press—R
Jesus Filled Day (books)
JourneyForth/BJU
(s)-Kindred Books—R
Life Changing Media
Lift Every Voice—R
Lighthouse Publishing—R
Lion and Lamb
(s)-McDougal Publishing—R
(s)-MileStones Intl.
Monarch Books
NavPress
New Hope—R
Nordskog Publishing—R
(s)-One World—R
On My Own Now—R
Pacific Press
Parson Place—R
Parsons Publishing—R
Pauline Books—R
Pilgrim Press—R
(s)-Pleasant Word—R
Power Publishing—R
(s)-Providence House—R
Quintessential Books—R
Ravenhawk Books—R
Resource Public.
Revival Nation
(s)-Rill & Associates
Samaritan Press—R
St. Anthony Mess. Press—R
(s)-Star Bible Public.
Strang Book—R
(s)-Tate Publishing—R

(s)-TEACH Services—R
Th1nk/NavPress—R
Third World Press—R
(s)-Trafford Publishing—R
(s)-WinePress—R
(s)-Word Alive
Xyzzy Press

PERSONAL RENEWAL
(a)-Baker Books
(a)-HarperOne
(a)-Kregel—R
(a)-Regal
(a)-Tyndale House—R

Aaron Book—R
(s)-ACW Press—R
(s)-American Binding—R
Barbour
(s)-Bfree Publishing
(s)-Black Forest—R
Blue Dolphin
BMH Books—R
(s)-Booklocker.com—R
(s)-Bookstand Publishing—R
Bridge Logos—R
Canticle Books—R
CharismaKids
Christian Writer's Ebook—R
Cladach Publishing
CLC Publications—R
Comfort Publishing
Conari Press
(s)-Creation House—R
Crossroad Publishing—R
(s)-DCTS Publishers
(s)-Deep River Books
Destiny Image (gifts)—R
(s)-Destiny Image (books)—R
(s)-E.F.S. Online Pub.
(s)-Elderberry Press
Emmaus Road
(s)-Essence—R
Evangelical Press
Evergreen Press
(s)-Fairway Press—R
(s)-Faith Books & More—R
FaithWalk
(s)-Forever Books—R
Forward Movement
Fresh Air Books

Gentle Path Press
GRQ—R
(s)-Halo Publishing Intl.
Hannibal Books
Health Commun.
Hensley Publishing
Hidden Brook Press—R
(s)-Holy Fire Publishing—R
(s)-House of Ali
Howard Books
(s)-IMD Press—R
(s)-Impact Christian—R
(s)-Insight Publishing—R
Intl. Awakening—R
Kirk House
Life Changing Media
Lift Every Voice—R
Lighthouse Publishing—R
Lion and Lamb
(s)-McDougal Publishing—R
(s)-MileStones Intl.
Monarch Books
NavPress
New Hope—R
Nordskog Publishing—R
(s)-One World—R
On My Own Now—R
Pacific Press
Pilgrim Press—R
(s)-Pleasant Word—R
Power Publishing—R
(s)-Providence House—R
Ravenhawk Books—R
Revival Nation
(s)-Rill & Associates
(s)-Star Bible Public.
Strang Book—R
(s)-Tate Publishing—R
(s)-TEACH Services—R
Th1nk/NavPress—R
(s)-Trafford Publishing—R
(s)-WinePress—R
(s)-Word Alive
(s)-Zoë Life Publishing

PHILOSOPHY

(a)-Baker Books
(a)-Doubleday Relig.—R
(a)-HarperOne
(a)-Kregel—R

(a)-One World/Ballantine
Aaron Book—R
(s)-ACW Press—R
(s)-American Binding—R
Baylor Univ. Press
(s)-Bfree Publishing
(s)-Black Forest—R
Blue Dolphin
(s)-Booklocker.com—R
(s)-Bookstand Publishing—R
Branden Publishing—R
(s)-Brentwood—R
Cambridge Scholars
Cambridge Univ. Press
Christian Writer's Ebook—R
Clarke & Co., James—R
Continuum Intl.—R
(s)-Creation House—R
Crossroad Publishing—R
(s)-Deep River Books
Dover Publications—R
Eerdmans Pub., Wm. B.—R
(s)-E.F.S. Online Pub.
(s)-Elderberry Press
(s)-Essence—R
Evangelical Press
(s)-Fairway Press—R
(s)-Faith Books & More—R
FaithWalk
Fordham Univ. Press—R
(s)-Forever Books—R
GRQ—R
Hidden Brook Press—R
(s)-Holy Fire Publishing—R
Inkling Books—R
(s)-Insight Publishing—R
InterVarsity Press—R
Larson Publications—R
Lighthouse Publishing—R
Lutheran Univ. Press
Lutterworth Press—R
Mercer Univ. Press—R
Monarch Books
Nordskog Publishing—R
(s)-One World—R
Palgrave Macmillan—R
Paragon House—R
(s)-Pleasant Word—R
(s)-Port Hole Public.

Power Publishing—R
(s)-Providence House—R
Quintessential Books—R
(s)-Salt Works—R
(s)-Star Bible Public.
St. Augustine's Press—R
St. Pauls/Alba—R
Still Waters Revival—R
Tarcher, Jeremy P.—R
(s)-Tate Publishing—R
(s)-TEACH Services—R
Third World Press—R
(s)-Trafford Publishing—R
Trinity Foundation—R
Univ. Press of America—R
(s)-WinePress—R
Wipf and Stock
(s)-Word Alive
Xyzzy Press
(s)-Zoë Life Publishing

PHOTOGRAPHS (FOR COVERS)

Aadeon Publishing—R
Abingdon Press
Ambassador Books
Ambassador Intl.—R
(s)-American Binding—R
(s)-Black Forest—R
Blue Dolphin
(s)-Booklocker.com—R
(s)-Book Publishers Net.—R
(s)-Bookstand Publishing—R
(s)-Brentwood—R
Bridge Logos—R
Cambridge Scholars
Canadian Inst. for Law—R
CarePoint Publishing—R
Carey Library, Wm.—R
Catholic Answers—R
Catholic Univ. of Amer. Press
Christian Focus—R
Church Growth Inst.
Cistercian—R
Comfort Publishing
Conciliar Press—R
Continuum Intl.—R
(s)-Creation House—R
(s)-CrossHouse—R
CrossLink Publishing

(s)-Dean Press, Robbie—R
Earthen Vessel—R
(s)-Essence—R
ETC Publications
Fair Havens—R
(s)-Faith Books & More—R
FaithWalk
Father's Press
(s)-Forever Books—R
Four Craftsmen—R
(s)-Fruitbearer Pub.
Georgetown Univ. Press
Guardian Angel
Guernica Editions—R
(s)-House of Ali
(s)-IMD Press—R
Intl. Awakening—R
Jebaire
JourneyStone—R
Jubilant Press—R
Kingsley Pub., Jessica—R
Knight George Pub.
Life Changing Media
Lift Every Voice—R
Lighthouse Publishing—R
Lion and Lamb
Liturgy Training—R
Lutheran Univ. Press
Marcher Lord Press
Monarch Books
MountainView
Neibauer Press—R
New Canaan—R
New Hope—R
Nordskog Publishing—R
(s)-One World—R
Oregon Catholic
Our Sunday Visitor—R
Parson Place—R
Pauline Kids—R
Paulist Press
Pilgrim Press—R
Players Press—R
(s)-Pleasant Word—R
Power Publishing—R
Quintessential Books—R
Ravenhawk Books—R
Reformation Heritage—R
(s)-Rill & Associates
Samaritan Press—R

(s)-Selah Publishing—R
Sheed & Ward
(s)-Star Bible Public.
Strang Book—R
Sunpenny Publishing
(s)-Tate Publishing—R
Tau-Publishing—R
(s)-TEACH Services—R
Touch Publications—R
(s)-Trafford Publishing—R
Treble Heart—R
Trinity Foundation—R
Troitsa Books
Two Fish Publishing—R
United Methodist
Univ. of AR Press—R
Wilshire Book—R
(s)-WinePress—R
(s)-Zoë Life Publishing

POETRY

Aaron Book—R
(s)-ACW Press—R
(s)-American Binding—R
Ancient Paths—R
(s)-Bfree Publishing
(s)-Black Forest—R
Blue Dolphin
(s)-Booklocker.com—R
(s)-Bookstand Publishing—R
Boyds Mills Press—R
Branden Publishing—R
(s)-Brentwood—R
Christian Writer's Ebook—R
Conquest Publishers
(s)-Creation House—R
(s)-Dean Press, Robbie—R
DiskUs Publishing
Earthen Vessel—R
Eerdmans Pub., Wm. B.—R
(s)-E.F.S. Online Pub.
(s)-Elderberry Press
(s)-Essence—R
(s)-Fairway Press—R
(s)-Faith Books & More—R
(s)-Forever Books—R
Guernica Editions—R
(s)-Halo Publishing Intl.
Hidden Brook Press—R
(s)-Holy Fire Publishing—R

(s)-IMD Press—R
(s)-Insight Publishing—R
(s)-LifeVest Publishing
Lighthouse Publishing—R
Lutterworth Press—R
More Than Novellas
(s)-One World—R
(s)-Pleasant Word—R
(s)-Poems By Me—R
(s)-Poet's Cove Press
(s)-Port Hole Public.
Power Publishing—R
(s)-Providence House—R
(s)-Rill & Associates
(s)-Selah Publishing—R
(s)-So. Baptist Press—R
(s)-Tate Publishing—R
Third World Press—R
(s)-Trafford Publishing—R
(s)-WinePress—R
(s)-Word Alive
Xyzzy Press
(s)-Zoë Life Publishing

POLITICS

(a)-Baker Books
(a)-Doubleday Relig.—R
(a)-HarperOne
(a)-Harvest House
(a)-Nelson, Thomas
(a)-One World/Ballantine

Aadeon Publishing—R
Aaron Book—R
(s)-ACW Press—R
(s)-American Binding—R
AMG Publishers—R
Baylor Univ. Press
(s)-Bfree Publishing
(s)-Black Forest—R
Blue Dolphin
(s)-Booklocker.com—R
Branden Publishing—R
(s)-Brentwood—R
Cambridge Scholars
Canadian Inst. for Law—R
Carson-Dellosa
Chalice Press—R
Christian Writer's Ebook—R
Church Publishing
(s)-Creation House—R

Crossroad Publishing—R
(s)-Deep River Books
Eerdmans Pub., Wm. B.—R
(s)-E.F.S. Online Pub.
(s)-Elderberry Press
(s)-Essence—R
(s)-Fairway Press—R
(s)-Faith Books & More—R
Fordham Univ. Press—R
(s)-Forever Books—R
Georgetown Univ. Press
Hidden Brook Press—R
(s)-Holy Fire Publishing—R
Howard Books
Inkling Books—R
(s)-Insight Publishing—R
Lighthouse Publishing—R
Mercer Univ. Press—R
New Canaan—R
Nordskog Publishing—R
(s)-One World—R
Palgrave Macmillan—R
Pilgrim Press—R
(s)-Pleasant Word—R
Power Publishing—R
Praeger Publishers
(s)-Providence House—R
Ravenhawk Books—R
(s)-Salt Works—R
Still Waters Revival—R
Strang Book—R
(s)-Tate Publishing—R
Third World Press—R
(s)-Trafford Publishing—R
Trinity Foundation—R
Univ. Press of America—R
(s)-WinePress—R
(s)-Word Alive
Yale Univ. Press
(s)-Zoë Life Publishing

POPULAR CULTURE

Chalice Press—R
(s)-Essence—R
(s)-IMD Press—R
Mercer Univ. Press—R
Palgrave Macmillan—R
Pauline Books—R
Third World Press—R
(s)-Zoë Life Publishing

POSTMODERNISM

Chalice Press—R
(s)-Essence—R
GRQ—R
(s)-IMD Press—R
Leafwood
Palgrave Macmillan—R
(s)-Zoë Life Publishing

PRAYER

(a)-Baker Books
(a)-Bethany House—R
(a)-Cook, David C.
(a)-Doubleday Relig.—R
(a)-FaithWords
(a)-HarperOne
(a)-Harvest House
(a)-Kregel—R
(a)-Nelson, Thomas
(a)-Regal
(a)-Tyndale House—R
(a)-WaterBrook Press—R
(a)-W Publishing

Aaron Book—R
Abingdon Press
ACTA Publications
(s)-ACW Press—R
Ambassador Books
Ambassador Intl.—R
(s)-American Binding—R
(s)-Ampelos Press
Anglicans United—R
Barbour
Beacon Hill Press—R
(s)-Bfree Publishing
(s)-Black Forest—R
Blue Dolphin
BMH Books—R
(s)-Booklocker.com—R
(s)-Bookstand Publishing—R
(s)-Brentwood—R
Bridge Logos—R
Catholic Book
Chalice Press—R
CharismaKids
Christian Family—R
Christian Focus—R
Christian Heritage—R
Christian Writer's Ebook—R

Church Publishing
Cistercian—R
CLC Publications—R
College Press—R
Conquest Publishers
Continuum Intl.—R
(s)-Creation House—R
(s)-CrossHouse—R
CrossLink Publishing
Crossroad Publishing—R
CSS Publishing—R
(s)-DCTS Publishers
(s)-Deep River Books
Destiny Image (gifts)—R
(s)-Destiny Image (books)—R
Discovery House—R
Earthen Vessel—R
Eerdmans Pub., Wm. B.—R
(s)-E.F.S. Online Pub.
(s)-Elderberry Press
Emmaus Road
(s)-Essence—R
Evangelical Press
Evergreen Press
Fair Havens—R
(s)-Fairway Press—R
Faith Alive
(s)-Faith Books & More—R
FaithWalk
Father's Press
(s)-Forever Books—R
Forward Movement
Four Craftsmen—R
(s)-Fruitbearer Pub.
Good Book—R
Gospel Publishing
GRQ—R
Guideposts Books
(s)-Halo Publishing Intl.
Harrison House
Hensley Publishing
Hidden Brook Press—R
(s)-Holy Fire Publishing—R
Hope Publishing—R
Howard Books
(s)-IMD Press—R
(s)-Impact Christian—R
(s)-Insight Publishing—R
InterVarsity Press—R
Intl. Awakening—R

Jebaire
Jesus Filled Day (books)
JourneyForth/BJU
Legacy Press—R
Libros Liguori
Lift Every Voice—R
Lighthouse Publishing—R
Liguori Public.—R
Lion and Lamb
Liturgy Training—R
Loyola Press
Lutheran Univ. Press
Lutterworth Press—R
(s)-McDougal Publishing—R
Messianic Jewish—R
(s)-MileStones Intl.
Monarch Books
Moody Publishers
Nordskog Publishing—R
(s)-One World—R
On My Own Now—R
Our Sunday Visitor—R
Pacific Press
Paradise Research—R
Pauline Books—R
Pauline Kids—R
Paulist Press
Pflaum Publishing
Pilgrim Press—R
(s)-Pleasant Word—R
(s)-Port Hole Public.
Power Publishing—R
Praxis Press
(s)-Providence House—R
Quintessential Books—R
Reformation Heritage—R
Revival Nation
(s)-Rill & Associates
Rose Publishing
(s)-Salvation Publisher—R
Samaritan Press—R
Scepter Publishers—R
(s)-Selah Publishing—R
Smyth & Helwys
(s)-So. Baptist Press—R
Standard Publishing
St. Anthony Mess. Press—R
(s)-Star Bible Public.
St. Bede's Public.—R
St. Pauls/Alba—R

Still Waters Revival—R
Strang Book—R
(s)-Tate Publishing—R
(s)-TEACH Services—R
Th1nk/NavPress—R
(s)-Trafford Publishing—R
VBC Publishing
Wesleyan Publishing
Westminster John Knox
Whitaker House
(s)-WinePress—R
(s)-Word Alive
(s)-Zoë Life Publishing

PRINT-ON-DEMAND

Aadeon Publishing—R
Aaron Book—R
(s)-ACW Press—R
(s)-American Binding—R
(s)-Black Forest—R
Blue Dolphin
(s)-Booklocker.com—R
(s)-Brentwood—R
Bridge Logos—R
Christian Writer's Ebook—R
Continuum Intl.—R
CrossLink Publishing
Crossroad Publishing—R
CSS Publishing—R
(s)-Dean Press, Robbie—R
Doulos Resources—R
Editorial Portavoz
(s)-Elderberry Press
Encore Performance
Evangelical Press
Evergreen Press
(s)-Faith Books & More—R
(s)-Forever Books—R
Four Craftsmen—R
Georgetown Univ. Press
Hannibal Books
Hidden Brook Press—R
(s)-Holy Fire Publishing—R
(s)-IMD Press—R
(s)-Infinity Publishing
Inkling Books—R
(s)-Insight Publishing—R
(s)-Kindred Books—R
Lighthouse Publishing—R
Lion and Lamb

Lutterworth Press—R
Nordskog Publishing—R
OakTara—R
(s)-One World—R
Players Press—R
(s)-Pleasant Word—R
(s)-Poems By Me—R
Power Publishing—R
Randall House Digital
Ravenhawk Books—R
(s)-Rill & Associates
(s)-Salvation Publisher—R
(s)-Self Publish Press—R
Sheed & Ward
(s)-Strong Tower—R
(s)-Trafford Publishing—R
Univ. Press of America—R
VBC Publishing
(s)-Word Alive

PROPHECY

(a)-Baker Books
(a)-Harvest House
(a)-Kregel—R
(a)-W Publishing

Aaron Book—R
(s)-ACW Press—R
(s)-American Binding—R
(s)-Bfree Publishing
(s)-Black Forest—R
Blue Dolphin
BMH Books—R
(s)-Booklocker.com—R
(s)-Bookstand Publishing—R
(s)-Brentwood—R
Bridge Logos—R
Chapter Two—R
CharismaKids
Christian Writer's Ebook—R
Comfort Publishing
(s)-Creation House—R
CSS Publishing—R
(s)-Deep River Books
(s)-Destiny Image (books)—R
Eerdmans Pub., Wm. B.—R
(s)-Elderberry Press
(s)-Essence—R
Evangelical Press
Fair Havens—R

(s)-Fairway Press—R
(s)-Faith Books & More—R
FaithWalk
Father's Press
(s)-Forever Books—R
Four Craftsmen—R
GRQ—R
Harrison House
Hidden Brook Press—R
(s)-Holy Fire Publishing—R
(s)-IMD Press—R
(s)-Insight Publishing—R
Lighthouse Publishing—R
Lutheran Univ. Press
(s)-McDougal Publishing—R
Monarch Books
Nordskog Publishing—R
(s)-One World—R
Pacific Press
Parson Place—R
Parsons Publishing—R
(s)-Pleasant Word—R
Power Publishing—R
(s)-Providence House—R
Ravenhawk Books—R
Revival Nation
(s)-Rill & Associates
(s)-Salvation Publisher—R
Samaritan Press—R
(s)-Selah Publishing—R
(s)-So. Baptist Press—R
(s)-Star Bible Public.
Still Waters Revival—R
Strang Book—R
(s)-Tate Publishing—R
(s)-TEACH Services—R
(s)-Trafford Publishing—R
(s)-WinePress—R
(s)-Word Alive
(s)-Zoë Life Publishing

PSYCHOLOGY

(a)-Baker Academic
(a)-Kregel—R
(a)-One World/Ballantine
(a)-Tyndale House—R

Aaron Book—R
(s)-ACW Press—R
Adams Media

(s)-American Binding—R
Blue Dolphin
(s)-Booklocker.com—R
(s)-Book Publishers Net.—R
(s)-Bookstand Publishing—R
(s)-Brentwood—R
Cambridge Scholars
CarePoint Publishing—R
Chalice Press—R
Christian Writer's Ebook—R
(s)-Creation House—R
(s)-Deep River Books
Eerdmans Pub., Wm. B.—R
(s)-E.F.S. Online Pub.
(s)-Elderberry Press
(s)-Essence—R
Evangelical Press
Evergreen Press
(s)-Fairway Press—R
(s)-Faith Books & More—R
FaithWalk
(s)-Forever Books—R
Gentle Path Press
GRQ—R
Health Commun.
Hidden Brook Press—R
(s)-Holy Fire Publishing—R
Hope Publishing—R
(s)-Insight Publishing—R
InterVarsity Press—R
Larson Publications—R
Life Changing Media
Lighthouse Publishing—R
Lion and Lamb
Monarch Books
MountainView
Nordskog Publishing—R
(s)-One World—R
On My Own Now—R
Palgrave Macmillan—R
Paragon House—R
(s)-Pleasant Word—R
Power Publishing—R
(s)-Providence House—R
Quintessential Books—R
(s)-Recovery Commun.
Samaritan Press—R
Siloam
(s)-So. Baptist Press—R
(s)-Star Bible Public.

Tarcher, Jeremy P.—R
(s)-Tate Publishing—R
(s)-TEACH Services—R
(s)-Trafford Publishing—R
Treble Heart—R
Univ. Press of America—R
Wilshire Book—R
(s)-WinePress—R
(s)-Word Alive
(s)-Zoë Life Publishing

RACISM

(a)-Baker Books

Aaron Book—R
(s)-ACW Press—R
(s)-American Binding—R
(s)-Black Forest—R
Blue Dolphin
(s)-Booklocker.com—R
(s)-Book Publishers Net.—R
(s)-Bookstand Publishing—R
Cambridge Scholars
Chalice Press—R
Christian Writer's Ebook—R
(s)-DCTS Publishers
(s)-Deep River Books
Destiny Image (gifts)—R
Eerdmans Pub., Wm. B.—R
(s)-E.F.S. Online Pub.
(s)-Elderberry Press
(s)-Essence—R
Evangelical Press
(s)-Fairway Press—R
(s)-Faith Books & More—R
FaithWalk
(s)-Forever Books—R
Forward Movement
Guernica Editions—R
Hidden Brook Press—R
(s)-Holy Fire Publishing—R
(s)-House of Ali
Howard Books
(s)-Insight Publishing—R
InterVarsity Press—R
Judson Press—R
Kirk House
Lift Every Voice—R
Lighthouse Publishing—R
Monarch Books

New Hope—R
Nordskog Publishing—R
(s)-One World—R
Palgrave Macmillan—R
Pilgrim Press—R
(s)-Pleasant Word—R
Power Publishing—R
(s)-Providence House—R
(s)-Salt Works—R
(s)-Star Bible Public.
Strang Book—R
(s)-Tate Publishing—R
Third World Press—R
(s)-Trafford Publishing—R
Univ. Press of America—R
(s)-WinePress—R
(s)-Word Alive
(s)-Zoë Life Publishing

RECOVERY

(a)-Baker Books
(a)-HarperOne
(a)-Tyndale House—R
(a)-WaterBrook Press—R

Aaron Book—R
(s)-ACW Press—R
Ambassador Books
(s)-American Binding—R
(s)-Bfree Publishing
(s)-Black Forest—R
Blue Dolphin
(s)-Booklocker.com—R
(s)-Book Publishers Net.—R
(s)-Bookstand Publishing—R
(s)-Brown Books
CarePoint Publishing—R
Chalice Press—R
Christian Writer's Ebook—R
Comfort Publishing
 (s)-Creation House—R
CSS Publishing—R
(s)-Deep River Books
Earthen Vessel—R
Eerdmans Pub., Wm. B.—R
(s)-E.F.S. Online Pub.
(s)-Elderberry Press
(s)-Essence—R
Evangelical Press
Evergreen Press

(s)-Fairway Press—R
(s)-Faith Books & More—R
Faith Communications
FaithWalk
(s)-Forever Books—R
Four Craftsmen—R
Gentle Path Press
Good Book—R
GRQ—R
(s)-Halo Publishing Intl.
Hannibal Books
Health Commun.
Hidden Brook Press—R
(s)-Holy Fire Publishing—R
Hope Publishing—R
Howard Books
(s)-IMD Press—R
(s)-Insight Publishing—R
Langmarc
Lighthouse Publishing—R
Lion and Lamb
(s)-McDougal Publishing—R
Monarch Books
Nordskog Publishing—R
(s)-One World—R
Paradise Research—R
Parsons Publishing—R
Pauline Books—R
(s)-Pleasant Word—R
Power Publishing—R
Randall House
(s)-Recovery Commun.
Siloam
(s)-Star Bible Public.
Strang Book—R
(s)-Tate Publishing—R
(s)-Trafford Publishing—R
VBC Publishing
Wilshire Book—R
(s)-WinePress—R
(s)-Word Alive
(s)-Zoë Life Publishing

REFERENCE

(a)-Baker Academic
(a)-Baker Books
(a)-Bethany House—R
(a)-Cook, David C.
(a)-Doubleday Relig.—R
(a)-HarperOne

(a)-Kregel—R
(a)-Tyndale House—R

Aaron Book—R
Abingdon Press
(s)-ACW Press—R
Ambassador Intl.—R
(s)-American Binding—R
AMG Publishers—R
Barbour
(s)-Bfree Publishing
BMH Books—R
(s)-Booklocker.com—R
(s)-Bookstand Publishing—R
Branden Publishing—R
(s)-Brentwood—R
Bridge Logos—R
Cambridge Scholars
Christian Heritage—R
Christian Writer's Ebook—R
Clarke & Co., James—R
College Press—R
(s)-Creation House—R
CrossLink Publishing
Crossroad Publishing—R
Dover Publications—R
Editorial Portavoz
Eerdmans Pub., Wm. B.—R
(s)-E.F.S. Online Pub.
(s)-Elderberry Press
Emmaus Road
(s)-Essence—R
Evangelical Press
Facts On File
(s)-Fairway Press—R
(s)-Faith Books & More—R
FaithWalk
(s)-Forever Books—R
GRQ—R
Grupo Nelson
Guardian Angel
Hendrickson—R
Hidden Brook Press—R
(s)-Holy Fire Publishing—R
(s)-IMD Press—R
(s)-Impact Christian—R
InterVarsity Press—R
Intl. Awakening—R
Life Cycle Books—R
Lighthouse Publishing—R

Lion and Lamb
Lutterworth Press—R
Monarch Books
Nordskog Publishing—R
(s)-One World—R
Our Sunday Visitor—R
Paragon House—R
Power Publishing—R
(s)-Providence House—R
Reference Service
Rose Publishing
Sheed & Ward
(s)-So. Baptist Press—R
(s)-Star Bible Public.
Starik Publishing
Still Waters Revival—R
(s)-Tate Publishing—R
(s)-TEACH Services—R
(s)-Trafford Publishing—R
Univ. Press of America—R
VBC Publishing
(s)-WinePress—R
(s)-Word Alive
(s)-Zoë Life Publishing
Zondervan

RELATIONSHIPS
(a)-Bethany House—R
(a)-FaithWords
(a)-Harvest House
(a)-Kregel—R
(a)-Nelson, Thomas
(a)-Regal

Aaron Book—R
(s)-ACW Press—R
Adams Media
Ambassador Books
Ambassador Intl.—R
(s)-American Binding—R
Barbour
(s)-Bfree Publishing
(s)-Black Forest—R
Blue Dolphin
(s)-Booklocker.com—R
(s)-Bookstand Publishing—R
Bridge Logos—R
(s)-Brown Books
CarePoint Publishing—R
Chalice Press—R

Christian Focus—R
Church Growth Inst.
Cladach Publishing
CLC Publications—R
Comfort Publishing
(s)-Creation House—R
(s)-CrossHouse—R
CrossLink Publishing
Crossroad Publishing—R
Discovery House—R
Eerdmans Pub., Wm. B.—R
(s)-E.F.S. Online Pub.
(s)-Elderberry Press
(s)-Essence—R
Evangelical Press
Evergreen Press
Extreme Diva
(s)-Faith Books & More—R
(s)-Forever Books—R
Forward Movement
Fresh Air Books
Gentle Path Press
GRQ—R
(s)-Halo Publishing Intl.
Hannibal Books
Health Commun.
Hensley Publishing
Hidden Brook Press—R
(s)-Holy Fire Publishing—R
Howard Books
(s)-IMD Press—R
(s)-Insight Publishing—R
InterVarsity Press—R
Judson Press—R
Life Changing Media
Lift Every Voice—R
Lighthouse Publishing—R
Lion and Lamb
Lutterworth Press—R
(s)-MileStones Intl.
Monarch Books
MOPS Intl.
NavPress
New Hope—R
New Leaf
Nordskog Publishing—R
On My Own Now—R
P & R Publishing—R
Pauline Books—R
(s)-Port Hole Public.

Power Publishing—R
(s)-Providence House—R
Quintessential Books—R
Randall House
Ravenhawk Books—R
(s)-Rill & Associates
(s)-Salt Works—R
Samaritan Press—R
(s)-Star Bible Public.
Strang Book—R
(s)-Tate Publishing—R
(s)-TEACH Services—R
Th1nk/NavPress—R
Torch Legacy
(s)-Trafford Publishing—R
Whitaker House
(s)-WinePress—R
(s)-Zoë Life Publishing

RELIGION
(a)-B & H Publishing
(a)-Baker Academic
(a)-Baker Books
(a)-Ballantine
(a)-Doubleday Relig.—R
(a)-FaithWords
(a)-HarperOne
(a)-Nelson, Thomas
(a)-Revell
(a)-Tyndale House—R
(a)-W Publishing
(a)-WaterBrook Press—R

Aaron Book—R
Abingdon Press
ACTA Publications
(s)-ACW Press—R
Ambassador Books
Ambassador Intl.—R
(s)-American Binding—R
American Cath. Press—R
Baylor Univ. Press
(s)-Bfree Publishing
(s)-Black Forest—R
Blue Dolphin
(s)-Booklocker.com—R
(s)-Bookstand Publishing—R
Boyds Mills Press—R
Branden Publishing—R
(s)-Brentwood—R

(s)-Brown Books
Cambridge Scholars
Cambridge Univ. Press
Catholic Answers—R
Catholic Univ. of Amer. Press
Chalice Press—R
Chapter Two—R
Chelsea House—R
Christian Family—R
Christian Heritage—R
Christian Writer's Ebook—R
Church Growth Inst.
Clarke & Co., James—R
CLC Publications—R
Continuum Intl.—R
(s)-Creation House—R
CrossLink Publishing
Crossroad Publishing—R
CSS Publishing—R
(s)-Deep River Books
Eerdmans Pub., Wm. B.—R
(s)-E.F.S. Online Pub.
(s)-Elderberry Press
Emmaus Road
(s)-Essence—R
Evangelical Press
Facts On File
(s)-Fairway Press—R
(s)-Faith Books & More—R
FaithWalk
Father's Press
Fordham Univ. Press—R
(s)-Forever Books—R
Fortress Press
Forward Movement
Georgetown Univ. Press
(s)-Grace Acres Press—R
GRQ—R
(s)-Halo Publishing Intl.
Harrison House
Hendrickson—R
Hidden Brook Press—R
His Work Christian Pub.—R
(s)-Holy Fire Publishing—R
(s)-House of Ali
(s)-IMD Press—R
(s)-Impact Christian—R
(s)-Insight Publishing—R
InterVarsity Press—R
Kirk House

Larson Publications—R
Libros Liguori
Life Changing Media
Life Cycle Books—R
Lighthouse Publishing—R
Lion and Lamb
Liturgy Training—R
Loyola Press
Lutheran Univ. Press
Lutterworth Press—R
(s)-McDougal Publishing—R
Mercer Univ. Press—R
Monarch Books
Mountain Church Books—R
New Leaf
New York Univ. Press
Nordskog Publishing—R
(s)-One World—R
Oregon Catholic
Our Sunday Visitor—R
Pacific Press
Palgrave Macmillan—R
Paradise Research—R
Parsons Publishing—R
Pauline Books—R
Paulist Press
Pflaum Publishing
Pilgrim Press—R
(s)-Pleasant Word—R
Power Publishing—R
Praeger Publishers
(s)-Providence House—R
Quintessential Books—R
Ragged Edge—R
Rose Publishing
(s)-Salt Works—R
Sheed & Ward
Smyth & Helwys
(s)-So. Baptist Press—R
(s)-Star Bible Public.
St. Bede's Public.—R
St. Pauls/Alba—R
Still Waters Revival—R
Strang Book—R
Tarcher, Jeremy P.—R
(s)-Tate Publishing—R
Tau-Publishing—R
(s)-TEACH Services—R
Th1nk/NavPress—R
Torch Legacy

(s)-Trafford Publishing—R
Trinity Foundation—R
Univ. of AR Press—R
Univ. Press of America—R
Westminster John Knox
Whitaker House
(s)-WinePress—R
(s)-Word Alive
Xyzzy Press
Yale Univ. Press
(s)-Zoë Life Publishing

RELIGIOUS TOLERANCE
(a)-Baker Books
(a)-FaithWords

Aaron Book—R
(s)-ACW Press—R
(s)-American Binding—R
Baylor Univ. Press
(s)-Black Forest—R
Blue Dolphin
(s)-Booklocker.com—R
Boyds Mills Press—R
Cambridge Scholars
Chalice Press—R
Christian Writer's Ebook—R
(s)-Creation House—R
(s)-Deep River Books
Eerdmans Pub., Wm. B.—R
(s)-E.F.S. Online Pub.
(s)-Elderberry Press
(s)-Essence—R
Evangelical Press
(s)-Fairway Press—R
(s)-Faith Books & More—R
FaithWalk
(s)-Forever Books—R
Forward Movement
Hidden Brook Press—R
(s)-Holy Fire Publishing—R
Howard Books
(s)-Insight Publishing—R
Judson Press—R
Lighthouse Publishing—R
Lion and Lamb
Mercer Univ. Press—R
Monarch Books
New Canaan—R
Nordskog Publishing—R

(s)-One World—R
On My Own Now—R
Palgrave Macmillan—R
Paragon House—R
(s)-Pleasant Word—R
Power Publishing—R
(s)-Providence House—R
(s)-Star Bible Public.
Strang Book—R
(s)-Tate Publishing—R
(s)-TEACH Services—R
(s)-Trafford Publishing—R
Westminster John Knox
(s)-WinePress—R
(s)-Word Alive
Yale Univ. Press
(s)-Zoë Life Publishing

RETIREMENT
(a)-Baker Books
(a)-Harvest House

Aaron Book—R
(s)-ACW Press—R
(s)-American Binding—R
(s)-Bfree Publishing
(s)-Black Forest—R
Blue Dolphin
(s)-Booklocker.com—R
Christian Writer's Ebook—R
Cladach Publishing
College Press—R
Eerdmans Pub., Wm. B.—R
(s)-E.F.S. Online Pub.
(s)-Elderberry Press
(s)-Essence—R
Evangelical Press
(s)-Fairway Press—R
(s)-Faith Books & More—R
(s)-Forever Books—R
Forward Movement
Health Commun.
Hidden Brook Press—R
(s)-Holy Fire Publishing—R
(s)-Insight Publishing—R
Kirk House
Lighthouse Publishing—R
Lion and Lamb
Monarch Books
Nordskog Publishing—R

(s)-One World—R
(s)-Pleasant Word—R
Power Publishing—R
(s)-Providence House—R
(s)-So. Baptist Press—R
(s)-Star Bible Public.
Strang Book—R
(s)-Tate Publishing—R
(s)-TEACH Services—R
(s)-Trafford Publishing—R
(s)-WinePress—R
(s)-Word Alive
(s)-Zoë Life Publishing

SCHOLARLY
(a)-Baker Academic
(a)-Baker Books
(a)-Cook, David C.
(a)-Doubleday Relig.—R
(a)-Kregel—R

Aaron Book—R
Abingdon Press
(s)-ACW Press—R
(s)-American Binding—R
Baylor Univ. Press
(s)-Bfree Publishing
Blue Dolphin
(s)-Booklocker.com—R
Branden Publishing—R
Cambridge Scholars
Cambridge Univ. Press
Chalice Press—R
Christian Heritage—R
Christian Writer's Ebook—R
Cistercian—R
Clarke & Co., James—R
Concordia Academic
Continuum Intl.—R
Crossroad Publishing—R
(s)-Deep River Books
Eerdmans Pub., Wm. B.—R
(s)-E.F.S. Online Pub.
(s)-Elderberry Press
(s)-Essence—R
ETC Publications
Evangelical Press
Facts On File
(s)-Fairway Press—R
(s)-Faith Books & More—R

Fordham Univ. Press—R
(s)-Forever Books—R
Fortress Press
Georgetown Univ. Press
(s)-Grace Acres Press—R
Guardian Angel
Hendrickson—R
Hidden Brook Press—R
(s)-Holy Fire Publishing—R
(s)-IMD Press—R
(s)-Impact Christian—R
Inkling Books—R
(s)-Insight Publishing—R
InterVarsity Press—R
Intl. Awakening—R
Life Cycle Books—R
Lighthouse Publishing—R
Lion and Lamb
Liturgy Training—R
Lutheran Univ. Press
Lutterworth Press—R
Mercer Univ. Press—R
Millennium III—R
New York Univ. Press
Nordskog Publishing—R
(s)-One World—R
Palgrave Macmillan—R
Paragon House—R
Pilgrim Press—R
(s)-Pleasant Word—R
Power Publishing—R
(s)-Providence House—R
Quintessential Books—R
Smyth & Helwys
(s)-Star Bible Public.
St. Augustine's Press—R
St. Bede's Public.—R
(s)-Tate Publishing—R
Third World Press—R
(s)-Trafford Publishing—R
Trinity Foundation—R
Univ. of AR Press—R
Univ. Press of America—R
VBC Publishing
Westminster John Knox
(s)-WinePress—R
Wipf and Stock
(s)-Word Alive
Yale Univ. Press
Youth Specialties

(s)-Zoë Life Publishing
Zondervan

SCIENCE
(a)-Baker Books
(a)-Doubleday Relig.—R

Aaron Book—R
(s)-ACW Press—R
(s)-American Binding—R
(s)-Bfree Publishing
(s)-Black Forest—R
Blue Dolphin
(s)-Booklocker.com—R
Boyds Mills Press—R
Cambridge Scholars
Chalice Press—R
Christian Family—R
Christian Writer's Ebook—R
Eerdmans Pub., Wm. B.—R
(s)-E.F.S. Online Pub.
(s)-Elderberry Press
(s)-Essence—R
Evangelical Press
Facts On File
(s)-Fairway Press—R
(s)-Faith Books & More—R
Fordham Univ. Press—R
(s)-Forever Books—R
Forward Movement
Guardian Angel
Heart of Wisdom
Hidden Brook Press—R
(s)-Holy Fire Publishing—R
Inkling Books—R
(s)-Insight Publishing—R
InterVarsity Press—R
Knight George Pub.
Lighthouse Publishing—R
Lion and Lamb
Master Books
(s)-MileStones Intl.
Monarch Books
New Leaf
Nordskog Publishing—R
(s)-One World—R
Palgrave Macmillan—R
Parsons Publishing—R
(s)-Pleasant Word—R
Power Publishing—R

Quintessential Books—R
Review and Herald
(s)-Rill & Associates
(s)-Salt Works—R
(s)-Star Bible Public.
(s)-Tate Publishing—R
(s)-TEACH Services—R
(s)-Trafford Publishing—R
Trinity Foundation—R
Troitsa Books
(s)-WinePress—R
(s)-Word Alive
(s)-Zoë Life Publishing

SELF-HELP
(a)-Baker Books
(a)-Ballantine
(a)-HarperOne
(a)-Harvest House
(a)-Hay House
(a)-Nelson, Thomas
(a)-One World/Ballantine
(a)-Revell
(a)-Tyndale House—R
(a)-WaterBrook Press—R

Aaron Book—R
(s)-ACW Press—R
Adams Media
Ambassador Books
(s)-American Binding—R
(s)-Bfree Publishing
(s)-Black Forest—R
Blue Dolphin
(s)-Booklocker.com—R
(s)-Book Publishers Net.—R
(s)-Bookstand Publishing—R
Bridge Logos—R
(s)-Brown Books
CarePoint Publishing—R
Chalice Press—R
Christian Writer's Ebook—R
CLC Publications—R
(s)-Creation House—R
CrossLink Publishing
Crossroad Publishing—R
(s)-DCTS Publishers
(s)-Dean Press, Robbie—R
(s)-Deep River Books
Destiny Image (gifts)—R

Dimensions for Living
(s)-E.F.S. Online Pub.
(s)-Elderberry Press
(s)-Essence—R
Evangelical Press
Evergreen Press
Extreme Diva
Fair Havens—R
(s)-Fairway Press—R
(s)-Faith Books & More—R
FaithWalk
Fell, Frederick—R
(s)-Forever Books—R
Gentle Path Press
Good Book—R
GRQ—R
Grupo Nelson
Guideposts Books
(s)-Halo Publishing Intl.
Health Commun.
Hidden Brook Press—R
His Work Christian Pub.—R
(s)-Holy Fire Publishing—R
(s)-House of Ali
Howard Books
(s)-Insight Publishing—R
Langmarc
Life Changing Media
Lighthouse Publishing—R
(s)-MileStones Intl.
Monarch Books
MountainView
Nordskog Publishing—R
(s)-One World—R
On My Own Now—R
Paradise Research—R
Perigee Books
Pilgrim Press—R
(s)-Pleasant Word—R
Power Publishing—R
PREP Publishing—R
(s)-Providence House—R
Quintessential Books—R
Ragged Edge—R
(s)-Rill & Associates
(s)-Salvation Publisher—R
(s)-Selah Publishing—R
St. Anthony Mess. Press—R
(s)-Star Bible Public.
Starik Publishing

Strang Book—R
Tarcher, Jeremy P.—R
(s)-Tate Publishing—R
Third World Press—R
Torch Legacy
(s)-Trafford Publishing—R
Treble Heart—R
VBC Publishing
Wilshire Book—R
(s)-WinePress—R
(s)-Word Alive
(s)-Zoë Life Publishing

SENIOR ADULT CONCERNS
(a)-Baker Books
(a)-Cook, David C.
(a)-Harvest House

Aaron Book—R
(s)-ACW Press—R
(s)-American Binding—R
(s)-Bfree Publishing
(s)-Black Forest—R
Blue Dolphin
(s)-Booklocker.com—R
Christian Writer's Ebook—R
(s)-Deep River Books
Discovery House—R
Eerdmans Pub., Wm. B.—R
(s)-E.F.S. Online Pub.
(s)-Elderberry Press
(s)-Essence—R
Evangelical Press
Evergreen Press
Fair Havens—R
(s)-Fairway Press—R
(s)-Faith Books & More—R
Focus on the Family—R
(s)-Forever Books—R
Hidden Brook Press—R
(s)-Holy Fire Publishing—R
(s)-Insight Publishing—R
Langmarc
Lighthouse Publishing—R
Lion and Lamb
Monarch Books
New Hope—R
Nordskog Publishing—R
(s)-One World—R

(s)-Pleasant Word—R
Power Publishing—R
(s)-Providence House—R
Samaritan Press—R
(s)-So. Baptist Press—R
(s)-Star Bible Public.
Strang Book—R
(s)-Tate Publishing—R
(s)-Trafford Publishing—R
(s)-WinePress—R
(s)-Word Alive
(s)-Zoë Life Publishing

SERMONS
(a)-Baker Books
(a)-Kregel—R

Aaron Book—R
Abingdon Press
(s)-ACW Press—R
(s)-American Binding—R
(s)-Bfree Publishing
(s)-Black Forest—R
(s)-Booklocker.com—R
(s)-Bookstand Publishing—R
(s)-Brentwood—R
Chalice Press—R
Chapter Two—R
Christian Family—R
Christian Focus—R
Christian Writer's Ebook—R
Church Growth Inst.
Continuum Intl.—R
CrossLink Publishing
CSS Publishing—R
(s)-DCTS Publishers
(s)-Deep River Books
Earthen Vessel—R
Editorial Portavoz
Eerdmans Pub., Wm. B.—R
(s)-E.F.S. Online Pub.
(s)-Elderberry Press
(s)-Essence—R
Evangelical Press
(s)-Fairway Press—R
(s)-Faith Books & More—R
(s)-Forever Books—R
Group Publishing
Hidden Brook Press—R
(s)-Holy Fire Publishing—R

(s)-IMD Press—R
(s)-Insight Publishing—R
Judson Press—R
Lighthouse Publishing—R
Lion and Lamb
Liturgical Press
Lutterworth Press—R
(s)-McDougal Publishing—R
Mercer Univ. Press—R
Monarch Books
MountainView
(s)-One World—R
Pacific Press
(s)-Pleasant Word—R
Power Publishing—R
(s)-Providence House—R
Reformation Heritage—R
(s)-Salt Works—R
(s)-Salvation Publisher—R
Samaritan Press—R
(s)-Sermon Select Press
(s)-So. Baptist Press—R
(s)-Star Bible Public.
Still Waters Revival—R
St. Pauls/Alba—R
(s)-Tate Publishing—R
(s)-TEACH Services—R
Torch Legacy
(s)-Trafford Publishing—R
(s)-WinePress—R
(s)-Word Alive
(s)-Zoë Life Publishing

SINGLES' ISSUES
(a)-Baker Books
(a)-Bethany House—R
(a)-Cook, David C.
(a)-FaithWords
(a)-Harvest House
(a)-Kregel—R

Aaron Book—R
(s)-ACW Press—R
Ambassador Books
(s)-American Binding—R
Barbour
(s)-Bfree Publishing
(s)-Black Forest—R
Blue Dolphin
(s)-Booklocker.com—R

(s)-Brentwood—R
Christian Focus—R
Christian Writer's Ebook—R
(s)-Creation House—R
(s)-Dean Press, Robbie—R
(s)-Deep River Books
Destiny Image (gifts)—R
Eerdmans Pub., Wm. B.—R
(s)-E.F.S. Online Pub.
(s)-Elderberry Press
(s)-Essence—R
Evangelical Press
Evergreen Press
Fair Havens—R
(s)-Fairway Press—R
(s)-Faith Books & More—R
FaithWalk
(s)-Forever Books—R
(s)-Fruitbearer Pub.
Health Commun.
Hensley Publishing
Hidden Brook Press—R
(s)-Holy Fire Publishing—R
(s)-Insight Publishing—R
InterVarsity Press—R
Judson Press—R
Lift Every Voice—R
Lighthouse Publishing—R
Lion and Lamb
(s)-McDougal Publishing—R
Messianic Jewish—R
(s)-MileStones Intl.
Monarch Books
New Hope—R
Nordskog Publishing—R
(s)-One World—R
On My Own Now—R
P & R Publishing—R
Pacific Press
Parsons Publishing—R
Pauline Books—R
Perigee Books
(s)-Pleasant Word—R
Power Publishing—R
(s)-Providence House—R
Quintessential Books—R
Review and Herald
(s)-Rill & Associates
(s)-Salt Works—R
Samaritan Press—R

(s)-Star Bible Public.
Strang Book—R
(s)-Tate Publishing—R
Th1nk/NavPress—R
(s)-Trafford Publishing—R
VBC Publishing
Whitaker House
(s)-WinePress—R
(s)-Word Alive
(s)-Zoë Life Publishing

SMALL-GROUP RESOURCES*

(s)-Bfree Publishing
(s)-Essence—R
Four Craftsmen—R
(s)-Grace Acres Press—R
(s)-IMD Press—R
Praxis Press
Randall House
St. Anthony Mess. Press—R
Touch Publications—R
(s)-Zoë Life Publishing

SOCIAL JUSTICE ISSUES

(a)-Baker Books
(a)-FaithWords
(a)-HarperOne
(a)-Nelson, Thomas

Aaron Book—R
(s)-ACW Press—R
(s)-American Binding—R
(s)-Ampelos Press
(s)-Bfree Publishing
(s)-Black Forest—R
Blue Dolphin
(s)-Booklocker.com—R
(s)-Brentwood—R
Canadian Inst. for Law—R
Chalice Press—R
Christian Writer's Ebook—R
Church Publishing
(s)-DCTS Publishers
(s)-Deep River Books
Destiny Image (gifts)—R
(s)-Destiny Image (books)—R
Eerdmans Pub., Wm. B.—R
(s)-E.F.S. Online Pub.
(s)-Elderberry Press

(s)-Essence—R
Evangelical Press
(s)-Fairway Press—R
(s)-Faith Books & More—R
(s)-Forever Books—R
Forward Movement
Georgetown Univ. Press
Hendrickson—R
Hidden Brook Press—R
(s)-Holy Fire Publishing—R
Hope Publishing—R
Howard Books
Inkling Books—R
(s)-Insight Publishing—R
InterVarsity Press—R
Judson Press—R
Kingsley Pub., Jessica—R
Libros Liguori
Life Cycle Books—R
Lift Every Voice—R
Lighthouse Publishing—R
Monarch Books
NavPress
New Hope—R
Nordskog Publishing—R
(s)-One World—R
On My Own Now—R
Our Sunday Visitor—R
Palgrave Macmillan—R
Paulist Press
Pilgrim Press—R
(s)-Pleasant Word—R
Power Publishing—R
(s)-Providence House—R
Quintessential Books—R
Ravenhawk Books—R
Sheed & Ward
(s)-Star Bible Public.
Still Waters Revival—R
Strang Book—R
(s)-Tate Publishing—R
Th1nk/NavPress—R
Third World Press—R
(s)-Trafford Publishing—R
(s)-WinePress—R
(s)-Word Alive
Yale Univ. Press
Youth Specialties
(s)-Zoë Life Publishing

SOCIOLOGY
(a)-Baker Books

Aaron Book—R
(s)-ACW Press—R
(s)-American Binding—R
(s)-Bfree Publishing
(s)-Black Forest—R
Blue Dolphin
(s)-Booklocker.com—R
(s)-Brentwood—R
Cambridge Scholars
Carey Library, Wm.—R
Christian Writer's Ebook—R
(s)-Deep River Books
Eerdmans Pub., Wm. B.—R
(s)-E.F.S. Online Pub.
(s)-Elderberry Press
(s)-Essence—R
Evangelical Press
(s)-Fairway Press—R
(s)-Faith Books & More—R
FaithWalk
Fordham Univ. Press—R
(s)-Forever Books—R
Hidden Brook Press—R
(s)-Holy Fire Publishing—R
(s)-IMD Press—R
(s)-Insight Publishing—R
InterVarsity Press—R
Life Cycle Books—R
Lighthouse Publishing—R
Lion and Lamb
Lutterworth Press—R
(s)-McDougal Publishing—R
Mercer Univ. Press—R
Monarch Books
New York Univ. Press
Nordskog Publishing—R
(s)-One World—R
On My Own Now—R
(s)-Pleasant Word—R
Power Publishing—R
(s)-Providence House—R
Review and Herald
(s)-Star Bible Public.
Still Waters Revival—R
Strang Book—R
(s)-Tate Publishing—R
Third World Press—R

(s)-Trafford Publishing—R
Univ. Press of America—R
(s)-WinePress—R
(s)-Word Alive
(s)-Zoë Life Publishing

SPIRITUAL GIFTS
(a)-B & H Publishing
(a)-Baker Books
(a)-Kregel—R
(a)-Nelson, Thomas
(a)-Regal
(a)-W Publishing

Aaron Book—R
(s)-ACW Press—R
Ambassador Books
(s)-American Binding—R
(s)-Bfree Publishing
(s)-Black Forest—R
Blue Dolphin
(s)-Booklocker.com—R
Bridge Logos—R
(s)-Brown Books
Canticle Books—R
Chapter Two—R
Christian Writer's Ebook—R
Church Growth Inst.
CLC Publications—R
Comfort Publishing
(s)-Creation House—R
(s)-CrossHouse—R
CrossLink Publishing
CSS Publishing—R
(s)-Dean Press, Robbie—R
(s)-Deep River Books
Destiny Image (gifts)—R
(s)-Destiny Image (books)—R
Eerdmans Pub., Wm. B.—R
(s)-E.F.S. Online Pub.
(s)-Elderberry Press
(s)-Essence—R
Evangelical Press
(s)-Fairway Press—R
(s)-Faith Books & More—R
FaithWalk
Father's Press
(s)-Forever Books—R
Forward Movement
Four Craftsmen—R

Gospel Publishing
(s)-Grace Acres Press—R
Group Publishing
Grupo Nelson
Guardian Angel
(s)-Halo Publishing Intl.
Harrison House
Hensley Publishing
Hidden Brook Press—R
(s)-Holy Fire Publishing—R
Howard Books
(s)-IMD Press—R
(s)-Insight Publishing—R
InterVarsity Press—R
Lift Every Voice—R
Lighthouse Publishing—R
Lion and Lamb
Lutheran Univ. Press
Magnus Press—R
(s)-MileStones Intl.
Monarch Books
New Hope—R
Nordskog Publishing—R
(s)-One World—R
Pacific Press
Parson Place—R
Parsons Publishing—R
(s)-Pleasant Word—R
Power Publishing—R
(s)-Providence House—R
Revival Nation
(s)-Rill & Associates
Rose Publishing
(s)-Salvation Publisher—R
(s)-Selah Publishing—R
(s)-Star Bible Public.
St. Bede's Public.—R
Strang Book—R
(s)-Tate Publishing—R
Tau-Publishing—R
(s)-TEACH Services—R
(s)-Trafford Publishing—R
Whitaker House
(s)-WinePress—R
(s)-Word Alive
(s)-Zoë Life Publishing

SPIRITUALITY
(a)-Baker Books
(a)-Ballantine

(a)-Bethany House—R
(a)-Doubleday Relig.—R
(a)-FaithWords
(a)-HarperOne
(a)-Hay House
(a)-Kregel—R
(a)-Nelson, Thomas
(a)-Tyndale House—R
(a)-WaterBrook Press—R
(a)-W Publishing

Aaron Book—R
Abingdon Press
ACTA Publications
(s)-ACW Press—R
Ambassador Books
(s)-American Binding—R
(s)-Bfree Publishing
(s)-Black Forest—R
Blue Dolphin
(s)-Booklocker.com—R
(s)-Book Publishers Net.—R
(s)-Bookstand Publishing—R
(s)-Brentwood—R
Bridge Logos—R
(s)-Brown Books
Cambridge Scholars
Canticle Books—R
Chapter Two—R
Christian Heritage—R
Christian Writer's Ebook—R
Church Publishing
Cistercian—R
Clarke & Co., James—R
CLC Publications—R
Comfort Publishing
Conari Press
Continuum Intl.—R
(s)-Creation House—R
CrossLink Publishing
Crossroad Publishing—R
CSS Publishing—R
(s)-Deep River Books
Destiny Image (gifts)—R
(s)-Destiny Image (books)—R
Discovery House—R
Eerdmans Pub., Wm. B.—R
(s)-E.F.S. Online Pub.
(s)-Elderberry Press
Emmaus Road

(s)-Essence—R
Evangelical Press
Evergreen Press
Fair Havens—R
(s)-Fairway Press—R
(s)-Faith Books & More—R
Faith Communications
FaithWalk
Fell, Frederick—R
(s)-Forever Books—R
Forward Movement
Gentle Path Press
Good Book—R
(s)-Grace Acres Press—R
GRQ—R
Guardian Angel
(s)-Halo Publishing Intl.
Hidden Brook Press—R
(s)-Holy Fire Publishing—R
(s)-House of Ali
Howard Books
(s)-IMD Press—R
(s)-Impact Christian—R
(s)-Insight Publishing—R
InterVarsity Press—R
Kingsley Pub., Jessica—R
Kirk House
Larson Publications—R
Libros Liguori
Lighthouse Publishing—R
Liguori Public.—R
Lion and Lamb
Loyola Press
Lutheran Univ. Press
Magnus Press—R
Monarch Books
New Hope—R
Nordskog Publishing—R
(s)-One World—R
On My Own Now—R
Pacific Press
Paradise Research—R
Paragon House—R
Parsons Publishing—R
Pauline Books—R
Paulist Press
Perigee Books
Pilgrim Press—R
(s)-Pleasant Word—R
Power Publishing—R

(s)-Providence House—R
Quintessential Books—R
Ragged Edge—R
Ravenhawk Books—R
Resource Public.
Revival Nation
(s)-Salt Works—R
(s)-Selah Publishing—R
Sheed & Ward
Smyth & Helwys
(s)-So. Baptist Press—R
St. Anthony Mess. Press—R
(s)-Star Bible Public.
St. Bede's Public.—R
St. Pauls/Alba—R
Strang Book—R
Sunpenny Publishing
(s)-Tate Publishing—R
Tau-Publishing—R
(s)-TEACH Services—R
Th1nk/NavPress—R
(s)-Trafford Publishing—R
Treble Heart—R
(s)-WinePress—R
(s)-Word Alive
(s)-Zoë Life Publishing

SPIRITUAL LIFE

(a)-B & H Publishing
(a)-Bethany House—R
(a)-FaithWords
(a)-HarperOne
(a)-Kregel—R
(a)-Nelson, Thomas
(a)-Regal
(a)-WaterBrook Press—R

Aadeon Publishing—R
Aaron Book—R
Abingdon Press
ACTA Publications
(s)-ACW Press—R
Ambassador Books
(s)-American Binding—R
Anglicans United—R
Barbour
Beacon Hill Press—R
(s)-Bfree Publishing
(s)-Black Forest—R
Blue Dolphin

BMH Books—R
(s)-Booklocker.com—R
(s)-Bookstand Publishing—R
Bridge Logos—R
(s)-Brown Books
Canticle Books—R
Chalice Press—R
Chapter Two—R
Christian Family—R
Christian Focus—R
Christian Writer's Ebook—R
Church Growth Inst.
Church Publishing
CLC Publications—R
Comfort Publishing
Congregational Life
Continuum Intl.—R
(s)-Creation House—R
(s)-CrossHouse—R
CrossLink Publishing
CSS Publishing—R
(s)-Deep River Books
(s)-Destiny Image (books)—R
Eerdmans Pub., Wm. B.—R
(s)-E.F.S. Online Pub.
(s)-Elderberry Press
Eldridge Plays
Elijah Press
Emmaus Road
(s)-Essence—R
Evangelical Press
Evergreen Press
(s)-Fairway Press—R
(s)-Faith Books & More—R
FaithWalk
Father's Press
(s)-Forever Books—R
Forward Movement
Gentle Path Press
(s)-Grace Acres Press—R
GRQ—R
Guardian Angel
(s)-Halo Publishing Intl.
Harrison House
Hidden Brook Press—R
(s)-Holy Fire Publishing—R
Howard Books
(s)-IMD Press—R
Inheritance Press
(s)-Insight Publishing—R

InterVarsity Press—R
JourneyForth/BJU
Judson Press—R
Life Changing Media
(s)-LifeVest Publishing
Lift Every Voice—R
Lighthouse Publishing—R
Lion and Lamb
Master Books
(s)-MileStones Intl.
Monarch Books
NavPress
New Hope—R
New Leaf
Nordskog Publishing—R
(s)-One World—R
On My Own Now—R
Parsons Publishing—R
Pauline Books—R
Paulist Press
Pilgrim Press—R
(s)-Pleasant Word—R
(s)-Port Hole Public.
Power Publishing—R
(s)-Providence House—R
Quintessential Books—R
Randall House
Reformation Trust
Review and Herald
Revival Nation
(s)-Rill & Associates
Rose Publishing
(s)-Salvation Publisher—R
Samaritan Press—R
(s)-Star Bible Public.
St. Bede's Public.—R
Strang Book—R
(s)-Tate Publishing—R
(s)-TEACH Services—R
Th1nk/NavPress—R
(s)-Trafford Publishing—R
Treble Heart—R
Wesleyan Publishing
Whitaker House
(s)-WinePress—R
(s)-Word Alive
(s)-Zoë Life Publishing

SPIRITUAL WARFARE
(a)-B & H Publishing

(a)-Baker Books
(a)-Nelson, Thomas
(a)-Regal
(a)-W Publishing

Aadeon Publishing—R
Aaron Book—R
(s)-ACW Press—R
(s)-American Binding—R
Anglicans United—R
(s)-Bfree Publishing
(s)-Black Forest—R
Blue Dolphin
(s)-Booklocker.com—R
(s)-Bookstand Publishing—R
Bridge Logos—R
(s)-Brown Books
Carey Library, Wm.—R
Chapter Two—R
Christian Family—R
Christian Focus—R
Christian Writer's Ebook—R
CLC Publications—R
Comfort Publishing
(s)-Creation House—R
CrossLink Publishing
Destiny Image (gifts)—R
(s)-Destiny Image (books)—R
Earthen Vessel—R
Editorial Portavoz
Eerdmans Pub., Wm. B.—R
(s)-E.F.S. Online Pub.
(s)-Elderberry Press
Emmaus Road
(s)-Essence—R
Evangelical Press
Evergreen Press
(s)-Fairway Press—R
(s)-Faith Books & More—R
FaithWalk
Father's Press
(s)-Forever Books—R
Four Craftsmen—R
(s)-Grace Acres Press—R
Grupo Nelson
Harrison House
Hensley Publishing
Hidden Brook Press—R
(s)-Holy Fire Publishing—R
(s)-IMD Press—R

(s)-Impact Christian—R
(s)-Insight Publishing—R
Lighthouse Publishing—R
Lion and Lamb
(s)-McDougal Publishing—R
Messianic Jewish—R
(s)-MileStones Intl.
Monarch Books
New Hope—R
Nordskog Publishing—R
(s)-One World—R
On My Own Now—R
Parson Place—R
Parsons Publishing—R
(s)-Pleasant Word—R
Power Publishing—R
(s)-Providence House—R
Revival Nation
(s)-Rill & Associates
(s)-Salvation Publisher—R
Samaritan Press—R
(s)-Selah Publishing—R
(s)-Star Bible Public.
Strang Book—R
(s)-Tate Publishing—R
(s)-TEACH Services—R
Th1nk/NavPress—R
(s)-Trafford Publishing—R
Treble Heart—R
VBC Publishing
Whitaker House
(s)-WinePress—R
(s)-Word Alive
(s)-Zoë Life Publishing

SPORTS/RECREATION

(a)-Baker Books
(a)-Ballantine
(a)-One World/Ballantine

Aaron Book—R
ACTA Publications
(s)-ACW Press—R
Ambassador Books
(s)-American Binding—R
(s)-Bfree Publishing
Blue Dolphin
(s)-Booklocker.com—R
(s)-Bookstand Publishing—R
Boyds Mills Press—R
(s)-Brown Books

Christian Writer's Ebook—R
Cladach Publishing
Comfort Publishing
Cross Training
(s)-Deep River Books
Earthen Vessel—R
(s)-E.F.S. Online Pub.
(s)-Elderberry Press
(s)-Essence—R
Evangelical Press
Evergreen Press
Facts On File
(s)-Fairway Press—R
(s)-Faith Books & More—R
(s)-Forever Books—R
Guardian Angel
(s)-Halo Publishing Intl.
Hidden Brook Press—R
His Work Christian Pub.—R
(s)-Holy Fire Publishing—R
(s)-IMD Press—R
(s)-Insight Publishing—R
Judson Press—R
Lighthouse Publishing—R
Lion and Lamb
Monarch Books
Nordskog Publishing—R
(s)-One World—R
(s)-Pleasant Word—R
Power Publishing—R
(s)-Providence House—R
Ravenhawk Books—R
Reference Service
Strang Book—R
Sunpenny Publishing
(s)-Tate Publishing—R
Third World Press—R
(s)-Trafford Publishing—R
(s)-WinePress—R
(s)-Word Alive
Xyzzy Press
(s)-Zoë Life Publishing

STEWARDSHIP

(a)-Baker Books
(a)-Bethany House—R
(a)-Kregel—R

Aaron Book—R
(s)-ACW Press—R

Ambassador Intl.—R
(s)-American Binding—R
Anglicans United—R
(s)-Bfree Publishing
(s)-Black Forest—R
Blue Dolphin
BMH Books—R
(s)-Booklocker.com—R
(s)-Brown Books
Chalice Press—R
Christian Focus—R
Christian Writer's Ebook—R
Church Growth Inst.
CLC Publications—R
College Press—R
(s)-Creation House—R
CrossLink Publishing
CSS Publishing—R
(s)-Deep River Books
Eerdmans Pub., Wm. B.—R
(s)-E.F.S. Online Pub.
(s)-Elderberry Press
Emmaus Road
(s)-Essence—R
Evangelical Press
Evergreen Press
(s)-Fairway Press—R
(s)-Faith Books & More—R
FaithWalk
Father's Press
(s)-Forever Books—R
Forward Movement
(s)-Grace Acres Press—R
Group Publishing
Hensley Publishing
Hidden Brook Press—R
(s)-Holy Fire Publishing—R
Hope Publishing—R
(s)-IMD Press—R
(s)-Insight Publishing—R
InterVarsity Press—R
Jebaire
Judson Press—R
Kirk House
Lift Every Voice—R
Lighthouse Publishing—R
Lion and Lamb
Lutheran Univ. Press
(s)-McDougal Publishing—R
Monarch Books

Neibauer Press—R
New Hope—R
Nordskog Publishing—R
(s)-One World—R
On My Own Now—R
Our Sunday Visitor—R
Pacific Press
Parson Place—R
Parsons Publishing—R
Pilgrim Press—R
(s)-Pleasant Word—R
Power Publishing—R
(s)-Providence House—R
Randall House
Revival Nation
Rose Publishing
(s)-Salvation Publisher—R
(s)-Star Bible Public.
(s)-Tate Publishing—R
(s)-TEACH Services—R
(s)-Trafford Publishing—R
VBC Publishing
Westminster John Knox
(s)-WinePress—R
(s)-Word Alive
(s)-Zoë Life Publishing

THEOLOGY
(a)-Baker Books
(a)-Bethany House—R
(a)-Cook, David C.
(a)-Doubleday Relig.—R
(a)-HarperOne
(a)-Kregel—R
(a)-Multnomah
(a)-Nelson, Thomas
(a)-Tyndale House—R

Aaron Book—R
Abingdon Press
(s)-ACW Press—R
Ambassador Intl.—R
(s)-American Binding—R
American Cath. Press—R
(s)-Bfree Publishing
Blue Dolphin
BMH Books—R
(s)-Booklocker.com—R
(s)-Bookstand Publishing—R
(s)-Brentwood—R
(s)-Brown Books

Canticle Books—R
Catholic Answers—R
Catholic Univ. of Amer. Press
Chalice Press—R
Chapter Two—R
Christian Family—R
Christian Focus—R
Christian Heritage—R
Christian Writer's Ebook—R
Church Publishing
Cistercian—R
Clarke & Co., James—R
CLC Publications—R
College Press—R
Conciliar Press—R
Concordia Academic
Continuum Intl.—R
(s)-Creation House—R
CrossLink Publishing
Crossroad Publishing—R
Crossway
CSS Publishing—R
(s)-Deep River Books
(s)-Deo Volente
Earthen Vessel—R
Eerdmans Pub., Wm. B.—R
(s)-E.F.S. Online Pub.
(s)-Elderberry Press
Emmaus Road
(s)-Essence—R
Evangelical Press
(s)-Fairway Press—R
(s)-Faith Books & More—R
FaithWalk
Father's Press
First Fruits of Zion
(s)-Forever Books—R
Fortress Press
Forward Movement
Founders Press
Georgetown Univ. Press
(s)-Grace Acres Press—R
Hidden Brook Press—R
(s)-Holy Fire Publishing—R
(s)-IMD Press—R
(s)-Impact Christian—R
Inkling Books—R
(s)-Insight Publishing—R
InterVarsity Press—R
Intl. Awakening—R

Kingsley Pub., Jessica—R
Kirk House
Leafwood
Lift Every Voice—R
Lighthouse Publishing—R
Lighthouse Trails—R
Lion and Lamb
Liturgical Press
Lutheran Univ. Press
Lutheran Voices
Lutterworth Press—R
Magnus Press—R
Mercer Univ. Press—R
Meriwether
Millennium III—R
Monarch Books
Nordskog Publishing—R
(s)-One World—R
Pacific Press
Palgrave Macmillan—R
Paulist Press
Pflaum Publishing
Pilgrim Press—R
(s)-Pleasant Word—R
Power Publishing—R
(s)-Providence House—R
Randall House
Ravenhawk Books—R
Reformation Heritage—R
Reformation Trust
Resource Public.
Review and Herald
Rose Publishing
Sheed & Ward
Smyth & Helwys
(s)-So. Baptist Press—R
(s)-Star Bible Public.
St. Augustine's Press—R
St. Bede's Public.—R
Still Waters Revival—R
St. Pauls/Alba—R
(s)-Tate Publishing—R
(s)-TEACH Services—R
Th1nk/NavPress—R
(s)-Trafford Publishing—R
Trinity Foundation—R
UMI Publishing—R
Univ. Press of America—R
VBC Publishing
Wesleyan Publishing

Westminster John Knox
(s)-WinePress—R
Wipf and Stock
(s)-Word Alive
Yale Univ. Press
(s)-Zoë Life Publishing
Zondervan

TIME MANAGEMENT
(a)-Baker Books
(a)-Cook, David C.
(a)-Nelson, Thomas

Aaron Book—R
(s)-ACW Press—R
(s)-American Binding—R
Barbour
(s)-Bfree Publishing
(s)-Black Forest—R
Blue Dolphin
(s)-Booklocker.com—R
(s)-Bookstand Publishing—R
(s)-Brown Books
Christian Writer's Ebook—R
(s)-CrossHouse—R
Crossroad Publishing—R
(s)-DCTS Publishers
(s)-Deep River Books
(s)-E.F.S. Online Pub.
(s)-Elderberry Press
(s)-Essence—R
Evangelical Press
Evergreen Press
(s)-Fairway Press—R
(s)-Faith Books & More—R
(s)-Forever Books—R
Forward Movement
(s)-Grace Acres Press—R
GRQ—R
Health Commun.
Hensley Publishing
Hidden Brook Press—R
(s)-Holy Fire Publishing—R
(s)-IMD Press—R
(s)-Insight Publishing—R
Judson Press—R
Kirk House
Lighthouse Publishing—R
Lion and Lamb
Monarch Books
New Hope—R

Nordskog Publishing—R
(s)-One World—R
On My Own Now—R
(s)-Pleasant Word—R
Power Publishing—R
(s)-Providence House—R
(s)-Salvation Publisher—R
(s)-Star Bible Public.
Strang Book—R
(s)-Tate Publishing—R
(s)-Trafford Publishing—R
VBC Publishing
(s)-WinePress—R
(s)-Word Alive
(s)-Zoë Life Publishing

TRACTS
(s)-Bfree Publishing
Chapter Two—R
Christian Writer's Ebook—R
(s)-Essence—R
Evangelical Press
Forward Movement
(s)-Fruitbearer Pub.
(s)-Holy Fire Publishing—R
Intl. Awakening—R
Libros Liguori
Life Cycle Books—R
Liguori Public.—R
Neibauer Press—R
(s)-One World—R
Praxis Press
Rose Publishing
Tract League
Trinity Foundation—R
(s)-Word Alive

TRAVEL
(a)-Baker Books
(a)-Ballantine
(a)-One World/Ballantine

Aaron Book—R
(s)-ACW Press—R
(s)-American Binding—R
(s)-Bfree Publishing
(s)-Booklocker.com—R
(s)-Book Publishers Net.—R
(s)-Brentwood—R
(s)-Brown Books
Cambridge Scholars

Chapter Two—R
Christian Heritage—R
Christian Writer's Ebook—R
Cladach Publishing
(s)-E.F.S. Online Pub.
(s)-Elderberry Press
(s)-Essence—R
(s)-Fairway Press—R
(s)-Faith Books & More—R
FaithWalk
(s)-Forever Books—R
Hidden Brook Press—R
(s)-Holy Fire Publishing—R
Hope Publishing—R
(s)-IMD Press—R
(s)-Insight Publishing—R
(s)-LifeVest Publishing
Lighthouse Publishing—R
Liguori Public.—R
Lion and Lamb
Master Books
Monarch Books
New Leaf
(s)-One World—R
(s)-Pleasant Word—R
Power Publishing—R
(s)-Providence House—R
Sunpenny Publishing
(s)-Tate Publishing—R
(s)-Trafford Publishing—R
(s)-WinePress—R
(s)-Word Alive
Xyzzy Press
(s)-Zoë Life Publishing

TWEEN BOOKS
Aaron Book—R
(s)-ACW Press—R
Ambassador Books
Ambassador Intl.—R
(s)-American Binding—R
Barbour
(s)-Bfree Publishing
(s)-Black Forest—R
(s)-Booklocker.com—R
(s)-Bookstand Publishing—R
Eerdmans Pub., Wm. B.—R
(s)-E.F.S. Online Pub.
(s)-Elderberry Press
Eldridge Plays

(s)-Essence—R
(s)-Faith Books & More—R
(s)-Forever Books—R
(s)-Fruitbearer Pub.
Hidden Brook Press—R
(s)-Holy Fire Publishing—R
(s)-Insight Publishing—R
JourneyStone—R
(s)-Kindred Books—R
Legacy Press—R
Lighthouse Publishing—R
Lion and Lamb
Messianic Jewish—R
(s)-MileStones Intl.
Mission City Press
Parsons Publishing—R
Pauline Books—R
Power Publishing—R
Putnam/Young Readers
(s)-Rill & Associates
(s)-Tate Publishing—R
(s)-Trafford Publishing—R
(s)-WinePress—R
(s)-Zoë Life Publishing

WOMEN'S ISSUES

(a)-B & H Publishing
(a)-Baker Academic
(a)-Baker Books
(a)-Ballantine
(a)-Bethany House—R
(a)-Cook, David C.
(a)-Doubleday Relig.—R
(a)-FaithWords
(a)-HarperOne
(a)-Harvest House
(a)-Kregel—R
(a)-Nelson, Thomas
(a)-One World/Ballantine
(a)-Regal
(a)-W Publishing

Aaron Book—R
ACTA Publications
(s)-ACW Press—R
Adams Media
Ambassador Books
(s)-American Binding—R
AMG Publishers—R
Barbour
Beacon Hill Press—R

(s)-Bfree Publishing
(s)-Black Forest—R
Blue Dolphin
BMH Books—R
(s)-Booklocker.com—R
(s)-Book Publishers Net.—R
(s)-Bookstand Publishing—R
Branden Publishing—R
Bridge Logos—R
(s)-Brown Books
Chalice Press—R
Christian Writer's Ebook—R
Church Publishing
College Press—R
Comfort Publishing
(s)-Creation House—R
(s)-CrossHouse—R
CrossLink Publishing
Crossway
(s)-Dean Press, Robbie—R
(s)-Deep River Books
Destiny Image (gifts)—R
Discovery House—R
Eerdmans Pub., Wm. B.—R
(s)-E.F.S. Online Pub.
(s)-Elderberry Press
Eldridge Plays
Emmaus Road
(s)-Essence—R
Evangelical Press
Evergreen Press
Facts On File
Fair Havens—R
(s)-Fairway Press—R
(s)-Faith Books & More—R
Faith Communications
FaithWalk
Focus on the Family—R
(s)-Forever Books—R
Fortress Press
(s)-Fruitbearer Pub.
Gentle Path Press
GRQ—R
Guernica Editions—R
(s)-Halo Publishing Intl.
Health Commun.
Hensley Publishing
Hidden Brook Press—R
(s)-Holy Fire Publishing—R
Hope Publishing—R

Howard Books
(s)-IMD Press—R
Inkling Books—R
(s)-Insight Publishing—R
InterVarsity Press—R
JourneyForth/BJU
Jubilant Press—R
Judson Press—R
Kirk House
Langmarc
Life Cycle Books—R
Lift Every Voice—R
Lighthouse Publishing—R
Lion and Lamb
Loyola Press
(s)-McDougal Publishing—R
Messianic Jewish—R
Monarch Books
Moody Publishers
NavPress
New Hope—R
New York Univ. Press
Nordskog Publishing—R
(s)-One World—R
On My Own Now—R
Palgrave Macmillan—R
Parson Place—R
Pauline Books—R
Perigee Books
Pilgrim Press—R
(s)-Pleasant Word—R
(s)-Port Hole Public.
Power Publishing—R
Praeger Publishers
(s)-Providence House—R
Ravenhawk Books—R
Reference Service
Review and Herald
Revival Nation
(s)-Rill & Associates
Samaritan Press—R
(s)-Selah Publishing—R
Sheed & Ward
(s)-So. Baptist Press—R
St. Anthony Mess. Press—R
(s)-Star Bible Public.
Still Waters Revival—R
Strang Book—R
Sunpenny Publishing
Tarcher, Jeremy P.—R

(s)-Tate Publishing—R
(s)-TEACH Services—R
Th1nk/NavPress—R
Third World Press—R
(s)-Trafford Publishing—R
Univ. of AR Press—R
VBC Publishing
Whitaker House
(s)-WinePress—R
(s)-Word Alive
(s)-Zoë Life Publishing

WORLD ISSUES
(a)-Baker Books
(a)-Doubleday Relig.—R
(a)-HarperOne
(a)-Kregel—R
(a)-Tyndale House—R

Aadeon Publishing—R
Aaron Book—R
(s)-ACW Press—R
(s)-American Binding—R
AMG Publishers—R
(s)-Ampelos Press
(s)-Bfree Publishing
(s)-Black Forest—R
Blue Dolphin
(s)-Booklocker.com—R
Boyds Mills Press—R
Branden Publishing—R
Bridge Logos—R
Carey Library, Wm.—R
Chalice Press—R
Christian Writer's Ebook—R
Comfort Publishing
(s)-Creation House—R
CrossLink Publishing
(s)-Deep River Books
Eerdmans Pub., Wm. B.—R
(s)-E.E.S. Online Pub.
(s)-Elderberry Press
(s)-Essence—R
Evangelical Press
(s)-Fairway Press—R
(s)-Faith Books & More—R
FaithWalk
First Fruits of Zion
(s)-Forever Books—R
Georgetown Univ. Press

Guernica Editions—R
(s)-Halo Publishing Intl.
Hidden Brook Press—R
(s)-Holy Fire Publishing—R
(s)-IMD Press—R
(s)-Insight Publishing—R
InterVarsity Press—R
Kirk House
Lift Every Voice—R
Lighthouse Publishing—R
Lion and Lamb
Monarch Books
NavPress
New Hope—R
Nordskog Publishing—R
(s)-One World—R
Palgrave Macmillan—R
Pilgrim Press—R
(s)-Pleasant Word—R
Power Publishing—R
(s)-Providence House—R
Quintessential Books—R
Ravenhawk Books—R
Revival Nation
(s)-Salt Works—R
(s)-Selah Publishing—R
(s)-Star Bible Public.
Still Waters Revival—R
Strang Book—R
(s)-Tate Publishing—R
Th1nk/NavPress—R
Third World Press—R
(s)-Trafford Publishing—R
VBC Publishing
(s)-WinePress—R
(s)-Word Alive
Yale Univ. Press
(s)-Zoë Life Publishing

WORSHIP
(a)-B & H Publishing
(a)-Bethany House—R
(a)-Cook, David C.
(a)-Kregel—R
(a)-Nelson, Thomas
(a)-Regal
(a)-W Publishing

Aaron Book—R
Abingdon Press

(s)-ACW Press—R
(s)-American Binding—R
Barbour
(s)-Bfree Publishing
(s)-Black Forest—R
BMH Books—R
(s)-Booklocker.com—R
Bridge Logos—R
Chalice Press—R
Chapter Two—R
CharismaKids
Christian Focus—R
Christian Heritage—R
Christian Writer's Ebook—R
Church Publishing
Clarke & Co., James—R
CLC Publications—R
College Press—R
Conquest Publishers
Continuum Intl.—R
(s)-Creation House—R
CrossLink Publishing
CSS Publishing—R
(s)-Deep River Books
(s)-Deo Volente
Destiny Image (gifts)—R
Eerdmans Pub., Wm. B.—R
(s)-E.E.S. Online Pub.
(s)-Elderberry Press
Eldridge Plays
Emmaus Road
(s)-Essence—R
Evangelical Press
(s)-Fairway Press—R
Faith Alive
(s)-Faith Books & More—R
FaithWalk
Father's Press
(s)-Forever Books—R
Forward Movement
Founders Press
(s)-Grace Acres Press—R
Group Publishing
GRQ—R
(s)-Halo Publishing Intl.
Harrison House
Hidden Brook Press—R
(s)-Holy Fire Publishing—R
(s)-IMD Press—R
(s)-Insight Publishing—R

InterVarsity Press—R
Jebaire
JourneyForth/BJU
Judson Press—R
Leafwood
Lift Every Voice—R
Lighthouse Publishing—R
Lion and Lamb
Liturgy Training—R
Lutheran Univ. Press
Lutterworth Press—R
Mercer Univ. Press—R
Messianic Jewish—R
(s)-MileStones Intl.
Monarch Books
National Drama
New Hope—R
Nordskog Publishing—R
(s)-One World—R
Oregon Catholic
Pacific Press
Parsons Publishing—R
Pilgrim Press—R
(s)-Pleasant Word—R
Power Publishing—R
(s)-Providence House—R
Reformation Trust
Resource Public.
Revival Nation
(s)-Rill & Associates
Rose Publishing
(s)-Salt Works—R
Samaritan Press—R
(s)-Selah Publishing—R
(s)-Star Bible Public.
Strang Book—R
(s)-Tate Publishing—R
(s)-TEACH Services—R
Th1nk/NavPress—R
(s)-Trafford Publishing—R
VBC Publishing
Westminster John Knox
(s)-WinePress—R
(s)-Word Alive

WORSHIP RESOURCES

(a)-B & H Publishing
(a)-Baker Books
(a)-Kregel—R

Aaron Book—R
Abingdon Press
(s)-ACW Press—R
(s)-American Binding—R
American Cath. Press—R
(s)-Bfree Publishing
(s)-Black Forest—R
(s)-Booklocker.com—R
(s)-Bookstand Publishing—R
Catholic Book
Chalice Press—R
Christian Writer's Ebook—R
Church Publishing
CSS Publishing—R
(s)-DCTS Publishers
(s)-Deep River Books
Eerdmans Pub., Wm. B.—R
(s)-E.F.S. Online Pub.
(s)-Elderberry Press
Eldridge Plays
Emmaus Road
(s)-Essence—R
Evangelical Press
(s)-Fairway Press—R
Faith Alive
(s)-Faith Books & More—R
FaithWalk
(s)-Forever Books—R
Forward Movement
Founders Press
Group Publishing
Hidden Brook Press—R
(s)-Holy Fire Publishing—R
(s)-IMD Press—R
(s)-Insight Publishing—R
InterVarsity Press—R
Judson Press—R
Lighthouse Publishing—R
Lion and Lamb
Liturgical Press
Liturgy Training—R
Lutheran Univ. Press
Meriwether
Monarch Books
National Drama
(s)-One World—R
Our Sunday Visitor—R
Parsons Publishing—R
Pilgrim Press—R
(s)-Pleasant Word—R

Power Publishing—R
(s)-Providence House—R
Resource Public.
(s)-Salt Works—R
Smyth & Helwys
Standard Publishing
(s)-Tate Publishing—R
(s)-TEACH Services—R
(s)-Trafford Publishing—R
Westminster John Knox
(s)-WinePress—R
(s)-Word Alive
(s)-Zoë Life Publishing

WRITING HOW-TO

Aaron Book—R
(s)-American Binding—R
(s)-Bfree Publishing
(s)-Booklocker.com—R
(s)-Bookstand Publishing—R
Christian Writer's Ebook—R
(s)-Deep River Books
(s)-E.F.S. Online Pub.
(s)-Elderberry Press
(s)-Essence—R
Evergreen Press
Fair Havens—R
(s)-Fairway Press—R
(s)-Faith Books & More—R
FaithWalk
(s)-Forever Books—R
Hidden Brook Press—R
(s)-Holy Fire Publishing—R
(s)-IMD Press—R
Jubilant Press—R
Lighthouse Publishing—R
Lion and Lamb
(s)-MileStones Intl.
Mission City Press
Nordskog Publishing—R
(s)-One World—R
Parson Place—R
(s)-Pleasant Word—R
Ponder Publishing
Power Publishing—R
(s)-Providence House—R
(s)-Selah Publishing—R
(s)-Tate Publishing—R
(s)-Trafford Publishing—R
Treble Heart—R

(s)-WinePress—R
(s)-Word Alive
Write Now—R
(s)-Zoë Life Publishing

YOUTH BOOKS (NONFICTION)

Note: Listing denotes books for 8- to 12-year-olds, junior highs, or senior highs. If all three, it will say "all." If no age group is listed, they did not specify.

(a)-Baker Books
(a)-WaterBrook Press—R (All)

Aaron Book—R (8-12/Jr. High)
(s)-ACW Press—R (All)
Ambassador Books (All)
(s)-American Binding—R
(Jr./Sr. High)
Anglicans United—R
(8-12/Jr. High)
Barbour (8-12/Jr. High)
(s)-Bfree Publishing (All)
(s)-Black Forest—R (All)
(s)-Booklocker.com—R (All)
(s)-Bookstand Publishing—R
(All)
(s)-Book Publishers Net.—R
(All)
Boyds Mills Press—R (All)
(s)-Brown Books (All)
Carson-Dellosa (8-12)
CharismaKids (8-12/Jr. High)
Chelsea House—R (Jr./Sr. High)
Christian Ed. Pub.
Christian Focus—R (All)
Christian Liberty Press (All)
Christian Writer's Ebook—R
(All)
Comfort Publishing (All)
Conciliar Press—R (8-12)
Contemporary Drama
(s)-Creation House—R (All)
(s)-CrossHouse—R (All)
Dawn Publications (Jr. High)
(s)-Deep River Books (All)
Eerdmans Pub., Wm. B.—R (All)
(s)-E.F.S. Online Pub. (All)
(s)-Elderberry Press (All)

Emmaus Road (All)
(s)-Essence—R (All)
Evergreen Press
Facts On File
(s)-Faith Books & More—R (All)
Father's Press (All)
Focus on the Family—R
(Sr. High)
(s)-Forever Books—R (All)
Grupo Nelson (Jr. High)
Guardian Angel (8-12)
(s)-Halo Publishing Intl. (All)
Health Commun. (Jr./Sr. High)
Hidden Brook Press—R (All)
(s)-Holy Fire Publishing—R
(All)
(s)-Insight Publishing—R (All)
JourneyStone—R
(8-12/Jr. High)
(s)-Kindred Books—R (All)
Knight George Pub. (All)
Legacy Press—R (8-12)
Life Cycle Books—R (8-12)
Lift Every Voice—R (All)
Lighthouse Publishing—R (All)
Lighthouse Trails—R (All)
Lion and Lamb (All)
Master Books (All)
McRuffy Press (8-12)
Meriwether (Jr./Sr. High)
Messianic Jewish—R
(s)-MileStones Intl. (Sr. High)
Mission City Press (8-12)
Monarch Books (All)
Moody Publishers
NavPress (Sr. High)
New Canaan—R (All)
New Leaf (All)
Nordskog Publishing—R (All)
(s)-One World—R (All)
On My Own Now—R (Sr. High)
P & R Publishing—R (All)
Pacific Press
Pauline Kids—R (8-12)
Pflaum Publishing (All)
(s)-Pleasant Word—R (All)
Power Publishing—R (All)
Putnam/Young Readers (All)
Ravenhawk Books—R
(Jr./Sr. High)

Starik Publishing (Sr. High)
(s)-Tate Publishing—R (All)
Th1nk/NavPress—R (Sr. High)
Third World Press—R (All)
(s)-Trafford Publishing—R (All)
Treble Heart—R (Jr./Sr. High)
Warner Press (All)
(s)-WinePress—R (All)
(s)-Word Alive (All)
Youth Specialties (Jr./Sr. High)
(s)-Zoë Life Publishing

YOUTH PROGRAMS

(a)-Baker Books
(a)-Kregel—R

(s)-ACW Press—R
(s)-American Binding—R
(s)-Bfree Publishing
Carson-Dellosa
Christian Liberty Press
Christian Writer's Ebook—R
Church Growth Inst.
Contemporary Drama
CrossLink Publishing
(s)-E.F.S. Online Pub.
Eldridge Plays
(s)-Fairway Press—R
Faith Alive
(s)-Forever Books—R
Gospel Publishing
Group Publishing
(s)-Holy Fire Publishing—R
(s)-IMD Press—R
(s)-Insight Publishing—R
Knight George Pub.
Lion and Lamb
Mission City Press
Monarch Books
(s)-One World—R
Pilgrim Press—R
Ponder Publishing
Power Publishing—R
(s)-Providence House—R
Randall House Digital
Standard Publishing
(s)-Tate Publishing—R
Th1nk/NavPress—R
(s)-Zoë Life Publishing

2

Alphabetical Listings of Book Publishers

If you do not find the publisher you are looking for, check the "General Index." See the introduction to that index for the codes used to identify the current status of each unlisted publisher. If you do not understand all the terms or abbreviations used in these listings, read the "How to Use This Book" section.

AADEON PUBLISHING COMPANY, PO Box 223, Hartford CT 06141. Fax (206) 666-5132. E-mail: submissions@aadeon.com. Website: www.aadeon.com. Submit to The Editor. Addresses spiritual issues, touching on social, and cultural issues related primarily toward the United States of America. Publishes 1 title/yr.; trade paperback. Accepts mss through agents or authors. Does print-on-demand. Reprints books. Requires 160,000 wds. or more. **Royalty 8% on net; no advance.** Average first printing 25-100. Publication within 1 yr. Considers simultaneous submissions. Requires accepted ms on disk in Microsoft Word. Responds in 1-4 mos. Requires NKJV. Guidelines on Website ("Submissions"); no catalog.

> **Nonfiction:** Proposal/3 chapters or complete ms; no phone/fax/e-query.
> **Tips:** "We are particularly interested in manuscripts that challenge average people to confront and overcome the negative influences of an increasingly secular and godless society. Manuscripts must be well organized, professionally edited, easy to understand, biblically based, and scripturally supported (frequent quotations from the Bible—chapter and verse—to support writings). Manuscripts must clearly speak to both a Christian and non-Christian audience."

AARON BOOK PUBLISHING, 1093 Bristol Caverns Hwy., Bristol TN 37620. (423) 212-1208. E-mail: info@aaronbookpublishing.com. Website: www.AaronBookPublishing.com. Imprint of Black Forest Press. Tim Rouse, ed. Honesty, uniqueness, service. Publishes hardcover, mass-market, coffee-table books. Some subsidy; does print-on-demand. Reprints books. Any length. **Royalty on retail.** Considers simultaneous submissions. Prefers mss by e-mail. Prefers KJV. Guidelines by mail; catalog for 9 x 12 SAE/5 stamps.

> **Nonfiction/Fiction:** Query first; proposal/2-3 chapters; phone/e-query OK.
> **Special Needs:** Books of good content. Strong characters and a great story line.
> **Artwork:** Open to queries from freelance artists.
> **Contest:** Sponsors contests occasionally.
> **Tips:** Open to almost any topic.

ABINGDON PRESS, 201—8th Ave. S., PO Box 801, Nashville TN 37202. (615) 749-6000. Fax: (615) 749-6512. E-mail: [first initial and last name]@umpublishing.org. Website: www.abing donpress.com. United Methodist Publishing House/Cokesbury. Editors: Mary C. Dean, ed-in-chief; Barbara Scott, fiction; Ron Kidd, study resources; Robert Ratcliff, professional and academic bks.; John Kutsko, dir. of acq.; Joseph A. Crowe, gen. interest bks. Books and church supplies directed primarily to a mainline religious market. Publishes 120 titles/yr.; hardcover, trade paperbacks. Receives 3,000 submissions annually. Less than 5% of books from first-time authors. Accepts mss through agents or authors. No reprints. Prefers 144 pgs. **Royalty 7.5% on retail.** Average first printing 3,500-4,000. Publication within 18 mos. No simultaneous submissions. Requires requested ms on disk. Responds in 2 mos. Prefers NRSV or a variety of which NRSV is one. Guidelines on Website ("Submissions" at bottom of page); free catalog.

Nonfiction: Proposal/2 chapters; no phone/fax/e-query.
Fiction: Solicited or agented material only.
Ethnic Books: African American, Hispanic, Native American, Korean.
Music: Submit to Gary Alan Smith. See guidelines on Website.
Photos: Accepts freelance photos for book covers.
Tips: "We develop and produce materials to help more people in more places come to know and love God through Jesus Christ and to choose to serve God and neighbor."
**Note: This publisher serviced by ChristianManuscriptSubmissions.com.

ACTA PUBLICATIONS, 484 N. Clark St., Chicago IL 60640. Toll-free (800) 397-2282. (847) 676-2282. Toll-free fax (800) 397-0079. (847) 676-2287. E-mail: acta@actapublications.com. Website: www.actapublications.com. Catholic. Gregory F. Augustine Pierce, pres. & co-pub.; submit to Andrew Yankech. Wants books that successfully integrate daily life and spirituality. Publishes 12 titles/yr.; hardcover, trade paperbacks, coffee-table books. Receives 150 submissions annually. 50% of books from first-time authors. Accepts mss through agents or authors. Prefers 150-200 pgs. **Royalty 10-12% of net; no advance.** Average first printing 3,000. Publication within 1 yr. Responds in 1-2 mos. Prefers NRSV. Guidelines on Website ("Submissions Guidelines"); catalog for 9 x 12 SAE/2 stamps.

Nonfiction: Query or proposal/1 chapter; no phone/fax/e-query.
Tips: "Most open to books that are useful to a large number of average Christians. Read our catalog and one of our books first."

ADAMS MEDIA CORP., 57 Littlefield St., Avon MA 02322. (508) 427-7100. Toll-free fax (800) 872-5628. Website: www.adamsmedia.com. Division of F + W Publications. Jill Alexander, sr. ed.; submit to Paula Munier. Publishes 250 titles/yr. Receives 6,500 submissions annually. 40% of books from first-time authors. Accepts mss through agents or authors. **Royalty; variable advance; or outright purchase.** Publication within 12-18 mos. Considers simultaneous submissions. Responds in 3 mos. to queries. No mss accepted by e-mail. Guidelines on Website ("Submissions"); catalog for 9 x 12 SAE/5 stamps.

Nonfiction: Query first by mail; no phone/fax/e-query.
Tips: General publisher that does some inspirational books.

AMBASSADOR BOOKS INC., 997 Macarthur Blvd., Mahwah NJ 07430. Toll-free (800) 218-1903. (201) 825-7300. Toll-free fax (800) 836-3161. Fax (201) 825-8345. E-mail: info@paulistpress .com. Website: www.paulistpress.com. Catholic/Paulist Press. Gerry Goggins, adult ed. (ggoggins@ paulistpress.com); Jennifer Conlan, children's ed. (jconlan@paulistpress.com). Books of intellectual and spiritual excellence. Publishes 12 titles/yr.; hardcover, trade paperbacks. Receives 1,000 submissions annually. 50% of books from first-time authors. Accepts mss through agents or authors. No reprints. **Royalty 8-10% of net; advance $500-1,000.** Publication within 1 yr. Considers simultaneous submissions. Responds in 3-4 mos. Prefers NSRV. Guidelines by mail/e-mail/Website ("Manuscript Submission"); free catalog (or on Website).

Nonfiction: Query; no phone/fax/e-query.
Fiction: Query. Juvenile, young adult, adult; picture books & board books.
Photos/Artwork: Accepts freelance photos for book covers; open to queries from freelance artists.

Tips: "Our mission for adult books is to celebrate the spiritual dimension of this world by witnessing to the reality of the Way, the Truth, and the Life. For children, it is to foster the knowledge that they are precious to the Lord while encouraging a friendship with Him that will last a lifetime."

@AMBASSADOR INTERNATIONAL (formerly Ambassador-Emerald, Intl.), 427 Wade Hampton Blvd., Greenville SC 29609. (864) 235-2434. Fax (864) 235-2491. E-mail: publisher@emerald house.com. Website: www.ambassador-international.com. Sam Lowry, ed. Dedicated to spreading the gospel of Christ and empowering Christians through the written word. Publishes 30+ titles/yr.; hardcover, trade paperbacks, mass-market paperbacks, coffee-table books, digital. Receives 350-400 submissions annually. 65% of books from first-time authors. Accepts mss through agents or authors. Subsidy publishes 40-50%; no print-on-demand. No reprints. Prefers 30,000+ wds. or 100-250 pgs. **Royalty 10-18% of net; no advance.** Average first printing 2,000-3,000. Publication within 3 mos. Considers simultaneous submissions. Prefers requested ms by e-mail. Responds in up to 30 days. Prefers KJV, NIV, ESV, NKJV, NASB. Guidelines by mail/e-mail/Website ("Get Published"/"submission guidelines" in text); free catalog.

   Nonfiction: E-mail proposal/3 chapters; phone/fax/e-query OK.

   Fiction: E-mail proposal/3chapters; phone/fax/e-query OK. For adults.

   Special Needs: Business, finance, biographies, novels, inspirational, devotional, topical, Bible studies.

   Also Does: DVDs.

   Photos/Artwork: Accepts freelance photos for book covers; open to queries from freelance artists.

   Tips: "We're most open to a book which has a clearly defined market and the author's total commitment to the project. We do well with first-time authors. We have full international coverage. Many of our titles sell globally."

AMERICAN CATHOLIC PRESS, 16565 State St., South Holland IL 60473-2025. (708) 331-5485. Fax (708) 331-5484. E-mail: acp@acpress.org. Website: www.acpress.org or www.leafletmissal .com. Catholic worship resources. Father Michael Gilligan, ed. dir. Publishes 4 titles/yr.; hardcover. Receives 10 submissions annually. Reprints books. **Pays $25-100 for outright purchases only.** Average first printing 3,000. Publication within 1 yr. No simultaneous submissions. Responds in 2 mos. Prefers NAS. No guidelines; catalog for SASE.

   Nonfiction: Query first; no phone/fax/e-query.

   Tips: "We publish only materials on the Roman Catholic liturgy. Especially interested in new music for church services. No poetry or fiction."

AMG PUBLISHERS/LIVING INK BOOKS, 6815 Shallowford Rd., Chattanooga TN 37421. Toll-free (800) 266-4977. (423) 894-6060. Toll-free fax (800) 265-6690. (423) 648-2244. E-mail: ricks@ amgpublishers.com, info@amgpublishers.com, or through Website: www.amgpublishers.com. AMG International. Rick Steele, product development & acquisitions; Dr. Warren Baker, sr. ed. To provide biblically oriented books for reference, learning, and personal growth. Imprints: Living Ink Books; God and Country Press. Publishes 30-35 titles/yr.; hardcover, trade paperbacks, and oversized Bible studies. Receives 2,500 submissions annually. 30% of books from first-time authors. Accepts mss through agents or authors. Reprints books. Prefers 40,000-60,000 wds. or 176-224 pgs. **Royalty 10-16% of net; average advance $2,000.** Average first printing 3,500. Publication within 18 mos. Accepts simultaneous submissions. Prefers accepted ms by e-mail. Responds in 1-4 mos. Prefers KJV, NASB, NIV, NKJV, NLT. Guidelines by e-mail/Website; catalog for 9 x 12 SAE/5 stamps.

   Nonfiction: Query letter first; e-query preferred. "Looking for historical fiction and nonfiction for our God and Country Press imprint. Need more reference-type works; Bible studies 4-8 weeks in length; and YA fiction."

Fiction: Query letter first; e-query preferred. "Always looking for YA fantasy and historical fiction for adults."

Special Needs: Bible studies and reference—especially reference.

Also Does: Bible software, Bible audio cassettes, CD-ROMs.

Artwork: Open to queries from freelance artists.

Tips: "Most open to a book that is well thought out, clearly written, and finely edited. A professional proposal, following our specific guidelines, has the best chance of acceptance. Spend extra time in developing a good proposal. AMG is always looking for something new and different—with a niche. Write, and rewrite, and rewrite, and rewrite again."

**Note: This publisher serviced by The Writer's Edge and ChristianManuscriptSubmissions.com.

+ANCIENT PATHS PUBLICATIONS, PO Box 7505, Fairfax Station VA 22039. E-mail: ssburris@cox.net. Skylar H. Burris, ed. Will publish one poetry chapbook every two years. Prefers 60-100 pgs. **Pays $50, plus one free chapbook.** No more than 25% of the content can be previously published. Guidelines by mail or e-mail.

Poetry: Query first by mail or e-mail. Have a 60-100 pg. chapbook ready to submit (maximum of 1 poem/pg.). Each poem a minimum of 8 lines.

Publication Schedule: March 1, 2011: Query period for poetry opens; February 1, 2012: Query period closes. July 1, 2012: One book will be chosen for first chapbook; September 1, 2012: Publication of first chapbook.

Tips: "All poems in your collection should have either Christian themes or universal religious themes."

ANGLICANS UNITED/LATIMER PRESS, PO Box 763217, Dallas TX 75376. (972) 293-7443. Fax (972) 293-7559. E-mail: anglicansunited@sbcglobal.net. Website: www.anglicansunited.com; www.latimerpress.com. Episcopal Church USA. Cheryl M. Wetzel, ed. Provides educational materials for biblically orthodox Anglicans and Episcopalians. Publishes 2 titles/yr.; trade paperbacks. Receives 30 submissions annually. 90% of books from first-time authors. Accepts mss through authors only. Some subsidy. Reprints out-of-print classics. Prefers up to 225 pgs. **Outright purchase for $100-500.** Average first printing 1,500-2,000. Publication within 6 mos. Considers simultaneous submissions. Prefers ms by disk or e-mail. Responds in 1 mo. Prefers NIV.

Nonfiction: Query letter only first; no phone query. "Looking for Anglican history and practice; adult and teen education."

Ethnic Books: Beginning to translate classical Anglican books into Spanish for Latin American market.

Also Does: Booklets; Videos/DVDs.

Artwork: Open to queries from freelance artists.

Tips: "Most open to (1) a book (60-110 pgs. total) used in Christian education classes for adults and teens; (2) a book (60 pgs.) on baptism, marriage, grief, confirmation, or stewardship."

**Note: This publisher serviced by The Writer's Edge.

AVON INSPIRE, HarperCollins, 10 E. 53rd St., New York NY 10022. (212) 207-7000. Website: www.harpercollins.com. Cynthia DiTiberio, ed. Inspirational women's fiction. Publishes 8-10 titles/yr. Agented submissions only.

Fiction: Historical & contemporary; Amish.

BAKER ACADEMIC, 6030 E. Fulton Rd., Ada MI 49301. (616) 676-9185. Fax (616) 676-9573. E-mail: submissions@bakeracademic.com. Website: www.bakeracademic.com. Imprint of Baker Publishing Group. Jim Kinney, ed. dir. Publishes religious academic books and professional books for students and church leaders. Publishes 50 titles/yr.; hardcover, trade paperbacks. 10% of books from first-time authors. Accepts mss through agents, submission services, or editor's personal contacts at writers' conferences. **Royalty; advance.** Publication within 1 yr. Guidelines on Website ("Contact"/"Submit a Manuscript or Proposal"); catalog for 10 x 13 SAE/3 stamps.

Nonfiction: No unsolicited queries.

**Note: This publisher serviced by The Writer's Edge and ChristianManuscriptSubmissions.org.

BAKER BOOKS, 6030 E. Fulton Rd., Ada MI 49301. (616) 676-9185. Fax (616) 676-2315. Website: www.bakerbooks.com. Imprint of Baker Publishing Group. Ministry titles for the church. Publishes hardcover, trade paperbacks. No unsolicited proposals. Catalog for 10 x 13 SAE/3 stamps. Submit only through an agent, The Writer's Edge, Authonomy.com, or ChristianManuscriptSubmissions.com.

BAKER'S PLAYS, 45 W. 25th St., New York NY 10010-2035. West coast: 7623 W. Sunset Blvd., Los Angeles CA 90046-2714. (212) 206-8990. E-mail: publications@bakersplays.com. Website: www. bakersplays.com. Samuel French, Inc. Roxane Heinze-Bradshaw, mng. ed. Publishes 30-40 titles/yr. Receives 800 submissions annually. 60% of plays from first-time authors. Accepts mss through agents or authors. **Book royalty 10% on retail; amateur performance royalty 70%; professional performance royalty 80%; no advance.** Considers simultaneous submissions. Accepts requested ms by e-mail. Responds in 6-8 mos. Guidelines available on Website ("Play Submissions").

Plays: E-query. For all ages. "Most open to plays that deal with modern Christian life."

Tips: "We currently publish full-length plays, one-act plays for young audiences, musicals, plays written by high schoolers, and religious plays. We consider plays year round." If your play has been produced, send copies of press clippings. If sending music, you must include a CD.

BALLANTINE PUBLISHING GROUP, 1745 Broadway, 18th Fl., New York NY 10019. (212) 782-9000. Website: www.randomhouse.com/BB. A Division of Random House. Submit to Religion Editor. General publisher that does a few religious books. Mss from agents only. No e-query. **Royalty 8-15%; variable advances.** Nonfiction & fiction. Guidelines on Website; no catalog.

@B & H PUBLISHING GROUP, 127—9th Ave. N., Nashville TN 37234-0115. (615) 251-2438. Fax (615) 251-1413. E-mail: pat.carter@bhpublishinggroup.com, or through Website: www.bhpub lishinggroup.com. Book and Bible division of LifeWay Christian Resources. Ricky King, assoc. pub.; Thomas Walters, sr. acq. ed. (nonfiction); Karen Ball, exec. ed. (fiction); Ray Clendenen, sr. academic acq. ed. (ray.clendenen@bhpublishinggroup.com). Imprints: B & H Books, B & H Academic, Holman Bible Publishers, Holman Reference, Broadman supplies, B & H Español. Publishes books in the conservative, evangelical tradition by and for the larger Christian world. Publishes 90-100 titles/yr.; hardcover, trade paperback. Receives 3,000 submissions annually. 10% of books from first-time authors. Requires submissions through agents. **Royalty on net; advance.** Publication within 18 mos. Considers simultaneous submissions. Responds in 9-12 mos. Prefers HCSB, NIV, NASB. Guidelines by mail/e-mail; free catalog.

Nonfiction: Query first; no phone/fax query.

Fiction: Query first; no phone/fax query. Adult.

Ethnic: Spanish translations.

Also Does: Licensing, Kindle Reader, some audio.

Blog: www.holmantv.com. A series of weekly video episodes for high school and college students.

Tips: "Follow guidelines when submitting. Be informed that the market in general is very crowded with the book you might want to write. Do the research before submitting."

**Note: This publisher serviced by The Writer's Edge and ChristianManuscriptSubmissions.com.

BANTAM BOOKS—See Doubleday Religious.

BARBOUR PUBLISHING INC., 1810 Barbour Dr., PO Box 719, Uhrichsville OH 44683. (740) 922-6045. Fax (740) 922-5948. E-mail: editors@barbourbooks.com or through Website: www .barbourbooks.com. Paul Muckley (pmuckley@barbourbooks.com), sr. ed./nonfiction; Rebecca Germany (rgermany@barbourbooks.com), sr. ed./romance and women's fiction (novels &

novellas); Kelly Williams (kwilliams@barbourbooks.com), mng. ed. and youth/children/gift acquisitions. To publish and distribute inspirational products offering exceptional value and biblical encouragement to the masses. Imprints: Barbour Books (fiction and nonfiction) and Heartsong Presents (romance: see separate listing). Publishes 200 titles/yr.; hardcover, trade paperbacks, mass-market paperbacks. Receives 1,500 submissions annually. 40% of books from first-time authors. Accepts mss through agents or authors. No subsidy. Prefers 50,000 wds. (nonfiction), or 80,000-100,000 wds. (fiction). **Royalty 8-12% of net; outright purchases $500-5,000; advance $500-5,000.** Average first printing 15,000-20,000. Publication within 24 mos. Considers simultaneous submissions & reprints. Responds in 1 mo. to queries. Prefers NIV, KJV. Guidelines by mail/Website (click on "Contact Us"/"How do I submit my manuscript for publishing?"); catalog for 9 x 12 SAE/2 stamps.

Nonfiction: Proposal/3 chapters; no phone/fax query; e-query OK. E-mail: submissions@ barbourbooks.com.

Fiction: Proposal/3 chapters to Rebecca Germany, fiction ed. Novellas 20,000 wds. For all ages. "We are interested in a mystery/romance series." E-mail: fictionsubmit@barbourbooks.com. See separate listing for Heartsong Presents & Heartsong Presents—Mysteries.

Tips: "We seek solid, evangelical books with the greatest mass appeal. A good title on practical Christian living will go much farther with Barbour than will a commentary on Jude. Do your homework before sending us a manuscript; send material that will work well within our publishing philosophy."

**Note: This publisher serviced by The Writer's Edge and ChristianManuscriptSubmissions.com.

BARCLAY PRESS, 211 N. Meridian St., Ste. 101, Newberg OR 97132. (503) 538-9775. Fax (503) 554-8597. E-mail: info@barclaypress.com. Website: www.barclaypress.com. Friends/Quaker. Dan McCracken, gen. mngr. No unsolicited manuscripts.

**Note: This publisher serviced by The Writer's Edge.

BAYLOR UNIVERSITY PRESS, One Bear Pl., #97363, Waco TX 76798-7308. (254) 710-3164. Fax (254) 710-3440. Website: www.baylorpress.com. Baptist. Dr. Carey C. Newman, dir., (254) 710-3522, carey_newman@baylor.edu. Imprint: Markham Press Fund. Academic press producing scholarly books on religion and social sciences; church-state studies. Publishes 30 academic titles/ yr.; hardcover, trade paperback. Receives 100+ submissions annually. 10% of books from first-time authors. Accepts mss through agents or authors. No subsidy publishing. No reprints. **Royalty 10% on net; no advance.** Average first printing 1,000. Publication within 12 mos. Accepts simultaneous submissions. Responds in 2 mos. Guidelines on Website ("Submit a Manuscript for Publication"); free catalog.

Nonfiction: Query only first; no phone/fax query, e-query OK. "Looking for academic books; religion and public life."

BEACON HILL PRESS OF KANSAS CITY, PO Box 419527, Kansas City MO 64141. (816) 931-1900. Fax (816) 753-4071. E-mail: jap@bhillkc.com. Website: www.bhillkc.com. Nazarene Publishing House/Church of the Nazarene. Bonnie Perry, pub. dir.; Richard Buckner, ministry line ed.; Judi Perry, consumer ed. A Christ-centered publisher that provides authentically Christian resources that are faithful to God's Word and relevant to life. Imprint: Beacon Hill Books. Publishes 30 titles/ yr.; hardcover, trade paperbacks. Accepts mss through agents or authors. Reprints books. Prefers 30,000-60,000 wds. or 250 pgs. **Royalty 12-14% of net; advance; some outright purchases.** Average first printing 5,000. Publication within 2 yrs. Considers simultaneous submissions. Responds in 3 mos. or longer. Guidelines on Website ("Writers Guidelines"); catalog by mail.

Nonfiction: Detailed proposal/2 chapters; no phone/fax query. "Looking for practical Christian living, felt needs, Christian care, spiritual growth, and ministry resources."

Tips: "Nearly all our titles come through acquisitions, and the number of freelance

submissions has declined dramatically. If you wish to submit, follow guidelines above. You are always welcome to submit after sending for guidelines."
Note: This publisher serviced by The Writer's Edge.

BELIEVE BOOKS, 13 S Street NW, Washington DC 20001. Phone/fax (202) 787-1532. E-mail: BelieveBooks@gmail.com. Website: www.BelieveBooks.com. Diane Haskett, pres. & ed-in-chief. Publishes inspirational life stories of people from around the world. E-query.

BETHANY HOUSE PUBLISHERS, 6030 E. Fulton Rd., Ada MI 49301. Website: www.bethanyhouse .com. Imprint of Baker Publishing Group. To help Christians apply biblical truth in all areas of life— whether through a well-told story, a challenging devotional, or the message of an illustrated children's book. Publishes 90-100 titles/yr.; hardcover, trade paperbacks. 2% of books from first-time authors. Accepts mss through agents only. Reprints on mass-market paperbacks. **Negotiable royalty on net; negotiable advance.** Publication within 1 yr. Considers simultaneous submissions. Responds in 3 mos. Guidelines on Website ("Contact us"/"Submit a Manuscript or Proposal"). Catalog for 9 x 12 SAE/5 stamps.

Nonfiction: "Seeking well-planned and developed books in the following categories: personal growth, deeper-life spirituality, contemporary issues, women's issues, reference, applied theology, and inspirational."
Fiction: See Website for current acquisitions needs.
Tips: "We do not accept unsolicited queries or proposals."
Note: This publisher serviced by The Writer's Edge, Authonomy.com, and Christian ManuscriptSubmissions.com.

@BLUE DOLPHIN PUBLISHING INC., PO Box 8, Nevada City CA 95959. (530) 477-1503. Fax (530) 477-8342. E-mail: Bdolphin@bluedolphinpublishing.com. Website: www.bluedolphinpub lishing.com. Paul M. Clemens, pub. Imprint: Pelican Pond (fiction & poetry), Papillon Publishing (juvenile), and Symposium Publishing (nonfiction). Books that help people grow in their social and spiritual awareness. Publishes 20-24 titles/yr. (includes 10-12 print-on-demand). Receives 4,800 submissions annually. 90% of books from first-time authors. Prefers about 60,000 wds. or 200-300 pgs. **Royalty 10-15% of net; no advance.** Average first printing 300, then on demand. Publication within 10 mos. Considers simultaneous submissions. Requires requested ms on disk. Responds in 3-6 mos. Guidelines by e-mail/Website (scroll down right side to "About Blue Dolphin"/"Guidance for Authors"); catalog for 8.5 x 11 SAE/2 stamps.

Nonfiction: Query or proposal/1 chapter; no phone/e-query. "Looking for books that will increase people's spiritual and social awareness. We will consider all topics."
Fiction: Query/2-pg. synopsis. Pelican Pond Imprint. For teens and adults; no children's board books or picture books.
Also Does: E-books.
Photos/Artwork: Accepts freelance photos for book covers; open to queries from freelance artists.
Tips: "Looking for mature writers whose focus is to help people lead better lives. Our authors are generally professionals who write for others—not just for themselves. We look for topics that would appeal to the general market, are interesting, different, and will aid in the growth and development of humanity. See Website before submitting."
Note: This publisher also publishes books on a range of topics, including cross-cultural spirituality. They also may offer a co-publishing arrangement, not necessarily a royalty deal.

BMH BOOKS, PO Box 544, Winona Lake IN 46590. (574) 268-1122. Fax (574) 268-5384. E-mail: tdwhite@bmhbooks.com. Website: www.BMHbooks.com. Blog: www.fgbcworld-blog.com. Fellow- ship of Grace Brethren Churches. Terry White, ed./pub. Trinitarian theology; dispensational escha- tology; emphasis on exegesis. Publishes 10-15 titles/yr.; hardcover, trade paperbacks. Receives

30 submissions annually. 50% of books from first-time authors. Accepts mss through agents or authors. Seldom reprints books. Prefers 50,000-75,000 wds. or 128-256 pgs. **Royalty 8-10% on retail; rarely pays an advance.** Average first printing 2,000. Publication within 1 yr. Prefers not to consider simultaneous submissions. Responds in 3 mos. Prefers KJV or NIV. Requires accepted mss by e-mail. Guidelines by mail/e-mail; free catalog.

>   **Nonfiction:** Proposal/2 chapters; no phone/fax query; e-query OK. "Most open to a small-group study book or text for Bible College/Bible Institute."
>   **Tips:** "Most open to biblically based, timeless, discipleship material."

BOYDS MILLS PRESS, 815 Church St., Honesdale PA 18431. (570) 253-1164. E-mail: contact@boydsmillspress.com. Website: www.boydsmillspress.com. General publisher. Submit to Manuscript Submissions. Publishes a wide range of literary children's titles, for preschool through young adult; very few religious. Imprint: Calkins Creek (American history). Publishes 80 titles/yr.; hardcover, trade paperbacks. Receives 15,000 submissions annually. 40% of books from first-time authors. Reprints books. **Royalty 4-12% on retail; advances vary.** Considers simultaneous submissions. Guidelines on Website ("Submissions") or by mail.

>   **Nonfiction:** Query/proposal package, outline, 3 sample chapters (expert review/edit of manuscript recommended).
>   **Fiction:** Outline/synopsis/first 3 chapters for novels; complete ms for picture books. "We are always interested in multicultural settings."
>   **Tips:** "We look for a broad range of books with fresh voices for children and young adults. We publish very few specifically religious books that are not multicultural or otherwise of broad appeal. Please consult our Website for the types of books we publish before submitting your manuscript." All submissions evaluated for all our imprints.

BRANDEN PUBLISHING CO., PO Box 812094, Wellesley MA 02482. (781) 235-3634. Fax (781) 790-1056. E-mail: branden@brandenbooks.com. Website: www.brandenbooks.com. Adolph Caso, ed. Books by or about women, children, military, Italian American or African American themes; religious fiction. Publishes 15 titles/yr.; hardcover, trade paperbacks, coffee-table books. Receives 1,000 submissions annually. 80% of books from first-time authors. Accepts mss through agents or authors. Reprints books. **Royalty based on profits; no advance.** Publication within 10 mos. No simultaneous submissions. Responds within days. Prefers accepted mss by disk or e-mail. Guidelines by mail; no catalog.

>   **Nonfiction:** Query only with SASE; no phone/fax queries; e-query OK.
>   **Fiction:** Query only with SASE. Ethnic, religious fiction. For adults.
>   **Ethnic Books:** African American & Italian.

BRIDGE LOGOS, 17750 N.W. 115th Ave., Bldg. 200, Ste. 220, Alachua FL 32615. (386) 462-2525. Fax (586) 462-2535. E-mail: editorial@bridgelogos.com or phildebrand@bridgelogos.com. Website: www.bridgelogos.com. Peggy Hildebrand, acq. ed. Publishes classics, books by Spirit-filled authors, and inspirational books that appeal to the general evangelical market. Imprint: Synergy. Publishes 40 titles/yr.; hardcover, trade paperbacks, mass-market paperbacks. Receives 200+ submissions annually. 30% of books from first-time authors. Accepts mss through agents or authors. Subsidy publishes to 5%; does very little print-on-demand. Reprints books. Prefers 250 pgs. **Royalty 10% on net; rarely pays $500 advance.** Average first printing 4,000-5,000. Publication within 6-12 mos. Considers simultaneous submissions. Responds in 6 wks. Prefers accepted mss by e-mail. Guidelines on Website ("Information"/"Manuscript Submission"); free catalog.

>   **Nonfiction:** Proposal/3-5 chapters; no phone/fax query; e-query OK. "Most open to evangelism, spiritual growth, self-help, and education." Charges a $50 manuscript submission/evaluation fee.
>   **Fiction:** Proposal/3-5 chapters; no phone/fax query; e-query OK.

Special Needs: Reference, biography, current issues, controversial issues, church renewal, women's issues, and Bible commentary. Also teen, preteen, and kid's books.

Ethnic Books: African American & Hispanic.

Photos: Accepts freelance photos for book covers.

Tips: "Looking for well-written, timely books that are aimed at the needs of people and that glorify God. Have a great message, a well-written manuscript, and a specific plan and willingness to market your book. Looking for previously published authors with an active ministry who are experts on their subject."

**Note: This publisher serviced by The Writer's Edge.

CAMBRIDGE SCHOLARS PUBLISHING, 12 Back Chapman St., Newcastle Upon Tyne NE6 2XX, United Kingdom. Fax +44 191 265 2056. E-mail: admin@c-s-p.org. Website: www.c-s-p.org. Dr. Andy Nercessian and other editors. Publishes 600 titles/yr.; 15 religious titles. Receives 1,500 submissions annually; 100 religious. 70% of books from first-time authors. No mss through agents. No reprints. No subsidy or print-on-demand. Prefers 100-500 pgs. **Royalty 15%; no advance.** Average first printing 500. Publication within 3 mos. Considers simultaneous submissions. Responds in 3 mos. Prefers accepted ms on disk. Guidelines on Website (under "Most Popular"/"Submission Guidelines"); free catalog.

Nonfiction: Proposal/1 chapter; e-query OK.

Ethnic Books: African American, Hispanic, and others.

Photos/Artwork: Accepts freelance photos for book covers; open to queries from freelance artists.

Tips: "We will consider very specialized books which others are likely to reject on the grounds of an absence of market, but they must be of a scholarly nature. We will only occasionally venture outside of the Arts, Humanities, and Social Sciences, but queries in all subjects are welcome. Our titles are mostly of interest to scholars and university academic staff."

CAMBRIDGE UNIVERSITY PRESS, 32 Avenue of the Americas, New York NY 10013-2473. Toll-free (800) 872-7423. (212) 924-3900. Fax (212) 691-3239. E-mail: newyork@cambridge.org. Website: www.cambridge.org/us. University of Cambridge. Submit to Humanities ed. (humanitiesed@cup.org); Social Science ed. (socialscienceed@cup.org); editors for other topics listed on Website. Guidelines on Website (down left-hand side, "Find Out More"/"Editorial Contacts").

Nonfiction: Proposal; no complete mss. Scholarly nonfiction.

CANADIAN INSTITUTE FOR LAW, THEOLOGY & PUBLIC POLICY INC., 89 Douglasview Rise S.E., Calgary AB T2Z 2P5, Canada. (403) 720-8714. Fax (403) 720-8746. E-mail: ciltpp@cs.com. Website: www.ciltpp.com. Will Moore, pres. Integrating Christianity with the study of law and political science. Publishes 2-4 titles/yr.; trade paperbacks. Receives 4-5 submissions annually. 1% of books from first-time authors. Accepts mss through agents or authors. Reprints books. **Royalty 7% on retail; no advance.** Average first printing 1,000. Publication within 12-24 mos. No simultaneous submissions. Responds in 6-12 mos. Prefers NIV. Guidelines by mail/e-mail; free catalog.

Nonfiction: Proposal/1 chapter. "Looking for books integrating Christianity with law and political science."

Photos: Accepts freelance photos for book covers.

CANDY CANE PRESS—See Ideals Publications (no freelance for now).

CANTICLE BOOKS, PO Box 2666, Carlsbad CA 92018. (760) 806-3743. Fax (760) 806-3689. E-mail: magnuspress@aol.com. Website: www.magnuspress.com. Imprint of Magnus Press. Warren Angel, ed. dir. To publish biblical studies by Catholic authors that are written for the average person and that minister life to Christ's Church. Publishes 2 titles/yr.; trade paperbacks. Receives 60 submissions annually. 50% of books from first-time authors. Accepts mss through agents or authors.

Reprints books. Prefers 105-300 pgs. **Royalty 6-12% on retail; no advance.** Average first printing 2,500. Publication within 1 yr. Considers simultaneous submissions. Accepts requested ms on disk. Responds in 1 mo. Guidelines by mail/e-mail/Website ("Canticle Book Submissions"); free catalog.

Nonfiction: Query or proposal/3 chapters; fax query OK. "Looking for spirituality, thematic biblical studies, unique inspirational/devotional books."

Tips: "Our writers need solid knowledge of the Bible and a mature spirituality that reflects a profound relationship with Jesus Christ. Most open to well-researched, popularly written biblical studies geared to Catholics, or personal experience books that share/emphasize a person's relationship with Christ."

CAREPOINT PUBLISHING, PO Box 870490, Stone Mountain GA 30087. Toll-free (800) 378-9584. (404) 625-9217. E-mail: info@carepointministry.com. Website: www.christiancarepoint.org. Independent Christian publisher. Dr. Scott Philip Stewart, ed. Publishes Christian care books and software to help 21st-century Christians and seekers and those who minister to them. Imprint: Two Fish Publishing (novellas; see separate listing). Publishes 12 titles/yr.; trade paperbacks. Receives 100+ submissions annually. 75% of books from first-time authors. Accepts mss through agents or authors. Reprints books. **Royalty 10-15% of net; no advance.** Publication within 6 mos. Considers simultaneous submissions, if notified. Accepts requested manuscript on disk or by e-mail. Responds in 4 wks. Guidelines on Website.

Nonfiction: Proposal/2-3 chapters; prefers e-mail query. "Looking for support-group resources."

Photos: Accepts freelance photos for book covers.

Special Needs: Self-help, personal growth, counseling aids, resources for peer and professional Christian caregivers and counselors.

Also Does: Interactive multimedia; book/CD sets.

Tips: "We are restructuring our company and are coming out with two new imprints: Way Out Books and Five Loaves Press."

WILLIAM CAREY LIBRARY PUBLISHERS & DISTRIBUTORS, 1605 E. Elizabeth St., Pasadena CA 91104. (626) 720-8210. E-mail through Website: www.missionbooks.org. A ministry of the U.S. Center for World Mission (www.uscwm.org). Attn: Editor (626-720-8202). Purpose is to publish the latest insights on frontier Christian missions. Publishes 10-15 titles/yr.; trade paperbacks. Reprints books. Variable lengths. **Royalty 10% on net; no advance.** Publication time varies. Guidelines on Website ("Submissions"); free catalog.

Nonfiction: Query only (2 pgs. max.); e-query OK. No unsolicited mss. "We are a specialized publisher focusing on books and studies of church growth, missions, world issues, and ethnic/cultural issues."

Special Needs: Anthropology and cross-cultural.

Photos: Accepts freelance photos for book covers.

Tips: "We mostly publish books on missions, evangelization, and unreached people groups. We welcome books that missionaries and mission-minded people would find useful and encouraging. For more information, please click on 'Publishing' on our Website."

CARSON-DELLOSA CHRISTIAN EDUCATION, PO Box 35665, Greensboro NC 27425-5665. (336) 632-0084. Fax (336) 632-0087. E-mail: clayton@carsondellosa.com. Website: www.carsondellosa .com. Carson-Dellosa Publishing Inc. Carol Layton, ed. dir. Creates high-quality children's products (interactive activities) that teach the Word of God, share His love and goodness, assist in faith development, and glorify His Son, Jesus Christ. Publishes 12 titles/yr.; soft-cover, reproducible, 8.5 x 11, teacher-resource books. Receives 50 submissions annually. 25% of books from first-time authors. No reprints. Prefers 64 pgs. **Royalty & advance confidential.** Publication within 18 mos.

Considers simultaneous submissions. Responds in 12 wks. Prefers NIV. Guidelines on Website ("About Us"/"Submissions"); free catalog.

Nonfiction: No unsolicited manuscripts (see Website for what you can send). "Looking for books that teach the Word of God to children in an engaging and fun way, particularly in a classroom setting."

Fiction: No unsolicited manuscripts (see Website for what you can send). "Fiction must be suited for classroom use."

Artwork: Accepts queries from freelance artists.

Also Does: Board games, teaching beach balls.

Tips: "Understand the type of books we publish and submit an engaging, well-written proposal. Most open to lesson and activity books that are fun for students and teachers."

**Note: This publisher serviced by ChristianManuscriptSubmissions.com.

CASCADIA PUBLISHING HOUSE LLC., 126 Klingerman Rd., Telford PA 18969. (215) 723-9125. E-mail: editor@cascadiapublishinghouse.com. Website: www.cascadiapublishinghouse.com. Mennonite. Michael A. King, ed. Imprint: DreamSeeker Books. Open to freelance; uses little unsolicited. Some books are subsidized by interested institutions. Guidelines/catalog on Website ("Submissions"). Not included in topical listings.

Nonfiction: Query only/vita; e-query OK.

CATHOLIC ANSWERS, 2020 Gillespie Way, El Cajon CA 92020. (619) 387-7200. Fax (619) 387-0042. E-mail through Website: www.catholic.com. Karl Keating, pres.; Mary Jane O'Brien, submissions ed. Publishes 10 titles/yr. Receives 10-15 submissions annually. 1% of books from first-time authors. No mss through agents. No subsidy. Reprints books. Prefers 40,000 wds. **Royalty on retail; negotiable advance.** Average first printing 5,000. Publication within 12 mos. Accepts simultaneous submissions. Responds in 1-3 mos. Prefers RSV—Catholic edition. Guidelines by e-mail; free catalog.

Nonfiction: Query first; no phone/fax/e-query.

Photos: Accepts freelance photos for book covers.

Tips: "Most open to Catholic apologetics and evangelization."

CATHOLIC BOOK PUBLISHING CO., 77 West End Rd., Totowa NJ 07512. (973) 890-2400. Fax (973) 890-2410. E-mail: info@catholicbookpublishing.com or through Website: www.catholic bookpublishing.com. Catholic. Anthony Buono, mng. ed. Inspirational books for Catholic Christians. Acquired Resurrection Press and World Catholic Press. Publishes 15-20 titles/yr. Receives 75 submissions annually. 30% of books from first-time authors. No mss through agents. **Variable royalty or outright purchases; no advance.** Average first printing 3,000. Publication within 12-15 mos. No simultaneous submissions. Responds in 2-3 mos. Guidelines on Website ("FAQ"/"Manuscript Submissions"); catalog for 9x12 SAE/5 stamps.

Nonfiction: Query letter only; no phone/fax query.

Tips: "We publish mainly liturgical books, Bibles, missals, and prayer books. Most of the books are composed in-house or by direct commission with particular guidelines. We strongly prefer query letters in place of full manuscripts."

CATHOLIC UNIVERSITY OF AMERICA PRESS, 620 Michigan Ave. N.E., Washington DC 20064. (202) 319-5052. Fax (202) 319-4985. E-mail: cua-press@cua.edu. Website: http://cuapress.cua .edu. David J. McGonagle, editor; submit to James Kruggel. Works of original scholarship and works intended for the college/university classroom in various fields, including theology and religious studies. Publishes 10 titles/yr.; hardcover & trade paperback. Receives 230 submissions annually. 25% of books from first-time authors. No mss through agents. No reprints. Prefers 200-300 pgs. **Royalty 10% on net; no advance.** Average first printing 750. Publication within 6 mos. Considers simultaneous submissions. Responds as soon as possible. Guidelines by mail/e-mail/Website ("For Prospective Authors"); free catalog.

Nonfiction: Query first; no phone/fax/e-query.

Special Needs: Works of original scholarship and works intended for the college and university classroom in theology.

Photos: Accepts freelance photos for book covers.

@CHALICE PRESS, 1221 Locust St., Ste. 670, St. Louis MO 63103-2381. (314) 231-8500. E-mail: submissions@chalicepress.com. Website: www.chalicepress.com. Christian Church (Disciples of Christ)/Christian Board of Publication. Submit to Editor. Books for a thinking, caring church; in Bible, theology, ethics, homiletics, pastoral care, Christian education, Christian living, and spiritual growth. Publishes 35 titles/yr.; hardcover, trade paperbacks, digital. Receives 500+ submissions annually. 20% of books from first-time authors. No mss through agents. Does some print-on-demand. Reprints books. Prefers 144-240 pgs. for general books, 160-300 pgs. for academic books. **Royalty 14% of net; no advance.** Average first printing 2,500-3,000. Publication within 1 yr. Rarely considers simultaneous submissions. Requires requested proposal and ms by e-mail. Responds in up to 30 days. Prefers NRSV or NIV. Guidelines on Website ("Author Guidelines" on left side); order catalog on Website or view online.

Nonfiction: Query only first, e-query OK; e-proposal upon publisher's request. "Looking for books on evangelism, leadership, and spiritual growth."

Fiction: Query only first, e-query OK; e-proposal upon publisher's request. For adults.

Also Does: Pamphlets.

Tips: "Looking for books for general readers that invite people into a deeper relationship with God, equipping them as disciples or sending them into missions locally or globally."

CHAPTER TWO, Fountain House, Conduit Mews, London SE18 7AP, United Kingdom. Phone ++44 (0) 20 8316 5389. Fax ++44 (0) 20 8854 5963. E-mail: chapter2uk@aol.com or through Website: www.chaptertwobooks.org.uk. Plymouth Brethren. Mr. E. Cross, ed. Publishing Plymouth Brethren titles and evangelistic materials to promote New Testament faith and practice. Publishes 20-30 titles/yr.; hardcover, trade paperbacks. No mss through agents. Reprints books. **Royalty 0-10% on retail (most authors donate their work).** Average first printing 3,000. Publication within 12 mos. No simultaneous submissions. Prefers KJV, NKJV. No guidelines; free catalog online.

Nonfiction: Query first; phone/e-query OK.

Special Needs: Plymouth Brethren commentaries.

Ethnic Books: Hispanic.

Tips: "Writer must be in a Plymouth Brethren assembly and have orthodox Christian doctrine."

CHARISMAKIDS, 600 Rinehart Rd., Lake Mary FL 32746. (407) 333-0600. Fax (407) 333-7100. E-mail: Custsvc@strang.com. Website: www.charismakids.com. Strang Book Group. Submit to The Editor. Books to help children experience God's presence, find His purpose for their lives, and receive the power of the Holy Spirit. Publishes 12 titles/yr. Receives hundreds of submissions annually. 10% of books from first-time authors. Prefers mss through agents. No reprints. Prefers 2,400 wds. or 32 pgs. **Royalty on net; pays an advance.** Average first printing 10,000. Publication within 1 yr. Considers simultaneous submissions. Responds in 6 mos. Catalog on Website.

Nonfiction: Proposal/1 chapter; fax/e-query OK.

Fiction: Proposal/1 chapter. Charismatic children's books; for children 4-8 years. Does not publish 24- to 32-page picture books.

Ethnic Books: African American, Charismatic.

Tips: "Most open to books with a Charismatic worldview for children."

**Note: This publisher serviced by ChristianManuscriptSubmissions.com.

THE CHARLES PRESS, PUBLISHERS, 230 N. 21st St., Ste. 202, Philadelphia PA 19103-1095. (215) 561-2786. Fax (215) 561-0191. E-mail: mailbox@charlespresspub.com. Website: www .charlespresspub.com. Lauren Metzler, pub. (lauren@charlespresspub.com). Responds in 4-16 wks. Guidelines on Website ("Manuscript Submissions Guidelines"); catalog.

Nonfiction: Proposal (to 10 pgs.); no fax submissions.

CHELSEA HOUSE PUBLISHERS, 132 W. 31st St., Fl. 17, New York NY 10001. Toll-free (800) 322-8755. (212) 896-4211. Toll-free fax (800) 678-3633. E-mail: editorial@factsonfile.com. Website: www.chelseahouse.com. Imprint of Infobase Publishing Group. Submit to Editorial Director. Publishes curriculum-based nonfiction books for middle school and high school students, including on religion. Publishes in hardcover. Reprints books. Considers simultaneous submissions. Responds in 3-4 wks. Guidelines/catalog on Website (click on "Contact Us"/down left-hand side to "Other Departments"/"Author submissions").

Nonfiction: Query or proposal/2-3 chapters.

Artwork: Open to queries from freelance artists; send photocopies.

CHICKEN SOUP FOR THE SOUL BOOKS—See listing in Periodical section.

CHOSEN BOOKS, Division of Baker Publishing Group, 3985 Bradwater St., Fairfax VA 22031-3702. (703) 764-8250. E-mail: jcampbell@chosenbooks.com. Website: www.chosenbooks.com. Jane Campbell, editorial dir. Charismatic; Spirit-filled-life titles. No unsolicited mss, but will respond to e-mail queries.

CHRISTIAN ED. PUBLISHERS, Box 26639, San Diego CA 92196. (858) 578-4700. Fax (858) 578-2431 (for queries only). E-mail: Editor@cehouse.com. Website: www.ChristianEdWarehouse .com. Blog: www.ceministry.blogspot.com, and vbstips.blogspot.com. Janet Ackelson, asst. ed. An evangelical publisher of Bible Club materials for ages two through high school, church special-event programs, and online Bible lessons. Publishes 80 curriculum titles/yr. Receives 150 submissions annually. 10% of books from first-time authors. No mss through agents. **Outright purchases for .03/ wd.; no advance.** Publication within 1 yr. Accepts requested ms on disk or by e-mail. Responds in 3-5 mos. No simultaneous submissions or reprints. Prefers NIV, KJV. Guidelines by mail/e-mail; catalog for 9 x 12 SAE/4 stamps.

Nonfiction: Query only; phone/fax/e-query OK. Children's Bible studies, curriculum, and take-home papers.

Fiction: For children; on assignment only.

Artwork: Open to freelance illustrators. Send files in Adobe Illustrator.

Tips: "All writing done on assignment. Request our guidelines; then complete a writer application before submitting. Need Bible-teaching ideas for preschool through sixth grade. Also publishes Bible stories for preschool and primary take-home papers, 200 wds." Using freelance writers mostly for Bible stories rather than fiction.

CHRISTIAN FAMILY PUBLICATIONS, 1854 Makarios Dr., St. Augustine FL 32080. (904) 471-4307. E-mail: christianfamily@mail.com. Website: www.christianfamilybooks.com. Gene Fedele, ed./pub. Imprints: Christian Family Library, Christian Heritage Classics, Great Christian Biographies. Publishes 1-3 titles/yr.; hardcover, trade paperbacks. Receives 30-40 submissions annually. 50% of books from first-time authors. No mss through agents. Reprints books. Prefers KJV or NKJV. Accepted mss on disk or by e-mail. Free catalog by mail.

Tips: "Most open to books from a Reformed theological position."

CHRISTIAN FOCUS PUBLICATIONS, LTD., Geanies House, Fearn, Tain, Ross-shire IV20 1TW, Scotland, UK. Phone 01862 871011. Fax 01862 871699. E-mail: info@christianfocus.com. Website: www.christianfocus.com. Submit adult material to Director of Publishing; children's material to Children's Editor. Focuses on having strong biblical content. Imprints: Mentor, Christian Heritage,

Christian Focus, Christian Focus 4 Kids. Publishes 90 titles/yr.; hardcover, trade paperbacks, mass-market paperbacks. Receives 300+ submissions annually. 10% of books from first-time authors. Accepts mss through agents or authors. Reprints books. **Royalty on net or outright purchase.** Publication within 24 mos. Considers simultaneous submissions. Accepts requested ms on disk. Responds typically in 4 mos. Guidelines on Website ("Submissions"); free catalog.

Nonfiction: Proposal/2 chapters; fax/e-query OK.

Fiction: Complete ms. For children and teens only. See guidelines for descriptions of children's fiction lines.

Photos: Accepts freelance photos for book covers.

Tips: "We are 'reformed,' though we don't insist all our authors would consider themselves reformed." Most open to issues-based popular books and children's fiction and biography. A prize-winning British publisher with good worldwide coverage.

CHRISTIAN HERITAGE SOCIETY, Box 519, Baldwin Place NY 10505. Phone/fax (914) 962-3287. E-mail: gtkurian@aol.com. Website: www.enyclopediasociety.com. George Kurian, ed. Publishes 6 titles/yr.; hardcover, trade paperbacks. Receives 100 submissions annually. 50% of books from first-time authors. Prefers mss through agents. No subsidy. Reprints books. Prefers 120,000 wds. **Royalty 10-15% on net; no advance.** Average first printing 10,000. Publication within 1 yr. Considers simultaneous submissions. Responds in 3 mos. Guidelines by mail; free catalog.

Nonfiction: Query; e-query OK. "Looking for Christian history, reference books, memoirs, devotionals, and evangelism."

CHRISTIAN LIBERTY PRESS, 502 W. Euclid Ave., Arlington Heights IL 60004. (847) 259-4444. Fax (847) 259-2941. E-mail: custserv@christianlibertypress.com or larsj@christianlibertypress.com. Website: www.christianlibertypress.com. Publishing arm of Christian Liberty Academy and Christian Liberty Academy School System (CLASS). Lars Johnson, admin. dir. Dedicated to publishing works that are consistent with the Word of God. Curriculum for kindergarten through high school.

Nonfiction: Proposal/2 chapters. A variety of enrichment and support books, including biographies, education resources, and Bible study materials.

Fiction: Proposal/2 chapters. Christian and historical.

@CHRISTIAN WRITER'S EBOOK NET, PO Box 446, Ft. Duchesne UT 84026. (435) 772-3429. E-mail: editor@writersebook.com or through Website: www.writersebook.com. Nondenominational/ Evangelical Christian. Linda Kay Stewart Whitsitt, ed-in-chief (linda@webtechdg.com); M. P. Whitsitt, asst. ed. (MPW@webtechdg.com); Terry Gordon Whitsitt, asst. to ed. (terry@webtechdg.com). Gives first-time authors the opportunity to bring their God-given writing talent to the Christian market. Publishes 15 titles/yr. Receives 100 submissions annually. 95% of books from first-time authors. Accepts mss through agents or authors. Subsidy publishes 25%. Reprints books. Prefers 60+ pgs. **Royalty 35-50%; no advance.** E-Books only. Publication within 6 mos. Considers simultaneous submissions. Electronic queries and submissions only; mss need to be in electronic form (MS Word, WordPerfect, ASCII, etc.) to be published; send by e-mail (preferred). No mail submissions accepted without contact by e-mail first. Responds in 1-2 mos. Guidelines on Website ("Publishing" on right side).

Nonfiction/Fiction: E-query only. Any topic or genre.

Also Does: Booklets, pamphlets, tracts. E-books.

Tips: "Make sure your work is polished and ready for print. The books we publish are sold in our online store. If you are not sure what an e-book is, check out our Website's FAQ page."

CHURCH GROWTH INSTITUTE, PO Box 7, Elkton MD 21922-0007. (434) 525-0022. Fax (434) 525-0608. E-mail: info@churchgrowth.org. Website: www.churchgrowth.org. Ephesians Four Ministries. Cindy G. Spear, resource development dir. Providing practical tools for leadership, evangelism, and church growth. Publishes 3 titles/yr.; trade paperbacks. Receives 40 submissions annually. 7% of books from first-time authors. No mss through agents. Prefers 64-160 pgs. **Royalty 6%**

on retail or outright purchase; no advance. Average first printing 100. Publication within 1 yr. Considers simultaneous submissions. Responds in 3 mos. Requires requested ms on disk. Guidelines sent after query/outline is received; catalog for 9 x 12 SAE/4 stamps, or on Website.

Nonfiction: Query; no phone/fax query; e-query OK. "We prefer our writers to be experienced in what they write about, to be experts in the field."

Special Needs: Topics that help churches grow spiritually and numerically; leadership training; attendance and stewardship programs; new or unique ministries (how-to). Self-discovery and evaluation tools, such as our Spiritual Gifts Inventory and Spiritual Growth Survey.

Photos: Accepts freelance photos for book covers.

Tips: "Most open to a practical manual or audio album (CDs/audiotapes and workbooks) for the pastor or other church leaders—something unique with a special niche. Must be practical and different from anything else on the same subject—or must be a topic/slant few others have published. Also very interested in evaluation tools as mentioned above. Please no devotionals, life testimonies, commentaries, or studies on books of the Bible."

CHURCH PUBLISHING, INC., (formerly listed as Morehouse Publishing Co.), 4775 Linglestown Rd., Harrisburg PA 17112. Toll-free (800) 242-1918. (212) 592-1800. Fax (717) 541-8136. E-mail: churchpublishing@cpg.org, or through Website: www.churchpublishing.org. Episcopal/Church Publishing Inc./Church Pension Group. Frank Tedeschi, sr. exec. ed. (445 Fifth Ave., New York NY 10016). Publishes thought-provoking books that serve the Episcopal Church and bring people of faith closer to God. Imprints: Morehouse Publishing, Seabury Books & Church Publishing. Publishes 30-40 titles/yr.; hardcover, trade paperbacks. Receives 500 submissions annually. 10% of books from first-time authors. Accepts mss through agents or authors. No subsidy or print-on-demand. No reprints. Prefers 100-200 pgs. **Royalty 10% of net; advance varies.** Average first printing varies. Publication within 18 mos. Considers simultaneous submissions. Responds in 3-4 mos. Prefers NRSV. Guidelines on Website; free catalog by mail.

Nonfiction: Proposal/1 chapter by mail; no phone/fax/e-query.

Special Needs: Women's issues, social justice, liturgics—all from an Episcopal/RC/mainline perspective.

Tips: "Please review our Website or catalog before sending proposal. We primarily accept books in our stated categories that are written by Episcopalians and written from an Anglican perspective. Not currently accepting children's book manuscripts."

CISTERCIAN PUBLICATIONS INC., The Abbey of Gethsemani, 3642 Monks Rd., Trappist KY 40051. Website: www.cistercianpublications.org. Fr. Mark Scott, OCSO, ed. dir. Works of monastic tradition and studies that foster renewal, spirituality, and ongoing formation of monastics. Publishes 8-14 titles/yr.; hardcover, trade paperbacks, some coffee-table books. Receives 30 submissions annually. 50% of books from first-time authors. No mss through agents. Reprints books. Prefers 204-286 pgs. **Royalty on net; no advance.** Average first printing 1,500. Publication within 2-10 yrs. Requires requested ms on disk. Guidelines on Website (scroll to bottom "Cistercian Publications"/"Manuscript Submission"); free style sheet/catalog.

Nonfiction: Query only by filling out the project summary form on the Website. History, spirituality, and theology.

Photos: Accepts freelance photos for book covers.

Tips: "We publish only on the Christian Monastic Tradition. Most open to a translation of a monastic text, or study of a monastic movement, author, or subject.

**Note: "Before submitting a manuscript, please request our Style Sheet and instructions. Manuscripts not conforming to our Style Sheet may be returned for revision."

CLADACH PUBLISHING, PO Box 336144, Greeley CO 80633. (970) 371-9530. E-mail: staff@ cladach.com. Website: www.cladach.com. Independent Christian publisher. Catherine Lawton, pub.

(cathyl@cladach.com); Hannah Lawton, submissions ed. Seeks to influence those inside and outside the body of Christ by giving a voice to talented writers with a clear, articulate, and Christ-honoring vision. Publishes 2-3 titles/yr.; trade paperbacks. Receives 200 submissions annually. 60% of books from first-time authors. Accepts proposals through agents or authors. No subsidy, print-on-demand, or reprints. Prefers 160-256 pgs. **Royalty 7% on net; no advance.** Average first printing 1,000. Publication within 1 yr. Considers simultaneous submissions. Accepted mss by e-mail. Responds in 3-6 mos. Prefers NIV, NRSV. Guidelines on Website ("For Authors"); free catalog.

> **Nonfiction:** Query letter only first (we're very selective); e-query OK. "Interested in books about God in creation."
>
> **Fiction:** Query letter only first (1-2 pgs.); e-query OK (copied into message). For adults. "Prefers gripping stories depicting inner struggles and real-life issues; well crafted. Would like to see Christian worldview, literary fiction."
>
> **Tips:** "We want writing that shows God active in our world and that helps readers experience His presence and power in their lives. Check out our Website for current guidelines and published books to see whether your book is a fit for Cladach." Unsolicited mss are returned unopened.

JAMES CLARKE & CO. LTD., PO Box 60, Cambridge CB1 2NT, England. Phone +44 (0) 1223 350865. Fax +44 (0) 1223 366951. E-mail: publishing@jamesclarke.co.uk. Website: www.james clarke.co.uk. Adrian Brink, ed. Publishes scholarly and reference titles in the areas of History & Biography, Biblical Studies and Theology. Imprints: The Lutterworth Press (general books: see separate listing). Publishes 25 titles/yr. (5 reprints, 20 new); hardcover & trade paperbacks. Receives 100 submissions annually. 90% of books from first-time authors. Accepts mss through agents or authors. Does print-on-demand. Reprints books. Subsidy publishes 2%. **Royalty on retail; pays an advance.** Publication within 18 mos. No simultaneous submissions. Responds in 3 mos. Requested ms by mail. Guidelines on Website ("Author Guidelines"); free catalog by mail.

> **Nonfiction:** Proposal/2 chapters; e-query OK.
>
> **Tips:** "For full author guidelines, visit our Website."

CLC PUBLICATIONS, PO Box 1449, Fort Washington PA 19034. (215) 542-1242. E-mail: sub missions@clcpublications.com. Website: www.clcpublications.com. CLC Ministries Intl. David Fessenden, mng. ed.; Becky English, assoc. ed. Books that reflect a passion for the topic and a depth of spirituality—a book that grows out of a fervent relationship with Christ. Publishes 12 titles/yr.; hardcover, trade paperbacks, mass-market paperbacks. Receives 200+ submissions annually. 80% of books from first-time authors. Accepts mss through agents or authors. Reprints books. Prefers under 60,000 wds. or under 300 pgs. **Royalty 10-12% of net; pays an advance.** Average first printing 3,000. Publication within 1 yr. Considers simultaneous submissions. Responds in 2-3 mos. Requires accepted mss on disk or by e-mail. Prefers NKJV. Guidelines by mail/e-mail/Website (at top "Writers Guidelines"); catalog for 9 x 12 SAE/2 stamps.

> **Nonfiction:** Query first; proposal/2-3 chapters; e-query OK. Books for the deeper life.
>
> **Special Needs:** A fresh approach to deepening one's relationship with God.
>
> **Ethnic Books:** African American.
>
> ****Note:** This publisher serviced by ChristianManuscriptSubmissions.com.

@COLLEGE PRESS PUBLISHING CO. INC., 223 W. Third St., Joplin MO 64801. Toll-free (800) 289-3300. (417) 623-6280. Fax (417) 623-8250. E-mail through Website: www.collegepress.com. Christian Church/Church of Christ. Submit to Acquisitions Editor. Christian materials that will help fulfill the Great Commission and promote unity on the basis of biblical truth and intent. Imprint: HeartSpring Publishing (see separate listing). Publishes 15-20 titles/yr.; hardcover, trade paperbacks. Receives 700 submissions annually. 25% of books from first-time authors. Accepts mss through agents or authors. Reprints books. Prefers 250-300 pgs. (paperback) or 300-600 pgs.

(hardback). **Royalty 5-15% of net; no advance.** Average first printing 3,000. Publication within 6 mos. Considers simultaneous submissions. Requires requested ms on disk; no e-mail submissions. Responds in 2-3 mos. Prefers NIV, NASB, NAS. Guidelines on Website ("For Authors"/"Publishing Guidelines"); catalog for 9 x 12 SAE/5 stamps.

Nonfiction: Query or proposal/2-3 chapters; no phone/fax query. "Looking for Bible study, reference, divorced leaders, blended families, and leadership." Expanding search for new authors, especially in women's ministry.

Ethnic Books: Reprints their own books in Spanish.

Also Does: E-books.

Tips: "We develop and supply Christian resources for use by individuals, churches, colleges/ universities/seminaries, and small groups. We are interested in biblical studies and resources that come from an 'Arminian' view and/or 'amillennial' slant."

**Note: This publisher serviced by ChristianManuscriptSubmissions.com.

@COMFORT PUBLISHING, 8410 Pit Stop Ct., Ste. 132, Concord NC 28027. (704) 979-9994. Fax (704) 979-9993. E-mail: jhuddle@comfortpublishing.com. Website: www.comfortpublishing.com. Comfort Publishing Services, LLC. Pamilla S. Tolen, sr. vp. (ptolen@comfortpublishing.com); submit to Kristy Huddle (khuddle@comfortpublishing.com). To promote Christian literature in a manner that is easy to read and understand, with a message that either teaches a principle or supports the truth of Christian faith. Publishes 10 titles/yr.; hardcover, trade paperbacks, digital. Receives 50 submissions annually. 50% of books from first-time authors. Prefers mss through agents; will accept from authors. No subsidy or print-on-demand. No reprints. Prefers 80,000 wds. or 200 pgs. **Royalty 8-12% on retail; some advances $100-2,000.** Average first printing 2,000. Publication within 12 mos. Considers simultaneous submissions. Responds in 6-9 mos. Accepts requested mss by e-mail. Guidelines by mail/e-mail/Website ("Submission Guidelines"); digital catalog.

Nonfiction: Proposal/3 chapters, or complete ms; e-query OK. Women's true stories.

Fiction: Proposal/3 chapters, or complete ms; e-query OK. For teens & adults. "Looking for young-adult or adult fiction."

Special Needs: Adult fiction or nonfiction, women's true stories, young-adult fiction.

Also Does: E-books.

Photos: Accepts freelance photos for book covers.

Tips: "Most open to fiction based on true stories; any well-written book with a message relevant to modern-day Christians."

CONARI PRESS, 500 Third St., Ste. 230, San Francisco CA 94107. E-mail: submissions@redwheel weiser.com. Website: www.conari.com or www.redwheelweiser.com. An imprint of Red Wheel/Weiser, LLC. Ms. Pat Bryce, acq. ed. Books on spirituality, personal growth, parenting, and social issues. Publishes 30 titles/yr. Responds in up to 3 mos. Guidelines and catalog on Website ("Submission Guidelines"). Incomplete topical listings.

CONCILIAR PRESS, Ben Lomand CA. E-mail: khyde@conciliarmedia.com. Website: www.concil iarpress.com. Antiochian Orthodox Christian Archdiocese of N.A. Katherine Hyde, acq. ed. Publishes 8-18 titles/yr. Receives 100 submissions annually. 20% of books from first-time authors. Accepts mss through agents or authors. Reprints books. **Royalty; no or small advance.** Average first printing 2,000. Accepts simultaneous submissions. E-mail submissions only. Responds in 1-3 mos. Prefers NKJV. Guidelines on Website (scroll to bottom "Submissions"); catalog on Website.

Nonfiction: E-query only. Accepts Eastern Orthodox material only.

Children's Books: E-query only. Send full manuscript for picture books under 2,000 wds.

Photos: Accepts freelance photos for book covers.

Tips: "Please explore our Website before submitting and carefully follow posted guidelines.

We accept only material by Eastern Orthodox Christians with specifically Orthodox content. We reserve the right not to respond to inappropriate submissions."

CONCORDIA ACADEMIC PRESS, 3558 S. Jefferson Ave., St. Louis MO 63118-3968. (314) 268-1080. E-mail: ed.engelbrecht@cph.org. Website: www.cph.org. Lutheran Church/Missouri Synod. Imprint of Concordia Publishing House. Rev. Edward A. Engelbrecht, STM, sr. ed. Scholarly and professional books in biblical studies, 16th-century studies, historical theology, and theology and culture. Publication within 2 yrs. Responds in 8-12 wks. Guidelines on Website (at bottom under "Service & Shopping Tools"/"Manuscript Submissions").

Nonfiction: Proposal/sample chapters.

Tips: "Freelance submissions are welcome. Prospective authors should consult the guidelines on the Website for an author prospectus and submission guidelines."

CONCORDIA PUBLISHING HOUSE, 3558 S. Jefferson Ave., St. Louis MO 63118-3968. (314) 268-1000. Website: www.cph.org. Lutheran Church/Missouri Synod. Rev. Paul T. McCain, pub. (paul .mccain@cph.org). Publishes 50 titles/yr.; hardcover, trade paperbacks. Does not consider unsolicited manuscripts.

CONGREGATIONAL LIFE AND LEARNING, Augsburg Fortress Canada, 500 Trillium Dr., Box 9940, Kitchener ON N2G 4Y4, Canada. E-mail: cllsub@augsburgfortress.org. Website: www.afcanada.com. Evangelical Lutheran Church in Canada. Submit using online form. Works to provide congregations with materials and resources for group and individual use that nurture faith, foster learning, and promote spiritual renewal among children, youth, and adults. **All material is work-for-hire.** Responds in 16 wks. Guidelines at www.afcanada.com/company/submitcongregational.jsp.

Nonfiction: Query first; e-query OK. "Looking for Sunday school materials, Bible study materials, and devotionals."

CONQUEST PUBLISHERS, PO Box 611, Washington DC 20710. (240) 342-3293. Fax (240) 342-3293. E-mail: info@conquestpublishers.com. Website: www.conquestpublishers.com. Louis N. Jones, publisher. To produce books and annuals to encourage, educate, exhort, and edify those who live an active, vibrant Christian lifestyle. Publishes hardcover & trade paperbacks. Royalty and subsidy publisher (publisher pays production costs but author may have to pay for some additional services—see guidelines). Prefers 32,000 wds. **Royalty 30% of retail if sold through their Website; 15% if sold through a distributor.** Considers simultaneous submissions; no reprints. Guidelines by e-mail/Website (inside box at bottom "Download Our Writers' Guidelines").

Nonfiction: E-mail query. See guidelines for required proposal contents.

Fiction: E-mail query. See guidelines for required proposal contents.

Tips: "We welcome first-time authors."

CONTEMPORARY DRAMA SERVICE, Meriwether Publishing Co., 885 Elkton Dr., Colorado Springs CO 80907. E-mail: editor@meriwether.com. Website: www.meriwetherpublishing.com. Publishes Christian plays for mainline churches. Also supplemental textbooks on theatrical subjects. Prefers comedy but does publish some serious works. Accepts full-length or one-act plays—comedy or musical. General and Christian. Publishes 30 plays/yr. Responds in 4-6 wks. See the Meriwether Publishing listing or Website for additional details ("Author's Corner" at top of list).

@CONTINUUM INTERNATIONAL PUBLISHING, 80 Maiden Lane, Rm. 704, New York NY 10038-4814. Toll-free (800) 561-7704. (212) 953-5858. Fax (212) 953-5944. E-mail: info@continuum books.com. Website: www.continuumbooks.com. Dr. David Barker, U.S. ed. dir. Imprints: T and T Clark; Burns & Oates. Publishes 60 titles/yr.; hardcover, trade paperbacks. Receives 500 submissions annually. 10% of books from first-time authors. Accepts mss through agents or authors. Subsidy publishes 5%. Does print-on-demand. Reprints books. **Royalty to 15%; pays an advance.** Prefers

60,000-120,000 wds. Publication within 9 mos. No simultaneous submissions. Responds in 1 mo. Guidelines by e-mail/Website ("Authors"/"How to Submit a Book Proposal"); free catalog.

Nonfiction: Query, proposal/1 chapter, or complete ms; phone/fax/e-query OK.

Photos: Accepts freelance photos for book covers.

Contest: Trinity Prize.

DAVID C. COOK, 4050 Lee Vance View, Colorado Springs CO 80918. (719) 536-0100. Fax (719) 536-3269. Website: www.cookministries.com. Dan Rich, sr. vp & pub.; Ingrid Beck, mng. ed. Discipleship is foundational; everything we publish needs to move the reader one step closer to maturity in Christ. Brands: David C. Cook (for teachers or program leaders who want Bible-based discipleship resources; Bible and study resources for serious Bible students; books for Christian families seeking biblical answers to life problems; books to equip kids—birth to age 12—for life); and fiction (inspiring fiction for mature believers). Publishes 85 titles/yr.; hardcover, trade paperbacks. 10% of books from first-time authors. Requires mss through agents. Publication within 1-2 yrs. Considers simultaneous submissions. Responds in 3-6 mos. Prefers requested ms by e-mail. Prefers NIV. Guidelines by mail/e-mail/Website ("Contact Information"/"Writers Guidelines" on left).

Nonfiction/Fiction: Accepts submissions only through agents or on request of one of their editors at a writers' conference.

**Note: This publisher serviced by The Writer's Edge and ChristianManuscriptSubmissions.com.

J. COUNTRYMAN, PO Box 141000, Nashville TN 37214-1000. (615) 902-3134. Fax (615) 902-3200. Website: www.jcountryman.com. Thomas Nelson Inc. Gift-book imprint. No longer accepting unsolicited manuscripts or proposals.

**Note: This publisher serviced by The Writer's Edge.

CROSSLINK PUBLISHING, PO Box 1232, Rapid City SD 57709. Toll-free (800) 323-0853. Toll-free fax (800) 934-6762. E-mail: publisher@crosslink.org. Website: www.crosslink.org. Christian Church/Church of Christ. Rick Bates, dir. Focused on providing valuable resources to authors as well as bringing vibrant and helpful resources to the Christian community. Estab. 2008. Publishes 6-8 titles/yr.; trade paperbacks. Receives 20 submissions annually. 25% of books from first-time authors. Prefers mss through agents. No subsidy; does print-on-demand. No reprints. Prefers 200-300 pgs. **Royalty 10% of retail; no advance.** Average first printing 750. Publication within 3 mos. Considers simultaneous submissions. Responds in 7 days. Requires accepted mss by e-mail. Guidelines on Website ("Publishing").

Nonfiction: Complete ms; e-query OK.

Special Needs: Devotionals and small group studies.

Photos/Artwork: Accepts freelance photos for book covers; open to queries from freelance artists.

Tips: "We are particularly interested in providing books that help Christians succeed in their daily walk (inspirational, devotional, small groups, etc.)."

THE CROSSROAD PUBLISHING CO., 831 Chestnut Ridge Rd., Chestnut Ridge NY 10977-6356. (845) 517-0180. Fax (845) 517-0181. E-mail: info@crossroadpublishing.com. Website: www.cpc books.com, or www.crossroadpublishing.com. Dr. John Jones, ed. dir. Books on religion, spirituality, and personal growth that speak to the diversity of backgrounds and beliefs; hopeful books that inform, enlighten, and heal; particular strengths in Catholic and Anglican titles as well as Christian spirituality and leadership. Imprints: Herder & Herder. Publishes 45 titles/yr.; hardcover, trade paperbacks. Receives 1,200 submissions annually. 10% of books from first-time authors. Accepts mss through agents or authors. Does print-on-demand. Reprints books. Prefers 50,000-60,000 wds. or 160-176 pgs. **Royalty 6-14% of net; small advance (more for established authors).** Average first printing 4,000. Publication within 14 mos. Considers simultaneous submissions. Responds in 6 wks. Accepts requested ms on disk. Guidelines on Website ("Contact Us"/"Submissions"); free catalog.

Nonfiction: Query letter only first; e-query required. Books that explore and celebrate the Christian life.

Tips: "Most authors need some combination of (1) exceptional writing ability, (2) expertise or authority in a field, (3) an existing platform for sales (speaking engagements, etc.). We are independent of all churches yet part of a 200-year tradition of excellent books for enriching Christian life."

Herder & Herder: 200 years of international publishing in the service of theology and church. Monographs, reference works, theological, and philosophical discourse. Special focus on younger and emerging theologians as well as the Christian spiritual disciplines.

CROSS TRAINING PUBLISHING, PO Box 1874, Kearney NE 68848. Toll-free (800) 430-8588. Fax (308) 338-2058. E-mail: gordon@crosstrainingpublishing.com. Website: www.crosstrainingpub lishing.com. Gordon Thiessen, pub. Sports books for children and adults. Catalog on Website.

CROSSWAY, 1300 Crescent St., Wheaton IL 60174. (630) 682-4300. Fax (630) 682-4785. E-mail: editorial@crossway.org. Website: www.crossway.org. A publishing ministry of Good News Publishers. Allan Fisher, sr. vp for book publishing; submit to Jill Carter, editorial administrator. Publishes books that combine the truth of God's Word with a passion to live it out, with unique and compelling Christian content. Publishes 70 titles/yr.; hardcover, trade paperbacks. Receives 1,000 submissions annually. 1% of books from first-time authors. Accepts mss through agents or authors. No reprints. Prefers 25,000 wds & up. **Royalty 10-21% of net; advance varies.** Average first printing 5,000-10,000. Publication within 18 mos. Considers simultaneous submissions. Responds in 6-8 wks. Prefers ESV. Guidelines by e-mail; free catalog.

Nonfiction: Currently not accepting unsolicited submissions.

Also Does: Tracts. See Good News Publishers.

**Note: This publisher serviced by The Writer's Edge and ChristianManuscriptSubmissions.com.

**Recipient of five 2006 Silver Angel Awards from Excellence in Media.

@CSS PUBLISHING GROUP INC., 5450 N. Dixie Hwy, Lima OH 45807-9559. (419) 227-1818. Fax (513) 297-1179. E-mail: editor@csspub.com, or through Website: www.csspub.com. Serves the needs of pastors, worship leaders, and parish program planners in the broad Christian mainline of the American church. Imprints: Fairway Press (subsidy—see separate listing); B.O.D. (Books On Demand); FaithWalk Books. Publishes 30-40 titles/yr.; trade paperbacks, digital. Receives 500-1,000 submissions annually. 50% of books from first-time authors. Subsidy publishes 50-60% through Fairway Press; does print-on-demand. Reprints books. Prefers 100-125 pgs. **No royalty or advance.** Average first printing 1,000. Publication within 12 mos. Considers simultaneous submissions. Responds in 3 wks. to 3 mos.; final decision within 12 mos. Requires requested ms on disk and in hard copy. Prefers NRSV. Guidelines by e-mail/Website ("Contact Us"/"Submissions Guidelines"); no catalog.

Nonfiction: Query or proposal/3 chapters; phone/e-query OK; complete ms for short works. "Looking for pastoral resources for ministry; lectionary sermons. Our material is practical in nature."

Fiction: Complete ms. Easy-to-perform dramas and pageants for all age groups. "Our drama interest primarily includes Advent, Christmas, Epiphany, Lent, and Easter. We do not publish long plays." Subsidy-only for fiction.

Tips: "We're looking for authors who will help with the marketing of their books."

CUSTOM BOOK, 77 Main St., Tappan NY 10983. Toll-free (800) 631-1362. (845) 365-0414. Fax (845) 365-0864. E-mail: customusa@aol.com or through Website: www.customstudios.com. Norman Shaifer, pres. Publishes 50-75 titles/yr. 50% of books from first-time authors. No mss through agents. **Royalty on net; some outright purchases for specific assignments.** Publication within 6 mos. Responds in 1 mo. Guidelines by mail.

Nonfiction: Query/proposal/chapters. "Histories of individual congregations, denominations, or districts."

Tips: "Find stories of larger congregations (750 or more households) who have played a role in the historic growth and development of the community or region."

+DAN RIVER PRESS, Conservatory of American Letters, PO Box 298, Thomaston ME 04861-0298. (207) 226-7428. E-mail: cal@americanletters.org. Website: www.americanletters.org. Richard S. Danbury, fiction ed. Publishes 6-8 titles/yr.; hardcover & trade paperbacks. **Royalty 10-15%.; pays some advances.** Publication within 3-4 mos. Considers simultaneous submissions. Responds in 2-3 days to queries. Guidelines on Website (scroll down and click on "Dan River Press").

   Fiction: Query/proposal. Does general religious fiction, inspirational, religious mystery/suspense, religious thrillers, and religious romance.

DAWN PUBLICATIONS, 12402 Bitney Springs Rd., Nevada City CA 95959. (530) 274-7775. Fax (530) 274-7778. E-mail: submission@dawnpub.com. Website: www.dawnpub.com. Glenn Hovemann, acq. ed. Dedicated to inspiring in children a sense of appreciation for all of life on earth. Publishes 6 titles/yr.; hardcover, trade paperbacks. Receives 3,050 submissions annually. 15% of books from first-time authors. Accepts mss through agents or authors. No reprints. **Royalty on net; pays an advance.** Publication within 1-2 yrs. Considers simultaneous submissions. Responds in 2 mos. Guidelines/catalog on Website ("Submissions").

   Nonfiction: Complete manuscript by mail or e-mail.

   Artwork: Open to queries from freelance artists (send sample c/o Muffy Weaver).

   Tips: "Most open to creative nonfiction. We look for nature awareness and appreciation titles that promote a relationship with the natural world and specific habitats, usually through inspiring treatment and nonfiction."

+DESERT BREEZE PUBLISHING, E-mail: submissions@desertbreezepublishing.com. Website: www.desertbreezepublishing.com. Gail Delaney, ed. Goal is to publish exceptionally crafted and captivating romance novels in multiple genres. Accepts 50,000 wds. or over 100,000 wds. (prefers 75,000-100,000). No simultaneous submissions. Guidelines on Website (click on "Submissions"); catalog online.

   Fiction: See guidelines.

   Special Needs: Historical romance set in the first half of the 20th century. See guidelines for other specific genres.

   Tips: "If you have questions about the guidelines, e-mail us at submissionsquestions@ desertbreezepublishing.com."

DIMENSIONS FOR LIVING, 201—8th Ave. S., Nashville TN 37203. Fax (615) 749-6512. E-mail: sbriese@umpublishing.org. Website: www.abingdonpress.com. United Methodist Publishing House. Joseph A. Crowe, ed.; submit to Manuscript Submissions (by mail only). Books for the general Christian reader. Publishes 120 titles/yr. Receives 2,000 submissions annually. Less than 1% of books from first-time authors. No reprints. Prefers 144 pgs. **Royalty 7.5% on retail; some outright purchases; no advance.** Average first printing 3,000. Publication within 2 yrs. Requires requested ms on disk. Responds in 8 wks. Guidelines on Website (scroll to bottom "Submissions"); free catalog.

   Nonfiction: Proposal/2 chapters; no phone query. Open to inspiration/devotion, self-help, home/family, special-occasion gift books.

DISCOVERY HOUSE PUBLISHERS, PO Box 3566, Grand Rapids MI 49501. Toll-free (800) 653-8333. (616) 942-9218. Fax (616) 974-2224. E-mail: dhptc@rbc.org. Website: www.dhp.org. RBC Ministries. Carol Holquist, pub.; submit to Manuscript Review Editor. Publishes books that foster Christian growth and godliness. Publishes 12-18 titles/yr.; hardcover, trade paperbacks, mass-market paperbacks. Accepts mss through agents or authors. Reprints books. **Royalty 10-14% on**

net; no advance. Publication within 12-18 mos. Considers simultaneous submissions. Requires accepted mss on disk or by e-mail. Responds in 4-6 wks. Guidelines by mail/e-mail/Website (FAQ #4); free catalog.

Nonfiction: Query letter only. If by e-mail, "Attn: Ms Review Editor" in subject line.

**Note: This publisher serviced by The Writer's Edge and ChristianManuscriptSubmissions.com.

@DISKUS PUBLISHING, PO Box 43, Albany IN 47320. E-mail: editor@diskuspublishing.com. Submissions to: editor@diskuspublishing.com or submissions@diskuspublishing.com. Website: www.diskuspublishing.com. Marilyn Nesbitt, ed-in-chief; Joyce McLaughlin, inspirational ed. E-book & print publisher. Publishes 50 titles/yr. **Royalty 40%.** Publication within 6-8 mos. Considers simultaneous submissions if noted. Prefers manuscripts by e-mail (be sure to put "Diskus" in the subject line). Guidelines by mail/Website; catalog online.

Nonfiction: Complete ms or query by mail or e-mail.

Fiction: Complete ms by e-mail. Includes religious fiction.

Tips: This publisher is currently closed to submissions. Check Website under submission guidelines to see when they are going to again open up to submissions.

DOUBLEDAY RELIGIOUS PUBLISHING, 1745 Broadway, New York NY 10019. (212) 782-9000. Fax (212) 782-8338. E-mail: tmurphy@randomhouse.com. Website: www.randomhouse.com. Imprint of Random House, Inc. Trace Murphy, editorial dir. Imprints: Image, Galilee, New Jerusalem Bible, Three Leaves Press, Anchor Bible Commentaries, Anchor Bible Reference Library. Publishes 45-50 titles/yr.; hardcover, trade paperbacks. Receives 1,500 submissions annually. 10% of books from first-time authors. Requires mss through agents. Reprints books. **Royalty 7.5-15% on retail; pays an advance.** Average first printing varies. Publication within 8 mos. Considers simultaneous submissions. Responds in 4 mos. No disk. Guidelines on Website ("About Random House"/"Manuscript Submissions"); catalog for 9 x 12 SASE/3 stamps.

Nonfiction: Agented submissions only. Proposal/3 chapters; no phone query.

Fiction: Religious fiction. Agented submissions only.

Ethnic Books: African American; Hispanic.

Tips: "Most open to a book that has a big and well-defined audience. Have a clear proposal, lucid thesis, and specified audience."

**Note: This publisher serviced by ChristianManuscriptSubmissions.com.

+DOULOS RESOURCES, 195 Mack Edwards Dr., Oakland TN 38060. (901) 451-0356. E-mail: info@doulosresources.org. Website: www.doulosresources.org. Reformed/Presbyterian. Ed Eubanks Jr., ed. dir. Resources designed to "prepare God's people for works of service, so that the body of Christ may be built up" (Ephesians 4:12). Publishes 4-5 titles/yr. Receives up to 50 submissions annually. 50% of books from first-time authors. Reprints books. **No advance.** Publication within 3-6 mos. Responds in 2-3 wks. Prefers NIV, ESV. Guidelines & catalog on Website ("About Us"/"May I Submit a Manuscript for Publication?"). Incomplete topical listings.

Nonfiction: Proposal/2-3 chapters; e-query only (attached as PDF/Word); no phone/fax query.

Also Does: E-books, booklets & pamphlets.

Tips: "Our resources are characterized by a thoughtful, biblical, and theologically-Reformed approach to resources that will serve the Church and advance the Kingdom. We publish materials aimed at pastors, church leaders, and lay-level readership. Our interest is to serve the Church and Kingdom, and we are happy for any opportunity to do so. While we won't lay aside our Presbyterian and Reformed identity, we believe that many of our resources may be useful to those outside of our theological and ecclesiastical circles."

DOVE INSPIRATIONAL PRESS, 1000 Burmaster St., Gretna LA 70053. (504) 368-1175. Fax (504) 368-1195. E-mail: editorial@pelicanpub.com. Website: www.pelicanpub.com. Nina Kooij, ed-in-chief. To publish books of quality and permanence that enrich the lives of those who read them. Imprint of Pelican Publishing. Publishes 1 title/yr.; hardcover, trade paperbacks. Receives 250 submissions annually. No books from first-time authors. Accepts mss through agents or authors. Reprints books. Prefers 200+ pgs. **Royalty; some advances.** Publication within 9-18 mos. No simultaneous submissions. Responds in 1 mo. on queries. Requires accepted ms on disk. Prefers KJV. Guidelines on Website ("About Us"/"Submissions"); catalog for 9 x 12 SAE/6 stamps.

Nonfiction: Proposal/2 chapters; no phone/fax/e-query.

Fiction: Children's picture books only.

Artwork: Open to queries from freelance artists.

DOVER PUBLICATIONS INC., 31 E. 2nd St., Mineola NY 11501-3852. (516) 294-7000, ext. 173. Fax (516) 873-1401 or (516) 742-6953. E-mail: mwaldrep@doverpublications.com. Website: www .doverpublications.com. Attn: Editorial Dept. Publishes some religious titles, reprints only. **Makes outright purchases.** Does not return submissions. Guidelines (under Customer Service) & free catalog on Website.

Nonfiction: Proposal with synopsis, contents, & 1 chapter; no submissions by e-mail. Religion topics.

+EARTHEN VESSEL PUBLISHING, 9 Sunny Oaks Dr., San Raphael CA 94903. (415) 302-1199. Fax (415) 499-8199. E-mail: kentphilpott@comcast.net. Website: www.earthenvessel.net. Evangelical/ Baptist. Kent & Katie Philpott, eds. Our goal is to preach Jesus Christ and Him crucified. Imprint: Siloam Springs Press. Publishes 3 titles/yr.; trade paperbacks. Receives 15 submissions annually. 50% of books from first-time authors. Prefers mss through agents; accepts through author. Reprints books. No subsidy or POD for now. Any length. **Royalty on retail price; no advance.** Average first printing varies. Publication within 6 mos. Considers simultaneous submissions. Accepted mss by disk or e-mail. Responds in 1 wk. to 1 mo. Guidelines on Website; no catalog.

Nonfiction: Query first by phone or e-mail; proposal/1 chapter.

Fiction: Query first by phone or e-mail; proposal/1 chapter.

Special Needs: Books of a solid biblical nature, Christ-centered, perhaps of a Reformed nature, but not limited to this theology. Special interest in awakenings and a special interest in pastors of small churches and their congregations.

Photos/Artwork: Accepts freelance photos for book covers; open to queries from freelance artists.

Tips: "Well-written and edited work is best. Not able to do major rewriting or editing. Lean toward, but not exclusively, Reformed thought. Our goal is to present the Gospel to unbelievers and the Scriptures to believers. We are small and can do very little, but we look forward to working with the print-on-demand format."

EDITORIAL PORTAVOZ, PO Box 2607, Grand Rapids MI 49501-2607. Toll-free (800) 733-2607. (616) 451-4775. Fax (616) 451-9330. E-mail: editor@portavoz.com or portavoz@portavoz.com. Website: www.portavoz.com. Spanish Division of Kregel Publishing. Submit to The Editor. To provide trusted, biblically based resources that challenge and encourage Spanish-speaking individuals in their Christian lives and service. Publishes 40+ titles/yr. 2-5% of books from first-time authors. Accepts mss through agents or authors. Does print-on-demand. No reprints. **Negotiable royalty on net; negotiable advance.** Average first printing 5,000. Publication within 13 mos. Considers simultaneous submissions. Responds in 2-4 mos. Guidelines on Website.

Nonfiction: Send proposal by e-mail or CD-ROM, with 2-3 chapters. "Looking for original Spanish reference works."

Artwork: Purchases artwork outright.

EDITORIAL UNILIT, 1360 N.W. 88th Ave., Miami FL 33172-3093. Toll-free (800) 767-7726. (305) 592-6136. Fax (305) 592-0087. E-mail: info@editorialunilit.com. Website: www.editorialunilit.com.

Spanish House. Submit to The Editor. To glorify God by providing the church and Spanish-speaking people with the tools to communicate clearly the gospel of Jesus Christ and help them grow in their relationship with Him and His church.

EERDMANS BOOKS FOR YOUNG READERS, 2140 Oak Industrial Dr. N.E., Grand Rapids MI 49505. Toll-free (800) 253-7521. (616) 459-4591. Fax (616) 459-6540. E-mail: youngreaders@eerdmans.com or info@eerdmans.com. Website: www.eerdmans.com/youngreaders. Wm. B. Eerdmans Publishing. Submit to Acquisitions Editor. Produces books for general trade, school, and library markets. Publishes 12-15 titles/yr.; hardcover, trade paperbacks. Receives 5,000 submissions annually. 3% of books from first-time authors. Prefers mss through agents. Age-appropriate length. **Royalty & advance vary.** Average first printing varies. Publication within 36 mos. No simultaneous submissions (mark "Exclusive" on envelope). Responds in 3 mos. Guidelines by mail/e-mail/Website ("Submission Guidelines"); catalog for 9 x 12 SAE/4 stamps.

> **Fiction:** Proposal/3 chapters for book length; complete ms for picture books. For children and teens. No e-mail or fax submissions.

> **Artwork:** Please do not send illustrations with picture-book manuscripts unless you are a professional illustrator. When submitting artwork, send color copies, not originals. Send illustrations sample to Gayle Brown, art dir.

> **Tips:** "Most open to thoughtful submissions that address needs in children's literature. We are not looking for Christmas stories at this time."

WM. B. EERDMANS PUBLISHING CO., 2140 Oak Industrial Dr. N.E., Grand Rapids MI 49505. Toll-free (800) 253-7521. (616) 459-4591. Fax (616) 459-6540. E-mail: info@eerdmans.com. Website: www.eerdmans.com. Protestant/Academic/Theological. Jon Pott, ed-in-chief. Imprint: Eerdmans Books for Young Readers (see separate listing). Publishes 120-130 titles/yr.; hardcover, trade paperbacks. Receives 3,000-4,000 submissions annually. 10% of books from first-time authors. Accepts mss through agents or authors. Reprints books. **Royalty; occasional advance.** Average first printing 4,000. Publication within 1 yr. Considers simultaneous submissions. Responds in 4 wks. to query; several months for mss. Guidelines by mail/Website (www.eerdmans.com/submit .htm); free catalog.

> **Nonfiction:** Proposal/2-3 chapters; no fax/e-query. "Looking for religious approaches to contemporary issues, spiritual growth, scholarly works."

> **Fiction:** Proposal/chapter; no fax/e-query. For all ages. "We are looking for adult novels with high literary merit."

> **Tips:** "Most open to material with general appeal, but well-researched, cutting-edge material that bridges the gap between evangelical and mainline worlds. Please include e-mail and/or SASE for a response."

> ****Note:** This publisher serviced by The Writer's Edge.

ELDRIDGE CHRISTIAN PLAYS & MUSICALS, PO Box 14367, Tallahassee FL 32317. (850) 385-2463. Fax (850) 385-2463. E-mail: info@histage.com. Website: www.95church.com. Independent Christian drama publisher. Susan Shore, new plays ed. To provide superior religious drama to enhance preaching and teaching, whatever your Christian denomination. Publishes 15 plays and 2 musicals/yr. Receives 350-400 plays annually. 75% of plays from first-time authors. One-act to full-length plays. **Outright purchases of $100-1,000 on publication; no advance.** Publication within 1 yr. Considers simultaneous submissions. Responds in 2 mos. Requires requested ms on disk or by e-mail. Free guidelines by mail/e-mail/Website ("Submission Guidelines"); catalog by mail.

> **Plays:** Complete ms; e-query OK. For children, teens, and adults. Send by e-mail to NewWorks@95church.com, or by mail to editor and address above.

> **Special Needs:** Always looking for high-quality Christmas and Easter plays but open to other

holiday and "anytime" Christian plays too. Can be biblical or contemporary, for performance by all ages, children through adult.

Tips: "Have play produced at your church and others prior to submission, to get out the bugs. At least try a stage reading."

ELIJAH PRESS, Meadow House Communications Inc., PO Box 317628, Cincinnati OH 45231-7628. (513) 521-7362. Fax (513) 521-7364. Website: www.elijahpress.com. Division of Meadow House Communications, Inc. Publishes quality religious/spiritual fiction and nonfiction books and tapes on and related to Christian living, church history, and spiritual reflection. S. R. Davis, ed. Publishes 3-5 titles/yr. Prefers 50,000-100,000 wds. Responds in 1 mo. Guidelines on Website ("Submissions"). Incomplete topical listings.

Nonfiction: One-page query; must have completed ms; no phone/e-query.

Fiction: Accepts fiction.

+ELLECHOR PUBLISHING HOUSE, LLC, PO Box 5489, Beaverton OR 97006. (559) 744-3553. Fax (206) 339-2483. E-mail: info@ellechor.org. Website: www.ellechorpublishing.com. Blog: www .ellechorpublishing.com/blog. Non-denominational. Olson Perry, Sr./VP of Publishing Accounts & Acquisitions. Publishes 4 titles/yr.; hardback, trade paperback, coffee-table books, and digital. Receives about 200 submissions annually. 85% of books from first-time authors. Prefers mss through agents. No subsidy or print on demand. Prefers 50,000+ wds. or 200+ pgs. **Royalty 10-25% on net; advance $1,500.** Average first printing 1,500. Publication within 9 mos. Discourages simultaneous submissions. Responds in 3-4 wks. Prefers KJV. Guidelines by e-mail; catalog $2.

Nonfiction: Submit by e-mail or through Website only; no phone, fax submissions.

Fiction: Submit by e-mail or through Website only; no phone, fax submissions.

Tips: Get your book professionally edited. Start a blog. We love Bible-based stories.

**Note: This publisher serviced by The Writer's Edge.

@EMMAUS ROAD PUBLISHING, 827 N. Fourth St., Steubenville OH 43952. Toll-free (800) 398-5470. (740) 283-2484. Fax (740) 283-4011. E-mail: questions@emmausroad.org. Website: www .emmausroad.org. Catholics United for the Faith. Shannon Minch-Hughes, V.P. Operations. To produce solid Catholic resources. Publishes 10-12 titles/yr.; hardcover, trade paperbacks, mass-market paperbacks, digital. Receives 50 submissions annually. 5% of books from first-time authors. No mss through agents. No subsidy, print-on-demand, or reprints. Prefers 200 pgs. **Royalty on net; pays an advance.** Average first printing 2,500. Publication within 18 mos. Considers simultaneous submissions. Guidelines on Website (scroll to bottom "Manuscript Submission Guidelines"); free catalog.

Nonfiction: Query.

Special Needs: Bible studies.

Also Does: Booklets.

ENCORE PERFORMANCE PUBLISHING, PO Box 14367, Tallahassee FL 32317. Phone/fax (850) 385-2463. E-mail: info@encoreplay.com. Website: www.encoreplay.com. Eldridge Publishing. Meredith Edwards, mng. dir. Specializes in children's plays and musicals and wholesome family entertainment for schools and churches. Publishes 5-10 titles/yr. Receives 75 submissions annually. **Royalty 10% on copy sales; 50% performance royalty; $100-1,000 for outright purchases; no advance.** Print-on-demand. Publication within 6 mos. Considers simultaneous submissions. Responds in 2 mos. Prefers accepted mss by e-mail. Guidelines on Website ("FAQ"/"How Can I submit My Play?" near the bottom of list); catalog.

Nonfiction: Submit synopsis to NewWorks@encoreplay.com. Publishes resource books for all ages on such topics as theatre arts, acting, auditions, improvisation, stage management, etc.

Fiction: Submit synopsis and production history to NewWorks@encoreplay.com. Publishes full-length plays and musicals, skits, and monologue collections, from elementary school through high school. Genres include comedy and drama, multicultural and Christian.

Tips: "We're especially interested in plays and musicals for children, tweens, and teens to help them navigate through the perilous waters of middle school and high school. We're looking for honest but entertaining works."

ETC PUBLICATIONS, 1456 Rodeo Rd., Palm Springs CA 92262. Toll-free (866) 514-9969. (760) 316-9695. Fax (760) 316-9681. Website: www.etcpublications.com. Education Technology Communications. Dr. Richard W. Hostrop, pub.; Lee Ona S. Hostrop, ed. dir. Publishes textbooks for the Christian and general markets at all levels of education. Publishes 6-12 titles/yr.; hardcover, trade paperbacks. Receives 50 submissions annually. 75% of books from first-time authors. Accepts mss through agents or authors. No reprints. Prefers 128-256 pgs. **Royalty 5-15% on net or retail; no advance.** Average first printing 1,500-2,500. Publication within 9 mos. No simultaneous submissions. Responds in 10 days. No guidelines (use Chicago Manual of Style); catalog for #10 SAE/1 stamp.

Nonfiction: Complete ms; e-query OK. "We are interested only in Christian-oriented, state history textbooks to be used in Christian schools and by homeschoolers."

Photos: Accepts freelance photos for book covers.

Tips: "Open only to state histories that are required at a specific grade level and are Christian oriented, with illustrations."

@EVANGELICAL PRESS, PO Box 614, Carlisle PA 17013-0614. Toll-free phone/fax (866) 588-6778. E-mail: editor@evangelicalpress.org. Website: www.evangelicalpress.org. Evangelical Press and Services Ltd. Submit to Book Editor. Committed to the dissemination of biblical Christianity throughout the world in numerous languages; and to support local Christians in local churches to live lives that glorify God. Publishes 24 titles/yr.; hardcover, trade paperbacks, mass-market paperbacks. Receives 300+ submissions annually. 80% of books from first-time authors. No mss through agents. Does print-on-demand. No reprints. **Royalty on net; no advance.** Average first printing 3,000. Publication within 12-18 mos. No simultaneous submissions. Accepts requested mss by e-mail. Responds within 3 mos. Prefers NIV/ESV/NKJV. Guidelines by e-mail/Website ("FAQ"/"How can I get my manuscript reviewed by EP?"); free catalog by mail.

Nonfiction: Query, proposal/2 chapters or complete ms; phone/e-query OK.

Also Does: E-books.

Tips: "Understand what our publishing company stands for."

EVERGREEN PRESS, 115 Beauregard St., Dauphin Island AL 36528-4519. (251) 973-0680. Fax (251) 973-0682. E-mail: Brian@evergreenpress.com. Website: www.evergreenpress.com. Genesis Communications. Brian Banashak, pub.; Kathy Banashak, ed-in-chief. Publishes books that empower people for breakthrough living by being practical, biblical, and engaging. Imprints: Evergreen Press, Gazelle Press, Axiom Press (print-on-demand). Publishes 30 titles/yr. Receives 250 submissions annually. 40% of books from first-time authors. Accepts mss through agents or authors. Subsidy publishes 35%. Does print-on-demand. No reprints. Prefers 96-160 pgs. **Royalty on net; no advance.** Average first printing 4,000. Publication within 6 mos. Considers simultaneous submissions. Requires requested ms on disk or by e-mail. Responds in 4-6 wks. Guidelines on Website ("Get Published"/"Book Submissions"); free catalog.

Nonfiction: Complete ms; fax/e-query OK. Submission form on Website.

Fiction: For all ages. Complete ms; phone/fax/e-query OK. Submission form on Website.

Special Needs: Business, finance, personal growth, women's issues, family/parenting, relationships, prayer, humor, and angels.

Also Does: Booklets.

Tips: "Most open to books with a specific market (targeted, not general) that the author is qualified to write for and that is relevant to today's believers and seekers. Author must also be open to editorial direction."

EXTREME DIVA MEDIA, INC., E-mail: query@extremedivamedia.com. Website: www.extremediva media.com. Jean Ann Duckworth, ed./pub. Publishes books in 4 areas: reducing stress, increasing joy, simplifying life, and enhancing relationships. Guidelines on Website.

Nonfiction: E-query only. Full manuscripts will be discarded unless requested.

Special Needs: Devotions to Go (30-day devotionals); Self Improvement; Cookbooks/ Entertainment Guides. New series "Girlfriends On . . ." was introduced in 2009. Now accepting submissions. Guidelines on Website ("Extreme Diva Media"/"Submission guidelines").

Tips: "We create books to help women live better lives. Show us how your book contributes to this mission."

FACTS ON FILE INC., 132 W. 31st St., 17th Fl., New York NY 10001. Toll-free (800) 322-8755. (212) 967-8800. Toll-free fax (800) 678-3633. E-mail: editorial@factsonfile.com. Website: www .factsonfile.com. Infobase Publishing. Submit to Editorial Director. School and library reference and trade books (for middle- to high-school students) tied to curriculum and areas of cross-cultural studies, including religion. Imprint: Checkmark Books. Publishes 3-5 religious titles/yr. Receives 10-20 submissions annually. 2% of books from first-time authors. Accepts mss through agents or authors. No reprints. Prefers 224-480 pgs. **Royalty 10% on retail; outright purchases of $2,000-10,000; advance $5,000-10,000.** Some work-for-hire. Average first printing 2,500. Publication within 9-12 mos. Considers simultaneous submissions. Responds in 2 mos. Requires requested ms on disk. Guidelines by mail/Website ("Contact Us"/"Other Departments"/"Author Submissions"); free catalog by mail.

Nonfiction: Query or proposal/1 chapter; fax/e-query OK.

Tips: "Most open to reference books tied to curriculum subjects or disciplines."

FAIR HAVENS PUBLICATIONS, PO Box 1238, Gainesville TX 76241-1238. Toll-free (800) 771-4861. (940) 668-6044. Fax (940) 668-6984. E-mail through Website: www.fairhavenspub.com. Submit to Acquisitions Department. Produces quality books, teaching and evangelistic literature, audiotapes and videotapes, CD-ROMs, dramas, and artworks that inspire faith and courage. Publishes 1-2 titles/yr.; hardcover, trade paperbacks. Receives 100 submissions annually. No first-time authors. Accepts mss through agents or authors. Subsidy publishes 25%; does print-on-demand. Reprints books. Prefers 250-300 pgs. **Royalty 10-18% on net; no advance (negotiable for published authors).** Average first printing 3,000-12,000. Publication within 8 mos. Considers simultaneous submissions. Responds in 12 or more wks. Requires requested ms on disk. Prefers NKJV. Guidelines on Website ("Authors"); no catalog.

Nonfiction: Proposal/3 chapters; no phone/fax/e-query. "We are interested in books based on original research based on compiled data, case studies, etc."

Special Needs: Nonfiction; personal experience; how-to books packed with practical information relating to a felt need.

Also Does: Booklets, audio- & videotapes, CD-ROMs, dramas.

Photos/Artwork: Accepts freelance photos for book covers; open to queries from freelance artists.

Tips: "We are flexible and work closely with our authors. We will help authors to self-publish if we do not elect to publish their manuscripts."

FAITH ALIVE CHRISTIAN RESOURCES, 2850 Kalamazoo Ave. S.E., Grand Rapids MI 49560. Toll-free (800) 333-8300. (616) 224-0819 or (616) 224-0728. Toll-free fax (888) 642-8606. E-mail: editors@faithaliveresources.org. Website: www.faithaliveresources.org. CRC Publications/Christian Reformed Church. Ruth Vanderhart, mng. ed. (rvanderhart@crcna.org). Guidelines on Website (scroll to bottom "Submission Guidelines").

Artwork: Open to queries from freelance artists; contact Dean Heetderks, art dir.

FAITH COMMUNICATIONS—See Health Communications.

FAITHWALK PUBLISHING, 5450 N. Dixie Hwy, Lima OH 45807-9559. Toll-free (800) 537-1030. (419) 227-1818. Fax (419) 228-9184. E-mail: submissions@faithwalkpub.com. Website: www.faith walkpub.com. Imprint of CSS Publishing. Dirk Wierenga, ed. (Send submission c/o Dirk Wierenga, 14140 Payne Forest, Grand Haven MI 49417 or e-query to dirkbw@gmail.com.) Called to publish books that appeal to seekers and believers who might otherwise never purchase a religious book. Publishes 10 titles/yr. Receives 500+ submissions annually. 10% of books from first-time authors. Accepts mss through agents or authors. No reprints. Prefers 160-356 pgs. **Royalty 6-10% on retail; no advance.** Average first printing 2,000-5,000. Publication within 12-18 mos. Considers simultaneous submissions (if indicated). Does not respond to submissions unless interested (no SASE needed). Prefers NIV, NRSV. Guidelines by mail/e-mail/Website ("Contact"); catalog online.
> **Nonfiction:** Proposal/1-2 chapters; no fax submissions; e-query OK. No children's or gift books.
> **Fiction:** Proposal/1-2 chapters; e-query OK. Adult; adventure, contemporary, and literary.
> **Photos:** Accepts freelance photos for book covers.

FAITHWORDS/HACHETTE BOOK GROUP, 10 Cadillac Dr., Ste. 220, Brentwood TN 37027. (615) 221-0996, ext. 221. Fax (615) 221-0962. Website: www.faithwords.com. Hachette Book Group USA. Anne Horch, ed. Publishes 35 titles/yr.; hardcover, trade paperbacks, mass-market paperbacks. Few books from first-time authors. Requires mss through agents. Prefers 60,000-90,000 wds. **Royalty on retail; pays an advance.** Publication within 12 mos. Considers simultaneous submissions. Prefers proposals & accepted ms by e-mail. Guidelines on Website ("Manuscript submissions" on right side).
> **Nonfiction:** Proposal with table of contents & 3 chapters from agents only. No phone/fax query; e-query OK.
> **Fiction:** For teens and adults. Proposal/3 chapters.
> ****Note:** This publisher serviced by ChristianManuscriptSubmissions.com.

FATHER'S PRESS, 2424 S.E. 6th St., Lee's Summit MO 64063. Phone/fax (816) 600-6288. E-mail: fatherspress@yahoo.com. Website: www.fatherspress.com. Mike Smitley, owner (mike@father spress.com). Publishes controversial and risky books that present the biblical truth about issues facing Christians and nonbelievers today. Publishes 6-10 titles/yr.; hardcover, trade paperbacks, mass-market paperbacks, coffee-table books. Receives 800-1,000 submissions annually. 50% of books from first-time authors. No mss through agents. No subsidy or print-on-demand. No reprints. Prefers 100 pgs. & up. **Royalty 10-15% on net; no advance.** Average first printing 500. Publication within 6 mos. Considers simultaneous submissions. Accepted mss by disk or e-mail. Responds in 7 days. Prefers KJV. Guidelines by mail/e-mail/Website ("About Us"/scroll down to "Submission Guidelines"); no catalog.
> **Nonfiction:** Query first; proposal/1 chapter; phone/e-query OK.
> **Fiction:** For all ages. Query first; phone/fax/e-query OK.
> **Special Needs:** Books that deal with issues that contribute to the decline of our economy and culture.
> **Photos:** Accepts freelance photos for book covers.
> **Tips:** "We prefer books with strong social, economic, and religious relevance. We like writers with a clear marketing strategy with strong sales leads and endorsements."

FREDERICK FELL PUBLISHERS INC., 2131 Hollywood Blvd., Ste. 305, Hollywood FL 33020. (954) 925-5242. Fax (954) 455-4243. E-mail through Website: www.fellpub.com. Submit to Editorial Dept. General publisher that publishes 2-4 religious titles/yr.; hardcover, trade paperbacks. Receives 4,000 submissions annually. 95% of books from first-time authors. Reprints books. Prefers 60,000 wds. or 200-300 pgs. **Royalty 6-15% on retail; advance $500-10,000.** Average first printing 7,500. Publication within 1 yr. Considers simultaneous submissions. Responds in 5-13 wks. Requires submissions by e-mail. Guidelines on Website ("Submission Guides").

Nonfiction: Proposal/2 chapters; no phone/fax/e-query. Looking for self-help and how-to books. Include a clear marketing and promotional strategy.

Fiction: Complete ms; no phone/fax/e-query. For adults; adventure and historical. "Looking for great storylines, with potential movie prospects."

Tips: "Spirituality, optimism, and a positive attitude have international appeal. Steer clear of doom and gloom; less sadness and more gladness benefits all." Also publishes New Age books. SASE required.

FIRST FRUITS OF ZION, PO Box 649, Marshfield MO 65706-0649. Toll-free (800) 775-4807. (417) 468-2741. Fax (417) 468-2745. E-mail through Website: www.FFOZ.org. Hope Egan, ed. A nonprofit ministry devoted to strengthening the love and appreciation of the Body of Messiah for the land, people, and Scripture of Israel. Publishes 2-6 titles/yr.; trade paperbacks. No mss through agents. **Royalty; no advance.** Publication within 6 mos. Considers simultaneous submissions. Responds in 1 mo. Prefers NASB.

Nonfiction: Query first; no phone/fax/e-query.

Special Needs: Books on Jewish or Hebraic roots only.

Tips: "Be very familiar with our material before submitting to us."

FOCUS ON THE FAMILY BOOK PUBLISHING AND RESOURCE DEVELOPMENT, (street address not required), Colorado Springs CO 80995. (719) 531-3400. Fax (719) 531-3448. E-mail through Website: www.focusonthefamily.com. Exists to support the family; all our products are about topics pertaining to families. Publishes 30-40 titles/yr.; hardcover, trade paperbacks, mass-market paperbacks (rarely). 12% of books from first-time authors. Rarely reprints books. Length depends on genre. **Royalty or work-for-hire; advance varies.** Average first printing varies. Publication within 18 mos. No longer considers unsolicited submissions. Responds in 1-3 mos. Prefers NIV (but accepts 10 others). Guidelines by e-mail/Website; no catalog.

Nonfiction: Query letter only through an agent or writers' conference contact with a Focus editor. "Most open to family advice topics. We look for excellent writing and topics that haven't been done to death—or that have a unique angle."

Fiction: Query letter only through an agent or writers' conference contact with a Focus editor. Stories must incorporate traditional family values or family issues; from 1900 to present day. Also does Mom Lit.

Artwork: Open to queries from freelance artists (but not for specific projects).

****Note:** This publisher serviced by The Writer's Edge and ChristianManuscriptSubmissions.com.

FORDHAM UNIVERSITY PRESS, 2546 Belmont Ave., University Box L, Bronx NY 10458. (718) 817-4795. Fax (718) 817-4785. E-mail: tartar@fordham.edu. Website: www.fordhampress.com. Helen Tartar, ed. dir.; Eric Newman, mng. ed. Publishes for both an academic and general audience; includes religion. Publishes hardcover & trade paperbacks. Reprints books. Guidelines on Website (under "Resources"); catalog.

Nonfiction: Query; no e-query.

FORTRESS PRESS, Box 1209, Minneapolis MN 55440-1209. (612) 330-3300. Fax (612) 330-3215. E-mail: booksub@augsburgfortress.org. Website: www.fortresspress.com. Submit to Book Submissions. Publishes religious academic books. Publishes 60 titles/yr.; hardcover, trade paperbacks. Receives 1,000 submissions annually. 10% of books from first-time authors. Accepts mss through agents or authors. No reprints. **Royalty on net.** Considers simultaneous submissions. Responds in 3 mos. Guidelines on Website ("Contact Us"/"Submission Guidelines"); free catalog (call 1-800-328-4648).

Nonfiction: Query/sample pgs. "Please study guidelines before submitting."

Ethnic Books: African American studies.

FORWARD MOVEMENT, 412 Sycamore St., Cincinnati OH 45202. Toll-free (800) 543-1813. (513) 721-6659. E-mail: rschmidt@forwarddaybyday.com. Website: www.forwardmovement.org. Episcopal. Submit to Editor and Director. Provides resources to support persons in their lives of prayer and faith. Publishes 30 books/yr. and 25 tracts & booklets. Receives 150 submissions annually. 20% of books from first-time authors. No mss through agents. No reprints. Prefers up to 200 pgs. **Onetime honorarium; no advance.** Average first printing 5,000. Publication within 9 mos. Considers simultaneous submissions. Prefers requested ms on disk as an RTF file. Responds in 1 mo. Prefers NRSV. Guidelines by mail/e-mail/Website ("About Us"/"Writers Guidelines"); free catalog.

Nonfiction: Query for book, complete ms if short; phone/e-query OK. "Looking for books on prayer and spirituality, devotionals, Christian living, and spiritual life."

Ethnic Books: African American & Hispanic (pamphlets).

Also Does: Booklets, 4-32 pgs.; pamphlets, 4-8 pgs.; tracts.

Tips: "We sell primarily to a mainline Protestant audience. Most open to books that deal with the central doctrines of the Christian faith. Spirituality and Christian living. We specialize in tracts and pamphlets."

FOUNDERS PRESS, PO Box 150931, Cape Coral FL 33915. (239) 772-1400. Fax (239) 772-1140. E-mail through Website: www.founders.org. Founders Ministries/Southern Baptist. Kenneth Puls, ed. Committed to producing and distributing books, pamphlets, and other materials that are consistent with the doctrines of grace and that speak from a historic Southern Baptist perspective. Responds in 4 mos. (or contact them). Guidelines & catalog on Website. Incomplete topical listings.

Nonfiction: Proposal plus completed author information sheet (available on the Website).

Also Does: Pamphlets.

+@FOUR CRAFTSMEN PUBLISHING, PO Box U, 1293 W. Apache Ln., Lakeside AZ 85929-0585. (928) 367-2076. Fax (928) 367-5223. E-mail: info@fourcraftsmen.com. Website: www.fourcrafts men.com. Cecelia Jackson, chief ed. A very small traditional publisher with an unconventional distribution system, just venturing into e-books; has two lines, one on Tennessee Walking horses and one on explicit Christian teaching. Publishes 1-5 titles/yr.; hard cover, trade paperbacks, and digital. Receives 2-5 submissions annually. 100% of books from first-time authors. Accepts mss through agents or authors. Rarely reprints books. Does print-on-demand. Prefers 40,000-80,000 wds. **Royalty 10-50%; no advance.** Average first printing 500. Publication within 4 mos. No simultaneous submissions. Responds in 3 wks. Prefers NAS, NKJ, NIV. Guidelines by e-mail/Website ("Info for Writers/Photographers"); free catalog.

Nonfiction: Proposal/5 chapters; phone/fax/e-query OK.

Special Needs: New outlooks on healing.

Photos/Artwork: Accepts freelance photos for book covers; open to queries from freelance artists.

Tips: "Experience illuminating Scripture truth and encouraging hope and faith and active participation in walking by/with the Holy Spirit."

FOURSQUARE MEDIA, 1910 W. Sunset Blvd., Ste. 200, Los Angeles CA 90026-0176. (213) 989-4494. E-mail: media@foursquare.org or through Website: www.foursquare.org/landing_pages/83,3 .html. The Foursquare Church; in partnership with Creation House (Strang Communications). Rick Wulfestieg, dir.; Larry Libby, sr. ed. To capture Foursquare history, vision, and values; for cell study groups, church ministry institutes, and pastoral-led congregational studies. Publishes 4+ titles/yr.

Nonfiction: E-query.

Also Does: Will host writers' conferences in the future to encourage ministry leaders in developing writing and publishing skills.

FRESH AIR BOOKS, PO Box 340004, Nashville TN 37203-0004. E-mail through Website: www .freshairbooks.org. Imprint of Upper Room Books. Submit to Acquisitions Editor. Books that inspire readers to explore Christian faith in a fresh, experimental way. Accepts mss through agents or author. **Royalty.** Guidelines on Website (scroll to bottom "Writers Guidelines"). Incomplete topical listings.

Nonfiction: Proposal/1 chapter by mail; no e-query.

Tips: "Rather than telling readers what to do, our books show the way, mostly through stories of people who live out authentic, compassionate faith in the real world. We believe that faith influences everything we do, and therefore, we consider manuscripts that address most areas of life. Currently we do not publish fiction or poetry, nor do we publish scholarly or academic works."

FRIENDS UNITED PRESS, 101 Quaker Hill Dr., Richmond IN 47374. (765) 962-7573. Fax (765) 966-1293. E-mail: friendspress@fum.org. Website: www.fum.org/shop. Friends United Meeting (Quaker). Katie Terrell, ed. To gather persons into a fellowship where Jesus Christ is known as Lord and Teacher. Publishes 3 titles/yr. Receives 25 submissions annually. 50% of books from first-time authors. No mss through agents. Does print-on-demand. Prefers 150-200 pgs. **Royalty 7.5% of net; no advance.** Publication within 1 yr. Considers simultaneous submissions; e-mail submissions preferred. Responds in 6 mos. Prefers requested ms by e-mail. Guidelines by mail/e-mail/Website; free catalog.

Nonfiction: Proposal/2 chapters; e-query preferred.

Ethnic Books: Howard Thurman Books (African American), Underground Railroad.

Tips: "Primarily open to Quaker authors. Looking for Quaker-related spirituality, or current faith issues/practice addressed from a Christian Quaker experience or practice."

**Note: Accepting no freelance submissions during 2011.

GENTLE PATH PRESS, PO Box 3172, Carefree AZ 85377. Toll-free (800) 708-1796. (480) 488-9303. E-mail: info@gentlepath.com or through Website: www.GentlePath.com. Attn: Submissions. Focuses on addiction and recovery from both a secular and spiritual point of view. Imprints: Gentle Path Press, Seasons of Hope. Publishes 2-5 titles/yr.; hardcover, trade paperbacks. Receives 6-12 submissions annually. 75% of books from first-time authors. Accepts mss through agents or authors. No subsidy or print-on-demand. No reprints. Prefers 200-350 pgs. **Royalty 8-12% of net; no advance.** Average first printing 2,000-5,000. Publication within 6 mos. Considers simultaneous submissions. Responds in 120 days. Guidelines by e-mail/Website ("About Us"); free catalog.

Nonfiction: Proposal/3 chapters or complete ms; no phone/fax/e-query.

Special Needs: "Good material on recovery (personal experience OK). Also spirituality, family issues, women's issues, and grief."

GEORGETOWN UNIVERSITY PRESS, 3240 Prospect St. N.W., Washington DC 20007. (202) 687-5889. Fax (202) 687-6340. E-mail: reb7@georgetown.edu or gupress@georgetown.edu. Website: www.press.georgetown.edu. Georgetown University. Richard Brown, dir. Scholarly books in religion, theology, ethics, and other fields, with an emphasis on cross-disciplinary and cross-cultural studies. Publishes 10 titles/yr. Receives 100 submissions annually. 10% of books from first-time authors. Accepts mss through agents or authors. No reprints. Prefers 80,000 wds. **Royalty 8-12% on net; negotiable advance.** Average first printing 2,000-3,000. Publication within 9-10 mos. Considers simultaneous submissions. Requires requested ms on disk. Responds in 6-8 wks. Prefers NRSV. Does print-on-demand. Guidelines on Website (scroll to bottom "Publishing with GUP"); free catalog.

Nonfiction: Guidelines for submitting a proposal are posted on Website. "Should be thoroughly researched and original."

Special Needs: Work relations, theology, ethics—with scholarly bent.

Ethnic Books: Hispanic.

Also Does: CD-ROMs.

Photos: Accepts freelance photos for book covers.

GOOD BOOK PUBLISHING COMPANY, PO Box 837, Kihei HI 96753-0837. Phone/fax (808) 874-4876. E-mail: dickb@dickb.com. Website: www.dickb.com/index.shtml. Christian/Protestant/ Bible Fellowship. Ken Burns, pres. Researches and publishes books on the biblical/Christian roots of Alcoholics Anonymous. Publishes 1 title/yr.; publishes trade paperbacks, mass-market paperbacks. Receives 8 submissions annually. 80% of books from first-time authors. No mss through agents. Reprints books. Prefers 250 pgs. **Royalty 10%; no advance.** Average first printing 3,000. Publication within 2 mos. Considers simultaneous submissions. Responds in 1 wk. No disk. Prefers KJV. No guidelines; free catalog.

> **Nonfiction:** Proposal; no phone/fax/e-query. Books on the spiritual history and success of AA; 12-step spiritual roots; Bible study.
> **Also Does:** Pamphlets, booklets.

GOSPEL LIGHT, 1957 Eastman Ave., Ventura CA 93003. Toll-free (800) 4-GOSPEL. (805) 644-9721, ext. 1223. Website: www.gospellight.com. Anita Griggs, ed. Accepts proposals for Sunday school and Vacation Bible School curriculum and related resources for children from birth through the preteen years; also teacher resources. Guidelines on Website (scroll to bottom "Submissions").

> **Also Does:** Sometimes has openings for readers of new curriculum projects. See Website for how to apply.
> **Tips:** "All our curriculum is written and field-tested by experienced teachers; most of our writers are on staff."
> ****Note:** This publisher serviced by ChristianManuscriptSubmissions.com.

GOSPEL PUBLISHING HOUSE, 1445 N. Boonville Ave., Springfield MO 65802. Toll-free (800) 641-4310. (417) 831-8000. E-mail: newproducts@gph.org. Website: www.gospelpublishing .com. Assemblies of God. Julie Horner, research & development dir. The majority of titles specifically address Pentecostal audiences in a variety of ministries in the local church. Publishes 5-10 titles/yr. Receives 250 submissions annually. 5% of books from first-time authors. Accepts mss through agents or authors. No reprints. **Royalty 5-10% of retail; no advance.** Average first printing 2,000. Publication within 1 yr. Considers simultaneous submissions. Responds in 4 mos. Requires accepted mss on disk or by e-mail. Guidelines on Website (scroll to bottom "Writers Guides"); free catalog.

> **Nonfiction:** Proposal/1 chapter; no phone query, e-query OK. "Looking for Holy Spirit; Pentecostal focus for pastors, local church lay leaders, and individuals; children's ministry programs and resources; small group resources."
> **Tips:** "Most open to a new program or resource for small groups, children's ministry, compassion ministry, or evangelistic outreach, written by someone who is actively leading it at the local church."

GROUP PUBLISHING INC., 1515 Cascade Ave., Loveland CO 80539-0481. Toll-free (800) 447-1070. (970) 292-4243. Fax (970) 622-4370. E-mail: kloesche@group.com. Website: www.group .com. Nondenominational. Kerri Loesche, contract & copyright administrator. Imprint: Group Books. To equip churches to help children, youth, and adults grow in their relationship with Jesus. Publishes 65 titles/yr.; trade paperbacks. Receives 1,000+ submissions annually. 5% of books from first-time authors. Accepts mss through agents or authors. Some subsidy. No reprints. Prefers 128-250 pgs. **Outright purchases of $25-3,000 or royalty of 8-10% of net; advance $3,000.** Average first printing 5,000. Publication within 12-18 mos. Considers simultaneous submissions. Responds in 6 mos. Requires requested ms in Word or by e-mail. Prefers NLT. Guidelines by mail (2 stamps)/e-mail/Website; catalog.

> **Nonfiction:** Query or proposal/2 chapters/intro/cover letter/SASE; no phone/fax query; e-query OK. "Looking for practical ministry tools for youth workers, C. E. directors, and teachers with an emphasis on active learning."

Artwork: Open to queries from freelance artists.

Tips: "Most open to a practical resource that will help church leaders change lives; innovative, active/interactive learning. Tell our readers something they don't already know, in a way that they've not seen before."

**Note: This publisher serviced by The Writer's Edge and ChristianManuscriptSubmissions.com.

GRQ INC., PO Box 1067, Brentwood TN 37024. (615) 776-3275. Fax (615) 507-1709. E-mail: rzaloba@comcast.net. Robert Zaloba, pres. A book packager. Publishes 40-50 titles/yr.; hardcover, trade paperbacks, coffee-table books. 70% of books from first-time authors. **Does mostly work-for-hire; rates depend on project; ranges from $1,500-$20,000; advance.** Average first printing varies, 10,000-50,000. Publication within 10 mos. Requires accepted ms on disk. No guidelines or catalog.

Nonfiction: Query only first; no phone/fax query; e-query OK.

Tips: "We are a book packager who produces books that speak to the Christian market at large. Our books are found outside of the traditional CBA market. They are uniquely formatted and targeted for an 'average' reader. Most open to practical, unique self-help; unique devotions."

GRUPO NELSON, PO Box 141000, Nashville TN 37214. Toll-free (800) 322-7423. (615) 902-2372/2375. Fax (615) 883-9376. E-mail: storres@thomasnelson.com. Website: www.gruponelson.com. Thomas Nelson has reformed its Spanish division into Grupo Nelson, with five Spanish-language imprints listed below. Larry Downs, VP/Publisher. Targets the needs and wants of the Hispanic community. Publishes 65-80 titles/yr. Receives 50 submissions annually. 90% of books from first-time authors. No mss through agents. Prefers 192 pgs. **Royalty on net; advance $500.** Average first printing 4,000. Publication within 15 mos. Accepts e-mail submissions. No guidelines; free catalog.

Nonfiction: Query letter only; no phone/fax/e-query.

Ethnic Books: Hispanic imprints.

Also Does: Computer games.

Tips: "Most open to Christian books based on the Bible."

Editorial Diez Puntos: Specializes in parenting & family, personal finance, health and fitness, self-help, and popular culture.

Leader Latino: Business & leadership.

Editorial Caribe: Bibles, Bible reference, and electronic products.

Editorial Betania: Inspirational, popular religious, and children's.

Editorial Catolica: Catholic books and Bibles.

@GUARDIAN ANGEL PUBLISHING INC., 12430 Tesson Ferry Rd., #186, St. Louis MO 63128. (314) 276-8482. Fax (314) 843-8517. E-mail: publisher@guardianangelpublishing.com. Website: www.guardianangelpublishing.com. Lynda S. Burch, pub. Goal is to inspire children to learn and grow and develop character skills to instill a Christian and healthy attitude of learning, caring, and sharing. Imprints: Wings of Faith, Angel to Angel, Angelic Harmony, Littlest Angels, Academic Wings, Guardian Angel Pets, Guardian Angel Health & Hygiene. Publishes 24-36 titles/yr.; trade paperbacks. Receives 300-600 submissions annually. 75% of books from first-time authors. No subsidy; does print-on-demand. Prefers 100-5,000 wds. or 32 pgs. **Royalty 30-50% on download; no advance.** Average first printing 50-100. Print books are wholesaled and distributed; e-books are sold through many distribution networks. Publication within 12 mos. No simultaneous submissions. Responds in 1 wk.-1 mo. Accepted mss by e-mail only. Guidelines on Website ("Submissions" on left side); catalog as e-book PDF.

Nonfiction: Complete ms; no phone/fax query; e-query OK. "Looking for all kinds of kids' books."

Fiction: Complete ms; no phone/fax query; e-query OK.

Also Does: E-books.

Photos/Artwork: Accepts freelance photos for book covers; open to queries from freelance artists.

Contest: Sponsors children's writing contest for schools.

Tips: "Most open to books that teach children to read and love books; to learn or grow from books."

GUERNICA EDITIONS, 489 Strathmore Blvd., Toronto ON M4C 1N8, Canada. E-mail through Website: www.guernicaeditions.com. Antonio D'Alfonso, ed. Deals with cultural bridging; interested in the next generation of writers. Publishes 1 religious title/yr.; trade paperbacks, mass-market paperbacks. Receives 100 submissions annually. 5% of books from first-time authors. No mss through agents. Reprints books. Prefers 100 pgs. **Royalty 8-10% of retail; some outright purchases of $200-5,000; advance $200-2,000.** Average first printing 1,500. Publication within 10 mos. Responds in 1-6 mos. Requires requested ms on disk; no e-mail. No guidelines (read one of our books to see what we like); catalog online.

> **Nonfiction:** Query only first by mail; no phone/fax/e-query. "Looking for books on world issues."
>
> **Fiction:** Query only first by mail. "Looking for short and profound literary works."
>
> **Ethnic Books:** Concentration on other cultures. "We are involved in translations and ethnic issues."
>
> **Photos:** Accepts freelance photos for book covers.
>
> **Tips:** "Know what we publish. We're interested in books that bridge time and space; works that fit our editorial literary policies." Responds only if you include International Reply Coupons.

GUIDEPOSTS BOOKS, 16 E. 34th St., 12th Fl., New York NY 10016-4397. (212) 251-8143. Website: www.guidepostsbooks.com. Guideposts Inc. Linda Raglan Cunningham, VP/ed-in-chief; Andrew Attaway, sr. acq. ed. Focuses on inspirational fiction, memoirs, story collections, devotionals, and faith-based true stories. Publishes 20 titles/yr.

> ****Note:** This publisher serviced by ChristianManuscriptSubmissions.com.

HANNIBAL BOOKS, PO Box 461592, Garland TX 75046-1592. Toll-free (800) 747-0738. Toll-free fax (888) 252-3022. E-mail: hannibalbooks@earthlink.net. Website: www.hannibalbooks .com. KLMK Communications Inc. Louis Moore, pub. Evangelical Christian publisher specializing in missions, marriage and family, critical issues, and Bible-study curriculum. Publishes 8-10 titles/yr.; trade paperbacks, mass-market paperbacks. Receives 300 submissions annually. 80% of books from first-time authors. Accepts mss from authors only. Some print-on-demand. Prefers 50,000-60,000 wds. **Royalty on net or outright purchase; no advance.** Average first printing 2,000-10,000. Publication within 3 mos. No simultaneous submissions. Responds in 3 mos. Prefers NIV. Guidelines on Website ("Become an Author"/ "Writers Guidelines"); free catalog by mail.

> **Nonfiction:** Book proposal/1-3 chapters; no phone/fax/e-query. "Looking for missionary, marriage restoration, homeschooling, and devotionals."
>
> **Fiction:** Book proposal/1-3 chapters; no phone/fax/e-query.
>
> **Tips:** "We are looking for go-get-'em new authors with a passion to be published. Most open to missionary life and Bible studies. Obtain our guidelines and answer each question thoroughly."

+HARBOURLIGHT BOOKS, PO Box 1738, Aztec NM 87410. E-mail: inquiry@harbourlightbooks .com. Website: www.harbourlightbooks.com. Division of Pelican Ventures, LLC. Christian fiction 25,000-80,000 wds. Action-adventure, mystery (cozy or other), suspense, crime drama, police procedural, speculative, sci-fi, futuristic, family saga, westerns, women's fiction. E-mail submissions only; see Website for submission form and procedure.

HARPERONE, 353 Sacramento St., #500, San Francisco CA 94111-3653. (415) 477-4400. Fax (415) 477-4444. E-mail: hcsanfrancisco@harpercollins.com. Website: www.harpercollins.com. Religious division of HarperCollins. Michael G. Maudlin, ed. dir. Strives to be the preeminent publisher of the most important books across the full spectrum of religion and spiritual literature, adding to the wealth of the world's wisdom by respecting all traditions and favoring none; emphasis on quality Christian spirituality and literary fiction. Publishes 75 titles/yr.; hardcover, trade paperbacks. Receives 10,000 submissions annually. 5% of books from first-time authors. Requires mss through agents. No reprints. Prefers 160-256 pgs. **Royalty 7.5-15% on retail; advance $20,000-100,000.** Average first printing 10,000. Publication within 18 mos. Considers simultaneous submissions. Responds in 3 mos. Requires requested ms on disk. Guidelines on Website ("About Us"/"Manuscript Submissions"); catalog.

   Nonfiction: Proposal/1 chapter; fax query OK.
   Fiction: Complete ms; contemporary adult fiction, literary, fables & parables, spiritual.
   Tips: "Agented proposals only."

HARRISON HOUSE PUBLISHERS, Box 35035, Tulsa OK 74153. Toll-free (800) 888-4126. (918) 523-5400. E-mail: customerservice@harrisonhouse.com. Website: www.harrisonhouse.com. Evangelical/charismatic. Julie Lechlider, mng. ed. To challenge Christians to live victoriously, grow spiritually, and know God intimately. Publishes 20 titles/yr.; hardcover, trade paperbacks, mass-market paperbacks. 5% of books from first-time authors. No mss through agents. No reprints. **Royalty on net or retail; no advance.** Average first printing 5,000. Publication within 12-24 mos. Responds in 6 mos. Accepts requested ms by e-mail. No guidelines or catalog. Not currently accepting any proposals or manuscripts.

   Nonfiction: Query first; then proposal/table of contents/1 chapter; no phone/fax query; e-query OK.
   **Note: This publisher serviced by ChristianManuscriptSubmissions.com.

HARVEST HOUSE PUBLISHERS, 990 Owen Loop N., Eugene OR 97402. (541) 343-0123. E-mail: admin@harvesthousepublishers.com. Website: www.harvesthousepublishers.com. Evangelical. Books and products that affirm biblical values and help people grow spiritually strong. Publishes 170 titles/yr.; hardcover, trade paperbacks, mass-market paperbacks, gift books. No longer accepting unsolicited submissions, proposals, queries, etc. Requires mss through agents. No guidelines/catalog.

   Nonfiction: Self-help; Christian living.
   Fiction: Historical romance.
   Tips: "Find a good agent."
   **Note: This publisher serviced by The Writer's Edge and ChristianManuscriptSubmissions.com.

HAY HOUSE INC., PO Box 5100, Carlsbad CA 92018-5100. (760) 431-7695. Fax (760) 431-6948. E-mail:editorial@hayhouse.com. Website: www.hayhouse.com. Jill Kramer, ed. dir.; Alex Freemon, submissions ed. Books to help heal the planet. Publishes 1 religious title/yr.; hardcover, trade paperbacks. Receives 50 religious submissions annually. 5% of books from first-time authors. Accepts mss through agents only. Prefers 70,000 wds. or 250 pgs. **Royalty.** Average first printing 5,000. Publication within 12-15 mos. Considers simultaneous submissions. Responds in 1-2 mos. Guidelines (www.hayhouse.com/guides.php).

   Nonfiction: Proposal/3 chapters. "Looking for self-help/spiritual with a unique ecumenical angle."
   Tips: "We are looking for books with a unique slant, ecumenical, but not overly religious. We want an open-minded approach." Includes a broad range of religious titles, including New Age.

HEALTH COMMUNICATIONS INC., 3201 S.W. 15th St., Deerfield Beach FL 33442. Toll-free (800) 441-5569. (954) 360-0909 (no phone calls). Fax (954) 360-0034. Website: www.hci-online.com or www.hcibooks.com. Submit to Editorial Committee. Nonfiction that emphasizes self-improvement, personal motivation, psychological health, and overall wellness; recovery/addiction, self-help/ psychology, soul/spirituality, inspiration, women's issues, relationships, and family. Imprint: HCI Teens. Publishes 50 titles/yr.; hard cover, trade paperbacks. 20% of books from first-time authors. Accepts mss through agents or authors. Prefers 250 pgs. **Royalty 15% of net.** Publication within 9 mos. Considers simultaneous submissions. Responds in 3 mos. Follow guidelines for submission. Guidelines on Website (scroll to bottom "Submissions"); catalog for 9 x 12 SASE.

Nonfiction: Query/outline and 2 chapters; no phone/fax/e-query. Needs books for Christian teens.

HEART OF WISDOM PUBLISHERS, 299 Coble Rd., Shelbyville TN 37160-6353. E-mail: info@ heartofwisdom.com or through Website: www.heartofwisdom.com. Publishes a variety of academic materials to help Christian families bring up children with a heart's desire for and knowledge of the Lord. Robin Sampson, ed. Query only. Guidelines on Website.

Special Needs: Currently accepting queries for high-quality history, science, and life skills unit studies for grades 4-12. Not accepting any other titles.

Tips: "We market to home educators and Christian schools."

HEARTSONG PRESENTS, Imprint of Barbour Publishing Inc., PO Box 721, 1810 Barbour Dr., Uhrichsville, OH 44683. E-mail: fictionsubmit@barbourbooks.com. Website: www.heartsongpre sents.com. JoAnne Simmons, ed. Produces affordable, wholesome entertainment through a book club that also helps to enhance and spread the gospel. Publishes 52 titles/yr.; mass-market paperbacks. Receives 1,000 submissions annually. 10% of books from first-time authors. Accepts mss through agents or authors. Prefers 45,000-50,000 wds. **Royalty 8% of net; advance $2,200.** Average first printing 20,000. Publication within 1 yr. Considers simultaneous submissions. Responds in 6-12 mos. Requires electronic submissions; no proposals via regular mail. Prefers KJV for historicals; NIV for contemporary. Guidelines by mail/e-mail; no catalog.

Fiction: Proposal/3 chapters; electronic submissions only (fictionsubmit@barbourbooks.com). Adult. "We publish 2 contemporary and 2 historical romances every 4 weeks. We cover all topics and settings. Specific guidelines available."

Tips: "Romance only, with a strong conservative-Christian theme. Read our books and study our style before submitting."

**Note: This publisher serviced by The Writer's Edge.

HEARTSONG PRESENTS/MYSTERIES, Imprint of Barbour Publishing Inc., PO Box 719, 1810 Barbour Dr., Uhrichsville, OH 44683. (740) 922-6045. Fax (740) 922-5948. E-mail: acquisitions@bar bourbooks.com. Website: www.barbourbooks.com. Editor's blog: www.editcafe.blogspot.com. JoAnne Simmons, acq. ed. Produces affordable, wholesome entertainment through a book club that also helps to enhance and spread the gospel. Publishes 32 titles/yr.; mass-market paperbacks. 25% of books from first-time authors. Accepts mss through agents or authors. No subsidy. Prefers 45,000-50,000 wds. **Royalty or outright purchase; pays an advance.** Average first printing 15,000-20,000. Publication within 9-12 mos. Considers simultaneous submissions. Responds in 3-6 mos. Accepts mss by e-mail. Guidelines by mail/e-mail/Website ("Contact Us"/"How do I submit my manuscript for publishing?").

Fiction: Proposal/3 chapters; no phone/fax query; e-query OK. Accepts only cozy mysteries with a romance plot thread.

Tips: "Cozy mysteries should feature an amateur sleuth in a setting that has a small-town 'feel.' The inciting crime should occur in the first chapter or two so the majority of the plot focuses on solving the 'whodunit' of the mystery. Study our specific guidelines thoroughly prior to proposal submission."

**Note: This publisher serviced by The Writer's Edge.

HEARTSPRING PUBLISHING, 223 W. Third St. (64801), PO Box 1132, Joplin MO 64802. Toll-free (800) 289-3300. (417) 623-6280. Fax (417) 623-8250. E-mail through Website: www.college

press.com. Christian Church/Church of Christ. Submit to Acquisitions Editor. Nonacademic imprint of College Press Publishing Co. Publishes 15-20 titles/yr.; trade paperbacks. Receives 700 submissions annually. 25% of books from first-time authors. Accepts mss through agents or authors. Reprints books. Prefers 250-300 pgs. **Royalty 5-15% of net; no advance.** Average first printing 3,000. Publication within 6 mos. Considers simultaneous submissions. Requires requested ms on disk; no e-mail submissions. Responds in 2-3 mos. Prefers NIV, NASB, NAS. Guidelines ("For Authors"/"Publishing Guidelines") & catalog on Website.

Nonfiction: Query first, then proposal/2-3 chapters; no phone/fax query.

Fiction: Christian fiction.

HENDRICKSON PUBLISHERS, 140 Summit St., PO Box 3473, Peabody MA 01961-3473. (978) 573-2276. Fax (978) 573-8276. E-mail: editorial@hendrickson.com. Website: www.hendrickson .com. No longer open to any freelance submissions.

HENSLEY PUBLISHING, 6116 E. 32nd St., Tulsa OK 74135. (918) 664-8520. Fax (918) 664-8562. E-mail: editorial@hensleypublishing.com. Website: www.hensleypublishing.com. Terri Kalfas, dir. of publishing. Goal is to get people studying the Bible instead of just reading books about the Bible; Bible study only. Publishes 5-10 titles/yr.; trade paperbacks. Receives 800 submissions annually. 50% of books from first-time authors. No mss through agents. No reprints. **Royalty on net; some outright purchases; no advance.** Average first printing 2,500. Publication within 12-18 mos. Considers simultaneous submissions. Requires requested ms in MAC format. Responds in 2 mos. Guidelines ("Writers' Corner") & catalog on Website.

Nonfiction: Query first, then proposal/first 3 chapters; no phone/fax query. "Looking for Bible studies of varying length for use by small or large groups, or individuals."

**Note: This publisher serviced by The Writer's Edge.

HIDDEN BROOK PRESS, 109 Bayshore Rd., RR #4, Brighton ON K0K 1H0, Canada. (613) 475-2368. E-mail: writers@hiddenbrookpress.com. Website: www.hiddenbrookpress.com. Richard M. Grove, ed./pub. Imprints: Hidden Brook Press, Arc Communications. Does hardcover, trade paperbacks, coffee-table books. Receives 1,000 submissions annually. 98% of books from first-time authors. Accepts mss through agents or authors. Does subsidy and print-on-demand, as well as royalty contracts. Reprints books. **Royalty on retail or net; no advance.** Average first printing 50-5,000. Accepts simultaneous submissions. Guidelines by e-mail/Website (scroll down to "Hidden Brook Submission Guidelines").

Nonfiction/Fiction: E-query or e-submissions. All topics; all genres.

HIS WORK CHRISTIAN PUBLISHING, PO Box 5732, Ketchikan AK 99901. (206) 274-8474. Fax (614) 388-0664. E-mail: editor@hisworkpub.com, or through Website: www.hisworkpub.com. Angela J. Perez, acq. ed. Books that glorify and honor God. Publishes 4-8 titles/yr.; hardcover, trade paperbacks, electronic. Receives 100+ submissions annually. 95% of books from first-time authors. Accepts mss through agents or authors. Reprints books. **Royalty 10-20% on net.** Publication within 2 yrs. Considers simultaneous submissions. Responds in 1-3 mos. Guidelines (under "Submissions")/ current needs/catalog on Website.

Nonfiction: Query with marketing proposal/3 chapters.

Fiction: Religious fiction. Query with marketing proposal/3 chapters.

Tips: "We accept no queries or submissions by e-mail."

HOPE PUBLISHING HOUSE, PO Box 60008, Pasadena CA 91106. (626) 792-6123. Fax (626) 792-2121. E-mail: hopepublishinghouse@gmail.com. Website: www.hope-pub.com. Southern California Ecumenical Council. Faith A. Sand, pub. Produces thinking books that challenge the faith community to be serious about their pilgrimage of faith. Imprint: New Paradigm Books. Publishes 6 titles/ yr. Receives 40 submissions annually. 30% of books from first-time authors. No mss through agents.

Reprints books. Prefers 200 pgs. **Royalty 10% on net; no advance.** Average first printing 3,000. Publication within 6 mos. No simultaneous submissions. Accepts mss by disk or e-mail. Responds in 3 mos. Prefers NRSV. No guidelines; catalog for 7 x 10 SAE/4 stamps.

Nonfiction: Query only first; no phone/fax query; e-query OK.

Tips: "Most open to a well-written manuscript, with correct grammar, that is provocative, original, challenging, and informative."

HOURGLASS BOOKS, 387 Northgate Rd., Lindenhurst IL 60046. E-mail: editor@hourglassbooks .org. Website: www.hourglassbooks.org/submissions.html. Gina Frangello & Molly McQuade, eds. Publishes anthologies of short stories assembled around a common theme. Accepts simultaneous submissions & reprints. **Shared royalties for contributors to the anthologies.** Guidelines on Website indicated above.

Fiction: Submit by e-mail (copied into message). Literary fiction only. Currently working on Occupational Hazards: Stories from the World of Work. No word limits, or fixed closing dates.

HOWARD BOOKS, 216 Centreville Dr., Ste. 303, Brentwood TN 37027-3226. (615) 873-2080. E-mail through Website: http://christian.simonandschuster.com/howard. Becky Nesbitt, vp & ed.-in-chief; submit to Manuscript Review Committee. A division of Simon & Schuster Inc. Publishes 65 titles/yr.; hardcover, trade paperbacks. Receives 1,000 submissions annually. 5% of books from first-time authors. Prefers 200-250 pgs. **Negotiable royalty & advance.** Average first printing 10,000. Publication within 16 mos. Considers simultaneous submissions. Accepted ms by e-mail. Responds in 6-8 mos. No disk. Prefers NIV. Guidelines on Website (scroll to bottom of page/click on "Divisions & Imprints"/click on Howard Books logo/"Author Resources"/"Manuscript Submission"); catalog.

Nonfiction: Accepting queries by e-mail from agents only.

Fiction: Proposal/3 chapters from agents only. Adult.

Tips: "Our authors must first be Christ-centered in their lives and writing, then qualified to write on the subject of choice. Public name recognition is a plus. Authors who are also public speakers usually have a ready-made audience."

**Note: This publisher serviced by The Writer's Edge and ChristianManuscriptSubmissions.com.

IDEALS PUBLICATIONS, 2636 Elm Hill Pike, Ste. 120, Nashville TN 37214. E-mail: pjay@guide posts.org. Website: www.idealsbooks.com. A Guideposts company. Peggy Schaefer, pub. Not currently accepting unsolicited mss.

+INHERITANCE PRESS, LLC, PO Box 950477, Lake Mary FL 32795. (407) 474-0483. E-mail: submissions@inheritancepress.com. Website: www.inheritancepress.com. Independent publisher. Monique Donahue, ed. **No advance.** Responds in 60 days. Guidelines on Website ("Submissions"). Incomplete topical listings.

Nonfiction: Proposal by mail or e-mail; no phone query.

INKLING BOOKS, 6528 Phinney Ave. N., Seattle WA 98103. (206) 365-1624. E-mail: editor@ inklingbooks.com. Website: www.InklingBooks.com. Michael W. Perry, pub. Publishes 6 titles/ yr.; hardcover, trade paperbacks. No mss through agents. Reprints books. Prefers 150-400 pgs. **No advance.** Print-on-demand. Publication within 2 mos. No guidelines or catalog. Not currently accepting submissions.

INTERNATIONAL AWAKENING PRESS, 139 N. Washington (60187), PO Box 232, Wheaton IL 60189-0232. (630) 653-8616. E-mail: info@internationalawakening.org. Website: www.interna tionalawakening.org. Intl. Awakening Ministries Inc. Richard Owen Roberts, ed./pres. Scholarly books on religious awakenings or revivals. Publishes 4 titles/yr. Receives 12 submissions annually. Reprints books. **Royalty negotiated; no advance.** Average first printing 3,000. Publication within 6 mos. Responds in 3 mos. Prefers requested ms on disk. Any translation; no paraphrases. No guidelines; free catalog.

Nonfiction: Query only; no phone/fax/e-query. "Looking for scholarly theology, especially Bible commentaries, church history, and revival-related material."
Also Does: Booklets, pamphlets, tracts.
Photos: Accepts freelance photos for book covers.
Tips: "Most open to scholarly books."

@INTERVARSITY PRESS, Box 1400, Downers Grove IL 60515-1426. Receptionist: (630) 734-4000. Fax (630) 734-4200. E-mail: email@ivpress.com. Website: www.ivpress.com. InterVarsity Christian Fellowship. Andrew T. LePeau, ed. dir.; submit to General Book Editor or Academic Editor. IVP books are characterized by a thoughtful, biblical approach to the Christian life that transforms the hearts, souls, and minds of readers in the university, church, and the world, on topics ranging from spiritual disciplines to apologetics, to current issues, to theology. Imprints: IVP Academic (Gary Deddo, ed.), IVP Connect (Cindy Bunch, ed.), IVP Books (Al Hsu, ed.). Publishes 110-120 titles/yr.; hardcover, trade paperbacks, mass-market paperbacks. Receives 1,300 submissions annually. 15% of books from first-time authors. Accepts mss through agents or authors. Reprints books. Prefers 50,000 wds. or 200 pgs. **Negotiable royalty on retail or outright purchase; negotiable advance.** Average first printing 5,000. Publication within 12 mos. Considers simultaneous submissions. Responds in 3 mos. Prefers NIV, NRSV. Accepts e-mail submissions after acceptance. Guidelines on Website (scroll to bottom "Submissions"); catalog for 9 x 12 SAE/5 stamps.
Nonfiction: Query only first, with detailed letter according to submissions guidelines, then proposal with 2 chapters; no phone/fax/e-query.
Ethnic Books: Especially looking for ethnic writers (African American, Hispanic, Asian American).
Also Does: Booklets, 5,000 wds.; e-books.
Blogs: www.ivpress.com/blogs/behindthebooks; www.ivpress.com/blogs/andyunedited; www.ivpress.com/blogs/addenda-errata.
Tips: "Most open to books written by pastors (though not collections of sermons) or other church staff, by professors, by leaders in Christian organizations. Authors need to bring resources for publicizing and selling their own books, such as a Website, an organization they are part of that will promote their books, speaking engagements, well-known people they know personally who will endorse and promote their book, writing articles for national publication, etc."
**Note: This publisher serviced by The Writer's Edge and ChristianManuscriptSubmissions.com.

@JEBAIRE PUBLISHING, PO Box 843, Snellville GA 30078-0843. (678) 325-1183. E-mail: info@jebairepublishing.com. Website: www.jebairepublishing.com. Shannon Clark, ed-in-chief. Our mission is "to give gifted writers a voice and hungry souls a full meal." Publishes 4-6 titles/yr.; trade paperbacks, e-books. 75% of books from first-time authors. No mss through agents. No subsidy, print-on-demand, or reprints. Prefers 35,000-60,000 wds. **Royalty 12-15% on net; no advance.** Average first printing 1,000. Publication within 12-15 mos. Considers simultaneous submissions. Responds in 6-8 weeks (to proposals). Requires accepted mss on disk or by e-mail. Guidelines by mail/e-mail; no catalog.
Nonfiction: E-query only first; do not send sample chapters by e-mail unless requested.
Photos/Artwork: Accepts freelance photos for book covers; open to queries from freelance artists.
Tips: "We look for writers who have an 'approachable' writing style. We want our readers to feel uplifted and encouraged rather than 'talked down to' or discouraged."

JESUS FILLED DAY PUBLISHING, PO Box 34, Houston TX 77001. (281) 399-4011. Fax (281) 399-3840. E-mail: team@haveajesusfilledday.com. Website: www.haveajesusfilledday.com. Ann

Chapman, VP. Publishes 1 title every 2 yrs.; trade paperback. Receives no submissions. No mss through agents. No reprints.

Nonfiction: Query first; no phone/fax/e-query.

JOURNEYFORTH/BJU PRESS, 1700 Wade Hampton Blvd., Greenville SC 29614. (864) 370-1800. Fax (864) 298-0268, ext. 4324. E-mail: jb@bju.edu. Website: www.bjupress.com. Bob Jones University Press. Nancy Lohr, youth ed.; Suzette Jordan, adult ed. Our goal is to publish excellent, trustworthy books for children and Christian-living titles for adults. Publishes 15-25 titles/yr.; hardcover, trade paperbacks. Receives 500 submissions annually (100 Christian living/400 youth novels). 10% of books from first-time authors. Accepts mss through agents or authors. **Royalty.** Average first printing varies. Publication within 12-18 mos. Considers simultaneous submissions. No submissions by disk or e-mail. Responds in 8-12 wks. Requires KJV. Guidelines by mail/e-mail; free catalog.

Nonfiction: Proposal/3-5 chapters; e-query OK.

Fiction: Proposal/5 chapters or complete ms. For children & teens. "Fiction must have a Christian worldview."

Artwork: Open to queries from freelance artists.

Tips: "The pre-college, homeschool market welcomes print-rich, well-written novels. No picture books, please, but compelling novels for early readers are always good for us, as are biographies on the lives of Christian heroes and statesmen. We focus on conservative biblical books for all ages that will help to develop skill with the written word as well as discernment as a believer; we complement the educational goals of BJU Press, our K-12 textbook division."
**Note: This publisher serviced by The Writer's Edge.

JOURNEY STONE CREATIONS, 3533 Danbury Rd., Fairfield OH 45014. (513) 860-0176. E-mail: pat@jscbooks.com. Website: www.jscbooks.com. Not currently accepting submissions; check Website for current status.

@JUBILANT PRESS: An Electronic & Print Publisher, PO Box 6421, Longmont CO 80501. E-mail: jubilantpress@aol.com. Website: www.JubilantPress.com. Supports Right to the Heart Ministries. Linda Shepherd & Rebekah Montgomery, pubs. Publishes downloadable e-books with instant information to change your life. Publishes 10 e-titles/yr., plus 1 print bk. Acquires print & e-books by invitation only. 0% of books from first-time authors. Accepts mss through agents or authors. Reprints books. Prefers 20-100 pgs. **Pays for the right to publish, plus a percentage of author's online sales (author must have an active Web page); variable advance.** Publication within 6 mos. Prefers NIV. Guidelines provided for specific projects.

Nonfiction: Brief e-mail query only; no phone/fax query.

Special Needs: Women's ministry helps, banquet-planning helps, speaking and writing helps.

Photos: Accepts freelance photos for book covers.

Tips: "Submissions accepted by invitation only. Best to send a brief e-mail with description of your idea. Please see our Web page to best understand our publishing program. Most open to a how-to, informational book with a need-to-know marketability."

JUDSON PRESS, PO Box 851, Valley Forge PA 19482-0851. Toll-free (800) 458-3766. Fax (610) 768-2107. E-mail: acquisitions@judsonpress.com. Website: www.judsonpress.com. American Baptist Churches USA/National Ministries. Rebecca Irwin-Diehl, ed. We are theologically moderate, historically Baptist, and in ministry to empower, enrich, and equip the disciples of Jesus and leaders in Christ's church. Publishes 12-15 titles/yr.; hardcover, trade paperbacks. Receives 800 submissions annually. 20% of books from first-time authors. Accepts mss through agents or authors. No subsidy; rarely does print-on-demand or reprints. Prefers 100-200 pgs. or 30,000-75,000 wds. **Royalty 10-15% on net; some work-for-hire agreements or outright purchases; occasional advance $300.** Average first printing 3,000. Publication within 18 mos. Considers simultaneous submissions. Requires accepted submissions on disk or by e-mail. Responds in 4-6 mos. Prefers NRSV. Guidelines on Website (under "Contact Us"); catalog online.

Nonfiction: Query or proposal/2 chapters; e-query OK. Practical books for today's church and leaders.

Ethnic Books: African American & Hispanic.

Artwork: Open to queries from freelance artists. Attn: Wendy Ronga, creative dir.

Tips: "Most open to books that are unique, compelling, and practical. Theologically and socially we are a moderate publisher. And we like to see a detailed marketing plan from an author committed to partnering with us."

**Note: This publisher serviced by The Writer's Edge.

JESSICA KINGSLEY PUBLISHERS, 116 Pentonville Rd., London N1 9JB, United Kingdom. U.S. address: 400 Market St., Ste. 400, Philadelphia PA 19106 (they will forward your proposal). Phone +44 (020) 7833 2307. Fax +44 (020) 7837 2917. E-mail: post@jkp.com. Website: www.jkp.com. Jessica Kingsley, CEO; submit to: New Book Proposals at JKP. Recognized as the leading publisher on autism and Asperger Syndrome, we publish in a range of areas including social work, education, arts therapies, and spirituality. Imprint: Singing Dragon. Publishes 45+ titles/yr.; hardcover, trade paperbacks. Receives 300+ submissions annually. 60% of books from first-time authors. Accepts mss through agents or authors. Print-on-demand for older books. Reprints books. Any length. **Royalty 5-10% on net; no advance.** Average first printing 1,500. Publication within 6 mos. No simultaneous submissions. Responds in up to 6 mos. Requires accepted mss on disk or by e-mail. Prefers NIV. Guidelines on Website (under "Authors"); free catalog by mail.

Nonfiction: Proposal/2 chapters; no phone/fax query; e-query OK.

Special Needs: Practical theology.

Photos: Accepts freelance photos for book covers.

Tips: "Most open to books that combine theory with practice; books for practitioners."

KIRK HOUSE PUBLISHERS, PO Box 390759, Minneapolis MN 55439. Toll-free (888) 696-1828. (952) 835-1828. Fax (952) 835-2613. E-mail: publisher@kirkhouse.com. Website: www.kirk house.com. Leonard Flachman, pub. Imprints: Lutheran University Press, Quill House Publishers. Publishes 6-8 titles/yr.; hardcover, trade paperbacks, coffee-table books. Receives hundreds of submissions annually. 95% of books from first-time authors. No mss through agents. No reprints. **Royalty 10-15% on net; no advance.** Average first printing 500-3,000. Publication within 6 mos. No simultaneous submissions. Requires disk or e-mail submission. Responds in 2-3 wks. Guidelines by e-mail/Website ("Submissions"); free catalog by mail.

Nonfiction: Proposal/1-2 chapters.

Tips: "Our catalog is eclectic; send a query. Our imprint, Quill House Publishers, accepts adult fiction."

KNIGHT GEORGE PUBLISHING HOUSE, LLC, 3310 Warringham, Waterford MI 48329. (586) 481-0466. E-mail: authors@knightgeorge.com. Website: www.KnightGeorge.com. Lutheran. Matt Jones, pres. A privately-owned, independent provider of innovative Christian educational materials to Lutheran schools. New publisher; hardcover, trade paperbacks. Receives 100+ submissions annually. 16% of books from first-time authors. No mss through agents. No subsidy or print-on-demand. No reprints. **Royalty 2-15% of net; no advance.** Considers simultaneous submissions. Responds in 6-8 mos. Accepted mss on disk. Guidelines by mail/e-mail/Website; no catalog.

Nonfiction: Proposal/2 chapters; no phone/fax query; e-query OK.

Fiction: Query only first. Children's stories and classroom reading books. "We seek to compete with Golden Books."

Special Needs: Classroom materials: textbooks, workbooks, hands-on learning aids, story books for lower elementary. Innovative teaching methods and newest technology are preferred.

Also Does: Board games, computer games, all hands-on learning methods.

Photos/Artwork: Accepts freelance photos for book covers (focus on academic subject); open to queries from freelance artists.

Tips: "We prefer books be submitted complete with original artwork. Most open to textbooks (teacher's editions should contain full student's edition within them), workbooks (as applicable), and projects, preferably as a package. Find new and creative ways to teach. We are a publishing house, but will consider any other products (within pricing limits) that educate. Of course, God should be at least implicit, but don't force biblical examples in your work. Write to meet the needs of the market."

KREGEL PUBLICATIONS, PO Box 2607, Grand Rapids MI 49501-2607. (616) 451-4775. Fax (616) 451-9330. E-mail: kregelbooks@kregel.com. Website: www.kregelpublications.com. Blog: www .kregelpublications.blogspot.com. Evangelical/Conservative. Dennis R. Hillman, pub.; Jim Weaver, academic & professional books ed.; submissions policy on Website. To provide tools for ministry and Christian growth from a conservative, evangelical perspective. Imprints: Kregel Kidzone, Kregel Academic and Professional, Kregel Classics. Publishes 75 titles/yr.; hardcover, trade paperbacks. 20% of books from first-time authors. Prefers mss through agents. Reprints books. **Royalty 8-16% of net; some outright purchases; pays advances.** Average first printing 5,000. Publication within 12 mos. Considers simultaneous submissions. Responds in 4 mos. Guidelines by e-mail; catalog for 9 x 12 SAE/3 stamps. No longer reviewing unsolicited queries, proposals, or manuscripts, except through agents, Writer's Edge, or ChristianManuscriptSubmissions.com.

> **Nonfiction:** "Most open to contemporary issues or academic works."
>
> **Fiction:** For all ages. "Looking for high-quality contemporary fiction with strong Christian themes and characters."
>
> **Tips:** "We are very selective. Strong story lines with an evident spiritual emphasis are required."
>
> ****Note:** This publisher serviced by The Writer's Edge and ChristianManuscriptSubmissions.com.

LANGMARC PUBLISHING, PO Box 90488, Austin TX 78709-0488. (512) 394-0989. Fax (512) 394-0829. E-mail: langmarc@booksails.com. Website: www.langmarc.com. Lutheran. Lois Qualben, pub. Focuses on spiritual growth of readers. Publishes 3-5 titles/yr.; hardcover, trade paperbacks. Receives 230 submissions annually. 60% of books from first-time authors. Accepts mss through agents or authors. No reprints. Prefers 150-300 pgs. **Royalty 10-14% on net; no advance.** Average first printing varies. Publication usually within 18 mos. Considers simultaneous submissions. Responds in 3 mos. Requires requested ms on disk. Prefers NIV. Guidelines on Website ("Guidelines for Nonfiction Authors"); free catalog.

> **Nonfiction:** Proposal/3 chapters; no phone query. "Most open to inspirational books."

LARSON PUBLICATIONS/PBPF, 4936 NYS Rte. 414, Burdett NY 14818-9729. (607) 546-9342. Fax (607) 546-9344. E-mail: larson@lightlink.com. Website: www.larsonpublications.org. Paul Cash, dir. Books cover philosophy, psychology, religion, and spirituality. Publishes 4-5 titles/yr.; hardcover, trade paperbacks. Receives 1,000 submissions annually. 5% of books from first-time authors. Some reprints. **Variable royalty; rarely gives an advance.** Publication within 1-2 yrs. Considers simultaneous submissions. Requires accepted mss on disk. Responds in 8 wks. Prefers NIV. Guidelines on Website (under "For Author"); no catalog.

> **Nonfiction:** Query by mail/outline & SASE; no phone/fax/e-query.

+LEAFWOOD PUBLISHERS, 1626 Campus Ct., Abilene TX 79601. Toll-free (877) 816-4455. (325) 674-2720. Fax (325) 674-6471. E-mail through Website: www.leafwoodpublishers.com. Seeks to publish books that speak to the spiritual hungers of people today and empower Christians to enjoy their faith; reflect biblical theology and are evangelical in spirit; address the new challenges to Christians presented by the emerging new era in Western culture that many are calling "postmodern," and maintain strong literary standards and are sensitive to the broad stream of Christian life and thought today.

An imprint of Abilene Christian University Press. Dr. Leonard Allen, dir. Guidelines on Website (bottom right-hand side "New Authors").

LEGACY PRESS, PO Box 261129, San Diego CA 92196. Toll-free (800) 323-7337. Toll-free fax (800) 331-0297. E-mail: editor@rainbowpublishers.com. Website: www.LegacyExpress.com. Rainbow Publishers. Submit to Manuscript Submissions. Publishes nondenominational nonfiction and fiction for children in the evangelical Christian market. Publishes 15 titles/yr. Receives 250 submissions annually. 50% of books from first-time authors. Reprints books. Prefers 150 pgs. & up. **Royalty 8% & up on net; advance $500+.** Average first printing 5,000. Publication within 2 yrs. Considers simultaneous submissions. Prefers requested ms on disk. Responds in 2-8 wks. Prefers NIV. Guidelines (go to bottom "Submissions") & catalog on Website.

> **Nonfiction:** Proposal/3-5 chapters; no e-queries. "Looking for nonfiction for girls and boys ages 2-12."
> **Fiction:** Proposal/3 chapters. For ages 2-12 only. Must include an additional component beyond fiction (e.g., devotional, Bible activities, etc.).
> **Special Needs:** Nonfiction for ages 10-12, particularly Christian twists on current favorites, such as cooking, jewelry making, games, etc.
> **Artwork:** Open to queries from freelance artists.
> **Tips:** "All books must offer solid Bible teaching in a fun, meaningful way that appeals to kids. Research popular nonfiction for kids in the general market, then figure out how to present those fun ideas in ways that teach the Bible. As a smaller publisher, we seek to publish unique niche books that stand out in the market."

LIBROS LIGUORI, 1 Liguori Dr., Liguori MO 63057-9999. Toll-free (800) 325-9521. (636) 464-2500. Fax (636) 464-8449. E-mail: manuscript_submission@liguori.org. Website: www.liguori.org. Spanish division of Liguori Publications. To spread the gospel in the Hispanic community by means of low-cost publications. Publishes 5 titles/yr. Receives 6-8 submissions annually. 5% of books from first-time authors. Prefers up to 30,000 wds. **Royalty 8-10% of net or outright purchases of $450 (book and booklet authors get royalties; pamphlet authors get $400 on acceptance); pays an advance.** Average first printing 3,500-5,000. Publication within 18 mos. No simultaneous submissions. Requires accepted mss on electronic file. Responds in 4-8 wks. Guidelines on Website (under "Company Info"); free catalog.

> **Nonfiction:** Four-page summary/1 chapter; fax/e-query OK. "Looking for issues families face today—substance abuse, unwanted pregnancies, etc.; family relations; religion's role in immigrants' experiences, pastoral Catholic faith."
> **Ethnic Books:** Focuses on Spanish-language products.
> **Also Does:** Pamphlets, booklets, tracts, PC software, clip art.
> **Tips:** "Contact us before writing. It's much easier to work together from the beginning of a project. We need books on the Hispanic experience in the U.S. Keep it concise, avoid academic/theological jargon, and stick to the tenets of the Catholic faith. Avoid abstract arguments."

@LIFE CHANGING MEDIA, 10777 W. Sample Rd., Unit 302, Coral Springs FL 33065-3768. (954) 554-1921. E-mail through Website: www.lifechangingmedia.net. Life Changing Publications. Paul Gundotra, pres.; Sindhu Roy, chief ed. Mass-market paperbacks. **Royalty on retail; no advance.** Average first print run varies. Publication within 3 mos. Considers simultaneous submissions (if indicated). Prefers accepted mss by e-mail. Responds in 30-60 days. Guidelines by e-mail/Website ("Submissions Guidelines"); no catalog.

> **Nonfiction:** Query first; e-query OK. "Please include a description of the book project, brief bio including publishing history. Let us know if you have the ability for public speaking."
> **Also Does:** E-books.

Photos: Accepts freelance photos for book covers.

Tips: "Looking for books that entertain, inform, but most of all that are life changing."

LIFE CYCLE BOOKS, PO Box 1008, Niagara Falls NY 14304-1008. Toll-free (800) 214-5849. (416) 690-5860. Toll-free fax (888) 690-8532. (416) 690-8532. E-mail: paulb@lifecyclebooks.com. Website: www.lifecyclebooks.com. Paul Broughton, gen. mngr.; submit to Attention: The Editor. Canadian office: 1149 Bellamy Rd. N., Unit 20, Toronto ON M1H 1H7 Canada. Toll-free (866) 880-5860. Toll-free fax (866) 690-8532. Attn: The Editor. Specializes in pro-life material. Publishes 6 titles/yr.; trade paperbacks. Receives 100 submissions annually. No mss through agents. 50% of books from first-time authors. Reprints books. **Royalty 8-10% of net; outright purchase of brochure material, $250+; advance $250-1,000.** Subsidy publishes 10%. Publication within 1 yr. No simultaneous submissions. Responds in 3-5 wks. Catalog on Website.

Nonfiction: Query or complete ms. "Our emphasis is on pro-life and pro-family titles."

Tips: "We are most involved in publishing leaflets of about 1,500 wds., and we welcome submissions of manuscripts of this length." No fiction or poetry.

LIFESONG PUBLISHERS, PO Box 183, Somis CA 93066. (805) 504-3916. Fax (614) 455-5030. E-mail: mailbox@lifesongpublishers.com or through Website: www.lifesongpublishers.com. Laurie Donahue, pub. Provides Christian families with tools that will aid in spiritual development of family members. Publishes 1-4 titles/yr.; trade paperbacks. No mss through agents. No reprints. Would consider subsidy publishing. **Royalty 10% on net; small advance.** Publication within 12 mos. Considers simultaneous submissions. Responds in 2-4 wks. No guidelines; catalog for 9 x 12 SAE/2 stamps. Not included in nonfiction topical listings.

Nonfiction: Proposal/3 chapters; e-query OK. "Looking for an author with an existing ministry."

LIFT EVERY VOICE BOOKS, 820 N. LaSalle Blvd., Chicago IL 60610. (312) 329-2140. Fax (312) 329-4157. E-mail: lifteveryvoice@moody.edu. Website: www.lifteveryvoicebooks.com. African American imprint of Moody Publishers. Moody Bible Institute. Cynthia Ballenger, acq. ed. To publish culturally relevant books and promote other resources that will help millions of African Americans experience the power and amazement of a fresh encounter with Jesus Christ. Publishes 10 titles/yr. Receives 50-75 submissions annually. 98% of books from first-time authors. Accepts mss through agents or authors. No subsidy. Reprints books. Prefers minimum of 50,000 wds. or 250 pgs. **Royalty on retail; pays an advance.** Average first printing 5,000. Publication within 12 mos. Considers simultaneous submissions. Responds quarterly. Accepts requested ms by e-mail. Prefers KJV, NASB, NKJV. Guidelines by e-mail; free catalog.

Nonfiction: Proposal/3 chapters; e-query OK.

Fiction: Proposal/3 chapters; e-query OK. For all ages. Send for fiction writers' guidelines.

Special Needs: Children's fiction, especially for boys; nonfiction & fiction for teen girls; also marriage books.

Ethnic Books: African American imprint.

Photos: Accepts freelance photos for book covers.

Tips: "Looking for quality fiction and nonfiction. LEVB is looking for good, strong, and focused writing that is Christ-centered and speaks to the African American community."

@LIGHTHOUSE PUBLISHING, 251 Overlook Park Ln., Lawrenceville GA 30043-7355. E-mail: AndyOverett@lighthousechristianpublishing.com. Website: www.lighthousechristianpublishing.com. Nondenominational. Andy Overett, ed.; submit to Chris Wright, sr. ed. To distribute a wide variety of Christian media to vast parts of the globe so people can hear about the gospel for free or very inexpensively (e-books, comics, movies, and online radio). Imprints: Lighthouse Publishing, Lighthouse Music Publishing. Publishes 20-30 titles/yr.; hardcover, trade paperbacks, mass-market paperbacks. Receives 100-150 submissions annually. 60% of books from first-time authors. Accepts mss through agents or authors. Subsidy publishes 15-20%. Does print-on-demand. Reprints books. Any length. **Royalty on net; no advance.** Average first printing 300-400. Publication within 6 mos. Considers simultaneous submissions. Prefers submissions by e-mail. Responds in 6-8 wks. Prefers NAS. Guidelines on Website ("Submissions"); catalog $5.

Nonfiction: Complete ms by e-mail only (info@lighthousechristianpublishing.com). Any topic. "Looking for children's books, Intelligent Design, and science."

Fiction: Complete ms by e-mail only. Any genre, for all ages.

Ethnic Books: Publishes books for almost all foreign-language markets.

Also Does: Comics, animation on CD, music CDs, plans to do Christian computer games in the future. E-books.

Photos/Artwork: Accepts freelance photos for book covers; open to queries from freelance artists.

Tips: "Most open to children's books, comics, and graphic novels; scientific and academic works with a Christian perspective."

LIGHTHOUSE TRAILS PUBLISHING LLC, PO Box 908, Eureka MT 59917. (406) 297-7756. Fax (406) 297-7762. E-mail: editors@lighthousetrails.com. Website: www.lighthousetrails.com. Blog: www.lighthousetrailsresearch.com/blog. David Dombrowski, acq. ed. We publish books that bring clarity and light to areas of spiritual darkness or deception, and we seek to preserve the integrity of God's Word in all our books. Imprint: Falling Sparrow Series. Publishes 4 titles/yr. Receives 100-150 submissions annually. 35% of books from first-time authors. Accepts mss through agents or authors. No subsidy or print-on-demand. Reprints books. Prefers 160-300 pgs. **Royalty 12-17% of net or 20% of retail; advance $750-1,000.** Average first printing 2,500. Publication within 6-9 mos. Considers simultaneous submissions. Requires accepted ms on disk or by e-mail. Responds in 8 wks. Prefers KJV. Guidelines on Website ("Publishing Info"/"Author Guidelines" on right); free catalog by mail.

Nonfiction: Proposal/2 chapters; no phone/fax query; e-query OK.

Fiction: Proposal/2-3 chapters. For all ages. "We are looking for a fiction book or fiction series that would include elements from our books exposing the emerging church and mystical spirituality; bible prophecy/eschatological."

Special Needs: Will look at autobiographies or biographies about people who have courageously endured through overwhelming circumstances (Holocaust survivors, child-abuse survivors, etc.) with a definite emphasis on the Lord's grace and faithfulness.

Artwork: Open to queries from freelance artists.

Tips: "No poetry at this time. Any book we consider will not only challenge the more scholarly reader, but also be able to reach those who may have less experience and comprehension. Our books will include human interest and personal experience scenarios as a means of getting the point across. Read a couple of our books to better understand the style of writing we are looking for. Also check our research Website for an in-depth look at who we are (www .lighthousetrailsresearch.com)."

LIGUORI PUBLICATIONS, 1 Liguori Dr., Liguori MO 63057-9999. Toll-free (800) 325-9521. (636) 464-2500. Fax (636) 464-8449. E-mail: manuscript_submission@liguori.org or through Website: www .liguori.org. Catholic/Redemptorists. Submit by e-mail. Spreading the Good News of the gospel by means of low-cost publications. Imprints: Libros Liguori (Spanish language), Liguori Books. Publishes 50 titles/yr.; trade paperbacks. Receives 20-30 submissions annually. 5% of books from first-time authors. Reprints books. Prefers up to 30,000 wds. for books; 40-100 pgs. for booklets; pamphlets 16-18 pgs. **Book & booklet authors get royalties; pamphlet authors get flat fee on acceptance; advance varies.** No simultaneous submissions. Requires requested ms by e-mail attachment. Responds in 4-8 wks. Requires NRSV. Guidelines on Website (under "Contact Us"); free catalog by mail.

Nonfiction: Send 4-page summary/1 chapter; fax/e-query OK. "Looking for issues families face today—substance abuse, unwanted pregnancies, etc.; family relations; pastoral Catholic faith."

Ethnic Books: Publishes books in Spanish. See separate listing for Libros Liguori.
Also Does: Booklets, pamphlets, tracts; books on Catholic faith.
Tips: "Keep it concise, avoid academic/theological jargon, and stick to the tenets of the Catholic faith. Avoid abstract arguments. Manuscripts accepted by us must have strong, middle-of-the-road, practical spirituality."

LION AND LAMB PUBLICATIONS, 8 Three Coins Ct., Fountain Inn SC 29644. (864) 409-0015. E-mail: info@LionandLambPublications.com. Website: www.LionandLambPublications.com. Andriea Chenot, ed.; submit to: submissions@LionandLambPublications.com. To win souls, equip saints, and strengthen faith through the power of God's Word; and be a part of God's opening doors for new authors. Publishes 25 titles/yr.; hardcover. Receives 300 submissions annually. 80% of books from first-time authors. Accepts mss through agents or authors. Does some print-on-demand. No reprints. **Royalty 10-15% on retail; variable advance.** Average first printing 5,000. Publication within 6-12 mos. Considers simultaneous submissions. Responds in 2-4 wks. Accepted mss on disk or by e-mail. Prefers NIV or Good News. Guidelines on Website (click on "Submissions").
    Nonfiction: Proposal/6 chapters; e-query OK. See Website for current needs.
    Fiction: Not currently accepting fiction submissions.
    Special Needs: Ministry resources primarily for children and youth ministries; Sunday school curriculum; Christian homeschool curriculum.
    Also Does: Computer games and other specialty products.
    Photos/Artwork: Accepts freelance photos for book covers; open to queries from freelance artists.
    Tips: "We are most open to ministry resources, and most concerned with books that help win souls, equip saints, and strengthen faith."

LION PUBLISHING, 4050 Lee Vance View, Colorado Springs CO 80918-7102. (719) 536-3271. David C. Cook. Accepts no freelance submissions.

@LITURGICAL PRESS, PO Box 7500, St. John's Abbey, Collegeville MN 56321-7500. Toll-free (800) 858-5450, ext. 2218. (320) 363-2213. Toll-free fax (800) 445-5899. (320) 363-3299. E-mail: Sales@litpress.org. Website: www.litpress.org. Order of St. Benedict, Inc. Imprints: Liturgical Press Books, Michael Glazier Books, Pueblo Books, Cistercian Publications. Peter Dwyer, dir.; submit to Hans Christoffersen, ed. dir. (hchristoffe@csbsju.edu). Publishes 75 titles/yr.; hardcover, trade paperbacks, coffee-table books, and digital. Does print-on-demand. Prefers 100-300 pgs. **Royalty 10% of net; some outright purchases; no advance.** No simultaneous submissions. Responds in 3 mos. Guidelines by mail/Website ("Author Information"/"Submit a Manuscript" on left); free catalog by mail.
    Nonfiction: Query/proposal. Adult only.
    Tips: "We publish liturgical, scriptural, theological, pastoral, and monastic wisdom resources."

LITURGY TRAINING PUBLICATIONS, Archdiocese of Chicago, 3949 S. Racine Ave., Chicago IL 60609-2523. Toll-free (800) 933-1800. (773) 486-8970. Fax (773) 486-7094. E-mail: editorialmanager@ltp.org. Website: www.LTP.org. Catholic/Archdiocese of Chicago. Mary Ehle & Mary Fox, eds. Resources for liturgy in Christian life. Imprint: Hillenbrand Books (Kevin Thornton, ed.). Publishes 25 titles/yr.; hardcover, trade paperbacks, coffee-table books. Receives 150 submissions annually. 25% of books from first-time authors. Accepts mss through agents or authors. No subsidy or print-on-demand. Reprints books. **Variable royalty on net or work-for-hire; advance.** Average first printing 2,000-5,000. Publication within 18 mos. Considers simultaneous submissions. Accepts full mss by e-mail. Responds in 3 mos. Prefers RNAB, NRSV Catholic edition. Guidelines by mail/e-mail/Website; free catalog by mail.
    Nonfiction: Proposal/1 chapter; no phone/fax/e-query.
    Ethnic Books: Hispanic.

Photos/Artwork: Accepts freelance photos for book covers; open to queries from freelance artists.

Tips: "Our focus is on providing materials to aid in participation in Catholic worship."

LOYOLA PRESS, 3441 N. Ashland Ave., Chicago IL 60657. Toll-free (800) 621-1008. (773) 281-1818. Fax (773) 281-0152. E-mail: editorial@loyolapress.com. Website: www.loyolabooks.org. Catholic. Joseph Durepos, acq. ed. (durepos@loyolapress.com). Publishes in the Jesuit and Ignatian Spirituality tradition. Publishes 20-30 titles/yr.; hardcover, trade paperbacks. Receives 500 submissions annually. Accepts mss through agents or authors. Prefers 25,000-75,000 wds. or 150-300 pgs. **Standard royalty; reasonable advance.** Average first printing 7,500-10,000. Considers simultaneous submissions and first-time authors without agents. Responds in 10-12 wks. Prefers NRSV (Catholic Edition). Guidelines/catalog on Website (under "Contact Us"/"Submissions").

Nonfiction: E-query first; proposal/sample chapters; no phone query.

Tips: "Looking for books and authors that help make Catholic faith relevant and offer practical tools for the well-lived spiritual life."

LUTHERAN UNIVERSITY PRESS, PO Box 390759, Minneapolis MN 55439. Toll-free (888) 696-1828. (952) 835-1828. Fax (952) 835-2613. E-mail: publisher@lutheranupress.org. Website: www .lutheranupress.org. Leonard Flachman, pub.; Karen Walhof, ed. Publishes 8-10 titles/yr.; hardcover, trade paperbacks, coffee-table books. Receives dozens of submissions annually. Subsidy publishes 25%. No print-on-demand or reprints. **Royalty 10-15% of net; no advance.** Average first printing 500-2,000. Publication within 6 mos. No simultaneous submissions. Responds in 3 wks. Guidelines by e-mail/Website ("Submissions"); free catalog by mail.

Nonfiction: Proposal/sample chapters in electronic format.

Photos: Accepts freelance photos for book covers.

Tips: "We accept manuscripts only from faculty of Lutheran colleges, universities, seminaries, and Lutheran faculty from other institutions."

LUTHERAN VOICES, Book Submissions, Augsburg Fortress, PO Box 1209, Minneapolis MN 55440-1209. E-mail through Website: www.augsburgfortress.org. Evangelical Lutheran Church in America. Develops quality, accessible books written primarily by ELCA authors that inform, teach, inspire, and renew. Series of books; 96 pgs. ea. **Royalty.** Responds in 8-12 wks. Guidelines on Website ("Contact Us"/"Submission Guidelines").

Nonfiction: Proposal.

Tips: "We are seeking prophets and preachers, politicians and pastors; educators and scientists; caregivers and counselors; professors and students; scholars and homemakers— people who have a story to tell, topics to illumine, and ideas to explore. It is expected that authors will write out of a foundational understanding of Lutheran theology and practice, though topics may be of interest to a wider Christian audience."

@LUTTERWORTH PRESS, PO Box 60, Cambridge CB1 2NT, England. Phone +44 (0) 1223 350865. Fax +44 (0) 1223 366951. E-mail: publishing@lutterworth.com. Website: www.lutterworth.com. Imprint of James Clarke & Co. Adrian Brink, ed. Publishes nonfiction, academic and educational titles in the areas of Art, History & Biography, Literary Criticism, Religion, Biblical Studies, and Theology. Imprints: Patrick Hardy Books, Acorn Editions. Publishes 25 titles/yr.; hardcover, trade paperbacks, & digital. Receives 100 submissions annually. 90% of books from first-time authors. Accepts mss through agents or authors. Subsidy publishes 2%. Does print-on-demand. **Royalty on retail; pays an advance.** Average first printing 250. Publication within 18 mos. No simultaneous submissions. Responds in 3 mos. Requested ms by mail. Guidelines on Website (scroll down to "Author Guidelines"); free catalog by mail.

Nonfiction: Proposal/2 chapters; e-query OK.

Tips: "For full author guidelines, visit our Website."

MACALESTER PARK PUBLISHING, 24558—546th Ave., Austin MN 55912. Toll-free fax (800) 407-9078. (507) 396-0135. E-mail: Macalesterpark@macalesterpark.com or through Website: www.macalesterpark.com. Focuses on reprinting books. Sue Franklin, owner.

MAGNUS PRESS, PO Box 2666, Carlsbad CA 92018. (760) 806-3743. Fax (760) 806-3689. E-mail: magnuspres@aol.com. Website: www.magnuspress.com. Warren Angel, ed. dir. All books must reflect a strong belief in Christ, solid biblical understanding, and the author's ability to relate to the average person. Imprint: Canticle Books. Publishes 3 titles/yr.; trade paperbacks. Receives 60 submissions annually. 50% of books from first-time authors. Accepts mss through agents or authors. Reprints books. Prefers 105-300 pgs. **Graduated royalty on retail; no advance.** Average first printing 2,500. Publication within 1 yr. Considers simultaneous submissions. Accepts requested ms on disk. Responds in 1 mo. Guidelines by mail/e-mail/Website ("Magnus Press Submissions"); free catalog by mail.
> **Nonfiction:** Query or proposal/3 chapters; fax query OK. "Looking for spirituality, thematic biblical studies, unique inspirational/devotional books, e.g. Adventures of an Alaskan Preacher."
> **Tips:** "Our writers need solid knowledge of the Bible and a mature spirituality that reflects a profound relationship with Jesus Christ. Most open to a popularly written biblical study that addresses a real concern/issue in the church at large today; or a unique inspirational book. Study the market; know what we do and don't publish."
> ****Note:** This publisher serviced by The Writer's Edge.

MARCHER LORD PRESS, 8345 Pepperridge Dr., Colorado Springs CO 80920. (719) 266-8874. E-mail: Jeff@marcherlordpress.com. Website: www.marcherlordpress.com. Jeff Gerke, pub. Premier publisher of Christian speculative fiction—it's all they do. Publishes 6-8 titles/yr.; trade paperbacks. Receives 200 submissions annually. 70% of books from first-time authors. Accepts mss through agents or authors. No subsidy; does print-on-demand. No reprints. Prefers 90,000 wds. **Author receives 50% after development costs are recouped; advance.** Publication within 6 mos. Considers simultaneous submissions. Responds in 6-12 mos. Guidelines/catalog on Website ("Write for Us").
> **Fiction:** Submit only through acquisitions form on Website.
> **Special Needs:** Full-length, Christian speculative fiction for an adult and older teen audience.
> **Photos/Artwork:** Accepts freelance photos for book covers; open to queries from freelance artists.
> **Tips:** "I'm most open to high fiction craftsmanship and a story that sweeps me away."

MASON CREST PUBLISHERS, 370 Reed Rd., Ste. 302, Broomall PA 19008. Toll-free (866)MCP-BOOK. (610) 543-6200. Fax (610) 543-3878. Website: www.masoncrest.com. Publishes core-related materials for grades K-12; includes religious materials.

MASTER BOOKS, PO Box 726, Green Forest AR 72638. (870) 438-5288. Fax (870) 438-5120. E-mail: submissions@newleafpress.net or through Website: www.masterbooks.net. Imprint of New Leaf Press. Craig Froman, asst. ed. Publisher of creation science books; all books are completely evolution free. Publishes 15-20 titles/yr.; hardcover, trade paperbacks. Receives 1,200 submissions annually. 10% of books from first-time authors. Accepts mss through agents or authors. No subsidy, print-on-demand, or reprints. Prefers 140-240 pgs. **Variable royalty; no advance.** Average first printing 5,000. Publication within 12 mos. Considers simultaneous submissions. Responds in 3 mos. Guidelines by mail/e-mail/Website; catalog for 9 x 12 SAE/5 stamps.
> **Nonfiction:** Must complete Author Proposal Form (available on Website). Accepts e-queries. "Looking for biblical creationism, biblical science, creation/evolution debate material."
> **Fiction:** Must complete Author Proposal Form (available on Website). Accepts e-queries.
> **Special Needs:** Creation science books and books for the Christian Education/homeschool markets.
> **Contest:** Master Books Scholarship Essay contest; $3,000 college scholarship; www.newleaf publishinggroup.com/store/scholarship.htm.

Artwork: Open to queries from freelance artists.

Tips: "Most open to books for education with lots of hands-on activities."

**Note: This publisher serviced by The Writers' Edge.

MCRUFFY PRESS, PO Box 212, Raymore MO 64083. (816) 331-7831. Fax (480) 772-4376. E-mail: brian@mcruffy.com. Website: www.mcruffy.com. Brian Davis, ed. Christian publisher of children's trade books, children's audio, and homeschool materials. Open to freelance. Requires e-query. Incomplete topical listings.

Tips: "Most open to seeing elementary educational materials, any subject area. Not currently accepting picture book manuscripts."

MERCER UNIVERSITY PRESS, 1400 Coleman Ave., Macon GA 31207-0003. (478) 301-2880. Fax (478) 301-2264. E-mail: jolley_ma@mercer.edu. Website: www.mupress.org. Baptist. Submit to Editor-in-Chief. Publishes 35 titles/yr. Receives 300 submissions annually. 40% of books from first-time authors. Accepts some mss through agents. Some reprints. **Royalty on net; no advance.** Average first printing 800-1,200. Publication within 24 mos. Prefers requested ms in hard copy; no disk or e-mail submissions. Responds in 3-4 mos. Guidelines by mail/e-mail/Website ("Information"/"For Authors"/"Submission Guidelines").

Nonfiction: Proposal/2 chapters; fax/e-query OK. "We are looking for books on history, philosophy, theology, literary studies, and religion, including history of religion, philosophy of religion, Bible studies, and ethics."

Fiction: No religious fiction, only Southern literary. Author information form on Website.

MERIWETHER PUBLISHING LTD./CONTEMPORARY DRAMA SERVICE, 885 Elkton Dr., Colorado Springs CO 80907. (719) 594-4422. Fax (719) 594-9916. E-mail: MerPCDS@aol.com, or editor@meriwether.com. Website: www.meriwetherpublishing.com. Nondenominational. Arthur L. Zapel, exec. ed.; submit to Rhonda Wray, assoc. ed. Publishes 30-45 plays & books/yr. Primarily a publisher of plays for Christian and general markets; must be acceptable for use in a wide variety of Christian denominations. Imprint: Contemporary Drama Service. Publishes 3 bks./25 plays/yr. Receives 1,200 submissions annually (mostly plays). 75% of submissions from first-time authors. Accepts mss through agents or authors. No reprints. Prefers 225 pgs. **Royalty 10% of net or retail; no advance.** Average first printing of books 1,500-2,500, plays 500. Publication within 6 mos. Considers simultaneous submissions. No e-mail submissions. Responds in up to 3 mos. Any Bible version. Guidelines by mail/e-mail/Website ("Writers Guidelines"); catalog for 9 x 12 SASE.

Nonfiction: Table of contents/1 chapter; fax/e-query OK. "Looking for creative worship books, i.e., drama, using the arts in worship, how-to books with ideas for Christian education." Submit books to Meriwether.

Fiction: Complete ms for plays. Plays only, for all ages. Always looking for Christmas and Easter plays (1 hr. maximum). Submit plays to Contemporary Drama.

Special Needs: Religious drama—or religious plays—mainstream theology. We prefer plays that can be staged during a worship service.

Tips: "Our books are on drama or any creative, artistic area that can be a part of worship. Writers should familiarize themselves with our catalog before submitting to ensure that their manuscript fits with the list we've already published." Contemporary Drama Service wants easy-to-stage comedies, skits, one-act plays, large-cast musicals, and full-length comedies for schools (junior high through college), and churches (including chancel dramas for Christmas and Easter). Most open to anything drama-related. "Study our catalog so you'll know what we publish and what would fit our list."

MESSIANIC JEWISH PUBLISHERS, 6120 Day Long Ln., Clarksville MD 21029. (410) 531-6644. Fax (410) 531-9440. E-mail: editor@messianicjewish.net. Website: www.MessianicJewish.net. Lederer/Messianic Jewish Communications. Submit to The Editor. Books that build up the Messianic

Jewish community, witness to unbelieving Jewish people, or help Christians understand their Jewish roots. Imprints: Lederer Books. Publishes 6-12 titles/yr.; hardcover, trade paperbacks. Receives 100+ submissions annually. 50% of books from first-time authors. No mss through agents. Reprints books. Prefers 50,000-88,000 wds. **Royalty 7-15% on net.** Average first printing 5,000. Publication within 12-24 mos. No simultaneous submissions. Responds in 3-6 mos. Requires requested ms on disk. Prefers Complete Jewish Bible. Guidelines on Website; free catalog by mail.

Nonfiction: Read submission guidelines first; then query. Messianic Judaism, Jewish evangelism, or Jewish roots of Christian faith. "Must have Messianic Jewish theme and demonstrate familiarity with Jewish culture and thought."

Fiction: Read submission guidelines first. For adults. Jewish themes only.

Special Needs: Messianic Jewish commentaries.

Ethnic Books: Jewish; Messianic Jewish.

Artwork: Open to queries from freelance artists.

Tips: "Must request guidelines before submitting book proposal; all submissions must meet our requirements. Looking for Messianic Jewish commentaries. Books must address one of the following: Jewish evangelism, Jewish roots of Christianity, or Messianic Judaism."

MILLENNIUM III PUBLISHERS, 174 N. Moore Rd., Simpsonville SC 29680. Toll-free (800) 967-7345. Robyn Grage, ed. To define the cause of the moral and spiritual decline, and to help restore Christian influence, in our national culture—especially in public schools. Publishes 4-5 titles/yr.; hardcover, trade paperbacks. Receives 100+ submissions annually. 30% of books from first-time authors. Accepts mss through agents or authors. Reprints books. Subsidy publishes 10-15%. Prefers 200-300 pgs. **Royalty 10-15% on net; some advances.** Publication within 10-12 mos. Considers simultaneous submissions. Prefers accepted mss on disk. Responds in 6-8 wks. Prefers NKJV. Guidelines by mail or e-mail; no catalog.

Nonfiction: Query only; no phone/fax/e-query.

Fiction: Query only; no phone/fax/e-query. For adults.

Special Needs: Serious critique of public schools regarding: underlying principles, morality, educationally, and Christian solutions.

Tips: "Most open to nonfiction books applying Christian solutions to contemporary cultural problems."

MISSION CITY PRESS, 8122 Datapoint Dr., Ste. 1000, San Antonio TX 78229-3273. E-mail: info@missioncitypress.com. Website: www.missioncitypress.com or www.alifeoffaith.com. Wendy Witherow, ed. coordinator. Provides nondenominational Christian print, gift, and toy products that help young people develop a strong foundation of faith in God. Imprints: A Life of Faith, Faith & Friends. Publishes 5 titles/yr.; hardcover, trade paperbacks. 50% of books from first-time authors. Prefers mss through agents. No subsidy publishing or reprints. Prefers 50,000 wds./224 pgs.; or 25,000 wds./112 pgs. **Outright purchases.** Publication within 6 months. Free catalog.

Nonfiction: Query only first. All topics indicated are for children and youth only.

Fiction: Proposal/2 chapters. A Life of Faith uses life stories of fictional girls living in the 19th and early 20th centuries to help today's 8- to 14-year-old girls learn to live a lifestyle of faith.

Also Does: Board games, dolls, and accessories.

Artwork: Open to queries from freelance artists.

Contest: Sponsors a contest (see Website).

Tips: "Spend a lot of time on our Website first and only pitch us things that fit our brand."

**Note: This publisher serviced by ChristianManuscriptSubmissions.com.

MONARCH BOOKS, Wilkinson House, Jordan Hill Rd., Oxford OX2 8DR, England. Phone 01144 0 1865 302750. Fax 01144 0 1865 302757. E-mail: info@lionhudson.com. Website: www.lion hudson.com. Lion Hudson PLC. Tony Collins, pub. The largest independent British publisher of books inspired by the Christian faith. Imprints: Monarch, Candle, Lion, Lion Children's. Publishes 160 titles/yr.; hardcover, trade paperbacks, mass-market paperbacks, coffee-table books. Receives 750 submissions annually. 20% of books from first-time authors. Accepts mss through agents or authors. No subsidy, print-on-demand, or reprints. Prefers 30,000 wds. & up. **Royalty 12.5-15% on net; pays an advance.** Average first printing 6,000. Publication within 9 mos. Considers simultaneous submissions. Prefers accepted mss by e-mail. Responds in 4-6 wks. Any Bible version. Guidelines on Website ("FAQs"/scroll down to "Prospective Authors and Illustrators"); free catalog (don't send U.S. stamps).

Nonfiction: Proposal/2 chapters; phone/fax/e-query OK.

Fiction: Only Lion Hudson imprint printing any fiction.

Special Needs: Original, saleable books with integrity and Christian core.

Photos/Artwork: Accepts freelance photos for book covers; open to queries from freelance artists.

Tips: "Most open to original, energetic, Spirit-filled books."

MOODY PUBLISHERS, 820 N. LaSalle Blvd., Chicago IL 60610. Fax (312) 329-2144. Send e-mails to pressinfo@moody.edu. Website: www.moodypublishers.org. Imprints: Northfield Publishing, Lift Every Voice (African American). Moody Bible Institute. Submit to Acquisitions Coordinator. To provide books that evangelize, edify the believer, and educate concerning the Christian life. Publishes 65-70 titles/yr.; hardcover, trade paperbacks, mass-market paperbacks. Receives 3,500 submissions annually. 1% of books from first-time authors. Accepts mss through agents or authors. **Royalty on net; advance $500-50,000.** Average first printing 10,000. Publication within 1 yr. No simultaneous submissions. Requires requested ms on disk. Responds in 2-3 mos. Prefers NAS, NLT, NIV. Guidelines on Website (under "Frequently Asked Questions #1"); catalog for 9 x 12 SAE/$2.38 postage (mark "Media Mail").

Nonfiction: Considers agented proposals only; no phone/fax/e-query. "For nonfiction, we review only those proposals that come from professional literary agents." Closed to all other unsolicited mss.

Fiction: Proposal/3-5 chapters; for all ages. "We are looking for stories that glorify God both in content and style. We believe that God gives some of his children the talents to write beautiful works of fiction, and we will seek out those artists and the stories they create. We wish to direct people toward God through beauty and truth." No picture books or romance genre fiction.

Ethnic Books: African American.

Tips: "Most open to books where the writer is a recognized expert and already has a platform to promote the book."

**Note: This publisher serviced by The Writer's Edge and ChristianManuscriptSubmissions.com.

MOPS INTERNATIONAL, 2370 S. Trenton Way, Denver CO 80231-3822. (303) 733-5353. Fax (303) 733-5770. E-mail: jblackmer@MOPS.org. Website: www.MOPS.org. Jean Blackmer, pub. mngr.; Carla Foote, dir. of media. Publishes books dealing with the needs and interests of mothers with young children, who may or may not be Christians. Publishes 2-3 titles/yr. Catalog on Website.

Nonfiction: Query or proposal/3 chapters; by mail, fax, or e-mail.

Tips: "Review existing titles on our Website to avoid duplication."

@MORE THAN NOVELLAS.COM, E-mail: lizdelayne@hotmail.com. Website: www.MoreThanNovellas.com. Liz DeLayne, ed. To promote and build a library of family-friendly fiction—with values that exemplify the teachings and walk of Christ—for people to read on the Web. Novellas online. **No payment.** Guidelines on Website ("How to Submit").

Nonfiction: Some romantic poetry.

Fiction: Complete ms by e-mail (attached or copied into the message).

Also Does: E-books.

WILLIAM MORROW, 10 E. 53rd St., New York NY 10022. (212) 207-7000. Fax (212) 207-7145. Website: www.harpercollins.com. Imprint of HarperCollins Publishers. General trade imprint; religious titles published by HarperOne. Submit to Acquisitions Editor. **Royalty on retail; advance.** Agented submissions only.

MOUNTAIN CHURCH BOOKS, an imprint of Alexander Books, 65 Macedonia Rd., Alexander NC 28701. (828) 252-9515. Fax (828) 255-8719. E-mail: pat@abooks.com or through Website. Website: www.abooks.com (being revamped). Submit to Editor. Christian books from a mainly Protestant viewpoint. Publishes hardcover & trade paperbacks. Reprints books. **Royalty on net.** Guidelines/catalog on Website. Incomplete topical listings.

> **Nonfiction:** Query or proposal/3 sample chapters first; no phone/fax/e-query.

@MOUNTAINVIEW PUBLISHING, 1284 Overlook Dr., Sierra Vista AZ 85635-5512. (520) 458-5602. Fax (520) 459-0162. E-mail: leeemory@earthlink.net. Website: www.trebleheartbooks.com. Christian division of Treble Heart Books. Ms. Lee Emory, ed./pub. Online Christian publisher; books never have to go out of print as long as they're being marketed and are selling. Imprints: Treble Heart (see separate listing), Sundowners, Whoodo Mysteries. Publishes 12-24 titles/yr; trade paperbacks. Receives 350 submissions annually. 30% of books from first-time authors. Accepts mss through agents or authors. No reprints. No word-length preference. **Royalty 35% of net on most sales; no advance.** Books are published electronically; average first printing 30-500. Publication usually within 1 yr. No simultaneous submissions (a 90-day exclusive is required on all submissions, plus a marketing plan). Responds in 90 days to submissions, 1-2 wks. to queries. Guidelines on Website ("Submissions Guidelines" right side).

> **Nonfiction:** Complete ms (by e-mail only) to: 1thbsubmissions2@earthlink.net. Submissions are now open between the 1st and 14th of each month. Excellent nonfiction, inspirational books are highly desired here.
>
> **Fiction:** Complete ms (by e-mail only). Genres: Historical romances; contemporary romances; novellas; mainstream and traditional inspirations in most categories; also Christian mysteries, Christian horror, and Christian westerns, and some outstanding short stories.
>
> **Photos:** Accepts high-quality freelance photos for book covers.
>
> **Tips:** "All inspirational fiction should contain faith elements. Challenge the reader to think, to look at things through different eyes. Avoid point-of-view head hopping and clichés; avoid heavy-handed preaching. No dark angel stories, hardcore science fiction/fantasy, though will consider futuristic Christian works. Send consecutive chapters, not random. A well-developed marketing plan must accompany all submissions, and no submissions will be accepted for consideration unless guidelines are followed. Actively seeking more nonfiction at this time."

MULTNOMAH BOOKS, 12265 Oracle Blvd., Ste. 200, Colorado Springs CO 80921. (719) 590-4999. Fax (719) 590-8977. E-mail: info@waterbrookmultnomah.com. Website: www.waterbrook multnomah.com. Part of WaterBrook Multnomah, a division of Random House Inc. Ken Petersen, VP/pub.dir. Imprint information listed below. Publishes 75 titles/yr.; hardcover, trade paperbacks. **Royalty on net; advance.** Multnomah is currently not accepting unsolicited manuscripts, proposals, or queries; no proposals for biographies, poetry, or children's books. Queries will be accepted through literary agents and at writers' conferences at which a Multnomah representative is present. Catalog on Website.

> **Multnomah Books:** Christian living and popular theology books.
>
> **Multnomah Fiction:** Well-crafted fiction that uses truth to change lives.

NATIONAL BLACK THEATRE INC., 2031-33 National Black Theatre Way, Fifth Ave. (between 125th & 126th Sts.), Harlem NY 10035. (212) 722-3800. E-mail: info@nationalblacktheatre.org or through Website: www.nationalblacktheatre.org. Does drama, musicals, and children's plays. Scripts need to reflect an African or African American lifestyle. Especially open to historical or inspirational forms. Also holds workshops and readings.

NATIONAL DRAMA SERVICE, LifeWay Christian Resources, One Lifeway Plaza, Nashville TN 37234. E-mail: terry@lifeway.com. Website: www.lifeway.com. Publishes dramatic material for use in Christian ministry: drama in worship, puppet & clown scripts, Christian comedy, mime/movement scripts, readers theater, creative worship services, monologues. Open to scripts 2-10 minutes long. E-mail for specific submissions guidelines.

NAVPRESS, Box 35001, Colorado Springs CO 80935. Website: www.navpress.com. To advance the calling of the Navigators by publishing life-transforming products that are biblically rooted, culturally relevant, and that glorify the gospel of Jesus Christ and His Kingdom. This company is restructuring and creating a two-pronged structure, dividing the team into trade publishing and direct publishing groups. Sue Kline leads the trade group. Mike Linder the direct team.
    **Note: This publisher serviced by The Writer's Edge and ChristianManuscriptSubmissions.com.

NAZARENE PUBLISHING HOUSE—See Beacon Hill Press of Kansas City.

NEIBAUER PRESS, 20 Industrial Dr., Warminster PA 18974. (215) 322-6200, ext. 255. Fax (215) 322-2495. E-mail: Nathan@Neibauer.com. Website: www.Neibauer.com. Nathan Neibauer, ed. For Evangelical/Protestant clergy and church leaders. Publishes 8 titles/yr. Receives 100 submissions annually. 5% of books from first-time authors. No mss through agents. Reprints books. Prefers 200 pgs. **Royalty on net; some outright purchases; no advance.** Average first printing 1,500. Publication within 6 mos. Considers simultaneous submissions. Responds in 4 wks. Prefers e-mail submissions. Prefers NIV. No guidelines/catalog.
    Nonfiction: Query or proposal/2 chapters; fax query OK.
    Also Does: Pamphlets, tracts.
    Photos: Accepts freelance photos for book covers.
    Tips: "Publishes only religious books on stewardship and church enrollment, stewardship and tithing, and church enrollment tracts."

TOMMY NELSON—See Thomas Nelson Publishers.

THOMAS NELSON, FICTION, PO Box 141000, Nashville TN 37215. (615) 889-9000. Website: www.ThomasNelson.com. Thomas Nelson Inc. Ami McConnell, sr. acq. ed.; Amanda Bostic, acq. ed. Fiction from a Christian worldview. Publishes fewer than 70 titles/yr.; hardcover, trade paperbacks, mass-market paperbacks. Requires mss through agents; does not accept unsolicited manuscripts. Prefers 80,000-100,000 wds. **Royalty on net; pays an advance.** Publication within 12 mos. Accepts simultaneous submissions. Responds in about 60 days. No guidelines; free catalog by mail.
    Fiction: Proposal/3 chapters. For teens and adults. Unsolicited queries are not considered and are not returned.

THOMAS NELSON PUBLISHERS, PO Box 141000, Nashville TN 37214-1000. (615) 889-9000. Fax (615) 902-2745. Website: www.thomasnelson.com. Does not accept or review any unsolicited queries, proposals, or manuscripts.
    **Note: This publisher serviced by The Writer's Edge and ChristianManuscriptSubmissions.com.

NEW CANAAN PUBLISHING CO. INC., 7906 Cove Ridge Dr., Hixon TN 37343-1808. E-mail: info@ newcanaanpublishing.com. Website: www.newcanaanpublishing.com. Kathy Mittelstadt, ed. Children's books with strong educational and moral content, for grades 1-9 (ages 5-16); also aggressively building its Christian titles list. Publishes 3-4 titles/yr.; hardcover, trade paperbacks. Receives 120 submissions annually. 50% of books from first-time authors. Accepts mss through agents or authors. Reprints books. Prefers 20,000-50,000 wds. or 120-250 pgs. **Royalty 8-10% of net; occasional advance.** Average first printing 500-5,000. Publication within 1 yr. No simultaneous submissions.

Responds in 3-4 mos. Requires requested ms on disk; no e-mail submissions. Guidelines/catalog on Website ("Writers' Info" at bottom), or for #10 SASE.

Nonfiction: Proposal/2 chapters or complete ms; no e-query. Does not return submissions.

Fiction: Proposal/2 chapters or complete ms; no e-query. For children and teens, 6-14 yrs. "We want children's books with strong educational and moral content; 10,000-20,000 wds." Now accepts picture books.

Special Needs: Middle-school-level educational books.

Photos: Accepts freelance photos for book covers.

NEW HOPE PUBLISHERS, Box 12065, Birmingham AL 35202-2065. (205) 991-8100. Fax (205) 991-4015. Website: www.newhopepublishers.com. Division of WMU. Imprints: New Hope Impact (missional community, social, personal-commitment, church-growth, and leadership issues); New Hope Arise (inspiring women, changing lives); New Hope Grow (Bible-study & teaching resources). Publishes 20-28 titles/yr.; hardcover, trade paperbacks. No unsolicited queries, proposals, or manuscripts.

**Note: This publisher serviced by The Writer's Edge and ChristianManuscriptSubmissions.com.

NEW LEAF PUBLISHING GROUP, PO Box 726, Green Forest AR 72638-0726. (870) 438-5288. Fax (870) 438-5120. E-mail: submissions@newleafpress.net or through Website: www.nlpg.com. Craig Froman, acq. ed. The world's largest creation-based publisher. Imprints: New Leaf Press, Master Books, Attic Books. Publishes 25-30 titles/yr.; hardcover, trade paperbacks, occasionally high-end gift titles, digital. Receives 1,200 submissions annually. 15% of books from first-time authors. Accepts mss through agents or authors. No subsidy, print-on-demand, or reprints. No length preference. **Variable royalty on net; no advance.** Average first printing varies. Publication within 8 mos. Considers simultaneous submissions. Responds within 3 mos. Requires accepted ms on disk. Guidelines by mail/e-mail/Website; free catalog by mail.

Nonfiction: Must complete Author's Proposal form; no phone/fax query; e-query OK. Accepts mss by e-mail. "Looking for books for the homeschool market, especially grades 1-8."

Fiction: Must complete Author Proposal Form. Query letter only first. Adult.

Special Needs: Stewardship of the earth; ancient man technology, inventions, etc.; educational products for grades K-6.

Contest: Master Books Scholarship Essay Contest; $3,000 college scholarship; www.newleaf publishinggroup.com/store/scholarship.htm.

Artwork: Open to queries from freelance artists.

Tips: "Accepts submissions only with Author's Proposal form available by e-mail or on our Website."

**Note: This publisher serviced by The Writer's Edge.

NEW YORK UNIVERSITY PRESS, 838 Broadway, 3rd Fl., New York NY 10003-4812. (212) 998-2575. Fax (212) 995-3833. E-mail: information@nyupress.org. Website: www.nyupress.org. Jennifer Hammer, religion ed. (jennifer.hammer@nyupress.org). Embraces ideological diversity. Publishes 100 titles/yr.; hardcover, trade paperbacks. Receives 800-1,000 submissions annually. 30% of books from first-time authors. Few mss through agents. **Royalty on net.** Publication within 10-12 mos. Considers simultaneous submissions. Initial response usually within 1 mo. (peer reviewed). Guidelines on Website (under "For Authors").

Nonfiction: Query or proposal/1 chapter.

Tips: "As a university press, we primarily publish works with a scholarly foundation written by PhDs affiliated with a university department. Our focus within religious studies is on religion in American history, culture, and politics. We do not publish liturgical studies, pastoral care, spiritual guides, or exegesis. If you are not a university or seminary-affiliated scholar (or a professional journalist) it is unlikely that your work will be appropriate for our list."

NORDSKOG PUBLISHING, 4562 Westinghouse St., Ste. E, Ventura CA 93003. (805) 642-2070. Fax (805) 642-1862. E-mail: jerry@NordskogPublishing.com. Website: www.NordskogPublishing.com. Jerry Nordskog, pub. Driven by a passion to honor God, edify His people, and advance Christ's cause. Imprint: Noble Novels. Publishes 8-12 titles/yr. Receives 25+ submissions annually. 33% of books from first-time authors. Prefers mss through agents. Often does print-on-demand. Does hardcover, trade paperbacks, mass-market paperbacks & coffee-table books. Reprints books. Prefers 200-300 pgs. **Royalty 10-25%; no advance unless well-known author.** Average first printing 500-1,000. Publication within 10+ mos. Sometimes considers simultaneous submissions. Accepted ms on disk. Responds in 60-90 days. Guidelines by e-mail/Website ("Contact"/"Publishers Guidelines"); free catalog.

> **Nonfiction:** Proposal with contents & author bio, or complete ms; fax query OK. "We accept anything that is thoroughly biblical, sound theologically, especially if unique and especially if 'meaty.'"
>
> **Fiction:** Proposal with contents & author bio, or complete ms; fax query OK. Any genre.
>
> **Photos/Artwork:** Accepts freelance photos for book covers; considers queries from freelance artists.
>
> **Tips:** "We look for sound theological doctrine and unique topics."

NORTHWESTERN PUBLISHING HOUSE, 1250 N. 113th St., Milwaukee WI 53226-3284. Toll-free (800) 662-6022. Fax (414) 475-7684. E-mail: braunj@nph.wels.net. Website: www.nph.net. Lutheran. Rev. John A. Braun, VP of publishing services. Open to freelance. Responds in 2-3 mos. Guidelines on Website ("Contact Us"/scroll down to "Questions regarding writing your own manuscript"/click on the word "manuscript"). Incomplete topical listings.

> **Nonfiction:** Complete ms/cover letter; or query letter/outline.

OAKTARA PUBLISHERS, PO Box 8, Waterford VA 20197. (540) 882-9062. Fax (540) 882-3719. E-mail: jnesbitt@oaktara.com or rtucker@oaktara.com. Website: www.oaktara.com. Jeff Nesbitt, mng. dir. (jnesbit@oaktara.com); Ramona Tucker, ed. dir. (rtucker@oatara.com). To create opportunities for new, talented Christian writers and to promote leading-edge fiction by established Christian authors; inspirational fiction only. Does print-on-demand. Reprints books. **Royalty; no advance.** Guidelines on Website (scroll to bottom "Writers Guidelines").

> **Fiction:** Submit by e-mail (attached file) in one Word file. For all ages.

ONE WORLD/BALLANTINE BOOKS, 1745 Broadway, New York NY 10036. (212) 782-9000. Fax (212) 572-4949. Website: www.randomhouse.com. Submit to Senior Editor. Imprint of Ballantine Books. Books are written by and focus on African Americans but from an American perspective. Publishes 24 titles/yr.; hardcover, trade paperbacks, mass-market paperbacks. Receives 850 submissions annually. 50% of books from first-time authors. Submissions from agents only. No reprints. Prefers 80,000 wds. **Royalty 7.5-15% on retail; advance $40,000-200,000.** Average first printing 10,000. Publication within 18 mos. Considers simultaneous submissions. Responds in 2 mos. No disk or e-mail. Guidelines on Website (scroll to bottom/"About Random House"/"Manuscript Submissions"); catalog. Note: No unsolicited submissions, proposals, manuscripts, or queries at this time.

> **Nonfiction:** Agented submissions only.
>
> **Fiction:** Agented submissions only. "Contemporary/ethnic novels for African American women."
>
> **Ethnic Books:** All are ethnic books.
>
> **Tips:** "You must understand African American culture and avoid timeworn stereotypes."

ON MY OWN NOW MINISTRIES (formerly The Quilldriver), PO Box 573, Clarksville AR 72830. Phone/fax (479) 497-0321. E-mail: donna@onmyownnow.com. Website: www.onmyownnow.com. Donna Lee Schillinger, pub. Inspirational nonfiction directed at young adults (17-25). Imprint: Two-Faced Books. Publishes 3 titles/yr. Receives 12 submissions annually. 67% of books from first-time authors. No mss through agents. Would consider reprinting books. Prefers 200 pgs. **Royalties; $500 advance.** Average first printing 2,000. Publication within 18 mos. Considers simultaneous submissions. Responds in 8 wks. Prefers NIV. Guidelines by e-mail; catalog for #10 SAE/1 stamp.

Nonfiction: Query first; or proposal/2 chapters; e-query OK.

Tips: "Most open to books that are hip and biblically sound—must resonate with young adults."

OREGON CATHOLIC PRESS, PO Box 18030, Portland OR 97218-0030. Toll-free (800) 548-8749. (503) 281-1191. Toll-free fax (800) 462-7329. E-mail: submissions@ocp.org. Website: www.ocp .org. Bari Colombari, sr. ed. To enhance the worship in the Catholic Church in the United States. Imprint: Pastoral Press. Publishes 5 titles/yr. Receives 80 submissions annually. 5% of books from first-time authors. No mss through agents. No reprints. Prefers 192 pgs. **Royalty 5-12% of net; no advance.** Average first printing 500. Publication within 12 mos. Considers simultaneous submissions. Prefers requested ms on disk; no e-mail submissions. Responds in 3 mos. Prefers NAB. Guidelines on Website ("About OCP"/"Music Submissions"); free catalog by mail.

Nonfiction: Proposal/1 chapter; no phone/fax/e-query. "Looking for liturgical ministries."

Ethnic Books: Hispanic/Spanish language.

Photos: Accepts freelance photos for book covers.

Tips: "Most open to Catholic liturgical works."

OUR SUNDAY VISITOR INC., 200 Noll Plaza, Huntington IN 46750-4303. Toll-free (800) 348-2440. (260) 356-8400. Fax (260) 356-8472. E-mail: booksed@osv.com. Website: www.osv.com. Catholic. Submit to Acquisitions Editor. To assist Catholics to be more aware and secure in their faith and capable of relating their faith to others. Publishes 30-40 titles/yr.; hardcover, trade paperbacks. Receives 500+ submissions annually. 10% of books from first-time authors. Prefers not to work through agents. Reprints books. **Royalty 10-12% of net; average advance $1,500.** Average first printing 5,000. Publication within 1-2 yrs. No simultaneous submissions. Responds in 3 mos. Requires requested ms on disk. Guidelines on Website ("About Us"/"Writers Guidelines"); catalog for 9 x 12 SASE.

Nonfiction: Proposal/2 chapters; e-query OK. "Most open to devotional books (not first person), church history, heritage and saints, the parish, prayer, and family."

Also Does: Pamphlets, booklets.

Photos: Occasionally accepts freelance photos for book covers.

Tips: "All books published must relate to the Catholic Church; unique books aimed at our audience. Give as much background information as possible on author qualification, why the topic was chosen, and unique aspects of the project. Follow our guidelines. We are expanding our religious education product line and programs."

PACIFIC PRESS PUBLISHING ASSN., Box 5353, Nampa ID 83653-5353. (208) 465-2500. Fax (208) 465-2531. E-mail: booksubmissions@pacificpress.com. Website: www.pacificpress.com. Seventh-day Adventist. David Jarnes, book ed.; submit to Scott Cady, acq. ed. Books of interest and importance to Seventh-day Adventists and other Christians of all ages. Publishes 35-40 titles/yr.; hardcover, trade paperbacks. Receives 500 submissions annually. 5% of books from first-time authors. Accepts mss through agents or authors. No reprints. Prefers 50,000-130,000 wds. or 160-400 pgs. **Royalty 12-15% of net; advance $1,500.** Average first printing 5,000. Publication within 6 mos. Considers simultaneous submissions. Responds in 1 mo. Requires requested ms on disk or by e-mail. Guidelines at www.pacificpress.com/index/php?pgName=newSubGuides; no catalog.

Nonfiction: Query only; e-query OK.

Fiction: Query only; almost none accepted; mainly biblical. Children's books: "Must be on a uniquely Seventh-day Adventist topic. No talking animals or fantasy."

Ethnic Books: Hispanic.

Also Does: Booklets.

Tips: "Most open to spirituality, inspirational, and Christian living. Our Website has the most up-to-date information, including samples of recent publications. For more information, see www.adventistbookcenter.com. Do not send full manuscript unless we request it after reviewing your proposal."

+@PALGRAVE MACMILLAN, 175 Fifth Ave., New York NY 10010. (646) 307-5097. E-mail: colleen.lawrie@palgrave-usa.com. Website: www.palgrave-usa.com. Colleen Lawrie, ed. A global, cross-market specializing in quality trade nonfiction and cutting-edge academic books. Publishes 5-8 titles/yr.; hardcover, trade paperbacks, digital. 50% of books from first-time authors. Accepts mss through agents or authors. Reprints books. **Royalty; advance.** Publication within 10 months. Considers simultaneous submissions. Guidelines by mail/e-mail/Website ("About Palgrave Macmillan"/"Author Guidelines").

Nonfiction: Proposal/2 chapters; e-query OK. Prefers accepted mss by e-mail.

P & R PUBLISHING CO., PO Box 817, Phillipsburg NJ 08865. (908) 454-0505. Fax (908) 859-2390. E-mail: editorial@prpbooks.com. Website: www.prpbooks.com. Marvin Padgett, ed. dir.; Melissa Craig, acq. ed. Mission is to publish Reformed material that is consistent with biblical teaching, as summarized in the Westminster Standards. Publishes 40 titles/yr.; hardcover, trade paperbacks. Receives 400 submissions annually. 5% of books from first-time authors; electronic submissions only. Accepts mss through agents or authors. Reprints books. Prefers 140-240 pgs. **Royalty 10-14% of net; rarely offers an advance.** Average first printing 4,000. Publication within 10-12 mos. Considers simultaneous submissions. Responds in 2 mos. to proposals. Guidelines by e-mail/Website (Potential Authors section); catalog by mail.

Nonfiction: Only accepts e-submissions with completion of online author guidelines (hard copy mss not returned).

Fiction: Only accepts e-submissions with completion of online author guidelines (hard copy mss not returned). For children or teens.

Also Does: Booklets.

Tips: "Direct biblical/Reformed content. Clear, engaging, and insightful applications of Reformed theology to life. Offer us fully developed proposals and polished sample chapters. All books must be consistent with the Westminster Confession of Faith."

**Note: This publisher serviced by The Writer's Edge and ChristianManuscriptSubmissions.com.

@PARADISE RESEARCH PUBLICATIONS INC., PO Box 837, Kihei HI 96753-0837. Phone/fax (808) 874-4876. E-mail: dickb@dickb.com. Website: www.dickb.com/index.shtml. Ken Burns, VP. Imprint: Tincture of Time Press. Publishes 5 titles/yr.; trade paperbacks. Receives 8 submissions annually. 80% of books from first-time authors. No mss through agents. Reprints books. Prefers 250 pgs. **Royalty 10% of retail; no advance.** Average first printing 5,000. Publication within 2 mos. Considers simultaneous submissions. Responds in 1 wk. No disk. Prefers KJV. No guidelines; free catalog.

Nonfiction: Query only; no phone/fax/e-query. Books on the biblical/Christian history of early Alcoholics Anonymous.

Also Does: Pamphlets, booklets, e-books.

Tips: "Most open to the history of early AA Christian Fellowship Program; healing of alcoholism/addiction by power of God."

PARAGON HOUSE, 1925 Oakcrest Ave., Ste. 7, St. Paul MN 55113-2619. (651) 644-3087. Fax (651) 644-0997. E-mail: submissions@paragonhouse.com. Website: www.paragonhouse.com. Rosemary Yokoi, acq. ed. Serious nonfiction and texts with an emphasis on religion, philosophy, and society. Imprints: Omega, Vision of. . . . Publishes 12-15 titles/yr.; hardcover, trade paperbacks. Receives 1,200 submissions annually. 20% of books from first-time authors. Accepts mss through agents or author. Reprints books. Prefers average 250 pgs. **Royalty 7-10% of net; advance $1,000.** Average first printing 1,500-3,000. Publication within 12-18 mos. Considers few simultaneous submissions.

Accepts e-mail submissions (attached file). Responds in 2-3 mos. Guidelines/catalog on Website ("Help"/"Authors Guidelines" on left).

Nonfiction: Query; proposal/2-3 chapters or complete ms; no phone/fax query. "Looking for scholarly overviews of topics in religion and society; textbooks in philosophy; ecumenical subjects; and reference books."

PARSON PLACE PRESS LLC, PO Box 8277, Mobile AL 36689-0277. (251) 645-9803. E-mail: info@parsonplacepress.com. Website: www.parsonplacepress.com. Michael L. White, mng. ed. Devoted to giving both Christian authors and Christian readers a fair deal. Publishes 2-5 titles/ yr.; hardcover, trade paperbacks. Receives 60 submissions annually. 80% of books from first-time authors. Accepts mss through agents or authors. Does print-on-demand. Reprints books. Prefers 100-200 pgs. **Royalty 50% of net; no advance.** Average first printing 4 (because of print-on-demand capabilities). Publication within 3 mos. No simultaneous submissions. Responds in 4-6 wks. Requested mss by e-mail (attached file). Prefers NKJV or NASB. Guidelines on Website ("Author Guidelines"); no catalog.

Nonfiction: Proposal/2 chapters; e-query OK. Christian topic/content only.

Fiction: Proposal/2 chapters; e-query OK. For all ages.

Special Needs: In nonfiction: end-times prophecy, evangelism, and Bible studies. In fiction: mystery, romance, historical.

Contests: Sponsors a poetry contest; guidelines on Website.

Photos/Artwork: Accepts freelance photos for book covers; open to queries from freelance artists.

Tips: "Most open to conservative, biblically based content that ministers to Christians. Write intelligently, clearly, sincerely, and engagingly."

PARSONS PUBLISHING HOUSE, PO Box 488, Stafford VA 22554. (850) 867-3061. Fax (540) 659-9043. E-mail: info@parsonspublishinghouse.com. Website: www.parsonspublishinghouse.com. Nondenominational. Diane Parsons, chief ed. Exists to partner with authors to release their voice into their world. Publishes 5 titles/yr.; hardcover, trade paperbacks. Receives 40 submissions annually. 85% of books from first-time authors. No mss through agents; accepts from authors. Reprints books. Prefers 120-160 pgs. **Royalty 10% on net; no advance.** Average first printing 300. Publication within 9 mos. Considers simultaneous submissions. Responds in 60 days. Prefers accepted mss by e-mail. Guidelines by e-mail/Website ("Submissions"); no catalog.

Nonfiction: Query; e-query OK.

Fiction: Query; proposal/3 chapters; e-query OK. For teens & adults.

Ethnic Books: Hispanic.

Artwork: Open to queries from freelance artists.

Tips: "Most open to Christian living and worship."

PAULINE BOOKS & MEDIA, Daughters of St. Paul, 50 Saint Pauls Ave., Jamaica Plain MA 02130-3491. (617) 522-8911. E-mail: editorial@paulinemedia.com. Website: www.pauline.org. Catholic/ Daughters of St. Paul. Sr. Maria Grace Dateno, FSP, and Sr. Sean Mayer, FSP, acq. eds.; Submit to Lauren Koehler, ed. asst. Responds to the hopes and needs of their readers with the Word of God and in the spirit of St. Paul, utilizing all available forms of media so others can find and develop faith in Jesus within the current culture. Imprint: Pauline Kids (see separate listing). Publishes 20 titles/ yr.; hardcover & trade paperbacks. Receives 350-400 submissions annually. 10% of books from first-time authors. Accepts mss through agents or authors. No subsidy or print-on-demand. Reprints books. Prefers 10,000-60,000 wds. **Royalty 5-10% on net; offers an advance.** Average first printing 4,000-10,000. Publication within 12 mos. Considers simultaneous submissions. Responds in 2-3 mos. Prefers requested ms by e-mail. Prefers NRSV. Guidelines by mail/e-mail/Website (scroll to bottom "Manuscript Submissions"); free catalog by mail.

Nonfiction: Proposal/2 chapters; complete ms; e-query OK.
Fiction: Proposal/2 chapters; complete ms; e-query OK. For children only. "Looking for middle-reader chapter fiction with a Catholic worldview and values."
Special Needs: "Spirituality (prayer/holiness of life/seasonal titles), faith formation (religious instruction/catechesis), family life (marriage/parenting issues), biographies of the saints, prayer books. Of particular interest is our faith and culture line, which includes titles that show how Christ is present and may be more fully embraced and proclaimed within our media culture."
Tips: "Submissions are evaluated on adherence to gospel values, harmony with the Catholic tradition, relevance of topic, and quality of writing.
Note: This publisher serviced by The Writer's Edge.

PAULINE KIDS, 50 St. Paul's Ave., Boston MA 02130. (617) 522-8911. Fax (617) 524-9805. E-mail: editorial@paulinemedia.com. Website: www.pauline.org. Pauline Books & Media/Catholic. Christina M. Wegendt FSP, children's ed.; submit to Lauren Koehler, ed. asst. Seeks to provide wholesome and entertaining reading that can help children develop strong Christian values. Publishes 20-25 titles/yr.; hardcover, trade paperbacks. Receives 300-450 submissions annually. 10% of books from first-time authors. Accepts mss through agents or authors. Reprints books. **Royalty 5-10% on net; pays an advance.** Average first printing 4,000-5,000. Publication within 24 mos. Considers simultaneous submissions. Responds in 2-3 mos. Prefers accepted ms by e-mail. Prefers NRSV. Guidelines by mail/e-mail/Website (scroll to bottom "Manuscript Submissions"); free catalog by mail.
Nonfiction/Fiction: Proposal/2 chapters for easy-to-read & middle-grade readers; complete ms for board and picture books; e-query OK.
Special Needs: Easy-to-read and middle-reader chapter fiction.
Photos/Artwork: Accepts freelance photos for book covers; open to queries from freelance artists.
Note: This publisher serviced by The Writer's Edge.

PAULIST PRESS, 997 Macarthur Blvd., Mahwah NJ 07430. Toll-free (800) 218-1903. (201) 825-7300. Toll-free fax (800) 836-3161. Fax (201) 825-8345. E-mail: info@paulistpress.com. Website: www.paulistpress.com. Catholic. Lawrence Boadt, ed. dir.; Jennifer Conlan, children's ed. To bring Catholic values and beliefs into dialogue with the North American culture. Imprints: Newman Press, HiddenSpring, Stimulus. Publishes 80 titles/yr. Receives 1,000 submissions annually. 15% of books from first-time authors. Accepts mss through agents or authors. Prefers 150-250 pgs. **Royalty 7-10% of net; advance $500-1,000.** Average first printing 2,000-2,500. Publication within 18-24 mos. Considers simultaneous submissions (prefers 1st option). Requires requested ms on disk. Responds in 2 mos. Prefers NRSV. Guidelines by mail/e-mail/Website ("Manuscript Submission"); free catalog by mail.
Nonfiction: Proposal/2 chapters or complete ms; e-query OK. "Looking for theology (Catholic and ecumenical Christian), popular spirituality, liturgy, and religious education texts." Children's books for 2-5, 5-8, 8-12, 9-14 years, as per guidelines; complete ms.
Ethnic Books: A few Hispanic.
Also Does: Booklets, pamphlets.
Photos: Accepts freelance photos for book covers.
Tips: "Most open to good spirituality books that have solid input and a clear sense of tradition behind them. Demonstrate grounded convictions. Stay well read. Pay attention to contemporary social needs."

PELICAN PUBLISHING CO. INC., 1000 Burmaster St., Gretna LA 70053. (504) 368-1175. Fax (504) 368-1195. E-mail: editorial@pelicanpub.com. Website: www.pelicanpub.com. Nina Kooij, ed-in-chief. To publish books of quality and permanence that enrich the lives of those who read them. Imprints: Firebird Press, Jackson Square Press, Dove Inspirational Press (see separate listing). Publishes 3 titles/yr.; hardcover, trade paperbacks. Receives 250 submissions annually. No books from first-time authors. Accepts mss through agents or authors. Reprints books. Prefers 200+ pgs. **Royalty; pays some advances.** Publication within 9-18 mos. No simultaneous submissions. Responds in 1 mo. on queries. Requires accepted ms on disk. Prefers KJV. Guidelines on Website ("About Us"/"Submissions"); catalog for 9 x 12 SAE/6 stamps.

Nonfiction: Proposal/2 chapters; no phone/fax/e-query. Children's picture books to 1,100 wds. (send complete ms); middle readers about Louisiana (ages 8 & up) at least 25,000 wds.; cookbooks at least 200 recipes.

Fiction: Complete ms. Children's picture books only. For ages 5-8 only.

Artwork: Open to queries from freelance artists.

Tips: "On inspirational titles we need a high-profile author who already has an established speaking circuit so books can be sold at these appearances."

PENGUIN PRAISE, 375 Hudson St., New York NY 10014. (212) 366-2000. Website: www.penguin .com. Joel Fotinos, pub.; Denise Silvestro, exec. ed. Christian publishing imprint of Penguin Group (USA). Will publish books by top-tier Christian authors. Does not usually accept unsolicited mss. Distribution handled by Strang Communications and Noble sales group.

PERIGEE BOOKS, 375 Hudson St., New York NY 10014. (212) 366-2000. Fax (212) 366-2365. Website: www.penguingroup.com. Penguin Group (USA) Inc. John Duff, pub./sr. ed. Publishes 3-5 spirituality titles out of 55-60 titles/yr. Receives 300 submissions annually. 30% of books from first-time authors. Strongly prefers mss through agents (but accepts freelance). Prefers 60,000-80,000 wds. **Royalty 6-7.5%; advance $5,000-150,000.** Average first printing varies. Publication within 18 mos. Considers simultaneous submissions. Responds in 2 mos. Guidelines available with contract; free catalog.

Nonfiction: Query only; no phone/e-query; fax query OK. "Looking for spiritual, prescriptive, self-help, and women's issues; no memoirs or personal histories."

PFLAUM PUBLISHING GROUP, 2621 Dryden Rd., Ste. 300, Dayton OH 45439. (937) 293-1415. Fax (937) 293-1310. E-mail: kcannizzo@pflaum.com or jeanlarkin@pflaum.com. Website: www.pflaum .com. Peter Li Education Group/Catholic. Karen Cannizzo, ed. dir., or Jean Larkin, ed. dir. Weekly lectionary-based magazines for pre-K through 8; sacramental preparation programs for primary, junior high, and high school; catechetical resources for pre-K through 12, and religious educators. Publishes about 20 titles/yr. Receives 25 submissions annually. 10% of books from first-time authors. No reprints. **Royalty on net or outright purchase; advance depends on author arrangement.** Average first printing 2,000. Publication within 9 mos. No simultaneous submissions. Requires accepted ms on disk or by e-mail. Responds as soon as possible. Prefers NRSV. Free guidelines/catalog.

Nonfiction: Proposal with at least 1 chapter; e-query OK. "We like user-friendly resources."

Tips: "We are looking for user-friendly, field-tested resources, particularly related to sacramental preparation and lectionary-based catechesis. We specialize in consumable resources—one book per user—that need to be replaced every year, for example, for Lent and Advent."

THE PILGRIM PRESS, 700 Prospect Ave. E., Cleveland OH 44115-1100. (216) 736-3755. Fax (216) 736-2207. E-mail: sadlerk@ucc.org or stavetet@ucc.org. Website: www.thepilgrimpress .com. United Church of Christ. Timothy G. Staveteig, pub.; Kim Sadler, ed. dir. Church and educational resources. Publishes 55 titles/yr. Receives 500 submissions annually. 60% of books from first-time authors. Prefers mss through agents. Reprints books. **Royalty 10% of net; or work-for-hire, onetime fee; negotiable advance.** Average first printing 2,000. Publication within 18 mos. No simultaneous submissions. Responds in 13 wks. Accepts submissions on disk or by e-mail. Guidelines/catalog on Website ("Writer's Submission Guidelines").

Nonfiction: Query first. Proposal/2 chapters; e-mail to proposals@thepilgrimpress.com.

Special Needs: Children's sermons, worship resources, youth materials, and religious materials for ethnic groups.

Ethnic Books: African American, Native American, Asian American, Pacific Islanders, and Hispanic.

Photos: Accepts freelance photos for book covers.

Tips: "Most open to well-written manuscripts that address mainline Protestant-Christian needs and that use inclusive language and follow the *Chicago Manual of Style*. The Pilgrim Press currently does not review the following genres: autobiographies, biographies, children's (Bible) stories, fiction, memoirs, poetry, repurposed collections of newspaper articles, or sermon collections. If your proposal falls into any of these genres, please do not contact us."

PLAYERS PRESS INC., PO Box 1132, Studio City CA 91614-0132. (818) 789-4980. E-mail: players press@att.net. Website: www.ppeps.com. Players Press Inc. Robert W. Gordon, ed. To create is to live life's purpose. Publishes only dramatic works; prides themselves on high-quality titles. Imprints: Phantom Publications; Showcase. Publishes 1-6 religious titles/yr.; hardcover, trade paperbacks, mass-market paperbacks, coffee-table books. Receives 50-80 religious submissions annually. 90% of books from first-time authors. Accepts mss through agents or authors. No subsidy publishing. Does print-on-demand with older titles. Sometimes reprints books. Variable length. **Royalty 10% on net; pays some advances.** Average first printing 1,000-10,000. Publication within 12 mos. No simultaneous submissions. No submissions by e-mail. Responds in 1-3 wks. on query; 3-12 mos. on ms. Guidelines by mail; catalog for 9 x 12 SAE/11 stamps or $4.50.

   Nonfiction/Plays: Query letter only; no phone/fax/e-query. "Always looking for plays and musicals, books on theatre, film, and/or television. Good plays; all categories. For all ages." Likes religious, romantic plays.

   Contests: Sometimes sponsors a contest.

   Photos/Artwork: Accepts freelance photos for book covers; open to queries from freelance artists.

   Tips: "Most open to plays, musicals, books on theatre, film, television, and supporting areas: cameras, lighting, costumes, etc."

PONDER PUBLISHING, 15128—27B Ave., Surrey BC V4P 1P2, Canada. E-mail: info@ponderpub lishing.ca. or through Website: www.PonderPublishing.ca. Darian Kovacs, pub. Focuses on Canadian writers primarily, writing material for youth and youth workers. Submit proposal through online form (see Website).

+PORT YONDER PRESS, 6332—33rd Ave. Dr., Shellsburg IA 52332. (319) 436-3015. E-mail: contact@portyonderpress.com. Website: www.PortYonderPress.com. C. Maggie Woychik, ed-in-chief. Crossover publisher of both Christian and general books. Publishes 6-12 titles/yr. Receives 200+ submissions annually. 15% of books from first-time authors. Accepts mss through agents or authors. Prefers 150-300 pgs. **Royalty 40-50% on net; small advance.** Does books-on-demand. Publication within 2 yrs. No simultaneous submissions. Accepts submissions only in January or at conferences where publisher/editor attends. Requires accepted mss by e-mail. Responds in 2 mos. Guidelines on Website (click on "Getting Published"). Not included in topical listings.

   Nonfiction & Fiction: Query in January.

   Tips: "We love a sea theme, literary books, unique, niche. Family-friendly books only. See Website for specifics."

@POWER PUBLISHING, 13680 N. Duncan Dr., Camby IN 46113. (317) 347-1051. Fax (317) 347-1068. E-mail: info@powerpublishinginc.com. Website: www.powerpublishinginc.com. Janet Schwind, ed.; submit by mail or through Website. Our innovative culture is author-focused, assuming great care and consideration with each manuscript, and offering a unique line of publishing programs to meet the needs of nearly every author. Publishes hardcover, trade paperbacks, mass-market paperbacks. Receives 7,200 submissions annually. 50% of books from first-time authors. Accepts mss through agents or authors. Subsidy/co-op publishes 10%; print-on-demand up to

10%. Reprints books. Prefers 150+ pgs. **Royalty on net.** Publication within 6 mos. Considers simultaneous submissions. Responds in 2 wks. to initial review; 60-90 days for second review. Prefers accepted mss by e-mail. Prefers NIV. Guidelines by mail/e-mail/Website (under "For Author"); no catalog.

Nonfiction: Proposal/3-6 chapters; complete ms; phone/fax/e-query OK.

Fiction: Proposal/3-6 chapters; complete ms; phone/fax/e-query OK. For all ages.

Special Needs: Christian leadership, emergent church, church/pastor resources, and general Christian living.

Also Does: E-books.

Photos/Artwork: Accepts freelance photos for book covers; open to queries from freelance artists.

Tips: "Most open to nonfiction—inspiring and written to appeal to a mass market, as well as spiritual-growth related, or church resources. We require all authors to complete and submit a New Author form with each manuscript submission. Form available by e-mail: info@powerpublishing.com or on the Website."

PRAEGER PUBLISHERS, 130 Cremona Dr., Santa Barbara CA 93117. (805) 968-1911. E-mail: mwilt@abc-clio.com. Website: www.praeger.com or www.abc-clio.com. Imprint of ABC-CLIO. Michael Wilt, sr. acq. ed. Primary markets are public and university libraries; no trade distribution. Publishes 5-25 titles/yr.; hardcover. Receives 100-120 submissions annually. Accepts mss through agents or authors. No subsidy or reprints. Prefers up to 100,000 wds. **Variable royalty on net; pays some advances**. Average first printing 1,500. Publication within 8-12 mos. Considers simultaneous submissions. Responds in 2-4 mos. Guidelines by e-mail; catalog on Website.

Nonfiction: Book proposal/1-3 chapters or all chapters available; e-query preferred.

Special Needs: General religious studies; religion & society/culture; religion & contemporary issues.

Ethnic Books: African American studies (general interest); Islamic studies; Jewish studies; Native American studies; Hispanic/Latino studies.

Tips: "Most open to general interest topics; accessible vocabulary and writing style. No self-help or how-to books."

+PRAXIS PRESS, 1515 Skelton Rd., Gainesville GA 30504. Toll-free (888) 816-9068. E-mail: clint@praxispress.org. Website: www.praxispress.org. Clint Bokelman, pub. **Outright purchase: buys all rights on acceptance.** Responds in 2+ mos. Guidelines on Website (scroll to bottom of page and click on "Contact Praxis Publishing").

PREP PUBLISHING, 1110½ Hay St., Fayetteville NC 28305. (910) 483-2336. Fax (910) 483-2439. E-mail: preppub@aol.com. Website: www.prep-pub.com. PREP Inc. Anne McKinney, mng. ed. (mckinney@prep-pub.com). Books to enrich people's lives and help them find joy in the human experience. Publishes 10 titles/yr.; hardcover, trade paperbacks. Receives 1,500+ submissions annually. 85% of books from first-time authors. Reprints books. Prefers 250 pgs. **Royalty 6-10% of retail; pays an advance.** Average first printing 3,000-5,000. Publication within 18 mos. Considers simultaneous submissions. Responds in 1 mo. Guidelines by mail/Website; catalog for #10 SAE/2 stamps.

Nonfiction: Query only; no phone query. Charges a $350 nonrefundable reading fee.

Fiction: Query only (cover letter and up to 3-page synopsis). All ages. "We are attempting to grow our Judeo-Christian fiction imprint."

Tips: "Rewrite, rewrite, rewrite with your reader clearly in focus."

G. P. PUTNAM'S SONS BOOKS FOR YOUNG READERS, 345 Hudson St., 14th Fl., New York NY 10014. (212) 414-3610. Website: www.penguingroup.com. Submit to Children's Manuscript Editor. Imprint: Penguin Group USA. Publishes 45 titles/yr.; hardcover. Accepts mss through agents or authors. No reprints. **Variable royalty on retail; negotiable advance.** Considers simultaneous submissions. No disk or e-mail submissions. Responds in 6 mos. Guidelines for SASE.

Nonfiction: Proposal/1-2 chapters. "We publish some religious/inspirational books and books for ages 2-18."

Fiction: For children or teens. Complete ms for picture books; proposal/3 chapters for novels. Primarily picture books or middle-grade novels.

QUIET WATERS PUBLICATIONS, PO Box 34, Bolivar MO 65613-0034. (417) 326-5001. E-mail: QWP@usa.net. Website: www.QuietWatersPub.com. Stephen Trobisch, ed. Books on marriage, family, and missions. Publishes 5-10 titles/yr.; hardcover, trade paperbacks. Prefers mss through agents. No subsidy; does print-on-demand. Reprints books. No length preference. **Royalty 8% on retail; no advance.** Publication within 6 mos. Considers simultaneous submissions. Guidelines on Website; catalog for 9 x 12 SAE/5 stamps.

Nonfiction/Fiction: Query letter first. Fiction for all ages.

QUINTESSENTIAL BOOKS, PO Box 8755, Kansas City MO 64114-0755. (816) 561-1555. E-mail: support@quintessentialbooks.com. Website: www.quintessentialbooks.com. Laura C. Joyce, ed. dir. Books that challenge people to think deeply and live passionately in accordance with sound principles. Publishes 5-10 titles/yr.; hardcover, trade paperbacks, mass-market paperbacks. Receives 150 submissions annually. 25% of books from first-time authors. Prefers mss through agents. Reprints books. Prefers 60,000-70,000 wds. or 224 pgs. **Royalty on net; negotiable advance.** Average first printing varies. Publication within 18 mos. Considers simultaneous submissions. Responds in 3-4 mos. Requires requested ms by e-mail. Prefers NIV or NLT. Guidelines by mail/Website.

Nonfiction: Query only; no phone/fax/e-query. "Nonfiction books must address significant topics in a fresh way, must speak boldly on controversial issues, and must be clear and accurate. Manuscripts on medicine, mental health, and nutrition will only be accepted from credentialed health professionals."

Fiction: Query only; no phone/fax/e-query. For adults. "Fiction must exhibit an understanding of human hearts and relationships, must create a complete and credible world for the reader, and must have multifaceted characters and aesthetic depth."

Photos/Artwork: Accepts freelance photos for book covers; open to queries from freelance artists.

Tips: "We are interested in reaching an intelligent, widely read audience. Avoid submitting simplistic material."

**Note: This publisher serviced by The Writer's Edge.

RAGGED EDGE PRESS, 73 W. Burd St., PO Box 708, Shippenburg PA 17257. (717) 532-2237. Fax (717) 532-6110. E-mail: marketing@whitemane.com or editorial@whitemane.com. Website: www.whitemane.com. White Mane Publishing Co. Inc. Harold E. Collier, acq. ed. Christian, social science, and self-help books that make a difference in people's lives. Publishes 10-15 titles/yr. Receives 50-75 submissions annually. 50% of books from first-time authors. Subsidy publishes 20%. Reprints books. Prefers 200 pgs. **Variable royalty on net; no advance.** Average first printing 3,000. Publication within 12-18 mos. Considers simultaneous submissions. Responds in 30-90 days. Guidelines by mail/e-mail; catalog online.

Nonfiction: Query only; fax/e-query OK.

Tips: "Most open to a Protestant book in the middle of the spectrum."

RAINBOW PUBLISHERS, PO Box 261129, San Diego CA 92196. Toll-free (800) 323-7337. Toll-free fax (800) 331-0297. E-mail: editor@rainbowpublishers.com. Website: www.rainbowpublishers.com. Submit to The Editor. Publishes Bible-teaching, reproducible books for children's teachers. Publishes 20 titles/yr. Receives 250 submissions annually. 50% of books from first-time authors. Reprints books. Prefers 96 pgs. **Outright purchases $640 & up.** Average first printing 2,500. Publication within

2 yrs. Considers simultaneous submissions. Responds in 3 mos. No disk or e-mail submissions. Prefers NIV. Guidelines/catalog on Website ("Submissions" at bottom).

Nonfiction: Proposal/2-5 chapters; no phone/e-query. "Looking for fun and easy ways to teach Bible concepts to kids, ages 2-12."

Special Needs: Creative puzzles and unique games.

Artwork: Open to queries from freelance artists.

Tips: "Visit your Christian bookstore or our Website to see what we have already published. We have over 100 titles and do not like to repeat topics, so a proposal needs to be unique for us but not necessarily unique in the market. Most open to writing that appeals to teachers who work with kids and Bible activities that have been tried and tested on today's kids."

@RANDALL HOUSE DIGITAL, 114 Bush Rd., PO Box 17306, Nashville TN 37217. Toll-free (800) 877-7030. (615) 361-1221. Fax (615) 367-0535. E-mail through Website: www.randallhouse.com. National Assn. of Free Will Baptists. Alan Clagg, dir. Produces curriculum-on-demand via the Internet, and electronic resources to supplement existing printed curriculum. Guidelines on Website (click on "Contact Us"/"Book Proposal Guide").

Nonfiction: Query first; e-query OK.

Special Needs: Teacher-training material (personal or group), elective Bible studies for adults, children's curriculum (other than Sunday school), and elective materials for teens.

Also Does: Digital books.

Tips: "We are looking for writers with vision for worldwide ministry who would like to see their works help a greater section of the Body of Christ than served by the conventionally printed products."

@RANDALL HOUSE PUBLICATIONS, 114 Bush Rd., Nashville TN 37217. Toll-free (800) 877-7030. (615) 361-1221. Fax (615) 367-0535. E-mail: michelle.orr@randallhouse.com. Website: www.randallhouse.com. Free Will Baptist. Michelle Orr, sr. acq. ed. Publishes Sunday school and Christian education materials to make Christ known, from a conservative perspective. Publishes 10-15 titles/yr.; hardcover, trade paperbacks, digital. Receives 300-500 submissions annually. 40% of books from first-time authors. Accepts mss through agents or authors. No subsidy or reprints. Prefers 40,000 wds. **Royalty 12-18% on net; pays an advance.** Average first printing 5,000. Publication within 18 mos. Considers simultaneous submissions. Accepts requested mss by e-mail. Responds in 10-12 wks. Guidelines by e-mail/Website ("Contact"/click on "Book Proposal Guide" in text); no catalog.

Nonfiction: Query; e-query OK; proposal/2 chapters. Must fill out book proposal form they provide.

Artwork: Open to queries from freelance artists (andrea.young@randallhouse.com).

Tips: "We are expanding our book division with a conservative perspective. We have a very conservative view as a publisher."

**Note: This publisher serviced by ChristianManuscriptSubmissions.com.

RAVENHAWK BOOKS, 7739 E. Broadway Blvd., #95, Tucson AZ 85710. E-mail: ravenhawk6dof@ yahoo.com. Website: www.6dofsolutions.com. Blog: see Website. The 6DOF Group. Karl Lasky, pub.; Shelly Geraci, submissions ed. Publishes variable number of titles/yr.; hardcover, trade paperbacks. Receives 1,000-1,500 submissions annually. 70% of books from first-time authors. Print-on-demand. Reprints books. **Royalty 40-50% on gross profits; no advance.** Average first printing 2,500. Publication in up to 18 mos. Considers simultaneous submissions. Responds in 6 wks., if interested. Catalog on Website.

Nonfiction: Query first; e-query OK. "Looking for profitable books from talented writers."

Fiction: Query first. For all ages. Unsolicited full mss returned unopened.

Special Needs: Looking for books from young authors, 16-22 years old.

Photos/Artwork: Accepts freelance photos for book covers; open to queries from freelance artists.

Tips: "Most open to crisp, creative, entertaining writing that also informs and educates. Writing, as any creative art, is a gift from God. Not everyone has the innate talent to do it well. We are author-oriented. We don't play games with the numbers."

REALMS—Fiction for all ages. See Strang Book Group.

REFERENCE SERVICE PRESS, 5000 Windplay Dr., Ste. 4, El Dorado Hills CA 95762. (916) 939-9620. Fax (916) 939-9626. E-mail: info@rspfunding.com. Website: www.rspfunding.com. R. David Weber, ed. Books related to financial aid and Christian higher education. Publishes 1 title/yr.; hardcover, trade paperbacks. Receives 3-5 submissions annually. Most books from first-time authors. No reprints. **Royalty 10% of net; usually no advance.** Publication within 5 mos. May consider simultaneous submissions. No guidelines; free catalog for 2 stamps.

> **Nonfiction:** Proposal/several chapters.

> **Special Needs:** Financial aid directories for Christian college students.

+REFORMATION HERITAGE BOOKS, 2965 Leonard St. N.E., Grand Rapids MI 49525. (616) 977-0889. Fax (616) 285-3246. E-mail: orders@heritagebooks.org. Website: www.heritagebooks.org. Dr. Joel Beeke, ed.; submit to Jay Collier. To glorify God and strengthen His church through the publication and distribution of Puritan and Reformed literature. Imprint: Soli Deo Gloria. Publishes 24 titles/yr.; hardcover, trade paperbacks. Receives 100 submissions annually. 25% of books from first-time authors. Prefers mss through agents. No subsidy. Reprints books. **Royalty 10-12%; no advance.** Average first printing 1,000. Publication within 8 mos. Considers simultaneous submissions. Accepted mss by e-mail. Responds in 2 mos. Prefers KJV. Guidelines by mail; free catalog.

> **Nonfiction:** Proposal/2 chapters; no phone/fax query; e-query OK. Looking for Puritan and Reformed books.

> **Photos:** Accepts freelance photos for book covers; open to queries from freelance artists.

REFORMATION TRUST PUBLISHING, Editorial Dept., 400 Technology Park, Lake Mary FL 32746. Toll-free (800) 435-4343. (407) 333-4244. Fax (407) 333-4233. E-mail: gbailey@ligonier.org. Website: www.reformationtrust.com. Imprint of Ligonier Ministries. Greg Bailey, dir. of publications. Exists to publish books true to the historic Christian faith from the best of today's pastors and scholars. Publishes 10-12 titles/yr.; hard cover, trade paperbacks. Receives 100 submissions annually. Open to first-time authors. Accepts mss through agents or authors. No subsidy or reprints. Prefers 40,000-80,000 wds. **Royalty on net; no advance.** Average first printing 5,000. Publication within 10 mos. Considers simultaneous submissions. Responds in 3 mos. Prefers ESV. Guidelines on Website; free catalog.

> **Nonfiction:** Proposal/2 chapters; no complete mss. Accepted ms by disk or e-mail.

> **Fiction:** Proposal/2 chapters. Children's fiction only. "As in all our titles, we want our children's books to touch the deep truths of the Christian faith."

> **Tips:** "We are looking for books that teach the historic Christian faith in layman's language. Our books are not academic, but good scholarship is important. Above all, our books must be based on Scripture. Our theological stance is Reformed/Calvinist."

> ****Note:** This publisher serviced by The Writer's Edge & ChristianManuscriptSubmissions.com.

REGAL BOOKS, 1957 Eastman Ave., Ventura CA 93003. (805) 644-9721. Fax (805) 644-9728. E-mail: editors@gospellight.com. Website: www.regalbooks.com. Gospel Light. Submit to The Editor. To know Christ and to make Him known; publishing resources to create meaningful dialogue. Publishes 50 titles/yr.; hardcover, trade paperbacks. Receives 1,000 submissions annually. 20% of books from first-time authors. Requires mss through agents. No subsidy, print-on-demand, or reprints. **Royalty.** Publication within 18 mos. Considers simultaneous submissions. Prefers NIV. No guidelines or catalog.

Nonfiction: All unsolicited mss returned unread, if SASE provided.

Tips: "Most open to books that are well-written; unique in some way. Work through an agent."

**Note: This publisher serviced by The Writer's Edge.

@RESOURCE PUBLICATIONS INC., 160 E. Virginia St., Ste. 290, San Jose CA 95112-5876. (408) 286-8505. Fax (408) 287-8748. E-mail: info@rpinet.com. Website: www.rpinet.com. William Burns, pub. Publishes 10 titles/yr.; trade paperbacks. Receives 450 submissions annually. 30% of books from first-time authors. Prefers 50,000 wds. **Royalty 8% of net; rare advance.** Average first printing 2,000. Publication within 1 yr. Responds in 10 wks. Prefers requested ms on disk. Guidelines by e-mail/Website ("Authors & Writers" left side); catalog on Website.

Nonfiction: Proposal/1 chapter; phone/fax/e-query OK.

Fiction: Proposal/2-3 chapters. Adult. Only read-aloud stories for storytellers; fables and parables. "Must be useful in ministerial, counseling, or educational settings."

Also Does: Computer programs; aids to ministry or education. E-books.

Tips: "Know our market. We cater to ministers in Catholic and mainstream Protestant settings. We are not an evangelical house or general interest publisher. Looking for nonfiction ideas that save people time, save money, or help people do their jobs better. Most open to a book that will help a practicing minister understand and deal with a pressing problem he or she faces."

REVELL BOOKS, Fleming H. Revell, Box 6287, Grand Rapids MI 49516. (616) 676-9185. Fax (616) 676-2315. Website: www.revellbooks.com. Imprint of Baker Publishing Group. Publishes inspirational fiction and nonfiction for the broadest Christian market. Catalog on Website. No unsolicited mss. Submit only through an agent, the Writer's Edge, Authonomy.com, or ChristianManuscriptSubmissions.com.

REVIEW AND HERALD PUBLISHING ASSN., 55 W. Oak Ridge Dr., Hagerstown MD 21740-7390. (301) 393-3000. Fax (301) 393-4055. E-mail: editorial@rhpa.org. Website: www.rhpa.org. Seventh-day Adventist. JoAlyse Waugh, acq. ed. (jwaugh@rhpa.org; 301-393-4050). **Royalty 12% of net on paperbacks; 14% of net on hard cover.** Responds in 3-4 mos. Any Bible version. Guidelines on Website ("Writer's Guidelines").

Nonfiction: Proposal.

REVIVAL NATION PUBLISHING, 218 Christina St., Sarnia ON N7T 5V2, Canada. (519) 339-7206. Fax (519) 339-7213. E-mail: publishing@revivalnation.com. Website: www.revivalnationpublishing.com. Revival Nation Evangelistic Ministries. Greg Holmes, pres. A not-for-profit publisher; all publishing revenue goes back to building God's Kingdom. Imprint: Revival Nation Kids. Publishes 30-50 titles/yr.; trade paperbacks. Receives 300-500 submissions annually. 90% of books from first-time authors. Accepts mss through agents or authors. No subsidy. No reprints. Prefers 200-250 pgs. **Royalty 10-25% on net; no advance.** Average first printing 1,000. Publication within 6 mos. Accepts simultaneous submissions. Responds in 1-2 mos. Prefers e-mail submissions (attached file in Word). Prefers NIV. Guidelines on Website ("Submissions"); free catalog.

Nonfiction: Complete ms; submit with online form via Website only. "We look for passion in the writing—something the author would die for."

Fiction: Complete ms; submit with online form via Website only. For children & adults.

Special Needs: Looking for revival, renewal, holiness, Holy Spirit, prayer, and Charismatic.

Tips: Gives preference to Canadian authors or those actively involved in ministry, but open to all. Only considers unpublished work; does not accept self-published books. This is a not-for-profit publisher.

ROSE PUBLISHING, 4733 Torrance Blvd., #259, Torrance CA 90503. Toll-free (800) 532-4278. (310) 353-2100. Fax (310) 353-2116. E-mail: rosepubl@aol.com. Website: www.rose-publishing

.com. Nondenominational. Lynnette Pennings, acq./mng. ed. Publishes primarily Bible studies, apologetics; Sunday school wall charts and visual aids. Publishes 30-40 titles/yr. 2% of projects from first-time authors. No mss through agents. No reprints. **Outright purchases.** Publication within 18 mos. Considers simultaneous submissions. Requires accepted mss by disk or e-mail. Responds in 2-3 mos. Catalog for 9 x 12 SAE/4 stamps.

Nonfiction: Query or proposal. No books, mainly booklets/pamphlets, wall charts/posters, or PowerPoints.

Special Needs: Query with sketch of proposed chart or poster (nonreturnable); fax query OK; e-query OK if less than 100 wds. (copied into message). Open to material that makes difficult Bible topics or theological topics easier; wall charts, study guides and worksheets on sharing your faith and salvation with skeptics. Typical subjects include: cults, books of the Bible, church history, world religions, discipleship, angels, prayer, teens, hot topics.

Also Does: PowerPoint presentations for biblical subjects.

Artwork: Open to queries from freelance artists.

Tips: "Now accepting more freelance submissions. No fiction." Publishes a unique format that makes difficult Bible topics easy to understand.

**Note: This publisher serviced by ChristianManuscriptSubmissions.com.

+ROYALTY BOOKS INTERNATIONAL, 2046 Gees Mill Rd., Ste. 210, Conyers GA 30013. (678) 923-3732. E-mail through Website: www.royaltybooksonline.com. **Royalty; pays an advance.**

SAINT CATHERINE OF SIENA PRESS, 4812 N. Park Ave., Indianapolis IN 46205. Toll-free (888) 232-1492. E-mail: service@saintcatherineofsienapress.com. Website: www.saintcatherineofsiena press.com. Catholic. Jean Zander, ed. dir. Established to promote "excellence in catechesis . . . in faithfulness to Rome." Responds in up to 2 mos. Guidelines/catalog on Website (scroll down to "Attention Authors").

Nonfiction: Proposal/2 chapters.

@SAMARITAN PRESS, PO Box 14451, Knoxville TN 37914. (865) 335-0072. Fax (865) 249-7206. E-mail: ihp@samaritanpress.com. Website: www.samaritanpress.com. R. Michael Henegar, ed.; submit to Kristy Lynn. Believes that every person has a story to tell and readers to enjoy that story. Publishes 15-20 titles/yr.; hardcover, mass-market paperbacks, coffee-table books. Receives 300 submissions annually. 70% of books from first-time authors. Accepts mss through agents or authors. Subsidy publishes 10%; does print-on-demand. Reprints books. Prefers 80+ pgs. **Royalty 10-15% on retail; no advance.** Average first printing 5,000. Publication within 12 mos. No simultaneous submissions. Responds in 3 mos. Wants accepted mss on disk. Prefers NKJV. Guidelines on Website; no catalog.

Nonfiction/Fiction: Query first or complete ms; e-query OK. Fiction for all ages.

Special Needs: All genres of fiction, Christian living, Bible study, and personal experience.

Also Does: E-books.

Photos/Artwork: Accepts freelance photos for book covers; open to queries from freelance artists.

Tips: "All types of fiction are considered, and we enjoy regular people submitting regular stories that can become great lessons of faith and devotion to Jesus Christ."

SCEPTER PUBLISHERS INC., PO Box 211, New York NY 10018. Toll-free (800) 322-8773. (212) 354-0670. Fax (212) 354-0736. E-mail: info@scepterpublishers.org. Website: www.scepterpublish ers.org. Catholic. John Powers, ed. Books on how to struggle to live faith and virtue in one's daily life. Publishes 15 titles/yr. 0-2% of books from first-time authors. Reprints books. Prefers 200 pgs. **Royalty on net; advance $1,000-2,000.** Average first printing 2,000. Publication within 24 mos. No simultaneous submissions. Responds within 1 mo. Guidelines on Website ("Contact"/scroll down to "Authors"); free catalog.

Nonfiction: Query only first with a 1-2 pg. synopsis; no phone/fax/e-query. Does not return material.

Fiction: Query only first; no phone/fax/e-query.

Tips: "Looking for books that help readers struggle better to live Christian virtues and seriously practice their faith."

SCRIPTURE PRESS—See David C. Cook.

SHEED & WARD, 4501 Forbes Blvd., Ste. 200, Lanham MD 20706. Toll-free (800) 462-6420. (301) 459-3366. Fax (301) 429-5747. Website: www.sheedandward.com. Imprint of Rowman & Littlefield Publishers Inc. Marcus Boggs, pub. (mboggs@rowman.com); submit to Sarah Stanton, acq. ed. (sstanton@rowman.com). Publishes books of contemporary impact and enduring merit in Catholic-Christian thought and action. Publishes 10-20 titles/yr.; hardcover, trade paperbacks. Receives 2,000 submissions annually. 25% of books from first-time authors. Prefers 50,000-80,000 wds. **Royalty 6-12% on retail; $2,000 advance.** Average first printing 3,000. Publication within 8 mos. Accepts simultaneous submissions. Responds in 2-3 mos. Requires requested ms on disk. Prefers NAB, NRSV (Catholic editions). Guidelines/catalog on Website ("Submissions").

> **Nonfiction:** Proposal/1-2 chapters; e-query OK. "Looking for parish ministry (health care, spirituality, leadership, general trade books for mass audiences, sacraments, small group, or priestless parish facilitating books), Catholic history, Catholic studies."
>
> **Photos/Artwork:** Considers photos/artwork as part of book package.
>
> **Tips:** "Looking for general trade titles and academic titles (oriented toward the classroom) in areas of spirituality, parish ministry, leadership, sacraments, prayer, faith formation, church history, and Scripture."

SILOAM—See Strang Book Group.

@SMYTH & HELWYS PUBLISHING INC., 6316 Peake Rd., Macon GA 31210-3960. Toll-free (800) 747-3016. (478) 757-0564. Fax (478) 757-1305. E-mail: Proposals@helwys.com. Website: www .helwys.com. Submit to Book Editor. Quality resources for the church, the academy, and individual Christians who are nurtured by faith and informed by scholarship. Publishes 25-30 titles/yr. Receives 600 submissions annually. 40% of books from first-time authors. Prefers 144 pgs. **Royalty 7%.** Considers simultaneous submissions. Responds in 3 mos. Guidelines by mail/e-mail/Website (under "How to Publish"); free catalog.

> **Nonfiction:** Hard copy of proposal with 2-4 sample chapters. "Manuscripts requested for topics appropriate for mainline church and seminary/university textbook market."
>
> **Also Does:** E-books. Copies of print books and original books. Go to: www.nextsunday.com.
>
> **Tips:** "Most open to books with a strong secondary or special market. Niche titles and short-run options available for specialty subjects."

+SOLID GROUND CHRISTIAN BOOKS, PO Box 660132, Vestavia Hills AL 35266. Toll-free (866) 789-7423. (205) 443-0311. Fax (775) 822-5917. E-mail: Mike.sgcb@charter.net. Website: www.solid-ground-books.com. Committed to the presentation of the cardinal doctrines of Holy Scripture.

STANDARD PUBLISHING, 8805 Governor's Hill Dr., Ste. 400, Cincinnati OH 45249. (513) 931-4050. Fax (513) 931-0950. Website: www.standardpub.com. CFM Religion Publishing Group LLC. Provides true-to-the-Bible resources that inspire, educate, and motivate Christians to a growing relationship with Jesus Christ. Accepts mss through agents or authors. Hardcover & trade paperbacks. No reprints. **Royalty or outright purchase; advance.** No simultaneous submissions. Responds in 3-6 mos. Prefers NIV/KJV. Guidelines on Website (www.standardpub.com/writers).

> **Nonfiction:** Query only; e-query OK.
>
> **Fiction:** Query only; e-query OK. Children's picture or board books; juvenile novels.

Special Needs: Adult and youth ministry resources; children's ministry resources.

**Note: This publisher serviced by The Writer's Edge and ChristianManuscriptSubmissions.com.

ST. ANTHONY MESSENGER PRESS and FRANCISCAN COMMUNICATIONS, 28 W. Liberty St., Cincinnati OH 45202. Toll-free (800) 488-0488. (513) 241-5615. Fax (513) 241-0399. E-mail: StAnthony@AmericanCatholic.org. Websites: www.AmericanCatholic.org; www.sampbooks.org; www .servantbooks.org. Catholic. Lisa Biedenbach, dir. of product development, SAMP (lisab@American Catholic.org); Cynthia Cavnar, dir. of product development, Servant (cynthiac@americancatholic. org); Louise Pore, dir. of development, Servant (lpore@AmericanCatholic.org); Jeanne Hunt, dir. of product development, Institutional (jeanneh@americancatholic.org); Katie Carroll, mng. ed. Seeks to publish affordable resources for living a Catholic-Christian lifestyle. Imprints: Servant Books, Franciscan Communications, Fischer Productions, Ikonographics (videos). SAMP publishes 20-35 titles/yr.; Servant publishes 15-18 titles/yr.; trade paperbacks (mostly). Receives 450 submissions annually. 5% of books from first-time authors. Accepts mss through agents or authors. Reprints books (seldom). Prefers 25,000-50,000 wds. or 100-250 pgs. **Royalty 10-14% on net; advance $1,000-3,000.** Average first printing 4,000. Publication within 18 mos. No simultaneous submissions. Accepts requested mss by e-mail. Responds in 5-9 wks. Prefers NRSV. Guidelines on Website ("Contact Us"/"Writer's Guidelines"); catalog for 9 x 12 SAE/4 stamps.

> **Nonfiction:** Proposal/1-2 chapters; fax/e-query OK. "Looking for resources for living the Catholic-Christian life at home and in workplace, pastoral resources for parishes and small groups; spiritual self-help from a Catholic perspective; prayer resources; saints and inspirational people; applied Scripture; and support for marriage."
>
> **Special Needs:** Spiritual role models, Catholic teaching/identity, marriage enrichment, personal growth/self help, spirituality, Catholic inspiration.
>
> **Ethnic Books:** Hispanic, African American occasionally.
>
> **Tips:** "Most open to books with sound Catholic doctrine that include personal experiences or anecdotes applicable to today's culture. Our books are decidedly Catholic. Content that can be produced in multiple formats is best, such as book, newsletter or magazine article, Web feature, radio feature, etc."

STARIK PUBLISHING, PO Box 307, Slaton TX 79364. E-mail: submissions@starikpublishing.com. Website: www.starikpublishing.com. Blog: www.starikpublishing.com/wordpress. Stacie Craig, exec. ed. A family-oriented publishing house seeking to improve families through literature. Publishes 1-3 titles/yr.; trade paperbacks. Receives 75 submissions annually. 30% of books from first-time authors. No books through agents. No subsidy or reprints. Prefers 100-400 pgs. **Royalty; no advance.** Average first print run 2,000. Considers simultaneous submissions. Responds in 6-8 wks. Guidelines by mail/e-mail/Website ("Submission Guidelines"); no catalog.

> **Nonfiction:** Proposal/3 chapters & short author bio; e-query OK. Accepts disk or e-mail submissions.
>
> **Fiction:** Proposal/3 chapters & short author bio; e-query OK. Teen/young adult & adult Christian fiction.
>
> **Artwork:** Open to queries from freelance artists.

ST. AUGUSTINE'S PRESS, PO Box 2285, South Bend IN 46680. (574) 291-3500. Fax (574) 291-3700. E-mail: bruce@staugustine.net. Website: www.staugustine.net. A conservative, non-denominational (although mostly Catholic) scholarly publisher of academic titles, mainly in academic philosophy, theology, and cultural history. Bruce Fingerhut, pres. Publishes 20-40 titles/yr.; hardcover, trade paperbacks. Receives 100+ submissions annually. 5% of books from first-time authors. Accepts mss through agents or authors. Reprints books. **Royalty 6-15% of net; advance $1,000.** Average first printing 1,000. Publication within 1 yr. Considers simultaneous submissions. Responds in 3 mos. No guidelines; free catalog.

Nonfiction: Query or proposal/chapters. "Most of our titles are philosophy." Cultural history. **Tips:** "Most open to books on subjects or by authors similar to what/who we already publish."

ST. BEDE'S PUBLICATIONS, St. Scholastica Priory, PO Box 545, Petersham MA 01366-0545. (978) 724-3213. Fax (978) 724-3216. E-mail: vincentclare@aol.com. Catholic/St. Scholastica Priory. Sr. Maryclare Vincent, pres.; submit to Acquisitions Editor. Publishes 3-4 titles/yr.; hardcover & trade paperbacks. 30-40% of books from first-time authors. Accepts mss through agents or authors. Reprints books. **Royalty 5-10% of net or retail.** Publication within 2 yrs. Considers simultaneous submissions. Responds in 2 mos. Prefers NIV. Catalog & guidelines for 9 x 12 SAE/2 stamps.

    Nonfiction: Has a heavy backlog so not accepting freelance submissions for now.

STEEPLE HILL, 233 Broadway, Ste. 1001, New York NY 10279-0001. (212) 553-4200. Fax (212) 277-8969. Website: www.SteepleHill.com. Harlequin Enterprises. Submit to any of the following: Joan Marlow Golan, exec. ed.; Melissa Endlich, sr. ed.; Tina James, sr. ed.; Emily Rodmell, asst. ed.; Rachel Burkot, ed. asst.; Elizabeth Mazer, asst. ed. Lines: Love Inspired (mass-market category romances), see listing below; Love Inspired Suspense; Love Inspired Historical, see listing below. Publishes 154 titles/yr.; mass-market paperbacks. Receives 500-1,000 submissions annually. 15% of books from first-time authors. Accepts mss through agents or authors. No reprints. **Royalty on retail; competitive advance.** Publication within 12-24 mos. No simultaneous submissions. Requires accepted ms on disk/hard copy. Responds in 3 mos. Prefers KJV. Guidelines by mail/Website (click on "Steeple Hill"/"scroll down right side to "Write"/"Writers Guidelines"); no catalog.

    Fiction: Complete ms for series; no phone/fax/e-query.

STEEPLE HILL LOVE INSPIRED, 233 Broadway, Ste. 1001, New York NY 10279-0001. (212) 553-4200. Fax (212) 277-8969. E-mail: rachel_burkot@harlequin.ca. Website: www.SteepleHill.com. Harlequin Enterprises. Submit to any of the following: Joan Marlow Golan, exec. ed.; Melissa Endlich, sr. ed.; Emily Rodmell, asst. ed.; Rachel Burkot, ed. asst. Mass-market Christian romance novels. Publishes 72 titles/yr.; mass-market paperbacks. Receives 500-1,000 submissions annually. 15% of books from first-time authors. Accepts mss through agents or authors. No reprints. Prefers 55,000-60,000 wds. **Royalty on retail; competitive advance.** Publication within 12-24 mos. Requires ms on disk/hard copy. Responds in 3 mos. Prefers KJV. Guidelines by mail/Website (click on "Steeple Hill"/scroll down right side to "Write"/"Writers Guidelines"); no catalog.

    Fiction: Query letter or 3 chapters and up to 5-page synopsis; no phone/fax/e-query.

    Tips: "We want character-driven romance with an author voice that inspires."

    **Note: This publisher serviced by ChristianManuscriptSubmissions.com.

STEEPLE HILL LOVE INSPIRED HISTORICAL, 233 Broadway, Ste. 1001, New York NY 10279-0001. (212) 553-4200. Fax (212) 227-8969. Website: www.SteepleHill.com. Harlequin Enterprises. Submit to any of the following: Joan Marlow Golan, exec. ed.; Tina James, sr. ed. in charge of line; Melissa Endlich, sr. ed.; Emily Rodmell, asst. ed.; Rachel Burkot, ed. asst.; Elizabeth Mazer, asst. ed. Mass-market Christian historical romance novels. Publishes 24 titles/yr.; mass-market paperbacks. Receives 500-1,000 submissions annually. 15% of books from first-time authors. Accepts mss through agents or authors. No reprints. Prefers 70,000-75,000 wds. **Royalty on retail; competitive advance.** Publication within 12-36 mos. No simultaneous submissions. Responds in 3 mos. Prefers KJV. Guidelines on Website (click on "Steeple Hill"/scroll down right side to "Write"/"Writers Guidelines"); no catalog.

    Fiction: Proposal/3 chapters. Historical romances featuring Christian characters facing the many challenges of life and love in a variety of historical time periods: biblical fiction, Americana (e.g., westerns, post–Civil War, etc.), European historical eras (e.g., Tudor, Regency, and Victorian England, 18th-century Scotland, etc.), and 20th century (turn-of-the-century through World War II).

STEEPLE HILL LOVE INSPIRED SUSPENSE, 233 Broadway, Ste. 1001, New York NY 10279-0001. (212) 553-4200. Fax (212) 277-8969. E-mail: Sarah_McDaniel@harlequin.ca. Website: www .SteepleHill.com. Harlequin Enterprises. Submit to any of the following: Joan Marlow Golan, exec. ed.; Tina James, sr. ed. in charge of line; Melissa Endlich, sr. ed.; Emily Rodmell, asst. ed.; Rachel Burkot, ed. asst.; Elizabeth Mazer, asst. ed. Mass-market inspirational Christian romantic suspense novels. Publishes 48 titles/yr.; mass-market paperbacks. Receives 500-1,000 submissions annually. 15% of books from first-time authors. Accepts mss through agents or authors. No reprints. Prefers 55,000-60,000 wds. **Royalty on retail; competitive advance.** Publication within 12-24 mos. No simultaneous submissions. Responds in 3 mos. Prefers KJV. Guidelines on Website (click on "Steeple Hill"/scroll down right side to "Write"/"Writers Guidelines"); no catalog.

Fiction: Proposal/3 chapters and up to 5-page synopsis; no phone/fax/e-query.

Special Needs: "We offer edge-of-the-seat, contemporary romantic suspense tales of intrigue and romance featuring Christian characters facing challenges to their faith and to their lives. Each story should have a compelling mystery or a suspenseful situation threatening the hero and the heroine, combined with an emotional, satisfying, and mature romance. Stories should focus equally on romance and suspense."

STILL WATERS REVIVAL BOOKS, 4710—37A Ave., Edmonton AB T6L 3T5, Canada. (708) 450-3730. Fax (708) 468-1096. E-mail: swrb@swrb.com. Website: www.swrb.com. Covenanter Church. Reg Barrow, pres. Publishes 100 titles/yr. Receives few submissions. Very few books from first-time authors. Reprints books. Prefers 128-160 pgs. **Negotiated royalty or outright purchase.** Considers simultaneous submissions. Catalog for 9 x 12 SAE/2 stamps.

Nonfiction: Proposal/2 chapters.

Tips: "Only open to books defending the Covenanted Reformation, nothing else."

ST. PAULS/ALBA HOUSE, 2187 Victory Blvd., Staten Island NY 10314-6603. (718) 761-0047. Fax (718) 761-0057. E-mail: Edmund_Lane@juno.com. Website: www.stpauls.us. Catholic/Society of St. Paul. Edmund C. Lane, SSP, ed-in-chief; Frank Sadowski, SSP, ed. Imprint: St. Pauls. Publishes 24 titles/yr.; trade paperbacks. Receives 450 submissions annually. 20% of books from first-time authors. No mss through agents. Reprints books. Prefers 124 pgs. **Royalty 7-10% on retail; no advance.** Average first printing 3,500. Publication within 9 mos. Prefers requested ms on disk. Responds in 1-2 mos. Free guidelines/catalog by mail.

Nonfiction: Query.

Special Needs: Spirituality in the Roman Catholic tradition; lives of the saints.

STRANG BOOK GROUP, 600 Rinehart Rd., Lake Mary FL 32746. (407) 333-0600. Fax (407) 333-7100. E-mail: creationhouse@strang.com or charismahouse@strang.com. Website: www.strang.com. Strang Communications. Submit to Acquisitions Assistant. To inspire and equip people to live a Spirit-led life and walk in the divine purpose for which they were called. This house has 8 imprints, which are listed with descriptions/details. Publishes 150 titles/yr.; hardcover, trade paperbacks, mass-market paperbacks. Receives 1,500 submissions annually. 65% of books from first-time authors. Prefers mss through agents. Reprints books. Prefers 55,000 wds. **Royalty on net or outright purchase; advance.** Average first printing 7,500. Publication within 9 mos. Considers simultaneous submissions. Accepts requested ms on disk or on Website. Responds in 6-10 wks. Guidelines by mail/e-mail/Website (under "Submit Book Proposal"); free catalog.

Nonfiction: Proposal or complete ms; by mail or e-query OK; no phone query. Book proposal application on Website. "Open to any books that are well-written and glorify Jesus Christ."

Fiction: Proposal or complete ms; by mail or e-query OK; no phone query. Book proposal application on Website. "For all ages. Fiction must have a biblical worldview and point the reader to Christ."

Photos: Accepts freelance photos for book covers.

Charisma House: Books on Christian living, mainly from a Charismatic/Pentecostal perspective. Topics: Christian living, work of the Holy Spirit, prophecy, prayer, Scripture, adventures in evangelism and missions, popular theology.

Siloam: Books about living in good health—body, mind, and spirit. Topics: alternative medicine; diet and nutrition; and physical, emotional, and psychological wellness. We prefer manuscripts from certified doctors, nutritionists, trainers, and other medical professionals. Proof of credentials may be required.

Frontline: Books on contemporary political and social issues from a Christian perspective.

Creation house: Co-publishing imprint for a wide variety of Christian books. Author is required to buy a quantity of books from the first press run. This is not self-publishing or print-on-demand.

Realms: Christian fiction in the supernatural, speculative genre. Full-length adult novels, 80,000-120,000 wds. Will also consider historical or biblical fiction if supernatural element is substantial.

Excel: Publishes books that are targeted toward success in the workplace and businesses.

Casa Creacion: Publishes and translates books into Spanish. (800) 987-8432. E-mail: casacreacion@strang.com. Website: www.casacreacion.com.

Publicaciones Casa: Publishes the same as Creation House and is for people who like to co-publish in Spanish. Contact info same as Casa Creacion.

**Note: This publisher serviced by ChristianManuscriptSubmissions.com.

SUMMERSIDE PRESS/LOVE FINDS YOU, 11024 Quebec Cir., Bloomington MN 55438. (612) 321-1015. E-mail: info@summersidepress.com. Website: www.summersidepress.com. Rachel Meisel, fiction ed. Inspirational romance fiction series. Accepts mss through agents only. Publishes 12 titles/yr. Prefers 80,000 wds. or 320 pgs. Guidelines on Website ("Submissions").

Fiction: Send a paragraph overview, plus a 2-3 page synopsis by e-mail (attached file).

Tips: "This series features inspirational romance novels set in actual cities and towns across the U.S."

+SUNPENNY PUBLISHING, Church Cottage N., Ferry Rd., Carleton St. Peter Norfolk NR1-7BD, United Kingdom. E-mail: info@sunpenny.com. Website: www.sunpenny.com. Jo Holloway, ed. Publishes 3-5 titles/yr.; hardcover, trade paperbacks, mass-market paperbacks, electronic originals. 50% of books from first-time authors. Accepts mss through agents or authors. **Royalty 50% of net.** Considers simultaneous submissions. Responds in 1-2 wks. to queries; 1-2 mos. to proposals; 2-3 mos. to manuscripts. Guidelines ("Submissions") & catalog on Website.

Nonfiction: Query, proposal, or complete ms. Christian/inspirational books.

Fiction: Query, proposal, or complete ms. Christian/inspirational books.

Photos/Artwork: Accepts freelance photos for book covers; open to queries from freelance artists.

TAN BOOKS AND PUBLISHERS INC., PO Box 410487, Charlotte NC 28241-0487. Toll-free (800) 437-5876, ext. 205. E-mail: taneditor@tanbooks.com. Website: www.TanBooks.com, or www.saint benedictpress.com. Catholic/Saint Benedict Press LLC. Thomas A. Nelson, ed. Accepts e-queries. Guidelines on Website (scroll to bottom "Manuscript submissions"). Not included in topical listings.

JEREMY P. TARCHER, 375 Hudson St., New York NY 10014. (212) 366-2000. Fax (212) 366-2670. Website: www.penguinputnam.com. Imprint of Penguin Group. Joel Fotinos, VP/pres. Publishes ideas and works about human consciousness that are large enough to include matters of spirit and religion. Publishes 40-50 titles/yr.; hardcover, trade paperbacks. Receives 2,000 submissions annually. 20% of books from first-time authors. Accepts mss through agents or authors. Reprints books. **Royalty 5-8% of retail; advance.** Considers simultaneous submissions. Free catalog.

   Nonfiction: Query. Religion.

TAU-PUBLISHING, 1422 E. Edgemont Ave., Phoenix AZ 85006. (602) 264-4828. Fax (602) 248-9656. E-mail: phoenixartist@msn.com or through Website: www.tau-publishing.org. Catholic. Jeffrey Campbell, pub. Imprint: Aleph-First. Publishes 15-20 titles/yr. Receives 25 submissions annually. 50% of books from first-time authors. Prefers mss through agents. Does some subsidy. Reprints books. Prefers 25,000-50,000 wds. or 100-200 pgs. **Royalty on net or a set fee; no advance.** Average first printing 3,000. Publication within 8 mos. Considers simultaneous submissions. Responds in 4-6 mos. Guidelines on Website ("Submissions Guidelines"); no catalog.

   Nonfiction: Query with a 1-2 pg. summary first; fax/e-query OK. "Looking for Catholic inspirational material; reflections and meditations."

   Photos: Accepts freelance photos for book covers.

TH1NK/NAVPRESS, 3820 N. 30th St., Colorado Springs CO 80904. Fax (719) 260-7223. E-mail: rebekah.guzman@navpress.com. Website: www.navpress.com. NavPress Publishing. Submit to The Editor. Nonfiction/fiction books and Bible studies for the teen/YA market (ages 16-21).

THIRD WORLD PRESS, PO Box 19730, 7822 S. Dobson Ave., Chicago IL 60619. (773) 651-0700. Fax (773) 651-7286. E-mail: GwenMTWP@aol.com or through Website: www.ThirdWorldPressInc .com. Submit to Asst. to the Publisher. Books that deal with African American and Third World people—their stories, experiences, and concerns. Publishes 20 titles/yr.; hard cover, trade paperbacks. Receives 400-500 submissions annually. 20% of books from first-time authors. Accepts mss through agents or authors. Reprints books. **Royalty on retail; advance varies.** Publication within 18 mos. Considers simultaneous submissions. Accepts requested mss on disk or by e-mail. Responds in 5-6 mos. Guidelines on Website ("Submission Guidelines"); free catalog.

   Nonfiction: Query by mail, phone, fax, or e-mail; or send proposal/1-2 chapters.

   Fiction: Query by mail, phone, fax, or e-mail; or send proposal/1-2 chapters. For all ages.

   Ethnic Books: African American, Hispanic, and Third World people.

   Tips: "Submit complete manuscript for poetry." This company is open to submissions in July only. Submissions are not returned.

TORCH LEGACY PUBLICATIONS, PO Box 1733, Joshua TX 76058-1733. (877)TORCHLP or (404) 348-4478. Fax (817) 887-3089. E-mail: info@torchlegacy.com. Website: www.torchlegacy.com. Daniel Whyte III, pres. Dedicated to publishing Bible-based books of all genres by and for African Americans and whosoever will. Publishes 7+ titles/yr. 80% of books from first-time authors. **Royalty 10% of net; no advance.** Average first printing 5,000. Publication within 12 mos. No simultaneous submissions. Responds in 2 mos.

   Nonfiction: Query first; e-query preferred. "We are especially interested in Christian self-help books for the African-American community for all age groups. Outright submissions in all categories are welcome."

   Ethnic Books: African American.

   Also Does: "We also handle the production and publishing of sermon books by local pastors for local churches, and we transcribe sermons for pastors under our imprint, St. Paul Press."

   Tips: "We are looking for books that are Bible-based but at the same time are exciting and life changing. Our mission is to 'turn many from darkness to light' in the Black community in America through presenting a clear, understandable presentation of the gospel of Jesus Christ."

THE TRACT LEAGUE, 2627 Elmridge Dr., Grand Rapids MI 49534-1329. (616) 453-7695. Fax (616) 453-2460. E-mail: info@tractleague.com. Website: www.tractleague.com. Publishes very few tracts from outside writers, but willing to look at ideas. Submit to General Manager.

TREBLE HEART BOOKS, 1284 Overlook Dr., Sierra Vista AZ 85635. (520) 458-5602. Fax (520) 459-0162. E-mail: leeemory@earthlink.net. Website: www.trebleheartbooks.com. Ms. Lee Emory, ed./pub. Faith-based books without heavy-handed preaching. Online publisher offers four divisions: Romance, Christian, Westerns, Mystery/Suspense. Imprint: MountainView (Christian division—see separate listing). Receives 100 submissions annually. 20% of books from first-time authors. No word length preference. Reprints few books. **Royalty 35% of net on most sales.** Publication within 12 mos. Books are published electronically in trade-size print. No simultaneous submissions (a 90-day exclusive is required on all submissions, and a viable marketing plan must accompany every submission). Responds in 90 days. Guidelines on Website ("Submissions Guidelines" right side).

Nonfiction: Submit by e-mail only (with separate marketing plan) to: 1thbsubmissions2@ earthlink.net. Submissions open the 1st-14th of each month. Excellent nonfiction books are highly desired here. Looking for nonfiction.

Fiction: E-mail submissions only. Welcomes most genres for their imprints, but no poetry, alternative life style, porno/erotica, or small children's books. We accept outstanding young adult material.

Photos/Artwork: Accepts high-quality freelance photos for book covers; rarely open to queries from freelance artists.

Tips: "All fiction should be fresh and intriguing. Challenge the reader to think, to look at things through different eyes. Avoid point of view head-hopping and clichés. Send consecutive chapters, not random. A well-developed marketing plan must accompany all submissions. You must follow our guidelines."

THE TRINITY FOUNDATION, PO Box 68, Unicoi TN 37692. (423) 743-0199. Fax (423) 743-2005. E-mail: tjtrinityfound@aol.com. Website: www.trinityfoundation.org. Thomas W. Juodaitis, ed. To promote the logical system of truth found in the Bible. Publishes 5 titles/yr.; hardcover, trade paperbacks. Receives 3 submissions annually. No books from first-time authors. No mss through agents. Reprints books. Prefers 200 pgs. **Outright purchases up to $1,500; free books; no advance.** Average first printing 2,000. Publication within 9 mos. No simultaneous submissions. Requires requested ms on disk. Responds in 2-3 mos. No guidelines; catalog on Website.

Nonfiction: Query letter only. Open to Calvinist/Clarkian books, Christian philosophy, economics, and politics.

Also Does: Pamphlets, booklets, tracts.

Photos: Accepts freelance photos for book covers.

Tips: "Most open to doctrinal books that conform to the Westminster Confession of Faith; nonfiction, biblical, and well-reasoned books, theologically sound, clearly written, and well organized."

TROITSA BOOKS, 400 Oser Ave., Ste. 1600, Hauppauge NY 11788-3619. (631) 231-7269. Fax (631) 231-8175. E-mail: Novaeditorial@earthlink.net, or through Website: www.novapublishers .com. Religious imprint of Nova Science Publishers Inc. Submit to Editor-in-Chief. Publishes 5-20 titles/yr. Receives 50-100 submissions annually. No mss through agents. Various lengths. **Royalty; no advance.** Publication within 6-18 mos. Considers simultaneous submissions. Accepts requested ms on disk or by e-mail (prefers e-mail for all submissions and correspondence). Responds in 1 mo. Guidelines on Website (under "For Authors"/"Form & Style for Manuscripts"); free catalog.

Nonfiction: Proposal/2 chapters by e-mail. Send to above e-mail with a copy to novascil@ aol.com.

Fiction: Proposal/2 chapters by e-mail. For adults.

Photos: Accepts freelance photos for book covers.

+TWO FISH PUBLISHING, PO Box 870490, Stone Mountain GA 30087. Toll-free (800) 378-9584. E-mail: info@carepointministry.com. Website: www.twofishpublishing.com. CarePoint Publishing.

Dr. Scott Philip Stewart, ed. "Our mission is to publish transformational novellas that minister God's grace, love, mercy, and healing power to deliver those who are hurting." Publishes 12 titles/yr.; trade paperbacks. 50% of books from first-time authors. Accepts mss through agents or authors. Reprints books. Prefers 20,000-30,000 wds. **Royalty 10-15% on net.** Average first printing varies. Publication within 6 mos. Considers simultaneous submissions. Responds in 4 wks. Guidelines on Website; no catalog.

> **Fiction:** Proposal/2-3 chapters, or complete ms. Novellas for teens and adults. "We accept only 'self-help' fiction—what we call care-lit."
>
> **Special Needs:** "We publish only novella-length fiction that features a main character finding freedom from a life-challenge (such as depression, anxiety, eating disorder, addiction, guilt, etc.) via God's grace and the resources of faith."
>
> **Photos/Artwork:** Accepts freelance photos for book covers; open to queries from freelance artists.
>
> **Tips:** "We are looking for well-crafted stories that are edgy, relevant page-turners with well-drawn characters and credible plots of deliverance. We are at the intersection of Christian fiction and self-help."
>
> ****Note:** This publisher serviced by The Writer's Edge.

TYNDALE ESPAÑOL, 351 Executive Dr., Carol Stream IL 60188. (630) 784-5272. Fax (630) 344-0943. E-mail: andresschwartz@tyndale.com. Website: www.tyndale.com. Andres Schwartz, dir. Spanish division of Tyndale House Publishers.

@TYNDALE HOUSE PUBLISHERS, INC. 351 Executive Dr., Carol Stream IL 60188. Toll-free (800) 323-9400. (630) 668-8300. Toll-free fax (800) 684-0247. E-mail through Website: www.tyndale.com. Submit to Manuscript Review Committee. Practical Christian books for home and family. Imprints: Tyndale Español (Spanish imprint); Picket Fence Press (resources for women juggling multiple priorities in and outside the home). Publishes 225-250 titles/yr.; hardcover, trade paperbacks, mass-market paperbacks (reprints). 5% of books from first-time authors. Requires mss through agents. Reprints books. **Royalty negotiable; outright purchase of some children's books; advance negotiable.** Average first printing 5,000-10,000. Publication within 9 mos. Considers simultaneous submissions. Responds in 3-6 mos. Prefers NLT. No unsolicited mss. Guidelines/catalog on Website (under "Site Map"/"Authors"/"Manuscript Policy").

> **Nonfiction:** Query from agents or published authors only; no phone/fax query. No unsolicited mss (they will not be acknowledged or returned).
>
> **Fiction:** "We accept queries only from agents, Tyndale authors, authors known to us from other publishers, or other people in the publishing industry. Novellas 25,000-30,000 wds.; novels 75,000-100,000 wds. All must have an evangelical Christian message."
>
> **Also Does:** E-books.
>
> ****Note:** This publisher serviced by The Writer's Edge and ChristianManuscriptSubmissions.com.

UMI PUBLISHING, 1551 Regency Court, Calumet IL 60409. Toll-free (800) 860-8642. (708) 868-7100. Fax (708) 868-6759. E-mail: customerservice@urbanministries.com or through Website: www.urbanministries.com. Urban Ministries Inc. Not currently accepting unsolicited manuscripts.

UNITED METHODIST PUBLISHING HOUSE—See Abingdon Press or Dimensions for Living.

UNIVERSITY OF ARKANSAS PRESS, McIlroy House, 105 N. McIlroy Ave., Fayetteville AR 72701. Toll-free (800) 626-0090. (479) 575-3246. Fax (479) 575-6044. E-mail: uapress@uark.edu. Website: www.uapress.com. Lawrence J. Malley, ed-in-chief. (lmalley@uark.edu). Academic publisher. Publishes 30 titles/yr.; hardcover, trade paperbacks. Receives 1,000 submissions annually. 30% of books from first-time authors. Accepts mss through agents or authors. Reprints books. Prefers 300 pgs. **Royalty on net; no advance.** Average first printing 1,000-2,000. Publication within 1 yr. Reluctantly considers simultaneous submissions. Responds in 3 mos. Requires accepted ms on disk. Guidelines on Website ("Submissions"); free catalog.

Nonfiction: Query. "All our books are scholarly." Looking for regional books.

Photos: Accepts freelance photos for book covers.

UNIVERSITY PRESS OF AMERICA, 4501 Forbes Blvd., Ste. 200, Lanham MD 20706. (301) 459-3366. Fax (301) 429-5748. E-mail: submitupa@univpress.com. Website: www.univpress.com. Rowman & Littlefield Publishing Group/Academic. Acq. eds.: Brooke Bascietto (bbascietto@univpress.com) and Samantha Kirk (skirk@univpress.com). Publishes scholarly works in the social sciences and humanities; established by academics for academics. Imprint: Hamilton Books (biographies & memoirs). Publishes 75 religion titles/yr. Receives 700 submissions annually. 75% of books from first-time authors. Accepts mss through agents or authors. Some subsidy. Does digital printing. Reprints books. Prefers 90-300 pgs. **Royalty up to 12% of net; no advance.** Average first printing 200-300. Publication within 4-6 mos. Considers simultaneous submissions. Accepts e-mail submissions. Responds in 2 wks. Accepts requested ms on disk or by e-mail. Guidelines on Website (click on "Submit Manuscript" in box); free catalog.

Nonfiction: Fill out online form to introduce your project. Proposal/3 chapters or complete ms; phone/fax/e-query OK. "Looking for scholarly manuscripts."

Ethnic Books: African studies; black studies.

Tips: "Most open to timely, thoroughly researched, and well-documented books. Moderately controversial topics. We publish academic and scholarly books only. Authors are typically affiliated with a college, university, or seminary."

VBC PUBLISHING, PO Box 9101, Vallejo CA 94591. (707) 315-1219. Fax (707) 648-2169. E-mail: akgordon1991@att.net. Vallejo Bible College. Kevin Gordon, pres. To glorify the Lord through Christian literature; to provide the Christian community with material to aid them in their personal studies and to help in their life and ministry. New publisher; plans 1-5 titles/yr.; hardcover, trade paperbacks. Receives 10 submissions annually. Plans to publish 50% of books from first-time authors. Accepts mss through agents or authors. Print-on-demand publisher. No reprints. Prefers 100+ pgs. **Royalty 8-12% on net; no advance.** Publication within 8 mos. Considers simultaneous submissions. Responds in 2-6 wks. Accepted mss on disk. Prefers KJV, NKJV, NASB, NIV. Guidelines by mail; no catalog.

Nonfiction: Proposal/2 chapters or complete ms; phone/e-query OK; no fax query.

Special Needs: Biblical theology, Bible study, and Christian living.

Artwork: Open to queries from freelance artists.

Tips: "Most open to doctrinally sound and relevant manuscripts. Have a well-written manuscript and a plan to market your book. Follow guidelines when submitting and trust in the Lord!"

@VIRTUAL TALES, E-mail through Website: www.virtualtales.com. P. June Diel, sr. ed.; Jake George, acq. ed. Produces e-book and paperback novels and novellas of at least 30,000 wds.; also open to short story collections. Requires e-mail submissions through Website form. Accepts reprints. Guidelines on Website ("About Us"/"Come Work for Us"/"Apply to Join Our Staff" #1). Incomplete topical listings.

THE VISION FORUM, 4719 Blanco Rd., San Antonio TX 78212. (210) 340-5250. Fax (210) 340-8577. Website: www.visionforum.com. Douglas W. Phillips, pres. Dedicated to the restoration of the biblical family. Historical fiction.

WARNER PRESS INC., 1201 E. 5th St., Anderson IN 46012. Toll-free (800) 741-7721. Fax (765) 640-8005. E-mail: rfogle@warnerpress.org. Website: www.warnerpress.org. Church of God. Karen Rhodes, sr. ed.; submit to Robin Fogle, asst. product ed. Committed to excellence in developing and marketing products and services based on scriptural truths to energize, educate, nurture, inspire, and unite the whole people of God. Hardcover books. Receives 100+ submissions annually. Rarely accepts mss through agents. No subsidy. No reprints. Prefers 32 pgs. for kid's books; 250-350 pgs.

for teen books. **Royalty & advance based on the author and type of book.** Publication within 12 mos. Considers simultaneous submissions. Responds in 6-8 wks. Prefers KJV or NIV. Guidelines on Website (scroll to bottom "Submissions Guidelines"); no catalog.

Nonfiction: Complete ms; fax/e-query OK. Accepts e-mail submissions.

Fiction: Query first, then complete ms; fax/e-query OK. Accepts e-mail submissions. For children & teens. "We want our books to be biblically sound but with a nondenominational viewpoint/bias."

Artwork: Send to Curtis Corzine, Creative Art Director (curtis@warnerpress.org).

Tips: "We primarily create books for ages 6-10 (picture books) and 8-12 (fantasy fiction). We are looking for books that are not preachy but do contain a biblical or moral foundation. Well-written, creative books by writers who have done their market research."

WATERBROOK PRESS, 12265 Oracle Blvd., Ste. 200, Colorado Springs CO 80921. (719) 590-4999. Fax (719) 590-8977. E-mail: info@waterbrookmultnomah.com. Website: www.waterbrook multnomah.com. Part of WaterBrook Multnomah, a division of Random House Inc. Ken Petersen, VP/ed. dir.; Laura Barker, mng. ed. Publishes 75 titles/yr.; hardcover, trade paperbacks. **Royalty on net; advance.** WaterBrook is currently not accepting unsolicited manuscripts, proposals, or queries; no proposals for biographies or poetry. Queries will be accepted though literary agents and at writers' conferences at which a WaterBrook representative is present. Catalog on Website.

Nonfiction/Fiction: Agented submissions only.

WESLEYAN PUBLISHING HOUSE, PO Box 50434, Indianapolis IN 46250-0434. (317) 774-7900. E-mail: wph@wesleyan.org. Website: www.wesleyan.org/wph. The Wesleyan Church. Attn: Editorial Director. Communicates the life-transforming message of holiness to the world. Publishes 15 titles/yr.; hardcover, trade paperbacks. Receives 150 submissions annually. 20% of books from first-time authors. Accepts mss through agents or authors. No reprints. Prefers 25,000-40,000 wds. **Royalty and advance.** Average first printing 4,000. Publication within 9-12 mos. Considers simultaneous submissions. Prefers requested ms by e-mail. Responds within 2 mos. Prefers NIV. Guidelines by mail/e-mail/Website ("Inside WPH"/"Writers Guidelines"); free catalog.

Nonfiction: Proposal/3-5 chapters; no phone/fax/e-query. "Looking for books that help Christians understand the faith and apply it to their lives."

**Note: This publisher serviced by ChristianManuscriptSubmissions.com.

WESTMINSTER JOHN KNOX PRESS—See Presbyterian Publishing Corporation.

WHITAKER HOUSE, 1030 Hunt Valley Cir., New Kensington PA 15068. (724) 334-7000. (724) 334-1200. E-mail: publisher@whitakerhouse.com. Website: www.whitakerhouse.com. Whitaker Corp. Tom Cox, sr. ed. To advance God's Kingdom by providing biblically based products that proclaim the power of the gospel and minister to the spiritual needs of people around the world. Publishes 30-40 titles/yr.; hardcover, trade paperbacks, mass-market paperbacks. Receives 500 submissions annually. 15% of books from first-time authors. Accepts mss through agents or authors. No subsidy, print-on-demand, or reprints. Prefers 50,000 wds. **Royalty 6-15% on net; some variable advances.** Average first printing 5,000. Publication within 10 mos. Considers simultaneous submissions. Prefers accepted ms by e-mail. Responds in 4 mos. Prefers NIV. Guidelines on Website ("Submissions Guidelines" center); no catalog.

Nonfiction/Fiction: Query only first; no phone/fax query; e-query OK.

Special Needs: Charismatic nonfiction, Christian historical romance, Amish romance, Christian African American romance.

Ethnic Books: Hispanic translations of current English titles.

Tips: "Looking for quality nonfiction and fiction by authors with a national marketing platform. Most open to high-quality, well-thought-out, compelling pieces of work. Review the guidelines and submit details as thoroughly as possible for publication consideration."

@WHITE ROSE PUBLISHING, PO Box 1738, Aztec NM 87410. E-mail: titleadmin@whiterose publishing.com. Website: www.whiterosepublishing.com. Nicola Martinez, ed.-in-chief. Publishes Christian romances or any romance subgenre. Publishes about 40 titles/yr; limited-edition hardcover, trade paperbacks, and e-books. Receives 1,000 submissions annually. 30% of books from first-time authors. Accepts mss through agents or authors. Does print-on-demand. Considers reprints, but publishes few. Prefers between 7,500 and 100,000 wds. **Royalty 40% on download; 7% on print.** Nominal advance. Publication in up to 12 mos. Considers simultaneous submissions reluctantly. Responds to proposals in 30 days; full mss within 90 days. Guidelines on Website ("Submissions Guidelines"); no catalog.

> **Fiction:** Query only first, via the submission form available on Website; romance only. "We are also very interested in series ideas in both short story and full novel length."
>
> **Also Does:** E-books. Short stories published in e-books only.
>
> **Contest:** We also sponsor programs such as Cover Stories and one to two contests per year. These are a great way for first-time authors to catch our attention."
>
> **Tips:** "We see a lot of submissions that are not romance. Please submit only romance."

WILSHIRE BOOK COMPANY, 9731 Variel Ave., Chatsworth CA 91311-4315. (818) 700-1522. Fax (818) 700-1527. E-mail: mpowers@mpowers.com or through Website: www.mpowers.com. A general publisher of motivational books. Melvin Powers, pres.; Marcia Powers, ed. Books that help you become who you choose to be tomorrow. Publishes 6 titles/yr. 80% of books from first-time authors. Accepts mss through agents or authors. Reprints books. Prefers 30,000 wds. or 128-160 pgs. **Royalty 5% on retail; variable advance.** Average first printing 5,000. Publication within 6 mos. Considers simultaneous submissions. No disk or e-mail submissions. Responds in 2 mos. Guidelines on Website (under "Become a Published Author").

> **Nonfiction:** Query or proposal/3 chapters; phone/e-query OK.
>
> **Fiction:** Allegory for adults that teaches principles of psychological/spiritual growth.
>
> **Photos/Artwork:** Accepts freelance photos for book covers; open to queries from freelance artists.
>
> **Tips:** "We are looking for adult allegories such as *Illusions,* by Richard Bach, *The Little Prince,* by Antoine de Saint Exupery, and *The Greatest Salesman in the World,* by Og Mandino. Analyze each one to discover what elements make it a winner. Duplicate those elements in your own style, using a creative, new approach and fresh material. We need 30,000-60,000 wds."

WIPF AND STOCK PUBLISHERS, 199 W. 8th Ave., Ste. 3. Eugene OR 97401-2960. (541) 344-1528. Fax (541) 344-1506. E-mail: proposal@wipfandstock.com. Website: www.wipfandstock.com. Submit to Attn: Editorial/Proposals. Specializes in new and reprinted academic books. Imprints: Cascade Books, Pickwick Publications, and Resource Publications. Guidelines/catalog on Website ("Submitting a Book Proposal"). Incomplete topical listings.

W PUBLISHING GROUP, PO Box 141000, Nashville TN 37214. (615) 889-9000. Fax (615) 902-2112. Website: www.Wpublishinggroup.com. Thomas Nelson Inc. David Moberg, pub.; Greg Daniel, assoc. pub. Publishes 75 titles/yr. Less than 3% of books from first-time authors. Requires mss through agents. No reprints. Does not accept unsolicited manuscripts. Prefers 65,000-95,000 wds. **Royalty.** No guidelines.

> **Nonfiction:** Query letter only first; no unsolicited ms. "Nonfiction dealing with the relationship and/or application of biblical principles to everyday life; 65,000-95,000 wds."
>
> ****Note:** This publisher serviced by The Writer's Edge & ManuscriptSubmissions.com.

WRITE NOW PUBLICATIONS, PO Box 110390, Nashville TN 37222. Toll-free (800) 21-WRITE. E-mail: RegAForder@aol.com. Website: www.writenowpublications.com. Reg A. Forder, exec. ed. To train and develop quality Christian writers; books on writing and speaking for writers and speakers. Royalty division of ACW Press. Publishes 1-2 titles/yr.; trade paperbacks. Receives 6 submissions annually. 0% from first-time authors. Accepts mss through agents or authors. Reprints books. **Royalty 10% of net.** Average first printing 2,000. Publication within 12 mos. Considers simultaneous submissions. Requires requested ms on disk. No guidelines/catalog.

Nonfiction: Writing how-to only. Query letter only; e-query OK.

XYZZY PRESS, E-mail: acquisitions@xyzzypress.com. Website: www.xyzzypress.com. Responds in several wks. Guidelines on Website.

Nonfiction/Fiction: Not accepting submissions at this time; check Website for any change in policy.

YALE UNIVERSITY PRESS, PO Box 209040, New Haven CT 06518-9040. (203) 432-6807. Fax (203) 436-1064. E-mail: jennifer.banks@yale.edu. Website: www.yalepress.yale.edu. Jennifer Banks, ed. Publishes scholarly and general-interest books, including religion. Publishes 15 religious titles/yr.; hardcover, trade paperbacks. Receives 1,000 submissions annually. 10% of books from first-time authors. Accepts mss through agents or authors. **Royalty from 0% to standard trade royalties; advance $0-100,000.** Average first printing 12 mos. Publication within 1 yr. Considers simultaneous submissions. Requires requested ms on hard copy; no e-mail submissions. Responds in 2 mos. Guidelines/catalog on Website (www.yalebooks.com).

Nonfiction: Query or proposal/sample chapters; fax query OK; no e-query. "Excellent and salable scholarly books."

Contest: Yale Series of Younger Poets competition. Open to poets under 40 who have not had a book of poetry published. Submit manuscripts of 48-64 pgs. by November 15. Entry fee $15. Send SASE for guidelines (also on Website). Send complete manuscript.

YOUTH SPECIALTIES, 1890 Cordell Ct., Ste. 105, El Cajon CA 92020. Toll-free (888) 346-4179. (619) 440-2333. Fax (619) 440-4939. E-mail: ideas@youthspecialties.com. Website: www.youthspecialties.com. YouthWorks! Inc. Submit to Attn: Ideas. Books for youth workers and teenagers. Imprint: Invert Books. Publishes 30 titles/yr. Accepts mss through agents or authors. No reprints. Prefers 35,000 wds. **Royalty on net or outright purchase of $3,000-8,000; pays an advance.** Publication within 18 mos. Considers simultaneous submissions. Responds in 4-6 wks. Prefers NIV. Guidelines by e-mail/Website (under "About Us"/"Write for Us"); free catalog.

Nonfiction: Proposal/2 chapters.

Tips: "We prefer books from youth workers who are in the trenches working with students."

ZONDERKIDZ, 5300 Patterson S.E., Grand Rapids MI 49530-0002. (616) 698-6900. Fax (616) 698-3578. E-mail: zpub@zondervan.com. Website: www.zonderkidz.com. Zondervan/HarperCollins. Children's book line of Zondervan; ages 12 & under. Not currently accepting proposals.

**Note: This publisher serviced by ChristianManuscriptSubmissions.com.

ZONDERVAN, General Trade Books; Academic and Professional Books, 5300 Patterson S.E., Grand Rapids MI 49530-0002. (616) 698-6900. Manuscript submission line: (616) 698-3447. E-mail through Website: www.zondervan.com. HarperCollins Publishers. Mission is to be the leading Christian communications company meeting the needs of people with resources that glorify Jesus Christ and promote biblical principles. Publishes 120 trade titles/yr.; hardcover, trade paperbacks, mass-market paperbacks. Few books from first-time authors. Accepts mss through agents or authors. No subsidy or reprints. **Royalty 12-14% of net; variable advance.** Publication within 12-18 mos. Considers simultaneous submissions. Requires requested ms by e-mail. Prefers NIV. Guidelines on Website (under "About Us"/"Manuscript Submissions"); catalog online.

Nonfiction: Submissions only by e-mail and only certain types of mss. See Website for e-mail address and submission guidelines.

Fiction: No fiction at this time; refer to Website for updates.

Special Needs: Currently accepting unsolicited book proposals in academic, reference, or ministry resources only (see guidelines).

Children's Lines: ZonderKidz and Faithgirlz (not currently accepting new products).

Ethnic Books: Vida Publishers division: Spanish and Portuguese.

Tips: "Almost no unsolicited manuscripts are published. Book proposals should be single-spaced with one-inch margins on all sides."

**Note: This publisher serviced by ChristianManuscriptSubmissions.com.

3

Subsidy Publishers

In this section you will find publishers who do 50% or more subsidy publishing. For our purposes, I am defining a subsidy publisher as any publisher that requires the author to pay for any part of the publishing costs. They may call themselves by a variety of names, such as book packager, cooperative publisher, self-publisher, or simply someone who helps authors get their books published. Print-on-demand (POD) businesses publish books one at a time and usually print books much faster than typical publishers. Another designation is custom publisher, which refers to a publisher that develops new authors to eventually work with royalty publishers.

To my knowledge the following publishers are legitimate subsidy publishers (as opposed to companies that are simply out to take your money and offer little in return), but I cannot guarantee that. It is important for you to understand that any time you are asked to pay for any part of the production of your book, you are entering into a nontraditional relationship with a publisher. This also applies to being asked to buy a certain number of books or to pay for services typically covered by a royalty publisher. Note that some subsidy publishers also do royalty publishing, so you could approach them as a royalty publisher. You just need to realize that they are likely to offer you a subsidy deal, so if you are interested only in a royalty arrangement, indicate that in your cover letter.

Some subsidy publishers will publish any book, as long as the author is willing to pay for it. Others are as selective about what they publish as a royalty publisher would be. As subsidy publishers become more selective, the professional quality of subsidy books is improving overall. Many will publish only nonfiction—no novels or children's books. These distinctions will be important as you seek the right publisher.

Subsidy publishing can be confusing, and many authors go into agreements with these publishers having little or no knowledge of what to expect. As a result, they come away unhappy or disillusioned; I frequently get complaints from authors who feel they have been cheated or taken advantage of. Each complaint brings with it an expectation that I should drop that publisher from this book. Although I am sensitive to these complaints, I also realize that I am not in a position to pass judgment on which publishers should be dropped. It has been my experience that for every complaint I get about a publisher, I find several other authors who sing the praises of that publisher. For that reason, I feel I can serve the needs of authors better by giving a brief overview of what to expect from a subsidy publisher and what kinds of terms should send up a red flag.

First, unless you know your book has a limited audience or you have your own method of distribution (such as having your own ministry or being a speaker who can sell your own books when you speak), I recommend that you try all the appropriate royalty publishers before considering a subsidy house.

If you are unsuccessful with the royalty publishers but still feel strongly about seeing your book published, a subsidy publisher may be able to help you. A subsidy publisher has the contacts, know-how, and resources to make printing your book easier and often less expensive than doing it yourself.

It is always good to get more than one bid to determine whether the terms you are being offered are competitive with those of other such publishers. A legitimate subsidy publisher will be happy to provide you with a list of former clients as references. Don't just ask for that list; follow through and contact more than one of those references. Get a catalog of the publisher's books or a list of those books, and then review a few of them yourself to check the quality of the work, the bindings, etc. See if the books are available through Amazon.com or similar online services. (It's important to understand that the majority of Christian or general bookstores will not carry a self-published book.) Get answers to all your questions before you commit yourself to anything. Also have someone review your contract before you sign it. I do such reviews, as do a number of others listed in the "Editorial Services" section of this book. Be sure that any terms agreed upon are in writing. The listings below include printers who could help you complete the printing process yourself, so you will want to check out those as well.

Keep in mind that the more copies of a book you have printed, the lower the cost per copy. But never let a publisher talk you into publishing more copies than you think is reasonable for your situation. Also, find out up front, and have included in the contract, how much promotion, if any, the publisher is going to do. Some will do as much as a royalty publisher; others do none at all. If the publisher is not doing promotion and you don't have any means of distribution yourself, it may not be a good idea to pursue subsidy publication. You don't want to end up with a garage full of books you can't sell.

Here are some definitions that will help you identify the different types of publishers. Just note that not all publishers may interpret their services as indicated below, so be sure you know what to expect before signing a contract.

Commercial/Mainstream/Traditional Publisher: One who pays all the costs of producing your book (see previous book section).

Vanity Publisher: Prints the books at the author's expense. Will print any book the author is willing to pay for. May offer marketing help, warehousing, editing, or promotion of some sort at the author's expense.

Subsidy Publisher: Shares the cost of printing and binding a book. Often more selective, but the completed books belong to the publisher, not the author. Author may buy books from the publisher and may also collect a royalty for books the publisher sells.

Self-Publishing: Author pays all the costs of publishing the book and is responsible for all the marketing, distribution, promotion, etc. Author may select a service package that defines the cost and services to be rendered. The books belong to the author and he/she keeps all the income from the sale of the books.

Following this section I include the names and addresses of Christian book distributors. I have asked them if they will consider distributing a subsidy-published book, and some have responded positively. You may want to contact some of them to find out their interest before you sign a contract with a subsidy publisher. For more help on self-publishing, go to: www.bookmarket.com/index.html.

+ A plus sign before a listing indicates it is a new listing this year or was not included last year.

@ Indicates the publisher produces e-books.

ACW PRESS, American Christian Writers, PO Box 110390, Nashville TN 37222. Toll-free (800) 21-WRITE. E-mail: Jim@JamesWatkins.com. Website: www.acwpress.com. Reg A. Forder, owner; Jim Watkins, editorial advisor. A self-publishing book packager. Imprint: Write Now Publications (see separate listing). Publishes 40 titles/yr.; hardcover, trade paperbacks, mass-market paperbacks, coffee-table books. Reprints books. SUBSIDY PUBLISHES 95%; does print-on-demand. Average first printing 2,500. Publication within 4-6 mos. Responds in 48-72 hrs. Request for estimate form available on Website. Not in topical listings; will consider any nonfiction or fiction topic. Guidelines by e-mail/Website.

Nonfiction/Fiction: All types considered.

Tips: "We offer a high quality publishing alternative to help Christian authors get their material into print. High standards, high quality. If authors have a built-in audience, they have the best chance to make self-publishing a success." Has a marketing program available to authors.

Note: This publisher serviced by The Writer's Edge and ChristianManuscriptSubmissions.com.

+ADVANTAGE BOOKS, PO Box 160847, Altamonte Springs FL 32716. Toll-free (888) 383-3110. (407) 788-3110. Fax (407) 788-3592. E-mail through Website: http://advbooks.com. Mike Janiczek, pub. SUBSIDY PUBLISHER. Digital books. Not included in topical listings.

AMERICAN BINDING & PUBLISHING CO., PO Box 60049, Corpus Christi TX 78466-0049. Toll-free (800) 863-3708. (361) 658-4221. E-mail: rmagner@grandecom.net. Website: www.american bindingpublishing.com. Rose Magner, pub. Publishes 60 titles/yr. Receives 200 submissions annually. 95% of books from first-time authors. No mss through agents. Reprints books. SUBSIDY PUBLISHES 100%; does print-on-demand. Prefers 200 pgs. **Royalty 15% on retail; no advance.** Publication within 2 wks. Considers simultaneous submissions. Requires requested ms on disk (Microsoft Word format). Responds in 2 wks. Any Bible version. Guidelines by mail/e-mail; free catalog.

Nonfiction: Complete ms; phone/e-query OK. Will consider any topic.

Fiction: Complete ms; phone/e-query OK. For all ages; all genres.

Ethnic Books: Black and Hispanic.

Photos: Accepts freelance photos for book covers.

Tips: "We are print-on-demand; authors are responsible for their own marketing. We will consider any topic—nonfiction or fiction, but most open to fiction."

AMPELOS PRESS, 951 Anders Rd., Lansdale PA 19446. Phone/fax (484) 991-8581. E-mail: mbagnull@aol.com. Website: www.writehisanswer.com. Marlene Bagnull, LittD, pub./ed. Services (depending on what is needed) include critiquing, editing, proofreading, typesetting, and cover design. Publishes 1-3 titles/yr. SUBSIDY PUBLISHES 100%. Query only. Not included in topical listings (see Tips).

Special Needs: Books about missions and meeting the needs of children both at home and abroad.

Tips: "Our vision statement reads: 'Strongly, unashamedly, uncompromisingly Christ-centered. Exalting the name of Jesus Christ. Seeking to teach His ways through holding up the Word of God as the Standard.' (*Ampelos* is the Greek word for 'vine' in John 15:5.)"

@BELIEVERSPRESS, 6820 W. 115th St., Bloomington MN 55438. Toll-free (800) 341-4192. (304) 719-0226. E-mail: info@believerspress.com. Website: www.believerspress.com. A division of Bethany Press International. Andrew Mackay, ed. Submit through Website. To provide Christian authors with a trustworthy team to help them successfully navigate their publishing dreams. Offers solutions to fit every budget. Authors pay only for services they need and are in full control. All work done as work-for-hire. Includes: editorial, typesetting, cover design, digital/conventional book production, e-books, distribution, marketing/publicity, author e-store book sales, and blog articles by industry professionals.

+BFREE PUBLISHING, 3443 S. State St. #6, Salt Lake City UT 84115. Toll free: (888) 230-8440. Fax (206) 350-8600 (no unsolicited phone calls). Website: www.bfree.org. Submit to Book Editor (does not wish editors' names or e-mails to be listed). We publish voices others in the publishing "establishment" overlook. Imprint: Zarach (Messianic books/no fiction). Publishes Christian books; hardcover, trade paperbacks, mass-market paperbacks, and digital. Prefers accepted mss on disk. Guidelines on Website ("Services and Price List").

Nonfiction: Query first or proposal with sample chapters.

Fiction: Query only first.

Special Needs: Titles that honor the God of the Bible, His Son, and the Bible itself.

Artwork: Open to queries from freelance artists.

+BIOGRAPHICAL PUBLISHING CO., 95 Sycamore Dr., Prospect CT 06712-1493. (203) 758-3661. Fax (253) 793-2618. E-mail: biopub@aol.com. Website: www.biopub.co.cc. John R. Guevin, ed. Provides services to get books published and to help market and sell them. Publishes 1-4 religious titles/yr.; hardcover, trade paperbacks, digital. Receives 50 submissions annually. 75% of books from first-time authors. Accepts mss through agents. No print on demand. Reprints books. Prefers 50-500 pgs. Author receives 95% of sales amount after expenses; no advance. Average first printing 100-1,000. Publication within 2 mos. Considers simultaneous submissions. Responds in 1 wk. Guidelines by mail/e-mail/Website; free catalog.

Nonfiction: Query letter only first. Most open to topical issues.

Fiction: Query letter only first. Any genre.

Photos/Artwork: Accepts freelance photos for book covers; open to queries from freelance artists.

BLACK FOREST PRESS/TENNESSEE PUBLISHING HOUSE/SOUTHERN HERITAGE BOOKS, Belle Arden Run Estate, 488 MountainView Dr., Mosheim TN 37818-3524. Phone/fax (423) 212-1208 (call ahead for fax). E-mail: authorinfo@blackforestpress.net. Website: www.blackforestpress.net. Covenant Christian Healing Ministries. Dr. Dahk Knox, pub.; Dr. Jan Knox, CFO; Mary Inbody, sr. ed. Provides truthful information about an author's book; whether you publish with them or not, you get free help and advice. Imprints: Recht Books, World Truth Publishing House, Abenteure Books, Kinder Books, Sonnerschein Books, Dichter Books, Segen Books. Publishes up to 35 titles/yr.; hardcover, trade paperbacks, coffee-table books. Receives 100 submissions annually. 70% of books from first-time authors. Accepts mss through agents. SUBSIDY PUBLISHES 50%; does print-on-demand. Reprints books (with permission). Prefers 120-325 pgs. **Royalty on net (100% of sales, minus $1/bk., unless other arrangements made), or outright purchase; no advance.** Average first printing 2,000, or 250 POD. Publication within 2 mos. Considers simultaneous submissions. Requires accepted ms by e-mail (attached). Responds in 2 wks. Prefers NIV/NKJV. Guidelines on Website; no catalog.

Nonfiction: Complete ms by e-mail (attached); phone/e-query OK.

Fiction: Complete ms. All genres for all ages.

Special Needs: Historical fiction, nonfiction biographies, religious books of any kind.

Photos/Artwork: Accepts freelance photos for book covers; open to queries from freelance artists.

Tips: "Most open to well-written nonfiction or historical novels. Our imprint, Tennessee Publishing House, provides tax-exemption write-offs with certain religious book offerings."

@BOOKLOCKER.COM INC., PO Box 2399, Bangor ME 04402-2399. (207) 262-9696. Fax (207) 262-5544. E-mail: angela@booklocker.com. Website: www.booklocker.com. Angela Hoy, pub. We seek unique, eclectic, and different manuscripts. Publishes 300 titles/yr.; hardcover, trade paperbacks, e-books. 70% of books from first-time authors. No mss through agents. SUBSIDY PUBLISHES 100%; does print-on-demand. Reprints books. Prefers 48-740 pgs.; less for children's books. **Royalty 35% on retail (15% on wholesale orders; 35% on booklocker.com orders; 50-70% for e-books); no advance.** Publication within 4-6 wks. Considers simultaneous submissions. Responds in less than a week. Bible version is author's choice. Guidelines on Website; no catalog.

Nonfiction: Complete ms; e-query OK. "We're open to all unique ideas."

Fiction: Complete ms; e-query OK. All genres for all ages.

Ethnic Books: Publishes for all ethnic groups.

Photos/Artwork: Uses stock photos or author-supplied photos/artwork.

Contest: The WritersWeekly.com 24-Hour Short Story Contest is held quarterly.

BOOK PUBLISHERS NETWORK, PO Box 2256, Bothell WA 98041. (425) 483-3040. Fax (425) 483-3098. E-mail: sherynhara@earthlink.net. Website: www.bookpublishersnetwork.com. Sheryn Hara, ed. Publishes 5-8 titles/yr.; hardcover, trade paperbacks. Receives 20 submissions annually.

100% of books from first-time authors. Accepts mss through agents. SUBSIDY PUBLISHES 100%. Reprints books. No preference on length. **No royalty/advance.** Publication within 3 mos. Considers simultaneous submissions. Responds in 1 mo. Guidelines on Website; no catalog.

Nonfiction: Proposal or complete ms; phone/fax/e-query OK.

Fiction: Proposal or complete ms; phone/fax/e-query OK. For all ages.

Photos: Accepts freelance photos for book covers.

Tips: "We take good care of our authors. We work hand-in-hand with them to produce a quality product."

BOOKS JUST BOOKS.COM, 51 E. 42nd St., Ste. 1202, New York NY 10017. Toll-free (800) 621-2556. Fax (212) 681-8002. E-mail: ron@rjcom.com or through Website: www.booksjustbooks.com. R J Communications. Ron Pramschufer, pub. SUBSIDY PUBLISHES 100%. Guidelines on Website. Not included in topical listings.

@BOOKSTAND PUBLISHING, 305 Vineyard Town Center, Ste. 302, Morgan Hill CA 95037. Toll-free (866) 793-9365. (408) 852-1832. Fax (650) 653-2509. E-mail: support@bookstandpublishing .com or authorservices@bookstandpublishing.com. Website: www.bookstandpublishing.com. Fast Press Publishing Inc. Kari Baldwin, ed. A POD publisher helping authors get published. Publishes 20+ titles/yr. Receives 20+ submissions annually. 80% of books from first-time authors. Accepts mss through agents. 100% PRINT-ON-DEMAND. Reprints books. **Royalty 10-30% on retail; no advance.** Average first printing 48. Publication within 2 mos. Considers simultaneous submissions. Responds immediately. Guidelines by mail/e-mail/Website; free catalog.

Nonfiction: Complete ms. Christian topics.

Fiction: Complete ms. For all ages. All genres.

Special Needs: Niche books, memoirs, Bible studies.

Photos: Accepts freelance photos for book covers.

+BOOKSURGE LLC. 7290 B Investment Dr., Charleston NC 29418. (866) 308-6235. Fax (843) 760-7506. E-mail: travis.craine@booksurge.com. Website: www.booksurge.com. Owned by Amazon .com. Travis Craine, publishing consultant. SUBSIDY PUBLISHER. **Royalty 35%.**

BRENTWOOD CHRISTIAN PRESS, 4000 Beallwood Ave., Columbus GA 31904. Toll-free (800) 334-8861. (706) 576-5787. Fax (706) 317-5808. E-mail: Brentwood@aol.com. Website: www .BrentwoodBooks.com. Mainline. U. D. Roberts, exec. ed. Publishes 267 titles/yr. Receives 2,000 submissions annually. Reprints books. SUBSIDY PUBLISHES 95%. Offers InstaBooks and Just in Time publishing (print-on-demand). Average first printing 500. Publication within 1 mo. Considers simultaneous submissions. Responds in 2 days. Guidelines by mail.

Nonfiction: Complete ms. "Collection of sermons on family topics, poetry, relation of Bible to current day."

Fiction: Complete ms. "Stories that show how faith helps overcome small, day-to-day problems."

Photos: Accepts freelance photos for book covers.

Tips: "Keep it short; support facts with reference." This publisher specializes in small print runs of 300-1,000. Can best serve the writer who has a completed manuscript.

BROWN BOOKS PUBLISHING GROUP, 16200 N. Dallas Pkwy., Ste. 170, Dallas TX 75248. (972) 381-0009. Fax (972) 248-4336. E-mail: joyce.springer@brownbooks.com. Website: www.brown books.com. Milli A. Brown, pub.; submit to Joyce Springer, dir. of Christian div. Publishes books in the areas of self-help, religion/inspirational, relationships, business, mind/body/spirit, and women's issues; we build relationships with our authors. Imprints: Personal Profiles, The P3 Press. Publishes 150 titles/yr.; hardcover, trade paperbacks, coffee-table books. Receives 4,000 submissions annually. 70% of books from first-time authors. No mss through agents. SUBSIDY PUBLISHES 100% through

Personal Profiles & P3 imprints. **Royalty 100% of retail; no advance.** Authors retain rights to their work. Average first printing 3,000-5,000. Publication in 6 mos. Accepts simultaneous submissions. Responds in 2 wks. Requires mss on disk or by e-mail. Responds in 2 wks. Guidelines on Website.

Nonfiction: Complete ms; phone/e-query preferred.

Fiction: Complete ms; phone/e-query OK. For all ages.

Tips: "We publish all genres with an emphasis on business, self-help, children's, and general Christian topics."

CHRISTIAN SERVICES NETWORK, 1975 Janich Ranch Ct., El Cajon CA 92019-1150. Toll-free (800) 636-7276. Fax (619) 579-0685. E-mail through Website: www.csnbooks.com. Michael Wourms, ed. SELF-PUBLISHING COMPANY. Details on Website.

CREATION HOUSE, 600 Rinehart Rd., Lake Mary FL 32746-4872. (407) 333-0600. Fax (407) 333-7100. E-mail: creationhouse@strang.com. Website: www.creationhouse.com. Strang Communications Co. Submit to Acquisitions Editor. To inspire and equip people to live a Spirit-led life and to walk in the divine purpose for which they were created. Publishes 125 titles/yr.; hardcover, trade paperbacks, mass-market paperbacks, coffee-table books. Receives 1,500 submissions annually. 80% of books from first-time authors. Accepts mss through agents. Reprints books. Prefers 25,000+ wds. or 100-200 pgs. **Royalty 12-15% of net; no advance.** Average first printing 2,000. Publication within 2-4 mos. Considers simultaneous submissions. Responds in 10-12 wks. Open to submissions on disk or by e-mail. Guidelines by mail/e-mail; free catalog.

Nonfiction: Proposal/complete ms; no phone/fax query; e-query OK. "Open to any books that are well written and glorify Jesus Christ."

Fiction: Proposal/complete ms; no phone/fax query; e-query OK. For all ages. "Fiction must have a biblical worldview and point the reader to Christ."

Photos: Accepts freelance photos for book covers.

Tips: "We use the term co-publishing to describe a hybrid between conventional royalty publishing and self- or subsidy publishing, utilizing the best of both worlds. We produce a high quality book for our own inventory, market it, distribute it, and pay the author a royalty on every copy sold. In return, the author agrees to buy, at a deep discount, a portion of the first print run."

CREDO HOUSE PUBLISHERS, 3148 Plainfield Ave. NE, Ste. 111, Grand Rapids MI 49525-3285. (616) 363-2686. E-mail: connect@credocommunications.net. Website: www.credocommunications .net. A division of Credo Communications LLC. Timothy J. Beals, pres. Works with Christian ministry leaders and organizations to develop life-changing books, Bible-related products, and other Christian resources. CUSTOM PUBLISHER. Publishes 6-12 titles/yr. Publication within 60-90 days. Average first printing 2,500. Guidelines on Website. Not included in topical listings.

Nonfiction/Fiction: Complete online author survey.

+*CROSSBOOKS, 1663 Liberty Dr., Ste. 200, Bloomington IN 47403. Toll-free (866) 879-0502. E-mail: customerservice@crossbooks.com. Website: www.crossbooks.com. SUBSIDY OR CO-OP PUBLISHER. Open to freelance submissions. Not included in topical listings.

CROSSHOUSE PUBLISHING, PO Box 461592, Garland TX 75046. Toll-free (877) 212-0933. Fax (877) 212-0933. E-mail: crosshousepublishing@earthlink.net or through Website: www.cross housepublishing.org. Self-publishing branch of KLMK Communications. Katie Welch, pub. To achieve excellence in Christian self-publishing without sacrificing personal interest and care for customers. Publishes hardcover, trade paperbacks. No mss through agents. SUBSIDY PUBLISHER. **Royalty 25% on net; no advance.** Publication within 3 mos. Guidelines on Website (under "Downloads").

Nonfiction/Fiction: Accepts fiction for all ages.

Photos: Accepts freelance photos for book covers.

Tips: "We provide authors the opportunity to have their books distributed through a wide array of Christian and general bookstores. We aspire to offer the marketplace superior Christian literature that will impact readers' lives."

+DAN RIVER PRESS, PO Box 298, Thomaston ME 04861. E-mail: cal@americanletters.org. Website: www.americanletter.org/danriverpress.htm. Bob Olmsted, pres. Estab. 1976. Requires $3,500 advance sales or donation. Royalty 10% on first 2,500 copies; 15% on additional sales. Discourages simultaneous submissions. Guidelines on Website. Not included in topical listings.

DCTS PUBLISHING, PO Box 40276, Santa Barbara CA 93140. Toll-free (800) 965-8150. Fax (805) 653-6522. E-mail: dennis@dctspub.com. Website: www.dctspub.com. Dennis Stephen Hamilton, ed. Books are designed to enrich the mind, encourage the heart, and empower the spirit. Publishes 5 titles/yr. Receives 25 submissions annually. 35% of books from first-time authors. No mss through agents. SUBSIDY PUBLISHES 70%. No reprints. Prefers 100-300 pgs. **Royalty 17% of retail; no advance.** Average first printing 3,500. Publication within 6-8 mos. No simultaneous submissions. Prefers KJV. Guidelines by mail; free catalog/brochure.

   Nonfiction: Query or proposal/2-3 chapters; e-query OK.

@ROBBIE DEAN PRESS, 2910 E. Eisenhower Parkway, Ann Arbor MI 48108. (734) 973-9511. Fax (734) 973-9475. E-mail: Fairyha@aol.com. Website: www.RobbieDeanPress.com. Interested in works that are multiculturally appealing and that approach a topic in a unique manner. Dr. Fairy C. Hayes-Scott, owner. Publishes 1 title/yr. Receives 20 submissions annually. 100% of books from first-time authors. Accepts mss through agents. SUBSIDY PUBLISHES 75%; does print-on-demand. Reprints books. Length flexible. **Royalty 10-20%; no advance.** Average first printing 250. Publication within 6 mos. Considers simultaneous submissions. Responds in 2-6 wks. Guidelines by e-mail; free catalog.

   Nonfiction: Query first. "We're open to new ideas."
   Fiction: "We seldom do fiction." For children only.
   Ethnic Books: Multicultural.
   Also Does: Booklets; e-books; computer games.
   Photos: Accepts freelance photos for book covers.
   Tips: "Most open to self-help, reference, senior adult topics, and parenting."

DEEPER REVELATION BOOKS, PO Box 4260, Cleveland TN 37320-4260. (423) 478-2843. Fax (423) 479-2980. E-mail through Website: www.deeperrevelationbooks.org. Mike Shreve, founder/dir. Publishing in-depth and edifying literature for the body of Christ; producing loving presentations of the gospel to followers of other worldviews. All submissions that match one or both of these descriptions are welcome. (Send $30 with unsolicited submissions.) Responds in 3-6 mos. A partnership publishing house. Authors are partners and associates who fund the printing of their works but own their books. DRB oversees the project to help authors learn the art of publishing, achieve their goals, produce works of excellence, and more easily receive national and international distribution. Does large print runs or print-on-demand. Average print run 2,000-3,000. Publishes 5 titles/yr. All books carry Deeper Revelation Books imprint. Guidelines on Website (under "Authors"/"Publish with Us").

DEEP RIVER BOOKS (formerly VMI Publishers), 26306 Metolius Meadows Dr., Camp Sherman OR 97730. E-mail: bill@deepriverbooks.com, nancie@deepriverbooks.com. Website: www.deepriver books.com. Virtue Ministries Inc. Bill and Nancie Carmichael, pubs. Partnering with new authors. Publishes 35 titles/yr.; hardback, trade paperbacks, coffee-table books. Receives hundreds of submissions annually. 90% of books from first-time authors. Accepts mss through agents. No reprints. Prefers 65,000+ wds. or 192-400 pgs. **Royalty 12-18% of net; no advance.** CUSTOM PUBLISHER; see Website for details. Average first printing 2,500+. Publication within 9-12 mos. Considers simultaneous submissions. Requires accepted ms by e-mail. Responds in 2 mos. Guidelines on Website.

   Nonfiction: Query first by e-mail only; proposal/2-3 chapters.

Fiction: Query first by e-mail only; proposal/2-3 chapters. For all ages. "Anything Christian or inspirational that is well written, especially from new authors."

Tips: "Go to our Website first, and read how we partner with new authors. Then, if you feel Deep River Books would be a good fit for you, e-mail your proposal."

**Note: This publisher serviced by ChristianManuscriptSubmissions.com.

DEO VOLENTE PUBLISHING, 1970 Gadsden Todd Levee Rd., Humboldt TN 38343. (731) 824-2919. Fax (731) 824-2526. E-mail: books@delvolente.net. Website: www.deovolente.net. Larry Byars, owner. Books that are consistent with Reformed theology and promote and assist the Christian walk. SUBSIDY PUBLISHER. Publishes 2-3 titles/yr.; trade paperbacks. Receives 10-20 submissions annually. Accepts mss through agents or authors. **Royalty 8-10% on retail; no advance.** Considers simultaneous submissions. Send accepted mss by disk or e-mail. Guidelines on Website; no catalog.

   Nonfiction: Query first; fax/e-query OK.

   Fiction: Proposal/3 chapters.

DESTINY IMAGE PUBLISHERS, PO Box 310, Shippensburg PA 17257. Toll-free (800) 722-6774. (717) 532-3040. Fax (717) 532-9291. E-mail: rrr@destinyimage.com or through Website: www .destinyimage.com. Ronda Ranalli, ed. mngr. To help people grow deeper in their relationship with God and others. Imprints: Destiny Image Fiction, Destiny Image Dark Matter. Publishes 100 titles/yr. Receives 1,500 submissions annually. 10% of books from first-time authors. Accepts mss through agents or authors. Reprints books. Prefers 190-220 pgs. **Royalty 10-15% on net; no advance.** Average first printing 10,000. Publication within 9-12 mos. Considers simultaneous submissions. Send unsolicited mss via their online Manuscript Submission Form. Responds in up to 6 mos. Guidelines on Website; free catalog.

   Nonfiction: Query or proposal/chapters; no e-query. Charges a $25 fee for unsolicited manuscripts (enclose with submission). Requires author to buy 5,000 copies of their book for $20,000.

   Fiction: Proposal/1-2 chapters. Adult.

   Tips: "Most open to books on the deeper life, or of Charismatic interest." Some authors report this publisher requires them to buy $20,000 worth of their own books—which would make this a subsidy publisher.

E.F.S. ONLINE PUBLISHING, 2844 Eighth Ave., Ste. 6E, New York NY 10039. (212) 283-8899. E-mail: efsenterprises@hotmail.com. Website: www.efs-enterprises.com. E.F.S. Enterprises Inc. Zeritha Jenkins, ed.; submit to Rita Baxter. Focuses on extremely well-written fiction and nonfiction that can compete with books published by larger houses; quality work that can stand the test of time. Imprints: E.F.S. Books & E.F.S. Drama Series. Publishes 10-20 titles/yr.; hardcover, trade paper-backs, mass-market paperbacks. Receives 200-250 submissions annually. 90% of books from first-time authors. Accepts mss through agents or authors. SUBSIDY PUBLISHER. No reprints. **Royalty 20-30% on net; advance considered for established authors.** Average first printing 100-300. Publication within 4-5 mos. No simultaneous submissions. Responds in 1-2 mos. Guidelines on Website (click on "EFS Publishing"); catalog online.

   Nonfiction: Query first (complete ms for subsidy deals); e-query OK.

   Fiction: Query first (complete ms for subsidy deals); e-query OK. "Looking for adult religious fiction; ethnic fiction; contemporary fiction; well-written, clean fiction."

   Special Needs: Very well-written inspirational fiction and nonfiction with a 21st-century flair.

   Ethnic Books: Black and other ethnicities.

   Artwork: Accepts queries from freelance artists.

   Contest: Sponsors three contests: Women's Empowerment Awards Writing Competition; Annual Writing Competition; and Religious Fiction & Nonfiction Writing Competition. See Website for details.

Tips: "(1) Most open to a well-written book that's plot-driven and supported by a dynamic cast of characters. (2) Proofread your manuscript before submitting. (3) Learn as much as possible about contemporary publishing."

ELDERBERRY PRESS INC., 1393 Old Homestead Rd., 2nd Fl., Oakland OR 97462. (541) 459-6043. Toll-free fax (888) 259-5484. E-mail: editor@elderberrypress.com. Website: www.elder berrypress.com. David W. St. John, exec. ed. Publishes 15 titles/yr. Receives 150-250 submissions annually. 90% of books from first-time authors. No mss through agents. SUBSIDY PUBLISHES 50%; does print-on-demand. **Royalty 10-25%; no advance.** Publication within 3 mos. Considers simultaneous submissions. Accepts disk or e-mail submissions. Responds in 1 mo. Guidelines on Website; free catalog.

   Nonfiction: Complete ms; phone/fax/e-query OK. "We consider all topics."

   Fiction: Complete ms; phone/fax/e-query OK. All genres for all ages.

ESSENCE PUBLISHING CO. INC., 20 Hanna Ct., Belleville ON K8P 5J2, Canada. Toll-free (800) 238-6376. (613) 962-2360. Fax (613) 962-3055. E-mail: info@essence-publishing.com. Website: www.essence-publishing.com. David Visser, mng. ed.; Sherrill Brunton, acqs. mgr.; (sbruton@ essence-publishing.com). Provides affordable, short-run book publishing to the Christian community; dedicated to furthering the work of Christ through the written word. Imprints: Guardian Books, Epic Press. Publishes 100-150+ titles/yr.; hardcover, trade paperbacks, mass-market paperbacks, coffee-table books. Receives 250+ submissions annually. 75% of books from first-time authors. Accepts mss from agents or authors. SUBSIDY PUBLISHES 100%. Does print-on-demand. Reprints books. Any length. **Royalty.** Average first printing 500-1,000. Publication within 3 mos. Considers simultaneous submissions. Responds in 2 wks. Prefers requested ms on disk or by e-mail. Bible version is author's choice. Guidelines by mail/e-mail; catalog online (www.essencebookstore.com).

   Nonfiction: Complete ms; phone/fax/e-query OK. Accepts all topics.

   Fiction: Complete ms. All genres for all ages. Also picture books.

   Also Does: Pamphlets, booklets, tracts.

   Photos/Artwork: Accepts freelance photos for book covers; open to queries from freelance artists.

FAIRWAY PRESS, subsidy division for CSS Publishing Company, 5450 N. Dixie Hwy., Lima OH 45807-9559. Toll-free (800) 241-4056. (419) 227-1818. Fax (419) 224-4647. E-mail: editor@csspub .com or through Website: www.fairwaypress.com. David Runk, ed. (david@csspub.com); submit to Attn: Sales Representative. Imprint: Express Press. Publishes 100 titles/yr. Receives 200-300 submissions annually. 80% of books from first-time authors. Reprints books. SUBSIDY PUBLISHES 100%. **Royalty to 50%; no advance.** Average first printing 500-1,000. Publication within 6-9 mos. Considers simultaneous submissions. Responds in up to 1 mo. Prefers requested ms on disk; no e-mail submissions. Prefers NRSV. Guidelines on Website ("Submit Your Manuscript"); catalog for 9 x 12 SAE.

   Nonfiction: Complete ms; phone/fax/e-query OK. All types. "Looking for manuscripts with a Christian theme, and seasonal material."

   Fiction: Complete ms. For adults, teens, or children; all types. No longer producing anything in full color or with four-color illustrations.

@FAITH BOOKS & MORE, 3255 Lawrenceville-Suwanee Rd., Ste. P250, Suwanee GA 30024. (678) 232-6156. Toll-free fax (888) 479-4540. E-mail: publishing@faithbooksandmore.com. Website: www.faithbooksandmore.com. 100% custom publishing. Nicole Smith, mng. ed. Survivors of Abuse, Health & Wellness, Teens. Baptist. Imprints: Faith Books & More; Friends of Faith, Corporate Connoisseur. Publishes 100 titles/yr; hardcover, trade paperbacks, and e-books. Receives 200 submissions annually. 90% of books from first-time authors. Accepts mss through agents or authors. SUBSIDY PUBLISHES 50%; does print-on-demand and off-set. Reprints books. Any length; no less than 4 pages. **Royalty; no advance.** Publication within 2 mos. Considers simultaneous submissions. Responds in 1 mo. Prefers NKJ or NIV. Guidelines by e-mail/Website; no catalog.

Nonfiction: Complete ms; phone/e-query OK. Any topic.

Fiction: Complete ms; phone/e-query OK. Any genre, for all ages.

Photos/Artwork: Accepts freelance photos for book covers; considers queries from freelance artists.

+FAITHFUL LIFE PUBLISHERS. 3335 Galaxy Way, North Fort Myers FL 33903-1419. Toll-free (888) 720-0950. (239) 652-0135. E-mail: JimWendorf@hotmail.com. Website: http://FLPublishers .com. Jim Wendorf, pub. SUBSIDY PUBLISHER. Not included in topical listings.

FOREVER BOOKS, 1405-77 University Crescent, Winnipeg MB R3T 3N8, Canada. Toll-free phone/ fax (888) 485-2224. E-mail: info@foreverbooks.ca. Website: www.foreverbooks.ca. Beryl Henne, mng. ed.; Gus Henne, acq. ed. Helping others tell their stories. Publishes 24+ titles/yr.; hardcover, trade paperbacks, mass-market paperbacks, coffee-table books. Receives 30+ submissions annually. 80% of books from first-time authors. Accepts mss through agents. SUBSIDY PUBLISHES 85%; does print-on-demand. Reprints books. Any length. A contract book publisher; author pays 100%. Average first printing 100-1,000. Publication within 4 mos. Considers simultaneous submissions. Responds in 2-3 wks. Accepts mss on disk or by e-mail. Guidelines by mail/e-mail; no catalog.

Nonfiction: Complete ms; e-query OK. All topics.

Fiction: Complete ms; e-query OK. All genres for all ages.

Photos/Artwork: Accepts freelance photos for book covers; open to queries from freelance artists.

FRUITBEARER PUBLISHING LLC, PO Box 777, Georgetown DE 19947. (302) 856-6649. Fax (302) 856-7742. E-mail: cfa@candyabbott.com or through Website: www.fruitbearer.com. Candy Abbott, mng. partner. Offers editing services and advice for self-publishers. Publishes 5-10 titles/ yr.; hardcover, picture books. Receives 10-20 submissions annually. 90% of books from first-time authors. SUBSIDY PUBLISHES 100%. No reprints. Average first printing 500-5,000. Publication within 1-6 mos. Responds in 3 mos. Guidelines by mail/e-mail; brochure for #10 SAE/1 stamp.

Nonfiction: Proposal/2 chapters; phone/fax/e-query OK.

Fiction: For all ages.

Also Does: Pamphlets, booklets, tracts.

Photos: Accepts freelance photos for book covers.

Tips: "Accepting limited submissions."

+GOOD IMPRESSIONS AUDIO BOOKS, 616 Sommerset Rd., Woodland WA 98674. E-mail: published@myaudiobook.org or through Website: www.myaudiobook.org. Publishes audio books. Guidelines on Website.

+@GRACE ACRES PRESS, PO Box 22, Larkspur CO 80118. (303) 681-9995. Fax (303) 681-9996. E-mail: info@GraceAcresPress.com. Website: www.GraceAcresPress.com. Grace Acres, Inc. Anne R. Fenske, ed./pub. A conservative publisher with an emphasis on dispensational theology. Publishes 4-6 titles/yr.; hardcover, trade paperbacks, digital. Receives 50-100 submissions annually. 80-90% of books from first-time authors. Accepts mss through agents or authors. SUBSIDY PUBLISHER. Reprints books. **Royalty 10-15% on net; no advance.** Average first printing 1,500-2,500. Publication within 6 mos. Considers simultaneous submissions. Responds in 3 mos. Guidelines by e-mail; free catalog.

Nonfiction: Query first; e-query OK. Requires accepted mss on disk.

Artwork: Open to queries from freelance artists.

Tips: "Most open to a book with a built-in audience/buyer; i.e. speaker, textbook."

+HALO PUBLISHING INTL., 5549 Canal Rd., Valley View OH 44125. (216) 255-6756. Fax (216)

255-6758. E-mail: contact@halopublishing.com. Website: www.halopublishing.com. Blog: www .halopublishing.blogspot.com. Kristin Maurice, chief ed. Publishes unique subject matter that most publishers turn away. Publishes 25-30 titles/yr.; hardcover, trade paperbacks, and coffee-table books. Receives 750-1,000 submissions annually. 99% of books from first-time authors. No mss through agents. No reprints. SUBSIDY PUBLISHES 85%; does print-on-demand. Prefers 3,000 wds. or 200 pgs. **Royalty 90-95%; no advance.** Average first printing 1,000. Publication within 2 mos. Considers simultaneous submissions. Responds in 1 mo. Guidelines by e-mail/Website; no catalog.

   Nonfiction: Proposal/3 chapters; phone/e-query OK.

   Fiction: Proposal/3 chapters; phone/e-query OK. For all ages.

   Special Needs: Educational books.

   Artwork: Open to queries from freelance artists.

HOLY FIRE PUBLISHING, 717 Old Trolley Rd., Ste. 6, Unit 116, Summerville SC 29485. (843) 628-0319. E-mail: publisher@christianpublish.com. Website: www.christianpublish.com. Venessa Hensel, COO. Important that everything we publish be clean and honoring to Christ and be in line with core Christian beliefs. Publishes 200 titles/yr.; hardcover, trade paperbacks. Receives 3,000 submissions annually. 50% of books from first-time authors. Accepts mss through agents. DOES ONLY PRINT-ON-DEMAND. Reprints books. Prefers 48-750 pgs. **Royalty, discounts, and retail price set by author; no advance.** Publication within 2 mos. Prefers submissions on disk or by e-mail. Guidelines by mail/e-mail/Website; no catalog.

   Nonfiction: Proposal/1 chapter; phone/fax/e-query OK. "Looking for Christian Living or Christian poetry." All topics.

   Fiction: Proposal/1 chapter; phone/fax/e-query OK. For all ages. All genres.

   Artwork: Open to queries from freelance artists.

THE HOUSE OF ALI (formerly Alfred Ali Literary Works), PO Box 582, Southfield MI 48076. (248) 356-5111. Fax (248) 356-1367. E-mail: AALiterary@aol.com. Website: www.AlfredAli.com. Alfred Ali, pub.; San Serif, ed. Spreading the word on how the Word of God can change and improve lives (1 Corinthians 3:16). Publishes 1 title/yr.; trade paperback. Receives 5 submissions annually. 80% of books from first-time authors. Accepts mss through agents. No reprints. SUBSIDY PUBLISHES 70%. Prefers 100-200 pgs. **Royalty 25% of retail; no advance.** Average first printing 1,000-5,000. Publication within 9 mos. Accepts e-mail submissions. Guidelines by mail; catalog $3.

   Nonfiction: Query only; fax query OK.

   Ethnic Books: Publishes for the African American market.

   Photos: Accepts freelance photos for book covers.

   Tips: "Most open to books that are based on inspiration that leads to self-awareness."

@IMD PRESS, 7140 Hooker St., Westminster CO 80030-5459. (303) 232-4779. Fax (303) 232-5009. E-mail: plargent@imdpress.com. Website: www.imdpress.com. IMD International. Phil Largent, pres.; Jim Hawley, IMD Press project mngr. (jimh@imdpress.com). To build up the Body of Christ through printed resources, while providing a "tentmaking" income/resource to fulfill our international mission. Publishes 10 titles/yr.; hardcover, mostly trade paperbacks, digital. Receives 10-15 submissions annually. 75% of books from first-time authors. Accepts mss through agents or authors. SUBSIDY PUBLISHES 100%; does print-on-demand. Reprints books. Any length. **Author pays all expenses.** Average first printing 1,000 (100-5,000+). Publication within 1 mo. Considers simultaneous submissions. Prefers accepted mss by e-mail. Responds in 1 mo. or less. Prefers NIV. Guidelines on Website; no catalog.

   Nonfiction: Complete ms; phone/e-query OK. Generally adult; curriculum for all ages.

   Special Needs: Bible studies, spiritual leadership development, small group Bible studies, encouragement for believers, faith building, and adult Bible study training or curriculum.

   Ethnic Books: Translation services for worldwide languages, esp. Indian, Africa, and SE Asia.

Photos: Accepts freelance photos for book covers.

Tips: "We do not buy mss or retain your rights; 15 years editing and 25 years design experience gives you publishing with integrity and excellence. Submit only completed mss. We do not edit." Also prints periodicals.

IMPACT CHRISTIAN BOOKS INC., 332 Leffingwell Ave., Ste. 101, Kirkwood MO 63122. (314) 822-3309. Fax (314) 822-3325. E-mail: info@impactchristianbooks.com or through Website: www.impactchristianbooks.com. William D. Banks, pres. Books of healing, miraculous deliverance, and spiritual warfare, drawing individuals into a deeper walk with God. Publishes 20+ titles/yr. Receives 20-50 submissions annually. 50-70% of books from first-time authors. No mss through agents. SUBSIDY PUBLISHES 50-70%. Reprints books. Average first printing 5,000. Publication within 2 mos. Considers simultaneous submissions. Responds by prior arrangement in 30 days. Requires requested ms on disk. Guidelines by mail; catalog for 9 x 12 SAE/5 stamps. Not in topical listings.

    Nonfiction: Query only; phone/fax query OK. Outstanding personal testimonies and Christ-centered books.

INFINITY PUBLISHING, 1094 New Dehaven St., Ste. 100, West Conshohocken PA 19428-2713. Toll-free (877) 289-2665. (610) 941-9999. Fax (610) 941-9959. E-mail: info@infinitypublishing.com. Website: www.infinitypublishing.com. 100% PRINT-ON-DEMAND. Charges $400 up-front fee. First order of books is at 50% discount; additional orders 40% discount. **Royalty 10-30%; no advance.** 70% of books from first-time authors. Prefers mss through agents. Publication within 3 mos. Considers simultaneous submissions. Prefers accepted ms on disk. Guidelines by mail/Website (under "Book Publishing"); no catalog.

    Nonfiction: Complete ms.

    Fiction: Complete ms. All genres; for all ages.

    Photos: Accepts freelance photos for book covers.

INSIGHT PUBLISHING GROUP, 8810 S. Yale, Ste. 410, Tulsa OK 74137. (918) 493-1718. Fax (918) 493-2219. E-mail: mail@freshword.com. Website: www.freshword.com. Christian Publisher. John Mason, ed. Owned by a best-selling author and publishing industry executive who established the company to serve authors. Publishes 50 titles/yr.; hardcover, trade paperbacks. Receives 50 submissions annually. 75% of books from first-time authors. Accepts mss through agents. 60% PRINT-ON-DEMAND; 40% SUBSIDY. Reprints books. Prefers 160 pgs. **Royalty 15-17% on net; no advance.** Average first printing 5,000. Publication within 3 mos. Considers simultaneous submissions. Requires disk or e-mail submission. Responds in 1 wk. Guidelines by e-mail.

    Nonfiction: Complete ms; phone/fax/e-query OK. Will consider most nonfiction topics.

    Fiction: Complete ms; phone/fax/e-query OK. Will consider most fiction topics.

    Also Does: Booklets.

    Tips: "Our team offers more than 30 years of expertise and a unique approach to publishing, creating a rewarding experience for each author who publishes with us. Our services include professional editing, typesetting, cover design, book coaching through John Mason, author tools, and extensive distribution. Most open to books that bear fruit, are unique, authentic, and relevant."

KINDRED BOOKS, 1310 Taylor Ave., Winnipeg MB R3M 3Z6, Canada. Toll-free (800) 545-7322. (204) 669-6575. Fax (204) 654-1865. E-mail: kindred@mbconf.ca. Website: www.kindredproductions.com. Mennonite Brethren/Imprint of Kindred Productions. Submit to: Attn. Manager. Publisher for the Mennonite Brethren Church in North America. Publishes 3-4 titles/yr.; hardcover, trade paperbacks. Receives 20 submissions annually. 95% of books from first-time authors. No mss through agents. SUBSIDY PUBLISHES 100%; does print-on-demand. Reprints books. Prefers 60,000 wds. or 200 pgs. Average first printing 1,000-2,000. Publication within 18 mos. Considers simultaneous submissions. Responds in 4 mos. Accepts requested ms by e-mail. Prefers NIV. Guidelines by mail/e-mail/Website; free catalog.

Nonfiction: Proposal/2-3 chapters; no phone query, fax/e-query OK. "Looking for Christian living and inspirational books."

Fiction: Proposal/2-3 chapters. For children & teens.

Tips: "Most open to Christian living or inspirational books that help everyday people grow in their relationship with Jesus. Books that help meet basic church needs. Material submitted should be in line with the Christian/evangelical faith."

LIFEVEST PUBLISHING INC., 4901 E. Dry Creek Rd., #170, Centennial CO 80122. Toll-free (877) 843-1007. (303) 221-1007. Website: www.lifevestpublishing.com. Ric Simmons, CEO. Specializes in children's books, educational literature, inspirational works, family/personal histories, and poetry. SUBSIDY PUBLISHES 100%. Submission form on Website.

MARKETINGNEWAUTHORS.COM, 2910 E. Eisenhower Pkwy., Ann Arbor MI 48108. Toll-free (800) 431-1579. (734) 975-0028. Fax (734) 973-9475. E-mail: info@marketingnewauthors.com or MarketingNewAuth@aol.com. Website: www.MarketingNewAuthors.com. Imprint of Robbie Dean Press. To primarily serve authors who wish to self-publish. Dr. Fairy C. Hayes-Scott, owner. 100% of books from first-time authors. Accepts mss through agents. SUBSIDY PUBLISHES 100%. Reprints books. Length flexible. Publication within 6 mos. Considers simultaneous submissions. Responds in 2-6 wks. Guidelines by e-mail/Website (under "Self-Publishing with MANA"). Offers 7 different marketing plans; see Website.

MCDOUGAL PUBLISHING, PO Box 3595, Hagerstown MD 21742. (301) 797-6637. Fax (301) 733-2767. E-mail: publishing@mcdougal.org. Website: www.mcdougalpublishing.com. McDougal Foundation/Evangelical. Diane McDougal, pres. Publishes books for the body of Christ. Imprints: McDougal Publishing, Fairmont Books, Parable Publishing, and Serenity Books. Publishes 10-15 titles/yr. Receives 150 submissions annually. 70% of books from first-time authors. Accepts mss through agents or authors. SUBSIDY PUBLISHES 20%. Does print-on-demand (author charged for print setup). Reprints books. Prefers 80-192 pgs. **Royalty 10-15% of net; no advance.** Requires authors to buy minimum of 2,000 copies of their book. Average first printing 3,000-5,000. Publication within 6 mos. Considers simultaneous submissions. Responds in 2 mos. Guidelines by mail/Website; free catalog by mail.

Nonfiction: Proposal/1-2 chapters (preferred); phone/fax/e-query OK. "Looking for titles on all topics relevant to the Christian life."

Fiction: Complete ms. "Now considering adult fiction from authors with an established market; no romance."

Tips: "Know who your audience is, and write to that audience. Also, keep focused on one central theme." Charges a $35 review fee for unsolicited manuscripts.

@MILESTONES INTERNATIONAL PUBLISHERS, PO Box 104, Newburg PA 17240. (717) 477-2230. Fax (717) 477-2261. E-mail: jimrill@milestonesintl.com or milestoneintl@bellsouth.net. Website: www.milestonesintl.com. Submit to: Jim Rill, pres., 9593 Possum Hollow Rd., Shippensburg PA 17257. Bringing significance to life's journey. Publishes 24-30 titles/yr.; hardcover, trade paperbacks, coffee-table books, digital. 75% of books from first-time authors. No mss through agents. Prefers 35,000-65,000+ wds. **Royalty 12-16+% on net; or outright purchase of $8,500-$18,000+; rarely pays an advance.** A multi-level publisher with many publishing packages available; many price breaks. Average first printing 2,500-10,000. Publication in 3 mos. Responds in 30 days. Prefers KJV, NKJV. Guidelines by phone consultation.

Nonfiction: Proposal/2-3 chapters (no returns). Phone query OK.

Fiction: Proposal/2-3 chapters (no returns); phone query OK. Simple living, Amish, Mennonite, basics.

Special Needs: Novels, Christian living, deeper walk, relationships, health (including homeopathic), issues, and events.

Photos/Artwork: Accepts freelance photos for book covers; open to queries from freelance artists.

Tips: "We use our distribution power to help bring a new level of visibility to an author—both domestic and international. Price structures have come down. With the number of books being published, it is important for the publisher to know an author's willingness to help support."

@ONE WORLD PRESS, 890 Staley Ln., Chino Valley AZ 86323. Toll-free (800) 250-8171. (928) 445-2081. Fax (928) 636-3331. E-mail: PrintMyBook@oneworldpress.com. Website: www.one worldpress.com. Joe Zuccarello, operations mngr. Publishes many titles/yr. Receives 25-50 submissions annually. 50% of books from first-time authors. Accepts mss through agents. SUBSIDY PUBLISHES 100%; does print-on-demand. Reprints books. Average first printing up to author. Publication within 2 mos. Considers simultaneous submissions. Responds in 2-4 wks. No guidelines or catalog.

   Nonfiction: Complete manuscript. All ages. "We publish about anything within decency and reason."

   Also Does: Booklets, e-books, pamphlets, tracts.

OUTSKIRTS PRESS, INC., 10940 S. Parker Rd. - 515, Parker CO 80134. Toll-free (888) OP-BOOKS. E-mail: info@outskirtspress.com. Website: www.outskirtspress.com. Submit to Book Editor. Open to unsolicited freelance. CUSTOM/SUBSIDY PUBLISHER. Not included in topical listings.

PATH PUBLISHING INC., Not accepting freelance submissions during 2011.

PATH PUBLISHING IN CHRIST, Accepting no freelance submissions during 2011.

PECAN TREE PUBLISHING, Toll-free (877) 207-2442. Fax (954) 272-7041. E-mail: submissions@ pecantreepress.com or through Website: www.pecantreepress.com. Submit to Book Editor. Prefers 85,000-120,000 wds. for fiction; 65,000-85,000 for nonfiction. SUBSIDY PUBLISHER. Responds in 8 wks. min. Guidelines on Website.

   Nonfiction/Fiction: Query/5 or more chapters through e-mail only.

   Tips: "All material must be legally copyrighted with the Library of Congress (www.loc.gov). Do not call about your manuscript."

PLEASANT WORD, See the WinePress Publishing listing.

POEMS BY ME, 4000 Beallwood Ave., Columbus GA 31904. Toll-free (800) 334-8861. E-mail: Brentwood@aol.com. Website: www.PoemsByMe.com. Brentwood Christian Press. U. D. Roberts, ed. Poetry that is spiritual, personal, emotional. Receives 80 submissions annually. 75% of books from first-time authors. Accepts mss through agents. SUBSIDY PUBLISHES 100%; does print-on-demand. Reprints books. Need at least 40 poems for a book. Same-week response.

POET'S COVE PRESS, 4000 Beallwood Ave., Columbus GA 31904. Toll-free (800) 334-8861. (706) 576-5787. E-mail: Brentwood@aol.com. Website: www.BrentwoodBooks.com. Subsidiary of Brentwood Publishers Group. U. D. Roberts, exec. dir. Publishes 75 titles/yr. SUBSIDY OR CUSTOM PUBLISHES 100%. Specializes in self-publishing books of religious or inspirational poetry, in small press runs of under 500 copies. Publication in 45 days. Same-day response.

   Tips: "Type one poem per page; include short bio and photo with first submission."

PORT HOLE PUBLICATIONS, PO Box 205, Westlake OR 97493. (541) 902-9091. E-mail: info@ellentraylor.com. Website: http://ellentraylor.com. Ellen Traylor, ed./pub. A COOPERATIVE

PUBLISHER requiring a financial investment on the part of the author, along with a standard contract and optional marketing package.

Nonfiction/Fiction: Query first.

Tips: "We are open to publishing family-friendly and/or Christian content books of any length or genre. We are especially open to thought-provoking books on being a Christian in this difficult world, terrific fiction, Christian philosophy, short-story collections, and poetry (no sermons, please)."

PROVIDENCE HOUSE PUBLISHERS, 238 Seaboard Ln., Franklin TN 37174. Toll-free (800) 321-5692. (615) 771-2020. Fax (615) 771-2002. E-mail: books@providencehouse.com. Website: www.providencehouse.com. Mary Lawson, acq. & development ed. (mlawson@providencehouse.com). Produces books that honor God and reflect the knowledge, commitment, and accomplishments of His people. Publishes 20+ religious titles/yr.; hardcover, trade paperbacks, coffee-table books. Receives 100+ submissions annually. 90% of books from first-time authors. No mss through agents. SUBSIDY PUBLISHES 90%; no print-on-demand. Reprints books. Prefers 96-512 pgs. **Author receives 100% income from sales.** Average first printing 3,000. Publication within 9-10 mos. Considers simultaneous submissions. Responds in up to 6 mos. Prefers accepted ms on disk. Prefers NIV, NKJV. Guidelines by mail; no catalog (see Website).

Nonfiction: Proposal/2 chapters or complete ms.; phone/fax/e-query OK. Accepts requested ms by e-mail. Fill out and send the Manuscript Submission Questionnaire Form (see Website).

Fiction: Proposal/2 chapters or complete ms. For all ages. "Looking for Christian suspense."

Special Needs: Biography, church histories, ministry histories, missionary memoirs.

Artwork: Open to queries from freelance artists.

Tips: "Most open to biblically based books; history or memoir; those with a speaking ministry tend to receive more attention. Well-written texts only."

RECOVERY COMMUNICATIONS INC., PO Box 19910, Baltimore MD 21211. (410) 243-8352. Fax (410) 243-8558. E-mail: tdrews3879@aol.com. Website: www.GettingThemSober.com. Toby R. Drews, ed. Publishes 4-6 titles/yr. No mss through agents. SUBSIDY PUBLISHER. Prefers 110 pgs. **Co-op projects; no royalty or advance.** Average first printing 5,000. Publication within 9 mos. Excellent nationwide distribution and marketing in bookstores. Send for their free information packet.

Nonfiction: Query only.

Tips: "Although technically we are a subsidy publisher, we are more of a hybrid publisher in that we give the author enough free books to sell in the back of the room to totally recoup all the money they have paid; plus we share 50/50 on net sales at bookstores. Over half of our authors have gotten their money back and made a great profit. We are also aggressive in our pursuit of catalog sales and foreign rights sales (we recently sold to a German publisher). We also individually coach all our authors, at no cost to them, to help them successfully obtain speaking engagements."

+RILL & ASSOCIATES, 9593 Possum Hollow Rd. Shippensburg PA 17257, and PO Box 119, Orrstown PA 17244. (303) 503-7257. Fax (717) 477-2261. E-mail: rillandassociates@gmail.com. Website: www.rillandassociates.com. Jim Rill, pub. To help, especially first-time authors, through the process of publishing; full service; no hidden fees; includes domestic and international marketing. Publishes 12-24 titles/yr.; hardcover, trade paperbacks. SUBSIDY PUBLISHER. Receives 100+ submissions annually. 75% of books from first-time authors. No mss through agents. Does short & long run POD, as well as large press. Prefers 35,000-80,000+ wds. **Royalty 12-18% on net; seldom gives an advance ($2,500-5,000).** Average first printing 5,000+. Publication within 3 mos. Considers simultaneous submissions. Responds in 1 mo. Takes accepted mss by disk or e-mail. Prefers KJV, NKJV. Catalog on Website.

Nonfiction: Proposal/2-3 chapters; phone/e-query OK.

Fiction: Proposal/2-3 chapters; phone/e-query OK. Clean, wholesome, Christian fiction. Also wants Amish/Mennonite fiction.

Special Needs: True stories, novels, relationships, deeper living, health, holistic, inspirational.

Ethnic Books: Black; Hispanic. "We have a large multicultural audience."

Photos/Artwork: Accepts freelance photos for book covers; open to queries from freelance artists.

Contest: Sometimes sponsors a contest.

THE SALT WORKS, 1655 Booth Rd., Roseville CA 95747. (916) 784-0500. Fax (916) 773-7421. E-mail: books@publishersdesign.com. Website: www.publishersdesign.com. Division of Publishers Design Group Inc. Robert Brekke, pub.; submit to Project Manager. Seeks to demonstrate through books that God is sovereign, just, and merciful in all He does. Imprint: Salty's Books (children's— see separate listing), PDG, Humpback Books. Publishes 3-5 titles/yr.; hard cover, trade paperbacks, coffee-table books. Receives 100+ submissions annually. 90% of Christian books from first-time authors. No mss through agents. SUBSIDY PUBLISHES 85%; no print-on-demand. Reprints books. Prefers 95,000-150,000 wds. **Rarely pays royalty of 7-12% on net; occasional advance.** Average first printing 2,500-10,000. Publication within 4-12 mos. Considers simultaneous submissions. Responds within 45 days. Prefers ESV/NASB/NKJV/NIV (in that order). Guidelines by mail/e-mail/Website (click on "Submissions" at bottom of home page); free catalog when available.

Nonfiction: E-query only first; after query & phone meeting, send proposal. Unsolicited mss returned unopened.

Fiction: E-query only first; after query & phone meeting, send proposal. Unsolicited mss returned unopened. For adults and children. "Looking for titles that help believers in exploring and facing common issues surrounding God's sovereignty, His grace and forgiveness, their own sin and idolatry, and the areas where pop culture has influenced the church. Characters are blatantly human."

Special Needs: Looking for titles that communicate a biblical Christian worldview without promoting overly simplistic, idealistic, or theoretical solutions to life's biggest questions; books that honestly show no timidity in addressing our humanness. Looking for manuscripts that demonstrate that society's problems are rooted in the personal and spiritual, not in the political, educational, moral, and financial realms.

Also Does: Board games and other specialty products: fitness products, art projects and products, interactive projects for children.

Photos/Artwork: Rarely accepts freelance photos for book covers; open to queries from freelance artists.

Tips: "Most open to books that look at the Christian experience through a realistic biblical and Reformed perspective. Books that address the Christian's real problems as a 'heart' problem—not a theological problem; not from a victim mind-set, not a mental or logical one; not from a perspective of merely needing another program, pep talk, or the latest rehash of formulas for victorious living. Books that show the author understands that unless God changes the heart and brings a person to repentance, there are no real and lasting answers."

**Note: This publisher serviced by The Writer's Edge and ChristianManuscriptSubmissions.com.

SALTY'S BOOKS, 1655 Booth Rd., Roseville CA 95678. Toll-free (800) 587-6666. (916) 784-0500. Fax (916) 773-7421. E-mail: books@publishersdesign.com. Website: www.publishersdesign.com. Imprint of The Salt Works/Division of Publishers Design Group Inc. Robert Brekke, pub.; submit to Project Mngr. Imprint for children's Christian books. Publishes 2-5 titles/yr.; hardcover, trade paperbacks, coffee-table books. Receives 50+ submissions annually. 90% of books from first-time authors. No mss through agents. SUBSIDY PUBLISHES 75%. Reprints books. Prefers 450-3,500 wds.

for picture books; 8,000-40,000 wds. for early readers. **Royalty 7-12% on net; no advance.** Average first print run for children's books 2,000. Publication within 4-12 mos. Considers simultaneous submissions. Responds within 45 days. Prefers ESV/NASB/NKJV/NIV in that order. Guidelines by mail/e-mail/Website; free catalog when available.

Nonfiction: Query letter only first; after query and phone meeting, send a proposal.

Fiction: Query letter only first; after query and phone meeting, send a proposal. "Looking for titles that help kids in exploring and facing common issues surrounding God's sovereignty."

Special Needs: Looking for manuscripts that offer kids answers from a biblically orthodox Reformed perspective.

Also Does: Board games; books with packaged products; etc.

Artwork: Open to queries from freelance artists.

Tips: "Deal with the difficult issues or subject areas that most Sunday school teachers and youth leaders are either afraid to deal with or incapable of dealing with. Ask librarians or bookstore owners which books are most popular and why."

**Note: This publisher serviced by The Writer's Edge and ChristianManuscriptSubmissions.com.

SALVATION PUBLISHER AND MARKETING GROUP, PO Box 40860, Santa Barbara CA 93140. (805) 682-0316. Fax (call first). E-mail: opalmaedailey@aol.com. Wisdom Today Ministries. Opal Mae Dailey, ed-in-chief. We encourage, inspire, and educate; author has the choice to be involved as much or little as desired—which gives the opportunity to control income; personal coaching and collective marketing available. Publishes 5-7 titles/yr.; hardcover, trade paperbacks, mass-market paperbacks. 60% of books from first-time authors. No mss through agents. SUBSIDY PUBLISHES 80%; does print-on-demand. Reprints books. Prefers 96-224 pgs. Average first printing 1,000. Publication within 3-4 mos. No simultaneous submissions. Accepts requested ms on disk or by e-mail (not attachments). Responds in 1 mo. Prefers KJV. Guidelines (also by e-mail).

Nonfiction: Query only first; phone/fax/e-query OK.

Tips: "Turning taped messages into book form for pastors is a specialty of ours. We do not accept any manuscript that we would be ashamed to put our name on."

SEED FAITH BOOKS LLC, PO Box 230913, Tigard OR 97281. (503) 718-7911. E-mail: helen@ seedfaithbooks.com. Website: www.seedfaithbooks.com. David & Helen Haidle, eds. Publishes resources (curriculum, evangelism tools, and mission outreach) for Christian schools, churches, homeschooling families, and for distribution to nonprofit ministries. Not currently accepting submissions, except by request. Contact us via e-mail if you have written materials that complement what we are already publishing.

Tips: "We produce children's big books and picture books, as well as pocketbooks and booklets for needy children and adults. We are interested in more teaching resources and ideas that would supplement what we are already producing. (See our Website.) We also can help other writers self-publish their ministry ideas. Minimal fee for services."

@SELAH PUBLISHING GROUP LLC., 162 Crescent Dr., Bristol TN 37620. Toll-free (877) 616-6451. E-mail: info@selahbooks.com. Website: www.selahbooks.com. Garlen Jackson, pub. A publisher that does not water down the author's message. Publishes 45 titles/yr. Receives 20 submissions annually. 75% of books from first-time authors. Prefers mss through agents. Reprints books. Prefers 40,000 wds. or 144 pgs. SUBSIDY PUBLISHER/BOOK PACKAGER. **Royalty 12-18% of net; no advance.** Average first printing 2,500. Publication within 6 mos. No simultaneous submissions. Prefers requested ms on disk. Responds in 2 mos. Prefers ASV. Guidelines by e-mail; free catalog.

Nonfiction: Complete ms; no phone/fax/e-query.

Fiction: Complete ms; no phone/fax/e-query. For all ages.

Also Does: E-books.

Photos: Accepts freelance photos for book covers.

Tips: "Most open to time-sensitive, current events, and controversial books. Writers should spend more time selling who they are in regard to character and integrity."
**Note: This publisher serviced by ChristianManuscriptSubmissions.com.

SELF PUBLISH PRESS, 4000 Beallwood Ave., Columbus GA 31904. Toll-free (800) 334-8861. (706) 576-5787. Fax (706) 317-5808. E-mail: Brentwood@aol.com. Website: www.PublishMyBook.com. Brentwood Publishing Group. U. D. Roberts, exec. ed.; submit to Marie Warren, ed. All books must be family suitable. Receives 100 submissions annually. 98% of books from first-time authors. Accepts mss through agents. SUBSIDY PUBLISHES 98%; does print-on-demand. Offers InstaBooks and Just in Time publishing (print-on-demand). Reprints books. Prefers 64-300 pgs. Publication within 1 mo. Considers simultaneous submissions. Responds in 3 days. Guidelines on Website; no catalog.

Nonfiction: Complete ms/disk; no phone/fax/e-query. All religious—for family or youth.

Fiction: Complete ms/disk; no phone/fax/e-query. For all ages.

SERMON SELECT PRESS, 4000 Beallwood Ave., Columbus GA 31904. Toll-free (800) 334-8861. (706) 576-5787. Fax (706) 317-5808. E-mail: Brentwood@aol.com. Website: www.BrentwoodBooks.com. Subsidiary of Brentwood Publishers Group. U. D. Roberts, exec. dir. SUBSIDY OR CUSTOM PUBLISHES 100%. Focus is on sermon notes, outlines, illustrations, plus news that pastors would find interesting. Publishes 100 copies. Cost of about $3-4/book. Publication in 45 days. Same-day response.

+SONFIRE MEDIA, 411 N. Main St., Galax VA 24333. Toll-free (800) 890-7744. (276) 236-1085. E-mail: info@sonfiremedia.com or through Website: www.sonfiremedia.com. Vie Herlocker, ed. (vie@sonfiremedia.com). Offers partnership contracts & traditional ones. **Royalty 15% on traditional contracts; no advance; 100% on partnership contracts.** Guidelines on Website (click on "submission link" in text). Not included in topical listings.

Nonfiction & Fiction: Follow online guidelines.

SOUTHERN BAPTIST PRESS, 4000 Beallwood, Columbus GA 31904. Toll-free (800) 334-8861. (706) 576-5787. E-mail: Brentwood@aol.com. Website: www.SouthernBaptistPress.com. U. D. Roberts, exec. ed. Publishes 25 books/yr. Receives 600 submissions annually. Reprints books. SUBSIDY OR CUSTOM PUBLISHES 95%. Average first printing 500. Publication within 2 mos. Considers simultaneous submissions. Responds in 1 week. Guidelines by mail.

Nonfiction: Complete ms. "Collections of sermons on family topics; poetry; relation of Bible to current day."

Fiction: Complete ms. "Stories that show how faith helps overcome small, day-to-day problems."

Tips: "Keep it short; support facts with reference."

SPARROWCROWNE PRESS, PO Box 172282, Arlington TX 7600392282. E-mail: AngelBeQuick@gmail.com. Rachel St. John, ed; submit to January Keck, acq. ed. Large enough to provide quality printing; small enough to form an old-fashioned business. Publishes 5 titles/yr.; hardcover, coffee-table books. Receives 200 submissions annually. 60% of books from first-time authors. No mss through agents.; does print-on-demand. SUBSIDY PUBLISHES 50%. Reprints books. Prefers 25,000-50,000 words, or up to 300 pgs. **Subsidy contracts vary; no advance.** Average first printing 100-1,000. No simultaneous submissions. Responds within 60 days. Requires accepted mss on disk. Prefers KJV, NKJV. Intl. guidelines by mail; no catalog.

Nonfiction: Query first; no phone/fax query; e-query OK. Send SASE; not responsible for unsolicited mss.

Tips: "We do buy certain mss, but they are a rarity. We are mainly self-publish/subsidy and print-on-demand."

STAR BIBLE PUBLICATIONS, 1105 S. Airport Cir., Ste. C, Euless TX 76040. Toll-free (800) 433-7507. (817) 354-6000. Fax (817) 354-6006. E-mail: service@starbible.com. Website: www.star

bible.com. Church of Christ. Books that will be in harmony with New Testament principles and useful among general audience markets and among Churches of Christ. Publishes 10-15 titles/yr.; mass-market paperbacks. Receives 20-25 submissions annually. 50% of books from first-time authors. No mss through agents. CO-OP PUBLISHER. No reprints. Prefers 110 pgs. **Royalty on retail; no advance.** Average first printing 1,000-1,500. Publication within 2 mos. No simultaneous submissions. Responds in 1 mo. Accepts mss on disk or by e-mail. Prefers ASV, KJV, NIV. Guidelines by mail/e-mail/Website; catalog on Website.

Nonfiction: Complete ms; phone/fax/e-query OK.

Fiction: Complete ms. For adults.

Photos: Accepts freelance photos for book covers.

Tips: "We are looking for general audience books that focus on the gospel and encourage readers to read the Bible, books that encourage people in their Christian walk, books on doctrine, studies on the Bible or specific books of the Bible, and topical studies."

+STONEHOUSE INK, (208) 514-6631. E-mail: stonehousepress@hotmail.com. Website: www .thestonepublishinghouse.com. Clean-fiction imprint of Ampelon Press (www.ampelonpublishing .com). Aaron Patterson, ed./pub. Also open to reprinting out-of-print books.

STRONG TOWER PUBLISHING, PO Box 973, Milesburg PA 16853. E-mail: strongtowerpubs@ aol.com. Website: www.strongtowerpublishing.com. Heidi L. Nigro, pub. Specializes in eschatology and books that challenge the reader to think more deeply about their faith and scriptural truths; must be biblically responsible, doctrinally defensible, and consistent with their statement of faith. Publishes 1-2 titles/yr.; trade paperbacks. 50% of books from first-time authors. No mss through agents. Reprints books. PRINT-ON-DEMAND 100%. **Royalty 25% of net; no advance.** Average first printing 50. Publication within 3-4 mos. Guidelines/information/prices on Website.

Nonfiction: Query. Eschatology.

Tips: "We recommend that all first-time authors have their manuscripts professionally edited. We will consider putting first-time authors into print, but by invitation only. That invitation comes only after the manuscript has been thoroughly evaluated and we have discussed the pros and cons of our unique on-demand publishing model with the author."

TATE PUBLISHING & ENTERPRISES LLC., Tate Publishing Bldg., 127 E. Trade Center Ter., Mustang OK 73064-4421. Toll-free (888) 361-9473. Fax (405) 376-4401. E-mail: publish@tate publishing.com. Website: www.tatepublishing.com. Curtis Winkle, sr. ed.; Dr. Richard Tate, dir. of acquisitions. Owns and operates their own, state-of-the-art printing plant facility; pays to produce audiobook. Publishes 120 titles/yr.; hardcover, trade paperbacks, mass-market paperbacks. Receives 60,000-75,000 contacts annually. 60% of books from first-time authors. Accepts mss through agents. SUBSIDY LIKELY (most authors asked to contribute $3,985.50 toward promotion—refunded if book does well). No print-on-demand. Accepts reprints. Prefers 115,000 wds. **Royalty 15-40% of net; negotiable advance with requirements.** Average first printing 5,000. Publication within 4-6 mos. Considers simultaneous submissions. Responds in 3-6 wks. Accepts submissions by disk or e-mail. Any Bible version. Guidelines by mail/e-mail/Website; free catalog.

Nonfiction: Proposal with synopsis & any number of chapters, or complete ms; phone/ fax/e-query OK. Any topic. "Looking for books that sell."

Fiction: Proposal with synopsis & any number of chapters or complete ms; phone/fax/ e-query OK. For all ages. Any genre.

Ethnic Books: For all ethnic markets.

Contest: For those in author pool.

Artwork: Has 31 full-time artists on staff; open to queries from freelance artists.

Tips: "We invest resources in every work we accept, and accept first-time authors."

**Note: This publisher serviced by The Writer's Edge.

TEACH SERVICES INC., 254 Donovan Rd., Brushton NY 12916. (518) 358-3494. Fax (518) 358-3028. E-mail: publishing@TEACHservices.com. Website: www.teachservices.com. Seventh-day Adventist. Timothy Hullquist, pres.; submit to Jennifer Aiken, acq. ed. To publish uplifting books for the lowest price. Publishes 48 titles/yr.; hardcover, trade paperbacks, coffee-table books. Receives 100+ submissions annually. 35% of books from first-time authors. No mss through agents. SUBSIDY PUBLISHES 75% (author has to pay for first printing, then publisher keeps it in print); limited print-on-demand. Reprints books. Prefers 40,000 wds. or 96 pgs. **Royalty 10% of retail; no advance.** Average first printing 2,000. Publication within 6 mos. Considers simultaneous submissions. Responds in 3 wks. Prefers accepted mss by e-mail. Prefers KJV. Guidelines by mail/e-mail/Website; catalog on Website.

Nonfiction: Complete ms; no phone/fax query.

Fiction: Complete ms; allegory and historical. For all ages.

Photos/Artwork: Accepts freelance photos for book covers; open to queries from freelance artists.

TRAFFORD PUBLISHING, 1663 Liberty Dr., Bloomington IN 47403. Toll-free (888) 232-4444. (250) 383-6864. Fax (250) 383-6804. E-mail: info@trafford.com or through Website: www.trafford.com. Trafford Holdings Ltd. Your book, your way. Publishes 100-200 titles/yr.; hardcover, trade paperbacks, mass-market paperbacks, coffee-table books. Receives 1,000-2,000 submissions annually. 90% of books from first-time authors. No mss through agents. 100% PRINT-ON-DEMAND; no subsidy. Reprints books. Prefers less than 700 pgs. **Royalty 60%; no advance.** Average first printing 40. Publication within 1 mo. Considers simultaneous submissions. Responds immediately. Prefers accepted mss on disk. Guidelines by mail/e-mail/Website; catalog $7.

Nonfiction: Any appropriate topic.

Fiction: All genres for all ages.

Photos: Accepts freelance photos for book covers.

Tips: "Authors choose the retail price for their books, and their royalty is 60% of the gross margin."

+WESTBOW PRESS, 1663 Liberty Dr., Bloomington IN 47403. Toll-free (866) 928-1240. Website: www.westbowpress.com. Subsidy division of Thomas Nelson Publishers. Kevin A. Gray, news media contact. Estab. 2009. Does print-on-demand and digital formats. Fill out online form to receive information on their publishing program. Guidelines on Website (click on "FAQ").

@WINEPRESS PUBLISHING, PO Box 428, 1730 Railroad St., Enumclaw WA 98022. Toll-free (800) 326-4674. (360) 802-9758. Fax (360) 802-9992. E-mail: acquisitions@winepressgroup .com. Website: www.winepresspub.com. Blog: www.winepressofwords.com. The WinePress Group. Submit via Website, or call acquisitions department. To ensure the highest quality and service, WP uses custom online software that allows you to track your book project from beginning to end. Imprints: WinePress Publishing, WinePress Kids (children's books), Annotation Press (general market, family friendly), UpWrite Books (writers resources), and WinePress POD. Publishes 75 titles/yr.; hardcover, trade paperbacks, mass-market paperbacks, coffee-table books. Receives 700+ submissions annually. 70% of books from first-time authors. Accepts mss through agents. BOOK PACKAGER/CUSTOM PUBLISHER 100%. Reprints books. Lengths range from 10,000-150,000 wds. or 48-1,300 pgs. **Author pays production costs, keeps all profit from sales.** Average first printing 3,000 (2,500 min.). Publication in 6-9 mos. Considers simultaneous submissions. Responds in 48 hrs. Accepts requested ms on disk. Any Bible version. Guidelines by e-mail; free catalog.

Nonfiction: Complete ms; e-query OK. Publishes all family-friendly, biblically oriented topics.

Fiction: Complete ms. Publishes all family-friendly, biblically oriented material and genres. For all ages.

Print-On-Demand: "In an industry where POD publishers will print almost anything,

WinePress's POD has high standards for both design and content." Prints 300 POD books and 75 off-set books annually.

Also Does: Audio books, e-books, multimedia, Website design & hosting, blogs, DVD production, CD/book packages, manuals, genuine leather Bibles, full-color children's books, board books, full publicity and marketing campaigns, book trailers, market consultation, blog and social network consultations, and advertising campaigns.

Photos/Artwork: Accepts copyright-free photos and artwork.

Tips: "Since 1991, WinePress has been an innovator in the Christian custom printing market. We partner with authors through a wide range of services provided by our in-house departments: including production, design, video, multimedia, Internet, publicity, promotions, warehousing fulfillment, and distribution departments. To ensure the highest quality, everything is coordinated by our unique online Co-C.A.P.T.A.I.N. software and friendly staff. We do not accept all manuscripts for publication and advise potential authors to first review our doctrinal standards on our Website."

**Note: This publisher serviced by The Writer's Edge and ChristianManuscriptSubmissions.com.

@WORD ALIVE PRESS, 131 Cordite Rd., Winnipeg MB R3W 1S1, Canada. Toll-free (866) 967-3782. (204) 777-7100. Toll-free fax (800) 352-9272. (204) 669-0947. E-mail: publishing@wordalivepress.ca. Website: www.wordalivepress.ca. C. Schmidt, publishing consultant. SUBSIDY PUBLISHER. Off-set printing, print-on-demand, editing services, sales, marketing and distribution services, Website development, professional custom cover design, Adobe and Kindle e-books, audio-books, and MP3 book files. Guidelines and price list available. Request their Free Guide to Publishing brochure from their Website.

Nonfiction/Fiction: All genres. Fiction for all ages.

@ZOË LIFE PUBLISHING, 9282 General Dr., Suite 150, Plymouth MI 48170. (734) 254-1043. Fax (734) 254-1063. E-mail: info@zoelifepub.com. Website: www.zoelifepub.com. Zoe Life Industries LLC. Sabrina Adams, ed. Books that help people live better, more productive lives while growing closer to God. Imprints: Pen of a Ready Writer, Titus, Business Builders. Publishes 40 titles/yr.; hardcover, trade paperbacks, mass-market paperbacks, coffee-table books, digital. 50+% of books from first-time authors. Accepts mss through authors or agents. SUBSIDY PUBLISHES 50%; no print-on-demand or reprints. Length open. **Royalty 10-25% of net; usually no advance.** Average first printing 3,000. Publication within 12 mos. Responds in 21-40 days. Open on Bible version. Guidelines by e-mail/Website; free catalog.

Nonfiction: Proposal/ 3 chapters + final chapter; phone/fax/e-query OK.

Fiction: Proposal/ 3 chapters + final chapter; phone/fax/e-query OK. For all ages; all genres. Complete mss for picture books.

Special Needs: Children's books, tweens, women's issues, Bible studies, and Christian living.

Photos: Accepts freelance photos for book covers.

4

Distributors

LISTING OF CHRISTIAN BOOK/MUSIC/GIFT DISTRIBUTORS

ALLIANCE—MUSIC, 4250 Coral Ridge Dr., Coral Springs FL 33065-7615. Toll-free (800) 329-7664. (954) 255-4600. Fax (954) 255-4825. E-mail: custsvc@aent.com. Website: www.aent.com. Alliance Entertainment Corp. Music.

AMAZON ADVANTAGE PROGRAM, Go to Amazon.com, scroll down to "Features & Services," click on "Selling with Amazon," and on the drop-down menu, click on "Advantage Program" in left-hand column. This is the site to contact if you want Amazon to distribute your book.

ANCHOR-WHITAKER DISTRIBUTORS, 1030 Hunt Valley Cir., New Kensington PA 15068. Toll-free (800) 444-4484. (724) 334-7000. Toll-free fax (800) 765-1960. (724) 334-1200. E-mail: purchasing@anchordistributors.com or marketing@anchordistributors.com. Website: www.anchordistributors.com. Christian books, Bibles, music, and gifts. Distributes self-published books on a contract distribution basis. Mail a copy of the book and all pertinent information to John Whitaker.

BLACK CHRISTIAN BOOK DISTRIBUTORS, LLC, 8528 Davis Blvd., Ste. 134, N. Richlands TX 76180. (817) 240-1256. Fax (817) 887-3089. Website: www.BlackCBD.com.

B. BROUGHTON CO., LTD., 322 Consumers Rd., North York ON M2J 1P8, Canada. Toll-free (800) 268-4449 (Canada only). (416) 690-4777. Fax (416) 690-5357. E-mail: sales@bbroughton.com. Website: www.bbroughton.com. Brian Broughton, owner. Canadian distributor. Distributes books, DVDs, gifts, greeting cards. Does not distribute self-published books.

CAMPUS CRUSADE FOR CHRIST/NEW LIFE RESOURCES, 375 Hwy. 74 S., Ste. A, Peachtree City GA 30269. Toll-free (800) 827-2788. Fax (770) 631-9916. E-mail: pat.pearce@campuscrusade.org. Website: www.campuscrusade.org. Contact: Pat Pearce. Resources for evangelism, discipleship, and spiritual multiplication; books, tracts, Bible studies, and training resources. Does not distribute self-published books.

CBA MAILING LISTS OF CHRISTIAN BOOKSTORES, PO Box 62000, Colorado Springs CO 80962-2000. (719) 265-9895. Fax (719) 272-3510. E-mail: cbender@cbaonline.org. Website: www.cbaonline.org. Available for rental. Three different lists available, including nonmember stores, 4,700 addresses ($249); member stores, 1,275 addresses ($599); or a combined list of all stores, 5,800 addresses ($699). Prices and numbers available subject to change. Call toll-free (800) 252-1950 for full details.

CENTRAL SOUTH DISTRIBUTION, 3730 Vulcan Dr., Nashville TN 37211. Toll-free (800) 251-3052. (615) 833-5960. Fax (615) 331-2501. E-mail through Website: www.centralsouthdistribution.com. Contact: Terry Woods. Distributes African American music and devotionals.

CHRISTIAN BOOK DISTRIBUTORS, PO Box 7000, Peabody MA 01961-7000. Toll-free (800) 247-4784. (978) 977-5000. Fax (978) 977-5010. E-mail through Website: www.christianbooks.com. Does not distribute self-published books.

CONSORTIUM BOOK SALES & DISTRIBUTION INC., 34—13th Ave. N.E., Ste. 101, Minneapolis MN 55413. (612) 746-2600. Fax (612) 746-2606. E-mail: info@cbsd.com. Website: www.cbsd

.com. Distributes a small number of religion titles—more ecumenical in nature than Christian. Does not distribute self-published books.

CORNERSTONE FULFILLMENT SERVICE, LLC, 2915 Chinook Ln., Box 14, Steamboat Springs CO 80487. (970) 870-1518. E-mail: ContactUs@cornerstonefulfillmentservice.com. Website: www .CornerstoneFulFillmentService.com. Blog: http://allthingsfulfilling.wordpress.com. Sue Leonard, owner. Distributes self- and independently published books, videos, DVDs, CDs. E-marketing services also available. Contact by phone/e-mail.

CROWN DISTRIBUTION, Toll-free (800) 661-9467. (780) 471-1417. Distributes Christian film & video in U.S., Canada, and around the world.

+DICKSONS, 709 B Avenue E., Seymour IN 47274. (815) 522-1308. Fax (812) 522-1319. E-mail: sflinn@discksonsgifts.com. Website: www.dicksonsgifts.com. Contact: Stephanie Flinn. Distributes wall art, tabletop gifts, garden, baby, Mother's Day, Father's Day, communion, confirmation, jewelry, Bible aids, Christmas, harvest, bookmarks, auto emblems. Does not distribute self-published books.

E-FULFILLMENT SERVICE INC., 807 Airport Access Rd., Traverse City MI 49686-3594. Toll-free (866) 922-6783. (231) 276-5057, ext. 100. Fax (231) 276-5074. E-mail: info@efulfillmentservice .com or through Website: www.efulfillmentservice.com. John Lindberg, pres. Services include storage and order fulfillment.

FOUNDATION DISTRIBUTING INC., 9 Cobbledick St., PO Box 98, Orono ON L0B 1M0, Canada. Toll-free (877) 368-3600. (905) 983-1188. Toll-free fax (877) 368-6399. Fax (905) 983-1190. E-mail: info@fdi.ca or WebHelp@fdi.ca. Website: www.fdi.ca. Canadian distributor.

GENESIS MARKETING, 850 Wade Hampton Blvd., Bldg. A, Ste. 100, Greenville SC 29609. Toll-free (800) 627-2651. (864) 233-2651. Toll-free fax (800) 849-4363. (869) 232-0059. Website: www .genesislink.com.

DOT GIBSON DISTRIBUTION, PO Box 117, Waycross GA 31502. Toll-free: (800) 336-8095. (912) 285-2848. Fax (912) 285-0349. E-mail: info@dotgibson.com. Website: www.dotgibson.com. Dot Gibson, owner (dot@dotgibson.com). Distributes cookbooks, children's books, gift books— humorous and inspirational.

GL SERVICES, 1957 Eastman Ave., Ventura CA 93003. Toll-free (888) 610-8011. (805) 677-6815. Fax (805) 644-4729. E-mail through Website: www.GospelLight.com. A division of Gospel Light. Does not distribute books for individual authors.

INDEPENDENT BOOK PUBLISHERS ASSOC., 627 Aviation Way, Manhattan Beach CA 90266-7107. (310) 372-2732. Fax (310) 374-3342. E-mail: info@ibpa-online.org. Website: www.ibpa-online .org. Trade association of independent publishers. Provides low-cost educational and marketing programs for independent book publishers. Terry Nathan, exec. dir. (terry@ibpa-online.org).

INGRAM BOOK GROUP/DISTRIBUTION, One Ingram Blvd., La Vergne TN 37086-1986. Toll-free (800) 937-8000. (615) 793-5000. Website: www.ingrambookgroup.com. The best way to have your book/product distributed by this company is to go through one of their trading partners. For a list of distributing partners and more information, visit their Website.

KEY MARKETING GROUP, 2448 E. 81st St., Ste. 4802, Jenks OK 74137. Toll-free (877) 727-0697. (918) 298-0232. Fax (918) 299-5912. E-mail through Website: www.keymgc.com. Bryan Norris, owner (bryan@keymgc.com).

LIGHTNING SOURCE INC., 1246 Heil Quaker Blvd., La Vergne TN 37086. (615) 213-5815. Fax (615) 213-4725. E-mail: inquiry@lightningsource.com, or new accounts@lightningsource.com. Website: www.lightningsource.com.

MALACO CHRISTIAN DISTRIBUTION, PO Box 9287, Jackson MS 39286-9287. Toll-free (877) 462-3623. (601) 982-4522. Fax (877) 270-4508. E-mail: malaco@malaco.com or through Website: www.malaco.com. Tony Goodwin, mng. dir. of sales (tgoodwin@malaco.com). Music distributor.

MCBETH CORP., Fulfillment and Distribution Headquarters, PO Box 400, Chambersburg PA 17201. Toll-free (800) 876-5112. (717) 263-5600. Fax (717) 263-5909. E-mail: mcbethcorp@supernet .com. Distributes Christian gifts, boxed cards, and napkins.

NEW DAY CHRISTIAN DISTRIBUTORS, 126 Shivel Dr., Hendersonville TN 37075. Toll-free (800) 251-3633. (615) 822-3633. Toll-free fax (800) 361-2533. E-mail: help@newdaychristian.com. Website: www.newdaychristian.com. Contact: Jeff Stangenberg (jstangenberg@newdaychristian. com). Music (primarily), books, Bibles, gift items. Distributes self-published books. Contact by e-mail.

NOAH'S ARK DISTRIBUTION, 28545 Felix Valdez Ave., Ste. B4, Temecula CA 92590-1859. Toll-free (800) 562-8093. (951) 693-0306. Fax (951) 693-2747. E-mail: slvanyo@msn.com or through Website: www.christianbooksanddvds.com. Contact: Scott Vanyo, mngr.

+OSMANGO DISTRIBUTION, Global Distributor of Quality Christian Media Products, 5251 W. 73rd St., Ste. C., Edina MN 55439. (719) 352-1864. Fax (952) 831-5809. Website: www.osman go.com.

THE PARABLE GROUP, 3563 Empleo St., San Luis Obispo CA 93401. (805) 543-2644. Fax (805) 545-8688. E-mail: info@parable.com or through Website: www.parable.com. Contact: Randy Maricle. "We are not a distributor, but a marketing group offering business solutions to locally-owned Christian bookstores."

PUBLISHERS GROUP WEST, National Headquarters: 1700 Fourth St., Berkeley CA 94710. (510) 809-3700. Fax (510) 809-3777. E-mail: info@pgw.com. Website: www.pgw.com. Submissions inquiries to: rose.anderson@pgw.com.

QUALITY BOOKS, 1003 W. Pines Rd., Oregon IL 61061. Toll-free (800) 323-4241. (815) 732-4450. Fax (815) 732-4499. E-mail: publisher.relations@quality-books.com. Website: www.quality books.com. Distributes small press books, audios, DVDs, CD-ROMs, and Blu-ray to public libraries. Distributes self-published books; asks for 1 copy of your book.

RANDOLF PRODUCTIONS INC., 18005 Sky Park Cir., Ste. K, Irvine CA 92614-6514. Toll-free (800) 266-7741. (949) 794-9109. Fax (949) 794-9117. E-mail: sales@go2rpi.com. Website: www .go2rpi.com and www.goccc.com. Distributor of Christian DVDs, books, and music. A subsidiary of Campus Crusade for Christ. Contact: Randy Ray, pres. (randy@go2rpi.com).

SPRING ARBOR DISTRIBUTORS, PO Box 3006, One Ingram Blvd., Mailstop 671, La Vergne TN 37086. Toll-free (800) 395-4340. Toll-free fax (800) 876-0186. (615) 213-5192. E-mail: cust serv@springarbor.com or through Website: www.springarbor.com. Contact: Mary Lou Alexander (800) 395-4340, ext. 33319; e-mail: marylou.alexander@springarbor.com. Books, music, Bibles; no gift items or church supplies.

STL DISTRIBUTION, NORTH AMERICA, 522 Princeton Rd., Johnson City TN 37601. Toll-free (800) 289-2772. Fax (800) 759-2779. Website: www.STL-Distribution.com. Distributes books, Bibles, CDs, audio books, DVDs, homeschool, gifts, church supplies, marketing materials and services, including the homeschool market and Catholic products.

WORD ALIVE, INC., 131 Cordite Rd., Winnipeg MB R3W 1S1, Canada. Toll-free (800) 665-1468. (204) 667-1400. Toll-free fax (800) 352-9272. (204) 669-0947. E-mail: orderdesk@wordalive. ca. Website: www.wordalive.ca. Distributes Christian books. Contact: Caroline Schmidt. Distributes self-published books. Contact by mail.

5

Market Analysis: Books

PUBLISHERS IN ORDER OF MOST BOOKS PUBLISHED PER YEAR

Adams Media 230
Tyndale House 225-250
Barbour Publishing 200
Harvest House 170
Monarch Books 160
Steeple Hill 154
Strang Book Group 150
Zonderkidz 150
Eerdmans, Wm. B. 120-130
Abingdon Press 120
Dimensions for Living 120
Zondervan 120
InterVarsity Press 110-120
Destiny Image 100
New York Univ. Press 100
Still Waters Revival 100
Bethany House 90-120
B & H Publishing 90-100
Christian Focus 90
David C. Cook 85
Boyds Mills Press 80
Christian Ed. Publishers 80
Paulist Press 80
HarperOne 75
Kregel 75
Liturgical Press 75
Multnomah Books 75
Univ. Press/America 75
W Publishing Group 75
Love Inspired 72
Crossway 70
Thomas Nelson, Fiction 70
WaterBrook Press 70
Grupo Nelson 65-80
Moody Publishers 65-70
Group Publishing 65
Howard Books 65
NavPress 60-65
Continuum Intl. 60
Fortress Press 60

Pilgrim Press 55
Heartsong Presents 52
T & T Clark 50-60
Baker Academic 50
Concordia 50
DiskUs Publishing 50
Liguori Publications 50
Regal Books 50
Love Inspired Suspense 48
Doubleday Religious 45-50
Jessica Kingsley Pub. 45+
Crossroad Publishing 45
G. P. Putnam/Young Readers 45
GRQ 40-50
Jeremy P. Tarcher 40-50
Editorial Portavoz 40+
Bridge Logos 40
FaithWords 40
P & R Publishing 40
White Rose 40
Pacific Press 35-40
Chalice Press 35
Mercer Univ. Press 35
Heartsong Presents/
  Mysteries 32
Revival Nation 30-50
Meriwether Publishing 30-45
Baker's Plays 30-40
Church Publishing 30-40
CSS Publishing 30-40
Focus on the Family 30-40
Our Sunday Visitor 30-40
Rose Publishing 30-40
Whitaker House 30-40
AMG Publishers 30-35
Ambassador International 30+
Baylor Univ. Press 30
Beacon Hill Press 30
Conari Press 30
Contemporary Drama 30 (plays)

Evergreen Press 30
Forward Movement 30
Jossey-Bass 30
Univ. of AR Press 30
Youth Specialties 30
Halo Publishing 25-30
New Leaf Press 25-30
Smyth & Helwys 25-30
James Clarke 25
Lion and Lamb 25
Liturgy Training 25
Lutterworth Press 25
Meriwether (plays) 25
Guardian Angel Pub. 24-36
Milestones Intl. Publishers 24-30
Alba House 24
Evangelical Press 24
Love Inspired Historical 24
One World 24
Reformation Heritage Books 24
St. Anthony Mess. Press 20-35
St. Augustine's Press 20-40
Chapter Two 20-30
Lighthouse Publishing 20-30
Loyola Press 20-30
New Hope 20-28
Pauline Kids 20-25
Blue Dolphin 20-24
Guideposts Books 20
Harrison House 20
Pauline Books 20
Pflaum Publishing 20
Rainbow Publishers 20
Third World Press 20
Eldridge (plays) 17
JourneyForth 15-25
Catholic Book Publishing 15-20
College Press 15-20
HeartSpring Publishing 15-20
Master Books 15-20

Samaritan Press 15-20
Branden Publishing 15
Cambridge Scholars Pub. 15
Christian Writers Ebook 15
Legacy Press 15
Scepter Publishers 15
Wesleyan Publishing House 15
Yale Univ. Press 15
MountainView Pub. 12-24
Discovery House 12-18
Eerdmans/Young Readers 12-15
Judson Press 12-15
Paragon House 12-15
CarePoint 12
Carson-Dellosa Christian 12
CharismaKids 12
CLC Publications 12
Two Fish Publishing 12
E.F.S. Online Publishing 10-20
Sheed & Ward 10-20
BMH Books 10-15
Wm. Carey Library 10-15
McDougal Publishing 10-15
Ragged Edge 10-15
Randall House 10-15
Emmaus Road 10-12
Reformation Trust 10-12
ACTA Publications 10
Catholic Answers 10
Catholic Univ./America Press 10
Comfort Publishing 10
FaithWalk Publishing 10
Georgetown University
    Press 10
Jubilant Press 10 (e-books)
Lift Every Voice 10
PREP Publishing 10
Resource Publications 10
Ambassador Books 9
Cistercian Publications 8-14
Conciliar Press 8-12
Avon Inspire 8-10
Hannibal Books 8-10
Lutheran University Press 8-10
Neibauer Press 8
Torch Legacy 7+
ETC Publications 6-12
Messianic Jewish 6-12
Father's Press 6-10
CrossLink Publishing 6-8

Kirk House Publishers 6-8
Christian Heritage 6
Dawn Publications 6
Hope Publishing 6
Inkling Books 6
Life Cycle Books 6
Wilshire Book Co. 6
Praeger Publishers 5-25
Troitsa Books 5-20
Encore Performance 5-10
Gospel Publishing House 5-10
Hensley Publishing 5-10
Quiet Waters 5-10
Quintessential Books 5-10
Palgrave Macmillan 5-8
Libros Liguori 5
Mission City Press 5
Mt. Olive College Press 5
Oregon Catholic Press 5
Paradise Research 5
Parsons Publishing 5
Trinity Foundation 5
His Work 4-8
Grace Acres Press 4-6
Jebaire Publishing 4-6
Larson Publications 4-5
Millennium III 4-5
Foursquare Media 4+
American Catholic Press 4
HCI Books 4
Intl. Awakening Press 4
Lighthouse Trails 4
Elijah Press 3-5
Facts On File 3-5
Langmarc Publishing 3-5
Perigee Books 3-5
Salt Works 3-5
Gollehon Press 3-4
New Canaan 3-4
St. Bede's 3-4
Tau-Publishing 3-4
Church Growth Institute 3
Earthen Vessel 3
Magnus Press 3
Pelican Publishing 3
On My Own Now 3
First Fruits of Zion 2-6
Gentle Path Press 2-5
Parson Place Press 2-5
Canadian Institute for Law 2-4

Frederick Fell 2-4
Cladach Publishing 2-3
Deo Volente 2-3
MOPS Intl. 2-3
Anglicans United 2
Canticle Books 2
Players Press 1-6
Four Craftsmen 1-5
VBC Publishing 1-5
LifeSong Publishers 1-4
Christian Family 1-3
Starik Publishing 1-3
Fair Havens Publications 1-2
Write Now! 1-2
Aadeon Publishing 1
Ancient Paths 1
Dove Inspirational 1
Good Book 1
Guernica Editions 1
Hay House 1
Reference Service 1

SUBSIDY PUBLISHERS
Xulon Press 1,500
Pleasant Word 300
Brentwood 267
Holy Fire 200
Brown Books 150
Creation House 125
Tate Publishing 120
Trafford Publishing 100-200
Essence Publishing 100-150+
Fairway Press 100
Poet's Cove 75
WinePress 75
American Binding 60
Insight Publishing 50
TEACH Services 48
Selah Publishing 45
Booklocker.com 40-50
ACW Press 40
Zoë Life 40
Black Forest Press 35
Deep River Books 35
Southern Baptist Press 25
Forever Books 24+
Bookstand Publishing 20+
Impact Christian Books 20+
Providence House 20+
Elderberry Press 15

Rill & Associates 12-24
Star Bible 10-15
IMD Press 10
Credo House 6-12
CrossLink Publishing 6-8
Fruitbearer Publishing 5-10

Book Publishers Network 5-8
Salvation Publisher 5-7
DCTS Publishers 5
Deeper Revelation Books 5
Recovery Communications 4-6
Kindred Books 3-4

Salt Works 3-5

Salty's Books 2-5

Ampelos Press 1-3

Strong Tower Publishing 1-2

BOOK TOPICS MOST POPULAR WITH PUBLISHERS

Note: Following is a list of topics in order by popularity. To find the list of publishers interested in each of these topics, go to the Topical Listings for Books (see Contents). An asterisk (*) indicates it was a new topic this year so may not yet accurately reflect industry-wide interest.

MISCELLANEOUS TALLIES
Art-Freelance 76
Booklets 46
Canadian/Foreign 21
Coffee-table books 35
E-books 54
Minibooks 18
Pamphlets 26
Photographs for covers 96
Print-on-demand 54
Tracts 19

TOPICS BY POPULARITY
1. Christian Living 152
2. Prayer 152
3. Family Life 151
4. Bible/Biblical Studies 150
5. Inspirational 146
6. Faith 142
7. Religion 140
8. Women's Issues 135
9. Devotional 131
10. Discipleship 131
11. Marriage 129
12. Theology 129
13. Spirituality 127
14. Fiction: Adult/Religious 126
15. Parenting 124
16. Spiritual Life 118
17. Biography 117
18. Current/Social Issues 114
19. Church History 113
20. Evangelism/Witnessing 111
21. Historical 111
22. Leadership 111
23. Personal Growth 108
24. Forgiveness 104

25. Worship 103
26. Church Life 102
27. Christian Education 100
28. Fiction: Historical 99
29. Ethics 97
30. Self-Help 96
31. Apologetics 95
32. Bible Commentary 95
33. Fiction: Contemporary 94
34. Men's 94
35. Ethnic/Cultural 92
36. Health 92
37. Christ 91
38. Relationships 91
39. Church Renewal 89
40. Healing 89
41. Youth: Nonfiction 89
42. Spiritual Gifts 88
43. Fiction: Juvenile
    (ages 8-12) 87
44. Fiction: Mystery/
    Suspense 86
45. Scholarly 86
46. Personal Renewal 85
47. Controversial Issues 84
48. Death/Dying 84
49. Missions/Missionary 84
50. Spiritual Warfare 84
51. How-To 83
52. Fiction: Biblical 82
53. Autobiography 81
54. Holy Spirit 81
55. Stewardship 81
56. Fiction: Adventure 80
57. Reference 80
58. Doctrinal 79

59. Fiction: Teen/Young
    Adult 79
60. Personal Experience 79
61. Christian Business 78
62. Humor 78
63. Money Management 77
64. Pastors' Helps 77
65. Church Traditions 75
66. Group Study 75
67. Singles' Issues 75
68. Counseling Aids 74
69. Encouragement 74
70. World Issues 74
71. Philosophy 73
72. Social Justice Issues 73
73. Divorce 72
74. Children's Picture Books 70
75. Dating/Sex 69
76. Memoirs 69
77. Eschatology 68
78. Prophecy 68
79. Recovery 68
80. Psychology 68
81. Sermons 67
82. Christian Homeschooling 66
83. Exegesis 66
84. Worship Resources 66
85. Politics 65
86. Fiction: Literary 64
87. Miracles 64
88. Fiction: Historical
    Romance 63
89. Fiction: Humor 63
90. Fiction: Romance 63
91. Fiction: Mystery/
    Romance 61
92. Environmental Issues 60

93. Holiday/Seasonal 60
94. Homeschooling
    Resources 60
95. Children's Easy Readers 59
96. Church Management 59
97. Holiness 59
98. Archaeology 58
99. Fiction: Fantasy 58
100. Science 58
101. Christian School 57
102. Cookbooks 57
103. Liturgical Studies 57
104. Grief 56
105. Sports/Recreation 56
106. Time Management 56
107. Creation Science 55
108. Fiction: Frontier/
    Romance 55
109. Racism 55
110. *Grandparenting 54
111. Economics 53
112. Religious Tolerance 53

113. Sociology 53
114. Curriculum 52
115. Fiction: Frontier 52
116. Poetry 52
117. Charismatic 51
118. Fiction: Allegory 51
119. Homiletics 51
120. Fiction: Adult/General 48
121. Fiction: Science Fiction 48
122. Cults/Occult 47
123. Fiction: Short Story
    Collection 47
124. Compilations 46
125. Drama 46
126. Fiction: Ethnic 46
127. Senior Adult Concerns 46
128. Travel 46
129. Music-Related 44
130. Retirement 43
131. Celebrity Profiles 42
132. Fiction: Westerns 42
133. *Church Growth 40

134. Fiction: Chick Lit 40
135. Writing How-to 39
136. Tween 38
137. Fiction: Novellas 36
138. Fiction: Fables/Parables 35
139. Fiction: Speculative 35
140. Youth Programs 35
141. Exposés 33
142. Gift Books 32
143. Games/Crafts 31
144. Fiction: Plays 26
145. Novelty Books for Kids 23
146. Children's Board Books 15
147. Children's Devotionals 13
148. *Small Group Resources 10
149. Christmas 9
150. Lifestyle 9
151. Popular Culture 8
152. Post Modernism 7
153. Fiction: Cozy Mysteries 6
154. Recovery 6
155. Lay counseling 4

BOOK PUBLISHERS WITH THE MOST BOOKS ON THE BESTSELLER LIST FOR THE PREVIOUS YEAR

This tally is based on actual sales in Christian bookstores reported from May 2009 through April 2010. Numbers behind the names indicate the number of titles each publisher had on that particular bestseller list during that time. Note that complete information in some categories was not available.

BIBLE STUDIES/ THEOLOGY/MINISTRY (INCOMPLETE)
1. Thomas Nelson 5
2. Harvest House 2
3. Zondervan 2
4. B & H Publishing 1
5. Concordia 1
6. Group Publications 1
7. HarperOne 1
8. Outreach Inc. 1
9. Penguin Group 1
10. WaterBrook Multnomah 1

CHILDREN'S BOOKS
1. Zondervan/Zonderkidz 26
2. Thomas Nelson 17
3. Standard 10

4. Barbour 5
5. Tyndale House 4
6. Baker Books 2
7. Bethany House 2
8. Gospel Light 2
9. Concordia 1
10. Ideals Publications 1

CHRISTIAN LIVING
1. Thomas Nelson 26
2. Zondervan 11
3. Harvest House 8
4. Strang 5
5. Tyndale House 5
6. David C. Cook 3
7. Moody Publications 3
8. FaithWords 2
9. Revell/Baker 2

10. WaterBrook/Multnomah 2
11. Abingdon Press 1
12. CLC Publications 1
13. Intervarsity Press 1
14. Outreach Inc. 1
15. Penguin Group 1
16. Random House 1

FICTION
1. Thomas Nelson 36
2. Bethany House 25
3. Zondervan 13
4. Tyndale House 8
5. Harvest House 7
6. Revell 7
7. Barbour Books 5
8. WaterBrook/Multnomah 3
9. Center Street 2

10. David C. Cook 2
11. Doubleday Religious 1
12. FaithWords 1
13. Howard Books 1
14. Penguin Group 1
15. Windblown Media 1

INSPIRATIONAL/ GENERAL INTEREST (INCOMPLETE)

1. Thomas Nelson 22
2. Barbour 5
3. Zondervan 5
4. Strang 4
5. Tyndale House 4
6. B & H Publishing 3
7. David C. Cook 2
8. FaithWords 2
9. Howard Publishing 2
10. Revell/Baker 2
11. Abingdon Press 1
12. Crossway Books 1
13. Doubleday Religious1
14. HarperCollins 1
15. Ideal Publications 1
16. Northfield 1
17. Outreach Inc. 1

18. Simon & Schuster 1
19. Whitaker House 1

YOUNG ADULT BOOKS (INCOMPLETE)

1.Thomas Nelson 6
2. Revell/Baker 2
3. WaterBrook/Multnomah 2
4. Bethany House 1
5. FaithWords 1
6. Harvest House 1
7. Moody Publications 1
8. NavPress 1
9. Regal Books 1
10. Tyndale House 1
11. Zondervan 1

COMBINED BESTSELLER LISTS

1. Thomas Nelson 112
2. Zondervan 58
3. Bethany House 28
4. Tyndale House 22
5. Harvest House 18
6. Barbour Books 15
7. Revell/Baker 15
8. Standard 10
9. Strang 9

10. WaterBrook/Multnomah 8
11. David C. Cook 7
12. FaithWords 6
13. B & H Publishing 4
14. Moody Publishing 4
15. Howard 3
16. Outreach Inc. 3
17. Penguin Group 3
18. Abingdon Press 2
19. Center Street 2
20. Concordia 2
21. Doubleday Religious 2
22. Gospel Light 2
23. Ideals 2
24. CLC Publications 1
25. Crossway Books 1
26. Group 1
27. HarperCollins 1
28. HarperOne 1
29. InterVarsity Press 1
30. NavPress 1
31. Northfield 1
32. Random House 1
33. Regal Books 1
34. Simon & Schuster 1
35. Whitaker House 1
36. Windblown Media 1

TOP 50 BESTSELLERS

This list is based on which publishers had the most books on the list of the Top 50 books each month. It tracks the top 50 sellers regardless of genre (those listed above are in specific genres). It is interesting to note that there were 29 publishers with books on this list during the last year (only 2 more than last year)—and the field is again dominated by the same top two publishers—although Thomas Nelson has almost twice the number on the list as last year.

1. Thomas Nelson 68
2. Zondervan 34
3. Bethany House 18
4. Tyndale House 14
5. Harvest House 12
6. WaterBrook/Multnomah 10
7. Barbour 8
8. FaithWords 6
9. Revell (Baker) 6
10. B & H Publishing 5

11. Strang 5
12. Penguin Group 4
13. David C. Cook 3
14. Moody Publishers 3
15. Center Street 2
16. Doubleday Religious 2
17. Harper Collins 2
18. Howard Books 2
19. NavPress 2
20. Standard 2

21. CLC Publications 1
22. Crossway Books 1
23. Group Publishing 1
24. Ideals Publications 1
25. InterVarsity Press 1
26. Outreach Inc. 1
27. Random House 1
28. Simon & Schuster 1
29. Windblown Media 1

PART 2

Periodical Publishers

6

Topical Listings of Periodicals

As soon as you have an article or story idea, look up that topic in the following topical listings (see table of contents for a full list of topics). Study the appropriate periodicals in the primary/alphabetical listings (as well as their writers' guidelines and sample copies) and select those that are most likely targets for the piece you are writing.

Note that most ideas can be written for more than one periodical if you slant them to the needs of different audiences, for example, current events for teens, or pastors, or women. Have a target periodical and audience in mind before you start writing. Each topic is divided by age group/audience, so you can pick appropriate markets for your particular slant.

If the magazine prefers or requires a query letter, be sure to write that letter first, and then follow any guidelines or suggestions they make if they give you a go-ahead.

R-Takes reprints
(*)-Indicates new topic this year
$-Indicates a paying market
($)-Indicates a paying-sometimes market

APOLOGETICS
ADULT/GENERAL
$-Arkansas Catholic—R
$-Aujourd'hui Credo—R
$-Bible Advocate—R
Bread of Life—R
$-Brink Magazine—R
$-Catholic Insight
CBN.com—R
$-Celebrate Life—R
$-Christianity Today—R
Christian Online
Christian Ranchman
$-Christian Research
$-Christian Standard—R
Church of England News
$-Columbia—R
Desert Call—R
Desert Voice—R
$-Earthen Vessel Online—R
E-Channels—R
$-Homeschooling Today—R
($)-Impact Magazine—R
$-In His Presence—R

$-In Touch
Koinonia
$-Lifeglow—R
$-Live—R
$-Lookout
$-Manna—R
Messianic Perspectives—R
$-Mother's Heart—R
Movieguide
$-On Mission
$-Our Sunday Visitor—R
$-Pathway—R
Perspectives—R
Perspectives/Science
PrayerWorks—R
$-Precepts for Living
Priscilla Papers
SCP Journal
$-Seek—R
$-Social Justice—R
Sword and Trumpet
Sword of the Lord—R
$-Way of St. Francis—R
Wisconsin Christian

CHILDREN
$-SHINE brightly—R

DAILY DEVOTIONALS
$-Brink Magazine—R
Penned from the Heart—R

MISSIONS
$-Associated Content—R
$-Drama Ministry—R
East-West Church
$-New Wineskins—R
Studio—R

PASTORS/LEADERS
$-Catholic Servant
$-Christian Century—R
Disciple Magazine—R
$-Enrichment—R
$-Outreach—R
$-Small Groups.com—R
Theological Digest—R

TEEN/YOUNG ADULT
$-Boundless Webzine—R
$-Direction Student
$-Horizon Student

$-TG Magazine
$-Young Christian Writers
$-Young Salvationist—R

ARTS/ENTERTAINMENT*
ADULT/GENERAL
$-Guide—R
Hope for Women
Unrecognized Woman—R
$-Upscale
$-Young Christian—R

CHILDREN
$-Guide—R

MUSIC
Gospel USA
Path MEGAzine
($)-TCP Magazine

PASTORS/LEADERS
$-Brink Magazine—R
$-Immerse

TEEN/YOUNG ADULT
Susie
$-TC Magazine

WOMEN
Empowering Everyday Women
Onyx Woman
Take Root & Write

BEAUTY/FASHION*
ADULT/GENERAL
$-Guide—R
Hope for Women
Unrecognized Woman—R
$-Upscale

CHILDREN
$-Guide—R

TEEN/YOUNG ADULT
Susie

WOMEN
Empowering Everyday Women
Life Tools for Women
Onyx Woman
Precious Times—R
Take Root & Write

BIBLE STUDIES
ADULT/GENERAL
$-Alive Now—R
$-Arlington Catholic
$-Aujourd'hui Credo—R
Bible Study Mag.
Bread of Life—R
Breakthrough Intercessor—R
$-Catholic Peace Voice—R
$-Catholic Yearbook—R
CBN.com—R
Christian Computing—R
Christian Motorsports
Christian Online
Christian Ranchman
$-Christian Research
$-Christian Standard—R
Church Herald & Holiness—R
$-Churchmouse Public.—R
$-Columbia—R
Connecting Point—R
Creation Care—R
$-Culture Wars—R
Desert Call—R
$-DreamSeeker—R
$-Earthen Vessel Online—R
Eternal Ink—R
Faithwebbin—R
Foursquare Leader
$-Gem—R
Gospel Herald
HEARTLIGHT Internet—R
$-Homeschooling Today—R
($)-HopeKeepers—R
$-In His Presence—R
$-In Touch
Koinonia
$-Kyria—R
$-Lifeglow—R
$-Lutheran Journal—R
$-Lutheran Witness
$-Mature Years—R
Messianic Perspectives—R
Methodist History
$-New Wineskins—R
$-Our Sunday Visitor—R
Perspectives—R
PrayerWorks—R
$-Precepts for Living
Priscilla Papers

$-Purpose—R
Quaker Life—R
$-Seek—R
$-Social Justice—R
Spirituality for Today
$-Spiritual Life
$-St. Anthony Messenger
Sword and Trumpet
Sword of the Lord—R
Trumpeter—R
Victory Herald—R
$-War Cry—R
$-Way of St. Francis—R
Wisconsin Christian

CHILDREN
$-Archaeology—R
$-Primary Street
$-SHINE brightly—R

CHRISTIAN EDUCATION/LIBRARY
$-Catechist
$-Children's Ministry
Congregational Libraries
$-Group
$-Preschool Playhouse (CE)

MISSIONS
Railroad Evangelist—R
Women of the Harvest

PASTORS/LEADERS
$-Catholic Servant
Disciple Magazine—R
$-Let's Worship
Sewanee Theo. Review
Sharing the Practice—R
$-SmallGroups.com—R
Theological Digest—R
$-Word & World

TEEN/YOUNG ADULT
$-Sharing the Victory—R
TeensForJC—R

WOMEN
($)-Beyond the Bend—R
Extreme Woman
For Every Woman—R
$-Mother's Heart—R
Precious Times—R
Virtuous Woman—R
Women's Ministry

BOOK EXCERPTS
ADULT/GENERAL
$-Alive Now—R
$-Associated Content—R
Books & Culture
Bread of Life—R
$-Catholic Digest—R
CBN.com—R
$-Charisma
$-Chicken Soup Books—R
$-Christianity Today—R
Christian Observer
$-Christian Renewal—R
$-Christian Retailing
Church of England News
$-Columbia—R
$-Covenant Companion—R
Creation Care—R
$-Culture Wars—R
E-Channels—R
Faithwebbin—R
Gospel Herald
$-Homeschooling Today—R
($)-HopeKeepers—R
$-Indian Life—R
$-Interim—R
Island Catholic—R
$-JC Town Reporter—R
$-KD Gospel Media
Koinonia
Messianic Perspectives—R
New Heart—R
New Identity—R
$-New Wineskins—R
$-Point—R
$-Power for Living—R
Priscilla Papers
$-Prism
Quaker Life—R
Regent Global—R
Single Again Mag.—R
Spirituality for Today
Trumpeter—R
$-United Church Observer—R
Unrecognized Woman—R
$-Upscale
$-U.S. Catholic—R
Wisconsin Christian
$-Written

CHRISTIAN EDUCATION/LIBRARY
Christian Early Ed.—R
Christian Library Jour.
$-Journal/Adventist Ed.—R

MISSIONS
East-West Church
Intl. Jour./Frontier—R

PASTORS/LEADERS
$-Christian Century—R
Great Comm. Research—R
$-Ministry Today
$-Outreach—R
Rick Warren's Ministry—R

TEEN/YOUNG ADULT
$-Boundless Webzine—R
$-J.A.M.
TeensForJC—R

WOMEN
($)-Beyond the Bend—R
Extreme Woman
$-Heart & Soul
$-Link & Visitor—R
Share
$-SpiritLed Woman
Unrecognized Woman—R
Virtuous Woman—R

WRITERS
$-Freelance Writer's Report—R
$-Writer

BOOK REVIEWS
ADULT/GENERAL
$-Abilities
African Voices—R
$-America
$-Anglican Journal
$-Arkansas Catholic—R
$-Arlington Catholic
$-Associated Content—R
$-Atlantic Catholic
$-Aujourd'hui Credo—R
Books & Culture
Bread of Life—R
Breakthrough Intercessor—R
$-Brink Magazine—R
byFaith

($)-Canadian Mennonite—R
Carolina Christian
$-Cathedral Age
$-Catholic Insight
$-Catholic Peace Voice—R
CBN.com—R
$-Charisma
$-Christian Citizen USA
Christian Computing—R
$-Christian Courier/Canada—R
Christian Family Jour.
$-Christian Herald—R
$-Christianity Today—R
Christian Journal—R
Christian Media—R
Christian Observer
Christian Press
Christian Ranchman
$-Christian Renewal—R
$-Christian Research
$-Christian Retailing
$-ChristianWeek—R
$-City Light News—R
Creation Care—R
$-Cresset
$-Culture Wars—R
Desert Voice—R
Divine Ascent
$-Earthen Vessel Online—R
E-Channels—R
$-Episcopal Life—R
Eternal Ink—R
$-Eureka Street
$-Faith & Family
$-Faith & Friends—R
$-Faith Today—R
Founders Journal
Foursquare Leader
Good News!
Good News Today
Gospel Herald
Halo Magazine—R
$-Haruah—R
Heartland Gatekeeper—R
$-Homeschooling Today—R
$-Home Times—R
($)-HopeKeepers—R
$-Image
$-Imagine
($)-Impact Magazine—R

$-Indian Life—R
$-Interim—R
Island Catholic—R
$-JC Town Reporter—R
$-KD Gospel Media
Koinonia
($)-Mennonite Historian—R
Methodist History
Movieguide
($)-Mutuality—R
New Christian Voices
New Frontier
$-New Wineskins—R
$-Our Sunday Visitor—R
Ozarks Christian
Penwood Review
Perspectives/Science
$-Prairie Messenger—R
$-Presbyterian Outlook
Priscilla Papers
$-Prism
Purpose Magazine—R
Quaker Life—R
Radix Magazine
Regent Global—R
$-Search
$-Significant Living—R
Single Again Mag.—R
$-Social Justice—R
$-Spiritual Life
Studio—R
$-Testimony—R
Time of Singing—R
Trumpeter—R
Unrecognized Woman—R
$-Upscale
$-U.S. Catholic—R
Victory Herald—R
$-Way of St. Francis—R
$-Weavings—R
Wisconsin Christian
$-World & I—R
$-Written
Xavier Review

CHILDREN

$-New Moon—R
$-SHINE brightly—R
$-Sparkle—R

CHRISTIAN EDUCATION/ LIBRARY

Christian Early Ed.—R
Christian Librarian—R
Christian School Ed.—R
$-Church Libraries—R
Congregational Libraries
$-Group
Jour./Ed. & Christian Belief—R
Jour. of Christian Ed.
Jour. of Christianity—R
$-Journal/Adventist Ed.—R
Jour./Research on Christian Ed.
$-Momentum
$-Teachers of Vision—R

MISSIONS

East-West Church
$-Evangelical Missions—R
$-Glad Tidings—R
Intl. Jour./Frontier—R
Missiology
($)-Operation Reveille—R
Women of the Harvest

MUSIC

$-Creator—R
Hymn

PASTORS/LEADERS

$-Catechumenate
$-Christian Century—R
CrossCurrents
$-Diocesan Dialogue—R
Disciple Magazine—R
$-Emmanuel
$-Enrichment—R
Foursquare Leader
Great Comm. Research—R
$-Interpreter
Jour./Pastoral Care
$-Leadership—R
$-Let's Worship
$-Ministry
Ministry in Motion—R
$-Ministry Today
$-Reformed Worship—R
Sharing the Practice—R
Theological Digest—R
$-Word & World
$-Worship Leader
$-Your Church—R

TEEN/YOUNG ADULT

$-Boundless Webzine—R
$-Devo'Zine—R
$-Direction Student
G4T Ink—R
$-Horizon Student
$-J.A.M.
TeensForJC—R
$-TG Magazine
$-Young Christian Writers

WOMEN

($)-Beyond the Bend—R
Chris. Work at Home Moms—R
$-Dabbling Mum—R
Empowering Everyday Women
Extreme Woman
Glory & Strength—R
$-Heart & Soul
Hope for Women
$-Horizons—R
$-inSpirit—R
Live Magazine
$-Mother's Heart—R
$-Pauses . . .
Precious Times—R
Share
Unrecognized Woman—R
Virtuous Woman—R
Women's Ministry

WRITERS

$-Adv. Christian Writer—R
Areopagus
$-Christian Communicator—R
$-Cross & Quill—R
Esdras' Scroll—R
$-Fellowscript—R
NW Christian Author—R
$-Tickled by Thunder
Write Connection
$-Writer
$-Writers' Journal

CANADIAN/FOREIGN MARKETS
ADULT/GENERAL

$-Abilities
$-Anglican Journal
$-Atlantic Catholic
$-Aujourd'hui Credo—R

$-Australian Catholics—R
$-B.C. Catholic—R
Bread of Life—R
$-Canada Lutheran—R
CanadianChristianity
Canadian Lutheran
($)-Canadian Mennonite—R
$-Catholic Insight
Catholic Register
Challenge Weekly
$-Christian Courier/Canada—R
Christian Courier/WI—R
$-Christian Herald—R
Christian Outlook
$-Christian Renewal—R
$-ChristianWeek—R
Church of England News
$-City Light News—R
$-Common Ground—R
Creation
E-Channels—R
$-Eureka Street
Evangelical Times
$-Faith & Friends—R
$-Faith Today—R
Fellowship
Gospel Herald
($)-Impact Magazine—R
$-Indian Life—R
Insights Mag./Canada
$-Interim—R
Island Catholic—R
LifeSite News
$-Living Light—R
($)-Mennonite Historian—R
$-Messenger
$-Messenger/Sacred Heart
$-Messenger/St. Anthony
$-Prairie Messenger—R
$-Seven Magazine—R
Studio—R
$-Testimony—R
$-United Church Observer—R

CHRISTIAN EDUCATION/ LIBRARY
$-Christian Educators—R
Jour./Ed. & Christian Belief—R
Jour. of Christian Ed.

DAILY DEVOTIONALS
$-Rejoice!

MISSIONS
$-Glad Tidings—R
Koinonia

MUSIC
Church Music

PASTORS/LEADERS
$-Evangelical Baptist
Technologies for Worship—R
Theological Digest—R

WOMEN
Christian Woman
Christian Women Today—R
Life Tools for Women
$-Link & Visitor—R
Women Today—R

WRITERS
Areopagus
$-Canadian Writer's Jour.—R
$-Fellowscript—R
$-Tickled by Thunder
Writers Manual

CELEBRITY PIECES
ADULT/GENERAL
American Tract—R
$-Angels on Earth
$-Arlington Catholic
$-Associated Content—R
$-Australian Catholics—R
Breakthrough
$-Brink Magazine—R
$-Catholic Digest—R
CBN.com—R
$-Celebrate Life—R
Christian Family Jour.
$-Christian Herald—R
$-Christianity Today Movies—R
Christian Journal—R
Christian Motorsports
Christian Online
Christian Ranchman
$-Churchmouse Public.—R
Church of England News
$-City Light News—R
$-Episcopal Life—R

Good News Journal—R
$-Good News, Etc.—R
$-Good News, The—R
Gospel Herald
$-Guideposts—R
Halo Magazine—R
Heartland Gatekeeper—R
HEARTLIGHT Internet—R
$-Home Times—R
($)-HopeKeepers—R
$-Imagine
($)-Impact Magazine—R
$-Indian Life—R
$-In Touch
$-JC Town Reporter—R
$-KD Gospel Media
$-Kindred Spirit—R
Koinonia
$-Living Light—R
$-Miracles, Healings—R
Movieguide
($)-Mutuality—R
$-New Wineskins—R
$-Our Sunday Visitor—R
$-Power for Living—R
$-Priority!—R
$-Prism
$-Significant Living—R
$-St. Anthony Messenger
Tri-State Voice
Trumpeter—R
$-Vibrant Life—R
$-War Cry—R
Wisconsin Christian

CHILDREN
$-American Girl—R
$-Cadet Quest—R
$-SHINE brightly—R
$-Sparkle—R

MUSIC
Christian Music—R

PASTORS/LEADERS
$-Catholic Servant
$-Ministry Today

TEEN/YOUNG ADULT
$-Essential Connection
G4T Ink—R
$-J.A.M.

$-Listen—R
$-Sharing the Victory—R
$-TC Magazine
TeensForJC—R
$-Young Salvationist—R

WOMEN
($)-Beyond the Bend—R
Empowering Everyday Women
Extreme Woman
$-Heart & Soul
$-Journey
More to Life
Precious Times—R
Virtuous Woman—R

WRITERS
$-Cross & Quill—R
NW Christian Author—R
$-Writer's Chronicle

CHRISTIAN BUSINESS
ADULT/GENERAL
$-Angels on Earth
Bread of Life—R
$-Brink Magazine—R
$-CBA Retailers
CBN.com—R
Christian Business
$-Christian Citizen USA
$-Christian Courier/Canada—R
Christian Family Jour.
Christian Motorsports
Christian News NW—R
Christian Online
Christian Ranchman
$-Christian Retailing
$-ChristianWeek—R
$-Churchmouse Public.—R
$-City Light News—R
Creation Care—R
Desert Call—R
Desert Voice—R
Disciple's Journal—R
Evangel/OR—R
$-Faith Today—R
$-Gem—R
Good News Journal—R
Gospel Herald
$-Gospel Today—R
$-Guideposts—R

Halo Magazine—R
Heartland Gatekeeper—R
HEARTLIGHT Internet—R
Highway News—R
$-Home Times—R
$-In Touch
$-JC Town Reporter—R
$-KD Gospel Media
Koinonia
Light of the World
$-Living—R
$-Lookout
$-Manna—R
Marketplace
MissionWares
New Identity—R
($)-NRB Magazine—R
$-Our Sunday Visitor—R
$-Pathway—R
$-Power for Living—R
$-Prism
$-Purpose—R
Purpose Magazine—R
Regent Global—R
$-Search
$-Significant Living—R
Single Again Mag.—R
$-St. Anthony Messenger
$-Together—R
Trumpeter—R
$-War Cry—R
Wisconsin Christian

CHRISTIAN EDUCATION/ LIBRARY
Christian School Ed.—R

MISSIONS
$-Evangelical Missions—R
Lausanne World—R

PASTORS/LEADERS
$-Catholic Servant
Church Executive
$-Clergy Journal—R
$-InSite—R
$-Interpreter
Ministry in Motion—R
Rick Warren's Ministry—R
Technologies for Worship—R
$-Today's Parish
$-Your Church—R

TEEN/YOUNG ADULT
$-Boundless Webzine—R
$-J.A.M.

WOMEN
($)-Beyond the Bend—R
Christian Women Today—R
Chris. Work at Home Moms—R
$-Dabbling Mum—R
Empowering Everyday Women
$-Heart & Soul
Onyx Woman
Precious Times—R
Virtuous Woman—R
Women Today—R

WRITERS
Writing Corner—R

CHRISTIAN EDUCATION
ADULT/GENERAL
African Voices—R
$-America
$-Anglican Journal
$-Animal Trails—R
$-Arlington Catholic
$-Atlantic Catholic
$-Aujourd'hui Credo—R
$-B.C. Catholic—R
Bread of Life—R
($)-Canadian Mennonite—R
$-Catholic Peace Voice—R
$-Celebrate Life—R
$-Christian Citizen USA
$-Christian Courier/Canada—R
$-Christian Examiner
Christian Family Jour.
$-Christian Home & School
$-Christianity Today—R
Christian News NW—R
Christian Observer
Christian Online
Christian Ranchman
$-Christian Renewal—R
$-Christian Retailing
$-Christian Standard—R
$-ChristianWeek—R
$-Churchmouse Public.—R
$-City Light News—R
$-Columbia—R
$-Company Magazine—R

Creation Care—R
$-Cresset
$-Culture Wars—R
Desert Call—R
Desert Voice—R
$-Direction
E-Channels—R
Eternal Ink—R
$-Faith & Family
$-Faith Today—R
Faithwebbin—R
Foursquare Leader
$-Gem—R
$-Good News, Etc.—R
Good News Journal—R
Gospel Herald
$-Gospel Today—R
$-Guide—R
Halo Magazine—R
HEARTLIGHT Internet—R
Highway News—R
$-Homeschooling Today—R
$-Home Times—R
$-In His Presence—R
$-JC Town Reporter—R
$-KD Gospel Media
Koinonia
$-Lifeglow—R
Light of the World
$-Live—R
$-Living Church
$-Lookout
$-Lutheran Witness
$-Manna—R
$-Messenger/Sacred Heart
Methodist History
Movieguide
New Identity—R
$-New Wineskins—R
Nostalgia—R
$-Our Sunday Visitor—R
$-ParentLife
Penned from the Heart—R
Perspectives—R
PrayerWorks—R
$-Precepts for Living
$-Presbyterian Outlook
$-Presbyterians Today—R
$-Prism
$-Purpose—R

$-Seek—R
Single Again Mag.—R
Spirituality for Today
$-St. Anthony Messenger
Sword and Trumpet
Sword of the Lord—R
$-Testimony—R
$-Together—R
Trumpeter—R
Victory Herald—R
$-War Cry—R
$-Way of St. Francis—R
Wisconsin Christian

CHILDREN
$-Guide—R
$-JuniorWay
$-Primary Street
$-Sparkle—R

CHRISTIAN EDUCATION/ LIBRARY
$-Catechist
$-Children's Ministry
Christian Early Ed.—R
$-Christian Educators—R
Christian Librarian—R
Christian School Ed.—R
$-Group
$-Journal/Adventist Ed.—R
Jour./Ed. & Christian Belief—R
Jour. of Christian Ed.
Jour. of Christianity—R
Jour./Research on Christian Ed.
$-Momentum
$-Preschool Playhouse (CE)
$-Teachers of Vision—R
$-Today's Catholic Teacher—R
$-Youth & CE Leadership

MISSIONS
East-West Church
$-Evangelical Missions—R
$-Glad Tidings—R

PASTORS/LEADERS
$-Catechumenate
$-Catholic Servant
$-Christian Century—R
Christian Education Jour.—R
$-Clergy Journal—R
CrossCurrents

Disciple Magazine—R
$-Enrichment—R
$-Immerse
$-Interpreter
Ministry in Motion—R
$-Ministry Today
$-RevWriter Resource
Rick Warren's Ministry—R
$-SmallGroups.com—R
Technologies for Worship—R
$-Today's Parish
$-Word & World
$-YouthWorker

TEEN/YOUNG ADULT
$-Boundless Webzine—R
$-Insight—R
$-J.A.M.
TeensForJC—R
$-TG Magazine
$-Young Adult Today

WOMEN
Christian Woman's Page—R
$-Horizons—R
$-inSpirit—R
$-Pauses . . .
Precious Times—R
Right to the Heart—R
Share

CHRISTIAN LIVING
ADULT/GENERAL
$-Alive Now—R
$-America
American Tract—R
$-Angels on Earth
$-Arkansas Catholic—R
$-Arlington Catholic
$-Atlantic Catholic
$-Aujourd'hui Credo—R
$-Australian Catholics—R
$-B.C. Catholic—R
$-Bible Advocate—R
Bread of Life—R
Breakthrough Intercessor—R
$-Brink Magazine—R
$-Canada Lutheran—R
$-Cathedral Age
$-Catholic Digest—R
$-Catholic Forester—R

$-Catholic New York
$-Catholic Yearbook—R
CBN.com—R
$-Celebrate Life—R
Central FL Episcopalian
$-CGA World—R
$-Charisma
$-Chicken Soup Books—R
$-Christian Citizen USA
$-Christian Courier/Canada—R
Christian Courier/WI—R
$-Christian Examiner
Christian Family Jour.
$-Christian Home & School
$-Christianity Today—R
Christian Journal—R
Christian Observer
Christian Online
Christian Quarterly—R
Christian Ranchman
$-Christian Research
$-Christian Standard—R
$-ChristianWeek—R
Church Herald & Holiness—R
$-Churchmouse Public.—R
Church of England News
$-City Light News—R
$-Columbia—R
Connecting Point—R
$-Covenant Companion—R
Creation Care—R
$-Culture Wars—R
Desert Call—R
Desert Voice—R
Divine Ascent
$-DreamSeeker—R
E-Channels—R
$-Enfoque a la Familia
Eternal Ink—R
$-Evangel/IN—R
Evangel/OR—R
$-Faith & Family
$-Faith & Friends—R
$-Faith Today—R
Faithwebbin—R
$-Family Digest—R
Fit Christian
Florida Baptist Witness
Foursquare Leader
$-Gem—R

$-Gems of Truth—R
$-Good News—R
$-Good News, Etc.—R
Good News Journal—R
$-Good News, The—R
Gospel Herald
$-Gospel Today—R
$-Guide—R
$-Guideposts—R
Halo Magazine—R
$-Haruah—R
HEARTLIGHT Internet—R
Highway News—R
$-Holiness Today
$-Homeschooling Today—R
$-Home Times—R
($)-HopeKeepers—R
$-Imagine
($)-Impact Magazine—R
$-Indian Life—R
$-In His Presence—R
$-In Touch
Island Catholic—R
$-JC Town Reporter—R
$-KD Gospel Media
Keys to Living—R
Koinonia
$-Kyria—R
Leaves—R
$-Lifeglow—R
$-Light & Life
Light of the World
$-Liguorian
$-Live—R
$-Living—R
$-Living Church
$-Lookout
$-Lutheran Digest—R
$-Lutheran Journal—R
$-Lutheran Witness
$-Manna—R
$-Marian Helper
$-Mature Living
$-Mature Years—R
Men.AG.org—R
$-Men of Integrity—R
Men of the Cross
MESSAGE/Open Bible—R
$-Messenger/Sacred Heart
Methodist History

$-Miracles, Healings—R
MissionWares
($)-Mutuality—R
New Heart—R
New Identity—R
$-New Wineskins—R
Nostalgia—R
$-Our Sunday Visitor—R
$-Over the Back Fence—R
$-Ozarks Senior Living—R
$-ParentLife
Penned from the Heart—R
$-Pentecostal Evangel—R
Perspectives—R
$-Point—R
$-Power for Living—R
PrayerWorks—R
$-Presbyterians Today—R
$-Psychology for Living—R
$-Purpose—R
Quaker Life—R
Regent Global—R
$-River Region's Journey
Saved Magazine
$-Search
$-Seek—R
Sharing—R
$-Significant Living—R
Single Again Mag.—R
Spirituality for Today
$-Spiritual Life
$-St. Anthony Messenger
$-Storyteller—R
SW Kansas Faith
Sword and Trumpet
Sword of the Lord—R
$-Testimony—R
$-Together—R
Trumpeter—R
$-United Church Observer—R
$-U.S. Catholic—R
$-Vibrant Life—R
Victory Herald—R
$-Victory in Grace—R
$-Vision—R
$-Vista—R
$-War Cry—R
$-Way of St. Francis—R
$-Wesleyan Life—R
Wisconsin Christian

CHILDREN
$-BREAD/God's Children—R
$-Cadet Quest—R
$-Focus/Clubhouse Jr.
$-Guide—R
$-JuniorWay
$-Partners—R
$-Pockets—R
$-Primary Street

CHRISTIAN EDUCATION/ LIBRARY
Congregational Libraries
$-Group
$-Kids' Ministry Ideas—R
$-Teachers of Vision—R
$-Youth & CE Leadership

DAILY DEVOTIONALS
$-Brink Magazine—R
Penned from the Heart—R

MISSIONS
$-Evangelical Missions—R
$-Glad Tidings—R
WEC.go
Women of the Harvest

PASTORS/LEADERS
$-Barefoot—R
$-Catechumenate
$-Catholic Servant
$-Christian Century—R
Disciple Magazine—R
Foursquare Leader
$-Immerse
$-Interpreter
$-Net Results
$-Preaching Well—R
$-Proclaim—R
$-Review for Religious
$-RevWriter Resource
Rick Warren's Ministry—R
Technologies for Worship—R
$-Word & World

TEEN/YOUNG ADULT
$-Boundless Webzine—R
$-Devo'Zine—R
$-Direction Student
$-Essential Connection
G4T Ink—R

$-Horizon Student
$-Insight—R
$-J.A.M.
$-Sharing the Victory—R
$-TC Magazine
TeensForJC—R
$-TG Magazine
$-Young Christian Writers
$-Young Salvationist—R

WOMEN
($)-Beyond the Bend—R
Christian Woman's Page—R
Chris. Work at Home Moms—R
Extreme Woman
First Lady
Glory & Strength—R
Handmaidens
Hope for Women
$-Horizons—R
Inspired Women
$-inSpirit—R
$-Journey
Just Between Us—R
$-Link & Visitor—R
Love, Pearls & Swine
Lutheran Woman's Quar.
$-MomSense—R
$-Mother's Heart—R
P31 Woman—R
$-Pauses . . .
Precious Times—R
Right to the Heart—R
Share
$-SpiritLed Woman
Together with God—R
Unrecognized Woman—R
Virtuous Woman—R
Women of the Cross
Women's Ministry
Women Today—R

CHURCH GROWTH
ADULT/GENERAL
$-America
$-Atlantic Catholic
Bread of Life—R
Breakthrough Intercessor—R
$-Catholic Peace Voice—R
$-Christian Examiner

Christian News NW—R
Christian Online
Christian Quarterly—R
$-Christian Standard—R
$-ChristianWeek—R
Church of England News
$-City Light News—R
$-Columbia—R
$-Culture Wars—R
Desert Call—R
E-Channels—R
$-EFCA Today
$-Evangel/IN—R
$-Faith & Family
$-Gem—R
$-Good News—R
$-Good News, Etc.—R
Gospel Herald
Halo Magazine—R
$-Holiness Today
$-In His Presence—R
$-In Touch
$-JC Town Reporter—R
$-KD Gospel Media
Koinonia
$-Liguorian
$-Live—R
$-Living Church
$-Lookout
Men.AG.org—R
MESSAGE/Open Bible—R
$-Messenger/Sacred Heart
$-Miracles, Healings—R
New Identity—R
$-New Wineskins—R
$-Our Sunday Visitor—R
Penned from the Heart—R
$-Presbyterian Outlook
$-Presbyterians Today—R
$-Purpose—R
Quaker Life—R
$-Seek—R
$-Significant Living—R
Spirituality for Today
$-St. Anthony Messenger
Sword and Trumpet
Sword of the Lord—R
$-Testimony—R
Trumpeter—R
Victory Herald—R

$-Victory in Grace—R
$-Way of St. Francis—R
$-Wesleyan Life—R
Wisconsin Christian

CHRISTIAN EDUCATION/ LIBRARY

$-Children's Ministry
Congregational Libraries
$-Group
$-Kids' Ministry Ideas—R
$-Youth & CE Leadership

MISSIONS

East-West Church
$-Evangelical Missions—R
$-Glad Tidings—R
Lausanne World—R
Missiology
($)-Operation Reveille—R

MUSIC

$-Creator—R
($)-TCP Magazine

PASTORS/LEADERS

$-Catechumenate
$-Catholic Servant
$-Christian Century—R
Christian Education Jour.—R
Church Executive
$-Clergy Journal—R
$-Enrichment—R
Foursquare Leader
Great Comm. Research—R
$-Growth Points—R
$-Immerse
$-Interpreter
$-Leadership—R
$-Let's Worship
Ministry in Motion—R
$-Ministry Today
$-Net Results
$-Outreach—R
Rick Warren's Ministry—R
Sharing the Practice—R
Technologies for Worship—R
Theological Digest—R
$-Worship Leader
$-Your Church—R

TEEN/YOUNG ADULT

$-Direction Student
$-Horizon Student
$-J.A.M.
TeensForJC—R

WOMEN

($)-Beyond the Bend—R
ChurchWoman
Hope for Women
$-inSpirit—R
Share

CHURCH HISTORY
ADULT/GENERAL

African Voices—R
$-America
$-Atlantic Catholic
$-Aujourd'hui Credo—R
Bread of Life—R
$-Catholic Digest—R
$-Catholic Insight
$-Catholic Peace Voice—R
$-Catholic Sentinel
$-Catholic Yearbook—R
CBN.com—R
$-Christian History—R
Christian Online
$-Christian Renewal—R
$-Christian Standard—R
Church of England News
$-City Light News—R
$-Columbia—R
$-Company Magazine—R
Creation Care—R
$-Cresset
Desert Call—R
Desert Voice—R
Divine Ascent
$-Earthen Vessel Online—R
E-Channels—R
$-Faith Today—R
$-Family Digest—R
Founders Journal
Friends Journal—R
Gospel Herald
$-Guide—R
Halo Magazine—R
$-Holiness Today
$-Homeschooling Today—R

$-In Touch
Island Catholic—R
$-JC Town Reporter—R
Koinonia
$-Leben—R
$-Liguorian
$-Lookout
$-Lutheran Journal—R
$-Lutheran Witness
($)-Mennonite Historian—R
$-Messiah Journal
Methodist History
Movieguide
$-New Wineskins—R
Nostalgia—R
$-Our Sunday Visitor—R
$-Pathway—R
PrayerWorks—R
$-Presbyterian Outlook
$-Presbyterians Today—R
Priscilla Papers
$-Purpose—R
$-Search
$-Social Justice—R
Spirituality for Today
$-St. Anthony Messenger
Sword and Trumpet
Sword of the Lord—R
Trumpeter—R
$-U.S. Catholic—R
$-Way of St. Francis—R
$-Wesleyan Life—R
Wisconsin Christian

CHILDREN

$-Archaeology—R

CHRISTIAN EDUCATION/ LIBRARY

$-Catechist
Catholic Library
$-Group

DAILY DEVOTIONALS

Penned from the Heart—R

MISSIONS

East-West Church
$-Evangelical Missions—R
$-Glad Tidings—R
Lausanne World—R

Missiology
($)-Operation Reveille—R
Railroad Evangelist—R

PASTORS/LEADERS
$-Catechumenate
$-Christian Century—R
$-Clergy Journal—R
CrossCurrents
Disciple Magazine—R
$-Enrichment—R
Foursquare Leader
$-Immerse
$-Leadership—R
Lutheran Forum
Sharing the Practice—R
Theological Digest—R

TEEN/YOUNG ADULT
$-Boundless Webzine—R
$-Essential Connection
$-J.A.M.
TeensForJC—R
$-Young Christian Writers

WOMEN
($)-Beyond the Bend—R
($)-History's Women—R
$-Horizons—R
$-Link & Visitor—R
Share

CHURCH LIFE
ADULT/GENERAL
$-America
$-Arkansas Catholic—R
$-Atlantic Catholic
$-Aujourd'hui Credo—R
$-Australian Catholics—R
$-Bible Advocate—R
Bread of Life—R
Breakthrough Intercessor—R
$-Canada Lutheran—R
$-Cathedral Age
$-Catholic Digest—R
$-Catholic Insight
$-Catholic Sentinel
$-Catholic Yearbook—R
CBN.com—R
$-Christian Home & School
$-Christianity Today—R

Christian Journal—R
Christian News NW—R
Christian Online
$-Christian Standard—R
$-ChristianWeek—R
$-Churchmouse Public.—R
Church of England News
$-Columbia—R
$-Company Magazine—R
$-Covenant Companion—R
Creation Care—R
Desert Call—R
Desert Voice—R
$-DreamSeeker—R
E-Channels—R
$-EFCA Today
Encompass
Eternal Ink—R
$-Evangel/IN—R
Evangel/OR—R
$-Faith & Family
$-Faith Today—R
$-FGBC World—R
$-Gem—R
$-Good News—R
$-Good News, Etc.—R
$-Good News, The—R
Gospel Herald
Halo Magazine—R
$-Holiness Today
$-Home Times—R
$-In His Presence—R
$-In Touch
Island Catholic—R
$-JC Town Reporter—R
Just Between Us—R
$-KD Gospel Media
Koinonia
Leaves—R
$-Lifeglow—R
$-Light & Life
$-Liguorian
$-Live—R
$-Living Church
$-Lookout
$-Lutheran Journal—R
$-Lutheran Witness
Men.AG.org—R
($)-Mennonite Historian—R
$-Messenger/St. Anthony

($)-Mutuality—R
New Identity—R
$-New Wineskins—R
Nostalgia—R
$-Our Sunday Visitor—R
$-Pathway—R
Penned from the Heart—R
$-Pentecostal Evangel—R
$-Presbyterian Outlook
$-Presbyterians Today—R
Priscilla Papers
$-Purpose—R
$-Seek—R
Spirituality for Today
$-St. Anthony Messenger
Sword of the Lord—R
$-Testimony—R
Trumpeter—R
$-U.S. Catholic—R
Victory Herald—R
$-War Cry—R
$-Way of St. Francis—R
$-Wesleyan Life—R
Wisconsin Christian

CHILDREN
$-Archaeology—R
$-BREAD/God's Children—R
$-Primary Street

CHRISTIAN EDUCATION/ LIBRARY
$-Children's Ministry
$-Group
$-Kids' Ministry Ideas—R
$-Youth & CE Leadership

DAILY DEVOTIONALS
Penned from the Heart—R

MISSIONS
East-West Church
$-Evangelical Missions—R
$-Glad Tidings—R

PASTORS/LEADERS
$-Catholic Servant
$-Christian Century—R
Church Executive
Disciple Magazine—R
$-Enrichment—R

Foursquare Leader
$-Immerse
$-Interpreter
$-Leadership—R
$-Ministry
$-Ministry & Liturgy—R
Ministry in Motion—R
$-Ministry Today
$-Net Results
$-Parish Liturgy—R
$-Priest
$-RevWriter Resource
Rick Warren's Ministry—R
Sharing the Practice—R
Technologies for Worship—R
$-Worship Leader
$-YouthWorker

TEEN/YOUNG ADULT
$-Boundless Webzine—R
$-Direction Student
$-Horizon Student
$-J.A.M.

WOMEN
($)-Beyond the Bend—R
Christian Woman's Page—R
ChurchWoman
For Every Woman—R
Hope for Women
$-Horizons—R
$-inSpirit—R
$-Pauses . . .
Share

CHURCH MANAGEMENT
ADULT/GENERAL
$-America
$-Atlantic Catholic
Bread of Life—R
$-Canada Lutheran—R
Christian Computing—R
Christian News NW—R
Christian Online
$-Christian Standard—R
$-ChristianWeek—R
$-Churchmouse Public.—R
Church of England News
$-Covenant Companion—R
Creation Care—R
$-Culture Wars—R

Disciple's Journal—R
E-Channels—R
$-EFCA Today
$-Faith Today—R
$-Gem—R
Gospel Herald
$-Gospel Today—R
Halo Magazine—R
$-KD Gospel Media
Koinonia
$-Living Church
$-Lookout
$-Our Sunday Visitor—R
$-Pathway—R
$-Presbyterian Outlook
Priscilla Papers
$-Purpose—R
Regent Global—R
$-St. Anthony Messenger
Sword of the Lord—R
Trumpeter—R
Wisconsin Christian

CHRISTIAN EDUCATION/ LIBRARY
$-Children's Ministry
$-Group
$-Kids' Ministry Ideas—R
$-Youth & CE Leadership

DAILY DEVOTIONALS
Penned from the Heart—R

MISSIONS
$-Evangelical Missions—R

PASTORS/LEADERS
$-Catholic Servant
Christian Education Jour.—R
Church Executive
$-Clergy Journal—R
Disciple Magazine—R
$-Enrichment—R
Foursquare Leader
Great Comm. Research—R
$-Growth Points—R
$-Immerse
$-Interpreter
$-Leadership—R
$-Ministry
Ministry in Motion—R
$-Ministry Today

$-Net Results
$-RevWriter Resource
Rick Warren's Ministry—R
Sharing the Practice—R
Technologies for Worship—R
$-Word & World
$-Worship Leader
$-Your Church—R

WOMEN
Share
Women's Ministry

CHURCH OUTREACH
ADULT/GENERAL
$-America
$-Atlantic Catholic
$-Bible Advocate—R
Bread of Life—R
$-Canada Lutheran—R
$-Catholic Sentinel
CBN.com—R
Christian Family Jour.
$-Christian Home & School
Christian News NW—R
Christian Online
$-Christian Research
$-Christian Standard—R
$-ChristianWeek—R
$-Churchmouse Public.—R
Church of England News
$-City Light News—R
$-Columbia—R
$-Company Magazine—R
$-Covenant Companion—R
Creation Care—R
$-Culture Wars—R
Desert Call—R
Desert Voice—R
$-Earthen Vessel Online—R
E-Channels—R
$-EFCA Today
$-Episcopal Life—R
Eternal Ink—R
$-Evangel/IN—R
Evangel/OR—R
$-Faith & Friends—R
$-Faith Today—R
$-FGBC World—R
$-Gem—R
$-Good News—R

$-Good News, Etc.—R
$-Good News, The—R
Gospel Herald
Halo Magazine—R
Heartland Gatekeeper—R
$-Holiness Today
$-Home Times—R
($)-HopeKeepers—R
$-In His Presence—R
$-In Touch
$-JC Town Reporter—R
Just Between Us—R
$-KD Gospel Media
Koinonia
$-Light & Life
$-Living Church
$-Lookout
$-Lutheran Witness
Men.AG.org—R
MESSAGE/Open Bible—R
$-Miracles, Healings—R
$-Montana Catholic
Network
New Identity—R
$-New Wineskins—R
$-On Mission
$-Our Sunday Visitor—R
$-Pathway—R
$-Point—R
$-Presbyterian Outlook
$-Presbyterians Today—R
$-Priority!—R
Priscilla Papers
$-Prism
$-Purpose—R
Quaker Life—R
$-Search
$-Seek—R
Spirituality for Today
$-St. Anthony Messenger
Sword of the Lord—R
$-Testimony—R
Trumpeter—R
Victory Herald—R
$-Wesleyan Life—R
Wisconsin Christian

CHILDREN
$-Primary Street

CHRISTIAN EDUCATION/ LIBRARY
$-Children's Ministry
$-Group
$-Journal/Adventist Ed.—R
$-Youth & CE Leadership

MISSIONS
East-West Church
$-Evangelical Missions—R
$-Glad Tidings—R
Lausanne World—R
Missiology
Railroad Evangelist—R

PASTORS/LEADERS
$-Catholic Servant
$-Christian Century—R
Church Executive
$-Clergy Journal—R
Disciple Magazine—R
$-Enrichment—R
Foursquare Leader
Great Comm. Research—R
$-Growth Points—R
$-Immerse
$-Insight Youth—R
$-Interpreter
$-Leadership—R
$-Let's Worship
$-Ministry
Ministry in Motion—R
$-Ministry Today
$-Net Results
$-Outreach—R
$-RevWriter Resource
Rick Warren's Ministry—R
Sharing the Practice—R
$-Small Groups.com—R
Technologies for Worship—R
$-Today's Parish
$-Word & World
$-Worship Leader
$-YouthWorker

TEEN/YOUNG ADULT
$-Direction Student
$-Horizon Student
$-Insight—R
TeensForJC—R
$-TG Magazine

WOMEN
Christian Woman's Page—R
Hope for Women
$-inSpirit—R
Just Between Us—R
$-Pauses . . .
Share
Women's Ministry

CHURCH TRADITIONS
ADULT/GENERAL
$-America
$-Arkansas Catholic—R
$-Atlantic Catholic
$-Aujourd'hui Credo—R
Bread of Life—R
$-Brink Magazine—R
$-Canada Lutheran—R
$-Catholic Digest—R
$-Catholic Yearbook—R
CBN.com—R
$-Celebrate Life—R
$-CGA World—R
$-Christian Examiner
$-Christian History—R
Christian Online
$-Christian Research
$-Christian Standard—R
$-Churchmouse Public.—R
Church of England News
$-Columbia—R
$-Cresset
Desert Call—R
E-Channels—R
Encompass
Eternal Ink—R
$-Faith & Family
$-Faith Today—R
$-Family Digest—R
$-FGBC World—R
$-Gem—R
Gospel Herald
$-Gospel Today—R
Halo Magazine—R
$-Holiness Today
$-Homeschooling Today—R
$-KD Gospel Media
Koinonia
$-Light & Life
$-Liguorian

$-Living Church
$-Lutheran Journal—R
$-Lutheran Witness
($)-Mennonite Historian—R
$-New Wineskins—R
Nostalgia—R
$-Our Sunday Visitor—R
Perspectives—R
$-Presbyterians Today—R
Priscilla Papers
$-Purpose—R
$-Search
Spirituality for Today
$-St. Anthony Messenger
$-Testimony—R
$-Together—R
Trumpeter—R
$-U.S. Catholic—R
Victory Herald—R
$-Way of St. Francis—R
Wisconsin Christian

CHILDREN
$-Archaeology—R

CHRISTIAN EDUCATION/
LIBRARY
$-Catechist
$-Children's Ministry
$-Group
$-Momentum

DAILY DEVOTIONALS
Penned from the Heart—R

MISSIONS
East-West Church
$-Glad Tidings—R

PASTORS/LEADERS
$-Barefoot—R
$-Catechumenate
$-Christian Century—R
$-Clergy Journal—R
Disciple Magazine—R
Foursquare Leader
$-Immerse
$-Interpreter
$-Leadership—R
Lutheran Forum
$-Ministry Today
$-Parish Liturgy—R

$-Reformed Worship—R
Rick Warren's Ministry—R
Sharing the Practice—R
Theological Digest—R

TEEN/YOUNG ADULT
$-J.A.M.
TeensForJC—R
$-TG Magazine

WOMEN
$-Horizons—R
$-Pauses . . .
Share

CONTROVERSIAL ISSUES
ADULT/GENERAL
American Tract—R
$-Animal Trails—R
$-Associated Content—R
$-Aujourd'hui Credo—R
$-Bible Advocate—R
Biblical Recorder
$-Brink Magazine—R
$-Canada Lutheran—R
CanadianChristianity
$-Catholic Insight
$-Catholic Peace Voice—R
CBN.com—R
$-Celebrate Life—R
Challenge Weekly
$-Christian Citizen USA
$-Christian Courier/Canada—R
$-Christian Examiner
$-Christian Home & School
$-Christianity Today—R
$-Christianity Today Movies—R
Christian Media—R
Christian Online
$-Christian Renewal—R
$-Christian Response—R
$-Christian Standard—R
$-ChristianWeek—R
Church of England News
$-City Light News—R
$-Columbia—R
Creation Care—R
$-Creative Nonfiction
$-Culture Wars—R
Desert Christian
Desert Voice—R

$-DreamSeeker—R
E-Channels—R
$-EFCA Today
Encompass
$-Enfoque a la Familia
Eternal Ink—R
$-Eureka Street
Evangelical Times
$-Faith Today—R
Faithwebbin—R
$-Good News—R
$-Good News, Etc.—R
$-Good News, The—R
Good News!
Good News Today
Gospel Herald
$-Gospel Today—R
Halo Magazine—R
Heartland Gatekeeper—R
$-Homeschooling Today—R
$-Home Times—R
($)-Impact Magazine—R
$-Indian Life—R
$-Interim—R
$-In Touch
$-KD Gospel Media
Koinonia
$-Lifeglow—R
$-Light & Life
$-Live—R
$-Living Church
$-Lookout
$-Manna—R
Movieguide
($)-Mutuality—R
New Identity—R
$-New Wineskins—R
$-Now What?—R
$-Our Sunday Visitor—R
Perspectives—R
$-Prairie Messenger—R
Priscilla Papers
$-Prism
$-Psychology for Living—R
$-Purpose—R
$-Search
Single Again Mag.—R
$-Social Justice—R
$-St. Anthony Messenger
Sword of the Lord—R

Tri-State Voice
Trumpeter—R
Unrecognized Woman—R
$-U.S. Catholic—R
Victory Herald—R
$-War Cry—R
$-Way of St. Francis—R
Wisconsin Christian
$-World & I—R
Xavier Review

CHILDREN
$-New Moon—R
Skipping Stones

CHRISTIAN EDUCATION/ LIBRARY
$-Group
$-Teachers of Vision—R
$-Today's Catholic Teacher—R

MISSIONS
East-West Church
$-Evangelical Missions—R
Intl. Jour./Frontier—R
($)-Operation Reveille—R

MUSIC
Hymn

PASTORS/LEADERS
$-Christian Century—R
Church Executive
$-Clergy Journal—R
CrossCurrents
Disciple Magazine—R
$-Enrichment—R
$-Immerse
$-InSite—R
$-Interpreter
Jour./Pastoral Care
$-Let's Worship
$-Ministry & Liturgy—R
$-Ministry Today
$-Outreach—R
$-Word & World
$-Worship Leader

TEEN/YOUNG ADULT
$-Boundless Webzine—R
$-Focus/Dare 2 Dig Deeper
$-J.A.M.
$-Sharing the Victory—R

$-TC Magazine
TeensForJC—R
$-TG Magazine
$-Young Salvationist—R

WOMEN
($)-Beyond the Bend—R
Extreme Woman
For Every Woman—R
Glory & Strength—R
Grace Today
$-Heart & Soul
Hope for Women
$-inSpirit—R
Precious Times—R
Take Root & Write
Unrecognized Woman—R

WRITERS
Areopagus

CRAFTS
ADULT/GENERAL
$-Associated Content—R
$-Atlantic Catholic
$-CGA World—R
Christian Online
$-Faith & Family
Gospel Herald
$-Guide—R
$-Imagine
$-Indian Life—R
Koinonia
$-Living—R
$-Mature Living
$-ParentLife
Sword of the Lord—R
$-World & I—R

CHILDREN
$-Adventures
$-American Girl—R
$-BREAD/God's Children—R
$-Cadet Quest—R
$-Celebrate
$-Focus/Clubhouse
$-Focus/Clubhouse Jr.
$-Guide—R
$-Junior Companion—R
$-JuniorWay
$-Pockets—R

$-Preschool Playhouse
$-SHINE brightly—R
$-Sparkle—R
$-Story Mates—R

CHRISTIAN EDUCATION/ LIBRARY
$-Catechist
$-Children's Ministry
$-Kids' Ministry Ideas—R
$-Youth & CE Leadership

PASTORS/LEADERS
$-Interpreter

TEEN/YOUNG ADULT
$-J.A.M.
TeensForJC—R
$-TG Magazine

WOMEN
Christian Woman's Page—R
Chris. Work at Home Moms—R
$-MomSense—R
$-Mother's Heart—R
P31 Woman—R
Take Root & Write
Virtuous Woman—R
Women's Ministry

CREATION SCIENCE
ADULT/GENERAL
Answers Magazine
$-Bible Advocate—R
CBN.com—R
$-Christian Citizen USA
$-Christian Courier/Canada—R
$-Christian Examiner
Christian Observer
$-Christian Renewal—R
$-Christian Research
$-Creation Illust.—R
Desert Voice—R
$-Good News, The—R
Gospel Herald
$-Guide—R
$-Haruah—R
$-Homeschooling Today—R
$-Home Times—R
$-Indian Life—R
$-JC Town Reporter—R
Koinonia

$-Lifeglow—R
$-Light & Life
$-Live—R
$-Living—R
$-Lookout
$-Pathway—R
Perspectives/Science
$-Salvo
$-St. Anthony Messenger
Sword and Trumpet
Sword of the Lord—R
Trumpeter—R
$-War Cry—R
$-Way of St. Francis—R
Wisconsin Christian

CHILDREN
$-Guide—R
$-Nature Friend—R
$-Sparkle—R

**CHRISTIAN EDUCATION/
LIBRARY**
$-Journal/Adventist Ed.—R

PASTORS/LEADERS
CrossCurrents
Disciple Magazine—R

TEEN/YOUNG ADULT
$-Boundless Webzine—R
$-J.A.M.
$-Young Christian Writers
$-Young Salvationist—R

WOMEN
$-Mother's Heart—R

CULTS/OCCULT
ADULT/GENERAL
American Tract—R
$-Bible Advocate—R
CBN.com—R
$-Christian Examiner
$-Christian Renewal—R
$-Christian Research
$-Creative Nonfiction
$-Culture Wars—R
Desert Voice—R
Gospel Herald
$-Guide—R
Halo Magazine—R

$-In His Presence—R
$-In Touch
$-JC Town Reporter—R
Koinonia
$-Light & Life
$-Lookout
New Heart—R
$-Now What?—R
SCP Journal
Sword of the Lord—R
Trumpeter—R
Wisconsin Christian

CHILDREN
$-Guide—R

MISSIONS
East-West Church
Intl. Jour./Frontier—R

PASTORS/LEADERS
$-Ministry Today
$-Word & World

TEEN/YOUNG ADULT
$-Boundless Webzine—R
$-TC Magazine
TeensForJC—R
$-Young Salvationist—R

WOMEN
For Every Woman—R
$-Journey

CURRENT/SOCIAL ISSUES
ADULT/GENERAL
American Tract—R
$-Anglican Journal
$-Apocalypse Chronicles—R
$-Arlington Catholic
$-Associated Content—R
$-Aujourd'hui Credo—R
$-B.C. Catholic—R
$-Bible Advocate—R
Biblical Recorder
Breakthrough Intercessor—R
$-Brink Magazine—R
Brink Online—R
$-Canada Lutheran—R
CanadianChristianity
$-Catholic Insight
$-Catholic New York

$-Catholic Peace Voice—R
CBN.com—R
Challenge Weekly
$-Christian Citizen USA
$-Christian Courier/Canada—R
Christian Courier/WI—R
$-Christian Examiner
$-Christian Home & School
$-Christianity Today—R
$-Christianity Today Movies—R
Christian Journal—R
Christian Observer
Christian Online
Christian Outlook
Christian Ranchman
$-Christian Renewal—R
$-Christian Research
$-Christian Standard—R
$-ChristianWeek—R
$-Churchmouse Public.—R
Church of England News
$-City Light News—R
$-Columbia—R
$-Covenant Companion—R
Creation Care—R
$-Creative Nonfiction
$-Cresset
$-Culture Wars—R
Desert Call—R
Desert Christian
$-Direction
$-Disaster News
$-DreamSeeker—R
E-Channels—R
Encompass
$-Enfoque a la Familia
$-Eureka Street
Evangelical Times
Evangel/OR—R
$-Faith Today—R
Faithwebbin—R
Foursquare Leader
Friends Journal—R
$-Gem—R
$-Good News—R
Good News Connection
$-Good News, Etc.—R
$-Good News, The—R
Good News Today
Gospel Herald

$-Guide—R
Halo Magazine—R
Heartland Gatekeeper—R
HEARTLIGHT Internet—R
$-Homeschooling Today—R
$-Home Times—R
$-Indian Life—R
$-In Touch
Island Catholic—R
$-JC Town Reporter—R
$-KD Gospel Media
Koinonia
$-Liberty
$-Lifeglow—R
LifeSite News
$-Light & Life
$-Liguorian
$-Live—R
$-Living—R
$-Lookout
$-Lutheran Witness
$-Manna—R
$-Marian Helper
Men.AG.org—R
$-Men of Integrity—R
$-MESSAGE
$-Messenger/St. Anthony
Messianic Perspectives—R
More Excellent Way—R
Movieguide
($)-Mutuality—R
New Christian Voices
New Heart—R
New Identity—R
$-New Wineskins—R
$-Now What?—R
$-Our Sunday Visitor—R
$-Ozarks Senior Living—R
$-ParentLife
$-Pathway—R
Perspectives—R
$-Point—R
$-Prairie Messenger—R
PrayerWorks—R
$-Priority!—R
Priscilla Papers
$-Prism
$-Psychology for Living—R
$-River Region's Journey
SCP Journal

$-Seek—R
Single Again Mag.—R
$-Social Justice—R
$-Special Living—R
$-St. Anthony Messenger
$-Storyteller—R
Sword of the Lord—R
$-Together—R
Tri-State Voice
Trumpeter—R
Unrecognized Woman—R
$-U.S. Catholic—R
$-War Cry—R
$-Way of St. Francis—R
Wisconsin Christian
$-World & I—R
$-Written

CHILDREN
$-BREAD/God's Children—R
$-Guide—R
$-JuniorWay
$-New Moon—R
$-SHINE brightly—R
Skipping Stones
$-Sparkle—R

CHRISTIAN EDUCATION/
LIBRARY
$-Children's Ministry
$-Momentum

DAILY DEVOTIONALS
$-Brink Magazine—R
Penned from the Heart—R

MISSIONS
East-West Church
$-Glad Tidings—R
$-New World Outlook
$-One
($)-Operation Reveille—R
Women of the Harvest

PASTORS/LEADERS
$-Barefoot—R
$-Catholic Servant
$-Christian Century—R
Disciple Magazine—R
$-Enrichment—R
$-InSite—R
$-Interpreter

$-Leadership—R
Lutheran Forum
$-Ministry & Liturgy—R
$-Ministry Today
$-Outreach—R
$-Word & World

TEEN/YOUNG ADULT
$-Boundless Webzine—R
$-Devo'Zine—R
$-Direction Student
$-Focus/Dare 2 Dig Deeper
$-Horizon Student
$-Insight—R
$-J.A.M.
$-Listen—R
$-Risen
$-Sharing the Victory—R
$-TC Magazine
TeensForJC—R
$-TG Magazine
$-Young Adult Today
$-Young Salvationist—R

WOMEN
$-At the Center—R
($)-Beyond the Bend—R
Chris. Work at Home Moms—R
Extreme Woman
For Every Woman—R
$-Fullfill
Glory & Strength—R
$-Heart & Soul
Hope for Women
$-Horizons—R
$-inSpirit—R
$-Link & Visitor—R
$-Mother's Heart—R
$-SpiritLed Woman
Unrecognized Woman—R
Virtuous Woman—R
Women Today—R

WRITERS
Areopagus

DEATH/DYING
ADULT/GENERAL
$-America
American Tract—R
$-Arlington Catholic
$-Associated Content—R

$-Atlantic Catholic
$-Aujourd'hui Credo—R
$-Bible Advocate—R
Bread of Life—R
$-Brink Magazine—R
CBN.com—R
$-Celebrate Life—R
$-Chicken Soup Books—R
$-Christian Citizen USA
$-Christianity Today—R
Christian Online
Christian Quarterly—R
Christian Ranchman
$-ChristianWeek—R
$-Churchmouse Public.—R
$-Columbia—R
$-Creative Nonfiction
Desert Call—R
E-Channels—R
Faithwebbin—R
$-Gem—R
$-Good News, Etc.—R
$-Guide—R
$-Guideposts—R
Halo Magazine—R
HEARTLIGHT Internet—R
($)-HopeKeepers—R
$-Indian Life—R
$-In His Presence—R
$-In Touch
Island Catholic—R
$-JC Town Reporter—R
$-KD Gospel Media
Koinonia
$-Light & Life
$-Liguorian
$-Live—R
$-Lookout
$-Men of Integrity—R
$-Messenger/Sacred Heart
New Heart—R
$-New Wineskins—R
$-Now What?—R
$-Our Sunday Visitor—R
$-ParentLife
Perspectives/Science
$-Point—R
$-Prairie Messenger—R
PrayerWorks—R
$-Presbyterian Outlook

$-Presbyterians Today—R
$-Psychology for Living—R
$-Seek—R
Single Again Mag.—R
$-Social Justice—R
Spirituality for Today
$-St. Anthony Messenger
$-Storyteller—R
Sword of the Lord—R
$-Testimony—R
Trumpeter—R
$-U.S. Catholic—R
$-War Cry—R
$-Way of St. Francis—R
Wisconsin Christian

CHILDREN
$-Guide—R
$-New Moon—R
Skipping Stones
$-Sparkle—R

CHRISTIAN EDUCATION/ LIBRARY
$-Momentum

DAILY DEVOTIONALS
Penned from the Heart—R

PASTORS/LEADERS
$-Catholic Servant
$-Christian Century—R
$-Clergy Journal—R
Disciple Magazine—R
$-Enrichment—R
$-InSite—R
$-Interpreter
Jour./Pastoral Care
$-Leadership—R
$-RevWriter Resource
Sharing the Practice—R

TEEN/YOUNG ADULT
$-Boundless Webzine—R
$-J.A.M.
TeensForJC—R
$-TG Magazine

WOMEN
($)-Beyond the Bend—R
For Every Woman—R
Glory & Strength—R
Hope for Women

$-inSpirit—R
$-Pauses . . .
Precious Times—R
Take Root & Write
Virtuous Woman—R
Women Today—R

DEPRESSION*
ADULT/GENERAL
$-Bible Advocate—R
$-Churchmouse Public.—R
Just Between Us—R
$-Lifeglow—R
$-Mother's Heart—R
$-Now What?—R
$-U.S. Catholic—R

WOMEN
$-Brink Magazine—R
Glory & Strength—R
Take Root & Write

DEVOTIONALS/ MEDITATIONS
ADULT/GENERAL
$-Alive Now—R
$-America
$-Arlington Catholic
$-Aujourd'hui Credo—R
$-Australian Catholics—R
Breakthrough Intercessor—R
$-Catholic Peace Voice—R
CBN.com—R
$-Chicken Soup Books—R
$-Christian Home & School
Christian Journal—R
Christian Online
Christian Quarterly—R
Christian Ranchman
$-Churchmouse Public.—R
$-Columbia—R
$-Covenant Companion—R
Creation Care—R
Desert Call—R
Divine Ascent
Eternal Ink—R
$-Evangel/IN—R
Evangelical Times
$-Faith & Family

$-Faith & Friends—R
Faithwebbin—R
$-Family Digest—R
Founders Journal
Foursquare Leader
$-Gem—R
$-Good News—R
Good News Journal—R
Halo Magazine—R
$-Haruah—R
HEARTLIGHT Internet—R
($)-HopeKeepers—R
$-In His Presence—R
$-In Touch
Just Between Us—R
$-KD Gospel Media
Keys to Living—R
Koinonia
$-Kyria—R
Leaves—R
$-Lifeglow—R
LifeTimes Catholic
$-Liguorian
$-Live—R
$-Living Church
$-Lutheran Digest—R
$-Mature Living
$-Messenger/Sacred Heart
$-Messenger/St. Anthony
($)-Mutuality—R
New Christian Voices
New Heart—R
$-New Wineskins—R
$-ParentLife
Penned from the Heart—R
$-Pentecostal Evangel—R
Perspectives—R
PrayerWorks—R
Quaker Life—R
Radix Magazine
$-Sports Spectrum
$-St. Anthony Messenger
Sword of the Lord—R
Trumpeter—R
Unrecognized Woman—R
Victory Herald—R
$-Victory in Grace—R
$-Vision—R
$-War Cry—R
$-Way of St. Francis—R

$-Weavings—R
$-Wesleyan Life—R
$-Written

CHILDREN
$-Keys for Kids—R
$-Pockets—R
$-Sparkle—R

CHRISTIAN EDUCATION/ LIBRARY
Congregational Libraries
$-Group

DAILY DEVOTIONALS
$-Brink Magazine—R
Christian Devotions—R
Daily Dev. for Deaf
$-Devotions
$-Forward Day by Day
Fruit of the Vine—R
Fusion
$-God's Word For Today
$-Light from the Word
($)-Mustard Seed
$-My Daily Visitor
Our Daily Journey
Penned from the Heart—R
$-Quiet Hour
$-Rejoice!
$-Secret Place
$-These Days
$-Upper Room
Word Among Us
$-Word in Season

MISSIONS
$-Glad Tidings—R
$-One
Women of the Harvest

PASTORS/LEADERS
$-Catholic Servant
Disciple Magazine—R
$-Emmanuel
$-Ministry Today
$-RevWriter Resource

TEEN/YOUNG ADULT
$-Devo'Zine—R
G4T Ink—R
$-J.A.M.
$-Take Five Plus

TeensForJC—R
$-TG Magazine
$-Young Adult Today

WOMEN
($)-Beyond the Bend—R
Christian Woman's Page—R
Chris. Work at Home Moms—R
$-Dabbling Mum—R
Extreme Woman
Glory & Strength—R
Handmaidens
$-Horizons—R
$-InspiredMoms—R
$-Journey
$-Melody of the Heart
$-Mother's Heart—R
$-Pauses . . .
Precious Times—R
$-SpiritLed Woman
Take Root & Write
Together with God—R
Truth Media
Unrecognized Woman—R
Virtuous Woman—R

WRITERS
ChristianWriters.com
$-Cross & Quill—R
$-Fellowscript—R
$-Shades of Romance—R

DISCIPLESHIP
ADULT/GENERAL
$-Alive Now—R
$-Arlington Catholic
$-Aujourd'hui Credo—R
$-Bible Advocate—R
$-Canada Lutheran—R
CBN.com—R
Christian Journal—R
Christian Motorsports
Christian Online
Christian Ranchman
$-Christian Research
$-Christian Standard—R
$-ChristianWeek—R
$-Churchmouse Public.—R
Church of England News
$-Columbia—R

$-Covenant Companion—R
$-Decision
Desert Call—R
$-EFCA Today
Eternal Ink—R
$-Evangel/IN—R
$-Faith & Family
$-Faith & Friends—R
$-Faith Today—R
Faithwebbin—R
$-Family Digest—R
$-Gem—R
$-Good News—R
Gospel Herald
$-Guide—R
Halo Magazine—R
HEARTLIGHT Internet—R
Highway News—R
$-Homeschooling Today—R
$-In His Presence—R
$-In Touch
$-JC Town Reporter—R
Just Between Us—R
$-KD Gospel Media
Koinonia
$-Kyria—R
$-Lifeglow—R
$-Light & Life
$-Liguorian
$-Live—R
$-Lookout
$-Manna—R
Men.AG.org—R
$-Men of Integrity—R
Men of the Cross
MissionWares
Movieguide
$-New Wineskins—R
($)-NRB Magazine—R
$-Pathway—R
Penned from the Heart—R
Perspectives—R
Regent Global—R
$-Seek—R
$-Significant Living—R
$-St. Anthony Messenger
$-Stewardship—R
Sword of the Lord—R
Trumpeter—R
Unrecognized Woman—R

Victory Herald—R
$-War Cry—R
$-Way of St. Francis—R
$-Wesleyan Life—R
Wisconsin Christian

CHILDREN
$-BREAD/God's Children—R
$-Guide—R
$-Primary Street
$-SHINE brightly—R
$-Sparkle—R

CHRISTIAN EDUCATION/ LIBRARY
$-Group
$-Youth & CE Leadership

DAILY DEVOTIONALS
$-Brink Magazine—R
Penned from the Heart—R

MISSIONS
$-Glad Tidings—R
Lausanne World—R

PASTORS/LEADERS
$-Barefoot—R
$-Catholic Servant
$-Christian Century—R
Christian Education Jour.—R
Disciple Magazine—R
$-Enrichment—R
Great Comm. Research—R
$-Growth Points—R
$-InSite—R
$-Interpreter
$-Leadership—R
Ministry in Motion—R
$-Net Results
$-Proclaim—R
$-RevWriter Resource
$-SmallGroups.com—R
Theological Digest—R
$-Word & World

TEEN/YOUNG ADULT
$-Boundless Webzine—R
$-Devo'Zine—R
$-Direction Student
$-Horizon Student
$-Insight—R

$-J.A.M.
$-TC Magazine
TeensForJC—R
$-Young Salvationist—R

WOMEN
($)-Beyond the Bend—R
Christian Woman's Page—R
Christian Women Today—R
Glory & Strength—R
$-Horizons—R
$-inSpirit—R
$-Journey
Just Between Us—R
$-Link & Visitor—R
$-Mother's Heart—R
P31 Woman—R
Precious Times—R
Virtuous Woman—R
Women of the Cross

DIVORCE
ADULT/GENERAL
American Tract—R
$-Angels on Earth
$-Arlington Catholic
$-Associated Content—R
$-Aujourd'hui Credo—R
$-Bible Advocate—R
$-Catholic Digest—R
CBN.com—R
$-Christian Examiner
Christian Motorsports
Christian Online
Christian Quarterly—R
Christian Ranchman
$-ChristianWeek—R
$-Churchmouse Public.—R
Church of England News
$-Columbia—R
$-Culture Wars—R
$-Earthen Vessel Online—R
Faithwebbin—R
$-Family Smart E-tips—R
$-Gem—R
$-Good News, Etc.—R
Gospel Herald
$-Guide—R
$-Guideposts—R
Halo Magazine—R

$-Home Times—R
($)-HopeKeepers—R
$-In His Presence—R
$-In Touch
Island Catholic—R
$-JC Town Reporter—R
$-KD Gospel Media
Koinonia
$-Kyria—R
$-Lifeglow—R
$-Light & Life
$-Live—R
$-Living—R
$-Living Church
$-Lookout
$-Manna—R
New Heart—R
$-New Wineskins—R
$-Our Sunday Visitor—R
$-ParentLife
Perspectives—R
Priscilla Papers
$-Psychology for Living—R
$-Seek—R
Single Again Mag.—R
$-St. Anthony Messenger
$-Storyteller—R
Trumpeter—R
Unrecognized Woman—R
$-U.S. Catholic—R
$-War Cry—R
Wisconsin Christian
$-World & I—R

CHILDREN
$-Guide—R

MISSIONS
$-Glad Tidings—R

PASTORS/LEADERS
$-Christian Century—R
$-Immerse
$-Interpreter
$-Word & World

TEEN/YOUNG ADULT
$-Direction Student
$-Horizon Student
$-J.A.M.
$-Young Salvationist—R

WOMEN
($)-Beyond the Bend—R
For Every Woman—R
Glory & Strength—R
Hope for Women
$-InspiredMoms—R
$-inSpirit—R
$-Journey
Precious Times—R
Take Root & Write
Unrecognized Woman—R
Women Today—R

DOCTRINAL
ADULT/GENERAL
$-Anglican Journal
$-Atlantic Catholic
$-Aujourd'hui Credo—R
$-B.C. Catholic—R
$-Bible Advocate—R
Bread of Life—R
$-Catholic Insight
CBN.com—R
Christian Media—R
Christian Online
$-Christian Research
$-Christian Standard—R
Creation Care—R
$-Culture Wars—R
$-Earthen Vessel Online—R
E-Channels—R
Evangelical Times
$-Faith & Family
Founders Journal
Gospel Herald
$-Guide—R
Halo Magazine—R
($)-Impact Magazine—R
$-In Touch
$-JC Town Reporter—R
$-KD Gospel Media
Koinonia
Movieguide
$-New Wineskins—R
$-Our Sunday Visitor—R
$-Pathway—R
Perspectives—R
Priscilla Papers
$-Social Justice—R

$-St. Anthony Messenger
Sword and Trumpet
Sword of the Lord—R
Trumpeter—R
$-U.S. Catholic—R
$-Way of St. Francis—R
$-Wesleyan Life—R
Wisconsin Christian

CHILDREN
$-Guide—R

MISSIONS
Intl. Jour./Frontier—R
Missiology

PASTORS/LEADERS
$-Catholic Servant
Disciple Magazine—R
$-Interpreter
Lutheran Forum
Sewanee Theo. Review
Sharing the Practice—R
Theological Digest—R
$-Word & World
$-Worship Leader

TEEN/YOUNG ADULT
$-Direction Student
$-Essential Connection
$-Horizon Student
$-J.A.M.

DVD REVIEWS
ADULT/GENERAL
$-Homeschooling Today—R
$-Mother's Heart—R

WOMEN
$-Brink Magazine—R
Glory & Strength—R

ECONOMICS
ADULT/GENERAL
$-America
$-Associated Content—R
$-Aujourd'hui Credo—R
Brink Online—R
$-Catholic Peace Voice—R
$-CBA Retailers
CBN.com—R

Christian Business
Christian Media—R
Christian Motorsports
Christian Online
Christian Ranchman
$-Christian Renewal—R
$-Christian Retailing
$-ChristianWeek—R
$-City Light News—R
$-Creative Nonfiction
$-Culture Wars—R
Faithwebbin—R
Gospel Herald
Halo Magazine—R
$-Homeschooling Today—R
$-Home Times—R
$-In Touch
Island Catholic—R
$-JC Town Reporter—R
Koinonia
$-Light & Life
$-Live—R
$-Living—R
Men.AG.org—R
Movieguide
($)-NRB E-Magazine—R
$-Our Sunday Visitor—R
Perspectives—R
Regent Global—R
$-Social Justice—R
$-St. Anthony Messenger
Trumpeter—R
Unrecognized Woman—R
Wisconsin Christian
$-World & I—R

PASTORS/LEADERS
$-Today's Parish
$-Word & World

TEEN/YOUNG ADULT
$-Boundless Webzine—R
$-J.A.M.
TeensForJC—R

WOMEN
Empowering Everyday Women
Live Magazine
$-Mother's Heart—R
Unrecognized Woman—R

ENCOURAGEMENT
ADULT/GENERAL
Ambassador
$-Bible Advocate—R
Breakthrough Intercessor—R
$-Bridal Guides—R
$-Brink Magazine—R
$-Catholic Digest—R
$-Catholic Forester—R
CBN.com—R
Central FL Episcopalian
Christian Family Jour.
$-Christian Home & School
Christian Journal—R
Christian Online
Christian Quarterly—R
Christian Ranchman
$-Christian Standard—R
$-Churchmouse Public.—R
$-City Light News—R
Connections Ldrship/MOPS
E-Channels—R
$-Evangel/IN—R
$-Faith & Family
$-Faith & Friends—R
Faithwebbin—R
$-Family Digest—R
$-Gems of Truth—R
Good News Journal—R
Gospel Herald
Halo Magazine—R
$-Homeschooling Today—R
$-Home Times—R
($)-HopeKeepers—R
$-Indian Life—R
$-In His Presence—R
$-In Touch
$-JC Town Reporter—R
Just Between Us—R
$-KD Gospel Media
Keys to Living—R
Koinonia
$-Kyria—R
Leaves—R
$-Lifeglow—R
$-Light & Life
$-Liguorian
$-Live—R
$-Lookout
$-Lutheran Digest—R

$-Manna—R
$-Mature Living
Men of the Cross
MissionWares
($)-Mutuality—R
New Heart—R
New Identity—R
$-New Wineskins—R
$-Ozarks Senior Living—R
$-ParentLife
Pegasus Review—R
Penned from the Heart—R
$-Point—R
PrayerWorks—R
Prison Victory
Regent Global—R
$-River Region's Journey
$-Seek—R
$-Significant Living—R
$-Storyteller—R
Sword of the Lord—R
$-Together—R
Unrecognized Woman—R
Victory Herald—R
$-Victory in Grace—R
$-Vision—R
$-Vista—R
$-Way of St. Francis—R
$-Wesleyan Life—R

CHILDREN
$-BREAD/God's Children—R
$-Cadet Quest—R
$-SHINE brightly—R
Skipping Stones
$-Sparkle—R

CHRISTIAN EDUCATION/ LIBRARY
$-Teachers of Vision—R
$-Youth & CE Leadership

DAILY DEVOTIONALS
$-Brink Magazine—R
Penned from the Heart—R

MISSIONS
$-Glad Tidings—R

PASTORS/LEADERS
Ministry in Motion—R

TEEN/YOUNG ADULT
$-Boundless Webzine—R
$-Direction Student
G4T Ink—R
$-Horizon Student
$-Insight—R
$-J.A.M.
$-Young Christian Writers
$-Young Salvationist—R

WOMEN
Empowering Everyday Women
Extreme Woman
First Lady
For Every Woman—R
Glory & Strength—R
Hope for Women
$-inSpirit—R
$-Journey
Just Between Us—R
$-Mother's Heart—R
P31 Woman—R
$-Pauses . . .
Precious Times—R
Take Root & Write
Together with God—R
Unrecognized Woman—R
Virtuous Woman—R
Women of the Cross

WRITERS
$-Christian Communicator—R
$-Cross & Quill—R
$-Fellowscript—R

ENVIRONMENTAL ISSUES
ADULT/GENERAL
$-America
$-Anglican Journal
$-Animal Trails—R
$-Associated Content—R
$-Aujourd'hui Credo—R
$-Bible Advocate—R
$-Brink Magazine—R
$-Cathedral Age
$-Catholic Peace Voice—R
$-Christian Courier/Canada—R
Christian Online
Christian Outlook
$-ChristianWeek—R
$-Churchmouse Public.—R

$-Common Ground—R
$-Covenant Companion—R
Creation Care—R
$-Creation Illust.—R
$-Creative Nonfiction
Desert Call—R
$-Disaster News
$-Faith Today—R
Gospel Herald
$-Guide—R
Halo Magazine—R
($)-HopeKeepers—R
$-In Touch
$-JC Town Reporter—R
$-KD Gospel Media
Koinonia
$-Light & Life
$-Liguorian
$-Living—R
$-Living Church
$-Lookout
New Identity—R
$-New Wineskins—R
$-Our Sunday Visitor—R
$-ParentLife
Pegasus Review—R
Perspectives—R
Perspectives/Science
$-Prairie Messenger—R
$-Presbyterian Outlook
$-Prism
Ruminate
$-Search
$-Seek—R
$-St. Anthony Messenger
Trumpeter—R
Unrecognized Woman—R
$-U.S. Catholic—R
$-War Cry—R
$-Way of St. Francis—R
Wisconsin Christian
$-World & I—R

CHILDREN
$-Guide—R
$-New Moon—R
$-Pockets—R
$-SHINE brightly—R
Skipping Stones
$-Sparkle—R

CHRISTIAN EDUCATION/ LIBRARY
Jour./Research on Christian Ed.
$-Momentum

PASTORS/LEADERS
$-Christian Century—R
$-InSite—R
$-Interpreter
$-RevWriter Resource
$-Word & World

TEEN/YOUNG ADULT
$-Boundless Webzine—R
$-Devo'Zine—R
$-J.A.M.
$-TC Magazine
TeensForJC—R
$-Young Salvationist—R

WOMEN
$-Horizons—R
$-inSpirit—R
Share
Unrecognized Woman—R

ESSAYS
ADULT/GENERAL
African Voices—R
$-America
$-Arlington Catholic
$-Associated Content—R
Books & Culture
$-Cathedral Age
$-Catholic Digest—R
$-Catholic Peace Voice—R
$-Chicken Soup Books—R
$-Christian Courier/Canada—R
$-Christianity Today—R
Christian Online
$-Christian Renewal—R
$-Churchmouse Public.—R
$-Columbia—R
$-Company Magazine—R
$-Covenant Companion—R
Creation Care—R
$-Creative Nonfiction
$-Culture Wars—R
$-Direction
$-Earthen Vessel Online—R
$-Faith Today—R

Faithwebbin—R
$-Gem—R
Gospel Herald
Halo Magazine—R
Heartland Gatekeeper—R
($)-HopeKeepers—R
($)-Impact Magazine—R
$-In Touch
Island Catholic—R
$-JC Town Reporter—R
Koinonia
$-Lifeglow—R
$-Liguorian
$-Lutheran Digest—R
$-Marriage Partnership
($)-Mutuality—R
New Christian Voices
$-New Wineskins—R
Nostalgia—R
$-Our Sunday Visitor—R
$-Ozarks Senior Living—R
Penwood Review
$-Precepts for Living
$-Prism
Ruminate
$-Search
$-Seek—R
Spirituality for Today
$-Spiritual Life
$-St. Anthony Messenger
$-Storyteller—R
$-This I Believe
Tiferet—R
Tri-State Voice
Trumpeter—R
$-U.S. Catholic—R
$-War Cry—R
$-Way of St. Francis—R
$-World & I—R
$-Written
Xavier Review

CHILDREN
$-Nature Friend—R
$-New Moon—R
Skipping Stones

CHRISTIAN EDUCATION/ LIBRARY
$-Journal/Adventist Ed.—R

MISSIONS
$-Evangelical Missions—R
$-Glad Tidings—R
$-PFI Global—R
Railroad Evangelist—R

MUSIC
$-Creator—R

PASTORS/LEADERS
$-Catholic Servant
$-Christian Century—R
CrossCurrents
$-Immerse
Jour./Pastoral Care
Lutheran Forum
$-Priest
Theological Digest—R
$-Torch Legacy Leader
$-Word & World
$-YouthWorker

TEEN/YOUNG ADULT
$-TC Magazine
TeensForJC—R
$-Young Christian Writers

WOMEN
Christian Woman's Page—R
$-Dabbling Mum—R
Extreme Woman
Handmaidens
$-Horizons—R
$-Pauses . . .

WRITERS
$-Adv. Christian Writer—R
$-Christian Communicator—R
$-Writer
$-Writer's Chronicle
$-Writer's Digest

ETHICS
ADULT/GENERAL
$-America
$-Angels on Earth
$-Associated Content—R
$-Aujourd'hui Credo—R
$-Brink Magazine—R
$-Cathedral Age
$-Catholic Digest—R

$-Catholic Insight
$-Catholic Peace Voice—R
CBN.com—R
$-Celebrate Life—R
$-Christian Courier/Canada—R
$-Christian Examiner
Christian Media—R
Christian Observer
Christian Online
Christian Ranchman
$-Christian Renewal—R
$-Christian Research
$-Christian Standard—R
$-ChristianWeek—R
$-Churchmouse Public.—R
Church of England News
$-Columbia—R
Creation Care—R
$-Creative Nonfiction
$-Cresset
$-Culture Wars—R
Desert Call—R
Desert Voice—R
E-Channels—R
$-Eureka Street
$-Faith Today—R
$-Good News, Etc.—R
Gospel Herald
Halo Magazine—R
$-In His Presence—R
$-Interim—R
$-In Touch
Island Catholic—R
$-JC Town Reporter—R
Koinonia
$-Lifeglow—R
$-Light & Life
$-Liguorian
$-Live—R
$-Living Church
$-Lookout
$-Manna—R
Men.AG.org—R
$-Men of Integrity—R
MissionWares
Movieguide
New Heart—R
$-New Wineskins—R
Nostalgia—R
($)-NRB E-Magazine—R

$-Our Sunday Visitor—R
$-Pathway—R
Perspectives—R
Perspectives/Science
$-Prairie Messenger—R
$-Presbyterian Outlook
Priscilla Papers
$-Prism
Regent Global—R
$-Search
$-Seek—R
$-Social Justice—R
$-St. Anthony Messenger
Trumpeter—R
Unrecognized Woman—R
$-War Cry—R
$-Way of St. Francis—R
$-World & I—R

CHILDREN
$-BREAD/God's Children—R
$-New Moon—R
Skipping Stones

CHRISTIAN EDUCATION/ LIBRARY
Christian Librarian—R
Jour./Research on Christian Ed.

DAILY DEVOTIONALS
$-Brink Magazine—R
Penned from the Heart—R

MISSIONS
$-Glad Tidings—R

PASTORS/LEADERS
$-Christian Century—R
$-Clergy Journal—R
CrossCurrents
Disciple Magazine—R
$-Enrichment—R
$-Immerse
$-Interpreter
Jour./Pastoral Care
Lutheran Forum
$-Ministry Today
Sewanee Theo. Review
Sharing the Practice—R
Theological Digest—R
$-Word & World

TEEN/YOUNG ADULT
$-Boundless Webzine—R
$-Devo'Zine—R
$-Direction Student
$-Horizon Student
$-Risen
TeensForJC—R
$-Young Salvationist—R

WOMEN
$-At the Center—R
Women Today—R

ETHNIC/CULTURAL PIECES
ADULT/GENERAL
African Voices—R
$-America
$-Arlington Catholic
$-Associated Content—R
$-Aujourd'hui Credo—R
$-Brink Magazine—R
$-Canada Lutheran—R
$-Catholic Digest—R
$-Catholic Peace Voice—R
$-CBA Retailers
CBN.com—R
$-Celebrate Life—R
$-Christian Citizen USA
$-Christian Courier/Canada—R
$-Christian Home & School
Christian Online
$-ChristianWeek—R
$-Churchmouse Public.—R
$-Columbia—R
$-Commonweal
$-Creative Nonfiction
Desert Call—R
Desert Voice—R
E-Channels—R
$-EFCA Today
Encompass
$-Enfoque a la Familia
$-Episcopal Life—R
$-Eureka Street
$-Faith Today—R
Faithwebbin—R
Foursquare Leader
$-Gem—R

$-Good News—R
Good News!
$-Good News, Etc.—R
$-Good News, The—R
Gospel Herald
$-Gospel Today—R
$-Guide—R
Halo Magazine—R
$-Haruah—R
($)-Impact Magazine—R
$-Indian Life—R
$-In Touch
$-JC Town Reporter—R
$-KD Gospel Media
Koinonia
$-Lifeglow—R
$-Light & Life
$-Live—R
$-Lookout
$-Manna—R
$-Men of Integrity—R
$-MESSAGE
Messianic Perspectives—R
Movieguide
($)-Mutuality—R
New Identity—R
$-New Wineskins—R
Nostalgia—R
$-Our Sunday Visitor—R
$-ParentLife
Penned from the Heart—R
$-Prairie Messenger—R
Priscilla Papers
$-Prism
Purpose Magazine—R
$-Salvo
Saved Magazine
SCP Journal
$-Search
$-Seek—R
Spirituality for Today
$-St. Anthony Messenger
$-Together—R
Trumpeter—R
Unrecognized Woman—R
$-Upscale
$-War Cry—R
$-Way of St. Francis—R
$-Wesleyan Life—R
$-World & I—R

$-Written
Xavier Review

CHILDREN
$-BREAD/God's Children—R
$-Faces
$-Guide—R
$-New Moon—R
Skipping Stones
$-Sparkle—R

CHRISTIAN EDUCATION/ LIBRARY
$-Momentum
$-Teachers of Vision—R

DAILY DEVOTIONALS
$-Brink Magazine—R
Penned from the Heart—R

MISSIONS
East-West Church
$-Evangelical Missions—R
$-Glad Tidings—R
Intl. Jour./Frontier—R
Missiology
($)-Operation Reveille—R
Women of the Harvest

PASTORS/LEADERS
$-Barefoot—R
$-Christian Century—R
Disciple Magazine—R
$-Enrichment—R
$-Interpreter
Jour./Pastoral Care
$-Ministry Today
$-Net Results
$-Torch Legacy Leader
$-Worship Leader

TEEN/YOUNG ADULT
$-Boundless Webzine—R
$-Devo'Zine—R
$-Essential Connection
TeensForJC—R
$-Young Salvationist—R

WOMEN
Grace Today
$-Heart & Soul
$-Horizons—R
$-inSpirit—R
$-Link & Visitor—R

Precious Times—R
$-SpiritLed Woman

EVANGELISM/ WITNESSING
ADULT/GENERAL
Ambassador
$-America
American Tract—R
$-Anglican Journal
$-Aujourd'hui Credo—R
$-Bible Advocate—R
Breakthrough Intercessor—R
$-Brink Magazine—R
$-Catholic Telegraph
$-Catholic Yearbook—R
CBN.com—R
Central FL Episcopalian
Christian Courier/WI—R
$-Christian Home & School
$-Christianity Today—R
Christian Online
Christian Ranchman
$-Christian Research
$-Christian Standard—R
$-Churchmouse Public.—R
Church of England News
$-Columbia—R
$-Decision
$-Earthen Vessel Online—R
E-Channels—R
$-Episcopal Life—R
$-Evangel/IN—R
$-Faith & Family
$-Faith Today—R
Florida Baptist Witness
$-Gem—R
$-Good News—R
$-Good News, Etc.—R
Good News Today
Gospel Herald
$-Guide—R
Halo Magazine—R
Heartbeat/CMA
$-In His Presence—R
$-In Touch
$-JC Town Reporter—R
$-KD Gospel Media
Koinonia
Leaves—R

$-Light & Life
$-Live—R
$-Living Church
$-Lookout
$-Lutheran Journal—R
$-Manna—R
Men.AG.org—R
$-Men of Integrity—R
MESSAGE/Open Bible—R
Messianic Perspectives—R
New Heart—R
$-New Wineskins—R
$-On Mission
$-Our Sunday Visitor—R
$-ParentLife
$-Pathway—R
Penned from the Heart—R
$-Point—R
$-Power for Living—R
PrayerWorks—R
$-Priority!—R
Regent Global—R
$-Seek—R
Sharing—R
Spirituality for Today
$-St. Anthony Messenger
Sword of the Lord—R
$-Testimony—R
Trumpeter—R
Victory Herald—R
$-War Cry—R
$-Way of St. Francis—R
$-Wesleyan Life—R
Wisconsin Christian

CHILDREN
$-BREAD/God's Children—R
$-Focus/Clubhouse Jr.
$-Guide—R
$-JuniorWay
$-Sparkle—R

CHRISTIAN EDUCATION/ LIBRARY
$-Group
$-Kids' Ministry Ideas—R
$-Youth & CE Leadership

DAILY DEVOTIONALS
$-Brink Magazine—R
Penned from the Heart—R

MISSIONS

East-West Church
$-Evangelical Missions—R
$-Glad Tidings—R
Intl. Jour./Frontier—R
Lausanne World—R
$-Leaders for Today
Missiology
($)-Operation Reveille—R

MUSIC

Christian Music—R

PASTORS/LEADERS

$-Catholic Servant
$-Cook Partners
Disciple Magazine—R
$-Enrichment—R
Great Comm. Research—R
$-Growth Points—R
$-Immerse
$-Interpreter
$-Leadership—R
$-Let's Worship
Ministry in Motion—R
$-Ministry Today
$-Outreach—R
$-RevWriter Resource
Rick Warren's Ministry—R
$-SmallGroups.com—R

TEEN/YOUNG ADULT

$-Boundless Webzine—R
$-Devo'Zine—R
$-Essential Connection
$-Insight—R
$-J.A.M.
$-TC Magazine
TeensForJC—R
$-TG Magazine
$-Young Salvationist—R

WOMEN

Extreme Woman
$-inSpirit—R
$-Journey
Just Between Us—R
$-Link & Visitor—R
P31 Woman—R
Precious Times—R
Share
$-SpiritLed Woman

EXEGESIS

ADULT/GENERAL

$-Alive Now—R
$-Aujourd'hui Credo—R
$-Bible Advocate—R
$-Catholic Insight
CBN.com—R
Christian Ranchman
$-Christian Standard—R
$-Earthen Vessel Online—R
E-Channels—R
Halo Magazine—R
$-In Touch
$-JC Town Reporter—R
Koinonia
$-Lifeglow—R
$-Living Church
Messianic Perspectives—R
$-Our Sunday Visitor—R
Perspectives—R
Priscilla Papers
Regent Global—R
$-Social Justice—R
$-St. Anthony Messenger
Sword and Trumpet
Sword of the Lord—R
Trumpeter—R
$-U.S. Catholic—R
$-Way of St. Francis—R
$-Wesleyan Life—R
Wisconsin Christian

MISSIONS

$-Glad Tidings—R

PASTORS/LEADERS

Disciple Magazine—R
$-Enrichment—R
$-Immerse
Lutheran Forum
Theological Digest—R

TEEN/YOUNG ADULT

$-Boundless Webzine—R
$-Young Adult Today

FAITH

ADULT/GENERAL

African Voices—R
$-America
$-Arkansas Catholic—R

$-Aujourd'hui Credo—R
Believer's Bay
$-Bible Advocate—R
Bread of Life—R
Breakthrough Intercessor—R
$-Brink Magazine—R
Brink Online—R
byFaith
$-Canada Lutheran—R
($)-Canadian Mennonite—R
$-Catholic Digest—R
$-Catholic Insight
$-Catholic Peace Voice—R
$-Catholic Yearbook—R
CBN.com—R
$-Christian Courier/Canada—R
Christian Family Jour.
$-Christian Home & School
$-Christianity Today—R
Christian Journal—R
Christian Online
Christian Quarterly—R
$-Christian Research
$-Christian Retailing
$-Christian Standard—R
$-ChristianWeek—R
Church Herald & Holiness—R
$-Churchmouse Public.—R
Church of England News
$-City Light News—R
$-Columbia—R
$-Covenant Companion—R
Desert Call—R
Desert Voice—R
$-Direction
Disciple's Journal—R
$-Earthen Vessel Online—R
E-Channels—R
Eternal Ink—R
$-Faith & Family
$-Faith & Friends—R
$-Family Digest—R
$-Gem—R
$-Good News, The—R
Gospel Herald
$-Guide—R
Halo Magazine—R
$-Haruah—R
Highway News—R
$-Home Times—R

Hope for Women
($)-HopeKeepers—R
$-Indian Life—R
$-In His Presence—R
$-In Touch
$-JC Town Reporter—R
Just Between Us—R
$-KD Gospel Media
Koinonia
$-Kyria—R
$-Lifeglow—R
LifeTimes Catholic
$-Light & Life
$-Liguorian
$-Live—R
$-Lookout
$-Lutheran Digest—R
$-Lutheran Journal—R
$-Manna—R
Men.AG.org—R
$-Men of Integrity—R
Messianic Perspectives—R
$-Miracles, Healings—R
New Christian Voices
New Heart—R
New Identity—R
$-New Wineskins—R
$-Now What?—R
$-Our Sunday Visitor—R
$-ParentLife
Pegasus Review—R
Penned from the Heart—R
$-Point—R
$-Prairie Messenger—R
PrayerWorks—R
Priscilla Papers
Prison Victory
$-Psychology for Living—R
$-Purpose—R
$-Seek—R
$-Social Justice—R
Spirituality for Today
$-St. Anthony Messenger
SW Kansas Faith
Sword and Trumpet
Sword of the Lord—R
$-Testimony—R
$-Together—R
Trumpeter—R
$-United Church Observer—R

Unrecognized Woman—R
$-Victory in Grace—R
$-Vista—R
$-Way of St. Francis—R
$-Weavings—R
$-Wesleyan Life—R
$-World & I—R

CHILDREN
$-BREAD/God's Children—R
$-Focus/Clubhouse Jr.
$-Guide—R
$-JuniorWay
$-Our Little Friend—R
$-Primary Street
$-Primary Treasure—R
$-SHINE brightly—R
$-Sparkle—R

CHRISTIAN EDUCATION/ LIBRARY
Catholic Library
$-Children's Ministry
Christian Librarian—R
$-Group
$-Momentum
$-Youth & CE Leadership

DAILY DEVOTIONALS
$-Brink Magazine—R
Penned from the Heart—R

MISSIONS
East-West Church
$-Glad Tidings—R
Lausanne World—R

MUSIC
Christian Music—R

PASTORS/LEADERS
Disciple Magazine—R
$-Immerse
$-Interpreter
$-Ministry Today
Plugged In
$-Proclaim—R
$-RevWriter Resource
$-SmallGroups.com—R
$-Worship Leader

TEEN/YOUNG ADULT
$-Boundless Webzine—R
$-Devo'Zine—R

$-Direction Student
G4T Ink—R
$-Horizon Student
$-Insight—R
$-J.A.M.
$-Risen
$-TC Magazine
TeensForJC—R
$-TG Magazine
$-Young Adult Today
$-Young Christian Writers
$-Young Salvationist—R

WOMEN
($)-Beyond the Bend—R
Christian Woman's Page—R
Chris. Work at Home Moms—R
Extreme Woman
For Every Woman—R
Glory & Strength—R
Hope for Women
$-Horizons—R
$-inSpirit—R
$-Journey
Just Between Us—R
Life Tools for Women
Love, Pearls & Swine
$-Mother's Heart—R
P31 Woman—R
$-Pauses . . .
$-SpiritLed Woman
Take Root & Write
Unrecognized Woman—R
Virtuous Woman—R
Women of the Cross
Women Today—R

WRITERS
Areopagus

FAMILY LIFE
ADULT/GENERAL
$-Abilities
African Voices—R
$-America
$-Angels on Earth
Anointed Pages
$-Arkansas Catholic—R
$-Arlington Catholic
$-Associated Content—R

$-Atlantic Catholic
$-Aujourd'hui Credo—R
$-Australian Catholics—R
$-B.C. Catholic—R
Believer's Bay
Bread of Life—R
$-Brink Magazine—R
byFaith
$-Canada Lutheran—R
$-Catholic Digest—R
$-Catholic Forester—R
$-Catholic Insight
CBN.com—R
$-Chicken Soup Books—R
$-Christian Courier/Canada—R
Christian Courier/WI—R
Christian Family Jour.
$-Christian Home & School
Christian Journal—R
Christian Online
Christian Quarterly—R
Christian Ranchman
$-Christian Renewal—R
$-ChristianWeek—R
Church Herald & Holiness—R
$-Churchmouse Public.—R
$-City Light News—R
$-Columbia—R
Connecting Point—R
$-Covenant Companion—R
Creation Care—R
$-Creative Nonfiction
$-Culture Wars—R
Desert Call—R
Desert Voice—R
Disciple's Journal—R
E-Channels—R
Eternal Ink—R
$-Faith & Family
$-Faith & Friends—R
Faithwebbin—R
$-Family Digest—R
$-Family Smart E-tips—R
Foursquare Leader
$-Gem—R
$-Good News, Etc.—R
Good News Journal—R
$-Good News, The—R
Gospel Herald
$-Guide—R

$-Guideposts—R
Halo Magazine—R
HEARTLIGHT Internet—R
Highway News—R
$-Homeschooling Today—R
$-Home Times—R
$-Indian Life—R
$-In His Presence—R
$-In Touch
$-JC Town Reporter—R
Just Between Us—R
$-KD Gospel Media
Keys to Living—R
Koinonia
$-Kyria—R
$-Lifeglow—R
LifeSite News
LifeTimes Catholic
$-Liguorian
$-Live—R
$-Living—R
$-Living Church
$-Living Light—R
$-Lookout
$-Lutheran Digest—R
$-Lutheran Witness
$-Manna—R
$-Marriage Partnership
$-Mature Years—R
Men.AG.org—R
$-Men of Integrity—R
Men of the Cross
($)-Mennonite Historian—R
$-Messenger/St. Anthony
($)-Mutuality—R
New Christian Voices
New Identity—R
$-New Wineskins—R
Nostalgia—R
$-Our Sunday Visitor—R
$-Over the Back Fence—R
$-ParentLife
$-Pathway—R
Pegasus Review—R
Penned from the Heart—R
$-Pentecostal Evangel—R
$-Point—R
$-Power for Living—R
$-Prairie Messenger—R
PrayerWorks—R

Priscilla Papers
Prison Victory
$-Psychology for Living—R
$-Purpose—R
Quaker Life—R
$-Rev Up Your Life
$-River Region's Journey
$-Search
$-Seek—R
$-Significant Living—R
Single Again Mag.—R
$-Social Justice—R
$-Special Living—R
Spirituality for Today
$-St. Anthony Messenger
$-Storyteller—R
SW Kansas Faith
Sword and Trumpet
Sword of the Lord—R
$-Testimony—R
$-Thriving Family
$-Together—R
Trumpeter—R
$-United Church Observer—R
Unrecognized Woman—R
$-Vibrant Life—R
$-Victory in Grace—R
$-Vision—R
$-Vista—R
$-War Cry—R
$-Way of St. Francis—R
$-Wesleyan Life—R
Wisconsin Christian
$-World & I—R

CHILDREN
$-BREAD/God's Children—R
$-Focus/Clubhouse
$-Focus/Clubhouse Jr.
$-Guide—R
$-JuniorWay
$-New Moon—R
$-Pockets—R
$-Sparkle—R

CHRISTIAN EDUCATION/ LIBRARY
$-Children's Ministry
$-Group
$-Youth & CE Leadership

DAILY DEVOTIONALS
Penned from the Heart—R

MISSIONS
$-Glad Tidings—R
Women of the Harvest

PASTORS/LEADERS
$-Catholic Servant
$-Enrichment—R
$-Immerse
$-InSite—R
$-Interpreter
Jour./Pastoral Care
Ministry in Motion—R
$-Ministry Today
$-Preaching Well—R
$-RevWriter Resource
$-Today's Parish
$-Word & World

TEEN/YOUNG ADULT
$-Direction Student
$-Horizon Student
$-Insight—R
$-J.A.M.
$-TC Magazine
TeensForJC—R
$-Young Adult Today
$-Young Christian Writers
$-Young Salvationist—R

WOMEN
Christian Woman
Christian Woman's Page—R
Chris. Work at Home Moms—R
$-Dabbling Mum—R
Extreme Woman
For Every Woman—R
$-Girlfriend 2 Girlfriend
Glory & Strength—R
Hope for Women
$-Horizons—R
$-InspiredMoms—R
$-inSpirit—R
$-Journey
Just Between Us—R
Life Tools for Women
$-Link & Visitor—R
Live Magazine
Lutheran Woman's Quar.
$-MomSense—R

$-Mother's Heart—R
P31 Woman—R
$-Pauses . . .
Precious Times—R
Share
$-SpiritLed Woman
Take Root & Write
Together with God—R
Unrecognized Woman—R
Virtuous Woman—R
Women of the Cross
Women Today—R

FEATURE ARTICLES
ADULT/GENERAL
$-Bible Advocate—R
Breakthrough Intercessor—R
$-Canada Lutheran—R
$-Churchmouse Public.—R
$-Columbia—R
$-Earthen Vessel Online—R
$-Faith Today—R
Just Between Us—R
$-Lifeglow—R
$-Mother's Heart—R
Unrecognized Woman—R

CHILDREN
$-Sparkle—R

CHRISTIAN EDUCATION/
LIBRARY
$-Animal Trails—R
$-Churchmouse Public.—R
$-EFCA Today
Koinonia
$-Momentum
$-Precepts for Living
$-Seek—R

WOMEN
$-Brink Magazine—R
Glory & Strength—R
Onyx Woman
Take Root & Write

FILLERS: ANECDOTES
ADULT/GENERAL
$-Alive Now—R
$-Angels on Earth
$-Animal Trails—R
Breakthrough Intercessor—R

$-Bridal Guides—R
$-Catholic Digest—R
$-Catholic Yearbook—R
Christian Journal—R
Christian Motorsports
Christian Quarterly—R
Christian Ranchman
$-Christian Response—R
Church Herald & Holiness—R
$-City Light News—R
Desert Call—R
Disciple's Journal—R
E-Channels—R
Eternal Ink—R
$-Family Digest—R
Foursquare Leader
$-Gem—R
Good News Journal—R
Halo Magazine—R
HEARTLIGHT Internet—R
Highway News—R
$-Homeschooling Today—R
$-Home Times—R
($)-Impact Magazine—R
$-In His Presence—R
$-JC Town Reporter—R
$-Lutheran Digest—R
$-Lutheran Journal—R
$-Manna—R
Movieguide
New Heart—R
$-Pentecostal Evangel—R
Prison Victory
$-Purpose—R
$-Significant Living—R
Single Again Mag.—R
Spirituality for Today
$-St. Anthony Messenger
Victory Herald—R
$-Vista—R
$-War Cry—R

CHILDREN
Skipping Stones

CHRISTIAN EDUCATION/
LIBRARY
Christian Librarian—R

MISSIONS
Railroad Evangelist—R

MUSIC
$-Creator—R

PASTORS/LEADERS
$-Barefoot—R
$-Enrichment—R
$-Leadership—R
$-PreachingToday.com
$-Preaching Well—R
Sharing the Practice—R
$-Sunday Sermons—R

TEEN/YOUNG ADULT
$-Young Christian—R
$-Young Salvationist—R

WOMEN
($)-Beyond the Bend—R
Christian Woman's Page—R
Extreme Woman
Glory & Strength—R
Just Between Us—R
$-Mother's Heart—R
Right to the Heart—R
Virtuous Woman—R

WRITERS
$-Canadian Writer's Jour.—R
$-Cross & Quill—R
$-Fellowscript—R
$-New Writer's Mag.
NW Christian Author—R
$-Tickled by Thunder
Write Connection
$-Writers' Journal

FILLERS: CARTOONS
ADULT/GENERAL
African Voices—R
American Tract—R
$-Angels on Earth
$-Animal Trails—R
$-Bridal Guides—R
$-Catholic Digest—R
$-Christian Citizen USA
Christian Computing—R
$-Christian Herald—R
Christian Journal—R
Christian Motorsports
Christian Quarterly—R
Christian Ranchman
$-Churchmouse Public.—R

$-City Light News—R
Connecting Point—R
$-Culture Wars—R
Disciple's Journal—R
E-Channels—R
$-Eureka Street
$-Evangel/IN—R
Evangel/OR—R
$-Faith & Friends—R
Foursquare Leader
$-Gem—R
Good News Journal—R
$-Gospel Today—R
$-Guide—R
Halo Magazine—R
HEARTLIGHT Internet—R
Highway News—R
$-Homeschooling Today—R
$-Home Times—R
 ($)-Impact Magazine—R
$-In His Presence—R
$-Interchange
$-Interim—R
$-JC Town Reporter—R
Light of the World
$-Liguorian
$-Lutheran Digest—R
$-Mature Years—R
Movieguide
New Heart—R
Pegasus Review—R
$-Power for Living—R
$-Presbyterians Today—R
Prison Victory
$-Significant Living—R
$-Special Living—R
$-St. Anthony Messenger
$-Storyteller—R
Trumpeter—R
$-United Church Observer—R

CHILDREN
$-American Girl—R
$-Guide—R
$-SHINE brightly—R
Skipping Stones

CHRISTIAN EDUCATION/ LIBRARY
$-Children's Ministry
Christian Librarian—R

$-Group
$-Journal/Adventist Ed.—R
$-Teachers of Vision—R
$-Today's Catholic Teacher—R
$-Youth & CE Leadership

MISSIONS
$-Glad Tidings—R
Mission Frontiers
Railroad Evangelist—R

MUSIC
Christian Music—R
$-Creator—R

PASTORS/LEADERS
$-Barefoot—R
$-Catholic Servant
$-Christian Century—R
$-Diocesan Dialogue—R
$-Enrichment—R
$-Leadership—R
$-Priest
Sharing the Practice—R
$-SmallGroups.com—R
$-Your Church—R

TEEN/YOUNG ADULT
G4T Ink—R
$-Listen—R
TeensForJC—R
$-Young Christian—R
$-Young Salvationist—R

WOMEN
Extreme Woman
Glory & Strength—R
Take Root & Write

WRITERS
$-Canadian Writer's Jour.—R
$-Cross & Quill—R
$-New Writer's Mag.
$-Writer
$-Writers' Journal

FILLERS: FACTS
ADULT/GENERAL
$-Animal Trails—R
Bread of Life—R
$-Bridal Guides—R
$-Catholic Digest—R
$-Catholic Yearbook—R

$-Christian Herald—R
Christian Motorsports
Christian Ranchman
$-Christian Response—R
$-City Light News—R
Desert Call—R
Disciple's Journal—R
$-Gem—R
Halo Magazine—R
Highway News—R
$-Homeschooling Today—R
$-Home Times—R
$-Interchange
$-JC Town Reporter—R
$-Lutheran Digest—R
$-Lutheran Journal—R
MESSAGE/Open Bible—R
Movieguide
$-Pentecostal Evangel—R
PrayerWorks—R
Prison Victory
$-Significant Living—R
Single Again Mag.—R
$-St. Anthony Messenger
Sword and Trumpet
Sword of the Lord—R
Unrecognized Woman—R
$-Vista—R
$-Written

CHILDREN
$-Nature Friend—R

*CHRISTIAN EDUCATION/
LIBRARY*
$-Kids' Ministry Ideas—R
$-Teachers of Vision—R
$-Today's Catholic Teacher—R

MISSIONS
$-Boundless Webzine—R
($)-Operation Reveille—R

PASTORS/LEADERS
$-Enrichment—R
$-Interpreter

TEEN/YOUNG ADULT
TeensForJC—R
$-TG Magazine
$-Young Christian—R
$-Young Salvationist—R

WOMEN
($)-Beyond the Bend—R
Christian Woman's Page—R
Extreme Woman
Glory & Strength—R
$-Mother's Heart—R
Unrecognized Woman—R
Virtuous Woman—R

WRITERS
Areopagus
$-New Writer's Mag.
Write Connection
$-Writers' Journal

FILLERS: GAMES
ADULT/GENERAL
$-Catholic Yearbook—R
$-CGA World—R
$-Christian Citizen USA
$-Christian Herald—R
Christian Motorsports
Christian Ranchman
Connecting Point—R
Disciple's Journal—R
$-Faith & Friends—R
$-Family Smart E-tips—R
$-Gem—R
$-Guide—R
Halo Magazine—R
HEARTLIGHT Internet—R
$-JC Town Reporter—R
$-Lutheran Journal—R
Movieguide
Prison Victory
Victory Herald—R

CHILDREN
$-American Girl—R
$-Guide—R
$-Pockets—R
$-SHINE brightly—R
$-Sparkle—R

*CHRISTIAN EDUCATION/
LIBRARY*
$-Group
$-Kids' Ministry Ideas—R

MISSIONS
$-Glad Tidings—R

PASTORS/LEADERS
$-Barefoot—R

TEEN/YOUNG ADULT
$-Listen—R
TeensForJC—R
$-Young Salvationist—R

FILLERS: IDEAS
ADULT/GENERAL
$-Animal Trails—R
$-Bridal Guides—R
$-CGA World—R
$-Christian Home & School
Christian Motorsports
Christian Quarterly—R
Christian Ranchman
Disciple's Journal—R
Evangel/OR—R
$-Family Smart E-tips—R
$-Gem—R
Halo Magazine—R
HEARTLIGHT Internet—R
Highway News—R
$-Homeschooling Today—R
$-Home Times—R
$-JC Town Reporter—R
Just Between Us—R
$-KD Gospel Media
$-Manna—R
Movieguide
New Identity—R
Prison Victory
$-Seek—R
Single Again Mag.—R

*CHRISTIAN EDUCATION/
LIBRARY*
$-Children's Ministry
Christian Librarian—R
Congregational Libraries
$-Group
$-Preschool Playhouse (CE)
$-Youth & CE Leadership

MISSIONS
$-Evangelical Missions—R
Mission Connection

MUSIC
$-Creator—R

PASTORS/LEADERS
$-Barefoot—R
$-Interpreter
$-Preaching Well—R
$-RevWriter Resource
$-Small Groups.com—R

TEEN/YOUNG ADULT
$-Young Christian—R

WOMEN
($)-Beyond the Bend—R
Christian Woman's Page—R
Empowering Everyday Women
Just Between Us—R
$-Mother's Heart—R
P31 Woman—R
Right to the Heart—R
Virtuous Woman—R

WRITERS
Areopagus
$-Canadian Writer's Jour.—R
Dedicated Author
$-Tickled by Thunder
Write Connection
$-Writers' Journal

FILLERS: JOKES
ADULT/GENERAL
$-Catholic Digest—R
Christian Journal—R
Christian Motorsports
Christian Ranchman
$-City Light News—R
Desert Voice—R
Disciple's Journal—R
Eternal Ink—R
$-Faith & Friends—R
$-Gem—R
Good News Journal—R
Halo Magazine—R
HEARTLIGHT Internet—R
$-Home Times—R
($)-Impact Magazine—R
$-In His Presence—R
$-Interchange
$-JC Town Reporter—R
Light of the World
$-Liguorian
$-Lutheran Digest—R

$-Mature Years—R
$-Miracles, Healings—R
Movieguide
New Heart—R
PrayerWorks—R
Prison Victory
$-Significant Living—R
Single Again Mag.—R
$-St. Anthony Messenger

MUSIC
$-Creator—R

PASTORS/LEADERS
$-Preaching Well—R
Sharing the Practice—R

TEEN/YOUNG ADULT
G4T Ink—R
TeensForJC—R

WOMEN
Extreme Woman
Virtuous Woman—R

WRITERS
Write Connection
$-Writers' Journal

FILLERS: KID QUOTES
ADULT/GENERAL
$-Animal Trails—R
$-Bridal Guides—R
Christian Journal—R
Desert Voice—R
Eternal Ink—R
Halo Magazine—R
Highway News—R
$-Home Times—R
$-Indian Life—R
$-JC Town Reporter—R
$-KD Gospel Media
Movieguide
Single Again Mag.—R
$-Upscale
Victory Herald—R

CHRISTIAN EDUCATION/ LIBRARY
$-Children's Ministry
Christian Early Ed.—R

WOMEN
$-Mother's Heart—R

FILLERS: NEWSBREAKS
ADULT/GENERAL
$-Anglican Journal
$-Arkansas Catholic—R
$-B.C. Catholic—R
$-Catholic Telegraph
Christian Journal—R
Christian Motorsports
Christian Ranchman
$-Christian Renewal—R
$-City Light News—R
Disciple's Journal—R
Evangel/OR—R
Friends Journal—R
$-Gem—R
Halo Magazine—R
HEARTLIGHT Internet—R
Highway News—R
$-Home Times—R
$-JC Town Reporter—R
$-KD Gospel Media
Movieguide
New Identity—R
($)-NRB E-Magazine—R
Prison Victory
Sword and Trumpet
Sword of the Lord—R
$-Vista—R

CHRISTIAN EDUCATION/ LIBRARY
Christian Librarian—R

MISSIONS
($)-Operation Reveille—R

PASTORS/LEADERS
$-Preaching Well—R

WOMEN
Hope for Women

WRITERS
Areopagus
$-New Writer's Mag.
$-Writers' Journal

FILLERS: PARTY IDEAS
ADULT/GENERAL
$-Animal Trails—R
$-Bridal Guides—R
Christian Ranchman

Disciple's Journal—R
Halo Magazine—R
Highway News—R
$-JC Town Reporter—R
$-KD Gospel Media
$-Manna—R
Movieguide
Victory Herald—R

CHILDREN
$-Sparkle—R

**CHRISTIAN EDUCATION/
LIBRARY**
$-Kids' Ministry Ideas—R
$-Youth & CE Leadership

MUSIC
$-Creator—R

PASTORS/LEADERS
$-Barefoot—R

TEEN/YOUNG ADULT
TeensForJC—R
$-Young Christian—R

WOMEN
Hope for Women
P31 Woman—R
Right to the Heart—R
Virtuous Woman—R

FILLERS: PRAYERS
ADULT/GENERAL
$-Alive Now—R
$-Angels on Earth
$-Animal Trails—R
Breakthrough Intercessor—R
$-Bridal Guides—R
$-Catholic Yearbook—R
$-CGA World—R
$-Christian Herald—R
Christian Journal—R
Christian Motorsports
Christian Online
Christian Ranchman
Desert Call—R
Disciple's Journal—R
E-Channels—R
Eternal Ink—R
$-Family Digest—R
$-Gem—R

Good News Journal—R
Halo Magazine—R
HEARTLIGHT Internet—R
Highway News—R
$-Homeschooling Today—R
$-Home Times—R
$-JC Town Reporter—R
LifeTimes Catholic
$-Mature Years—R
Movieguide
PrayerWorks—R
Prison Victory
Single Again Mag.—R
Spirituality for Today
Victory Herald—R
$-Vista—R

CHILDREN
$-SHINE brightly—R
$-Sparkle—R

DAILY DEVOTIONALS
$-Word in Season

MISSIONS
$-Glad Tidings—R

TEEN/YOUNG ADULT
G4T Ink—R
TeensForJC—R
$-TG Magazine
$-Young Christian—R
$-Young Salvationist—R

WOMEN
Glory & Strength—R
Just Between Us—R
Right to the Heart—R
Unrecognized Woman—R
Virtuous Woman—R

WRITERS
$-Cross & Quill—R
Write Connection
$-Writers' Journal

FILLERS: PROSE
ADULT/GENERAL
$-Animal Trails—R
$-Bible Advocate—R
Bread of Life—R
$-Bridal Guides—R
Christian Motorsports

Christian Online
Christian Ranchman
$-Decision
Desert Call—R
Disciple's Journal—R
Eternal Ink—R
Evangel/OR—R
$-Gem—R
Halo Magazine—R
HEARTLIGHT Internet—R
Highway News—R
$-Homeschooling Today—R
$-JC Town Reporter—R
Movieguide
Pegasus Review—R
$-Pentecostal Evangel—R
Prison Victory
$-Purpose—R
Single Again Mag.—R
Sword and Trumpet
Sword of the Lord—R
Victory Herald—R

CHILDREN
$-Partners—R

PASTORS/LEADERS
$-Preaching Well—R

TEEN/YOUNG ADULT
$-Listen—R
TeensForJC—R
$-Young Christian—R

WOMEN
$-Melody of the Heart

WRITERS
Areopagus
$-Freelance Writer's Report—R
Write Connection
$-Writer
$-Writers' Journal

FILLERS: QUIZZES
ADULT/GENERAL
$-Animal Trails—R
$-Bridal Guides—R
$-Catholic Yearbook—R
Christian Motorsports
Christian Online
Christian Ranchman

Church Herald & Holiness—R
Disciple's Journal—R
$-Faith & Friends—R
$-Gem—R
$-Guide—R
Halo Magazine—R
$-Homeschooling Today—R
($)-Impact Magazine—R
$-JC Town Reporter—R
Light of the World
$-Lutheran Journal—R
Movieguide
Prison Victory

CHILDREN
$-Cadet Quest—R
$-Focus/Clubhouse
$-Guide—R
$-Nature Friend—R
$-Partners—R
$-SHINE brightly—R
Skipping Stones
$-Sparkle—R
$-Story Mates—R

CHRISTIAN EDUCATION/ LIBRARY
Christian Education Jour.—R
Disciple Magazine—R
$-Kids' Ministry Ideas—R
Ministry in Motion—R
$-Ministry Today

TEEN/YOUNG ADULT
G4T Ink—R
$-Listen—R
TeensForJC—R
$-TG Magazine
$-Young Christian—R
$-Young Salvationist—R

WOMEN
$-Melody of the Heart
Virtuous Woman—R

WRITERS
$-Writers' Journal

FILLERS: QUOTES
ADULT/GENERAL
$-Alive Now—R
$-Animal Trails—R

Bread of Life—R
$-Bridal Guides—R
$-Catholic Digest—R
$-Catholic Yearbook—R
$-Christian Herald—R
Christian Journal—R
Christian Motorsports
Christian Quarterly—R
Christian Ranchman
$-Christian Response—R
$-Culture Wars—R
Desert Call—R
Desert Voice—R
Disciple's Journal—R
$-Faith & Friends—R
$-Family Smart E-tips—R
$-Gem—R
Halo Magazine—R
HEARTLIGHT Internet—R
$-Homeschooling Today—R
$-Home Times—R
$-Indian Life—R
$-JC Town Reporter—R
$-Lutheran Journal—R
MESSAGE/Open Bible—R
Movieguide
New Identity—R
Pegasus Review—R
PrayerWorks—R
Prison Victory
$-Seek—R
Spirituality for Today
$-St. Anthony Messenger
$-Storyteller—R
Unrecognized Woman—R
$-Vista—R
$-Written

CHILDREN
$-Partners—R
Skipping Stones

MISSIONS
Railroad Evangelist—R

TEEN/YOUNG ADULT
$-TG Magazine
$-Young Christian—R

WOMEN
($)-Beyond the Bend—R
Glory & Strength—R

Just Between Us—R
Right to the Heart—R
Unrecognized Woman—R

WRITERS
$-Canadian Writer's Jour.—R
$-Fellowscript—R
Write Connection
$-Writers' Journal

FILLERS: SERMON ILLUSTRATIONS
ADULT/GENERAL
$-Churchmouse Public.—R
Halo Magazine—R
$-JC Town Reporter—R

PASTORS/LEADERS
$-PreachingToday.com
$-Preaching Well—R
$-RevWriter Resource
$-Sunday Sermons—R

WOMEN
($)-Beyond the Bend—R

FILLERS: SHORT HUMOR
ADULT/GENERAL
$-JC Town Reporter—R
$-Angels on Earth
$-Animal Trails—R
$-Bridal Guides—R
$-Christian Citizen USA
Christian Journal—R
Christian Motorsports
Christian Online
Christian Quarterly—R
Christian Ranchman
$-Churchmouse Public.—R
$-City Light News—R
Disciple's Journal—R
Eternal Ink—R
$-Family Digest—R
Friends Journal—R
$-Gem—R
Good News Journal—R
Halo Magazine—R
HEARTLIGHT Internet—R
Highway News—R
$-Homeschooling Today—R
$-Home Times—R

($)-Impact Magazine—R
$-Indian Life—R
$-In His Presence—R
Just Between Us—R
$-Leben—R
$-Lutheran Digest—R
$-Manna—R
$-Mature Living
MESSAGE/Open Bible—R
Movieguide
New Heart—R
PrayerWorks—R
$-Presbyterians Today—R
Prison Victory
$-Seek—R
$-Significant Living—R
Single Again Mag.—R
Unrecognized Woman—R
Victory Herald—R

CHILDREN
$-SHINE brightly—R
$-Sparkle—R

**CHRISTIAN EDUCATION/
LIBRARY**
Christian Librarian—R

MISSIONS
$-Glad Tidings—R

MUSIC
Christian Music—R
$-Creator—R

PASTORS/LEADERS
$-Barefoot—R
$-Catholic Servant
$-Enrichment—R
$-Interpreter
$-Leadership—R
$-Preaching Well—R
Sharing the Practice—R

TEEN/YOUNG ADULT
G4T Ink—R
TeensForJC—R
$-Young Christian—R
$-Young Salvationist—R

WOMEN
($)-Beyond the Bend—R
Christian Woman's Page—R

Extreme Woman
Glory & Strength—R
Just Between Us—R
$-Melody of the Heart
$-Mother's Heart—R
Unrecognized Woman—R

WRITERS
Areopagus
$-Christian Communicator—R
$-Fellowscript—R
$-New Writer's Mag.
$-Tickled by Thunder
Write Connection
$-Writers' Journal

FILLERS: TIPS
ADULT/GENERAL
$-Animal Trails—R
$-Bridal Guides—R
Christian Ranchman
Good News Journal—R
Halo Magazine—R
Highway News—R
$-Homeschooling Today—R
$-Home Times—R
$-JC Town Reporter—R
Just Between Us—R
$-KD Gospel Media
$-Manna—R
Movieguide
New Identity—R
Single Again Mag.—R
$-Special Living—R
$-Storyteller—R
Unrecognized Woman—R
Victory Herald—R
$-Written

CHILDREN
$-Cadet Quest—R

**CHRISTIAN EDUCATION/
LIBRARY**
$-Kids' Ministry Ideas—R
$-Youth & CE Leadership

PASTORS/LEADERS
$-Barefoot—R
$-Enrichment—R
$-Your Church—R

TEEN/YOUNG ADULT
TeensForJC—R
$-Young Christian—R

WOMEN
($)-Beyond the Bend—R
Christian Woman's Page—R
Glory & Strength—R
Hope for Women
$-MomSense—R
$-Mother's Heart—R
Unrecognized Woman—R
Virtuous Woman—R
Women's Ministry

WRITERS
$-Fellowscript—R
$-Freelance Writer's Report—R
NW Christian Author—R
Write Connection
$-Writers' Journal

FILLERS: WORD PUZZLES
ADULT/GENERAL
$-Animal Trails—R
$-Bridal Guides—R
$-Catholic Yearbook—R
$-CGA World—R
$-Christian Citizen USA
$-Christian Herald—R
Christian Journal—R
Christian Quarterly—R
Christian Ranchman
$-Churchmouse Public.—R
Connecting Point—R
Desert Voice—R
Disciple's Journal—R
$-Evangel/IN—R
$-Faith & Friends—R
Friends Journal—R
$-Gem—R
$-Gospel Today—R
$-Guide—R
Halo Magazine—R
HEARTLIGHT Internet—R
($)-Impact Magazine—R
$-JC Town Reporter—R
Light of the World
$-Mature Years—R
Movieguide

$-Power for Living—R
$-Significant Living—R

CHILDREN
$-Adventures
$-American Girl—R
$-Cadet Quest—R
$-Faces
$-Focus/Clubhouse
$-Guide—R
$-Nature Friend—R
$-Our Little Friend—R
$-Partners—R
$-Pockets—R
$-SHINE brightly—R
Skipping Stones
$-Story Mates—R

CHRISTIAN EDUCATION/
LIBRARY
$-Kids' Ministry Ideas—R
$-Youth & CE Leadership

MISSIONS
$-Glad Tidings—R

TEEN/YOUNG ADULT
G4T Ink—R
TeensForJC—R
$-TG Magazine
$-Young Christian—R
$-Young Salvationist—R

WOMEN
$-Melody of the Heart
Take Root & Write

WRITERS
$-Writers' Journal

FOOD/RECIPES
ADULT/GENERAL
$-Animal Trails—R
$-Associated Content—R
$-Bridal Guides—R
CBN.com—R
Christian Online
Christian Quarterly—R
$-Faith & Family
Good News Journal—R
Gospel Herald
$-Homeschooling Today—R
($)-HopeKeepers—R

($)-Impact Magazine—R
$-Indian Life—R
$-In His Presence—R
Just Between Us—R
$-KD Gospel Media
Koinonia
$-Mature Living
New Identity—R
$-ParentLife
$-Significant Living—R
$-St. Anthony Messenger
Unrecognized Woman—R
$-World & I—R
$-Written

CHILDREN
$-Adventures
$-American Girl—R
$-Celebrate
$-Faces
$-Focus/Clubhouse
$-Focus/Clubhouse Jr.
$-Pockets—R
$-SHINE brightly—R
$-Sparkle—R

MISSIONS
$-Glad Tidings—R
Women of the Harvest

TEEN/YOUNG ADULT
$-Boundless Webzine—R
$-J.A.M.
TeensForJC—R

WOMEN
($)-Beyond the Bend—R
Christian Women Today—R
Chris. Work at Home Moms—R
$-Dabbling Mum—R
Empowering Everyday Women
First Lady
For Every Woman—R
$-Girlfriend 2 Girlfriend
Glory & Strength—R
Hope for Women
$-Melody of the Heart
$-Mother's Heart—R
Precious Times—R
Take Root & Write
Unrecognized Woman—R

Virtuous Woman—R
Women Today—R

GRANDPARENTING
ADULT/GENERAL
$-Christian Standard—R
$-Churchmouse Public.—R
$-Columbia—R
$-Good News, The—R
Gospel Herald
$-In Touch
$-KD Gospel Media
Koinonia
$-Lifeglow—R
$-Mother's Heart—R
$-Seek—R
Unrecognized Woman—R

WOMEN
$-Brink Magazine—R
Glory & Strength—R
Take Root & Write

HEALING
ADULT/GENERAL
$-America
$-Angels on Earth
Anointed Pages
$-Associated Content—R
CBN.com—R
$-Celebrate Life—R
$-Christian Home & School
Christian Motorsports
Christian Online
Christian Quarterly—R
Christian Ranchman
$-ChristianWeek—R
$-Churchmouse Public.—R
Connecting Point—R
E-Channels—R
Foursquare Leader
$-Gem—R
$-Good News—R
Gospel Herald
$-Guideposts—R
Halo Magazine—R
$-Home Times—R
($)-HopeKeepers—R
Island Catholic—R
$-JC Town Reporter—R

$-KD Gospel Media
Koinonia
$-Lifeglow—R
$-Light & Life
$-Live—R
$-Miracles, Healings—R
New Heart—R
New Identity—R
$-Our Sunday Visitor—R
Perspectives—R
Prayer Closet
$-Seek—R
Sharing—R
Single Again Mag.—R
$-Sound Body—R
$-Spiritual Life
$-St. Anthony Messenger
$-Testimony—R
Trumpeter—R
$-United Church Observer—R
$-Way of St. Francis—R
$-World & I—R

CHILDREN
$-BREAD/God's Children—R
Skipping Stones

DAILY DEVOTIONALS
Penned from the Heart—R

PASTORS/LEADERS
$-Immerse
$-Word & World

TEEN/YOUNG ADULT
$-Boundless Webzine—R
$-J.A.M.

WOMEN
Christian Woman's Page—R
Extreme Woman
Glory & Strength—R
Hope for Women
$-Mother's Heart—R
$-Pauses . . .
Precious Times—R
Share
$-SpiritLed Woman
Unrecognized Woman—R
Virtuous Woman—R

WRITERS
Areopagus

HEALTH
ADULT/GENERAL
$-Abilities
$-Angels on Earth
$-Anglican Journal
Anointed Pages
$-Apocalypse Chronicles—R
$-Associated Content—R
$-Aujourd'hui Credo—R
$-B.C. Catholic—R
$-Brink Magazine—R
$-Catholic Forester—R
CBN.com—R
$-Celebrate Life—R
$-CGA World—R
$-Christian Courier/Canada—R
Christian Courier/WI—R
Christian Health Care
$-Christian Home & School
Christian Online
Christian Quarterly—R
Christian Ranchman
$-ChristianWeek—R
$-Churchmouse Public.—R
$-Common Ground—R
$-Creative Nonfiction
Disciple's Journal—R
E-Channels—R
Faithwebbin—R
Fit Christian
Gospel Herald
$-Gospel Today—R
$-Guide—R
$-Guideposts—R
Halo Magazine—R
$-Home Times—R
Hope for Women
($)-HopeKeepers—R
$-In His Presence—R
Island Catholic—R
$-JC Town Reporter—R
Just Between Us—R
$-KD Gospel Media
Koinonia
$-Lifeglow—R
$-Light & Life
$-Live—R
$-Lookout
$-Mature Years—R
$-MESSAGE

MESSAGE/Open Bible—R
New Heart—R
New Identity—R
$-Our Sunday Visitor—R
$-Ozarks Senior Living—R
$-ParentLife
Penned from the Heart—R
$-Pentecostal Evangel—R
Perspectives/Science
Purpose Magazine—R
$-Rev Up Your Life
Single Again Mag.—R
$-Sound Body—R
$-Special Living—R
$-St. Anthony Messenger
$-Testimony—R
Trumpeter—R
Unrecognized Woman—R
$-Upscale
$-Vibrant Life—R
$-Vista—R
$-War Cry—R
Wisconsin Christian
$-World & I—R
$-Written

CHILDREN
$-American Girl—R
$-BREAD/God's Children—R
$-Guide—R
$-New Moon—R
Skipping Stones
$-Sparkle—R

DAILY DEVOTIONALS
Penned from the Heart—R

PASTORS/LEADERS
$-Christian Century—R
$-Immerse
$-InSite—R
$-Interpreter
$-Word & World

TEEN/YOUNG ADULT
$-Boundless Webzine—R
$-Devo'Zine—R
G4T Ink—R
$-J.A.M.
$-Listen—R
TeensForJC—R
$-TG Magazine

WOMEN
$-At the Center—R
Christian Woman
Christian Woman's Page—R
Christian Women Today—R
$-Dabbling Mum—R
Empowering Everyday Women
Extreme Woman
Glory & Strength—R
$-Heart & Soul
$-Horizons—R
$-InspiredMoms—R
$-inSpirit—R
$-Journey
Life Tools for Women
Live Magazine
Lutheran Woman's Quar.
$-Mother's Heart—R
$-Pauses . . .
Precious Times—R
Share
$-SpiritLed Woman
Take Root & Write
Unrecognized Woman—R
Virtuous Woman—R
Women Today—R

HISTORICAL
ADULT/GENERAL
$-Angels on Earth
$-Arlington Catholic
$-Associated Content—R
$-Capper's
$-Catholic Peace Voice—R
CBN.com—R
$-Celebrate Life—R
$-Christian Citizen USA
$-Christian Courier/Canada—R
$-Christian History—R
Christian Motorsports
Christian Observer
Christian Online
$-Christian Renewal—R
$-Columbia—R
$-Company Magazine—R
Creation Care—R
E-Channels—R
$-Eureka Street
Evangelical Times
$-Faith Today—R

$-Family Digest—R
$-FGBC World—R
Gospel Herald
$-Guide—R
Halo Magazine—R
$-Haruah—R
$-Homeschooling Today—R
$-Home Times—R
$-Indian Life—R
$-In His Presence—R
$-In Touch
Island Catholic—R
$-JC Town Reporter—R
$-KD Gospel Media
Koinonia
$-Leben—R
$-Light & Life
$-Lutheran Digest—R
($)-Mennonite Historian—R
$-Messiah Journal
Messianic Times
Methodist History
New Identity—R
$-New Wineskins—R
Nostalgia—R
$-Our Sunday Visitor—R
$-Over the Back Fence—R
Perspectives—R
Perspectives/Science
$-Power for Living—R
PrayerWorks—R
$-Presbyterian Outlook
Priscilla Papers
Sharing—R
$-Social Justice—R
$-St. Anthony Messenger
$-Storyteller—R
Sword of the Lord—R
Trumpeter—R
Unrecognized Woman—R
$-Upscale
$-Way of St. Francis—R
$-Wesleyan Life—R
Wisconsin Christian
$-World & I—R

CHILDREN
$-Archaeology—R
$-BREAD/God's Children—R
$-Faces

$-Focus/Clubhouse Jr.
$-Guide—R
$-New Moon—R
$-Sparkle—R

MISSIONS
East-West Church
$-Glad Tidings—R
$-One
Women of the Harvest

MUSIC
$-Creator—R
Hymn

PASTORS/LEADERS
$-Leadership—R
Lutheran Forum
$-Ministry Today
$-Priest
Sewanee Theo. Review
Theological Digest—R
$-Today's Parish
$-Word & World

TEEN/YOUNG ADULT
$-Boundless Webzine—R
$-J.A.M.
TeensForJC—R
$-Young Adult Today
$-Young Christian Writers

WOMEN
($)-History's Women—R
$-SpiritLed Woman

WRITERS
Areopagus
$-Tickled by Thunder

HOLIDAY/SEASONAL
ADULT/GENERAL
$-Alive Now—R
American Tract—R
$-Angels on Earth
$-Animal Trails—R
$-Arlington Catholic
Bread of Life—R
$-Brink Magazine—R
$-Capper's
$-Cathedral Age
$-Catholic Digest—R
$-Catholic New York

CBN.com—R
$-CGA World—R
$-Chicken Soup Books—R
$-Christian Courier/Canada—R
Christian Courier/WI—R
Christian Family Jour.
$-Christian Home & School
Christian Journal—R
Christian Online
$-Christian Renewal—R
$-Christian Retailing
$-ChristianWeek—R
$-Churchmouse Public.—R
$-City Light News—R
$-Columbia—R
Connecting Point—R
$-Covenant Companion—R
Desert Call—R
E-Channels—R
Eternal Ink—R
$-Faith & Family
Faithwebbin—R
$-Family Digest—R
$-Family Smart E-tips—R
Foursquare Leader
$-Gem—R
$-Gems of Truth—R
$-Good News, Etc.—R
Good News Journal—R
$-Good News, The—R
Gospel Herald
$-Guide—R
$-Guideposts—R
Halo Magazine—R
HEARTLIGHT Internet—R
$-Homeschooling Today—R
$-Home Times—R
 ($)-HopeKeepers—R
$-In His Presence—R
$-In Touch
$-JC Town Reporter—R
Just Between Us—R
$-KD Gospel Media
Koinonia
$-Lifeglow—R
$-Light & Life
$-Liguorian
$-Live—R
$-Living—R
$-Living Church

$-Living Light—R
$-Lookout
$-Manna—R
$-Mature Living
$-Mature Years—R
Messianic Perspectives—R
$-Miraculous Medal
$-Montana Catholic
$-On Mission
$-Our Sunday Visitor—R
$-Over the Back Fence—R
$-ParentLife
Penned from the Heart—R
$-Point—R
$-Power for Living—R
$-Prairie Messenger—R
PrayerWorks—R
$-Psychology for Living—R
$-Purpose—R
$-Rev Up Your Life
$-River Region's Journey
$-Seek—R
Sharing—R
$-Special Living—R
$-St. Anthony Messenger
Sword of the Lord—R
$-Together—R
Trumpeter—R
$-United Church Observer—R
Unrecognized Woman—R
$-U.S. Catholic—R
$-Vibrant Life—R
Victory Herald—R
$-Victory in Grace—R
$-Vision—R
$-Vista—R
$-War Cry—R
$-Way of St. Francis—R
$-Wesleyan Life—R
$-World & I—R

CHILDREN
$-Archaeology—R
$-Focus/Clubhouse
$-Focus/Clubhouse Jr.
$-Guide—R
$-Junior Companion—R
$-JuniorWay
$-Nature Friend—R
$-Pockets—R

$-Primary Street
$-SHINE brightly—R
Skipping Stones
$-Sparkle—R

CHRISTIAN EDUCATION/ LIBRARY
$-Group
$-Today's Catholic Teacher—R
$-Youth & CE Leadership

DAILY DEVOTIONALS
$-Brink Magazine—R
Penned from the Heart—R
$-These Days

MISSIONS
$-Glad Tidings—R
Railroad Evangelist—R
Women of the Harvest

MUSIC
$-Creator—R

PASTORS/LEADERS
$-Catholic Servant
Disciple Magazine—R
$-Interpreter
$-Preaching Well—R
$-Sunday Sermons—R

TEEN/YOUNG ADULT
$-Boundless Webzine—R
$-Essential Connection
$-J.A.M.
TeensForJC—R
$-TG Magazine
$-Young Christian—R
$-Young Christian Writers
$-Young Salvationist—R

WOMEN
($)-Beyond the Bend—R
Christian Women Today—R
For Every Woman—R
Glory & Strength—R
($)-History's Women—R
Hope for Women
$-InspiredMoms—R
$-inSpirit—R
$-Journey
Just Between Us—R
Lutheran Woman's Quar.

$-Mother's Heart—R
P31 Woman—R
$-Pauses . . .
Precious Times—R
Take Root & Write
Together with God—R
Unrecognized Woman—R
Virtuous Woman—R

WRITERS
Areopagus
$-Cross & Quill—R

HOLY SPIRIT*
ADULT/GENERAL
Breakthrough Intercessor—R
$-Churchmouse Public.—R
$-Columbia—R
$-Earthen Vessel Online—R
Just Between Us—R
$-Kyria—R
$-Lifeglow—R
Unrecognized Woman—R

PASTORS/LEADERS
$-Brink Magazine—R
$-Immerse

HOMESCHOOLING
ADULT/GENERAL
$-Animal Trails—R
Christian Family Jour.
$-Churchmouse Public.—R
$-Columbia—R
Desert Voice—R
Faithwebbin—R
$-Good News, Etc.—R
$-Good News, The—R
Gospel Herald
$-Guide—R
$-Homeschooling Today—R
$-Home Times—R
$-In His Presence—R
$-In Touch
$-JC Town Reporter—R
$-KD Gospel Media
Koinonia
$-Our Sunday Visitor—R
$-ParentLife
Unrecognized Woman—R
Wisconsin Christian

CHILDREN
$-Archaeology—R
$-BREAD/God's Children—R
$-Guide—R
$-New Moon—R
Skipping Stones

CHRISTIAN EDUCATION/ LIBRARY
Jour./Ed. & Christian Belief—R

MISSIONS
$-Glad Tidings—R
Women of the Harvest

TEEN/YOUNG ADULT
$-Boundless Webzine—R
$-Insight—R
$-J.A.M.
$-TG Magazine
$-Young Christian—R

WOMEN
Christian Woman's Page—R
Chris. Work at Home Moms—R
For Every Woman—R
Hope for Women
$-InspiredMoms—R
$-inSpirit—R
$-Journey
$-Mother's Heart—R
Take Root & Write
Unrecognized Woman—R
Virtuous Woman—R

HOMILETICS
ADULT/GENERAL
CBN.com—R
Christian Ranchman
$-Columbia—R
$-Earthen Vessel Online—R
E-Channels—R
Gospel Herald
Halo Magazine—R
$-In Touch
Koinonia
$-New Wineskins—R
Perspectives—R
Priscilla Papers
$-Social Justice—R
$-St. Anthony Messenger
$-Stewardship—R

$-Testimony—R
Trumpeter—R
$-Wesleyan Life—R

PASTORS/LEADERS
$-Christian Century—R
$-Clergy Journal—R
$-Enrichment—R
$-Ministry & Liturgy—R
Preaching
$-Preaching Well—R
$-Priest
$-Proclaim—R
Sewanee Theo. Review

WOMEN
$-SpiritLed Woman
Unrecognized Woman—R

HOW-TO
ADULT/GENERAL
$-Animal Trails—R
$-Associated Content—R
$-Bridal Guides—R
$-Brink Magazine—R
$-Canada Lutheran—R
$-CBA Retailers
CBN.com—R
$-Celebrate Life—R
$-CGA World—R
Christian Motorsports
Christian Observer
Christian Online
$-Christian Retailing
Connecting Point—R
$-Direction
E-Channels—R
$-Faith & Family
$-Faith Today—R
$-Family Digest—R
$-Family Smart E-tips—R
$-Good News, Etc.—R
Gospel Herald
Halo Magazine—R
$-Home Times—R
($)-HopeKeepers—R
$-Imagine
$-In Touch
$-JC Town Reporter—R
Just Between Us—R
Koinonia

$-Lifeglow—R
$-Live—R
$-Living—R
$-Living Church
$-Marriage Partnership
$-MESSAGE
($)-Mutuality—R
$-On Mission
$-ParentLife
PrayerWorks—R
$-Presbyterians Today—R
Regent Global—R
$-Significant Living—R
$-St. Anthony Messenger
$-Testimony—R
Trumpeter—R
$-Vibrant Life—R
Victory Herald—R
$-Vista—R
$-World & I—R
$-Written

CHILDREN
$-Archaeology—R
$-Cadet Quest—R
$-Sparkle—R

CHRISTIAN EDUCATION/ LIBRARY
$-Catechist
$-Christian Educators—R
Christian Librarian—R
$-Church Libraries—R
Congregational Libraries
$-Group
$-Journal/Adventist Ed.—R
$-Kids' Ministry Ideas—R
$-Preschool Playhouse (CE)
$-Teachers of Vision—R
$-Today's Catholic Teacher—R
$-Youth & CE Leadership

MISSIONS
$-Glad Tidings—R
$-PFI Global—R

PASTORS/LEADERS
$-Insight Youth—R
$-Lead Magazine—R
$-Ministry
$-Ministry & Liturgy—R
$-Ministry Today

$-Net Results
$-Newsletter Newsletter
$-Outreach—R
$-RevWriter Resource
$-Worship Leader
$-Your Church—R

TEEN/YOUNG ADULT
$-Listen—R
TeensForJC—R
$-TG Magazine

WOMEN
($)-Beyond the Bend—R
Christian Woman's Page—R
Christian Women Today—R
Chris. Work at Home Moms—R
$-Dabbling Mum—R
Extreme Woman
Hope for Women
Just Between Us—R
$-Melody of the Heart
$-Mother's Heart—R
Precious Times—R
Take Root & Write
Unrecognized Woman—R
Virtuous Woman—R

WRITERS
$-Adv. Christian Writer—R
$-Cross & Quill—R
Esdras' Scroll—R
$-Fellowscript—R
$-Freelance Writer's Report—R
$-Poets & Writers
$-Writer's Digest

HOW-TO ACTIVITIES (JUV.)
ADULT/GENERAL
$-Animal Trails—R
$-Associated Content—R
$-Christian Home & School
Christian Online
E-Channels—R
$-Faith & Family
$-Family Smart E-tips—R
$-JC Town Reporter—R
Keys to Living—R
Koinonia
$-On Mission
$-ParentLife

$-St. Anthony Messenger
$-World & I—R

CHILDREN
$-Adventures
$-American Girl—R
$-Archaeology—R
$-BREAD/God's Children—R
$-Cadet Quest—R
$-Celebrate
$-Faces
$-Focus/Clubhouse
$-Focus/Clubhouse Jr.
$-Guide—R
$-Junior Companion—R
$-JuniorWay
$-Nature Friend—R
$-Pockets—R
$-Preschool Playhouse
$-Preschool Playhouse (CE)
$-Seeds
$-SHINE brightly—R
$-Sparkle—R

CHRISTIAN EDUCATION/ LIBRARY
$-Children's Ministry
Christian Early Ed.—R
$-Group
$-Kids' Ministry Ideas—R
$-Preschool Playhouse (CE)

PASTORS/LEADERS
$-Interpreter

TEEN/YOUNG ADULT
$-Listen—R
$-TG Magazine
$-Young Christian—R

WOMEN
Chris. Work at Home Moms—R
$-Mother's Heart—R

HUMOR
ADULT/GENERAL
$-Abilities
American Tract—R
$-Angels on Earth
$-Associated Content—R
$-Brink Magazine—R
$-Catholic Digest—R

$-Catholic Forester—R
$-Catholic Peace Voice—R
CBN.com—R
$-CGA World—R
$-Chicken Soup Books—R
Christian Computing—R
$-Christian Courier/Canada—R
$-Christian Home & School
$-Christianity Today—R
Christian Journal—R
Christian Online
Christian Quarterly—R
Christian Ranchman
$-Churchmouse Public.—R
$-City Light News—R
Connecting Point—R
Creation Care—R
$-Creative Nonfiction
Desert Voice—R
Disciple's Journal—R
E-Channels—R
Eternal Ink—R
$-Faith & Family
$-Family Smart E-tips—R
$-Gem—R
$-Good News, Etc.—R
Good News Journal—R
$-Good News, The—R
Gospel Herald
$-Guide—R
Halo Magazine—R
$-Haruah—R
Highway News—R
$-Homeschooling Today—R
$-Home Times—R
 ($)-HopeKeepers—R
$-Indian Life—R
$-In His Presence—R
$-In Touch
Island Catholic—R
$-JC Town Reporter—R
$-KD Gospel Media
Koinonia
$-Lifeglow—R
$-Liguorian
$-Living—R
$-Living Church
$-Living Light—R
$-Lookout
$-Manna—R

$-Marriage Partnership
$-Mature Living
Men.AG.org—R
$-Miracles, Healings—R
More Excellent Way—R
New Christian Voices
New Heart—R
$-New Wineskins—R
Nostalgia—R
$-Our Sunday Visitor—R
$-Over the Back Fence—R
$-Ozarks Senior Living—R
Pegasus Review—R
Penned from the Heart—R
PrayerWorks—R
$-Psychology for Living—R
Ruminate
$-Seek—R
$-Significant Living—R
$-St. Anthony Messenger
$-Storyteller—R
$-Testimony—R
$-Thriving Family
$-Together—R
Trumpeter—R
Unrecognized Woman—R
$-U.S. Catholic—R
Victory Herald—R
$-Victory in Grace—R
$-Vista—R
$-War Cry—R
$-Way of St. Francis—R
$-Weavings—R
$-Wildwood Reader—R
$-World & I—R
Xavier Review

CHILDREN
$-Cadet Quest—R
$-Faces
$-Focus/Clubhouse Jr.
$-Guide—R
$-SHINE brightly—R
$-Sparkle—R

CHRISTIAN EDUCATION/ LIBRARY
$-Children's Ministry

DAILY DEVOTIONALS
Penned from the Heart—R

MISSIONS
$-Glad Tidings—R
Women of the Harvest

MUSIC
Christian Music—R
$-Creator—R

PASTORS/LEADERS
$-Catholic Servant
$-Enrichment—R
$-Leadership—R
Ministry in Motion—R
$-Preaching Well—R
$-Priest
$-Today's Parish

TEEN/YOUNG ADULT
$-Boundless Webzine—R
$-Direction Student
$-Essential Connection
G4T Ink—R
$-Horizon Student
$-TC Magazine
TeensForJC—R
$-Young Christian Writers
$-Young Salvationist—R

WOMEN
($)-Beyond the Bend—R
Extreme Woman
Glory & Strength—R
Hope for Women
$-Horizons—R
$-Journey
Lutheran Woman's Quar.
$-Melody of the Heart
$-MomSense—R
$-Mother's Heart—R
$-SpiritLed Woman
Take Root & Write
Unrecognized Woman—R

WRITERS
Areopagus
$-Christian Communicator—R
$-New Writer's Mag.

INNER LIFE
ADULT/GENERAL
$-Canada Lutheran—R
$-Catholic Digest—R

CBN.com—R
Christian Journal—R
Christian Ranchman
$-ChristianWeek—R
$-Churchmouse Public.—R
Divine Ascent
E-Channels—R
$-Faith & Family
Gospel Herald
Halo Magazine—R
Hope for Women
$-In Touch
Island Catholic—R
$-JC Town Reporter—R
Just Between Us—R
Koinonia
$-Kyria—R
LifeTimes Catholic
$-Light & Life
$-Live—R
$-Living—R
$-Mature Years—R
$-Men of Integrity—R
$-New Wineskins—R
$-Our Sunday Visitor—R
Penned from the Heart—R
$-Presbyterians Today—R
Regent Global—R
$-Seek—R
Spirituality for Today
$-Testimony—R
$-Together—R
Unrecognized Woman—R
Victory Herald—R
$-Way of St. Francis—R
$-Weavings—R
$-Wildwood Reader—R
$-World & I—R

PASTORS/LEADERS
$-Immerse
$-Interpreter
Jour./Pastoral Care

TEEN/YOUNG ADULT
$-Boundless Webzine—R
$-TC Magazine
TeensForJC—R
$-Young Salvationist—R

WOMEN
Christian Woman's Page—R
Empowering Everyday Women
$-Fullfill
Glory & Strength—R
$-Journey
Just Between Us—R
$-Mother's Heart—R
$-Pauses . . .
Take Root & Write
Unrecognized Woman—R
Women Today—R

INSPIRATIONAL
ADULT/GENERAL
African Voices—R
$-Alive Now—R
$-Angels on Earth
$-Animal Trails—R
$-Arlington Catholic
$-Associated Content—R
$-Aujourd'hui Credo—R
Bread of Life—R
Breakthrough Intercessor—R
$-Bridal Guides—R
$-Brink Magazine—R
($)-Canadian Mennonite—R
$-Capper's
$-Catholic Forester—R
$-Catholic Peace Voice—R
CBN.com—R
$-Celebrate Life—R
$-CGA World—R
$-Chicken Soup Books—R
Christian Family Jour.
$-Christian Home & School
Christian Journal—R
Christian Motorsports
Christian Online
Christian Quarterly—R
Christian Ranchman
$-Churchmouse Public.—R
$-Columbia—R
Connecting Point—R
$-Covenant Companion—R
$-Decision
$-Direction
Divine Ascent
$-DreamSeeker—R

E-Channels—R
Eternal Ink—R
$-Evangel/IN—R
$-Faith & Family
Faithwebbin—R
$-Family Digest—R
Foursquare Leader
$-Gem—R
$-Good News—R
Good News Journal—R
$-Good News, The—R
Gospel Herald
$-Gospel Today—R
$-Guideposts—R
Halo Magazine—R
HEARTLIGHT Internet—R
Highway News—R
$-Homeschooling Today—R
$-Home Times—R
Hope for Women
($)-HopeKeepers—R
$-Indian Life—R
$-In His Presence—R
$-In Touch
$-JC Town Reporter—R
Just Between Us—R
$-KD Gospel Media
Keys to Living—R
Koinonia
Leaves—R
$-Lifeglow—R
$-Liguorian
$-Live—R
$-Living—R
$-Living Church
$-Lookout
$-Lutheran Digest—R
$-Marian Helper
$-Mature Living
($)-Mennonite Historian—R
$-MESSAGE
MESSAGE/Open Bible—R
$-Messenger/Sacred Heart
Messianic Perspectives—R
$-Miracles, Healings—R
($)-Mutuality—R
New Heart—R
New Identity—R
Nostalgia—R
$-ParentLife

$-Partners—R
Pegasus Review—R
Penned from the Heart—R
$-Power for Living—R
$-Prairie Messenger—R
PrayerWorks—R
$-Precepts for Living
$-Presbyterians Today—R
$-Priority!—R
Prison Victory
$-Psychology for Living—R
$-Purpose—R
Quaker Life—R
$-Seek—R
$-Significant Living—R
Single Again Mag.—R
Spirituality for Today
$-St. Anthony Messenger
$-Stewardship—R
$-Storyteller—R
SW Kansas Faith
Sword and Trumpet
Sword of the Lord—R
$-Testimony—R
$-Together—R
Trumpeter—R
$-United Church Observer—R
Unrecognized Woman—R
$-Upscale
Victory Herald—R
$-Victory in Grace—R
$-Vista—R
$-War Cry—R
$-Way of St. Francis—R
$-Wesleyan Life—R
$-Wildwood Reader—R
$-World & I—R

CHILDREN
$-Archaeology—R
$-BREAD/God's Children—R
$-Cadet Quest—R
$-Partners—R
$-Primary Street
$-SHINE brightly—R
$-Sparkle—R

CHRISTIAN EDUCATION/ LIBRARY
$-Children's Ministry
Congregational Libraries

$-Journal/Adventist Ed.—R
$-Youth & CE Leadership

DAILY DEVOTIONALS
$-Brink Magazine—R
Penned from the Heart—R
$-Rejoice!

MISSIONS
$-Glad Tidings—R
($)-Operation Reveille—R
Women of the Harvest

MUSIC
$-Creator—R
($)-TCP Magazine

PASTORS/LEADERS
$-Catholic Servant
$-Interpreter
$-Let's Worship
$-Ministry Today
$-Preaching Well—R
$-Priest
Technologies for Worship—R

TEEN/YOUNG ADULT
$-Boundless Webzine—R
$-Devo'Zine—R
$-Direction Student
G4T Ink—R
$-Horizon Student
$-Insight—R
$-J.A.M.
TeensForJC—R
$-TG Magazine
$-Young Christian—R
$-Young Christian Writers
$-Young Salvationist—R

WOMEN
($)-Beyond the Bend—R
Christian Women Today—R
Empowering Everyday Women
Extreme Woman
For Every Woman—R
$-Fullfill
Glory & Strength—R
Hope for Women
$-Horizons—R
$-InspiredMoms—R
$-inSpirit—R
$-Journey

Life Tools for Women
$-Link & Visitor—R
Love, Pearls & Swine
Lutheran Woman's Quar.
$-MomSense—R
$-Mother's Heart—R
P31 Woman—R
$-Pauses . . .
Precious Times—R
Right to the Heart—R
Share
$-SpiritLed Woman
Take Root & Write
Unrecognized Woman—R
Virtuous Woman—R

WRITERS
Areopagus
NW Christian Author—R
$-Writer's Digest

INTERVIEWS/PROFILES
ADULT/GENERAL
$-Abilities
American Tract—R
$-Anglican Journal
Anointed Pages
$-Arkansas Catholic—R
$-Arlington Catholic
$-Associated Content—R
$-Australian Catholics—R
Baptist Standard
Biblical Recorder
Books & Culture
Breakthrough Intercessor—R
$-Brink Magazine—R
CanadianChristianity
($)-Canadian Mennonite—R
$-Cathedral Age
$-Catholic New York
$-Catholic Peace Voice—R
CBN.com—R
$-Celebrate Life—R
Challenge Weekly
$-Charisma
Christian Business
Christian Chronicle
Christian Courier/WI—R
$-Christian Herald—R
$-Christianity Today—R

$-Christianity Today Movies—R
Christian Motorsports
Christian Observer
Christian Online
Christian Ranchman
$-ChristianWeek—R
Church of England News
$-Churchmouse Public.—R
$-City Light News—R
$-Columbia—R
Creation Care—R
$-Culture Wars—R
Desert Call—R
Desert Christian
Divine Ascent
E-Channels—R
Encompass
$-Episcopal Life—R
Eternal Ink—R
Evangel/OR—R
$-Faith Today—R
Faithwebbin—R
$-FGBC World—R
$-Gem—R
$-Good News—R
Good News Connection
$-Good News, Etc.—R
$-Good News, The—R
Good News Today
Gospel Herald
$-Gospel Today—R
$-Guideposts—R
Halo Magazine—R
Heartland Gatekeeper—R
HEARTLIGHT Internet—R
$-Home Times—R
($)-HopeKeepers—R
$-Indian Life—R
$-In His Presence—R
$-Interim—R
$-In Touch
$-JC Town Reporter—R
Just Between Us—R
$-KD Gospel Media
$-Kindred Spirit—R
Koinonia
LifeSite News
$-Light & Life
$-Liguorian
$-Living Church

$-Lookout
$-Manna—R
$-Marriage Partnership
$-MESSAGE
Messianic Perspectives—R
More Excellent Way—R
($)-Mutuality—R
New Heart—R
New Identity—R
$-On Mission
$-Our Sunday Visitor—R
$-Ozarks Senior Living—R
$-ParentLife
$-Power for Living—R
PrayerWorks—R
$-Presbyterian Outlook
$-Priority!—R
$-Prism
Regent Global—R
$-Search
$-St. Anthony Messenger
$-Stewardship—R
$-Testimony—R
Tri-State Voice
Trumpeter—R
$-United Church Observer—R
Unrecognized Woman—R
$-Upscale
$-Vibrant Life—R
$-War Cry—R
$-Way of St. Francis—R
$-Weavings—R
Wisconsin Christian
$-World & I—R

CHILDREN
$-American Girl—R
$-Cadet Quest—R
$-Faces
$-New Moon—R
$-Pockets—R
$-Primary Street
$-SHINE brightly—R
Skipping Stones
$-Sparkle—R

CHRISTIAN EDUCATION/
LIBRARY
$-Children's Ministry
$-Church Libraries—R
$-Youth & CE Leadership

MISSIONS
East-West Church
$-Evangelical Missions—R
$-Glad Tidings—R
$-Leaders for Today
($)-Operation Reveille—R
$-PFI Global—R

PASTORS/LEADERS
$-Catholic Servant
$-Christian Century—R
$-Enrichment—R
$-InSite—R
Ministry in Motion—R
$-Ministry Today
$-Outreach—R
$-Priest

TEEN/YOUNG ADULT
$-Boundless Webzine—R
$-Direction Student
$-Essential Connection
$-Horizon Student
$-J.A.M.
$-Listen—R
$-Risen
$-Spirit
$-TC Magazine
TeensForJC—R
$-TG Magazine
$-Young Salvationist—R
$-YouthWalk

WOMEN
Chris. Work at Home Moms—R
Empowering Everyday Women
Extreme Woman
Glory & Strength—R
$-Horizons—R
$-Journey
Just Between Us—R
$-Link & Visitor—R
Love, Pearls & Swine
More to Life
$-Pauses . . .
Precious Times—R
Unrecognized Woman—R
Virtuous Woman—R

WRITERS
$-Adv. Christian Writer—R
Areopagus

$-Christian Communicator—R
$-Cross & Quill—R
$-Fellowscript—R
$-New Writer's Mag.
$-Poets & Writers
Write Connection
$-Writer
$-Writer's Chronicle
$-Writer's Digest
$-Writers' Journal
Writers Manual

LEADERSHIP
ADULT/GENERAL
African Voices—R
$-Angels on Earth
CBN.com—R
Christian Business
$-Christian Courier/Canada—R
$-Christian Home & School
Christian Motorsports
$-Christian Retailing
$-Christian Standard—R
$-ChristianWeek—R
$-Churchmouse Public.—R
$-Columbia—R
Connections Ldrship/MOPS
$-Culture Wars—R
Desert Voice—R
Disciple's Journal—R
E-Channels—R
$-EFCA Today
Encompass
$-Faith Today—R
Foursquare Leader
$-Gem—R
$-Good News—R
$-Good News, Etc.—R
Good News Journal—R
Gospel Herald
Halo Magazine—R
HEARTLIGHT Internet—R
($)-HopeKeepers—R
$-In Touch
$-JC Town Reporter—R
Just Between Us—R
$-KD Gospel Media
Koinonia
$-Kyria—R
$-Light & Life

$-Living Church
$-Lookout
$-Manna—R
Men.AG.org—R
$-Men of Integrity—R
Men of the Cross
MissionWares
($)-Mutuality—R
$-New Wineskins—R
($)-NRB E-Magazine—R
$-Our Sunday Visitor—R
$-Presbyterian Outlook
Priscilla Papers
Quaker Life—R
Regent Global—R
$-St. Anthony Messenger
$-Stewardship—R
$-Testimony—R
Trumpeter—R
$-United Church Observer—R
Victory Herald—R
$-Vista—R
$-Way of St. Francis—R
Wisconsin Christian
$-World & I—R

CHILDREN
$-BREAD/God's Children—R

CHRISTIAN EDUCATION/ LIBRARY
$-Children's Ministry
Christian Early Ed.—R
Christian Librarian—R
Christian School Ed.—R
$-Group
Jour./Research on Christian Ed.
$-Momentum
$-Teachers of Vision—R
$-Today's Catholic Teacher—R
$-Youth & CE Leadership

MISSIONS
East-West Church
$-Glad Tidings—R
$-Leaders for Today
Mission Connection

PASTORS/LEADERS
$-Catholic Servant
$-Christian Century—R
Christian Education Jour.—R

$-Clergy Journal—R
Disciple Magazine—R
$-Enrichment—R
Great Comm. Research—R
$-Growth Points—R
$-Immerse
$-InSite—R
$-Interpreter
$-Leadership—R
$-Lead Magazine—R
$-Ministry
Ministry in Motion—R
$-Ministry Today
$-Net Results
$-Outreach—R
Plugged In
$-RevWriter Resource
Rick Warren's Ministry—R
$-SmallGroups.com—R
Theological Digest—R
$-Word & World
$-Worship Leader
$-Your Church—R

TEEN/YOUNG ADULT
$-Boundless Webzine—R
$-Direction Student
$-Horizon Student
TeensForJC—R

WOMEN
($)-Beyond the Bend—R
For Every Woman—R
$-Horizons—R
Just Between Us—R
Precious Times—R
Right to the Heart—R
Share
$-SpiritLed Woman
Take Root & Write
Unrecognized Woman—R
Women of the Cross
Women Today—R

LIFESTYLE ARTICLES
ADULT/GENERAL
Anointed Pages
Breakthrough
$-Brink Magazine—R
Brink Online—R
byFaith

$-Canada Lutheran—R
$-Catholic Insight
CBN.com—R
Christian Family Jour.
Christian Journal—R
Christian Ranchman
$-ChristianWeek—R
$-Churchmouse Public.—R
$-City Light News—R
Connections Ldrship/MOPS
Creation Care—R
$-Faith Today—R
$-FGBC World—R
Fit Christian
$-Good News, Etc.—R
$-Good News, The—R
Gospel Herald
Halo Magazine—R
$-Home Times—R
Hope for Women
$-In His Presence—R
$-In Touch
Island Catholic—R
$-JC Town Reporter—R
$-KD Gospel Media
Koinonia
$-Lifeglow—R
$-Light & Life
$-Liguorian
$-Live—R
$-Lookout
$-Manna—R
$-Mature Living
Men.AG.org—R
New Identity—R
Nostalgia—R
$-Our Sunday Visitor—R
Ozarks Christian
$-ParentLife
$-Priority!—R
$-Rev Up Your Life
$-River Region's Journey
Saved Magazine
$-Seek—R
Share
Unrecognized Woman—R
$-Upscale
$-U.S. Catholic—R
$-Vibrant Life—R
$-Way of St. Francis—R

TEEN/YOUNG ADULT
$-Boundless Webzine—R
$-Direction Student
$-Horizon Student
$-Insight—R
$-TC Magazine

WOMEN
($)-Beyond the Bend—R
Christian Woman's Page—R
Empowering Everyday Women
For Every Woman—R
$-Fullfill
Glory & Strength—R
Grace Today
Hope for Women
Live Magazine
Love, Pearls & Swine
$-Mother's Heart—R
Onyx Woman
Take Root & Write
Truth Media
Unrecognized Woman—R
Women Today—R
You Can Live Again

LITURGICAL
ADULT/GENERAL
$-Alive Now—R
$-Arlington Catholic
$-Aujourd'hui Credo—R
$-Cathedral Age
$-Catholic Yearbook—R
$-Columbia—R
$-Culture Wars—R
Divine Ascent
E-Channels—R
$-Episcopal Life—R
Gospel Herald
Halo Magazine—R
Island Catholic—R
Koinonia
$-Living Church
$-Lutheran Journal—R
$-Messenger/Sacred Heart
$-New Wineskins—R
$-Our Sunday Visitor—R
Perspectives—R
$-Prairie Messenger—R
$-Social Justice—R

$-St. Anthony Messenger
$-Testimony—R
$-U.S. Catholic—R
$-Way of St. Francis—R

CHRISTIAN EDUCATION/ LIBRARY
Catholic Library

PASTORS/LEADERS
$-Barefoot—R
$-Catholic Servant
$-Christian Century—R
$-Clergy Journal—R
CrossCurrents
$-Diocesan Dialogue—R
Lutheran Forum
$-Ministry & Liturgy—R
$-Parish Liturgy—R
$-Preaching Well—R
$-Reformed Worship—R
Rick Warren's Ministry—R
Sewanee Theo. Review
$-Today's Parish
$-Word & World

WOMEN
$-Horizons—R

MARRIAGE
ADULT/GENERAL
$-Angels on Earth
Anointed Pages
$-Arlington Catholic
$-Associated Content—R
$-Atlantic Catholic
$-Bible Advocate—R
$-Bridal Guides—R
$-Brink Magazine—R
$-Catholic Digest—R
CBN.com—R
$-Celebrate Life—R
$-Christian Courier/Canada—R
$-Christian Examiner
Christian Family Jour.
$-Christian Home & School
Christian Journal—R
Christian Motorsports
Christian Online
Christian Quarterly—R
Christian Ranchman
$-Christian Research

$-Christian Standard—R
$-ChristianWeek—R
Church Herald & Holiness—R
$-Churchmouse Public.—R
$-Columbia—R
$-Culture Wars—R
$-Decision
Desert Voice—R
Disciple's Journal—R
E-Channels—R
$-Evangel/IN—R
$-Faith & Family
Faithwebbin—R
$-Family Digest—R
$-Family Smart E-tips—R
Foursquare Leader
$-Gem—R
$-Good News, Etc.—R
Good News Journal—R
$-Good News, The—R
Gospel Herald
$-Guideposts—R
Halo Magazine—R
HEARTLIGHT Internet—R
$-Home Times—R
($)-HopeKeepers—R
$-Indian Life—R
$-In His Presence—R
$-In Touch
Island Catholic—R
$-JC Town Reporter—R
Just Between Us—R
$-KD Gospel Media
Koinonia
$-Kyria—R
$-Lifeglow—R
$-Light & Life
$-Liguorian
$-Live—R
$-Living—R
$-Living Church
$-Living Light—R
$-Lookout
$-Manna—R
$-Marriage Partnership
$-Mature Living
Men.AG.org—R
$-Men of Integrity—R
Men of the Cross
More Excellent Way—R

($)-Mutuality—R
New Christian Voices
New Identity—R
$-New Wineskins—R
$-Our Sunday Visitor—R
$-ParentLife
Pegasus Review—R
Penned from the Heart—R
Perspectives—R
$-Point—R
$-Prairie Messenger—R
PrayerWorks—R
Priscilla Papers
$-Psychology for Living—R
$-Purpose—R
$-River Region's Journey
$-Seek—R
$-Significant Living—R
Single Again Mag.—R
Spirituality for Today
$-St. Anthony Messenger
$-Testimony—R
$-Thriving Family
$-Together—R
Trumpeter—R
Unrecognized Woman—R
$-U.S. Catholic—R
$-Vibrant Life—R
$-Vista—R
$-War Cry—R
$-Way of St. Francis—R
$-Wesleyan Life—R
$-Wildwood Reader—R
Wisconsin Christian
$-World & I—R

DAILY DEVOTIONALS
Penned from the Heart—R

MISSIONS
$-Glad Tidings—R

PASTORS/LEADERS
$-Catholic Servant
$-Christian Century—R
Disciple Magazine—R
$-Interpreter
Jour./Pastoral Care
$-Ministry & Liturgy—R
$-Ministry Today
$-Preaching Well—R

$-SmallGroups.com—R
Theological Digest—R
$-Today's Parish
$-Word & World

TEEN/YOUNG ADULT
$-Boundless Webzine—R
TeensForJC—R
$-Young Adult Today

WOMEN
Christian Woman
Christian Woman's Page—R
Chris. Work at Home Moms—R
$-Dabbling Mum—R
Empowering Everyday Women
Extreme Woman
First Lady
For Every Woman—R
$-Girlfriend 2 Girlfriend
Glory & Strength—R
Grace Today
$-Heart & Soul
Hope for Women
$-Horizons—R
$-inSpirit—R
$-Journey
Lutheran Woman's Quar.
$-MomSense—R
$-Mother's Heart—R
P31 Woman—R
$-Pauses…
Precious Times—R
$-SpiritLed Woman
Take Root & Write
Unrecognized Woman—R
Virtuous Woman—R
Women of the Cross
Women Today—R

MEN'S ISSUES
ADULT/GENERAL
$-Arlington Catholic
$-Associated Content—R
$-Brink Magazine—R
CBN.com—R
$-Chicken Soup Books—R
$-Christian Examiner
Christian Journal—R
Christian News NW—R
Christian Online

Christian Quarterly—R
Christian Ranchman
$-ChristianWeek—R
$-Churchmouse Public.—R
$-Columbia—R
$-Creative Nonfiction
Desert Voice—R
Disciple's Journal—R
E-Channels—R
$-EFCA Today
$-Evangel/IN—R
Faithwebbin—R
$-Family Digest—R
$-Family Smart E-tips—R
Foursquare Leader
$-Gem—R
$-Good News, Etc.—R
$-Good News, The—R
Gospel Herald
Halo Magazine—R
HEARTLIGHT Internet—R
Highway News—R
$-Home Times—R
($)-HopeKeepers—R
$-Indian Life—R
$-In His Presence—R
$-In Touch
$-JC Town Reporter—R
$-KD Gospel Media
Koinonia
$-Lifeglow—R
$-Light & Life
$-Live—R
$-Living—R
$-Lookout
$-Manna—R
Men.AG.org—R
$-Men of Integrity—R
Men of the Cross
MissionWares
($)-Mutuality—R
New Identity—R
$-Our Sunday Visitor—R
Penned from the Heart—R
Perspectives—R
$-Point—R
PrayerWorks—R
$-Presbyterian Outlook
Priscilla Papers
Prison Victory

$-Psychology for Living—R
$-Purpose—R
Regent Global—R
$-River Region's Journey
$-Seven Magazine—R
$-Significant Living—R
Single Again Mag.—R
$-St. Anthony Messenger
$-Testimony—R
$-Together—R
Trumpeter—R
$-United Church Observer—R
$-Vibrant Life—R
$-Wesleyan Life—R
Wisconsin Christian
$-World & I—R
$-Written

PASTORS/LEADERS
$-Interpreter
$-SmallGroups.com—R
$-Word & World

TEEN/YOUNG ADULT
$-Boundless Webzine—R
TeensForJC—R

WOMEN
Hope for Women
$-Mother's Heart—R
Unrecognized Woman—R

MIRACLES
ADULT/GENERAL
$-Angels on Earth
$-Anglican Journal
$-Animal Trails—R
$-Aujourd'hui Credo—R
$-B.C. Catholic—R
Breakthrough Intercessor—R
$-Catholic Yearbook—R
CBN.com—R
$-CGA World—R
$-Chicken Soup Books—R
$-Christian Home & School
$-Christianity Today—R
Christian Motorsports
Christian Online
Christian Quarterly—R
Christian Ranchman
$-Christian Standard—R

$-ChristianWeek—R
$-Churchmouse Public.—R
$-Columbia—R
Connecting Point—R
$-Culture Wars—R
$-Decision
Disciple's Journal—R
Divine Ascent
E-Channels—R
$-Episcopal Life—R
$-Gem—R
$-Good News—R
Gospel Herald
$-Guide—R
$-Guideposts—R
Halo Magazine—R
$-Home Times—R
($)-HopeKeepers—R
$-In His Presence—R
$-In Touch
$-JC Town Reporter—R
$-KD Gospel Media
Koinonia
$-Lifeglow—R
$-Light & Life
$-Live—R
$-Living Church
$-Lookout
$-Lutheran Journal—R
$-Men of Integrity—R
$-Miracles, Healings—R
New Heart—R
$-New Wineskins—R
$-Now What?—R
$-Our Sunday Visitor—R
Pegasus Review—R
Penned from the Heart—R
Perspectives—R
$-Power for Living—R
PrayerWorks—R
$-Presbyterian Outlook
$-Priority!—R
Priscilla Papers
$-Seek—R
$-Significant Living—R
Spirituality for Today
$-St. Anthony Messenger
$-Storyteller—R
Sword and Trumpet
Sword of the Lord—R

$-Testimony—R
Trumpeter—R
Unrecognized Woman—R
Wisconsin Christian

CHILDREN
$-BREAD/God's Children—R
$-Guide—R
$-Sparkle—R

DAILY DEVOTIONALS
Penned from the Heart—R

PASTORS/LEADERS
$-Clergy Journal—R
Great Comm. Research—R
$-Interpreter
$-Ministry Today
Rick Warren's Ministry—R
$-Word & World

TEEN/YOUNG ADULT
$-Boundless Webzine—R
$-Devo'Zine—R
G4T Ink—R
$-Insight—R
$-Young Salvationist—R

WOMEN
Glory & Strength—R
Hope for Women
$-Horizons—R
$-Journey
$-Link & Visitor—R
$-Mother's Heart—R
$-SpiritLed Woman
Unrecognized Woman—R

MISSIONS
ADULT/GENERAL
Breakthrough Intercessor—R
$-Brink Magazine—R
$-Canada Lutheran—R
$-Christian Home & School
Christian Ranchman
Church Herald & Holiness—R
$-Churchmouse Public.—R
$-City Light News—R
$-Columbia—R
$-EFCA Today
$-Faith Today—R
$-Good News, Etc.—R

$-Good News, The—R
Gospel Herald
$-Guide—R
Halo Magazine—R
$-In Touch
$-KD Gospel Media
Koinonia
$-Live—R
Messianic Perspectives—R
New Identity—R
$-On Mission
$-Our Sunday Visitor—R
$-ParentLife
PrayerWorks—R
Quaker Life—R
Spirituality for Today
Victory Herald—R
$-Way of St. Francis—R

CHILDREN
$-BREAD/God's Children—R
$-Guide—R

CHRISTIAN EDUCATION/ LIBRARY
Christian Librarian—R

DAILY DEVOTIONALS
$-Brink Magazine—R

MISSIONS
Action Magazine
East-West Church
$-Evangelical Missions—R
$-Glad Tidings—R
Intl. Jour./Frontier—R
Lausanne World—R
$-Leaders for Today
Missiology
Mission Connection
Mission Frontiers
$-New World Outlook
$-One
($)-Operation Reveille—R
$-PFI Global—R
Railroad Evangelist—R
WEC.go
Women of the Harvest

PASTORS/LEADERS
Church Executive
Disciple Magazine—R

$-Enrichment—R
$-Immerse
Ministry in Motion—R

TEEN/YOUNG ADULT
$-Direction Student
$-Horizon Student

WOMEN
$-Mother's Heart—R
Take Root & Write

MONEY MANAGEMENT
ADULT/GENERAL
$-Anglican Journal
$-Associated Content—R
$-Bridal Guides—R
$-Brink Magazine—R
Brink Online—R
byFaith
$-Catholic Forester—R
$-CBA Retailers
CBN.com—R
Christian Journal—R
Christian Motorsports
Christian Online
Christian Quarterly—R
Christian Ranchman
$-ChristianWeek—R
$-Churchmouse Public.—R
Connecting Point—R
$-Creative Nonfiction
Disciple's Journal—R
E-Channels—R
$-Faith & Family
Faithwebbin—R
$-Family Smart E-tips—R
$-Gem—R
Gospel Herald
Halo Magazine—R
HEARTLIGHT Internet—R
Highway News—R
$-Home Times—R
Hope for Women
$-In His Presence—R
$-In Touch
$-JC Town Reporter—R
Just Between Us—R
$-KD Gospel Media
Koinonia
$-Lifeglow—R

$-Live—R
$-Lookout
$-Manna—R
$-Marriage Partnership
$-Mature Years—R
Men.AG.org—R
($)-NRB E-Magazine—R
$-Our Sunday Visitor—R
$-ParentLife
Penned from the Heart—R
$-Rev Up Your Life
$-Significant Living—R
Single Again Mag.—R
$-St. Anthony Messenger
$-Testimony—R
$-Together—R
Trumpeter—R
Unrecognized Woman—R
$-War Cry—R
Wisconsin Christian
$-World & I—R

CHILDREN
$-BREAD/God's Children—R
$-SHINE brightly—R

DAILY DEVOTIONALS
Penned from the Heart—R

PASTORS/LEADERS
$-Clergy Journal—R
$-Enrichment—R
$-Immerse
$-Interpreter
Ministry in Motion—R
Rick Warren's Ministry—R
$-SmallGroups.com—R
$-Today's Parish
$-Your Church—R

TEEN/YOUNG ADULT
$-Boundless Webzine—R
$-Direction Student
$-Horizon Student

WOMEN
Christian Women Today—R
Chris. Work at Home Moms—R
Empowering Everyday Women
Glory & Strength—R
$-Heart & Soul
Hope for Women
$-Horizons—R

$-InspiredMoms—R
$-Journey
Life Tools for Women
More to Life
$-Mother's Heart—R
Precious Times—R
Unrecognized Woman—R
Virtuous Woman—R
Women Today—R

MOVIE REVIEWS
ADULT/GENERAL
$-Abilities
$-Associated Content—R
$-Atlantic Catholic
byFaith
CBN.com—R
Christian Family Jour.
$-Christian Herald—R
$-Christianity Today Movies—R
Christian Journal—R
$-Churchmouse Public.—R
$-City Light News—R
Creation Care—R
$-Cresset
$-Eureka Street
$-Faith & Friends—R
$-Good News, The—R
Good News Today
Gospel Herald
Heartland Gatekeeper—R
$-Home Times—R
$-Interim—R
Island Catholic—R
$-JC Town Reporter—R
$-KD Gospel Media
Movieguide
New Christian Voices
$-Our Sunday Visitor—R
Perspectives—R
$-Prairie Messenger—R

MUSIC
Hymn

TEEN/YOUNG ADULT
$-Risen
$-TC Magazine

WOMEN
Chris. Work at Home Moms—R
Empowering Everyday Women

Extreme Woman
Glory & Strength—R
Hope for Women
Virtuous Woman—R

MUSIC REVIEWS
ADULT/GENERAL
$-Arlington Catholic
$-Associated Content—R
$-Atlantic Catholic
$-Aujourd'hui Credo—R
($)-Canadian Mennonite—R
$-Catholic Peace Voice—R
CBN.com—R
$-Charisma
Christian Family Jour.
$-Christian Herald—R
Christian Journal—R
Christian Media—R
$-Christian Renewal—R
$-Christian Retailing
$-City Light News—R
$-Cresset
Desert Voice—R
E-Channels—R
$-Eureka Street
$-Faith & Family
$-Faith Today—R
Faithwebbin—R
Foursquare Leader
$-Good News, The—R
Gospel Herald
Halo Magazine—R
$-Haruah—R
Heartland Gatekeeper—R
HEARTLIGHT Internet—R
$-Interim—R
$-JC Town Reporter—R
$-KD Gospel Media
Movieguide
New Christian Voices
$-Our Sunday Visitor—R
$-Prairie Messenger—R
$-Presbyterians Today—R
$-Prism
$-Testimony—R
Trumpeter—R
$-World & I—R

CHILDREN
$-Sparkle—R

CHRISTIAN EDUCATION/ LIBRARY
$-Church Libraries—R

MISSIONS
$-Glad Tidings—R
Women of the Harvest

MUSIC
Christian Music—R
$-Creator—R
Gospel USA
Path Megazine
($)-TCP Magazine

PASTORS/LEADERS
$-Barefoot—R
$-Christian Century—R
Foursquare Leader
$-Interpreter
$-Ministry Today
$-Parish Liturgy—R
$-Reformed Worship—R
Technologies for Worship—R
$-Worship Leader

TEEN/YOUNG ADULT
$-Devo'Zine—R
$-Risen
$-Sharing the Victory—R
$-TC Magazine
TeensForJC—R
$-TG Magazine

WOMEN
Chris. Work at Home Moms—R
Empowering Everyday Women
Extreme Woman
Glory & Strength—R
Hope for Women
Precious Times—R
Virtuous Woman—R

NATURE
ADULT/GENERAL
$-Animal Trails—R
$-Associated Content—R
$-Aujourd'hui Credo—R
$-Brink Magazine—R
CBN.com—R
$-Christian Courier/Canada—R
$-Christian Renewal—R

$-Churchmouse Public.—R
Creation
Creation Care—R
$-Creation Illust.—R
$-Creative Nonfiction
$-Gem—R
Gospel Herald
$-Guide—R
Halo Magazine—R
$-In Touch
$-JC Town Reporter—R
$-KD Gospel Media
Keys to Living—R
Koinonia
$-Lifeglow—R
$-Lutheran Digest—R
New Identity—R
$-Our Sunday Visitor—R
$-Over the Back Fence—R
$-Partners—R
Pegasus Review—R
Penned from the Heart—R
PrayerWorks—R
Ruminate
$-Salvo
$-Search
$-Seek—R
$-St. Anthony Messenger
$-Storyteller—R
$-Testimony—R
Trumpeter—R
$-Way of St. Francis—R
$-Wildwood Reader—R
Wisconsin Christian
$-World & I—R

CHILDREN
$-Archaeology—R
$-BREAD/God's Children—R
$-Cadet Quest—R
$-Focus/Clubhouse Jr.
$-Guide—R
$-Nature Friend—R
$-Partners—R
$-SHINE brightly—R
Skipping Stones
$-Sparkle—R

PASTORS/LEADERS
$-Word & World

TEEN/YOUNG ADULT
$-Boundless Webzine—R
$-Devo'Zine—R
$-Young Christian Writers

WOMEN
Virtuous Woman—R

NEWS FEATURES
ADULT/GENERAL
Ambassador
$-Arkansas Catholic—R
$-Associated Content—R
$-Atlantic Catholic
Baptist Standard
Biblical Recorder
CanadianChristianity
($)-Canadian Mennonite—R
Carolina Christian
$-Cathedral Age
$-Catholic Insight
$-Catholic New York
$-Catholic Peace Voice—R
$-Catholic Sentinel
CBN.com—R
Challenge Weekly
$-Charisma
Christian Chronicle
Christian Courier/WI—R
$-Christian Examiner
$-Christianity Today Movies—R
Christian News NW—R
Christian Press
Christian Ranchman
$-Christian Renewal—R
$-Christian Research
$-Christian Response—R
$-Christian Retailing
$-ChristianWeek—R
$-Churchmouse Public.—R
Church of England News
$-City Light News—R
$-Commonweal
$-Compass Direct
Creation Care—R
Desert Christian
Desert Voice—R
$-Disaster News
Encompass
$-Eureka Street

Evangel/OR—R
$-Faith Today—R
Florida Baptist Witness
Founders Journal
Good News!
Good News Connection
$-Good News, Etc.—R
Good News Today
Gospel Herald
Heartland Gatekeeper—R
$-Home Times—R
($)-HopeKeepers—R
($)-Impact Magazine—R
$-Indian Life—R
$-Interchange
Island Catholic—R
$-JC Town Reporter—R
$-KD Gospel Media
$-Liberty
LifeSite News
Louisiana Baptist
$-Manna—R
Messianic Perspectives—R
$-Miracles, Healings—R
$-Montana Catholic
More Excellent Way—R
Movieguide
Network
$-Our Sunday Visitor—R
Ozarks Christian
$-Partners—R
$-Priority!—R
$-Search
$-St. Anthony Messenger
Sword and Trumpet
$-Testimony—R
Tri-State Voice
Trumpeter—R
$-Upscale
$-War Cry—R
$-World & I—R

CHILDREN
$-Partners—R
$-Pockets—R

MISSIONS
East-West Church
$-Glad Tidings—R
($)-Operation Reveille—R

PASTORS/LEADERS
$-Christian Century—R
Church Executive
Disciple Magazine—R
$-Ministry Today
Rick Warren's Ministry—R

TEEN/YOUNG ADULT
$-Listen—R
$-Young Christian Writers

WOMEN
Empowering Everyday Women
Hope for Women

WRITERS
$-Poets & Writers

NEWSPAPERS/TABLOIDS
Ambassador
$-Anglican Journal
$-Arkansas Catholic—R
$-Arlington Catholic
$-Atlantic Catholic
Baptist Standard
$-B.C. Catholic—R
Biblical Recorder
CanadianChristianity
Carolina Christian
$-Catholic New York
Catholic Register
$-Catholic Sentinel
$-Catholic Servant
$-Catholic Telegraph
Challenge Weekly
Christian Chronicle
$-Christian Citizen USA
$-Christian Courier/Canada—R
Christian Courier/WI—R
$-Christian Examiner
$-Christian Herald—R
Christian Journal—R
Christian Media—R
Christian News NW—R
Christian Observer
Christian Press
Christian Ranchman
$-Christian Renewal—R
$-ChristianWeek—R
Church of England News
$-City Light News—R

$-Common Ground—R
Desert Christian
Desert Voice—R
Disciple's Journal—R
$-Episcopal Life—R
Evangelical Times
Florida Baptist Witness
Good News!
Good News Connection
$-Good News, Etc.—R
Good News Today
Heartland Gatekeeper—R
$-Home Times—R
$-Indian Life—R
$-In His Presence—R
$-Interchange
$-Interim—R
Island Catholic—R
$-JC Town Reporter—R
$-Layman
LifeSite News
Light of the World
$-Living—R
$-Living Light—R
Living Stones
Louisiana Baptist
$-Manna—R
Messianic Times
$-Montana Catholic
Network
New Frontier
$-Our Sunday Visitor—R
Ozarks Christian
$-Ozarks Senior Living—R
$-Prairie Messenger—R
PrayerWorks—R
Senior Connection
SW Kansas Faith
Sword of the Lord—R
$-Together—R
Tri-State Voice
Wisconsin Christian

NOSTALGIA
ADULT/GENERAL
$-Associated Content—R
$-Catholic Forester—R
$-Good News, Etc.—R
Gospel Herald
Halo Magazine—R

$-Home Times—R
$-In Touch
Koinonia
$-Lutheran Digest—R
$-Mature Living
Nostalgia—R
$-Over the Back Fence—R
PrayerWorks—R
$-Seek—R
$-Storyteller—R
$-Testimony—R

CHILDREN
$-Faces

PASTORS/LEADERS
$-Priest

WOMEN
Glory & Strength—R
$-Journey

ONLINE PUBLICATIONS
ADULT/GENERAL
$-America
$-Anglican Journal
Answers Magazine
$-Apocalypse Chronicles—R
$-Associated Content—R
Behind the Hammer
Believer's Bay
Books & Culture
Breakthrough
$-Brink Magazine—R
CanadianChristianity
$-Cathedral Age
$-Catholic Digest—R
CBN.com—R
Challenge Weekly
$-Charisma
Christian Chronicle
Christian Computing—R
$-Christian Examiner
$-Christianity Today—R
$-Christianity Today Movies—R
Christian Journal—R
Christian Media—R
Christian Observer
Christian Online
Christian Outlook
$-Christian Standard—R

$-Churchmouse Public.—R
$-Columbia—R
$-Company Magazine—R
$-Compass Direct
$-Decision
$-Disaster News
Disciple's Journal—R
Divine Ascent
$-Drama Ministry—R
$-DreamSeeker—R
Eternal Ink—R
$-Eureka Street
$-Faith Today—R
Faithwebbin—R
$-Family Smart E-tips—R
Foursquare Leader
Good News!
Good News Connection
$-Good News, The—R
Gospel Herald
Haiku Hippodrome
Halo Magazine—R
$-Haruah—R
HEARTLIGHT Internet—R
$-Homeschooling Today—R
($)-Impact Magazine—R
$-Interim—R
$-JC Town Reporter—R
$-KD Gospel Media
Koinonia
$-Kyria—R
$-Layman
$-Leben—R
LifeSite News
LifeTimes Catholic
$-Lookout
$-Manna—R
$-Marian Helper
Men.AG.org—R
Men of the Cross
$-Messenger/St. Anthony
MissionWares
More Excellent Way—R
$-New Wineskins—R
$-Now What?—R
($)-NRB E-Magazine—R
$-On Mission
$-Pentecostal Evangel—R
Perspectives—R
PrayerWorks—R

$-Priority!—R
Regent Global—R
$-Relevant
Single Again Mag.—R
$-Sound Body—R
$-St. Anthony Messenger
$-Testimony—R
Touched By the Hand
Trumpeter—R
Unrecognized Woman—R
$-U.S. Catholic—R
Victory Herald—R
$-World & I—R

CHILDREN
$-American Girl—R
$-Archaeology—R
$-Focus/Clubhouse
$-Focus/Clubhouse Jr.
Girls Connection
$-Keys for Kids—R
$-Kids' Ark—R

DAILY DEVOTIONALS
$-Forward Day by Day

MISSIONS
Mission Frontiers
($)-Operation Reveille—R
Women of the Harvest

MUSIC
$-Creator—R

PASTORS/LEADERS
$-Barefoot—R
$-Cook Partners
Disciple Magazine—R
$-Immerse
$-InSite—R
$-Interpreter
$-Leadership—R
$-Living Church
Ministry in Motion—R
$-Net Results
$-Newsletter Newsletter
Preaching
$-PreachingToday.com
$-Reformed Worship—R
$-RevWriter Resource
Rick Warren's Ministry—R
$-SmallGroups.com—R
$-Sunday Sermons—R

Technologies for Worship—R
$-YouthWorker

TEEN/YOUNG ADULT
$-Boundless Webzine—R
Connected
StudentLife
TeensForJC—R
$-Young Salvationist—R

WOMEN
$-At the Center—R
Breathe Again
Christian Ladies Connect
Christian Woman's Page—R
Christian Women Today—R
Chris. Work at Home Moms—R
$-Dabbling Mum—R
Empowering Everyday Women
For Every Woman—R
$-Fullfill
$-Girlfriend 2 Girlfriend
Glory & Strength—R
Handmaidens
($)-History's Women—R
Hope for Women
$-InspiredMoms—R
Inspired Women
Life Tools for Women
Live Magazine
$-Melody of the Heart
Right to the Heart—R
Take Root & Write
Virtuous Woman—R
Women of the Cross
Women's Ministry
Women Today—R

WRITERS
Author-Me
ChristianWriters.com
Dedicated Author
Esdras' Scroll—R
$-Freelance Writer's Report—R
$-Shades of Romance—R
WriteToInspire.com
Writing Corner—R

OPINION PIECES
ADULT/GENERAL
$-Arkansas Catholic—R
$-Arlington Catholic

$-Associated Content—R
$-B.C. Catholic—R
$-Brink Magazine—R
$-Catholic New York
$-Catholic Peace Voice—R
CBN.com—R
$-Christian Citizen USA
$-Christian Courier/Canada—R
$-Christian Examiner
$-Christianity Today—R
$-Christianity Today Movies—R
Christian News NW—R
$-Christian Renewal—R
$-Christian Research
$-ChristianWeek—R
$-Churchmouse Public.—R
Church of England News
$-Culture Wars—R
$-Episcopal Life—R
$-Eureka Street
Faithwebbin—R
$-Good News, Etc.—R
$-Good News, The—R
Gospel Herald
Halo Magazine—R
$-Home Times—R
($)-HopeKeepers—R
$-Indian Life—R
$-Interim—R
$-In Touch
Island Catholic—R
$-JC Town Reporter—R
Koinonia
$-Lifeglow—R
$-Living Church
$-Lookout
Movieguide
($)-NRB E-Magazine—R
$-Our Sunday Visitor—R
Perspectives—R
$-Prairie Messenger—R
$-Presbyterian Outlook
Regent Global—R
$-Salvo
$-Social Justice—R
$-St. Anthony Messenger
$-Testimony—R
Trumpeter—R
$-United Church Observer—R
Unrecognized Woman—R

$-World & I—R
$-Written

CHILDREN
$-New Moon—R
Skipping Stones

CHRISTIAN EDUCATION/ LIBRARY
$-Group
Jour. of Christianity—R
$-Teachers of Vision—R

MISSIONS
$-Evangelical Missions—R
$-Glad Tidings—R
($)-Operation Reveille—R

PASTORS/LEADERS
$-Catholic Servant
$-Ministry Today
$-Priest
$-Word & World
$-Worship Leader

TEEN/YOUNG ADULT
TeensForJC—R
$-Young Christian Writers

WOMEN
($)-Beyond the Bend—R
Hope for Women
Unrecognized Woman—R

WRITERS
$-Adv. Christian Writer—R
Areopagus
$-New Writer's Mag.

PARENTING
ADULT/GENERAL
American Tract—R
$-Angels on Earth
$-Arkansas Catholic—R
$-Arlington Catholic
$-Associated Content—R
$-Atlantic Catholic
$-Canada Lutheran—R
$-Catholic Digest—R
$-Catholic Yearbook—R
CBN.com—R
$-Celebrate Life—R
$-Chicken Soup Books—R

$-Christian Courier/Canada—R
Christian Family Jour.
$-Christian Home & School
Christian Motorsports
Christian Observer
Christian Quarterly—R
Christian Ranchman
$-Christian Renewal—R
$-Christian Research
$-ChristianWeek—R
$-Churchmouse Public.—R
$-Columbia—R
Creation Care—R
$-Culture Wars—R
Disciple's Journal—R
$-Faith & Family
Faithwebbin—R
$-Family Digest—R
$-Family Smart E-tips—R
Foursquare Leader
$-Gem—R
$-Good News, Etc.—R
Good News Journal—R
$-Good News, The—R
Gospel Herald
Halo Magazine—R
HEARTLIGHT Internet—R
Highway News—R
$-Homeschooling Today—R
$-Home Times—R
($)-HopeKeepers—R
$-Indian Life—R
$-In His Presence—R
$-In Touch
$-JC Town Reporter—R
Just Between Us—R
$-KD Gospel Media
Koinonia
$-Lifeglow—R
$-Light & Life
$-Liguorian
$-Live—R
$-Living—R
$-Living Light—R
$-Lookout
$-Lutheran Journal—R
$-Manna—R
$-Marriage Partnership
Men.AG.org—R
$-Men of Integrity—R

Movieguide
($)-Mutuality—R
New Christian Voices
$-New Wineskins—R
$-Our Sunday Visitor—R
$-ParentLife
Pegasus Review—R
Penned from the Heart—R
$-Pentecostal Evangel—R
$-Point—R
$-Power for Living—R
$-Prairie Messenger—R
$-Psychology for Living—R
$-Purpose—R
$-River Region's Journey
$-Seek—R
Single Again Mag.—R
$-Special Living—R
Spirituality for Today
$-St. Anthony Messenger
SW Kansas Faith
$-Testimony—R
$-Thriving Family
$-Together—R
Trumpeter—R
$-Vibrant Life—R
Victory Herald—R
$-Vista—R
$-War Cry—R
$-Wesleyan Life—R
Wisconsin Christian
$-World & I—R

CHRISTIAN EDUCATION/
LIBRARY
$-Children's Ministry

DAILY DEVOTIONALS
Penned from the Heart—R

MISSIONS
$-Glad Tidings—R

PASTORS/LEADERS
$-Catholic Servant
$-Interpreter
Plugged In

WOMEN
Christian Woman's Page—R
Chris. Work at Home Moms—R
$-Dabbling Mum—R

Extreme Woman
For Every Woman—R
$-Girlfriend 2 Girlfriend
Glory & Strength—R
$-Heart & Soul
Hope for Women
$-InspiredMoms—R
$-inSpirit—R
$-Journey
Just Between Us—R
$-Link & Visitor—R
Lutheran Woman's Quar.
$-MomSense—R
$-Mother's Heart—R
P31 Woman—R
$-Pauses...
Precious Times—R
$-SpiritLed Woman
Take Root & Write
Unrecognized Woman—R
Virtuous Woman—R
Women Today—R

PASTORS' HELPS*
PASTORS/LEADERS
$-Barefoot—R
$-Catechumenate
$-Catholic Servant
$-Christian Century—R
Christian Education Jour.—R
Church Executive
$-Clergy Journal—R
$-Cook Partners
CrossCurrents
$-Diocesan Dialogue—R
Disciple Magazine—R
$-Emmanuel
$-Enrichment—R
$-Evangelical Baptist
Foursquare Leader
Great Comm. Research—R
$-Growth Points—R
$-Immerse
$-InSite—R
Jour./Pastoral Care
$-Leadership—R
$-Lead Magazine—R
$-Let's Worship
$-Living Church

Lutheran Forum
$-Ministry
$-Ministry & Liturgy—R
Ministry in Motion—R
$-Ministry Today
$-Net Results
$-Newsletter Newsletter
$-Outreach—R
$-Parish Liturgy—R
Plugged In
Preaching
$-PreachingToday.com
$-Preaching Well—R
$-Proclaim—R
Purpose Driven Conn.
$-Reformed Worship—R
$-Review for Religious
$-RevWriter Resource
Rick Warren's Ministry—R
Sewanee Theo. Review
Sharing the Practice—R
$-SmallGroups.com—R
$-Sunday Sermons—R
Technologies for Worship—R
Theological Digest—R
$-Today's Parish
$-Torch Legacy Leader
$-Word & World

PEACE ISSUES
ADULT/GENERAL
$-Associated Content—R
$-Aujourd'hui Credo—R
$-Cathedral Age
CBN.com—R
$-ChristianWeek—R
$-Columbia—R
$-Eureka Street
Evangel/OR—R
Gospel Herald
Halo Magazine—R
$-In Touch
Island Catholic—R
$-JC Town Reporter—R
Koinonia
$-Liguorian
$-Living—R
$-Lookout
($)-Mennonite Historian—R
Messianic Perspectives—R

$-Our Sunday Visitor—R
Penned from the Heart—R
Perspectives—R
$-Purpose—R
Quaker Life—R
$-Seek—R
Spirituality for Today
$-Testimony—R
$-Together—R
$-U.S. Catholic—R
$-Way of St. Francis—R

CHILDREN
$-New Moon—R
$-Pockets—R
Skipping Stones

MISSIONS
$-Glad Tidings—R

PASTORS/LEADERS
$-Christian Century—R
$-Clergy Journal—R
$-Immerse
$-Interpreter

TEEN/YOUNG ADULT
$-TG Magazine

WOMEN
Extreme Woman
$-Horizons—R
$-Pauses…
Unrecognized Woman—R
Women Today—R

PERSONAL EXPERIENCE
ADULT/GENERAL
African Voices—R
$-Alive Now—R
$-Angels on Earth
$-Associated Content—R
$-Australian Catholics—R
$-B.C. Catholic—R
Behind the Hammer
$-Bible Advocate—R
Breakthrough
$-Bridal Guides—R
$-Brink Magazine—R
$-Catholic Digest—R
$-Catholic New York
$-Catholic Peace Voice—R
$-Catholic Yearbook—R

CBN.com—R
$-Celebrate Life—R
$-CGA World—R
$-Chicken Soup Books—R
$-Christian Courier/Canada—R
$-Christianity Today—R
Christian Journal—R
Christian Motorsports
Christian Observer
Christian Online
Christian Quarterly—R
$-ChristianWeek—R
$-Churchmouse Public.—R
$-Columbia—R
$-Commonweal
$-Creative Nonfiction
$-Decision
$-Earthen Vessel Online—R
E-Channels—R
$-Evangel/IN—R
Faithwebbin—R
$-Family Digest—R
$-Gem—R
$-Good News, Etc.—R
Gospel Herald
$-Guide—R
$-Guideposts—R
Halo Magazine—R
Highway News—R
$-Home Times—R
($)-HopeKeepers—R
$-In His Presence—R
$-In Touch
Island Catholic—R
$-JC Town Reporter—R
Just Between Us—R
$-KD Gospel Media
Keys to Living—R
Koinonia
$-Kyria—R
Leaves—R
$-Light & Life
$-Liguorian
$-Live—R
$-Living—R
$-Living Church
$-Lookout
$-Lutheran Journal—R
$-Marian Helper
$-Mature Living

$-MESSAGE
More Excellent Way—R
($)-Mutuality—R
New Heart—R
New Identity—R
$-New Wineskins—R
Nostalgia—R
$-Now What?—R
$-On Mission
$-Ozarks Senior Living—R
$-ParentLife
$-Partners—R
Penned from the Heart—R
$-Point—R
$-Power for Living—R
PrayerWorks—R
$-Psychology for Living—R
Quaker Life—R
Ruminate
$-Seek—R
Sharing—R
$-Spiritual Life
$-St. Anthony Messenger
$-Storyteller—R
$-Testimony—R
$-Together—R
Trumpeter—R
Unrecognized Woman—R
$-Upscale
$-U.S. Catholic—R
Victory Herald—R
$-Victory in Grace—R
$-Vision—R
$-War Cry—R
$-Way of St. Francis—R
$-Wesleyan Life—R
$-World & I—R

CHILDREN
$-BREAD/God's Children—R
$-Faces
$-Guide—R
$-New Moon—R
$-Partners—R
Skipping Stones
$-Sparkle—R

CHRISTIAN EDUCATION/ LIBRARY
$-Children's Ministry
$-Group

$-Journal/Adventist Ed.—R
$-Teachers of Vision—R

DAILY DEVOTIONALS
Penned from the Heart—R
$-Rejoice!

MISSIONS
$-Evangelical Missions—R
$-Glad Tidings—R
Railroad Evangelist—R
Women of the Harvest

PASTORS/LEADERS
$-Catholic Servant
Jour./Pastoral Care
$-Lead Magazine—R
$-Priest
$-Today's Parish
$-Worship Leader
$-YouthWorker

TEEN/YOUNG ADULT
$-Boundless Webzine—R
$-Devo'Zine—R
$-Direction Student
$-Horizon Student
$-Insight—R
$-Spirit
$-TC Magazine
TeensForJC—R
$-TG Magazine
$-Young Salvationist—R

WOMEN
Christian Woman's Page—R
Chris. Work at Home Moms—R
Empowering Everyday Women
Extreme Woman
Glory & Strength—R
Hope for Women
Inspired Women
$-Journey
Just Between Us—R
$-Melody of the Heart
$-MomSense—R
$-Mother's Heart—R
$-Pauses…
Precious Times—R
$-SpiritLed Woman
Unrecognized Woman—R
Virtuous Woman—R
Women Today—R

WRITERS
Areopagus
$-New Writer's Mag.
NW Christian Author—R

PERSONAL GROWTH
ADULT/GENERAL
$-Alive Now—R
$-Associated Content—R
$-Bible Advocate—R
$-Catholic Digest—R
$-Catholic Forester—R
$-Catholic Peace Voice—R
CBN.com—R
$-Christian Courier/Canada—R
Christian Journal—R
Christian Online
Christian Quarterly—R
Christian Ranchman
$-Churchmouse Public.—R
$-Columbia—R
$-Common Ground—R
Connections Ldrship/MOPS
$-Decision
Divine Ascent
$-Earthen Vessel Online—R
E-Channels—R
$-Evangel/IN—R
$-Faith & Family
$-Faith & Friends—R
Faithwebbin—R
$-Family Digest—R
$-Gem—R
$-Good News, Etc.—R
$-Good News, The—R
Gospel Herald
$-Guide—R
Halo Magazine—R
$-Home Times—R
($)-HopeKeepers—R
$-Indian Life—R
$-In His Presence—R
$-In Touch
Island Catholic—R
$-JC Town Reporter—R
Just Between Us—R
$-KD Gospel Media
Keys to Living—R
Koinonia

$-Kyria—R
Leaves—R
$-Lifeglow—R
$-Light & Life
$-Liguorian
$-Live—R
$-Living—R
$-Living Church
$-Lookout
$-Lutheran Digest—R
$-Manna—R
$-Mature Living
$-Mature Years—R
$-Men of Integrity—R
More Excellent Way—R
($)-Mutuality—R
New Heart—R
New Identity—R
$-New Wineskins—R
$-Now What?—R
$-ParentLife
Penned from the Heart—R
$-Prairie Messenger—R
PrayerWorks—R
Prison Victory
$-Psychology for Living—R
$-Purpose—R
Regent Global—R
$-Rev Up Your Life
$-River Region's Journey
$-Seek—R
Share
Single Again Mag.—R
$-St. Anthony Messenger
$-Stewardship—R
$-Testimony—R
$-Together—R
Trumpeter—R
Unrecognized Woman—R
$-U.S. Catholic—R
Victory Herald—R
$-Victory in Grace—R
$-War Cry—R
$-Way of St. Francis—R
$-Wildwood Reader—R
$-World & I—R

CHILDREN
$-BREAD/God's Children—R
$-Guide—R

Skipping Stones
$-Sparkle—R

CHRISTIAN EDUCATION/ LIBRARY
$-Children's Ministry
$-Youth & CE Leadership

DAILY DEVOTIONALS
Penned from the Heart—R

MISSIONS
$-Glad Tidings—R
Women of the Harvest

PASTORS/LEADERS
$-Ministry Today

TEEN/YOUNG ADULT
$-Boundless Webzine—R
$-Direction Student
$-Horizon Student
$-Insight—R
TeensForJC—R
$-TG Magazine
$-Young Adult Today
$-Young Salvationist—R

WOMEN
Christian Woman's Page—R
$-Dabbling Mum—R
Empowering Everyday Women
Extreme Woman
$-Fullfill
Glory & Strength—R
Hope for Women
$-Horizons—R
$-inSpirit—R
$-Journey
Just Between Us—R
Life Tools for Women
Love, Pearls & Swine
$-MomSense—R
$-Mother's Heart—R
Onyx Woman
P31 Woman—R
$-Pauses…
Precious Times—R
$-SpiritLed Woman
Take Root & Write
Unrecognized Woman—R
Virtuous Woman—R
Women Today—R

WRITERS
Areopagus

PHOTO ESSAYS
ADULT/GENERAL
$-Associated Content—R
$-Cathedral Age
Christian Motorsports
Creation Care—R
Desert Voice—R
$-Faith & Family
$-Good News, Etc.—R
$-Good News, The—R
$-Imagine
Island Catholic—R
$-KD Gospel Media
Nostalgia—R
$-Our Sunday Visitor—R
$-Ozarks Senior Living—R
$-Priority!—R
$-Prism
$-Salvo
$-St. Anthony Messenger
$-U.S. Catholic—R
$-Wildwood Reader—R
$-World & I—R

CHILDREN
$-Faces
Skipping Stones

CHRISTIAN EDUCATION/ LIBRARY
$-Journal/Adventist Ed.—R

MISSIONS
$-Glad Tidings—R

PASTORS/LEADERS
Church Executive
$-Outreach—R
$-Priest
$-YouthWorker

TEEN/YOUNG ADULT
TeensForJC—R

WOMEN
Christian Woman's Page—R
$-Horizons—R

PHOTOGRAPHS

Note: "Reprint" indicators (R) have been deleted from this section and "B" for black & white glossy prints or "C" for color transparencies inserted. An asterisk (*) before a listing indicates they buy photos with articles only.

ADULT/GENERAL

African Voices—B
American Tract
Anglican Journal—B/C
*Animal Trails—B/C
*Arkansas Catholic—C
Arlington Catholic—B
Associated Content—C
Bible Advocate—C
*Breakthrough Intercessor—C
*Bridal Guides—B/C
Canada Lutheran—B
*Catholic Digest—B/C
Catholic Forester—B/C
*Catholic Insight
Catholic New York—B
Catholic Peace Voice—B/C
Catholic Sentinel—B/C
Catholic Telegraph—B
Catholic Yearbook—C
CBA Retailers—C
*Celebrate Life—C
*Charisma—C
*Christian Citizen USA—C
*Christian Courier/Canada—B
*Christian Examiner—C
Christian Family Jour.—C
Christian Herald—C
*Christian History—B/C
Christian Home & School—C
*Christianity Today—C
*Christian Motorsports—B
*Christian Online
Christian Retailing—C
*Christian Standard—B/C
ChristianWeek—B/C
Churchmouse Public.—B/C
*Church of England News
City Light News—B/C
*Commonweal—B/C
Connecting Point—B

Covenant Companion—B/C
Culture Wars—B/C
Decision
*Desert Voice
Divine Ascent—B
*Earthen Vessel Online—B/C
Episcopal Life—B
Eureka Street—B/C
*Evangel/IN—B
*Evangel/OR—B/C
Faith & Family—C
*Faith & Friends—C
FGBC World—C
*Foursquare Leader
*Good News Journal
*Good News, The—C
Gospel Herald—C
Gospel Today
*Guideposts—B/C
Halo Magazine
Highway News—B
Holy House Ministries—B
*Homeschooling Today—B/C
*Home Times—B/C
*HopeKeepers—B/C
Imagine—C
*Impact Magazine—C
Indian Life—B/C
*In His Presence
Interchange—B
*Interim—B/C
*In Touch
Island Catholic—B/C
KD Gospel Media—B/C
*Layman—B
Leaves—B/C
*Leben—C
Liberty—B/C
*Lifeglow—B/C
Light & Life—B/C
*Liguorian—C
*Live—B/C
Living—B/C
Living Church—B/C
*Living Light—B/C
*Lookout—B/C
*Lutheran Journal—C
Lutheran Witness
*Manna—C
Marian Helper—B/C

*Mature Living
*Mature Years—C
Messianic Perspectives—B
Miracles, Healings—B
Montana Catholic
Mutuality—B/C
*New Heart—C
*New Identity—C
New Wineskins—B/C
Nostalgia—B/C
On Mission—B/C
Our Sunday Visitor—B/C
Over the Back Fence—C
*Pathway
Pentecostal Evangel—B/C
*Perspectives—B
*Point—C
Power for Living—B
Presbyterian Outlook—B/C
*Presbyterians Today—B/C
*Prism—B/C
*Psychology for Living—C
*Purpose—B
*Quaker Life—B/C
River Region's Journey
Salvo—C
*Seek—C
*Special Living—B/C
Spiritual Life—B
Sports Spectrum—C
*St. Anthony Messenger—B/C
*Storyteller—B
*Testimony—B/C
Tiferet—B/C
*Together—B/C
*United Church Observer—B/C
*Unrecognized Woman—C
Upscale
*Vibrant Life—C
Vision—B/C
*War Cry—B/C
Way of St. Francis—B/C
*World & I—B/C

CHILDREN

American Girl—C
Cadet Quest—C
Celebrate—C
*Focus/Clubhouse—C
*Focus/Clubhouse Jr.—C

Nature Friend—B/C
*Pockets—C
SHINE brightly—C
Skipping Stones

CHRISTIAN EDUCATION/
LIBRARY
*Christian Early Ed.—C
Christian Librarian—B
*Church Libraries—B/C
Journal/Adventist Ed.—B
*Kids' Ministry Ideas
*Momentum—C
*Teachers of Vision—C
*Today's Catholic Teacher—C
*Youth & CE Leadership—C

DAILY DEVOTIONALS
Our Daily Journey—C
Secret Place—B
Upper Room

MISSIONS
Evangelical Missions
*Glad Tidings—C
Intl. Jour./Frontier
*New World Outlook—C
*One—C
Operation Reveille—B/C
PFI Global

MUSIC
Christian Music—B
*Creator—B/C

PASTORS/LEADERS
Catechumenate—C
Catholic Servant
Christian Century—B/C
*Church Executive—C
*Disciple Magazine—B/C
*Foursquare Leader
Immerse—C
*InSite—C
*Leadership—B
Ministry—B
Priest
Reformed Worship—C
Today's Parish—B/C
*Worship Leader—C
*Your Church—C
*YouthWorker

TEEN/YOUNG ADULT
*Direction Student—B/C
Essential Connection—B/C
Listen—B/C
*Sharing the Victory—C
*Spirit
Take Five Plus—B/C
Young Adult Today—B
*Young Christian—B/C

WOMEN
At the Center—C
Beyond the Bend—B/C
Glory & Strength
Handmaidens
*Link & Visitor—B
*Mother's Heart—C
*Precious Times—C
Right to the Heart
*Unrecognized Woman—C

WRITERS
Best New Writing—C
*Cross & Quill—B
Esdras' Scroll—B/C
*New Writer's Mag.
*Poets & Writers
Tickled by Thunder
Write Connection—B
*Writer's Chronicle—B
*Writer's Digest—B

POETRY
ADULT/GENERAL
African Voices—R
$-Alive Now—R
$-America
$-Associated Content—R
$-Aujourd'hui Credo—R
$-Bible Advocate—R
Bread of Life—R
Breakthrough Intercessor—R
$-Bridal Guides—R
$-Catholic Peace Voice—R
$-Catholic Yearbook—R
$-Christian Courier/Canada—R
Christian Journal—R
Christian Motorsports
$-Christian Research
$-Churchmouse Public.—R
$-Commonweal

Connecting Point—R
Creation Care—R
$-Creation Illust.—R
$-Cresset
$-Culture Wars—R
Desert Call—R
E-Channels—R
Eternal Ink—R
$-Eureka Street
$-Evangel/IN—R
Evangel/OR—R
Friends Journal—R
$-Gem—R
Good News Journal—R
Haiku Hippodrome
Halo Magazine—R
$-Haruah—R
Highway News—R
$-Homeschooling Today—R
$-Home Times—R
$-Image
($)-Impact Magazine—R
$-Indian Life—R
$-In His Presence—R
Island Catholic—R
$-JC Town Reporter—R
$-KD Gospel Media
Keys to Living—R
Leaves—R
$-Liberty
LifeTimes Catholic
$-Light & Life
Light of the World
$-Live—R
$-Lutheran Digest—R
$-Lutheran Journal—R
$-Mature Living
$-Mature Years—R
Men of the Cross
$-Miraculous Medal
New Heart—R
New Identity—R
$-New Wineskins—R
Pegasus Review—R
Penned from the Heart—R
Penwood Review
Perspectives—R
$-Prairie Messenger—R
Priscilla Papers
$-Purpose—R

Quaker Life—R
Radix Magazine
Relief Journal—R
Ruminate
Sharing—R
Silver Wings—R
Single Again Mag.—R
$-St. Anthony Messenger
$-Storyteller—R
Studio—R
Sword and Trumpet
Sword of the Lord—R
$-Testimony—R
$-Thomas Ink
Tiferet—R
Time of Singing—R
$-U.S. Catholic—R
Victory Herald—R
$-Vision—R
$-Way of St. Francis—R
$-Weavings—R
$-World & I—R
Xavier Review

CHILDREN
$-American Girl—R
$-Faces
$-Focus/Clubhouse Jr.
$-Partners—R
$-Pockets—R
$-SHINE brightly—R
Skipping Stones
$-Story Mates—R

CHRISTIAN EDUCATION/ LIBRARY
$-Teachers of Vision—R
$-Today's Catholic Teacher—R

DAILY DEVOTIONALS
Christian Devotions—R
$-God's Word For Today
Penned from the Heart—R
$-Secret Place
$-These Days

MISSIONS
$-Glad Tidings—R
Railroad Evangelist—R

PASTORS/LEADERS
$-Catechumenate
$-Christian Century—R

CrossCurrents
$-Emmanuel
Jour./Pastoral Care
Lutheran Forum
$-Preaching Well—R
$-Review for Religious
Sharing the Practice—R

TEEN/YOUNG ADULT
$-Devo'Zine—R
$-Essential Connection
G4T Ink—R
$-Insight—R
$-Take Five Plus
TeensForJC—R
$-Young Christian—R
$-Young Christian Writers
$-Young Salvationist—R

WOMEN
Christian Woman's Page—R
Glory & Strength—R
Handmaidens
$-Link & Visitor—R
$-Melody of the Heart
$-MomSense—R
Unrecognized Woman—R
Virtuous Woman—R

WRITERS
Areopagus
$-Best New Writing
$-Canadian Writer's Jour.—R
$-Christian Communicator—R
ChristianWriters.com
$-Cross & Quill—R
Esdras' Scroll—R
$-New Writer's Mag.
NW Christian Author—R
$-Tickled by Thunder
Write Connection
$-Writer's Digest
$-Writers' Journal

POLITICS
ADULT/GENERAL
African Voices—R
$-Anglican Journal
$-Arlington Catholic
$-Associated Content—R
$-Brink Magazine—R

Brink Online—R
$-Cathedral Age
$-Catholic Insight
$-Catholic Peace Voice—R
CBN.com—R
Christian Business
$-Christian Courier/Canada—R
Christian Courier/WI—R
$-Christian Examiner
$-Christianity Today—R
Christian Media—R
$-Christian Renewal—R
$-ChristianWeek—R
$-Churchmouse Public.—R
Church of England News
$-Commonweal
Creation Care—R
$-Creative Nonfiction
$-Cresset
Desert Voice—R
$-Faith Today—R
$-Good News, Etc.—R
$-Good News, The—R
Gospel Herald
Halo Magazine—R
$-Home Times—R
$-In Touch
Island Catholic—R
$-JC Town Reporter—R
$-KD Gospel Media
Koinonia
$-Light & Life
Movieguide
Network
New Christian Voices
$-New Wineskins—R
$-Our Sunday Visitor—R
Perspectives—R
$-Presbyterian Outlook
$-Social Justice—R
$-St. Anthony Messenger
$-Testimony—R
Tri-State Voice
Trumpeter—R
$-U.S. Catholic—R
Wisconsin Christian
$-World & I—R

CHILDREN
$-New Moon—R

MISSIONS
East-West Church
$-One

PASTORS/LEADERS
$-Christian Century—R
$-Immerse
$-Interpreter
$-Word & World

TEEN/YOUNG ADULT
$-Boundless Webzine—R
$-InTeen—R

WOMEN
Empowering Everyday Women
$-inSpirit—R

PRAISE*
ADULT/GENERAL
Breakthrough Intercessor—R
$-Churchmouse Public.—R
$-Kyria—R
$-Mother's Heart—R

PASTORS/LEADERS
Christian Early Ed.—R
Christian School Ed.—R
Disciple Magazine—R

WOMEN
$-Brink Magazine—R
Glory & Strength—R

PRAYER
ADULT/GENERAL
African Voices—R
$-Alive Now—R
$-Angels on Earth
Believer's Bay
$-Bible Advocate—R
Breakthrough Intercessor—R
$-Brink Magazine—R
$-Cathedral Age
$-Catholic Digest—R
$-Catholic Peace Voice—R
$-Catholic Yearbook—R
CBN.com—R
$-Celebrate Life—R
$-CGA World—R
$-Christian Home & School
$-Christianity Today—R
Christian Journal—R

Christian Online
Christian Quarterly—R
Christian Ranchman
$-Christian Research
$-Christian Standard—R
$-ChristianWeek—R
$-Churchmouse Public.—R
$-Columbia—R
Connecting Point—R
$-Covenant Companion—R
$-Culture Wars—R
$-Decision
Desert Call—R
Desert Voice—R
Divine Ascent
$-Earthen Vessel Online—R
$-Episcopal Life—R
$-Evangel/IN—R
$-Faith & Family
Faithwebbin—R
$-Family Digest—R
Foursquare Leader
$-Gem—R
$-Good News—R
$-Good News, Etc.—R
$-Good News, The—R
Gospel Herald
$-Guide—R
Halo Magazine—R
HEARTLIGHT Internet—R
Holy House Ministries—R
$-Home Times—R
($)-HopeKeepers—R
$-In His Presence—R
$-In Touch
Island Catholic—R
$-JC Town Reporter—R
Just Between Us—R
$-KD Gospel Media
Koinonia
$-Kyria—R
Leaves—R
$-Lifeglow—R
$-Light & Life
$-Liguorian
$-Live—R
$-Living Church
$-Lookout
$-Lutheran Digest—R
$-Lutheran Journal—R

$-Lutheran Witness
$-Manna—R
$-Marian Helper
$-Mature Years—R
Men.AG.org—R
$-Men of Integrity—R
MESSAGE/Open Bible—R
$-New Wineskins—R
$-Our Sunday Visitor—R
$-ParentLife
Pegasus Review—R
Penned from the Heart—R
$-Pentecostal Evangel—R
Perspectives—R
$-Point—R
Prayer Closet
PrayerWorks—R
$-Presbyterian Outlook
$-Presbyterians Today—R
$-Priority!—R
$-River Region's Journey
$-Seek—R
$-Spiritual Life
$-St. Anthony Messenger
Sword of the Lord—R
$-Testimony—R
Trumpeter—R
Unrecognized Woman—R
$-U.S. Catholic—R
Victory Herald—R
$-War Cry—R
$-Way of St. Francis—R
$-Wesleyan Life—R
Wisconsin Christian

CHILDREN
$-BREAD/God's Children—R
$-Guide—R
$-Primary Street
$-Sparkle—R

CHRISTIAN EDUCATION/ LIBRARY
$-Children's Ministry
$-Group
$-Teachers of Vision—R
$-Youth & CE Leadership

DAILY DEVOTIONALS
$-Brink Magazine—R
Penned from the Heart—R

MISSIONS
$-Glad Tidings—R
Intl. Jour./Frontier—R
$-PFI Global—R
Railroad Evangelist—R

MUSIC
$-Creator—R

PASTORS/LEADERS
$-Catholic Servant
$-Clergy Journal—R
$-Diocesan Dialogue—R
Disciple Magazine—R
$-Emmanuel
$-Immerse
$-Interpreter
$-Leadership—R
$-Ministry & Liturgy—R
$-Ministry Today
$-Proclaim—R
$-Reformed Worship—R
$-Review for Religious
Rick Warren's Ministry—R
Sewanee Theo. Review
$-SmallGroups.com—R
Theological Digest—R
$-Today's Parish
$-Word & World
$-Worship Leader

TEEN/YOUNG ADULT
$-Boundless Webzine—R
$-Devo'Zine—R
$-Direction Student
$-Horizon Student
$-Insight—R
$-InTeen—R
$-J.A.M.
TeensForJC—R
$-TG Magazine
$-Young Salvationist—R

WOMEN
($)-Beyond the Bend—R
Christian Woman's Page—R
Extreme Woman
For Every Woman—R
Glory & Strength—R
Hope for Women
$-Horizons—R
$-InspiredMoms—R

$-inSpirit—R
$-Journey
Just Between Us—R
Lutheran Woman's Quar.
$-Mother's Heart—R
P31 Woman—R
Precious Times—R
Right to the Heart—R
$-SpiritLed Woman
Unrecognized Woman—R
Virtuous Woman—R
Women Today—R

WRITERS
Areopagus

PROPHECY
ADULT/GENERAL
$-Apocalypse Chronicles—R
Believer's Bay
$-Bible Advocate—R
CBN.com—R
Christian Media—R
Christian Online
Christian Quarterly—R
$-Christian Research
Faithwebbin—R
Foursquare Leader
Gospel Herald
Halo Magazine—R
$-In His Presence—R
$-In Touch
$-JC Town Reporter—R
$-KD Gospel Media
Koinonia
$-Light & Life
$-Live—R
Midnight Call
$-Our Sunday Visitor—R
Single Again Mag.—R
$-St. Anthony Messenger
Sword of the Lord—R
$-Testimony—R
Trumpeter—R
Unrecognized Woman—R

PASTORS/LEADERS
$-Ministry Today
Rick Warren's Ministry—R
$-Word & World

TEEN/YOUNG ADULT
$-InTeen—R
TeensForJC—R
$-Young Salvationist—R

WOMEN
$-SpiritLed Woman
Unrecognized Woman—R

PSYCHOLOGY
ADULT/GENERAL
$-Associated Content—R
$-Aujourd'hui Credo—R
$-Catholic Peace Voice—R
CBN.com—R
$-Christian Courier/Canada—R
Christian Online
$-Creative Nonfiction
$-Gem—R
Gospel Herald
Halo Magazine—R
$-In Touch
Island Catholic—R
$-JC Town Reporter—R
$-KD Gospel Media
Koinonia
$-Light & Life
More Excellent Way—R
$-Mother's Heart—R
$-Our Sunday Visitor—R
Perspectives/Science
$-Psychology for Living—R
$-Search
$-Spiritual Life
$-St. Anthony Messenger
$-Testimony—R
Trumpeter—R
$-Vibrant Life—R
$-World & I—R

CHILDREN
$-New Moon—R

PASTORS/LEADERS
$-Immerse
Jour./Pastoral Care
$-Word & World

WOMEN
($)-Beyond the Bend—R
Glory & Strength—R

PUPPET PLAYS

$-Children's Ministry
Christian Early Ed.—R
$-Churchmouse Public.—R
$-Imagine
$-JC Town Reporter—R

RACISM
ADULT/GENERAL
$-Aujourd'hui Credo—R
$-Brink Magazine—R
$-Catholic Peace Voice—R
CBN.com—R
$-Christian Citizen USA
$-Christianity Today—R
$-ChristianWeek—R
$-Columbia—R
$-Creative Nonfiction
$-Eureka Street
$-Faith Today—R
Faithwebbin—R
Gospel Herald
$-Guide—R
Halo Magazine—R
$-In Touch
Island Catholic—R
$-JC Town Reporter—R
$-KD Gospel Media
Koinonia
$-Light & Life
$-Live—R
$-Lookout
$-Manna—R
$-Men of Integrity—R
($)-Mutuality—R
$-New Wineskins—R
$-Our Sunday Visitor—R
Perspectives—R
Priscilla Papers
$-Prism
$-St. Anthony Messenger
$-Testimony—R
$-Together—R
Trumpeter—R
$-Upscale
$-U.S. Catholic—R
$-Way of St. Francis—R
$-World & I—R

CHILDREN
$-Guide—R
$-New Moon—R
$-Our Little Friend—R
$-Primary Treasure—R
Skipping Stones
$-Sparkle—R

MISSIONS
East-West Church

PASTORS/LEADERS
$-Clergy Journal—R
CrossCurrents
Jour./Pastoral Care
$-Ministry Today

TEEN/YOUNG ADULT
$-Boundless Webzine—R
$-Direction Student
$-Horizon Student
TeensForJC—R
$-TG Magazine
$-Young Salvationist—R

WOMEN
$-Horizons—R
$-SpiritLed Woman

RECOVERY
ADULT/GENERAL
$-Bible Advocate—R
CBN.com—R
Christian Journal—R
$-Churchmouse Public.—R
$-Creative Nonfiction
$-Disaster News
$-Earthen Vessel Online—R
$-Good News, The—R
Gospel Herald
Halo Magazine—R
$-Home Times—R
($)-HopeKeepers—R
$-In Touch
$-JC Town Reporter—R
$-KD Gospel Media
Koinonia
$-Kyria—R
$-Light & Life
$-Live—R
$-Lookout

$-Manna—R
Men.AG.org—R
$-Men of Integrity—R
$-Miracles, Healings—R
$-Our Sunday Visitor—R
$-Priority!—R
$-Prism
Prison Victory
Ruminate
$-Seek—R
Unrecognized Woman—R
$-Way of St. Francis—R
$-Wildwood Reader—R
Wisconsin Christian
$-Written

PASTORS/LEADERS
Jour./Pastoral Care
$-Ministry Today

TEEN/YOUNG ADULT
$-Boundless Webzine—R

WOMEN
($)-Beyond the Bend—R
Glory & Strength—R
$-inSpirit—R
Right to the Heart—R
Take Root & Write
Women Today—R

RELATIONSHIPS
ADULT/GENERAL
$-Angels on Earth
Anointed Pages
$-Associated Content—R
$-Aujourd'hui Credo—R
$-Bridal Guides—R
$-Brink Magazine—R
$-Canada Lutheran—R
($)-Canadian Mennonite—R
$-Catholic Digest—R
$-Catholic Forester—R
CBN.com—R
$-Celebrate Life—R
$-Chicken Soup Books—R
Christian Family Jour.
$-Christian Home & School
Christian Journal—R
Christian Online

Christian Quarterly—R
Christian Ranchman
$-ChristianWeek—R
$-Churchmouse Public.—R
$-Creative Nonfiction
Desert Call—R
E-Channels—R
Eternal Ink—R
$-Evangel/IN—R
$-Faith Today—R
Faithwebbin—R
$-Family Digest—R
$-Family Smart E-tips—R
Foursquare Leader
$-Gem—R
$-Gems of Truth—R
Good News Journal—R
$-Good News, The—R
Gospel Herald
$-Gospel Today—R
$-Guideposts—R
Halo Magazine—R
HEARTLIGHT Internet—R
Highway News—R
$-Homeschooling Today—R
$-Home Times—R
Hope for Women
($)-HopeKeepers—R
$-In His Presence—R
$-In Touch
Island Catholic—R
$-JC Town Reporter—R
Just Between Us—R
$-KD Gospel Media
Keys to Living—R
Koinonia
$-Kyria—R
$-Lifeglow—R
$-Light & Life
$-Liguorian
$-Live—R
$-Living—R
$-Lookout
$-Manna—R
$-Mature Years—R
Men.AG.org—R
$-Men of Integrity—R
Men of the Cross
More Excellent Way—R
($)-Mutuality—R

New Heart—R
New Identity—R
$-New Wineskins—R
$-Our Sunday Visitor—R
Ozarks Christian
$-ParentLife
Pegasus Review—R
Penned from the Heart—R
$-Pentecostal Evangel—R
Perspectives—R
$-Point—R
PrayerWorks—R
Priscilla Papers
$-River Region's Journey
$-Search
$-Seek—R
Single Again Mag.—R
$-Special Living—R
Spirituality for Today
$-St. Anthony Messenger
$-Storyteller—R
$-Testimony—R
$-Together—R
Trumpeter—R
Unrecognized Woman—R
$-Upscale
$-Vibrant Life—R
$-Vision—R
$-Vista—R
$-War Cry—R
$-Way of St. Francis—R
$-Wesleyan Life—R
$-Wildwood Reader—R
$-World & I—R

CHILDREN
$-BREAD/God's Children—R
$-Cadet Quest—R
$-New Moon—R
$-SHINE brightly—R
Skipping Stones
$-Sparkle—R

CHRISTIAN EDUCATION/ LIBRARY
$-Group
$-Teachers of Vision—R
$-Youth & CE Leadership

MISSIONS
$-Glad Tidings—R

PASTORS/LEADERS
$-Leadership—R
$-SmallGroups.com—R
$-Word & World

TEEN/YOUNG ADULT
$-Boundless Webzine—R
$-Direction Student
G4T Ink—R
$-Horizon Student
$-Insight—R
$-Listen—R
$-TC Magazine
TeensForJC—R
$-TG Magazine
$-Young Salvationist—R

WOMEN
$-At the Center—R
($)-Beyond the Bend—R
Christian Woman's Page—R
$-Dabbling Mum—R
Empowering Everyday Women
Extreme Woman
First Lady
For Every Woman—R
$-Girlfriend 2 Girlfriend
Glory & Strength—R
$-Heart & Soul
Hope for Women
$-InspiredMoms—R
$-inSpirit—R
$-Journey
Just Between Us—R
Life Tools for Women
$-Link & Visitor—R
Live Magazine
Love, Pearls & Swine
Lutheran Woman's Quar.
$-MomSense—R
$-Mother's Heart—R
P31 Woman—R
$-Pauses…
Precious Times—R
$-SpiritLed Woman
Take Root & Write
Unrecognized Woman—R
Virtuous Woman—R
Women Today—R

RELIGIOUS FREEDOM
ADULT/GENERAL
$-Arlington Catholic
$-Aujourd'hui Credo—R
$-Brink Magazine—R
$-Catholic Peace Voice—R
CBN.com—R
Christian Courier/WI—R
$-Christian Examiner
$-Christian Home & School
$-Christianity Today—R
Christian Observer
Christian Online
Christian Ranchman
$-Christian Response—R
$-ChristianWeek—R
$-Churchmouse Public.—R
Church of England News
$-Columbia—R
$-Commonweal
$-Compass Direct
Connecting Point—R
Desert Voice—R
E-Channels—R
$-Episcopal Life—R
$-Eureka Street
$-Faith Today—R
$-Gem—R
$-Good News, The—R
Good News Today
Gospel Herald
$-Guide—R
Halo Magazine—R
$-Home Times—R
$-In His Presence—R
$-Interim—R
$-In Touch
Island Catholic—R
$-JC Town Reporter—R
$-KD Gospel Media
Koinonia
$-Liberty
$-Lifeglow—R
$-Light & Life
$-Live—R
$-Lookout
$-Manna—R
MESSAGE/Open Bible—R
Messianic Perspectives—R
$-New Wineskins—R

$-Our Sunday Visitor—R
$-Pathway—R
Pegasus Review—R
Perspectives—R
$-Prairie Messenger—R
$-Presbyterian Outlook
$-Prism
$-Salvo
$-Search
$-Seek—R
Spirituality for Today
$-Spiritual Life
$-St. Anthony Messenger
$-Testimony—R
Trumpeter—R
$-U.S. Catholic—R
Victory Herald—R
$-Way of St. Francis—R
Wisconsin Christian
$-World & I—R

CHILDREN
$-Guide—R
$-New Moon—R
Skipping Stones

CHRISTIAN EDUCATION/ LIBRARY
$-Teachers of Vision—R

MISSIONS
East-West Church
$-Evangelical Missions—R
$-Glad Tidings—R
Lausanne World—R
($)-Operation Reveille—R
WEC.go

PASTORS/LEADERS
$-Catholic Servant
$-Christian Century—R
CrossCurrents
$-Word & World

TEEN/YOUNG ADULT
$-Boundless Webzine—R
$-Direction Student
$-Horizon Student
$-InTeen—R
TeensForJC—R

WOMEN
$-SpiritLed Woman

RELIGIOUS TOLERANCE
ADULT/GENERAL
$-Aujourd'hui Credo—R
$-Brink Magazine—R
$-Catholic Peace Voice—R
CBN.com—R
$-Christian Examiner
$-Christian Home & School
Christian Online
$-Christianity Today—R
$-ChristianWeek—R
Church of England News
$-Columbia—R
$-Compass Direct
E-Channels—R
$-Eureka Street
$-Faith Today—R
$-Good News, Etc.—R
Gospel Herald
Halo Magazine—R
$-Interim—R
$-In Touch
Island Catholic—R
$-JC Town Reporter—R
$-KD Gospel Media
Koinonia
$-Light & Life
$-Live—R
$-Lookout
$-Manna—R
Messianic Perspectives—R
More Excellent Way—R
$-New Wineskins—R
$-Our Sunday Visitor—R
Perspectives—R
$-Prairie Messenger—R
$-Search
$-Seek—R
Spirituality for Today
$-St. Anthony Messenger
$-Testimony—R
Trumpeter—R
$-U.S. Catholic—R
$-Way of St. Francis—R
$-World & I—R

CHILDREN
$-New Moon—R
$-Primary Treasure—R
Skipping Stones

MISSIONS
East-West Church
$-Glad Tidings—R
($)-Operation Reveille—R

PASTORS/LEADERS
$-Christian Century—R
Church Executive
$-Clergy Journal—R
CrossCurrents

TEEN/YOUNG ADULT
$-Boundless Webzine—R
$-Direction Student
$-Horizon Student
TeensForJC—R

WOMEN
Hope for Women

REVIVAL
ADULT/GENERAL
$-Bible Advocate—R
Breakthrough Intercessor—R
CBN.com—R
$-Christian Home & School
Christian Quarterly—R
Christian Ranchman
$-Churchmouse Public.—R
$-Columbia—R
$-Earthen Vessel Online—R
$-Good News, Etc.—R
Gospel Herald
Halo Magazine—R
$-Home Times—R
$-In His Presence—R
$-In Touch
$-KD Gospel Media
Koinonia
$-Light & Life
$-Live—R
$-Lookout
$-Manna—R
$-Point—R

PASTORS/LEADERS
Great Comm. Research—R
$-Ministry Today

TEEN/YOUNG ADULT
$-Boundless Webzine—R
$-Insight—R

WOMEN
Hope for Women

SALVATION TESTIMONIES
ADULT/GENERAL
American Tract—R
Believer's Bay
CBN.com—R
$-Christian Home & School
Christian Journal—R
Christian Motorsports
Christian Online
Christian Quarterly—R
Christian Ranchman
$-Christian Research
$-Churchmouse Public.—R
$-Columbia—R
Connecting Point—R
$-Decision
$-Earthen Vessel Online—R
E-Channels—R
$-Evangel/IN—R
$-FGBC World—R
$-Gem—R
$-Good News, Etc.—R
Gospel Herald
$-Guide—R
$-Guideposts—R
Halo Magazine—R
Heartbeat/CMA
Highway News—R
$-Home Times—R
$-In His Presence—R
$-In Touch
$-JC Town Reporter—R
$-KD Gospel Media
Koinonia
Leaves—R
$-Lifeglow—R
$-Light & Life
$-Live—R
$-Men of Integrity—R
$-MESSAGE
Messianic Perspectives—R
New Heart—R
New Identity—R
$-Now What?—R
$-On Mission
$-Pathway—R
$-Point—R

$-Power for Living—R
PrayerWorks—R
$-Priority!—R
$-Seek—R
$-St. Anthony Messenger
Sword of the Lord—R
$-Testimony—R
$-Together—R
Trumpeter—R
$-War Cry—R
$-Wesleyan Life—R
Wisconsin Christian

CHILDREN
$-Guide—R
$-Sparkle—R

CHRISTIAN EDUCATION/ LIBRARY
$-Group

MISSIONS
Railroad Evangelist—R

TEEN/YOUNG ADULT
$-Boundless Webzine—R
$-Direction Student
$-Horizon Student
$-InTeen—R
TeensForJC—R

WOMEN
($)-History's Women—R
Hope for Women
$-Journey
Precious Times—R
$-SpiritLed Woman
Unrecognized Woman—R
Women Today—R

WRITERS
Areopagus

SCIENCE
ADULT/GENERAL
$-Animal Trails—R
Answers Magazine
$-Associated Content—R
$-Aujourd'hui Credo—R
CBN.com—R
$-Christian Courier/Canada—R
$-Churchmouse Public.—R
Creation

Creation Care—R
$-Creation Illust.—R
$-Creative Nonfiction
$-Eureka Street
$-Faith Today—R
Gospel Herald
$-Guide—R
$-Home Times—R
$-In Touch
Island Catholic—R
Koinonia
$-Light & Life
$-Our Sunday Visitor—R
Perspectives—R
Perspectives/Science
$-Salvo
$-Search
$-St. Anthony Messenger
$-Testimony—R
Trumpeter—R
$-U.S. Catholic—R
$-World & I—R

CHILDREN
$-Archaeology—R
$-Cadet Quest—R
$-Guide—R
$-Nature Friend—R
$-New Moon—R
Skipping Stones
$-Sparkle—R

MISSIONS
Intl. Jour./Frontier—R

PASTORS/LEADERS
$-Immerse
$-Word & World

TEEN/YOUNG ADULT
$-InTeen—R
TeensForJC—R

WOMEN
$-Mother's Heart—R

SELF-HELP
ADULT/GENERAL
$-Associated Content—R
$-Catholic Digest—R
CBN.com—R

$-CGA World—R
Disciple's Journal—R
$-Family Smart E-tips—R
Gospel Herald
Halo Magazine—R
$-Home Times—R
($)-HopeKeepers—R
$-In Touch
$-JC Town Reporter—R
$-KD Gospel Media
Koinonia
$-Lifeglow—R
$-Light & Life
$-Liguorian
$-Lookout
$-Manna—R
Men of the Cross
$-Seek—R
$-Significant Living—R
Single Again Mag.—R
$-Special Living—R
$-St. Anthony Messenger
$-Testimony—R
Trumpeter—R
$-Vibrant Life—R
$-World & I—R

CHILDREN
Skipping Stones

MISSIONS
$-Glad Tidings—R
Women of the Harvest

PASTORS/LEADERS
$-Interpreter

TEEN/YOUNG ADULT
$-Listen—R
TeensForJC—R

WOMEN
Christian Woman's Page—R
Extreme Woman
For Every Woman—R
$-Fullfill
Glory & Strength—R
$-Journey
Take Root & Write
Women of the Cross

SENIOR ADULT ISSUES
ADULT/GENERAL
$-Angels on Earth
$-Anglican Journal
$-Arkansas Catholic—R
$-Associated Content—R
$-B.C. Catholic—R
Breakthrough Intercessor—R
byFaith
$-Catholic Forester—R
CBN.com—R
$-CGA World—R
Christian Quarterly—R
Christian Ranchman
$-Christian Standard—R
$-ChristianWeek—R
$-Churchmouse Public.—R
$-City Light News—R
$-Columbia—R
Desert Voice—R
$-Evangel/IN—R
$-Faith Today—R
$-Family Digest—R
$-Family Smart E-tips—R
$-Gem—R
$-Good News, The—R
Gospel Herald
Halo Magazine—R
$-Home Times—R
($)-HopeKeepers—R
$-In His Presence—R
$-In Touch
Island Catholic—R
$-JC Town Reporter—R
Koinonia
$-Lifeglow—R
$-Light & Life
$-Liguorian
$-Live—R
$-Mature Living
$-Mature Years—R
$-Our Sunday Visitor—R
$-Ozarks Senior Living—R
Penned from the Heart—R
$-Point—R
$-Power for Living—R
PrayerWorks—R
$-River Region's Journey
$-Seek—R
Senior Connection

$-Significant Living—R
Single Again Mag.—R
$-St. Anthony Messenger
$-Testimony—R
Trumpeter—R
Unrecognized Woman—R
$-U.S. Catholic—R
$-War Cry—R
$-Way of St. Francis—R
$-Wesleyan Life—R

CHRISTIAN EDUCATION/ LIBRARY
$-Youth & CE Leadership

DAILY DEVOTIONALS
Penned from the Heart—R

MISSIONS
$-Glad Tidings—R

PASTORS/LEADERS
$-Diocesan Dialogue—R
$-Interpreter
$-Word & World

WOMEN
For Every Woman—R
$-inSpirit—R
Unrecognized Woman—R

SERMONS
ADULT/GENERAL
$-Arlington Catholic
Breakthrough Intercessor—R
$-Catholic Yearbook—R
$-Earthen Vessel Online—R
Gospel Herald
$-In His Presence—R
$-KD Gospel Media
Koinonia
$-Lutheran Journal—R
Pegasus Review—R
$-St. Anthony Messenger
$-Stewardship—R
Sword of the Lord—R
$-Testimony—R
Trumpeter—R
Victory Herald—R
$-Weavings—R
Wisconsin Christian

PASTORS/LEADERS
$-Clergy Journal—R
$-Ministry Today
Preaching
$-Preaching Well—R
$-Proclaim—R
Sharing the Practice—R
$-Sunday Sermons—R
$-Today's Parish
$-Torch Legacy Leader

SHORT STORY: ADULT/GENERAL
$-Best New Writing
CBN.com—R
$-Churchmouse Public.—R
Desert Call—R
Desert Voice—R
$-Earthen Vessel Online—R
Faithwebbin—R
$-Glad Tidings—R
Halo Magazine—R
Handmaidens
$-Haruah—R
$-Imagine
$-In His Presence—R
$-Liguorian
$-Ministry & Liturgy—R
$-Miraculous Medal
$-New Writer's Mag.
$-Over the Back Fence—R
Perspectives—R
PrayerWorks—R
$-Preaching Well—R
$-Purpose—R
Ruminate
$-Seek—R
$-Significant Living—R
Tiferet—R
Unrecognized Woman—R
$-Wildwood Reader—R

SHORT STORY: ADULT/RELIGIOUS
$-Alive Now—R
$-Angels on Earth
$-Anglican Journal
Areopagus
$-Associated Content—R
$-Aujourd'hui Credo—R

$-Bridal Guides—R
$-Canadian Writer's Jour.—R
$-Catholic Forester—R
$-Catholic Yearbook—R
CBN.com—R
$-CGA World—R
$-Christian Century—R
$-Christian Courier/Canada—R
$-Christian Educators—R
$-Christian Home & School
Christian Journal—R
Christian Online
Christian Ranchman
$-Christian Renewal—R
$-Christian Research
Christian Woman's Page—R
$-Churchmouse Public.—R
$-City Light News—R
Connecting Point—R
$-Covenant Companion—R
CrossCurrents
Desert Voice—R
$-Earthen Vessel Online—R
Esdras' Scroll—R
$-Eureka Street
$-Evangel/IN—R
$-Faith & Family
Faithwebbin—R
Foursquare Leader
$-Gem—R
$-Gems of Truth—R
$-Glad Tidings—R
Glory & Strength—R
Handmaidens
$-Haruah—R
HEARTLIGHT Internet—R
$-Homeschooling Today—R
$-Home Times—R
$-Horizons—R
$-Image
$-Imagine
($)-Impact Magazine—R
$-Indian Life—R
$-In His Presence—R
$-inSpirit—R
Intl. Jour./Frontier—R
Island Catholic—R
$-JC Town Reporter—R
Koinonia
$-Liguorian

$-Live—R
$-Lutheran Journal—R
Lutheran Woman's Quar.
$-Melody of the Heart
$-Messenger/Sacred Heart
$-Messenger/St. Anthony
$-Miraculous Medal
$-New Wineskins—R
$-On Mission
Perspectives—R
PrayerWorks—R
Precious Times—R
$-Presbyterian Outlook
$-Proclaim—R
$-Purpose—R
Railroad Evangelist—R
Relief Journal—R
Ruminate
Seeds of Hope
$-Seek—R
$-Shades of Romance—R
$-Significant Living—R
Spirituality for Today
$-St. Anthony Messenger
Studio—R
$-Testimony—R
Tiferet—R
Unrecognized Woman—R
$-U.S. Catholic—R
$-Vision—R
$-Vista—R
$-Way of St. Francis—R
$-Wesleyan Life—R
$-Written

SHORT STORY: ADVENTURE
ADULT
$-Angels on Earth
$-Animal Trails—R
$-Associated Content—R
$-Best New Writing
CBN.com—R
$-Churchmouse Public.—R
Desert Voice—R
Esdras' Scroll—R
$-Gem—R
$-Glad Tidings—R
Halo Magazine—R
$-Haruah—R

HEARTLIGHT Internet—R
$-Indian Life—R
$-In His Presence—R
$-JC Town Reporter—R
$-Liguorian
($)-Midnight Diner
$-Partners—R
PrayerWorks—R
$-Storyteller—R
Studio—R
Unrecognized Woman—R
$-Vision—R
$-Weavings—R

CHILDREN
$-American Girl—R
$-Animal Trails—R
$-Archaeology—R
$-BREAD/God's Children—R
$-Cadet Quest—R
Connecting Point—R
Eternal Ink—R
$-Focus/Clubhouse Jr.
$-Junior Companion—R
$-Kids' Ark—R
$-New Moon—R
$-Partners—R
$-SHINE brightly—R
Skipping Stones
$-Sparkle—R
Sword of the Lord—R
$-Young Christian—R

TEEN/YOUNG ADULT
$-Animal Trails—R
$-Archaeology—R
$-BREAD/God's Children—R
$-Cadet Quest—R
$-Direction Student
$-Horizon Student
$-InTeen—R
$-Partners—R
$-SHINE brightly—R
$-Storyteller—R
Sword of the Lord—R
TeensForJC—R
$-Young Adult Today
$-Young Christian—R
$-Young Christian Writers

SHORT STORY: ALLEGORY
ADULT
$-Alive Now—R
$-Associated Content—R
CBN.com—R
Christian Journal—R
Christian Woman's Page—R
$-Churchmouse Public.—R
$-City Light News—R
$-Covenant Companion—R
Esdras' Scroll—R
$-Gem—R
$-Glad Tidings—R
Glory & Strength—R
Halo Magazine—R
HEARTLIGHT Internet—R
$-Home Times—R
$-Imagine
$-Indian Life—R
$-In His Presence—R
$-JC Town Reporter—R
$-Liguorian
Men of the Cross
$-New Wineskins—R
PrayerWorks—R
Railroad Evangelist—R
Studio—R
$-Vision—R
$-Way of St. Francis—R
Women of the Cross

CHILDREN
$-Animal Trails—R
$-Nature Friend—R
Sword of the Lord—R
$-Young Christian—R

TEEN/YOUNG ADULT
$-Animal Trails—R
$-Direction Student
$-Home Times—R
$-Horizon Student
Sword of the Lord—R
$-Young Christian Writers

SHORT STORY: BIBLICAL
ADULT
$-Alive Now—R
$-Anglican Journal
$-Aujourd'hui Credo—R

Bread of Life—R
$-Catholic Yearbook—R
CBN.com—R
$-CGA World—R
Christian Journal—R
Christian Online
Christian Ranchman
Christian Woman's Page—R
Congregational Libraries
Connecting Point—R
Desert Call—R
Desert Voice—R
$-Earthen Vessel Online—R
Esdras' Scroll—R
$-Evangel/IN—R
Faithwebbin—R
$-Gem—R
$-Glad Tidings—R
Halo Magazine—R
$-Haruah—R
HEARTLIGHT Internet—R
$-Homeschooling Today—R
$-Horizons—R
$-In His Presence—R
$-JC Town Reporter—R
$-Kindred Spirit—R
$-Lutheran Journal—R
Lutheran Woman's Quar.
$-New Wineskins—R
PrayerWorks—R
$-Purpose—R
Railroad Evangelist—R
$-Seek—R
Spirituality for Today
Studio—R
Victory Herald—R
$-Vista—R
$-Way of St. Francis—R
$-Wesleyan Life—R

CHILDREN
$-Adventures
$-Animal Trails—R
$-BREAD/God's Children—R
Christian Ranchman
Eternal Ink—R
Faithwebbin—R
$-Focus/Clubhouse
$-Nature Friend—R
$-Pockets—R

$-Sparkle—R
Sword of the Lord—R
Victory Herald—R
$-Young Christian—R

TEEN/YOUNG ADULT
$-Anglican Journal
$-Animal Trails—R
$-BREAD/God's Children—R
Christian Ranchman
$-Direction Student
$-Essential Connection
Faithwebbin—R
$-Home Times—R
$-Horizon Student
$-InTeen—R
Spirituality for Today
Sword of the Lord—R
TeensForJC—R
Victory Herald—R
$-Young Adult Today

SHORT STORY: CONTEMPORARY
ADULT
African Voices—R
$-Alive Now—R
$-Angels on Earth
$-Associated Content—R
$-Aujourd'hui Credo—R
CBN.com—R
$-Christian Century—R
$-Christian Courier/Canada—R
$-Christian Home & School
$-Christian Renewal—R
Christian Woman's Page—R
Connecting Point—R
$-Covenant Companion—R
Esdras' Scroll—R
$-Eureka Street
$-Evangel/IN—R
Faithwebbin—R
$-Gem—R
$-Glad Tidings—R
Halo Magazine—R
$-Haruah—R
HEARTLIGHT Internet—R
$-Indian Life—R
$-In His Presence—R
$-JC Town Reporter—R

$-Liguorian
$-Mature Living
$-New Wineskins—R
$-New Writer's Mag.
$-Partners—R
Perspectives—R
PrayerWorks—R
Precious Times—R
Railroad Evangelist—R
Relief Journal—R
Ruminate
$-Seek—R
$-Shades of Romance—R
Spirituality for Today
$-Storyteller—R
Studio—R
Tiferet—R
$-U.S. Catholic—R
$-Vision—R
$-Wildwood Reader—R
$-Written
Xavier Review

CHILDREN
$-Adventures
$-American Girl—R
$-Animal Trails—R
$-BREAD/God's Children—R
$-Cadet Quest—R
Faithwebbin—R
$-Focus/Clubhouse
$-Focus/Clubhouse Jr.
$-Kids' Ark—R
$-New Moon—R
$-Partners—R
$-Pockets—R
$-SHINE brightly—R
$-Sparkle—R
$-Story Mates—R
$-Young Christian—R

TEEN/YOUNG ADULT
$-Animal Trails—R
$-Cadet Quest—R
$-Direction Student
$-Essential Connection
Faithwebbin—R
$-Home Times—R
$-Horizon Student
$-Partners—R
$-Spirit

$-Storyteller—R
TeensForJC—R
$-Young Christian Writers

SHORT STORY: ETHNIC
ADULT
African Voices—R
$-Associated Content—R
$-CGA World—R
Esdras' Scroll—R
$-Eureka Street
Faithwebbin—R
$-Gem—R
$-Glad Tidings—R
Halo Magazine—R
$-Haruah—R
$-Indian Life—R
$-JC Town Reporter—R
PrayerWorks—R
Relief Journal—R
$-Seek—R
Spirituality for Today
Studio—R
Unrecognized Woman—R
$-U.S. Catholic—R
Xavier Review

CHILDREN
$-American Girl—R
$-Animal Trails—R
Faithwebbin—R
$-Focus/Clubhouse
$-Kids' Ark—R
$-New Moon—R
Skipping Stones
$-Sparkle—R
$-Young Christian—R

TEEN/YOUNG ADULT
$-Animal Trails—R
Faithwebbin—R
$-SHINE brightly—R
TeensForJC—R
$-Young Christian—R

SHORT STORY: FANTASY
ADULT
$-Associated Content—R
Connecting Point—R
$-Eureka Street
Faithwebbin—R

$-Gem—R
$-Glad Tidings—R
Halo Magazine—R
($)-Impact Magazine—R
$-In His Presence—R
$-JC Town Reporter—R
$-Storyteller—R
Studio—R
$-Tickled by Thunder
$-Written

CHILDREN
Faithwebbin—R
$-Focus/Clubhouse
$-New Moon—R
$-SHINE brightly—R
$-Sparkle—R
Sword of the Lord—R

TEEN/YOUNG ADULT
Faithwebbin—R
$-InTeen—R
$-SHINE brightly—R
$-Storyteller—R
Sword of the Lord—R
TeensForJC—R
$-Young Adult Today
$-Young Christian Writers

SHORT STORY: FRONTIER
ADULT
$-Associated Content—R
Connecting Point—R
Desert Voice—R
$-Gem—R
$-Glad Tidings—R
Halo Magazine—R
$-Haruah—R
$-Indian Life—R
$-In His Presence—R
$-JC Town Reporter—R
PrayerWorks—R
$-Storyteller—R
Studio—R

CHILDREN
$-Animal Trails—R
Eternal Ink—R
$-Kids' Ark—R
$-New Moon—R
$-SHINE brightly—R

Sword of the Lord—R
$-Young Christian—R

TEEN/YOUNG ADULT
$-Home Times—R
$-Storyteller—R
Sword of the Lord—R
$-Young Christian Writers

SHORT STORY:
FRONTIER/ROMANCE
$-Associated Content—R
Connecting Point—R
$-Gem—R
Halo Magazine—R
$-Haruah—R
$-JC Town Reporter—R
$-Shades of Romance—R
Studio—R
Unrecognized Woman—R

SHORT STORY:
HISTORICAL
ADULT
$-Alive Now—R
$-Associated Content—R
$-Aujourd'hui Credo—R
CBN.com—R
$-Christian Renewal—R
$-City Light News—R
Connecting Point—R
Desert Voice—R
$-Earthen Vessel Online—R
Faithwebbin—R
$-Gem—R
$-Glad Tidings—R
Halo Magazine—R
$-Haruah—R
HEARTLIGHT Internet—R
$-Homeschooling Today—R
$-Home Times—R
$-Imagine
$-Indian Life—R
$-In His Presence—R
$-JC Town Reporter—R
Lutheran Woman's Quar.
$-New Writer's Mag.
$-Partners—R
$-Purpose—R
Railroad Evangelist—R
$-Seek—R

Spirituality for Today
$-Storyteller—R
Studio—R

CHILDREN

$-American Girl—R
$-Animal Trails—R
$-Archaeology—R
$-BREAD/God's Children—R
Christian Ranchman
Faithwebbin—R
$-Focus/Clubhouse
$-Focus/Clubhouse Jr.
$-Home Times—R
$-Kids' Ark—R
$-Nature Friend—R
$-New Moon—R
$-Partners—R
$-SHINE brightly—R
$-Sparkle—R
Sword of the Lord—R
$-Young Christian—R

TEEN/YOUNG ADULT

$-Animal Trails—R
$-Archaeology—R
$-BREAD/God's Children—R
Christian Ranchman
Faithwebbin—R
$-Home Times—R
$-InTeen—R
$-Partners—R
$-SHINE brightly—R
Spirituality for Today
$-Storyteller—R
Sword of the Lord—R
$-Young Adult Today
$-Young Christian Writers

SHORT STORY: HISTORICAL/ROMANCE

Areopagus
$-Associated Content—R
CBN.com—R
Connecting Point—R
Faithwebbin—R
$-Gem—R
Halo Magazine—R
$-Haruah—R
$-JC Town Reporter—R
$-Liguorian

$-Shades of Romance—R
Studio—R
Unrecognized Woman—R
$-Written

SHORT STORY: HUMOROUS

ADULT

African Voices—R
$-Associated Content—R
$-Catholic Forester—R
CBN.com—R
$-CGA World—R
$-Christian Courier/Canada—R
Christian Journal—R
$-Churchmouse Public.—R
$-City Light News—R
Congregational Libraries
Connecting Point—R
$-Covenant Companion—R
$-Eureka Street
$-Gem—R
$-Glad Tidings—R
Glory & Strength—R
Halo Magazine—R
$-Haruah—R
HEARTLIGHT Internet—R
$-Home Times—R
$-Imagine
$-In His Presence—R
$-JC Town Reporter—R
$-Liguorian
$-Mature Living
$-Mature Years—R
Men of the Cross
$-Miraculous Medal
$-New Writer's Mag.
$-Over the Back Fence—R
Pegasus Review—R
PrayerWorks—R
$-Presbyterian Outlook
$-Seek—R
$-Significant Living—R
Spirituality for Today
$-Storyteller—R
Studio—R
Unrecognized Woman—R
$-U.S. Catholic—R
$-Vista—R

CHILDREN

$-Cadet Quest—R
Christian Ranchman
Congregational Libraries
Eternal Ink—R
$-Focus/Clubhouse
$-Home Times—R
$-New Moon—R
$-SHINE brightly—R
Skipping Stones
$-Sparkle—R
$-Story Mates—R
Sword of the Lord—R
$-Young Christian—R

TEEN/YOUNG ADULT

$-Animal Trails—R
$-Cadet Quest—R
Christian Ranchman
$-Direction Student
$-Essential Connection
$-Home Times—R
$-Horizon Student
$-InTeen—R
Pegasus Review—R
$-Storyteller—R
Sword of the Lord—R
TeensForJC—R
$-Young Adult Today
$-Young Christian Writers

SHORT STORY: JUVENILE

$-Adventures
African Voices—R
$-American Girl—R
Areopagus
$-Associated Content—R
$-Beginner's Friend—R
$-Cadet Quest—R
$-Catholic Forester—R
CBN.com—R
$-Christian Renewal—R
Church Herald & Holiness—R
$-Churchmouse Public.—R
Congregational Libraries
Desert Voice—R
Esdras' Scroll—R
$-Faces
$-Faith & Family
$-Focus/Clubhouse

$-Focus/Clubhouse Jr.
Halo Magazine—R
$-In His Presence—R
$-Junior Companion—R
$-Keys for Kids—R
$-Kids' Ark—R
$-Nature Friend—R
$-New Moon—R
$-Partners—R
$-Pockets—R
$-Primary Pal—R
$-Seek—R
$-SHINE brightly—R
Skipping Stones
$-Sparkle—R
$-Story Mates—R
TeensForJC—R
$-United Church Observer—R

SHORT STORY: LITERARY
ADULT
African Voices—R
$-Associated Content—R
$-Christian Courier/Canada—R
$-Covenant Companion—R
Esdras' Scroll—R
$-Eureka Street
Faithwebbin—R
$-Gem—R
$-Glad Tidings—R
Halo Magazine—R
Handmaidens
$-Haruah—R
$-Imagine
$-JC Town Reporter—R
$-New Wineskins—R
Pegasus Review—R
Perspectives—R
Relief Journal—R
Ruminate
$-Seek—R
$-Storyteller—R
Studio—R
$-Tickled by Thunder
Tiferet—R
$-U.S. Catholic—R
$-Wildwood Reader—R
$-Written
Xavier Review

CHILDREN
$-New Moon—R
Skipping Stones

TEEN/YOUNG ADULT
Faithwebbin—R
$-Home Times—R
Pegasus Review—R
Spirituality for Today
$-Storyteller—R

SHORT STORY: MYSTERY/ROMANCE
$-Associated Content—R
$-Churchmouse Public.—R
Connecting Point—R
$-Direction Student
Faithwebbin—R
$-Gem—R
Halo Magazine—R
$-Haruah—R
$-Horizon Student
$-JC Town Reporter—R
$-Shades of Romance—R
Studio—R
TeensForJC—R
Unrecognized Woman—R

SHORT STORY: MYSTERY/SUSPENSE
ADULT
$-Associated Content—R
$-Best New Writing
CBN.com—R
Connecting Point—R
Desert Voice—R
Esdras' Scroll—R
Faithwebbin—R
$-Gem—R
$-Glad Tidings—R
Halo Magazine—R
$-Haruah—R
HEARTLIGHT Internet—R
$-JC Town Reporter—R
($)-Midnight Diner
Relief Journal—R
$-Storyteller—R
Studio—R
$-Tickled by Thunder
Unrecognized Woman—R

CHILDREN
$-American Girl—R
$-Animal Trails—R
Faithwebbin—R
$-Kids' Ark—R
$-New Moon—R
$-SHINE brightly—R
$-Sparkle—R
Sword of the Lord—R
$-Young Christian—R

TEEN/YOUNG ADULT
$-Animal Trails—R
$-Direction Student
Faithwebbin—R
$-Horizon Student
$-InTeen—R
$-SHINE brightly—R
$-Storyteller—R
Sword of the Lord—R
TeensForJC—R
$-Young Adult Today
$-Young Christian Writers

SHORT STORY: PARABLES
ADULT
$-Associated Content—R
$-Catholic Yearbook—R
$-Christian Courier/Canada—R
Christian Journal—R
$-Covenant Companion—R
$-Earthen Vessel Online—R
Esdras' Scroll—R
$-Gem—R
$-Glad Tidings—R
Glory & Strength—R
HEARTLIGHT Internet—R
$-Imagine
($)-Impact Magazine—R
$-In His Presence—R
$-JC Town Reporter—R
$-Liguorian
$-Lutheran Journal—R
$-Ministry & Liturgy—R
$-New Wineskins—R
Perspectives—R
$-Preaching Well—R
Railroad Evangelist—R
$-Seek—R
Studio—R

$-Testimony—R
$-Way of St. Francis—R

CHILDREN
$-Animal Trails—R
$-Archaeology—R
Eternal Ink—R
$-Faces
$-Focus/Clubhouse Jr.
$-Sparkle—R
$-Young Christian—R

TEEN/YOUNG ADULT
$-Animal Trails—R
$-Archaeology—R
$-Home Times—R
$-InTeen—R
$-SHINE brightly—R
TeensForJC—R
$-Testimony—R
$-Young Adult Today
$-Young Christian Writers

SHORT STORY: PLAYS
Areopagus
$-Churchmouse Public.—R
$-Drama Ministry—R
Esdras' Scroll—R
$-Faces
$-Imagine
$-J.A.M.
$-New Wineskins—R
$-SHINE brightly—R
Studio—R
TeensForJC—R
Unrecognized Woman—R

SHORT STORY: ROMANCE
ADULT
$-Associated Content—R
$-Bridal Guides—R
CBN.com—R
$-Churchmouse Public.—R
Connecting Point—R
Faithwebbin—R
$-Gem—R
Halo Magazine—R
$-Haruah—R
$-JC Town Reporter—R
Precious Times—R
$-Shades of Romance—R

$-Storyteller—R
Studio—R
Unrecognized Woman—R
$-Wildwood Reader—R
$-Written

TEEN/YOUNG ADULT
$-Animal Trails—R
$-Direction Student
$-Horizon Student
TeensForJC—R

SHORT STORY: SCIENCE FICTION
ADULT
African Voices—R
$-Associated Content—R
$-Churchmouse Public.—R
Connecting Point—R
$-Eureka Street
Faithwebbin—R
$-Gem—R
$-Glad Tidings—R
Halo Magazine—R
$-JC Town Reporter—R
$-Storyteller—R
Studio—R
$-Tickled by Thunder
$-Written

CHILDREN
Faithwebbin—R
$-Kids' Ark—R
$-New Moon—R
$-SHINE brightly—R
$-Sparkle—R
Sword of the Lord—R

TEEN/YOUNG ADULT
$-Direction Student
Faithwebbin—R
$-Home Times—R
$-Horizon Student
$-InTeen—R
$-J.A.M.
$-SHINE brightly—R
$-Storyteller—R
Sword of the Lord—R
$-Young Adult Today

SHORT STORY: SENIOR ADULT FICTION
ADULT
$-Churchmouse Public.—R
Desert Voice—R
$-Earthen Vessel Online—R
$-Glad Tidings—R
Halo Magazine—R
$-Imagine
$-In His Presence—R
$-Liguorian
$-Live—R
$-Mature Living
$-Mature Years—R
PrayerWorks—R
$-Seek—R
$-St. Anthony Messenger
Unrecognized Woman—R
$-Vista—R

SHORT STORY: SKITS
$-Churchmouse Public.—R
Desert Voice—R
$-Drama Ministry—R
Esdras' Scroll—R
$-Imagine

CHILDREN
$-Drama Ministry—R
$-Focus/Clubhouse Jr.
$-SHINE brightly—R
Sword of the Lord—R

TEEN/YOUNG ADULT
$-Drama Ministry—R
$-J.A.M.
$-SHINE brightly—R
Sword of the Lord—R
TeensForJC—R

SHORT STORY: SPECULATIVE
ADULT
$-Associated Content—R
$-Churchmouse Public.—R
$-Eureka Street
Faithwebbin—R
Halo Magazine—R
$-JC Town Reporter—R
($)-Midnight Diner
Relief Journal—R

Studio—R
$-Tickled by Thunder
$-Written

CHILDREN
$-New Moon—R

TEEN/YOUNG ADULT
Faithwebbin—R
$-Home Times—R
TeensForJC—R
$-Young Christian Writers

SHORT STORY: TEEN/ YOUNG ADULT
$-Anglican Journal
$-Animal Trails—R
$-BREAD/God's Children—R
$-Catholic Forester—R
CBN.com—R
$-Churchmouse Public.—R
Desert Voice—R
$-Direction Student
Esdras' Scroll—R
$-Essential Connection
Halo Magazine—R
$-Horizon Student
$-In His Presence—R
$-InTeen—R
$-J.A.M.
$-New Moon—R
Pegasus Review—R
Precious Times—R
$-Seek—R
$-Sharing the Victory—R
Skipping Stones
$-Spirit
$-Storyteller—R
TeensForJC—R
$-Testimony—R
Tiferet—R
Unrecognized Woman—R
Victory Herald—R
$-Written
$-Young Adult Today
$-Young Christian—R
$-Young Christian Writers
$-Youth Compass—R

SHORT STORY: WESTERNS
ADULT
$-Associated Content—R
$-Bridal Guides—R
$-JC Town Reporter—R
($)-Midnight Diner
$-Storyteller—R
Studio—R
$-Tickled by Thunder

CHILDREN
$-Animal Trails—R
Christian Ranchman
$-Kids' Ark—R
$-Sparkle—R
Sword of the Lord—R
$-Young Christian—R

TEEN/YOUNG ADULT
$-Animal Trails—R
Christian Ranchman
$-Storyteller—R
Sword of the Lord—R

SINGLES' ISSUES
ADULT/GENERAL
African Voices—R
Anointed Pages
$-Associated Content—R
$-Brink Magazine—R
CBN.com—R
$-Christian Examiner
Christian Family Jour.
Christian Online
Christian Ranchman
$-ChristianWeek—R
$-Churchmouse Public.—R
$-Columbia—R
Desert Voice—R
Disciple's Journal—R
E-Channels—R
$-Evangel/IN—R
$-Faith Today—R
Faithwebbin—R
$-Family Smart E-tips—R
Foursquare Leader
$-Gem—R
$-Good News, The—R
Gospel Herald

Halo Magazine—R
HEARTLIGHT Internet—R
$-Home Times—R
($)-HopeKeepers—R
$-In His Presence—R
$-In Touch
$-JC Town Reporter—R
$-KD Gospel Media
Koinonia
$-Kyria—R
$-Light & Life
$-Live—R
$-Lookout
Men.AG.org—R
($)-Mutuality—R
New Identity—R
$-Our Sunday Visitor—R
$-ParentLife
Penned from the Heart—R
$-Point—R
$-Power for Living—R
Priscilla Papers
$-Psychology for Living—R
$-River Region's Journey
$-Seek—R
Single Again Mag.—R
$-St. Anthony Messenger
$-Testimony—R
$-Together—R
Trumpeter—R
Unrecognized Woman—R
$-U.S. Catholic—R
$-Vibrant Life—R
$-War Cry—R
$-Wesleyan Life—R
$-Wildwood Reader—R
Wisconsin Christian
$-World & I—R

CHRISTIAN EDUCATION/ LIBRARY
$-Youth & CE Leadership

DAILY DEVOTIONALS
$-Brink Magazine—R
Penned from the Heart—R

MISSIONS
$-Glad Tidings—R
Women of the Harvest

PASTORS/LEADERS
$-Interpreter
$-Ministry Today
$-Word & World

TEEN/YOUNG ADULT
$-Boundless Webzine—R
$-InTeen—R
$-TC Magazine
TeensForJC—R
$-Young Salvationist—R

WOMEN
Christian Woman's Page—R
Christian Women Today—R
Glory & Strength—R
Hope for Women
$-inSpirit—R
$-Mother's Heart—R
$-SpiritLed Woman
Take Root & Write
Unrecognized Woman—R
Women of the Cross
Women Today—R

SMALL-GROUP HELPS
ADULT/GENERAL
$-Churchmouse Public.—R
Disciple Magazine—R
$-Kyria—R
Ministry in Motion—R
$-Ministry Today
$-RevWriter Resource
$-SmallGroups.com—R

SOCIAL JUSTICE
ADULT/GENERAL
$-Arkansas Catholic—R
$-Arlington Catholic
$-Associated Content—R
$-Aujourd'hui Credo—R
$-Brink Magazine—R
Brink Online—R
$-Canada Lutheran—R
$-Catholic Peace Voice—R
CBN.com—R
$-Christian Citizen USA
$-Christian Courier/Canada—R
$-Christianity Today—R
Christian Online

$-Christian Response—R
$-Christian Standard—R
$-ChristianWeek—R
$-Columbia—R
$-Commonweal
$-Company Magazine—R
$-Covenant Companion—R
Creation Care—R
$-Creative Nonfiction
$-Cresset
$-Culture Wars—R
Desert Call—R
Desert Voice—R
$-Disaster News
E-Channels—R
$-Eureka Street
Evangel/OR—R
$-Faith & Family
$-Faith Today—R
Foursquare Leader
$-Gem—R
$-Good News, The—R
Gospel Herald
$-Guide—R
Halo Magazine—R
$-Indian Life—R
$-In Touch
Island Catholic—R
$-JC Town Reporter—R
$-KD Gospel Media
Koinonia
$-Kyria—R
$-Light & Life
$-Liguorian
$-Lookout
$-Men of Integrity—R
More Excellent Way—R
($)-Mutuality—R
New Identity—R
$-New Wineskins—R
$-Our Sunday Visitor—R
Penned from the Heart—R
Perspectives—R
$-Prairie Messenger—R
$-Precepts for Living
Priscilla Papers
$-Prism
$-Salvo
$-Search
$-Seek—R

$-Social Justice—R
Spirituality for Today
$-Spiritual Life
$-St. Anthony Messenger
$-Testimony—R
$-Together—R
Trumpeter—R
$-United Church Observer—R
$-Way of St. Francis—R
$-World & I—R

CHILDREN
$-Guide—R
$-Pockets—R
Skipping Stones

CHRISTIAN EDUCATION/
LIBRARY
$-Journal/Adventist Ed.—R

MISSIONS
East-West Church
$-Glad Tidings—R
Lausanne World—R
Missiology

PASTORS/LEADERS
$-Barefoot—R
$-Christian Century—R
$-Clergy Journal—R
$-Immerse
$-Interpreter
Jour./Pastoral Care
Sharing the Practice—R
Theological Digest—R
$-Torch Legacy Leader

TEEN/YOUNG ADULT
$-Boundless Webzine—R
$-Devo'Zine—R
$-Spirit
$-TC Magazine
TeensForJC—R
$-TG Magazine
$-Young Salvationist—R

WOMEN
$-Horizons—R
$-inSpirit—R

SOCIOLOGY
ADULT/GENERAL
$-Anglican Journal
$-Associated Content—R

$-Catholic Peace Voice—R
$-Christian Courier/Canada—R
Christian Online
$-Creative Nonfiction
$-Culture Wars—R
$-Gem—R
Gospel Herald
Halo Magazine—R
$-In Touch
Island Catholic—R
$-JC Town Reporter—R
$-KD Gospel Media
Koinonia
$-Light & Life
More Excellent Way—R
$-Our Sunday Visitor—R
Perspectives—R
Perspectives/Science
Priscilla Papers
$-Salvo
$-Search
$-Social Justice—R
$-St. Anthony Messenger
$-Testimony—R
Trumpeter—R
$-World & I—R

PASTORS/LEADERS
Great Comm. Research—R
$-Immerse
$-Torch Legacy Leader
$-Word & World

TEEN/YOUNG ADULT
$-Boundless Webzine—R
$-InTeen—R
TeensForJC—R

WOMEN
($)-Beyond the Bend—R
Women of the Cross

SPIRITUAL GIFTS
ADULT/GENERAL
African Voices—R
$-Bible Advocate—R
Bread of Life—R
$-Brink Magazine—R
CBN.com—R
$-Christian Home & School
$-Christianity Today—R

Christian Motorsports
Christian Online
Christian Quarterly—R
Christian Ranchman
$-Christian Standard—R
$-ChristianWeek—R
$-Churchmouse Public.—R
$-Columbia—R
$-Covenant Companion—R
E-Channels—R
$-Faith & Family
$-Faith & Friends—R
Faithwebbin—R
Gospel Herald
$-Guide—R
Halo Magazine—R
$-Home Times—R
($)-HopeKeepers—R
$-In Touch
Island Catholic—R
$-JC Town Reporter—R
Just Between Us—R
$-KD Gospel Media
Koinonia
$-Kyria—R
$-Light & Life
$-Live—R
$-Mature Years—R
$-Men of Integrity—R
$-Miracles, Healings—R
($)-Mutuality—R
$-New Wineskins—R
Penned from the Heart—R
PrayerWorks—R
Priscilla Papers
Regent Global—R
$-Seek—R
Spirituality for Today
$-St. Anthony Messenger
$-Stewardship—R
Sword and Trumpet
$-Testimony—R
$-Together—R
Trumpeter—R
Unrecognized Woman—R
Victory Herald—R
$-Vista—R
$-Way of St. Francis—R
Wisconsin Christian

CHILDREN
$-BREAD/God's Children—R
$-Guide—R
$-Our Little Friend—R
$-Primary Treasure—R
$-Sparkle—R

DAILY DEVOTIONALS
Penned from the Heart—R

PASTORS/LEADERS
$-Immerse
$-Interpreter
$-Ministry Today
$-RevWriter Resource
$-Worship Leader

TEEN/YOUNG ADULT
$-Direction Student
$-Horizon Student
$-TC Magazine
TeensForJC—R

WOMEN
($)-Beyond the Bend—R
Christian Woman's Page—R
Extreme Woman
For Every Woman—R
Hope for Women
$-inSpirit—R
$-Journey
Just Between Us—R
P31 Woman—R
Precious Times—R
$-SpiritLed Woman
Unrecognized Woman—R
Virtuous Woman—R
Women Today—R

SPIRITUALITY
ADULT/GENERAL
African Voices—R
$-Alive Now—R
American Tract—R
$-Angels on Earth
Anointed Pages
$-Arkansas Catholic—R
$-Arlington Catholic
$-Associated Content—R
$-Atlantic Catholic
$-Aujourd'hui Credo—R

$-Bible Advocate—R
Bread of Life—R
Breakthrough Intercessor—R
$-Brink Magazine—R
$-Catholic Digest—R
$-Catholic Peace Voice—R
CBN.com—R
$-CGA World—R
$-Christian Courier/Canada—R
$-Christianity Today—R
Christian Journal—R
Christian Online
$-ChristianWeek—R
$-Churchmouse Public.—R
Church of England News
$-Columbia—R
$-Common Ground—R
$-Covenant Companion—R
$-Culture Wars—R
Desert Call—R
Divine Ascent
E-Channels—R
$-Episcopal Life—R
$-Eureka Street
$-Faith & Family
$-Faith & Friends—R
$-Faith Today—R
Faithwebbin—R
$-Family Digest—R
$-Gem—R
$-Good News—R
$-Good News, The—R
Gospel Herald
$-Guideposts—R
Halo Magazine—R
HEARTLIGHT Internet—R
$-Indian Life—R
$-In Touch
Island Catholic—R
$-JC Town Reporter—R
Just Between Us—R
$-KD Gospel Media
Koinonia
Leaves—R
$-Lifeglow—R
LifeTimes Catholic
$-Light & Life
$-Live—R
$-Living Church
$-Lookout

$-Mature Years—R
$-Men of Integrity—R
$-Messenger/Sacred Heart
$-Messenger/St. Anthony
Messianic Perspectives—R
New Heart—R
$-New Wineskins—R
$-Our Sunday Visitor—R
Pegasus Review—R
Penned from the Heart—R
Penwood Review
$-Prairie Messenger—R
$-Presbyterian Outlook
$-Presbyterians Today—R
Priscilla Papers
Quaker Life—R
$-Seek—R
Single Again Mag.—R
Spirituality for Today
$-Spiritual Life
$-St. Anthony Messenger
$-Stewardship—R
Sword and Trumpet
$-Testimony—R
$-Together—R
Trumpeter—R
Unrecognized Woman—R
$-U.S. Catholic—R
Victory Herald—R
$-Vista—R
$-War Cry—R
$-Way of St. Francis—R
$-Weavings—R
Wisconsin Christian
$-World & I—R

CHILDREN
$-BREAD/God's Children—R
$-New Moon—R
Skipping Stones

CHRISTIAN EDUCATION/ LIBRARY
Catholic Library
$-Children's Ministry
Jour./Ed. & Christian Belief—R
Jour./Research on Christian Ed.

DAILY DEVOTIONALS
Penned from the Heart—R

MISSIONS
$-Evangelical Missions—R
$-Glad Tidings—R
Missiology

PASTORS/LEADERS
$-Christian Century—R
$-Diocesan Dialogue—R
Disciple Magazine—R
$-Emmanuel
$-Immerse
$-Interpreter
Jour./Pastoral Care
$-Leadership—R
$-Ministry & Liturgy—R
$-Ministry Today
$-Proclaim—R
$-Review for Religious
$-RevWriter Resource
Rick Warren's Ministry—R
Sharing the Practice—R
Theological Digest—R
$-Today's Parish
$-Word & World
$-Worship Leader

TEEN/YOUNG ADULT
$-Boundless Webzine—R
$-Direction Student
$-Horizon Student
$-InTeen—R
$-TC Magazine
TeensForJC—R
$-TG Magazine
$-Young Adult Today

WOMEN
($)-Beyond the Bend—R
Christian Woman's Page—R
Extreme Woman
$-Heart & Soul
Hope for Women
$-Horizons—R
$-inSpirit—R
$-Journey
Lutheran Woman's Quar.
$-Pauses . . .
Precious Times—R
$-SpiritLed Woman
Unrecognized Woman—R
Women of the Cross
Women Today—R

WRITERS
Areopagus

SPIRITUAL LIFE
ADULT/GENERAL
$-Arkansas Catholic—R
$-Associated Content—R
$-Atlantic Catholic
$-Aujourd'hui Credo—R
$-Bible Advocate—R
Bread of Life—R
Breakthrough Intercessor—R
$-Brink Magazine—R
$-Cathedral Age
$-Catholic Digest—R
$-Catholic Peace Voice—R
$-Catholic Yearbook—R
CBN.com—R
$-Christian Examiner
$-Christian Home & School
Christian Journal—R
Christian Online
Christian Quarterly—R
Christian Ranchman
$-Christian Research
$-ChristianWeek—R
$-Churchmouse Public.—R
$-Columbia—R
Connections Ldrship/MOPS
$-Covenant Companion—R
Divine Ascent
E-Channels—R
$-Enfoque a la Familia
Eternal Ink—R
$-Faith & Family
$-Faith & Friends—R
$-Faith Today—R
Faithwebbin—R
$-Family Digest—R
$-Good News, The—R
Gospel Herald
$-Guide—R
Halo Magazine—R
$-Home Times—R
$-In His Presence—R
$-In Touch
Island Catholic—R
$-JC Town Reporter—R
Just Between Us—R

$-KD Gospel Media
Koinonia
$-Light & Life
$-Liguorian
$-Live—R
$-Lookout
$-Lutheran Journal—R
$-Mature Living
$-Men of Integrity—R
Messianic Perspectives—R
New Heart—R
New Identity—R
$-New Wineskins—R
$-Our Sunday Visitor—R
$-ParentLife
Penned from the Heart—R
Perspectives—R
PrayerWorks—R
$-Presbyterians Today—R
Priscilla Papers
Regent Global—R
Ruminate
$-Search
$-Seek—R
$-Significant Living—R
Single Again Mag.—R
Spirituality for Today
$-St. Anthony Messenger
$-Stewardship—R
Sword and Trumpet
$-Testimony—R
$-Together—R
Unrecognized Woman—R
Victory Herald—R
$-Way of St. Francis—R
$-Weavings—R
$-Wildwood Reader—R

CHILDREN
$-BREAD/God's Children—R
$-Guide—R
$-Sparkle—R

CHRISTIAN EDUCATION/ LIBRARY
$-Teachers of Vision—R
$-Youth & CE Leadership

DAILY DEVOTIONALS
$-Brink Magazine—R
Penned from the Heart—R

MISSIONS
$-Glad Tidings—R
WEC.go

PASTORS/LEADERS
$-Barefoot—R
Christian Education Jour.—R
$-Immerse
$-Interpreter
Jour./Pastoral Care
$-Leadership—R
$-Ministry
$-Ministry & Liturgy—R
Ministry in Motion—R
$-Ministry Today
$-Review for Religious
$-RevWriter Resource
$-SmallGroups.com—R

TEEN/YOUNG ADULT
$-Boundless Webzine—R
$-Direction Student
G4T Ink—R
$-Horizon Student
$-TC Magazine
$-TG Magazine
$-Young Salvationist—R

WOMEN
Christian Woman's Page—R
Chris. Work at Home Moms—R
Extreme Woman
First Lady
$-Fullfill
Glory & Strength—R
Hope for Women
$-Horizons—R
$-inSpirit—R
$-Journey
Just Between Us—R
More to Life
$-Mother's Heart—R
P31 Woman—R
$-Pauses...
Precious Times—R
Right to the Heart—R
Take Root & Write
Unrecognized Woman—R
Women Today—R

SPIRITUAL RENEWAL
ADULT/GENERAL
$-Arkansas Catholic—R
$-Associated Content—R
$-Bible Advocate—R
Bread of Life—R
Breakthrough Intercessor—R
$-Brink Magazine—R
$-Canada Lutheran—R
CBN.com—R
Christian Family Jour.
$-Christian Home & School
Christian Online
Christian Quarterly—R
Christian Ranchman
$-ChristianWeek—R
$-Churchmouse Public.—R
$-Columbia—R
Eternal Ink—R
$-Evangel/IN—R
$-Faith Today—R
Faithwebbin—R
$-Good News, Etc.—R
Gospel Herald
Halo Magazine—R
$-Home Times—R
$-In His Presence—R
$-In Touch
Island Catholic—R
$-JC Town Reporter—R
Just Between Us—R
$-KD Gospel Media
Koinonia
$-Light & Life
$-Liguorian
$-Live—R
$-Lookout
$-Manna—R
$-Men of Integrity—R
Messianic Perspectives—R
New Identity—R
$-New Wineskins—R
$-ParentLife
$-Pentecostal Evangel—R
$-Point—R
PrayerWorks—R
$-Seek—R
Spirituality for Today
Sword and Trumpet
$-Testimony—R

Unrecognized Woman—R
Victory Herald—R
$-Way of St. Francis—R
$-Wildwood Reader—R
Wisconsin Christian

CHILDREN
$-BREAD/God's Children—R
$-Sparkle—R

PASTORS/LEADERS
$-Christian Century—R
Christian Education Jour.—R
$-Immerse
$-Interpreter
$-Leadership—R
$-Ministry & Liturgy—R
Ministry in Motion—R
$-Ministry Today
Theological Digest—R

TEEN/YOUNG ADULT
$-Boundless Webzine—R
$-Direction Student
$-Horizon Student
$-TC Magazine
$-TG Magazine
$-Young Salvationist—R

WOMEN
Christian Woman's Page—R
Extreme Woman
Glory & Strength—R
Hope for Women
$-Horizons—R
$-inSpirit—R
$-Journey
Just Between Us—R
$-Pauses . . .
Precious Times—R
Right to the Heart—R
Take Root & Write
Unrecognized Woman—R
Virtuous Woman—R
Women Today—R

SPIRITUAL WARFARE
ADULT/GENERAL
$-Angels on Earth
$-Associated Content—R
Believer's Bay

$-Bible Advocate—R
Bread of Life—R
Breakthrough Intercessor—R
$-Brink Magazine—R
CBN.com—R
$-Celebrate Life—R
$-CGA World—R
$-Christian Home & School
$-Christianity Today—R
Christian Online
Christian Quarterly—R
Christian Ranchman
$-Christian Research
$-ChristianWeek—R
$-Churchmouse Public.—R
$-Columbia—R
$-Earthen Vessel Online—R
E-Channels—R
$-Faith & Friends—R
Faithwebbin—R
$-Gem—R
$-Good News—R
$-Good News, Etc.—R
Gospel Herald
Halo Magazine—R
HEARTLIGHT Internet—R
$-In His Presence—R
$-JC Town Reporter—R
Just Between Us—R
$-KD Gospel Media
Koinonia
Leaves—R
$-Light & Life
$-Live—R
$-Lookout
$-Manna—R
$-Men of Integrity—R
Messianic Perspectives—R
New Heart—R
$-New Wineskins—R
Penned from the Heart—R
Prayer Closet
PrayerWorks—R
Prison Victory
$-Seek—R
$-St. Anthony Messenger
Sword and Trumpet
Sword of the Lord—R
$-Testimony—R
Trumpeter—R

Victory Herald—R
Wisconsin Christian

CHILDREN
$-BREAD/God's Children—R

DAILY DEVOTIONALS
Penned from the Heart—R

MISSIONS
($)-Operation Reveille—R
Railroad Evangelist—R

PASTORS/LEADERS
Disciple Magazine—R
$-Growth Points—R
$-Let's Worship
$-Ministry Today
Rick Warren's Ministry—R
$-Small Groups.com—R

TEEN/YOUNG ADULT
TeensForJC—R
$-Young Salvationist—R

WOMEN
$-At the Center—R
Extreme Woman
Glory & Strength—R
Hope for Women
$-inSpirit—R
$-Journey
Just Between Us—R
$-Mother's Heart—R
Precious Times—R
Unrecognized Woman—R
Women Today—R

SPORTS/RECREATION
ADULT/GENERAL
$-Abilities
$-Angels on Earth
$-Arlington Catholic
$-Associated Content—R
CBN.com—R
$-Christian Citizen USA
Christian Courier/WI—R
$-Christian Renewal—R
$-Churchmouse Public.—R
$-City Light News—R
Connecting Point—R
Creation Care—R
$-Earthen Vessel Online—R

$-Eureka Street
$-Family Smart E-tips—R
$-Gem—R
$-Good News, Etc.—R
Gospel Herald
$-Gospel Today—R
$-Guide—R
$-Guideposts—R
Heartbeat/CMA
Heartland Gatekeeper—R
$-Home Times—R
$-In His Presence—R
$-In Touch
$-JC Town Reporter—R
$-KD Gospel Media
Koinonia
$-Lifeglow—R
$-Living Light—R
$-Lookout
$-Miracles, Healings—R
$-Our Sunday Visitor—R
$-Over the Back Fence—R
$-Rev Up Your Life
$-Sports Spectrum
$-St. Anthony Messenger
$-Storyteller—R
$-Testimony—R
$-U.S. Catholic—R
$-Vibrant Life—R
Wisconsin Christian
$-World & I—R

CHILDREN
$-American Girl—R
$-Cadet Quest—R
$-Guide—R
$-SHINE brightly—R
$-Sparkle—R

**CHRISTIAN EDUCATION/
LIBRARY**
$-Teachers of Vision—R

MISSIONS
$-Glad Tidings—R

PASTORS/LEADERS
$-Insight Youth—R

TEEN/YOUNG ADULT
$-Boundless Webzine—R
$-Direction Student

G4T Ink—R
$-InTeen—R
$-Listen—R
$-Sharing the Victory—R
$-TC Magazine
TeensForJC—R
$-Young Salvationist—R

WOMEN
Hope for Women
$-Mother's Heart—R
Take Root & Write

STEWARDSHIP
ADULT/GENERAL
$-Angels on Earth
$-Bible Advocate—R
$-Canada Lutheran—R
$-Catholic Yearbook—R
CBN.com—R
$-Celebrate Life—R
$-Christian Courier/Canada—R
Christian News NW—R
Christian Online
Christian Ranchman
$-Christian Standard—R
$-ChristianWeek—R
$-Churchmouse Public.—R
$-Columbia—R
Creation Care—R
E-Channels—R
$-Evangel/IN—R
$-Faith Today—R
$-Family Digest—R
$-Gem—R
$-Good News, The—R
Gospel Herald
$-Guide—R
Halo Magazine—R
Highway News—R
$-Home Times—R
$-In His Presence—R
$-In Touch
$-JC Town Reporter—R
$-KD Gospel Media
Koinonia
$-Lifeglow—R
$-Light & Life
$-Liguorian
$-Live—R

$-Living Church
$-Lookout
$-Lutheran Journal—R
$-Lutheran Witness
$-Manna—R
New Identity—R
($)-NRB E-Magazine—R
$-Our Sunday Visitor—R
Penned from the Heart—R
Perspectives—R
$-Power for Living—R
$-Presbyterian Outlook
$-Prism
$-Purpose—R
Quaker Life—R
Regent Global—R
$-Seek—R
$-St. Anthony Messenger
$-Stewardship—R
$-Testimony—R
Trumpeter—R
$-United Church Observer—R
$-U.S. Catholic—R
$-Way of St. Francis—R
$-Wesleyan Life—R
Wisconsin Christian
$-Written

CHILDREN
$-BREAD/God's Children—R
$-Guide—R
$-SHINE brightly—R
$-Sparkle—R

CHRISTIAN EDUCATION/ LIBRARY
$-Momentum

DAILY DEVOTIONALS
Penned from the Heart—R

MISSIONS
East-West Church
$-Glad Tidings—R

PASTORS/LEADERS
$-Clergy Journal—R
Disciple Magazine—R
$-InSite—R
$-Interpreter
$-Let's Worship
Ministry in Motion—R

$-Ministry Today
$-Net Results
$-Preaching Well—R
$-RevWriter Resource
Sharing the Practice—R
$-Your Church—R

TEEN/YOUNG ADULT
$-Boundless Webzine—R
$-Direction Student
$-Horizon Student
$-TC Magazine
TeensForJC—R
$-Young Salvationist—R

WOMEN
Hope for Women
$-Horizons—R
$-Journey
$-Mother's Heart—R
P31 Woman—R
Precious Times—R

TAKE-HOME PAPERS
ADULT/GENERAL
$-Evangel/IN—R
$-Gem—R
$-Gems of Truth—R
$-Live—R
$-Power for Living—R
$-Purpose—R
$-Seek—R
$-Vision—R
$-Vista—R

CHILDREN
$-Adventures
$-Beginner's Friend—R
$-Celebrate
$-Good News—R
$-Good News (child)
$-Guide—R
$-Junior Companion—R
$-JuniorWay
$-Our Little Friend—R
$-Partners—R
$-Preschool Playhouse
$-Primary Pal—R
$-Primary Street
$-Primary Treasure—R
$-Promise

$-Seeds
$-Story Mates—R
$-Venture

TEEN/YOUNG ADULT
$-Insight—R
$-Spirit
$-Visions
$-Youth Compass—R

THEOLOGICAL
ADULT/GENERAL
$-Alive Now—R
$-America
$-Anglican Journal
$-Arkansas Catholic—R
$-Arlington Catholic
$-Atlantic Catholic
$-Aujourd'hui Credo—R
$-B.C. Catholic—R
$-Bible Advocate—R
Bread of Life—R
$-Brink Magazine—R
byFaith
$-Cathedral Age
$-Catholic Peace Voice—R
$-Catholic Yearbook—R
CBN.com—R
$-Christian Courier/Canada—R
$-Christianity Today—R
Christian Online
Christian Ranchman
$-Christian Renewal—R
$-Christian Research
$-Christian Standard—R
$-Churchmouse Public.—R
Church of England News
Creation Care—R
$-Cresset
$-Culture Wars—R
Divine Ascent
$-Earthen Vessel Online—R
E-Channels—R
$-Episcopal Life—R
$-Eureka Street
Evangelical Times
$-Faith Today—R
Founders Journal
$-Good News—R
Gospel Herald

Halo Magazine—R
$-In His Presence—R
$-In Touch
Koinonia
$-Light & Life
$-Living Church
$-Lookout
$-Lutheran Journal—R
$-Messenger/Sacred Heart
Messianic Perspectives—R
Movieguide
$-New Wineskins—R
$-Our Sunday Visitor—R
Perspectives—R
Perspectives/Science
$-Prairie Messenger—R
PrayerWorks—R
$-Presbyterian Outlook
Priscilla Papers
Purpose Magazine—R
Quaker Life—R
$-Search
$-Social Justice—R
$-Spiritual Life
$-St. Anthony Messenger
$-Testimony—R
Trumpeter—R
$-United Church Observer—R
$-U.S. Catholic—R
$-Way of St. Francis—R

CHRISTIAN EDUCATION/ LIBRARY
Catholic Library
Jour. of Christianity—R

DAILY DEVOTIONALS
$-Brink Magazine—R
Penned from the Heart—R

MISSIONS
East-West Church
$-Glad Tidings—R
Lausanne World—R
Missiology

PASTORS/LEADERS
$-Catechumenate
$-Christian Century—R
$-Clergy Journal—R
CrossCurrents
$-Diocesan Dialogue—R

Disciple Magazine—R
Great Comm. Research—R
$-Growth Points—R
$-Immerse
Jour./Pastoral Care
Lutheran Forum
$-Ministry & Liturgy—R
$-Preaching Well—R
$-Proclaim—R
$-Reformed Worship—R
$-RevWriter Resource
Rick Warren's Ministry—R
Sewanee Theo. Review
Sharing the Practice—R
$-SmallGroups.com—R
$-Today's Parish
$-Word & World
$-Worship Leader

TEEN/YOUNG ADULT
$-Boundless Webzine—R
$-InTeen—R
TeensForJC—R
$-Young Salvationist—R

WOMEN
$-Horizons—R

THINK PIECES
ADULT/GENERAL
$-Alive Now—R
$-Associated Content—R
Baptist Standard
$-Brink Magazine—R
$-Catholic Forester—R
$-Catholic Peace Voice—R
$-CGA World—R
$-Christian Courier/Canada—R
$-Christianity Today—R
Christian Online
$-ChristianWeek—R
$-Churchmouse Public.—R
$-City Light News—R
Desert Call—R
$-Earthen Vessel Online—R
$-Episcopal Life—R
$-Eureka Street
$-Faith Today—R
$-Gem—R
Gospel Herald
Halo Magazine—R

$-Haruah—R
HEARTLIGHT Internet—R
$-In Touch
Island Catholic—R
$-JC Town Reporter—R
$-KD Gospel Media
Koinonia
$-Lifeglow—R
$-Light & Life
$-Lookout
$-Manna—R
Men of the Cross
New Identity—R
$-New Wineskins—R
$-Our Sunday Visitor—R
Pegasus Review—R
Penned from the Heart—R
Penwood Review
PrayerWorks—R
$-Presbyterian Outlook
Purpose Magazine—R
$-Search
$-Seek—R
$-St. Anthony Messenger
$-Stewardship—R
$-Testimony—R
Trumpeter—R
Unrecognized Woman—R
$-World & I—R

CHILDREN
Skipping Stones

CHRISTIAN EDUCATION/ LIBRARY
$-Children's Ministry

PASTORS/LEADERS
$-Catholic Servant
$-Enrichment—R
$-Ministry Today
Rick Warren's Ministry—R
$-Word & World

TEEN/YOUNG ADULT
$-Boundless Webzine—R
$-TC Magazine
TeensForJC—R
$-Young Salvationist—R

WOMEN
$-MomSense—R

$-Mother's Heart—R
Take Root & Write
Unrecognized Woman—R
Women of the Cross

WRITERS
Areopagus

TIME MANAGEMENT
ADULT/GENERAL
$-Associated Content—R
$-Bridal Guides—R
$-Brink Magazine—R
$-Catholic Forester—R
$-CBA Retailers
CBN.com—R
Christian Business
Christian Online
$-ChristianWeek—R
$-Churchmouse Public.—R
Disciple's Journal—R
Faithwebbin—R
$-Gem—R
Gospel Herald
Halo Magazine—R
$-Home Times—R
($)-HopeKeepers—R
$-In Touch
$-JC Town Reporter—R
Just Between Us—R
$-KD Gospel Media
Koinonia
$-Lifeglow—R
$-Light & Life
$-Live—R
$-Living Light—R
$-Lookout
Men of the Cross
MissionWares
($)-NRB E-Magazine—R
$-ParentLife
Penned from the Heart—R
Regent Global—R
$-St. Anthony Messenger
$-Stewardship—R
$-Testimony—R
$-Together—R
Trumpeter—R
$-Victory in Grace—R
$-World & I—R

CHRISTIAN EDUCATION/ LIBRARY
Christian Librarian—R
Christian School Ed.—R
$-Youth & CE Leadership

DAILY DEVOTIONALS
$-Brink Magazine—R
Penned from the Heart—R

PASTORS/LEADERS
$-Enrichment—R
$-Interpreter
Ministry in Motion—R
Rick Warren's Ministry—R
$-Your Church—R

TEEN/YOUNG ADULT
$-Boundless Webzine—R
$-Direction Student
$-Horizon Student
TeensForJC—R
$-TG Magazine
$-Young Christian Writers

WOMEN
Christian Woman
Christian Woman's Page—R
Chris. Work at Home Moms—R
$-Girlfriend 2 Girlfriend
Glory & Strength—R
Hope for Women
$-InspiredMoms—R
$-inSpirit—R
$-Journey
Just Between Us—R
Life Tools for Women
$-Mother's Heart—R
P31 Woman—R
Precious Times—R
Take Root & Write
Unrecognized Woman—R
Virtuous Woman—R
Women Today—R

WRITERS
$-Adv. Christian Writer—R
$-Christian Communicator—R
$-Fellowscript—R
Write Connection
$-Writer
$-Writers' Journal

TRAVEL
ADULT/GENERAL
$-Abilities
$-Angels on Earth
$-Arlington Catholic
$-Associated Content—R
$-Bridal Guides—R
$-Brink Magazine—R
$-Capper's
CBN.com—R
Christian Family Jour.
$-Churchmouse Public.—R
$-City Light News—R
$-Common Ground—R
Creation Care—R
$-Creative Nonfiction
Desert Voice—R
$-Family Digest—R
$-Gem—R
Gospel Herald
Halo Magazine—R
($)-HopeKeepers—R
$-In His Presence—R
$-In Touch
Island Catholic—R
$-JC Town Reporter—R
$-KD Gospel Media
Koinonia
$-Lifeglow—R
$-Mature Living
$-Mature Years—R
Movieguide
New Identity—R
$-Over the Back Fence—R
$-Ozarks Senior Living—R
$-ParentLife
$-Seek—R
Single Again Mag.—R
$-Special Living—R
$-Testimony—R
$-Upscale
$-Way of St. Francis—R
Wisconsin Christian
$-World & I—R

CHILDREN
$-Archaeology—R
$-Faces
$-SHINE brightly—R
Skipping Stones
$-Sparkle—R

MISSIONS
$-Glad Tidings—R

TEEN/YOUNG ADULT
$-Boundless Webzine—R
TeensForJC—R

WOMEN
Hope for Women
$-InspiredMoms—R
Live Magazine
Precious Times—R
Take Root & Write
Unrecognized Woman—R

TRUE STORIES
ADULT/GENERAL
African Voices—R
$-Angels on Earth
Baptist Standard
Behind the Hammer
Biblical Recorder
Breakthrough Intercessor—R
$-Bridal Guides—R
$-Brink Magazine—R
byFaith
$-Catholic Digest—R
CBN.com—R
$-Celebrate Life—R
Challenge Weekly
Christian Observer
Christian Online
Christian Quarterly—R
Christian Ranchman
$-City Light News—R
$-Columbia—R
$-Creative Nonfiction
$-Culture Wars—R
$-Disaster News
$-Earthen Vessel Online—R
E-Channels—R
$-Enfoque a la Familia
Eternal Ink—R
Evangelical Times
$-Faith & Family
$-Family Digest—R
Foursquare Leader
$-Gem—R
$-Gems of Truth—R
$-Good News, Etc.—R
$-Good News, The—R

Good News Today
Gospel Herald
$-Guide—R
$-Guideposts—R
Halo Magazine—R
$-Haruah—R
Heartland Gatekeeper—R
HEARTLIGHT Internet—R
Highway News—R
$-Home Times—R
($)-HopeKeepers—R
$-Indian Life—R
$-In His Presence—R
$-In Touch
$-JC Town Reporter—R
$-KD Gospel Media
Koinonia
$-Kyria—R
$-Lifeglow—R
$-Light & Life
$-Live—R
$-Lutheran Digest—R
$-Marriage Partnership
$-Mature Living
Men of the Cross
MESSAGE/Open Bible—R
Messianic Perspectives—R
MissionWares
New Heart—R
New Identity—R
$-New Wineskins—R
Nostalgia—R
$-Now What?—R
$-On Mission
$-ParentLife
$-Partners—R
Penned from the Heart—R
$-Pentecostal Evangel—R
$-Power for Living—R
PrayerWorks—R
$-Priority!—R
$-Search
$-Seek—R
$-St. Anthony Messenger
$-Storyteller—R
$-Testimony—R
Tri-State Voice
Trumpeter—R
Unrecognized Woman—R
Victory Herald—R

$-Victory in Grace—R
$-Vision—R
$-Vista—R
$-War Cry—R
$-Way of St. Francis—R
$-Written

CHILDREN
$-BREAD/God's Children—R
$-Cadet Quest—R
$-Focus/Clubhouse Jr.
$-Guide—R
$-Nature Friend—R
$-New Moon—R
$-Our Little Friend—R
$-Partners—R
$-Pockets—R
$-Primary Treasure—R
$-SHINE brightly—R
Skipping Stones
$-Sparkle—R
$-Story Mates—R

CHRISTIAN EDUCATION/
LIBRARY
$-Children's Ministry
Christian Early Ed.—R

MISSIONS
$-Glad Tidings—R
$-Leaders for Today
($)-Operation Reveille—R

PASTORS/LEADERS
$-Leadership—R
$-Preaching Well—R
Sharing the Practice—R

TEEN/YOUNG ADULT
$-Boundless Webzine—R
$-Direction Student
$-Essential Connection
$-Horizon Student
$-Insight—R
$-Listen—R
$-Sharing the Victory—R
$-Spirit
$-TC Magazine
TeensForJC—R
$-TG Magazine
$-Young Christian—R
$-Young Christian Writers

$-Young Salvationist—R
$-YouthWalk

WOMEN
Empowering Everyday Women
Extreme Woman
For Every Woman—R
Glory & Strength—R
($)-History's Women—R
Hope for Women
$-Journey
$-MomSense—R
$-Mother's Heart—R
$-Pauses . . .
Precious Times—R
Unrecognized Woman—R
Women Today—R

WRITERS
Areopagus

VIDEO REVIEWS
ADULT/GENERAL
$-Arlington Catholic
$-Atlantic Catholic
($)-Canadian Mennonite—R
$-Catholic Peace Voice—R
CBN.com—R
$-Christian Citizen USA
Christian Family Jour.
$-Christian Renewal—R
$-Christianity Today Movies—R
Creation Care—R
Desert Call—R
Desert Voice—R
E-Channels—R
Eternal Ink—R
$-Eureka Street
$-Faith & Family
Foursquare Leader
Gospel Herald
Halo Magazine—R
Heartland Gatekeeper—R
$-Home Times—R
$-Imagine
$-Interim—R
$-JC Town Reporter—R
$-KD Gospel Media
Movieguide
New Christian Voices
$-Our Sunday Visitor—R

$-Presbyterians Today—R
Quaker Life—R
Single Again Mag.—R
$-Testimony—R
Trumpeter—R

CHILDREN
$-Sparkle—R

**CHRISTIAN EDUCATION/
LIBRARY**
$-Church Libraries—R
Congregational Libraries
Jour. of Christianity—R

MISSIONS
East-West Church
$-Glad Tidings—R

PASTORS/LEADERS
$-Christian Century—R
Foursquare Leader
$-Interpreter
$-Ministry Today
Technologies for Worship—R
$-Worship Leader

TEEN/YOUNG ADULT
$-Devo'Zine—R
TeensForJC—R
$-TG Magazine

WOMEN
Christian Woman's Page—R
$-Dabbling Mum—R
Empowering Everyday Women
Extreme Woman
Glory & Strength—R
Hope for Women
$-Mother's Heart—R
Precious Times—R
Virtuous Woman—R

WEBSITE REVIEWS
ADULT/GENERAL
$-Atlantic Catholic
Brink Online—R
$-Catholic Peace Voice—R
CBN.com—R
$-Christian Citizen USA
$-Christianity Today—R
Eternal Ink—R
Gospel Herald

Heartland Gatekeeper—R
($)-HopeKeepers—R
$-JC Town Reporter—R
New Christian Voices
New Identity—R
$-New Wineskins—R
($)-NRB E-Magazine—R
$-On Mission
$-Our Sunday Visitor—R
Single Again Mag.—R
$-Upscale
$-World & I—R

MISSIONS
East-West Church
($)-Operation Reveille—R

PASTORS/LEADERS
$-Interpreter
Ministry in Motion—R

TEEN/YOUNG ADULT
TeensForJC—R
$-TG Magazine

WOMEN
Empowering Everyday Women
Glory & Strength—R
Hope for Women
$-Mother's Heart—R

WRITERS
NW Christian Author—R
$-Writers' Journal

WOMEN'S ISSUES
ADULT/GENERAL
$-Abilities
$-Alive Now—R
$-Anglican Journal
$-Arlington Catholic
$-Associated Content—R
$-Brink Magazine—R
$-Catholic Forester—R
$-Catholic Peace Voice—R
$-CBA Retailers
CBN.com—R
$-Celebrate Life—R
$-CGA World—R
$-Chicken Soup Books—R
$-Christian Citizen USA
$-Christian Courier/Canada—R
$-Christian Examiner

Christian Family Jour.
Christian Journal—R
Christian News NW—R
Christian Online
Christian Quarterly—R
Christian Ranchman
$-ChristianWeek—R
$-Churchmouse Public.—R
Church of England News
$-Columbia—R
$-Creative Nonfiction
Desert Voice—R
Disciple's Journal—R
$-EFCA Today
$-Episcopal Life—R
$-Evangel/IN—R
$-Faith & Family
$-Faith Today—R
$-Family Smart E-tips—R
Foursquare Leader
$-Gem—R
$-Good News, The—R
Gospel Herald
$-Gospel Today—R
Halo Magazine—R
HEARTLIGHT Internet—R
Holy House Ministries—R
Hope for Women
($)-HopeKeepers—R
$-Indian Life—R
$-In His Presence—R
$-In Touch
Island Catholic—R
$-JC Town Reporter—R
$-KD Gospel Media
Koinonia
$-Kyria—R
$-Light & Life
$-Liguorian
$-Live—R
$-Lookout
$-Manna—R
More Excellent Way—R
($)-Mutuality—R
New Identity—R
$-New Wineskins—R
$-Our Sunday Visitor—R
$-ParentLife
Penned from the Heart—R
Perspectives—R

$-Point—R
$-Prairie Messenger—R
PrayerWorks—R
$-Presbyterian Outlook
Priscilla Papers
$-Psychology for Living—R
$-Purpose—R
Purpose Magazine—R
$-River Region's Journey
$-Seek—R
Share
$-St. Anthony Messenger
$-Storyteller—R
$-Testimony—R
$-Together—R
Trumpeter—R
$-United Church Observer—R
Unrecognized Woman—R
$-U.S. Catholic—R
$-Vibrant Life—R
$-War Cry—R
$-Wesleyan Life—R
$-World & I—R
$-Written

CHILDREN
$-New Moon—R
Skipping Stones

CHRISTIAN EDUCATION/ LIBRARY
$-Teachers of Vision—R

DAILY DEVOTIONALS
Penned from the Heart—R

MISSIONS
$-Glad Tidings—R
Women of the Harvest

PASTORS/LEADERS
$-Interpreter
$-SmallGroups.com—R
$-Word & World

TEEN/YOUNG ADULT
$-Boundless Webzine—R
TeensForJC—R
$-TG Magazine

WOMEN
$-At the Center—R
($)-Beyond the Bend—R
Breathe Again

Christian Ladies Connect
Christian Woman
Christian Woman's Page—R
Christian Women Today—R
Chris. Work at Home Moms—R
ChurchWoman
$-Dabbling Mum—R
Empowering Everyday Women
Extreme Woman
First Lady
For Every Woman—R
$-Fullfill
$-Girlfriend 2 Girlfriend
Glory & Strength—R
Grace Today
Handmaidens
$-Heart & Soul
Hope for Women
$-Horizons—R
$-InspiredMoms—R
Inspired Women
$-inSpirit—R
$-Journey
Just Between Us—R
Life Tools for Women
$-Link & Visitor—R
Live Magazine
Love, Pearls & Swine
Lutheran Woman's Quar.
$-Melody of the Heart
$-MomSense—R
More to Life
$-Mother's Heart—R
Onyx Woman
Oregon Womens Report
P31 Woman—R
$-Pauses…
Precious Times—R
Right to the Heart—R
Share
$-SpiritLed Woman
Take Root & Write
Together with God—R
Truth Media
Unrecognized Woman—R
Virtuous Woman—R
Women of the Cross
Women Today—R
Women's Ministry
You Can Live Again

WORKPLACE ISSUES
ADULT/GENERAL
$-Associated Content—R
byFaith
CBN.com—R
Christian Business
$-Christian Examiner
Christian Online
Christian Ranchman
$-Christian Retailing
$-ChristianWeek—R
$-Churchmouse Public.—R
Desert Voice—R
E-Channels—R
$-Eureka Street
$-Evangel/IN—R
$-Faith & Friends—R
$-Faith Today—R
$-Good News, Etc.—R
$-Good News, The—R
Good News Today
Gospel Herald
$-Gospel Today—R
Halo Magazine—R
Highway News—R
Hope for Women
($)-HopeKeepers—R
$-In His Presence—R
$-In Touch
Island Catholic—R
$-JC Town Reporter—R
$-KD Gospel Media
Koinonia
$-Light & Life
$-Live—R
$-Lookout
$-Manna—R
$-Marriage Partnership
$-Men of Integrity—R
$-Montana Catholic
More Excellent Way—R
New Christian Voices
New Heart—R
$-Our Sunday Visitor—R
$-ParentLife
Penned from the Heart—R
Perspectives—R
$-Point—R
$-Purpose—R
Purpose Magazine—R

Regent Global—R
$-Rev Up Your Life
$-River Region's Journey
$-Seek—R
$-Testimony—R
$-Together—R
$-World & I—R

CHRISTIAN EDUCATION/ LIBRARY
Christian Librarian—R
$-Group
$-Teachers of Vision—R
$-Today's Catholic Teacher—R

MISSIONS
($)-Operation Reveille—R

PASTORS/LEADERS
Church Executive
$-Interpreter
$-Your Church—R

TEEN/YOUNG ADULT
$-Boundless Webzine—R

WOMEN
Empowering Everyday Women
$-Fullfill
Glory & Strength—R
Hope for Women
$-InspiredMoms—R
Inspired Women
$-Journey
Life Tools for Women
Live Magazine
More to Life
Oregon Women's Report
Unrecognized Woman—R
Women Today—R

WRITERS
$-Adv. Christian Writer—R

WORLD ISSUES
ADULT/GENERAL
American Tract—R
$-Arlington Catholic
$-Associated Content—R
$-Aujourd'hui Credo—R
Baptist Standard
Biblical Recorder
$-Brink Magazine—R
CanadianChristianity

$-Catholic Peace Voice—R
Catholic Register
CBN.com—R
$-CGA World—R
Challenge Weekly
Christian Chronicle
$-Christian Examiner
Christian Observer
Christian Online
$-Christian Renewal—R
$-ChristianWeek—R
$-Churchmouse Public.—R
$-Columbia—R
$-Compass Direct
$-Creative Nonfiction
$-Culture Wars—R
Desert Christian
Desert Voice—R
$-Eureka Street
$-Evangel/IN—R
Evangelical Times
$-Faith Today—R
Friends Journal—R
$-Gem—R
Good News Connection
$-Good News, Etc.—R
Good News Today
Gospel Herald
$-Guide—R
Halo Magazine—R
Heartland Gatekeeper—R
HEARTLIGHT Internet—R
$-Home Times—R
$-Indian Life—R
$-In Touch
$-JC Town Reporter—R
Jerusalem Connection
Koinonia
$-Liberty
LifeSite News
$-Light & Life
$-Living Church
$-Lookout
Messianic Perspectives—R
Movieguide
($)-Mutuality—R
New Identity—R
$-New Wineskins—R
$-Our Sunday Visitor—R
Penned from the Heart—R

Perspectives—R
$-Presbyterian Outlook
$-Prism
$-Purpose—R
Purpose Magazine—R
$-Salvo
$-Seek—R
$-Social Justice—R
$-St. Anthony Messenger
$-Testimony—R
Tri-State Voice
Trumpeter—R
$-United Church Observer—R
$-War Cry—R
$-Way of St. Francis—R
$-World & I—R

CHILDREN
$-Guide—R
$-New Moon—R
Skipping Stones

MISSIONS
East-West Church
$-Glad Tidings—R
Intl. Jour./Frontier—R
Lausanne World—R
$-Leaders for Today
Missiology
Mission Frontiers
$-New World Outlook
$-One
($)-Operation Reveille—R
$-PFI Global—R

PASTORS/LEADERS
$-Christian Century—R
$-Ministry Today
$-Word & World

TEEN/YOUNG ADULT
$-Boundless Webzine—R
$-TC Magazine
TeensForJC—R
$-TG Magazine

WOMEN
Hope for Women
$-Horizons—R
$-SpiritLed Woman

WRITERS
Areopagus

WORSHIP
ADULT/GENERAL
$-Angels on Earth
$-Arlington Catholic
$-Aujourd'hui Credo—R
$-Bible Advocate—R
Bread of Life—R
$-Brink Magazine—R
$-Canada Lutheran—R
$-Catholic Yearbook—R
CBN.com—R
$-CGA World—R
$-Christian Examiner
Christian Online
Christian Ranchman
$-Christian Standard—R
$-Christianity Today—R
$-ChristianWeek—R
$-Churchmouse Public.—R
$-Columbia—R
Creation Care—R
$-Culture Wars—R
E-Channels—R
Eternal Ink—R
$-Evangel/IN—R
Foursquare Leader
Gospel Herald
Halo Magazine—R
($)-HopeKeepers—R
$-Imagine
$-In His Presence—R
$-In Touch
Koinonia
$-Kyria—R
$-Lifeglow—R
$-Light & Life
$-Liguorian
$-Live—R
$-Living Church
$-Lookout
$-Lutheran Journal—R
$-Manna—R
New Identity—R
$-New Wineskins—R
Penned from the Heart—R
Perspectives—R
$-Point—R
$-Power for Living—R
PrayerWorks—R
$-Presbyterian Outlook

$-Presbyterians Today—R
Priscilla Papers
Purpose Magazine—R
Quaker Life—R
$-Seek—R
$-Spiritual Life
$-St. Anthony Messenger
$-Stewardship—R
Sword and Trumpet
Sword of the Lord—R
$-Testimony—R
Time of Singing—R
Trumpeter—R
$-United Church Observer—R
$-U.S. Catholic—R
$-Vista—R
$-War Cry—R
$-Way of St. Francis—R
$-Wesleyan Life—R
$-World & I—R

CHILDREN
$-BREAD/God's Children—R
$-Keys for Kids—R
$-Promise
$-Sparkle—R

**CHRISTIAN EDUCATION/
LIBRARY**
$-Group
$-Youth & CE Leadership

DAILY DEVOTIONALS
$-Brink Magazine—R
Penned from the Heart—R

MISSIONS
$-Glad Tidings—R
Lausanne World—R

MUSIC
Church Music
$-Creator—R

PASTORS/LEADERS
$-Barefoot—R
$-Clergy Journal—R
$-Enrichment—R
Great Comm. Research—R
$-Growth Points—R
$-Immerse
$-Interpreter

$-Leadership—R
$-Let's Worship
$-Ministry & Liturgy—R
$-Ministry Today
$-Parish Liturgy—R
Preaching
$-Reformed Worship—R
$-RevWriter Resource
Rick Warren's Ministry—R
Sharing the Practice—R
Theological Digest—R
$-Today's Parish
$-Word & World
$-Worship Leader
$-Your Church—R

TEEN/YOUNG ADULT
$-Boundless Webzine—R
$-Direction Student
$-Horizon Student
$-Insight—R
$-TC Magazine
TeensForJC—R
$-TG Magazine

WOMEN
Christian Woman's Page—R
Extreme Woman
For Every Woman—R
Glory & Strength—R
Hope for Women
$-Horizons—R
$-Journey
$-Mother's Heart—R
Take Root & Write
Virtuous Woman—R
Women Today—R

WRITING HOW-TO
ADULT/GENERAL
$-Associated Content—R
$-Canada Lutheran—R
$-CBA Retailers
CBN.com—R
Christian Observer
Christian Online
$-Haruah—R
$-Home Times—R
($)-HopeKeepers—R
Pegasus Review—R

Penwood Review
Single Again Mag.—R
$-St. Anthony Messenger
$-World & I—R

CHILDREN
Skipping Stones

CHRISTIAN EDUCATION/ LIBRARY
$-Group
$-Teachers of Vision—R

PASTORS/LEADERS
$-Newsletter Newsletter

TEEN/YOUNG ADULT
$-Boundless Webzine—R
TeensForJC—R
$-Young Christian Writers

WOMEN
$-Dabbling Mum—R
Extreme Woman
Hope for Women
$-Mother's Heart—R
Precious Times—R
Right to the Heart—R
Take Root & Write

WRITERS
$-Adv. Christian Writer—R
Areopagus
Author-Me
$-Best New Writing
$-Canadian Writer's Jour.—R
$-Christian Communicator—R
Christian Fiction Online
$-Cross & Quill—R
$-Fellowscript—R
Fiction Fix
$-Freelance Writer's Report—R
$-New Writer's Mag.
NW Christian Author—R
$-Poets & Writers
$-Shades of Romance—R
$-Tickled by Thunder
Write Connection
$-Writer
$-Writer's Chronicle
$-Writer's Digest
$-Writers' Journal
Writers Manual

WriteToInspire.com
Writing Corner—R

YOUNG-WRITER MARKETS
Note: These publications have indicated they will accept submissions from children or teens (C or T).

ADULT/GENERAL
African Voices
$-Animal Trails
Anointed Pages
$-Aujourd'hui Credo (C or T)
$-Bridal Guides (C or T)
$-Catholic Peace Voice (T)
$-Catholic Yearbook (C or T)
CBN.com (T)
$-Celebrate Life (C or T)
$-Christian Citizen USA (T)
$-Christian Herald (T)
$-Christian Home & School (C or T)
Christian Journal (C or T)
Christian Online (C or T)
$-ChristianWeek (T)
Church Herald & Holiness (C or T)
$-Churchmouse Public. (T)
$-City Light News (T)
$-Creative Nonfiction (T)
Desert Voice (T)
$-Drama Ministry (T)
$-DreamSeeker (C or T)
$-Earthen Vessel Online (C or T)
E-Channels (T)
Eternal Ink (C or T)
Gospel Herald (C or T)
$-Gospel Today
Haiku Hippodrome (C or T)
Halo Magazine
$-Haruah (T)
Holy House Ministries (C or T)
$-Homeschooling Today (C or T)
$-Home Times (T)
($)-HopeKeepers (T)
$-Indian Life (C or T)
$-In His Presence (C or T)
$-Interchange (C or T)

Island Catholic (C or T)
$-KD Gospel Media (T)
$-Leben (T)
LifeTimes Catholic (T)
$-Light & Life (C or T)
$-Lutheran Journal (C or T)
$-Manna (C or T)
Men of the Cross (T)
$-Miracles, Healings (C or T)
MissionWares (T)
$-New Wineskins (C or T)
Pegasus Review (T)
Penned from the Heart (C or T)
$-Priority! (C or T)
Purpose Magazine (C or T)
Quaker Life (C or T)
$-River Region's Journey (T)
$-Significant Living
Silver Wings (C or T)
$-Storyteller (C or T)
Victory Herald (C or T)
$-Vista (C or T)
$-Way of St. Francis (C or T)
Wisconsin Christian (C or T)

CHILDREN
$-American Girl
$-Archaeology (C or T)
$-Focus/Clubhouse (C)
$-Kids' Ark (C or T)
$-New Moon (C or T)
$-Pockets (C)

CHRISTIAN EDUCATION/ LIBRARY
$-Children's Ministry (C or T)

DAILY DEVOTIONALS
Penned from the Heart (C or T)

MISSIONS
$-Glad Tidings (T)
Koinonia

PASTORS/LEADERS
$-Insight Youth (T)
$-Let's Worship
$-Reformed Worship (C or T)

TEEN/YOUNG ADULT
$-Boundless Webzine (T)
$-Direction Student (T)
$-Essential Connection

G4T Ink (T)
$-Horizon Student (T)
$-Insight (T)
$-Listen
$-Take Five Plus (T)
$-TC Magazine (T)
TeensForJC (T)
$-TG Magazine (T)
$-Young Christian (C or T)
$-Young Christian Writers (T)

WOMEN
$-Dabbling Mum (T)
Extreme Woman (T)
($)-History's Women (T)
$-Mother's Heart (T)
Precious Times (T)
Together with God (T)
Unrecognized Woman
Women of the Cross (T)
Women Today (T)

WRITERS
$-Canadian Writer's Jour. (T)
Esdras' Scroll (C or T)
$-Fellowscript (T)
NW Christian Author (T)
$-Tickled by Thunder (C or T)
Write Connection (T)
$-Writers' Journal (T)

YOUTH ISSUES
ADULT/GENERAL
American Tract—R
Anointed Pages
$-Arlington Catholic
$-Associated Content—R
$-Atlantic Catholic
$-Aujourd'hui Credo—R
$-Canada Lutheran—R
$-Catholic Forester—R
$-Catholic Peace Voice—R
CBN.com—R
$-Chicken Soup Books—R
$-Christian Citizen USA
$-Christian Examiner
Christian Family Jour.
$-Christian Home & School
Christian Motorsports
Christian News NW—R

Christian Online
Christian Ranchman
$-Christian Renewal—R
$-ChristianWeek—R
$-Churchmouse Public.—R
$-Columbia—R
$-Culture Wars—R
Desert Voice—R
E-Channels—R
$-EFCA Today
$-Eureka Street
$-Faith & Family
$-Family Smart E-tips—R
$-Good News, The—R
Gospel Herald
$-Guide—R
Halo Magazine—R
$-Homeschooling Today—R
$-Home Times—R
$-Indian Life—R
$-In His Presence—R
$-In Touch
Island Catholic—R
$-JC Town Reporter—R
$-KD Gospel Media
Koinonia
LifeTimes Catholic
$-Living Church
$-Lookout
$-Manna—R
MESSAGE/Open Bible—R
$-Our Sunday Visitor—R
Pegasus Review—R
Penned from the Heart—R
$-Point—R
$-Presbyterian Outlook
Quaker Life—R
$-Seek—R
Single Again Mag.—R
Spirituality for Today
$-St. Anthony Messenger
Sword of the Lord—R
$-Testimony—R
Trumpeter—R
Unrecognized Woman—R
$-U.S. Catholic—R
$-Way of St. Francis—R
$-Wesleyan Life—R
$-World & I—R

CHILDREN
$-American Girl—R
$-BREAD/God's Children—R
$-Cadet Quest—R
$-Guide—R
$-Keys for Kids—R
$-New Moon—R
$-SHINE brightly—R
Skipping Stones
$-Sparkle—R

CHRISTIAN EDUCATION/ LIBRARY
$-Group
$-Journal/Adventist Ed.—R
$-Teachers of Vision—R
$-Youth & CE Leadership

MISSIONS
East-West Church

PASTORS/LEADERS
$-Barefoot—R
$-Catholic Servant
$-Immerse
$-Insight Youth—R
$-InSite—R
$-Interpreter
Plugged In
$-Word & World
$-YouthWorker

TEEN/YOUNG ADULT
$-Boundless Webzine—R
Connected
$-Direction Student
$-Focus/Dare 2 Dig Deeper
G4T Ink—R
$-Horizon Student
$-Insight—R
$-Listen—R

$-Risen
$-Sharing the Victory—R
$-Spirit
StudentLife
Susie
$-TC Magazine
$-TG Magazine
$-Visions
$-Young Salvationist—R
$-YouthWalk

WOMEN
$-At the Center—R
Extreme Woman
$-Mother's Heart—R
P31 Woman—R
Take Root & Write
Together with God—R
Unrecognized Woman—R

7

Periodicals and E-zines

Following are the listings of periodicals. They are arranged alphabetically by type of periodical. (See table of contents for a list of types). Nonpaying markets are indicated in bold letters within those listings, e.g., **NO PAYMENT**. Paying markets are indicated with a $ in front of the listing, and starting this year the payment amount is also highlighted.

A plus sign (+) before an entry indicates that it is a new listing. It is important that freelance writers request writer's guidelines and a recent sample copy or visit a periodical's Website before submitting to any of these publications. This year you will find specific directions on how to locate the guidelines on their Website for many of the publishers.

If you do not find the publication you are looking for, look in the "General Index" in the back of the book. See the introduction of that index for the codes used to identify the current status of each unlisted publication.

For a detailed explanation of how to understand and get the most out of these listings, as well as solid marketing tips, see the "How to Use This Book" section at the front of the book. Unfamiliar terms are explained in the "Glossary."

+ A plus sign means it is a new listing.

$ A dollar sign before a listing indicates a paying market.

($)A dollar sign in parentheses before a listing indicates they sometimes pay, or pay in books or other merchandise.

@ Indicates an online publication.

ADULT/GENERAL MARKETS

$ABILITIES MAGAZINE, 401—340 College St., Toronto ON M5T 3A9, Canada. (416) 923-1885. Fax (416) 923-9829. E-mail: ray@abilities.ca. Website: www.abilities.ca. Canadian Abilities Foundation; general. Raymond Cohen, ed-in-chief. Canada's foremost cross-disabilities lifestyle magazine. Open to freelance. Query; e-query preferred. **Pays $50-250 Cdn.** for 1st rts. Articles 750-2,000 wds. No simultaneous submissions. Requires disk. Kill fee 50%. Guidelines/theme list on Website ("Abilities .ca Services"/"Write for Us" on right side). (Ads)

   Tips: "Ensure your query is strongly Canadian and includes strategies, news, or ideas on living with a disability. We don't publish material with an overtly religious tone. Articles must be disability-related with a positive tone and practical advice."

AFRICAN VOICES, 270 W. 96th St., New York NY 10025. (212) 865-2982. Fax (212) 316-3335. E-mail: africanvoices@aol.com or through Website: www.africanvoices.com. African Voices Communications Inc. Layding Kaliba, mng. ed.; Kim Horne, fiction ed.; Debbie Officer, book review ed. Publishes original fiction, nonfiction, and poetry by artists of color. Quarterly mag.; 48 pgs.; circ. 20,000. Subscription $12. 75% unsolicited freelance; 25% assigned. Query/clips; e-query OK. **PAYS IN COPIES** for 1st rts. Articles 500-2,500 wds. (25/yr.); fiction 500-2,000 wds. (20/yr.); book reviews 500-1,200 wds. Responds in 16 wks. Seasonal 4 mos. ahead. Accepts simultaneous submissions & reprints (tell when/where appeared). Requires accepted submissions by e-mail (copied into message). Uses some sidebars. Guidelines on Website ("Submissions"); copy $5/9x12 SAE/$2.38 postage (mark "Media Mail"). (Ads)

Poetry: Layding Kalbia, poetry ed. Accepts 75-80/yr. Avant-garde, free verse, light verse, haiku, traditional; to 3 pgs. Submit max. 3 poems.

Fillers: Accepts 10/yr. Cartoons.

$ALIVE NOW, PO Box 340004, Nashville TN 37203-0004. (615) 340-7218. Fax (615) 340-7267. E-mail: alivenow@upperroom.org. Website: www.alivenow.upperroom.org. The Upper Room. JoAnn Evans Miller, ed. Short, theme-based writings in attractive graphic setting for reflection and meditation. Bimonthly mag.; 48 pgs.; circ. 40,000. Subscription $17.95. 30% unsolicited freelance; 70% assigned. Complete ms/cover letter; e-query OK. **Pays $35-120** on acceptance for all rts. Articles 200-400 wds. (25/yr.); fiction 200-400 wds. Responds 13 wks. before issue date. Seasonal 6-8 mos. ahead. Accepts simultaneous submissions & reprints (tell when/where appeared). Accepts e-mail submissions (copied into message). Uses some sidebars. Prefers NRSV. Guidelines/theme list by mail/Website (scroll to bottom "Writers Guidelines"); copy for 6x9 SAE/4 stamps.

Poetry: Avant-garde, free verse, traditional; 10-45 lines; $25-100. Submit max. 5 poems. On issue's theme.

Fillers: Anecdotes, prayers, quotes; no payment.

Tips: "We can only accept submissions that fit with our themes. Write for our theme list and make your submission relevant to the topic. Avoid the obvious and heavy-handed preachiness."

** This periodical was #20 on the 2010 Top 50 Christian Publishers list (#46 in 2009, #46 in 2008).

THE AMBASSADOR, 1040 Lincoln Rd., Ste. A, #124, Yuba City CA 95991. (530) 933-1385. Fax (530) 564-1503. E-mail: editor@Ambassadornewspaper.com. Seth Halpern, ed./pub. To encourage the local Christian community. Monthly newspaper; circ. 6,000. Subscription $30. Open to unsolicited freelance. Query. Incomplete topical listings. (Ads)

$@AMERICA, 106 W. 56th St., New York NY 10019-3893. (212) 581-4640. Fax (212) 399-3596. E-mail: articles@americamagazine.org. Website: www.americamagazine.org. Catholic. Submit to Editor-in-Chief. For thinking Catholics and those who want to know what Catholics are thinking. Weekly mag. & online version; 32+ pgs.; circ. 46,000. Subscription $56. 100% unsolicited freelance. Complete ms/cover letter; fax/e-query OK. **Pays $150-300** on acceptance. Articles 1,500-2,000 wds. Responds in 6 wks. Seasonal 3 mos. ahead. Does not use sidebars. Guidelines by mail/Website; copy for 9x12 SAE. (Ads) Incomplete topical listings.

Poetry: Buys avant-garde, free verse, light verse, traditional; 20-35 lines; $2-3/line.

AMERICAN TRACT SOCIETY, Box 462008, Garland TX 75046-2008. (972) 276-9408. Fax (972) 272-9642. E-mail:chrisn@ATSmail.org. Website: www.ATStracts.org. Submit to Tract Ed. Majority of tracts written to win unbelievers. New tract releases bimonthly; 40 new titles produced annually. 5% unsolicited freelance; 2% assigned. Complete ms/cover letter; e-query OK. **PAYS IN COPIES** on publication for exclusive tract rts. Tracts 600-1,200 wds. Responds in 6-8 wks. Seasonal 1 yr. ahead. Accepts simultaneous submissions & reprints (tell when/where appeared). Accepts requested ms on disk or by e-mail (attached or copied into message). Prefers NIV, KJV. Guidelines by mail/e-mail/Website ("Ways to Contribute"/"How to write a tract"); free samples for #10 SAE/1 stamp. (No ads)

Special needs: Youth issues, African American, cartoonists, critical issues.

Tips: "Read our current tracts; submit polished writing; relate to people's needs and experiences. Follow guidelines—almost no one does."

$ANGELS ON EARTH, 16 E. 34th St., New York NY 10016. (212) 251-8100. Fax (212) 684-1311. E-mail: submissions@angelsonearth.com. Website: www.angelsonearth.com. Guideposts. Colleen Hughes, ed-in-chief; Meg Belviso, depts. ed. for features and fillers. Presents true stories about God's angels and humans who have played angelic roles on earth. Bimonthly mag.; 75 pgs.; circ. 550,000.

Subscription $19.95. 90% unsolicited freelance. Complete ms/cover letter; no phone/fax/e-query. **Pays $25-400** on publication for all rts. Articles 100-2,000 wds. (100/yr.); all stories must be true. Responds in 13 wks. Seasonal 6 mos. ahead. E-mail submissions from Website. Guidelines on Website (www.angelsonearth.com/writers_Guidelines.asp); copy for 7x10 SAE/4 stamps.

Fillers: Buys many. Anecdotal shorts of similar nature (angelic); 50-250 wds. $50-100.

Columns/Departments: Buys 50/yr. Messages (brief, mysterious happenings), $25. Earning Their Wings (good deeds), 150 wds. $50. Only Human? (human or angel?/mystery), 350 wds. $100. Complete ms.

Tips: "We are not limited to stories about heavenly angels. We also accept stories about human beings doing heavenly duties."

$ANGLICAN JOURNAL, 80 Hayden St., Toronto ON M4Y 2J6, Canada. (416) 924-9199, ext. 307. Fax (416) 921-4452. E-mail: editor@national.anglican.ca. Website: www.anglicanjournal.com. Anglican Church of Canada. Kristin Jenkins, ed. National newspaper of the Anglican Church of Canada; informs Canadian Anglicans about the church at home and overseas. Newspaper (10X/yr.) & online; 12-16 pgs.; circ. 200,000. Subscription $10 Cdn., $17 U.S. & foreign. 10% unsolicited freelance. Query only; fax/e-query OK. **Pays $150-250 for features; $150 for columns and reviews; or .25/wd. Cdn.**, on acceptance for 1st & electronic rts. Articles to 1,000 wds. (12-15/yr.); fiction for early teens, teens, and adults. Responds in 2 wks. Seasonal 2 mos. ahead. No reprints. Guidelines by e-mail/Website (click on "Writers Guidelines" at bottom of Home Page). (Ads)

Tips: "Select subject matter that would be of interest to a national audience."

$ANIMAL TRAILS, 2660 Peterborough St., Oak Hills VA 20171. E-mail: animaltrails@yahoo.com. Website: http://animaltrailsmagazine.doodlekit.com. Tellstar Publishing. Shannon Bridget Murphy, ed. Keeping animal memories alive through writing. Quarterly mag. 85% unsolicited freelance. Complete ms/cover letter; e-query OK. **Pays .02-.05/wd**. on acceptance for 1st, onetime, reprint, or simultaneous rts. Articles to 2,000 wds.; fiction to 2,000 wds. Responds in 2-8 wks. Seasonal 3 mos. ahead. Accepts simultaneous submissions & reprints (tell when/where appeared). Accepts disk or e-mail submissions (attached or copied into message). No kill fee. Regularly uses sidebars. Prefers KJV. Guidelines by e-mail. (No ads)

Poetry: Buys variable number. Avant-garde, free verse, haiku, light verse, traditional; any length. Pays variable rates. Submit any number.

Fillers: Buys most types, to 1,000 wds.

Tips: "Most open to articles, stories, poetry, and fillers that explain the value of animals and their relationship with God. The value of animals is the mission of Animal Trails. Include a Scripture reference."

ANOINTED PAGES MAGAZINE, 3900 W. Brown Deer Rd., Ste. A-149, Milwaukee WI 53209. (414) 517-8876 or (414) 759-4959. E-mail: info@anointedpages.com. Website: www.anointedpages.com. Interdenominational. Marvin Ivy, pub. (marvinivy@anointedpages.com); Jodine Ivy, editorial administrator (jodineive@anointedpages.com). To profile religious and community leaders and the lives that they are changing within their ministry and community, and to meet the needs of people with articles on the holistic lifestyle. Bimonthly mag. Subscription $19.99. Estab. 2007. Open to unsolicited freelance. Query. Articles. Also accepts submissions from teens.

@ANSWERS MAGAZINE & ANSWERSMAGAZINE.COM, PO Box 510, Hebron KY 41048. (859) 727-2222. Fax (859) 727-4888. E-mail: nationaleditor@answersmagazine.com. Website: www.answersmagazine.com. Answers in Genesis. Mike Matthews, exec. ed-in-chief. Bible-affirming, creation-based. Quarterly mag. Subscription $24. Articles 300-600 wds. Responds in 30 days. Details on Website ("Contact"/"Write for Answers Magazine"/"Writers Guidelines").

**2010 EPA Award of Merit: General.

$@THE APOCALYPSE CHRONICLES, Box 448, Jacksonville OR 97530. Phone/fax (541) 899-8888. E-mail: James@ChristianMediaNetwork.com. Website: www.Christianmedia.tv. Christian Media. James Lloyd, ed./pub. Deals with the apocalypse exclusively. Quarterly & online newsletter; circ. 2,000-3,000. Query; prefers phone query. **Payment negotiable** for reprint rts. Articles. Responds in 3 wks. Requires KJV. No guidelines; copy for #10 SAE/2 stamps.

   Tips: "It's helpful if you understand your own prophetic position and are aware of its name, i.e., Futurist, Historicist, etc."

$ARKANSAS CATHOLIC, PO Box 7417, Little Rock AR 72217. (501) 664-0125. Fax (501) 664-6572. E-mail: mhargett@dolr.org. Website: www.arkansas-catholic.org. Catholic Diocese of Little Rock. Malea Hargett, ed. Statewide newspaper for the local diocese. Weekly tabloid; 16 pgs.; circ. 7,700. Subscription $22. 1% unsolicited freelance; 10% assigned. Query/clips; e-query OK. **Pays .10-.12/wd.** on publication for 1st rts. Articles 1,000 wds. Accepts simultaneous submissions & reprints. Accepts requested ms by e-mail. Uses some sidebars. Prefers Catholic Bible. Guidelines by mail/e-mail; copy for 9x12 SAE/2 stamps. (Ads)

   Columns/Departments: Buys 2/yr. Seeds of Faith (education). Complete ms. Pays $20.
   Tips: "All stories and columns must have an Arkansas and Catholic connection."

$ARLINGTON CATHOLIC HERALD, 200 N. Glebe Rd., Ste. 600, Arlington VA 22203. (703) 841-2590. Fax (703) 524-2782. E-mail: editorial@catholicherald.com. Website: www.catholicherald.com. Catholic Diocese of Arlington. Michael F. Flach, ed., mflach@catholicherald.com or through Website. Regional, for the local diocese. Weekly newspaper; 28 pgs.; circ. 61,000. Subscription $14. 10% unsolicited freelance. Query; phone/fax/e-query OK. **Pays $50-150** on publication for one-time rts. Articles 500-1,500 wds. Responds in 2 wks. Seasonal 3 mos. ahead. Accepts simultaneous submissions. Prefers accepted ms on disk. Regular sidebars. Guidelines by mail/Website; copy for 11x17 SAE. (Ads)

   Columns/Departments: Sports; School News; Local Entertainment; 500 wds.
   Tips: "All submissions must be Catholic related. Avoid controversial issues within the church."

$@ASSOCIATED CONTENT, 88 Steele St., Ste. 400, Denver CO 80206-5715. (720) 255-9185. E-mail: miguel@associatedcontent.com or through Website: www.associatedcontent.com. Associated Content. Miguel Chacon, submissions mngr. Weekly e-zine; 1000+ pgs. Free online. 100% unsolicited freelance. Query online. **Pays $3-20** on acceptance for nonexclusive, electronic rts. Articles 400-5,000 wds. (1,000+/yr.); fiction 400-5,000 wds. (1,000+/yr.). Responds in 2 wks. Seasonal 1 mo. ahead. Accepts simultaneous submissions & reprints (tell when/where appeared). Accepts submissions online only. Guidelines on Website ("Sign Up/Publish"/"Join our community of contributors"/"Learn more about"/"Submission Guidelines"); copy online.

   Poetry: Avant-garde, free verse, haiku, light verse, traditional.
   Tips: "Look over Website and see what the other writers are doing. Sign up, fill out a profile, and submit your work."
   ** This periodical was #1 on the 2010 Top 50 Christian Publishers list (#6 in 2008, #6 in 2007, #7 in 2006).

$ATLANTIC CATHOLIC, 88 College St., Antigonish NS B2G 2L7, Canada. (902) 863-4370. Fax (902) 863-1943. E-mail: editor@thecasket.ca or atlanticcatholic@thecasket.ca. Website: www.thecasket.ca. The Casket Printing and Publishing Co. Ken Sims, pub.; Brian Lazzuri, mng. ed. Reports religious news that will inform, educate, and inspire Catholics. Biweekly tabloid; circ. 2,000. Subscription $28. Open to unsolicited freelance. **Pays $25/story.** Articles to 800 wds. Accepts e-mail submissions of mss up to 800 wds. (Ads)

   Tips: "Most open to book and movie reviews, less than 700 wds.; also celebrity profiles, less than 700 wds."

$AUJOURD'HUI CREDO, 1435 City Councillors, Montreal QC H3A 2E4, Canada. (514) 284-1675. Fax (514) 284-1672. E-mail: davidfines@egliseunie.org. Website: www.united-church.ca. United Church of Canada. David Fines, dir. The only French Reformed magazine in North America. Monthly mag.; 28 pgs.; circ. 350. Subscription $25 Cdn. 20% unsolicited freelance. Complete ms; fax/e-query OK. **Pays $150** on publication for nonexclusive rts. Not copyrighted. Articles 1,500 wds. (10/yr.); fiction 800 wds. (6/yr.); reviews 100 wds. Responds in 4 wks. Seasonal 2 mos. ahead. Accepts simultaneous submissions & reprints (tell when/where appeared). Requires e-mail submissions (attached or copied into message). No kill fee. Uses some sidebars. Also accepts submissions from children/teens. Prefers TOB. Guidelines/theme list by e-mail; free copy. (Ads)

Poetry: Accepts free verse.

Tips: "Most likely to break in by being inclusive and intelligent. Looking for theological reflection or social topics. Contact director. Must write in French."

$AUSTRALIAN CATHOLICS, PO Box 553, Richmond Victoria 3121, Australia. Phone (61) (3) 9421 9666. Fax (61) (3) 9421 9600. E-mail: auscaths@jespub.jesuit.org.au or through Website: www.australiancatholics.com.au. Jesuit Communications. Michael McVeigh, ed. Stories of faith and living for a contemporary Catholic audience. Mag. published 5X/yr.; 36 pgs.; circ. 200,000. Subscription $25. Open to unsolicited freelance. Query or complete ms; e-query OK. **Payment by negotiation** on publication for 1st rts. Articles 800-1,200 wds. Seasonal 4 mos. ahead. Accepts reprints (tell when/where appeared). Uses some sidebars.

Tips: "We generally prefer articles on people, either as interviews or reflections on personal experiences. We generally don't consider an overseas submission, unless it can be made relevant for an Australian audience."

THE BAPTIST STANDARD, PO Box 660267, Dallas TX 75266-0267. (214) 630-4571. Fax (214) 638-8535. E-mail: marvknox@baptiststandard.com or through Website: www.baptiststandard .com/postnuke/index.php. Marv Knox, ed. The Texas Baptist news journal. Biweekly newspaper. Subscription $20.50. Incomplete topical listings.

$B.C. CATHOLIC, 150 Robson St., Vancouver BC V6B 2A7, Canada. (604) 683-0281. Fax (604) 683-4288. E-mail: bcc@rcav.bc.ca. Website: www.rcav.org/bcc. Roman Catholic Archdiocese of Vancouver. Paul Schratz, ed. News, education, and inspiration for Canadian Catholics. Weekly (48X) newspaper; 20 pgs.; circ. 20,000. Subscription $32. 20% unsolicited freelance. Query; phone query OK. **Pays .15/wd.** on publication for 1st rts. **Photos $30.** Articles 300-3,000 wds. Responds in 6 wks. Seasonal 4 wks. ahead. Accepts simultaneous submissions & reprints (.05/wd.). Prefers e-mail submission (copied into message). Guidelines on Website ("Submissions" left side); free copy. (Ads)

Tips: "Items of relevance to Catholics in British Columbia are preferred."

@BEHIND THE HAMMER, 1018 Main St., Akron PA 17501. (717) 859-2210. Fax (717) 859-4910. E-mail: communications@mds.mennonite.net, or mdsus@mds.mennonite.net. Website: www.mds.mennonite.net. Mennonite Disaster Services. Scott Sundberg, ed. Quarterly & online mag. Subscription free. Open to freelance. Complete ms/cover letter. **NO PAYMENT.** Articles. Guidelines on Website; free copy. Not in topical listings.

Tips: "By sharing our stories we hope to encourage and motivate one another to continue expressing the love of God through MDS activity."

@BELIEVER'S BAY, 1202 S. Pennsylvania St., Marion IN 46953. (765) 997-1736. E-mail: publisher@BelieversBay.com. Website: www.BelieversBay.com. Tim Russ, pub. To share the love of God with common sense. Monthly online mag. Mostly freelance. Complete ms by e-mail only (attached); e-query OK. **NO PAYMENT** for 1st & electronic rts. (permanently archives pieces).

Articles 500-1,000 wds. Guidelines/monthly topical themes listed at www.believersbay.com/submis sion_guidelines.htm.

Columns/Departments: Columns 300-500 wds.

Special needs: Living in Responsible Grace.

Tips: "Only accepts e-mail submissions: submit@believersbay.com."

$BIBLE ADVOCATE, Box 33677, Denver CO 80233. (303) 452-7973. Fax (303) 452-0657. E-mail: bibleadvocate@cog7.org. Website: www.cog7.org/BA. Church of God (Seventh-day). Calvin Burrell, ed.; Sherri Langton, assoc. ed. Adult readers; 50% not members of the denomination. Bimonthly (6X) mag.; 32 pgs.; circ. 13,500. Subscription free. 25-35% unsolicited freelance. Complete ms/ cover letter; no phone/fax/e-query. **Pays $25-55** on publication for 1st, onetime, reprint, electronic, simultaneous rts. Articles 600-1,200 wds. (10-20/yr.). Responds in 4-10 wks. Seasonal 9 mos. ahead (no Christmas or Easter pieces). Accepts simultaneous submissions & reprints (tell when/where appeared). Accepts requested ms by e-mail (attached). Regularly uses sidebars. Prefers NIV, NKJV. Guidelines/theme list by mail/Website ("Writers Guidelines" right side); copy for 9x12 SAE/3 stamps. (No ads)

Poetry: Buys 6-10/yr. Free verse, traditional; 5-20 lines; $20. Submit max. 5 poems.

Fillers: Buys 5/yr. Prose; 100-400 wds. $20.

Special needs: Articles centering on upcoming themes (see Website).

Tips: "If you write well, all areas are open to freelance, especially personal experiences that tie in with the monthly themes. Articles that run 600-700 words are more likely to get in. Also, fresh writing with keen insight is most readily accepted."

+BIBLE STUDY MAGAZINE, 1313 Commercial St., Bellingham WA 98225-4307. (360) 527-1700. Fax (360) 527-1707. E-mail: sales@logos.com. Website: www.biblestudymagazine.com. John D. Barry, ed-in-chief (john@biblestudymagazine.com). Each issue provides tools and methods for Bible study, as well as insights from people like John Piper, Kay Arthur, Mark Driscoll, Randy Alcorn, John MacArthur, Barry Black, and more.

BIBLICAL RECORDER, PO Box 18808, Raleigh NC 27619-8808. (919) 847-2127. Fax (919) 847-6939. E-mail: editor@biblicalrecorder.org. Website: www.biblicalrecorder.org. Baptist. Norman Jameson, ed. Newspaper. Subscription $15.99. Incomplete topical listings.

@BOOKS & CULTURE, 465 Gundersen Dr., Carol Stream IL 60188. (630) 260-6200. Fax (630) 260-0114. E-mail: booksandculture@christianitytoday.com or through Website: www.booksand culture.com. Christianity Today Intl. John Wilson, ed. (jwilson@christianitytoday.com). To edify, sharpen, and nurture the evangelical intellectual community by engaging the world in all its complexity from a distinctly Christian perspective. Bimonthly & online newsletter.; circ. 12,000. Subscription $19.95. Open to freelance. Query. Articles & reviews. Incomplete topical listings. (Ads)

THE BREAD OF LIFE, 35—5100 S. Service Rd., PO Box 127, Burlington ON L7R 3X5, Canada. (905) 634-5433. E-mail: info@thebreadoflife.ca. Website: www.thebreadoflife.ca. Catholic. Paula Simmons-Wint, ed. Catholic Charismatic. To encourage spiritual growth in areas of renewal in the Catholic Church today. Bimonthly mag.; 48 pgs.; circ. 2,500. Subscription $35 Cdn.; $40 elsewhere. 5% unsolicited freelance. Complete ms/cover letter; fax query OK. **NO PAYMENT.** Articles 750 wds.; book reviews 250 wds. Responds in 4-6 wks. Seasonal 6 mos. ahead. Accepts reprints (tell when/ where appeared). No disk. Does not use sidebars. Prefers NAB, NJB. Guidelines; copy for 9x12 SAE/$2.38 postage (mark "Media Mail"). (Some ads)

Poetry: Accepts little.

Fillers: Accepts 10-12/yr. Facts, prose, quotes; to 250 wds.

Tips: "Most open to testimonies; contact managing editor. We do appreciate poetry submissions and 750-word testimonies of the power of Jesus/Holy spirit active in your life. It is best if a writer includes a 2-3 line biography and photo for publication."

THE BREAKTHROUGH INTERCESSOR, PO Box 121, Lincoln VA 20160-0121. (540) 338-5522. Fax (540) 338-1934. E-mail: editor@intercessors.org. Website: www.intercessors.org. Nondenominational. Cherise Ryan Curby, ed. Preparing and equipping people who pray; encouraging in prayer and faith. Quarterly mag.; 32 pgs.; circ. 4,000. Subscription $18. 85% unsolicited freelance. Complete ms; fax/e-query OK. Accepts full mss by e-mail. **PAYS 5 COPIES** for 1st, reprint rts. Articles 700-1,000 wds. (20-25/yr.); book reviews 300-600 wds.; music/video reviews 300 wds. Responds in 2-5 weeks. Seasonal 6 mos. ahead. Accepts simultaneous submissions and reprints (tell when/where appeared). Prefers requested ms by e-mail (attached file). Uses some sidebars. Also accepts submissions from children/teens. Any Bible version. Guidelines by e-mail/Website ("Publications"/"Writers Guidelines"); copy online. (No ads)

Poetry: Accepts 4/yr. Any type, 4-32 lines. Submit any number (as long as they're about prayer).

Fillers: Accepts 8/yr. Anecdotes, prayers; to 300 wds.

Special needs: Moving personal stories in how prayer has changed your life, or someone else's.

Tips: "Break in by submitting true articles/stories about prayer and its miraculous results, and articles that teach about an aspect of prayer using Scripture to support each point." Manuscripts acknowledged but not returned.

@BREAKTHROUGH MAGAZINE, (517) 882-3595. E-mail: editor@breakthroughonlinemag.com. Website: www.breakthroughonlinemag.com. Baraka Miller, ed. "Every struggle endures a breakthrough, every breakthrough endures a struggle." Showcases those who have made their breakthrough in life and who are impacting their communities; sharing the joy of life, family, success, and above all Christ, the one who gives us strength to "Breakthrough." Webzine.

$BRIDAL GUIDES, 2660 Peterborough St., Oak Hill VA 20171. E-mail: bridalguides@yahoo.com. Website: http://bridalguidesmagazineguidelines.doodlekit.com. Tellstar Publishing. Shannon Bridget Murphy, ed. Theme-based wedding/reception ideas and planning for Christian wedding planners. Quarterly mag. 85% unsolicited freelance. Complete ms/cover letter; e-query OK. **Pays .02-.05/wd.** on acceptance for 1st, onetime, reprint, simultaneous rts. Articles to 2,000 wds.; fiction to 2,000 wds. Responds in 2-8 wks. Seasonal 3 mos. ahead. Accepts simultaneous submissions & reprints (tell when/where appeared). Accepts disk or e-mail submissions (attached or copied into message). No kill fee. Regularly uses sidebars. Also accepts submissions from children/teens. Prefers KJV. Guidelines by e-mail. (No ads)

Poetry: Buys variable number. Avant-garde, free verse, haiku, light verse, traditional; any length. Pays variable rates. Submit any number.

Fillers: Buys most types, to 1,000 wds.; .02-.05/wd.

Special needs: "Most open to wedding and planning articles that show readers how to successfully complete plans for their events. Illustrations and art either with or without manuscript packages. Romance fiction related to weddings, travel, and home."

$@THE BRINK MAGAZINE, 114 Bush Rd., Nashville TN 37217. Toll-free (800) 877-7030. (615) 361-1221. Fax (615) 367-0535. E-mail: thebrink@randallhouse.com or through the Website: www.thebrinkonline.com. Randall House. Jacob Riggs, ed. Devotional magazine for young adults; focusing on Bible studies, life situations, discernment of culture, and relevant feature articles. Quarterly & online mag.; 64 pgs.; circ. 10,000. Subscription $6.99. Estab. 2008. 30% unsolicited freelance; 70% assigned. Query, query/clips; prefers e-query. Accepts full mss by e-mail. **Pays $50-150** on acceptance for all rts. Articles 500-1,500 wds. (10-15/yr.). Responds in 1-2 wks. Seasonal 6 mos. ahead. Accepts simultaneous submissions & reprints (tell when/where appeared). Requires accepted articles by e-mail (attached file). No kill fee. Regularly uses sidebars. Guidelines/theme list on Website (under "The Magazine"/"Write for the Brink"). (No ads)

Fillers: Buys 4/yr. Ideas, newsbreaks, quizzes; 50-100 wds. No payment.

Columns/Departments: Buys 4/yr.; query. What _____ Says about_____ (hot cultural topic, movie, song, event, or TV show is used to draw out a certain theme). Pays $50-100.

Tips: "A writer can best get in by writing for the online version by pitching the editor an idea. After familiarity has been built, the editor could contact the writer for printed pieces."

@THE BRINK ONLINE, 114 Bush Rd., Nashville TN 37217. Toll-free (800) 877-7030. (615) 361-1221. Fax (615) 367-0535. E-mail: thebrink@randallhouse.com. Website: www.thebrinkonline .com. Randall House. Jacob Riggs, ed. Webzine for twentysomethings, including articles focusing on but not limited to: faith, media, dating, culture, politics, religion, technology, social justice, and finance. Updated weekly. Articles 500-1,500 wds. Accepts reprints. Requires e-query. Guidelines on Website (scroll to bottom "The Magazine"/"Write for The Brink").

BYFAITH (byFaith), 1700 N. Brown Rd., Ste. 105, Lawrenceville GA 30043. (678) 825-1005. Fax (678) 825-1001. E-mail: editor@byfaithonline.com or through Website: www.byfaithonline.com. Presbyterian Church in America (PCA). Dick Doster, ed. (ddoster@byfaithonline.com). Provides news of the PCA; connects members, guests, and staff members to the denomination. Bimonthly mag.; 54 pgs. Subscription $19.95. Open to unsolicited freelance. Complete ms by e-mail ("Editorial Submission" in subject line). **NO MENTION OF PAYMENT.** Articles 500-3,000 wds. Guidelines on Website ("About byFaith"/scroll down to "Submitting Articles"). Incomplete topical listings.

Tips: "We publish in 5 areas: stories that provoke thinking and creativity; very practical theology; articles that help readers understand the arts and culture; sensible, down-to-earth information; and PCA news."

** 2008, 2006 EPA Award of Excellence—Denominational; 2007 EPA Award of Merit: Denominational.

$CANADA LUTHERAN, 302—393 Portage Ave., Winnipeg MB R3B 3H6, Canada. Toll-free (888) 786-6707, ext. 172. (204) 984-9172. Fax (204) 984-9185. E-mail: editor@elcic.ca, or canaluth@ elcic.ca. Website: www.elcic.ca/clweb. Evangelical Lutheran Church in Canada. Provides information and inspiration to help our lay readers relate their faith to everyday life and foster a connection with their congregation, synods, and national office. Trina Gallop, ed. dir. (tgallop@elcic.ca); Lucia Carruthers, ed. Denominational. Monthly (8X) mag.; 32 pgs.; circ. 14,000. Subscription $22.60 Cdn.; $42 U.S. 40% unsolicited freelance; 60% assigned. E-query or complete ms. **Pays $.20/wd. Cdn.** on publication for 1st rts. Articles 700-1,200 wds. (15/yr.). Responds in 1-2 wks. Seasonal 6 mos. ahead. No simultaneous submissions; accepts reprints (tell when/where appeared). Prefers e-mail submission (attached file). Sometimes pays kill fee. Regularly uses sidebars. Prefers NRSV. Guidelines on Website ("Contribute"/"Writing Guide"); no copy.(Ads)

Columns/Departments: Buys 16/yr. Practicing Our Faith (how-to piece to help readers deepen or live out their faith); 600 wds. Pays .20/wd.

Tips: "Canadians/Lutherans receive priority here; others considered but rarely used. Want material that is clear, concise, and fresh. Primarily looking for how-to articles."

@CANADIANCHRISTIANITY.COM, #200-20316—56 Ave., Langley BC V3A 3Y7, Canada. Toll-free (888) 899-3777. E-mail: editor@canadianchristianity.com. Website: www.CanadianChristianity .com. A ministry of the Christian Info Society. David Dawes, mng. ed. Online newspaper. Incomplete topical listings.

THE CANADIAN LUTHERAN, 3074 Portage Ave., Winnipeg MB R3K 0Y2, Canada. Toll-free (800) 588-4226. (204) 895-3433. Fax (204) 897-4319. E-mail: communications@lutheranchurch.ca or through Website: www.lutheranchurch.ca. Lutheran Church—Canada. Ian Adnams, ed. Monthly (10X) mag. Subscription $20. Open to unsolicited freelance. Not in topical listings. (Ads)

($)CANADIAN MENNONITE, 490 Dutton Dr., Unit C5, Waterloo ON N2L 6H7, Canada. Toll-free (800) 378-2524. (519) 884-3810. Fax (519) 884-3331. E-mail: submit@canadianmennonite.org. Website: www.canadianmennonite.org. Canadian Mennonite Publishing Service. Ross W. Muir, mng. ed. Seeks to promote covenantal relationships within the Mennonite Church Canada constituency (guided by Hebrews 10:23-25). Biweekly mag.; 32-40 pgs.; circ. 14,750. Subscription $32.50 Cdn.; $52.50 U.S. Open to unsolicited freelance. Query; phone/e-query OK. **Pays .10/wd. for solicited submissions only; .05/wd. for reprints**; for 1st rts. Articles 400-800 wds.; reviews 500 wds. (pays .10/wd.). Responds in 2-4 wks. Accepts reprints (tell when/where appeared). Prefers e-mail submissions (attached file). Some kill fees 50%. Uses some sidebars. Guidelines and past issues on Website ("Write"). Incomplete topical listings. (Ads)
> **Tips:** "We provide channels for sharing accurate and fair information, faith profiles, inspirational and educational materials, news, and analysis of issues facing the church. We use very little from outside the Mennonite Church."

$+CANTICLE MAGAZINE, 325 Scarlet Blvd., Oldsmar FL 34677. Toll-free (800) 558-5452. (813) 854-1518. Fax (813) 891-1267. E-mail: editor@canticlemagazine.com. Website: www.canticle magazine.com. Women of Grace/Catholic. Susan Brinkman, OCDS, ed. Dedicated solely to the woman's vocation within the church. Bimonthly jour.; 32 pgs.; circ. 4,000. Subscription $29.95. 75% unsolicited freelance; 25% assigned. Query or complete ms; e-query OK. **Pays $50-150** on publication for 1st rts. Articles 600 or 1,200 wds. Responds in 4-6 wks. Seasonal 4 mos. ahead. Requires e-mail submissions in attached file after acceptance. No kill fee. Regularly uses sidebars. Prefers NAB or RSV (Catholic version). Guidelines/theme list on Website (down to "Writers Guidelines"); copy online. (Ads)
> **Columns/Departments:** Buys 6/yr. Send complete ms. Solitary Genius (singles, widows; religious perspective), 600 words; pays $50-75. List of columns in guidelines; 500-750 words; $75 for assigned, less for unsolicited.
> **Tips:** "Read guidelines and theme list."

$CAPPER'S, 1503 S.W. 42nd St., Topeka KS 66609. (785) 274-4300. Fax (785) 274-4305. E-mail: cappers@cappers.com or through Website: www.cappers.com. Ogden Publications. K. C. Compton, ed-in-chief. Timely news-oriented features with positive messages. Monthly mag.; 40-56 pgs.; circ. 150,000. Subscription $18.95. 40% unsolicited freelance. Complete ms/cover letter by mail only. **Pays about $2.50/printed inch for nonfiction** on publication. Articles to 1,000 wds. (50/yr.). Responds in 2-6 mos. Seasonal 6 mos. ahead. No simultaneous submissions or reprints. Prefers requested ms by e-mail. Uses some sidebars. Guidelines by mail/Website; copy $4/9x12 SAE/4 stamps. (Ads)
> **Columns/Departments:** Buys 12/yr. Garden Path (gardens/gardening), 500-1,000 wds. Payment varies. This column most open.
> **Tips:** "Our publication is all original material either written by our readers/freelancers or occasionally by our staff. Every department, every article is open. Break in by reading at least 6 months of issues to know our special audience. Most open to nonfiction features and garden stories." Submissions are not acknowledged or status reports given.

CAROLINA CHRISTIAN NEWS (formerly *Blue Ridge Christian News*), 29 Crystal St., #101, Spruce Pine NC 28777. (828) 766-7048. Fax (828) 765-9128. E-mail: info@carolinachristiannews.com. Website: www.carolinachristiannews.com. Nondenominational. Steve Parker, ed./pub. Monthly newspaper, 2 editions: Metrolina Edition, circ. 30,000; Mountain Edition, circ. 20,000. Subscription $24. Open to unsolicited freelance. Query first. Articles. Incomplete topical listings. (Ads)
> **Tips:** "We are committed to bringing health, unity, and spiritual maturity to the Body of Christ

while releasing the power of the Holy Spirit into every segment of society: home, church, education, business, media, arts, and government."

$@CATHEDRAL AGE, 3101 Wisconsin Ave. N.W., Washington DC 20016. (202) 537-5681. Fax (202) 364-6600. E-mail: Cathedral_Age@cathedral.org. Website: www.cathedralage.org. Protestant Episcopal Cathedral Foundation. Craig W. Stapert, pub. mngr. News from Washington National Cathedral and stories of interest to friends and supporters of WNC. Quarterly & online mag.; 36 pgs.; circ. 30,000. Subscription $15. 50% assigned freelance. Query; e-query OK. **Pays to $750** on publication for all rts. Articles 1,200-1,500 wds. (10/yr.); book reviews 600 wds. ($250). Responds in 6 wks. Seasonal 6 mos. ahead. Requires requested ms on disk or by e-mail (attached file). Kill fee 50%. Uses some sidebars. Prefers NRSV. No guidelines; copy $5/9x12 SAE/5 stamps. (No ads)
   Special needs: Art, architecture, music.
   Tips: "We assign all articles, so query with clips first. Always write from the viewpoint of an individual first, then move into a more general discussion of the topic. Human-interest angle important."

$@CATHOLIC DIGEST, PO Box 6015, 1 Montauk Ave., Ste. 200, New London CT 06320-1789. (860) 437-3012. Fax (860) 536-5600. E-mail: cdfillers@bayard-us.com. Website: www.CatholicDigest .com. Catholic/Bayard Publications. Submit to Articles Editor. Readers have a stake in being Catholic and a wide range of interests: religion, family, health, human relationships, good works, nostalgia, and more. Monthly & online mag.; 128 pgs.; circ. 400,000. Subscription $19.95. 15% unsolicited freelance; 20% assigned. Complete ms (for original material)/cover letter, tear sheets for reprints; no e-query. **Pays $200-300 ($100 for reprints)** on acceptance for 1st rts. Online-only articles receive $100, plus half of any traceable revenue. Articles 1,000-2,000 wds.; feature articles 1,200-1,700 wds. (60/yr.). Responds in 6-8 wks. Seasonal 3-4 mos. ahead. Accepts reprints (tell when/ where appeared). Accepts requested ms on disk or by e-mail (copied into message). Regularly uses sidebars. Prefers NAB. Guidelines on Website ("About"/"Writers Guidelines"); copy for 7x10 SAE/2 stamps. (Ads)
   Fillers: Fillers Editor. Buys 200/yr. Anecdotes, cartoons, facts, jokes, quotes; 1 line to 300 wds. $2/published line on publication. Submit to cdfillers@bayard-inc.com.
   Columns/Departments: Buys 75/yr. Open Door (personal stories of conversion to Catholicism); 200-500 wds. $2/published line. See guidelines for full list.
   Special needs: Family and career concerns of Baby Boomers who have a stake in being Catholic.
   Contest: See Website for current contest, or send a SASE.
   Tips: "We favor the anecdotal approach. Stories must be strongly focused on a definitive topic that is illustrated for the reader with a well-developed series of true-life, interconnected vignettes."
   ** This periodical was #29 on the 2009 Top 50 Christian Publishers list (#31 in 2008, #37 in 2007, #31 in 2006).

$CATHOLIC FORESTER, Box 3012, Naperville IL 60566-7012. Toll-free (800) 552-0145. (630) 983-3381. Toll-free fax (800) 811-2140. (630) 983-3384. E-mail: magazine@catholicforester.com. Website: www.catholicforester.org. Catholic Order of Foresters. Mary Anne File, ed. For mixed audience, primarily parents and grandparents between the ages of 30 and 80+. Quarterly mag.; 40 pgs.; circ. 100,000. Free/membership. 20% unsolicited freelance. Complete ms/cover letter; no phone/ fax/e-query. **Pays .50/wd.** on acceptance for 1st rts. Articles 1,000-1,500 wds. (12-16/yr.); fiction for all ages 500-1,000 wds. (12-16/yr.). Responds in 3 mos. Accepts simultaneous submissions & reprints (tell when/where appeared). Accepts requested ms by e-mail. Uses some sidebars. Prefers Catholic Bible. Guidelines on Website; copy for 9x12 SAE/4 stamps. (No ads)

Tips: "Looking for informational, inspirational articles on finances and health. Writing should be energetic with good style and rhythm. Most open to general interest and fiction."
** This periodical was #36 on the 2009 Top 50 Christian Publishers list (#23 in 2008, #26 in 2007, #19 in 2006).

$CATHOLIC INSIGHT, PO Box 625, Adelaide Sta., 31 Adelaide St. E., Toronto ON M5C 2J8, Canada. (416) 204-9601. Fax (416) 204-1027. E-mail: reach@catholicinsight.com. Website: www.catholic insight.com. Life Ethics Information Center. Fr. Alphonse de Valk, ed./pub. News, analysis, and commentary on social, ethical, political, and moral issues from a Catholic perspective. Monthly (11X) mag.; 32 pgs.; circ. 3,400. Subscription $35 Cdn., $55 U.S. 2% unsolicited freelance; 98% assigned. Query preferred; phone/fax/e-query OK. **Pays $175 for 1,500 wds. ($200 for 2,000 wds.)** on publication for 1st rts. Articles 750-1,500 wds. (20-30/yr.); book reviews 750 wds. ($85). Responds in 6-8 wks. Seasonal 2 mos. ahead. Accepts requested ms on disk. Uses some sidebars. Prefers RSV (Catholic). Guidelines by mail/e-mail; copy $4.50 Cdn./9x12 SAE/$2 Cdn. postage or IRC. (Ads)

    Tips: "We are interested in intelligent, well-researched, well-presented commentary on a political, religious, social, or cultural matter from the viewpoint of the Catholic Church."

$CATHOLIC NEW YORK, 1011 First Ave., Ste. 1721, New York NY 10022. (212) 688-2399. Fax (212) 688-2642. E-mail: cny@cny.org. Website: www.cny.org. Catholic. John Woods, ed-in-chief. To inform New York Catholics. Biweekly newspaper; 40 pgs.; circ. 135,000. Subscription $24. 2% unsolicited freelance. Query or complete ms/cover letter. **Pays $15-100** on publication for onetime rts. Articles 500-800 wds. Responds in 5 wks. Copy $3.

    Tips: "Most open to columns about specific seasons of the Catholic Church, such as Advent, Christmas, Lent, and Easter."

$CATHOLIC PEACE VOICE, 532 W. 8th, Erie PA 16502-1343. (814) 453-4955, ext. 235. Fax (814) 452-4784. E-mail: info@paxchristiusa.org. Website: www.paxchristiusa.org. Dave Robinson, exec. dir. (Dave@paxchristiusa.org). For members of Pax Christi USA, the national Catholic Peace Movement. Bimonthly newsmag.; 16-20 pgs.; circ. 23,000. Subscription $20, free to members. 15-20% unsolicited freelance; 25-30% assigned. Complete ms; phone/fax/e-query OK. **Pays $50-75** on publication for all & electronic rts. Articles 500-1,500 wds. (10-15/yr.); reviews 750 wds. ($50). Responds in 1-2 wks. Accepts simultaneous submissions & reprints (tell when/where appeared). Accepted ms on disk or by e-mail (attached or copied into message). Uses some sidebars. Also accepts submissions from teens. Guidelines by mail/e-mail; copy for 9x12 SAE/2 stamps. (Ads)

    Poetry: Accepts 1-5/yr. Avant-garde, free verse, haiku, light verse, traditional. Submit max. 2 poems. No payment.

    Tips: "Most open to features and news, as well as reviews and resources. E-mailing us and pitching a story is the best way to break into our publication. Emphasis is on nonviolence. No sexist language."

THE CATHOLIC REGISTER, 1155 Yonge St., Ste. 401, Toronto ON M4T 1W2, Canada. (416) 934-3410. Fax (416) 934-3409. E-mail: editor@catholicregister.org, or news@catholicregister.org or through Website: www.catholicregister.org. Jim O'Leary, ed./pub.; Mickey Conlon, mng. ed. To provide reliable information about the world from a Catholic perspective. Weekly (47X) tabloid; circ. 33,000. Subscription $42.70. Open to unsolicited freelance. Not in topical listings. (Ads)

$CATHOLIC SENTINEL, 5536 N.E. Hassalo St., Portland OR 97213. (503) 281-1191. Fax (503) 460-5496. E-mail: sentinel@ocp.org or through Website: www.sentinel.org. Oregon Catholic Press. Bob Pfohman, ed. Weekly tabloid; 20 pgs.; circ. 16,000. Subscription $32. 2% unsolicited freelance; 0% assigned. Query/clips. **Payment negotiable** on publication for onetime rts. Articles 600-1,500 wds. Responds in 4 wks. Seasonal 2 mos. ahead. Accepts requested ms on disk or by e-mail (copied into message). Uses some sidebars. Prefers NAS. Incomplete topical listings. Guidelines on Website (under "About Us"/"Articles Submissions Guidelines"); copy for 9x12 SAE/3 stamps. (Ads)

Tips: "We're most open to local church news and feature articles."

$CATHOLIC TELEGRAPH, 100 E. 8th St., Cincinnati OH 45202. (513) 421-3131. Fax (513) 381-2242. E-mail: cteditorial@catholiccincinnati.org. Website: www.thecatholictelegraph.com. Tricia Hempel, ed. Diocese newspaper for Cincinnati area (all articles must have a Cincinnati or Ohio connection). Weekly newspaper; 24-28 pgs.; circ. 100,000. Subscription $24. Limited unsolicited freelance; mostly assigned. Send résumé and writing samples for assignment. **Pays varying rates** on publication for all rts. Articles. Responds in 2-3 wks. Kill fee. No guidelines; copy $2/#10 SASE.

Fillers: Newsbreaks (local).

Special needs: Personality features for "Everyday Evangelists" section. These are feature stories that offer a slice of life of a person who is making a difference as a Roman Catholic Christian in their community. Prefer to have a tie within the Archdiocese of Cincinnati; must be an Ohioan. Complete ms; 800 wds.; pays $40 (extra for photos of individual interviewed).

Tips: "Most likely to accept an article about a person, event, or ministry with an Ohio connection—Cincinnati-Dayton area."

$THE CATHOLIC YEARBOOK, 7010—6th St. N., Oakdale MN 55128. (651) 702-0086. Fax (651) 702-0074. E-mail: catholic2@msn.com. Apostolic Publishing Co. Inc. Roger Jensen, ed. Family magazine of articles and prayers, promoting the sharing of Christian fellowship among Catholics. Annual mag.; 68-72 pgs.; circ. 400,000. 60% unsolicited freelance; 40% assigned. Complete ms/cover letter. **Pays $5-50** on publication for 1st rts. Articles 750-1,500 wds. (20/yr.). Response time varies. No simultaneous submissions; accepts reprints. Accepts articles on disk or by e-mail (attached file). No kill fee. Uses some sidebars. Prefers NIV. Also accepts submissions from children/teens. Guidelines by mail. (Ads)

Poetry: Buys 10/yr. Light verse, traditional; 15-50 wds. up to 150 wds. Pays $8-30. Submit max. 3 poems.

Fillers: Buys 5-10/yr. Anecdotes, facts, games, prayers, quizzes, quotes, and word puzzles; 50-300 wds. Pays $5-30.

$@CBA RETAILERS + RESOURCES, 9240 Explorer Dr., Colorado Springs CO 80920. Toll-free (800) 252-1950. (719) 272-3555. Fax (719) 272-3510. E-mail: ksamuelson@cbaonline.org. Website: www.cbaonline.org. Christian Booksellers Assn. Submit queries to Kathleen Samuelson, publications dir. To provide Christian retail store owners and managers with professional retail skills, product information, and industry news. Monthly trade journal (also in digital edition); 48-100 pgs.; circ. 5,000. Subscription $59.95 (for nonmembers). 10% unsolicited freelance; 80% assigned. Query/clips; fax/e-query OK. **Pays .30/wd.** on publication for all rts. Articles 800-2,000 wds. (30/yr. assigned); book/music/video reviews, 150 wds. ($35). Responds in 8 wks. Seasonal 4-5 mos. ahead. Prefers requested ms mailed in MS Word file. Regularly uses sidebars. Accepts any modern Bible version. (Ads/Dunn & Dunn/856-582-0690)

Special needs: Trends in retail, consumer buying habits, market profiles. By assignment only.

Tips: "Looking for writers who have been owners/managers/buyers/sales staff in Christian retail stores. Most of our articles are by assignment and focus on producing and selling Christian products or conducting retail business. We also assign reviews of books, music, videos, giftware, kids products, and software to our regular reviewers."

@CBN.COM (CHRISTIAN BROADCASTING NETWORK), 977 Centerville Turnpike, Virginia Beach VA 23463. (757) 226-3557. Fax (757) 226-3575. E-mail: chris.carpenter@cbn.org or through Website: www.CBN.com. Christian Broadcasting Network. Chris Carpenter, dir. of internal programming; Belinda Elliott, books ed. Online mag.; 1.6 million users/mo. Free online. Open to unsolicited freelance. E-mail submissions (attached as a Word document). Query/clips; e-query OK.

NO PAYMENT. Devotions 500-700 wds. Spiritual Life Teaching, 700-1,500 wds. Living Features (Family, Entertainment, Health, Finance), 700-1,500 wds. Movie/TV/Music Reviews, 500-1,000 wds. Hard News, 300-700 wds. News Features, 700-1,500 wds. News Interviews, 1,000-2,000 words; fiction. Accepts reprints (tell when/where appeared). Also accepts submissions from teens. Prefers NLT/NASB/NKJV. Guidelines by e-mail; copy online. (No ads)

> **Special needs:** Adoption stories/references, world religions from Judeo/Christian perspective.
>
> **Tips:** "In lieu of payment, we link to author's Website and provide a link for people to purchase the author's materials in our Web store."

$CELEBRATE LIFE, PO Box 1350, Stafford VA 22555. (540) 659-4171. Fax (540) 659-2586. E-mail: CLMag@all.org. Website: www.clmagazine.org. American Life League. Rick Johnston, mng. ed. Covers all right-to-life matters according to Catholic teaching. Bimonthly mag.; 48 pgs.; circ. 70,000. Subscription $12.95. 50% unsolicited freelance; 50% assigned. E-query preferred. **Pays** on publication according to quality of article for 1st or reprint rts.; or work-for-hire assignments. Articles 400-1,600 wds. Seasonal 4 mos. ahead. Accepts few reprints. Prefers e-mail submissions or disk. No kill fee. Also accepts submissions from children/teens. Prefers Jerusalem Bible (Catholic). Guidelines/theme list on Website ("Writers Guidelines"). (No ads)

> **Special needs:** Personal experience about abortion, post-abortion stress/healing, adoption, activism/young people's involvement, death/dying, euthanasia, eugenics, special needs children, personhood, chastity, large families, stem-cell science, and other right-to-life topics.
>
> **Tips:** "We are no-exceptions pro-life in keeping with the Catholic Church. Looking for interviews with pro-life leaders and nonfiction stories about people who live according to pro-life ethics despite diversity. Photos are preferred for personal stories. No fiction or poetry. Break in by submitting work."
>
> ** This periodical was #43 on the 2007 Top 50 Christian Publishers list.

CENTRAL FLORIDA EPISCOPALIAN, 1017 E. Robinson St., Orlando FL 32801. Toll-free (800) 299-3567. (407) 423-3567. Fax (407) 872-0006. E-mail: joethoma@aol.com. Website: www.cfdiocese .org. Episcopal Diocese of Central Florida. Joe Thoma, ed. (faithdigest@aol.com). To spread the Good Word of Jesus Christ to the people of Central Florida, the U.S., and the world. Monthly mag.; circ. 24,000. Subscription $10. Open to unsolicited freelance. Articles. Incomplete topical listings. (Ads)

$CGA WORLD, PO Box 249, Olyphant PA 18447. Toll-free (800) 836-5699. (570) 586-1091. Fax (570) 586-7721. E-mail: cgaemail@aol.com. Website: www.catholicgoldenage.org. Catholic Golden Age. Barbara Pegula, mng. ed. For Catholics 50+. Quarterly newsletter. Subscription/membership $12. Uses little freelance. Query. **Pays .10/wd.** on publication for 1st, onetime, or reprint rts. Articles 600-1,000 wds.; fiction 600-1,000 wds. Responds in 6 wks. Seasonal 6 mos. ahead. Accepts reprints (tell when/where appeared). Accepts requested ms on disk. Guidelines by mail; copy for 9x12 SAE/3 stamps. (Ads)

@CHALLENGE WEEKLY, PO Box 68-800, Newton, Auckland, New Zealand 1032. Phone (64-9) 378 4052, or +64 027 271 2849. Fax (64-9) 376 3855. E-mail: editor@challengeweekly.co.nz or through Website: www.challengeweekly.co.nz. Challenge Publishing Society. Garth George, ed. New Zealand's Christian newspaper. Proclaiming the good news that Jesus is the Christ. Weekly online newspaper. Subscription $68. Incomplete topical listings.

$@CHARISMA, 600 Rinehart Rd., Lake Mary FL 32746. (407) 333-0600. Fax (407) 333-7100. E-mail: charisma@strang.com. Website: www.charismamag.com. Strang Communications. Marcus Yoars, ed.; Jimmy Stewart, mng. ed.; Felicia Mann, online ed.; submit to J. Lee Grady. Primarily for the Pentecostal and Charismatic Christian community. Monthly & online mag.; 100+ pgs.; circ. 250,000. Subscription $14.97. 80% assigned freelance. Query only; no phone query, e-query OK.

Pays up to $1,000 (for assigned) on publication for all rts. Articles 2,000-3,000 wds. (40/yr.); book/music reviews, 200 wds. ($20-35). Responds in 8-12 wks. Seasonal 5 mos. ahead. Kill fee $50. Prefers accepted ms by e-mail. Regularly uses sidebars. Guidelines on Website (click on "Writers Guidelines" at the bottom of Home Page); copy $4. (Ads)

Tips: "Most open to news section, reviews, or features. Query (published clips help a lot)."

$CHICKEN SOUP FOR THE SOUL BOOK SERIES, PO Box 700, Cos Cob CT 06807. Fax (203) 861-7194. E-mail: webmaster@chickensoupforthesoul.com. Website: www.chickensoup.com. Chicken Soup for the Soul Publishing, LLC. Submit to Webmaster's e-mail. A world leader in self-improvement, helps real people share real stories of hope, courage, inspiration, and love that is open to all ages, races, etc. Quarterly trade paperback books; 385 pgs.; circ. 60 million. $14.95/book. 98% unsolicited freelance. Make submissions via Website. **Pays $200 (plus 10 free copies of the book, worth more than $110)** on publication for reprint, electronic, and nonexclusive rts. Articles 300-1,200 wds. Seasonal anytime. Accepts simultaneous submissions & sometimes reprints (tell when/where appeared). Prefers e-mail submissions: Go to www.chickensoupforthesoul.com and click on "Submit Your Story" on the left tool bar. No kill fee. Accepts submissions from children & teens. Guidelines/themes on Website; free sample. (No ads)

Special needs: See Website for a list of upcoming titles.

Contest: See Website for list of current contests.

Tips: "Visit our Website and be familiar with our book series. Send in stories via our Website, complete with contact information. Submit story typed, double-spaced, max. 1,200 words, in a Word document."

+@CHRISTIAN BIBLE STUDIES.COM. 465 Gundersen Dr., Carol Stream IL 60188-2498. E-mail: cbsnewsletter@christianitytoday.com. Website: www.ChristianBibleStudies.com. Christianity Today Intl. JoHannah Reardon, mng. ed. Publishes Bible studies online for individuals and Bible study groups. Does not accept freelance Bible studies or articles, but if you are a published author and would like to promote your book, they will consider doing so by using an excerpt in their Featured Articles section. Send to editor at above e-mail. Guidelines on Website ("Who Are We?"/"Guidelines for Writers" left side).

@CHRISTIAN BUSINESS DAILY.COM, c/o Selling Among Wolves LLC, 7156 W. 127th St, #396, Palos Hts. IL 60463. E-mail: articles@christianbusinessdaily.com or through Website: www.christianbusinessdaily.com. Bob Regnerus, online dir. Business news from a Christian worldview. E-zine. Open to freelance. Query. **NO PAYMENT.** Articles. Incomplete topical listings. (Ads)

@THE CHRISTIAN CHRONICLE, PO Box 11000, Oklahoma City OK 73013. (405) 425-5070. Fax (405) 425-5076. E-mail: bailey.mcbride@oc.edu, or through Website: www.christianchronicle .org. Churches of Christ. Bobbie Ross Jr, ed.; Tamie Ross, online ed. An international newspaper for members of the Church of Christ. Monthly newspaper & online. Subscription $20 (onetime fee). Connection on Website ("You Share"/"Submit a Story"). Incomplete topical listings.

$CHRISTIAN CITIZEN USA, PO Box 49365 or 250 N. Cassel Rd., Dayton OH 45377. Toll-Free (877) 428-6397. (937) 233-6227. Fax (937) 233-6231. E-mail: editor@ccn-usa.net, or info@ ccn-usa.net. Website: www.citizenusa.us. Christian Media Group Inc. Pendra Lee Snyder, pub. Only Judeo-Christian newspaper in Ohio; news features, current events presented from Judeo-Christian worldview. Monthly newspaper; circ. 30,000. Subscription $50. 10% unsolicited freelance; 75% assigned. Query/clips; phone/fax/e-query OK. Accepts full mss by e-mail. **Pays up to $25** on publication for all (if assigned) or 1st rts. Articles 600-800 wds.; book reviews, 500-600 wds.; music reviews, 200-300 wds.; video reviews, 500 wds. (pays $20-25). Responds in 4 wks. Seasonal 2-3 mos. ahead. Prefers e-mail submissions (copied into message). No kill fee. Uses some sidebars. Also accepts submissions from teens. Prefers KJV. (Ads) Guidelines by e-mail/Website.

Fillers: Buys 4/yr. Cartoons, games, short humor, word puzzles. Pays $20-25.
Columns/Departments: Buys 4/yr. News features, under 800 wds. $20-50 or no payment. E-query.
Tips: "Most open to current news features, or current events/political."

@CHRISTIAN COMPUTING MAGAZINE, PO Box 319, Belton MO 64012. Toll-free phone/fax (800) 456-1868. (816) 331-8142. E-mail: steve@ccmag.com or through Website: www.ccmag .com. Steve Hewitt, ed-in-chief. For Christian/church computer users. Monthly (11X) & online mag.; 2 pgs.; circ. 30,000. Subscription $14.95, or free digital version. 40% unsolicited freelance. Query/ clips; fax/e-query OK. **NO PAYMENT** for all rts. Articles 1,000-1,800 wds. (12/yr.). Responds in 4 wks. Seasonal 2 mos. ahead. Accepts reprints. Requires requested ms on disk. Regularly uses sidebars. Guidelines by mail; copy for 9x12 SAE.
   Fillers: Accepts 6 cartoons/yr.
   Columns/Departments: Accepts 12/yr. Telecommunications (computer), 1,500-1,800 wds.
   Special needs: Articles on Internet, DTP, computing.

$CHRISTIAN COURIER (Canada), 5 Joanna Dr., St. Catherines ON L2N 1V1, Canada. (U.S. address: Box 110, Lewiston NY 14092-0110). Toll-free (800) 969-4838. (905) 682-8311. Toll-free fax (800) 969-4838. (905) 682-8313. E-mail: editor@christiancourier.ca or through Website: www.christian courier.ca. Reformed Faith Witness. Bert Witvoet, viewpoint ed.; Brett Alan Dewing, features ed. To present Canadian and international news, both religious and general, from a Reformed Christian perspective. Biweekly tabloid; 24-28 pgs.; circ. 4,000. Subscription $48 Cdn.; $40, U.S. 20% unsolicited freelance; 80% assigned. Complete ms/cover letter; fax/e-query OK. **Pays $75-120 U.S., up to .10/wd. for assigned ($50-100 for unsolicited)**; 30 days after publication for onetime, reprint, or simultaneous rts. Not copyrighted. Articles 700-1,200 wds. (40/yr.); fiction to 1,200-2,500 wds. (6/yr.); book reviews 800-1,200 wds. Responds in 1-3 wks. Seasonal 3 mos. ahead. Accepts simultaneous submissions & reprints (tell when/where appeared). Prefers accepted ms by e-mail (attached file). No kill fee. Uses some sidebars. Prefers NIV. Guidelines/deadlines on Website (under "Writers"); no copy. (Ads)
   Poetry: Buys 12/yr. Avant-garde, free verse, light verse, traditional; 10-30 lines; $20-30. Submit max. 5 poems.
   Tips: "Suggest an aspect of the theme which you believe you could cover well, have insight into, could treat humorously, etc. Show that you think clearly, write clearly, and have something to say that we should want to read. Have a strong biblical worldview and avoid moralism and sentimentality." Responds only if material is accepted.

@CHRISTIAN COURIER (WI), 1933 W. Wisconsin Ave., Milwaukee WI 53233. (414) 345-3545. Fax (414) 918-4503. E-mail: editor@ChristianCourierNewspaper.com. Website: www.christian couriernewspaper.com. Online site: www.christian-courier.com. ProBuColls Assn. Dr. Dennis Hill, ed. To propagate the gospel of Jesus Christ and cover those events which demonstrate Christian unity. Monthly & online newspaper; circ. 10,000. 10% freelance. Query; e-query OK. **PAYS IN COPIES,** for onetime rts. Not copyrighted. Articles 300-1,500 wds. (6/yr.). Responds in 4-8 wks. Seasonal 2 mos. ahead. Accepts reprints. Guidelines by mail; free copy. (Ads)
   Special needs: Human interest, special ministries; see editorial calendar for details.
   Tips: "We are looking for bloggers who can objectively cover nondenominational Christian events in Wisconsin, the U.S., and globally."

$@CHRISTIAN EXAMINER, PO Box 2606, El Cajon CA 92021. (619) 668-5100. Fax (619) 668-1115. E-mail: info@christianexaminer.com. Website: www.christianexaminer.com. Selah Media Group. Lori Arnold, ed. To report on current events from an evangelical Christian perspective, particularly traditional family values and church trends. Monthly & online newspaper; 24-36 pgs.; circ. 180,000. Subscription $19.95. 5% assigned. Query/clips. **Pays .10/wd.,** on publication for 1st

& electronic rts. Articles 600-900 wds. Responds in 4-5 wks. Seasonal 3 mos. ahead. No simultaneous submissions or reprints. Prefers e-mail submissions (copied into message). No kill fee. Uses some sidebars. Guidelines by e-mail; copy $1.50/9x12 SAE. (Ads)

Tips: "We prefer news stories."

** 2010 EPA Award of Merit: Online; 2007, 2006 EPA Award of Merit: Newspaper. Member of Fellowship of Christian Newspapers (FCN).

@CHRISTIAN FAMILY JOURNAL, 312 Point Pleasant Dr., St. Augustine FL 32086. (904) 471-4307. Website: www.christianfamilypublications.com. Providing positive, Christian information to families across the Southeast (more than one publication). Laurie Stroud, pub. (laurie@christianfamily publications.com); Julie Moore, ed. (julie@christianfamilypublications.com). Monthly & online mags.; 24-36 pgs; circ. 10,000-30,000/market. Subscription free or available for $25. Open to unsolicited freelance. Query; e-query OK. **NO PAYMENT.** Articles 500 wds. (150/yr.); reviews 300-500 wds.; rarely uses fiction. Responds in a few wks. Seasonal 3 mos. ahead. No simultaneous submissions or reprints. Prefers e-mail submission (attached file in Word doc.). Uses some sidebars. Guidelines by e-mail; copy for 9x12 SAE/$3 postage. (Ads)

Columns/Departments: Accepts 10-15/mo. Query.

CHRISTIAN HEALTH CARE NEWSLETTER, PO Box 3618, Peoria IL 61612-3618. Toll-free (888) 268-4377. Fax (309) 689-0764. Website: www.samaritanministries.org. Samaritan Ministries Intl. Ray King, ed. Health issues. Monthly newsletter; circ. 13,900. Subscription $12. Open to unsolicited freelance. Articles & reviews. Incomplete topical listings. (Ads)

$THE CHRISTIAN HERALD, PO Box 68526, Brampton ON L6R 0J8, Canada. (905) 874-1731. Fax (905) 874-1781. E-mail: info@christianherald.ca. Website: www.christianherald.ca. Covenant Communications. Fazal Karim Jr., ed-in-chief. A Canadian-Christian tabloid with a focus on Christian arts and entertainment. Monthly tabloid; 24 pgs.; circ. 30,000. Subscription free, or $25 if mailed (Canadian residents add 5% sales tax). 5% unsolicited freelance; 95% assigned. Query; fax/e-query OK. **Pays $20-100 or .10/wd.** on publication for 1st rts. Articles 500-1,500 wds.; product reviews 150-200 wds. Responds in 4 wks. Seasonal 3 mos. ahead. Accepts simultaneous submissions & reprints (tell when/where appeared). Prefers e-mail submissions (attached file). No kill fee. Uses some sidebars. Also accepts submissions from teens. Prefers ESV, KJV, NLT. Guidelines by mail/e-mail/ Website ("Submissions"/"Writers Guidelines"); copy for 9x12 SAE/$2 Canadian postage. (Ads)

Fillers: Accepts 10/yr. Cartoons, facts, games, jokes, prayers, quotes, and word puzzles; 20-100 wds. No payment.

Columns/Departments: Interviews (Christian newsmakers/personalities), 900 wds. $20-50.

Tips: "Most open to articles/columns with specific reference to Canadians, with Canadian quotes, relevance, etc."

$@CHRISTIAN HISTORY.NET (formerly *Christian History*), 465 Gundersen Dr., Carol Stream IL 60188. (630) 480-2004. Fax (630) 260-0114. E-mail: CHeditor@christianhistory.net. Website: www.christianhistory.net. Christianity Today Intl. Jennifer Trafton, mng. ed. To teach Christian history to educated readers in an engaging manner. Online magazine. Subscription $12. 5% unsolicited freelance; 95% assigned. Query only. **Pays .10-.25/wd.** on publication for 1st rts. Articles 500-3,000 wds. (1/yr.). Responds in 2 mos. Accepts reprints (tell when/where appeared). Prefers accepted ms by e-mail (attached or copied into message). Kill fee 50%. Regularly uses sidebars. Prefers NIV. Guidelines/theme list on Website (under "About Us"/ "Submissions"); copy for 9x12 SASE. (Ads)

Tips: Let us know your particular areas of specialization and any books or articles you have published in the area of Christian history. Theme-related articles are usually assigned. Most open to non-themed departments: Story Behind; People Worth Knowing; Turning Point. Please familiarize yourself with our magazine before querying.

** 2008 EPA Award of Merit: General.

$CHRISTIAN HOME & SCHOOL, 3350 East Paris Ave. S.E., Grand Rapids MI 49512. Toll-free (800) 635-8288. (616) 957-1070, ext. 239. Fax (616) 957-5022. E-mail: rheyboer@CSIonline.org. Website: www.CSIonline.org. Christian Schools Intl. Rachael Heyboer, mng. ed. For parents of children of all ages; offering a biblical perspective on all areas of parenting. Biannual mag.; 40 pgs.; circ. 67,000. Subscription $13.95. 25% unsolicited; 75% assigned. Complete ms or e-query. Accepts full mss by e-mail. **Pays $50-250** on publication for 1st rts. Articles 1,000-2,000 wds. (30/yr.); book reviews $25 (assigned). Responds in 4 wks. Seasonal 6 mos. ahead (no Christmas or summer). Accepts simultaneous query. Prefers mss by e-mail (attached). Regularly uses sidebars. Accepts submissions from children/teens. Prefers NIV. Guidelines/theme list by mail/Website ("About CSI"/ "What We Have to Offer"/"CSI Publications"/Christian Home & School"/ "Writers Guidelines"; copy for 7x10 SAE/4 stamps. (Ads)

   Tips: "Writers can break in by having articles written about parenting (at all stages of life), geared from a Christian perspective and current with the times."
   ** 2007 EPA Award of Merit: Organizational. This periodical was #46 on the 2010 Top 50 Christian Publishers list (#41 in 2009, #36 in 2008, #44 in 2007, #32 in 2006).

$@CHRISTIANITY TODAY, 465 Gundersen Dr., Carol Stream IL 60188-2498. (630) 260-6200. Fax (630) 260-8428. E-mail: cteditor@christianitytoday.com. Website: www.christianitytoday.com/ctmag. Christianity Today Int. Mark Galli, ed. For evangelical Christian thought leaders who seek to integrate their faith commitment with responsible action. Monthly & online mag.; 65-120 pgs.; circ. 155,000. Subscription $19.95. Prefers e-query or complete ms. **Pays .25-.35/wd.** on publication for 1st rts. Articles 1,000-4,000 wds. (60/yr.); book reviews 800-1,000 wds. (pays per-page rate). Responds in 13 wks. Seasonal 8 mos. ahead. Accepts reprints (tell when/where appeared—payment 25% of regular rate). Kill fee 50%. Does not use sidebars. Prefers NIV. Guidelines on Website ("Contact Us"/"Writers Guidelines"); copy for 9x12 SAE/3 stamps. (Ads)

   Tips: "Read the magazine." Does not return unsolicited manuscripts.
   ** 2010, 2006 EPA Award of Merit: Online (for Christianity Today Online); 2008, 2006 EPA Award of Excellence: General; 2010, 2009 EPA Award of Merit: General.

$@CHRISTIANITY TODAY MOVIES, 465 Gundersen Dr., Carol Stream IL 60188. (630) 260-6200. Fax (630) 260-8428. E-mail: CTmovies@christianitytoday.com. Website: www.Christianity TodayMovies.com. Christianity Today Intl. Mark Moring, ed. To inform and equip Christian moviegoers to make discerning choices about films, through timely coverage, insightful reviews and interviews, educated opinion, and relevant news, all from a Christian worldview. Weekly e-zine. Subscription free. 10% unsolicited freelance; 90% assigned. Query; fax/e-query OK. Accepts full mss by e-mail. **Pays $75-125** on acceptance for 1st rts. Articles 500-2,000 wds. (150/yr.) & movie reviews 700-1,000 wds. ($110). Responds in 2 wks. No seasonal. Sometimes accepts simultaneous submissions and reprints (tell when/where appeared). Prefers e-mail submissions (attached file). Some kill fees 50%. Uses some sidebars. Prefers NIV. No guidelines; copy online. (Ads)

   Tips: "Study our Website; know what we're doing. Always looking for commentaries and/or news pieces on trends in the industry, especially as they relate to a Christian audience."
   ** 2009, 2007 EPA Award of Merit: Online. This periodical was #39 on the 2010 Top 50 Christian Publishers list (#37 in 2009, #35 in 2008).

@THE CHRISTIAN JOURNAL, 1032 W. Main, Medford OR 97501. (541) 773-4004. Fax (541) 773-9917. E-mail: info@thechristianjournal.org. Website: www.TheChristianJournal.org. Lifting the Cross Ministries. Chad McComas, ed. Dedicated to sharing encouragement with the body of Christ in Southern Oregon and Northern California. Monthly & online newspaper; 16-24 pgs.; circ. 15,000. Subscription $20; most copies distributed free. 50% unsolicited freelance; 50% assigned. Complete ms; phone/fax query OK. **NO PAYMENT** for onetime rts. Articles & fiction to 500 words; reviews to 500 wds.; children's stories 500 wds. Prefers articles by e-mail to info@thechristianjournal.org (attached file). Also accepts submissions from children/teens. Guidelines/theme list by e-mail/ Website ("Writer's Info"); copy online. (Ads)

Poetry: Accepts 12-20/yr. Free verse, haiku, light verse, traditional; 4-12 lines. Submit max. 2 poems.

Fillers: Accepts 50/yr. Anecdotes, cartoons, jokes, kid quotes, newsbreaks, prayers, quotes, short humor, or word puzzles; 100-300 wds.

Columns/Departments: Accepts 6/yr. Youth; Seniors; Children's stories; all to 500 wds.

Tips: "Send articles on themes; each issue has a theme. Theme articles get first choice."

** This periodical was #40 on the 2010 Top 50 Christian Publishers list.

@CHRISTIAN MEDIA, Box 448, Jacksonville OR 97530. (541) 899-8888. E-mail: James@ ChristianMediaNetwork.com. Website: www.ChristianMediaDaily.com or www.ChristianMediaNet work.com. James Lloyd, ed./pub. Updates on world conditions, politics, economics, in the light of prophecy. Quarterly & online tabloid; 24 pgs.; circ. 25,000. Query; prefers phone query. **NO PAYMENT** for negotiable rts. Articles; book & music reviews, 3 paragraphs. Accepts simultaneous submissions & reprints. Prefers requested ms on disk. Requires KJV. Copy for 9x12 SAE/2 stamps.

Special needs: Particularly interested in stories that expose dirty practices in the industry— royalty rip-offs, misleading ads, financial misconduct, etc. No flowery pieces on celebrities; wants well-documented articles on abuse in the media.

CHRISTIAN MOTORSPORTS ILLUSTRATED, PO Box 790, Quinlan TX 754764. (607) 742-3407. E-mail: articles@christianmotorsports.com or through Website: www.christianmotorsports.com. CPO Publishing. Roland Osborne, pub. Covers the entire world of motorsports, from NASCAR to dirt, snowmobile, drag boat, NHRA, go-karts, Moto-X, car shows, bike rallies, lawnmower races, etc., with a unique Christian spin. Quarterly mag.; 64 pgs.; circ. 74,000. Subscription $20. 50% unsolicited freelance. Complete ms; e-query OK. **PAYS IN COPIES**. Articles 650-1,200 wds. (30/yr.). Seasonal 4 mos. ahead. Requires requested ms by e-mail or through Website. Regularly uses side-bars. Guidelines on Website ("Submit Your Story"). (Ads)

Fillers: Accepts 100/yr. Anecdotes, cartoons, facts, games, ideas, jokes, newsbreaks, prayers, prose, quizzes, quotes, short humor.

Columns/Departments: Accepts 10/yr.

Tips: "Christians involved in motorsports, tech-tips, bike ministries, etc. CMI is chrome, smoke, and big engines—with Jesus in the middle! If it relates to motorsports, try us. Relevant photos to accompany article required. Browse Website and read one of our mags to get a flavor for the publication."

CHRISTIAN NEWS NORTHWEST, PO Box 974, Newberg OR 97132. Phone/fax (503) 537-9220. E-mail: cnnw@cnnw.com. Website: www.cnnw.com. John Fortmeyer, ed./pub. News of ministry in the evangelical Christian community in western and central Oregon and southwest Washington; distributed primarily through evangelical churches. Monthly newspaper; 24-32 pgs.; circ. 29,000. Subscription $22. 10% unsolicited freelance; 5% assigned. Query; phone/fax/e-query OK. **NO PAYMENT.** Not copyrighted. Articles 300-400 wds. (100/yr.). Responds in 4 wks. Seasonal 3 mos. ahead. Accepts reprints (tell when/where appeared). Accepts e-mail submissions. Regularly uses sidebars. Guidelines by mail/e-mail; copy $1.50. (Ads)

Tips: "Most open to ministry-oriented features. Our space is always tight, but stories on lesser-known, Northwest-based ministries are encouraged. Keep it very concise. Since we focus on the Pacific Northwest, it would probably be difficult for anyone outside the region to break into our publication."

** 2006 EPA Award of Merit: Newspaper.

@THE CHRISTIAN OBSERVER, PO Box 1371, Lexington VA 24450. (703) 335-2844. Fax (703) 368-4817. E-mail: editor@christianobserver.org, or christianobserver@comcast.net. Website:

www.ChristianObserver.org. Christian Observer Foundation; Presbyterian Reformed. Bob Williams, mng. ed. To encourage and edify God's people and families. Internet versions of *Presbyterians Week* and the *Christian Observer*. Circ: 3,500 visits/month to Website; 900 e-mail subscriptions to Presbyterians Week. Query; e-query OK. **NO PAYMENT.** Accepts e-mail submissions. (Ads)

@CHRISTIAN ONLINE MAGAZINE, PO Box 262, Wolford VA 24658. E-mail: submissions@chris tianmagazine.org. Website: www.ChristianMagazine.org. Darlene Osborne, pub. (darlene@christian magazine.org). Strictly founded on the Word of God, this magazine endeavors to bring you the best Christian information on the net. Monthly e-zine. Subscription free. 10% unsolicited freelance; 90% assigned. E-query. Articles 500-700 wds. Responds in 1 wk. Seasonal 2 mos. ahead. Prefers accepted ms by e-mail (attached file). **NO PAYMENT.** Regularly uses sidebars. Also accepts submissions from children/teens. Prefers KJV. Guidelines on Website ("Submit an Article: Writer's Guidelines"). (Ads)
    Fillers: Accepts 50/yr. Prayers, prose, quizzes, short humor; 500 wds.
    Columns/Departments: Variety Column, 700-1,000 wds. Query.
    Tips: "Most open to solid Christian articles founded on the Word of God."

@THE CHRISTIAN OUTLOOK, 492 Hob Moor Rd., Yardley, Birmingham B25 8UB, United Kingdom. Phone +44 (0) 870 383 0197. Fax +44 (0) 870 199 2302. E-mail through Website: www .thechristianoutlook.net. Nondenominational. Issues on life and living from a Christian perspective. Online newspaper. Free online. Open to unsolicited freelance. Submit through Website. Incomplete topical listings.
    Tips: "We also maintain forums for online interaction among Christians, and between Christians and non-Christians."

CHRISTIAN PRESS NEWSPAPER, 504 N. Main St., Newton KS 67114. (316) 283-8300. Fax (316) 283-6090. E-mail: editor@christianpress.com. Website: www.christianpress.com. Russ Jones, pub. Monthly Newspaper; circ. 80,000. Articles/reviews. See Website for details ("Contact Us"/ "Writers Wanted").
    Tips: "We inform the public of issues that affect our decision-making, encourage and build up the body of Christ, and are a tool to bring others to a life-changing decision for Christ and give back to our community."

CHRISTIAN QUARTERLY, PO Box 311, Palo Cedro CA 97073. Phone/fax (530) 247-7500. E-mail: ChristQtly@aol.com. Nondenominational. Cathy Jansen, pub. Uplifting and encouraging articles. Quarterly tabloid; 28 pgs; circ. 15,000. Subscription free. 100% unsolicited freelance. Phone or e-query. Accepts full mss by e-mail. **NO PAYMENT.** Not copyrighted. Articles to 1,200 wds. Responds immediately. Accepts reprints (tell when/where appeared). Accepts e-mail (attached or copied into message). Never uses sidebars. Also accepts submissions from children/teens. Guidelines by e-mail; copy for 10x13 SAE/$2 postage. (Ads)
    Poetry: Accepts 6-10/yr. Free verse, traditional.
    Fillers: Accepts anecdotes, cartoons, ideas, quotes, short humor, and word puzzles.
    Columns/Departments: Uses many. Marriage & Family; Health; Financial; Testimonies.
    Special needs: "Articles helping people grow in their Christian walk."

THE CHRISTIAN RANCHMAN/COWBOYS FOR CHRIST, 3011 FM 718, Newark TX 76071, or PO Box 7557, Fort Worth TX 76111. (817) 236-0023. Fax (817) 236-0024. E-mail: cwb4christ@cowboys forchrist.net, or CFCmail@cowboysforchrist.net, or through Website: www.CowboysforChrist.net. Interdenominational. Ted Pressley, ed. Monthly tabloid; 20 pgs.; circ. 43,800. No subscription. 85% unsolicited freelance. Complete ms/cover letter. **NO PAYMENT** for all rts. Articles 350-1,000 wds.; book/video reviews (length open). Does not use sidebars. Guidelines on Website ("Contact Us"/ "Submit an Article"); sample copy.
    Poetry: Accepts 40/yr. Free verse. Submit max. 3 poems.

Fillers: Accepts all types.

Tips: "We're most open to true-life Christian stories, Christian testimonies, and Christian or livestock news. Contact us with your ideas first."

$CHRISTIAN RENEWAL, Box 770, Lewiston NY 14092-0770, or PO Box 777, Jordan Sta., ON L0R 1S0, Canada. (905) 562-5059. Fax (905) 562-1368. E-mail: JVANDYK@aol.com. Website: www.crmag.com. Reformed (Conservative). John Van Dyk, ed. Church-related and world news for members of the Reformed community of churches in North America. Biweekly newspaper; 48 pgs.; circ. 3,500. Subscription $42 U.S./$44 Cdn. (christianrenewal@hotmail.com). 2% unsolicited freelance; 50% assigned. Query/clips; e-query OK. **Pays $25-100** for onetime rts. Articles 500-3,000 wds.; fiction 2,000 wds. (6/yr.); book reviews 50-200 wds. Seasonal 2 mos. ahead. Accepts simultaneous submissions & reprints. Prefers e-mail submission. Uses some sidebars. Prefers NIV, ESV. No guidelines; copy $2. (Ads: christianrenewal@hotmail.com)

$CHRISTIAN RESEARCH JOURNAL, PO Box 8500, Charlotte NC 28271-8500. (704) 887-8200. Fax (704) 887-8299. E-mail: submissions@equip.org. Website: www.equip.org. Christian Research Institute. Elliot Miller, ed-in-chief; Melanie Cogdill, ed. Probing today's religious movements, promoting doctrinal discernment and critical thinking, and providing reasons for Christian faith and ethics. Quarterly mag.; 64 pgs.; circ. 30,000. Subscription $39.50. 75% freelance. Query or complete ms/cover letter; fax query OK; e-query & submissions OK. **Pays .16/wd.** on publication for 1st rts. Articles to 4,200 wds. (25/yr.); book reviews 1,100-2,500 wds. Responds in 4 mos. Accepts simultaneous submissions. Kill fee to 50%. Guidelines by mail/e-mail (guidelines@equip.org); copy $6. (Ads)

> **Columns/Departments:** Effective Evangelism, 1,700 wds. Viewpoint, 875 wds. News Watch, to 2,500 wds.
>
> **Special needs:** Viewpoint on Christian faith and ethics, 1,700 wds.; news pieces, 800-1,200 wds.
>
> **Tips:** "Be familiar with the Journal in order to know what we are looking for. We accept freelance articles in all sections (features and departments). E-mail for writer's guidelines."

$THE CHRISTIAN RESPONSE, PO Box 125, Staples MN 56479-0125. (218) 894-1165. E-mail: happy2@arvig.net. HAPCO Industries. Hap Corbett, ed./pub. Exposes antireligious bias in America and encourages readers to write letters against such bias. Bimonthly newsletter; 6 pgs. Subscription $13. 10% unsolicited freelance. Complete ms/cover letter; e-query OK. Accepts full mss by e-mail after acceptance. **Pays $5-20** on acceptance for onetime rts. Articles 50-700 wds. (4-6/yr.). Responds in 2 wks. Seasonal 6 mos. ahead. Accepts simultaneous submissions & reprints. Does not use sidebars. Guidelines; copy for $2 or 5 stamps. (Ads—classified only)

> **Fillers:** Buys 2-3/yr. Anecdotes, facts, quotes; up to 150 wds. $5-10.
>
> **Special needs:** Articles on antireligious bias; tips on writing effective letters to the editor; pieces on outstanding accomplishments of Christians in the secular media.
>
> **Tips:** "The best way to break in is to uncover an instance of a Christian being denied civil rights by any public unit or government agency because of being a Christian and writing a concise 500-700 word article about it."

$@CHRISTIAN RETAILING, 600 Rinehart Rd., Lake Mary FL 32746. (407) 333-0600. Fax (407) 333-7133. E-mail: Christian.Retailing@strang.com. Website: www.christianretailing.com. Strang Communications. Andy Butcher, ed. (andy.butcher@strang.com). For Christian product industry manufacturers, distributors, retailers. Trade & online journal published monthly; circ. 9,500 (print), 14,000 (digital). Subscription $75. 10% assigned. Query/clips; no phone/fax/e-query. **Pays .25/wd.** on publication for articles (various lengths); book reviews (no payment), 160 wds. No simultaneous submissions. Accepts requested mss by e-mail (attached file). Kill fee. Uses some sidebars. Prefers NIV. Guidelines by e-mail; catalogs primarily for assigned book reviews. (Ads)

> **Tips:** "Notify the managing editor, Christine D. Johnson (Chris.johnson@strang.com) of

your expertise in the Christian products industry." Also publishes 2 supplements: *The Church Bookstore* and *Inspirational Gift Trends*, both quarterly.

$@CHRISTIAN STANDARD, 8805 Governor's Hill Dr., Ste. 400, Cincinnati OH 45249. (513) 931-4050. Fax (513) 931-0950. E-mail: christianstandard@standardpub.com. Website: www.christianstandard.com. Standard Publishing/Christian Churches/Churches of Christ. Mark A. Taylor, ed. Devoted to the restoration of New Testament Christianity, its doctrines, its ordinances, and its fruits. Weekly & online mag.; 16 pgs.; circ. 30,000. Subscription $45. 40% unsolicited freelance; 60% assigned. Complete ms; no phone/fax/e-query. **Pays $20-200** on publication for onetime, reprint, & electronic rts. Articles 800-1,600 wds. (200/yr.). Responds in 9 wks. Seasonal 8-12 mos. ahead. Accepts reprints (tell when/where appeared). Guidelines/copy on Website. (Ads)
　　Tips: "We would like to hear ministers and elders tell about the efforts made in their churches. Has the church grown? developed spiritually? overcome adversity? succeeded in missions?"

$CHRISTIANWEEK, Box 725, Winnipeg MB R3C 2K3, Canada. Toll-free (800) 263-6695. (204) 982-2060. Fax (204) 947-5632. E-mail: admin@christianweek.org. Website: www.christianweek.org. Fellowship for Print Witness. Doug Koop, edit. dir.; Jerrad Peters, mng. ed. Canada's leading Christian news source; telling the stories of God and His people in Canada. Biweekly tabloid newspaper; 8-24 pgs.; circ. 2,000-42,000. Subscription $44.95 (Cdn.), $65.95 (U.S.). Query; phone/fax/e-query OK. Accepts full mss by e-mail. **Pays .10/wd.** on publication for onetime & electronic rts. Not copyrighted. Articles 400-1,500 wds. (200/yr.); book reviews 400 wds. (pays free book). Responds in 1-2 wks. Seasonal 4 mos. ahead. Accepts simultaneous submissions & reprints (tell when/where appeared). Prefers accepted ms by e-mail (attached). Sometimes pays kill fee. Uses some sidebars. Prefers NRSV. Guidelines on Website; copy for 9x12 SASE. (Ads)
　　Tips: "Most open to general news, profiles, and features. Writers are encouraged to query first with ideas about people or news events in their own community (Canadian angles, please) or denomination that would be of interest to readers in other denominations or in other areas of the country."
　　** This periodical was #27 on the 2010 Top 50 Christian Publishers List.

CHURCH HERALD AND HOLINESS BANNER, 7407 Metcalf, Overland Park KS 66212. Fax (913) 722-0351. E-mail: HBeditor@juno.com. Website: www.heraldandbanner.com. Church of God (Holiness)/Herald and Banner Press. Mark D. Avery, gen mngr. Offers the conservative holiness movement a positive outlook on their church, doctrine, future ministry, and movement. Monthly mag.; 24 pgs.; circ. 1,100. Subscription $12.50. 5% unsolicited freelance; 50% assigned. Query; e-query OK. Accepts full mss by e-mail. **NO PAYMENT** for onetime, reprint, or simultaneous rts. Not copyrighted. Articles 600-1,200 wds. (3-5/yr.). Responds in 9 wks. Seasonal 6 mos. ahead. Accepts simultaneous submissions & reprints (tell when/where appeared). Accepts requested ms on disk or by e-mail (attached file). Uses some sidebars. Prefers KJV. Also accepts submissions from children/teens. No guidelines; copy for 9x12 SAE/2 stamps. (No ads)
　　Fillers: Anecdotes, quizzes; 150-400 wds.
　　Tips: "Most open to short inspirational/devotional articles. Must be concise, well written, and get one main point across; 200-600 wds. Be well acquainted with the Wesleyan/Holiness doctrine and tradition. Articles which are well written and express this conviction are very likely to be used."

$@CHURCHMOUSE PUBLICATIONS LLC, PO Box 9, Hudson NH 03051. (610) 357-4462 or (603) 318-8366. E-mail: admin@churchmousepublications.com. Website: www.churchmousepublications.com. Estab. 2008. Clarice G. James, mng. ed.; Susan W. Loud, nonfiction ed. Web-based Christian publishing syndicate serving the Christian community. Online publishing syndicate. 70% unsolicited freelance; 30% assigned. E-query; register online, then upload feature. Markets to periodicals, newspapers, churches, faith-based organizations. **Payment split 50/50 between**

syndicate and author; for 1st, onetime, reprint, simultaneous, or syndication rts. Pays monthly or quarterly depending on sales online. Articles 500-1,200 wds.; fiction 800-2,000 wds. Seasonal 2 mos. ahead. Accepts simultaneous submissions & reprints (tell when/where appeared). No kill fee. Regularly uses sidebars. Accepts submissions from teens (if well written). Prefers NIV, NAS, NKJV, KJV. Guidelines/theme list on Website. (Ads)

Poetry: Open to free verse, haiku, light verse, traditional, 8-24 lines. Submit max. 4 poems.

Fillers: Cartoons, sermon illustrations, short humor, word puzzles; 250-350 wds.

Columns/Departments: Open to columns; 500-750 wds. Sermon illustrations 100-700 wds. "We are open to new columnists in a variety of topics. Need columns from seniors, Christian business leaders, and youth ministries. Send a few samples through Website."

Special needs: Christian business stories or articles; sports celebrities' testimonies; more articles from younger generation. News/political column; children's stories; fillers (200-350 wds. for their Bulletin Boosters).

Tips: "We are a web-based publishing syndicate and online source for Christian articles, columns, devotionals, cartoons, and more. To submit features for review by our Editorial Advisory Board (EAB), you should: (1) register as a producer on our Website; (2) review our submissions guidelines and our current features categories; (3) upload a sampling of your work (1-3 features) for review by the EAB. If you are excellent at what you do, and if we believe others will be willing to pay their good, hard-earned money for the right to use your features, then we are more interested in accepting your work than rejecting it."

@CHURCH OF ENGLAND NEWSPAPER, Religious Intelligence Ltd., 14 Great College St., London SW1P 3RX, England. Phone +44 20 7878 1001. Fax +44 20 7878 1031. E-mail: CEN@church newspaper.com. Website: www.churchnewspaper.com. Religious Intelligence LTD. Colin Blakely, ed. Weekly & online newspaper; circ. 25,000. Subscription 60 pounds (UK); 100 dollars (U.S.). Query: phone/e-query OK. Accepts e-mail submissions (attached file). Uses some sidebars. Guidelines by e-mail/Website ("Add Your Story"). (Ads)

Tips: "Most open to news reports and general features."

$CITY LIGHT NEWS, 459 Astoria Cres. S.E., Calgary AB T2J 0Y6, Canada. (403) 640-2011. Fax (403) 640-2000. E-mail: info@calgarychristian.com. Website: www.calgarychristian.com. CLN Productions. Peter McManus, ed./pub. A Christian newspaper serving the church audience in Central and Southern Alberta and Southeastern BC. Monthly tabloid; 20-36 pgs.; circ. 11,000+. Subscription $24.95 Cdn. 10% unsolicited freelance; 60% assigned. Query/clips; phone/fax/e-query OK. **Pays .10-.15/wd. Cdn.,** on publication for 1st rts. Articles 550 wds.; fiction 300 wds.; reviews 300 wds. (.10/wd.). Responds in 2 wks. Seasonal 1 mo. ahead. Accepts simultaneous submissions & reprints (tell when/where appeared). Prefers e-mail submissions (attached file). Some kill fees 100%. Uses some sidebars. Also accepts submissions from teens. Prefers NIV. Guidelines by e-mail/Website ("Contact Us"/"Guidelines for Submitting Articles"); copy for 10x13 SAE/$3 postage. (Ads)

Fillers: Buys 24/yr. Anecdotes, cartoons, facts, jokes, newsbreaks, quotes, short humor; 100-150 wds. Pays .10/wd.

Columns/Departments: Query. Opinion column. Pays .10-.15/wd.

Special needs: Current blogs.

Tips: "Most open to uplifting, personal stories of real-life situations; upcoming events."

$@COLUMBIA, 1 Columbus Plaza, New Haven CT 06510-3326. (203) 752-4398. Fax (203) 752-4109. E-mail: columbia@kofc.org. Website: www.kofc.org/columbia. Knights of Columbus. Alton Pelowski, mng. ed. Geared to a general Catholic family audience; most stories must have a Knights of Columbus connection. Monthly & online mag.; 32 pgs.; circ. 1.6 million. Subscription $6; foreign $8. 25% unsolicited freelance; 75% assigned. Query; e-query OK. Accepts full mss by e-mail. **Pays $250-1,000** on acceptance for 1st & electronic rts. Articles 500-1,500 wds. (12/yr.). Responds in

4-6 wks. Seasonal 4 mos. ahead. Occasional reprint (tell when/where appeared). Accepts e-mail submission (copied into message). Sometimes pays kill fee. Regularly uses sidebars. Prefers NAS. Guidelines by mail/e-mail; free copy. (No ads)

Special needs: Essays on spirituality, personal conversion. Catholic preferred. Query first.

Tips: "We welcome contributions from freelancers in all subject areas. An interesting or different approach to a topic will get the writer at least a second look from an editor. Most open to feature writers who can handle church issues, social issues from an orthodox Roman Catholic perspective. Must be aggressive, fact-centered writers for these features."

** This periodical was #45 on the 2006 & 2007 Top 50 Christian Publishers list.

$COMMON GROUND, #204—4381 Fraser St., Vancouver BC V6V 4G4, Canada. (604) 733-2215. Fax (604) 733-4415. E-mail: editor@commonground.ca. Website: www.commonground.ca. Common Ground Publishing. Joseph Roberts, sr. ed. Covers health, environment, spirit, creativity, and wellness. Monthly tabloid; circ. 70,000. Subscription $60 Cdn.; U.S. $50. 10% unsolicited freelance. Query by e-mail. **Pays .10/wd. (Cdn.)** on publication (although most articles are donated) for onetime or reprint rts. Articles 600-1,500 wds. (to 2,500 wds.), (12/yr.). Responds in 6-13 wks. (returns material only if clearly specified). Seasonal 3 mos. ahead. Accepts simultaneous submissions & reprints. Requires requested ms by e-mail. Guidelines on Website ("Quick Links"/"Writers Guidelines" on left); copy $5. Incomplete topical listings. (Ads)

Tips: "Donated articles are given priority over paid articles. Once an article has been published, we will contact you with the final word count, after which you may submit an invoice."

$COMMONWEAL, 475 Riverside Dr., Rm. 405, New York NY 10115-0499. (212) 662-4200. Fax (212) 662-4183. E-mail: editors@commonwealmagazine.org. Website: www.commonwealmagazine.org. Commonweal Foundation/Catholic. Paul Baumann, ed. A review of public affairs, religion, literature, and the arts, for an intellectually engaged readership. Biweekly jour.; 32 pgs.; circ. 19,000. Subscription $55. 20% unsolicited freelance. Query/clips; phone query OK. **Pays $75-100** on publication for all rts. Articles 750-1,000 or 2,000-3,000 wds. (30/yr.). Responds in 3-4 wks. Seasonal 2 mos. ahead. Prefers requested ms by e-mail. Kill fee 2%. Uses some sidebars. Guidelines on Website (under "Contact Us"); free copy. (Ads)

Poetry: Rosemary Deen, poetry ed. Buys 30/yr. Free verse, traditional; to 75 lines; .75/line. Submit max. 5 poems. Submit October-May, by mail only.

Columns/Departments: Upfronts (brief, newsy facts and information behind the headlines), 750-1,000 wds. The Last Word (commentary based on insight from personal experience or reflection), 700 wds.

Tips: "Most open to meaningful articles on social, political, religious, and cultural topics; or columns."

$@COMPANY MAGAZINE: The World of Jesuits and Their Friends, 1016 16th St. N.W., Washington DC 20036-5703. (773) 761-9432. Fax (773) 761-9443. E-mail: editor@company magazine.org. Website: www.companymagazine.org. Martin McHugh, ed.; Megan Austin, asst. ed. For people interested in or involved with Jesuit ministries. Quarterly & online mag.; 32 pgs.; circ. 120,000. Free subscription. 40% unsolicited freelance; 60% assigned. Complete ms/cover letter; e-query OK. **Pays $250-450** on publication for onetime rts. Articles 1,500 wds. Responds in 6 wks. Seasonal 3 mos. ahead. Accepts simultaneous submissions & reprints (tell when/where appeared). Prefers e-mail submission (attached file). Prefers NRSV, NAB, NJB. Guidelines by mail/e-mail; copy for 9x12 SAE/4 stamps. (No ads)

Columns/Departments: Books with a Jesuit connection; Minims and Maxims (short items of interest to Jesuit world), 100-150 wds./photo; Letters to the Editor; Obituaries. No payment (usually).

Tips: "We welcome manuscripts as well as outlines of story ideas and indication of willingness to accept freelance assignments (please include résumé and writing samples with the latter two). Articles must be Jesuit-related, and writers usually have some prior association with and/or knowledge of the Jesuits. Looking for feature articles (Jesuit-related), historical, essays, or ministry-related articles."

$@COMPASS DIRECT NEWS, PO Box 27250, Santa Ana CA 92799. (949) 862-0304. Fax (949) 752-6536. E-mail: info@compassdirect.org. Website: www.compassdirect.org. Compass Direct. Jeff M. Sellers, ed. To raise awareness of and encourage prayer for Christians worldwide who are persecuted for their faith. Online news source; circ. 830. E-mail subscription $25; for reprint rights $40. Uses little unsolicited freelance. **Pays $125-175.** Articles 800-1,200 wds. No reviews. Query only. Guidelines by e-mail. (No ads)

> **Tips:** "An international journalist could submit an article query on a current/specific instance of Christian persecution in a country with religious liberty restrictions. Be on the scene where persecution of Christians is taking place, and report it thoroughly and professionally."

CONNECTING POINT, PO Box 685, Cocoa FL 32923. (321) 632-0130. Fax (321) 632-5540. E-mail: lhoward@specialgatherings.com or info@specialgatherings.com. Linda G. Howard, ed. For and by the mentally challenged (mentally retarded) community; primarily deals with spiritual and self-advocacy issues. Monthly mag.; 12 pgs.; circ. 1,000. Free. 75% unsolicited freelance. Complete ms; phone/fax/e-query OK. **NO PAYMENT** for 1st rts. Articles (24/yr.) & fiction (12/yr.), 250-300 wds. Responds in 3-6 wks. Seasonal 3 mos. ahead. Accepts simultaneous submissions & reprints. Guidelines by mail/e-mail; copy for 9x12 SAE/$2.38 postage (mark "Media Mail").

> **Poetry:** Accepts 4/yr. Any type; 4-30 lines. Submit max. 10 poems.
> **Fillers:** Accepts 12/yr. Cartoons, games, word puzzles; 50-250 wds.
> **Columns/Departments:** Accepts 24/yr. Devotion Page, 250 wds. Bible Study, 250 wds. Query.
> **Special needs:** Self-advocacy, integration/normalization, justice system.
> **Tips:** "All manuscripts need to be in primary vocabulary."

CONNECTIONS LEADERSHIP/MOPS, 2370 S. Tenton Way, Denver CO 80231. (303) 733-5353. Fax (303) 733-5770. E-mail: Connections@MOPS.org. Website: www.MOPS.org. MOPS Intl. Carla Foote, ed. To provide leadership training and encouragement for leaders of chartered MOPS groups (Mothers of Preschoolers). Quarterly; circ. 25,000. Subscription $10. Open to unsolicited freelance. Query. Articles. Guidelines on Website (under "MOM Resources"/"Writers Guidelines"). Incomplete topical listings.

$THE COVENANT COMPANION, 5101 N. Francisco Ave., Chicago IL 60625. (773) 907-3326. Fax (773) 784-4366. E-mail: communication@covchurch.org. Website: www.covchurch.org. Evangelical Covenant Church. Jane Swanson-Nystrom, ed. (jane.swanson@covchurch.org); Cathy Norman Peterson, features ed. Informs, stimulates thought, and encourages dialog on issues that affect the denomination. Monthly mag.; 40 pgs.; circ. 12,000. Subscription $19.95. 10-15% unsolicited freelance; 75% assigned. Query or complete ms/cover letter; fax/e-query OK. **Pays $35-100** after publication (within 3 wks.) for onetime or simultaneous rts. Articles 600-1,800 wds. (40/yr.). Prefers e-mail submission. Responds in 4 wks. Seasonal 4 mos. ahead. Accepts simultaneous submissions & reprints (tell when/where appeared). Some kill fees. Regularly uses sidebars. Prefers NRSV. Guidelines by mail/e-mail; copy for 9x12 SAE/5 stamps or $2.50. (Ads)

CREATION, PO Box 4545, Eight Mile Plains QLD 4113, Australia. Phone 07 3840 9888. Fax 07 3840 9889. E-mail: mail@creation.info. Website: www.creation.com. Creation Ministries Intl. Carl Wieland, managing dir. A family, nature, science magazine focusing on creation/evolution issues. Quarterly mag.; 56 pgs.; circ. 50,000. Subscription $28. 30% unsolicited freelance. Query; phone/fax/e-query OK. **NO PAYMENT** for all rts. Articles to 1,500 wds. (20/yr.). Responds in 2-3 wks.

Prefers requested ms on disk or by e-mail (attached file). Regularly uses sidebars. Guidelines by mail/e-mail; copy $7.50. (No ads)

Tips: "Get to know the basic content/style of the magazine and emulate. Send us a copy of your article, or contact us by phone."

CREATION CARE, 275 Edgewood Dr., Americus GA 31709. (678) 541-0747 (office), or (404) 414-7906 (direct). E-mail: een@creationcare.org. Website: www.creationcare.org/magazine. Evangelical Environmental Network. Rusty Prichard, PhD, ed. (submit to: rusty@creativecare.org). For Christians who care about stewardship of natural resources, environmental responsibility, sustainability, and simplicity. Quarterly mag.; 40 pgs.; circ. 6,000. Subscription $30 (free to supporters). 40% unsolicited freelance. Query; e-query OK. **NO PAYMENT.** Articles 750-2,100 wds. (20/yr.); book reviews 250 wds. Responds in 6-8 wks. Seasonal 4 mos. ahead. No simultaneous submissions. Accepts reprints (tell when/where appeared). Prefers accepted ms by e-mail. Regularly uses sidebars. Prefers NRSV, NIV. Guidelines on Website (under "Magazine"/"Writers Guidelines"). (Ads)

Tips: "Feature articles and reviews are often done by freelancers, also interviews/profiles, news features, essays. Writing is especially sought that conveys the concrete, real-life connections between care of creation, social justice, Christian ministry, personal discipleship, parenting, and community. Articles should focus on or appeal to evangelicals and other Christians with a vibrant, orthodox faith and a high view of Scripture."

$CREATION ILLUSTRATED, PO Box 7955, Auburn CA 95604. (530) 269-1424. Fax (530) 269-1428. E-mail: ci@creationillustrated.com. Website: www.creationillustrated.com. Tom Ish, ed./pub. An uplifting, Bible-based Christian nature magazine that glorifies God; for ages 9-99. Quarterly mag.; 68 pgs.; circ. 20,000. Subscription $19.95. 60% unsolicited freelance; 40% assigned. Query or query/clips; fax/e-query OK. **Pays $75-125** within 30 days of publication for 1st rts. (holds rts. for 6 mos.). Articles 1,000-2,000 wds. (20/yr.). Response time varies. Seasonal 6 mos. ahead. Accepts simultaneous submissions & reprints (tell when/where appeared). Prefers e-mail submission (attached file or copied into message). Kill fee 25%. Uses some sidebars. Prefers NKJV. Guidelines/theme list by mail/Website; copy $3/9x12 SAE/$2.38 postage (mark "Media Mail"). (Some ads)

Poetry: Short, usually 4-8 verses. Needs to have both nature and spiritual thoughts. Pays about $15.

Columns/Departments: Creation Up Close Feature, 1,500-2,000 wds. $100; Re-Creation and Restoration Through Outdoor Adventure, 1,500-2,000 wds. $100; Creatures Near and Dear to Us, 1,500-2,000 wds. $100; Children's Story, 500-1,000 wds. $50-75; My Walk with God, 1,000-1,500 wds. $75; Gardens from Eden Around the World, 1,000-1,500 wds., $75; Creation Day (a repeating series), 1,500-2,000 wds. $100.

Tips: "Most open to an experience with nature/creation that brought you closer to God and will inspire the reader to do the same. Include spiritual lessons and supporting Scriptures—at least 3 or 4 of each."

$CREATIVE NONFICTION, 5501 Walnut St., Ste. 202, Pittsburgh PA 15232. (412) 688-0304. Fax (412) 688-0262. E-mail: information@creativenonfiction.org. Website: www.creativenonfiction.org. Lee Gutkind, ed. Publishes compelling nonfiction stories with a strong narrative and research element. Quarterly mag.; 100 pgs.; circ. 6,000. Subscription $32 for 4 issues. 50% unsolicited freelance; 50% assigned. Complete ms/cover letter; no phone/fax/e-query. **Pays $10/published page** on publication for all rts. Articles to 5,000 wds. (30/yr.). Responds in 5 mos. Accepts simultaneous submissions; no reprints. No disk or e-mail submissions. No kill fee or sidebars. Also accepts submissions from teens. Guidelines by e-mail/Website ("Submission Guidelines"); copy $10/$3 postage. (Ads)

Contests: Sometimes sponsors contests; see Website for details.

$THE CRESSET: A Review of Arts, Literature & Public Affairs, Huegli Hall, Valparaiso University, 1409 Chapel Dr., Valparaiso IN 46383. (219) 464-6809. E-mail: cresset@valpo.edu. Website: www.valpo.edu/cresset. Valparaiso University/Lutheran. James Paul Old, ed. For college-educated, professors, pastors, laypeople; serious review essays on religious-cultural affairs. Mag. published 5X/yr.; 60 pgs.; circ. 4,500. Subscription $20. 10% unsolicited freelance; 90% assigned. Query; e-query OK. **Pays $100-500** on publication for all rts. Articles 2,000-4,500 wds. (2/yr.); book/music reviews, 1,000 wds. ($150). Responds in 15 wks. No simultaneous submissions or reprints. Prefers requested ms by e-mail (attached or copied into message). Regularly uses sidebars. Prefers NRSV. Guidelines on Website ("Contact"/"Submissions"); copy $4. (No ads)

   Poetry: John Ruff, poetry ed. Buys 20/yr. Avant-garde, free verse, light verse, traditional; to 40 lines; $15-25. Submit max. 4 poems.

   Columns/Departments: Buys 20/yr. Books; Music; Science & Technology; World Views; all 1,000 wds. $100-250. Query.

$CULTURE WARS, 206 Marquette Ave., South Bend IN 46617-1111. (574) 289-9786. Fax (574) 289-1461. E-mail: letters@culturewars.com or fidelitypress@sbcglobal.net. Website: www.culturewars.com. Ultramontagne Associates Inc. Dr. E. Michael Jones, ed. Issues relating to Catholic families and issues affecting America that affect all people. Monthly (11X) mag.; 48 pgs.; circ. 3,500. Subscription $39. 20% unsolicited freelance. Complete ms/cover letter; fax/e-query OK. **Pays $100 & up** on publication for all rts. Articles (25/yr.); book reviews $50. Responds in 12-24 wks. Query about reprints. Prefers requested ms on disk. Uses some sidebars. Developing guidelines; copy for 9x12 SAE/5 stamps.

   Poetry: Buys 15/yr. Free verse, light verse, traditional; 10-50 lines; $25. Submit max. 2 poems.

   Fillers: Buys 15/yr. Cartoons, quotes; 25 wds. & up; payment varies.

   Columns/Departments: Buys 25/yr. Commentary, 2,500 wds. Feature, 5,000 wds. $100-250.

   Tips: "All fairly open except cartoons. Single-spaced preferred; photocopies must be legible."

$@DECISION/DECISION ONLINE, 1 Billy Graham Pkwy., Charlotte NC 28201-0001. (704) 401-2432. Fax (704) 401-3009. E-mail: submissions@bgea.org. Website: www.decisionmag.org. Billy Graham Evangelistic Assn. Bob Paulson, ed. Evangelism/Christian nurture; all articles must have connection to BGEA. Monthly (11X) & online mag.; 44 pgs.; circ. 350,000. Subscription $15. 5% unsolicited freelance; written mostly in-house. Query preferred; no phone/fax/e-query. **Pays $200-500** on publication for 1st rts. Articles 400-1,000 wds. (8/yr.). Response time varies. Seasonal 3-5 mos. ahead. Accepts ms by e-mail (attached file). Uses some sidebars. Prefers NIV. Guidelines by mail/e-mail/Website ("Decision Magazine"/"Writers Guidelines"); copy for 10x13 SAE/3 stamps. (No ads)

   Columns/Departments: Buys 11/yr. Finding Jesus (people who have become Christians through Billy Graham ministries), 700-900 wds. $200. Complete ms.

   Special needs: Personal experience articles telling how a Billy Graham ministry helped you live out your faith.

   Tips: "Nearly all of our articles have some connection with a ministry of the Billy Graham Evangelistic Assn.—through the author's participation in the ministry or through the author's being touched by the ministry."

   ** 2010, 2009 EPA Award of Merit: Organizational.

DESERT CALL: Contemplative Christianity and Vital Culture, Box 219, Crestone CO 81131. (719) 256-4778. Fax (719) 256-4719. E-mail: nada@spirituallifeinstitute.org. Website: www.spirituallifeinstitute.org. Spiritual Life Institute/Catholic. Suzie Ryan, ed. Practical spirituality and contemplative prayer; interfaith/interreligious dialog, the arts and culture, fiction. Quarterly mag.; 32 pgs.; circ. 2,000. Subscription $20. 15% unsolicited freelance; 10% assigned. Complete ms/cover letter; no phone/fax/e-query. **PAYS 3 COPIES** for 1st rts. Articles 1,000-2,500 wds. (4/yr.); some fiction.

Responds in 15 wks. Seasonal 8 mos. ahead. Accepts reprints (tell when/where appeared). No disk or e-mail submissions. Uses some sidebars. No guidelines; copy $2.50/10x13 SAE. (No ads)

Poetry: Accepts 3/yr. Free verse, haiku, traditional; to 25 lines.

Fillers: Accepts 3/yr. Anecdotes, facts, prayers, prose, quotes; 50-250 wds.

DESERT CHRISTIAN NEWS, PO Box 4196, Palm Desert CA 92261. (760) 772-2027. E-mail: smiller@desertchristiannews.org. Website: www.desertchristiannews.org. Susan Miller, ed. To encourage communication and unity among Christians in the Coachella Valley by sharing inspiring local news stories, feature articles, and information. Monthly newspaper; weekly TV/radio programs. Subscription $49.95. Open to freelance. Articles to 500 wds. Query preferred. Articles; reviews. Guidelines on Website ("Submit Article"). Incomplete topical listings. (Ads)

THE DESERT VOICE, PO Box 567, Imperial CA 92251. (760) 337-9200. Fax (760) 355-0197. E-mail: editor@desertvoice.info. Website: www.desertvoice.info. Witness Publishing Inc. Alex Arroyave, ed. To reach the lost and to provide family-friendly news not found elsewhere by bias or neglect, or simply because they don't feel it's important. Monthly newspaper; 20 pgs.; circ. 5,200. No subscriptions. Open to freelance. Complete ms/cover letter. **NO PAYMENT.** Articles & fiction 500-800 wds.; reviews 300 wds. Seasonal 2 mos. ahead. Accepts simultaneous submissions & reprints (tell when/where appeared). Prefers e-mail submissions (attached file). Uses some sidebars. Occasionally accepts submissions from teens. No guidelines or copy. (Ads)

Fillers: Jokes, kid quotes, quotes, word puzzles.

Special needs: News.

$DIRECTION, PO Box 436987, Chicago IL 60643. (708) 868-7100, ext. 236. Fax (708) 868-6759. E-mail: ecarey@urbanministries.com. Website: www.urbanministries.com. Urban Ministries Inc. Submit to Evangeline Carey, developmental ed. An adult-level Sunday school quarterly publication consisting of student book and teacher's guide. Quarterly mag; 64 pgs.; $19.45 (student) and $29.45 (teacher). 100% assigned. Query or query/clips; phone/fax/e-query OK. Accepts full manuscripts by e-mail. **Pays to $200 ($300 for lessons)** on acceptance, for all rts. Articles 1,500-3,500 wds. Responds in 4 wks. Seasonal 12 mos. ahead. No simultaneous submissions or reprints. Requires accepted ms on disk or by e-mail (attached or copied into message). Kill fee 50%. Does not use sidebars. Prefers KJV. Guidelines by e-mail; copy for SASE. (No ads)

Tips: "Send query with a writing sample, or attend our annual conference on the first weekend in November each year."

$@DISASTER NEWS NETWORK, PO Box 1746, Ellicott City MD 21041. (443) 393-3330. Fax (443) 420-0085. E-mail: info@villagelife.org. Website: www.disasternews.net. Village Life Co. Submit to Editor. Online; an interactive daily news site on the World Wide Web. Query by e-mail only. **Pays $100-150** after publication for all rts. Articles 1,000 wds. (varies). Requires accepted ms by e-mail. Guidelines on Website. (Ads)

Tips: "Most open to 'people stories' related to faith-based disaster response and/or mitigation. Also, faith-based response to incidents of public violence, and volunteer stories. Authors are expected to have an e-mail submission address. Check our Website." Authors must be DNN pre-approved contractor writers. This publication is moving so check Website for new address.

@DISCIPLE'S JOURNAL, 10 Fiorenza Dr., Wilmington MA 01887-4421. Toll-free (800) 696-2344. (978) 657-7373. Fax (978) 657-5411. E-mail: kadorothy@yahoo.com. Website: www.disciples directory.com. Kenneth A. Dorothy, ed. To strengthen, edify, inform, and unite the body of Christ. Monthly & online newspaper; 24-32 pgs.; circ. 8,000. Subscription $14.95. 5% unsolicited freelance. Query; fax/e-query OK. **NO PAYMENT** for onetime rts. Articles 400 wds. (24/yr.); book/music/video reviews 200 wds. Responds in 2 wks. Seasonal 2 mos. ahead. Accepts simultaneous submissions &

reprints (tell when/where appeared). Prefers requested ms on disk or by e-mail (attached file). Uses some sidebars. Prefers NIV. Guidelines/theme list by mail/e-mail; copy for 9x12 SAE/$2.38 postage (mark "Media Mail"). (Ads)

Fillers: Accepts 12/yr. All types; 100-400 wds.

Columns/Departments: Financial; Singles; Men; Women; Business; Parenting; all 400 wds.

Tips: "Most open to men's, women's, or singles' issues; missions; or homeschooling. Send sample of articles for review."

@DIVINE ASCENT: A Journal of Orthodox Faith, PO Box 439, 21770 Ponderosa Way, Manton CA 96059. (530) 474-5964. Fax (530) 474-3564. E-mail: office@monasteryofstjohn.org. Website: www.monasteryofstjohn.org. Monastery of St. John of Shanghai & San Francisco/Orthodox Church in America. Archimandrite Memetios, abbot & ed-in-chief. Focuses on contemporary Orthodox spirituality as seen in the lives and writings of saints, and holy men and women of our own time. Semiannual & online jour.; 150 pgs. Subscription $25/2 yrs. 20% unsolicited freelance; 65% assigned. Query. **NO PAYMENT** for all rts. Articles (6/yr.); book reviews 500 wds. Responds in 4-8 wks. No reprints. Prefers disk or e-mail submissions (attached file). Does not use sidebars. Prefers RSV, KJV, NKJV. Guidelines by e-mail. (Ads, from Orthodox Christian businesses)

Tips: "Nothing Protestant."

$@DRAMA MINISTRY, PO Box 40387, Nashville TN 37204. Toll-free (866) 859-7622. Fax (615) 463-9139 E-mail: service@dramaministry.com or through Website: www.dramaministry.com. Belden Street Music Company. Regi Stone, pub. Mag. published 4X/yr. & online; page count varies. Subscription $119.95. 75% unsolicited freelance; 25% assigned. Complete ms/cover letter for scripts; query for articles; e-query OK. Accepts full scripts by e-mail. **Pays $100** for scripts on publication for onetime & online rts. Articles 500-700 wds. (80/yr.); scripts 2-10 minutes (80/yr.). Responds in 6-8 wks. Seasonal 6 mos. ahead. Accepts simultaneous submissions & reprints (tell when/where appeared). Requires submissions by e-mail (attached file or copied into message). No kill fee or sidebars. Also accepts submissions from teens. Any Bible version. Guidelines on Website ("Writers Needed" right side orange box). (No ads)

Tips: "If your script is well written and you have a true understanding of what works within the church drama ministry, then you will break into our publication easily. Please adhere to and read writers' guidelines thoroughly (see Website). We do not respond unless we choose to publish your script. All scripts written by freelancers."

$@DREAMSEEKER MAGAZINE, 126 Klingerman Rd., Telford PA 18969. (215) 723-9125. E-mail: DSM@CascadiaPublishingHouse.com or editor@CascadiaPublishingHouse.com. Website: www .CascadiaPublishingHouse.com. Cascadia Publishing House. Submit to The Editor. For readers committed to exploring from the heart, with passion, depth, and flair, their own visions and issues of the day. Quarterly print & online mag.; 52 pgs.; circ. 1,000 (including online). Subscription $14.95. 10% unsolicited freelance; 90% assigned. Query; e-query OK. Accepts full mss by e-mail. **Pays $5 or .01/wd.** on publication for 1st or onetime rts. Articles 750-1,000 wds. (preferred; 1,500-2,000 wds.); short pcs. 350-400 wds. (10/yr.). Responds in 8 wks. No seasonal. No simultaneous submissions; rarely buys reprints (tell when/where appeared). Prefers submissions on disk or by e-mail (attached file). No kill fee or sidebars. Also accepts submissions from children/ teens. Guidelines on Website (click on "Submissions"/"Mission Statement" highlighted in 1st paragraph/"Submissions"); copy online. Incomplete topical listings.

$+@EARTHEN VESSEL ONLINE MAGAZINE, 9 Sunny Oaks Dr., San Rafael CA 94903. (415) 302-1199. Fax (415) 499-8199. E-mail: kentphilpott@comcast.net. Website: www.earthenvessel .net. Earthen Vessel Publishing. Kent & Katie Philpott, co-editors. An unusual variety of topics for Christians who have a broad interest in the world around them, with the goal that they may be equipped to present the person and work of Jesus Christ in a biblically faithful manner. Monthly e-zine; 23 pgs. Subscription free online (donations accepted). Estab. 2010. 10% unsolicited freelance; 90% assigned. Complete ms/cover letter; phone/e-query OK. Accepts full mss by e-mail. **Pays 5% of income for that month** for 12 feature writers; one week after end of each month; for one-time rts. Not copyrighted. Articles 300-800 wds.; accepts fiction; book reviews 400 wds. Responds in 2 wks. Accepts simultaneous submissions & reprints. Accepts e-mail submissions (attached file). No kill fee. No sidebars. Also accepts submissions from children/teens. Any Bible version. Guidelines by e-mail. (No ads)

> **Tips:** "Our interests are broad.; it's best to study our online magazine to see those areas we're interested in. The subject matter is not so much a concern as is a careful and thoughtful presentation of the person and work of Jesus Christ. We have a Reformed theology but are not rigid or exclusive."

@E-CHANNELS, 3819 Bloor St. W., Toronto ON M9P 1K7, Canada. Phone/fax (519) 651-2232. E-mail: cbbrown@bell.net. Website: http://renewalfellowship.presbyterian.ca. The Renewal Fellowship/Presbyterian (P.C.C.). Calvin Brown, ed. For Presbyterians seeking spiritual renewal and biblical orthodoxy. Online mag.; 20 pgs.; circ. 2,000. Subscription $12. 10% unsolicited freelance; 90% assigned. Query; e-query OK. **PAYS IN COPIES** for onetime rts. Articles 1,000-1,500 wds. (15/yr.); book reviews 300 wds. Responds in 4 wks. Seasonal 4-6 mos. ahead. Accepts reprints (tell when/where appeared). Prefers mss by e-mail (attached file/RTF). Regularly uses sidebars. Also accepts submissions from teens. No guidelines; copy for #10 SAE/3 stamps. (Ads)

> **Poetry:** Accepts 3/yr. Free verse, haiku, light verse, traditional; 3 lines & up. Submit max. 6 poems.
> **Fillers:** Accepts 4/yr. Anecdotes, cartoons, prayers.; 6-100 wds.

$EFCA TODAY, 418 Fourth St. N.E., PO Box 315, Charlottesville VA 22902. (434) 961-2500. Fax (434) 961-2507. E-mail: Today@EFCA.org, or DianeMc@journeygroup.com. Website: www.efcatoday.org. Evangelical Free Church of America/Journey Group. Diane McDougall, ed. Denominational. Quarterly mag.; 32 pgs.; circ. 44,000. Subscription $10. 5% unsolicited freelance; 95% assigned. Query (preferred) or complete ms/cover letter; fax/e-query OK. **Pays .23/wd.** on acceptance for 1st and subsidiary rts. (free use on EFCA Website or church bulletins). Articles 300-800 wds. (4/yr.). Responds in 6 wks. Seasonal 6 mos. ahead. Prefers e-mail (attached file) or hard copy. Kill fee 50%. Regularly uses sidebars. Guidelines by mail/e-mail/Website ("Quick Links"/"Writers Guidelines" right side); copy $1/10x13 SAE/$2.38 postage (mark "Media Mail"). (Ads)

> **Special needs:** Stories of EFCA churches in action.
> **Tips:** "Read samples—really can't beat it—and make sure the articles are about EFCA vision and/or activities, geared to leaders, not pew-sitters. We are not a general-interest publication. 'Inspirational' pieces are not applicable."
> ** 2010, 2008, 2007, 2006 EPA Award of Merit: Denominational; 2009 EPA Award of Excellence: Denominational. This periodical was #43 on the 2010 Top 50 Christian Publishers list (#39 in 2009, #41 in 2007, #50 in 2006).

$EL HERALDO CRISTIANO (THE CHRISTIAN HERALD), PO Box 2955, 639 Cleveland St., Ste. 245, Clearwater FL 33755. (813) 200-7055. E-mail: info@elheraldocristiano.org. Website: www.elheraldocristiano.org. Pentecostal/published in Spanish. Joseph Diaz, ed./pub. Embracing the family for Christ. Estab. 2007; 36 pgs. Distributed in Tampa Bay area but nationwide eventually. **Pays.** Call or e-mail. Incomplete topical listings.

ENCOMPASS, 2296 Henderson Mill Rd. N.E., Ste. 406, Atlanta GA 30345-2739. Toll-free (800) 914-2000. (770) 414-1515. Fax (770) 414-1518. E-mail: rlundy@americananglican.org. Website: www.americananglican.org. The American Anglican Council. Robert Lundy, ed. To provide news and information regarding the Episcopal Church and worldwide Anglican Communion; to provide inspirational articles for the spread of Christ's kingdom; to offer encouragement and challenge to the larger church. Bimonthly newsletter; 4-6 pgs.; circ. 45,000. Subscription free. Open to freelance. Query preferred; phone/e-query OK. **NO PAYMENT.** Articles 200-2,000 wds. Responds in 2 wks. Accepts articles by e-mail (attached file). Uses some sidebars. No guidelines; copy for 9x12 SAE/2 stamps.

Tips: "Most open to features or aspects of important people in the Anglican scene in America; commentary on current events in the Anglican community from the orthodox point of view."

$ENFOQUE A LA FAMILIA, 8675 Explorer Dr., Colorado Springs CO 80920. Toll-free (800) 434-2345. (719) 548-4660. Fax (719) 531-3383. E-mail: info@enfoquealafamilia.com. Website: www.enfoque.org. Focus on the Family. Submit to The Editor. To provide family-friendly material to our domestic Spanish constituents and inform the Hispanic community of culturally relevant issues that affect their families. Bimonthly mag.; circ. 30,000. Subscription free. Open to freelance. Complete ms/cover letter. **Pays.** Articles; no reviews. Incomplete topical listings. (No ads)

$@EPISCOPAL LIFE ONLINE, 815—2nd Ave., New York NY 10017. Toll-free (800) 334-7626. (212) 716-6000. Fax (212) 949-8059. E-mail: mdavies@episcopalchurch.org or elife@aflweb printing.com. Website: www.episcopal-life.org. Episcopal Church. Solange De Santis, newspaper ed.; Matthew Davies, online ed. Denominational. Monthly newspaper; 28 pgs.; circ. 200,000. Subscription $27.00. 10% assigned. Query/clips or complete ms/cover letter; phone query on breaking news only; e-query OK. **Pays $50-300** on publication for 1st, onetime, or simultaneous rts. Articles 800 wds. (24/yr.); assigned book reviews 200-300 wds. ($50). Responds in 1-4 wks. Seasonal 3 mos. ahead. Accepts simultaneous submissions & reprints. Accepts e-mail submission. Kill fee 50%. No guidelines; free copy. (Ads)

Columns/Departments: Commentary on political/religious topics; 300-600 wds. $35-75. Query.

Tips: "All articles must have Episcopal Church slant or specifics. We need topical/issues, not devotional stuff. Most open to feature stories about Episcopalians—clergy, lay, churches, involvement in local efforts, movements, ministries."

** This periodical was #50 on the 2009 Top 50 Christian Publishers list (#50 in 2008).

@ESDRAS' SCROLL, 35 Trace Dr., Stockbridge GA 30281-1346. (678) 826-0648. Fax (928) 563-3225. E-mail: submissions@voicesofchrist.org. Website: www.voicesofchrist.org. Voices of Christ Literary Ministries. Theresa H. Johnson, ed. We prefer poetry, and creative writing that is relevant to time/seasons in which we live. Seasonal e-zine/literary mag.; circ. 5,000. Subscription free. 100% unsolicited freelance. Call or query; e-query OK. Accepts full mss by e-mail. **NO PAYMENT** for onetime, reprint, electronic rts. Articles & fiction 500-1,500 wds.; book reviews 250 wds. Responds in 6 wks. Seasonal 2 mos. ahead. Accepts simultaneous submissions & reprints (tell when/where appeared). Prefers e-mail submissions (attached). Uses some sidebars. Also accepts submissions from children/teens. Prefers KJV. Guidelines on Website; copy online. (Ads)

Poetry: Accepts up to 100/yr. Any type; 3-30 lines. Submit max. 3-5 poems. "Poetry is our main focus, specifically poetry that addresses social issues."

Fillers: Accepts up to 20/yr. Cartoons, sermon illustrations, short humor; 250 wds.

Tips: "Submit creative work that is relevant to the times/seasons in which we live. In particular, writings that address social, government, educational, or even religious issues from a spiritual perspective. We readily review and accept poetry that addresses current social issues of concern to the church and society that uphold Christian principles. In addition, we actively seek poetry that deals with end-time ministry." Fiction for children and teens, 12 years and up.

@ETERNAL INK, 4706 Fantasy Ln., Alton IL 62002. E-mail: eternallyours8@yahoo.com. Non-denominational. E-mail publication; open to any serious effort or submission. Mary-Ellen Grisham, ed. (meginrose@gmail.com); Ivie Bozeman, features ed. (CarlPhil10@aol.com); Pat Earl, devotions ed. Biweekly e-zine; 1 pg.; circ. 450. Subscription free. 25% unsolicited freelance; 75% assigned. Complete ms/cover letter by e-mail only. **NO PAYMENT** for onetime rts. Not copyrighted. Articles/ devotions 300-500 wds. (26/yr.); reviews 300-500 wds. Responds in 6 wks. Seasonal 2 mos. ahead. Accepts simultaneous submissions & reprints. Accepts e-mail submissions (copied into message). No kill fee or sidebars. Prefers NIV. Occasionally accepts submissions from children/teens. Guidelines/ copy by e-mail. (No ads)

> **Poetry:** Elizabeth Pearson, poetry ed. (roybet@sbcglobal.net). Accepts 24-30/yr. Free verse, traditional, inspirational; to 30 lines. Submit max. 3 poems.
>
> **Fillers:** Ivie Bozeman, fillers ed. (ivie@rose.net). Accepts 24-30/yr. Anecdotes, jokes, kid quotes, prayers, prose, short humor; 150-250 wds.
>
> **Columns/Departments:** Accepts many/yr. See information on Website. Query.
>
> **Contest:** Annual Prose/Poetry Contest in November-December, with 1st, 2nd, and 3rd-place winners in each category. Book awards for first-place winners. See Website.
>
> **Tips:** "Please contact Mary-Ellen Grisham by e-mail with questions."

$@EUREKA STREET: An Online Magazine of Public Affairs, the Arts and Theology, PO Box 553, Richmond VIC 3121, Australia. Tel.: +61 3 9421 9666 or 1300 72 88 46. Fax +61 3 9421 9600. E-mail: eureka@eurekastreet.com.au or through Website: www.eurekastreet.com.au. Jesuit Communications. Michael Mullins, ed.; submit to Tim Kroenert, asst. ed. An online magazine of public affairs, the arts, and theology. Daily e-zine; circ. 30,000. Subscription free. 35% unsolicited freelance; 35% assigned. Query; phone/e-query OK (complete ms for fiction). Accepts full mss by e-mail (submissions@eurekastreet.com.au). **Pays $200** on publication for onetime rts. Articles 600-800 wds.; fiction 700-800 wds.; reviews 400 wds. (pays $100). Responds in 1 wk. Seasonal 1 mo. ahead. No simultaneous submissions or reprints. Requires submissions by e-mail (attached). Uses some sidebars. Guidelines on Website (go to bottom of Home Page & click on "Advertise & Contribute").

> **Poetry:** Philip Harvey (poetry@eurekastreet.com.au). Buys 50/yr. Avant-garde, free verse, haiku, light verse, traditional. Pays $50 for a set of 4 poems. Submit max. 3 poems.
>
> **Contest:** Eureka Street/Reader's Feast Award for social justice/human rights writing; and Margaret Dooley Award for Young Writers. Website: www.crimeandjusticefestival.com/eureka.
>
> ****This periodical was #12 on the 2009 Top 50 Christian Publishers list.

$EVANGEL (IN), Box 535002, Indianapolis IN 46253-5002. (317) 244-3660. E-mail: evangel editor@fmcna.org. Free Methodist/Light and Life Communications. Julie Innes, ed. For young to middle-aged adults; encourages spiritual growth. Weekly take-home paper (published quarterly); 8 pgs.; circ. 11,000. Subscription $9. 100% unsolicited freelance. Complete ms/cover letter; no e-query. **Pays .04/wd. ($10 min.)** on publication for onetime rts. Articles 1,200 wds. (100/yr.); fiction 1,200 wds. (100/yr.). Responds in 6-8 wks. Seasonal 12-15 mos. ahead. Accepts some simultaneous submissions & reprints (tell when/where appeared). Accepts requested mss by e-mail. Some sidebars. Prefers NIV. Guidelines by mail/e-mail; copy for #10 SAE/1 stamp. (No ads)

> **Poetry:** Buys 40+/yr. Free verse, light verse, traditional; 3-16 lines; $10. Submit max. 5 poems. Rhyming poetry not usually taken seriously.
>
> **Fillers:** Buys 20/yr. Cartoons, crypto-word puzzles; to 100 words; $10.
>
> **Tips:** "Bring fresh insight to a topic. Submit material appropriate for the market and audience. Although we will cover a specific issue of concern to men or to women, we prefer that the problem be addressed universally. Don't ramble; stick to one thesis. A returned manuscript isn't always because of poor writing. Can also use short devotional material, 600 words or less."

@EVANGEL (OR), PO Box 301036, Portland OR 97294. Toll-free (888) 492-4216. Fax (503) 665-9235. E-mail: brenda@pnmc.com. Website: www.pnmc.org. Pacific Northwest Mennonite Conference. Brenda Zook Friesen, ed. Official publication of the Pacific Northwest Mennonite

Conference, featuring news and features about the churches, organizations, and people of the Mennonite Church USA in WA, OR, ID, AK, and W. MT. Quarterly online mag.; 8 pgs.; circ. 25,000. Subscription free. 5% unsolicited freelance; 50% assigned. Query; fax/e-query OK. Accepts full mss by e-mail. **PAYS IN COPIES** for onetime rts. Not copyrighted. Articles 500-1,000 wds. (4/yr.). Responds in 2-4 wks. Seasonal 4 mos. ahead. No simultaneous submissions; accepts reprints (tell when/where appeared). Accepts requested mss on disk or by e-mail (attached file). Uses some sidebars. Guidelines by mail/e-mail; copy for 9x12 SAE/$1.05 postage. (No ads)

Fillers: Accepts 2-4/yr. Newsbreaks, prose, 50-150 wds.

Special needs: Features on local congregational activities.

Tips: "Become familiar with the views, beliefs of Mennonite Church USA. Visiting www.men noniteusa.org is a good place to start. Please address issues from a Mennonite perspective. Check our Website."

@EVANGELICAL TIMES, Faverdale North Industrial Estate, Darlington DL3 0PH, United Kingdom. Tel: +44 1325 380232. E-mail: theeditors@evangelicaltimes.org or through Website: www.evangel ical-times.org. Edgar Andrews & Roger Fay, eds. For churches who hold a biblical, Christ-centered theology and the doctrines of grace; circulated worldwide. Monthly & online tabloid newspaper; 32 pgs.; circ. 40,000. Subscription $18 (surface), $28 (airmail). Incomplete topical listings.

Tips: "Our paper offers UK and world news, Christian comment, and a wide variety of articles (biblical, devotional, practical, topical, doctrinal, and historical), with a strong missionary dimension."

$FAITH & FAMILY: The Magazine of Catholic Living, 432 Washington Ave., North Haven CT 06473. (203) 230-3800. Fax (203) 230-3838. E-mail: editor@faithandfamilylive.com. Website: www.faithandfamilylive.com. Catholic/Circle Media Inc. Danielle Bean, ed. dir.; submit to Robyn B. Lee, mng. ed. Features writing for Catholics and/or Christian families of all ages. Quarterly mag.; 100 pgs.; circ. 32,000. Subscription $17.95. 10% unsolicited freelance; 90% assigned. Query/clips; e-query preferred; no phone query. **Pays** on publication for 1st rts. (payment depends on section). Articles 700-3,000 wds. (35/yr.); brief reviews. Responds in 6-8 wks. Seasonal 6-9 mos. ahead. No reprints. Prefers e-mail submission (attached file). Kill fee. Regularly uses sidebars. Accepts illustrations from children. Prefers NAB. Guidelines by mail/Website; copy $4.50/10x13 SAE. (Ads)

Tips: "Most open to well-written feature articles employing good quotations, anecdotes, and transitions about an interesting aspect of family life; departments; news items. To break in, submit ideas for The Home Front." Wants only Catholic theme-related material.

** This periodical was #22 on the 2008 Top 50 Christian Publishers list (#33 in 2007).

$FAITH & FRIENDS, 2 Overlea Blvd., Toronto ON M4H 1P4, Canada. (416) 422-6226. Fax (416) 422-6120. E-mail: faithandfriends@can.salvationarmy.org or through Website: www.faithandfriends .ca. The Salvation Army. Submit to: Editor. Monthly mag.; 32 pgs.; circ. 50,000. Subscription $17 Cdn. 90% assigned. Query/clips; e-query preferred. **Pays up to $200 Cdn.** on publication for onetime rts. Articles 500-1,000 wds. Responds in 2 wks. Seasonal 6 mos. ahead. Accepts simultaneous submissions & reprints (tell when/where appeared). Prefers accepted ms by e-mail (attached file). Uses some sidebars. Prefers TNIV. Guidelines by mail/Website (click on "Magazine"/"Writers Guidelines"); free copy. (No ads)

Fillers: Buys 10/yr. Cartoons, games, jokes, quizzes, quotes, word puzzles; 50 wds. $25.

Columns/Departments: God in My Life (how Christians in the workplace find faith relevant), 600 wds. Words to Live By (simple Bible studies/discussions of faith), 600 wds. Faith Builders (movie & TV reviews from a spiritual and faith perspective), 750-1,000 wds. Between the Lines (book reviews), 500 wds. Someone Cares.

** This periodical was #30 on the 2010 Top 50 Christian Publishers list.

$@FAITH TODAY: To Connect, Equip and Inform Evangelical Christians in Canada, M.I.P.

Box 3745, Markham ON L3R 0Y4, Canada. (905) 479-5885. Fax (905) 479-4742. E-mail: editor@ faithtoday.ca. Website: www.faithtoday.ca. Evangelical Fellowship of Canada. Gail Reid, mng. ed.; Bill Fledderus, sr. ed.; Karen Stiller, assoc. ed. A general-interest publication for Christians in Canada; almost exclusively about Canadians, including Canadians abroad. Bimonthly & online mag.; 56 pgs.; circ. 18,000. U.S. print subscription $34.98, digital only $17.39. 20% unsolicited freelance; 80% assigned. Query only; fax/e-query preferred. **Pays $80-500 (.20-.25 Cdn./wd.)** on publication for 1st & electronic rts.; reprints .15/wd. Features 800-1,700 words; cover stories 2,000 wds.; essays 650-1,200 wds.; profiles 900 words; reviews 300 wds. (75-100/yr.). Responds in 6 wks. Prefers e-mail submission. Kill fee 30-50%. Regularly uses sidebars. Any Bible version. Guidelines at www. faithtoday.ca/writers; copy at www.faithtoday.ca/digitalsample. (Ads)

Columns/Departments: Guest column (a kind of essay/Canadian focus), 650 wds. Buys 2/yr. Pays $150.

Special needs: Canadian-related content.

Tips: "Most open to short, colorful items, statistics, stories, profiles for Kingdom Matters department. Content (not author) must be Canadian." Unsolicited manuscripts will not be returned.

** This periodical was #42 on the 2006 Top 50 Christian Publishers list.

@FAITHWEBBIN ONLINE MAGAZINE, PO Box 8732, Columbia SC 29202. Fax (775) 908-9660. E-mail: editor@faithwebbin.net. Website: www.faithwebbin.net. Tywebbin Creations. Mrs. Tyora Moody, ed. For Christian families. Monthly online mag. 100% unsolicited freelance. Complete ms by e-mail only; e-query OK. **NO PAYMENT.** Articles 800-1,000 wds. (15-20/yr.). Responds in 1-2 wks. Seasonal 2 mos. ahead. Accepts reprints (tell when/where appeared). Requires e-mail submission (attached file). Regularly uses sidebars. Any Bible version. Guidelines/theme list on Website ("Writer's Guidelines"). (No ads)

Columns/Departments: Accepts 12/yr. Seek (original Bible study lessons and devotions), 1,000-1,200 wds. Grow (Christian living: family, finance, marriage, etc.), 800-1,000 wds. Needs more health and finance articles.

Special needs: Book reviews and author interviews.

Tips: "The two areas exclusively open to freelancers are Seek and Grow. Articles are normally accepted if they meet the length requirement and are not similar to what is already included on the site. Looking for fresh articles; love testimonial type devotions or articles that encourage and motivate the reader. Devotions are accepted frequently."

$THE FAMILY DIGEST, PO Box 40137, Fort Wayne IN 46804. Catholic. Corine B. Erlandson, manuscript ed. Dedicated to the joy and fulfillment of Catholic family life and its relationship to the Catholic parish. Quarterly booklet; 48 pgs.; circ. 150,000. Distributed through parishes. 95% unsolicited freelance. Complete ms/cover letter; no phone/fax/e-query. **Pays $50-60,** 4-9 wks. after acceptance, for 1st NA rts. Articles 700-1,200 wds. (40/yr.). Responds in 4-9 wks. Seasonal 7 mos. ahead. Occasionally buys reprints (tell when/where appeared). Prefers hard copy by mail. Uses some sidebars. Prefers NAB. Guidelines by mail; copy for 6x9 SAE/2 stamps. (Ads)

Fillers: Buys 12/yr. Anecdotes drawn from experience, prayers, short humor; 25-100 wds. pays $25.

Tips: "Prospective freelance writers should be familiar with the types of articles we accept and publish. We are looking for upbeat articles which affirm the simple ways in which the Catholic faith is expressed in daily life. Articles on family life, parish life, seasonal articles, how-to pieces, inspirational, prayer, spiritual life, and church traditions will be gladly reviewed for possible acceptance and publication."

$@FAMILY SMART E-TIPS, PO Box 1125, Murrietta CA 92564-1125. (858) 513-7150. Fax (951) 461-3526. E-mail: plewis@smartfamilies.com or info@smartfamilies.com. Website: www.smart

families.com. Smart Families Inc. Paul Lewis, ed./pub. Christian parenting, with strong crossover to general families. Bimonthly e-newsletter. 20% unsolicited freelance. Complete ms preferred; fax/e-query OK. **Pays $50-250** on publication for 1st rts. Articles 200-1,000 wds. Responds in 1-3 wks. Seasonal 4 mos. ahead. Accepts simultaneous submissions & reprints. Prefers e-mail submission (attached file). Uses some sidebars. Prefers NIV. Limited guidelines on Website (Click on "About the Program"/"Editorial Guidelines & Privacy Policy"). (No ads)

Fillers: Games, ideas, quotes.

Tips: "We are not a typical 'magazine' and have tight length requirements. Because of crossover audience, we do not regularly print Scripture references or use traditional God-word language."

FELLOWSHIP MAGAZINE, PO Box 412, 1109 Garner Ave., Fenwick ON L0S 1C0, Canada. Toll-free (800) 678-2607. (905) 892-1441. Website: www.fellowshipmagazine.org. Fellowship Publications/United Church of Canada. Diane Walker, sr. ed. (pmiller17@cogeco.ca). To provide a positive voice for orthodoxy and uphold the historic Christian faith within the denomination; general lay audience. Quarterly mag.; circ. 9,000. Subscription free for donation. Open to unsolicited freelance. **NO PAYMENT.** Not in topical listings. (Ads)

$FGBC WORLD, PO Box 544, Winona Lake IN 46590. (574) 268-1122. Fax (574) 268-5384. E-mail: lcgates@bmhbooks.com. Website: www.fgbcworld.com. Brethren Missionary Herald Co. Liz Cutler Gates, ed. Connecting people and churches of the Fellowship of Grace Brethren Churches. Bimonthly magazine; 16 pgs.; circ. 16,000. Subscription free. Open to unsolicited freelance; 10% assigned. Query/clips; fax/e-query OK. Accepts full mss by e-mail. **Pays to $100** on publication. Seasonal 4-5 months ahead. No simultaneous submissions; accepts reprints (tell when/where appeared). Prefers accepted articles on disk or by e-mail (attached file). Uses some sidebars. Theme list; no guidelines; copy on Website. (Ads)

Tips: "Articles must have a Grace Brethren connection."

THE FIT CHRISTIAN, PO Box 5732, Ketchikan AK 99901. (206) 274-8474. Fax (614) 388-0664. E-mail: editor@fitchristian.com. Website: www.fitchristian.com. His Work Christian Publishing. Angela J. Perez, ed. A Christian health and fitness magazine. Bimonthly mag. Subscription free. Open to unsolicited freelance. Articles. Incomplete topical listings. (Ads)

FLORIDA BAPTIST WITNESS, 1230 Hendricks Ave., Ste. 514, Jacksonville FL 32207. (904) 596-3165. Fax (904) 346-0696. E-mail: jhannigan@floridabaptistwitness.com, info@goFBW.com, or through Website: www.floridabaptistwitness.com. Florida Baptist Witness Inc./Southern Baptist. Joni B. Hannigan, mng. ed. (904-596-3167). Publishes Good News about God's work that edifies, exhorts, and empowers Florida Baptists to exalt God and extend his Kingdom. Biweekly newspaper; circ. 33,000. Subscription $17.95. Open to unsolicited freelance. Query, query/clips; e-query OK; no calls. Articles. Incomplete topical listings. (Ads)

Tips: "Submit queries on ideas for specific articles, interviews, Q & A's of particular personalities, conferences, topics related to Southern Baptist or evangelical interest. This is a denominational publication. No columns or fiction; follow AP style."

THE FOUNDERS JOURNAL, PO Box 150931, Cape Coral FL 33915. (239) 772-1400. Fax (239) 772-1140. E-mail from Website: www.founders.org. Founders Ministries/Southern Baptist. Kenneth Puls, ed. Consistent with the doctrines of grace that speak from a historic Southern Baptist perspective. Quarterly jour. Subscription $20. Complete ms/cover letter and completed author-information form from Website. Articles & book reviews. Responds in 4 mos. or you may contact them. Guidelines on Website (click on "FAQ"/"The Founders Journal"/"Guidelines for Submitting"). Incomplete topical listings.

FRIENDS JOURNAL: Quaker Thought and Life Today, 1216 Arch St., #2A, Philadelphia PA

19107-2835. (215) 563-8629. Fax (215) 568-1377. E-mail: info@friendsjournal.org. Website: www.friendsjournal.org. Quaker. Robert Dockhorn, sr. ed. Reflects Quaker life with commentary on social issues, spiritual reflection, Quaker history, and world affairs. Monthly mag.; circ. 8,000. Subscription $39. 70% freelance. Complete ms by e-mail preferred. **NO PAYMENT.** Articles to 2,500 wds.; news items 50-200 wds.; reports of Quaker events 450 wds. Responds in 3-16 wks. Accepts simultaneous submissions or reprints, if notified. Guidelines on Website (click on "Contact"/"Submit an Article"); free copy. Incomplete topical listings.

Poetry: To 25 lines.

Fillers: Games, short humor, newsbreaks, and word puzzles.

$THE GEM, 700 E. Melrose Ave., Box 926, Findlay OH 45839-0926. (419) 424-1961. Fax (419) 424-3433. E-mail: communications@cggc.org, or through Website: www.cggc.org. Churches of God, General Conference. Rachel L. Foreman, ed. To encourage and motivate people in their Christian walk. Monthly (13X) take-home paper for adults; 8 pgs.; circ. 6,000. Subscription $14. 80% unsolicited freelance; 20% assigned. Complete ms/cover letter; phone/fax/e-query OK. **Pays $15** after publication for onetime rts. Articles 300-1,200 wds. (125/yr.); fiction 1,200 wds. (125/yr.). Responds in 12 wks. Seasonal 3 mos. ahead. Accepts simultaneous submissions & reprints (tell when/where appeared). Accepts requested ms on disk or by e-mail. Uses some sidebars. Prefers NIV. Guidelines on Website ("Information"/"Periodicals"/scroll down to "Gem Guidelines"); copy for #10 SAE/2 stamps. (No ads)

Poetry: Buys 100/yr. Any type, 3-40 lines; $5-15. Submit max. 3 poems.

Fillers: Buys 100/yr. All types except party ideas; 25-100 words; $5-10.

Special needs: Missions and true stories. Be sure that fiction has a clearly religious/ Christian theme.

Tips: "Most open to real-life experiences where you have clearly been led by God. Make the story interesting and Christian."

** This periodical was #13 on the 2010 Top 50 Christian Publishers list (#9 in 2009, #7 in 2008, #9 in 2007, #37 in 2006).

$GEMS OF TRUTH, PO Box 4060, 7407-7415 Metcalf Ave., Overland Park KS 66204. (913) 432-0331. Fax (913) 722-0351. E-mail: sseditor1@juno.com. Website: www.heraldandbanner.com. Church of God (Holiness)/Herald & Banner Press. Arlene McGehee, Sunday school ed. Denominational. Weekly adult take-home paper; 8 pgs.; circ. 14,000. Subscription $2.45. Complete ms/cover letter; phone/ fax/e-query OK (prefers mail or e-mail). **Pays .005/wd.** on publication for 1st rts. Fiction 1,000-2,000 wds. Seasonal 6-8 mos. ahead. Accepts simultaneous submissions & reprints (tell when/where appeared). Prefers KJV. Guidelines/theme list/copy by mail. Not in topical listings. (No ads)

$GOOD NEWS, PO Box 150, Wilmore KY 40390. (859) 858-4661. Fax (859) 858-4972. E-mail: steve@goodnewsmag.org or info@goodnewsmag.org. Website: www.goodnewsmag.org. United Methodist/Forum for Scriptural Christianity Inc. Steve Beard, ed. Focus is evangelical renewal within the denomination. Bimonthly mag.; 44 pgs.; circ. 100,000. Subscription $25. 20% unsolicited freelance. Query first; no phone/fax/e-query. **Pays $100-150** on publication for onetime rts. Articles 1,500-1,850 wds. (25/yr.). Responds in 24 wks. Seasonal 4-6 mos. ahead. Accepts simultaneous submissions & reprints (tell when/where appeared). Accepts requested ms on disk. Kill fee. Regularly uses sidebars. Prefers NIV. Guidelines by mail/Website; copy $2.75/9x12 SAE. (Ads)

Tips: "Most open to features."

@GOOD NEWS! 440 W. Nyack Rd., West Nyack NY 10994. (845) 620-7438, ext. 20438. Fax (845) 620-7723. E-mail: warren_maye@use.salvationarmy.org. Website: www.SAgoodnews.org. The Salvation Army. Warren Maye, ed. Monthly & online newspaper; 8 pgs.; circ. 30,000. 5% unsolicited freelance; 20% assigned. Guidelines in Website (scroll down left side to "Submissions Guidelines").

@GOOD NEWS CONNECTION, 105 Harris Ave., Portland ME 04103. Toll-free (800) 357-0203. (207) 797-4915. E-mail: goodnewsmaine@aol.com. Website: www.goodnewsconnection.com. Jim Duran, pub. Enriching thousands of families in Maine and New Hampshire, through churches, bookstores, numerous retail outlets, and on the Web. Bimonthly & online newspaper; circ. 6,000. Subscription $16.95. Query preferred. Articles; no reviews. Incomplete topical listings.

$GOOD NEWS, ETC., PO Box 2660, Vista CA 92085. (760) 724-3075. E-mail: goodnewseditor@ cox.net. Website: www.goodnewsetc.com. Good News Publishers Inc. of California. Rick Monroe, ed. Feature stories and local news of interest to Christians in San Diego County. Monthly tabloid; 20-28 pgs.; circ. 36,000. Subscription $30. 5% unsolicited freelance; 5% assigned. Query; e-query OK. **Pays $40-150** on publication for all, 1st, onetime, or reprint rts. Articles 500-900 wds. (15/yr.). Responds in 2 wks. Seasonal 2 mos. ahead. Accepts simultaneous submissions & reprints (tell when/ where appeared). Prefers accepted ms on disk. Regularly uses sidebars. Prefers NIV. No guidelines; copy for 9x12 SAE/4 stamps. (Ads)

Tips: "Most open to local (San Diego), personality-type articles. A San Diego connection is needed."

$@THE GOOD NEWS, (formerly *Good News in South Florida*), PO Box 935148, Margate FL 33093. (954) 564-5378. Fax (866) 587-2911. E-mail: editor@goodnewsfl.org. Website: www.good newsfl.org. Blackstone Media Group. Grif Blackstone, ed. To report truth, provoke thought, and honor Jesus Christ. Monthly & online newspaper; 24-56 pgs.; circ. 80,000. Subscription $19.95. Open to freelance. Query/published clips; e-query OK. Accepts full mss by e-mail. **Pays .10/wd.** for all, 1st, one-time rts. Articles 500-800 wds. Responds in 1 wk. Seasonal 2 mos. ahead. Accepts simultaneous submissions & reprints. Prefers e-mail submissions (attached file). Uses some side-bars. Prefers NLT. Guidelines on Website ("Writer's Guidelines"). (Ads)

** 2008, 2007 EPA Award of Merit: Newspaper.

THE GOOD NEWS JOURNAL, 9701 Copper Creek Dr., Austin TX 78729-3543. (512) 249-6535. Fax (512) 249-0018. E-mail: goodnewsjournal10@gmail.com. Website: www.thegoodnewsjournal.net. Evelyn W. Davison, pub. Christian paper for national circulation by subscription, and Central Texas by free distribution. Bimonthly journal; 24 pgs.; circ. 60,000. Subscription $29.95. 40% unsolicited freelance; 60% assigned. Query; e-query OK. **NO PAYMENT** for nonexclusive or reprint rts. Articles 350 wds. Seasonal 2 mos. ahead. Accepts reprints. Prefers accepted ms by e-mail (attached file). Uses some sidebars. Guidelines on Website; copy for 9x12 SAE/2 stamps. (Ads)

Poetry: Accepts 4-6/yr. Traditional.

Fillers: Accepts many. Anecdotes, cartoons, jokes, prayers, short humor, and tips; 10-50 wds.

Tips: "Most open to short help articles; hope articles; and humor articles."

THE GOOD NEWS TODAY, PO Box 161, Little Compton RI 02837. Phone/fax (401) 619-0418. E-mail: larry@thegoodnewstoday.org. Website: www.thegoodnewstoday.org. Good News Outreach. Lawrence L. Lepore, mng. ed. To evangelize the lost and unite the body of Christ in Rhode Island and S.E. Massachusetts. Monthly newspaper; circ. 16,000. Subscription $25. Open to unsolicited freelance. Complete ms. Articles; book & movie reviews. Starting a new Boston edition. Incomplete topical listings. (Ads)

@THE GOSPEL HERALD, 701 W. Georgia St., Ste. 1500, Vancouver BC V7Y 1C6, Canada. (604) 715-6288. Fax (604) 608-9152. E-mail: edward@gospelherald.com. Website: www.gospelherald .net. Interdenominational. Edward Shih, pub. The only global Chinese Christian daily news source in English. Daily online journal. All rts. Prefers e-mail submissions (attached or copied into message). Accepts submissions from children/teens. No guidelines; copy online. (Ads)

$@GOSPEL TODAY MAGAZINE, 115 Scarlett Oak Way, PO Box 800 (30213), Fairburn GA 30213-3448. (770) 719-4825. Fax (770) 716-2660. E-mail: gteditorial@aol.com or Gospeltodaymag@aol

.com. Website: www.gospeltoday.com. Horizon Concepts Inc. Dr. Teresa Hairston, pub. (drhairston@aol.com). Ministry/Christian lifestyle directed toward urban marketplace. Bimonthly (6X) digital mag.; 64-80 pgs.; circ. 200,000. Subscription $20. 5% unsolicited freelance; 90% assigned. Query; e-query OK. **Pays $75-250** on publication for all rts. Articles 1,000-3,500 wds. (4/yr.). Responds in 4-6 wks. Seasonal 3 mos. ahead. Accepts simultaneous submissions & reprints (tell when/where appeared). Prefers accepted ms by e-mail (attached file). Kill fee 15%. Uses some sidebars. Prefers NKJV. Guidelines on Website (click on Gospel Today Logo/"Editorial"); copy $3.50. (Ads)

Fillers: Accepts 2-3/yr. Cartoons, word puzzles. No payment.

Columns/Departments: Precious Memories (historic overview of renowned personality), 1,500-2,000 wds. From the Pulpit (issue-oriented observation from clergy), 2,500-3,000 wds. Life & Style (travel, health, beauty, fashion tip, etc.), 1,500-2,500 wds. Broken Chains (deliverance testimony), 1,200 wds. Query. Pays $50-75.

Tips: "Looking for great stories of great people doing great things to inspire others."

GREATER PHOENIX CHRISTIAN CHRONICLE, 7070 E. 3rd Ave., Scottsdale AZ 85251. (602) 980-0003. E-mail through Website: www.gpchristianchronicle.com. David Singer, pub.; Shana Thornton, ed. Monthly newspaper; circ. 25,000. Subscription $20. Open to unsolicited freelance. Query. Articles/reviews. Incomplete topical listings. (Ads)

Tips: "We exist to inform our readers from a biblical perspective, raising the standard for family values, sourcing and networking within the Phoenix community."

$GUIDEPOSTS, 16 E. 34th St., 21st Fl., New York NY 10016-4397. (212) 251-8100. E-mail: submissions@guideposts.com. Website: www.guideposts.com. Interfaith. Submit to Articles Editor. Personal faith stories showing how faith in God helps each person cope with life in some particular way. Monthly mag.; 86 pgs.; circ. 2.5 million. Subscription $13.94. 40% unsolicited freelance; 20% assigned. Complete ms/cover letter by e-mail (attached or copy into message). **Pays $100-500** on publication for all rts. Articles 750-1,500 wds. (40-60/yr.), shorter pieces 250-750 words ($100-250). Responds only to mss accepted for publication in 2 mos. Seasonal 6 mos. ahead. Accepts simultaneous submissions & reprints. Kill fee 20%. Uses some sidebars. Free guidelines on Website: www.guideposts.com/tellusyourstory; copy. (Ads)

Columns/Departments: Mysterious Ways (divine intervention), 250 wds. What Prayer Can Do, 250 wds. Angels Among Us, 400 wds. Divine Touch (tangible evidence of God's help), 400 wds.

Contest: Writers Workshop Contest held on even years with a late June deadline. Winners attend a week-long seminar in New York (all expenses paid) on how to write for *Guideposts*.

Tips: "Be able to tell a good story, with drama, suspense, description, and dialog. The point of the story should be some practical spiritual help that subjects learned through their experience. Use unique spiritual insights, strong and unusual dramatic details. We rarely present stories about deceased or professional religious people." First person only.

@HAIKU HIPPODROME, PO Box 2340, Clovis CA 93613-2340. (559) 347-0194. E-mail: clovis wings@aol.com. Poetry on Wings. Jackson Wilcox, ed. Bimonthly mag. & e-zine; 8 pgs.; circ. 100. Subscription by donation. 100% unsolicited freelance. Complete ms/cover letter; phone query OK. No full mss by e-mail. **PAYS 1 COPY & SUBSCRIPTION** on publication for 1st rts. Haiku 3 lines. Responds in 4 wks. Seasonal 3+ mos. ahead. No simultaneous submissions or reprints. Also accepts submissions from children/teens. Prefers KJV. Guidelines by mail; copy for #10 SAE/1 stamp. (No ads)

Poetry: Accepts 225/yr. Haiku; 3 lines. Submit max. 3 poems.

Contest: Every issue includes a Hippodrome Tanka: 3 lines (5-7-5) which are given. The contestant then provides 2 lines of 7 syllables each. Prize for best 2 is publication in next issue.

Tips: "We accept a broad range of what many call English Haiku: (3 lines—often 5-7-5 syllables). However we encourage the style of the early haiku poets—seizing the actuality of the moment in nature and expressing it in the purity of a word or phrase." Prefers no more than 2 haiku on a page.

@HALO MAGAZINE, 148 Banks Dr., Winchester VA 22602. (540) 877-3568. Fax (540) 877-3535. E-mail: halomag@aol.com. Website: www.halomag.com. Marian Newman Braxton, pres./ed. Designed to minister to the unsaved and encourage the Christian; reaches a wide audience, including churches, hospitals, and prison ministries across many states. Quarterly & online mag.; 40-54 pgs. Subscription $20. Open to unsolicited freelance. Fax or e-query; complete ms for fiction. Accepts full mss by e-mail. **NO PAYMENT.** Articles & fiction 600-1,500 wds. Submit seasonal 3-4 mos. ahead. Accepts simultaneous submissions & reprints. Prefers submissions by disk/e-mail (attached or copied into message). Uses some sidebars. Accepts submissions from children/teens. Prefers KJV. No guidelines; sample copy for 9x12 SAE/$2 postage. (Ads)

   Poetry: Accepts original poems; any type or length.

   Fillers: Any type or length.

   Contest: Sponsors some contests: Presidents' Day (your favorite president; why), Thanksgiving (what you're thankful for), etc.

   Tips: "Contact us via e-mail and sign up to write for regular columns such as marriage, death, dealing with illness, teen corner, caregiver's corner, women's corner, divorce, etc."

$@HARUAH: Breath of Heaven, 9618 Misty Brook Grove, Memphis TN 38016. (901) 213-3878. E-mail: editor@haruah.com. Website: www.haruah.com. Double-Edge Publishing. R. L. Copple, ed. A magazine dedicated to the art of writing; wanting to inspire and encourage our readers to think in new ways. Monthly e-zine; circ. 9,000. Subscription free online. 75% unsolicited freelance; 25% assigned. Complete ms/cover letter; no phone/fax query; e-query OK. Requires use of online submission form on Website. **Pays $5** for onetime & electronic rts. Articles to 1,000 wds. (20+/yr.) or fiction (60+/yr.); reviews 500 wds. Responds in 4-6 wks. Seasonal several mos. ahead. No simultaneous submissions; some reprints (tell when/where appeared). Submit through their online submissions system. Does not use sidebars. Also accepts submissions from teens (students). Any Bible version. Guidelines/copy on Website (scroll to bottom & click on "Information for Writers/Artists"). (No ads)

   Poetry: Rochita Loenen-Ruiz, poetry ed. Accepts 24+/yr. Free verse, light verse, traditional, literary; any number of lines. Pays $2. Submit max. 3 poems.

   Tips: "Your story doesn't have to mention God, but we would prefer it to point to Him in one way or another. We have a family atmosphere and love to help emerging writers. But be aware that we keep our expectations for our publication high, and do not settle just to fill space. If you are thinking of submitting and aren't sure if your submission fits our guidelines, always feel free to e-mail a query. We have wonderful forums to mingle with the staff. Take advantage of those and get to know us."

HEARTBEAT/CMA, PO Box 9, Hatfield AR 71945. (870) 389-6196. Fax (870) 389-6199. E-mail: heartbeat@cmausa.org or through Website: www.cmausa.org. Christian Motorcyclists Assn. Jennifer Hayes, ed. To encourage members and give them a tool when they are witnessing in the general world. Monthly; circ. 18,000. Subscription $20. Open to freelance. Complete ms/cover letter. Articles; no reviews. Incomplete topical listings. (Ads)

THE HEARTLAND GATEKEEPER, PO Box 34038, Omaha NE 68134. (402) 926-2633. Fax (402) 391-8744. E-mail: publisher@heartlandgatekeeper.org or through Website: www.heartlandgate keeper.org. Faith Missions Intl./nondenominational. Irene Jensen, ed./pub. To promote unity in the body of Christ, to encourage spiritual growth, to testify to the goodness of God through reporting from a Christian perspective, to reach those who have yet to know Jesus; for Omaha/Council Bluffs region. Monthly newspaper; circ. 10,000. Subscription $24. Open to freelance. Prefers query; e-query OK; use online submission form. **NO PAYMENT** for onetime or reprint rts. Articles 150-300 wds., 300-700 wds., or feature articles 500-1,000 wds. Accepts reprints (tell when/where appeared). E-mail submissions only. Guidelines on Website (click on "About Us"/"Submitting Articles"). Incomplete topical listings. (Ads)

@HEARTLIGHT INTERNET MAGAZINE, PO Box 7044, Abilene TX 79608. E-mail: phil@heart light.org or through Website: www.heartlight.org. Westover Hills Church of Christ. Phil Ware, ed. Offers positive Christian resources for living in today's world. Weekly online mag.; 20+ pgs.; circ. 70,000+. Subscription free. 20% unsolicited freelance. E-query. **NO PAYMENT** for electronic rts. Articles 300-450 wds. (25-35/yr.); fiction 500-700 wds. (12-15/yr.). Responds in 3 wks. Seasonal 2 mos. ahead. Accepts simultaneous submissions & reprints (tell when/where appeared). Prefers e-mail submission. Regularly uses sidebars. Prefers NIV. Copy on Website.

> **Fillers:** Accepts 12/yr. Anecdotes, cartoons, games, ideas, jokes, newsbreaks, prayers, prose, quotes, short humor, word puzzles; to 350 wds.
>
> **Tips:** "Most open to feature articles; Just for Men or Just for Women, or Heartlight for Children (columns)."

HIGHWAY NEWS AND GOOD NEWS, PO Box 117, Marietta PA 17547-0117. For UPS or FedEx: 1525 River Rd., Marietta PA 17547. (717) 426-9977. Fax (717) 426-9980. E-mail: editor@trans portforchrist.org. Website: www.transportforchrist.org. Transport for Christ. Inge Koenig, ed. For truck drivers and their families; evangelistic, with articles for Christian growth. Monthly mag.; 16 pgs.; circ. 35,000. Subscription $35 donation. 60% unsolicited freelance. Complete ms/cover letter; fax query OK; e-query preferred. **PAYS IN COPIES** for rights offered. Articles 600 or 1,500 wds. Seasonal 4 mos. ahead. Accepts simultaneous submissions & reprints (tell when/where appeared). Prefers requested ms by e-mail (attached or copied into message). Uses some sidebars. Prefers NIV. Guidelines/theme list by mail; free copy for 9x12 SAE. (No ads)

> **Poetry:** Accepts 2/yr.; any type; 3-20 lines. Submit max. 5 poems. Rarely uses poetry; should be related to the trucking life, with a Christian focus.
>
> **Fillers:** Accepts 12/yr. Anecdotes, cartoons, facts, ideas, prayers, prose, short humor, tips; to 100 wds.
>
> **Tips:** "Looking for items affecting the trucking industry. Need pieces, no longer than 800 words, on health, marriage, and fatherhood. Most open to features and true stories about truckers. Send pictures."

$HOLINESS TODAY, 17001 Prairie Star Pkwy., Lenexa KS 66220. (913) 577-0500. Fax (913) 577-0857. E-mail: HolinessToday@Nazarene.org. Website: www.holinesstoday.org. Church of the Nazarene. Carmen Ringhiser, mng. ed. Bimonthly mag.; circ. 40,000. Subscription $12. Accepts unsolicited freelance. Query first. **Pays.** Articles. Guidelines by e-mail. Incomplete topical listings. (No ads)

> **Tips:** "Keeps readers connected with the Nazarene experience and provides tools for everyday faith."

HOLY HOUSE MINISTRIES NEWSLETTER, 9641 Tujunga Canyon Blvd., Tujunga CA 91042. (818) 249-3477. Fax (818) 249-3432. E-mail: HolyHouse9@aol.com or through Website: http://holyhouseministries.tripod.com. Rev. Kimberlie Zakarian, pres. Ministers to the unity of families by writing to individual members. Bimonthly newsletter; 6 pgs. Subscription free. 20% unsolicited freelance; 80% assigned. Query; e-query OK. Prefers accepted ms by e-mail. **PAYS 5 COPIES** for onetime rts. Articles 300 wds. (50/yr.). Responds in 2 wks. Seasonal 3 mos. ahead. Accepts reprints (tell when/where appeared). Uses some sidebars. Also accepts submissions from children/teens. No guidelines; copy for $1.25. Incomplete topical listings.

> **Tips:** "Most open to women's issues and prayer tips."

$@HOMESCHOOLING TODAY, PO Box 244, Abingdon VA 24210. (276) 628-1686. Fax (276) 628-5811. E-mail: editor@homeschooltoday.com. Submit to management@homeschooltoday.com. Website: www.homeschoolingtoday.com. Nehemiah Four LLC. Steve Murphy, pub.; Marilyn Rockett, nonfiction ed. Practical articles, encouragement, news, and lessons for homeschoolers. Bimonthly & online mag.; 72 pgs.; circ. 10,000. Subscription $21.99. 40% unsolicited freelance; 60% assigned. Complete ms by e-mail (attached file) or disk; e-query OK. **Pays .10/published wd.** on publication for 1st rts. Feature articles 2,000-2,200 wds.; articles 700-1,100 wds. (30/yr.); book reviews 300 wds. (.10/wd.); fiction for adults. Responds in 10 wks. Seasonal 6 mos. ahead. Accepts simultaneous submissions; occasional reprints. Requires requested ms by e-mail (attached file). Kill fee 25%. Uses some sidebars, 200-400 wds. KJV, NKJV, ESV, or 1599 Geneva. Guidelines/theme list on Website ("Write for Us"); copy for 9x12 SAE/$2 postage & $5. (Ads)

Poetry: Accepts 12/yr. Traditional. Submit max. 2 poems. Pays .10/wd.

Fillers: Accepts 40/yr. Anecdotes, cartoons, facts, ideas, prayers, prose, quizzes, quotes, short humor, tips; 25-200 wds. Pays .10/wd.

Columns/Departments: Buys 20-24/yr. Living Literature (unit study with Living Books), 1,000 wds. Hearth and Homeschool (encouraging words for moms), 1,000 wds. Pays .10/wd. (See guidelines for additional departments.) Monthly e-newsletter: *Homeschooling Helper* (monthly e-newsletter encouraging homeschool moms), 800 wds. Semimonthly e-newsletter: *Father-Led Home Education* (encouragement for homeschool dads), 800 wds. Query.

Tips: "Most open to departments and features in the print edition; also e-newsletter is open to freelance for homeschooling dads and moms."

$HOME TIMES FAMILY NEWSPAPER, PO Box 22547, West Palm Beach FL 33416-2547. (561) 439-3509. Fax (561) 908-6701. E-mail: hometimes@aol.com. Website: www.hometimes.org. Neighbor News Inc. Dennis Lombard, ed./pub. Conservative, pro-Christian community newspaper. Monthly tabloid; 24 pgs.; circ. 4,000. Subscription $24. 15% unsolicited freelance; 25% assigned. Complete ms only/cover letter; no phone/fax/e-query. **Pays $5-25** on acceptance for onetime rts. Articles 100-1,000 wds. (15/yr.); fiction 300-1,500 wds. (3/yr.). Responds in 2-3 wks. Seasonal 2 mos. ahead. Accepts simultaneous submissions & reprints (tell when/where appeared). Accepts requested ms by e-mail. No kill fee. Regularly uses sidebars. Also accepts submissions from teens. Any Bible version. Guidelines by mail; 3 issues $3. (Ads)

Poetry: Buys almost none. Free verse, traditional; 2-16 lines; $5. Submit max. 3 poems.

Fillers: Uses a few/yr. Anecdotes, cartoons, facts, ideas, jokes, kid quotes, newsbreaks, prayers, quotes, short humor, tips; to 100 wds. pays 3-6 copies, if requested.

Columns/Departments: Buys 30/yr. See guidelines for departments, to 600 wds. $5-15.

Special needs: Good short stories (creative nonfiction, or fiction). More faith, miracles, personal experiences, people stories, and home & family articles.

Tips: "Most open to personal stories or home/family pieces. Very open to new writers, but study guidelines and sample first; we are different. Published by Christians, but not 'religious.' Looking for more positive articles and stories. Occasionally seeks stringers in multiple viable markets to write local people features with photos. Journalism experience is preferred. E-mail query for more info with your name, background, and address to hometimes2@aol.com. We strongly suggest you read *Home Times*. Also consider our manual for writers: *101 Reasons Why I Reject Your Manuscript* ($19)."

** This periodical was #47 on the 2010 Top 50 Christian Publishers list.

($)@HOPEKEEPERS MAGAZINE, PO Box 502928, San Diego CA 92150. Toll-free (888) 751-7378. (858) 486-4685. Toll-free fax (800) 933-1078. E-mail: rest@restministries.org. Website: www .hopekeepersmagazine.com. Rest Ministries Inc. Lisa Copen, ed. For people who live with chronic illness or pain; offers encouragement, support, and hope dealing with everyday issues. Quarterly mag.; 64 pgs.; digital only. Subscription $18. 60% unsolicited freelance; 40% assigned. Prefers e-mail queries. **PAYS IN COPIES.** Writers receive passwords to give to friends for digital access. Sometimes pay is determined for articles with extensive research; on publication. Articles 375-1,500 wds.; book reviews 300 wds. Responds in 6-8 wks. Seasonal 6 mos. ahead. Accepts simultaneous submissions &

reprints. Prefers e-mail submissions (attached or copied into message). Regularly uses sidebars. Also accepts submissions from teens. Guidelines by mail/e-mail/Website ("Writer's Guidelines" left side); Copy $3/6x9 SAE. (Ads)

Fillers: Accepts 25/yr. Facts, newsbreaks, tips; 40-90 wds.

Columns/Departments: Accepts 4/yr. Refreshments (devotional-style/journal writing); 350 wds.

Tips: "Topics should be 'attention grabbers' about specific emotions (Is it okay to be mad at God?), or experiences (parenting with a chronic illness), or helpful (5 things you should know about illness on the job). Most open to upbeat topical articles that give reader motivation to change/reflect; should be balanced with personal experience, others' experiences, facts, and Scripture. Devotionals or 'my illness story' not accepted. Please read guidelines; 90% of submissions ignore guidelines. Content also accepted for online publications. Fiction is considered but not used frequently."

$IMAGE, 3307 Third Ave. W., Seattle WA 98119. (206) 281-2988. Fax (206) 281-2979. E-mail: image@imagejournal.org. Website: www.imagejournal.org. Gregory Wolfe, pub./ed.; Mary Kenagy, mng. ed. Publishes the best literary fiction, poetry, nonfiction, and visual arts that engage the Judeo-Christian tradition. Quarterly jour.; 128 pgs.; circ. 5,200. Subscription $39.95. 50% unsolicited freelance; 50% assigned. Mailed queries preferred; no e-query. **Pays $10/pg. ($200 max.)** on acceptance for 1st rts. Articles/essays 4,000-6,000 wds. (10/yr.); fiction 4,000-6,000 wds. (8/yr.); book reviews 2,000 wds. Responds in 1-2 mos. No seasonal. Accepts simultaneous submissions; no reprints. No kill fees. Does not use sidebars. Any Bible version. Guidelines by mail/Website (click on "About"/"Submission Guidelines"); copy $16 (postpaid). (Ads)

Poetry: Buys 24/yr. Good poetry. Pays $2/line (up to $150). Submit max. 5 poems.

Tips: "Read the journal to understand what we publish. We're always thrilled to see high quality literary work in the unsolicited freelance pile, but we really can't typify what we're looking for other than good writing that's honest about faith and the life of faith. No genre fiction."

$IMAGINE: Arts Ministry Magazine for IMAGO DEI, 1015 Minnesota Ave., Kansas City KS 66101. Phone/fax (913) 233-0266. E-mail: lori@imagodeiarts.org. Website: www.imagodeiarts.org. IMAGO DEI: Friends of Christianity and the Arts. Calista Baker, submissions ed.; Lori L. Triplett, senior ed. For Christians interested in a broad view of the arts. Semiannual mag.; 48 pgs.; circ. 1,000. Estab. 2008. 100% unsolicited freelance. Complete ms/cover letter; no phone/fax query; e-query OK. No full mss by e-mail. **Pays $15-25** on publication for onetime rts. Articles/fiction/reviews 1,000-2,500 wds. Responds in 12 wks. Accepts simultaneous submissions; no reprints. Accepts e-mail submissions. No kill fee. Does not use sidebars. Also accepts submissions from children/teens. Any Bible version. Guidelines on Website; copy $9.95/9x12 SAE/$2 postage. (Ads)

Poetry: Marie Asner, poetry ed. Buys 25-50/yr. Avant-garde, free verse, light verse, traditional; to 40 lines. Pays $15-25. Submit max. 3 poems.

Special needs: Any type of art: songs, visual art, choreography, drama.

Tips: "Entire magazine is freelance written; open to any art form."

($)@IMPACT MAGAZINE, 301 Geylang Rd., #03-04 Geylang Centre, Singapore 389344. Tel. 65 6748 1244. Fax 65 748 3744. E-mail: editor@impact.com.sg or through Website: www.impact.com .sg. Impact Christian Comm. Ltd. Andrew Goh, ed.; Loy Chin Fen, copy ed. To help young working adults apply Christian principles to contemporary issues. Bimonthly & online mag.; 56 pgs.; circ. 6,000. Subscription $20. 10% unsolicited freelance. Query or complete ms/cover letter; phone/fax/e-query OK. Accepts full ms by e-mail. **Ranges from no payment up to $40/pg.,** for all rts. Articles 1,200-1,500 wds. (12/yr.) & fiction 1,000-2,000 wds. (6/yr.). Seasonal 2 mos. ahead. Accepts reprints. Prefers e-mail submission (attached file). Uses some sidebars. Prefers NIV. Guidelines by mail/e-mail; copy for $4/$3 postage (surface mail). (Ads)

Poetry: Accepts 2-3 poems/yr. Free verse, 20-40 lines. Submit max. 3 poems.

Fillers: Accepts 6/yr. Anecdotes, cartoons, jokes, quizzes, short humor, and word puzzles.

Columns/Departments: Closing Thoughts (current social issues), 600-800 wds. Testimony (personal experience), 1,500-2,000 wds. Parenting (Asian context), 1,000-1,500 wds. Faith Seeks Understanding (answers to tough questions of faith/Scripture), 80-1,000 wds.

Tips: "We're most open to fillers and testimonies."

$INDIAN LIFE, PO Box 3765, Redwood Post Office, Winnipeg MB R2W 3R6, Canada. U.S. address: PO Box 32, Pembina ND 58271. (204) 661-9333. Fax (204) 661-3982. E-mail: joanne.data@indian life.org or through Website: www.indianlife.org. Indian Life Ministries/nondenominational. Jim Uttley, ed. An evangelistic publication for English-speaking aboriginal people in North America. Bimonthly tabloid newspaper; 16 pgs.; circ. 16,000. Subscription $15. 5% unsolicited freelance; 5% assigned. Query (query or complete ms for fiction); phone/fax/e-query OK. **Pays .15/wd (to $200)** on publication for 1st rts. Articles 150-2,500 wds. (20/yr.); fiction 500-2,000 wds. (8/yr.); reviews, 250 wds. ($40). Responds in 6 wks. Seasonal 4 mos. ahead. Accepts simultaneous submissions & reprints (tell when/where appeared). Accepts requested ms by e-mail (copied into message preferred). Some kill fees 50%. Uses some sidebars. Accepts submissions from children/teens. Prefers New Life Version, NIV. Guidelines by mail/e-mail/Website; copy for 9x12 SAE/$2 postage (check or money order). (Ads)

Poetry: Buys 4 poems/yr.; free verse, light verse, traditional, 10-100 wds. pays $40. Submit max. 5 poems.

Fillers: Kid quotes, quotes, short humor, 50-200 wds. $10-25.

Special needs: Celebrity pieces must be aboriginal only. Looking for legends.

Tips: "Most open to testimonies from Native Americans/Canadians—either first person or third person—news features, or historical fiction with strong and accurate portrayal of Native American life from the Indian perspective. A writer should have understanding of some Native American history and culture. We suggest reading some Native American authors. Native authors preferred, but some others are published. Aim at a 10th-grade reading level; short paragraphs; avoid multisyllable words and long sentences."

**2010 EPA Award of Merit: Newspaper. This periodical was #6 on the 2010 Top 50 Christian Publishers list (#30 in 2009).

$IN HIS PRESENCE, PO Box 14451, Knoxville TN 37914. (865) 335-0072. Fax (865) 524-5277. E-mail: ihp@samaritanpress.com. Website: www.samaritanpress.com. Samaritan Press. R. Michael Henegar, pres. Offers ongoing serial-form stories and new articles and interviews to interest Christian communities. Monthly tabloid; 36+ pgs; circ. 25,000. Subscription $25. 80% unsolicited freelance; 20% assigned. Query; e-query OK. **Pay negotiable** on publication. Articles 600-1,200 wds.; fiction 2,000+ wds. Responds in 4-6 wks. Seasonal 3 mos. ahead. Accepts simultaneous submissions & reprints (tell when/where appeared). Wants accepted mss by e-mail. Sometimes pays kill fee. Also accepts submissions from children/teens. Prefers NKJV. Guidelines (also by e-mail/Website); copy for 9x12 SAE/$2 postage. (Ads)

Poetry: Buys 10-15/yr. Light verse, traditional; 12-36 lines. Pay negotiable. Submit max. 2 poems.

Fillers: Buys 12-15/yr. Anecdotes, cartoons, jokes, short humor; 60-600 wds. Pay negotiable.

Tips: "All sections and departments are open to new writers and freelancers. Just let us see your work and have confidence in yourself and your ability."

+INSIGHTS MAGAZINE CANADA, PO Box 2510, Vancouver BC V6B 3W7, Canada. Toll-free (800) 663-7639. Fax (604) 870-8743. E-mail: info@insightforliving.ca, or through Website: www.insight forliving.ca. Insight for Living Canada. Submit to Robyn Roste (robynr@insightforliving.ca). Monthly mag.; 20 pgs. Subscription free. Open to freelance submissions.

$INTERCHANGE, 412 Sycamore St., Cincinnati OH 45202-4179. Toll-free (800) 582-1712. (513)

421-0311. Fax (513) 421-0315. E-mail: rthompson@diosohio.org or through Website: www.epis copal-dso.org. Episcopal Diocese of Southern Ohio. Richelle Thompson, dir. of communications. Regional paper for the Episcopal and Anglican Church in southern Ohio. Monthly (11X) newspaper; 16 pgs.; circ. 12,000. Free. 20% unsolicited freelance. Query or complete ms/cover letter. **Pays $50-150** on acceptance for all rts. Articles 500-2,000 wds. (8-10/yr.). Responds in 4 wks. Accepts simultaneous submissions. Prefers requested ms on disk/CD. Regularly uses sidebars. Also accepts submissions from children/teens. Copy for 9x12 SASE.

Fillers: Cartoons, facts, jokes.

Tips: "Most open to features, especially with a local angle."

$@THE INTERIM, 104 Bond St., Third Floor, Toronto ON M5B 1X9, Canada. (416) 204-1687. Fax (416) 204-1027. E-mail: ptuns@theinterim.com. Website: www.theinterim.com. The Interim Publishing Co. Paul Tuns, ed. Abortion, euthanasia, pornography, feminism, and religion from a pro-life perspective; Catholic and evangelical Protestant audience. Monthly & online newspaper; 24 pgs.; circ. 20,000. Subscription $40 Cdn. or U.S. 60% unsolicited freelance. Query; phone/e-query OK. **Pays $50-150 Cdn.,** on publication. Articles 400-750 wds.; book, music, video reviews, 500 wds. ($50-75 Cdn.). Responds in 2 wks. Seasonal 2 mos. ahead. Accepts simultaneous submissions & reprints (tell when/where appeared). Prefers e-mail submission (copied into message). Kill fee. Uses some sidebars. Prefers RSV & others. No guidelines; catalog by mail. (Ads)

Fillers: Cartoons.

Tips: "We are most open to news on life, family, and moral issues; informative commentary."

$IN TOUCH, 3836 DeKalb Technology Pkwy., Atlanta GA 30340. (770) 451-1001. E-mail: writers@ intouch.org. Website: www.intouch.org. In Touch Ministries. Tonya Stoneman, ed. Publishing arm of Dr. Charles Stanley's international ministry. Monthly mag.; 48 pgs.; circ. 1 million. Subscription free. 25% unsolicited freelance; 25% assigned. Query, e-query OK. No full mss by e-mail. **Pays varying rates** on acceptance for 1st, electronic, nonexclusive rts. Articles 800-2,000 wds. (60/yr.). Responds in 6-8 wks. Seasonal 6 mos. ahead. No simultaneous submissions or reprints. Prefers e-mail submissions (attached or copied into message). Uses some sidebars. Prefers NASB. Guidelines by e-mail/ Website; copy for 6x9 SAE. (No ads)

Columns/Departments: Strong in Spirit (exegetical), 1,200 wds. Family Room (family topics), 800-1,200 wds. By Faith (profiles), 800-1,200 wds. Solving Problems (life issues), 800-1,200 wds. Payment varies.

** 2010 EPA Award of Excellence: Devotional; 2007 EPA Award of Merit: Devotional.

ISLAND CATHOLIC NEWS, PO Box 5424, Sta. B, Victoria BC V8R 6S4, Canada. (250) 727-9429. Fax (250) 727-3647. E-mail: Icn@telus.net. Island Catholic News Society. Patrick Jamieson, mng. ed., submit to Louise Beinhauer (250-727-3247). Dissenting but concerned Catholics critical of the institution of the Catholic Church. Monthly tabloid; 12-16 pgs.; circ. 2,000. Subscription $35 Cdn./U.S. 90% unsolicited freelance; 10% assigned. Query; phone/fax/e-query OK. Accepts full mss by e-mail. **PAYS IN COPIES OR AD SPACE** on publication for 1st, onetime or reprint rts. Articles 250/350/500 wds. (2-4/yr.); fiction 1,500 wds. (1-2/yr.); reviews 250-750 wds. Responds in 4 wks. Seasonal 2 mos. ahead. Accepts simultaneous submissions & reprints (tell when/where appeared). Accepts e-mail submissions. Regularly uses sidebars. Prefers Jerusalem Bible. Also accepts submissions from children/teens. Guidelines by mail; copy for #10 SAE/3 stamps. (Ads)

Poetry: Accepts 10-20/yr. Avant-garde, free verse, haiku; 5-20 lines. Submit max. 4 poems.

Fillers: Prayers, prose, quotes.

Tips: "Call to chat."

$@THE JC TOWN REPORTER, (formerly *The JC Reporter*) 3190 Lancaster Dr. N.E., Salem OR 97305. (503) 316-1220. Fax (503) 585-7228. E-mail: editor@thejctown.com. Website: www.thejc town.com. The JC Media Group. Cindy Smith, pres./pub. Combined with radio & Web, we spread the Word and encourage, equip, and unite the local body of Christ. Monthly & online newspaper; 24-32 pgs; circ. 20,000. Subscription $20. Estab. 2007. 70% unsolicited freelance; 30% assigned. Query/clips; fax/e-query OK. Accepts full mss by e-mail (attached file). **Pays $25-75** for onetime rts. Not copyrighted. Articles to 700 wds. (100/yr.); fiction to 700 wds. (100/yr.); reviews 200 wds., pays $10. Responds in 4-6 wks. Seasonal 2 mos. ahead. Accepts simultaneous submissions & reprints (tell when/where appeared). No kill fee. Uses some sidebars. Guidelines by e-mail; copy for 10x13 SAE/$2 postage. (Ads)

> **Poetry:** Accepts 24/yr. Any type. No payment. Submit any number.
> **Fillers:** Accepts many/yr. All types; 300-500 wds.
> **Columns/Departments:** Buys many/yr. Query or complete ms, $20-50.
> ** This periodical was # 7 on the 2010 Top 50 Christian Publishers list.

THE JERUSALEM CONNECTION, PO Box 20295, Washington DC 20041. (703) 707-0014. Fax (703) 707-9514. E-mail: editor@tjci.org. Website: www.tjci.org. The Jerusalem Connection Intl. James M. Hutchens, ed. (jmh@tjci.org). To inform, educate, and activate support for Israel and Jewish people; advocates for Christian Zionism. Bimonthly mag.; circ. 3,500. Subscription $30. Open to unsolicited freelance. Query. Articles. Incomplete topical listings. (Ads)

+JOBTOJOY.US, 5042 E. Cherry Hills Blvd., Springfield, MO 65809. (417) 832-8409. Fax (206) 350-8652. E-mail: editor@JobToJoy.us, e-mail submissions preferred (attachment formats include Word, Word Perfect, Works, or Sun's free OpenOffice; not PDF files). Also attach a brief author's bio, and digital photo if available. E-query OK. Open to 90% unsolicited freelance. Reprints fine, electronic rights. J. R. Chrystie, director of online website. All submissions should have a positive focus. **NO PAYMENT.** In lieu of payment, accepted authors will be featured on Our Authors page with their bio, photo, and link to their Website. Devotions 300-500 words; Book Reviews (query first) 400-600 words; Inspiring Testimonials (successful job change, career change, new retirement years' career transition into ministry or volunteerism) 600-1000 words. Some poetry. Keep it positive.

> **Fillers:** Inspiring quotations 20-75 words; humorous short stories about a job change 70-150 words; positive job change how-to tips 50-150 words; review of helpful job-related website 30-50 words; a Bible verse that helped you through a job change 20-50 words; cartoons should be attached as a jpg file (remember this is a Christian site).
> **Special Needs:** Feature Articles (query first) such as how to know when God wants you elsewhere, what is the difference between a job and a ministry, and relevant interviews. Read our mission statement and be creative.

$@KD GOSPEL MEDIA MAGAZINE, PO Box 1211, Hartford CT 06143-1211. (860) 833-2360. Fax (860) 461-7928. E-mail: deanne@kdgmmag.com or through Website: www.kdgmmag.com. To bring the God perspective into the homes of our readers in a motivating and encouraging way. Deanne Williams, chief ed. Quarterly & online mag.; 84 pgs. Subscription $14.50. Estab. 2009. 20% unsolicited freelance; 80% assigned. Query/clips; e-query OK. Accepts full mss by e-mail. **Pays $100-200** on publication for all rts. Articles 1,050 wds.; reviews 500 wds. Responds in 3-6 wks. Seasonal 4 mos. ahead. Accepts simultaneous submissions. Accepts articles on disk or by e-mail (attached file). No kill fee. Uses some sidebars. Also accepts submissions from teens. Guidelines by e-mail/Website (go to bottom of home page); theme list online; no copy. (Ads)

> **Poetry:** Buys 6/yr. Any type of religious poetry; 15-20 lines. Pays $50. Submit max. 2 poems.
> **Fillers:** Buys 12/yr. Ideas, kid quotes, newsbreaks, party ideas, tips; 200-300 wds. Pays $25.
> **Columns/Departments:** Buys 12/yr., 500-1,000 wds. $100-200. Complete ms.
> **Special needs:** Beauty, fashion, missions, sports, men's/women's/youth issues, holiday/seasonal, movie reviews, time management, food/recipes, and politics.
> **Contest:** Sponsors a poetry contest once a year from January 1 to August 30. Winner published in October issue.

Tips: "Creativity is a huge plus. Sending photos with queries helps a lot. Be clear in what you are offering because you never know when we will be looking to fill a position. Be sure to check your facts and reference others' work. All articles should be positive, educational, and/ or faith based."

KEYS TO LIVING, 105 Steffens Rd., Danville PA 17821. (570) 437-2891. E-mail: owcam@verizon .net. Website: http://keystoliving.homestead.com. Connie Mertz, ed./pub. Educates, encourages, and challenges readers through devotional and inspirational writings; also nature articles, focusing primarily on wildlife in eastern U.S. Quarterly newsletter; 12 pgs. Subscription $10. 30% unsolicited freelance (needs freelance). Complete ms/cover letter; prefers e-mail submissions; no phone query. **PAYS 2 COPIES** for onetime or reprint rts. Articles 350-500 wds. Responds in 4 wks. Accepts reprints. No disk; e-mail submission OK (copied into message). Prefers NIV. Guidelines/theme list on Website ("Guidelines/Subscription"); copy for 7x10 SAE/2 stamps. (No ads)

> **Poetry:** Accepts if geared to family, nature, personal living, or current theme. Traditional with an obvious message.
>
> **Special needs:** More freelance submissions on themes only.
>
> **Tips:** "We are a Christ-centered family publication. Seldom is freelance material used unless it pertains to a current theme. No holiday material accepted. Stay within word count."

$@KINDRED SPIRIT, 3909 Swiss Ave., Dallas TX 75204. (214) 841-3556. Fax (972) 222-1544. E-mail: sglahn@dts.edu. Website: www.dts.edu/ks. Dallas Theological Seminary. Sandra Glahn, ed-in-chief. Publication of Dallas Theological Seminary. Tri-annual & online mag.; 16-20 pgs.; circ. 30,000. Subscription free. 75% unsolicited freelance. Query/clips; fax/e-query OK. **Pays $300 flat fee** on publication for 1st & electronic rts. Articles 1,100 wds.; also accepts biblical fiction. Responds in 6 wks. Seasonal 8 mos. ahead. No simultaneous submissions; accepts reprints. Requires accepted mss by e-mail (attached or copied into message). Regularly uses sidebars. Prefers NIV. Guidelines on Website ("Submissions"); copy by mail. (No ads)

> **Special needs:** Profiles/interviews of DTS grads and faculty are open to anyone.
>
> **Tips:** "Any news or profiles or expositions of Scripture with a link to DTS will receive top consideration; all topics other than interviews need to come from DTS graduates."
>
> ** 2009 Award of Merit: Online.

@KOINONIA, 8107 Holmes Rd., Kansas City MO 64131. (816) 361-7242. Fax (816) 361-2144. E-mail: koinoniaemail@gmail.com. Website: www.holycatholicanglican.net. Holy Catholic Church/ Anglican Rite. Holly Michael, ed. Seeks a variety of articles pertaining to the orthodox Christian faith. Quarterly & online newsletter/journal; 16-20 pgs. Subscription $10. Complete ms/cover letter; fax/e-query OK. Accepts full mss by e-mail. **PAYS IN COPIES & SUBSCRIPTION** for one-time rts. Articles/short stories to 2,000 wds. Guidelines by e-mail; copy online. (Ads)

> **Tips:** "All sections open."

$@THE LAYMAN, 136 Tremont Park Dr. N.E., PO Box 2210, Lenoir NC 28645. (828) 758-8716. Fax (828) 758-0920. E-mail: laymanletters@layman.org. Website: www.layman.org. Presbyterian Lay Committee. Carman Fowler, pres. & exec. dir.; Parker T. Williamson, ed. emeritus; Paula R. Kincaid, ed. of *The Layman* & *The Layman Online*. For evangelical Christians interested in the Presbyterian and Reformed denominations. Bimonthly & online newspaper; 24 pgs.; circ. 100,000. No subscriptions. 10% unsolicited freelance. Query. **Pays negotiable rates** on publication for 1st rts. Articles 800-1,200 wds. (12/yr.). Responds in 2 wks. Seasonal 2 mos. ahead. Prefers requested ms on disk. Regularly uses sidebars. Copy for 9x12 SAE/3 stamps. (No ads)

LEAVES, PO Box 87, Dearborn MI 48121-0087. (313) 561-2330. Fax (313) 561-9486. E-mail: leaves -mag@juno.com. Website: www.rc.net/detroit/mariannhill/leaves.htm. Catholic/Mariannhill Fathers of Michigan. Jacquelyn M. Lindsey, ed. For all Catholics; promotes devotion to God and his saints and publishes readers' spiritual experiences, petitions, and thanksgivings. Bimonthly mag.; 24 pgs.; circ. 35,000. Subscription free. 50% unsolicited freelance. Complete ms/cover letter; phone/fax/e-query OK. **NO PAYMENT** for 1st or reprint rts. Not copyrighted. Articles 500 wds. (6-12/yr.). Responds in 4 wks. Seasonal 4 mos. ahead. Accepts reprints. Accepts e-mail submissions (copied into message). Does not use sidebars. Prefers NAB, RSV (Catholic edition). No guidelines or copy. (No ads)

Poetry: Accepts 6-12/yr. Traditional; 8-20 lines. Submit max. 4 poems.

Special needs: Testimonies of conversion or reversion to Catholicism.

Tips: "Besides being interestingly and attractively written, an article should be confidently and reverently grounded in traditional Catholic doctrine and spirituality. The purpose of our magazine is to edify our readers."

$@LEBEN, 2150 River Plaza Dr., Ste. 150, Sacramento CA 95833. (916) 473-8866, ext. 4. E-mail: editor@Leben.us or through Website: www.Leben.us. City Seminary Press. Wayne Johnson, ed. Focuses on Protestant Christian history and biography. Quarterly & online mag.; 24 pgs.; circ. 5,000. Subscription $9.95. 20% unsolicited freelance; 80% assigned. Complete ms; e-query OK. Accepts full mss by e-mail. **Pays $175 or .05/wd.** (copies & subscription) on acceptance for 1st & electronic rts. Articles 500-2,500 wds. (4/yr.). Responds in 2 wks. Accepts simultaneous submissions & reprints (tell when/where appeared). Prefers e-mail submissions (attached file). Uses some sidebars. Also accepts submissions from teens. Prefers KJV. Guidelines on Website ("Write for Leben"); copy for 9x12 SAE/$2 postage. (Ads)

Fillers: Buys 4-6/yr. Short humor. Pays $5-10.

Special needs: Reprints from old publications; historical, humor, etc.

Tips: "We feature stories that are biographical, historically accurate, and interesting—about Protestant martyrs, patriots, missionaries, etc., with a 'Reformed' slant."

$LIBERTY, Dept. of Public Affairs and Religious Liberty, 12501 Old Columbia Pike, Silver Springs MD 20904-1608. (301) 680-6690. Fax (301) 680-6695. E-mail: Lincoln.Steed@nad.adventist.org. Website: www.libertymagazine.org. Seventh-day Adventist. Lincoln Steed, ed. (lincoln.steed@nad .adventist.org). Deals with religious-liberty issues for government officials, civic leaders, and laymen. Bimonthly mag.; 32 pgs.; circ. 200,000. Subscription $7.95. 95% unsolicited freelance. Query/clips; phone/fax/e-query OK. **Pays $100-500** on acceptance for 1st rts. Articles & essays 1,000-2,500 wds. Responds in 5-13 wks. Requires requested ms on disk or by e-mail. Guidelines/copy by mail.

$LIFEGLOW, Box 6097, Lincoln NE 68506-0097. (402) 448-0981. Fax (402) 488-7582. E-mail: info@christianrecord.org. Website: www.christianrecord.org. Christian Record Services for the Blind. Bert Williams, ed. For sight-impaired adults; interdenominational Christian audience. Bimonthly large-print mag.; 51 pgs.; circ. 13,000+. Subscription free to the sight-impaired. 90% unsolicited freelance; 10% assigned. Query or complete ms/cover letter; e-query OK. Accepts full mss by e-mail. **Pays $50-100** on publication for 1st rts. Articles 800-1,400 wds. (12-15/yr). Responds in 12 wks. Seasonal 6 mos. ahead. No simultaneous submissions; occasionally accepts reprints. Requires accepted mss by e-mail (attached or copied into message). No kill fee. Uses some sidebars. Prefers NKJV, NIV. Guidelines/theme list by e-mail; no copy. (No ads)

Columns/Departments: Query; pays $75.

LIFESITENEWS.COM, Canadian address: 104 Bond St. E., Third Fl., Toronto ON M5B 1X9, Canada. U.S. address: 4 Family Life Ln., Front Royal VA 22630. Toll-free (888) 678-6008. E-mail: editor@ lifesitenews.com or lsn@lifesitenews.com. Website: www.lifesitenews.com. An originally written online daily news service covering life, faith, family, and freedom. John-Henry Westen, cofounder & ed-in-chief. With reporters in Europe, Latin America, Canada, and United States. Free subscription at www.lifesite.net/ldn/subscribe. Incomplete topical listings.

Tips: "Highly regarded as a leader in the field of pro-life and pro-family news."

@LIFETIMES CATHOLIC EZINE, (877) 585-3816. E-mail: bjubar@parishwebmaster.com (see guidelines for e-mail address for each department) or through Website: www.ParishWebmaster.com/writers.htm. Catholic. Brandon Jubar, ed. Designed to spread the Good News and minister to people online. Weekly online publication. Open to submissions. Send complete ms in body of e-mail using online form. **NO PAYMENT.** Articles 300-600 wds. (300/yr.). Also accepts submissions from teens. Guidelines on Website (scroll down to "Guidelines").

   Columns: Weekly Reflection; Catholic Life; Faith & Spirituality; Family; Self-Improvement; Teen Issues; Teen 2 Teen.

$LIGHT & LIFE, Box 535002, Indianapolis IN 46253-5002. (317) 244-3660. Fax (317) 244-1247. E-mail: LLMAuthors@fmcna.org. Website: www.freemethodistchurch.org/Magazine. Free Methodist Church of North America. Cynthia Schnereger, mng. ed.; submit to Margie Newton, ms manager. Interactive magazine for maturing Christians; contemporary-issues oriented, thought-provoking; emphasizes spiritual growth, discipline, holiness as a lifestyle. Bimonthly mag.; 32 pgs. (plus pull-outs); circ. 13,000. Subscription $16. 95% unsolicited freelance. Query first; e-query OK. **Pays .15/wd.** on acceptance for 1st rts. Articles 800-1,500 wds. (24/yr.). Responds in 8-12 wks. Seasonal 12 mos. ahead. No simultaneous submissions. Prefers e-mail submission (attached file) after acceptance. No kill fee. Uses some sidebars. Prefers NIV. Also accepts submissions from children/teens. Guidelines on Website ("Writer's Guides"); copy $4. (Ads)

   Tips: "Best to write a query letter. We are emphasizing contemporary issues articles, well researched. Ask the question, 'What topics are not receiving adequate coverage in the church and Christian periodicals?' Seeking unique angles on everyday topics."

   ** This periodical was #48 on the 2010 Top 50 Christian Publishers list.

LIGHT OF THE WORLD NEWSPAPER, 177—34 Troutville Rd., Jamaica NY 11434. (718) 938-7966. E-mail: Christislight@aol.com. Julius Ogunnaya, ed. Primarily targets African Christians and non-Christians. Monthly newspaper; 28 pgs.; circ. 20,000. Open to unsolicited freelance. E-query. **NO PAYMENT.** Articles 2 pgs. max. Guidelines by e-mail. Incomplete topical listings. (Ads)

   Poetry: Accepts poetry.
   Fillers: Cartoons, jokes, quizzes, and word puzzles.
   Contest: Youth Annual Essay Competition.

$LIGUORIAN, One Liguori Dr., Liguori MO 63057-9999. Toll-free (800) 464-2555. (636) 464-2500. Toll-free fax (800) 325-9526. (636) 464-8449. E-mail: liguorianeditor@liguori.org. Website: www.liguorian.org. Catholic/Liguori Publications. Jay Staten, ed. dir.; Cheryl Plass, mng. ed. To help Catholics of all ages better understand the gospel and church teachings and to show how these teachings apply to life and the problems confronting them as members of families, the church, and society. Monthly (10X) mag.; 40 pgs.; circ. 100,000. Subscription $20. 30-40% unsolicited freelance; 60% assigned. Query, query/clips, or complete ms; phone/fax/e-query OK. **Pays .12-.15/wd.** on acceptance for 1st rts. Articles 1,200-2,200 wds. (30-50/yr.); fiction 1,800-2,000 wds. (10/yr.). No simultaneous submissions or reprints. Responds in 8-12 wks. Seasonal 6-8 mos. ahead. Prefers requested ms by e-mail (attached file). Sometimes pays kill fee. Uses some sidebars. Prefers NRSV. Guidelines by mail/e-mail/Website ("About Liguorian"/"Author Guidelines"); copy for 9x12 SAE/3 stamps. (Ads)

   Fillers: Buys 10/yr. Cartoons, jokes.
   Tips: "Most open to 1,000-word meditations; 1,800-word fiction; or 1,500-word personal testimonies. Send complete manuscript for fiction. Polish your own manuscript."

   ** This periodical was #16 on the 2009 Top 50 Christian Publishers list (#13 in 2008, #16 in 2007, #22 in 2006).

$LIVE, 1445 N. Boonville Ave., Springfield MO 65802-1894. (417) 862-2781. Fax (417) 863-1874. E-mail: rl-live@gph.org. Website: www.gospelpublishing.com. Assemblies of God/Gospel Publishing

House. Richard Bennett, adult ed. Inspiration and encouragement for adults. Weekly take-home paper; 8 pgs.; circ. 38,000. Subscription $14.80. 100% unsolicited freelance. Complete ms/cover letter; no phone/fax query; e-query OK. **Pays .10/wd. (.07/wd. for reprints)** on acceptance for one-time or reprint rts. Articles 400-1,100 wds. (80-90/yr.); fiction 400-1,100 wds. (20/yr.). Responds in 4-6 wks. Seasonal 18 mos. ahead. Accepts simultaneous submissions & reprints (tell when/where appeared). Accepts e-mail submissions (attached file). No kill fees. Few sidebars. Prefers NIV, KJV. Guidelines by mail/e-mail/Website ("Writer's Guides"); copy for #10 SAE/1 stamp. (No ads)

> **Poetry:** Buys 12-18/yr. Free verse, light verse, traditional; 8-25 lines; $60 ($35 for reprints) when scheduled. Submit max. 3 poems.

> **Tips:** "We are often in need of good shorter stories (400-600 wds.), especially true stories or based on true stories. Often need holiday stories that are not 'how-to' stories, particularly for patriotic or nonreligious holidays. All areas open to freelance—human interest, inspirational, and difficulties overcome with God's help. Fiction must be especially good with biblical application. Follow our guidelines. Most open to well-written personal experience with biblical application. Send no more than two articles in the same envelope and send a SASE."
> ** This periodical was #10 on the 2010 Top 50 Christian Publishers list (#3 in 2009, #5 in 2008, #1 in 2007, #8 in 2006).

$LIVING FOR THE WHOLE FAMILY, 1251 Virginia Ave., Harrisonburg VA 22802. (540) 433-5351. Fax (540) 434-0247. E-mail: Mediaforliving.gmail.com. Website: www.livingforthewholefamily.com. Media for Living. Melodie M. Davis, ed. (melodiemd@msn.com). A positive, practical, and uplifting publication for the whole family; mass distribution. Quarterly tabloid; 28-36 pgs.; circ. 50,000. Subscription free. 95% unsolicited freelance. Query or complete ms/cover letter; e-query OK. **Pays $50-60; $35-45 for shorter pcs.** about 3 mos. after publication for onetime rts. Articles 1,000-1,200 wds.; shorter features 250-550 wds. (40-50/yr.). Responds in 3-4 mos. Seasonal 4 mos. ahead. Accepts simultaneous submissions & reprints (tell when/where appeared). Accepts requested ms by e-mail (copied into message; include e-mail address in message). Uses some sidebars. Prefers NIV. Guidelines on Website (click on "Contact" and scroll down); copy for 9x12 SAE/4 stamps. (Ads)

> **Tips:** "We are directed toward the general public, many of whom have no Christian interests, and we're trying to publish high-quality writing on family issues/concerns from a Christian perspective. That means religious language must be low key. Too much of what we receive is directed toward a Christian reader. We get far more than we can use, so something really has to stand out. Please carefully consider before sending. Need more articles of interest to men. Our articles need to have a family slant or fit the descriptor 'encouragement for families.'"
> When submitting by e-mail, put title of magazine and title of your piece in subject line. Also include your e-mail address in body of message.

$LIVING LIGHT NEWS, #200, 5306—89th St., Edmonton AB T6E 5P9, Canada. (780) 468-6397. Fax (780) 468-6872. E-mail: shine@livinglightnews.com. Website: www.livinglightnews.com. Living Light Ministries. Jeff Caporale, ed. To motivate and encourage Christians; witnessing tool to the lost. Bimonthly tabloid; 36 pgs.; circ. 75,000. Subscription $24.95 U.S. 40% unsolicited freelance; 60% assigned. Query; e-query OK. **Pays $20-125 (.05-.10/wd. Cdn. or .10/wd. U.S.)** on publication for all, 1st, onetime, simultaneous, or reprint rts. Articles 350-700 wds. (75/yr.). Responds in 4 wks. Seasonal 3-4 mos. ahead. Accepts simultaneous submissions & reprints (tell when/where appeared). Guidelines by e-mail/Website ("More"/"Writing Guidelines" left side); copy for 9x12 SAE/$2.50 Cdn. postage or IRCs (no U.S. postage). (Ads)

> **Columns/Departments:** Buys 20/yr., 450-600 wds. $10-30 Cdn. Parenting; relationships. Query.

> **Special needs:** Celebrity interviews/testimonials of well-known personalities. Fun or informative articles (250-700 wds.) for Christian-education supplement.

Tips: "Most open to a timely article about someone who is well known in North America, in sports or entertainment, and has a strong Christian walk."
** This periodical was #34 on the 2007 Top 50 Christian Publishers list (#38 in 2006).

LIVING STONES NEWS, 2031 E. First St., Duluth MN 55812. (218) 728-4945. E-mail: corinne@livingstonesnews.com, editor@livingstonesnews.com or through Website: www.livingstonesnews.com. Corinne E. Scott, pub. To glorify God, to reach out to the unsaved, and to bring hope, encouragement, peace, and the unconditional love of Jesus Christ to our readers. Monthly newspaper; circ. 15,000. Distributed free through churches & businesses; $18 for individual subscriptions. Open to freelance. Query preferred. Articles. (Ads) Not included in topical listings.

$@THE LOOKOUT, 8805 Governor's Hill Dr., Ste. 400, Cincinnati OH 45249. (513) 931-4050. Fax (513) 931-0950. E-mail: lookout@standardpub.com. Website: www.lookoutmag.com. Standard Publishing. Shawn McMullen, ed. For adults who are interested in learning more about applying the gospel to their lives. Weekly & online mag.; 16 pgs.; circ. 52,000. Subscription $45. 40% unsolicited freelance; 60% assigned. Query for theme articles; e-query OK. **Pays $145-225** on acceptance (after contract is signed), for 1st rts. Articles 1,000-1,600 wds. Responds in 10 wks. Seasonal 9-12 mos. ahead. Accepts simultaneous submissions; no reprints. No disks or e-mail submissions. Kill fee 50%. Regularly uses sidebars. Prefers NIV. Guidelines/theme list by e-mail/Website: www.lookout mag.com/write/default.asp); copy for #10 SAE/$1. (Ads)

   Columns/Departments: Buys 24/yr. Outlook (personal opinion); Salt & Light (innovative ways to reach out into the community); Faith Around the World; all 800 wds. Pays $125. Query.

   Tips: "Most open to feature articles according to our theme list. Get a copy of our theme list and query about a theme-related article at least six months in advance. Request sample copies of our magazine to familiarize yourself with our publishing needs (also available online)."
   ** This periodical was #22 on the 2010 Top 50 Christian Publishers list (#10 in 2009, #17 in 2008, #10 in 2007, #30 in 2006).

@LOUISIANA BAPTIST MESSAGE, PO Box 311, Alexandria LA 71309. (318) 442-7728. Fax (318) 445-8328. E-mail: editor@baptistmessage.com. Website: www.baptistmessage.com. Louisiana Southern Baptists. Kelly Boggs, ed. To report the news of what God is doing through Southern Baptists in Louisiana. Weekly & online newspaper; circ. 45,000. Subscription $14. Open to unsolicited freelance. Complete ms. Articles & reviews. Incomplete topical listings. (Ads)

$THE LUTHERAN DIGEST, 6160 Carmen Ave. E., Inver Grove MN 55076. (651) 451-9945. E-mail: editor@lutherandigest.com. Website: www.lutherandigest.com. The Lutheran Digest Inc. Nick Skapyak, ed. Blend of general and light theological material used to win nonbelievers to the Lutheran faith. Quarterly literary mag.; 64 pgs.; circ. 60,000. Subscription $16. 100% unsolicited freelance. Query or complete ms/cover letter; phone/fax/e-query OK. **Pays $35-100+ ($25-50 for reprints)** on acceptance for onetime & reprint rts. Articles to 1,000 wds. or no more than 7,000 characters—3,000 preferred (25-30/yr.). Accepts full mss by e-mail. Responds in 4-9 wks. Seasonal 6-9 mos. ahead. Accepts simultaneous submissions & reprints (tell when/where appeared). Accepts e-mail submissions (attached). No kill fee. Uses some sidebars. Rarely accepts submissions from children/teens. Guidelines by mail/Website ("Write for Us"); copy $3.50/6x9 SAE. (Ads)

   Poetry: Accepts 20+/yr. Light verse, traditional; short/varies; no payment. Submit max. 3 poems/mo.

   Fillers: Anecdotes, facts, short humor, tips; length varies; no payment.

   Tips: "We want our readers to feel uplifted after reading our magazine. Therefore, short, hopeful pieces are encouraged. We need well-written short articles that would be of interest to middle-aged and senior Christians—and also acceptable to Lutheran Church pastors. We prefer real-life stories over theoretical essays. Personal tributes and testimony articles are discouraged. Please read sample articles and follow our writers' guidelines prior to submission—a little research goes a long way. Too much inappropriate and irrelevant material received."

**This periodical was #31 on the 2010 Top 50 Christian Publishers list (#24 in 2009).

$THE LUTHERAN JOURNAL, PO Box 28158, Oakdale MN 55128. (651) 702-0086. Fax (651) 702-0074. E-mail: christianad2@msn.com. Vance Lichty, pub.; Roger S. Jensen, ed.; submit to Editorial Assistant. Family magazine for, by, and about Lutherans, and God at work in the Lutheran world. Annual mag.; 48 pgs.; circ. 200,000. Subscription $6. 60% unsolicited freelance; 40% assigned. Complete ms/cover letter; fax query OK. **Pays .01-.04/wd.** on publication for all or 1st rts. Articles 750-1,500 wds. (25-30/yr.); fiction 1,000-1,500 wds. Response time varies. Seasonal 4-5 mos. ahead. Accepts reprints. Uses some sidebars. Prefers NIV, NAS, KJV. Accepts requested ms on disk. Also accepts submissions from children/teens. Guidelines by mail; copy for 9x12 SAE/2 stamps. (Ads)

Poetry: Buys 4-6/yr. Light verse, traditional; 50-150 wds. $10-30. Submit max. 3 poems.

Fillers: Buys 5-10/yr. Anecdotes, facts, games, prayers, quizzes, quotes; 50-300 wds. $5-30.

Columns/Departments: Buys 40/yr. Apron Strings (short recipes); About Books (reviews), 50-150 wds. $5-25.

Tips: "Most open to Lutheran lifestyles or Lutherans in action." Does not return rejected manuscripts.

$THE LUTHERAN WITNESS, 1333 S. Kirkwood Rd., St. Louis MO 63122-7295. (314) 996-1202. Fax (314) 996-1126. E-mail: james.heine@lcms.org. Website: www.lcms.org/witness. The Lutheran Church Missouri Synod. Jim Heine, executive ed. Official periodical of the denomination, for lay members of its congregations; to encourage responsible Christian action in church and society. Monthly mag.; 28 pgs.; circ. 200,000. Subscription $22. 25% unsolicited freelance; 75% assigned. Complete ms/cover letter; no phone/fax query; e-query OK. Accepts full mss by e-mail. **Pays $150-500** on publication for 1st & electronic rts. Articles to 1,500 wds. (20/yr.). Responds in 8-15 wks. Seasonal 6 mos. ahead. Accepts simultaneous submissions; no reprints. Accepts fax or e-mail submissions (attached). Sometimes pays 50% kill fee. Regularly uses sidebars. Prefers ESV. Guidelines on Website ("Writer's Guidelines" small print); copy for 9x12 SASE. (Ads)

Columns/Departments: Buys 11/yr. Pays $150.

$@THE MANNA, PO Box 130, Princess Anne MD 21853. (410) 543-9652. Fax (410) 651-9652. E-mail: wolc@wolc.org. Website: www.wolc.org. Maranatha Inc. Debbie Byrd, ed-in-chief. A free monthly tabloid featuring evangelical articles, and distributed in the marketplace in Delaware, Maryland, and Virginia. Digital online tabloid; 32-40 pgs; circ. 42,000. Subscription free. 10-15% unsolicited freelance; 15% assigned. Query/clips; e-query OK. No full mss by e-mail. **Pays $30-50** on publication for 1st, onetime, or reprint rts. Articles 1,000-1,200 wds. Responds in 1-2 wks. Seasonal 3-4 mos. ahead. No simultaneous submissions. Accepts reprints (tell when/where appeared). Accepted articles on disk or by e-mail (copied into message). Uses some sidebars. Also accepts submissions from children/teens. No guidelines; copy for 9x12 SAE/2 stamps. (Ads)

Fillers: Anecdotes, ideas, party ideas, short humor, and tips. No payment.

Columns/Departments: Accepts up to 12/yr. Finances (business or personal); Counseling (Q & A); Personal Integrity (scriptural); all 800 wds. No payment.

Special needs: Themes: marital fidelity, conquering fear, hypocrites, heaven, showing compassion, and What Is Your Hope? Most open to these theme pieces.

Tips: "E-mail your query."

** 2010 Award of Merit: Newspaper; 2009 Award of Excellence: Newspaper.

$@MARIAN HELPER, Marian Helpers Center, Eden Hill, Stockbridge MA 01263. (413) 298-3691. Fax (413) 298-3583. E-mail: came@marian.org. Website: www.marian.org. Catholic/Marians of the

Immaculate Conception. Dave Came, exec. ed.; Felix Carroll, review ed. Quarterly & online mag.; circ. 500,000. Rarely uses unsolicited; 25% assigned freelance. Query/clips or complete ms/cover letter. **Pays $250** for 1,000-1,200 wds. (2-page feature), for 1st rts. Articles 500-900 wds. Responds in 6 wks. Seasonal 6 mos. ahead. Kill fee 30%. Guidelines/copy for #10 SAE. (No ads)

> **Tips:** "Write about God's mercy touching people's everyday lives or about devotion to the Blessed Virgin Mary in a practical, inspirational, or fresh way."

MARKETPLACE, 2001 W. Plano Pkwy., Ste. 3200, Plano TX 75075-8646. Toll-free (800) 775-7657. (972) 941-4400. Fax (972) 578-5754. E-mail: artstricklin@mchapusa.com. Website: www.mcha pusa.com. Marketplace Chaplains USA. Art Stricklin, VP/Public Relations. Focus is on working in the corporate workplace. Triennial literary mag.; 12-18 pgs.; circ. 16,000. Subscription free. 10% assigned. Query; e-query OK. Accepts full mss by e-mail. **NO PAYMENT** for all rts. Articles. Prefers e-mail submission. No copy. Incomplete topical listings. (No ads)

> **Tips:** "We are attempting to cut back on freelance and use only assigned stories."

$+@MARRIAGE PARTNERSHIP, 465 Gundersen Dr., Carol Stream IL 60188. E-mail: mp@ marriagepartnership.com. Website: www.marriagepartnership.com. Christianity Today Inc. Ginger Kolbaba, ed. To provide realistic, challenging, and practical insights into healthy Christian marriage; for middle-class, college-educated Christians in their 20s, 30s, and 40s (median age 36). E-zine. Query only; prefers e-query. **Pays $50-150** on acceptance for exclusive online rts. (with the exception of using your material on your own site). Articles. Responds in 10-12 wks. No simultaneous submissions. Guidelines on Website ("Contact Us"/ "Writer's Guidelines"); copy on Website. Incomplete topical listings.

> **Tips:** "Writers who can communicate with freshness, clarity, and insight will receive serious consideration. We are looking for writers who are willing to speak candidly about marriages, including their own."

$MATURE LIVING, One Lifeway Plaza, MSN 175, Nashville TN 37234-0175. (615) 251-5677. E-mail: matureliving@lifeway.com. Website: www.lifeway.com. LifeWay Christian Resources/Southern Baptist. Rene Holt, content ed. Christian leisure reading for 55+ adults, characterized by human interest and Christian warmth. Monthly mag.; 60 pgs.; circ. 318,000. Subscription $22.50. 90% unsolicited freelance; 10% assigned. Complete ms/cover letter; no phone/fax/e-query. Accepts full mss by e-mail (attached or copied into message). **Pays $85-115** for feature articles ($105-115 for fiction) on acceptance for all rts. Articles 400-1,200 wds. (85/yr.); senior adult fiction 900-1,200 wds. (12/yr.). Responds in 6-8 wks. Seasonal 6-8 mos. ahead. No simultaneous submissions or reprints. No kill fee. Uses some sidebars. Prefers KJV, HCSB. Guidelines by mail/e-mail (rene.holt@ lifeway.com); copy for 9x12 SAE/4 stamps. (Ads)

> **Poetry:** Buys 24-30/yr. Light verse, traditional; 12-16 lines; $35. Submit max. 3 poems.
>
> **Fillers:** Accepts 144/yr. Grandchildren stories, 50-100 wds. no payment.
>
> **Columns/Departments:** Buys 300+/yr. Cracker Barrel, 4-line verse, $15; Grandparent's Brag Board, 50-100 wds. $15; Over the Garden Fence (gardening), 300-350 wds. Communing with God (devotional), 125-200 wds. Fun 'n Games (wordsearch/crossword puzzles), 300-350 wds. Crafts; Recipes; $15-50. Complete ms. See guidelines for full list.
>
> **Tips:** "Almost all areas open to freelancers except medical and financial matters. Study the magazine for its style. Write for our readers' pleasure and inspiration. Fiction for 55+ adults needs to underscore a biblical truth."
>
> ** This periodical was #12 on the 2010 Top 50 Christian Publishers list (#22 in 2009, #44 in 2008, #13 in 2007, #10 in 2006).

$MATURE YEARS, Box 801, Nashville TN 37202. (615) 749-6292. Fax (615) 749-6512. E-mail: matureyears@umpublishing.org. United Methodist. Marvin W. Cropsey, ed. To help persons in and nearing retirement years understand and appropriate the resources of the Christian faith in dealing with specific problems and opportunities related to aging. Quarterly mag.; 112 pgs.; circ. 55,000. Subscription $24. 60% unsolicited freelance; 40% assigned. Complete ms/cover letter; fax/e-query OK. **Pays .07/wd.** on acceptance for onetime rts. Articles 900-2,000 wds. (60/yr.); fiction 1,200-2,000 wds. (4/yr.). Responds in 9 wks. Seasonal 14 mos. ahead. Accepts reprints. Prefers accepted ms by e-mail (copied into message). Regularly uses sidebars. Prefers NRSV, NIV. Guidelines by mail/e-mail; copy $5. (No ads)

   Poetry: Buys 24/yr. Free verse, haiku, light verse, traditional; 4-16 lines; .50-1.00/line. Submit max. 6 poems.

   Fillers: Buys 20/yr. Anecdotes (to 300 wds.), cartoons, jokes, prayers, word puzzles (religious only); to 30 wds. $5-25.

   Columns/Departments: Buys 20/yr. Health Hints, 900-1,200 wds. Modern Revelations (inspirational), 900-1,100 wds. Fragments of Life (true-life inspirational), 250-600 wds. Going Places (travel), 1,000-1,500 wds. Money Matters, 1,200-1,800 wds.

   Special needs: Articles on crafts and pets. Fiction on older adult situations. All areas open except Bible studies.

   ** This periodical was #36 on the 2010 Top 50 Christian Publishers list (#30 in 2007, #35 in 2006).

@MEN.AG.ORG, 1445 N. Boonville Ave., Springfield MO 65802. (417) 862-2781. Fax (417) 832-0574. E-mail: men@ag.org. Website: www.men.ag.org. Assemblies of God. Darian Amsler, field & commun. coord. Targeting men, ages 25-60; Christian/Pentecostal distinctive. Weekly E-zine. 10% unsolicited freelance; 90% assigned. Prefers e-query. **No payment** for 1st rts. Articles 600-1,000 wds. Responds in 1 wk. Seasonal 5 mos. ahead. Accepts simultaneous submissions & reprints (tell when/where appeared). Prefers e-mail submissions (attached file). Prefers NIV. Guidelines by e-mail/Website ("Write for Men.ag.org" in bottom, right-hand corner of Home Page); copy online. (Ads)

   Tips: "In being familiar with Website, submit articles (by e-mail) relevant to the faith, life, and culture. "

($)MENNONITE HISTORIAN, 600 Shaftesbury Blvd., Winnipeg MB R3P 0M4, Canada. (204) 888-6781. E-mail: aredekopp@mennonitechurch.ca. Or, 1310 Taylor Ave., Winnipeg MB R3M 3Z6, Canada. (204) 669-6575. E-mail: dheidebrecht@mbconf.ca. Website: www.mennonitechurch.ca/programs. Mennonite Heritage Centre of Mennonite Church Canada, and the Centre for Mennonite Brethren Studies of the Canadian Conference of Mennonite Brethren churches. Alf Redekopp (MHC), and Doug Heidebrecht (CMBS), co-eds; Conrad Stoesz (CMBS/MHC), assoc. ed. Gathers and shares historical material related to Mennonites; focus on North America, but also beyond. Quarterly newsletter; 8-12 pgs.; circ. 600. Subscription $13. 40% unsolicited freelance; 20% assigned. Complete ms/cover letter; phone/e-query OK. **NO PAYMENT EXCEPT BY SPECIAL ARRANGEMENT** for 1st rts. Articles 250-1,000 wds. Accepts simultaneous submissions & reprints (tell when/where appeared). Prefers e-mail submission (attached file). Does not use sidebars. Limited guidelines on Website; copy for 9x12 SASE.

   Tips: "Must be Mennonite related (i.e., related to the life and history of the denomination, its people, organizations, and activities). Most open to lead articles. Write us with your ideas. Also genealogical articles."

$MEN OF INTEGRITY, 465 Gundersen Dr., Carol Stream IL 60188. (630) 260-6200. Fax (630) 260-0451. E-mail: mail@menofintegrity.net. Website: www.MenofIntegrity.net. Christianity Today Intl. Christopher Lutes, ed. Uses narrative to apply biblical truth to specific gritty issues men face. Bimonthly pocket-size mag.; 64 pgs.; circ. 70,000. Subscription $19.95. 10% unsolicited freelance. Complete ms. **Pays $50** on acceptance for onetime & electronic rts. Articles 225 wds. (15/yr.). Responds in 6 wks. Accepts simultaneous submissions & reprints (tell when/where appeared).

Accepts requested ms on disk or e-mail (attached file or copied into message). Does not use sidebars. Prefers NLT. Guidelines/theme list by mail/e-mail; copy $4/#10 SAE. (Ads)
  ** 2006 EPA Award of Merit: Devotional

@MEN OF THE CROSS, 920 Sweetgum Creek, Plano TX 75023. (972) 517-8553. E-mail: info@ menofthecross.com. Website: www.menofthecross.com. Greg Paskal, content mngr. (greg@greg paskal.com). Encouraging men in their walk with the Lord; strong emphasis on discipleship and relationship. Online community. 50% unsolicited freelance. Query by e-mail. **NO PAYMENT**. Not copyrighted. Articles 500-1,500 wds. (10/yr.). Responds in 2-4 wks. Seasonal 3 mos. ahead. Accepts simultaneous submissions; no reprints. Prefers e-mail submissions (attached or copied into message). Uses some sidebars. Prefers NIV, NKJV, NASB. Also accepts submissions from teens. Guidelines by e-mail; copy online. (No ads)
  Poetry: Accepts 1/yr. Avant-garde, free verse; 50-250 lines. Submit max. 1 poem.
  Special needs: Christian living in the workplace.
  Tips: "Appropriate topic could be a real, first-hand account of how God worked in the author's life. We are looking for humble honesty in hopes it will minister to those in similar circumstances. View online forums for specific topics."

$MESSAGE MAGAZINE, Review and Herald Pub. Assn., 55 W. Oak Ridge Dr., Hagerstown MD 21740. (301) 393-4100. Fax (301) 393-4103. E-mail: message@RHPA.org. Website: www.mes sagemagazine.org. Review & Herald/Seventh-day Adventist. Washington Johnson II, ed. (wjohnson@ rhpa.org). Pat Harris, assoc. ed. (pharris@rhpa.org). For African Americans and all people seeking practical Christian guidance on current events and a better lifestyle. Bimonthly mag.; 32 pgs.; circ. 125,000. Subscription $17.95. 10-20% freelance written. Query or complete ms/cover letter; fax/e-query OK. **Pays $300** on acceptance for 1st rts. Articles 700-800 wds.; fiction for children (ages 5-8), 500 wds. Responds in 6-10 wks. Seasonal 6 mos. ahead. Prefers requested ms by e-mail. Regularly uses sidebars. Prefers KJV. Guidelines on Website ("Writer's Guidelines"); copy for 9x12 SAE/2 stamps. (Ads)
  Columns/Departments: Buys for each issue. Healthspan (health issues), 700 wds.
  MESSAGE Jr. (biblical stories or stories with clear-cut moral for ages 5-8), 500 wds. $50-300.
  Tips: "As with any publication, writers should have a working knowledge of *MESSAGE*. They should have some knowledge of our style and our readers."

MESSAGE OF THE OPEN BIBLE, 2020 Bell Ave., Des Moines IA 50315-1096. (515) 288-6761. Fax (515) 288-2510. E-mail: message@openbible.org. Website: www.openbible.org. Open Bible Standard Churches. Andrea Johnson, mng. ed. To inspire, inform, and educate the Open Bible family. Bimonthly mag.; 16 pgs.; circ. 2,500. Subscription $9.95. 3% unsolicited freelance; 3% assigned. Query or complete ms/cover letter; e-query OK. **PAYS 5 COPIES.** Not copyrighted. Articles 750 wds. (2/yr.). Responds in 4 wks. Seasonal 4 mos. ahead. Accepts simultaneous submissions & reprints (tell when/where appeared). Accepts requested ms on disk or by e-mail. Regularly uses sidebars. Prefers NIV. Guidelines/theme list by mail/e-mail; copy for 9x12 SAE/2 stamps. (No ads)
  Fillers: Accepts 6/yr. Facts, quotes, short humor; 50 wds.
  Tips: "A writer can best break in by giving us material for an upcoming theme, or something inspiring, specifically as it would relate to an Open Bible layperson."

$THE MESSENGER, 440 Main St., Steinbach MB R5G 1Z5, Canada. (204) 326-6401. Fax (204) 326-1613. E-mail: messenger@emconf.ca or through Website: www.emconf.ca/Messenger. Evangelical Mennonite Conference. Terry M. Smith, ed.; Rebecca Roman, asst. ed. Serves Evangelical Mennonite Conference members and general readers. Monthly mag.; 36 pgs. Subscription $24. Uses little freelance, but open. Query preferred; phone/fax/e-query OK. Accepts full mss by e-mail. **Pays $50-120** on publication for 1st rts. only. Articles. Brief guidelines on Website ("Subscriptions, Article Submission Information"). Not included in topical listings.

$@THE MESSENGER OF SAINT ANTHONY, Via Orto Botanico 11, 35123 Padova, Italy (U.S. address: Anthonian Assn., 101 Saint Anthony Dr., Mt. Saint Francis IN 47146). (812) 923-6356 or 049 8229924. Fax (812) 923-3200 or 049 8225651. E-mail: m.conte@santonio.org (editor); messenger @santantonio.org (ed. sec.); or info@santantonio.org. Website: www.saintanthonyofpadua.net. Catholic/Provincia Padovana F.M.C. Fr. Mario Conte OFM, ed.; Corrado Roeper, ed. sec. For middle-aged and older Catholics in English-speaking world; articles that address current issues. Monthly & online mag.; 50 pgs.; circ. 45,000. Subscription $25 U.S. 10% unsolicited freelance; 90% assigned. Query (complete ms for fiction); phone/fax/e-query OK. **Pays $40/pg.** (600 wds./pg.) for onetime rts. Articles 600-2,400 wds. (40/yr.); fiction 900-1,200 wds. (11/yr.). Responds in 8-10 wks. Seasonal 3 mos. ahead. Prefers e-mail submission (attached file or copied into message). Regularly uses side-bars. Prefers NEB (Oxford Study Edition). Guidelines by mail/e-mail; free copy. (No ads)
>   **Columns/Departments:** Buys 50-60/yr. Documentary (issues), 600-2,000 wds. Spirituality, 600-2,000 wds. Church Life, 600-2,000 wds. Saint Anthony (devotional), 600-1,400 wds. Living Today (family life), 600-1,400 wds. $55-200. Complete ms.
>   **Special needs:** Short story of a moral or religious nature; St. Anthony.
>   **Tips:** "Most open to short stories; Saint Anthony, and devotional articles on parishes named after Saint Anthony, local feasts/shrines in Saint Anthony's honour. All writers should bring a uniquely Catholic perspective to their articles."

$MESSENGER OF THE SACRED HEART, 661 Greenwood Ave., Toronto ON M4J 4B3, Canada. (416) 466-1195. Catholic/Apostleship of Prayer. Rev. F. J. Power, S.J., ed. Help for daily living on a spiritual level. Monthly mag.; 32 pgs.; circ. 11,000. Subscription $14. 20% freelance. Complete ms; no phone query. **Pays .10/wd.** on acceptance for 1st rts. Articles 700-1,500 wds. (30/yr.); fiction 700-1,500 wds. (12/yr.). Responds in 5 wks. Seasonal 5 mos. ahead. No disk. Does not use sidebars. Guidelines by mail; no copy. (No ads)
>   **Tips:** "Most open to inspirational stories and articles."

$MESSIAH JOURNAL, PO Box 649, Marshfield MO 65706-0649. (417) 468-2741. Fax (417) 468-2745. E-mail: amber@ffoz.org or through Website: www.ffoz.org. First Fruits of Zion. Boaz Michael, ed. Dedicated to the study, exploration, and celebration of our righteous and sinless Torah-observant King—Yeshua of Nazareth. Quarterly mag.; 34 pgs.; circ. 10,000. Subscription $35.Open to free-lance. Query; fax query OK. **Pays** on acceptance for all rts. Articles (15-20/yr.). Responds in 3 wks. Seasonal 6 mos. ahead. Accepts simultaneous submissions; no reprints. Requires e-mail submissions (attached file). Does not use sidebars. Prefers NASB. Copy for $4/9x12 SAE/5 stamps. Incomplete topical listings. (No ads)
>   **Tips:** "F.F.O.Z. is a nonprofit ministry devoted to strengthening the love and appreciation of the Body of the Messiah for the land, people, and Scriptures of Israel. Since our focus is unique, please be very familiar with our magazine before submitting your query. Our Torah Testimony column is always open, as are some of the others. Looking for something on Hebrew roots."

MESSIANIC PERSPECTIVES, PO Box 345, San Antonio TX 78292-0345. (210) 226-0421. Fax (210) 226-2140. E-mail: rachelz@cjfm.org. Website: www.cjfm.org. CJF Ministries. Rachel Zanardi, ed. To provide for our constituency ministry-related news along with Bible teaching from a messianic perspective. Bimonthly newspaper; 20 pgs.; circ. 30,000. Subscription $10. Open to unsolicited freelance. Query; e-query OK. Accepts full mss by e-mail. Articles & reviews. Responds in 4 wks. Seasonal 4 mos. ahead. Accepts simultaneous submissions & reprints (tell when/where appeared). Prefers e-mail submissions (attached file). Regularly uses sidebars. Prefers NKJV. No guidelines or copy. (No ads)

THE MESSIANIC TIMES, PO Box 2096, Niagara Falls NY 14302. (760) 329-5399. Fax (760) 329-4877. E-mail: editor@messianictimes.com, or through Website: www.messianictimes.com. Times of the Messiah Ministries. Paul Liberman, pub.; Karen S. Meissner, ed. To unify the Messianic Jewish community around the world, to serve as an evangelistic tool to the Jewish community, and to educate Christians about the Jewish roots of their faith. Bimonthly newspaper; circ. 35,000. Subscription $21.99. Accepts freelance. Query preferred. Articles & reviews. Not in topical listings. (Ads)

METHODIST HISTORY, PO Box 127, Madison NJ 07940. (973) 408-3189. Fax (973) 408-3909. E-mail: RWilliams@gcah.org. Website: www.gcah.org. United Methodist. Robert J. Williams, ed. History of the United Methodism and Methodist/Wesleyan churches. Quarterly jour.; 64 pgs.; circ. 800. Subscription $20. 100% unsolicited freelance. Query; phone/fax/e-query OK. **PAYS 3 COPIES** for all rts. Historical articles to 5,000 wds. (15/yr.); book reviews 500 wds. Responds in 8 wks. Requires requested ms on disk. Does not use sidebars. Guidelines by mail/Website; no copy. (Ads)
    Special needs: United Methodist church history.

MIDNIGHT CALL MAGAZINE, PO Box 280008, Columbia SC 29228. Toll-free (800) 845-2420. (803) 755-0733. Fax (803) 755-6002. E-mail: info@midnightcall.com. Website: www.midnightcall .com. Arno Froese, ed. The world's only international voice of prophecy regarding end-time events. Subscription $22.50.

($)+THE MIDNIGHT DINER, 60 W. Terra Cotta Ave., Ste. B, #156, Crystal Lake IL 60014-3548. E-mail: michelle@reliefjournal.com. Website: http://themidnightdiner.com. CC Publishing. Michelle Pendergrass, ed-in-chief. Annual jour.; 175 pgs; circ. 300. Estab. 2008. 90% unsolicited freelance; 10% assigned. Complete ms/cover letter; no phone/fax/e-query. Use online submission system only. **PAYS IN COPIES ($100 to editor's choice story)** on publication for 1st rts. No articles. Fiction up to 10,000 wds. (15-20/yr.). Responds in 16-20 wks. Accepts simultaneous submissions; no reprints. Any Bible version. Guidelines on Website (scroll down to "Writer's Guidelines"); no copy. (Ads)
    Special needs: Also open to horror, crime, and UFO/alien fiction.

$MIRACLES, HEALINGS, & THE UNEXPLAINED, 13527 N.E. Rose Pkwy., Portland OR 97230. (503) 793-3026. Fax (503) 206-4792. E-mail: solidgoldpub@comcast.net. Website: www.miracles magazine.com. Sue Wade, ed. Showing through the overwhelming evidence of miracles that Jesus is healing and revealing himself to people every day. Semiannual mag./booklet, 35-50 pgs. Estab. 2007. 99% freelance. Complete ms by mail/cover letter or through Website; e-query OK. Accepts full mss by e-mail. **Pays $10-25** on publication for onetime & reprint rts. Not copyrighted. Articles 100-2,000 wds. Responds in 8 wks. Seasonal 6 mos. ahead. Accepts simultaneous submissions & reprints. Accepts articles by e-mail (attached or copied into message). Uses some sidebars. Also accepts submissions from children/teens. Any Bible version. Guidelines by e-mail/Website ("Submit a Story"); no copy. (Ads)
    Fillers: Accepts 20/yr. Anecdotes, cartoons, facts, ideas, jokes, kid quotes, short humor; 50-60 wds. Pays $10.
    Contest: Sometimes holds a contest for the most unique miracle story.
    Tips: "Keep stories active, yet brief. Use description such as time of day, atmosphere, people around, what it smelled like, witnesses (if any), what you look like, colors you remember, etc. Express your feelings and the importance to you. Include a picture of yourself or those in the story. The stories must be true and can be verified if necessary. Stories are meant to increase faith and hope in those who read them."

$THE MIRACULOUS MEDAL, 475 E. Chelten Ave., Philadelphia PA 19144-5785. Toll-free (800) 523-3674. (215) 848-1010. Fax (215) 848-1014. E-mail through Website: www.cammonline.org. Catholic. Rev. James O. Kiernan, C.M., ed. Fiction and poetry for Catholic adults, mostly women. Quarterly mag.; 36 pgs.; circ. 200,000. Subscription free to members. 40% unsolicited freelance. Query by mail only. **Pays .03/wd. and up** on acceptance, for 1st rts. Religious fiction 1,000-2,000 wds. some 1,000-1,500 wds. (6/yr.). Responds in 13 wks. Seasonal anytime. Accepts simultaneous submissions. Guidelines by mail/e-mail; copy for 6x9 SAE/2 stamps. Incomplete topical listings. (No ads)

Poetry: Buys 6/yr. Free verse, traditional; to 20 lines; $1 & up/line. Send any number. "Must have religious theme, preferably about the Blessed Virgin Mary."

Tips: "Most open to good short stories, 1,500-2,500 wds. or poetry, with light religious theme."

@MISSIONWARES.COM, 920 Sweetgum Creek, Plano TX 75023. (972) 517-8553. E-mail: info@missionwares.com. Website: www.missionwares.com. Greg Paskal, owner. Website targeted toward Christian technologists. E-zine. 50% unsolicited freelance. Complete ms; e-query OK. Accepts full mss by e-mail. **NO PAYMENT** for onetime rts. Not copyrighted. Articles 1,500-5,000 wds. (3-5/yr.). Responds in 3-4 wks. No seasonal. No simultaneous submissions or reprints. Accepts e-mail submissions (attached file in Word or PDF). Does not use sidebars. Also accepts submissions from teens. Prefers NIV, NKJV, NLT. Guidelines by e-mail; copy online. (No ads)

Special needs: Technical White Papers. Best practices in technology as outlined by biblical precedence.

Tips: "We are looking for out-of-the-box thinking when it comes to the usage of current and new technologies."

$THE MONTANA CATHOLIC, PO Box 1729, Helena MT 59624. (406) 442-5820. Fax (406) 442-5191. E-mail: rstmartin@diocesehelena.org. Website: www.diocesehelena.org. Catholic Diocese of Helena. Renee St. Martin Wizeman, ed. Publishes news and features from a Catholic perspective, particularly as they pertain to the church in western Montana. Monthly tabloid; 20 pgs.; circ. 9,000. Subscription $12-16. 5% freelance. Query or complete ms; e-query OK. **Pays .05-.10/wd.** on acceptance for 1st, onetime, simultaneous rts. Articles 400-650 wds. (5/yr.). Responds in 5 wks. Accepts simultaneous submissions. Kill fee 25%. Guidelines on Website (click on "News & Events"/"Montana Catholic Newspaper"/"Writers Guidelines"). Incomplete topical listings. (Ads)

Tips: "Most open to seasonal pieces or articles with a tie to western Montana. Must have a Catholic angle."

@THE MORE EXCELLENT WAY (formerly Society for the Prevention of Cruelty to Humans), PO Box 3032, Clackamas OR 97015. E-mail: spch.email@yahoo.com. Website: www.preventcrueltytohumans.com. Stan Baldwin, ed/pub. To encourage personal acts of decency and kindness; to challenge and change the prevailing culture of cruelty. Mostly e-zine. Subscription free. Open to unsolicited freelance. Complete ms/cover letter; no phone/fax query; e-query preferred. Submit by e-mail. **PAYS COPIES & SUBSCRIPTION** for onetime rts. Not copyrighted. Articles 350-800 wds. (18/yr.) Responds in 1 wk. Accepts reprints (tell when/where appeared). No sidebars. Accepts submissions from teens. Guidelines by e-mail; copy on Website. (No ads)

Columns/Departments: Accepts 24/yr. Friends of the Dolphin (profile/experience of service, compassion, kindness); Mom Factor (teaching children in the home, character building). Complete ms.

Tips: "Write to touch the heart. Nonfiction with a fictional story style. Everything must encourage others to love their neighbors. Minimize the religious talk."

MOVIEGUIDE, 1151 Avenida Acaso, Camarillo CA 93012. Toll-free (800) 577-6684. (770) 825-0084. Fax (805) 383-4089. E-mail through Website: www.movieguide.org. Good News Communications/Christian Film & Television Commission. Dr. Theodore Baehr, pub. Family guide to media entertainment from a biblical perspective. Monthly mag.; 48 pgs.; circ. 2,500. Subscription $40. 40% unsolicited freelance. Query/clips. **PAYS IN COPIES** for all rts. Articles 1,000 wds. (100/yr.); book/music/video/movie reviews, 750-1,000 wds. Responds in 6 wks. Seasonal 6 mos. ahead. Accepts requested ms on disk. Regularly uses sidebars. Guidelines/theme list; copy for SAE/4 stamps. (Ads)

Fillers: Accepts 1,000/yr.; all types; 20-150 wds.

Columns/Departments: Movieguide; Travelguide; Videoguide; CDguide, etc.; 1,200 wds.

Contest: Scriptwriting contest for movies with positive Christian content. Go to www.kairos prize.com.

Tips: "Most open to articles on movies and entertainment, especially trends, media literacy, historical, and hot topics."

($)MUTUALITY, 122 W. Franklin Ave., Ste. 218, Minneapolis MN 55404-2451. (612) 872-6898. Fax (612) 872-6891. E-mail: mgreulich@cbeinternational.org or cbe@cbeinternational.org. Website: www.cbeinternational.org. Christians for Biblical Equality. Megan Greulich, ed. Seeks to provide inspiration, encouragement, and information about equality within the Christian church around the world. Quarterly mag.; 32 pgs.; circ. 2,000. Subscription $40/free to members. 80% assigned freelance. Query/clips; fax/e-query OK. **PAYS A GIFT CERTIFICATE TO THEIR BOOKSTORE** on publication for 1st or electronic rts. Articles 1,000-2,000 wds. (12/yr.); book reviews 500-800 wds. Responds in 6 wks. Accepts reprints (tell when/where appeared). Accepts requested ms on disk or by e-mail (attached file). Regularly uses sidebars. Prefers NRSV, TNIV. Guidelines by mail/Website ("Resources"/"Mutuality Magazine"/"Writers Guidelines"); copy for 9x12 SAE/3 stamps. (Ads)

** 2009 Award of Merit: Most Improved Publication.

@NASHVILLE CHRISTIAN TIMES, 455 Sam Ridley Blvd., Ste. 263, Smyrna TN 37167. E-mail: nashvillechristiantimes@gmail.com. Website: www.nashvillechristiantimes.com. Nashville Christian Writers Assn. Carol Harper, exec. ed. An online resource for Nashville's Christian Community. E-zine. Project is associated with the Nashville Christian Writers Assn. and REST Ministries. Welcomes submissions for The Christian View department.

NETWORK, PO Box 131165, Birmingham AL 35213-6165. (205) 328-7112. E-mail: dolores@net worknewspaper.org. Website: www.networknewspaper.org. Interdenominational. Dolores Milazzo-Hicks, ed./pub. To encourage and nurture dialog, understanding, and unity in Christian communities. Monthly tabloid; 12-16 pgs.; circ. 10,000. Subscription $17.50. 50% unsolicited freelance. Phone/fax/e-query OK. **NO PAYMENT.** Not copyrighted. Articles to 500 wds. Accepts simultaneous submissions. Articles and news.

Tips: "Most open to feature stories that express the unity of the body of Christ and articles that encourage and uplift our readers. We also cover state, local, national, and international news."

@NEW CHRISTIAN VOICES.COM., E-mail: editor@newchristianvoices.com. Website: www .NewChristianVoices.com. Nondenominational. Joanne Brokaw, ed. Humor/lifestyle Website. Open to unsolicited freelance. **Pays** on acceptance for all rts. (but will negotiate on rts.); pay based on experience and quality of work. Articles 300-600 wds.; devotionals 150-250 wds. (buys all rts. to devotionals). Responds in 1-4 wks. Guidelines on Website ("NCV's Writer's Guidelines"). Incomplete topical listings.

Special needs: Looking for bloggers. Put "Blog Query" in subject line of e-mail.

Tips: "We're looking for good writers who can write funny (amusing to hilarious) essays, commentaries, editorials, and columnlike material for our channels. We're interested in creating relationships with writers who will write for us regularly. "

NEW FRONTIER, 180 E. Ocean Blvd., 4th Fl., Long Beach CA 90802. (562) 491-8331. Fax (562) 491-8791. E-mail: New.frontier@usw.salvationarmy.org. Website: www.salvationarmy.usawest .org/newfrontier. Salvation Army Western Territory. Robert L. Docter, ed. To share the Good News of the gospel and the work of The Salvation Army in the western territory with Salvationists and friends. Biweekly newspaper; circ. 25,500. Subscription $15. Open to freelance. Prefers query. **NO PAYMENT.** Articles & reviews; no fiction. Not in topical listings. (Ads)

A NEW HEART, PO Box 4004, San Clemente CA 92674-4004. (949) 496-7655. Fax (949) 496-8465. E-mail: HCFUSA@gmail.com. Website: www.HCFUSA.com. Aubrey Beauchamp, ed. For Christian healthcare givers; information regarding medical/Christian issues. Quarterly mag.; 16 pgs.;

circ. 5,000. Subscription $25. 20% unsolicited freelance; 10% assigned. Complete ms/cover letter; phone/fax/e-query OK. **PAYS 2 COPIES** for onetime rts. Not copyrighted. Articles 600-1,800 wds. (20-25/yr.). Responds in 2-3 wks. Accepts simultaneous submissions & reprints. Accepts e-mail submission. Does not use sidebars. Guidelines by mail/fax; copy for 9x12 SAE/3 stamps. (Ads)

Poetry: Accepts 1-2/yr. Submit max. 1-3 poems.

Fillers: Accepts 3-4/yr. Anecdotes, cartoons, facts, jokes, short humor; 100-120 wds.

Columns/Departments: Accepts 20-25/yr. Chaplain's Corner, 200-250 wds. Physician's Corner, 200-250 wds.

Tips: "Most open to real-life situations which may benefit and encourage healthcare givers and patients. True stories with medical and evangelical emphasis."

@NEW IDENTITY MAGAZINE, PO Box 375, Torrrance CA 90508. (310) 947-8707. E-mail: inquiry@newidentitymagazine.com. Website: www.newidentitymagazine.com. Cailin Henson, ed-in-chief. To help new Christians with their new identity in Christ. Quarterly & online mag.; 48-52 pgs. Subscription free online. 50% unsolicited freelance; 50% assigned. Query; e-query OK. Accepts full mss by e-mail. **NO PAYMENT** for 1st rts. Articles 500-4,000 wds. Responds in 1-4 wks. No simultaneous submissions; accepts reprints (tell when/where appeared). Accepts e-mail submissions (attached or copied into message). Uses some sidebars. Prefers NIV, The Message, AMP. Guidelines/copy on Website (scroll to bottom "Writer's Guidelines"). (Ads)

Poetry: Accepts 4-8/yr. Any type or length. Submit max. 4 poems.

Fillers: Ideas, newsbreaks, quotes, tips, events, ordinary Christians doing extraordinary things.

Columns/Departments: See guidelines.

Tips: "Share your perspective, your story or how you're living out your passions and using your gifts."

$@NEW WINESKINS, PO Box 41028, Nashville TN 37204-1028. (615) 292-2940. Fax (615) 292-2931. E-mail: info@wineskins.org. Website: www.wineskins.org. The ZOE Group Inc. Greg Taylor, sr. ed. Combines biblical and cultural scholarly focus with popular-level articles and art for a powerful journal/magazine hybrid. Bimonthly e-zine; 15-20 articles/mo. 50% unsolicited freelance; 50% assigned. Query; e-query preferred. **Pays $50** for online articles by year-end, for onetime and electronic rts. Articles 800-2,500 wds. (100/yr.); fiction 1,000-2,500 wds. (10/yr.); book reviews 800-1,200 wds. ($50). Responds in 1-2 mos. Seasonal 6 mos. ahead. Accepts simultaneous submissions & reprints (tell when/where appeared). Prefers e-mail submissions (attached or copied into message). No kill fee. Sometimes uses sidebars. Also accepts submissions from children/teens. Prefers NIV or NRSV. Guidelines by e-mail/Website ("About Us"/"Writer's Guidelines"); copy on Website. (Ads)

Poetry: Buys 4-5/yr. Avant-garde, free verse, light verse; 100-2,000 wds. Pays $50. Submit max. 1 poem.

Tips: "Best way to break in is by reviewing books, specifically ones we request. Also by writing well-shaped and well-researched pieces that are more than just opinions."

**This periodical was #24 on the 2010 Top 50 Christian Publishers list (#38 in 2009).

NOSTALGIA, PO Box 203, Spokane WA 99210-0203. (509) 299-4041. E-mail: editor@NostalgiaMagazine.net. Website: www.nostalgiamagazine.net. King's Publishing Group Inc. Mark Carter, ed. We provide a forum for baby boomers and before to share photos and stories of yesterday that enrich life today; we use exclusively dated images/photos. Bimonthly mag.; 48 pgs. Subscription $19.95. 90% unsolicited freelance; 10% assigned. Complete ms/cover letter; e-query OK. **PAYS COPIES** on publication for 1st, onetime, reprint, simultaneous, or electronic rts. Articles 400-1,500 wds. (150/yr.). Responds in up to 1 yr. Seasonal 4 mos. ahead. Accepts simultaneous submissions & reprints (tell when/where appeared). Prefers e-mail submissions (attached or copied into message). No kill fee. Regularly uses sidebars. Guidelines by mail/e-mail/Website ("Send Us Your Story"/"Writer's Guidelines"); query for themes/topics; copy $5/9x12 SAE. (Ads)

Special needs: Photos and family memories from 1940s, 1950s, and 1960s.

Tips: "Looking for personal family memories with interesting photos: traveling, camping, working together. Specific episodes are better than generalities (400-2,000 wds., 1 photo/400 wds.). Dig out a great fun photo showing people engaged in life, write a caption, submit. No genealogies. Send us a first-person account showing everyday life from the years 1950-1968, with great photos."

$@NOW WHAT? Box 33677, Denver CO 80233. (303) 452-7973. Fax (303) 452-0657. E-mail: now what@cog7.org. Website: http://nowwhat.cog7.org. Church of God (Seventh-day). Sherri Langton, assoc. ed. Articles on salvation, Jesus, social issues, life problems, that are seeker sensitive. Monthly online mag.; available only online. 100% unsolicited freelance. Complete ms/cover letter; no query. **Pays $25-55** on publication for first, onetime, electronic, simultaneous, or reprint rts. Articles 1,000-1,500 wds. (20/yr.). Responds in 4-10 wks. Accepts simultaneous submissions & reprints (tell when/where appeared). Accepts requested ms by e-mail. Regularly uses sidebars. Prefers NIV. Guidelines by mail/Website ("Send Us Your Story"); copy of online article for #10 SAE/1 stamp. (No ads)

    Special needs: "Personal experiences must show a person's struggle that either brought him/her to Christ or deepened faith in God. The entire Now What? site is built around a personal experience each month."

    Tips: "The whole e-zine is open to freelance. Think how you can explain your faith, or how you overcame a problem, to a non-Christian. It's a real plus for writers submitting a personal experience to also submit an objective article related to their story. Or they can contact Sherri Langton for upcoming personal experiences that need related articles."

($)@NRB MAGAZINE, 9510 Technology Dr., Manassas VA 20110-4167. (703) 330-7000. Fax (703) 330-7100. E-mail: info@nrb.org or through Website: www.nrb.org. National Religious Broadcasters. Laurel MacLeod, sr. ed. Topics relate to Christian radio, television, satellite, church media, Internet, and all forms of communication; promoting access and excellence in Christian communications. Monthly (9X) & online mag.; 52 pgs.; circ. 9,300. Subscription $24; Canadians add $6 U.S.; foreign add $24 U.S. 70% unsolicited freelance. Complete ms/cover letter; fax/e-query OK. **PAYS 6 COPIES ($100-200 for assigned)** on publication for 1st or reprint rts. Articles 1,000-2,000 wds. (30/yr.). Responds in 6 wks. Seasonal 6 mos. ahead. Accepts simultaneous submissions & reprints (tell when/where appeared). Prefers accepted ms by e-mail. Regularly uses sidebars. Prefers NAS. Guidelines/theme list by mail/e-mail; free copy. (Ads)

    Columns/Departments: Valerie Fraedrich, asst. ed. Accepts 9/yr. Trade Talk (summary paragraphs of news items/events in Christian broadcasting), 50 wds. Opinion (social issues), 750 wds. Columns coordinated in-house, 500 wds.

    Special needs: Electronic media; education. All articles must relate in some way to broadcasting: radio, TV, programs on radio/TV, or Internet.

    Tips: "Most open to feature articles relevant to Christian communicators. Become acquainted with broadcasters in your area and note their struggles, concerns, and victories. Find out what they would like to know, research the topic, then write about it." Contact assistant editor for guidelines, reprint permission, classified ads, additional copies, etc.

$@ON MISSION, 4200 North Point Pkwy., Alpharetta GA 30022-4176. (770) 410-6382. Fax (770) 410-6105. E-mail: onmission@namb.net. Website: www.onmission.com. North American Mission Board, Southern Baptist. Carol Pipes, ed. Helping readers share Christ in the real world. Quarterly & online mag.; 32 pgs.; circ. 200,000. Subscription free. 1-5% unsolicited freelance; 50-60% assigned. Query (complete ms for fiction); no phone/fax query; e-query OK. Accepts full mss by e-mail. **Pays .25/wd.** on acceptance for 1st rts. Articles 500-1,000 wds. (20/yr.). Responds in 8 wks. Seasonal 8 mos. ahead. No simultaneous submissions or reprints. Accepts e-mail submissions (attached or copied into message). Kill fee. Regularly uses sidebars. Prefers HCSB. Guidelines by mail/e-mail/ Website (put "Writers Guidelines" in search box); copy for 9x12 SAE/$2.38 postage. (Ads)

Columns/Departments: Buys 4-8/yr. The Pulse (outreach/missions ideas); 500 wds. Query. **Special needs:** Needs articles on these topics: sharing your faith, interviews/profiles of missionaries, starting churches, volunteering in missions, sending missionaries.

Tips: "We are primarily a Southern Baptist publication reaching out to Southern Baptist pastors and laypeople, equipping them to share Christ, start churches, volunteer in missions, and impact the culture. Write a solid, 750-word, how-to article geared to 20- to 40-year-old men and women who want fresh ideas and insight into sharing Christ in the real world in which they live, work, and play. Send a résumé, along with your best writing samples. We are an on-assignment magazine, but occasionally a well-written manuscript gets published." ** 2010, 2007, 2006 EPA Award of Merit: Missionary.

@OREGON FAITH REPORT.COM., (503) 644-1300. E-mail: oregon@oregonreport.com. Website: www.oregonfaithreport.com. A daily Web magazine that features the latest local religion news that is missed by the local newspaper. Jason Williams, pub. Online. Open to unsolicited freelance. **NO PAYMENT.** Articles. Complete mss by e-mail.

Tips: "We're looking for guest opinion pieces on news related to topics and insightful commentary on the issues facing Oregonians. This is an opportunity for Oregon writers to get their articles circulated and build a support base of readers."

$OUR SUNDAY VISITOR, 200 Noll Plaza, Huntington IN 46750. Toll-free (800) 348-2440. (260) 356-8400. Fax (260) 356-8472. E-mail: oursunvis@osv.com. Website: www.osv.com. Catholic. John Norton, ed.; Sarah Hayes, article ed. Vital news analysis, perspective, spirituality for today's Catholic. Weekly newspaper; 24 pgs.; circ. 68,000. 10% unsolicited freelance; 90% assigned. Query or complete ms; fax/e-query OK. **Pays $100-800** within 4 wks. of acceptance for 1st & electronic rts. Articles 500-3,500 wds. (25/yr.). Responds in 4-6 wks. Seasonal 2 mos. ahead. No simultaneous submissions; rarely accepts reprints (tell when/where appeared). Kill fee. Regularly uses sidebars. Prefers RSV. Guidelines by mail/e-mail/Website (click on "About Us"/"Writers' Guidelines" in left column); copy for $2/10x13 SAE/$1 postage. (Ads)

Columns/Departments: Faith; Family; Trends; Profile; Heritage; Media; Q & A. See guidelines for details.

Tips: "Our mission is to examine the news, culture, and trends of the day from a faithful and sound Catholic perspective—to see the world through the eyes of faith. Especially interested in writers able to do news analysis (with a minimum of 3 sources), or news features." ** This periodical was #11 on the 2009 Top 50 Christian Publishers list (#48 in 2006).

+OVERFLOW MAGAZINE, PO Box 842197, Houston TX 77284-2197. E-mail: allthat3@peoplepc .com. Deborah Elum, ed.

$OVER THE BACK FENCE, PO Box 756, Chillicothe OH 45601. Toll-free (800) 718-5727. Fax (330) 220-3083. E-mail: SWilliamson@glpublishing.com or through Website: www.backfencemagazine .com. Long Point Media. Sarah Williamson, ed. Positive news about southern Ohio. Bimonthly mag.; 74 pgs.; circ. 15,000. Subscription $13.95. 60% unsolicited freelance. Query/clips; fax/e-query OK. **Pays .15-.20/wd. (.10/wd. for fiction)** on publication for onetime rts. Articles 750-1,000 wds. (9-12/yr.); fiction 300-850 wds. (8/yr.). Responds in 12 wks. Seasonal 1 yr. ahead. Accepts simultaneous submissions & reprints (tell when/where appeared). Requires requested ms on disk or by e-mail (copied into message). Regularly uses sidebars. Guidelines by mail/Website ("Submissions"); copy $4/9x12 SAE or on Website. (Ads)

Columns/Departments: Buys 8/yr. Memory Lane (interesting history that never made the headlines), 800-1,000 wds. Heartstrings (touching essays), 800 wds. Shorts (humorous essays), 800 wds. Complete ms. Pays $80-120.

Special needs: Think upbeat and positive. Articles on nature, history, travel, nostalgia, and family.

Tips: "We need material for our columns most often—Humorous Shorts, Memory Lane, and Heartstrings. It is best for writers to send things with appeal for Midwest readers and be generally positive. We do not publish articles that criticize or create a negative feeling about a geographical area or people."

** This periodical was #49 on the 2010 Top 50 Christian Publishers list.

THE OZARKS CHRISTIAN NEWS, 149 Grand Ave., Branson MO 65616. Phone/fax (417) 336-3636. E-mail: editor@ozarkschristiannews.com. Website: www.OzarksChristianNews.com. John Sacoulas, ed. Celebrating the common ground in the body of Christ. Monthly newspaper; circ. 20,000. Subscription $30. Open to unsolicited freelance. Complete ms. Articles & reviews. Incomplete topical listings. (Ads)

$OZARKS SENIOR LIVING NEWSPAPER, 2010 S. Steward, Springfield MO 65804. (417) 862-0852. Fax (417) 862-9079. E-mail: seniorliving@sbcglobal.net. Website: www.slnewspaper.net. Metropolitan Radio Group Inc. Joyce Yonker O'Neal, mng. ed. Positive, upbeat paper for people 55+; includes religious articles. Monthly newspaper; 40 pgs.; circ. 40,000. 25-50% unsolicited freelance. Query or complete ms/cover letter; no phone/fax/e-query. **Pays $20-35 for assigned; $5-35 for unsolicited**; 30 days after publication for 1st, reprint, electronic rts. Articles 600 wds. (65/yr.). Responds in 2-5 wks. Seasonal 4 mos. ahead. Guidelines by mail/Website ("Writer's Guides" left side); copy for 9x12 SAE/5 stamps.

$@PARENTLIFE and PARENTLIFE ONLINE, One Lifeway Plaza, Nashville TN 37234-0172. (615) 251-2196. Fax (615) 277-8142. E-mail: parentlife@lifeway.com. Website: www.lifeway.com/parent life. Blog: www.lifeway.com/parentlifeblog. LifeWay Christian Resources. Jodi Skulley, ed. (jodi.skul ley@lifeway.com). A child-centered magazine for parents of children 12 and under. Monthly & online mag.; 52 pgs.; circ. 72,000. Subscription $22.95. 5% unsolicited freelance; 95% assigned. Query; e-query OK. Accepts full mss by e-mail. **Pays $150-500** on acceptance for nonexclusive rts. Articles 500-1,500 wds. (60/yr.). Responds in 6 mos. Seasonal 1 yr. ahead. Accepts simultaneous submissions; no reprints. Prefers e-mail submissions (attached file). No kill fee. Regularly uses sidebars. Prefers HCSB. Guidelines/theme list by mail/e-mail/Website; copy for 10x13 SASE. (Ads)

Columns/Departments: Buys 60/yr. A Healthy Life (parent health issues), to 500 wds. On the Way (expectant-parent topics), to 500 wds. The Funny Life (funny family stories), 100 wds. Single Parent Life, to 500 wds. Working Life, to 500 wds. Pays $20-150. Query.

Tips: "Most open to feature articles, articles on single parents, working parents, expectant parents. Fill out the online application: www.lifeway.com/people, and then submit article ideas to editor after application is completed."

**This periodical was #14 on the 2010 Top 50 Christian Publishers list (#13 in 2009).

$@THE PATHWAY, 400 E. High St., Jefferson City MO 65101. (573) 635-7931. Toll-free fax (800) 736-6227, ext. 230. E-mail: dhinkle@mobaptist.org. Website: www.mbcpathway.com. Missouri Baptist Convention. Don Hinkle, ed. For Missouri Southern Baptists. Biweekly & online tabloid; 20 pgs; circ. 15,000. Subscription $10. 1% unsolicited freelance; 20% assigned. Query; phone/fax/e-query OK. **Pays $50-200** for all rts. Articles 700-800 wds. (30/yr.). Responds in 2 wks. Seasonal 2 mos. ahead. Accepts simultaneous submissions & reprints (tell when/where appeared). Accepts disk or e-mail submissions (attached or copied into message). No kill fee. Uses some sidebars. Prefers NIV/KJV/NAS.

THE PEGASUS REVIEW, PO Box 88, Henderson MD 21640-0088. (410) 482-6736. E-mail: editor @pegasus review.com. Art Bounds, ed. Theme-oriented poetry, short fiction, and essays; not necessarily religious; in calligraphy format. Quarterly mag.; 12-14 pgs.; circ. 150. Subscription $12. 100%

unsolicited freelance. Query or complete ms/cover letter (include background); e-query OK. No complete mss by e-mail. **PAYS 2 COPIES** for onetime rts. Fiction (2.5 pgs.) is ideal, single-spaced (6-10/yr.); also one-page essays. Responds in 4 wks. Accepts simultaneous submissions & reprints (tell when/where appeared). No disk or e-mail submissions. Does not use sidebars. Also accepts submissions from teens. Prefers KJV. Guidelines/theme list by e-mail; copy $2.50. (No ads)

Poetry: Accepts 40-50/yr. Free verse, haiku, traditional; 5-25 lines (shorter the better; pay attention to line length). Theme oriented. Submit max. 3 poems.

Fillers: Accepts 20/yr. Cartoons, prose, quotes; 100-150 wds.

Special needs: 2011 themes: January—Memories; April—Parents; July—Our Earth; October—On Poetry and Reading. (These are subject to change.)

Tips: "Keep improving your craft and adhere to guidelines. Things change, but quality survives. Continue to persevere."

$@PENTECOSTAL EVANGEL, (formerly *Today's Pentecostal Evangel*), 1445 N. Boonville, Springfield MO 65802-1894. (417) 862-2781. Fax (417) 862-0416. E-mail: pe@ag.org. Website: www.pe.ag.org. Assemblies of God. Ken Horn, ed.; submit to Scott Harrup, sr. assoc. ed. Assemblies of God. Weekly & online mag.; 32 pgs.; circ. 170,000. Subscription $28.99. 5% unsolicited freelance; 95% assigned. Complete ms/cover letter; no phone/fax/e-query. Accepts full mss by e-mail. **Pays .06/ wd. (.04/wd. for reprints)** on acceptance for 1st & electronic rts. Articles 500-1,200 wds. (10-15/yr.); testimonies 200-300 wds. Responds in 6-8 wks. Seasonal 6-8 mos. ahead. No simultaneous submissions; accepts reprints (tell when/where appeared). Kill fee 100%. Prefers e-mail submissions (attached file). Uses some sidebars. Prefers NIV, KJV. Guidelines on Website (click on "Writer's Guidelines" just under "Customer Service" & "Media"); copy for 9x12 SAE/$1.39 postage. (Ads)

Fillers: Anecdotes, facts, personal experience, testimonies; 250-500 wds. Practical, how-to pieces on family life, devotions, evangelism, seasonal, current issues, Christian living; 250 wds. Pays about $25.

Special needs: "The *Pentecostal Evangel* offers a free e-mail/online devotional, *Daily Boost.* Contributors are not paid, but a number of these writers have been published in the magazine."

Tips: "True, first-person inspirational material is the best bet for a first-time contributor. We reserve any controversial subjects for writers we're familiar with. Positive family-life articles work well near Father's Day, Mother's Day, and holidays."
**2010 EPA Award of Excellence: Denominational.

THE PENTECOSTAL MESSENGER, PO Box 850, Joplin MO 64802. (417) 624-7050. Fax (417) 624-7102. E-mail: charlotteb@pcg.org, or johnm@pcg.org. Website: www.pcg.org. Pentecostal Church of God. General Bishop Charles G. Scott, ed-in-chief; General Secretary Wayman C. Ming Jr., exec. ed.; Brian Ramos, production mngr.; Peggy Allen, Charlotte Beal, Rebecca Bogle, Bret Lyerla, John Mallinak, Kimberly Ming, Brooke Skiles, Scott Yearton, editorial/production staff. Denominational publication; ministry resource. Monthly (11X) mag.; circ. 5,000. Subscription $12. Accepts freelance. Prefers query. Complete ms. Articles. Copy $1.50. Not in topical listings. (Ads)
** 2009 Award of Excellence: Most Improved Publication.

THE PENWOOD REVIEW, PO Box 862, Los Alamitos CA 90720-0862. E-mail: submissions@ penwoodreview.com. Website: www.penwoodreview.com. Lori Cameron, ed. Poetry, plus thought-provoking essays on poetry, literature, and the role of spirituality and religion in the literary arts. Biannual jour.; 40+ pgs.; circ. 80-100. Subscription $16. 100% unsolicited freelance. Complete ms; no e-query. **NO PAYMENT** ($2 off subscription & 1 free copy), for onetime and electronic rts. Articles 1 pg. (single-spaced). Responds in 9-12 wks. Prefers requested ms by e-mail (copied into message). Guidelines by mail/e-mail/Website ("Info"/"Submissions"); copy $8.

Poetry: Accepts 120-160/yr. Any type, including formalist; to 2 pgs. Submit max. 5 poems.

Special needs: Faith and the literary arts; religion and literature. Needs essays (up to 2 pgs., single-spaced).

Tips: "We publish poetry almost exclusively and are looking for well-crafted, disciplined poetry, not doggerel or greeting-card-style poetry. Poets should study poetry, read it extensively, and send us their best, most original work. Visit our Website or buy a copy for an idea of what we publish."

@PERSPECTIVES: A Journal of Reformed Thought, 4500—60th Ave. S.E., Grand Rapids MI 49512. (616) 392-8555, ext. 131. Fax (616) 392-7717. E-mail: perspectives@rca.org. Website: www.perspectivesjournal.org. Reformed Church Press. Dr. Scott Hoezee, Dr. James Bratt, and Steve Mathonnet-VanderWell, eds. To express the Reformed faith theologically; to engage issues that Reformed Christians meet in personal, ecclesiastical, and societal life; and thus to contribute to the mission of the church of Jesus Christ. Monthly (10X) & online mag.; 24 pgs.; circ. 3,000. Subscription $30. 75% unsolicited freelance; 25% assigned. Complete ms/cover letter or query; fax/e-query OK. **PAYS 6 COPIES** for 1st rts. Articles (10/yr.) and fiction (3/yr.), 2,500-3,000 wds.; reviews 1,000 wds. Responds in 20 wks. Seasonal 10 mos. ahead. Accepts reprints (tell when/ where appeared). Prefers requested ms by e-mail (attached file). Uses some sidebars. Prefers NRSV. Guidelines on Website ("About Us"/"Writer's Guidelines"); no copy. (Ads)

> **Poetry:** Accepts 2-3/yr. Traditional. Submit max. 3 poems. Hard copy only to above address.
> **Columns/Departments:** Accepts 12/yr. As We See It (editorial/opinion), 750-1,000 wds. Inside Out (biblical exegesis), 750 wds. Complete ms.
> **Tips:** "Most open to feature-length articles. Must be theologically informed, whatever the topic. Avoid party-line thinking and culture-war approaches. I would say that a reading of past issues and a desire to join in a contemporary conversation on the Christian faith would help you break in here. Also the 'As We See It' column is a good place to start."

PERSPECTIVES ON SCIENCE & CHRISTIAN FAITH, PO Box 668, Ipswich MA 01938. (978) 356-5656. Fax (978) 356-4375. E-mail: asa@asa3.org. Website: www.asa3.org. American Scientific Affiliation. Submit to Arie Leegwater, ed. (Calvin College, 1726 Knollcrest Cir. S.E., Grand Rapids MI 49546; leeg@calvin.edu). Quarterly journal; 72 pgs.; circ. 2,000+. Subscription $40/yr. 75% unsolicited freelance; 25% assigned. E-query. Accepts full mss by e-mail. **NO PAYMENT.** Articles 6,000 wds. (20/yr.). Responds in 2 wks. Seasonal 4 mos. ahead. No simultaneous submissions or reprints. Accepts submissions by disk or e-mail (attached file). Regularly uses sidebars. Guidelines on Website (click on "Publications"/"ASA Journal PSCF"/"About PSCF"/"Instructions to Authors").

> **Special needs:** Science and faith; bioethics.
> **Tips:** "Freelancers must have credentials to write about their subjects, i.e., advanced degree in science or theology. Article must be well-researched and will be peer-reviewed."

$POINT, 2002 S. Arlington Heights Rd., Arlington Heights IL 60005-4102. Toll-free (800) 323-4215, ext. 3217. (847) 879-3217. Fax (847) 228-5376. E-mail: bobputman@convergeworldwide .org. Website: www.convergeworldwide.org. Converge Worldwide/Baptist General Conference. Bob Putman, ed. Almost exclusively by, for, and about the people and ministries of the Converge Worldwide (Baptist General Conference). Bimonthly mag.; 16 pgs.; circ. 45,000. Subscription free. 5% unsolicited freelance; 95% assigned. Query/clips; e-query preferred. **Pays $60-280** on publication for 1st, reprint, electronic rts. Articles 300-1,400 wds. (20-30/yr.). Responds in 5-9 wks. Seasonal 6 mos. ahead. Accepts simultaneous submissions & reprints (tell when/where appeared). Prefers accepted mss by e-mail (attached file). Kill fee 50%. No sidebars. Prefers NIV. Guidelines/ theme list by mail/e-mail; free copy for #10 SAE. (Ads)

> **Columns/Departments:** Buys 30/yr. Converge Connection (short news blurbs of happenings in Converge churches), 75-250 wds. New Life (first-person or "as-told-to" story of Converge church member transformation or church transformation), 750-1,400 wds.

Tips: "To break in, report on interesting happenings/ministry in Converge (BGC) churches close to you for our Converge Connection column."
** 2007 EPA Award of Excellence: Denominational. This periodical was #37 on the 2010 Top 50 Christian Publishers list (#47 in 2008, #50 in 2007).

$POWER FOR LIVING, MS #104—Manuscript Submission, 4050 Lee Vance View, Colorado Springs CO 80918. Toll-free (800) 708-5550. (719) 536-0100. Fax (719) 535-2928. Website: www.cook ministries.org. Cook Communications/Scripture Press Publications. Don Alban Jr., ed. To expressly demonstrate the relevance of specific biblical teachings to everyday life via reader-captivating profiles of exceptional Christians. Weekly take-home paper; 8 pgs.; circ. 250,000. Subscription $3.99/quarter. 15% unsolicited freelance; 85% assigned. Complete ms; no phone/fax/e-query. **Pays up to .15/wd. (reprints up to .10/wd.)** on acceptance for onetime rts. Profiles 700-1,500 wds. (20/yr.). Responds in 10 wks. Seasonal 1 yr. ahead. Accepts simultaneous submissions & reprints (tell when/where appeared). Accepts requested ms on disk. Kill fee. Requires KJV. Guidelines on Website (click on "About David C. Cook"/"Writers Guidelines"); copy for #10 SAE/1 stamp (Use address above, but change to MS #205—Sample Request). (No ads)
> **Special needs:** "Third-person profiles of truly out-of-the-ordinary Christians who express their faith uniquely. We use very little of anything else."
> **Tips:** "Most open to vignettes, 450-1,500 wds. of prominent Christians with solid testimonies or profiles from church history. Focus on the unusual. Signed releases required." Not currently open to freelance submissions; check Website for any changes.

$PRAIRIE MESSENGER: Catholic Journal, PO Box 190, Muenster SK S0K 2Y0, Canada. (306) 682-1772. Fax (306) 682-5285. E-mail: pm.canadian@stpeterspress.ca. Website: www.prairiemes senger.ca. Catholic/Benedictine Monks of St. Peter's Abbey. Peter Novecosky, OSB, ed.; Maureen Weber, assoc. ed. For Catholics in Saskatchewan and Manitoba, and Christians in other faith communities. Weekly tabloid (46X); 20 pgs.; circ. 6,300. Subscription $32 Cdn. 10% unsolicited freelance; 90% assigned. Complete ms/cover letter; phone/fax/e-query OK. **Pays $55 ($2.75/column inch for news items)** on publication for 1st, onetime, simultaneous, reprint rts. Not copyrighted. Articles 800-900 wds. (15/yr.). Responds in 9 wks. Seasonal 3 mos. ahead. Accepts simultaneous submissions & reprints. Regularly uses sidebars. Guidelines by e-mail/Website (scroll down left side to "Writers' Guidelines"); copy for 9x12 SAE/$1 Cdn./$1.39 U.S. postage. (Ads)
> **Poetry:** Accepts 15/yr. Avant-garde, free verse, haiku, light verse; 3-30 lines. Pays $20 Cdn.
> **Columns/Departments:** Accepts 5/yr. Pays $55 Cdn.
> **Special needs:** Ecumenism; social justice; native concerns.
> **Tips:** "Comment/feature section is most open; send good reflection column of about 800 words; topic of concern or interest to Prairie readership. It's difficult to break into our publication. Piety not welcome." This publication is limited pretty much to Canadian writers only.

THE PRAYER CLOSET, PO Box 278, Hickory, MS 39332. (601) 646-2295. E-mail: info@prayercloset ministries.org. Website: www.prayerclosetministries.org. Dr. Kevin Meador, ed. Challenges and equips believers in the areas of prayer, fasting, spiritual warfare, journaling, and healing. Monthly newsletter; circ. 3,000. Free subscription online. **PAYS IN COPIES.** Prefers NKJV. Guidelines by mail.
> **Tips:** "We are looking for sound, biblically based articles concerning the indicated topics (see topical listings)."

@PRAYERWORKS, PO Box 301363, Portland OR 97294. (503) 761-2072. E-mail: VannM1@aol .com. Website: www.prayerworksnw.org. The Master's Work. V. Ann Mandeville, ed. For prayer warriors in retirement centers; focuses on prayer. Weekly newspaper and online (soon); 4 pgs.; circ. 1,500. Subscription free. 100% unsolicited freelance. Complete ms. **PAYS IN COPIES/SUBSCRIPTION** for onetime rts. Not copyrighted. Articles (30-40/yr.) & fiction (30/yr.); 350-500 wds. Responds in

3 wks. Seasonal 2 mos. ahead. Accepts simultaneous submissions & reprints. Does not use sidebars. Guidelines by mail; copy for #10 SAE/1 stamp. (No ads)

Poetry: Accepts 20-30/yr. Free verse, haiku, light verse, traditional. Submit max. 10 poems.

Fillers: Accepts up to 50/yr. Facts, jokes, prayers, quotes, short humor; to 50 wds.

Tips: "Write tight and well. Half our audience is over 70, but 30% is young families. Subject matter isn't important as long as it is scriptural and designed to help people pray. Have a strong, catchy takeaway."

$PRECEPTS FOR LIVING, Annual Sunday School Commentary, PO Box 436987, Chicago IL 60643. E-mail: ecarey@urbanministries.com. Website: www.urbanministries.com. Urban Ministries Inc. Dr. Vincent Bacote, ed; submit to Evangeline Carey, developmental ed. *Precepts for Living* is a verse-by-verse Sunday School commentary geared toward an African American adult audience. Word studies are presented in the original Greek and Hebrew languages to further illuminate understanding of the text. KJV Scriptures. 500 pgs. Strict adherence to guidelines. Query/writing samples & clips; e-query OK. Lessons are assigned. **Pays $200** per Bible Study lesson and $300 for More Light on the Text, a verse-by-verse commentary which includes Greek and Hebrew word studies, 120 days after acceptance, for all rts. Requires accepted ms by e-mail (attached).

Tips: "Must be able to write adult Christian curriculum. Send résumé, including educational experience. Should be astute in biblical education and how to correctly exegete Scripture."

$THE PRESBYTERIAN OUTLOOK, Box 85623, Richmond VA 23285-5623. Toll-free (800) 446-6008. (804) 359-8442. Fax (804) 353-6369. E-mail: jhaberer@pres-outlook.org. Website: www.pres-outlook.org. Presbyterian Church (USA)/Independent. Jack Haberer, ed.; Roy Howard, book review ed. For ministers, members, and staff of the denomination. Biweekly mag.; 32 pgs.; circ. 10,000. Subscription $49.95. 5% unsolicited freelance; 95% assigned. Query; phone/fax/e-query OK. **Payment varies** for all rts. Not copyrighted. Articles/fiction to 1,000 wds.; book reviews 1 pg. Responds in 1-2 wks. Seasonal 2 mos. ahead. Accepts e-mail submissions. Uses some sidebars. Prefers NRSV. Guidelines by mail/e-mail; free copy. (Ads)

Tips: "Correspond (mail or e-mail) with editor regarding current needs; most open to features. Most material is commissioned; anything submitted should be of interest to Presbyterian church leaders."

$PRESBYTERIANS TODAY, 100 Witherspoon St., Louisville KY 40202-1396. Toll-free (800) 227-2872. (502) 569-5000. Toll-free fax (800) 541-5113. (502) 569-8632. E-mail: today@pcusa.org. Website: www.pcusa.org/today. Presbyterian Church (USA). Eva Stimson, ed.; John Sniffen, assoc. ed. Denominational; not as conservative or evangelical as some. Monthly (10X) mag.; 48 pgs.; circ. 58,000. Subscription $19.95. 25% freelance. Query or complete ms/cover letter; phone/fax/e-query OK. **Pays $75-300** on acceptance for 1st rts. Articles 800-2,000 wds. (prefers 1,000-1,500); (20/yr.). Also uses short features 250-600 wds. Responds in 2-5 wks. Seasonal 3 mos. ahead. Few reprints. Accepts requested ms on disk or by e-mail. Kill fee 50%. Prefers NRSV. Guidelines on Website: www.pcusa.org/today/guidelines/guidelines.htm; free copy. (Ads)

Fillers: Cartoons, $25; and short humor to 150 wds. No payment.

Tips: "Most open to feature articles about Presbyterians—individuals, churches with special outreach, creative programs, or mission work. Do not often use inspirational or testimony-type articles."

** This periodical was #40 on the 2006 Top 50 Christian Publishers list.

$@PRIORITY! 440 W. Nyack Rd., West Nyack NY 10994. (845) 620-7450. Fax (845) 620-7723. E-mail: linda_johnson@use.salvationarmy.org. Website: www.prioritypeople.org. The Salvation Army. Linda D. Johnson, ed.; Robert Mitchell, assoc. ed. Quarterly & online mag.; 48-56 pgs.; circ. 28,000. Subscription $8.95. 50% assigned. Query/clips; e-query OK. **Pays $200-800** on acceptance for 1st rts. Articles 400-1,700 wds. (8-10/yr.). All articles assigned. Responds in 2 wks. Occasionally buys reprints (tell when/where appeared). Prefers accepted ms by e-mail (in Word or copied into message). Kill fee 50%. Regularly uses sidebars. Prefers NIV. Occasionally buys submissions from children/teens. Guidelines/theme list by e-mail; copy $1/9x12 SAE. (Ads)

> **Columns/Departments:** Buys 5-10/yr. Prayer Power (stories about answered prayer, or harnessing prayer power); Who's News (calling attention to specific accomplishments or missions); My Take (opinion essay); all 400-700 wds. $200-400. Query.
>
> **Special needs:** All articles must have a connection to The Salvation Army. Can be from any part of the U.S. Looking especially for freelancers with Salvation Army connections; Christmas recollections (by August 1); people/program features.
>
> **Tips:** "Most open to features on people. Every article, whether about people or programs, tells a story and must feature the Salvation Army. Stories focus on evangelism, holiness, prayer. The more a writer knows about The Salvation Army, the better."
>
> **This publication was #11 on the 2010 Top 50 Christian Publishers List.

PRISCILLA PAPERS, 122 W. Franklin Ave., Ste. 218, Minneapolis MN 55404-2451. Send submissions to editor at: 130 Essex St., Gordon-Conwell Theological Seminary, S. Hamilton MA 01982. (612) 872-6898. Fax (612) 872-6891. E-mail: debbeattymel@aol.com. Website: www.cbeinternational.org. Christians for Biblical Equality. William David Spencer, ed.; Deb Beatty Mel, assoc. ed. Addresses biblical interpretation and its relationship to women and men sharing authority and ministering together equally, not according to gender, ethnicity, or class but according to God's gifting. Quarterly jour.; 32 pgs.; circ. 2,000. Subscription $40 (includes subscription to *Mutuality*). 85% unsolicited freelance; 15% assigned. Query preferred; e-query OK. **PAYS 3 COPIES, PLUS A GIFT CERTIFICATE AT CBE'S MINISTRY** for 1st & electronic rts. Articles 600-5,000 wds. (1/yr.); no fiction; book reviews 600 wds. (free book). Slow and careful response. No reprints. Seasonal 12 mos. ahead. Prefers proposed ms on disk or by e-mail (attached file) with hard copy. No kill fee. Uses some sidebars. Guidelines on Website; copy for 9x12 SAE/$2.07 postage. (Ads)

> **Poetry:** Accepts 1/yr. Avant-garde, free verse, traditional (on biblical gender equality themes); pays a free book.
>
> **Tips:** "P.P. is the academic voice of CBE. Our target is the informed lay reader. All sections are open to freelancers. Any well-written, single-theme article (no potpourri) presenting a solid exegetical and hermeneutical approach to biblical equality from a high view of Scripture will be considered for publication." Seeks original cover art work. Use *Chicago Manual of Style*.

$PRISM: America's Alternative Evangelical Voice, 6 E. Lancaster Ave., Wynnewood PA 19096-3495. (484) 384-2990. Fax (610) 649-3834. E-mail: kristyn@esa-online.org. Website: www.esa-online.org/prism. Evangelicals for Social Action. Kristyn Komarnicki, ed. For Christians who are interested in the social and political dimensions of the gospel. Bimonthly mag.; 40 pgs.; circ. 2,500. Subscription $35. 50% unsolicited freelance. Complete ms/cover letter; e-query OK. Accepts full mss by e-mail (copied into message). **Pays $75-450** on publication for 1st & electronic rts. Articles 1,500-3,000 wds. (10-12/yr.); no fiction; book reviews, 500 wds. ($75). Responds within 12 wks. Seasonal 9 mos. ahead. No reprints. Regularly uses sidebars. Prefers NRSV. Guidelines by e-mail/Website ("Review Prism"/"Writers' Guidelines" right side); copy $3. (Ads)

> **Tips:** "Open to features on social justice issues (profiles of cutting-edge and/or particularly effective holistic ministries) and on living out the Christian faith within contemporary culture. Understand progressive evangelicals and E.S.A. Read Tony Campolo, Ron Sider, and Richard Foster. Most open to features. We don't assign work to writers we haven't published before, so send a full manuscript."
>
> ** 2008 Award of Merit: Organizational.

+PRISON VICTORY, PO Box 790, Quinlan TX 754764. (607) 742-3407. E-mail: articles@christianmotorsports.com, or through Website: www.prisonvictory.org. CPO Publishing. Roland Osborne, pub. A prison ministry of Christian Motorsports Magazine. 50% unsolicited freelance. Complete ms; e-query OK. **PAYS IN COPIES.** Articles 650-1,200 wds. (30/yr.). Seasonal 4 mos. ahead. Requires requested ms by e-mail or through Website. Regularly uses sidebars. Guidelines on Website ("Submit Your Story"). (Ads)

Fillers: Accepts 100/yr. Anecdotes, cartoons, facts, games, ideas, jokes, newsbreaks, prayers, prose, quizzes, quotes, short humor.

Columns/Departments: Accepts 10/yr.

Tips: "Relevant photos to accompany article required. Browse Website and read one of our mags. to get a flavor for the publication."

+@PRODIGAL MAGAZINE, E-mail: jasonwenell@gmail.com. Website: http://prodigalmagazine .com. Jason Wenell, ed-in-chief. Online mag. E-query editor with your writing history, topical interest, and short bio. A place for men after God's heart to find informative, relevant, cutting-edge information on lifestyle, relationships, career, pop culture, and their walk with God; primary target is 17- to 40-year-olds; secondary target 40+. **NO PAYMENT for now.** Profiles 300-1,000 wds.; Question of the Week, 500-1,500 wds.; devotions 500-1,000 wds.; relationships 500-1,500 wds.; Career & Money 500-1,000 wds.; news 500-1,500 wds.; reviews 400-1,000 wds. Guidelines at http://prodigal magazine.com/write; copy online.

$PSYCHOLOGY FOR LIVING, 250 W. Colorado Blvd., Ste. 200, Arcadia CA 91007. (626) 821-8400. Fax (626) 821-8409. E-mail: editor@ncfliving.org. Website: www.ncfliving.org. Narramore Christian Foundation. Robert & Melanie Whitcomb, eds. Addresses issues of everyday life from a Christian and psychological viewpoint. Quarterly mag.; 8 pgs. (one issue 24 pgs.); circ. 7,000. Subscription free to donors or for a $20 donation. Open to freelance. Complete ms/cover letter; fax OK, e-query preferred. **Pays $75-200,** plus a subscription, on publication for 1st, onetime, or reprint rts. Articles 1,000-1,700 wds. Responds in 2-4 wks. Seasonal 4 mos. ahead. Accepts reprints (tell when/where appeared). Prefers accepted ms by e-mail (attached file). Uses some sidebars. Prefers NIV. Guidelines on Website (click on "Printed Literature"/"Psychology for Living Magazine"/ scroll down to "Writers Guidelines" box); free copy. (No ads)

Tips: "Tell a story or illustration that shows how a psychological/emotional problem was dealt with in a biblical and psychologically sound manner. Not preachy."

$PURPOSE, 616 Walnut Ave., Scottdale PA 15683-1999. (620) 367-8432. Fax (724) 887-3111. E-mail: PurposeEditor@mpn.net. Website: www.mpn.net. Mennonite Publishing Network/Agency of Mennonite Church USA & Canada. Carol Duerksen, ed. Denominational, for older youth & adults. Monthly take-home paper; 32 pgs.; circ. 8,900. Subscription $22.65; $23.78 Cdn. 80% unsolicited freelance; 20% assigned. Complete ms (only)/cover letter; e-mail submissions preferred. **Pays $10-42 or .06-.07/wd.** on acceptance (or when editor chooses) for onetime rts. Articles & fiction, 400-600 wds. (95/yr.). Responds in 6 mos. Seasonal 1 yr. ahead. Accepts simultaneous submissions & reprints (tell when/where appeared). Regularly uses sidebars. Guidelines on Website (click on "Periodicals"/"Writers Guidelines"); copy $2/6x9 SAE/2 stamps. (No ads)

Poetry: Buys 120/yr. Free verse, haiku, traditional; 3-12 lines; up to $2/line ($7.50-20). Submit max. 5 poems.

Fillers: Buys 25/yr. Anecdotes, prose; up to 300 wds., up to .06/wd.

Tips: "Read our guidelines. All areas are open. Articles must carry a strong story line. First person is preferred. Don't exceed maximum word length, send no more than 3 works at a time."

** This periodical was #44 on the 2010 Top 50 Christian Publishers list (#25 in 2009, #19 in 2008, #38 in 2007, #43 in 2006).

PURPOSE MAGAZINE, PO Box 83020, Columbus OH 43203. (614) 530-4398. E-mail: purpose forlife@gmail.com. Website: www.purposemagazine.com. Blog: http://purposemagazine.com/blogs/

purpose-blog.aspx. Ellavation Enterprises Inc. Ella Coleman, pub./ed-in-chief. Christian magazine for a predominately African American audience; personal and family empowerment to inspire, motivate, and educate readers to live their God-given purpose. Bimonthly mag.; 32-40 pgs.; circ. 5,000. Subscription $25. 25% unsolicited freelance; 75% assigned. Query/clips; e-query OK. **PAYS A SUBSCRIPTION & PROMOTION**. Articles. Accepts reprints (tell when/where appeared). Prefers e-mail submissions (attached file in Word). Regularly uses sidebars. Also accepts submissions from children/teens. Prefers NKJV. Guidelines on Website; copy for 9x12 SASE. (Ads)

Poetry: Accepts very few; 30-40 lines. Submit max. 20 poems.

Fillers: Most types; 200-500 wds.

Columns/Departments: Financial wisdom. Complete ms.

Contests: Occasionally sponsors a contest.

QUAKER LIFE, 101 Quaker Hill Dr., Richmond IN 47374. (765) 962-7573. Fax (765) 962-1293. E-mail: quakerlife@fum.org. Website: www.fum.org. Friends United Meeting. Katie Wonsik, ed. For Christian Quakers, focusing on news around the world, peace and justice, simplicity, and inspiration. Bimonthly mag.; 48 pgs.; circ. 4,000. Subscription $24. 50% unsolicited freelance; 50% assigned. Query; fax/e-query OK. Accepts full ms by e-mail. **PAYS 3 COPIES** on publication for 1st rts. Articles to 1,500 wds. (40/yr.); book reviews 300 wds.; music/video reviews, 200 wds. Responds in 4 wks. Seasonal 4 mos. ahead. Accepts some reprints (tell when/where appeared). Accepts e-mail submissions (attached in Word or copied into message). No kill fee. Uses some sidebars. Prefers RSV. Also accepts submissions from children/teens. Guidelines/theme list by e-mail/Website; copy $2. (Ads)

Poetry: Accepts 2/yr.

Columns/Departments: Peace Notes (peace and justice news and ideas); Inspirations (1st person personal experience); Scripture for Living (applying biblical teachings); Perspectives (opinion); each 750 wds. Query or complete ms.

Special needs: Leadership, church growth, personal experience.

Tips: "All articles must fit within the theme (list on Website). Write on current issues or a personal spiritual experience from a Christian perspective. Be more practical than academic. For general readers who are Christian Quakers."

RADIX MAGAZINE, PO Box 4307, Berkeley CA 94704. (510) 548-5329. E-mail: RadixMag@aol .com. Website: www.RadixMagazine.com. Sharon Gallagher, ed.; Luci Shaw, poetry ed. Features in-depth articles for thoughtful Christians who are interested in engaging the culture. Quarterly mag.; 32 pgs. Subscription $15. 10% unsolicited freelance; 90% assigned. E-queries only. **PAYS IN COPIES** for 1st rts. Meditations, 300-500 wds. (2/yr.); book reviews 700 wds. Responds in 6 wks. to e-mail only. Seasonal 6 mos. ahead. No simultaneous submissions or reprints. Accepted submissions by e-mail only (attached file). Uses some sidebars. Prefers NRSV. Guidelines by e-mail; copy $5. (Ads)

Poetry: Accepts 12/yr. Avant-garde, free verse, haiku, traditional; 4-30 lines. Submit max. 1 poem.

Tips: "Most open to poetry, book reviews, meditations. Familiarity with the magazine is key."

@REGENT GLOBAL BUSINESS REVIEW, 1000 Regent University Dr., Virginia Beach VA 23464. (757) 226-4074. E-mail: rgbr@regent.edu. Website: www.regent.edu/rgbr. Regent University— School of Global Leadership & Entrepreneurship. Julianne R. Cenac, exec. ed. (Jcenac@regent .edu). For Christian leaders and managers who take their faith seriously and who give genuine thought to how to live out that faith in the workplace and everywhere else. Bimonthly e-zine; 30 pgs.; circ. 10,000. Free online. 25% unsolicited freelance; 75% assigned. Query/clips by e-mail only. **NO PAYMENT** for electronic rts. Feature articles 1,200-2,500 wds.; case studies 2,500-4,000 wds. (not including any data appendices); Tool Kit/Executive Summaries 250-500 wds. Responds in 2 wks. Seasonal 6 mos. ahead. No simultaneous submissions; accepts reprints. Requires accepted mss by e-mail (attached file). Regularly uses sidebars. Prefers NIV. Guidelines on Website (click on "Submissions").

Columns/Departments: Tool Kit (tips and resources), 250-500 wds. Research Translations, 1,000-1,500 wds.

Tips: "If you are interested in contributing to the exploration and advancement of global business, we are interested in hearing from you. We seek articles from contributors who are recognized experts in their fields or who have requisite experience and credentials to be qualified to speak authoritatively on the subject matter."

$@RELEVANT & RELEVANTMAGAZINE.COM, 1220 Alden Rd., Orlando FL 32803-2546. Toll-free (877) 538-4417. (407) 660-1411. Fax (407) 401-9100. E-mail: corene@relevantmediagroup.com. Website: www.RelevantMagazine.com. Relevant Media Group. Roxanne Wieman, ed. dir. (roxanne@ relevantmediagroup.com). Targets culture-savvy twentysomethings who are looking for purpose, depth, and spiritual truth. Bimonthly & online mag.; 100 pgs. Subscription $10. 80% freelance. Send a one-paragraph query/clips; prefers e-mail; no phone/fax query. **Pays $100-400** within 45 days of publication for 1st rts. & all electronic rts. for 6 mos.; nonexclusive rts. thereafter. Features 600-1,000 wds.; reviews 400-600 wds. Prefers submissions as Word attachments. Guidelines on Website (www.relevantmagazine.com/how-to-write-for-relevant); copy $2.98.

RELIEF JOURNAL, 60 W. Terra Cotta Ave, Ste. B, #156, Crystal Lake IL 60014-3548. E-mail: editor @reliefjournal.com. Website: www.reliefjournal.com. CC Publishing, NFP. Christopher Fisher, ed-in-chief; Lisa Ohlen Harris, nonfiction ed.; Chris Fisher, fiction ed. A Christian Literary Expression. Semiannual mag.; 175 pgs.; circ. 300. Subscription $48. 90% unsolicited freelance; 10% assigned. Use online submissions system only; no mail or e-mail submissions. Complete ms. **PAYS IN COPIES** for 1st rts. Creative nonfiction (20/yr.) & fiction (24/yr.) to 8,000 wds. Responds in 16 wks. Accepts simultaneous submissions & reprints (only when solicited). Any Bible version. Guidelines on Website ("Submit Your Work"). Incomplete topical listings. (Ads)

Poetry: Brad Fruhauff, poetry ed. Accepts 80-100/yr. Poetry that is well-written and makes sense; to 1,000 wds. Submit max. 5 poems.

$@RENEWED & READY: Adventist Living for Today, 16617 Kendle Rd., Williamsport MD 21795. (301) 223-6738. E-mail: editor@RenewedandReady.com. Website: www.RenewedandReady .com. Seventh-day Adventist. Ginger Church, Webmaster. To inspire Adventists, over 50, to have a zest for life. Online magazine. **Pays.**

$+REV UP YOUR LIFE, E-mail: submission@revupyrlife.com. Website: www.revupyrlife.com. General audience. Submit to The Editor. Practical, self-improvement articles for men. Bimonthly mag. Open to unsolicited freelance. **Pays a $10 honorarium** on acceptance. Articles 1,000 wds. Guidelines/theme list on Website ("Magazine Guidelines").

$RIVER REGION'S JOURNEY, (formerly *Montgomery's Journey*), 555 Farmington Rd., Montgomery AL 36109-4609. Phone/fax (334) 213-7940. E-mail: deanne@readjourneymagazine .com, or through Website: www.readjourneymagazine.com. Keep Sharing LLC. DeAnne Watson, ed. For Protestant Christians and Christian families. Monthly mag.; 60-72 pgs.; circ. 18,000. Open to freelance. Complete ms by e-mail. **Pays $25** on publication for onetime or reprint rts. Articles 900-1,500 wds. Seasonal 3 mos. ahead. Accepts requested ms on disk or by e-mail (attached file). No kill fee. Regularly uses sidebars. Also accepts submissions from teens. Guidelines by e-mail; no copy. (Ads)

Tips: "Most open to feature articles, instructional in nature, with subheaders and sidebars."

RUMINATE: Faith in Literature and Art, 140 N. Roosevelt Ave., Fort Collins CO 80521. (970) 449-2726. E-mail: editor@ruminatemagazine.com. Website: www.ruminatemagazine.com. Brianna Van Dyke, ed.; submit to submissions@ruminatemagazine.com. An intimate and hip publication of faith literature and art; publishes work with both subtle and overt associations to the Christian faith as well as work that has no direct association. Quarterly mag.; 70 pgs.; circ. 1,500. Subscription $28. 100% unsolicited freelance. Complete ms/cover letter by e-mail only. **PAYS 3 COPIES OR SUBSCRIPTION** for 1st rts. Articles to 5,000 wds. (4-8/yr.); fiction to 5,000 wds. (8-12/yr.). Responds in 16 wks. Accepts simultaneous submissions; no reprints. Requires disk or e-mail submissions (attached file). Does not use sidebars. Guidelines/theme list on Website ("Main Menu"/ "Get Involved"/"Submissions"); order copy on Website/$9. (Ads)

   Poetry: Lacee Perrin, poetry ed. (poetry@ruminatemagazine.com). Accepts 50/yr. Avant-garde, free verse, traditional; to 40 lines. Submit max. 4 poems.

   Contest: Annual poetry contest deadline is May 15. Annual fiction contest deadline is November 15. Entry fee: $15. Prizes: $300 1st prize; $150 to runner-up. Details on Website.

   Tips: "We are looking for writers and artists who are interested in the process of creating quality work that reveals the nature of Christ."

$SALVO MAGAZINE, PO Box 410788, Chicago IL 60641. (773) 481-1090. Fax (773) 481-1095. E-mail: editor@salvomag.com. Website: www.salvomag.com. Fellowship of St. James. Bobby Maddex, ed. Geared toward young adults, 25-45, who want to free themselves from the false worldviews emanating from Hollywood, the media, and the Academy. Quarterly mag.; 96 pgs.; circ. 2,800. Subscription $25.99. 25% unsolicited freelance; 75% assigned. Query/clips; no phone/fax query, e-query OK. Accepts full mss by e-mail. **Pays .20/wd.** on publication for 1st rts. Articles 600-2,500 wds. (16/yr.). Responds in 4 wks. No seasonal. No simultaneous submissions or reprints. Prefers e-mail submissions (attached file). Kill fee $100. Regularly uses sidebars. No Bible references. Guidelines/theme list on Website (click on "Magazine"/scroll all the way to the bottom and click on "Submission Guidelines"); copy $6.99. (Ads)

   Columns/Departments: Buys 12/yr. Dispatches (features) 2,000 wds. The Trenches (tales of academic bias) 1,200 wds. Random Flak (minifeatures) 1,200 wds. (.20/wd.)

   Tips: "We are most open for features on science, sex, and society—anything that deconstructs false ideology and worldviews, using reason and logic alone."

SAVED MAGAZINE, PO Box 22-2302, Hollywood FL 33022-3100. Toll-free (877) 34SAVED. (954) 921-4700. Fax (954) 921-4724. E-mail: editorial@savedmagazine.com. Website: www. savedmaga zine.com. Christian. Barbara Hall, ed. Targets diverse Christian population by infusing area businesses, neighborhoods, and ministries across economic and ethnic lines. Bimonthly mag. Subscription $15. Open to unsolicited freelance. **NO MENTION OF PAYMENT.** Articles. Editorial schedule on Website ("Editorial Schedule"), no guidelines. Incomplete topical listings. (Ads)

SCP JOURNAL, PO Box 4308, Berkeley CA 94704. (510) 540-0300. Fax (510) 540-1107. E-mail: scp@scp-inc.org. Website: www.scp-inc.org. Spiritual Counterfeits Project Inc. Tal Brooke, ed. Deals with topics from apologetics to New Age, new religions, cults, occult, and cultural trends. Quarterly jour.; circ. 15,000. Subscription $25. Open to queries only. Articles. Incomplete topical listings. Guidelines on Website (click on "SCP Publications"/scroll to bottom & click on "Information"/ "Writers Guidelines"). (No ads)

$SEARCH MAGAZINE, 1319 Eighteenth St. N.W., Washington DC 20036-1802. (202) 296-6267. E-mail: editors@searchmagazine.org. Website: www.searchmagazine.org. Science & Spirit Resources Inc./Heldref Publications. Peter Manseau, ed. For intellectually curious, educated readers who have an interest in how technology, faith, ethics, and the arts connect in both global affairs and their everyday lives. Bimonthly mag; 66 pgs.; circ. 7,500. Subscription $30. 20% freelance. Query by e-mail only. **Pays .20-.75/wd. for assigned, .20-.50/wd. for unsolicited** for articles on acceptance for all rts. Makes work-for-hire assignments. No reprints. Articles 1,200-2,500 wds. (40/yr.). Responds in 1 mo. Seasonal 6 mos. ahead. Guidelines on Website ("About Us/"Write for Us"); copy on Website.

Columns/Departments: Interlude (social/science environmental topic), 1,200-1,600 wds. Critical Mass (news briefs covering all areas of science—physics, gender, space, psychology, etc.); pays $200-300. See Website for samples of departments.

Tips: "Common mistakes include shallow reporting, lack of in-depth writing, lack of diversity in religious perspectives. We're looking for well-researched articles that include interviews with scientists, theologians, and everyday people. The best articles include citations for recent research and current books. Thoughtful leads, transitions, and conclusions based on the writer's research and insight are a must."

SEEDS OF HOPE: Hope for the Healing of Hunger and Poverty, 602 James Ave., Waco TX 76706-1476. (254) 755-7745. Fax (254) 753-1909. E-mail: Seedseditor@clearwire.net. Website: www.seedspublishers.org. Seeds of Hope Publishers. Katie Cook, ed. Committed to the healing of hunger and poverty in our world. Quarterly worship packet; 20 pgs. of camera-ready resources. Subscription $120. Individual packet $50. Back issues less expensive. Also quarterly newsletter, *Hunger News & Hope*, published through denominational offices of national churches. E-query OK. **NO PAYMENT.**

$SEEK, 8805 Governor's Hill Dr., Ste. 400, Cincinnati OH 45249. E-mail: seek@standardpub.com. Website: www.Standardpub.com. Standard Publishing. Margaret K. Williams, ed. Light, inspirational, take-home reading for young and middle-aged adults. Weekly take-home paper; 8 pgs.; circ. 29,000. Subscriptions $16.99 (sold only in sets of 5). 75% unsolicited freelance; 25% assigned. Complete ms; no phone/fax/e-query. **Pays .07/wd.** on acceptance for 1st rts., **.05/wd. for reprints**. Articles 500-1,200 wds. (150-200/yr.); fiction 500-1,200 wds. Responds in 18 wks. Seasonal 1 yr. ahead. Accepts reprints (tell when/where appeared). Prefers submissions by e-mail (attached file). Uses some sidebars. Guidelines/theme list by mail/Website ("About Standard Publishing"/"View Writer's Guidelines" left side); copy for 6x9 SAE/2 stamps. (No ads)

Fillers: Buys 50/yr. Ideas, short humor; $15.

Tips: "We now work with a theme list. Only articles tied to these themes will be considered for publication. Check Website for theme list and revised guidelines."

** This periodical was #19 on the 2010 Top 50 Christian Publishers list (#19 in 2009, #11 in 2008, #7 in 2007, #26 in 2006).

SENIOR CONNECTION, PO Box 38, Dundee IL 60118. (847) 428-0205. Fax (847) 428-5902. E-mail: srconn@yahoo.com. Website: www.seniorconnectionnewspaper.com. Churchill Publications/Catholic. Peter Rubino, ed. For Catholics ages 50 and up with ties to the Chicago area. Monthly newspaper; circ. 190,000. Subscription $20. Open to unsolicited freelance. Articles. Incomplete topical listings.

$+SEVEN MAGAZINE, PO Box 725, Winnipeg MB R3C 2K3, Canada. Toll-free (800) 263-6695. (204) 982-2060. Fax (204) 947-5632. E-mail: admin@christianweek.org. Website: www.christian week.org (click on "Also By Christian Week"). Fellowship for Print Witness. Submit to The Editor. A Canadian men's magazine. Bimonthly mag. Query; phone/fax/e-query OK. **Pays .10/wd.** on publication for onetime & electronic rts. Articles 400-1,500 wds. Responds in 1-2 wks. Seasonal 4-6 mos. ahead. Accepts simultaneous submissions & reprints (tell when/where appeared). Prefers accepted mss by e-mail. Uses some sidebars. Prefers NRSV. Copy on Website. Incomplete topical listings.

SHARING: A Journal of Christian Healing, PO Box 780909, San Antonio TX 78278-0909. (210) 681-5146. Fax (210) 681-5146. E-mail: Marjorie.George@dwtx.org or through Website: www .orderofstluke.org. Order of St. Luke the Physician. Marjorie George, ed. For Christians interested in spiritual and physical healing. Monthly (10X) jour.; 16 pgs.; circ. 9,000. Subscription $20. 100% unsolicited freelance. Complete ms/cover letter. **NO PAYMENT** for onetime or reprint rts. Articles 750-900 wds. (50/yr.). Responds in 3 wks. Seasonal 2 mos. ahead. Accepts simultaneous submissions

& reprints (tell when/where appeared). Prefers ms by e-mail. Some sidebars. Prefers RSV. Guidelines on Website (click on "Sharing Magazine"/"Submit an Idea"); copy for 8x10 SAE/2 stamps.

Poetry: Accepts 10-12/yr. Free verse, traditional; 6-14 lines.

Tips: "We're looking for crisp, clear, well-written articles on the theology of healing and personal witness of healing. We are totally open; best to send manuscript. We do not return manuscripts or poems, nor do we reply to inquiries regarding manuscript status."

$SIGNIFICANT LIVING: Celebrating Life and Faith for Today's Christian, 2800 Vision Ct., Aurora IL 60506. (815) 986-7337. Fax (866) 888-3072. E-mail: peg@pegshort.com. Website: www .significantliving.org. Peg Short, ed-in-chief. Dedicated to serving adults in the second half of life (boomers to seniors), empowering them to live with Christlike vitality, and inspiring them to serve others, so that our nation may be strengthened and God may be honored. Bimonthly mag.; 40 pgs.; circ. 25,000. Subscription by membership only, $19.95. Estab. 2007. 5-10% unsolicited freelance; 90-95% assigned. Query; e-query OK. Accepts full mss by e-mail. **Pays .20-.30/wd.** on acceptance for all rts. Articles & fiction 1,000-1,200 wds. Responds in up to 2-3 wks. Seasonal 6 mos. ahead. Accepts simultaneous submissions & reprints (tell when/where appeared). Prefers e-mail submissions (attached file). Kill fee $25. Uses some sidebars. Guidelines by e-mail/Website ("Magazines"/ "Writer's Guidelines"); free copy. (Ads)

Fillers: For boomers & seniors. Anecdotes, cartoons, facts, jokes, short humor, word puzzles.

Tips: "Most open to features—role-model stories that reflect issues for boomers and seniors. Open to celebrity and athlete stories, and features that are issue-oriented to boomers and seniors. Human interest and role-model stories of middle and senior adult issues."

** This periodical was #25 on the 2010 Top 50 Christian Publishers list (#14 in 2009).

SILVER WINGS, PO Box 2340, Clovis CA 93613-2340. (559) 347-0194. E-mail: cloviswings@aol .com. Poetry on Wings/Evangelical. Jackson Wilcox, ed. Christian understanding and uplift through poetry. Bimonthly mag.; 16 pgs.; circ. 300. Subscription free with donation. 100% unsolicited freelance. Query or complete ms; phone query OK. **PAYS ONE COPY & SUBSCRIPTION** for poetry only for 1st rts.; book reviews 200 wds. Not copyrighted. Poetry only. Responds in 3 wks. Seasonal 3-12 mos. ahead. No disk or e-mail submissions. Does not use sidebars. Prefers KJV. Also accepts submissions from children/teens. Guidelines by mail; copy for 6x9 SASE/2 stamps. (No ads)

Poetry: Accepts 175/yr. Free verse, haiku, light verse, traditional; 3-20 lines. Submit max. 3 poems. No payment. "Any poetry that conforms to Christian conduct, teaching, and morality. No profanity or mention of alcoholic beverages."

Contest: Annual poetry contest on a theme (December 31 deadline); send SASE for details. Winners published in March. $325 in prizes. $3 entry fee.

Tips: "We like poems with clear Christian message, observation, or description. Poetry should be easy to read and understand. Short poems get best attention. We are open to topics and material making a point that agrees with Christian teaching. We will even consider views that vary within the Christian community. Encourage submissions from teens." Poems must be original work of submitting poet and never previously published.

@SINGLE AGAIN MAGAZINE, 7405 Greenback Ln., #129, Citrus Heights CA 95610-5603. (916) 773-1111. Fax (916) 773-2999. E-mail: publisher@singleagainmagazine.com. Website: www.single again.com. Messenger Publishing Group. Rev. Paul V. Scholl, pub. Caters to people trying to put their lives back together after divorce, separation, or death of a significant other. Quarterly & online newsletter; 8-10 pgs. Subscription $12. Open to freelance. Complete ms/cover letter by mail or e-mail (preferred). **NO PAYMENT** for simultaneous rts. Articles 500 wds. and up (50-75/yr.). Responds in 6 wks. Accepts simultaneous submissions & reprints (tell when/where appeared). Accepts requested mss by e-mail (attached file in Word only). Does not use sidebars. Guidelines on Website. Incomplete topical listings. (Ads)

Poetry: Accepts 6-12/yr. Any type to 24 lines. Submit max. 6 poems.

Fillers: Accepts 15-12/yr. Anecdotes, facts, ideas, jokes, kid quotes, prayers, prose, short humor, tips.

Tips: "Write from your heart first. Don't worry about your article being perfect. We will help you with any final editing."

$SOCIAL JUSTICE REVIEW, 3835 Westminster Pl., St. Louis MO 63108-3472. (314) 371-1653. Fax (314) 371-0889. E-mail: centbur@sbcglobal.net. Website: www.socialjusticereview.org. Central Bureau of the Catholic Central Verein. Rev. Edward Krause, C.S.C., ed. For those interested in the social teaching of the Catholic Church. Bimonthly mag.; 32 pgs.; circ. 5,000. Subscription $20. 90% unsolicited freelance. Query or complete ms/cover letter; no phone/fax/e-query. **Pays .02/wd.** on publication for onetime rts. Not copyrighted. Articles 1,500-3,000 wds. (80/yr.); book reviews 500 wds. (no payment). Responds in 1 wk. Seasonal 3 mos. ahead. Accepts reprints (tell when/where appeared). Prefers submissions on disk. No kill fee. Does not use sidebars. No guidelines; copy for 9x12 SAE/3 stamps. (No ads)

> **Columns/Departments:** Virtue; Economic Justice (Catholic views); variable length. Query or complete ms. Pays .02/wd.
>
> **Tips:** "Articles and reviews open to freelancers. Fidelity to papal teaching and clarity and simplicity of style; thoughtful and thought-provoking writing."

$@SOUND BODY Newsletter, Radio & TV Program, Box 448, Jacksonville OR 97530. Phone/fax (541) 899-8888. E-mail: Susan@SoundBody.tv or susan@christianmedianetwork.com. Website: www.SoundBody.tv. Christian Media. James Lloyd, ed./pub. A health newsletter with an alternative slant. Quarterly & online newsletter. Query; prefers e-mail query. **Payment negotiable** for reprint rts. Articles. Responds in 3 wks. Requires KJV. No guidelines; copy for #10 SAE/2 stamps.

SOUTHWEST KANSAS FAITH AND FAMILY, PO Box 1454, Dodge City KS 67801. (620) 225-4677. Fax (620) 225-4625. E-mail: info@swkfaithandfamily.org. Website: www.swkfaithandfamily.org. Independent. Stan Wilson, pub. Dedicated to sharing the Word of God and news and information that honors Christian beliefs, family traditions, and values that are the cornerstone of our nation. Monthly newspaper; circ. 5,000. Subscription $18. Accepts freelance. Prefers e-query; complete ms OK. Articles; no reviews. Guidelines on Website ("Submit Articles"). Incomplete topical listings. (Ads)

$@SPECIAL LIVING, PO Box 1000, Bloomington IL 61702. (309) 962-2003. E-mail: gareeb@aol.com. Website: www.specialiving.com. Betty Garee, pub./ed. For and about physically disabled adults, mobility-impaired individuals. Quarterly online mag.; 80 pgs.; free online. 75% unsolicited freelance; 10% assigned. Query; phone/e-query OK. Accepts full mss by e-mail. **Pays .10/wd. ($80)** on publication for 1st rts. Articles 300-800 wds. (50/yr.). Responds in 3 wks. Seasonal 6 mos. ahead. Accepts simultaneous submissions & reprints (tell when/where appeared). Prefers requested ms on disk. No kill fee. Uses some sidebars. No guidelines. (Ads)

> **Fillers:** Buys 20/yr. Cartoons, tips.
>
> **Tips:** "Query with a specific idea. Have good photos to accompany your article. Most open to mobility-impaired concerns and successes."

SPIRITUALITY FOR TODAY, PO Box 7466, Greenwich CT 06836. (203) 316-9394. Fax (203) 316-9396. E-mail: Clemons10@aol.com. Website: www.spirituality.org. Clemons Productions Inc. Dorothy Riera, asst. ed. Adults' spiritual renewal with articles that challenge reflection. Monthly mag.; 13-15 pgs.; circ. 495,000. Subscription free. Open to freelance. E-query OK. **NO PAYMENT.** Articles & short stories 1,000 wds. Guidelines by e-mail. (Ads)

> **Fillers:** Accepts anecdotes, prayers, quotes.
>
> **Tips:** "Most open to human interest pertaining to the church (2 pgs.); and human values. Just submit an e-mail with article attached. We always respond to our e-mails."

$SPIRITUAL LIFE, 2131 Lincoln Rd. N.E., Washington DC 20002-1199. Toll-free (888) 616-1713. (202) 832-5505. Fax (202) 832-5711. E-mail: edodonnell@aol.com. Website: www.Spiritual-Life .org. Catholic. Edward O'Donnell, O.C.D., ed. Essays on Christian spirituality with a pastoral application to everyday life. Quarterly jour.; 64 pgs.; circ. 12,000. Subscription $22. 80% unsolicited freelance. Complete ms/cover letter; phone/fax/e-query OK. **Pays $50-250 ($50/pg.)** on acceptance for 1st rts. Articles/essays 3,000-5,000 wds. (20/yr.); book reviews 1,500 wds. ($15). Responds in 9 wks. Seasonal 9 mos. ahead. Accepts simultaneous submissions. Requires requested ms on disk. Does not use sidebars. Prefers NAB. Guidelines by mail; copy for 7x10 SAE/5 stamps.

   Tips: "No stories of personal healing, conversion, miracles, etc."

$SPORTS SPECTRUM, PO Box 2037, Indian Trail NC 28079. Toll-free (866) 821-2971. (704) 821-2971. Fax (704) 821-2669. E-mail: editor@sportsspectrum.com or info@sportsspectrum .com. Website: www.sportsspectrum.com. Sports Spectrum Publishing. Brett Honeycutt, mng. ed. (bhoneycutt@sportsspectrum.com). Designed to feature sports people and issues as a way of introducing the gospel to non-Christian sports fans and encouraging Christian sports fans. Quarterly mag.; 68 pgs.; circ. 20,000. Subscription $27.52. 80% assigned. Query/clips; e-query OK. **Pays .21/wd.** on acceptance for all rts. Not copyrighted. Articles 1,200-1,500 wds. (40/yr.). Responds in 3-4 wks. Requires accepted ms by e-mail (attached file). Kill fee 30-50%. Regularly uses sidebars. Prefers NIV. Guidelines by mail/e-mail/Website (click on "About SS"/"Writer's Guide"); no sample copy. (Ads)

   Tips: "The best thing a writer can do is to be aware of the special niche *Sports Spectrum* has developed in sports ministry. Then find athletes who fit that niche and who haven't been covered in the magazine."

   ** 2007, 2006 EPA Award of Merit: General.

$@ST. ANTHONY MESSENGER, 28 W. Liberty St., Cincinnati OH 45202-6498. (513) 241-5615. Fax (513) 241-0399. E-mail: StAnthony@AmericanCatholic.org. Website: www.AmericanCatholic .org. Fr. Pat McCloskey, O.F.M., ed. For Catholic adults & families. Monthly & online mag.; 64 pgs.; circ. 305,000. Subscription $28. 55% unsolicited freelance. Query/clips (complete ms for fiction); e-query OK. **Pays .20/wd.** on acceptance for 1st, reprint (right to reprint), and electronic rts. Articles 1,500-3,000 wds., prefers 1,500-2,500 (35-50/yr.); fiction 1,500-2,500 wds. (12/yr.); book reviews 500 wds. $50. Responds in 3-9 wks. Seasonal 6 mos. ahead. Kill fee. Uses some sidebars. Prefers NAB. Guidelines on Website ("Contact Us"/"Writer's Guidelines"); copy for 9x12 SAE/4 stamps. (Ads)

   Poetry: Christopher Heffron, poetry ed. Buys 20/yr. Free verse, haiku, traditional; 3-25 lines; $2/line ($20 min.). Submit max. 2 poems.

   Fillers: Cartoons.

   Tips: "Many submissions suggest that the writer has not read our guidelines or sample articles. Most open to articles, fiction, profiles, interviews of Catholic personalities, personal experiences, and prayer. Writing must be professional; use Catholic terminology and vocabulary. Writing must be faithful to Catholic belief and teaching, life, and experience. Our online writers' guidelines indicate the seven categories of articles. Texts of articles reflecting each category are linked to the online writers' guidelines for nonfiction articles."

   ** This periodical was #28 on the 2009 Top 50 Christian Publishers list (#25 in 2008, #22 in 2007, #33 in 2006).

$STEWARDSHIP, PO Box 1561, New Canaan CT 06840. Toll-free (888) 320-5576. (203) 966-6470. Fax (203) 966-4654. E-mail: guy@parishpublishing.org, or info@parishpublishing.org. Website: www.parishpublishing.org. Parish Publishing LLC. Guy Brossy, principal. Inspires parishioners to give to their church—abilities, time, and monies. Monthly newsletter; 4 pgs.; circ. 1 million. 50% unsolicited freelance; 50% assigned. Fax/e-query with cover letter. **Pays $50** on acceptance for all & reprint rts. Articles 150, 200, or 300 wds. (50/yr.). Responds in 2 wks. Seasonal 3 mos. ahead.

Accepts simultaneous submissions & reprints. Accepts e-mail submissions (attached or copied into message). Regularly uses sidebars. Free guidelines/copy by mail. (No ads)

   Tips: "Write articles that zero in on stewardship—general, time, talent, or treasure—as it relates to the local church."

$THE STORYTELLER, 2441 Washington Rd., Maynard AR 72444. (870) 647-2137. E-mail: story tellermag1@yahoo.com. Website: www.thestorytellermagazine.com. Fossil Creek Publishing. Regina Cook Williams, ed./pub.; Ruthan Riney, review ed. Family audience. Quarterly jour.; 72 pgs.; circ. 700. Subscription $20. 100% unsolicited freelance. Complete ms/cover letter; phone/e-query OK. **Pays .0025/wd.** on publication for 1st rts. Articles 2,500 wds. (60/yr.); fiction 2,500 wds. (100-125/yr.). Responds in 1 wk. Seasonal 3 mos. ahead. Accepts simultaneous submissions & reprints (tell when/ where appeared). Responds in 1-2 wks. No disk or e-mail submissions; does not use sidebars. Also accepts submissions from children/teens (not children's stories). Guidelines by mail/Website ("Guidelines"); copy $6/9x12 SAE/5 stamps. (Ads)

   Poetry: Jamie Johnson, poetry ed. Accepts 100/yr. Free verse, haiku, light verse, traditional; 5-40 lines. Submit max. 3 poems. Pays $1/poem.

   Fillers: Accepts 10-20/yr. Cartoons, quotes, tips; 25-50 wds. Writing-related only.

   Special needs: Original artwork. Funny or serious stories about growing up as a pastor's child or being a pastor's wife. Also westerns and mysteries.

   Contest: Offers 1 or 2 paying contests per year, along with People's Choice Awards, and Pushcart Prize nominations. Go to www.thestorytellermagazine.com, for announcements of all forthcoming contests for the year.

   Tips: "We look for stories that are written well, flow well, have believable dialogue, and good endings. So many writers write a good story but fizzle at the ending. All sections of the magazine are open except how-to articles. Study the craft of writing. Learn all you can before you send anything out. Pay attention to detail, make sure manuscripts are as free of mistakes as possible. Follow the guidelines—they aren't hard." Always looking for B & W photos for front cover.

   ** This periodical was #42 on the 2007 Top 50 Christian Publishers list.

STUDIO: A Journal of Christians Writing, 727 Peel St., Albury NSW 2640, Australia. Phone/ fax +61 2 6021 1135. E-mail: studio00@bigpond.net.au. Submit to Studio Editor. Quarterly jour.; 36 pgs.; circ. 300. Subscription $60 AUS. 90% unsolicited freelance; 10% assigned. Query. **PAYS IN COPIES** for onetime rts. Articles 3,000 wds. (15/yr.); fiction 3,000 wds. (50/yr.); book reviews 300 wds. Responds in 3 wks. Accepts simultaneous submissions & reprints (tell when/where appeared). No disks; e-mail submissions OK. Does not use sidebars. Guidelines by mail (send IRC); copy for $10 AUS. (Ads)

   Poetry: Accepts 200/yr. Any type; 4-100 lines. Submit max. 3 poems.

   Contest: See copy of journal for details.

   Tips: "We accept all types of fiction and literary article themes."

THE SWORD AND TRUMPET, PO Box 575, Harrisonburg VA 22803-0575. (540) 867-9444. Fax (540) 867-9419. E-mail: swandtrump@verizon.net or through Website: www.swordandtrumpet.org. Mennonite. Paul Emerson, ed. Primarily for conservative Bible believers. Monthly mag.; 37 pgs.; circ. 3,300. Subscription $15. **NO PAYMENT.** Articles. Prefers KJV. (No ads)

SWORD OF THE LORD NEWSPAPER, PO Box 1099, Murfreesboro TN 37133-1099. Toll-free (800) 247-9673. (615) 893-6700. Fax (615) 895-7447. E-mail: guyking@swordofthelord.com or through Website: www.swordofthelord.com. Independent Baptists and other fundamentalists. Dr. Shelton Smith, pres./ed.; submit to Guy King. Revival and soul-winning. Biweekly newspaper; 24 pgs.; circ. 70,000. Subscription $12. Open to freelance. Query; phone/fax/e-query OK. **NO PAYMENT.** Articles 500-1,000 wds.; fiction for 4-7 & 8-12 yrs. and teenagers. Responds in 13 wks.

Seasonal 3 mos. ahead. Accepts simultaneous submissions & reprints (tell when/where appeared). Accepts disk or e-mail submissions (attached file). No kill fee. Does not use sidebars. Requires KJV. Guidelines by mail/e-mail; no copy. (Ads)

Poetry: Accepts variable number. Free verse, light verse, traditional; any length.

Fillers: Accepts variable number. Facts, newsbreaks, prose.

Columns/Departments: Accepts variable number. Kid's Korner (children's stories); Teen Talk (teen issues); both 500-700 wds.

Tips: "Most open to Bible study, soul-winning material, Christian growth, and youth character building that does not stress graphic portrayals of 'what's really going on out there.' Only works from a fundamentalist viewpoint and using the KJV are considered." Does not reprint articles from Mennonite, Lutheran, or Catholic publications.

$@TESTIMONY, 2450 Milltower Ct., Mississauga ON L5N 5Z6, Canada. (905) 542-7400. Fax (905) 542-7313. E-mail: testimony@paoc.org. Website: www.testimonymag.com. The Pentecostal Assemblies of Canada. Steve Kennedy, ed. To encourage a Christian response to a wide range of issues and topics, including those that are peculiar to Pentecostals. Monthly & online mag.; 24 pgs.; circ. 14,000. Subscription $24 U.S./$19.05 Cdn. (includes GST). 10% unsolicited free-lance; 90% assigned. Query; fax/e-query OK. **Pays $20-75** on publication for 1st rts. (no pay for reprint rts.). Articles 700-900 wds. Responds in 6-8 wks. Seasonal 4 mos. ahead. Accepts reprints (tell when/where appeared). Prefers e-mail submission (copied into message). Regularly uses sidebars. Prefers NIV. Guidelines/theme list by mail/e-mail/Website (click on "Fellowship Servi ces"/"Publications"/"Testimony"/scroll down to "View our Submission Guidelines Here"); copy $2/9x12 SAE. (Ads)

Tips: "View theme list on our Website and query us about a potential article regarding one of our themes. Our readership is 98% Canadian. We prefer Canadian writers or at least writers who understand that Canadians are not Americans in long underwear. We also give preference to members of this denomination, since this is related to issues concerning our fellowship."

$THIS I BELIEVE ESSAYS, 2424 Frankfort Ave., Louisville KY 40206-3515. (502) 259-9889. E-mail through Website: www.npr.org/thisibelieve/guide.html. National Public Radio (NPR). Write and submit your own story of personal belief; those accepted will be recorded and read on the air. Guidelines & contract included on the Website. Complete ms. submitted through Website. **Pays $200,** 30 days after your essay is recorded. Personal essay 350-500 wds. Details on Website (see Website address above).

$THOMAS INK, (formerly listed as *Poetry Scout*), 2210 Weiss Ln., Georgetown TX 78626. E-mail: director@poetryscout-centreministry.com. Website: www.thomas-ink.com. Poetry Scout—Centre Ministry. T. L. Means, dir. Seeking Christian inspirational **poetry writers to cost-share in a part-nership book publishing contract**. Poetry only. (Ads only as Website links)

Poetry: Accepts 10 pages per poet per publishing contract; 10 pages of theme-oriented poetry, quotes, and elaborating thoughts. Free verse or traditional (theme oriented); up to 32 lines/poem. Payment is based on contractual agreement with affiliated publisher, and within a partnership cost-share plan. Prescreen required of a 10-line inspirational poem reflecting the "Trinity of God." Mail complete ms; send by e-mail; or submit through Website. Guidelines on Website (on home page).

$+@THRIVING FAMILY, 8605 Explorer Dr., Colorado Springs CO 80920. E-mail: thrivingfam ilysubmissions@family.org. Website: www.thrivingfamily.com. Focus on the Family. Submit to The Editor. Focuses on marriage and parenting from a biblical perspective; mostly for families with 4- to 12-year-olds in the family. Monthly & online mag. Open to unsolicited freelance. Complete ms or query; e-query OK (no attachments). **Pays .25/wd.** Feature articles 1,200-2,000 wds.; online articles 800-1,200 wds. Guidelines/theme list; copy online. Incomplete topical listings.

Columns/Departments: Family Stages (practical tips), 50-200 wds. For Fun (marriage or family humor articles), about 500 wds., pays $175; For Him (male perspective), 450 wds. For Her (female perspective), 450 wds. Blended Family (concerns of blended families), 800 wds. Extended Family (relationships with relatives), 450 wds.

TIFERET: A Journal of Spiritual Literature, 211 Dryden Rd., Bernardsville NJ 07924-1108. (908) 432-2149. E-mail: editors@tireretjournal.com. Website: www.tiferetjournal.com. Donna Baier Stein, pub./ed-in-chief. Publishes writings from authors of many faiths. Quarterly literary mag.; 176 pgs. Open to unsolicited freelance. Only accepts electronic submissions via Website. **NO PAYMENT** for 1st rts. Articles; fiction. Responds in 4 mos. Accepts simultaneous submissions & rarely reprints. Guidelines on Website ("Submit").

Poetry: Renee Ashley, poetry ed. Submit max. 6 poems.

Special needs: Accepts artwork, black & white for interior; color for cover.

TIME OF SINGING: A Magazine of Christian Poetry, PO Box 149, Conneaut Lake PA 16316. E-mail: timesing@zoominternet.net. Website: www.timeofsinging.com. Lora Zill, ed. We try to appeal to all poets and lovers of poetry. Quarterly booklet; 44 pgs.; circ. 250. Subscription $17. 95% unsolicited freelance; 5% assigned. Complete ms; e-query OK. **PAYS IN COPIES** for 1st, onetime, or reprint rts. Poetry only (some book reviews by assignment). Responds in 12 wks. Seasonal 6 mos. ahead. Accepts simultaneous submissions & reprints (tell when/where appeared). Accepts e-mail submission (attached file). Guidelines by mail/e-mail/Website ("Guidelines"); copy $4 ea. or 2/$6.

Poetry: Accepts 150-200/yr. Free verse, haiku, light verse, traditional; 3-60 lines. Submit max. 5 poems. Always need form poems (sonnets, villanelles, triolets, etc.) with Christian themes. Fresh rhyme. "Cover letter not needed; your work speaks for itself."

Contest: Sponsors 1-2 annual poetry contests on specific themes or forms ($2 entry fee/ poem) with cash prizes (see Website or send SASE for rules).

Tips: "Study poetry, read widely—both Christian and non-Christian. Work at the craft. Be open to suggestions and critique. If I have taken time to comment on your work, it is close to publication. If you don't agree, submit elsewhere. I appreciate poets who take chances, who write outside the box. Time of Singing is a literary poetry magazine, so I'm not looking for greeting card verse or sermons that rhyme."

$TOGETHER, 1251 Virginia Ave., Harrisonburg VA 22802. (540) 433-5351. Fax (540) 434-0247. E-mail: Tgether@aol.com. Website: www.churchoutreach.com. Media for Living. Melodie Davis, ed. (melodiemd@msn.com). An outreach magazine distributed by churches to attract the general public to Christian faith and life. Quarterly tabloid; 8 pgs.; circ. 25,000. Free. 90% unsolicited freelance. Complete ms/cover letter or query; e-query OK. **Pays $35-60** after publication for 1st & electronic rts. Articles 500-1,200 wds. (16/yr.). Responds in 9-17 wks. Seasonal 6 mos. ahead. Accepts simultaneous submissions & reprints. Accepts requested ms on disk or by e-mail (copied into message). Uses some sidebars. Prefers NIV. Guidelines/theme list by mail/e-mail/Website (click on "Together"/ scroll down box on right side to "Are you a writer?"); copy on Website. (No ads)

Tips: "Deal with contemporary themes with fresh style. We need a variety of salvation testimonies from all racial/ethnic groups, with excellent photos available (don't submit photos until requested)." When submitting by e-mail, put title of magazine and title of your piece in subject line. Also include your e-mail address in body of message.

@TOUCHED BY THE HAND OF GOD, Website: www.touchedbythehandofgod.com. Barrett Batson, ed. People share stories of how God has opened doors, hearts, or minds for them in remarkable ways and at just the right time. Website. Free online. Open to unsolicited freelance. Complete ms. Use submission form on Website. **NO PAYMENT** for onetime or reprint rts. Personal stories to 600 wds. Guidelines on Website ("Share a Story").

@TRI-STATE VOICE, 38 Sioux Ave., Oakland NJ 07436-2133. (201) 644-7062. E-mail: tristate voice@aol.com. Website: www.tristatevoice.com. Tom Campisi, ed. To be a voice to the Christian community in Greater NYC. Monthly & online newspaper; circ. 15,000. Subscription $24. Open to freelance. Query preferred. Articles; no reviews. Incomplete topical listings. (Ads)

@THE TRUMPETER, 20969 Certosa Ter., Boca Raton FL 33433. (305) 274-4880. Fax (302) 370-1485. E-mail: info@thetrumpeter.com. Website: www.thetrumpeter.com. Swanko Communications. Martiele Swanko, ed-in-chief. Unites all South Florida Christian denominations, ethnic groups, and cultures. Online mag.; 80+ pgs.; circ. 20,000. Subscription $19.95. 90% unsolicited freelance. Query; fax/e-query OK. **NO PAYMENT** for onetime rts. Features & sports, 900-1,000 wds.; articles 500-1,200 wds.; book/music/video reviews, 100 wds. Responds in 4 wks. Accepts reprints (tell when/where appeared). Requires requested ms on disk or by e-mail. Regularly uses sidebars. Prefers KJV. Guidelines/theme list by mail/e-mail/Website. (Ads)

> **Fillers:** Cartoons.
>
> **Columns/Departments:** Accepts 100/yr. Around Town (local talk), 100-125 wds. Arts & Entertainment, 400 wds. Legal, 450 wds. Political/Viewpoint, 100-125 wds.
>
> **Tips:** "Call us for a special feature assignment. Be a good writer. Know how to effectively write a paragraph by the rules and use active verbs instead of passive verbs or adjectives."

TRUTH TREASURES/COVENANT TREASURES, 1302 E. 30th, Apt. A, Texarkana AR 71854. E-mail: tonya@covenantculture.com. Website: www.truth-treasures.com. Blog: www.truth-treasures .com/blog. Covenant Treasures Ministries, Inc. Tonya Taylor, ed.; submit to Submission for Covenant Treasures. Devotionals, testimonials, and humor. Open to unsolicited freelance.

$THE UNITED CHURCH OBSERVER, 478 Huron St., Toronto ON M5R 2R3, Canada. (416) 960-8500. Fax (416) 960-8477. E-mail: dnwilson@ucobserver.org, or through Website: www.ucobserver .org. United Church of Canada. David Wilson, ed./pub. To voice hope for individual Christians, for the United Church, for God's world. Monthly (11X) mag.; circ. 70,000. Subscription $23 Cdn.; $30 U.S. 20% freelance written; uses a limited amount of material from non-United Church freelancers. **Pays variable rates** for 1st rts. (sometimes all rts.). Articles to 1,200 wds. Accepts reprints (tell when/where appeared). Guidelines on Website (click on "Faith"/scroll all the way to the bottom of the page, right-hand side, to "Writers Guidelines"). (Ads)

$UPSCALE MAGAZINE: Exposure to the World's Finest, 600 Bronner Brothers Way S.W., Atlanta GA 30310. (404) 758-7467. Fax (404) 755-9892. E-mail: features@upscalemag.com (department editors listed on Website). Website: www.upscalemagazine.com. Upscale Communications Inc. Joyce E. Davis, sr. ed. To inspire, inform, and entertain African Americans. Monthly mag.; circ. 250,000. Subscription $20. 75-80% unsolicited freelance. Query; fax/e-query OK. **Pays $100 & up** on publication for 1st rts. Articles (135/yr.); novel excerpts. Seasonal 6 mos. ahead. Accepts simultaneous submissions. Responds in 5-9 wks. Kill fee 25%. Guidelines/copy on Website (click on "Style & Beauty"/"Submit stories for this channel").

> **Columns/Departments:** Buys 6-10/yr. News & Business (factual, current); Lifestyle (travel, home, wellness, etc.); Beauty & Fashion (tips, trends, upscale fashion, hair); Arts & Entertainment. Query. Payment varies. These columns most open to freelance.
>
> **Tips:** "We are open to queries for exciting and informative nonfiction." Uses inspirational and religious articles.

$@U.S. CATHOLIC, 205 W. Monroe St., Chicago IL 60606. (312) 236-7782. Fax (312) 236-8207. E-mail: submissions@uscatholic.org. Website: www.uscatholic.org. The Claretians. Meinrad Schrer-Emunds, exec. ed. (emundsm@claretians.org); Rev. John Molyneau C.M.F., ed/pub.; Bryan Cones, mng. ed. (conesb@claretians.org). Devoted to starting and continuing a dialog with Catholics of diverse lifestyles and opinions about the way they live their faith. Monthly & online mag.; 52 pgs.;

circ. 28,000. Subscription $22. 20% unsolicited freelance; 80% assigned. Complete ms/cover letter; e-query OK. **Pays $200-1,000 (fiction $100-250)** on acceptance for 1st rts. Articles 700-2,500 wds.; fiction to 2,500 wds.; reviews 375 wds. (pays $75). Responds in 8 wks. Seasonal 6 mos. ahead. No simultaneous submissions. Accepts reprints (tell when/where appeared). Prefers requested ms by e-mail (attached file). Sometimes pays 25% kill fee. Regularly uses sidebars. Prefers NRSV. Guidelines on Website ("Write for Us"/"Writer's Guide" at bottom); copy for 10x13 SASE. (Ads: Fran Hurst 312-544-8145)

> **Poetry:** Buys 6/yr. Submit poetry (and fiction) to literaryeditor@uscatholic.org. Free verse, light verse, traditional; to 50 lines; pays $75.
>
> **Columns/Departments:** (See guidelines first.) Buys 10/yr.; pays $100-200. Sounding Board, 1,100-1,300 wds. $250; Practicing Catholic, 750 wds. $150. Opinion column.
>
> **Tips:** "Most open to features and essays. All manuscripts (except for fiction or poetry) should have an explicit religious dimension that enables readers to see the interaction between their faith and the issue at hand. Fiction should be well written, creative, with solid character development."
>
> ** This periodical was #31 on the 2009 Top 50 Christian Publishers list (#20 in 2008, #23 in 2007, #23 in 2006).

$VIBRANT LIFE, 55 W. Oak Ridge Dr., Hagerstown MD 21740-7390. (301) 393-4019. Fax (301) 393-4055. E-mail: vibrantlife@rhpa.org. Website: www.vibrantlife.com. Seventh-day Adventist/ Review & Herald. Heather Quintana, ed. Total health publication (physical, mental, and spiritual); plus articles on family and marriage improvement; ages 30-50. Bimonthly mag.; 32 pgs.; circ. 30,000. Subscription $20. 50% unsolicited freelance; 30% assigned. Query/clips; fax/e-query OK. **Pays $100-300** on acceptance for 1st, onetime, reprint, or electronic rts. Articles 450-650 wds.; feature articles to 1,000 wds. (50-60/yr.). Responds in 5 wks. Seasonal 9 mos. ahead. Accepts simultaneous submissions & reprints (tell when/where appeared). Accepts e-mail submissions (attached file). Kill fee 50%. Regularly uses sidebars. Prefers NIV. Guidelines/themes on Website ("Writer's Guidelines"); copy $1/9x12 SAE. (Ads)

> **Tips:** "Articles need to be very helpful, practical, and well documented. Don't be preachy. Sidebars are a real plus." See Website.
>
> ** This periodical was #9 on the 2010 Top 50 Christian Publishers list (#40 in 2009, #26 in 2007).

@VICTORY HERALD, Box 190, Tipton OK 73570. Phone/fax (580) 667-4178. E-mail:dsmith@ pldi.net. Website: www.victoryherald.com. To promote and encourage writers to submit works of inspirational content and purpose that will reach out and touch the hearts of readers. Donna Smith, ed. Monthly e-zine. 70% unsolicited freelance; 30% assigned. Complete ms; e-query OK. Accepts full mss by e-mail. **NO PAYMENT** for onetime rts. Articles 500-750 wds.; fiction 750-1,200 wds. Responds in 2 wks. Seasonal 2 mos. ahead. Accepts simultaneous submissions & reprints (tell when/ where appeared). Prefers submissions by e-mail (attached file or copied into message). Uses some sidebars. Also accepts submissions from children/teens. Guidelines/copy on Website. (No ads)

> **Poetry:** Accepts 24-36/yr. Free verse, haiku, traditional; 40-45 lines max. Submit max. 3 poems.
>
> **Fillers:** Accepts 24-36/yr. Anecdotes, games, kid quotes, party ideas, prayers, prose, short humor, tips; 50-150 wds.
>
> **Columns/Departments:** Complete ms; no payment.
>
> **Tips:** "More open to inspirational works; any writing that encourages and inspires one to live for Christ."

$@VICTORY IN GRACE, 60 Quentin Rd., Lake Zurich IL 60047. (847) 438-4494. Fax (847) 438-4232. E-mail: cameron@victoryingrace.org, or julie@victoryingrace.org. Website: www.victory ingrace.org. Teaching and print ministry of Dr. James Scudder. Cameron Edwards, mng. ed. Serves to help and inspire viewers and listeners of *Victory in Grace* with Dr. James Scudder. Online mag. 5% unsolicited freelance; 95% assigned/in-house. E-query only. **Pays .15/wd.** on publication for 1st rts. Not copyrighted. Articles 1,200-1,500 wds. (20/yr.). Responds in 4-6 wks. Seasonal 6 mos. ahead. Accepts simultaneous submissions & reprints (tell when/where appeared). Prefers e-mail submissions (attached file). Sometimes pays kill fee. Regularly uses sidebars. Prefers KJV. Guidelines by mail/e-mail; copy online.

Special needs: True stories of how someone's life has changed through the ministry of *Victory in Grace*.

Tips: "Most open to a strong story about how God helps His people to cope with or overcome obstacles."

+VINEYARDS: JOURNAL OF CHRISTIAN POETRY, Dept. of English, University of Southern Mississippi, Hattiesburg MS 39406-5037. Website: www.christwriters.info/index/vineyards-a-journal-of-christian-poetry. Philip C. Kolin, ed. Estab. 2010. **NO PAYMENT.** Website takes you directly to guidelines.

Poetry: Accepts poetry for the magazine.

$THE VISION, 8855 Dunn Rd., Hazelwood MO 63042-2299. (314) 837-7300. Fax (314) 837-1803. E-mail: WAP@upci.org. Website: www.upci.org/wap. United Pentecostal Church. Richard M. Davis, ed.; submit to Karen Myers, administrative aide. Denominational. Weekly take-home paper; 4 pgs.; circ. 6,000. Subscription $2.49/quarter. 95% unsolicited freelance. Complete ms/cover letter; no e-query. **Pays $8-25** on publication. Articles 500-1,600 wds. (to 120/yr.); fiction 1,200-1,600 wds. (to 120/yr.); devotionals 350-400 wds. Seasonal 9 months ahead. Accepts simultaneous submissions & reprints. Guidelines by mail/e-mail/Website ("Writer's Guidelines" left side); free copy/#10 SASE. (No ads)

Poetry: Buys 30/yr.; traditional; $3-12.

Columns/Departments: Devotionals 350-400 wds. Requires KJV.

Tips: "Most open to fiction short stories, real-life experiences, and short poems. Whether fiction or nonfiction, we are looking for stories depicting everyday life situations and how Christian principles are used to solve problems, resolve issues, or enhance one's spiritual growth. Be sure manuscript has a pertinent, spiritual application. Best way to break into our publication is to send a well-written article that meets our specifications."

$VISTA, PO Box 50434, Indianapolis IN 46250-0434. (317) 774-7900. E-mail: submissions@wesleyan.org. Website: www.wesleyan.org/wph. Wesleyan Publishing House. Jim Watkins, ed. Weekly take-home paper; 8 pgs. 62% unsolicited freelance; 38% assigned. Accepts full mss by e-mail. **Pays $5-35** on publication for onetime and reprint rts. Articles 500-550 wds.; fiction 500-550 wds.; humor 250 wds. Seasonal 9 mos. ahead. No simultaneous submissions. Requires e-mail submissions (attached). No kill fee. Regularly uses sidebars. Also accepts submissions from children/teens. Prefers NIV. Guidelines in Website (www.wesleyan.org/wg); copy $2.50. (No ads)

Fillers: Buys many/yr. Anecdotes, facts, newsbreaks, prayers, quotes; 30-75 wds.

Special needs: Book excerpts from WPH products.

Tips: "Great market for beginning writers. Any subject related to Christian growth."

THE VOICE OF GRACE & TRUTH, PO Box 43, Brandamore PA 19316. (610) 942-3053. E-mail: mail@thevoiceofgraceandtruth.com or through Website: www.thevoiceofgraceandtruth.com. A paper with purpose! Joyce Tilney, ed. Bimonthly newspaper; 16 pgs.; circ. 15,000. Subscription $19.95. Open to unsolicited freelance. Query first. Articles. Incomplete topical listings. (Ads)

Tips: "We offer teaching, news, and testimonies to inspire, educate, and challenge the Body of Christ, and to share Jesus with the world."

$WAR CRY, 615 Slaters Ln., Alexandria VA 22314. (703) 684-5500. Fax (703) 684-5539. E-mail: War_cry@USN.salvationarmy.org. Website: www.salvationarmypublications.org. The Salvation Army.

Maj. Ed Forster, ed-in-chief; Jeff McDonald, mng. ed. Pluralistic readership reaching all socio-economic strata and including distribution in institutions. Biweekly mag.; 24 pgs.; circ. 250,000. Subscription $10. 5% unsolicited freelance. Prefers to accept full mss by e-mail (attached or copied into message) or complete ms/brief cover letter; no phone/fax query; e-query OK. **Pays .15/wd.** on acceptance for 1st, onetime rts. Articles 500-1,000 wds.; no fiction or poetry. Responds in 3-4 wks. Seasonal 1 yr. ahead. Does not accept simultaneous submissions or reprints. Prefers accepted ms by e-mail (attached or copied into message). No kill fee. Uses some sidebars. Prefers NIV. Guidelines by mail/e-mail; copy for 9x12 SASE. (No ads)

Fillers: Buys 10/yr. Anecdotes (inspirational), 100-400 wds., .15/wd.

** This periodical was #38 on the 2010 Top 50 Christian Publishers list (#45 in 2009, #40 in 2008, #17 in 2006).

$THE WAY OF ST. FRANCIS, 1112—26th St., Sacramento CA 95816-5610. (916) 443-5717. Fax (916) 443-2019. E-mail: ofmcaway@att.net. Website: www.sbfranciscans.org. Franciscan Friars of California/Catholic. Sharon E. Melberg, mng. ed. For those interested in the message of St. Francis of Assisi as lived out by contemporary people. Bimonthly mag.; 49 pgs.; circ. 5,000. Subscription $15; $17 foreign. 60% unsolicited freelance; 40% assigned. Complete ms/cover letter; phone/fax/e-query OK. Accepts full mss by e-mail. **Pays $50 (or up to 10 copies & 2 subscriptions)** on publication for 1st rts. Articles 900-1,800 wds. (25/yr.); fiction 500-2,000 wds. (12/yr.); reviews 250 wds. Responds in 2 wks. Seasonal 6 mos. ahead. No simultaneous submissions; reprints accepted (tell when/where appeared). Prefers requested ms on disk or by e-mail (attached file). No kill fee. Uses some sidebars. Prefers NAB. Also accepts submissions from children/teens. Guidelines/theme list by mail/e-mail/Website; copy for 6x9 SAE/$2.77 postage (mark "Media Mail"). (No ads)

Poetry: Accepts 4-6 poems/yr.; any type; 4-50 lines; pays $50.

Tips: "Write a piece that explores an aspect of Franciscan spirituality that is fresh and provocative. All fiction must have a Franciscan tie-in."

**This periodical was #35 on the 2009 Top 50 Christian Publishers list.

$WEAVINGS, 1908 Grand Ave., PO Box 340004, Nashville TN 37203-0004. (615) 340-7200. E-mail: weavings@upperroom.org. Website: www.upperroom.org. The Upper Room. Submit to The Editor. For clergy, lay leaders, and all thoughtful seekers who want to deepen their understanding of, and response to, how God's life and human lives are being woven together. Quarterly mag. Subscription $28. Open to freelance. Complete ms. **Pays .12/wd. & up** on acceptance. Articles 1,250-2,000 wds.; sermons & meditations 500-2,000 wds.; stories (short vignettes or longer narratives) to 2,000 wds.; book reviews 750 wds. Responds within 13 wks. Accepts reprints. Accepts requested ms on disk or by e-mail. Guidelines/theme list on Website (click on "Weavings" under Publishing column on right side, then "Writing for Weavings"); copy for 7.5x10.5 SAE/5 stamps. Incomplete topical listings.

Poetry: Pays $75 & up.

Tips: Note that this publication is transitioning as we go to press and will likely be changing format, as well as other aspects of this listing. Check their Website for current information.

$@WESLEYAN LIFE ONLINE, Box 50434, Indianapolis IN 46250-0434. (317) 774-7909. Fax (317) 774-7913. E-mail: communications@wesleyan.org. Website: www.wesleyanlifeonline.com. The Wesleyan Church Corp. Dr. Ronald D. Kelly, gen. ed.; Jerry Brecheisen, mng. ed. Denominational. Online mag.; 40 pgs.; circ. 50,000. Subscription controlled. 10% freelance. E-mail submissions only. **Pays $50-80** for unsolicited on publication for 1st or simultaneous rts. Articles 400-500 wds. (50/yr.). Responds in 2 wks. Seasonal 6 mos. ahead. Accepts simultaneous submissions & reprints (tell when/where appeared). Guidelines by mail/e-mail/Website; copy $2. (Ads—limited)

Tips: "Most open to 400-500 word articles. Must be submitted electronically. No poetry."

$THE WILDWOOD READER, PO Box 55-0898, Jacksonville FL 32255. (904) 705-6806. E-mail: publisher@wildwoodreader.com. Website: www.wildwoodreader.com. Timson Edwards Co. Alex

Gonzalez, pub. Focus is on adult, literary short fiction that is uplifting and motivational for living life in wellness and spirit. Occasional short fiction magazine & annual anthology; 16 pgs.; circ. 100. Subscription $12. 100% unsolicited freelance. Query in writing. **Pays $10-75**, 60 days after publication for onetime rts. Fiction 800-2,400 wds. (18/yr.). Responds in 6 wks. Seasonal 4 mos. ahead. Accepts simultaneous submissions & reprints (tell when/where appeared). Requires CD by mail. Guidelines by mail; no copy. (Ads)

> **Contest:** Sponsors regular contests with winners being published. Readers pick the best of the year for an annual award.

> **Tips:** "Most open to good, solid, ready-to-print short stories that follow the indications above. I prefer new and emerging writers; we are not a high end publication yet, but working our way there. Your work must be edited and ready to publish."

WISCONSIN CHRISTIAN NEWS, PO Box 756, 1007 W. Arlington St., Marshfield WI 54449. (715) 486-8066. E-mail: christiannews@charter.net or through Website: www.wisconsinchristiannews .com. Rob E. Pue, ed. Regional Christian newspaper for all of Wisconsin; nondenominational/ evangelical. Monthly newspaper; 48 pgs.; circ. 10,000. Subscription $25. Open to freelance. **NO PAYMENT.** Articles 500-1,500 wds. Responds in 1 wk. Seasonal 2 mos. ahead. Accepts e-mail submissions (copied into message). Uses some sidebars. Also accepts submissions from children/teens. No guidelines; copy $2. (Ads)

WORD & WAY, 3236 Emerald Ln., Ste. 400, Jefferson City MO 65109-3700. (573) 635-5939, ext. 206. Fax (573) 635-1774. E-mail: wordandway@wordandway.org. Website: www.wordandway.org. Baptist. Bill Webb, ed. (bwebb@wordandway.org). Biweekly. Subscription $17.50. To glorify God.

$@THE WORLD & I ONLINE: The Magazine for Lifelong Learners, 3600 New York Ave. N.E., Washington DC 20002-1947. (202) 635-4054. Fax (202) 832-5780. E-mail: editors@worldandi .com. Website: www.worldandi.com. New World Communications. Charles Kim, pub. Scholarly and encyclopedic. Monthly online journal. Subscription rates on Website. 10-20% unsolicited freelance. Considers draft articles on speculation, or queries on specific topics (offer evidence of research/qualification on topic). E-query only. **Pays $25** following publication for onetime rts. **($100 for all electronic rights** may be offered to select authors). Articles 1,000-2,000 wds., no maximum limit (550-600/yr.). Requests free use of original photo(s) to illustrate, if available (digital only—no prints, slides, or returnable material). Responds in 6-10 wks. Query for seasonal 5 mos. ahead. No reprints. Prefers requested ms by e-mail (unformatted Word). Uses some sidebars. Guidelines on Website.

> **Special needs:** Areas of interest include Arts, Life, Travel (first person); Profiles [(a) individuals who make a difference in community; (b) successful first generation immigrants for ESL section; (c) exceptional writers, literary figures, artists, scientists, role models, etc.]; Culture (global cultural studies/peoples/societies/cultural practices, unique to specific countries, cultures, communities, worldwide; folklore and tales; American regional and ethnic heritage), Civil War. Other sections include Science, Analysis, Commentary on Current Affairs (specialist contributors only), and Book Reviews.

> **Tips:** "Life, Culture, Profiles areas most open to freelancers. Offer a great/original idea (with established background as a writer). Tone of essay should be objective. Avoid advocacy and undue partisanship. Audience is educated, nonspecialist, nonsectarian. We especially appreciate scholarly contributions."

> ** This periodical was #32 on the 2009 Top 50 Christian Publishers list (#34 in 2008, #32 in 2007, #41 in 2006).

WRECKED FOR THE ORDINARY, 1515 Skeleton Dr., Gainesville GA 30504. E-mail: editor@ wreckedfortheordinary.com. Website: www.wreckedfortheordinary.com. Jeff Goins, ed. Seeks to awake and challenge a generation of young adults to follow an unsafe Christ in a world numbed by pop Christianity. **NO PAYMENT.** Articles 600-800 wds. (longer pieces divided into 2-part series).

$WRITTEN, PO Box 250504, Atlanta GA 30325. (404) 753-8315. E-mail: editor@writtenmag.com. Website: www.writtenmag.com. Zipporah Publications LLC. Michelle Gipson, pub. Celebrates the word and the reader; nationally syndicated insert to African American newspapers across the country. Bimonthly tabloid; 12-16 pgs; circ. 130,000. Subscription $8. 20% unsolicited freelance; 80% assigned. Query/clips; e-query OK. **Pays $10-75 or .10/wd.** on publication for onetime rts. Articles 500-750 wds. (6-8/yr.); reviews 250 wds. ($75). Responds in 3 wks. Seasonal 3 mos. ahead. Accepts simultaneous submissions; no reprints. Requires e-mail submissions (attached file in Word). No kill fee. Regularly uses sidebars. Also accepts submissions from teens. Guidelines by mail/Website; copy for 9x12 SAE/$1 postage. (Ads—media kit available on Website)

> **Fillers:** Accepts 1-3/yr. Facts, quotes, tips.
> **Contest:** Next New Writer Contest.
> **Tips:** "Our column for freelancers is 'First Person Singular.' We look for heartfelt stories from writers who have something to share with readers. We look for moving stories that 'bleed on the page.'"

XAVIER REVIEW, 1 Drexel Dr., Box 110C, New Orleans LA 70125. (504) 520-7549 or (504) 520-7303. Fax (504) 520-7944. Website: www.xula.edu. Xavier University of Louisiana. Nicole Pepinster Greene, ed. (ngreene@xula.edu). Publishes nondogmatic, thought-provoking, and sometimes humorous and even irreverent work on religious subject matters. Semiannual literary jour.; 75 pgs.; circ. 300. Subscription $10 (individuals), $15(institutions). 90% unsolicited freelance; 10% assigned. Complete ms/cover letter; e-query OK. **PAYS IN COPIES** for 1st rts. Articles 250-5,000 wds. (3/yr.); fiction 250-5,000 wds. (6/yr.); book reviews 250-750 wds. Responds in 4 wks. Accepts simultaneous submissions; no reprints. Prefers accepted mss by e-mail (attached). No kill fee. Does not use sidebars. Guidelines on Website; copy for $2/7x10 SAE/3 stamps. (No ads)

> **Poetry:** Accepts 20/yr. Avant-garde, free verse, traditional; 5-60 lines. Submit max. 5 poems.

CHILDREN'S MARKETS

$ADVENTURES, 2923 Troost Ave., Kansas City MO 64109-1538. (816) 931-1900. Fax (816) 412-8306. E-mail through Website: www.wordaction.com. Donna Fillmore, ed. For 6- to 8-yr.-olds (1st & 2nd graders); emphasis on principles, character building. Weekly take-home paper; 4 pgs.; circ. 40,000. Subscription $11.96 ($2.99/child/quarter). 25% unsolicited freelance. Query; e-query OK. **Pays $15** on acceptance for multiple-use rts. Articles 200 wds. Responds in 4-6 wks. Accepts simultaneous submissions; no reprints. Accepts requested ms by e-mail (attached file). Prefers NIV. Guidelines/theme list by mail/e-mail; copy for #10 SAE/1 stamp. (No ads)

> **Special needs:** Recipes and crafts; activities.
> **Tips:** "Looking for creative activities that 1st and 2nd graders can do on their own at home; crafts, recipes, simple science projects that can be connected to the theme."

$@AMERICAN GIRL, PO Box 620497, Middleton WI 53562-0497. Toll-free (800) 360-1861. (608) 836-4848. Fax (608) 831-7089. E-mail: im_agmag_editor@pleasantco.com. Website: www .americangirl.com. Pleasant Company Publications. Kristi Thom, ed.; Barbara E. Stretchberry, mng. ed. General market; for girls ages 8-12 to recognize and celebrate girls' achievements yesterday and today, inspire their creativity, and nurture their hopes and dreams. Bimonthly & online mag.; 50 pgs.; circ. 700,000. Subscription $22.95. 5% unsolicited freelance; 10% assigned. Query (complete ms for fiction); no e-query. **Pays $1/wd. ($300 minimum)** on acceptance for 1st or all rts. Articles 150-1,000 wds. (10/yr.); fiction to 2,300 wds. (6/yr.; $500 min.). Responds in 13 wks. Seasonal 6 mos. ahead. Accepts simultaneous submissions & reprints. Kill fee 50%. Uses some sidebars.

Guidelines on Website ("Magazine"/"Contact Information"/"Our Company"/"Writer's Guidelines"); copy $3.95 (check/9x12 SAE/$2.38 postage (mark "Media Mail"). (No ads)

Poetry: All poetry is by children.

Fillers: Cartoons, puzzles, word games; $50.

Columns/Departments: Buys 10/yr. Girls Express (short profiles on girls), to 150 wds. (query); Giggle Gang (visual puzzles, mazes, word games, math puzzles, seasonal games/ puzzles), send complete ms. Pays $50-200.

Contest: Contests vary from issue to issue.

Tips: "Girls Express offers the most opportunities for freelancers. We're looking for short profiles of girls who are doing great and interesting things. Key: a girl must be the 'star' and the story written from her point of view. Be sure to include the ages of the girls you are pitching to us. Write for 8- to 12-year-olds—not teenagers."

$@ARCHAEOLOGY, E-mail: shannondustytrails@yahoo.com. Shannon Bridget Murphy, ed./ pub. Biblical archaeology for children and teens. Quarterly mag. Open to unsolicited freelance. Complete ms/cover letter; e-query OK. **Pays .02-.05/wd.** on acceptance for 1st, onetime rts. Articles 500-2,000 wds.; fiction 500-2,000 wds. Responds in 2-4 wks. Seasonal 6-8 mos. ahead. Accepts simultaneous submissions & reprints (tell when/where appeared). No kill fee. Regularly uses sidebars. Also accepts submissions from children/teens. Prefers KJV. Guidelines by e-mail.

Poetry: Open to any type of poetry from children and teens.

Fillers: Anecdotes, cartoons, facts, games, ideas, kid quotes, newsbreaks, party ideas, prayers, prose, quizzes, quotes, sermon illustrations, short humor, tips, and word puzzles.

$BEGINNER'S FRIEND, PO Box 4060, Overland Park KS 66204. (913) 432-0331. Fax (913) 722-0351. E-mail: sseditor1@juno.com. Website: www.heraldandbanner.com. Church of God (Holiness)/ Herald and Banner Press. Arlene McGehee, Sunday school ed. Denominational; for young children. Weekly take-home paper; 4 pgs.; circ. 2,700. Subscription $1.50. Complete ms/cover letter; phone/fax/e-query OK (prefers mail or e-mail). **Pays .005/wd.** on publication for 1st rts. Fiction 500-800 wds. Seasonal 6-8 mos. ahead. Accepts simultaneous submissions & reprints (tell when/ where appeared). Prefers KJV. Guidelines/theme list; copy. Not in topical listings.

$BREAD FOR GOD'S CHILDREN, Box 1017, Arcadia FL 34265-1017. (863) 494-6214. Fax (863) 993-0154. E-mail: Bread@breadministries.org. Website: www.breadministries.org. Bread Ministries Inc. Judith M. Gibbs, ed. A family magazine for serious Christians who are concerned about their children or grandchildren. Quarterly mag.; 32 pgs.; circ. 5,000. Subscription free. 20-25% unsolicited freelance. Complete ms; no e-query. **Pays $10-30 ($40-50 for fiction)** on publication for 1st rts. Not copyrighted. Articles 500-800 wds. (6/yr.); fiction & true stories 500-900 wds. for 4-10 yrs., 900-1,500 wds. for teens 13 and up (6/yr.). Responds in 8-12 wks. (may hold longer). Uses some simultaneous submissions & reprints (tell when/where appeared). Some sidebars. Prefers KJV. Guidelines by mail/e-mail; 3 copies for 9x12 SAE/5 stamps; 1 copy 3 stamps. (No ads)

Columns/Departments: Buys 5-8/yr. Let's Chat (discussion issues facing children), 500-800 wds. Teen Page (teen issues), 600-900 wds. and Idea Page (object lessons or crafts for children), 300-800 wds. $10-30.

Tips: "Most open to fiction and articles. Our child and youth fiction can always use a well-written piece about living out godly principles. We need good stories for the younger children—ages 4-10 years. Most open to fiction or real-life stories of overcoming through faith in Jesus Christ. No tag endings or adult solutions coming from children. Create realistic characters and situations. No 'sudden inspiration' solutions. Open to any areas of family life related from a godly perspective."

$CADET QUEST, PO Box 7259, Grand Rapids MI 49510. (616) 241-5616. Fax (616) 241-5558. E-mail: submissions@CalvinistCadets.org. Website: www.CalvinistCadets.org. Calvinist Cadet Corps.

G. Richard Broene, ed. To show boys ages 9-14 how God is at work in their lives and in the world around them. Mag. published 7X/yr.; 24 pgs.; circ. 7,500. Subscription $15.05. 35% unsolicited freelance. Complete ms/cover letter. **Pays .04-.06/wd.** on acceptance for 1st, onetime, or reprint rts. Articles 800-1,500 wds. (12/yr.); fiction 1,000-1,300 wds. (14/yr.). Responds in 4-6 wks. Accepts simultaneous submissions & reprints (tell when/where appeared). Accepts ms by e-mail (copied into message). Uses some sidebars. Prefers NIV. Guidelines/theme list by mail/Website ("Submissions/ Help"/"Cadet Quest Author's Info"); copy for 9x12 SAE/3 stamps. (Ads—limited)

Fillers: Buys several/yr. Quizzes, tips, puzzles; 20-200 wds. $5 & up.

Tips: "Most open to fiction or fillers tied to themes; request new theme list in January of each year (best to submit between February and April each year). Also looking for simple projects/ crafts, and puzzles (word, logic)."

$CELEBRATE, 2923 Troost Ave., Kansas City MO 64109. (816) 931-1900. Fax (816) 753-4071. E-mail through Website: www.wordaction.com. Word-Action Publishing Co./Church of the Nazarene. Melissa Hammer, sr. ed. Weekly activity/story paper connects Sunday school learning to life for preschoolers (3 & 4), kindergartners (5 & 6), and their families. Weekly take-home paper; 4 pgs.; circ. 40,000. Subscription $10. 50% unsolicited freelance. Query or complete ms/cover letter; e-query OK. **Pays $15 or .25/line** on acceptance for multiple-use rts. Articles 200 wds. Responds in 4-6 wks. No seasonal. Accepts simultaneous submissions; no reprints. Accepts e-mail submissions (attached file). Prefers NIV. Guidelines by e-mail; theme list/copy for #10 SAE/1 stamp. (No ads)

Special needs: Activities, recipes, poems, piggyback songs, and crafts for 3- to 6-year-olds.

Tips: "Activities should be something a preschooler or kindergartener can do mostly on their own at home. Supplies should be things commonly found around the house or easily obtained at craft stores."

$FACES, 30 Grove St., Ste. C, Peterborough NH 03458. Toll-free (800) 821-0115. (603) 924-7209. Fax (603) 924-7380. E-mail: facesmag@yahoo.com. Website: www.cobblestonepub.com. Cobblestone Publishing/general. Elizabeth Crooker Carpentiere, ed. Introduces young readers (ages 9-14) to different world cultures, religion, geography, government, and art. Monthly mag.; 52 pgs.; circ. 15,000. Subscription $29.95. 90-100% freelance. Query only; e-query OK. **Pays .20-.25/wd.** on publication for all rts. Articles 300-800 wds. (45-50/yr.); fiction to 800 wds. (retold folktales, legends, plays; related to theme). Responds in 4 wks. to 4 mos. Accepts simultaneous submissions. Prefers disk or hard copy. Kill fee 50%. Guidelines/themes by mail/Website (click on "Guidelines" then scroll down to "Cobblestone Publishings Group Magazines" and click on "Faces"); copy $4.95/9x12 SAE/$2.07 postage; also online.

Poetry: Any type to 100 wds.

Fillers: Activities, 100-600 wds. .20-.25/wd.

$@FOCUS ON THE FAMILY CLUBHOUSE, 8605 Explorer Dr., Colorado Springs CO 80920. (719) 531-3400. Website: www.clubhousemagazine.com. Focus on the Family. Jesse Florea, ed.; Joanna Lutz, asst. ed.; submit to Ashley Eiman, ed. asst. For children 8-12 years who desire to know more about God and the Bible. Monthly & online mag.; 32 pgs.; circ. 90,000. Subscription $19.99. 15% unsolicited freelance; 25% assigned. Complete ms/cover letter; no phone/fax/e-query. **Pays .15-.25/wd.** for articles, **up to $300 for fiction** on acceptance for nonexclusive license. Articles to 800 wds. (5/yr.); fiction 500-1,800 wds. (30/yr.). Responds in 8 wks. Seasonal 6 mos. ahead. Accepts simultaneous submissions; no reprints. No disk or e-mail submissions. Kill fee. Uses some sidebars. Prefers NIV. Also accepts submissions from children once a year. Guidelines by mail; copy (call 800-232-6459). (No ads)

Fillers: Buys 6-8/yr. Quizzes, word puzzles, recipes; 200-800 wds., .15-.25/wd.

Tips: "Most open to fiction, personality stories, quizzes, and how-to pieces with a theme. Avoid stories dealing with boy-girl relationships, poetry, and contemporary, middle-class

family settings (current authors meet this need). We look for fiction in exciting settings with ethnic characters. Creatively retold Bible stories and historical fiction are easy ways to break in. Send manuscripts with list of credentials. Read past issues."
** 2010, 2009, 2008, 2007, 2006 EPA Award of Merit: Youth.

$@FOCUS ON THE FAMILY CLUBHOUSE JR., 8605 Explorer Dr., Colorado Springs CO 80920. (719) 531-3400. Fax (719) 531-3499. E-mail: joanna.lutz@fotf.org. Website: www.clubhousemaga zine.com. Focus on the Family. Suzanne Hadley, ed.; Joanna Lutz, asst. ed.; submit to Ashley Eiman, ed. asst.; Suzanne Gosselin, nonfiction ed. For 3- to 7-year-olds growing up in a Christian family. Monthly & online mag.; 32 pgs.; circ. 80,000. Subscription $19.99. 25% unsolicited freelance; 50% assigned. Complete ms/cover letter; no phone/fax/e-query. **Pays $30-200 ($50-200 for fiction)** on accep- tance for nonexclusive rts. Articles 100-500 wds. (1-2/yr.); fiction 250-1,000 wds. (10/yr.); Bible stories 250-800 wds.; one-page rebus stories to 350 wds. Responds in 8 wks. Seasonal 6-9 mos. ahead. Kill fee 25%. Uses some sidebars. Guidelines by mail; copy (call 800-232-6459). (No ads)

Poetry: Buys 4-8/yr. Traditional; 10-25 lines (to 250 wds.); $50-100.

Fillers: Buys 4-8/yr. Recipes/crafts; 100-500 wds. $30-100.

Special needs: Bible stories, rebus, fiction, and crafts.

Tips: "Most open to short, nonpreachy fiction, beginning reader stories, and read-to-me. Be knowledgeable of our style and try it out on kids first. Looking for stories set in exotic places; nonwhite, middle-class characters; historical pieces; humorous quizzes; and craft and recipe features are most readily accepted."
** 2010 EPA Award of Excellence: Youth; 2007 EPA Award of Merit: Youth.

@GIRLS CONNECTION, 1445 N. Boonville Ave., Springfield MO 65802-1894. Website: http://mgc .ag.org/connection. Missionettes Girls Clubs/Assemblies of God. A program for winning girls to Jesus Christ through love and acceptance. Webzine.

$GOOD NEWS, 2621 Dryden Rd., Moraine OH 45439. (937) 293-1415. Fax (937) 293-1310. E-mail: service@pflaum.com. Website: www.pflaum.com. Catholic. Joan Mitchell CSJ, ed. For chil- dren in grades 2 and 3. Weekly (32X) take-home paper. **Pays.** Not in topical listings.

$GUIDE, 55 W. Oak Ridge Dr., Hagerstown MD 21740. (301) 393-4037. Fax (301) 393-4055. E-mail: Guide@rhpa.org. Website: www.guidemagazine.org. Seventh-day Adventist/Review and Herald Publishing. Rachel Whitaker, assoc. ed. A Christian journal for 10- to 14-yr.-olds, present- ing true stories relevant to their needs. Weekly mag.; 32 pgs.; circ. 26,000. Subscription $54.95/ yr. 75% unsolicited freelance; 20% assigned. Complete ms/cover letter; fax/e-query OK. **Pays .07- .10/wd. ($25-140)** on acceptance for 1st, reprint, simultaneous, and electronic rts. True stories only, 500-1,300 wds. (200/yr.). Responds in 4-6 wks. Seasonal 8 mos. ahead. Accepts simultaneous submissions & reprints (tell when/where appeared; pays 50% of standard rate). Prefers requested ms by e-mail (attached or copied into message). Kill fee 20-50%. Regularly uses sidebars. Accepts submissions from children/teens. Prefers NIV. Guidelines on Website ("Contact Us"/scroll down to "Writer's Guidelines") or by mail; copy for 6x9 SAE/2 stamps. (Ads)

Fillers: Buys 40-50/yr. Cartoons, games, quizzes, word puzzles on a spiritual theme; 20-50 wds. $20-40. Accepting very few games, only the most unusual concepts.

Columns/Departments: Accepts 5-10/yr. You Said It (100-300 wd. true stories written by kids 10-14). Complete ms. Pays a complimentary book.

Special needs: "Most open to true action/adventure, Christian humor, and true stories showing God at work in a 10- to 14-year-old's life. Stories must have energy and a high level of intrinsic interest to kids. Put it together with dialog and a spiritual slant, and you're on the 'write' track for our readers. School life."

Tips: "We are very open to freelancers. Use your best short-story techniques (dialogue, scenes, a sense of 'plot') to tell a true story starring a kid ages 10-14. Bring out a clear

spiritual/biblical message. We publish multipart true stories regularly; 3-12 chapters, 1,200 words each. We can no longer accept nature or historical stories without documentation. All topics indicated need to be addressed within the context of a true story."
** This periodical was #17 on the 2010 Top 50 Christian Publishers list (#23 in 2009, #24 in 2008, #27 in 2007, #44 in 2006).

$JUNIOR COMPANION, PO Box 4060, Overland Park KS 66204. (913) 432-0331. Fax (913) 722-0351. E-mail: sseditor1@juno.com. Website: www.heraldandbanner.com. Church of God (holiness)/ Herald and Banner Press. Arlene McGehee, Sunday school ed. Denominational; for 4th-6th graders. Weekly take-home paper; 4 pgs.; circ. 3,500. Subscription $1.50/quarter. Complete ms/cover letter; phone/fax/e-query OK (prefers mail or e-mail). **Pays .005/wd.** on publication for 1st rts. Fiction 500-1,200 wds. Seasonal 6-8 mos. ahead. Accepts simultaneous submissions & reprints (tell when/ where appeared). Prefers KJV. Guidelines/theme list/copy by mail. Not in topical listings.

$JUNIORWAY, PO Box 436987, Chicago IL 60643. Fax (708) 868-6759. Website: www.urbanmin istries.com. Urban Ministries Inc. K. Steward, ed. (ksteward@urbanministries.com). Sunday school magazine with accompanying teacher's guide and activity booklet for 4th-6th graders. Open to free-lance queries; 100% assigned. Query and/or e-query with writing sample and/or clips; no phone queries. **Pays $150** for curriculum, 120 days after acceptance for all rts. Articles 1,200 wds. (4/yr.), pays $80. Responds in 4 wks. No simultaneous submissions. Requires requested material by e-mail (attached file). Guidelines by e-mail. Incomplete topical listings. (No ads)

   Poetry: Buys 8/yr.; 200-400 wds. pays $40.

   Tips: *"Juniorway* principally serves an African American audience; editorial content addresses broad Christian issues. Looking for those with educational or Sunday school teaching experience who can actually explain Scriptures in an insightful and engaging way and apply those Scriptures to the lives of children 9-11 years old."

$@KEYS FOR KIDS, PO Box 1001, Grand Rapids MI 49501-1001. (616) 647-4971. Fax (616) 647-4950. E-mail: Hazel@cbhministries.org, or geri@cbhministries.org. Website: www.cbhministries.org. CBH Ministries. Hazel Marett, ed.; Geri Walcott, ed. A daily devotional booklet for children (8-14) or for family devotions. Bimonthly booklet & online version; 80 pgs.; circ. 70,000. Subscription free. 100% unsolicited freelance. Complete ms; e-query OK. Accepts full mss by e-mail. **Pays $25** on acceptance for 1st, reprint, or simultaneous rts. Devotionals (includes short fiction story) 375-425 wds. (60-70/yr.). Responds in 4-8 wks. Seasonal 4-5 mos. ahead. Accepts simultaneous submissions & reprints. Prefers NKJV. Guidelines by mail/e-mail; copy for $1.39 postage. (No ads)

   Tips: "We want children's devotions. If you are rejected, go back to the sample and study it some more. We use only devotionals, but they include a short fiction story. Any appropriate topic is fine."

$@THE KIDS' ARK CHILDREN'S CHRISTIAN MAGAZINE, PO Box 3160, Victoria TX 77903. Toll-free (800) 455-1770. (361) 485-1770. E-mail for queries: editor@thekidsark.com. Website: http://thekidsark.com. Interdenominational. Submit to: Joy Mygrants, sr. ed. To give kids, 6-12, a bib-lical foundation on which to base their choices in life. Quarterly & online mag.; 36 pgs.; circ. 8,000. 100% unsolicited freelance. Complete ms; e-query OK. Accepts full ms by e-mail. **Pays $100 max.** on publication for 1st, reprint ($25), electronic, worldwide rts. Fiction 600 wds. (Buys 4 stories/ issue—16/yr.); no articles. Responds in 3-4 wks. No reprints. Prefers accepted submissions by e-mail (attached file). Kill fee 15%. Uses some sidebars. Also accepts submissions from children/ teens. Prefers NIV. Guidelines/theme list on Website ("Writer's Guidelines"); copy for $1 postage. (Ads—limited)

   Tips: "Open to fiction only (any time period). Think outside the box! Must catch children's attention and hold it; be biblically based and related to theme. We want to teach God's principles in an exciting format. Every issue contains the Ten Commandments and the plan of salvation."

$NATURE FRIEND: Helping Children Explore the Wonders of God's Creation, 4253 Woodcock Ln., Dayton VA 22821. (540) 867-0764. Fax (540) 867-9516. E-mail: editor@nature friendmagazine.com. Website: www.naturefriendmagazine.com. Dogwood Ridge Outdoors. Kevin Shank, ed. For ages 6-16. Monthly mag.; 24 pgs.; circ. 13,000. Subscription $36. 50-80% freelance written. Complete ms/cover letter; no phone/fax/e-query. **Pays .05/wd.** on publication for 1st rts. Articles 250-900 wds. (50/yr.); or fiction 500-750 wds. (40/yr.). Responds in 12-13 wks. Seasonal 4 mos. ahead. Accepts simultaneous submissions & reprints. Submit accepted articles on disk (Word format) or by e-mail. Uses some sidebars. KJV only. Guidelines $5 (www.naturefriendmagazine.com/index.pl?linkid=12;class=gen); copy $5/ SAE/$2 postage. (No ads)

Fillers: Buys 12/yr. Quizzes, word puzzles; 100-500 wds. $10-15.

Columns/Departments: "Month" Nature Trails (seasonal, nature activity for each month); 100-450 wds. Write up as something you do each year, such as mushroom hunting, wildflower walk, snowshoeing, Christmas bird count, viewing a specific meteor shower, etc.

Tips: "We want to bring joy and knowledge to children by opening the world of God's creation to them. We endeavor to create a sense of awe about nature's Creator and a respect for His creation. I'd like to see more submissions of hands-on things to do with a nature theme. The best way to learn about the content we use is to be a current, active subscriber."

$@NEW MOON: The Magazine for Girls and Their Dreams, New Moon Girl Media, PO Box 161287, Duluth MN 56816. Toll-free (800) 381-4743. (218) 728-5507. Fax (218) 728-0314. E-mail: help@newmoon.com. Website: www.newmoon.org. New Moon Publishing. Submit to Editorial Dept. A feminist publication for girls 8-14 years of age; we value diversity and take girls seriously. Bimonthly & online mag.; 49 pgs.; circ. 30,000. Subscription $34.95. 40% unsolicited freelance; 50% assigned. Query or complete ms/cover letter; e-query OK. Accepts full mss by e-mail. **Pays .06/wd.** on publication for all rts. Articles 600-1,200 wds. (12/yr.); fiction 1,200-1,500 wds. (6/yr.); book reviews 300 wds. Responds in 24 wks. No seasonal/holiday. Accepts simultaneous submissions & reprints (tell when/where appeared). Prefers accepted articles by e-mail (copied into message). No kill fee. Regularly uses sidebars. Also accepts submissions from girls and teens. Guidelines/theme list on Website; copy $7/9x12 SAE. (No ads)

Poetry: Buys 12/yr. Poetry from girls 8-14 only. Pays $10. Submit any number/any length.

Columns/Departments: Buys 18/yr. Herstory (women from history), 600 wds. Women's Work (women in careers), 600 wds. Body Language (health & puberty issues for girls), 600 wds. Pays .06/wd.

Tips: "We accept work from girls and women only. Girls can submit to any department. Adults must limit their submissions to fiction and the columns listed above."

$OUR LITTLE FRIEND, 1350 N. Kings Rd., Nampa ID 83687. (208) 465-2500. Fax (208) 465-2531. E-mail: ailsox@pacificpress.com or through Website: www.pacificpress.com. Seventh-day Adventist. Aileen Andres Sox, ed. To help children understand their infinite value to their Creator and Redeemer; learn how to respond to God; show love to their family and friends; serve others in their world; find fulfillment participating in the Seventh-day Adventist Church. Weekly take-home paper for 1- to 6-yr.-olds; 8 pgs. Subscription $25.96. 25% unsolicited freelance (or reprints); 50% assigned. Complete ms by e-mail (attached file). **Pays $25-40** on acceptance for onetime or reprint rts. True stories 450-550 wds. (52/yr.); no articles. Responds in 26 wks. Seasonal 7 mos. ahead. Accepts simultaneous submissions & reprints; no serials. Prefers e-mail submissions (attached file). Guidelines by mail/Website (click on "Information"/"Submissions Guidelines"); copy for 9x12 SAE/2 stamps. (No ads)

$PARTNERS, Christian Light Publications Inc., Box 1212, Harrisonburg VA 22803-1212. (540) 434-0768. Fax (540) 433-8896. E-mail: partners@clp.org. Website: www.clp.org. Mennonite. Etta G. Martin, ed. Helping 9- to 14-yr.-olds to build strong Christian character. Weekly take-home paper;

4 pgs.; circ. 6,923. Subscription $11.45. 99% unsolicited freelance; 1% assigned. Complete ms; e-query OK. **Pays .04-.06/wd.** on acceptance for 1st, multiuse, or reprint rts. Articles 200-800 wds. (100/yr.); fiction & true stories 400-1,600 wds. (200/yr.); serial stories up to 1,600 wds./installment; short-short stories to 400 wds. Responds in 6 wks. Seasonal 6 mos. ahead. Accepts reprints only 5 yrs. or more after last publication (tell when/where appeared); serials 2 parts. Prefers e-mail submissions (attached or copied into message). No kill fee. Requires KJV. Guidelines/theme list by mail/e-mail; copy for 9x12 SAE/3 stamps. (No ads)

Poetry: Buys 250/yr. Traditional, story poems; 4-24 lines; .65-.75/line.

Fillers: Buys 275/yr. Prose, quizzes, quotes, word puzzles (Bible-related); 200-800 wds., .04-.06/wd.

Columns/Departments: Character Corner; Cultures & Customs; Historical Highlights; Maker's Masterpiece; Missionary Mail; Torches of Truth; or Nature Nook; all 200-800 wds.

Tips: "Most open to character-building articles and stories that teach a spiritual lesson. New approaches to old themes, or new theme relevant to age level. Please ask for our guidelines before submitting manuscripts. Write in a lively way (showing, not telling) and on a child's level of understanding (ages 9-14). We do not require that you be Mennonite, but we do send a questionnaire for you to fill out if you desire to write for us."

** This periodical was #3 on the 2010 Top 50 Christian Publishers list (#2 in 2009, #3 in 2008, #14 in 2007, #15 in 2006).

$POCKETS, PO Box 340004, Nashville TN 37203-0004. (615) 340-7333. Fax (615) 340-7267. E-mail: pockets@upperroom.org or through Website: www.pockets.upperroom.org. United Methodist/The Upper Room. Submit to Lynn W. Gilliam, ed. Devotional magazine for children (6-11 yrs.). Monthly (11X) mag.; 48 pgs.; circ. 67,000. Subscription $21.95. 75% unsolicited freelance. Complete ms/brief cover letter; no phone/fax/e-query. **Pays .14/wd.** on acceptance for onetime rts. Articles 400-800 wds. (10/yr.) & fiction 600-1,400 wds. (40/yr.). Responds in 8 wks. Seasonal 1 yr. ahead. Accepts simultaneous submissions & reprints (tell when/where appeared). No mss by e-mail. Uses some sidebars. Prefers NRSV. Also accepts submissions from children through age 12. Guidelines/theme list by mail/e-mail/Website (click on "Print Magazine"/"Write for Pockets"); copy for 9x12 SAE/4 stamps. (No ads)

Poetry: Buys 25/yr. Free verse, haiku, light verse, traditional; to 25 lines; $25-48. Submit max. 7 poems.

Fillers: Buys 50/yr. Games, word puzzles; $25-50.

Columns/Departments: Buys 20/yr. Complete ms. Kids Cook; Pocketsful of Love (ways to show love in your family), 200-300 wds. Peacemakers at Work (children involved in environmental, community, and peace/justice issues; include action photos and name of photographer), to 600 wds. Pocketsful of Prayer, 400-600 wds. Someone You'd Like to Know (preferably a child whose lifestyle demonstrates a strong faith perspective), 600 wds. Pays .14/wd.

Special needs: Two-page stories for ages 5-7, 600 words max. Need role model stories, retold biblical stories, Someone You'd Like to Know, and Peacemakers at Work.

Contest: Fiction-writing contest; submit between 3/1 & 8/15 every year. Prize $1,000 and publication in *Pockets*. Length 1,000-1,600 wds. Must be unpublished and not historical fiction. Previous winners not eligible. Send to Pockets Fiction Contest at above address, and include an SASE for return of manuscript and response. Write "Fiction Contest" on envelope and on title/first page of manuscript.

Tips: "Well-written fiction that fits our themes is always needed. Make stories relevant to the lives of today's children and show faith as a natural part of everyday life. All areas open to freelance. Nonfiction probably easiest to sell for columns (we get fewer submissions for those). Read, read, read, and study. Be attentive to guidelines, themes, and study past issues."

** This periodical was #8 on the 2010 Top 50 Christian Publishers list (#6 in 2009, #8 in 2008, #11 in 2007, #12 in 2006).

$PRESCHOOL PLAYHOUSE, PO Box 436987, Chicago IL 60643. (708) 868-7100. E-mail: jgrier@urbanministries.com. Website: www.urbanministries.com. Urban Ministries Inc. Janet Grier, ed. Quarterly Sunday school curriculum including student magazine, teacher's guide, and teaching resources for 2- to 5-year-olds. Open to freelance; 100% assigned. Query/clips and/or writing sample; no phone query. **Pays $150** for curriculum 120 days after acceptance for all rts. Assignments only. No simultaneous submissions or reprints. Requires accepted ms by e-mail only (attached file). No kill fee. Requires NIV. Include sample of age-appropriate curriculum writing/Bible explanation for children with request for guidelines. Guidelines for #10 SASE. (No ads)

> **Tips:** "*Preschool Playhouse* principally serves an urban, African American audience; editorial content addresses broad Christian issues. Looking for writers with educational or Sunday school teaching experience who can accurately explain Scripture in an insightful and engaging way and apply those Scriptures to the lives of children 2-5 years old."

$PRIMARY PAL, PO Box 4060, Overland Park KS 66204. (913) 432-0331. Fax (913) 722-0351. E-mail: sseditor1@juno.com. Website: www.heraldandbanner.com. Church of God (holiness)/Herald and Banner Press. Arlene McGehee, Sunday school ed. Denominational; for 1st-3rd graders. Weekly take-home paper; 4 pgs.; circ. 2,900. Subscription $1.50. Complete ms/cover letter; phone/fax/e-query OK (prefers mail or e-mail). **Pays .005/wd.** on publication for 1st rts. Fiction 500-1,000 wds. Seasonal 6-8 mos. ahead. Accepts simultaneous submissions & reprints (tell when/where appeared). Prefers KJV. Guidelines/theme list/copy by mail. Not in topical listings.

$PRIMARY STREET, PO Box 436987, Chicago IL 60643. (708) 868-7100. E-mail: jgrier@urbanministries.com. Website: www.urbanministries.com. Urban Ministries Inc. Janet Grier, ed. Quarterly Sunday school curriculum including student magazine, teacher's guide, and teaching resources for 6- to 8-year-olds. Open to freelance queries; 100% assigned. **Pays $150** for curriculum 120 days after acceptance for all rts. Assignments only. No simultaneous submissions or reprints. Requires accepted ms by e-mail only (attached file). No kill fee. Will accept sidebars on assigned educational topics; pay varies. Requires NIV. Include sample of age-appropriate curriculum writing/Bible explanation for children with request for guidelines. Guidelines for #10 SASE. (No ads)

> **Tips:** "*Primary Street* principally serves an urban, African American audience; editorial content addresses broad Christian issues. Looking for writers with educational or Sunday school teaching experience who can accurately explain Scripture in an insightful and engaging way and apply those Scriptures to the lives of children 6-8 years old."

$PRIMARY TREASURE, 1350 N. Kings Rd., Nampa ID 83687. (208) 465-2500. Fax (208) 465-2531. E-mail: ailsox@pacificpress.com or through Website: www.pacificpress.com. Seventh-day Adventist. Aileen Andres Sox, ed. To help children understand their infinite value to their Creator and Redeemer; learn how to respond to God; show love to their family and friends; serve others in their world; find fulfillment participating in the Seventh-day Adventist Church. Weekly take-home paper for 6- to 9-yr.-olds (1st-4th grades); 16 pgs. 50% freelance (assigned), 25% reprints or unsolicited. Complete ms by e-mail preferred (attached file). **Pays $25-50** on acceptance for onetime or reprint rts. True stories 900-1,000 wds. (52/yr.); articles used rarely (query). Responds in 13 wks. Seasonal 7 mos. ahead. For simultaneous submissions & reprints see guidelines; serials to 10 parts (query). Guidelines by mail/Website (click on "Information"/"Submissions Guidelines"); copy for 9x12 SAE/2 stamps. (No ads)

> **Tips:** "We need true adventure stories with a spiritual slant; positive, lively stories about children facing modern problems and making good choices. We always need strong stories about boys and stories featuring dads. We need a spiritual element that frequently is missing from submissions."

$PROMISE, 2621 Dryden Rd., Moraine OH 45439. Toll-free (800) 543-4383. (937) 293-1415. Fax (937) 293-1310. E-mail: service@pflaum.com. Website: www.pflaum.com. Catholic. Joan Mitchell CSJ, ed. For kindergarten and grade 1; encourages them to participate in parish worship. Weekly (32X) take-home paper. **Pays.** Not in topical listings.

$+REAL, 55 W. Oak Ridge Dr., Hagerstown MD 21740-7301. (301) 393-4037. E-mail: real@rhpa .org. Website: www.realmagazineonline.org. Seventh-day Adventist. Geared for children ages 9-15 outside the faith. Bimonthly mag. Subscription $18.95. **Pays.** Estab. 1/10.

$SEEDS, 2621 Dryden Rd., Moraine OH 45439. (937) 293-1415. Fax (937) 293-1310. E-mail: service@pflaum.com. Website: www.pflaum.com. Catholic. Joan Mitchell CSJ, ed. Prepares children to learn about God; for preschoolers. Weekly (32X) take-home paper; 4 pgs. **Pays.** Not in topical listings.

$SHINE BRIGHTLY, Box 7259, Grand Rapids MI 49510. (616) 241-5616, ext. 3034. Fax (616) 241-5558. E-mail: servicecenter@gemsgc.org. Website: www.gemsgc.org. GEMS Girls Clubs. Sara Hilton, ed. (734-478-1596; sara@gemsgc.org). To show girls ages 9-14 that God is at work in their lives and in the world around them. Monthly (9X) mag.; 24 pgs.; circ. 13,000. Subscription $13.25. 80% unsolicited freelance; 20% assigned. Complete ms; no e-query. **Pays .03-.05/wd.** on publication for 1st or reprint rts. Articles 100-400 wds. (35/yr.); fiction 400-900 wds. (30/yr.). Responds in 4-6 wks. Seasonal 10 mos. ahead. Accepts simultaneous submissions & reprints. Accepts requested ms on disk. Regularly uses sidebars. Prefers NIV. Guidelines/theme list on Website (click on "Girls" tab/"Shine Brightly"/Magazine cover for SB in the right-hand column/"Writers"); copy $1/9x12 SAE/3 stamps. (No ads)

    Fillers: Buys 10/yr. Cartoons, games, party ideas, prayers, quizzes, short humor, word puzzles; 50-200 wds. $5-10.

    Special needs: Craft ideas that can be used to help others. Articles on how words can help build others up or tear people down.

    Tips: "Be realistic—we get a lot of fluffy stories with Pollyanna endings. We are looking for real-life-type stories that girls relate to. We mostly publish short stories but are open to short reflective articles. Know what girls face today and how they cope in their daily lives. We need angles from home life and friendships, peer pressure, and the normal growing-up challenges girls deal with."

SKIPPING STONES: A Multicultural Magazine, PO Box 3939, Eugene OR 97403. (541) 342-4956. E-mail: editor@skippingstones.org. Website: www.skippingstones.org. Interfaith/multicultural. Arun N. Toké, exec. ed. A multicultural awareness and nature appreciation magazine for young people 7-17, worldwide. In 22nd year. Bimonthly (5X) mag.; 36 pgs.; circ. 2,500. Subscription $25. 85% unsolicited freelance; 15% assigned. Query or complete ms/cover letter; no phone query; e-query/submissions OK. **PAYS IN COPIES** (40% discount on extra issues) for 1st, electronic, and nonexclusive reprint rts. Articles (15-25/yr.) 750-1,000 wds.; fiction for teens, 750-1,000 wds. Responds in 9-13 wks. Seasonal 2-4 mos. ahead. Accepts simultaneous submissions. Accepts ms on disk or by e-mail. Regularly uses sidebars. Guidelines/theme list by mail/e-mail/Website ("Writing for Us"/"Guidelines" on left side); copy $6. (No ads)

    Poetry: Only from kids under 18. Accepts 100/yr. Any type; 3-30 lines. Submit max. 4-5 poems.

    Fillers: Accepts 10-20/yr. Anecdotes, cartoons, games, quizzes, short humor, word puzzles; to 250 wds.

    Columns/Departments: Accepts 10/yr. Noteworthy News (multicultural/nature/international/social, appropriate for youth), 200 wds.

    Special needs: Stories and articles on your community and country, peace, nonviolent communication, compassion, kindness, spirituality, tolerance, and giving.

    Contest: Annual Book Awards for published books and authors (deadline February 1);

Annual Youth Honor Awards for students 7-17 (deadline June 25). Send SASE for guidelines, or check the Website.

Tips: "Most of the magazine is open to freelance. We're seeking submissions by minority, multicultural, international, and/or youth writers. Do not be judgmental or preachy; be open or receptive to diverse opinions."

$SPARKLE, PO Box 7259, Grand Rapids MI 49510. (616) 241-5616. Fax (616) 241-5558. E-mail: amy@gemsgc.org, or servicecenter@gemsgc.org. Website: www.gemsgc.org. GEMS Girls' Clubs (nondenominational). Sara Hilton, ed. (734-478-1596/sara@gemsgc.org). To prepare girls, grades 1-3, to live out their faith and become world changers; to help girls make a difference in the world. Published 6X/yr. (October-March). Subscription $10.25. 80% unsolicited freelance; 20% assigned. Complete ms; no e-query. **Pays .03/wd.** on publication for 1st, reprint, or simultaneous rts. Articles 200-400 wds. (10/yr.); fiction 200-400 words (6/yr.). Responds in 6 wks. Seasonal 10 mos. ahead. Accepts simultaneous submissions & reprints. Accepts requested ms on disk. Regularly uses sidebars. Prefers NIV. Guidelines/theme list by mail/e-mail/Website (click on "Girls" tab/"Sparkle"/Magazine cover for *Sparkle* in right-hand column/"Writers"); copy $1/9x12 SAE/3 stamps. (No ads)

   Fillers: Buys 10/yr. Games, party ideas, prayers, quizzes, short humor; 50-200 wds. $5-15.

   Tips: "Send in pieces that teach girls how to be world-changers for Christ, or that fit our annual theme. We also are always looking for games, crafts, and recipes. Keep the writing simple. Keep activities short. Engage a 3rd grader, while being easy enough for a 1st grader to understand."

$STORY MATES, Box 1212, Harrisonburg VA 22803-1212. (540) 434-0750. Fax (540) 433-8896. E-mail: StoryMates@clp.org. Website: www.clp.org. Mennonite/Christian Light Publications Inc. Crystal Shank, ed. For 4- to 8-yr.-olds. Weekly take-home paper; 4 pgs.; circ. 6,500. Subscription $11.45. 90% unsolicited freelance. Complete ms. **Pays up to .05/wd.** on acceptance for 1st rts. **(.06/wd. for 1st rts., plus reprint rts.).** Realistic or true stories, 800-900 wds. (50-75/yr.); picture stories 120-150 wds. Responds in 6 wks. Seasonal 6 mos. ahead. Accepts simultaneous submissions & reprints (tell when/where appeared). No disk. Requires KJV. Guidelines/theme list by mail/e-mail; copy for 9x12 SAE/3 stamps. Will send questionnaire to fill out. (No ads)

   Poetry: Buys 25/yr. Traditional, any length. Few story poems. Pays up to .65/line.

   Fillers: Quizzes, word puzzles, craft ideas. "Need fillers that correlate with theme list; Bible related." Pays about $10.

   Special needs: True or true-to-life stories the children can relate to.

   Tips: "Carefully read our guidelines and understand our conservative Mennonite applications of Bible principles." Very conservative.

   ** This periodical was #49 on the 2007 Top 50 Christian Publishers list.

$VENTURE, 2621 Dryden Rd., Moraine OH 45439. (937) 293-1415. Fax (937) 293-1310. E-mail: service@pflaum.com. Website: www.pflaum.com. Catholic. Joan Mitchell CSJ, ed. For grades 4-6. Weekly (52X) take-home paper. **Pays.** Not in topical listings.

+THE VIRTUOUS GIRL, A Magazine by Girls for Girls, Website: www.thevirtuousgirl.org. Independent Seventh-day Adventist ministry. Quarterly magazine & e-zine.

CHRISTIAN EDUCATION/LIBRARY MARKETS

$CATECHIST, 2621 Dryden Rd., 3rd Fl., Dayton OH 45439. Toll-free (800) 523-4625. (937) 847-5900. Fax (314) 638-6812. E-mail: kdotterweich@peterli.com. Website: www.catechist.com. Catholic; Peter Li Education Group. Kass Dotterweich, ed. For Catholic school teachers and parish volunteer catechists. Mag. published 7X/yr.; 52 pgs.; circ. 52,000. Subscription $26.95. 30% unsolicited freelance; 70% assigned. Query (preferred) or complete ms. **Pays $25-150 (variable**

rates) on publication. Articles 1,200 wds. Responds in 9-18 wks. Guidelines by mail/Website (click on "About"/"Writers Guidelines"); copy $3.

Tips: "Most open to 'From the Field' column: Classroom ideas to 600 wds."

CATHOLIC LIBRARY WORLD, 100 North St., Ste. 224, Pittsfield MA 01201-5178. (413) 443-2252. Fax (413) 442-2252. E-mail: cla@cathla.org. Website: www.cathla.org. Catholic Library Assn. Sr. Mary E. Gallagher SSJ, gen. ed. For libraries at all levels—preschool to postsecondary to academic, parish, public, and private. Quarterly jour.; 80 pgs.; circ. 1,000. Subscription $60/$85 foreign. 90% unsolicited freelance; 10% assigned. Query or complete ms; phone/fax/e-query OK. **PAYS 1 COPY** for all rts. Articles (12-16/yr.); book/video reviews, 300-500 wds. Responds in 4-6 wks. No simultaneous submissions or reprints. Accepts requested ms on disk. Uses some sidebars. No guidelines; copy for 9x12 SAE. (Ads)

Special needs: Topics of interest to academic libraries, high school and children's libraries, parish and community libraries, archives, and library education. Reviewers cover areas such as theology, spirituality, pastoral, professional, juvenile books and material, and media.

Tips: "Review section considers taking on new reviewers who are experts in field of librarianship, theology, and professional studies. No payment except a free copy of the book or materials reviewed. Query us by mail or e-mail."

$@CHILDREN'S MINISTRY MAGAZINE, 1515 Cascade Ave., Loveland CO 80539. Toll-free (800) 447-1070. Fax (970) 292-4373. E-mail: jhooks@cmmag.com or info@group.com. Website: www .childrensministry.com. Group Publishing/nondenominational. Christine Yount Jones, exec. ed.; submit to Jennifer Hooks, mng. ed. (jhooks@cmmag.com). The leading resource for adults who work with children (ages 0-12) in the church. Bimonthly & online mag.; 140 pgs.; circ. 60,000. Subscription $29.95. 40% unsolicited freelance; 60% assigned. Complete ms/cover letter; e-query OK. **Pays $25-400** on acceptance for all & electronic rts. Articles 50-1,800 wds. (250-300/yr.). Responds in 8-10 wks. Seasonal 6-9 mos. ahead. No simultaneous submissions or reprints. Accepts requested ms by e-mail (attached or copied into message). Regularly uses sidebars. Also accepts submissions from children/teens. Sometimes pays kill fee. Prefers NLT. Guidelines by mail/e-mail/ Website; copy $2/9x12 SAE/$2.38 postage (mark Media Mail). (Ads)

Fillers: Buys 25-50/yr. Cartoons, kid quotes; 25-50 wds. $25-60.

Columns/Departments: Submit to Carmen Kamrath (ckamrath@cmmag.com). Buys 200+/yr. Age-level insights (age-appropriate ideas); Family Ministry (family ideas); Reaching Out (outreach ideas); 150-250 wds. Teacher Telegram (ideas for teachers); For Parents Only (parenting ideas); 150-300 wds. $40-150. Complete ms.

Special needs: Seasonal ideas, outreach ideas, volunteer management, and family ministry. Always looking for new ideas, crafts, games, and activities.

Tips: "All areas open to freelancers. Start small—ideas, activities, and personal essays. Or go big—wow us with a profoundly inspiring article that fits the magazine's makeup. We're looking for stand-out ideas and the very latest in this important ministry area. If you're in the trenches, we want to hear from you. We seek features from experts in practice or in theory. No poetry or fiction."

** This periodical was #4 on the 2010 Top 50 Christian Publishers list (#5 in 2009, #4 in 2008, #8 in 2007, #5 in 2006).

CHRISTIAN EARLY EDUCATION, PO Box 65130, Colorado Springs CO 80921. Toll-free (888) 892-4258. (719) 528-6906. Fax (719) 531-0631. E-mail: earlyeducation@acsi.org. Website: www .acsi.org. Assn. of Christian Schools Intl. D'Arcy Maher, sr. ed. Equips individuals serving children ages 0-5 from a biblical perspective. Quarterly mag.; 32 pgs.; circ. 6,000. Subscription $14. 10% unsolicited freelance; 90% assigned. Query; phone/fax/e-query OK. Accepts full mss by e-mail. **PAYS IN COPIES** for 1st, reprint rts. Articles 400-1,800 wds. (12-15/yr.); book reviews 100-300 wds.

Responds in 4 wks. Seasonal 10 mos. ahead. Accepts reprints (tell when/where appeared). Requires e-mail submissions (attached file). Uses some sidebars. Prefers NIV. Guidelines/theme list by e-mail; free copy. (Ads)

Fillers: Accepts 4/yr; kid quotes, 10-30 wds.

Columns/Departments: Accepts up to 10/yr. Staff Training (training for teachers of young children, to use in staff meeting), 400 wds. Parents' Place (material suitable for parents of young children), 400 wds. Complete ms.

Tips: "Most open to these columns: Unique Perspectives, Footprints in Development, Professional Edge, Resource Review, Heart 2 Heart, and Field Trip."

$CHRISTIAN EDUCATORS JOURNAL, 73 Highland Ave., St. Catherines ON L2R 4H9, Canada. Phone/fax (905) 684-3991. E-mail: bert.witvoet@sympatico.ca or through Website: www.CEJonline .com. Christian Educators Journal Assn. Bert Witvoet, mng. ed. For educators in Christian day schools at the elementary, secondary, and college levels. Quarterly jour.; 36 pgs.; circ. 4,200. Subscription $7.50 (c/o James Rauwerda, 2045 Boston St. S.E., Grand Rapids MI 49506, 616-243-2112). 50% unsolicited freelance; 50% assigned. Query; phone/e-query OK. **Pays $30** on publication for one-time rts. Articles 750-1,500 wds. (20/yr.); fiction 750-1,500 wds. Responds in 5 wks. Seasonal 4 mos. ahead. Accepts simultaneous submissions & reprints. Guidelines/theme list; copy $1.50 or 9x12 SAE/4 stamps. (Limited ads)

Poetry: Buys 6/yr. On teaching day school; 4-30 lines; $10. Submit max. 5 poems.

Tips: "No articles on Sunday school, only Christian day school. Most open to theme topics and features."

THE CHRISTIAN LIBRARIAN, Ryan Library, PLNU, 3600 Lomaland Dr., San Diego CA 92106. (619) 849-2208. Fax (619) 849-7024. E-mail: apowell@pointloma.edu. Website: www.acl.org. Assn. of Christian Librarians. Anne-Elizabeth Powell, ed-in-chief. Geared toward academic librarians of the Christian faith. Triennial jour.; 40 pgs.; circ. 800. Subscription $30. 50% unsolicited freelance; 50% assigned. E-mail; fax/e-query OK. **NO PAYMENT** for onetime rts. Not copyrighted. Articles 1,000-3,500 wds.; research articles to 5,000 wds. (6/yr.); reviews 150-300 wds. Responds in 5 wks. Accepts simultaneous submissions & reprints (tell when/where appeared). Prefers accepted ms by e-mail (attached file). Uses some sidebars. Guidelines by mail/e-mail/Website ("The Christian Librarian"/down to "Editorial Policies"); copy $5. (No ads)

Fillers: Anecdotes, ideas, short humor; 25-300 wds.

Special needs: Articles dealing with the intersection of faith and professional duties in libraries. Interviews with library leaders, profiles of Christian academic libraries, international librarianship. Deals with all topics as they can be applied to librarianship. Articles on Christian librarianship for peer review.

Tips: "Reviews are a good way to gain publication. Write a tight, well-researched article about a current 'hot topic' in librarianship as it is defined in a Christian setting; or ethics of librarianship. Articles on 'how we did it right' are good entry publications."

CHRISTIAN LIBRARY JOURNAL, 85785 Glenada Rd., Florence OR 97439. (541) 991-2407. Fax (866) 422-8356. E-mail: nlhesch@christianlibraryj.org. Website: www.christianlibraryj.org. Christian Library Services. Nancy L. Hesch, pub. Provides reviews from a Christian viewpoint of both Christian and non-Christian books for Christian schools, homeschools, and family libraries. Book reviews & some articles comparing books; to be posted on blog.

Tips: "If interested in doing reviews, send us your name, mailing address, phone number, and e-mail. We will respond with guidelines, and books will be sent from publisher."

CHRISTIAN SCHOOL EDUCATION, PO Box 65130, Colorado Springs CO 80962-5130. (719) 528-6906. Fax (719) 531-0631. E-mail: cse@acsi.org. Website: www.acsi.org. Association of Christian Schools Intl. Steven C. Babbitt, ed. To provide accurate information as well as provoke thought and reflection about the ministry of Christian school education worldwide. Quarterly mag.; 56 pgs.; circ. 70,000. Subscription $16. 2% unsolicited freelance; 98% assigned. Query preferred; phone query OK. **NO PAYMENT.** Asks for photocopy permission for member schools. Articles 650-2,600 wds.; book reviews 600 wds. Responds in 12 wks. No seasonal material. Accepts simultaneous submissions & reprints (tell when/where appeared). Requires submissions by disk or e-mail (attached file). Regularly uses sidebars. Prefers NIV, NKJV. Guidelines by mail/e-mail. (Ads)

> **Tips:** "Most articles for publication are solicited, therefore freelancers 'breaking into publication' is highly unlikely. Most open to Christian business and leadership."

$CHURCH LIBRARIES, 9118 W. Elmwood Dr., #1G, Niles IL 60714-5820. (847) 296-3964. Fax (847) 296-0754. E-mail: linjohnson@ECLAlibraries.org. Website: www.ECLAlibraries.org. Evangelical Church Library Assn. Lin Johnson, mng ed. To assist church librarians in setting up, maintaining, and promoting church libraries and media centers. Quarterly mag.; 32-36 pgs.; circ. 400. Subscription $35. 25% unsolicited freelance. Complete ms or queries by e-mail only. **Pays .05/wd.** on acceptance for 1st or reprint rts. Articles 500-1,000 wds. (24-30/yr.); book/music/DVD reviews by assignment, 75-150 wds. Free product. Responds in 4-6 wks. Seasonal 6 mos. ahead. Accepts reprints (tell when/where appeared). Requires e-mail submission. Regularly uses sidebars. Prefers NIV. Guidelines by mail/e-mail/Website ("Church Libraries Journal"/"Click for Writer's Guidelines"; copy for 9x12 SAE/4 stamps. (Ads)

> **Tips:** "Talk to church librarians or get involved in library or reading programs. Most open to articles and promotional ideas; profiles of church libraries. Book reviews assigned; need for reviewers fluctuates; if interested e-mail for availability."

CONGREGATIONAL LIBRARIES TODAY, 2920 S.W. Dolph Ct., Portland OR 97219-4055. (503) 244-6919. Fax (503) 977-3734. E-mail: csla@worldaccessnet.com. Website: www.cslainfo.org. Church and Synagogue Library Assn. Judith Janzen, exec. dir. To help librarians run congregational libraries. Quarterly; 28 pgs.; circ. 3,000. Subscription $40 U.S.; $50 Cdn. (USD), $60 foreign (USD). Query; no e-query. **NO PAYMENT.** Requires accepted ms on disk. Articles of variable lengths. Book & video reviews 1-2 paragraphs. Guidelines/copies by mail. (Ads)

> **Fillers:** Ideas.

$GROUP MAGAZINE, Box 481, Loveland CO 80539. (970) 669-3836. Fax (970) 292-4373. E-mail: rlawrence@group.com or sfirestone@group.com or info@group.com. Website: www.group.com or www.youthministry.com. Scott Firestone IV, ed.; submit to Kerri Loesch (kloesche@group.com). For leaders of Christian youth groups; to supply ideas, practical help, inspiration, and training for youth leaders. Bimonthly mag.; 85 pgs.; circ. 25,000. Subscription $29.95. 50% unsolicited freelance; 50% assigned. Query; fax/e-query OK. **Pays $150-350** on acceptance for all rts. Articles 175-2,000 wds. (100/yr.). Responds in 6-9 wks. Seasonal 5 mos. ahead. No simultaneous submissions or reprints. Accepts e-mail submissions (copied into message). No kill fee. Uses some sidebars. Any Bible version. Guidelines on Website (click on "Site Map" at bottom of page/scroll down to #27 "Submissions"); copy $2/9x12 SAE/3 stamps. (Ads)

> **Fillers:** Buys 5-10/yr. Cartoons, games, ideas; $40.
> **Columns/Departments:** Buys 30-40/yr. Try This One (youth group activities), to 300 wds. Hands-on-Help (tips for leaders), to 175 wds. Strange But True (profiles remarkable youth ministry experience), 500 wds. Pays $50. Complete ms.
> **Special needs:** Articles geared toward working with teens; programming ideas; youth-ministry issues.
> **Tips:** "We're always looking for effective youth-ministry ideas, especially those tested by youth leaders in the field. Most open to Hands-On-Help column (use real-life examples, personal experiences, practical tips, Scripture, and self-quizzes or checklists). We buy the idea, not the verbatim submission."

** This periodical was #28 on the 2010 Top 50 Christian Publishers list (#36 in 2007).

$THE JOURNAL OF ADVENTIST EDUCATION, 12501 Old Columbia Pike, Silver Spring MD 20904-6600. (301) 680-5069. Fax (301) 622-9627. E-mail: rumbleb@gc.adventist.org. Website: http://jae.adventist.org. General Conference of Seventh-day Adventists. Beverly J. Robinson-Rumble, ed. For Seventh-day teachers teaching in the church's school system, kindergarten to university and educational administrators. Bimonthly (5X) jour.; 48 pgs.; circ. 10,800. Selected articles are translated into French, Spanish, and Portuguese for a twice-yearly International Edition. Subscription $18.25 (add $3 outside U.S.). Percentage of freelance varies. Query or complete ms; phone/fax/e-query OK. **Pays $25-300** on publication for 1st North American and translation rts., and permission to post on Website. Articles 1,000-2,000 wds. (2-20/yr.). Responds in 6-17 wks. Seasonal 6 mos. ahead. Accepts reprints (tell when/where appeared). Accepts requested ms on disk. Regularly uses sidebars. Guidelines on Website ("For Authors"); copy for 10x12 SAE/5 stamps.

   Fillers: Cartoons only, no payment.

   Special needs: "All articles in the context of parochial schools (not Sunday school tips); professional enrichment and teaching tips for Christian teachers. Need feature articles and articles on the integration of faith and learning."

JOURNAL OF CHRISTIAN EDUCATION, PO Box 602, Epping NSW 1710, Australia. Phone/fax +612 9868 6644. E-mail: business@acfe.org.au, submit to editor@acfe.org.au. Website: www.jce.org.au. Australian Christian Forum on Education Inc. Dr. Grant Maple & Dr. Ian Lambert, eds. To consider the implications of the Christian faith for the entire field of education. Triannual jour.; 80 pgs.; circ. 400. Subscription $55 AUS, $55 U.S. for individuals; $70 AUS, $70 U.S. for institutions. 40% unsolicited freelance; 60% assigned. Complete ms/cover letter; phone/fax/e-query OK. **NO PAYMENT** for onetime rts. Articles 3,000-6,000 wds. (6/yr.); book reviews 400-600 wds. Responds in 4 wks. Seasonal 6 mos. ahead. Accepts requested ms on disk or by e-mail (attached file). Does not use sidebars. Guidelines by e-mail/Website (Click on "About the Journal"/ "Guidelines for Authors"); free copy. (No ads)

   Tips: "Send for a sample copy, study guidelines, and submit manuscript. Most open to articles or book reviews. Open to any educational issue from a Christian perspective."

JOURNAL OF CHRISTIANITY AND FOREIGN LANGUAGES, Dept. of Germanic and Asian Languages, Calvin College, 3201 Burton St. S.E., Grand Rapids MI 49546. (616) 957-8609. Fax (616) 526-8583. E-mail: dsmith@calvin.edu. Website: www.nacfla.net. North American Christian Foreign Language Assn. Dr. David Smith, ed. Scholarly articles dealing with the relationship between Christian belief and the teaching of foreign languages and literatures; mainly for college faculty. Annual jour.; 100 pgs.; circ. 100. Subscription $16 (indiv.), $27 (library). Open to freelance. Complete ms/cover letter; phone/fax/e-query OK. **PAYS IN COPIES/OFFPRINTS.** Articles 2,000-4,000 wds. (6/yr.); book/video reviews, 750 wds. Responds in 12-16 wks. Rarely accepts reprints (tell when/where appeared). Requires requested ms on disk or by e-mail (attached file). Does not use sidebars. Guidelines by mail/ Website; no copy. (Ads)

   Columns/Departments: Accepts 1-3/yr. Forum (position papers, pedagogical suggestions), 1,000-1,500 wds.

   Tips: "Most open to Forum column; guidelines at www.nacfla.net. Also see Website for abstracts and samples. Book reviews and opinion pieces must be related to Christianity and education in foreign languages and literature."

JOURNAL OF EDUCATION & CHRISTIAN BELIEF, Kuyers Institute, Calvin College, 3201 Burton St. S.E., Grand Rapids MI 49546. (616) 526-8609. Fax (616) 526-7502. E-mail: jecb@stapleford -centre.org. Website: www.jecb.org. Association of Christian Teachers; The Stapleford Centre; The Kuyers Institute for Christian Teaching and Learning. Editors: Dr. David Smith (use above address) & Dr. John Shortt, 1 Kiteleys Green, Leighton Buzzard, Beds LU7 3LD, United Kingdom. Phone +44 0 1525 379709. Semiannual jour.; 80 pgs.; circ. 400. Subscription $45. 80% unsolicited freelance;

20% assigned. Complete ms/cover letter; e-query OK. **NO PAYMENT** for 1st rts. Articles 5,000 wds. (12/yr.). Responds in 4-8 wks. Accepts reprints (tell when/where appeared). Prefers requested ms by e-mail (attached file). Does not use sidebars. Guidelines by e-mail/Website ("Notes for Contributors"); no copy. (No ads)

> **Tips:** "Most open to reviews of books related to education and Christian belief; should be expert reviews addressed to an academic audience. Must address Christian education in competent, scholarly manner."

JOURNAL OF RESEARCH ON CHRISTIAN EDUCATION, Andrews University, Information Services Bldg., Ste. 101, Berrien Springs MI 49104. (269) 471-6080. Fax (269) 471-6224. E-mail: jrce@andrews.edu. Website: www.andrews.edu/jrce. Andrews University. Larry D. Burton, ed.; Janet Mallory, book rev. ed. Research related to Christian schooling (all levels) within the Protestant tradition. Triennial jour.; 100+ pgs.; circ. 400. Subscription $60. 100% unsolicited freelance. Complete ms/cover letter; phone/fax/e-query OK. **NO PAYMENT.** Articles, 13-26 double-spaced pgs. (12-18/yr.); book reviews, 2-5 pgs. Responds in 1 wk.; decision within 6 mos. (goes through review board). No simultaneous submissions. Requires e-mail submissions. Does not use sidebars. Guidelines by mail/e-mail/Website ("Authors"). (No ads)

> **Tips:** "This is a research journal. All manuscripts should conform to standards of scholarly inquiry. Manuscripts are submitted to a panel of 3 experts for their review. Publication decision is based on recommendation of reviewers. Authors should submit manuscripts written in scholarly style and focused on Christian schooling. Submit an electronic copy along with a 100-word abstract and 30-word bio-sketch indicating institutional affiliation."

$KIDS' MINISTRY IDEAS, 55 W. Oak Ridge Dr., Hagerstown MD 21740. (301) 393-3178. Fax (301) 393-3209. E-mail: KidsMin@rhpa.org. Website: www.kidsministryideas.org. Seventh-day Adventist. Candace DeVore, ed. For adults leading children (birth-8th grade) to Christ. Quarterly mag.; 32 pgs.; circ. 2,500. Complete ms/cover letter; e-query OK. **Pays $20-100** within 5-6 wks. of acceptance for 1st rts. Articles 700 wds.; reviews 300 wds. ($50). Responds in 2 wks. Seasonal 6 mos. ahead. Accepts reprints (tell when/where appeared). Accepts full ms by e-mail (attached file). No kill fee. Regularly uses sidebars. Accepts submissions from children. Prefers NIV, NKJV, ICB. Guidelines on Website ("Writer's Guidelines"); theme list by request; copy for 9x12 SASE. (Ads)

> **Fillers:** Accepts 10/yr. Facts, games, party ideas, quizzes, tips, word puzzles; 300-500 wds. Pays $20-50.

> **Tips:** "Write editor—contact through Website."

$MOMENTUM, 1005 N. Glebe Rd., Ste. 525, Arlington VA 22201-5792. Toll-free (800) 711-6232. Fax (703) 243-0025. E-mail: momentum@ncea.org, or through Website: www.ncea.org/news/momentum/WritingforMomentum.asp. National Catholic Educational Assn. Brian Gray, ed. Features outstanding programs, issues, and research in Catholic education. Quarterly mag.; 80 pgs.; circ. 23,000. Subscription $20 (free to members). 50% unsolicited freelance; 30% assigned. Query or complete ms; phone/e-query OK. **Pays $50-100** on publication for 1st rts. Articles 500-1,500 wds. (25-30/yr.); research articles 3,500-5,000 wds.; book reviews 300 wds. ($50). No simultaneous submissions. Accepts full mss by e-mail (attached—preferred—or copied into message). Pays some kill fees. Regularly uses sidebars. Prefers NAB (Catholic). Guidelines/theme list by e-mail/Website (above Website opens to guidelines); copy $5/9x12 SAE/$2.38 postage (mark "Media Mail"). (Ads)

> **Columns/Departments:** From the Field (success ideas that can be used by other Catholic schools); DRE Directions (guidance for directors of religious education programs); both 700 wds.

> **Tips:** "All sections are open, but first visit our Website to understand the organization and then call or e-mail to discuss ideas. Much higher rate of acceptance when we've had a conversation first."

$PRESCHOOL PLAYHOUSE, PO Box 436987, Chicago IL 60643. E-mail: rsailes@urbanministries .com. Website: www.urbanministries.com. Urban Ministries Inc. Dr. R. Sailes, dir. of children's curriculum. Quarterly Sunday school curriculum for 2- to 5-year-olds with accompanying teacher's guide and curriculum resource materials. Open to freelance; 100% assigned. Query/clips and/or writing sample; no phone query. **Pays $150** for curriculum 120 days after acceptance for all rts. Articles accepted only on assignment. No simultaneous submissions or reprints. Requires accepted ms by e-mail only (attached file). No kill fee. Will accept sidebars on assigned educational topics; pay varies. Requires NIV. Guidelines for #10 SASE. (No ads)

> **Tips:** "Preschool Playhouse principally serves an African American audience; editorial content addresses broad Christian issues. Looking for those with educational or Sunday school teaching experience who can accurately explain Scripture in an insightful and engaging way and apply those Scriptures to the lives of preschool children."

$@TEACHERS OF VISION MAGAZINE, 227 N. Magnolia Ave., Ste. 2, Anaheim CA 92801. (714) 761-1476. Fax (714) 761-1679. E-mail: TOV@ceai.org. Website: www.ceai.org. Christian Educators Assn., Intl. Judy Turpen, contributing ed. To encourage, equip, and empower Christian educators serving in public and private schools. Bimonthly & online mag.; circ. 10,000. Subscription $20. 50% unsolicited freelance; 50% assigned. Query; prefers e-query (judy@ceai.org). **Pays $20-50 ($30 for reprints)** on publication for 1st or reprint rts. Articles 600-2,500 wds. (15-20/yr.); minifeatures 400-750 wds.; $25; very few book reviews 50 wds. (pays copies). Responds in 4-12 wks. Seasonal 4 mos. ahead. Accepts simultaneous submissions & reprints (tell when/where appeared). Accepts requested ms on disk or by e-mail (attached or copied into message). Regularly uses sidebars. Any Bible version. Guidelines/theme list on Website (www.ceai.org/fbenefits/teachers_of_vision/ tov_index_ed.htm); copy for 9x12 SAE/4 stamps. (Ads)

> **Poetry:** Accepts 2-3/yr. Free verse, haiku, light verse, traditional; 4-16 lines. Submit max. 3 poems.
> **Fillers:** Educational only.
> **Special needs:** Legal and other issues in public education. Interviews; classroom resource reviews; living out your faith in your work.
> **Tips:** "Know public education; write from a positive perspective as our readers are involved in public education by calling and choice. Most open to tips for teachers for living out their faith in the classroom in legally appropriate ways. No preachy articles."

$TODAY'S CATHOLIC TEACHER, 2621 Dryden Rd., Dayton OH 45439. Toll-free (800) 523-4625, ext. 1139. (937) 293-1415. Fax (937) 293-1310. E-mail: mnoschang@peterli.com. Website: www .catholicteacher.com. Catholic; Peter Li Education Group. Mary C. Noschang, ed-in-chief; submit to Betsy Shepard, mng. ed. (bshepard@peterli.com). Directed to personal and professional concerns of teachers and administrators in K-12 Catholic schools. Monthly mag. (6X during school yr.); 60 pgs.; circ. 45,000. Subscription $15.95. 30% unsolicited freelance; 30% assigned. Query; phone/fax/e-query OK. **Pays $100-250** on publication for 1st rts. Articles 600-800, 1,000-1,200, or 1,500-2,500 wds. (40-50/yr.). Responds in 18 wks. Seasonal 3 mos. ahead. Accepts simultaneous submissions & reprints (tell when/where appeared). Prefers requested ms by e-mail (attached file). Regularly uses sidebars. Guidelines/theme list on Website (click on "About"/"Writers Guidelines"); copy $3/9x12 SAE. (Ads)

> **Special needs:** Activity pages teachers can copy and pass out to students to work on. Try to provide classroom-ready material teachers can use to supplement curriculum.
> **Tips:** "Looking for material teachers in grades 3-9 can use to supplement curriculum material. Most open to articles related to school curriculum and other areas, or lesson plans."
> ** This periodical was #35 on the 2007 Top 50 Christian Publishers list.

$YOUTH AND CHRISTIAN EDUCATION LEADERSHIP, 1080 Montgomery Ave., Cleveland TN 37311. Toll-free (800) 553-8506. (423) 478-7597. Fax (423) 478-7616. E-mail: jonathanm@

renovatuscommunity.com or info@pathwaypress.org. Website: www.pathwaypress.org. Church of God/Pathway Press. Jonathan Martin, ed. To inform, equip, and inspire Christian education teachers and leaders. Quarterly mag.; 32 pgs.; circ. 10,000. Subscription $8. 10% unsolicited freelance; 90% assigned. Complete ms/cover letter; phone/e-query OK. Accepts full mss by e-mail (attached). **Pays $25-50** on publication for 1st or onetime rts. Articles 500-1,000 wds. (20/yr.). Responds in 2 wks. Seasonal 4 mos. ahead. Accepts simultaneous submissions; no reprints. Accepts requested ms on disk or by e-mail (attached file). No kill fee. Uses some sidebars. Prefers NIV. Guidelines on Website (click on "Leadership" in left-hand column/scroll down to "Writers Guidelines for Leadership"); copy $1.25/9x12 SAE. (No ads)

  Fillers: Buys 4/yr. Cartoons, ideas, party ideas, tips, word puzzles; 250-300 wds. Pays $35.

  Special needs: Most open to how-to articles relating to Christian education. Local church ministry stories; articles on youth ministry, children's ministry, Christian education, and Sunday school.

DAILY DEVOTIONAL MARKETS

Due to the nature of the daily devotional market, the following market listings give a limited amount of information. Because most of these markets assign all material, they do not wish to be listed in the usual way.

If you are interested in writing daily devotionals, send to the following markets for guidelines and sample copies, write up sample devotionals to fit each one's particular format, and send to the editor with a request for an assignment. **DO NOT** submit any other type of material to these markets unless indicated.

CHRISTIAN DEVOTIONS, PO Box 6494, Kingsport TN 37663. Fax (423) 239-7103. E-mail: cindy@ christiandevotions.us. Website: www.christiandevotions.us. Cindy Sproles & Eddie Jones, eds. Prefers completed devotions; 300-400 wds. **NOW PAYS $10/DEVOTION.** Accepts poetry. Accepts reprints & e-mail submissions. Guidelines on Website ("Write for Us").

DAILY DEVOTIONS FOR THE DEAF, 21199 Greenview Rd., Council Bluffs IA 51503-4190. (712) 322-5493. Fax (712) 322-7792. E-mail: JoKrueger@deafmissions.com. Website: www.deafmissions.com. Jo Krueger, ed. Published 3 times/yr. Circ. 26,000. Prefers to see completed devotionals; 225-250 wds. **NO PAYMENT.** E-mail submissions OK.

$DEVOTIONS, 8805 Governor's Hill Dr., Ste. 400, Cincinnati OH 45249-3319. (513) 931-4050. E-mail: mwilliams@standardpub.com. Website: www.standardpub.com. Gary Allen, ed.; Margaret Williams, project ed. Assigned by work-for-hire contract to previously published writers only. Query by e-mail only. **Pays $20/devotion.** Send list of credits rather than a sample.

$FORWARD DAY BY DAY, 412 Sycamore St. #2, Cincinnati OH 45202-4110. Toll-free (800) 543-1813. (513) 721-6659. Fax (513) 721-0729. E-mail: rschmidt@forwarddaybyday.com. Website: www.forwardmovement.org. Richard H. Schmidt, ed. Also online version. Send three sample devotions according to guidelines posted on Website. Likes author to complete an entire month's worth of devotions. Subscription $13. Accepts e-mail submissions. Length: 215 wds. **Pays $300 for a month of devotions.** No reprints. Guidelines on Website. ("About Us"/"Writers Guidelines"). (No ads)

FRUIT OF THE VINE, Barclay Press, 211 N. Meridian St., #101, Newberg OR 97132. (503) 538-9775. Fax (503) 554-8597. E-mail: info@barclaypress.com. E-mail submissions accepted at phampton@barclaypress.com. Website: www.barclaypress.com. Editorial team: Paula Hampton & Judy Woolsey. Send samples and request assignment. Accepts e-mail submissions & reprints. Subscription $18. Prefers 250-290 wds. **PAYS FREE SUBSCRIPTION & 6 COPIES.** Guidelines by mail/Website ("Information Desk"/"Writing Guidelines").

FUSION, 114 Bush Rd., Nashville TN 37217. (615) 361-1221. Fax (615) 367-0535. E-mail: jona than.yandell@randallhouse.com or through Website: www.randallhouse.com. Randall House. Jonathan Yandell, ed. For adults 30+, combines truth and faith in daily life. Encourages application of Scripture through devotions and experience; instructional, and inspirational articles. Quarterly mag.; circ. 20,000. Subscription $30. Open to freelance. Query with samples by e-mail.

　　**2010 EPA Award of Excellence: Most Improved Publication; 2010 EPA Award of Merit: Devotional.

$+GOD'S WORD FOR TODAY, 1445 N. Boonville Ave., Springfield MO 65802. (417) 831-8000. E-mail: rl-gwft@gph.org. Website: www.GospelPublishing.com. Assemblies of God. Paul W. Smith, dir., ed. services. Assigns all devotions. Contact to see if they are accepting new writers. New writers will need to write a sample. **Pays $25.** Accepts poetry and e-mail submissions. No reprints. Guidelines on Website ("God's Word for Today"/down to "Writers Guides").

$LIGHT FROM THE WORD, PO Box 50434, Indianapolis IN 46250-0434. (317) 774-7900. E-mail: submissions@wesleyan.org. Website: www.wesleyan.org/wph. Wesleyan. Craig A. Bubeck, ed. dir. Devotions 220-230 wds. **Pays $100 for seven devotions**. Electronic submissions only. Send a couple of sample devotions to fit their format and request an assignment. Accepts e-mail submissions. No reprints.

($)MUSTARD SEED MINISTRIES DEVOTIONAL, PO Box 501, Bluffton IN 46714. E-mail: devotionals@mustardseedministries.org. Website: www.mustardseedministries.org. MustardSeed Ministries Inc. Wayne Steffen, ed. (Wayne@mustardseedministries.org). Devotional mag. 100% unsolicited freelance. Complete ms; e-mail submissions preferred. **PAYS A UNIQUE, ATTRACTIVE PLAQUE**. Devotions 225-275 wds. Guidelines on Website.

　　Tips: "We do not return any submissions and prefer that they are e-mailed to us. We are looking for submissions that are biblically based. Sincerity is as important as your writing skills. Most of us have a story to tell about how Christ touched our life in some situation that others in this world would benefit from; please send this to us." Also looking for articles for their newsletter. Guidelines on Website.

$MY DAILY VISITOR, 200 Noll Plaza, Huntington IN 46750. Toll-free (800) 348-2440. (260) 356-8400. Fax (260) 356-8472. E-mail: mdvisitor@osv.com. Website: www.osv.com. Catholic. Submit to The Editor. Scripture meditations based on the day's Catholic Mass readings. Bimonthly devotional booklet. Open to freelance from Catholic writers only. **Pays $500 for a month's devotions** (28-31 days), plus 5 copies, on acceptance for onetime rts. Not copyrighted. Devotions 125-135 wds. ea. (assigns a full month at a time). Guidelines on Website (click on "About Us"/ "Writers Guidelines"/"My Daily Visitor").

OUR DAILY JOURNEY, 3000 Kraft Ave. S.E., Grand Rapids MI 49512. (616) 974-2663. Fax (616) 957-5741. E-mail: tfelten@rbc.org. Website: www.rbc.org. RBC Ministries. Tom Felten, ed. Devotionals for today's young adult; features meditations on God's leading through life and community participation (click on "Devotionals"/"Our Daily Journey"). This appears to now be a community of bloggers. Guidelines for posting on the blog on Website ("Comments Guidelines"). (No ads)

PENNED FROM THE HEART, 304 Stow Neck Rd., Salem NJ 08079-3431. (856) 339-9422. E-mail: ed4penned@gmail.com. Website: www.gloriaclover.com. Son-Rise Publications (toll-free 800-358-0777). Jana Carman, ed. Annual daily devotional book; about 240 pgs.; 5,000 copies/yr. 100% unsolicited freelance. Complete ms/cover letter; phone/e-query OK. **PAYS ONE COPY OF THE BOOK + A DISCOUNT TO RESELL BOOKS**. Onetime rts. Devotions up to 250 wds. (365/yr.). Responds in 9-13 wks. Considers simultaneous submissions; accepts reprints (tell when/where appeared). Prefers mss by e-mail (attached). Also accepts submissions from children/teens. Guidelines/examples on Website: www.gloriaclover.com/guidelines.html. (No ads)

Poetry: To 24 lines. Pays one copy.

Tips: "Devotions must be biblically based, and something with an unexpected 'punch' is preferred. Build faith, encourage, and glorify God. No New Age material. Follow guidelines, specifically 250 words or less."

$THE QUIET HOUR, 4050 Lee Vance View, Colorado Springs CO 80919. E-mail: gwilde@stmarys bonita.org. Website: www.davidccook.com/index.cfm. David C. Cook. Gary Wilde, ed. Subscription $3.49/quarter. 100% freelance (makes 13 assignments/yr.). **Pays $15-35/devotional** on acceptance. Send list of credits only, rather than a sample. Accepts e-mailed sample devotional. Responds in 3 mos. Currently using only writers previously published in this publication.

$REJOICE! 600 Shaftesbury Blvd., Winnipeg MB R3P 0M4, Canada. (204) 488-0610. Fax (204) 831-5675. E-mail: ByronRB@mph.org. Website: www.mpn.net/rejoice. Faith & Life Resources/ Mennonite Publishing Network. Byron Rempel-Burkholder, ed. Daily devotional magazine grounded in Anabaptist theology. Quarterly mag.; 112 pgs.; circ. 12,000. Subscription $29.60. 5% unsolicited freelance; 95% assigned. **Pays $100-125 for 7-day assigned meditations,** 250-300 wds. each; on publication for 1st rts. Also accepts testimonies 500-600 wds. (8/yr.). Prefers that you send a couple of sample devotions and inquire about assignment procedures; fax/e-query OK. Accepts assigned mss by e-mail (attached). Responds in 4 wks. Seasonal 8 mos. ahead. No simultaneous submissions or reprints. Some kill fees 50%. No sidebars. Prefers NRSV. Guidelines by e-mail/Website (scroll down to "Writing for Rejoice!" center).

Poetry: Buys 8/yr. Free verse, light verse; 60 characters. Pays $25. Submit max. 3 poems.

Tips: "Don't apply for assignment unless you are familiar with the publication and Anabaptist theology."

$THE SECRET PLACE, Box 851, Valley Forge PA 19482-0851. (610) 768-2434. Fax (610) 768-2441. E-mail: thesecretplace@abc-usa.org. Website: www.judsonpress.com. Kathleen Hayes, sr. ed. Prefers to see completed devotionals, 200 wds. (use unfamiliar Scripture passages). 64 pgs. Circ. 150,000. 100% freelance. **Pays $20** for 1st rts. Accepts poetry. Prefers e-mail submissions. No reprints. Guidelines by mail.

$THESE DAYS, 100 Witherspoon St., Louisville KY 40202-1396. (502) 569-5102. Fax (502) 569-5113. E-mail: vpatton@presbypub.com. Website: www.ppcpub.com. Presbyterian Publishing Corp. Vince Patton, ed. Quarterly booklet; circ. 200,000. Subscription $7.95. Query/samples. 95% unsolicited freelance. **Pays $14.25/devotion** on acceptance for 1st and nonexclusive reprint rts. (makes work-for-hire assignments); 200 wds. (including key verse and short prayer). Wants short, contemporary poetry ($15) on church holidays and seasons of the year—overtly religious (15 lines, 33-character/line maximum). Query for their two feature segments (short articles): "These Moments" and "These Times." Guidelines by mail; copy for 6x9 SAE/3 stamps.

Poetry: Accepts poetry.

Photos: Buys digital photos for the cover.

$THE UPPER ROOM, PO Box 340004, Nashville TN 37203-0004. (615) 340-7252. Fax (615) 340-7267. E-mail: TheUpperRoomMagazine@upperroom.org. Website: www.upperroom.org. Mary Lou Redding, ed. dir. 95% unsolicited freelance. **Pays $30/devotional** on publication. 72 pgs. This publication wants freelance submissions and does not make assignments. Phone/fax/e-query OK. Send devotionals up to 250 wds. Buys explicitly religious art, in various media, for use on covers only (transparencies/slides requested); buys onetime, worldwide publishing rts. Accepts e-mail submissions (copied into message). Guidelines by mail/Website ("Writers"); copy for 5x7 SAE/2 stamps. (No ads)

Tips: "We do not return submissions. Accepted submissions will be notified in 6-9 wks. Follow guidelines. Need meditations from men." Always include postal address with e-mail submissions.

@THE WORD AMONG US, 9639 Doctor Perry Rd., #126, Ijamsville MD 21754. Toll-free (800) 775-9673. (301) 831-1262. Fax (301) 831-1188. E-mail: lrz@wau.org. Website: www.wau.org. Catholic. Leo Zanchettin, ed. Daily meditations based on the Mass readings; inspirational essays; and stories of the saints and other heroes of the faith. Print & online mag.; circ. 500,000. Subscription $34.95 (print & online); $9.95 (online only).

$THE WORD IN SEASON, PO Box 1209, Minneapolis MN 55440-1209. Fax (612) 330-3215. E-mail: rochelle@rightnowcoach.com. Website: www.augsburgfortress.org. Augsburg Fortress. Rev. Rochelle Y. Melander, ed./mngr. 96 pgs. Devotions to 200 wds. **Pays $20/devotion**; $75 for prayers. Accepts e-mail submissions (copied into message) after reading guidelines. Guidelines at www.augsburgfortress.org, type "The Word in Season" in search box.

Tips: "We prefer that you write for guidelines. We will send instructions for preparing sample devotions. We accept new writers based on the sample devotions we request and make assignments after acceptance."

MISSIONS MARKETS

ACTION MAGAZINE: Men for Missions, PO Box A, Greenwood IN 46142. (317) 881-6752. Fax (317) 865-1076. E-mail: keller@omsinternational.org or w.hartig@mfmi.org. Website: www.mfmi .org. Kent Eller, dir. Articles 500-600 wds. Click on "DO"/"ACTION Magazine." Informs the public of ministry opportunities, as well as reporting on the various OMS mission teams. Triennial mag. Open to unsolicited freelance (on missions & salvation testimonies)/copy available. Complete ms.

@EAST-WEST CHURCH & MINISTRY REPORT, Asbury University, One Macklem Dr., Wilmore KY 40390. Phone/fax (859) 858-2427. E-mail: emark936@gmail.com. Website: www.eastwestreport .org. Dr. Mark R. Elliott, ed. Examines all aspects of church life and mission outreach in the former Soviet Union and Central and Eastern Europe as a service to both the church and academia. Quarterly newsletter; 16 pgs.; circ. 200. Print subscription $49.45; e-mail subscription $22.95. 20% unsolic-ited freelance; 80% assigned. Complete ms/cover letter; phone/fax/e-query OK. **PAYS 2 COPIES** for all rts. Articles 2,000 words average (4/yr.); book reviews, 400 wds. Responds in 4 wks. No simul-taneous submissions or reprints. Uses some sidebars. Prefers requested ms on disk or by e-mail. Regularly uses sidebars. Any Bible version. Guidelines on Website ("Author Guidelines" right side); no copy. (No ads)

Tips: "All submissions must relate to Central and Eastern Europe or the former Soviet Union."

$EVANGELICAL MISSIONS QUARTERLY, PO Box 794, Wheaton IL 60187. (630) 752-7158. Fax (630) 752-7155. E-mail: emq@wheaton.edu. Website: www.emisdirect.com. Evangelism and Missions Information Service (EMIS). A. Scott Moreau, ed.; Laurie Fortunak Nichols, mng. ed. & book review ed. For missionaries and others interested in missions trends, strategies, issues, prob-lems, and resources. Quarterly jour.; 136 pgs.; circ. 7,000. Subscription $24.95. 67% unsolicited; 33% assigned. Query; phone/fax/e-query OK. **Pays $100** on publication for all & electronic rts. Articles 3,000 wds. (30/yr.); book reviews 400 wds. (query/pays $25). Responds in 2 wks. Accepts few reprints (tell when/where appeared). Prefers requested ms on disk or by e-mail (copied into message). Uses some sidebars. Kill fee negotiable. Prefers NIV. Guidelines on Website ("Writers Guidelines"); free copy. (Ads)

Columns/Departments: Buys 8/yr. In the Workshop (tips to increase missionary effectiveness), 800-2,000 wds. Perspectives (opinion), 800 wds. Pays $50-100.

Tips: "We consider all submissions. It is best to check our Website for examples and guidelines.

Present an article idea and why you are qualified to write it. All articles must target evangelical, cross-cultural missionaries. 'In the Workshop' is most open to freelancers. Most authors have a credible connection to and experience in missions."

$GLAD TIDINGS, 50 Wynford Dr., Toronto ON M3C 1J7, Canada. Toll-free (800) 619-7301. (416) 441-1111. Fax (416) 441-2825. E-mail: cwood@presbyterian.ca. Website: www.presbyterian.ca. Women's Missionary Society/Presbyterian Church in Canada. Colleen Wood, ed. Challenges concerned Christians to reflect on their faith through articles and reports related to mission and social justice issues, locally, nationally, and internationally. Bimonthly mag.; 48 pgs.; circ. 4,000. Subscription $14 Cdn. 20% unsolicited freelance; 80% assigned. Query; e-query OK. Accepts full mss by e-mail. **Pays $15-50** on publication for onetime or reprint rts. Articles 800-1,600 wds. (2-4/yr.); fiction 400-1,200 wds. (6/yr.); reviews 200 wds. (no payment). Responds in 3 wks. Seasonal 3-4 mos. ahead. Accepts simultaneous submissions & reprints (tell when/where appeared). Prefers e-mail submissions (attached or copied into message). No kill fee. Uses some sidebars. Also accepts submissions from teens. Prefers NRSV. Guidelines by e-mail; no copy. (Ads—limited)

> **Poetry:** Buys 6/yr. Avant-garde, free verse, haiku, light verse, traditional; 5-100 wds. Pays $10-20. Submit max. 5 poems.
> **Fillers:** Buys 4-6/yr. cartoons, games, kid quotes, prayers, short humor, word puzzles; $10-20.
> **Tips:** "Writers can best break in with submissions of poetry, puzzles, or fiction. It is best to query as we often use themes."

INTERNATIONAL JOURNAL OF FRONTIER MISSIOLOGY, 1539 E. Howard St., Pasadena CA 91104. (626) 398-2108. Fax (626) 398-2185. E-mail: ijfm@wciu.edu. Website: www.ijfm.org. International Society of Frontier Missiology. Rory Clark, ed. Dedicated to frontiers in missions. Quarterly jour.; 48 pgs.; circ. 500. Subscription $18. 75% unsolicited freelance. Complete ms/cover letter; phone/fax/e-query OK. **NO PAYMENT** for onetime rts. Articles 2,000-6,000 wds. Seasonal 3 mos. ahead. Accepts simultaneous submissions & reprints. Accepts e-mail submissions. Does not use sidebars. Guidelines/theme list by e-mail/Website (scroll down to "Author Guidelines"); no copy. (Ads)

> **Special needs:** Contextualization, church in missions, training for missions, mission trends and paradigms, de-westernization of the gospel and missions from the Western world, biblical worldview development, mission theology, Animism, Islam, Buddhism, Hinduism, nonliterate peoples, tent making, mission member care, reaching nomadic peoples, mission history, new religious movements and missions, science and missions, etc.
> **Tips:** "Writers on specific issues we cover are always welcome. Although the circulation is small, the print run is 2,000 and used for promotional purposes. Highly recommended for mission schools, libraries, and mission executives."

@LAUSANNE WORLD PULSE, PO Box 794, Wheaton IL 60187. (630) 752-7158. Fax (630) 752-7155. E-mail: submissions@lausanneworldpulse.com. Website: www.lausanneworldpulse.com. Lausanne Committee for World Evangelism/Wheaton College. Laurie Fortunak Nichols, editorial coord. News and information on evangelism and missions from around the world. Monthly e-zine; 40 pgs.; circ. 8,000. Subscription free online. 20% unsolicited freelance; 80% assigned. Query or complete ms/cover letter; e-query OK. Accepts full mss by e-mail. **NO PAYMENT** for 1st, reprint, electronic, non-exclusive rts. Articles 600-1,500 wds. Responds in 2-3 wks. Seasonal 6 mos. ahead. Accepts simultaneous submissions; might accept reprints (tell when/where appeared). Prefers accepted mss by e-mail (attached file). Uses some sidebars. Guidelines/theme list on Website ("Submit an Article"). (No ads)

$LEADERS FOR TODAY, Box 13, Atlanta GA 30370. (770) 449-8869. Fax (770) 449-8457. E-mail: ingridalbuquerque@yahoo.com. Website: www.haggai-institute.com. Haggai Institute. Ingrid Albuquerque, ed. Primarily for donors to ministry; focus is alumni success stories. Quarterly mag.; 16 pgs.; circ. 7,500. Subscription free. 100% assigned to date. Query; fax query OK. **Pays .10-.25/wd.**

on acceptance for all rts. Articles 1,000-2,000 wds. Responds in 2-3 wks. Requires requested ms on disk or by e-mail (attached file). Kill fee 100%. Regularly uses sidebars. Prefers NIV. Guidelines/ theme list by mail; copy for 9x12 SAE/4 stamps. (No ads)

> **Tips:** "If traveling to a developing country, check well in advance regarding the possibility of doing an alumni story. All articles are preassigned; query first."

MISSIOLOGY: An International Review, Covenant Theological Seminary, 12330 Conway Rd., St. Louis MO 63141. (314) 434-4044, ext. 4207. Fax (314) 392-4212. E-mail: missiology@cov enantseminary.edu. Website: www.asmweb.org. American Society of Missiology/Asbury Theological Seminary. J. Nelson Jennings, ed. A scholarly journal for those who study and practice missions worldwide. Quarterly jour.; 128-136 pgs.; circ. 1,500. Subscription $26. 60% unsolicited freelance; 40% assigned. Complete ms/cover letter. **PAYS 20 COPIES** for 1st rts. Articles 3,000-5,000 wds. (20/yr.); book reviews 400 wds. Responds in 8 wks. No seasonal. No simultaneous submissions or reprints. Prefers requested ms by e-mail (attached file) or on disk. Uses some sidebars. Any Bible version. Guidelines on Website (click on "Missiology"/scroll down to "Style Guide" in text); copy for 6x9 SAE/$3.16 postage ($6 foreign). (Ads)

@MISSION CONNECTION, 17001 Prairie Star Pkwy., Lenexa KS 66220. (913) 577-2970. Fax (913) 577-0861. E-mail: missionconnection@nazarene.org. Website: www.nazarenemissions.org. Nazarene Missions Intl. Gail L. Sawrie, ed. A meeting place for equipping NMI leaders through interaction and resource exchange. Monthly e-zine. Subscription free. Open to unsolicited free-lance. Complete ms. **NO PAYMENT.** Not copyrighted. Articles to 400 wds. Guidelines on Website. Incomplete topical listings. (No ads)

@MISSION FRONTIERS, 1605 Elizabeth St., Pasadena CA 91104. (626) 797-1111. Fax (626) 398-2263. E-mail: mission.frontiers@uscwm.org. Website: www.missionfrontiers.org. U.S. Center for World Mission. Dr. Ralph Winter, ed.; Rick Wood, mng. ed. To stimulate a movement to establish indigenous churches where still needed around the world. Bimonthly & online mag.; 24 pgs.; circ. 100,000. Subscription free for $25 donation. No unsolicited freelance; 100% assigned. Query. **NO PAYMENT.** Articles & reviews. Rarely responds. Accepts requested ms on disk or by e-mail (cop-ied into message). Regularly uses sidebars. No guidelines; free copy. Incomplete topical listings. (Ads—MFAds@uscwm.org)

> **Fillers:** Cartoons.
>
> **Tips:** "Be a published missionary or former missionary. Be on the cutting edge of a strategic breakthrough or methods of reaching an unreached ethnic group." Looking for true-life, short sidebars of Muslims accepting Jesus, or impact of prayer in missions.

$NEW WORLD OUTLOOK, 475 Riverside Dr., Rm. 1476, New York NY 10115-0122. (212) 870-3765. Fax (212) 870-3940. E-mail: nwo@gbgm-umc.org. Website: http://gbgm-umc.org/nwo. United Methodist. Christie R. House, ed. Denominational missions. Bimonthly mag.; 48 pgs.; circ. 24,000. Subscription $10. 20% unsolicited freelance. Query; fax/e-query OK. **Pays $50-300** on publication for all & electronic rts. Articles 500-2,000 wds. (24/yr.); book reviews 200-500 wds. (assigned). No guaranteed response time. Seasonal 4 mos. ahead. Kill fee 50% or $100. Prefers e-mail submission (Word Perfect 6.1 or 8.1 in attached file). Regularly uses sidebars. Prefers NRSV. Guidelines by mail; copy $3. (Ads)

> **Tips:** "Ask for a list of United Methodist mission workers and projects in your area. Investigate them, propose a story, and consult with the editors before writing. Most open to articles and/or color photos of U.S. or foreign mission sites visited as a stringer, after consultation with the editor."

$ONE, 1011 First Ave., New York NY 10022-4195. Toll-free (800) 442-6392. (212) 826-1480. Fax (212) 826-8979. E-mail: cnewa@cnewa.org, or through Website: www.cnewa.org. Catholic Near

East Welfare Assn. Michael La Civita, exec. ed. Interest in cultural, religious, and human rights development in Middle East, N.E. Africa, India, or Eastern Europe. Bimonthly mag.; 40 pgs.; circ. 100,000. Subscription $24. 50% unsolicited freelance; 50% assigned. Query/clips; fax query OK. **Pays .20/edited wd. ($200)** on publication for all rts. Articles 1,200-1,800 wds. (15/yr.). Responds in 9 wks. Accepts requested ms on disk. Kill fee $200. Prefers NAS. Guidelines by mail/e-mail; copy for 8x11 SAE/2 stamps.

Tips: "We strive to educate our readers about the culture, faith, history, issues, and people who form the Eastern Christian churches. Anything on people in Palestine/Israel, Eastern Europe, or India. Material should not be academic. Include detailed photographs with story or article."

($)@OPERATION REVEILLE E-JOURNAL, PO Box 3488, Monument CO 80132-3488. (719) 572-5908. Fax (775) 248-8147. E-mail: bside@oprev.org. Website: www.oprev.org. Mission To Unreached Peoples. Bruce T. Sidebotham, dir. Provides information to equip U.S. military Christians for cross-cultural ministry. Bimonthly e-zine. Subscription free. 20% unsolicited freelance; 80% assigned. Query; e-query OK. Accepts full mss by e-mail. **PAYS IN COPIES or up to $99** for electronic, reprint, or nonexclusive rights (negotiable). Articles 500-2,500 wds. (2/yr.); book reviews 700 wds. Responds in 2 wks. Accepts simultaneous submissions & reprints (tell when/where appeared). Accepts requested ms by e-mail (attached file). Uses some sidebars. Prefers NIV. No guidelines; copy online. (Ads)

Fillers: Accepts 4/yr. Facts; newsbreaks; commentary, to 150 wds.

Columns/Departments: Accepts 4/yr. Agency Profile (describes a mission agency's history and work), 200-300 wds. Area Profile (describes spiritual landscape of a military theater of operations), 300-750 wds. Resource Review (describes a cross-cultural ministry tool), 100-200 wds. Query.

Special needs: Commentary on service personnel in cross-cultural ministry situations and relationships.

Tips: "We need insights for military personnel on understanding and relating the gospel to Muslims."

$PFI GLOBAL LINK JOURNAL, Box 17434, Washington DC 20041. (703) 481-0000. Fax (703) 481-0003. E-mail: communications@pfi.org. Website: www.pfi.org. Prison Fellowship Intl. Seldom uses freelance articles, but would consider articles with a direct connection to a Prison Fellowship organization outside of the United States.

THE RAILROAD EVANGELIST, PO Box 5026, Vancouver WA 98668-5026. (360) 699-7208. E-mail: rrjoe@comcast.net, or REA@comcast.net. Website: www.railroadevangelist.com. Railroad Evangelistic Assn. Joe Spooner, ed. For railroad and transportation employees and their families. Tri-annual mag.; 16 pgs.; circ. 2,500. Subscription $8. 100% unsolicited freelance. Complete ms/ no cover letter; phone query OK. **NO PAYMENT.** Articles 100-700 wds. (10-15/yr.); railroad-related fiction only, for children 5-12 yrs. Seasonal 4 mos. ahead. Accepts simultaneous submissions & reprints. Accepts e-mail submissions. Does not use sidebars. Guidelines by mail/e-mail/Website (scroll to bottom); copy for 9x12 SAE/2 stamps. (No ads)

Poetry: Accepts 4-8/yr. Traditional, any length. Send any number.

Fillers: Accepts many. Anecdotes, cartoons, quotes; to 100 wds.

Tips: "We need 400- to 700-word railroad-related salvation testimonies; or railroad-related human-interest stories; or model railroads. Since we publish only three times a year, we are focusing on railroad-related articles only. Just write and tell us or send us what you have. We'll let you know if we can use it or not."

@WEC.GO, PO Box 1707, Fort Washington PA 19034. (215) 646-2322. Fax (215) 646-6202. E-mail: wec.go@wec-usa.org. Website: www.wec-usa.org/wec.go. Worldwide Evangelism for Christ

International. Kay Negly, ed. Quarterly & online mag.; circ. 9,500. Subscription free. Open to unsolicited freelance. Query first. **NO PAYMENT.** Articles. Incomplete topical listings.

> **Tips:** "Our purpose is to inform the Christian public about WEC International, and missions in general—through life stories that challenge our readers spiritually and stir their hearts for His Great Commission."

@WOMEN OF THE HARVEST, PO Box 151297, Lakewood CO 80215-9297. Toll-free (877) 789-7778. (303) 985-2148. Fax (303) 989-4239. E-mail: editor@womenoftheharvest.com. Website: www.womenoftheharvest.com. Women of the Harvest Ministries Intl. Inc. Cindy Blomquist, ed. To support and encourage women serving in cross-cultural missions. Bimonthly e-zine; 35 pgs.; circ. 8,000. Free online. 90% unsolicited freelance; 10% assigned. Complete ms; e-query OK. Accepts full ms by e-mail. **NO PAYMENT** for onetime & electronic rts. Articles 300-800 wds. Responds in 2 wks. Seasonal 3 mos. ahead. No simultaneous submissions or reprints. Prefers requested ms by e-mail (copied into message or attached file). Uses some sidebars. Guidelines/theme list/copy on Website (click on "Publications" twice/"Writers Guidelines"). (No ads)

> **Tips:** "This is a magazine designed especially for women serving cross-culturally. We need articles, humor, and anecdotes related to this topic. Best way to break in is by having a cross-cultural missions experience or to be heading to the mission field."

** 2008 EPA Award of Excellence: Online; 2006 EPA Award of Merit: Online.

MUSIC MARKETS

@CHRISTIAN MUSIC WEEKLY, 7057 Bluffwood Ct., Brownsburg IN 46112-8650. (317) 892-5031. Fax (317) 892-5034. Canadian address: 775 Pam Cres, Newmarket ON L3Y 5B7, Canada. E-mail through Website: www.ChristianMusicWeekly.com. Joyful Sounds. Rob Green, ed. Trade paper for Worship, Inspirational, Adult Contemporary, and Southern Gospel Music radio formats. Weekly & online trade paper; 12 pgs.; circ. 300-1,200. Subscription $49 (paper) or free (PDF via e-mail). 25% unsolicited freelance; 75% assigned. Query by e-mail only. **PAYS IN COPIES** (will publish photo of writer and tiny bio). Articles 600-2,000 wds.; music reviews, 100-300 wds. Responds in 2 wks. Seasonal 2 mos. ahead. Accepts reprints. Requires requested ms on disk (DOS-ASCII), prefers e-mail submission. Guidelines by e-mail; copy for 9x12 SAE/2 stamps. (Ads)

> **Fillers:** Cartoons, short humor (particularly radio or music related).
>
> **Columns/Departments:** Insider (artist interview); Programming 101 (radio technique); retail, inspirational, especially for musicians and radio people; 600-2,000 wds.
>
> **Special needs:** Songwriting and performance.
>
> **Tips:** "Most open to artist interviews. Must be familiar with appropriate music formats."

@CHRISTIAN VOICE MAGAZINE, PO Box 147, Kennedy AL 35574. (205) 662-4826. Fax (205) 596-4375. E-mail: news@christianvoicemagazine.com or editor@christianvoicemagazine.com. Website: www.christianvoicemagazine.com. Published by Wilds & Assocs. John Lanier, exec. ed. Christian music news & information. Monthly print and digital mag. Estab. 2006. Subscription $20 print; $10 digital download. Open to unsolicited freelance. Complete ms/copy ready. Music-related news articles. Guidelines on Website (click on "Contact Us"/scroll down to "New Submission Guidelines"). Not included in topical listings.

$CHURCH MUSIC QUARTERLY, 19 The Close, Salisbury, Wiltshire, SP1 2EB, United Kingdom. Phone +44 (0) 1722 424848. Fax +44 1722 424849. E-mail: cmq@rscm.com. Website: www.rscm.com. Royal School of Church Music. Submit to: Cathy Markale, communications officer. Advice and inspiration for church musicians around the world. Quarterly mag.; 60 pgs; circ. 12,000. Subscription free with RSCM membership. 5% unsolicited freelance; 95% assigned. Query/clips; phone/fax/e-query OK. Accepts full mss by e-mail. **Pays** on publication. Articles. Incomplete topical listings. (Ads)

$@CREATOR MAGAZINE, PO Box 3538, Pismo Beach CA 93448. Toll-free (800) 777-6713. (707) 837-9071. E-mail: creator@creatormagazine.com. Website: www.creatormagazine.com. Rod Ellis, ed. For interdenominational music ministry; promoting quality, diverse music programs in the church. Bimonthly & online mag.; 48-56 pgs.; circ. 6,000. Subscription $32.95. 35% unsolicited freelance. Query or complete ms/cover letter; fax/e-query OK. **Pays $30-75** for assigned, $30-60 for unsolicited, on publication for 1st, onetime, reprint rts. Articles 1,000-10,000 wds. (20/yr.); book reviews ($20). Responds in 4-12 wks. Seasonal 4 mos. ahead. Accepts simultaneous submissions & reprints (tell when/where appeared). Prefers requested ms on disk. Regularly uses sidebars. Prefers NRSV. Guidelines/theme list/copy for 9x12 SAE/5 stamps. (Ads)

    Fillers: Buys 20/yr. Anecdotes, cartoons, ideas, jokes, party ideas, short humor; 10-75 wds. $5-25.

    Special needs: Articles on worship; staff relationships.

+GOSPEL USA MAGAZINE, PO Box 970704, Miami FL 33197-0704. (305) 234-8689. Fax (305) 234-0514. E-mail: cecilbrown@gospelusamagazine.com. Website: www.gospelusamagazine.com. Cecil Brown, ed. Gospel music and news magazine. Bimonthly. Subscription $15.

THE HYMN: A Journal of Congregational Song, Baptist Theological Seminary at Richmond, 3400 Brook Rd., Richmond VA 23227-4536. Toll-free (800) THEHYMN. Fax (804) 355-9208. E-mail: hymneditor@amural.com or office@thehymnsociety.org. Website: www.hymnsociety.org. Hymn Society in the U.S. & Canada. Nancy E. Hall, ed. For church musicians, hymnologists, scholars; articles related to the congregational song. Quarterly jour.; 60 pgs.; circ. 3,000. Subscription $75. 85% unsolicited freelance; 15% assigned. Query; phone/e-query OK. **NO PAYMENT** for all rts. Articles any length (12/yr.); book and music reviews any length. Responds in 6 wks. Seasonal 4 mos. ahead. Prefers requested ms on disk or by e-mail (attached file). Regularly uses sidebars. Any Bible version. Guidelines on Website ("Guidelines"); free copy. (Ads)

    Special needs: Articles on history of hymns or practical ways to teach or use hymns. Controversial issues as related to hymns and songs. Contact editor.

    Contest: Hymn text and tune contests for special occasions or themes.

    Tips: "Focus all articles on congregational song. No devotional material."

+@PATH MEGAZINE, 14880 Bellaire Blvd., Houston TX 77083. (407) 462-5550. E-mail: pathmagazine@hotmail.com, or through Website: www.pathmegazine.com. Your online path to Christian entertainment. Anissa King, mng. ed. Monthly online gospel video magazine. Free subscription.

($)TCP MAGAZINE, 181—104 Wind Chime Ct., Raleigh NC 27615. Phone/fax (919) 676-0263. E-mail: info@theconnectionplace.com. Website: www.theconnectionplace.com. The Connection Place Inc. Peggy Tatum, ed. To connect music, ministries, and Christian businesses. Quarterly mag.; 36 pgs; circ. 20,000. Subscription $15. 100% assigned. Query/clips; e-query OK. **PAYS IN COPIES & ADVERTISEMENT.** Articles 550 wds.; short story to 300 wds.

    Special needs: Trends in religion.

PASTOR/LEADERSHIP MARKETS

$BAREFOOT, 2923 Troost Ave., Kansas City MO 64109-1593. Toll-free (866) 355-9933. (816) 931-1900. Fax (816) 412-8306. E-mail: bfeditor@barefootministries.com or through Website: www.barefootministries.com. Mike Wonch, ed. Dedicated to resourcing and equipping youth workers. 10% unsolicited freelance; 90% assigned. E-query preferred; fax query OK. **Pays $50-100** on publication for all rts. Articles for youth workers 1,000-2,000 wds. (20-25/yr.); reviews 500 wds. ($25). Responds in 8 wks. Seasonal 6 mos. ahead. Accepts reprints (tell when/where appeared). Accepts e-mail submissions (attached or copied into message). Some kill fees. Does not use sidebars. Prefers NIV. Guidelines by e-mail; copy online. (No ads)

Fillers: Buys 20-40/yr. Anecdotes, cartoons, games, ideas, party ideas, short humor, and tips, 100-200 wds. $20-40.

Special needs: Youth worker and youth issues.

Tips: "We are most open to freelancers in the areas of product, music, and entertainment reviews. Where youth ministry articles and curricular pieces are concerned, we usually assign those to established youth ministry professionals."

$CATECHUMENATE: A Journal of Christian Initiation, 3949 S. Racine Ave., Chicago IL 60609-2523. Toll-free (800) 933-1800. (773) 486-8970. E-mail: editors@ltp.org. Website: www.LTP.org. Catholic. Mary Fox, ed. For clergy and laity who work with those who are planning to become Catholic. Bimonthly mag.; 48 pgs.; circ. 5,600. Subscription $20. 60% unsolicited freelance; 40% assigned. Query; phone/fax/e-query OK. Accepts full ms by e-mail. **Pays $100-300** on publication for all rts. Articles 2,000-3,000 wds. (10/yr.); book reviews 800 wds. Responds in 2 wks. Seasonal 6 mos. ahead. No simultaneous submissions or reprints. Requires requested ms by e-mail (attached). No kill fee. Use some sidebars. Guidelines by e-mail; copy for 6x9 SAE/4 stamps. (No ads)

   Poetry: Buys 6/yr. Any type; 5-20 lines; $75. Submit max. 5 poems. Onetime rts.

   Columns/Departments: Buys 26/yr. Sunday Word (Scripture reflection on Sunday readings, aimed at catechumen); 450 wds. $200-250. Query for assignment.

   Special needs: Christian initiation; reconciliation.

   Tips: "Writers should have worked at parishes or dioceses or taught in universities about Christian initiation."

$THE CATHOLIC SERVANT, PO Box 24142, Minneapolis MN 55424. (612) 729-7321. Cell (612) 275-0431. Fax (612) 724-8695. E-mail: JohnSondag@sainthelena.us. Catholic. John Sondag, ed./ pub. For Catholic evangelization, catechesis, and apologetics. Monthly tabloid; 12 pgs.; circ. 41,000 during school yr.; 33,000 summer. Query/clips; fax query OK. **Pays $60** on publication. Articles 750-1,000 wds. (12/yr.). Responds in 4 wks. Seasonal 3 mos. ahead. Requested mss by e-mail only. Uses some sidebars. (Ads)

   Fillers: Cartoons & short humor.

   Columns/Departments: Opinion column, 500-750 wds.

   Tips: "We buy features or columns only." Be sure to indicate "Ms for *Catholic Servant*" in subject line of e-mail.

$THE CHRISTIAN CENTURY, 104 S. Michigan Ave., Ste. 700, Chicago IL 60603. (312) 263-7510 (no phone calls). Website: http://christiancentury.org. Christian Century Foundation. Submit queries by e-mail to: submissions@christiancentury.org. For ministers, educators, and church leaders interested in events and theological issues of concern to the ecumenical church. Biweekly mag.; 48 pgs.; circ. 30,000. Subscription $59. 10% unsolicited freelance; 90% assigned. **Pays $125** on publication for all or onetime rts. Articles 1,500-3,000 wds. (150/yr.); book reviews, 800-1,500 wds.; music or film reviews 1,000 wds.; pays $0-75. No fiction submissions. Responds in 2-12 wks. Seasonal 4 mos. ahead. No simultaneous submissions. Accepts reprints (tell when/where appeared). No kill fee. Regularly uses sidebars. Prefers NRSV. Guidelines/theme list by e-mail/Website (scroll to bottom & click on "Submission Guidelines"); copy $5. (Ads)

   Poetry: Poetry Editor (poetry@christiancentury.org). Buys 50/yr. Any type (religious but not sentimental); to 20 lines; $50. Submit max. 10 poems.

   Special needs: Film, popular-culture commentary; news topics and analysis.

   Tips: "Keep in mind our audience of sophisticated readers, eager for analysis and critical perspective that goes beyond the obvious. We are open to all topics if written with appropriate style for our readers."

CHRISTIAN EDUCATION JOURNAL, 13800 Biola Ave., LaMirada CA 90639. (562) 903-6000, ext. 5528. Fax (562) 906-4502. E-mail: editor.cej@biola.edu. Website: www.biola.edu/cej. Talbot School of Theology, Biola University. Kevin E. Lawson, ed. Academic journal on the practice of Christian education; for students, professors, and thoughtful ministry leaders in Christian education. Semiannual jour.; 200-250 pgs.; circ. 750. Subscription $32. Open to freelance. Query; e-query OK. Accepts full mss by e-mail. **NO PAYMENT** for 1st rts. Articles 3,000-6,000 wds. (20/yr.); book reviews 2-5 pgs. Responds in 4-6 wks. No seasonal. Might accept simultaneous submissions & reprints (tell when/where appeared). Requires e-mail submissions (attached file in Word format). Does not use sidebars. Any Bible version. Guidelines on Website ("Publications Policy"/"Guidelines for writing and reviewing articles"); no copy. (Ads)

> **Tips:** "Focus on foundations and/or research with implications for the conception and practice of Christian education." Book reviews must be preassigned and approved by the editor; guidelines on Website.

CHURCH EXECUTIVE, 4742 N. 24th St., Ste. 340, Phoenix AZ 85016. (602) 265-7600. Fax (602) 265-4300. E-mail: ron@churchexecutive.com. Website: www.churchexecutive.com. Power Trade Media. Ronald E. Keener, ed. Business magazine for larger churches and megachurches, read by pastors, executive pastors, and business administrators. Monthly mag.; 52 pgs; circ. 20,000. Subscription $39. 5% unsolicited freelance; 95% assigned. Query; phone/e-query OK. Accepts full mss by e-mail. **NO PAYMENT.** Articles 1,200 wds. Responds in 2 wks. Seasonal 3 mos. ahead. Accepts simultaneous submissions; no reprints. Accepts e-mail submissions (attached file). Regularly uses sidebars. Prefers NIV. Guidelines/theme list by e-mail; copy for 9x12 SAE/$2 postage. (Ads)

> **Columns/Departments:** Accepts 5/yr. Query.
> **Special needs:** Church construction; economic impact on giving.
> **Tips:** "Relate your piece to our editorial calendar and product categories." Needs a lot of Website content.

$THE CLERGY JOURNAL, 6160 Carmen Ave. E., Inver Grove Heights MN 55076-4422. (651) 451-9945. Fax (651) 457-4617. E-mail: sfirle@logosstaff.com. Website: www.logosproductions.com. Logos Productions Inc. Sharon Firle, mng. ed. Directed mainly to clergy—a practical guide to church leadership and personal growth. Monthly (9X) mag.; 56 pgs.; circ. 6,000. Subscription $46.95. 5% unsolicited freelance; 95% assigned. Complete ms/cover letter; fax/e-query OK. **Pays $75-150** on publication for 1st rts. Articles 1,000-1,500 wds. (25/yr.). Responds in 4 wks. Seasonal 8 mos. ahead. Accepts simultaneous submissions & reprints (tell when/where appeared). Prefers requested ms by e-mail (attached file). No kill fee. Uses some sidebars. Prefers NRSV. Guidelines/theme list by mail/e-mail/Website; copy for 9x12 SAE/4 stamps. (Ads—struran@logosstaff.com)

> **Columns/Departments:** Ministry Issues; Preaching & Worship; Personal Issues; $75-150.
> **Special needs:** Church technology issues.
> **Tips:** "Our greatest need is sermon writers who can write on assigned texts. Instructions sent on request. Our readers are mainline Protestant. We are interested in meeting the personal and professional needs of clergy in areas like worship planning, church and personal finances, and self-care—spiritual, physical, and emotional."

$@COOK PARTNERS, 4050 Lee Vance View, Colorado Springs CO 80918. (719) 536-0100. Fax (719) 536-3266. E-mail: Marie.Chavez@davidccook.org. Website: www.cookinternational.org. Cook International. Submit to Marie Chavez. Seeks to encourage self-sufficient, effective indigenous Christian publishing worldwide to spread the life-giving message of the gospel. Bimonthly online publication; circ. 2,000. Subscription free. Open to unsolicited freelance. Query or complete ms. Articles & reviews 400-1,500 wds. Responds in 1-4 wks. **Most writers donate their work, but will negotiate for payment if asked.** Wants all rts. Incomplete topical listings. (No ads)

CROSSCURRENTS, 475 Riverside Dr., Ste. 1945, New York NY 10015. (212) 870-2544. Fax (212) 870-2539. cph@crosscurrents.org. Website: www.crosscurrents.org. Association for Religion and Intellectual Life. Charles P. Henderson, exec. dir.; submit to Managing Editor. For thoughtful activists for social justice and church reform. Quarterly mag.; 144 pgs.; circ. 5,000. Subscription $42. 25% unsolicited freelance; 75% assigned. Mostly written by academics. Complete ms/cover letter; e-query OK. **PAYS IN COPIES** for all rts. Articles 3,000-5,000 wds.; fiction 3,000 wds.; book reviews 1,000 wds. Responds in 4-8 wks. Seasonal 6 mos. ahead. No simultaneous submissions or reprints. Prefers requested ms on disk or by e-mail (attached file). Does not use sidebars. Guidelines on Website ("About Writing for CrossCurrents" center); no copy. (Ads)

    Poetry: Accepts 12/yr. Any type or length; no payment. Submit max. 5 poems.

    Tips: "Looking for focused, well-researched articles; creative fiction and poetry. Send two double-spaced copies; SASE; use *Chicago Manual of Style* and nonsexist language."

$DIOCESAN DIALOGUE, 16565 S. State St., South Holland IL 60473. (708) 331-5485. Fax (708) 331-5484. E-mail: acp@acpress.org. Website: www.americancatholicpress.org. American Catholic Press. Father Michael Gilligan, editorial dir. Targets Latin-Rite dioceses in the U.S. that sponsor a Mass broadcast on TV or radio. Annual newsletter; 8 pgs.; circ. 750. Free. 20% unsolicited freelance. Complete ms/cover letter; no phone/fax/e-query. Articles 200-1,000 wds. **Pays variable rates** on publication for all rts. Responds in 10 wks. Accepts simultaneous submissions & reprints. Uses some sidebars. Prefers NAB (Confraternity). No guidelines; copy $3/9x12 SAE/2 stamps. (No ads)

    Fillers: Cartoons, 2/yr.

    Tips: "Writers should be familiar with TV production of the Mass and/or the needs of senior citizens, especially shut-ins."

+@DISCIPLE MAGAZINE (replacing *Pulpit Helps*), 6815 Shallowford Rd., Chattanooga TN 37421. Toll-free (800) 251-7206. (423) 894-6060. Fax (423) 894-1055. E-mail: justinl@amginternational .org. Website: www.disciplemagazine.com. AMG International. Justin Lonas, ed/pub. Help for pastors with a focus on theology and discipleship. Biweekly e-zine; circ. 2,000. Subscription $15. Estab. 2009. 15% unsolicited freelance; 85% assigned. Query; e-query OK. Accepts full mss by e-mail. **NO PAYMENT** for all rts. Articles 1,000-1,200 wds. (5-10/yr.); reviews 350 wds. Responds in 1 wk. Seasonal 2 mos. ahead. Accepts simultaneous submissions & reprints (tell when/where appeared). Requires e-mail submission (attached file). Uses some sidebars. Prefers NASB. Guidelines by e-mail; copy online. (Ads)

    Special needs: Solid theology (exposition, exegesis), and discipleship.

    Tips: "Most open to thoughtful pieces on discipleship, showing insight and Christian maturity. Also open to stories/insights from missionaries and those proclaiming Christ around the world."

$EMMANUEL, 5384 Wilson Mills Rd., Cleveland OH 44143. (440) 449-2103. Fax (440) 449-3862. E-mail: emmanuel@blessedsacrament.com. Website: www.blessedsacrament.com. Catholic. Rev. Paul Bernier SSS, ed. (pbernier@blessedsacrament.com); Patrick Riley, book review ed. Eucharistic spirituality for priests and others in church ministry. Bimonthly mag.; 96 pgs.; circ. 3,000. Subscription $31; $36 foreign. 30% unsolicited freelance. Query or complete ms/cover letter; e-query OK. **Pays $75-150 for articles, $50 for meditations,** on publication for all rts. Articles 2,000-2,750 wds.; meditations 1,000-1,250 wds.; book reviews 500-750 wds. Responds in 2 wks. Seasonal 4 mos. ahead. Accepts manuscripts on disk or as e-mail attachments. Guidelines/theme list by mail/e-mail. (Ads)

    Poetry: Buys 6-10/yr. Free verse, light verse, traditional; 8 lines & up; $35. Submit max. 3 poems.

    Tips: "Most open to articles, meditations, poetry oriented toward Eucharistic spirituality, prayer, and ministry."

$ENRICHMENT: A Journal for Pentecostal Ministry, 1445 N. Boonville Ave., Springfield MO 65802. (417) 862-2781, ext. 4095. Fax (417) 862-0416. E-mail: enrichmentjournal@ag.org. Website: www.enrichmentjournal.ag.org. Assemblies of God. George P. Wood, exec. ed.; Rick Knoth, mng. ed. (rknoth@ag.org). Quarterly jour.; 144-160 pgs.; circ. 33,000. Subscription $24; foreign add $30. 15% unsolicited freelance. Complete ms/cover letter. **Pays up to .15/wd. ($75-350)** on acceptance for 1st rts. Articles 1,000-2,800 wds. (25/yr.); book reviews, 250 wds. ($25). Responds in 8-12 wks. Seasonal 1 yr. ahead. Accepts simultaneous submissions & reprints (tell when/where appeared). Requires requested ms by e-mail (copied into message or attached). Kill fee up to 50%. Regularly uses sidebars. Prefers NIV. Guidelines on Website; copy for $7/10x13 SAE. (Ads)

Fillers: Buys over 100/yr. Anecdotes, cartoons, facts, short humor, tips; $25-40, or .10-.20/wd.

Columns/Departments: Buys 40/yr. For Women in Ministry (leadership ideas), Associate Ministers (related issues), Managing Your Ministry (how-to), Financial Concepts (church stewardship issues), Family Life (minister's family), When Pews Are Few (ministry in smaller congregation), Worship in the Church, Leader's Edge, Preaching That Connects, Ministry & Medical Ethics; all 1,200-2,500 wds. $75-275. Query or complete ms.

Tips: "Most open to EShorts: short, 150-250 word, think pieces covering a wide range of topics related to ministry and church life, such as culture, worship, generational issues, church/community, trends, evangelism, surveys, time management, and humor."

** 2010, 2009 Award of Merit: Christian Ministries. 2008, 2007 EPA Award of Excellence: Christian Ministry. This periodical was #16 on the 2010 Top 50 Christian Publishers list (#15 in 2009, #43 in 2008, #47 in 2006).

$THE EVANGELICAL BAPTIST, PO Box 457, Guelph, ON N1H 6K9, Canada. (519) 821-4830, ext. 229. Fax (519) 821-9829. E-mail: eb@fellowship.ca or through Website: www.fellowship.ca. Fellowship of Evangelical Baptist Churches in Canada. Jennifer Bugg, mng. ed. To enhance the life and ministry of pastors and leaders in local churches. Quarterly mag. Subscription $12. Query preferred. **Pays .05/wd.** on publication for onetime rts. Articles 800-2,400 wds.; book reviews 200-500 wds. Guidelines on Website (click on "Connections & Resources"/"EB Magazine"/"Writers").

FOURSQUARE LEADER, 1910 W. Sunset Blvd., Ste. 400, PO Box 26902, Los Angeles CA 90026-0176. Toll-free (888) 635-4234. (213) 989-4230. Fax (213) 989-4590. E-mail: comm@foursquare .org, or through Website: www.foursquare.org. International Church of the Foursquare Gospel. Marcia Graham, ed. For credentialed Foursquare leaders. Quarterly mag.; 20 pgs.; circ. 10,000. Subscription free. Estab. 2009. 100% assigned. Query/clips. No full mss by e-mail. **NO PAYMENT** for all rts. Articles 500-1,000 wds.; book/music/video reviews 150 wds. Responds in 4 wks. Seasonal 4 mos. ahead. No simultaneous submissions or reprints. Requires e-mail submissions (attached file). Kill fee negotiable. Uses some sidebars. Prefers NKJV. Guidelines by mail/e-mail/Website; free copy on request. (No ads)

Tips: "Query only via e-mail on relevant real-life topics and related to Foursquare ministry."

THE GREAT COMMISSION RESEARCH JOURNAL, (formerly *Journal of the American Society for Church Growth*), Alan McMahan, ed., Biola School of Intercultural Studies, 13800 Biola Ave., LaMirada CA 90639. (562) 944-0351. Fax (562) 906-4502. E-mail: alan.mcmahan@biola.edu. Website: www.biola.edu/gcr. Biola University. Targets professors, pastors, denominational executives, and seminary students interested in church growth and evangelism. Biannual jour. (winter & summer); 150 pgs.; circ. 400. Subscription $24. 66% unsolicited freelance; 33% assigned. Complete ms/cover letter; phone/fax/e-query OK. **PAYS IN COPIES** for onetime rts. Not copyrighted. Articles 15 pgs. or 4,000-5,000 wds. (10/yr.); book reviews 750-2,000 wds. Responds in 8-12 wks. Accepts simultaneous submissions & reprints (tell when/where appeared). Prefers requested ms on disk or by e-mail. Does not use sidebars. Any Bible version. Guidelines by mail (also in journal) or on Website ("Submission Guidelines")/theme list; copy $10. (Ads)

Tips: "Provide well-researched and tightly written articles related to some aspect of church growth. Articles should be academic in nature, rather than popular in style. We're open to new writers at this time."

$GROWTH POINTS, PO Box 892589, Temecula CA 92589-2589. Phone/fax (951) 506-3086. E-mail: cgnet@earthlink.net. Website: www.churchgrowthnetwork.com. Dr. Gary L. McIntosh, ed.

For pastors and church leaders interested in church growth. Monthly newsletter; 2 pgs.; circ. 8,000. Subscription $16. 10% unsolicited freelance; 90% assigned. Query; fax/e-query OK. **Pays $25** for onetime rts. Not copyrighted. Articles 1,000-2,000 wds. (2/yr.). Responds in 4 wks. Accepts simultaneous submissions & reprints. Accepts requested ms on disk. Does not use sidebars. Guidelines by mail; copy for #10 SAE/1 stamp. (No ads)

> **Tips:** "Write articles that are short (1,200 words), crisp, clear, with very practical ideas that church leaders can put to use immediately. All articles must have a pro-church-growth slant, be very practical, have how-to material, and be very tightly written with bullets, etc."

$+IMMERSE: A Journal of Faith, Life and Youth Ministry, 2929 Troost Ave., Kansas city MO 64109. (816) 931-1900. E-mail: contact@immersejournal.com. Website: http://immersejournal .com. Barefoot Ministries/Nazarene Publishing House. Tim Baker, mng. ed. Offers a robust, holistic and earthy view of youth ministry, to help equip youth workers with innovative ways of viewing and being a part of youth ministry as a whole. Bimonthly jour.; 48 pgs; circ. 20,000. Subscription $39.99. 5% unsolicited freelance; 95% assigned. Query; e-query OK. **Pays** on acceptance for all rts. Not copyrighted. Articles 2,000-2,500 wds. Responds in 2 wks. Seasonal 6 mos. ahead. No simultaneous submissions or reprints. Prefers e-mail submissions (attached file). Kill fee $25. Uses some sidebars. Accepts submissions from teens. Guidelines/theme list by e-mail; copy for 9x12 SAE/3 stamps. (Ads)

> **Columns/Departments:** Buys 54/yr. Story (stories of the Gospel and modern-day examples of God's will); Gospel Theology (youth ministry is a theological endeavor); Arts & Culture (inspire and equip youth leaders to dive into art & culture); Spiritual Formation & Leadership Development (help shape the leadership of youth ministry); 2,000-2,500 wds. Query.
>
> **Tips:** "Read our publication to figure out the vibe we are looking for."

$INSIGHT YOUTH RESOURCE, 55 W. Oak Ridge Dr., Hagerstown MD 21740. E-mail: iyr_editor @yahoo.com. Seventh-day Adventist. Patricia Humphrey, ed. For Christian youth leaders; a practical resource filled with ideas for creative youth ministry and programming. Quarterly mag.; 48 pgs.; circ. 2,200. 5% unsolicited freelance; 95% assigned. Query/clips; fax query OK; best to e-mail, as editor lives in Texas. **Pays $25-350** on acceptance for nonexclusive full rts. Articles 700-900 wds. (16/yr.). Responds in 8-12 wks. Seasonal 12 mos. ahead. Accepts reprints (tell when/where appeared). Accepts e-mail submissions (attached file in Microsoft Word). No kill fee. Regularly uses sidebars. Prefers KJV, NKJV, NIV. Also accepts submissions from teens. Guidelines by mail/e-mail; copy for 9x12 SAE/$2.38 postage (mark "Media Mail"). (Ads)

> **Columns/Departments:** Outreach Ideas (service activity ideas for teens), 800-1,000 wds. Super Social Suggestions (social activities and games for teen groups), 800-1,000 wds. Program Ideas (creative youth programming ideas), variable lengths.
>
> **Special needs:** Articles dealing with understanding and teaching youth. Innovative concepts in youth ministry.
>
> **Tips:** "Areas most open to freelancers are the Super Social and Outreach Ideas. We are always looking for creative activity ideas that teen leaders can do with youth, ages 14-18. The activities should be fun to do and well written with clear, easy-to-follow instructions. Ideas that are tested and have worked well with your own youth group are preferred."

$INSITE, PO Box 62189, Colorado Springs CO 80962-2189. (719) 260-9400. Fax (719) 260-6398. E-mail: editor@ccca.org, or info@ccca.org. Website: www.ccca.org. Christian Camp and Conference Assn. Martha Krienke, ed. To inform and inspire professionals serving in the Christian camp and conference community. Bimonthly mag.; 52 pgs.; circ. 8,200. Subscription $29.95. 15% unsolicited freelance; 85% assigned. Query; e-query OK. **Pays .20/wd.** on publication for 1st and electronic rts. Cover articles 1,500-2,000 wds. (12/yr.); features 1,200-1,500 wds. (30/yr.); sidebars 250-500 wds. (15-20/yr.). Responds in 4 wks. Seasonal 6 mos. ahead. Accepts simultaneous submissions &

reprints (tell when/where appeared). Prefers e-mail submission (attached file). Kill fee. Regularly uses sidebars. Prefers NIV. Guidelines on Website; copy $4.99/9x12 SAE/$1.73 postage. (Ads)

Special needs: Outdoor setting; purpose and objectives; administration and organization; personnel development; camper/guest needs; programming; health and safety; food service; site/facilities maintenance; business/operations; marketing and PR; relevant spiritual issues; and fund-raising.

Tips: "Most open to how-to pieces; get guidelines, then query first. Don't send general camping-related articles. We print stories specifically related to Christian camp and conference facilities; innovative programs or policies; how a Christian camp or conference experience affected a present-day leader. Review several issues so you know what we're looking for."

** 2010, 2008, 2006 EPA Award of Merit: Christian Ministries; 2007 EPA Award of Excellence: Christian Ministries; 2006 EPA Award of Merit: Most Improved Publication.

$@INTERPRETER and INTERPRETER ONLINE, PO Box 320, Nashville TN 37202-0320. (615) 742-5407. Fax (615) 742-5460. E-mail: knoble@umcom.org, or through Website: www .InterpreterMagazine.org. United Methodist Church. Joey Butler, mng. ed.; Kathy Noble, ed. For lay leaders and pastors of the United Methodist Church; focus on ministry ideas and resources, spiritual-growth issues, with a practical slant. Bimonthly & online mag.; 44+ pgs.; circ. 225,000. Subscription $12. Some assigned freelance; very little unsolicited material. Query/clips. **Pays** on acceptance for all rts. Articles 500-1,000 wds. (6 print/yr.; some Web exclusive). Seasonal 6 mos. ahead. No simultaneous submissions or reprints. Use submission form on Website or submit via e-mail. No kill fee. Uses some sidebars. Prefers NRSV. Guidelines on Website; copy for 9x12 SAE/4 stamps. (Ads)

Columns/Departments: Lighter Fare (limited/occasional humor); Leadership Link (leadership theory & practice); IdeaMart (resources to support local church ministry); The World is My Parish (stories of United Methodists around the world); all 200-250 wds. Payment varies.

Tips: "All articles must have a specific and prominent United Methodist connection. Very difficult for unsolicited freelancers to break in, as we have an excellent pool and depend on them for referrals. No stories about organizations, ministries, missions with an official United Methodist equivalent. All writers must have an understanding of United Methodist organization."

** Received awards from the Associated Church Press in 2008 and United Methodist Assn. of Communicators in 2007.

THE JOURNAL OF PASTORAL CARE & COUNSELING, 1549 Clairmont Rd., Ste. 103, Decatur GA 30033-4635. (404) 320-0195. Fax (404) 320-0849. E-mail: MngEd@jpcp.org. Website: www.jpcp .org. Dr. Terry R. Bard, mng. ed. For chaplains/pastors/professionals involved with pastoral care and counseling in other than a church setting. Quarterly jour.; 116 pgs.; circ. 10,000. Subscription $35. 95% unsolicited freelance; 5% assigned. Query; phone/fax/e-query OK. **PAYS 10 COPIES** for 1st rts. Articles 5,000 wds. or 20 pgs. (30/yr.); book reviews 5 pgs. Responds in 8 wks. Accepts requested ms electronically (instructions on Website). Does not use sidebars. Guidelines on Website (click on "JPC & C Manuscripts for Review"/"Guidelines" in text); no copy. (Ads)

Poetry: Accepts 16/yr. Free verse; 5-16 lines. Submit max. 3 poems.

Special needs: "We publish brief (500-600 wds.) 'Personal Reflections,' but they need to deal with clinical experiences that have led the writer to reflect on the religious and/or theological meaning generated."

Tips: "Most open to poems and personal reflections. Readers are highly trained clinically, holding professional degrees in religion/theology. Writers need to be professionals on topics covered."

$@LEADERSHIP, 465 Gundersen Dr., Carol Stream IL 60188. (630) 260-6200. Fax (630) 260-0451. E-mail: LJEditor@LeadershipJournal.net. Website: www.leadershipjournal.net. Christianity Today Intl. Marshall Shelley, ed-in-chief. Practical help for pastors/church leaders, covering the spectrum of subjects from personal needs to professional skills. Quarterly & online jour.; 104 pgs.; circ. 48,000. Subscription $24.95. 20% unsolicited freelance; 80% assigned. Query or complete ms/cover letter; fax/e-query OK. Accepts full mss by e-mail. **Pays .15-20/wd.** on acceptance for 1st & electronic rts. Articles 500-3,000 wds. (10/yr.).; book reviews 100 wds. (pays $25-50). Responds in 6 wks. Seasonal 6 mos. ahead. Accepts reprints (tell when/where appeared). Accepts requested ms by e-mail (copied into message or attached Word doc). Kill fee 30%. Regularly uses sidebars. Prefers NLT. Guidelines on Website; copy for 9x12 SAE/$2 postage. (Ads)

> **Fillers:** Buys 80/yr. Cartoons, short humor; to 150 wds. $25-50.
>
> **Columns/Departments:** Skye Jethani, mng. ed. Buys 12/yr. Tool Kit (practical stories or resources for preaching, worship, outreach, pastoral care, spiritual formation, and administration); 100-700 wds. Complete ms. Pays $50-250.
>
> **Tips:** "*Leadership* is a practical journal for pastors. Tell real-life stories of church life—defining moments—dramatic events. What was learned the hard way—by experience. We look for articles that provide practical help for problems church leaders face, not essays expounding on a topic, editorials arguing a position, or homilies explaining biblical principles. We want 'how-to' articles based on first-person accounts of real-life experiences in ministry in the local church."
>
> ** 2010, 2006 EPA Award of Excellence: Christian Ministries; 2008 EPA Award of Merit: General; 2007 EPA Award of Merit: Christian Ministries. This periodical was #21 on the 2010 Top 50 Christian Publishers list (#21 in 2009, #18 in 2008, #15 in 2007, #14 in 2006).

$LEAD MAGAZINE, 55 W. Oak Ridge Dr., Hagerstown MD 21740. (301) 393-4095. Fax (301) 393-4055. E-mail: fcrumbly@rhpa.org, or sabbathschoolleadership@rhpa.org. Website: www.myleadmagazine.org. Seventh-day Adventist/Review & Herald. Faith Crumbly, ed. Nurtures, educates, and supports adult Bible study and program leaders by providing training in leadership and interpersonal skills, plus programs. Monthly mag.; 32 pgs.; circ. 8,100. Subscription $42.95 (add $6 for addresses outside U.S., Canada, and Bermuda). 10% unsolicited freelance; 90% assigned. Complete ms. **Pays $25-100** on acceptance for 1st rts. Articles 600-1,200 wds. (120-150/yr.). Responds in 1-2 wks. Seasonal 6-8 mos. ahead. Accepts reprints (tell when/where appeared). Prefers accepted ms by e-mail (attached file). Uses some sidebars. Guidelines/theme list on Website ("Writer's Guidelines" left side); copy for $2.36 in postage. (For ads, contact: Genia Blumenberg at gblumenberg@rhpa.org)

> **Columns/Departments:** Buys 5/yr. Tool Kit (interpersonal skills, organization, mentoring, training), 600-800 wds. Query. Pays $70-100.

$LET'S WORSHIP, One Lifeway Plaza, MSN 175, Nashville TN 37234-0170. (615) 251-3775. Fax (615) 251-2795. E-mail: craig.adams@lifeway.com. Website: www.lifeway.com. Southern Baptist/LifeWay Christian Resources. Craig Adams, ed-in-chief. Resources for pastors and worship leaders; countering the norm with contagious ideas. Quarterly mag.; 96 pgs.; circ. 5,500. Subscription $62.35. 10% unsolicited freelance; 90% assigned. Complete ms by e-mail only. **Pays .105/wd.** on acceptance for all, 1st, or onetime rts. Articles 1,500 wds. (50/yr.); book reviews 300 wds. ($50). Responds in 10 wks. Seasonal 10 mos. ahead. Accepts simultaneous submissions. Requires ms by e-mail (attached file or copied into message). Regularly uses sidebars. Prefers HCSB. No guidelines/copy. (No ads)

> **Columns/Departments:** Wednesday Words (4-week Bible study with listening sheets); Bible study, 625 wds.; church choir; instrumental music; worship media; student worship; children's worship; listening sheet, 200 wds. Drama (original scripts), 900 wds.
>
> **Special needs:** New worship songs, staff communication tools and tips, fresh hymn arrangements, children's worship ideas, media techniques and tools, drama scripts, puppet scripts, singing techniques and exercises, etc.

Tips: "This periodical exists to bring the entire church staff to the same page with regards to worship culture in the church community."

$@THE LIVING CHURCH, PO Box 514036, Milwaukee WI 53203-3436. (414) 276-5420. Fax (414) 276-7483. E-mail: tlc@livingchurch.org or through Website: www.livingchurch.org. Episcopal/The Living Church Foundation Inc. John Schuessler, mng. ed. Independent news coverage of the Episcopal Church for clergy and lay leaders. Weekly & online mag.; 24+ pgs.; circ. 9,000. Subscription $42.50. Open to freelance. Query; phone/fax/e-query OK. **Pays $25-100 (for solicited articles, nothing for unsolicited)** for onetime rts. Articles 1,000 wds. (10/yr.). Responds in 2-4 wks. Seasonal 2 mos. ahead. Prefers requested ms by e-mail (attached or copied into message). Uses some sidebars. Guidelines by mail/e-mail; free copy. (Ads)

   Columns/Departments: Accepts 5/yr. Benediction (devotional/inspirational), 200 wds. Complete ms. No payment.

   Tips: "Most open to features, as long as they have something to do with the Episcopal Church."

@LUTHERAN FORUM, PO Box 327, Delhi NY 13753-0327. (607) 746-7511. E-mail: dkralpb@aol.com. Website: www.lutheranforum.org. American Lutheran Publicity Bureau. Sarah Hinlicky Wilson, ed. (editor@lutheranforum.org). For church leadership—clerical and laity. Quarterly & online mag.; 64 pgs.; circ. 3,200. Subscription $26.95. 20% unsolicited freelance; 80% assigned. E-query only. **PAYS 2 COPIES** for onetime rts. Articles 2,000 wds. (48/yr.). Responds in 26-32 wks. No simultaneous submissions or reprints. Accepts full mss by e-mail only (attached file). No sidebars. Prefers ESV. Guidelines/theme list on Website ("Submissions Guidelines" in lower, right-hand column); copy for 9x12 SAE/$8. (Ads)

   Poetry: Accepts 2-8/yr. Avant-garde, free verse, traditional. Submit max. 5 poems.

   Special needs: Hymns written by Lutheran composers only. Submit to Sally Messner, messner@lutheranforum.org.

   Tips: "Review the departments on our Website and read back issues. 95% of material is by Lutheran writers. Clarity of expression and sophistication of theological analysis are essential. No devotions or personal essays."

$@MINISTRY & LITURGY, 160 E. Virginia St., #290, San Jose CA 95112. Toll-free (888) 273-7782. (408) 286-8505. Fax (408) 287-8748. E-mail: editor@rpinet.com. Website: www.rpinet.com/ml. Resource Publications Inc. Donna M. Cole, ed. dir. To help liturgists and ministers make the imaginative connection between liturgy and life. Monthly (10X) & online mag.; 50 pgs.; circ. 20,000. Subscription $50. 5% unsolicited freelance; 5% assigned. Query only; fax/e-query OK. **Pays $50-200** on publication for 1st rts. Articles & fiction 1,500 wds. (30/yr.). Responds in 4 wks. Seasonal 6 mos. ahead. Accepts reprints (tell when/where appeared). Requires requested ms on disk. Regularly uses sidebars. Guidelines/theme on Website (click on "Authors & Writers" in left-hand column); copy $4/11x14 SAE/2 stamps. (Ads)

   Special needs: The practice of ministry: music ministry, youth ministry, pastoral ministry, and liturgical ministry.

   Contest: Visual Arts Awards.

   Tips: "Writers need to be able to help our reader do his or her job better. Be familiar enough with contemporary issues in ministry to provide perceivable value to the reader. Provide new insight or valuable insight into issues of concern to members of a ministry team. Credibility (training and experience in ministry) is important."

@MINISTRY IN MOTION E-ZINE, 6275 Autumn Meadows, Dayton OH 45424. (937) 725-9485. E-mail: hanover@dmim.net. Website: www.ministryinmotion.net. Nondenominational. Thomas Hanover, ed. We seek to equip lay and clergy leaders for ministry in the 21st century through the resources of publications, coaching, consulting, and other Website tools. Bimonthly e-zine; circulation 1,000+. Subscription free online. 25% unsolicited freelance; 75% assigned. Query; e-query OK. Accepts full mss by e-mail. **NO PAYMENT** for onetime & electronic rts. Articles 1,000-1,200 wds. (10-12/yr.); book reviews 750 wds. Responds in 2 wks. Seasonal 3 mos. ahead. Accepts simultaneous submissions & reprints (tell when/where appeared). Prefers submissions by e-mail (attached file). Regularly uses sidebars. Prefers NIV or NRSV. Guidelines on Website; copy by e-mail/Website. (Ads)

Fillers: Short humor.

Columns/Departments: Accepts 4-6/yr. Ministry Employment (how to find employment in ministry field); Women's Ministries (how to lead effective women's ministries); 700-1,000 wds. Query.

Tips: "Share leadership tips and insights. The more practical and how-to, the better. No theology or heavily scholastic articles; we are for the everyday church worker. Avoid church culture terms and lingo related to your own denomination. If no experience, send us some samples. We'll work with you."

$MINISTRY MAGAZINE: International Journal for Pastors, 12501 Old Columbia Pike, Silver Spring MD 20904. (301) 680-6510. Fax (301) 680-6502. E-mail: MinistryMagazine@gc.adventist .org. Website: www.ministrymagazine.org. Seventh-day Adventist. Nikolaus Satelmajer, ed.; Willie E. Hucks II, assoc. ed. For pastors. Monthly jour.; 32 pgs.; circ. 19,000. Subscription $32.80. 90% unsolicited freelance. Query; fax/e-query OK. **Pays $50-300** on acceptance for all rts. Articles 1,000-1,500 wds.; book reviews 100-150 wds. ($25). Responds within 13 wks. Prefers requested ms by e-mail. Uses some sidebars. Guidelines/theme list by mail/Website ("Article Submissions"); copy for 9x12 SAE/5 stamps. (Ads)

$@MINISTRY TODAY, 600 Rinehart Rd., Lake Mary FL 32746. (407) 333-0600. Fax (407) 333-7133. E-mail: ministrytoday@strang.com. Website: www.ministrytodaymag.com. Strang Communications. Submit to The Editor. Helps for pastors and church leaders, primarily in Pentecostal/ Charismatic churches. Quarterly & online mag.; 112 pgs.; circ. 30,000. Subscription $14.97. 60-80% freelance. Query; fax/e-query preferred. **Pays $50 or $500-800** on publication for all rts. Articles 1,800-2,500 wds. (25/yr.); book/music/video reviews, 300 wds. $25. Responds in 4 wks. Prefers accepted ms by e-mail. Kill fee. Regularly uses sidebars. Prefers NIV. Guidelines on Website (scroll to bottom of Home Page & click on "Writers' Guidelines"); copy $6/9x12 SAE. For free subscription to online version go to: www.digital.ministrytoday.com/signup.(Ads)

Tips: "Most open to columns. Study guidelines and the magazine. Please correspond with editor before sending an article proposal."

$@NET RESULTS, 2101 W. Broadway, Ste. 103, Columbia MO 65203. (573) 234-4374. Fax (866) 834-1938. E-mail: submissions@netresults.org, or netresults@netresults.org. Website: www .netresults.org. Net Results Inc. Bill Tenny-Brittian, sr. ed. (billtb@netresults.org). Offers Christian church leaders practical, ministry-vitalization ideas and methods. Digital mag.; 32 pgs.; circ. 12,000. Subscription $49.95 for digital. 20% unsolicited freelance; 80% assigned. Query; fax/e-query OK. Accepts full ms through e-mail. **Now pays a small amount** on publication for onetime rts. Articles 1,000-2,000 wds. (20/yr.). Response time varies. Seasonal 6 mos. ahead. No simultaneous submissions or reprints. Requires accepted ms by e-mail (attached file). No kill fee. Regularly uses sidebars. Prefers TNIV. Guidelines on Website ("Writer's Information"). Copy for 9x12 SAE. (Limited ads)

Tips: "We prefer practical, how-to articles on ideas that have worked in a local church setting."

$@THE NEWSLETTER NEWSLETTER, PO Box 36269, Canton OH 44735. Toll-free (800) 992-2144. E-mail: service@comresources.com or through Website: www.newsletternewsletter.com. Communication Resources. Stephanie Martin, ed. To help church secretaries and church newsletter editors prepare their newsletter. Monthly & online newsletter; 14 pgs. Subscription $49.95. 100% assigned. Complete ms; e-query OK. **Pays $50-150** on acceptance for all rts. Articles 800-1,000 wds.

(12/yr.). Responds in 4 wks. Seasonal 4 mos. ahead. Accepts simultaneous submissions. Requires requested ms by e-mail. Kill fee. Guidelines by mail/e-mail.

Tips: "Most open to how-to articles on various aspects of newsletter production—writing, graphics, layout and design, postal, printing, etc."

$OUTREACH MAGAZINE, 2230 Oak Ridge Way, Vista CA 92081-8341. (760) 940-0600. Fax (760) 597-2314. E-mail: editor@outreach.com or through Website: www.outreachmagazine.com. Lindy Lowry, ed. (llowry@outreach.com). Tells the ideas, insights, and stories of today's outreach-focused churches and is designed to inspire, challenge, and equip churches to connect with their communities and show the love of God to people both locally and globally. Bimonthly mag.; 130 pgs.; circ. 35,000. Subscription $29.95. 20% unsolicited freelance; 80% assigned. Query/clips; e-query OK. **Pays $400** for articles; $700-1,000 for feature articles; on publication for 1st rts. Articles 1,200-2,500 wds. Responds in 8 wks. Seasonal 6 mos. ahead. No simultaneous submissions; rarely accepts reprints (tell when/where appeared). Prefers submissions by e-mail (attached file). Sometimes pays kill fee. Regularly uses sidebars. Guidelines on Website (click on "Writers Guidelines" near top of Home Page); free copy. (Ads)

   Columns/Departments: Accepts fewer than 10/yr. Pulse (tight and bright stories about churches finding unique ways to outreach), 50-250 wds. From the Frontline (profile of one church and the unique way it's reaching its community), 800 wds. SoulFires (as-told-to pieces from interview with someone doing outreach), 950 wds.; .30/wd. or flat fee. Query.

   Special needs: Interviews with non-Christians.

   Tips: "Most open to interviews/profiles (Soulfires, Frames, The Outreach Interview); church stories (Pulse, Idea Bank, From the Front Line); outreach ideas from churches (Idea Bank, Connections, Big Idea)."

$PARISH LITURGY, 16565 S. State St., South Holland IL 60473. (708) 331-5485. Fax (708) 331-5484. E-mail: acp@acpress.org. Website: www.americancatholicpress.org. American Catholic Press. Father Michael Gilligan, exec. dir. A planning tool for Sunday and holy day liturgy. Quarterly mag.; 40 pgs.; circ. 1,200. Subscription $24. 5% unsolicited freelance. Query; no phone/e-query. **Pays variable rates** for all rts. Articles 400 wds. Responds in 4 wks. Seasonal 4 mos. ahead. Accepts simultaneous submissions & reprints (tell when/where appeared). Uses some sidebars. Prefers NAB. No guidelines; copy available. (No ads)

   Tips: "We only use articles on the liturgy—period. Send us well-informed articles on the liturgy."

@PLUGGED IN ONLINE, Colorado Springs CO 80920 (no street address needed). Toll-free (800) 232-6459. (719) 531-3400. Fax (719) 548-5823. E-mail: waliszrs@fotf.org, or pluggedin@fam ily.org. Website: www.pluggedinonline.com. Focus on the Family. Steven Isaac, online ed.; Bob Smithhouser, sr. ed. To assist parents and youth leaders in better understanding popular youth culture and equip them to impart principles of discernment in young people. Online newsletter. Open to queries only. Articles. Incomplete topical listings. (No ads)

   **2010 EPA Award of Excellence: Online.

@PREACHING, PREACHING ONLINE & PREACHING NOW, 750 Old Hickory Blvd., Ste. 150-1, Brentwood TN 37027. (615) 386-3011. Fax (615) 312-4277. E-mail: editor@preaching.com or through Website: www.preaching.com. Salem Communications. Dr. Michael Duduit, ed. Bimonthly; circ. 9,000. Subscription $24.95/2 yrs. 50% unsolicited freelance; 50% assigned. Query; fax/e-query OK. **PAYS A SUBSCRIPTION** for onetime & electronic rts. Responds in 4-8 wks. Seasonal 10-12 mos. ahead. Reprints from books only. Prefers requested ms by e-mail (attached file). Uses some sidebars. Guidelines on Website; copy online. (ads). *Preaching Online* is a professional resource for pastors that supplements *Preaching* magazine. Includes all content from magazine, plus additional articles and sermons. Feature articles, 2,000-2,500, $50. Sermons 1,500-2,000 wds.

$35. *Preaching Now* is a weekly e-mail/e-zine; circ. 19,000. Subscription $39.95. Accepts books for review. Guidelines on Website (scroll down to bottom of Home Page and click on "Site Map"/scroll down to "Help"/ "Writing for Us"); Copy $8. (Ads)

$@PREACHINGTODAY.COM, 465 Gundersen Dr., Carol Stream IL 60188-2498. Toll-free (877) 247-4787. (630) 260-6200. Fax (630) 260-0451. E-mail: blarson@christianitytoday.com or through Website: www.preachingtoday.com. Christianity Today Intl. Brian Larson, ed. Open to fresh sermon illustrations from various sources for preachers (no recycled illustrations from other illustration sources). E-mail submissions only; use online submission form. Articles 250-500 wds. Responds in 1 mo. Guidelines on Website (click on "Contact"/scroll down to "Editorial"/click on "read the submission guidelines" in the text). Sermon illustrations only.

$PREACHING WELL, PO Box 3102, Margate NJ 08402. Toll-free (800) 827-9401. (609) 822-9401. Fax (609) 822-1638. E-mail: techsupport@voicings.com. Website: www.voicings.com. Voicings Publications. James Colaianni Jr., pub. Sermon illustration resource for professional clergy. Monthly newsletter, 8 pgs. Subscription $37.95. 5% unsolicited freelance. Complete ms; e-query OK. **Pays .10/wd.** on publication for any rts. Illustrations/anecdotes 50-250 wds. Responds in 6 wks. Seasonal 4 mos. ahead. Accepts reprints. Prefers requested ms on disk or by e-mail. Guidelines/topical index by mail/e-mail; copy for 9x12 SAE. (Ads)

Poetry: Light verse, traditional; 50-250 lines; .10/wd. Submit max. 3 poems.
Fillers: Various; sermon illustrations; 50-250 wds.; .10/wd.
Tips: "All sections open."

$THE PRIEST, 200 Noll Plaza, Huntington IN 46750-4304. Toll-free: (800) 348-2440. (260) 356-8400. Fax (260) 359-9117. E-mail: tpriest@osv.com. Website: www.osv.com. Catholic/Our Sunday Visitor Inc. Msgr. Owen F. Campion, ed.; submit to Murray Hubley, assoc. ed. For Catholic priests, deacons, and seminarians; to help in all aspects of ministry. Monthly jour.; 48 pgs.; circ. 6,500. Subscription $39.95. 40% unsolicited freelance. Query (preferred) or complete ms/cover letter; phone/fax/e-query OK. **Pays $50-250** on acceptance for 1st rts. Not copyrighted. Articles to 1,500 wds. (96/yr.); some 2-parts. Responds in 5-13 wks. Seasonal 3 mos. ahead. Uses some sidebars. Prefers disk or e-mail submissions (attached file). Prefers NAB. Guidelines on Website (click on "About Us"/"The Priest Writers' Guidelines"; free copy. (Ads)

Fillers: Murray Hubley, fillers ed. Cartoons; $35.
Columns/Departments: Buys 36/yr. Viewpoint, to 1,000 wds. $75.
Tips: "Write to the point, with interest. Most open to nuts-and-bolts issues for priests, or features. Keep the audience in mind; need articles or topics important to priests and parish life. Include Social Security number."

$@PROCLAIM, PO Box 1561, New Canaan CT 06840. Toll-free (888) 320-5576. Fax (203) 966-4654. E-mail: meg@parishpublishing.org, or info@parishpublishing.org. Website: www.parishpub lishing.org. Parish Publishing LLC. Meg Brossy, ed. The leading inspirational preaching resource for church leaders. Online subscription $59.95; print subscription $69.95. 20% unsolicited freelance; 80% assigned. Query/clips. **Pays to $100** on publication or acceptance for reprint rts. Responds in 2 wks. Seasonal 3 mos. ahead. Prefers accepted mss by e-mail (attached file). (No ads)

Tips: *"Proclaim* follows the Catholic Lectionary and the Revised Common Lectionary (RCL). Writers are usually priests and ministers, or in seminary."

+PURPOSE DRIVEN CONNECTION, 1 Saddleback Pkwy., Lake Forest CA 92630-2244. Toll-free (877) 727-8677. (949) 609-8703. E-mail: info@pastors.com. Website: www.purposedriven .com. Dr. Rick Warren/Saddleback Church. Offers hope, spiritual solutions to problems Americans face amidst national hunger for a deeper connection to God and others. Quarterly mag.; 146 pgs. Subscription $29.99.

$@REFORMED WORSHIP, 2850 Kalamazoo S.E., Grand Rapids MI 49560-0001. Toll-free (800) 777-7270. (616) 224-0763. Toll-free fax (888) 642-8606. (616) 224-0803. E-mail: info@reformed worship.org. Website: www.reformedworship.org. Faith Alive Christian Resources. Rev. Joyce Borger, ed. To provide worship leaders and committees with practical assistance in planning, structuring, and conducting congregational worship in the Reformed tradition. Quarterly & online mag.; 48 pgs.; circ. 4,600. Subscription $29.95. 30% unsolicited freelance; 70% assigned. Query; e-query OK. Accepts full mss by e-mail. **Pays .05/wd.** on publication for 1st & electronic rts. Articles 1,400 wds.; book reviews 200 wds. Responds in 2-4 wks. Seasonal 6-9 mos. ahead. Rarely accepts reprints (tell when/where appeared). Prefers e-mail submission (attached file). Uses some sidebars. Also accepts submissions from children/teens. Prefers NIV, TNIV, NRSV. Guidelines on Website ("About Us"/"Writer's Guidelines"); copy for 9x12 SAE/$2.38 postage (mark "Media Mail"). (No ads)

Columns/Departments: Songs for the Season (music and background notes, usually 3 songs), 2,000 wds. Worship Technology (intersection of worship and technology), 900 wds. Query.

Tips: "Most open to liturgies for worship, prayers. Practical themes or ideas for worship that have been tried. You need to understand and focus on the Reformed tradition of worship."

$REVIEW FOR RELIGIOUS, 3601 Lindell Blvd., St. Louis MO 63108-3393. (314) 633-4610. Fax (314) 633-4611. E-mail: reviewrfr@gmail.com. Website: www.reviewforreligious.org. Catholic/ Jesuits of Missouri Province. Rev. David L. Fleming, S.J., ed. A forum for shared reflection on the lives and experience of all who find that the church's rich heritages of spirituality support their personal and apostolic Christian lives. Quarterly mag.; 112 pgs.; circ. 4,000. Subscription $30. 100% unsolic- ited freelance. Complete ms/cover letter; no phone/fax/e-query. Accepts full ms by e-mail. **Pays $6/printed pg.** on publication for 1st rts. Articles 1,500-5,000 wds. (50/yr.). Responds in 9 wks. Seasonal 8 mos. ahead. Accepts requested ms on disk. Does not use sidebars. Prefers RSV, NAB. Guidelines on Website ("Writer's Guides" at bottom); copy for 10x13 SAE/5 stamps. (No ads)

Poetry: Buys 10/yr. Light verse, traditional; 3-12 lines; $6. Submit max. 4 poems.

Tips: "Read the journal. Do not submit an article without reading at least one issue. Submit an article based on our guidelines."

$@THE REVWRITER RESOURCE, PO Box 81, Perkasie PA 18944. Phone/fax (215) 453-8128. E-mail: editor@revwriter.com. Website: www.revwriter.com. Nondenominational/RevWriter Resources LLC. Rev. Susan M. Lang, ed. An electronic newsletter for busy lay and clergy congregational leaders. Monthly e-zine.; circ. 650. Subscription free. 90% unsolicited freelance; 10% assigned. Query; e-query preferred. **Pays $20** on publication for 1st electronic rts. & one-year archival rts.; $10 for devotions. Articles 1,500 wds.; questions or exercises for group use, 250-500 wds. No simultaneous submissions or reprints. Also accepts submissions from teens. Guidelines by e-mail/Website; copy online. (Ads)

Fillers: Buys 10/yr. Ministry ideas; Ministry Resources List to accompany article; 250-400 wds. These are usually written by the feature-article writer. Also Practical Wisdom section.

Tips: "I'm always looking for articles for the Practical Wisdom section, which focuses on program or ministry ideas that worked for you. This is an easy area to break into. They are short pieces, usually 250-400 wds. Articles should be practical how-tos for busy church leaders—materials they can use in their ministry settings. Be sure to read archived issues for previous formats and ministry resources already covered. Looking for a new approach to stewardship. Most open to devotion writing in Lent and Advent, and the monthly articles and discussion questions. Send me an e-query detailing the article you'd like to write and include your expertise in this area. The material must be practical and applicable to life as a busy congregational leader. They want information they can use."

SEWANEE THEOLOGICAL REVIEW, School of Theology, Box 46-W, Sewanee TN 37383-0001. (931) 598-1475. E-mail: STR@sewanee.edu. Website: www.sewanee.edu/theology/str/strhome .html. Anglican/Episcopal. Submit to Managing Editor. For Anglican/Episcopal clergy and interested laity. Quarterly jour.; 120 pgs. Subscription $24. Open to freelance. Complete ms/cover letter; no e-query. **NO PAYMENT** for all rts. Articles (24/yr.). Responds in 9-26 wks. Seasonal 24 mos. ahead. No simultaneous submissions or reprints. Prefers requested ms on disk or by e-mail (attached file). Prefers NRSV. No guidelines; copy $8. Incomplete topical listings. (Ads)

Special needs: Anglican and Episcopal theology, religion, history, doctrine, ethics, homiletics, liturgies, hermeneutics, biography, prayer, practice.

SHARING THE PRACTICE, c/o Central Woodward Christian Church, 3955 W. Big Beaver Rd., Troy MI 48084-2610. (248) 644-0512. Website: www.apclergy.org. Academy of Parish Clergy/Ecumenical/Interfaith. Rev. Dr. Robert Cornwall, ed-in-chief (drbobcornwall@msn.com); Dr. Forrest V. Fitzhugh, book rev. ed. (s.spade@att.net). Growth toward excellence through sharing the practice of parish ministry. Quarterly international jour.; 40 pgs.; circ. 250 (includes 80 seminary libraries & publishers). Subscription $30/yr. (send to APC, 2249 Florinda St., Sarasota FL 34231-1414). 100% unsolicited freelance. Complete ms/cover letter; e-query OK; query/clips for fiction. **NO PAYMENT** for 1st, reprint, simultaneous, or electronic rts. Articles 500-2,500 wds. (25/yr.); reviews 500-1,000 wds. Responds in 2 wks. Seasonal 6 mos. ahead. Accepts simultaneous submissions & reprints (tell when/where appeared). Prefers e-mail submissions (copied into message). Uses some sidebars. Prefers NRSV. Guidelines/theme list by mail/e-mail; free copy. (No ads)

Poetry: Accepts 12/yr. Any type; 25-35 lines. Submit max. 2 poems.

Fillers: Accepts 6/yr. Anecdotes, cartoons, jokes, short humor; 50-100 wds.

Columns/Departments: Academy News; President's.

Contest: Book of the Year Award ($100+), Top Ten Books of the Year list, Parish Pastor of the Year Award ($200+). Inquire by e-mail to DIELPADRE@aol.com.

Tips: "We desire articles and poetry by practicing clergy of all kinds who wish to share their practice of ministry. Join the Academy."

$@SMALLGROUPS.COM, 465 Gundersen Dr., Carol Steam IL 60188. (630) 260-6200. Fax (630) 260-0451. E-mail: smallgroups@christianitytoday.com. Website: www.smallgroups.com. Christianity Today Intl. Sam O'Neal, mng. ed. Serves small group leaders and churches and provides training and curriculum that is easy to use. Weekly e-zine; circ. 50,000. Subscription $99. 10% unsolicited freelance; 50% assigned. Complete ms/cover letter; e-query OK. Accepts full mss by e-mail. **Pays $75-150 for articles; $350-750 for curriculum**; on acceptance for electronic & nonexclusive rts. Articles 750-1,500 wds. (50/yr.). Responds in 2 wks. Seasonal 2 mos. ahead. Accepts simultaneous submissions & reprints (tell when/where appeared). Prefers requested ms by e-mail (attached file). Some kill fees 50%. No sidebars. Accepts reprints. Prefers NIV. Guidelines/copy by e-mail. (Ads)

Fillers: Icebreakers and other small-group learning activities.

Special needs: Video Bible studies.

Tips: "It's best to submit articles that you have used to train and support small groups and leaders in your own church."

**2010 EPA Award of Merit: Online.

$@SUNDAY SERMONS, PO Box 3102, Margate NJ 08402. Toll-free (800) 827-9401. (609) 822-9401. E-mail: sermons@voicings.com. Website: www.voicings.com. James Colaianni Jr., pub. Full-text sermon resource serving professional clergy since 1970. Exclusively online. Subscription $77.95. 15% unsolicited freelance. Complete ms; e-query OK. **Pays .10/wd.** on publication for any rts. Complete sermon manuscripts 1,200-1,500 wds.; illustrations/anecdotes 50-250 wds. Responds in 6 wks. Seasonal 4 mos. ahead. Accepts reprints. Prefers requested ms by e-mail. Guidelines/topical index by e-mail; copy online. Incomplete topical listings.

Fillers: Various; sermon illustrations; 50-250 wds., .10/wd.

Tips: "Submit complete sermon, 1,200-1,500 wds. Read sample sermons on our Website."

@TECHNOLOGIES FOR WORSHIP, 3891 Holborn Rd., Queensville ON L0G 1R0, Canada. (905) 473-9822. Fax (905) 473-9928. E-mail: krc@tfwm.com. Website: www.tfwm.com. ITC Inc. Kevin Rogers Cobus, ed. Monthly (10X) & online mag.; 92+ pgs.; circ. 35,000. Subscription $29.95. 100% unsolicited freelance. Query; phone/fax/e-query OK. **NO PAYMENT** for onetime rts. Articles 700-1,200 wds. Responds in 2 wks. Seasonal 2 mos. ahead. Accepts simultaneous submissions & reprints (tell when/where appeared). Prefers accepted ms by e-mail (attached or copied into message). Uses some sidebars. Guidelines/theme list by mail/Website; copy by mail. (Ads)

> **Special needs:** Website streaming resources for churches and ministries; technologies: audio, video, music, computers, broadcast, lighting, and drama; 750-2,500 wds.
>
> **Tips:** "Call/fax/e-mail the editor to discuss idea for article or column. The publication is open to technical, educational articles that can benefit the church, providing hints, tips, guidelines, examples, studies, tutorials, etc. on new technology and new uses for it in the church."

THEOLOGICAL DIGEST & OUTLOOK, 415 Linwell Rd., St. Catherines ON L2M 2P3, Canada. (905) 935-5369. Fax (905) 935-7134. E-mail: p-d@niagara.com. Website: www.ITCanada.com/~theology. United Church of Canada—Church Alive. Rev. Paul Miller, ed. For clergy and informed laity; evangelical/orthodox slant within denomination. Semiannual mag.; 36 pgs.; circ. 400. Subscription $15 Cdn., $19 U.S. 100% unsolicited freelance. Complete ms; phone/fax/e-query OK. **NO PAYMENT.** Articles 1,500-5,000 wds. (6-8/yr.). Deadlines for submissions are December 15 and May 15. Responds in 2 wks. Accepts reprints (tell when/where appeared). Prefers disk or e-mail submissions. Does not use sidebars. Any Bible version. No guidelines. (No ads)

> **Tips:** "Just submit."

$TODAY'S PARISH, 1 Montauk Ave., Ste. 200, New London CT 06320. Toll-free (800) 321-0411, ext. 188 (editor). (860) 536-2611. Fax (860) 536-5674. E-mail: NWagner@twentythirdpublica tions.com or nwagner@bayard-us.com. Websites: www.todaysparish.com or www.twentythirdpubli cations.com. Catholic/Twenty-Third Publications. Nick Wagner, ed. Practical ideas and issues relating to parish life, management, and ministry. Mag. published 7X/yr.; 40 pgs.; circ. 14,800. Subscription $24.95. Very little unsolicited freelance. Query or complete ms. **Pays $75-100** on publication for 1st rts. Articles 800-1,800 wds. (15/yr.). Responds in 13 wks. Seasonal 6 mos. ahead. Guidelines by mail; copy for 9x12 SASE.

$@TORCH LEGACY LEADER, PO Box 1733, Joshua TX 76058. Toll-free (877)TORCHLP. (404) 348-4478. Fax (817) 887-3089. E-mail: info@torchlegacy.com. Website: www.torchlegacy.com. Torch Ministries Intl. Daniel Whyte III, pres./ed. A biblically based journal for black church leaders and community leaders. Online jour. 60% unsolicited freelance; 40% assigned. Complete ms/cover letter; e-query OK. **Pays $50 (flat fee)** on publication for 1st rts. **Best Black Sermon of the quarter receives $100** on publication. Articles 1,500 wds. Responds in 12 wks. Seasonal 6 mos. ahead. Requires requested ms on disk. Uses some sidebars. Prefers KJV. Guidelines by mail/e-mail/ Website. Incomplete topical listings.

> **Special needs:** Sermons; articles; essays on the spiritual, social, and moral crisis facing the black community in America, with biblically based solutions.
>
> **Tips:** "We are looking for sound, biblically based material that can be used by God to help lift up black America to where it needs to be in every area of life."

@RICK WARREN'S MINISTRY TOOLBOX, 1 Saddleback Pkwy., Lake Forest CA 92630-2244. Toll-free (877) 727-8677. (949) 609-8703. E-mail: info@pastors.com. Website: www.pastors.com (archive: www.pastors.com/Legacy/RWMT/MTAchive.asp). Tobin Perry, ed. dir. To mentor pastors worldwide. Weekly e-zine; circ. 177,000. Free e-mail newsletter. 10% unsolicited freelance; 90% assigned. Query; e-query OK. **NO PAYMENT** for onetime, reprint, simultaneous, & electronic rts. Will link readers to your site or book on Amazon in exchange for article. Articles 800-1,000 wds. (250/yr.). Responds in 6-8 wks. Seasonal 4 mos. ahead. Accepts simultaneous submissions & reprints (tell when/where appeared). Prefers accepted ms by e-mail (attached file). Uses some sidebars. Guidelines/copy by e-mail. (No ads)

> **Special needs:** Issues facing pastors and other ministry leaders. Time management, conflict resolution, facilitating change, communication and preaching, stewardship, worship, lay ministry, temptation, spiritual vitality, family matters, finances, creative ideas for ministry, vision, power, authority, encouragement, ministry and missions mobilization, small group leadership, facilitating spiritual growth, missions (specifically battling spiritual lostness, egocentric leadership, poverty, disease, and illiteracy locally and globally). Uses a lot of church leadership and pastoral book excerpts and articles adapted from books. The key is that the submission relates to church leaders, specifically pastors.

> **Tips:** "We're very open to freelance contributions. Although we are unable to pay, this is a worldwide ministry to pastors."

$WORD & WORLD: Theology for Christian Ministry, 2481 Como Ave., St. Paul MN 55108. (651) 641-3210. Fax (651) 641-3354. Website: www.luthersem.edu/word&world. E.L.C.A./Luther Theological Seminary. Frederick J. Gaiser, ed. (fgaiser@luthersem.edu); Mark Thronveit, book rev. ed. (mthrontv@luthersem.edu). Addresses ecclesiastical and general issues from a theological perspective and addresses pastors and church leaders with the best fruits of theological research. Quarterly jour.; 104 pgs.; circ. 2,500. Subscription $28. 10% unsolicited freelance. Complete ms/ cover letter; phone query OK. **Pays $50** on publication for all rts. Articles 3,500 wds. Responds in 2-8 wks. Guidelines/theme list on Website (click on "Submissions & Style Sheet"); copy $7.

> **Tips:** "Most open to general articles. We look for serious theology addressed clearly and interestingly to people in the practice of ministry. Creativity and usefulness in ministry are highly valued."

$@WORSHIP LEADER, 32234 Paseo Adelanto, Ste. A, San Juan Capistrano CA 92675-3622. Toll-free (888) 881-5861. (949) 240-9339. Fax (949) 240-0038. E-mail: editor@wlmag.com. Website: www.worshipleader.com. The Worship Leader Partnership. Jeremy Armstrong, mng. ed. A resource for current trends, theological insights, and planning programs for all those involved in church worship. Bimonthly (8X) & digital mag.; 84-100 pgs.; circ. 40,000. Subscription $19.95. 20% unsolicited freelance; 80% assigned. Query/clips or complete ms by fax/e-mail OK. **Pays $200-800 for assigned, $200-500 for unsolicited,** on publication for all or 1st rts. Articles 1,200-2,000 wds. (15-30/yr.); reviews 300 wds. Responds in 6-13 wks. Seasonal 6 mos. ahead. Accepts e-mail submissions (attached file—MS Word). Kill fee 50%. Uses some sidebars. Prefers NIV. Guidelines/theme list on Website ("Contact"/"Submit an Article"); copy $5. (Ads)

> **Tips:** "Read our magazine. Become familiar with our themes. Submit for our Website; this is the first step towards a writing relationship."

$YOUR CHURCH, 465 Gundersen Dr., Carol Stream IL 60188. (630) 260-6200. Fax (630) 260-0114. E-mail: YCEditor@yourchurch.net. Website: www.yourchurch.net. Christianity Today Intl. Submit to Matt Branaugh, ed. We give pastors and church leaders practical information to help them in managing the business side of the church. Bimonthly trade journal; 44+ pgs. Subscription free to church administrators. 10% unsolicited freelance; 90% assigned. Query/clips; phone/fax/e-query OK. **Pays .20/wd.** on acceptance for 1st & electronic rts. Articles 1,000-2,000 wds. (10/yr.). Responds in 4 wks. Seasonal 6 mos. ahead. Accepts simultaneous submissions & reprints (tell when/where appeared). Prefers e-mail submission (attached file). Accepts full manuscripts by e-mail. Kill fee 50%. Regularly uses sidebars. Prefers NIV. Guidelines/theme list by e-mail/Website; copy for 9x12 SASE. (Ads: 630-260-6202)

> **Fillers:** Buys 12/yr. Cartoons, $125.

> **Columns/Departments:** Query. Ask the Experts (Q & A), 100-300 wds. $50-200.

> **Special needs:** Church management articles; audio/visual equipment; books/curriculum

resources; music equipment; church products; furnishings; office equipment; computers/software; transportation (bus, van); video projectors; church architecture/construction. **Tips:** "Write and ask to be considered for an assignment; tell of your background, experience, strengths, and writing history. All areas are open to freelancers—articles on every topic we cover. Writers who can research a topic, interview experts, and present clear, concise writing should persistently and consistently ask for assignments. It might take several months to get an assignment."
** 2010 EPA Award of Merit: Christian Ministries. This periodical was #18 on the 2010 Top 50 Christian Publishers list (#27 in 2009, #16 in 2008, #12 in 2007, #13 in 2006).

$@YOUTHWORKER JOURNAL, c/o Salem Publishing, 750 Old Hickory Blvd., Ste. 150-1, Brentwood TN 37027. (615) 386-3011. Fax (615) 386-3380. E-mail: proposals@youthworker.com. Website: www.Youthworker.com. Salem Communications. Steve & Lois Rabey, eds. For youth workers/church and parachurch. Bimonthly & online jour.; 72 pgs.; circ. 15,000. Subscription $39.95. 100% unsolicited freelance. Query or complete ms (only if already written); e-query preferred. **Pays $50-300** on publication for 1st/perpetual rts. Articles 250-3,000 wds. (30/yr.); length may vary. Responds in 26 wks. Seasonal 6 mos. ahead. No reprints. Kill fee $50. Guidelines/theme list on Website: www.youthworker.com/editorial_guidelines.php; copy $5/10x13 SAE. (Ads)
  Columns/Departments: Buys 10/yr. International Youth Ministry, and Technology in Youth Ministry.
  Tips: "Read *YouthWorker*; imbibe its tone (professional, though not academic; conversational, though not chatty). Query me with specific, focused ideas that conform to our editorial style. It helps if the writer is a youth minister, but it's not required. Check Website for additional info, upcoming themes, etc. WorldView column on mission activities and trips is about only one open to outsiders."

TEEN/YOUNG-ADULT MARKETS

$@BOUNDLESS WEBZINE, Focus on the Family, Colorado Springs CO 80995 (no street address needed). (719) 531-5181. Fax (719) 531-3349. E-mail: editor@boundless.org. Website: www.boundless.org. Focus on the Family. Ted Slater, ed. For Christian singles up to their mid-30s. Weekly e-zine; 200,000 visitors/mo.; 130 page views/mo. on blog. Free online. 5% unsolicited freelance; 95% assigned. Query/clips; e-query OK. Accepts full ms by e-mail. **Pays .30/wd.** on acceptance for nonexclusive rts. Articles 1,200-1,800 wds. (140/yr.). Responds in 4 wks. Seasonal 4 mos. ahead. Accepts simultaneous submissions & reprints (tell when/where appeared). Requires e-mail submission (attached—preferred—or copied into message). No kill fee. Does not use sidebars. Also accepts submissions from teens. Prefers ESV, NIV. Guidelines by mail/Website (click on "About Us"/scroll down to "Write for Us"/"Writers' Guidelines"); copy online. (No ads)
  Tips: "See author guidelines on our Website. Most open to conversational, winsome, descriptive, and biblical."
  ** This periodical was #15 on the 2010 Top 50 Christian Publishers list (#18 in 2009, #12 in 2008, #25 in 2007, #24 in 2006).

@CONNECTED, Box 6097, Lincoln NE 68506-0097. (402) 488-0981. Fax (402) 488-7582. E-mail: editor@christianrecord.org. Website: http://connected.christianrecord.org. Christian Record Services for the Blind. Bert Williams, ed. For visually impaired adults; for interdenominational Christian audience. E-zine. Guidelines by e-mail. Not included in topical listings.

$@DEVO'ZINE, PO Box 340004, Nashville TN 37203-0004. (615) 340-7247. Fax (615) 340-1783. E-mail: devozine@upperroom.org, or smiller@upperroom.org. Websites: www.devozine.org and www.devozine.info. Upper Room Ministries. Sandy Miller, ed. Devotional; to help teens (12-18) develop and maintain their connection with God and other Christians. Bimonthly online mag.;

80 pgs.; circ. 90,000. Subscription $21.95. 85% unsolicited freelance; 15% assigned. Query; phone/fax/e-query OK. **Pays $25 for meditations, $100 for feature articles (assigned)** on acceptance for these onetime rts.: newspaper, periodical, electronic, and software-driven rts., and the right to use in future anthologies. Meditations 150-250 wds. (350/yr.); articles 650-700 wds.; book/music/video reviews 650-700 wds. $100. Responds in 16 wks. Seasonal 6-8 mos. ahead. Accepts occasional reprints (tell when/where appeared). Accepts requested ms by e-mail or online submission. Regular sidebars. Prefers NRSV, NIV, CEV. Guidelines/theme list on Website (Click on "About Devo'zine"/ "Writers Corner"/"Writers Guidelines"); copy/7x10 SASE. (No ads)

Poetry: Buys 25-30/yr. Free verse, light verse, haiku, traditional; to 150 wds. or 10-20 lines; $25. Submit max. 1 poem/theme, 9 themes/issue.

Tips: "E-mail with ideas for weekend features related to specific themes."

** This periodical was #5 on the 2010 Top 50 Christian Publishers list (#1 in 2009, #2 in 2008, #3 in 2007, #1 in 2006).

$DIRECTION STUDENT MAGAZINE, PO Box 17306, Nashville TN 37217. (615) 361-1221. Fax (615) 367-0535. E-mail: direction@d6family.com. Website: www.randallhouse.com. Randall House. Jonathan Yandell, ed.; submit to Derek Lewis, ed. asst. Bringing junior high students to a closer relationship with Christ through devotionals, relevant articles, and pertinent topics. Quarterly mag.; 56 pgs.; circ. 5,300. Open to freelance. Complete ms/cover letter; query for fiction. Accepts full mss by e-mail. **Pays $35-150 for nonfiction; $35-125 for fiction**; on publication for 1st rts. Articles 600-1,500 wds. (35/yr.); book reviews 600-800 wds. ($35). Responds in 6 wks. Seasonal 6 mos. ahead. Accepts simultaneous submissions; no reprints. Prefers e-mail submissions (attached file). No kill fee. Regularly uses sidebars. Also accepts submissions from teens. Guidelines by e-mail/Website; copy for 9x12 SAE. (No ads)

Columns/Departments: Buys 10/yr. Changing Lanes (describe how God is changing you), 600-800 wds. Between the Lines (review of book selected by Randall House), 600-800 wds. $35-50.

Tips: "We are open to freelancers by way of articles and submissions to 'Changing Lanes' (600-800 wds.) and for feature articles (1,200-1,500 wds.). All articles should be about an aspect of the Christian life or contain a spiritual element, as the purpose of this magazine is to bring junior high students closer to Christ. We are happy to accept personal testimonies or knowledgeable articles on current hot topics and how they compare to biblical standards."

$ESSENTIAL CONNECTION (EC), One Lifeway Plaza, Nashville TN 37234-0174. (615) 251-2008. Fax (615) 277-8271. E-mail: ec@lifeway.com. Website: www.lifeway.com. LifeWay Christian Resources of the Southern Baptist Convention. Mandy Crow, ed. Christian leisure reading and devotional guide for 7th-12th graders. Monthly mag.; 60 pgs.; circ. 120,000. Subscription $24.95. 10% unsolicited freelance; 90% assigned. Query; e-query OK. **Pays $80-120** on acceptance for all rts. Articles 800-1,200 wds. (12/yr.); fiction 1,200 wds. (12/yr.). Responds in 10 wks. Seasonal 9 mos. ahead. No simultaneous submissions or reprints. Prefers e-mail submission (attached file or copied into message). No kill fee. Uses some sidebars. Prefers NIV. Guidelines by mail/e-mail; free copy. (No ads)

Poetry: Accepts 36/yr. All types. From teens only.

Special needs: Always in search of Christian humor; sports profiles. Most open to fiction (send complete ms).

Tips: "We generally prefer writers to complete the writer process at www.lifeway.com/people."

$FOCUS ON THE FAMILY DARE 2 DIG DEEPER SERIES, Youth Culture Dept., Colorado Springs CO 80995 (no street address needed). (719) 531-3400. Fax (719) 531-3448. Website: www.family.org. Submit to Acquisitions Editor. A series of small booklets that deal with hard topics that teens (ages 12-18) are struggling with. Query editor with your ideas to be sure they haven't already covered the topic. **Pays.**

G4T INK, 2401 Waterman Blvd., Fairfield CA 94534-1800. (707) 446-4463. E-mail: info@gen erations4truth.org. Website: www.generations4truth.org. Generations 4 Truth. Diana Ventura, dir. Ministry written for and by teens, college students, and adults who address teen issues. Quarterly mag.; 30-40 pgs; circ. 2,500. Estab. 2007. 70% unsolicited freelance; 30% assigned. Query/clips; e-query OK. **NO PAYMENT** for nonexclusive rts. Not copyrighted. Articles 200-400 wds. Responds in 4-6 wks. Accepts simultaneous submissions & reprints (tell when/where appeared). Accepts e-mail submissions (attached file in Word.doc). Uses some sidebars. Prefers NIV. Accepts submissions from teens. Guidelines on Website; copy for 9x12 SAE.

> **Poetry:** Accepts 4-8/yr.
> **Fillers:** Accepts cartoons, jokes, prayers, quizzes, short humor, and word puzzles.
> **Tips:** "Submit short articles that encourage teens. Issues pertinent to today's teens. Also, filler content such as poetry and cartoons."

$HORIZON STUDENT MAGAZINE (formerly *Clear Horizon*), PO Box 17306, Nashville TN 37217. (615) 361-1221. Fax (615) 367-0535. E-mail: horizon@d6family.com. Website: www.randallhouse .com. Randall House. Jonathan Yandell, ed.; submit to Derek Lewis, ed. asst. Bringing high school students to a closer relationship with Christ through devotionals, relevant articles, and pertinent topics. Quarterly mag.; 56 pgs. Open to freelance. Query or complete ms/cover letter; query for fiction; e-query OK. Accepts full mss by e-mail. **Pays $35-150** for articles, $50-125 for fiction, on publication for 1st rts. Articles 600-1,500 wds. (35/yr.); book reviews 600-800 wds. ($35). Responds in 6 wks. Seasonal 6 mos. ahead. Accepts simultaneous submissions; no reprints. Prefers e-mail submissions (attached file). No kill fee. Regularly uses sidebars. Also accepts submissions from teens. Guidelines by e-mail/Website; copy for 9x12 SAE. (No ads)

> **Columns/Departments:** Buys 10/yr. Changing Lanes (describe how God is changing you), 600-800 wds. Between the Lines (review of book selected by Randall House), 600-800 wds. $35-50.
> **Tips:** "We are open to freelancers by way of articles and submissions to 'Changing Lanes' (600-800 words). All articles should be about an aspect of the Christian life or contain a spiritual element, as the purpose of this magazine is to bring high school students closer to Christ. We are happy to accept personal testimonies or knowledgeable articles on current hot topics and how they compare to biblical standards."

$INSIGHT, 55 W. Oak Ridge Dr., Hagerstown MD 21740-7301. (301) 393-4038. Fax (301) 393-4055. E-mail: insight@rhpa.org. Website: www.insightmagazine.org. Review and Herald Publishing Assn./Seventh-day Adventist. Dwain Esmond, ed. A magazine of positive Christian living for Seventh-day Adventist high school students, ages 13-19. Weekly take-home mag.; 16 pgs.; circ. 20,000. Subscription $49.95. 80% unsolicited freelance. Complete ms/cover letter; fax/e-query OK. **Pays $50-85**, on publication for 1st rts. Not copyrighted. Articles 1,200-1,700 wds. (120/yr.). Seasonal 6 mos. ahead. Accepts reprints (tell when/where appeared). Prefers e-mail submission (attached file or copied into message). Kill fee. Uses some sidebars. Prefers NIV. Also accepts submissions from teens. Guidelines on Website (scroll down to "Writer's Guidelines" on left); copy $2/7x10 SASE. (No ads)

> **Poetry:** Buys to 36/yr. All types; to 1 pg.; $10. By high school and college students only.
> **Columns/Departments:** Buys 50/yr. On the Edge (drama in real life), 800-1,500 wds. $50-100; It Happened To Me (personal experience in first person), 600-900 wds. $50-75; Big Deal (big topics, such as prayer, premarital sex, knowing God's will, etc.) with sidebar, 1,200-1,700 wds. $75 + $25 for sidebar; So I Said (first-person opinion), 300-500 wds. $25-125. Complete ms.
> **Contest:** Sponsors a nonfiction and poetry contest; includes a category for students under 21. Prizes to $250. June deadline (varies). Send SASE for rules.
> **Tips:** "We look for teen-written or stories written from a teen perspective that are first-person accounts of experiencing God in everyday life. Also need stories by male authors, particularly

some humor. Also profiles of Seventh-day Adventist teenagers who are making a notable difference."

** This periodical was #43 on the 2009 Top 50 Christian Publishers list (#28 in 2006).

$INTEEN, PO Box 436987, Chicago IL 60643. (708) 868-7100, ext. 362. Fax (708) 868-6759. Website: www.urbanministries.com. Urban Ministries Inc. Submit to Editor. Teen curriculum for ages 15-17 (student and teacher manuals). Quarterly booklet; 32 pgs.; circ. 20,000. Subscription $11.25. 1% unsolicited freelance; 99% assigned. Query/clips; phone query OK; no e-query. **Pays $75-150** on acceptance for all rts. Articles & fiction 1,200 wds. Responds in 4 wks. Seasonal 9 mos. ahead. Accepts some reprints (tell when/where appeared). Accepts requested ms on disk or by e-mail (copied into message). Prefers NIV. Free guidelines/theme list/copy for 10x13 SAE. (No ads)

Poetry: Buys 4/yr. Free verse; variable length; $25-60.

Tips: "Write in with sample writings and be willing and ready to complete an assignment. We prefer to make assignments. Most open to Bible study guides applicable and interesting for teens. Writers who can accurately explain Scriptures to teens are always welcome."

$J.A.M.: JESUS AND ME, PO Box 436987, Chicago IL 60643. (708) 868-7100, ext. 373. Fax (708) 868-6759. E-mail: tlee@urbanministries.com. Website: www.urbanministries.com. Urban Ministries Inc. Timothy Lee, ed. Quarterly Sunday school magazine for 12- to 14-year-olds. Open to freelance. Query/clips; fax/e-query OK. **Pays up to $150** for curriculum 120 days after acceptance for all rts. Lessons up to 900 wds. which include a story approx. 250 wds. Responds in 4 wks. Seasonal 6 mos. ahead. No simultaneous submissions or reprints. Requires accepted ms by e-mail (attached file). Prefers NIV. Guidelines/copy for #10 SASE. (No ads)

Tips: "J.A.M. principally serves an African American audience; editorial content addresses broad Christian issues. Looking for those with educational or Sunday school teaching experience who can accurately explain Scripture in an insightful and engaging way and apply those Scriptures to the lives of 12- to 14-year-olds."

$LISTEN MAGAZINE, 55 W. Oak Ridge Dr., Hagerstown MD 21740. (301) 393-4019. E-mail: editor @listenmagazine.org. Website: www.listenmagazine.org. The Health Connection. Celeste Perrino-Walker, ed. Positive lifestyle magazine for teens/young adults; emphasizes values in a general tone. Monthly mag. (September-May); 16 pgs.; circ. 20,000/exposure 100,000. Subscription $26.95. 50% unsolicited freelance; 50% assigned. Query or complete ms; e-query OK. **Pays .06-.10/wd. ($80-250)** on acceptance for 1st or reprint rts. Articles 800 wds. (30-50/yr.). Responds in 2 wks. to 3 mos. Seasonal 1 yr. ahead. Accepts simultaneous submissions & reprints (tell when/where appeared). Accepts requested ms on CD or by e-mail (attached file). Guidelines/theme list on Website ("Writer's Guidelines" top right corner); copy $2/9x12 SAE/2 stamps. (No ads)

Special needs: Antidrug, antitobacco, anti-alcohol; positive role models. For true stories, need stories dealing with everyday problems: peer pressure, decision making, friendship, family conflict, self-discipline, divorce, abuse, anorexia/bulimia, and making positive choices. Need interesting, informative, and fresh topics for our life skills articles (which draws the same topics year after year). Another easy way to break in is to offer a new, emerging sport or hobby.

Tips: "Need celebrity features. We've stopped using fiction. While it isn't always possible, we like to feature stories about individuals who overcome the temptation to experiment with drugs and alcohol, and/or who find a creative way to deal with a bad situation. We have a narrow focus. By offering us cutting edge articles on our subjects, you'll have a greater chance of breaking in."

** This periodical was #39 on the 2008 Top 50 Christian Publishers list (#29 in 2007, #20 in 2006).

$@RISEN MAGAZINE: The Art & Soul of Pop Culture, 9171 Towne Centre Dr., Ste. 460, San Diego CA 92122-6217. (858) 481-5650. Fax (858) 481-5660. E-mail: matthew@risenmaga zine.com or chris@risenmagazine.com. Website: www.risenmagazine.com (online version of the magazine). Risen Media LLC. Submit to Managing Editor. Audience is 18- to 35-year-old seekers and new believers; original photos and one-on-one interviews cut to the heart of today's cultural icons. Bimonthly mag.; 34 pgs.; circ. 45,000+. Subscription $19.95. Open to freelance. Query; phone/e-query OK. **Pays $150-700.** Articles. (Ads)

$@SHARING THE VICTORY, 8701 Leeds Rd., Kansas City MO 64129-1680. Toll-free (800) 289-0909. (816) 921-0909. Fax (816) 921-8755. E-mail: stv@fca.org. Website: www.SharingTheVictory.com (online version of the magazine). Fellowship of Christian Athletes (Protestant and Catholic). Jill Ewert, ed. Equipping and encouraging athletes and coaches to take their faith seriously, in and out of competition. Monthly (9X—double issues in Jan., Jun. & Aug.) mag.; 32 pgs.; circ. 80,000. Subscription $19.95. 10% unsolicited freelance; 40% assigned. Query only/clips; e-query OK. **Pays $150-400** on publication for 1st rts. Articles 1,000 wds. (5-20/yr.). Responds in 13 wks. Seasonal 6 mos. ahead. Accepts reprints, pays 50% (tell when/where appeared). Accepts requested ms on disk or by e-mail (attached or copied into message). Kill fee .05%. Uses some sidebars. Prefers HCSB. Guidelines on Website; copy $1/9x12 SAE/3 stamps. (Ads)

   Special needs: Articles on FCA camp experiences. All articles must have an athletic angle. Need stories featuring Christian female professional athletes with an FCA connection.

   Tips: "FCA angle important; pro and college athletes and coaches giving solid Christian testimony; we run stories according to athletic season. Need articles on Christian pro athletes—all sports. It is suggested that the writer actually look at the magazine for general style and presentation."

$SPIRIT, 1884 Randolph Ave., St. Paul MN 55105-1700. (651) 690-7010. Fax (651) 690-7039. E-mail: jmcsj9@aol.com. Catholic/Good Ground Press. Joan Mitchell CSJ, ed. Religious education for Catholic high schoolers. Weekly newsletter; circ. 20,000. 50% freelance written. Complete ms/cover letter or query; fax/e-query OK. **Pays $250-300** on publication for all rts. Articles 1,000-1,200 wds. (4/yr.); fiction 1,000-1,200 wds. (10/yr.; $125-300). Responds in 5 wks. Seasonal 6 mos. ahead. Accepts simultaneous submissions. Free guidelines/copy by mail.

   Tips: "No born-again pieces. Articles about teens must be written from their point of view."

@STUDENTLIFE BIBLE STUDY, 2183 Parkway Lake Dr., Birmingham AL 35236. Toll-free (888) 811-9934. Fax (205) 403-3969. E-mail: slpublishing@studentlife.net. Website: www.studentlife.net. Andy Blanks, exec. ed. Bible study curriculum intended to take jr. high and sr. high school students through the Bible in 6 years. Ty Gullick, exec. ed. for new Bible study curriculum for adult learners. Weekly online. Subscriptions on a sliding scale. Open to freelance. Complete ms/cover letter. (No ads)

SUSIE: Magazine for Teen Girls, (615) 216-6147. E-mail: susieshell@comcast.net. Susie Shellenberger, owner. A publication appealing and relevant for today's girl. Estab. 2009. Monthly mag. Open to unsolicited freelance. E-mail complete manuscripts labeled "Free Freelance." **NO PAYMENT FOR THE FIRST YEAR.** Nonfiction & fiction. Not included in topical listings.

$TAKE FIVE PLUS YOUTH DEVOTIONAL GUIDE, 1445 N. Boonville Ave., Springfield MO 65802-1894. (417) 862-2781, ext. 4208. Fax (417) 862-6059. E-mail: rl-take5plus@gph.org. Assemblies of God. Glen Ellard, ed. Devotional for teens. By assignment only. Query. Accepts e-mail submissions. **Pays $25/devotion.** Devotions may range from 210 to 235 wds. (max.). Guidelines on request.

   Poetry: Accepts poetry from teens; no more than 25 lines.

   Tips: "The sample devotions need to be based on a Scripture reference available by query. You will not be paid for the sample devotions." Also accepts digital photos, and artwork from teens.

$TC MAGAZINE, 915 E. Market, Ste. 10750, Searcy AR 72149. (501) 279-4530. Fax (501) 279-4931. E-mail: editor@tcmagazine.org or info@TCmagazine.org. Website: www.tcmagazine.org. Institute for Church & Family. Laura Edwards, ed. To help teenagers (13-19) discover style in faith and love. Quarterly mag.; 52 pgs.; circ. 8,000. Subscription $12.95. 10% unsolicited freelance; 40% assigned. Complete ms; fax or e-query OK. Accepts full mss by e-mail. **Pays variable rates** on publication for all rts. Articles 500-1,200 wds. (10/yr.); no fiction. Responds only if chosen for publication. Seasonal 6 mos. ahead. No simultaneous submissions or reprints. No kill fee. Uses some sidebars. Also accepts submissions from teens. Guidelines on Website ("About Us"/"Writers Guidelines"); copy $3.95/9x12 SAE. (Ads—e-mail to request rate book & media kit)

> **Columns/Departments:** Buys 5/yr. Complete ms. College (college prep for high schoolers), 800-1,000 wds. Humor (funny article in first person), 800 wds.
>
> **Tips:** "We really look for teen writers. First-person articles about personal experience are desired. No fiction at this time."

@TEENS FOR JC.COM, 2855 Lawrenceville-Suwanee Rd., Ste. 760-355, Suwanee GA 30024. Phone/fax (770) 831-8622. E-mail: uvaldes@aol.com or info@teensforjc.com. Website: www.teensforjc.com or www.plgkmedia.com. PLGK Communications Inc. Quentin Plair, pres./CEO. Salutes the fun and exhilaration of being a Christian teen. Monthly e-zine. 90% unsolicited freelance; 10% assigned. Complete ms/cover letter; no phone/fax/e-query. Accepts requested ms on disk or by e-mail (attached file). **NO PAYMENT** for onetime rts. Not copyrighted. Articles 100-5,000 wds. (15/yr.) & fiction 100-5,000 wds. (12/yr.); reviews 200 wds. Responds in 12 weeks. Seasonal 4 mos. ahead. Accepts simultaneous submissions & reprints (tell when/where appeared). No kill fee. Uses some sidebars. Also accepts submissions from teens. Guidelines by mail/Website. (Ads)

> **Poetry:** Accepts many; any type; 1-200 lines.
>
> **Fillers:** Accepts many; cartoons, facts, games, jokes, party ideas, prayers, prose, quizzes, short humor, tips, word puzzles; 10-750 wds.
>
> **Columns/Departments:** Accepts 36/yr. School tips (teen tips for scholarly excellence); Scoop (current info); Music (music reviews/stories); Speak Out (opinion articles by teens); all 100-500 wds.
>
> **Tips:** "Provide information teens need to lay a foundation for a successful life. Looking for great stories."

$TG!: The Magazine for Catholic Teens, E-mail: editor@tgmagazine.net. Website: www.tgmaga zine.net. Catholic. Heather Gaffney, ed-in-chief. For Catholic teenage girls; covers faith, life, and fashion. Bimonthly mag.; 32 pgs.; circ. 3,500. Subscription $18.95. Open to freelance. E-query preferred; no phone/fax query. Accepts full mss by e-mail. **Pays .15-.20/wd.** for 1st & electronic rts. Articles 800-1,200 wds.; no fiction; reviews 50-100 wds. ($25). Responds in 4-6 wks. Seasonal 12 mos. ahead. No simultaneous submissions or reprints. Some kill fees. Regularly uses sidebars. Also accepts submissions from teens (no pay). Prefers NAB or NRSV (Catholic editions only). Guidelines by mail/e-mail; copy $4.99/7x10 SAE. (Ads)

> **Fillers:** Buys unlimited number. Facts, prayers, quizzes, quotes, word puzzles.
>
> **Columns/Departments:** Social Justice; Health/Hygiene/Beauty; Teen Issues; Life Plan; Entertainment; Make-It-Your-Own; True Girl Saint. Pays by the word.
>
> **Tips:** "Our feature articles are most open to freelancers. Reading back issues is imperative to understanding our mission, style, tone, and audience. A firm grasp of our readers' needs for educational, spiritual, and entertainment resources will help guide submissions."

$VISIONS, 2621 Dryden Rd., Moraine OH 45439. (937) 293-1415. Fax (937) 293-1310. E-mail: service@pflaum.com. Website: www.pflaum.com. Catholic. Joan Mitchell CSJ, ed. For grades 7 & 8. Weekly (32X) take-home paper. Not in topical listings.

$YOUNG ADULT TODAY, PO Box 436987, Chicago IL 60643. (708) 868-7100, ext. 362. Fax (708) 868-6759. Website: www.urbanministries.com. Urban Ministries Inc. Submit to Editor. Magazine for 18- to 24-year-olds. Open to freelance. Query/clips; fax/e-query OK. **Pays $75-150**, 120 days after acceptance for all rts. Articles 200-400 wds. Responds in 4 wks. Seasonal 6 mos. ahead. Accepts simultaneous submissions. Accepts requested ms on disk. Prefers NIV. Free guidelines/theme list/copy for #10 SASE. (No ads)

Poetry: Buys 4/yr. Free verse; variable length; $25-60.

Tips: "Send query with a writing sample, or attend our annual conference on the first weekend in November each year. Manuscripts are evaluated at the conference."

$YOUNG CHRISTIAN, 2660 Petersborough St., Oak Hill VA 20171. E-mail: youngchristianmagazine @yahoo.com. Website: http://youngchristianmagazineguidelines.doodlekit.com. Shannon Bridget Murphy, ed. Christian writing with the Lord's message for children and teens. Quarterly mag. 85% unsolicited freelance. Complete ms/cover letter; e-query OK. **Pays .02-.05/wd.** on acceptance for 1st or onetime rts. Articles 500-2,000 wds.; fiction 500-2,000 wds. Responds in 2-8 wks. Seasonal 3-6 mos. ahead. Accepts simultaneous submissions & reprints (tell when/where appeared). Accepts disk; prefers e-mail submissions (attached or copied into message). No kill fee. Regularly uses sidebars. Prefers KJV. Guidelines by e-mail/Website (Website above opens to writer's guidelines). (No ads)

Poetry: Buys variable number. Avant-garde, free verse, haiku, light verse, traditional; any length; variable rates. Submit any number.

Fillers: Buys anecdotes, cartoons, facts, ideas, kid quotes, party ideas, prayers, prose, quizzes, quotes, short humor, tips, and word puzzles; to 1,000 wds.

Tips: "Most open to nonfiction, fiction, poetry, and fillers written by children and teens. Include a Scripture reference. *Young Christian* will provide information to teachers and educational employees on request. Accepts books, CDs, or tapes to be reviewed, but no written reviews."

$YOUNG CHRISTIAN WRITERS MAGAZINE, PO Box 34116, Knoxville TN 37930. E-mail: editor @youngchristianwriters.com. Website: www.YoungChristianWriters.com. Pete Zanoni, dir.; Alicia Zanoni (age 16), ed. Publishes stories, essays, poems, comics, and book reviews written from a Christian worldview by students ages 12-18. Quarterly mag.; 20 pgs. Subscription $15. 80% unsolicited freelance; 20% assigned. Complete ms by mail or e-mail. Accepts full mss by e-mail. **Pays $10-15** on publication for all rts. (will negotiate, if asked). Articles/short stories/essays to 3,000 wds. Responds in 6 wks. if interested. Seasonal 2 mos. ahead. No simultaneous submissions or reprints. Prefers e-mail submissions (copied into message). Accepts submissions from teens, 12-18 years. Prefers KJV, NAS, NSV, NIV. Guidelines/themes by e-mail/Website ("Writer's Guidelines"); no copy. (No ads)

Poetry: Buys 12/yr.; free verse, haiku, light verse, traditional; to 300 wds. Pays $5-10. Submit max. 5 poems.

Special needs: Looking for creative, well-written work—fiction, essays (current issues, nature, history, true stories, biography, nature, creation science), book reviews of high quality literature, variety of poetry. Accurate, well-organized current news articles from a biblical worldview and analysis.

Tips: "Our vision is to inspire teens to honor God with their creative writing. If interested in being a book reviewer, send us a sample book review you have written (we'll contact you with a book to review if we're interested)."

$@YOUNG SALVATIONIST, PO Box 269, Alexandria VA 22313-0269. (703) 684-5500. Fax (703) 684-5539. E-mail: ys@usn.salvationarmy.org. Website: http://publications.salvationarmyusa.org. The Salvation Army. Amy Reardon, ed. For teens and young adults in the Salvation Army. Monthly (10X) & online mag.; 24 pgs.; circ. 48,000. Subscription $4.50. 20% unsolicited freelance; 80% assigned. Complete ms preferred; e-query OK. **Pays .15/wd. (.10/wd. for reprints)** on acceptance for 1st, onetime, or reprint rts. Articles (60/yr.); short evangelistic pieces, 350-600 wds. No fiction. Responds in 9 wks. Seasonal 6 mos. ahead. Accepts reprints (tell when/where appeared). Accepts requested ms on disk or by e-mail. Uses some sidebars. Prefers NIV. Guidelines/theme list by mail/Website; copy for 9x12 SAE/3 stamps. (No ads)

    ** This periodical was #2 on the 2010 Top 50 Christian Publishers list (#4 in 2009, # 9 in 2008, #5 in 2007, #3 in 2006).

$YOUTH COMPASS, PO Box 4060, Overland Park KS 66204. (913) 432-0331. Fax (913) 722-0351. E-mail: sseditor1@juno.com. Church of God (holiness)/Herald and Banner Press. Arlene McGehee, Sunday school ed. Denominational; for teens. Weekly take-home paper; 4 pgs.; circ. 4,800. Subscription $1.50. Complete ms/cover letter; phone/fax/e-query OK (prefers mail or e-mail). **Pays .005/wd.** on publication for 1st rts. Fiction 800-1,500 wds. Seasonal 6-8 mos. ahead. Accepts simultaneous submissions & reprints (tell when/where appeared). Prefers KJV. Guidelines/theme list/copy by mail. Not in topical listings.

$YOUTHWALK, 4201 N. Peachtree Rd., Atlanta GA 30341. (770) 451-9300. Fax (770) 454-9313. E-mail: yw@ywspace.org. Website: www.ywspace.org. Walk Thru the Bible Ministries. Laurin Makohon, ed. (laurin@ywspace.org). To help students navigate their Bibles, connect with God, and own their faith. Monthly devotional mag.; circ. 30,000. Subscription $22.95. 5% unsolicited freelance; 25% assigned. Complete ms. **Pays $50-250.** Articles 600-1,500 wds.; no reviews. Requires NIV. Brief guidelines on Website ("Contact Us"/"FAQs"). (No ads)

    Tips: "We accept freelance for feature articles only; no devotionals. Submit a complete manuscript of a real-life teen story."

    ** 2008, 2007 EPA Award of Excellence: Devotional; 2010, 2006 EPA Award of Merit: Devotional.

WOMEN'S MARKETS

$@AT THE CENTER, PO Box 309, Fleetwood PA 19522-0309. Toll-free phone/fax (800) 588-7744. (610) 944-7250. E-mail: info@atcmag.com. Website: www.atcmag.com. Right Ideas Inc. Jerry Thacker, ed. Designed to help staff, volunteers, and board members of Crisis Pregnancy Centers/Pregnancy Care Centers with relevant information and encouragement. Quarterly online mag. Subscription free. 20% unsolicited freelance; 80% assigned. Query/clips; e-query preferred. Accepts full mss by e-mail. **Pays $150** on publication for 1st, reprint, or simultaneous rts. Articles 1,000 wds. Responds in 4 wks. Seasonal 6 mos. ahead. Accepts simultaneous submissions & reprints (tell when/where appeared). Accepts e-mail submissions (attached file). No kill fee. Uses some sidebars. Accepts submissions from teens. Prefers ESV. Guidelines/idea list by e-mail; copy online. (Ads)

    Special needs: Stories of Christian leaders who were almost aborted.

    Tips: "Looking for practical articles of help and encouragement for those involved in the work of CPC/PCC ministry—center directors, staff, and volunteers. If someone has been involved in crisis pregnancy work, their insight into many areas of the ministry can be helpful to staff and board. Need good techniques for counseling abortion-minded clients."

($)@BEYOND THE BEND, 22 Williams St., Batavia NY 14020. (585) 343-2810. Fax (585) 343-3245. E-mail: submissions@beyondthebend.com. Website: www.beyondthebend.com. PC Publications. Patti Chadwick, ed. (Patti@beyondthebend.com). For women in midlife. Monthly e-zine. Subscription free online. 50% unsolicited freelance; 50% assigned. Complete ms/cover letter or query; e-query OK. **PAYS IN FREE BOOKS** for onetime and reprint rts. Articles 500-1,000 wds. (25/yr.); reviews 500 wds. Responds in 1 wk. Seasonal 6 mos. ahead. Accepts simultaneous submissions & reprints (tell when/where appeared). Prefers e-mail submissions (attached or copied into message). Uses some sidebars. Guidelines on Website ("Writers' Guidelines" left side); copy online. (Ads)

    Fillers: Accepts 20/yr. Anecdotes, facts, ideas, quotes, sermon illustrations, short humor, and tips; 25-50 wds.

    Tips: "Make sure articles pertain to issues of women in midlife."

@BREATHE AGAIN MAGAZINE, 222 W. 21st St., Ste. F126, Norfolk VA 23517. (757) 404-1582. Fax (757) 626-1669. E-mail: info@breatheagain.org. Website: www.breatheagainmagazine.com. Facebook page: www.facebook.com/pages/breatheagainmagazine/183998288878. Nicole Cleveland, ed./pub. (editor@breatheagain.org). Stirring stories about overcoming adversity and living triumphant, successful lives encourage and motivate women not only to endure but to overcome life's most challenging moments. Bimonthly digital mag. Open to stories of overcoming. Guidelines on Website ("Submit Your Stories"/down to "Writer's Guidelines" on right).

@CHRISTIAN LADIES CONNECT, E-mail: demetria@christianladies.net. Website: www.christianladies.net. Demetria Brown Zinga, pub. Online mag. Open to unsolicited freelance. Query by e-mail only. **NO PAYMENT** for onetime or reprint rts. Articles 500-1,500 wds. Responds in 4-6 wks. Seasonal 3-6 mos. ahead. Uses some sidebars. Guidelines & editorial calendar on Website. Incomplete topical listings.

+CHRISTIAN WOMAN, PO Box 163, North Sydney NSW 2059, Australia. (61) (2) 8437-3541. Fax (61) (2) 9999-2053. E-mail: jbaxter@mediaincorporated.org. Website: www.christianwoman.com .au. Inspired Media. Jenny Baxter, ed. Covers issues of importance to Christian women. Subscription $24.95. Open to unsolicited freelance. Guidelines on Website (click on "Christian Woman"/"Write For"). Incomplete topical listings.

Tips: "We give preference to Australian and New Zealand writers."

@CHRISTIAN WOMAN'S PAGE, E-mail: editor@christianwomanspage.org. Website: www.christianwomanspage.org. Nondenominational. Janel Messenger, ed./pub. Strives to provide women with the whys and hows to live Christianity lovingly and practically in day-to-day life. Monthly e-zine & weekly blog. Carries 12-16 articles/issue; 90,000 unique visitors/yr. 98% unsolicited freelance; 2% assigned. Complete ms/cover letter by e-mail only. **NO PAYMENT** for 1st, onetime, reprint, simultaneous, nonexclusive rts. Articles 1,200-1,700 wds.; devotions no less than 700 wds.; larger articles can be broken into parts; reviews 500-700 wds.; fiction 1,800 wds. Responds in 3-5 wks. Seasonal 2 mos. ahead. Accepts simultaneous submissions & reprints (tell when/where appeared). Requires e-mail submissions (copied into message). No sidebars. Prefers NIV. Guidelines/needs list/copy on Website ("Write for Us" at bottom). (No ads)

Poetry: Accepts 3-5/yr. Light verse, traditional. Submit max. 3 poems.

Fillers: Accepts several/yr. Anecdotes, facts, ideas, short humor, and tips.

Columns/Departments: No columns, but open to them.

Tips: "We are an excellent new writer's market. We will use almost every well-written article submitted if it fits with our mission—encouraging women to live with passion and love for Jesus Christ."

@CHRISTIAN WOMEN TODAY, Box 300, Sta. A, Vancouver BC V6C 2X3, Canada. (604) 514-2000. Fax (604) 514-2124. E-mail: editor@christianwomentoday.com. Website: www.christianwomentoday.com. French Website: www.chretiennes.com. Campus Crusade for Christ, Canada. Karen Schenk, pub.; Stacy Wiebe, ed. For Christian women, 20-60 yrs. Monthly online mag.; 2 million hits/mo. 30% unsolicited freelance. Query first; e-query preferred. **NO PAYMENT.** Lifestyle articles 200-500 wds.; features 500-1,000 wds.; life stories 500 wds. Seasonal 4 mos. ahead. Accepts simultaneous submissions & reprints (tell when/where appeared). Prefers e-mail submission (attached file). Guidelines/theme list on Website ("Contact" at bottom of page/"Submit an Article"/"content submissions page" in text). (Ads)

Tips: "The writer needs to have a global perspective, have a heart to build women in their faith, and help develop them to win others to Christ. Text should be written for online viewing with subheads and bullets in the body of the article."

@CHRISTIAN WORK AT HOME MOMS, PO Box 974, Bellevue NE 68005. Toll-free (888) 44-CWAHM. E-mail: jill@cwahm.com. Website: www.cwahm.com. Christian Work at Home Inc. Jill

Hart, pres. Primary audience is moms looking for information and advice about working from home. Weekly online mag.; 2,000 pgs. sitewide; circ. 15,000-20,000 unique visitors/mo. Subscription free online. 50% unsolicited freelance; 50% assigned. Query or complete ms; e-query OK. Accepts full mss by e-mail. **NO PAYMENT** for nonexclusive rts. Articles 600 wds. & up (50-75/yr.); reviews 300 wds. Responds in 2 wks. Seasonal 2 mos. ahead. Accepts reprints. Requires accepted mss by e-mail (copied into message). Uses some sidebars. Guidelines/theme list/copy on Website (scroll down to "Submit Your Article" in green circle on right). (Ads)

Special needs: More how-to on homeschooling with a home business.

Tips: "We are always looking for great devotions, recipes, and craft ideas. We also look for how-to articles related to running a home business, and profiles of successful work-at-home moms."

CHURCHWOMAN, 475 Riverside Dr., Ste. 1626A, New York NY 10115. Toll-free (800) 298-5551. (212) 870-2347. Fax (212) 870-2338. E-mail: cwu@churchwomen.org. Website: www.church women.org. Church Women United. Julie Drews, ed. Shares stories of women acting on their faith and engaging in the work for peace and justice around the world. Quarterly mag.; 28 pgs.; circ. 3,000. Subscription $10. 1% unsolicited freelance. Query. **PAYS IN COPIES.** Articles to 3 pgs. Prefers accepted ms by e-mail (copied into message). Guidelines by mail; copy $1.

$@THE DABBLING MUM, 508 W. Main St., Beresford SD 57004. (605) 763-2549. E-mail: dm@thed abblingmum.com. Website: www.thedabblingmum.com. Alyice Edrich, ed. Balance your life while you glean from successful entrepreneurs, parents, writers, cooks, and Christians—just like you. Biweekly e-zine; circ. 30,000-40,000. Subscription free online. 90% unsolicited freelance; 10% assigned. Complete ms submitted online; e-query OK. Accepts full mss by e-mail. **Pays $10-40 (reprints $5-10)** on acceptance for 1st & reprint rts, and nonexclusive indefinite archival rts. Articles 500-1,500 wds. (48-96/yr.); book & video reviews 500 wds. (no payment). Responds in 4-12 wks. Seasonal 1 mo. ahead. No simultaneous submissions; accepts reprints (tell when/where appeared). Accepts e-mail submissions (copied into message). No kill fee or sidebars. Also accepts submissions from teens. Prefers KJV or NAS. Guidelines/editorial calendar/copy on Website ("E-Magazine"/"Writing"). (Ads)

Special needs: Simple living articles; small-business ideas; healing art projects.

Columns/Departments: Query; pays $10-25. "We have a 'current needs' section and editorial calendar online that are updated frequently with columnists wanted, article needs, word count, and payment." Affiliate marketing columnist needed.

Tips: "Write something that is not readily available on the Internet. Add a personal twist to your how-to piece, and talk to readers in a conversational tone. Also write a business article—it's the most difficult area to fill. If we like what we see we'll consider more of your work outside that area."

** This periodical was #29 on the 2010 Top 50 Christian Publishers list (#49 in 2008, #39 in 2007).

@EMPOWERING EVERYDAY WOMEN, Toll-free (877) 419-6560, ext. 4. E-mail: submissions@ eewmagazine.com or articles@eewmagazine.com. Website: www.eewmagazine.com. Dianna Hobbs, ed-in-chief (dhobbs@eewmagazine.com). For African American Christian women. Online mag. Open to unsolicited freelance. Complete ms or query by e-mail only. **NO PAYMENT** for onetime electronic rights & right to archive. Articles 800-1,500 wds. Responds in up to 12 wks. Guidelines on Website ("Submissions" at bottom of page). Incomplete topical listings. (Ads)

Tips: "The EEW woman is a forward-thinking woman. She is looking for new information to help enhance her spiritually, emotionally, physically, and financially. When she logs onto our site she expects to carry away practical tools that can be applied to her daily life."

@EXTREME WOMAN MAGAZINE, 910 Saint Andrews Dr., Apt. 1-13, Murfreesboro TN 37128-6522. E-mail: eic@extremewomanmagazine.com. Website: www.extremewomanmagazine.com.

Rochelle L. Valasek, pub./ed-in-chief. Spotlights women (20-100 yrs.) who live extremely for God. Monthly & online mag. (also a quarterly PDF mag.); 32 pgs. Subscription free for now. 100% unsolicited freelance. Complete ms/cover letter; fax/e-query OK. **NO PAYMENT** for onetime rts. Articles 500-1,000 wds. (60/yr.); reviews up to 300 wds. Responds in 2-4 wks. Seasonal 6 mos. ahead. Accepts simultaneous submissions; no reprints (negotiable). Prefers e-mail submissions (attached file). Uses some sidebars. Also accepts submissions from teens. Prefers KJV. Guidelines/theme list by mail/e-mail/Website ("Writer's Guidelines" on left); copy by mail. (Ads)

   Poetry: Accepts 12/yr. Free verse, light verse, traditional; 5-20 lines. Submit max. 3 poems.

   Fillers: Accepts 12/yr. Anecdotes, cartoons, facts, jokes, quotes, short humor, and tips; 24+ wds.

   Tips: "As we revamp the magazine, we will look at all freelance to fit in. Best way to break in is to check out our online magazine."

FIRST LADY, PO Box 1233, Mableton GA 30126. E-mail: FLMezine@gmail.com. Website: www .firstladymagazine.com or www.FLMezine.com. Tracey L. Smith, pub. To educate, encourage, and inspire women about many aspects of life from a Christian viewpoint. Monthly mag.; circ. 30,000. Subscription $10. Articles.

@FOR EVERY WOMAN, 1445 N. Boonville Ave., Springfield MO 65802-1894. (417) 862-2781, ext. 4066. Fax (417) 862-0503. E-mail: dhampton@ag.org or womens@ag.org. Website: www.women .ag.org. Assemblies of God Women's Ministries Dept. D. Hampton, admin. coord. Inspirational online magazine for women. Ongoing Webzine. 20% unsolicited freelance. Complete ms; e-query OK. Accepts full mss by e-mail. **NO PAYMENT** for onetime rts. Articles 500-800 wds. (20/yr.). Responds within 1 yr. Seasonal 9-12 mos. ahead. Accepts reprints (tell when/where appeared). Accepts e-mail submissions (attached file). Uses some sidebars. Prefers NIV. Guidelines/theme list by e-mail/Website ("Writers' Guidelines" bottom of page); copy by e-mail. (Ads)

   Columns/Departments: Buys 30/yr. The Single Woman (never married, widowed, divorced), 400 wds. Family Matters (single or married moms); I Still Do! (marriage), 400 wds. See site for column information.

   Special needs: Prayer focus.

   Tips: "Always need articles that encourage and have biblical support text."

   ** 2008 EPA Award of Merit: General.

$@FULLFILL, 315 Bristol Rd., Chatham IL 62629. E-mail: writer@fullfill.org. Website: www.fullfill .org. MOPS Intl. Mary Byers, ed. Encourages women in all seasons of life to realize, utilize, and maximize their influence. Quarterly mag. & online community. Open to unsolicited freelance. Complete ms preferred; considers queries. **Pays varying amounts** on publication. Articles 1,000-1,500 wds. Requires e-mail submissions (attached or copied into message—writer@fullfill.org). Guidelines/themes on Website (click on "About Us," then "Write"). Incomplete topical listings.

   Columns/Departments: Coaching Corner (coaching on personal growth, life management, professional growth), 650 wds.

$@GIRLFRIEND 2 GIRLFRIEND, E-mail: submission@g2gzine.com. Website: www.g2gzine.com. Jean Ann Duckworth, pub.; submit to The Editor (editor@g2gzine.com). For women (target age 30-55) interested in a simpler way of life; general. 7X/yr. online mag. Open to freelance. Complete mss; e-query OK. **Pays $10 honorarium** on publication for articles to 1,000 wds. (72-120/yr.); within 60 days of publication; for onetime rts. Seasonal 4 mos. ahead. Prefers e-mail (attached file in Word format). Guidelines on Website ("Submission Guidelines"). Incomplete topical listings.

   Special needs: Focuses on 4 specific areas: reducing stress, enhancing joy, simplifying life, and building/strengthening relationships.

   Tips: "Read the current issue to better understand our mission and market. We like working with first-time authors."

+@GLORY AND STRENGTH, 3609 Gere Field Rd, B3, St. Joseph MO 64506. (816) 279-9673. E-mail: admin@gloryandstrength.com. Website: www.gloryandstrength.com. Debra L. Butterfield Ministries. Debra L. Butterfield, pub./ed. Ministers to those who have been impacted by such issues as sexual and physical abuse, pornography, substance abuse, and addictions; offering godly wisdom and practical advice for overcoming these issues. Bimonthly e-zine. Subscription free online. Estab. 2009. 100% unsolicited freelance. Query; phone/e-query OK. Accepts full mss by e-mail (after a query). **NO PAYMENT**, but provides a 50-word bio & link to your Website on publication for electronic rts. Articles 700-1,200 wds. (10-15/yr.); fiction 700-1,000 wds. (5-10/yr.); reviews 100 wds. Responds in 2 wks. Seasonal 4 mos. ahead. Accepts simultaneous submissions & reprints (tell when/ where appeared). Prefers articles by e-mail (attached file). Regularly uses sidebars. Guidelines/ theme list by e-mail/Website ("Writers" at bottom); copy on Website. (Ads)

Poetry: Accepts few; any type. Submit max. 3-4 poems.

Fillers: Anecdotes, cartoons, facts, prayers, quotes, short humor, and tips.

Columns/Departments: Accepts 10-15/yr. Cheerful Heart (humorous fiction or nonfiction), 700-1,000 wds. Words of Strength (devotional), about 700 wds.

Tips: "'Cheerful Heart' is best way to break in. Writers' guidelines list our themes for each issue. Follow those and query and you have a better chance at acceptance."

+GRACE TODAY, 17100 S. Halsted, Harvey IL 60426. E-mail: info@yourgracetoday.com, or through Website: www.yourgracetoday.com. Shawntrice Smith, ed. Deals with relevant issues that are cutting edge, taboo, and even controversial, while remaining positive, honest, and providing spiritual perspective; for African American women. Quarterly mag. Subscription $18.97.

@HANDMAIDENS, E-mail: iona@handmaidens.org or through Website: www.handmaidens.org. Iona Hoeppner, ed. For women of all (or no) denominations; consider the sensitivities of those whose theology may differ from your own. E-zine. Open to unsolicited freelance. Complete ms. **NO PAYMENT** for onetime rts. Articles; fiction. Requires e-mail submissions (copied into message). Guidelines on Website ("Guidelines" top of page).

Poetry: Accepts poetry.

Tips: "We welcome your art, photos, poetry, essays, articles, short stories, devotional material, links, almost anything of interest to Christian women."

$HEART & SOUL, 2514 Maryland Ave., Baltimore MD 21218. Toll-free (800) 834-8813, ext. 105. (410) 576-9199. Fax (410) 662-4596. E-mail: editor@heartandsoul.com. Website: www.heartand soul.com. General. Submit to Editorial Dept. The African American woman's ultimate guide to total well-being (body, mind, and spirit). Bimonthly mag.; 88-96 pgs.; circ. 300,000. Subscription $18. Open to unsolicited freelance. Query preferred. **Pays** on acceptance. Articles 800-1,500 wds. Guidelines on Website (Click on "About Us"/"Writers Guidelines"). (Ads) Incomplete topical listings.

($)@HISTORY'S WOMEN, 22 Williams St., Batavia NY 14020. (585) 343-2810. Fax (585) 343-3245. E-mail: submissions@historyswomen.com. Website: www.historyswomen.com. PC Publications. Patti Chadwick, ed. Online magazine highlighting the extraordinary achievements of women throughout history. Monthly e-zine; 20 pgs.; circ. 21,000. Subscription free online. 20% unsolicited freelance. E-query/e-submissions only. **PAYS IN COPIES & FREE E-BOOKS (occasionally pays $10, if budget permits)** for 1st, onetime, reprint, or electronic rts. Articles 400-1,200 wds. (20/yr.). Responds in 1-2 wks. Seasonal 3 mos. ahead. Accepts simultaneous submissions & reprints (tell when/where appeared). Prefers e-mail submission (copied into message). Does not use sidebars. Also accepts submissions from teens. Guidelines on Website ("Writers' Guidelines" bottom of page); copy on site archive. (Ads)

Columns/Departments: Buys 10-20/yr. Women to Admire, in these columns: Women of Faith; First Women (pioneers in their field); Social Reformers; Amazing Moms; Women Who Ruled (women rulers); Early America; all 500-1,000 wds. $10. Query or complete ms.

HOPE FOR WOMEN MAGAZINE, 110 Main St., 3rd Fl., Burlington VT 05401. (802) 861-8000 or (303) 324-6058. Fax (802) 861-8002. E-mail: Editor@hopeforwomenmag.com. Website: www .hopeforwomenmag.com. Virtuous Publications Inc. Submit to Editor. A Christian lifestyle magazine that celebrates the diversity of women of faith. Quarterly mag.; 72 pgs.; circ. 50,000. Subscription $14.95. 95% unsolicited freelance; 5% assigned. Query/clips; e-query OK. Accepts full mss by e-mail. **NO PAYMENT** for 1st rts. Articles 500-2,000 wds.; reviews 300 wds. Responds in 4-6 wks. Seasonal 2-3 mos. ahead. No simultaneous submissions or reprints. Accepts e-mail submissions (attached file). Guidelines/theme list by mail/e-mail; copy for #10 SASE. (Ads)

> **Fillers:** Newsbreaks, party ideas, tips; .10/wd.
>
> **Columns/Departments:** Relationships (nurturing and maintaining positive relationships), 800-1,200 wds. Light (tough issues usually kept quiet in the church), 800-1,000 wds. Journey (helps for a woman's life journey), 500-800 wds., .10-.15/wd. Query. Additional columns listed on Website.
>
> **Tips:** "Each issue features at least one interview with a woman of faith—often a celebrity— who has come through a difficult time and grown stronger in her faith because of it."

$HORIZONS, 100 Witherspoon St., Louisville KY 40202-1396. (502) 569-5897. Fax (502) 569-8085. E-mail: yhileman@ctr.pcusa.org, or sharon.gillies@pcusa.org or through Website: www .pcusa.org/horizons. Presbyterian Church (USA)/Presbyterian Women. Yvonne Hileman, asst. ed. Justice issues and spiritual life for Presbyterian women. Bimonthly mag. & annual Bible study; 40 pgs.; circ. 25,000. Subscription $24.95. 10% unsolicited freelance; 90% assigned. Complete ms preferred; fax/e-query OK. **Pays $50**/600 wds. on publication for all rts. Articles 600-1,800 wds. (10/yr.) & fiction 800-1,200 wds. (5/yr.); book reviews 100 wds. ($25). Responds in 3 mos. Seasonal 6 mos. ahead. Accepts simultaneous submissions & reprints (tell when/where appeared). Accepts requested ms on disk or by e-mail (attached file or copied into message). Kill fee. Regularly uses sidebars. Prefers NRSV. Guidelines/theme list by mail/e-mail/Website; copy $4/9x12 SAE. (No ads)

> **Poetry:** Buys 5/yr. All types; $50-100. Submit max. 5 poems.
>
> **Fillers:** Cartoons, church-related graphics; $50.
>
> **Tips:** "Most open to devotionals, mission stories, justice and peace issues. Writer should be familiar with constituency of Presbyterian women and life in the Presbyterian Church (USA)."
>
> ** This periodical was #6 on the 2006 Top 50 Christian Publishers list.

$@INSPIREDMOMS.COM, E-mail: wendy@inspiredmoms.com. Website: www.inspiredmoms .com. Wind Spirit Press. Wendy Hamilton, site ed. Bimonthly e-zine & resource Website for moms. Open to unsolicited freelance on themes. Complete ms/bio by e-mail only (indicate theme/edition for submission in e-mail subject line). **Pays $25/published article.** Articles to 1,000-1,200 wds. (48/yr.). Accepts reprints not published within previous 6 months. Responds in 2-3 wks. Guidelines/ theme list on Website or by e-mail.

> **Tips:** "We need writers skilled at conversational writing and approaching tough topics relevant to moms."

@INSPIRED WOMEN MAGAZINE, E-mail: publisher@inspiredwomenmagazine.com, or contact @inspiredwomenmagazine.com. Website: www.inspiredwomenmagazine.com. Christian. Adriana Zamot, pub. Offers the women of the world information about the issues that affect us every day. Monthly online mag. Open to unsolicited freelance. Query first; e-query preferred. **NO PAYMENT** for onetime rts. Articles. Guidelines/copy on Website ("Submission guidelines" at top of page). Incomplete topical listings.

$INSPIRIT MAGAZINE, 5101 N. Francisco Ave., Chicago IL 60625. (773) 907-3332. Fax (773) 784-4366. E-mail: wmc@covchurch.org. Website: www.covchurch.org/women. Dept. of Women Ministries. Ruth Hill, ed-in-chief (ruth.hill@covchurch.org). To inform and inspire women across the Evangelical Covenant denomination. Quarterly mag.; 50 pgs.; circ. 1,500. Subscription $12. 40% unsolicited freelance; 60% assigned. Complete ms/cover letter; fax/e-query OK. Must include e-mail contact address. **Pays $25** on publication. Articles about 750 wds. (4/yr.); fiction 750-800 wds. (4/yr.). Seasonal 2.5 mos. ahead. Accepts simultaneous submissions & reprints (tell when/where appeared). Prefers e-mail submissions (attached file). Uses some sidebars. Prefers TNIV or NIV. Guidelines/theme list on Website; copy for 6x9 SAE/$2.50 postage or $4. (Ads)

   Tips: "Follow themes printed in issues and guidelines posted on our Website."

$JOURNEY: A Woman's Guide to Intimacy with God, One Lifeway Plaza, Nashville TN 37234-0175. (615) 251-5659. E-mail: journey@lifeway.com. Website: www.lifeway.com. LifeWay Christian Resources. Articles to: Manuscript Submissions at address above. Devotional submissions to: Susan Nelson, Walk Through the Bible, 4201 N. Peachtree Rd., Atlanta GA 30341. Pamela Nixon, lead ed.; Tammy Drolsum, ed. Devotional magazine for women 30-50 years old. Monthly mag.; 44 pgs.; circ. 215,000. Subscription $24.95. 15% unsolicited freelance; 85% staff or assigned. Subscription $22.05. Query/clips or complete ms/cover letter; no phone/fax/e-query or e-submissions. **Pays $50-100** on acceptance for all rts. Articles 350-1,000 wds. (10-12/yr.). Responds in 8 wks. Seasonal 6-7 mos. ahead. Regularly uses sidebars. Prefers HCSB. Accepts requested ms on disk. Guidelines by mail; copy for 6x9 SAE/2 stamps.

   Special needs: Strong feature articles, 750-1,000 words (including sidebars) on topics of interest to women 30-50 years old ranging from practical applications of faith to spiritual growth, as well as profiles of Christian women in leadership positions.

   Tips: "Most open to feature articles that are well written with a thorough understanding of our magazine and target audience. Strong sample devotionals written in Journey style may be considered for assignment of a devotional."

JUST BETWEEN US, 777 S. Barker Rd., Brookfield WI 53045. Toll-free (800) 260-3342. (262) 786-6478. Fax (262) 796-5752. E-mail: jbu@elmbrook.org. Website: www.justbetweenus.org. Elmbrook Church Inc. Shelly Esser, ed. Ideas, encouragement, and resources for wives of evangelical ministers and women in leadership. Quarterly mag.; 40 pgs.; circ. 7,500. Subscription $19.95. 85% unsolicited freelance; 15% assigned. Query; phone/fax/e-query OK. **NO PAYMENT** for onetime rts. Articles 1,200-1,500 wds. or less (50/yr.). Responds in 8 wks. Accepts simultaneous submissions & reprints (tell when/where appeared). Accepts e-mail submissions (attached file). Regularly uses sidebars. Prefers NIV. Guidelines/theme list by e-mail/Website ("JBU Magazine"/"Writer's Guidelines"); no copy. (Ads)

   Fillers: Accepts 24/yr. Ideas, short humor, tips; 50-75 wds.

   Tips: "Most open to feature articles addressing the unique needs of women in leadership (Bible-study leaders, women's ministry directors, pastors' wives, missionary wives, etc.); or "Ideas to Inspire" column with short ministry tips for readers. Some of these needs would include relationship with God, staff, leadership skills, ministry how-tos, balancing ministry and family, and marriage. The best way to break in is to contact the editor with a query."

$+@KYRIA, 465 Gundersen Dr., Carol Stream IL 60188. (630) 260-6200. Fax (630) 260-0114. E-mail: Kyria@christianitytoday.com. Website: www.kyria.com. Christianity Today Intl. Submit to Acquisitions Editor. To equip and encourage women to use their gifts, take responsibility for their spiritual formation, and fulfill the work God has called them to—through the power of the life-transforming and life-sustaining Spirit. Women's online digizine. Subscription $14.95. Estab. 2009. Open to unsolicited freelance. Query; e-query OK. Does not accepts full mss by e-mail. **Pays $50-150** on acceptance for 1st or reprint rts. Articles 600-1,500 wds. Responds in 8-10 wks. Seasonal 4 mos. ahead. Accepts simultaneous submissions & reprints (tell when/where appeared). No kill fee. Uses some sidebars. Prefers NLT. Guidelines/theme list on Website ("Help & Info"/"FAQs"/"Kyria Writer's Guidelines"); no copy. (Ads)

   Fillers: Buys 12/yr. Devotions, 150-200 wds. pays $25-50.

Special needs: Spiritual disciplines.

Tips: "See our Website for more specifics: kyria.com/help/writersguidelines/kyriawritersguidelines.html."

@LIFE TOOLS FOR WOMEN: Online Women's Lifestyle Magazine, 40 MacEwan Park Rise, N.W., Calgary AB T3K 3Z9, Canada. (403) 295-1932. Fax (403) 291-2515. E-mail: editor@lifetoolsforwomen.com. Website: www.lifetoolsforwomen.com. Judy Rushfeldt, ed. Equipping women to reach their potential. Monthly online mag. Monthly page views: 45,000. Articles 500-1,200 wds. **NO PAYMENT.** Provides a byline and up to 50-word bio, including e-mail & Website link. Prefers e-query & e-submission (attached file). Guidelines on Website ("Writer Submissions" on left side).

$THE LINK & VISITOR, 100-304 The East Mall, Etobicoke ON M9B 6E2, Canada. (416) 651-8967. Fax (416) 622-2308. E-mail through Website: www.baptistwomen.com. Baptist Women of Ontario and Quebec. Renee James, ed. A positive, practical Baptist magazine for Canadian women who want to reach others for Christ. Bimonthly mag.; 24 pgs.; circ. 4,000. Subscription $17 Cdn., $17 U.S. 50% freelance. Complete ms; e-query OK. **Pays .06-.10/wd. Cdn.,** on publication for onetime or simultaneous rts.; some work-for-hire. Articles 600-1,000 wds. (30-35/yr.). Responds in 16 wks. Seasonal 4 mos. ahead. Accepts simultaneous submissions & reprints (tell when/where appeared). Requires e-mail submission (copied into message). No kill fee. Uses some sidebars. Prefers NIV (inclusive language), NRSV, NLT. Guidelines/theme list on Website ("Link & Visitor"/"Write"); copy for 9x12 SAE/2 Cdn. stamps. (Ads—limited/Canadian)

Poetry: Buys 6/yr. Free verse; 12-32 lines; pays $10-20. Submit max. 3 poems.

Tips: "Feature writers who know our magazine and our readers will know what topics and types of stories we are looking for. Canadian writers only, please."

@LIVE MAGAZINE, E-mail: info@liv-magazine.com. Website: www.liveinvictory.org. Suber Media Group. Cheryl A. Pullins, ed-in-chief. A Christian publication for the affluent Christian woman; dedicated to excellence, enlightenment, and empowerment. Online mag. Free subscription. Makes assignments. Send query by e-mail. E-mail for guidelines. (Ads—advertising@liv-magazine.com)

Tips: "Our mission is to promote the application of the principles of the Word of God by using the magazine as a tool to empower people to live in victory in every area of their lives! The magazine is a ministry. Through articles and imagery *LIVE Magazine* showcases, shares, and encourages people around the globe with the message of victory!"

+LOVE, PEARLS AND SWINE, E-mail: editor@lpsmag.com. Website: www.lpsmag.com. Abi Olukeye, ed-in-chief. Continually offers modern Christian women a virtual sanctuary that authentically represents their values. Quarterly mag. Open to unsolicited freelance. Articles 500-800 wds. Responds within 4 mos. Requires e-mail submissions. Guidelines on Website (scroll down to "Contribute"); copy online. Incomplete topical listings.

LUTHERAN WOMAN'S QUARTERLY, PO Box 411993, St. Louis MO 63141-1993. Toll-free (800) 252-5965. Fax (314) 268-1532. E-mail: editor@lwml.org or lwml@lwml.org. Website: www.lwml.org. Lutheran Women's Missionary League. Nancy Graf Peters, ed-in-chief. For women of the Lutheran Church—Missouri Synod. Quarterly mag.; 44 pgs.; circ. 200,000. Subscription $5.50. 25% unsolicited freelance; 75% assigned. Complete ms/cover letter. **NO PAYMENT.** Not copyrighted. Articles 750-1,200 wds. (4/yr.); fiction 750-1,200 wds. (4/yr.). Responds in 2 wks. Seasonal 5 mos. ahead. Regularly uses sidebars. Prefers NIV. Guidelines/theme list by mail/e-mail; no copy.

Tips: "Most open to articles. Must reflect the Missouri Synod teachings. Most of our writers are from the denomination. We set themes two years ahead. Contact us for themes and guidelines."

$@MELODY OF THE HEART: Reconciling Hearts; Offering Hope, 8409 S. Elder Ave., Broken Arrow, OK 74011-8286. (918) 451-4017. E-mail inquiries: Please use Online Contact Form (no mail submissions). Website: www.epistleworks.com/HeartMelody. Epistleworks Creations. JoAnn Reno Wray, ed./pub. Christian publication for women 30-65+ yrs.; heart-stirring, tight writing to bring practicality and joy to life. Bimonthly online publication; over 100,000 hits monthly. Open to freelance. Query with online form for most submissions (including short fiction). **Pays** on publication for reprint or 1st electronic rights: $40 for columnists (1st rights only. Currently filled; open to queries. Columnists commit to one year/6 columns); $20-25 for articles and short fiction. Published material includes short bio (150 words plus current photo—"JPG" format). Any rights purchased include one month exclusive publication in our online magazine, then may sell elsewhere. Pays by check or PayPal. After initial publication, articles archived for 6 months. Articles 750-900 words; short fiction under 1000 wds. Response only if work accepted due to high volume of submissions. Writers should check the online guidelines often to note any changes in editorial needs. Guidelines PDF available for download. Publisher has been on a health-related sabbatical; check Website for openness to submissions.

$MOMSENSE (MomSense), 2370 S. Trenton Way, Denver CO 80231. (303) 733-5353. Fax (303) 733-5770. E-mail: MomSense@mops.org or info@mops.org. Website: www.MomSense.org, or www .MOPS.org. MOPS Intl. Inc. (Mothers of Preschoolers). Mary Darr, ed. Nurtures mothers of preschoolers from a Christian perspective with articles that both inform and inspire on issues relating to womanhood and motherhood. Bimonthly mag.; 32 pgs.; circ. 120,000. Subscription $23.95. 20% unsolicited freelance; 30% assigned. Complete ms/cover letter & bio; e-query OK. Accepts full mss by e-mail. **Pays .15/wd.** on publication for 1st & reprint rts. Articles 450-650 wds. (15-20/yr.). Responds in 12 wks. Seasonal 6 mos. ahead. Accepts simultaneous submissions & reprints (tell when/ where appeared). Prefers requested ms by e-mail (attached file or copied into message). Some kill fees 10%. Uses some sidebars. Prefers NIV. Guidelines/theme list by mail/e-mail/or at www.MOPS.org/ write; copy for 9x12 SAE/$1.39 postage. (Ads)

Poetry: Buys 6/yr. Any type to 400 wds. Pays .15/wd. Submit max. 6 poems.

Fillers: Accepts 10/yr. Tips. No payment.

Special needs: "We always need practical articles to the woman as a woman, and to the woman as a mom."

Contest: Sponsors several contests per year for writing and photography. Check Website for details on current contests.

Tips: "Most open to theme-specific features. Writers are more seriously considered if they are a mother with some connection to MOPS (but not required). Looking for original content ideas that appeal to Christian and non-Christian readers."

** This periodical was #35 on the 2010 Top 50 Christian Publishers list (#34 in 2009, #14 in 2008, #21 in 2007).

@MORE TO LIFE (MTL), 415 Second St., Indian Rocks Beach FL 33785. (727) 596-7625. Fax (727) 593-3523. E-mail: info@munce.com. Website: www.MTLMagazine.com. The Munce Group. Andrea Stock, ed. Lifestyle magazine for women who are discovering their spiritual core and true purpose. Online mag.; circ. 250,000-2 million. Incomplete topical listings. (Ads)

Tips: "This magazine will draw attention to the quality, variety, and relevance of Christian products for everyday living and guide the readers back to Christian retail stores."

$@THE MOTHER'S HEART MAGAZINE, PO Box 231, Oxford MI 48370. E-mail: Editor@TMHMag .com, or kym@kymwright.com. Website: www.The-Mothers-Heart.com. alWright! Publishing. Kym Wright, ed. Serves and encourages mothers in the many facets of staying at home and raising a family. Bimonthly online mag.; 80-100 pgs; circ. 20,000. Subscription by donation. 40% unsolicited freelance; 60% assigned. Query or complete ms; e-query OK. **Pays $10-75** on publication for 1st, reprint, electronic rts. Articles 1,500-2,000 wds. (45/yr.); book & video reviews 150-200 wds. Responds in 3-6 wks. Seasonal 4-6 mos. ahead. No simultaneous submissions; possibly reprints (tell when/where appeared). Requires e-mail submissions, attached (.doc or .docx files only) or copied into message. No kill fee. Regularly uses sidebars. Prefers NIV. Also accepts submissions from teens. Guidelines by e-mail/Website (down to "Writer's Guide" on left); download copy from Website. (Ads)

Fillers: Buys up to 20/yr. Anecdotes, facts, ideas, kid quotes, short humor, and tips; 100-250 wds. Pays $10-20.

Columns/Departments: Query, then send complete ms/15 article ideas for column topic. Pays $50-75.

Special needs: Large families: how you do it, organization, travel. Money management in our economic times. Raising special-needs children. "Coming Home" stories about mothers who choose to stay home with their children. Homeocentric pieces. Homeschool unit studies.

Tips: "Editor will work with author to develop article idea. To break in, read back issues, then query with your idea. Inspirational, encouragement, upbeat pieces will be considered over others. Sound biblical concepts, articles based on and including Scripture. Write from an outline. Begin with a scenario, story, or hook to spark reader's interest." Open to almost any topic.

+ONYX WOMAN, PO Box 91362, Pittsburgh PA 15221. (412) 731-5159. E-mail: own@onyxwomannetwork.com. Website: www.ownonyxwomannetwork.com. Onyx Woman Network. A multimedia organization. Ola R. Jackson, pub. To provide you with information, resources, encouragement, and motivation that will help you make wise lifestyle choices. A business magazine for women of color.

@OREGON WOMENS REPORT.COM, (503) 644-1300. E-mail: Oregon@oregonreport.com. Website: www.OregonWomensReport.com. Online women's magazine that features intelligent ideas, thoughtful opinions, and real-life experiences of local women. Jason Williams, pub. Webzine. Open to freelance. Complete ms by e-mail. Articles. **NO PAYMENT.**

Tips: "Our open-comment webzine allows people to discuss articles and build an online community around our writers. We are seeking volunteer article submissions on topical issues, insightful commentary, and true-to-life testimonies."

$PAUSES . . . An Oasis to Nurture a Woman's Spirit, N1261Briarwood Ln., Merrill WI 54452. (715) 536-2450. E-mail: pausesforyou@verizon.net. Catholic. Sallie Bachar, ed. To inspire, encourage, and enable Christian women to reach the fullness of their authentic, God-given femininity. Quarterly journal; 28 pgs. Subscription $12. 100% unsolicited freelance. Complete ms/cover letter; e-query OK. **Pays $10** on publication for onetime rts. Articles 300-500 wds. (50/yr.); reviews 200 wds. Responds in 4 wks. Seasonal 3 mos. ahead. Accepts simultaneous submissions; no reprints. Accepts submissions by e-mail (attached). No sidebars. Guidelines by mail/e-mail; copy for 6x9 SAE/2 stamps. (Ads)

PRECIOUS TIMES, 3857 Birch St., Ste. 215, Newport Beach CA 92660. Toll-free (800) 299-0696. (714) 564-3949. E-mail: precioustimesmag@gmail.com or bookrevieweditor@precioustimesmag.com. Website: www.precioustimesmag.com. Independent. Marilyn White, pub/ed-in-chief. To help black women (ages 20-60) grow in their relationships with God, self, and others; biblical, but not preachy. Quarterly mag.; 76 pgs.; circ. 350,000. Subscription $18. 90% unsolicited freelance; 10% assigned. Complete ms; e-query OK. **PAYS 5 COPIES** for 1st rts. Personal testimonies, 1,800-2,000 wds.; everyday-life information, 1,200-2,400 wds.; health/fitness/beauty, 1,200 wds.; celebrity/personality interviews, 1,800-2,400 wds.; book reviews, 250-300 wds.; music reviews, 200-500 words; fiction, 2,400-3,200 wds. (20 articles/yr.; 4 fiction). Responds in 12 wks. Seasonal 10 mos. ahead. Accepts simultaneous submissions & reprints (tell when/where appeared). Requires e-mail submissions (attached or copied into message in Word only). Uses some sidebars. Prefers NIV. Also accepts submissions from teens. Guidelines by mail/e-mail/Website; copy $5/9x12 SAE. (Ads)

Columns/Departments: Business, Health, Beauty, Finance; 600 wds.

Tips: "Provide practical theology for contemporary issues. All articles should have a personal perspective, be relevant, and use real life anecdotes. We prefer a black woman's perspective on life issues."

P31 WOMAN, 616-G Matthews-Mint Hill Rd., Matthews NC 28105. (704) 849-2270. Fax (704) 849-7267. E-mail: editor@proverbs31.org. Website: www.proverbs31.org. Proverbs 31 Ministries. Glynnis Whitwer, ed.; submit to Janet Burke, asst. ed. (janet@proverbs31.org). Seeks to offer a godly woman's perspective on life. Monthly mag.; 16 pgs.; circ. 10,000. Subscription for donation. 50% unsolicited freelance; 50% assigned. Complete ms; e-query OK. **PAYS IN COPIES** for onetime rts. Not copyrighted. Articles 200-1,000 wds. (40/yr.). Responds in 4-6 wks. Seasonal 3 mos. ahead. Accepts simultaneous submissions & reprints (tell when/where appeared). Prefers accepted ms by e-mail (attached file or copied into message). Uses some sidebars. Prefers NIV. Guidelines/theme list by mail/Website; copy on Website. (No ads)

Fillers: Accepts 12/yr. Ideas, party ideas, prose; to 100 wds.

Tips: "Looking for articles that encourage women and offer practical advice as well."

@RIGHT TO THE HEART OF WOMEN E-ZINE, PO Box 6421, Longmont CO 80501. (303) 772-2035. Fax (303) 678-0260. E-mail: rtthwomen@aolo.com. Website: www.righttotheheartofwomen.com. Rebekah Montgomery, ed. (rmontgomery@rebekahmontgomery.com). Encouragement and helps for women in ministry. Weekly online e-zine; 5 pgs.; circ. 18,000. Subscription free. 10% unsolicited freelance; 90% assigned. Query; e-query OK. **NO PAYMENT** for nonexclusive rts. Articles 100-800 wds. (20/yr.). Responds in 2 wks. Seasonal 2 mos. ahead. Accepts simultaneous submissions & reprints (tell when/where appeared). Requires accepted mss by e-mail (copied into message). Does not use sidebars. No guidelines; copy on Website. (Ads)

Columns/Departments: Accepts 10/yr. Women Bible Teachers; Profiles of Women in Ministry; Women's Ministry Tips; Author's and Speaker's Tips; 100 wds. Query.

Special needs: Book reviews must be in first person, by the author. Looking for women's ministry event ideas. Topics related to women and women's ministries.

Tips: "For free subscription, subscribe at Website above; also view e-zine. We want to hear from those involved in women's ministry or leadership. Also accepts manuscripts from AWSAs (see www.awsawomen.com). Query with your ideas."

SHARE, 10 W. 71st St., New York NY 10023-4201. (212) 877-3041. Fax (212) 724-5923. E-mail: CDofANatl@aol.com. Website: www.catholicdaughters.org. Catholic Daughters of the Americas. Peggy O'Brien, exec. dir.; submit to Peggy Eastman, ed. For Catholic women. Quarterly mag.; circ. 85,000. Free with membership. Most articles come from membership, but is open. **NO PAYMENT.** Buys color photos & covers. Guidelines/copy by mail. (Ads)

Tips: "We use very little freelance material unless it is written by Catholic Daughters."

$SPIRITLED WOMAN, 600 Rinehart Rd., Lake Mary FL 32746. (407) 333-0600. Fax (407) 333-7100. E-mail: spiritledwoman@strang.com. Website: www.spiritledwoman.com. Strang Communications. Brenda J. Davis, ed. To call women, ages 20-60, into intimate fellowship with God so he can empower them to fulfill his purpose for their lives. Bimonthly mag.; 100 pgs.; circ. 100,000. Subscription $17.95. 1% unsolicited freelance; 99% assigned. Query (limit to 500 wds.); e-query OK. **Pays to $300 ($50 for humor, $75 for testimonies)** on publication for 1st and all electronic rts. Articles 1,200-2,000 wds. Responds in 18-26 wks. No simultaneous submissions. Guidelines by mail/e-mail; copy. (Ads)

Columns/Departments: Testimonies; Final Fun (funny stories or embarrassing moments, to 200 wds.); cartoons; $25-50.

Tips: "Most of our articles are commissioned. Mainly we want high-impact feature articles that depict a practical and spiritual application of scriptural teachings. Need brief testimonies of 350 words or less (open to all); profiles of women in ministry. Articles need to deal with the heart issues that hold a woman back. Also humorous anecdotes and book excerpts."

** 2007 EPA Award of Merit: Most Improved Publication.

+@TAKE ROOT AND WRITE, 111 Shellie Ct., Longwood FL 32779. (407) 619-5097. Fax (407) 788-5358. E-mail: noellemena@takerootandwrite.com. Website: www.takerootandwrite.com. Christian/nondenominational. Shona Neff, sr. ed. (senioreditor@takerootandwrite.com). Bimonthly & online mag.; 44 pgs; circ. 2,000. Subscription free. Estab. late 2008. Query; e-query with online submission form only. **NO PAYMENT** for onetime use (but expects credit if piece is published elsewhere on the Internet). Articles 600-800 wds. Responds in 2-3 wks. Seasonal 2 mos. ahead. No simultaneous submissions or reprints. Requires e-mail submissions. No sidebars. Prefers KJV/NIV/AB/Message. Guidelines/theme list on Website (scroll down to "Guest Writer Submissions" on left side); copy. (Ads—one sponsor/issue)

Fillers: Accepts 24/yr. Cartoons and word puzzles.

Columns/Departments: Accepts many (see Website).

Special needs: Filling columnist positions; growing guest writer submissions. Has a devotions-only site at www.takerootandwritedevotions.com. Open to submissions at: editor@takerootandwritedevotions.com.

Tips: "Most open to open columns. When there is not a current columnist, that column is open to guest submissions. Then we have a list of open categories that are always open to guest writer submissions. Of course, you can submit to become a columnist for any open column as well. We work with established writers as well as new and upcoming writers. Do not hesitate to contact us through our Writers Submissions Form on our Website."

TOGETHER WITH GOD, PO Box 5002, Antioch TN 37011. Toll-free (877) 767-7662. (615) 731-6812. Fax (615) 731-0771. E-mail: twg@wnac.org. Website: www.wnac.org. Women Nationally Active for Christ of National Assn. of Free Will Baptists. Sarah Fletcher, ed. A women's magazine with emphasis on fulfilling the Great Commission. Bimonthly mag.; 32 pgs.; circ. 7,500. Subscription $12. Estab. 2007. 25% unsolicited freelance; 75% assigned. Complete ms/cover letter. Accepts full ms by e-mail. **PAYS IN COPIES** for 1st rts. Articles 750-1,200 wds. (10/yr.). Responds in 8 wks. Seasonal 12 mos. ahead. No simultaneous submissions; accepts reprints (tell when/where appeared). Prefers e-mail submissions (attached file). Regularly uses sidebars. Also accepts submissions from teens. Prefers KJV. Guidelines/theme list by e-mail; copy for 10x13 SAE/$1. (No ads)

Columns/Departments: What Works (practical tips/lists about women's health, homes, fitness, fashion, or finances); My Mentor (women 13-40 write about older women's influence in life); 500-700 wds.

Special needs: Christian life, family issues, creative outreach.

Contest: Annual Creative Arts Contest. March 1 deadline. Categories include Programs, Articles, Poetry, Plays/Skits, Devotionals, Art/Photography. Open to our subscribers, Women Active for Christ, or any woman active in the Free Will Baptist Church.

Tips: "Most open to articles. Bulk of material comes from Women Active for Christ or Free Will Baptist writers."

+@TRUTH MEDIA, E-mail: devotions@truthmedia.com. Website: www.truthmedia.com. Nicole Wiebe, ed. Website for women. Devotions 400-500 wds. for women. Complete ms by e-mail. **NO PAYMENT.**

@THE UNRECOGNIZED WOMAN MAGAZINE, PO Box 122, Ashland VA 23005-2432. (804) 503-3680. Fax (804) 798-1048. E-mail: editor@theunrecognizedwomanmagazine.com. Website: www.the unrecognizedwomanmagazine.com. Outstretched Hands Publication. Joan Cook, ed./pub. Empowering and encouraging women (ages 23-65) with stories of hope, inspiration, and resourceful information for their lifestyles. Bimonthly e-zine; 40+ pgs; circ. 5,000. Subscription free. Estab. 2007. 50% unsolicited freelance; 50% assigned. Query with clips/e-query OK. Accepts full mss by e-mail. **NO PAYMENT** for onetime & electronic rts. Articles 800-1,200 wds. (4/yr.); fiction 800-1,000 wds. (3/yr.); book reviews 40-75 wds. Responds in 2 wks. Seasonal 3 mos. ahead. No simultaneous submissions. Accepts reprints (tell when/where appeared). Requires e-mail submissions (attached file). Uses some sidebars. Guidelines/theme list on Website ("The Magazine"/"About the Magazine"/"It's About You"/click on "submissions" in text on right); copy for 9x12 SAE/$2.50 postage. (Ads)

Poetry: Accepts 12/yr. Any type; 3-20 lines. Submit max. 2 poems.

Fillers: Accepts 30/yr.; facts, quotes, short humor, and tips, 8-50 wds.

Columns/Departments: Accepts 24/yr. Complete ms.

Special needs: Vegetarian recipes. Women's success stories in business or as entrepreneurs.

Tips: "We are most open to true stories, personal experiences, think pieces, opinion pieces, and spirituality. A writer can be a part of our publication if they have a willingness and the creativity to write to win souls or plant seeds. There is no special requirement but for the writer to believe in what he/she writes."

@A VIRTUOUS WOMAN, 594 Ivy Hill, Harlan KY 40831. (606) 573-6506. E-mail: submissions@ avirtuouswoman.org. Website: www.avirtuouswoman.org. Independent Seventh-day Adventist ministry. Melissa Ringstaff, dir./ed. Strives to provide practical articles for women ages 20-60 years; based on Proverbs 31. Monthly e-zine; circ. 20,000+ online. 80% unsolicited freelance; 20% assigned. Complete ms/cover letter; e-query OK. Accepts full mss by e-mail. **NO PAYMENT** for first, reprint, electronic, anthology rts. Articles 500-2,000 wds. (150+/yr.); reviews 500-1,000 wds. Responds in 6-8 wks. Seasonal 6 mos. ahead. No simultaneous submissions; accepts reprints (tell when/where appeared). Accepts e-mail submissions (attached file in .doc or .txt or copied into message). Uses some sidebars. Prefers KJV, NIV, NLT. Guidelines/theme list on Website (click on "Main"/"Writers' Guidelines"); copy for 9x12 SAE/$2.02 postage & $3.50. (Ads)

Poetry: Accepts 5/yr. Free verse, traditional. Submit max. 2 poems.

Fillers: Accepts 12/yr. Anecdotes, facts, ideas, jokes, party ideas, prayers, quizzes, and tips; to 200 wds.

Tips: "Write practical articles that appeal to the average woman—articles that women can identify with. Do not preach. Read our writer's helps for ideas."

@WOMEN OF THE CROSS, 920 Sweetgum Creek, Plano TX 75023. (972) 517-8553. Greg Paskal, content mngr. (greg@gregpaskal.com). Encouraging women in their walk with the Lord; strong emphasis on discipleship and relationship. Online community. 50% unsolicited freelance. Complete ms by e-mail; e-query OK. **NO PAYMENT.** Articles 500-1,500 wds. (10/yr.). Responds in 2-4 wks. Seasonal 3 mos. ahead. Accepts simultaneous submissions; no reprints. Prefers e-mail submissions (attached or copied into message). Uses some sidebars. Prefers NIV, NKJV, NASB. Also accepts submissions from teens. Guidelines by e-mail. (No ads)

Poetry: Accepts 2/yr. Avant-garde, free verse, haiku, or light verse; 50-250 lines. Submit max. 1 poem.

Columns/Departments: Accepts 10/yr. Features (Christian living, encouragement); Article (to other women); all 500-1,500 wds.

Special needs: Personal stories of growing in the Lord; faith-stretching stories about international adoption.

Tips: "Appropriate topics could be first-hand accounts of how God worked in the author's life through a personal or family experience. View online forum for specific topics."

@WOMEN'S MINISTRY MAGAZINE, 4319 S. National Ave., #303, Springfield MO 65810-2607. (417) 888-2067. Fax (866) 360-2611. E-mail: publisher@womensministry.net. Website: www .womensministry.net, or www.jenniferrothschild.com. Jennifer and Philip Rothschild, pubs. Where more than 25,000 women's ministry leaders find news, events, and tips for women's ministry in the local church. Online newsletter. Subscription free. Open to freelance. Use online submission form. Guidelines on Website (scroll down to "WM Get Published" on left side).

Special needs: Punchy, practical tips and ideas related to leading effective women's ministry.

@WOMEN TODAY MAGAZINE, Box 300, Sta. A, Vancouver BC V6C 2X3, Canada. Toll-free (800) 563-1106, ext. 252. (604) 514-2000 (no phone calls). Fax (604) 514-2002. E-mail: editor@ womentodaymagazine.com. Website: www.womentodaymagazine.com or http://truthmedia.com/ tem/writeforus. Campus Crusade for Christ, Canada. Karen Schenk, pub.; Claire Colvin, sr. ed. For the professional, preseeking woman, 20-60 years; provides quality information that leads into a discussion of spiritual things and a presentation of the gospel. Monthly e-zine; 1.5 million hits/ mo.; 100,000 unique visitors/mo. 60% unsolicited freelance; up to 10% assigned. Must use online submission system on Website; e-query OK. Accepts full ms by e-mail. **NO PAYMENT** for onetime or reprint rts. Articles 300-1,000 wds. (12-24/yr.). Responds in 8-12 wks. to accepted material only. Seasonal 4 mos. ahead. Accepts simultaneous submissions & reprints. Requires use of online submission form. Does not use sidebars. Also accepts submissions from teens. Guidelines/theme list on Website. (Ads)

Columns/Departments: Columns tend toward how-to; 600-1,000 wds. Beauty & Fashion; Health & Fitness; Food & Cooking; Advice.

Tips: "Write on a topic from the theme list 4-5 months in advance. Beauty/fashion, relationships, and self-esteem are big draws on our site, and we can always use more great content. To break in, make your article approachable to an unchurched audience, avoid Christian jargon, and speak the truth plainly."

+YOU CAN LIVE AGAIN, PO Box 2403, DeSoto TX 75123. (214) 875-6271. E-mail: yclamaga zine@yahoo.co, or through Website: www.yclamagazine.com. Women's magazine; includes a Teen Scene section. Kertrina Dauway, pub. To empower, guide, and encourage women who have allowed life's issues to distract them from fulfilling God's purpose in their lives. Bimonthly mag. Subscription $21.99.

WRITERS' MARKETS

$ADVANCED CHRISTIAN WRITER, 9118 W. Elmwood Dr., #1G, Niles IL 60714-5820. (847) 296-3964. Fax (847) 296-0754. E-mail: ljohnson@wordprocommunications.com. Website: www .ACWriters.com. American Christian Writers/Reg Forder, Box 110390, Nashville TN 37222. Toll-free (800) 21-WRITE. E-mail: ACWriters@aol.com (for samples, advertising, and subscriptions). Lin Johnson, mng. ed. A professional newsletter for published writers. Bimonthly newsletter; 8 pgs.; circ. 500. Subscription $19.95. 50% unsolicited freelance. Query or complete ms, correspondence, & mss by e-mail only. **Pays $20** on publication for 1st or reprint rts. Articles 500-1,200 wds. (18/yr.). Responds in 4-6 wks. Seasonal 6 mos. ahead. No simultaneous submissions. Accepts reprints (tell when/where appeared). Uses some sidebars. Requires e-mail submission (attached or copied into message). No kill fee. Prefers NIV. Guidelines by mail/e-mail; copy for #10 SAE/2 stamps. (Ads)

Special needs: Behind-the-scenes look at a publishing house (how it started, how editorial operates, current needs, submission procedures); how-to; opinion pieces; time management; workplace issues.

Tips: "We accept articles only from professional, well-published writers and from editors. We need manuscripts about all aspects of building a freelance career and how to increase sales and professionalism; on the advanced level; looking for depth beyond the basics."

AREOPAGUS MAGAZINE, E-mail: editor@areopagus.org.uk. Website: www.areopagus.org.uk. Areopagus Publications. Julian Barritt, ed. For amateur Christian writers, producing both general and Christian writing. Quarterly mag.; 32 pgs.; circ. 100. Subscription $22 U.S. 0% unsolicited freelance. Complete ms/cover letter (if subscriber); e-query OK. **NO PAYMENT.** Articles 1,800 wds. (6/ yr.); fiction 1,800 wds. (5/yr.); book reviews 300 wds. Responds in 1 mo. Seasonal 4 mos. ahead. Accepts e-mail submissions (attached or copied into message). Does not use sidebars. Any Bible version. Guidelines by mail; copy on Website.

Poetry: Accepts 40/yr.; any type; to 60 lines. Submit max. 3 poems.

Fillers: Accepts 10/yr. Facts, ideas, newsbreaks, prose, short humor, to 200 wds.

Contest: Sponsors a quarterly, subscribers-only, writing competition (fiction, nonfiction, or poetry).

Tips: "Items are selected by merit from subscribers only. If not accepted, a recommendation for resubmission is given if there is potential."

AUTHOR-ME.COM, 6086 Dunes Dr., Sanford NC 27332. E-mail: cookcomm@gte.net. Website: www.Author-Me.com. Independent. Bruce L. Cook, pub.; Adam W. Smith, ed. dir. (awsmith@patriot .net); Yvette Moore, mng. ed. (yvette.y.moore@gmail.com). Endeavors to encourage and nurture new writers in their craft. Accepts freelance. Complete ms. **NO PAYMENT.** No submissions from writers under age 14. Edit manuscripts before submitting. Staff of volunteer editors review your manuscript and request revisions before posting. Requires e-mail submissions from Website form. Guidelines on Website (scroll down to "Guidelines" on left side).

$BEST NEW WRITING, PO Box 11, Titusville NJ 08560. E-mail: cklim@bestnewwriting.com. Website: www.bestnewwriting.com. Christopher Klim, exec. ed.; Robert Gover, ed. This annual anthology carries the results of the Eric Hoffer Award for Books and Prose. Submit books via mail; no queries. Submit prose online. The prose category is for creative fiction and nonfiction less than 10,000 wds. Annual award for books features 14 categories. **Pays $500 for winning prose; $1,500 for winning book.** Guidelines at www.HofferAward.com.

$CANADIAN WRITER'S JOURNAL, White Mountain Publications, Box 1178, New Liskeard ON P0J 1P0, Canada. Canada-wide toll-free (800) 258-5451. (705) 647-5424. Fax (705) 647-8366. E-mail: cwj@cwj.ca. Website: www.cwj.ca. Deborah Ranchuk, ed./pub. How-to articles for writers. Bimonthly mag.; 64 pgs.; circ. 350. Subscription $35. 90% unsolicited freelance; 10% assigned. Complete ms/cover letter or query; phone/fax/e-query OK. **Pays $7.50 Cdn./**published pg. (about 450 wds.) on publication (2-9 mos. after acceptance) for onetime rts. Articles 400-2,000 wds. (200/yr.); fiction to 1,500 wds. (see contest below); book/music/video reviews 250-500 wds. ($7.50). Responds in 9 wks. Seasonal 3 mos. ahead. Accepts simultaneous submissions & reprints (tell when/where appeared). Prefers e-mail submission (copied into message only). Some sidebars. Prefers KJV. Also accepts submissions from teens. Guidelines by mail/e-mail/Website ("Submission Guidelines" on left); copy $9. (Ads)

Poetry: Buys 40-60/yr. All types; to 40 lines; $2-5. Submit max. 10 poems.

Fillers: Buys 15-20/yr. Anecdotes, cartoons, ideas, quotes; 20-200 wds. $3-5.

Contest: Sponsors annual short-fiction contest (April 30 and September 30 deadlines); to 1,200 wds. Entry fee $5. Prizes $150, $100, $50. All fiction needs are filled by this contest. E-mail: cwj@cwj.ca.

Tips: "Send clear, complete, concise how-to-write articles with a sense of humor and usefulness. Read the guidelines and follow them, please."

** This periodical was #23 on the 2010 Top 50 Christian Publishers list (#20 in 2009, #30 in 2008, #19 in 2007).

$CHRISTIAN COMMUNICATOR, 9118 W. Elmwood Dr., #1G, Niles, IL 60714-5820. (847) 296-3964. Fax (847) 296-0754. E-mail: ljohnson@wordprocommunications.com. Website: www .ACWriters.com. American Christian Writers/Reg Forder, Box 110390, Nashville TN 37222. Toll-free (800) 21-WRITE. Fax (615) 834-0450. E-mail: ACWriters@aol.com (for samples, advertising or subscriptions). Lin Johnson, mng. ed.; Sally Miller, poetry ed. For Christian writers/speakers who want to improve their writing craft and speaking ability, stay informed about writing markets, and be encouraged in their ministries. Monthly (11X) mag.; 20 pgs.; circ. 3,000. Subscription $29.95. 70% unsolicited freelance. Complete ms/queries by e-mail only. **Pays $5-10** on publication for 1st or reprint rts. Articles 650-1,000 wds. (90-100/yr.). Responds in 4-6 wks. Seasonal 6 mos. ahead. Accepts reprints (tell when/where appeared). Requires e-mail submission. Guidelines by e-mail; copy for 9x12 SAE/3 stamps to Nashville address. (Ads)

   Poetry: Buys 22/yr. Free verse, haiku, light verse, traditional; to 20 lines. Poems on writing or speaking; $5. Send to Sally Miller: sallymiller@ameritech.net.

   Columns/Departments: Buys 35/yr. A Funny Thing Happened on the Way to Becoming a Communicator (humor), 75-300 wds. Interviews (published authors or editors), 650-1,000 wds. Speaker's Corner (techniques for speakers), 650-1,000 wds.

   Tips: "I need anecdotes for the "Funny Thing Happened" column and articles on speaking, research, creativity."

+@CHRISTIAN FICTION ONLINE MAGAZINE, E-mail through Website: http://christianfiction onlinemagazine.com. Associated with Christian Fiction Blog Alliance. Bonnie Calhoun, pub. Articles. **NO PAYMENT.**

@CHRISTIANWRITERS.COM, Website: www.christianwriters.com. A free online writers' resource community to provide a supportive, family atmosphere where writers may easily access the tools and resources to create, market, and publish their work. Accepts articles, short fiction, poetry, and devotionals. Submit through Website. Guidelines on Website.

$FELLOWSCRIPT, Canada. E-mail: submissions@inscribe.org. Website: www.inscribe.org. Inscribe Christian Writers' Fellowship. Janet Sketchley, acq. ed. To provide encouragement, instruction, news, and helpful information for the membership of InScribe Christian Writers' Fellowship. Quarterly newsletter; 28-44 pgs.; circ. 150-200. Subscription $40 (includes membership). 45% unsolicited freelance; 55% assigned. Complete ms; e-query OK. **Pays $5 or .025/wd. Cdn.** on publication for 1st or onetime rts. or .015/wd. for reprint rts. Articles 600-1,200 wds. (70/yr.); book reviews (writing related), 300-500 wds. ($5). Responds in 4-6 wks. Seasonal 12 mos. ahead. Accepts simultaneous submissions & reprints (tell when/where appeared). Requires mss by e-mail (attached or copied into message). No kill fee. Uses some sidebars. Also accepts submissions from teens. Prefers NIV or NKJV. Guidelines on Website; for sample copy, e-mail them for mailing address (then send 9x12 SASE/3 Cdn. stamps and $3.50 in U.S. or Cdn. funds. (Ads if writing related)

   Fillers: Accepts 4-8/yr. Anecdotes, quotes, short humor, tips (all writing related); 300-600 wds. Pays $5.

   Special needs: Articles of practical help to writers, from beginners to advanced.

   Contest: Fall contest in conjunction with InScribe's Fall Conference every year in September (August deadline). Categories include fiction, poetry, children's stories, essays, and nonfiction. Details on Website, or write and ask to be put on mailing list.

   Tips: "The best submissions for us are practical articles on an aspect of writing, written in conversational style and with a good take-away."

FICTION FIX NEWSLETTER: The Nuts and Bolts of Crafting Better Fiction, E-mail: admin istration@coffeehouseforwriters.com. Website: www.coffeehouseforwriters.com/fictionfix. Carol Lindsay, ed. For writers and aspiring writers of short stories and novels. Monthly newsletter; circ. 5,000. To subscribe, go to the Website and click the subscribe link. E-query only. Responds in 2-3 wks. **NO PAYMENT**. "This is a newsletter for a community of writers. We are interested in hearing your writing and publication stories. Think: 'What should other writers know about my experience? What writing hints/tips work best for me?'" Guidelines on Website (down to "Writer Guide").

Tips: "Articles must be received by the 10th of the previous month. Articles received after the 10th will be considered for a later publication."

$FREELANCE WRITER'S REPORT, 45 Main St., PO Box A, North Stratford NH 03590-0167. (603) 922-8383. E-mail: editor@writers-editors.com. Website: www.writers-editors.com. General/CNW Publishing Inc. Dana K. Cassell, ed. Covers marketing and running a freelance writing business. Monthly newsletter; 8 pgs. 25% freelance. Complete ms via e-mail (attached or copied into message). **Pays .10/wd.** on publication for onetime rts. Articles to 900 wds. (50/yr.). Responds within 1 wk. Seasonal 2 mos. ahead. Accepts simultaneous submissions & reprints (tell when/where appeared). Does not use sidebars. Guidelines on Website; copy for 6x9 SAE/2 stamps (for back copy); $4 for current copy.

Fillers: Prose fillers to 400 wds.

Contest: Open to all writers. Deadline March 15, 2009. Nonfiction, fiction, children's, poetry. Prizes: $100, $75, $50. Details on Website.

Tips: "No articles on the basics of freelancing; our readers are established freelancers. Looking for marketing and business building for freelance writers/editors/book authors."

$NEW WRITER'S MAGAZINE, PO Box 5976, Sarasota FL 34277-5976. (941) 953-7903. E-mail: newriters@aol.com. General/Sarasota Bay Publishing. George S. Haborak, ed. Bimonthly mag.; circ. 5,000. 95% freelance. Query or complete ms by mail. **Pays $10-50 ($20-40 for fiction)** on publication for 1st rts. Articles 700-1,000 wds. (50/yr.); fiction 700-800 wds. (2-6/yr.). Responds in 5 wks. Guidelines by mail; copy $3.

Poetry: Buys 10-20/yr. Free verse, light verse; 8-20 lines. Pays $5 min. Submit max. 3 poems.

Fillers: Buys 25-45/yr. Writing-related cartoons; buys 20-30/yr.; pays $10 max. Anecdotes, facts, newsbreaks, short humor; 20-100 wds. buys 5-15/yr. Pays $5 max.

Tips: "We like interview articles with successful writers."

NORTHWEST CHRISTIAN AUTHOR, NCWA, PO Box 428, Enumclaw WA 98022. Toll-free (800) 731-6292. E-mail: acquisitions@nwchristianwriters.org. Website: www.nwchristianwriters.org. Northwest Christian Writers Assn. Carla Williams, mng. ed. & acquisitions. To encourage Christian authors to share the gospel through the written word and to promote excellence in writing. Bimonthly newsletter; 12 pgs.; circ. 200. Subscription $12 or $25 including membership. 40% unsolicited freelance; 60% assigned. Complete ms/cover letter; e-query OK. **NO PAYMENT;** digital copies; hard copies on request for onetime or reprint rts. Not copyrighted. Articles 300-1,000 wds. (20/yr.); book reviews 100 wds. Responds in 2 wks. Accepts simultaneous submissions & reprints (tell when/where appeared). Prefers e-mail submission (attached file). Uses some sidebars. Also accepts submissions from teens. Guidelines on Website; no copy. (Classified ads)

Poetry: Accepts 3/yr. Free verse, light verse. Submit max. 3 poems.

Fillers: Anecdotes, tips; 50-250 wds.

Profiles: Every issue includes a profile (800-1,000 wds.) of a NWCW member and short sample of their work.

Special needs: How-tos on nonfiction and fiction writing. Focus on genre techniques. Interviews with Christian authors.

Tips: "Most open to articles on writing techniques, particularly for specific genres. Stay within word count. E-queries should have 'NW Christian Author' in subject line. Include 1-3 sentence author bio with article."

$POETS & WRITERS MAGAZINE, 90 Broad St., Ste. 2100, New York NY 10004-2272. (212) 226-3586. Fax (212) 226-3963. E-mail: editor@pw.org. Website: www.pw.org. General. Submit to The Editors. Professional trade journal for poetry, fiction, and nonfiction writers. Subscription $19.95. Bimonthly mag.; circ. 60,000. Query/clips by mail; e-query OK. **Pays $150-500** on acceptance for 1st & nonexclusive rts. Articles 500-3,000 wds. (35/yr.). Responds in 4-6 wks. Seasonal 4 mos. ahead. Some kill fees 25%. Guidelines on Website; copy $5.95. (Ads)

Tips: "Most open to News & Trends, The Literary Life, and The Practical Writer (columns)."

$@SHADES OF ROMANCE MAGAZINE, 7127 Minnesota Ave., St. Louis MO 63111. E-mail: sormag@mail.com. Website: www.sormag.com. Blog: www.sormag.blogspot.com. LaShaunda Hoffman, ed. A guide for readers and writers of multicultural romance and fiction. Bimonthly e-zine. E-query only. **Pays $20 for articles, $25 for fiction** within 30 days of publication (through PayPal) for electronic rts. Articles 500-800 wds. (6/yr.); short stories 500-1,500 wds. (6/yr.); devotions 200-500 wds. Responds in 2-4 wks. Seasonal 2 mos. ahead. Accepts simultaneous submissions & reprints (tell when/where appeared; pays $10). Accepts e-mail submissions (attached file). Does not use sidebars. Guidelines/themes by e-mail/Website ("Submissions" at top of page); copy online. (Ads)

Note: Currently closed to submissions.

$@SPIRIT-LED WRITER, E-mail: query@spiritledwriter.com. Website: www.SpiritLedWriter.com. Lisa A. Crayton, pub./ed. Internet magazine for Christian beginning, intermediate, and advanced writers. Monthly e-zine. Query by e-mail (put "Query: [subject]" in subject line). **Pays $20** on publication for onetime, reprint, and electronic rts. Articles 800-1,200 wds. (70+/yr.); reviews to 500 wds. Responds in 6-8 wks. Accepts reprints. Submit accepted mss by e-mail (no attachments). Regularly uses sidebars. Also accepts submissions from teens. Guidelines by e-mail/Website ("Writer's Guidelines" at bottom); copy online. (Ads)

Columns/Departments: Buys several/yr. Musing Dept. (writing-related personal reflections), 700-900 wds. God's Glory Dept. (writing success stories), 500-700 wds. Business (articles on the business of writing), to 1,200 wds. Children's Column (how-to on writing for youth), to 1,200 wds. $10-20.

Special needs: Writing-related devotionals; conference coverage (700-900 wds.); and book reviews of writing books, 250-500 wds. ($5-10, depending on whether they supply the book). Also articles on writing for youth or on advanced writing topics.

Tips: "Easiest to break in with a success story (God's glory), musing article, or devotional. We seek how-to and feature articles with a writing theme. We are not a general, Christian-living publication. We reject many manuscripts because they are general, not writing-related. Make it relevant to writing and writers."

$TICKLED BY THUNDER, 14076—86A Ave., Surrey BC V3W 0V9, Canada. (604) 591-6095. E-mail: info@tickledbythunder.com. Website: www.tickledbythunder.com. Larry Lindner, ed. For writers wanting to better themselves. Quarterly chapbook (3-4X); 24 pgs.; circ. 1,000. Subscription $10 Cdn. or U.S. 90% unsolicited freelance; 10% assigned. Complete ms/cover letter; e-query OK from subscribers only (use online form). **Pays $2-5 (in Cdn. or U.S. stamps)** on publication for onetime rts. Articles 1,500 wds. (5/yr.); fiction 2,000 wds. (20/yr.); book/music/video reviews 1,000 wds. Responds in 16 wks. Seasonal 6 mos. ahead. Accepts simultaneous submissions. Prefers requested ms on disk, no e-mail submission. Uses some sidebars. Also accepts submissions from children/teens. Guidelines by mail/e-mail/Website (click on "Magazine" and scroll down to "Guidelines" in gold box); copy $2.50/6x9 SAE. (Ads)

Poetry: Accepts 20-40/yr. Any type; to 40 lines. Submit max. 5-7 poems. "Try sending seasonal poetry well in advance."

Contest: For fiction (February 15 annual deadline) and poetry (February 15, May 15, August 15, and October 15 annual deadlines). Article contests for subscribers only (February 15, May 15, August 15, and October 15 deadlines). Send SASE for guidelines.

Tips: "Write a 300-word article describing how you feel about your successes/failures as a writer. Be specific, and focus—don't be at all general or vague; tell what works for you. Be original; describe with action, concisely. Use imagery. For fiction, surprise me. Write to put me on the edge of my seat—hold my attention—then wrap it up with something unexpected. Need book reviews of writing books."

THE WRITE CONNECTION, 3706 N.E. Shady Lane Dr., Gladstone MO 64119. Phone/fax (816) 459-8016. E-mail: HACWN@earthlink.net. Website: www.hacwn.org. Heart of America Christian Writers' Network. Jeanette Littleton, exec. ed.; Pat Mitchell, ed. Monthly newsletter; 4 pgs.; circ. 150. Subscription free with HACWN membership $25. 50% unsolicited freelance; 50% assigned. Complete ms/cover letter; e-query OK. **NO PAYMENT** for 1st or reprint rts. Articles 400 wds. (12/yr.); book reviews 200 wds. Responds in 8 wks. Accepts simultaneous submissions; no reprints. Accepts requested mss by e-mail. Uses some sidebars. Also accepts submissions from teens. (Ads)

   Poetry: Accepts 5/yr. Free verse, light verse, traditional; to 12 lines. Submit max. 3 poems.

   Fillers: Accepts 25/yr. Anecdotes, facts, ideas, jokes, prayers, prose, quotes, short humor, tips—solely dealing with writing.

$THE WRITER, 21027 Crossroads Cir., Waukesha WI 53187. (262) 796-8776. Fax (262) 798-6468. E-mail: queries@writermag.com. Website: www.writermag.com. General. Jeff Reich, ed.; Ron Kovach, sr. ed. (rkovach@writermag.com); Sarah Lange, assoc. ed. (slange@writermag.com). How-to for writers; lists religious markets on Website. Monthly mag.; 60-68 pgs.; circ. 30,000. Subscription $32.95. 80% unsolicited freelance. Query; no phone/fax query (prefers hard copy or e-query). **Pays $300-500** for feature articles; book reviews ($40-80, varies); on acceptance for 1st rts. Features 600-3,500 wds. (60/yr.). Responds in 4-6 wks. Uses some sidebars. Guidelines by mail/Website ("The Magazine"/"Submissions"). (Ads)

   Fillers: Prose; writer-related cartoons $50. Send cartoons to slange@writermag.com.

   Columns/Departments: Buys 24+/yr. Freelance Success (shorter pieces on the business of writing); Off the Cuff (personal essays about writing; avoid writer's block stories). All 600-1,600 wds. Pays $100-300 for columns; $25-75 for Take Note. Query 4 months ahead. See guidelines for full list of columns.

   Special needs: How-to on the craft of writing only.

   Contests: Runs an annual short-story contest, as well as the Sylvia Burack scholarship contest for college students.

   Tips: "Get familiar first with our general mission, approach, tone, and the types of articles we do and don't do. Then, if you feel you have an article that is fresh and well suited to our mission, send us a query. Personal essays must provide takeaway advice and benefits for writers; we shun the 'navel-gazing' type of essay. Include plenty of how-to, advice, and tips on techniques. Be specific. Query for features six months ahead. All topics indicated must relate to writing."

   ** This periodical was #42 on the 2010 Top 50 Christian Publishers list (#17 in 2009, #45 in 2008).

$THE WRITER'S CHRONICLE: The Magazine for Serious Writers, The Association of Writers & Writing Programs, George Mason University, MSN 1E3, 4400 University Dr., Fairfax VA 22030-4444. (703) 993-4301. Fax (703) 993-4302. E-mail: awp@awpwriter.org. Website: www.awpwriter.org. Supriya Bhatnagar, ed. Magazine for serious writers; articles used as teaching tools. Mag. published 6X during academic yr.; 96 pgs.; circ. 33,000. Subscription $20. 80% unsolicited freelance; 20% assigned. Query; phone/fax/e-query OK. No full mss by e-mail. **Pays .11/wd.** on publication for 1st rts. Articles to 7,000 wds. max. Responds in 12 wks. Accepts simultaneous submissions. No reprints. No articles on disk or by e-mail. No kill fee. Uses some sidebars. Guidelines/theme list on Website ("Magazine"/"Editorial Guidelines"); copy for 10x13 SAE/first-class postage. (Ads)

   Special needs: Articles on the craft of writing and interviews with established writers from all over the world. Essays, trends, and literary controversies. No poetry or fiction.

Contests: Grace Paley Prize for Short Fiction, $4,000 & publication; AWP Prize for Creative Nonfiction, $2,000 & publication; Donald Hall Prize for Poetry, $4,000 & publication; AWP Prize for the Novel, $2,000 & publication. Website: www.awpwriter.org.

$WRITER'S DIGEST, 4700 E. Galbraith Rd., Cincinnati OH 45236. (513) 531-2690, ext. 11483. Fax (513) 891-7153. E-mail: wordsubmissions@fwmedia.com. Website: www.writersdigest.com. General/F & W Publications. Submit to Acquisitions Editor. To inform, instruct, or inspire the free-lancer and author. Monthly (8X) mag.; 84-92 pgs.; circ. 110,000. Subscription $19. 20% unsolicited; 60% assigned. E-mail submissions only. Responds in 8-16 wks. **Pays .30-.50/wd.** on acceptance for 1st & electronic rts. Articles 800-1,500 wds. (75/yr.). Seasonal 8 mos. ahead. Requires requested ms by e-mail (copied into message). Kill fee 25%. Regularly uses sidebars. Guidelines/editorial calendar on Website; no copy. (Ads)

> **Contests:** Sponsors annual contest for articles, short stories, poetry, and scripts. Also The International Self-Published Book Awards. Send SASE for rules.
>
> **Tips:** "We're looking for technique pieces by published authors."
>
> ** This periodical was #45 on the 2010 Top 50 Christian Publishers list (#49 in 2009, #38 in 2008).

$WRITERS' JOURNAL, PO Box 394, Perham MN 56573-0394. (218) 346-7921. Fax (218) 346-7924. E-mail: editor@writersjournal.com. Website: www.writersjournal.com. Val-Tech Media/General. Leon Ogroske, ed. Advice, tools, and markets for writers, communicators, and poets. Bimonthly mag.; 68 pgs.; circ. 10,000. Subscription $19.97. 90% unsolicited freelance; 10% assigned. Complete ms/cover letter; phone/fax/e-query OK. **Usually pays $30, plus subscription,** on publication for onetime rts. Articles 1,200-2,200 wds. (30-40/yr.); fiction 2,000 wds. (contest entries only). Responds in 6-28 wks. Accepts simultaneous submissions; no reprints. Accepts requested ms by e-mail (copied into message). No kill fee. Uses some sidebars. Also accepts submissions from teens. Guidelines on Website (scroll down left side to "Information"/"Writers' Guidelines"); copy $5/SASE/$1.82 postage. (Ads)

> **Poetry:** Esther M. Leiper, poetry ed. Buys 25/yr. All types; to 10 lines; $5/poem. Submit max. 4 poems.
>
> **Fillers:** Buys 20/yr. Any type, 10-200 wds. Pays $1-10.
>
> **Contest:** Runs several contests each year. Prizes up to $500. Categories are short story, horror/ghost, romance, travel writing, and fiction; 3 poetry; 2 photo. Guidelines on Website.
>
> **Tips:** "Be concise; no wordiness. Avoid personal essays. Write to the reader. We are looking for a well-written article on freelance income; articles on how to write better and how to sell what authors write. Also looking for articles on obscure income markets for writers. General story construction and grammar tips."

WRITERS MANUAL, Ste. 402, 7231—120th St., Delta BC V4C 6P5, Canada. E-mail: editor@writersmanual.com. Website: www.writersmanual.com (click on "Get Interviewed!"). Krista Barrett, ed-in-chief. Looking for author and/or freelance interviews. Onetime rts.

@WRITETOINSPIRE.COM, E-mail: editor@writetoinspire.com. Website: www.writetoinspire.com. Online publication. Provides good how-to information for Christian writers. **NO PAYMENT** for 1st or onetime rts. Articles 500-700 wds. written in an online style. Send submissions in body of e-mail (no attachments). Guidelines on Website ("Writers' Guidelines" on left-hand side).

@WRITING CORNER, E-mail through Website: www.writingcorner.com. Online publication. Open to unsolicited freelance. Query or complete ms by e-mail (no attachments). **NO PAYMENT** for nonexclusive rts. Articles 600-900 wds.; fiction 600-900 wds. Responds in 2 wks. Accepts reprints. Guidelines on Website: www.writingcorner.com/admin/sub-guidelines.htm.

8

Market Analysis for Periodicals

PERIODICALS IN ORDER BY CIRCULATION

ADULT/GENERAL
Guideposts 2,500,000
Columbia 1,600,000
In Touch 1,000,000
Stewardship 1,000,000
Focus on the Family 800,000
Angels on Earth 550,000
Marion Helpers 500,000
Spirituality for Today 495,000
Catholic Digest 400,000
Catholic Yearbook 400,000
Decision 350,000
Mature Living 318,000
St. Anthony Messenger 305,000
Charisma 250,000
Power for Living 250,000
Upscale Magazine 250,000
War Cry 250,000
Anglican Journal 215,000
Australian Catholics 200,000
Gospel Today 200,000
Liberty 200,000
Lutheran Journal 200,000
Lutheran Witness 200,000
Miraculous Medal 200,000
On Mission 200,000
Pentecostal Evangel 170,000
Christianity Today 155,000
Cappers 150,000
Family Digest 150,000
Written 130,000
MESSAGE 125,000
Company 120,000
Catholic Forester 100,000
CGA World 100,000
Good News (KY) 100,000
Liguorian 100,000
Christian Motorsports 74,000
ParentLife 72,000
HEARTLIGHT Internet 70,000+

Celebrate Life 70,000
Common Ground 70,000
Men of Integrity 70,000
United Church Observer 70,000
Christian Home & School 67,000
Lutheran Digest 60,000
Presbyterians Today 58,000
Mature Years 55,000
Arlington Catholic 53,000
Lookout 52,000
Christian History 50,000
Chronicle—IN Edition 50,000
Creation 50,000
Faith & Friends 50,000
Wesleyan Life 50,000
America 46,000
Encompass 45,000
Louisiana Baptist Message 45,000
Messenger of St. Anthony 45,000
Point 45,000
EFCA Today 44,000
The Manna 42,000
Alive Now 40,000
Holiness Today 40,000
Live 38,000
Highway News 35,000
Leaves 35,000
Florida Baptist Witness 33,000
Faith & Family 32,000
Cathedral Age 30,000
Christian Computing 30,000
Christian Research 30,000
Christian Standard 30,000
Eureka Street 30,000
Kindred Spirit 30,000
Messianic Perspectives 30,000
Vibrant Life 30,000
World & I 30,000
Christian News NW 29,000
Seek 29,000

Priority! 28,000
U.S. Catholic 28,000
Evangel (OR) 25,000
In His Presence 25,000
Significant Living 25,000
Central FL Episcopalian 24,000
Catholic Peace Voice 23,000
African Voices 20,000
Creation Illustrated 20,000
Interim 20,000
Ozarks Christian 20,000
Trumpeter 20,000
Commonweal 19,000
Faith Today 18,000
Heartbeat 18,000
Marketplace 16,000
Over the Back Fence 15,000
The Pathway 15,000
SCP Journal 15,000
Tri-State Voice 15,000
Victory in Grace 15,000
Canadian Mennonite 14,750
Canada Lutheran 14,000
Gems of Truth 14,000
Testimony 14,000
Bible Advocate 13,500
Lifeglow 13,000+
Light & Life 13,000
Books & Culture 12,000
Christian Health Care 12,000
Covenant Companion 12,000
Spiritual Life 12,000
Evangel 11,000
Messenger/Sacred Heart 11,000
Sports Spectrum 11,000
The Brink 10,000+
Homeschooling Today 10,000
Messiah Magazine 10,000
Presbyterian Outlook 10,000
Regent Global Bus. Rev. 10,000

Vision 10,000
Christian Retailing 9,500
NRB E-Magazine 9,300
Fellowship 9,000
Haruah 9,000
Living Church 9,000
Montana Catholic 9,000
Sharing 9,000
Purpose 8,900
Friends Journal 8,000
Arkansas Catholic 7,700
Science & Spirit 7,500
Psychology for Living 7,000
Creation Care 6,000
Creative Nonfiction 6,000
Gem 6,000
Impact 6,000
Vision 6,000
Image 5,200
AGAIN 5,000
Ambassador 5,000
CBA Retailers 5,000
CrossCurrents 5,000
Leben 5,000
New Heart 5,000
Pentecostal Messenger 5,000
Prism 5,000
Purpose Magazine 5,000
Review for Religious 5,000
Social Justice Review 5,000
Way of St. Francis 5,000
Maine Family Record 4,600
Cresset 4,500
Breakthrough Intercessor 4,000
Home Times 4,000
Quaker Life 4,000
Culture Wars 3,500
Evangel 3,500
JerUSAlem Connection 3,500
Catholic Insight 3,400
Sword and Trumpet 3,300
Perspectives 3,000
Prayer Closet 3,000
Salvo 2,800
Bread of Life 2,500
Message of the Open Bible 2,500
Movieguide 2,500
Railroad Evangelist 2,500
Apocalypse Chronicles
    2,000-3,000

Perspectives/Science & Chr.
    Faith 2,000+
Atlantic Catholic 2,000
E-Channels 2,000
Desert Call 2,000
Mutuality 2,000
Priscilla Papers 2,000
Mennonite Historian 1,600
Ruminate 1,500
Church Herald/Holiness
    Banner 1,100
Connecting Point 1,000
DreamSeeker 1,000
Methodist History 800
Compass Direct 785
Storyteller 700
Eternal Ink 450
Aujourd'hui Credo 350
Midnight Diner 300
Relief 300
Silver Wings 300
Studio 300
Xavier Review 300
Time of Singing 250
Pegasus Review 150
Reverent Submissions 125
Haiku Hippodrome 100
Wildwood Reader 100
Penwood Review 80-100

CHILDREN
American Girl 700,000
Focus/Clubhouse 90,000
Focus/Clubhouse Jr. 80,000
Keys for Kids 70,000
Pockets 67,000
Our Little Friend 45,000-50,000
Adventures 40,000
Celebrate 40,000
Primary Treasure 35,000
New Moon 30,000
Guide 26,000
Primary Street 20,000
Faces 15,000
Nature Friend 13,000
SHINE brightly 13,000
Bread for God's Children 10,000
Kids' Ark 8,000
Cadet Quest 7,500
Partners 6,923

Story Mates 6,500
Junior Companion 3,500
Primary Pal (KS) 2,900
Beginner's Friend 2,700
Skipping Stones 2,500

CHRISTIAN EDUCATION/ LIBRARY
Christian School Education
    70,000
Children's Ministry 60,000
Catechist 52,000
Today's Catholic Teacher 45,000
Group 25,000
Momentum 23,000
Jour./Adventist Education 10,800
Teachers of Vision 10,000
Youth & CE Leadership 10,000
Christian Early Education 6,000
Christian Educators Journal 4,200
Kids' Ministry Ideas 2,500
Catholic Library World 1,000
Christian Librarian 800
Jour./Christian Education 400
Jour./Education & Christian
    Belief 400
Jour./Research on Christian
    Education 400
Jour./Christianity & Foreign
    Lang. 100

DAILY DEVOTIONALS
These Days 200,000
Secret Place 150,000
Our Journey 80,000
Daily Devotions for the
    Deaf 26,000
Rejoice! 12,000
Penned from the Heart 5,000

MISSIONS
One 100,000
Mission Frontiers 75,000
New World Outlook 24,000
Montgomery's Journey 18,000
Mission Connection 14,400
WEC.go 9,500
Women of the Harvest 8,000
Leaders for Today 7,500
Evangelical Missions 7,000

Glad Tidings 4,500
Railroad Evangelist 2,500
Missiology 1,500
Intl. Jour./Frontier Missions 500
East-West Church & Ministry
    Report 200

MUSIC
TCP Magazine 20,000
I AM Magazine 15,000
Church Music 12,000
Creator 6,000
Hymn 3,000

NEWSPAPERS
Layman 450,000
Anglican Journal 200,000
Episcopal Life 200,000
Christian Examiner 180,000
Catholic New York 135,000
Catholic Telegraph 100,000
Christian Press 80,000
Good News in South Florida
    80,000
Living Light News 75,000
Common Ground 70,000
Sword of the Lord 70,000
Our Sunday Visitor 68,000
Good News Journal 60,000
Arlington Catholic Herald 53,000
Chronicle/Kansas 50,000
Christian Ranchman 43,800
Evangelical Times 40,000
Good News, Etc. 36,000
Messianic Times 35,000
Catholic Register 33,000
Christian Herald 30,000
Christian News NW 30,000
Citizen USA 30,000
Good News! 30,000
Interim 30,000
New Frontier 25,500
Christian Media 25,000
Greater Phoenix Christian
    Chronicle 25,000
Together 25,000
B.C. Catholic 20,000
Charlotte World 20,000
JC Town Reporter 20,000
Light of the World 20,000

HeartBeat/CMA 18,000
Catholic Sentinel 16,000
Good News Today 16,000
Indian Life 16,000
Christian Journal 15,000
Christian Quarterly 15,000
Christian Voice 15,000
Living Stones News 15,000
Voice of Grace & Truth 15,000
Interchange 12,000
City Light News 11,000+
Blue Ridge Christian News 11,000
Christian Courier (WI) 10,000
Heartland Gatekeeper 10,000
Network 10,000
Wisconsin Christian News 10,000
Disciple's Journal 8,000
Arkansas Catholic 7,700
Prairie Messenger 6,300
Home Times 6,000
Desert Voice 5,200
SW KS Faith & Family 5,000
Christian Courier (Canada) 4,000
Christian Renewal 3,500
Atlantic Catholic 2,000
ChristianWeek 2,000
Island Catholic News 2,000
PrayerWorks 1,500

PASTORS/LEADERS
Interpreter 225,000
Rick Warren's Ministry 177,000
SmallGroups.com 50,000
Worship Leader 50,000
Leadership 48,000
Plugged In 43,000
Catholic Servant 41,000
OUTreach 35,000
Technologies/Worship 35,000
Enrichment 33,000
Christian Century 30,000
Ministry Today 30,000
Torch Legacy Leader 22,000
Church Executive 20,000
Immerse 20,000
Ministry & Liturgy 20,000
Ministry 19,000
Preaching Now 19,000
YouthWorker 15,000
Today's Parish 14,800

Net Results 12,000
Foursquare Leader 10,000
Jour./Pastoral Care 10,000
Preaching 9,000
InSite 8,200
Lead 8,100
Growth Points 8,000
Priest 6,500
Clergy Journal 6,000
Catechumenate 5,600
Let's Worship 5,500
CrossCurrents 5,000
Reformed Worship 4,600
Review for Religious 4,000
Lutheran Forum 3,200
Emmanuel 3,000
Environment & Art 2,500
Word & World 2,500
Disciple Magazine 2,000
Parish Liturgy 1,200
Ministry in Motion 1,000+
Christian Ed. Jour. 750
Diocesan Dialogue 750
RevWriter Resource 650
Great Commission Research 400
Theological Digest 400
Sharing the Practice 250

TEEN/YOUNG ADULT
Essential Connection 120,000
Devo'zine 90,000
Sharing the Victory 80,000
Young Salvationist 48,000
Risen Magazine 45,000+
YouthWalk 30,000
Insight 20,000
InTeen 20,000
Listen 20,000
Spirit 20,000
TC Magazine 8,000
Direction Student 5,300
Youth Compass 4,800
True Girl 3,500
G4T Ink 2,500

WOMEN
Precious Times 350,000
Heart & Soul 300,000
More to Life 250,000-2,000,000
Journey 215,000

Lutheran Woman's Quarterly
200,000
Melody of the Heart 130,000
MomSense 120,000
SpiritLed Woman 100,000
Share 95,000
Hope for Women 50,000
Life Tools for Women 45,000
Dabbling Mum 30,000-40,000
First Lady 30,000
Connections Leadership/
MOPS 25,000
Horizons 25,000
Women's Ministry 25,000
History's Women 21,000
A Virtuous Woman 20,000+

A Woman of Worth 20,000
Right to the Heart 18,000
P31 Woman 10,000
Just Between Us 7,500
Together with God 7,500
Unrecognized Woman 5,000
Link & Visitor 4,000
ChurchWoman 3,000
Take Root and Write 2,000
inSpirit 1,500

WRITERS
Writer's Digest 110,000
Poets & Writers 60,000
Writer's Chronicle 33,000

The Writer 30,000
Writers' Journal 10,000
Fiction Fix 5,000
New Writer's 5,000
Poetic Voices 5,000
Christian Communicator 3,000
Cross & Quill 1,000+
Tickled by Thunder 1,000
Advanced Christian Writer 500
Canadian Writer's Journal 385
NW Christian Author 200
FellowScript 150-200
Write Connection 150
Areopagus (UK) 100
The Write Touch 40

PERIODICAL TOPICS IN ORDER OF POPULARITY

Note: Following is a list of topics in order by popularity. To find the list of publishers interested in each of these topics, go to the topical listings for periodicals and find the topic you are interested in. The numbers indicate how many periodical editors said they were interested in seeing something of that type or on that topic. An asterisk (*) indicates a new topic this year. Because those topics are new, the low numbers are not yet an accurate reflection of interest in the marketplace.

MISCELLANEOUS TALLIES
African American Markets 18
Canadian/Foreign 67
Newspapers/Tabloids 74
Online Publications 163
Photographs 205
Take-home Papers 31
Young Writer Markets 105

TOPICS BY POPULARITY
1. Christian Living 248
2. Family Life 209
3. Current/Social Issues 197
4. Book Reviews 196
5. Inspirational 191
6. Faith 179
7. Interviews/Profiles 179
8. Prayer 167
9. Personal Experience 158
10. Holiday/Seasonal 157
11. Women's Issues 156
12. Relationships 155
13. Marriage 152
14. Christian Education 150
15. Spirituality 149

16. Poetry 148
17. Devotionals/Meditations 142
18. Controversial Issues 141
19. True Stories 141
20. Church Life 138
21. Humor 136
22. Church Outreach 134
23. Personal Growth 132
24. Evangelism/Witnessing 131
25. Spiritual Life 131
26. Ethnic/Cultural Pieces 125
27. Parenting 125
28. Discipleship 124
29. Worship 121
30. Leadership 119
31. Encouragement 117
32. Health 117
33. Youth Issues 114
34. Church Growth 107
35. Ethics 106
36. How-to 105
37. Theological 105
38. Church History 103
39. Essays 101
40. Death/Dying 100

41. Social Justice 100
42. World Issues 99
43. Historical 96
44. News Features 96
45. Miracles 95
46. Stewardship 94
47. Fillers: Cartoons 93
48. Church Traditions 91
49. Short Story:
    Adult/Religious 91
50. Bible Studies 90
51. Money Management 90
52. Religious Freedom 88
53. Christian Business 87
54. Spiritual Renewal 86
55. Men's Issues 85
56. Singles' Issues 85
57. Spiritual Gifts 85
58. Celebrity Pieces 81
59. Divorce 81
60. Time Management 80
61. Environmental Issues 79
62. Spiritual Warfare 78
63. Workplace Issues 78
64. Lifestyle 77

65. Opinion Pieces 75
66. Short Story:
    Contemporary 75
67. Fillers: Anecdotes 74
68. Fillers: Short Humor 74
69. Salvation Testimonies 74
70. Music Reviews 72
71. Book Excerpts 71
72. Short Story: Biblical 70
73. Church Management 68
74. Short Story: Humorous 68
75. Think Pieces 68
76. Apologetics 67
77. Senior Adult Issues 67
78. Healing 66
79. Sports/Recreation 64
80. Politics 63
81. Short Story: Historical 62
82. Missions/Missionary 60
83. Inner Life 59
84. Doctrinal 58
85. Racism 58
86. Religious Tolerance 58
87. Short Story: Adventure 58
88. Fillers: Facts 57
89. Nature 57
90. Video Reviews 57
91. Food/Recipes 56
92. Travel 56
93. Fillers: Ideas 54
94. Fillers: Quotes 53
95. Pastors' Helps 53
96. Writing How-to 53
97. Fillers: Word Puzzles 52
98. Economics 51

99. Fillers: Prayers 51
100. Crafts 46
101. Creation Science 46
102. Homeschooling 45
103. Peace Issues 45
104. How-to Activities (juv.) 44
105. Liturgical 44
106. Recovery 44
107. Science 43
108. Self-help 43
109. Fillers: Quizzes 42
110. Fillers: Tips 42
111. Short Story: Parables 42
112. Short Story:
     Mystery/Suspense 40
113. Fillers: Jokes 39
114. Fillers: Prose 38
115. Movie Reviews 38
116. Short Story: Allegory 38
117. Exegesis 37
118. Sociology 37
119. Short Story: Juvenile 36
120. Cults/Occult 35
121. Prophecy 35
122. Short Story: Literary 35
123. Psychology 34
124. Short Story: Ethnic 34
125. Fillers: Newsbreaks 33
126. Short Story:
     Teen/Young Adult 33
127. Website Reviews 33
128. Photo Essays 32
129. Fillers: Games 31
130. Short Story:
     Science Fiction 31

131. Homiletics 30
132. Short Story: Fantasy 29
133. Sermons 28
134. Short Story:
     Adult/General 28
135. Revival 27
136. Short Story: Frontier 25
137. Feature Articles 23
138. Fillers: Party Ideas
139. Short Story: Romance
140. Nostalgia 20
141. Fillers: Kid Quotes 18
142. Short Story: Westerns 18
143. *Arts/Entertainment 16
144. Short Story:
     Senior Adult Fiction 16
145. Short Story: Speculative 16
146. Grandparenting 15
147. Short Story:
     Historical/Romance 15
148. Short Story:
     Mystery/Romance 15
149. Short Story: Skits 14
150. Short Story: Plays 12
151. *Beauty/Fashion 11
152. *Depression 10
153. Holy Spirit 10
154. Short Story:
     Frontier/Romance
155. Praise 9
156. Fillers:
     Sermon Illustrations 8
157. Small-Group Helps 7
158. Puppet Plays 5
159. DVD Reviews 4

SUMMARY OF INFORMATION ON CHRISTIAN PERIODICAL PUBLISHERS FOUND IN THE ALPHABETICAL LISTINGS

Note: Following is some general information based on typical averages of the information supplied by the periodical publishers in this guide. This information will be valuable in determining what numbers or percentages are typical in the various categories.

Wants Query or Complete Manuscript

Not all periodicals indicate a preference, but 45-50% prefer or accept a complete manuscript, 35-38% want or will accept a query, 3-5% require a query, and 12-15% will accept either.

Accepts Phone/Fax/E-mail Query

Every year fewer periodical publishers are accepting phone or fax queries, and at this point almost none do. The majority now prefer e-mail queries—either directly or through an online form available on their Website. It is suggested that you reserve phone queries for timely projects or assignments that require immediate answers to questions. If you call, be sure you have your question or idea well thought out and can present it succinctly and articulately. It is always important to use the form of communication they indicate in their listing.

Submissions by E-mail
This area continues to show some significant changes in editors' perceptions of e-mail submissions. When asked if they would accept submissions by e-mail, now more than half say yes. Of those, 40% wanted the article copied into the message, 42% wanted them sent as an attached file, and the last 18% would accept them either way. Generally speaking, those who prefer the article copied into the message fear viruses, while those who prefer an attached copy don't like losing the coding when you copy it into the message.

Pays on Acceptance or Publication
Of the publishers that indicated, 40% pay on acceptance, while 60% pay on publication.

Percentage of Freelance
Many of the publishers responded to the question about how much freelance material they use. Based on the figures we have, for the average publisher, 34% of the material purchased is unsolicited freelance, and 66% is assigned.

Circulation
In dividing the list of periodicals into three groups, according to size of circulation, the list comes out as follows: Publications with a circulation of 100,000 or more (up to 3,000,000) make up 15% of periodicals; publications with a circulation between 50,000 and 100,000, 10%; the remaining 75% have a circulation of 50,000 or less. If we break that last group into three more groups by circulation, we come out with circulations of 33,000-50,000 making up 10%; 18% with circulations of 17,000-32,000; and the remaining 72% with less than 17,000. That means that 52% of all the periodicals that reported their circulation are at a circulation of 17,000 or less. Not all publications update their circulation every year, but for those that did this year, 73% reported a decline in circulation, while 27% showed an increase.

Response Time
The average response time is just over eight weeks, one week longer than reported three or four years ago. Those who are writing and submitting regularly will have no problem confirming that most publishers are taking longer to respond to submissions—both for queries and complete manuscripts.

Reprints
Just over 48% of the periodicals included in the market guide accept reprints. Most Christian publishers now want a tear sheet of the original publication, or at least a cover letter telling when and where it appeared originally. Be sure to check the individual listings to see if a publisher wants to know when and where a piece has appeared previously. Most are also paying less for reprints than for original material.

Preferred Bible Version
The most preferred Bible version is the New International Version, the preference of more than half the publishers. Other preferred versions are the King James Version, the New Revised Standard Version, the New American Bible, New American Standard, Revised Standard Version, and New King James. The NIV seems a good choice for those who didn't indicate a preference, although the more conservative groups seem to favor the KJV.

PART 3
Specialty Markets

9

Greeting Card/Gift/Specialty Markets

This listing contains both Christian/religious card publishers and secular publishers that have religious lines or produce some religious or inspirational cards. Keep in mind that the secular companies may produce other lines of cards that are not consistent with your beliefs, and that for a secular company, inspirational cards usually do not include religious imagery. All of these are paying markets. A support group for greeting card writers can be found at http://groups.yahoo.com/group/GreetingCardWriters.

Note: See the end of this listing for specialty product topical lists.

CARD PUBLISHERS

AFRICAN AMERICAN EXPRESSIONS, 10266 Rockingham Dr., Sacramento CA 95827-2515. Toll-free (800) 684-1555. (916) 424-5000. Fax (916) 424-5053. E-mail: gperkins@black-gifts.com or info@black-gifts.com. Website: www.black-gifts.com. Greg Perkins, pres. Christian card publisher and specialty products. Open to freelance; buys 5-10 ideas/yr. Prefers outright submissions. Pays $35 on acceptance. No royalty. Responds in 2 wks. Uses rhymed, unrhymed, traditional, and light verse. Produces invitations and conventional, humorous, informal, inspirational, juvenile, novelty, and religious cards. Needs anniversary, birthday, Christmas, friendship, get well, graduation, keep in touch, love, miss you, Mother's Day, new baby, relatives (all occasions), sympathy, valentines, wedding, and pastor appreciation. Holiday/seasonal 9 mos. ahead. Open to ideas for new card lines, calendars/journals, novelty/gift items, magnets, and stationery. No guidelines; free catalog.

AMERICAN GREETINGS, One American Rd., Cleveland OH 44144-2398. (216) 252-7300. Fax (216) 252-6778. Website: www.americangreetings.com. Kathleen McKay, ed. No unsolicited material.

ARTBEAT OF AMERICA/GRACEFULLY YOURS, (formerly listed as Dickson's Life Publishing), 768 Bridger, Ste. 1, Lafayette CO 80026. (303) 664-1416. E-mail: gracefullyrick@gmail.com. Website: www.artbeatofamerica.com. Christian brand is www.gracefully-yours.com, published books and radio show branded as www.miss-takes.com. National radio show: www.blogtalkradio.com/search/rick-tocquigny-life-lessons. Rick Tocquigny, pub. Open to freelance design and editorial for social expression industry; also open to ideas for student-parent activity, coloring books, journals, Post-it notes, stationery, and life lessons content. No guidelines or catalog.

ARTFUL GREETINGS, PO Box 52428, Durham NC 27717. Toll-free (800) 638-2733. (919) 484-0100. Fax (919) 484-3099. E-mail: myw@artfulgreetings.com or through Website: www.artfulgreetings.com. Lonita Whitted, CEO. Black art greeting cards and gifts.

BLUE MOUNTAIN ARTS INC., PO Box 4549, Boulder CO 80306. (303) 449-0536. Fax (303) 447-0939. E-mail: editorial@sps.com. Website: www.sps.com. Submit to Editorial Department. General card publisher that does a few inspirational cards. Open to freelance; buys 50-100 ideas/yr. Prefers outright submissions. Pays $300 for all rts. for use on a greeting card, or $50 for onetime use in a book, on publication. No royalties. Responds in 12-16 wks. Uses unrhymed or traditional poetry; short or long, but no one-liners. Produces inspirational and sensitivity. Needs anniversary, birthday, Christmas, congratulations, Easter, Father's Day, friendship, get well, graduation, keep in touch, love, miss you, Mother's Day, new baby, please write, relatives, sympathy, thank you, valentines, wedding, reaching for dreams. Holiday/seasonal 3 mos. ahead. Open to ideas for new card lines. Send any number of ideas (1 per pg.). Open to ideas for gift books. Guidelines; no catalog.

Contest: Sponsors a poetry card contest online. Details on Website.

Tips: "We are interested in reviewing poetry and writings for greeting cards, and expanding our field of freelance poetry writers."

C4YOURSELF GREETING CARDS, 1342 Main St., Cincinnati OH 45202. (508) 608-1878. E-mail through Website: www.c4yourself.biz. Angela Morrow, creator. Christmas cards & cards for all occasions. Also does desk calendars. E-mail with card ideas.

CREATIVE CHRISTIAN GIFTS, PO Box 915441, Longwood FL 32791-5441. Toll-free (866) 325-1857. (407) 610-9535. E-mail: sales@creativechristiangifts.com. Website: www.creativechris tiangifts.com. Greeting cards & note cards.

CURRENT INC., PO Box 2559, Colorado Springs CO 80901. (719) 594-4100. Fax (719) 534-6259. No freelance.

DAYSPRING CARDS INC., Editorial Department, Box 1010, 21154 Hwy. 16 East, Siloam Springs AR 72761. Fax (479) 524-9477. E-mail: info@dayspring.com (type "write" in message or subject line). Website: www.dayspring.com. Attn: Freelance Editor. Christian/religious card publisher. Please read guidelines before submitting. Prefers outright submission. Pays $60/idea on acceptance for all rts. No royalty. Responds in 4-8 wks. Uses unrhymed, traditional, light verse, conversational, contemporary; various lengths. Looking for inspirational cards for all occasions, including anniversary, birthday, relative birthday, congratulations, encouragement, friendship, get well, new baby, sympathy, thank you, wedding. Also needs seasonal cards for friends and family members for Christmas, Valentine's Day, Easter, Mother's Day, Father's Day, Thanksgiving, graduation, and Clergy Appreciation Day. Include Scripture verse with each submission. Send 10 ideas or less. Guidelines by phone or e-mail; no catalog.

Tips: Prefers submissions on 8.5 x 11 inch sheets, not 3x5 cards (one idea per sheet).

DESIGN DESIGN INC., 19 La Grave S.E., Grand Rapids MI 49503. (616) 774-2448. Fax (616) 774-4020. Website: www.designdesign.us. Rebecca Cooper, text ed. (rebecca.cooper@designdesign.us); Susan Birnbaum, card editor (616-771-8359/susan.birnbaum@designdesign.us). A general card publisher that does a few inspirational and religious cards. Open to freelance submissions. Prefers outright submissions (but not of artwork). Rights purchased depend on product. Uses rhymed, unrhymed, traditional, and light verse. Produces anniversary, birthday, Christmas, congratulations, Easter, Father's Day, friendship, get well, graduation, Halloween, love, miss you, Mother's Day, new baby, relative (all occasions), St. Patrick's Day, sympathy, Thanksgiving, thank you, valentines, and wedding. Open to new card lines. Open to ideas for gift/novelty items, greeting books, magnets, and stationery. Guidelines on Website; no catalog.

HEAVENLY DESIGNS, 118 Burnell Pl. S.E., Leesburg VA 20175. Toll-free (866) 707-0113. Phone/fax (703) 737-0113. E-mails: cindyjames@birthverse.com, or bjames@birthverse.com. Website: www.birthverse.com. Bob & Cindy James, owners. Inspirational greeting cards.

HERMITAGE ART CO. INC., 5151 N. Ravenswood Ave., Chicago IL 60640-2722. Toll-free (800) 621-7992. (773) 561-3773. Fax (773) 561-4422. E-mail: Office@hermitageart.com. Website: www.hermitageart.com. Color bulletins, bookmarks, specialty items.

INSPIRATIONART & SCRIPTURE INC., PO Box 5550, Cedar Rapids IA 52406-5550. Toll-free (800) 728-5550. (319) 365-4350. Fax (319) 861-2103. E-mail: Customerservice@inspirationart.com.

Website: www.inspirationart.com. Publishes Christian posters only. Charles Edwards, creative dir. Open to freelance. Buys 20-30 ideas/yr. Prefers e-mail contact. Pays $150-250, 30 days after publication, for right to publish as a poster; or royalties 5% of net. Responds in 4 wks. Seasonal 6 mos. ahead. Open to new ideas for posters. Submit up to 3 ideas. Artist's guidelines on Website.

NORTHERN CARDS, Creative Department, 5035 Timberlea Blvd., Unit #9, Mississauga ON L4W 2W9, Canada. Toll-free (877) 627-7444. (905) 625-4944. Fax (905) 625-5995. E-mail: artists@ northerncards.com. Website: www.northerncards.com. Open to writers and artists. Greeting cards.

NOVO CARD PUBLISHERS INC., 7570 N. Croname Rd., Niles IL 60714-3904. Toll-free (800) 624-2426. (847) 588-3220. Fax (847) 588-3508. E-mail: art@novocard.net. Website: www.novocard .net. Submit to Art Production. General card publisher that does a few inspirational and religious cards. Open to freelance; buys 10 ideas/yr. Prefers outright submissions. Pays $2/line on acceptance for all rts. No royalties. Responds in 5 wks. Uses traditional and light verse; 5-20 lines (nothing too brief). Produces baby announcements, conventional, humorous, inspirational, invitations, juvenile, religious, studio. Needs anniversary, birthday, Christmas, congratulations, Easter, Father's Day, friendship, get well, congratulations, miss you, Mother's Day, new baby, relatives (all occasions), sympathy, Thanksgiving, thank you, valentines, wedding. Seasonal 6-8 mos. ahead. Open to ideas for new card lines. Submit enough ideas to show style. Guidelines/needs list on Website (click on "Contact"); no catalog.

    Tips: "We don't want anything too brief or too lengthy. We like verse that holds everyone's hearts, especially the male gender."

OATMEAL STUDIOS, PO Box 138CW, Rochester VT 05767. (802) 767-3171. E-mail: Dawn@oat mealstudios.com. Website: www.oatmealstudios.com. Dawn Abraham, editor. Always needs birthday ideas. No holiday copy needed. Guidelines for submitting on Website, or submit ideas on 3 x 5 index cards with your name and address on each one. Also see Artist's Guidelines.

PLESH CREATIVE GROUP INC., 165 Main St., Unit 209, Medway MA 02053-1584. (508) 359-6400. Fax (508) 359-6448. E-mail: pleshcreative@gmail.com. Website: www.PleshCreative.com. Submit to: Suzanne Comeau. General card publisher with a religious line. Open to freelance. Prefers outright submissions. Buys all rts. Pays $30-50 on acceptance. No royalties. Responds in several wks. Uses rhymed, unrhymed, traditional, and light verse; 8-10 lines or shorter. Produces conventional, humorous, inspirational, juvenile, religious.

P. S. GREETINGS/FANTUS PAPER PRODUCTS, 5730 N. Tripp Ave., Chicago IL 60646-6723. Toll-free (800) 621-8823. (773) 267-6150. Fax (773) 267-6055. E-mail: artdirector@psgreet ings.com or through Website: www.psgreetings.com. General card publisher with a religious line. Submit to Design Director; Re: Freelance Writer. Open to freelance. Holiday/seasonal 6 mos. ahead. Responds in 1 mo. Pays flat fee on publication; no royalty. Responds in 3-4 wks. Rhymed, unrhymed, traditional, light verse. Produces announcements, conventional, humorous, informal, inspirational, invitations, juvenile, novelty, religious, sensitivity, softline, studio. Not open to ideas for new card lines or specialty products. Guidelines on Website (under "Creative"/"Artist's Guidelines").

RED FARM STUDIO, 1135 Roosevelt Ave., Pawtucket RI 02861-0347. Toll-free (877) REDFARM. (401) 728-9300. Toll-free fax (888) 860-3276. E-mail: redfarm@quadrigaart.com. Website: www .redfarmstudio.com. Thomas Scott, pres.; Steven Scott, VP; submit to Production Coordinator. General card publisher with a religious line. 100% freelance; buys 100 ideas/yr. Outright submission. Pays variable rates (about $4/line) within 1 mo. of acceptance for exclusive rts. No royalties. Responds in 2 mos. Uses traditional and light verse; 1-4 lines. Produces announcements, invitations, religious. Needs anniversary, birthday, Christmas, friendship, get well, new baby, sympathy, wedding.

Holiday 6 mos. ahead. Not open to ideas for new card lines. Submit any number of ideas. Guidelines/needs list for SASE.

BOB SIEMON DESIGNS INC., 3501 W. Segerstrom Ave., Santa Ana CA 92704-6497. (714) 549-0678. Fax (714) 979-2627. Website: www.bobsiemon.com. No freelance.

SOLE SOURCE GREETINGS, Attn: Art Submissions or Attn: Copy Submissions, 1 Idea Way, Caldwell ID 83605-6902. Toll-free (800) 346-5860 or (800) 285-1657. Toll-free fax (800) 455-0642. E-mail through Website: www.solesourcegreetings.com. Send artwork via e-mail as a JPG or PDF file (see Website for size details). Check Website for samples of greetings. Open to: thinking of you, birthday, thank you, sympathy, new baby, congratulations, anniversary, wedding, etc. Also business-specific cards. Pays up to $500 for artwork; pays $25/message. Royalties 5% on retail sales; 2.5% on wholesale catalog sales.

WARNER PRESS INC., 1201 E. 5th St., PO Box 2499, Anderson IN 46018-9988. (765) 644-7721. Fax (765) 640-8005. E-mail: rfogle@warnerpress.org. Website: www.warnerpress.org. Karen Rhodes, product mktg. ed.; Robin Fogle, ed. asst. Producer of church resources (greeting cards, bulletins, coloring books, puzzle books). 30% freelance; buys 30-50 ideas/yr. Query for guidelines. Pays $30-35 on acceptance (for bulletins); material for bulletins cannot be sold elsewhere for bulletin use but may be sold in any other medium. No royalties. Responds in 6-8 wks. Uses rhymed, unrhymed, traditional verse, and devotionals for bulletins; 16-24 lines. Accepts 10 ideas/submission. Guidelines for bulletins; no catalog.

    Also Does: Also open to ideas for coloring books, bookmarks, charts, postcards, church-resource items.

    Photos/Artwork: Accepts freelance photos and queries from freelance artists.

WORLD LIBRARY PUBLICATIONS, 3708 River Rd., Ste. 400, Franklin Park IL 60131. Toll free (800) 621-5197, ext. 2800. (847) 233-2800. Fax (847) 233-2762. E-mail: odegardj@jspaluch.com. Website: www.wlpmusic.com. A division of J. S. Paluch Co. Jennifer Odegard, marketing dir. A music, liturgy, and art publisher with some greeting cards in their line. Open to freelance. Query. Pays on publication; pays some negotiable royalties. Traditional verse. Produces inspirational & religious cards; anniversary, birthday, Christmas, Easter, St. Patrick's Day, sympathy. Holiday/seasonal 10-12 mos. ahead. Not open to ideas for new card lines. Open to ideas for various specialty items; all religious themed. Also does books/CDs. Send any number of ideas. Guidelines; catalog for 9x12 SASE.

ADDITIONAL CARD PUBLISHERS

NOTE: Following is a list of card publishers who did not respond to our questionnaire. You may want to contact them on your own to see if they are open to freelance submissions.

BERG CHRISTIAN ENTERPRISES, 4525 S.E. 63rd Ave., Portland OR 97206. (503) 777-4101.

BLACK FAMILY GREETING CARDS, 20 Cortlandt Ave., New Rochelle NY 10801. Bill Harte, pres.

BLACKSMITH CARDS & PRINTS, 37535 Festival Dr., Palm Desert CA 92211. Bob Smith, pres.

CD GREETING CARDS, PO Box 5084, Brentwood TN 37024-5084.

+CHRISTIAN ART KIDS, 1025 N. Lombard Rd., Lombard IL 60148.

CRT CUSTOM PRODUCTS INC., 7532 Hickory Hills Ct., Whites Creek TN 37189.

DESIGNS FOR BETTER LIVING, 1716 N. Vista St., Los Angeles CA 90046.

KRISTIN ELLIOTT INC., 6030 N. Orchard Rd., Tucson AZ 85704-5310.

GOOD NEWS IN SIGHT, 2610 Mirror Lake Dr., Fayetteville NC 28303-5212.

GRACE PUBLICATIONS, PO Box 9432, Wyoming MI 49509-0432.

GREENLEAF INC., 951 S. Pine St., #250, Spartanburg SC 29302-3370. Greenleaf Foundation Inc.

HIGHER HORIZONS, PO Box 78399, Los Angeles CA 90016-0399.

+INNOVATIVE, 19840 Nordhoff Pl., Chatsworth CA 91311.

+KARDIA PRESS, PO Box 11314, Olympia WA 98508-1314.

LUCY & ME GALLERY, 13232 Riviera Pl. N.E., Seattle WA 98125-4645. Diane Roger, card ed.

+MOONLIGHTING CARDS, PO Box 4670, Vallejo CA 94590.

MORE THAN A CARD, 5010 Baltimore Ave., Bethesda MD 20816.

FREDERICK SINGER & SONS INC., 520 S. Fulton Ave, Mount Vernon NY 10550-5011.

RANDALL WILCOX PUBLISHING, 826 Orange Ave., #544, Coronado CA 92118.

CAROL WILSON FINE ARTS, PO Box 17394, Portland OR 97217. Gary Spector, ed.

GAME MARKETS
NOTE: Some of the following markets for games, gift items, and videos have not indicated their interest in receiving freelance submissions. Contact these markets on your own for information on submission procedures before sending them anything.

+ BIBLEQUEST, 6405 Tiffany Oaks, Arlington TX 76016. Toll-free (866) 248-4045. E-mail: cs@ biblequest.com. Website: www.biblequest.com. Produces board games, action figures, story cards, and puzzles.

GOODE GAMES INTERNATIONAL, Original Family Fun Games, PO Box 1099, Nicholasville KY 40356. Toll-free (800) 257-7767. (859) 881-4513. E-mail: info@goodegames.com. Website: www .goodegames.com. Contact: Mike Goode.

+THE LEARNING JOURNEY INTERNATIONAL, 4727 E. Union Hills Dr., Ste. 300, Phoenix AZ 85050. (602) 787-1115. Fax (602) 787-1114. E-mail: info@tlji.com. Website: www.thelearning journey.com. Games, puzzles, electronics.

+LEFT BEHIND GAMES INC./DIGITAL PRAISE, Inspired Media Entertainment, 25060 Hancock Ave., Ste. 103, Box 110, Murrieta CA 92562. (951) 894-6597. E-mail through Website: www.leftbe hindgames.com, or www.digitalpraise.com. Video games.

TALICOR, 901 Lincoln Pkwy., Plainwell MI 49080. (269) 685-2345. Fax (269) 685-6789. E-mail through Website: www.Talicor.com. Nicole Hancock, pres. Produces board games and puzzles. 100% freelance; buys 10 ideas/yr. Outright submissions. Pays variable rates on publication for all rts. Royalty 4-6%. Responds in 4 wks. Seasonal 6 mos. ahead. Open to new ideas for board games, novelty items, puzzles, or toys. Submit 1-4 ideas. No guidelines; catalog for 9x12 SAE/$2.38 postage (mark "Media Mail").

WISDOM TREE, PO Box 8682, Tucson AZ 85738-8682. Fax (520) 825-5702. E-mail: Thuff80691@ aol.com. Website: www.wisdomtreegames.com. Brenda Huff, owner. Produces Bible-based computer games and does sales and marketing of Bible-based and family-friendly educational games. Responds in 1-6 wks. Seasonal 8 mos. ahead. Open to review of beta versions of computer games, computer software, or video games. Also networks with Christian Game Developers Group to put projects together. Catalog on request.
   Special Needs: "Storybook/puzzle game engine."

GIFT/SPECIALTY-ITEM MARKETS

ANCHOR WALLACE PUBLISHERS, 1000 Hwy. 4 S., PO Box 7000, Sleepy Eye MN 56085-0007. Toll-free (800) 533-3570. Toll-free fax (800) 582-2352. E-mail: contactus@anchorwallace.com. Website: www.anchorwallace.com. Worship bulletins, foil & 4-color elegant certificates.

ARTBEATS, 129 Glover Ave., Norwalk CT 06850-1311, or 130 Scott Rd., Waterbury CT 06705. (203) 847-2000. Fax (203) 846-2105. E-mail: Richard@nygs.com or mail@nygs.com. Website: www.NYGS.com. New York Graphic Society. Richard Fleischmann, pub. Produces prints and posters. Open to freelancers; purchases 100 ideas/yr. Outright submissions. Pays on publication. Royalties 10%. Responds in 3 wks. Does conventional, inspirational, juvenile, religious, and sensitivity prints and posters. Open to new ideas. Guidelines on Website; no catalog.

ASHLEIGH MANOR, PO Box 3851, Frederick MD 21705-3851. Toll free (800) 327-4212. (301) 631-0106. Fax (301) 631-0108. E-mail: info@ashleighmanor.com. Website: www.ashleighmanor.com. Produces specialty products: religious frames & giftware, bookmarks, gift/novelty items. Free catalog.

BE ONE SPORTSWEAR, 3208 Merrywood Dr., Sacramento CA 95825. (916) 483-7630. E-mail: Blane@beone.com. Website: www.BeOne.com. Christian clothing (T-shirts), promo products.

CARPENTREE INC., Carpentree Design, 2724 N. Sheridan, Tulsa OK 74115. Toll-free (800) 736-2787. (918) 582-3600. Fax (918) 587-4329. E-mail through Website: www.carpentree.com. Submit to Design Dept. Produces framed art and verse. Buys several ideas/yr. Prefers outright submission. Rights purchased are negotiable. Pays on publication; negotiable royalty. Responds in 12-15 wks. Uses rhymed, unrhymed, and traditional verse for framed art; 4-16 lines. Open to ideas for new specialty items. Submit max 10 ideas. Open to ideas for framed art, tabletop items, and gift/novelty items. Guidelines; catalog $5/10x13 SAE.

+CELEBRATE YOUR FAITH, 7135 Shady Oak Rd., Eden Prairie MN 55344. (763) 477-4141. Fax (763) 477-5015. E-mail: customercare@celebrateyourfaith.com. Website: www.celebrateyourfaith .com. Submit to: New Product Selection Team. Producer of specialty products. Open to freelance submissions. Prefers e-mail contact. Details of purchases unknown at this time. Responds in 2 weeks. Produces bookmarks and gift/novelty items; open to ideas for these specialty products. No guidelines or catalog.

CHRISTIAN ART GIFTS, 1025 N. Lombard Rd., PO Box 1443, Lombard IL 60148. Toll-free (800) 521-7807. (630) 599-0240. Fax (630) 599-0245. Website: www.christianartgifts.com. Friendship cards, greeting books, bookmarks, mugs.

CROSS GIFT DIVISION/DICKSONS INC., 513 Warrenville Rd., Warren NJ 07059. Jewelry ideas. Website: www.dicksongifts.com/contact_us.aspx.

DESTINY IMAGE GIFTS, PO Box 310, Shippensburg PA 17257. (717) 532-3040. Fax (717) 532-9291. E-mail: rrr@destinyimage.com, or through Website: www.destinyimage.com. Ronda Ranalli, ed. mngr. No unsolicited e-mail submissions; use online submission form. Gift products. Guidelines on Website (under "Contact Us"/"Manuscript Submissions").

DEXSA: The Giving Company, PO Box 109, Hudson WI 54016. Toll-free (800) 933-3972. (715) 386-8701. Toll-free fax (888) 559-1603. E-mail through Website: www.dexsa.com. John Larson, owner. Gifts.

EAGLES WINGS, 2101 Old Hickory Tree Rd., St. Cloud FL 34772. (407) 892-6358. Fax (407) 892-6759. E-mail: info@eagleswings.com. Website: www.eagleswings.com. Apparel.

+P. GRAHAM DUNN, 1417 Zuercher Rd., Dalton OH 44618. Toll-free (800) 828-5260, or (866) 922-0306. (330) 857-5405. Fax (330) 857-5455. E-mail through Website: www.pgrahamdunn.com.

Open to samples from artists; send to: P. Graham Dunn, Attn: Art Review, 630 Henry St., Dalton OH 44618 (guidelines at "Attention Artists"). Produces cards, home decorations, gift items.

GREENACRE WORKSHOP, Toll-free (877) 733-3276. Toll-free fax (888) 860-3276. (401) 728-0350. E-mail: redfarm@designergreetings.com. Website: www.greenacreworkshop.com. Coloring/activity books; paintables.

HERITAGE PUZZLE INC., PO Box 328, Pfafftown NC 27040-0328. Toll-free (888) 348-3717. Toll-free fax (866) 727-8209. E-mail: heritagepuzzle@triad.rr.com. Website: www.heritagepuzzle.com. Religious jigsaw puzzles.

JODY HOUGHTON DESIGNS INC., 5434 River Rd. N., #135, Keizer OR 97303-4429. Toll-free (800) 733-8253. (503) 656-7748. E-mail: jody@jodyhoughton.com. Website: www.jodyhoughton.com.

+JESUS IN ME UNLTD., PO Box 1251, Gilroy CA 95021. Toll-free (888) 546-8583. Fax (408) 842-5005. Website: www.JesuInMeUnltd.com. Deborah Senior, pres. (Deborah@jesusinmeunltd.com). Christian clothing and accessories.

KNOW HIM CHRISTIAN GEAR, 6200 S. Troy Cir., Ste. 140, Englewood CO 80111-6474. Toll-free (888) 256-6944. (303) 662-9512. Fax (303) 662-9942. E-mail: Doug.Mckenna@knowhim.com or through Website: www.KnowHim.com. Doug McKenna, pres. Christian apparel.

JAMES LAWRENCE COMPANY, 1501 Livingstone Rd., PO Box 188, Hudson WI 54016. Toll-free (800) 546-3699. (715) 386-3082. Fax (715) 386-3699. E-mail: brian@jameslawrencecompany .com. Website: www.jameslawrencecompany.com. Brian Johnson, gen. mngr. Producer of specialty products. Open to freelance. Buys variable number/yr. Prefers e-mail contact. Prefers exclusive rts. Pays $50-100/verse on acceptance. Negotiable royalties. Responds in 3-4 wks. Inspirational verse no shorter than 4 lines and no longer than 5 stanzas of 4 lines ea. Holiday 6-9 mos. ahead. Open to new ideas for gift/novelty items, magnets, mugs, plaques. Send any number of ideas. No guidelines or catalog. View Website before submitting.

LIVING EPISTLES, 2232 S. Main St., #444, Ann Arbor MI 48103. Toll-free (800) 294-8637. Fax (205) 759-9889. E-mail: LivingEpistlesService@livingepistles.com, or through Website: www.liv ingepistles.com. Apparel.

LORENZ CORP., PO Box 802, Dayton OH 45401. Toll-free (800) 444-1144, ext. 1. (937) 228-6118. Fax (937) 223-2042. E-mail: submit@lorenz.com or through Website: www.lorenz.com. Attn: Editorial Coordinator. Gift products, stationery, bookmarks, buttons, postcards, posters, and more. Guidelines on Website (Under "Contact"). For music submissions, click on "Submitting Music Manuscripts."

MCBETH CORP., PO Box 400, Chambersburg PA 17201. Toll-free (800) 876-5112. (717) 263-5600. Fax (717) 263-5909. E-mail: mcbethcorp@supernet.com. Website: www.wholesalecentral.com/mcbethcorp. Gifts, jewelry, calendars, Christmas items, activity books, greeting cards, and more.

NOT OF THIS WORLD CLOTHING CO., 169 Radio Rd. #8, Corona CA 92879. Toll-free (866) 625-9069. (951) 354-9528. Fax (951) 354-9529. E-mail: info@notw.com, or info@c28.com. Website: www.notw.com. Shirts, wallets, belts, belt buckles.

RED LETTER 9, 2910 Kerry Forest Pkwy., #D4, Tallahassee FL 32309. Toll-free (866) 804-4833. Toll-free fax (866) 804-4832. E-mail: info@redletter9.com. Website: www.redletter9.com. Apparel and gift items. Not actively seeking freelance art, but will review artist's portfolios.

SERENDIPITY PUZZLE CO., a division of The Marek Group, W228 N821 Westmound Dr., Waukesha WI 53186. (262) 549-8930. Fax (262) 549-8910. E-mail: diane.bucher@serendipity puzzles.com. Website: www.serendipitypuzzles.com. Diane Bucher-Gilboy, dir. of sales. Produces specialty products. Open to freelance. Purchases 50+ ideas/yr. Prefers outright submissions through e-mail. Payment & royalty (decided case-by-case) on acceptance. Responds in 2 wks. Seasonal 2 mos. ahead. Open to new ideas for specialty items. Submit 2 or more ideas at a time. Manufactures custom orders. Free catalog.

Tips: "The Marek Group is a nationally recognized, high quality commercial printing and manufacturing company, specializing in catalogs, publications, direct mail, variable data, Web-to-print applications, and the manufacturing of puzzles and board games."

SONTEEZ CHRISTIAN T-SHIRTS, PO Box 44106, Phoenix AZ 85064. Toll-free (800) 874-4485. Fax (623) 792-5709. Website: www.sonteez.com. Sandy Shapiro, owner (sandy@sonteez.com).T-shirts.

VIDA ENTERTAINMENT, 201 East City Hall Ave., Norfolk VA 23451. Toll-free (877)YES-VIDA. (757) 626-3102. E-mail: sales@vidaentertainment.com. Website: www.vidaentertainment.com. Submit to D. Booth. Books, CDs, DVDs, comics, computer games. Open to freelance. Buys 2 ideas/yr.

+WITNESS, 2150 Valley Ridge Ct., Ste. 100, Highland Village TX 75077. Toll-free (888) 438-9486. Fax (972) 219-2220. E-mail: through Website: www.witnessline.com. Produces clothing and jewelry.

+YZ COMPANY INC., 2441 Tech Center Ct., Ste. 111, Las Vegas NV 89128. Toll-free (877) 422-5599. (702) 386-9926. Fax (702) 386-9925. E-mail through Website: www.yzcompany.com. Fashion jewelry/crosses.

SOFTWARE DEVELOPERS

AMG SOFTWARE, 6815 Shallowford Rd. (37421), PO Box 22000, Chattanooga TN 37422. Toll-free (800) 266-4977. (423) 894-6060, ext. 277. Toll-free fax (800) 265-6690. (423) 894-9511. Ricks@amgpublishers.com. Website: www.amgpublishers.com. AMG International. Contact: Rick Steele, Dir. of Electronic Media.

BAKER SOFTWARE, Box 6287, Grand Rapids MI 49516-6287. (616) 676-9185. Fax (616) 676-9573. Website: www.BakerBooks.com. Baker Publishing Group.

B & H SOFTWARE, 127 Ninth Ave. N., Nashville TN 37234. (615) 251-3638. Website: www .BHpublishinggroup.com.

ELLIS ENTERPRISES INC., 5100 N. Brookline, #465, Oklahoma City OK 73112. (405) 948-1766. Fax (405) 917-2250. E-mail: mail@ellisenterprises.com. Website: www.ellisenterprises.com or www.BibleLibrary.com. Contact: Dr. John Ellis. Produces the Micro Bible, Ultra Bible, Mega Bible, and Maxima Bible. Check out additional products on their Website.

LOGOS BIBLE SOFTWARE, 1313 Commercial St., Bellingham WA 98225-4307. (360) 527-1700. Fax (360) 527-1707. E-mail: sales@logos.com. Website: www.logos.com. Contact: Dan Pritchett (Dan@logos.com). Publishes the Logos Bible Software Scholar's Library, Leader's Library, Bible Study Library, and more. Over 10,000 titles from more than 100 publishers now compatible with the system. Now also runs *Bible Study Magazine* (see listing in periodical section).

NAVPRESS SOFTWARE, 16002 Pool Canyon Rd., Austin TX 78734. Website: www.navpress.com.

OLIVE TREE BIBLE SOFTWARE, PO Box 48271, Spokane WA 99228. (509) 466-5700. Fax (509) 467-4976. E-mail: support@olivetree.com. Website: www.OliveTree.com. Drew Haninger, pres. Bible software.

ZONDERVAN DIGITAL MEDIA, 5300 Patterson St. S.E., Grand Rapids MI 49530. Toll-free (800) 226-1122. (616) 698-6900. Fax (616) 698-3483. Website: www.zondervan.com. Contact: Jody DeNeef. Software.

VIDEO/CD/DVD MARKETS

ALL THAT PRODUCTIONS INC., PO Box 1594, Humble TX 77347-1594. (218) 878-2062. E-mail: thelma@itsathelma.com. Website: www.ItsAThelma.com. Deborah Elum, dir. Produces videos and movies of comedy series *It's a Thelma.* Not open to freelance.

ALPHA OMEGA PUBLICATIONS, 804 N. 2nd Ave. E., Rock Rapids IA 51246. Toll-free (800) 682-7391. Fax (712) 472-4856. Website: www.AOP.com. Videos & DVDs.

AMG PUBLISHERS/CDs/DVDs, 6815 Shallowford Rd. (37421), PO Box 22000, Chattanooga TN 37422. Toll-free (800) 266-4977. (423) 894-6060, ext. 277. Toll-free fax (800) 265-6690. (423) 894-9511. E-mail: ricks@amgpublishers.com. Website: www.amgpublishers.com. AMG International. Contact: Rick Steele, dir. of prod. dev./acq. Bible CD-ROMs.

CANDLELIGHT MEDIA GROUP, 3323 State Hwy. 276, Emory TX 75440. Toll-free (800) 747-2696. E-mail: info@candlelightmedia.com. Website: www.candlelightmedia.com. Videos, DVDs.

CLOUD TEN PICTURES, PO Box 1440, Niagara Falls NY 14302. (905) 684-5561. Fax (905) 684-7946. Website: www.cloudtenpictures.com. Film production and acquisition, video distribution, and marketing. Cloud Ten Pictures (maker of the Left Behind movies) is committed to making quality, Christian-themed films. For all inquiries, contact C.E.O.: Andre van Heerden; andrev@cloudtenpic tures.com.

DALLAS CHRISTIAN VIDEO, Toll-free (877) 516-2900. Fax (972) 644-5926. E-mail: DCV6681@ aol.com. Website: www.dallaschristianvideo.com. Contact: Bob Hill. Videos.

RUSS DOUGHTEN FILMS INC., 5907 Meredith Dr., Des Moines IA 50322. Toll-free (800) 247-3456. (515) 278-4737. Fax (515) 278-4738. E-mail: cneufeld@rdfilms.com. Website: www.rdfilms .com. Russell S. Doughton Jr., pres. Submit to Production Dept. Produces and distributes feature-length Christian movies. Open to ideas. Guidelines; free catalog.

TOMMY NELSON VIDEOS, PO Box 141000, Nashville TN 37214. Website: www.tommynelson.com or www.thomasnelson.com. Contact: Wayne Zeitner, dir. of brand development.

PROPHECY PUBLICATIONS, PO Box 7000, Oklahoma City OK 73153. (405) 634-1234. Fax (405) 636-1054. E-mail: Krissie@prophecyinthenews.com. Website: www.prophecyinthenews.com. Contact: J. R. Church. Religious education videos; fiction videos.

TYNDALE FAMILY VIDEO, 351 Executive Dr., Carol Stream IL 60188. (630) 668-8300. Website: www.tyndale.com. Videos.

VISION VIDEO/GATEWAY FILMS, PO Box 540, Worcester PA 19490-0540. Toll-free (800) 523-0226. (610) 584-3500. Fax (610) 584-6643. E-mail: info@VisionVideo.com. Website: www .VisionVideo.com. Contact: Karen Rutt.

WACKY WORLD STUDIOS, 148 E. Douglas Rd., Oldsmar FL 34677-2939. (813) 818-8277. Fax (813) 818-8396. E-mail: info@wackyworld.tv, or through Website: www.wackyworld.tv. Full service custom art and design studio. Videos, DVDs.

ZONDERVAN AUDIO AND VIDEO, 5300 Patterson St. S.E., Grand Rapids MI 49530. Toll-free (800) 226-1122. (616) 698-6900. Fax (616) 698-3483. Website: www.zondervan.com. Contact: T. J. Rathbun. Audio & video.

SPECIALTY-PRODUCTS TOPICAL LISTINGS

NOTE: Most of the following publishers are greeting card/specialty market publishers, but some will be found in the book publisher listings.

An A in parentheses (a) before a listing indicates an agent is required.
An asterisk (*) after a category name indicates the category is new this year.

ACTIVITY/COLORING BOOKS
(a)-Cook, David C.
Artbeat of America
Greenacre Workshop
Knight George Pub.
McBeth Corp.
Rainbow Publishers
Serendipity Puzzle
Warner Press
World Library Pub.

AUDIOTAPES
(a)-Tyndale House
(a)-W Publishing
AMG Publishers
AMG Software
Eldridge Plays
Fair Havens
McRuffy Press
Zondervan Audio/Video

BANNERS
Serendipity Puzzle
World Library Pub.

BOARD GAMES/GAMES
(a)-Cook, David C.
(a)-Tyndale House
Bethel Publishing
Biblequest
Carson-Dellosa
Goode Games
Knight George Pub.
Master Books
Mission City Press
Morris, William
Rainbow Publishers
Review and Herald
Salt Works
Serendipity Puzzle
Standard Publishing
Talicor

The Learning Journey Intl.
WinePress

BOOKMARKS
Ashleigh Manor
Blue Mountain Arts
Celebrate Your Faith
Christian Art Gifts
Hermitage Art
Lorenz
Serendipity Puzzle
Warner Press
World Library Pub.

BULLETINS
Hermitage Art

CALENDARS/DAILY JOURNALS
(a)-Tyndale House
Abingdon Press
African Amer. Expressions
Artbeat of America
Barbour
Blue Mountain Arts
C4Yourself Greetings
Group Publishing
McBeth Corp.
Neibauer Press
Serendipity Puzzle
Women of the Promise
World Library Pub.

CD-ROMs
(a)-Cook, David C.
AMG Publishers
AMG Video/CD
CarePoint Publishing
Fair Havens
Georgetown Univ. Press
Group Publishing
Lighthouse Publishing
Our Sunday Visitor

Vida Entertainment
World Library Pub.

CHARTS
Rose Publishing
Serendipity Puzzle
Warner Press

CLIP ART*
Libros Liguori

COMIC BOOKS
(a)-Nelson, Thomas
Lighthouse Publishing
Serendipity Puzzle
Vida Entertainment
ZonderKidz

COMPUTER GAMES
(a)-Cook, David C.
Dean Press, Robbie
Grupo Nelson
Knight George Pub.
Lighthouse Publishing
Lion and Lamb
Vida Entertainment
WinePress
Wisdom Tree

COMPUTER SOFTWARE
(a)-Regal
AMG Publishers
AMG Software
B & H Software
Baker Software
Ellis Enterprises
Libros Liguori
Logos Bible Software
NavPress Software
Olive Tree/Software
Resource Public.
Wisdom Tree
World Library Pub.
Zondervan Digital

DVDs
Ambassador Intl.
Anglicans United
Candlelight Media
Vida Entertainment
Wacky World
WinePress
World Library Pub.

GIFT BOOKS
(a)-B & H Publishing
(a)-Baker Books
(a)-Ballantine
(a)-Cook, David C.
(a)-Countryman, J.
(a)-HarperOne
(a)-Hay House
(a)-Regal
ACTA Publications
Adams Media
Ambassador Books
American Binding
Barbour
Black Forest
Blue Mountain Arts
Booklocker.com
Book Publishers Net.
Brown Books
Christian Writer's Ebook
Contemporary Drama
Creation House
DCTS Publishers
Dean Press, Robbie
Deep River Books
Dimensions for Living
Editorial Portavoz
Eerdmans Pub., Wm. B.
Elderberry Press
Essence
Evergreen Press
Fairway Press
Faith Communications
GRQ
Guardian Angel
Hidden Brook Press
Holy Fire Publishing
Howard Books
IMD Press
Lift Every Voice
Lighthouse Publishing

Mission City Press
Monarch Books
New Leaf
One World
Our Sunday Visitor
Pleasant Word
Providence House
Ravenhawk Books
Review and Herald
Rose Publishing
Salt Works
Serendipity Puzzle
Tate Publishing
Trafford Publishing
Vida Entertainment
WinePress
Word Alive
World Library Pub.

GIFT/NOVELTY ITEMS
(a)-Cook, David C.
Abingdon Press
African Amer. Expressions
Artbeat of America
Artful Greetings
Ashleigh Manor
Blue Mountain Arts
Carpentree
Celebrate Your Faith
Christian Art Gifts
Design Design
Destiny Image
Dexsa
Hermitage Art
Houghton Designs, Jody
Lawrence Co., James
Lion and Lamb
Lorenz
McBeth Corp.
Mission City Press
P. Graham Dunn
Red Letter 9
Salt Works
Serendipity Puzzle
Talicor

GREETING BOOKS
Blue Mountain Arts
Christian Art Gifts
Design Design

Houghton Designs, Jody
Serendipity Puzzle

JEWELRY*
Cross Gift Division
McBeth Corp.
Witness
Yz Company Inc.

MAGNETS
African Amer. Expressions
Blue Mountain Arts
Design Design
Houghton Designs, Jody
Lawrence Co., James
World Library Pub.

MUGS
Christian Art Gifts
Lawrence Co., James

NOTECARDS
Creative Christian Gifts

PLAQUES
Houghton Designs, Jody
Lawrence Co., James

POSTCARDS
Abingdon Press
Houghton Designs, Jody
Lorenz
Serendipity Puzzle
Warner Press
World Library Pub.

POSTERS
ArtBeats
InspirationArt
Life Cycle Books
Lorenz
Serendipity Puzzle
World Library Pub.

POWERPOINT*
Rose Publishing

PUZZLES
Biblequest
Christian Art Gifts
Heritage Puzzle
Rainbow Publishers
Serendipity Puzzle

Talicor
The Learning Journey Intl.

STATIONERY
African Amer. Expressions
Artbeat of America
Design Design
Lorenz
Serendipity Puzzle

STORY CARDS*
BibleQuest

SUNDAY BULLETINS
Anchor Wallace
Serendipity Puzzle
Warner Press
World Library Pub.

TOYS
BibleQuest
Mission City Press
Standard Publishing
Talicor

T-SHIRTS/APPAREL
Be One Sportswear
Eagles Wings
Jesus In Me Unltd.
Know Him
Living Epistles
Not of This World
Red Letter 9
SonTeez
Witness
World Library Pub.

VIDEOS/VIDEO GAMES
(a)-Cook, David C.
(a)-Regal
(a)-Tyndale House
(a)-W Publishing
Abingdon Press
Alpha Omega
AMG Video/CD
Anglicans United
Candlelight Media

Cloud Ten
Dallas Christian Video
Destiny Image
Doughten Films, Russ
Editorial Unilit
Fair Havens
Focus on the Family
Group Publishing
Howard Books
Left Behind Games Inc./
    Digital Praise
Master Books
Nelson Videos, Tommy
Pauline Books
Prophecy Publications
Tyndale Family Video
Vision Video
Wacky World
Wisdom Tree
Zondervan Audio/Video

PART 4

Helps for Writers

10

Christian Writers' Conferences and Workshops

Visit the following Websites for information on these and other conferences available across the country: www.freelancewriting.com/conferences or www.screenwriter.com/insider/WritersCalendar .html. Link to these conference Websites at www.stuartmarket.com. Because many of the conferences had not yet set 2011 dates, you will need to check their Websites for exact dates.

+ Indicates a new listing

ALABAMA

SOUTHERN CHRISTIAN WRITERS CONFERENCE. Tuscaloosa/First Baptist Church; early June 2011. Contact: Joanne Sloan, SCWC, PO Box 1106, Northport AL 35473. (205) 333-8603. E-mail: SCWCworkshop@bellsouth.net. Website: http://web.mac.com/wmdsloan/iweb/SCWC. Editors/agents in attendance. Attendance: 200+.

ARIZONA

AMERICAN CHRISTIAN WRITERS PHOENIX CONFERENCE. Grace Inn; October 28-29, 2011. Contact: Reg A. Forder, Box 110390, Nashville TN 37222. Toll-free (800) 21-WRITE. E-mail: ACWriters@aol.com. Website: www.ACWriters.com. Speakers: Chip MacGregor, Gail Martin, Steve Laube & Donna Goodrich. Attendance: 40-80.

CATHOLIC SCREENWRITERS WORKSHOP. Tucson; March 2011. Contact: Fr. Tom Santa, CssR, 7101 W. Picture Rocks Rd., Tucson AZ 85743-9645. Toll-free (866) 737-5751. (520) 744-3400. Fax (520) 744-8021. E-mail: office@desertrenewal.org. Website: www.desertrenewal.org. See Website for additional writers' events.

+HOW TO WRITE YOUR BOOK AND GET IT PUBLISHED. Location and date not set at this time. Contact: Larry Davis, PO Box 2825, Peoria AZ 85380. (623) 337-8710 or (623) 206-7144. E-mail: ldavis@intermediapub.com. Website: www.intermediapub.com. Speakers: Larry Davis and Eddie Smith. Editors in attendance.

ARKANSAS

SILOAM SPRINGS WRITERS' WORKSHOP. Siloam Springs; September (probably 3rd Saturday). Contact: Margaret Weathers, 716 W. University St., Siloam Springs AR 72761. (479) 524-6598. E-mail: rogeneo@centurytel.net. Sponsors a contest (6 categories of poetry & 6 categories of prose). No editors/agents in attendance. No scholarships. Attendance: 30.

CALIFORNIA

ACT ONE: WRITING PROGRAM. Hollywood; summer of 2011. Contact: Vicki Peterson, 2690 N. Beachwood Dr., Hollywood CA 90068. (323) 464-0815. Fax (323) 468-0315. E-mail: info@ actoneprogram.com. Website: www.ActOneProgram.com. These are intensive training sessions for screenwriters, taught by professionals working in Hollywood. Offers track for television writers. No editors/agents in attendance. Limited to 30 students (by application).

ANTELOPE VALLEY CHRISTIAN WRITERS' CONFERENCE. Lancaster (near Los Angeles); June 20-21, 2011. Presented by High Desert Christian Writer's Guild and Quartz Hill School of Theology. Faculty panel, group discounts, one free critique. Contact: Steve Hutson, dir., 4083 W. Avenue L, Ste. 255, Lancaster CA 93536. (661) 722-4896. Toll-free fax (866) 501-4280. E-mail: info@avwrit ers.com. Website:www.avwriters.com.

BIOLA MEDIA CONFERENCE. La Mirada; April or May 2011 (date varies). Contact: Craig Detweiler, Biola University, 13800 Biola Ave., La Mirada CA 90639. Toll-free (866) 334-2266. Website: www .biolamedia.com.

CASTRO VALLEY CHRISTIAN WRITERS SEMINAR. Castro Valley; February 2011. Contact: Pastor Jon Drury, 19300 Redwood Rd., Castro Valley CA 94546-3465. (510) 886-6300. Fax (510) 581-5022. E-mail: jdrury@redwoodchapel.org. Website: www.christianwriter.org. No editors/agents in attendance. Offers full or partial scholarships. Attendance: 200.

MOUNT HERMON CHRISTIAN SONGWRITERS CONFERENCE. Near Santa Cruz; August 29-September 1, 2011 (always the Monday-Thursday before Labor Day). Call (888)MH-CAMPS or visit Website: www.mounthermon.org/songwriters.

MOUNT HERMON CHRISTIAN WRITERS CONFERENCE. Mount Hermon (near Santa Cruz); April 15-19, 2011; March 30-April 3, 2012. Offers a Career Track for professional writers (details on Website); and a teen track. Contact: Rachel A. Williams, Box 413, Mount Hermon CA 95041-0413. (831) 430-1238. Fax (831) 335-9413. E-mail: rachel.williams@mounthermon.org. Website: www .mounthermon.org/writers (no brochure; all details on Website December 1). Keynote speaker for 2011: Bill Myers; for 2012: Liz Curtis Higgs. Many editors and agents in attendance. Offers partial scholarships on tuition only. Cash awards. Attendance: 425.

MOUNT HERMON HEAD-START MENTORING CLINIC. Mount Hermon, April 13-14, 2011. This mentoring session is held the two days prior to the regular spring conference. See the listing for Mount Hermon Christian Writers Conference for details or www.mounthermon.org.

NATIONAL CHRISTIAN WRITERS CONFERENCE. San Diego; March 2011. Contact: Antonio L. Crawford, PO Box 1458, National City CA 91951-1458. (619) 791-5810. E-mail: ncwcsd@yahoo .com. Website: www.nationalchristianwritersconference.com.

ORANGE COUNTY CHRISTIAN WRITERS FELLOWSHIP SPRING WRITERS DAY. Irvine; April 2011. Contact: John DeSimone, dir.; Peg Matthews, ed., PO Box 5056, Fullerton CA 92838. (714) 538-7070. Fax (949) 458-1807. E-mail: editor@occwf.org. Website: www.occwf.org. Editors and possibly agents in attendance. Offers full and partial scholarships. See Website for list of faculty and conference date. Attendance: 100-150+.

SAN DIEGO CHRISTIAN WRITER'S GUILD FALL CONFERENCE. San Diego; September 2011. Contact: Jennie Gillespie, PO Box 270403, San Diego CA 92198. (760) 294-3269. E-mail: info@ sandiegocwg.org. Website: www.sandiegocwg.org. Offers an advanced track. Editors/agents in attendance. Offers some scholarships. Attendance: 200.

SANTA BARBARA CHRISTIAN WRITERS CONFERENCE. Westmont College; October 2011. Contact: Opal Mae Dailey, PO Box 40860, Santa Barbara CA 93140. Phone/fax (805) 682-0316 (call first for fax). E-mail: opalmaedailey@aol.com. Website: www.sbwritersconference.com. Offers scholarships to students. Attendance: 50.

SOCIETY OF CHILDREN'S BOOK WRITERS & ILLUSTRATORS CONFERENCE IN CHILDREN'S LITERATURE. New York City, early February 2011; Los Angeles, early August 2011. Society of

Children's Book Writers & Illustrators. Contact: Lin Oliver, 8271 Beverly Blvd., Los Angeles CA 90048. (323) 782-1010. Fax (323) 782-1892. E-mail: scbwi@scbwi.org. Website: www.scbwi.org. Includes a track for professionals. Editors/agents in attendance. Attendance: 900.

+SIERRA FOOTHILLS CHRISTIAN WRITERS CONFERENCE. Auburn; October 2011. Contact: Debbie Fuller Thomas, PO Box 7013, Auburn CA 95604. (530) 889-9760. E-mail: sierrafoothillsconference@gmail.com. Website: http://sierrafoothillsconference.com. Affiliated with Novel Matters. Attendance: 65.

WRITER'S SYMPOSIUM BY THE SEA. San Diego/Point Loma Nazarene University; February 2011. Contact: Dean Nelson, Professor, Journalism Dept., PLNU, 3900 Lomaland Dr., San Diego CA 92106. (619) 849-2592. Fax (619) 849-2566. E-mail: deannelson@pointloma.edu. Website: www.pointloma.edu/writers. No editors/agents in attendance. No scholarships. Attendance: 500.

COLORADO

AD LIB CHRISTIAN ARTS RETREAT. Franciscan Retreat Center; Colorado Springs; September 2011 (tentative). Contact: Prof. Richard Terrell, 6905 Forest Lake Blvd., Lincoln NE 68516. (402) 486-4198. Cell (402) 440-8851. E-mail: richard.terrell@doane.edu. Website: www.adlibchristianarts.org. Gather for Sabbath, fellowship, display/discuss art/writing projects, and work on what we love to do. Guest artists are the editors of *Ruminate*, CO-based arts journal. No working editors/agents. Attendance: limited to 20.

COLORADO CHRISTIAN WRITERS CONFERENCE. Estes Park; May 11-14, 2011 at the YMCA of the Rockies. Director: Marlene Bagnull, LittD, 951 Anders Rd., Lansdale PA 19446. Phone/fax (484) 991-8581. E-mail: mbagnull@aol.com. Website: www.writehisanswer.com/Colorado. Conferees choose 6 hour-long workshops from 42 offered or a clinic (beginning novelists, advanced novelists, nonfiction, possibly one more—by application) plus one 6.5-hour continuing session from 8 offered. Four 15-minute one-on-one appointments, paid critiques, editors' panels, and general sessions. Early-bird workshops Wednesday afternoon. Teens Write Saturday afternoon, plus teens are welcome to attend the entire conference at 60% off. Contest for published and not-yet-published writers awards—two 50% off 2012 conference registration fee (registered conferees only). Faculty of 60 authors, editors, and agents. Attendance: 260.

GLEN EYRIE FICTION WRITER'S CONFERENCE. Colorado Springs; January 2011. Contact: Craig Dunham, 3820 N. 30th, Colorado Springs CO 80904. Toll-free (800) 944-4536. (719) 634-0808. Fax (719) 272-7448. Website: www.gleneyrie.org. Some editors/agents in attendance. Attendance: 100. Check Website for conferences and dates.

JERRY B. JENKINS CHRISTIAN WRITERS GUILD WRITING FOR THE SOUL CONFERENCE. Grand Hyatt, Denver; February 10-13, 2011. Sponsored by the Jerry B. Jenkins Christian Writers Guild. Host: Jerry B. Jenkins. Speakers for 2011 include: Liz Curtis Higgs, Ken Davis, and McNair Wilson. Appointments with publishers' reps & agents. More than 30 editors and agents in attendance. Payment plans available. Special meal rates offered for nonparticipating spouses or parents of teens. General sessions with national keynote speakers and in-depth workshops on 6 tracks. Contact: Admissions Manager, 5525 N. Union Blvd., Ste. 200, Colorado Springs CO 80918. Toll-free (866) 495-5177. Fax (719) 495-5181. E-mail: ContactUs@christianwritersguild.com. Website: www.christianwritersguild.com. Offers partial scholarships. Attendance: 400.

+SOUTHWEST CHRISTIAN WRITERS' 2011 WRITE FOR HIS GLORY CONFERENCE. Hesperus; September 2011. Contact: Barbara Kugle or Connie Peters, 240 Ash, Cortez CO 81321. (970) 564-9449 or (970) 946-1900. E-mail: barbkugle@gmail.com. Speaker: James Watkins. No editors or agents in attendance. Offers full and partial scholarships. Attendance: 30.

CONNECTICUT

WESLEYAN WRITERS CONFERENCE. Wesleyan University/Middletown; 55th year; June 2011 (5-day, long-weekend program; see Website for date). Contact: Anne Greene, Director, Wesleyan Writers Conference, Wesleyan University, 294 High St., Middletown CT 06459. (860) 685-3604. Fax (860) 685-2441. E-mail: agreene@wesleyan.edu. Website: www.wesleyan.edu/writers. Both new and experienced writers welcome. Editors/agents in attendance. Offers fellowship and scholarship awards. Attendance: 100.

FLORIDA

AMERICAN CHRISTIAN WRITERS ORLANDO CONFERENCE. November 19, 2011. Contact: Reg A. Forder, Box 110390, Nashville TN 37222. Toll-free (800) 21-WRITE. E-mail: ACWriters@aol.com. Website: www.ACWriters.com. Speaker: Roger Palms. Attendance: 40-80.

+DEEP THINKERS RETREAT. Orlando FL; February. Contact: Susan May Warren, PO Box 1290, Grand Marais MN 55604. (218) 387-2853. E-mail: retreats@mybooktherapy.com. Website: http:// deepthinkers.mybooktherapy.com. Offers an advanced track. Speaker: Susan May Warren. Agents in attendance. No scholarships. Each retreat attendee receives a private consultation about his or her writing. If ready for advanced writing techniques we teach them that. Sponsors the My Book Therapy Frasier Contest. Attendance: 16.

FLORIDA CHRISTIAN WRITERS CONFERENCE. Lake Yale Conference Center; Leesburg FL; March 2-6, 2011. Contact: Billie Wilson, 2344 Armour Ct., Titusville FL 32780. (321) 269-5831. Fax (321) 267-9654. E-mail: billiewilson@cfl.rr.com. Website: www.flwriters.org. Offers advanced track (15 hours of class time—by application only) & teen track. Editors and agents in attendance. Offers full & partial scholarships. Offers awards in 11 categories. Awards open to registrants; mss submitted to conference for review are considered for an award. Attendance: 275.

GEORGIA

AMERICAN CHRISTIAN WRITERS ATLANTA CONFERENCE. July 8-9, 2011. Contact: Reg Forder, Box 110390, Nashville TN 37222. Toll-free (800) 21-WRITE. E-mail: ACWriters@aol.com. Website: www.ACWriters.com. Speakers: Lin Johnson, Linda Canup & Bob Hostetler. Attendance: 40-80.

CATCH THE WAVE WRITERS CONFERENCE. Marietta; September 2011. See Website for conference details: www.christianauthorsguild.org. Sponsors a short-story contest and an article contest. Editors/agents in attendance. No scholarships. Attendance: 60.

EAST METRO ATLANTA CHRISTIAN WRITERS CONFERENCE. Covington; July 2011. Contact: Colleen Jackson, PO Box 2896, Covington GA 30015. (404) 444-7514. E-mail: cjac401992@aol .com. Website: www.emacw.org. Check Website for location and details.

GEORGIA CHRISTIAN WRITERS' SPRING FESTIVAL. Atlanta area; May 7, 2011 (first Saturday in May each year). Contact: Lloyd Blackwell, 3049 Scott Rd. N.E., Marietta GA 30066. (770) 421-1203. E-mail: lloydblackwell@worldnet.att.net.

+INTERNATIONAL CHRISTIAN RETAIL SHOW. (Held in a different location each year.); Atlanta; July 10-13, 2011. Contact: Scott Graham, Box 62000, Colorado Springs CO 80962-2000. Toll-free (800) 252-1950. (719) 265-9895. Fax (719) 272-3510. E-mail: info@cbaonline.org. Website: www.christianretailshow.com. Entrance badges available through book publishers or Christian bookstores. Attendance: 8,000.

SOUTHEASTERN WRITERS ASSN. ANNUAL WORKSHOP. St. Simons Island; June 2011. Contact: Sheila Hudson, registrar, 161 Woodstone Dr., Athens GA 30605. E-mails listed on Website: www

.southeasternwriters.com. Attendance: limited to 100. Sponsors contests on the Website. Agents/ editors in attendance. Evaluations with 3-day registrations.

ILLINOIS

KARITOS CHRISTIAN ARTS CONFERENCE. Bolingbrook; July or August 2011. Contact: Bob Hay, 1122 Brentwood Ln., Wheaton IL 60189. E-mail: bob@karitos.com. Website: www.karitos.com. Features workshops in all areas of the arts, including writing. Also general sessions and evening celebrations. Attendance: 300-400.

WRITE-TO-PUBLISH CONFERENCE. Wheaton (Chicago area); June 8-11, 2011. Contact: Lin Johnson, 9118 W. Elmwood Dr., #1G, Niles IL 60714-5820. (847) 296-3964. Fax (847) 296-0754. E-mail: lin@WriteToPublish.com. Website: www.WriteToPublish.com. Offers freelance career track (prerequisite: 1 published book). Speaker: Robin Jones Gunn. Majority of faculty are editors; also has agents. Offers full and partial scholarships. Attendance: 250.

INDIANA

AMERICAN CHRISTIAN WRITERS FORT WAYNE CONFERENCE. Clarion Downtown; April 1-2, 2011. Contact: Reg A. Forder, Box 110390, Nashville TN 37222. Toll-free (800) 21-WRITE. E-mail: ACWriters@aol.com. Website: www.ACWriters.com. Speakers: Dennis Hensley, Terry White, Bob Hostetler & Linda Wade. Attendance: 40-80.

BETHEL COLLEGE CHRISTIAN WRITERS' WORKSHOP. Bethel College/Mishawaka; Spring 2011. Contact: English Dept. Chair, 1001 W. McKinley Ave., Mishawaka IN 46544. (574) 257-3427. Website: www.BethelCollege.edu/writersworkshop. Editors sometimes in attendance; no agents. Sometimes offers full or partial scholarships. Attendance: 130.

EARLHAM SCHOOL OF RELIGION: THE MINISTRY OF WRITING COLLOQUIUM. Richmond; November 4-5, 2011. Contact: Susan Yanos, Earlham School of Religion, 228 College Ave., Richmond IN 47374-4095. Toll-free (800) 432-1377. (765) 983-1420. Fax (765) 983-1688. E-mail: yanossu@earlham.edu. Website: www.esr.earlham.edu. Editors in attendance. No scholarships. Attendance: 100.

MIDWEST WRITERS WORKSHOP. Muncie/Ball State University Alumni Center; July 28-30, 2011 (always the last Thursday, Friday, and Saturday of July). Contact: Dept. of Journalism, Ball State University, Muncie IN 47306-0484. Director: Jama Kehoe Bigger. (765) 282-1055. E-mail: midwest writers@yahoo.com. Website: www.midwestwriters.org. Sponsors a contest. Editors/agents in attendance. Offers full scholarships. Attendance: 150.

+WRITE 2 IGNITE! CONFERENCE. 1001 Bethel Cir., Mishawaka IN 46545; February 18-19, 2011. Contact: Cindy Lynn Jacobs (jacobsc@bethelcollege.edu). (574) 257-3409. E-mail: write2ignite@ jeanmatthewhall.com. Website: www.write2ignite.com. For Christian writers of children's literature (theme may change from year to year). Attendance: 30-50.

IOWA

+AMERICAN CHRISTIAN WRITERS DES MOINES CONFERENCE. August 13, 2011. Contact: Reg A. Forder, Box 110390, Nashville TN 37222. Toll-free (800) 21-WRITE. E-mail: ACWriters@aol .com. Website: www.ACWriters.com. Speaker: Jim Watkins. Attendance: 30-45.

CEDAR FALLS CHRISTIAN WRITERS' WORKSHOP. Riverview Conference Center/Cedar Falls; June 8-11, 2011. Contact: Jean Vaux, 1703 Sunnyside Dr., Cedar Falls IA 50613-4644. (319) 277-

7444. Fax (318) 277-1721. E-mail: vauxcom@cfu.net. Website: www.shellybeachonline.com. No editor/agents in attendance. Offers full & partial scholarships. Attendance: 35.

CHRISTIAN WRITERS SEMINAR. Arnolds Park; September 2011. Contact: Denise Triggs, PO Box 281, Okoboji IA 51355. (712) 332-7191. E-mail: waterfalls42@hotmail.com. Website: www.water fallsretreats.com. No editors/agents in attendance. No scholarships. Attendance: 20.

IOWA SUMMER WRITING FESTIVAL. University of Iowa/Iowa City; June/July 2011. This is a general writer's conference that comes highly recommended for good, solid instruction. Contact: Amy Margolis, Iowa Summer Writing Festival, C215 Seashore Hall, University of Iowa, Iowa City IA 52242-5000. (319) 335-4160. Fax (319) 335-4743. E-mail: iswfestival@uiowa.edu. Website: www.uiowa .edu/~iswfest. For two months, June and July, you can sign up for either one-week workshops or weekend workshops on a wide variety of topics. Write for a catalog of offerings (available in February).

QUAD-CITIES CHRISTIAN WRITERS' CONFERENCE. Eldridge; April 8-9, 2011. Contact: Twila Belk, 4350 Tanglewood Rd., Bettendorf IA 52722. (563) 332-1622. E-mail: Twilabelk@mchsi.com. Website: www.qccwc.com. Speakers: Cynthia Ruchti, Jim Pence, and others. No editors or agents in attendance. Offers full scholarships. Attendance 100.

KANSAS

CALLED TO WRITE. Pittsburg; April 1-2, 2011. Contact: Carol Russell, 894—165th St., Fort Scott KS 66701. (620) 547-2472. E-mail: rlrussell@ckt.net. Website: www.christianwritersfellowship .blogspot.com. Contest for attendees only. Offers full and partial scholarships. Attendance: 75.

KENTUCKY

+AMERICAN CHRISTIAN WRITERS LOUISVILLE CONFERENCE. September 10, 2011. Contact: Reg Forder, Box 110390, Nashville TN 37222. Toll-free (800) 21-WRITE. E-mail: ACWriters@aol .com. Website: www.ACWriters.com. Speaker: Dennis Hensley. Attendance: 40-80.

KENTUCKY CHRISTIAN WRITERS CONFERENCE. Elizabethtown; June 2011. E-mail: registrar@ kychristianwriters.com. Website: www.kychristianwriters.com. Editors in attendance. Workshops and appointments with faculty. Attendance: 100.

MASSACHUSETTS

CAPE COD ANNUAL SUMMER WRITERS CONFERENCE. Craigville Conference Center; third week in August 14-19, 2011. Contact: Nancy Rubin Stuart, conf. dir., PO Box 408, Osterville MA 02655-0408. (508) 420-0200. Fax (508) 420-0212. E-mail: writers@capecodwriterscenter.org. Website: www.capecodwriterscenter.org. Editors, publishers, and agents in attendance. Offering 5-day workshops, as well as shorter courses in all genres. Manuscript evaluations available. Deadline for registration is July 15. No registration fee for CCWC members; for nonmembers $35. Class prices vary.

MICHIGAN

AMERICAN CHRISTIAN WRITERS GRAND RAPIDS CONFERENCE. June 24-25, 2011. Contact: Reg Forder, Box 110390, Nashville TN 37222. Toll-free (800) 21-WRITE. E-mail: ACWriters@ aol.com. Website: www.ACWriters.com. Speakers: Dave Branson, Jim Watkins & Bob Hostetler. Attendance: 40-80.

+FAITH WRITERS CONFERENCE. Livonia; August 12-13, 2011. Contact: Deb Porter, C/O 15630 Williams, Livonia MI 48154. E-mail: dporter@faithwriters.com. Website: www.faithwriters.com/ page-turner.php. Attendance 75-100.

FESTIVAL OF FAITH & WRITING. Grand Rapids; April 2012 (held every other year). Contact: Shelly LeMahieu Dunn, 3201 Burton S.E., Grand Rapids MI 49546. (616) 526-6770. E-mail: ffw@calvin .edu. Website: www.calvin.edu/festival. Editors/agents in attendance; no scholarships. Attendance: 1,800.

MARANATHA CHRISTIAN WRITERS' SEMINAR. Maranatha Bible & Missionary Conference/ Muskegon; September 26-30, 2011; September 24-28, 2012. Contact: Verna Kokmeyer, 4759 Lake Harbor Rd., Muskegon MI 49441-5299. (231) 798-2161. Fax (231) 798-2152. E-mail: info@write withpurpose.org. Website: www.WriteWithPurpose.org. 2011 Speakers include: Robin Jones Gunn and Sally Stuart. Offers tracks for advanced writers and teens. Editors/agents in attendance. Offers partial scholarships. Attendance: 125.

MINNESOTA

AMERICAN CHRISTIAN WRITERS MINNEAPOLIS CONFERENCE. August 12-13, 2011. Contact: Reg Forder, Box 110390, Nashville TN 37222. Toll-free (800) 21-WRITE. Website: www.ACWriters .com. Speakers: Lin Johson, Joyce Ellis & Tama Westman. Attendance: 40-80.

MINNESOTA CHRISTIAN WRITERS GUILD SPRING & FALL SEMINARS. Minneapolis/St. Paul; spring seminar, March or April 2011; fall seminar, October or November 2011. Contact: Mrs. Pat Van der Merwe, 19820 Olde Sturbridge Rd., Corcoran MN 55340. (763) 478-6145. E-mail: pdvdm@ comcast.net. Website: www.mnchristianwriters.org. No editors/agents in attendance; no scholarships. Attendance: 50.

+STORYCRAFTERS RETREAT. Minneapolis MN; October 2011. Contact: Susan May Warren, PO Box 1290, Grand Marais MN 55604. (218) 387-2853. E-mail: retreats@mybooktherapy.com. Website: http://storycrafters.mybooktherapy.com. This retreat is for writers at all levels. We focus on storycrafting—starting with an idea, and leaving with a plotted story. Speaker: Susan May Warren. Agents in attendance; no editors. Sponsors the My Book Therapy Frasier Contest (winner attends retreat for free). Attendance: 16.

THE WRITING ACADEMY SEMINAR. Mount Olivet Retreat Center, south of Minneapolis; July 28-August 1, 2011. Sponsors year-round correspondence writing program and annual seminar. Contact: Nancy Remmert, 312 St. Louis Ave., St. Louis MO 63135-2756. (314) 522-3718. E-mail: rnremmert@att.net. Website: www.wams.org. Sponsors a writing contest open to members (rules are posted on Website). No editors or agents in attendance. No scholarships. Attendance: 30.

WRITING SEMINARS/NORTH HENNEPIN COMMUNITY COLLEGE. Minneapolis (7411 85th Ave. N., Brooklyn Park MN 55445); new classes every Monday and Thursday, year round. Instructor: Louise B. Wyly. Offers 27 different writing courses for all skill levels. Topics include Fiction Writing, Novel Writing, Mystery Novels, Writing for Children and Teens, The Artist's Way, Memoirs, and other beginning and advanced courses. Offers a Creative Writing Certificate and an Advanced Creative Writing Certificate. Contact: Louise Wyly, 6315—55th Ave. N., Minneapolis MN 55428-3581, or call (763) 533-6207. E-mail: Lsnowbunny@aol.com. Website: www.nhcc.edu. Go to adult education classes/creative writing.

MISSOURI

+AMERICAN CHRISTIAN WRITERS SPRINGFIELD CONFERENCE. Lamplighter North; August 6, 2011. Contact: Reg A. Forder, Box 110390, Nashville TN 37222. Toll-free (800) 21-WRITE. E-mail: ACWriters@aol.com. Website: www.ACWriters.com. Attendance: 40-80.

HEART OF AMERICA CHRISTIAN WRITERS NETWORK CONFERENCES. Kansas City; November 2011, check Website for dates of additional events. Contact: Jeanette Littleton, 3706 N.E. Shady Lane

Dr., Gladstone MO 64119. Phone/fax (816) 459-8016. E-mail: HACWN@earthlink.net. Website: www.HACWN.org. Offers classes for new and advanced writers. Editors/agents in attendance. Contest details on brochure. Attendance: 125.

NEBRASKA

+MY THOUGHTS EXACTLY WRITERS' RETREAT. Near Omaha; Spring 2011. Contact: C.A. Paden, PO Box 1073, Fremont NE 68925. (408) 727-6508. A self-guided writers' retreat with creative, inspirational, and writing prompts.

NEW HAMPSHIRE

WRITERS WORKSHOPS BY MARY EMMA ALLEN. Taught on request by writers' groups, conferences, schools, and libraries. Topics include: Workshops for Young Writers (for schools and home-parenting groups); Writing Your Family Stories; Blogging for Fun, Profit, & Promotion; Scrapbooking Your Stories. Contact: Mary Emma Allen (instructor), 55 Binks Hill Rd., Plymouth NH 03264. (603) 536-2641. E-mail: me.allen@juno.com. Blogs: http://maryemmallen.blogspot.com, http://bookbag blog.blogspot.com.

NEW MEXICO

CLASS CHRISTIAN WRITER'S CONFERENCE. Ghost Ranch/Abiquiu; October 2011. Editors and agents in attendance. Contact: Linda Gilden, dir., PO Box 52103, Albuquerque NM 87181-2103. E-mail: kaeporter@gmail.com. Website: www.classeminars.org. Editors/agents in attendance. Partial scholarships. Attendance: 400.

THE GLEN WORKSHOP. St. John's College/Santa Fe; first full week in August 2011. Includes fiction, poetry, nonfiction, memoir, on-site landscape painting, figure drawing, collage and mixed media, and several master classes. Contact: Julie Mullins, 3307 Third Ave. W., Seattle WA 98119. (206) 281-2988 (Image). Fax (206) 281-2979 (Image). E-mail: image@imagejournal.org. Website: www. imagejournal.org/page/events/the-glen-workshop. Two Image editors; no agents in attendance. Offers partial scholarships. Attendance: 200.

+SOUTHWEST CHRISTIAN WRITERS STUDIO. Glorieta; May 1-5, 2011; May 2012. Contact: Alton Gansky, 9983 Rose Dr., Oak Hills CA 92344-0220. (760) 220-1075. E-mail: alton@ganskycom munications.com. Website: www.swcws.com. Offers an advanced track. Speakers: Chip MacGregor, Jack Cavanaugh, and others. No editors or agents in attendance. Sponsors a contest (details at www .brmcwc.com). Offers full and partial scholarships. Attendance: Limited to first 100 registrants.

SOUTHWEST WRITERS MINI WORKSHOPS. Albuquerque; various times during the year (check Website for dates). Contact: Conference Chair, 3721 Morris St. N.E., Ste. A, Albuquerque NM 87111-3611. (505) 265-9485. E-mail: swwriters@juno.com. Website: www.southwestwriters.com. General conference. Sponsors the Southwest Writers Contests annually and quarterly (see Website). Agents/editors in attendance. Attendance: 50.

NEW YORK

INTERNATIONAL CONFERENCE ON HUMOR, HOPE AND HEALING/THE POSITIVE POWER OF HUMOR AND CREATIVITY. Silver Bay NY; June 2011. General. Contact: Dr. Joel Goodman, 10 Madison Ave., Saratoga Springs NY 12866-3406. (518) 587-8770. E-mail: info@humorproject.com. Website: www.humorproject.com. We have a drawing for humorous anecdotes/stories that focus on the positive power of humor, how people were able to turn a negative situation into a laughing matter. Attendance: 400.

NORTH CAROLINA

+AMERICAN CHRISTIAN WRITERS GREENSBORO CONFERENCE. April 30, 2011. Contact: Reg A. Forder, Box 110390, Nashville TN 37222. Toll-free (800) 21-WRITE. E-mail: ACWriters@aol.com. Website: www.ACWriters.com. Speakers: Jim Watkins & Thomas Smith. Attendance: 30-45.

BLUE RIDGE MOUNTAINS CHRISTIAN WRITERS CONFERENCE. LifeWay Ridgecrest Conference Center; May 1-5, 2011; May 2012. Contact: Alton Gansky, 9983 Rose Dr., Oak Hills CA 92344-0220. (760) 220-1075. E-mail: alton@ganskycommunications.com. Website: www.brmcwc.com, or www .Lifeway.com/christianwriters. Offers an advanced track. Editors and agents in attendance. Sponsors a contest (details at www.brmcwc.com). Offers full and partial scholarships. Attendance: 350.

SHE SPEAKS CONFERENCE. Concord; July 22-24, 2011; July 20-22, 2012. Contact: LeAnn Rice, 616-G Matthews-Mint Hill Rd., Charlotte NC 28105. (704) 849-2270. Fax (704) 849-7267. E-mail: office@Proverbs31.org. Website: www.SheSpeaksConference.com. Editors/agents in attendance; sometimes offers scholarships. Offers some advance-level sessions. Attendance: 600.

OHIO

AMERICAN CHRISTIAN WRITERS COLUMBUS CONFERENCE. June 11, 2011. Hosted by Columbus Christian Writers Assn./Pat Zell, (937) 593-9207. Contact: Reg Forder, Box 110390, Nashville TN 37222. Toll-free (800) 21-WRITE. E-mail: ACWriters@aol.com. Website: www .ACWriters.com. Speaker: Jim Watkins. Attendance: 40-80.

NORTHWEST OHIO CHRISTIAN WRITERS ONE-DAY SEMINAR. Toledo; October 16, 2011 (tentative). Contact: Kathy Douglas, 5702 Angola Rd., Lot 139, Toledo OH 43615. (419) 867-0805. E-mail: mlka@toast.net. Website: www.katherinedouglas.com. No editors/agents in attendance; no scholarships. Attendance: 50.

NORTHWEST OHIO CHRISTIAN WRITERS SPRING 2-DAY RETREAT. Lial Retreat Center/ Whitehouse; late April, early May 2011. Contact: Shelley Lee. E-mail: shelleyrlee@gmail.com. Website: www.nwocw.org. Advance registration required. Attendance: about 12.

PEN TO PAPER LITERARY SYMPOSIUM. Dayton; October 1, 2011; October 6, 2012. Contact: Valerie L. Coleman, Pen of the Writer, 893 S. Main St., PMB 175, Englewood OH 45322. (937) 307-0760. E-mail: info@penofthewriter.com. Website: www.penofthewriter.com. Editors in attendance. No scholarships. Attendance: 30.

WRITE ON! WORKSHOP. Dayton; March 26, 2011; March 31, 2012. Contact: Valerie Coleman, Pen of the Writer, PMB 175—893 S. Main St., Dayton OH 45322. (937) 307-0760. Fax (515) 474-3643. E-mail: info@penofthewriter.com. Website: www.penofthewriter.com. Speakers: Valerie Coleman, Earth Jallow, Wendy Hart Beckman. Editors in attendance; no agents. No scholarships. Attendance: 30.

OKLAHOMA

AMERICAN CHRISTIAN WRITERS OKLAHOMA CITY CONFERENCE. La Quinta Hotel; March 25-26, 2011. Contact: Reg Forder, Box 110390, Nashville TN 37222. Toll-free (800) 21-WRITE. E-mail: ACWriters@aol.com. Website: www.ACWriters.com. Speakers: John Riddle, Cris Bolley & Rene Gutteridge. Attendance: 40-80.

OREGON

HEART TALK. A workshop for people beginning to speak or write for publication. Portland/Western Seminary; March 2011 (may not be held/see Website). Contact: Kenine Stein, Women's Center for Ministry, Western Seminary, 5511 S.E. Hawthorne Blvd., Portland OR 97215-3367. (503) 517-1931.

Fax (503) 517-1889. E-mail: wcm@westernseminary.edu. Website: www.westernseminary.edu/women. Beverly Hislop, exec. dir. of Women's Center for Ministry. Attendance: 100. Offers partial scholarships based on need. Conference alternates between writing one year and speaking the next. Workshops and editors/publicists available for consultation. Check Website for details. Future of this conference uncertain at this time.

OREGON CHRISTIAN WRITERS COACHING CONFERENCE. Canby (near Portland); late July/early August. Contact: Sue Miholer, 1075 Willow Lake Rd. N., Keizer OR 97303-5790. (503) 393-3356. E-mail: scregistration@oregonchristianwriters.org. Website: www.OregonChristianWriters .org. Includes about 7 hours of training under a specific coach/topic. Offers advanced track. Editors/agents in attendance. Offers partial working scholarships. Attendance: 250.

PENNSYLVANIA

+CATHOLIC WRITERS CONFERENCE. Valley Forge (location may vary); August 2011. Contact: Ann Lewis, conference coordinator. E-mail: annlewis@joesystems.com. Held in conjunction with the Catholic Marketing Network Trade Show.

GREATER PHILADELPHIA CHRISTIAN WRITERS CONFERENCE. Philadelphia Biblical University, Langhorne; August 4-6 or 11-13, 2011 (tentative). Founder and director: Marlene Bagnull, LittD, 951 Anders Rd., Lansdale, PA 19446. Phone/fax (484) 991-8581. E-mail: mbagnull@aol.com. Website: www.writehisanswer.com/Philadelphia. Conferees choose 6 hour-long workshops from 42 offered or a clinic by application (beginning novelists, advanced novelists, nonfiction) plus one 6.5-hour continuing session from 8 offered. Four 15-minute one-on-one appointments, paid critiques, editors panels, and general sessions. Contest (registered conferees only) awards 50% off 2012 conference registration to a published and not-yet-published conferee. Especially encourages African American writers. Faculty of 50-60 authors, editors, and agents. Attendance: 250.

HIGHLIGHTS FOUNDATION FOUNDERS WORKSHOPS. Honesdale; February-December 2011. Contact: Kent Brown, Highlights Foundation, 814 Court St., Honesdale PA 18431. (570) 253-1192. Fax (570) 253-0179. E-mail: contact@highlightsfoundation.org. Website: www.HighlightsFoundation .org. Editors and agents in attendance. Modest grants may be available. For children's writers. Targeted workshops that allow you to select a topic that fits your writing needs—from sports to nature, from magazine to books, from fiction to nonfiction, and from picture books to young adult novels. Offers a track for advanced writers. General.

HIGHLIGHTS FOUNDATION WRITERS WORKSHOP AT CHAUTAUQUA. Chautauqua NY; July 2011. Contact: Kent Brown, Highlights Foundation, 814 Court St., Honesdale PA 18431. (570) 253-1192. Fax (570) 253-0179. E-mail: contact@highlightsfoundation.org. Website: www.highlights foundation.org. For children's writers and illustrators. Week-long conference. Choose workshops for your level, genre, and interests. Offers full and partial scholarships (applications received through January 2011). Editors/agents in attendance. General conference. Attendance 100.

MERCER COUNTY ANNUAL ONE-DAY WRITERS' WORKSHOP. (Sponsored by St. David's Writers' Conference); Stoneboro; April 20, 2011. Contact: Gloria Clover, 26 Everbreeze Dr., Hadley PA 16130, (724) 253-2635; gloworm@windstream.net. Websites: www.gloriaclover.com; www .stdavidswriters.com; www.writingsuccess.info. Teaching and motivational. Sponsors a contest and manuscript critique. No scholarships. Attendance: 120.

MONTROSE CHRISTIAN WRITERS CONFERENCE. Montrose; July 24-29, 2011. Patti Souder, dir.; contact: Donna Kosik, Montrose Bible Conference, 5 Locust St., Montrose PA 18801-1112. (570) 278-1001. Fax (570) 278-3061. E-mail: mbc@montrosebible.org. Website: www.montrosebible

.org. Tracks for advanced writers and teens (some years). Editors/agents in attendance. Attendance: 100. Provides a few partial scholarships.

ST. DAVIDS CHRISTIAN WRITERS' CONFERENCE. Grove City College, Grove City; June 2011 & 2012. Lora Zill, director. Contact: Audrey Stallsmith, registrar, 87 Pines Rd. E., Hadley PA 16130-1019. (724) 253-2738. E-mail: registrar@stdavidswriters.com. Website: www.stdavidswriters.com. Offers track for advanced writers. Contest for participants; guidelines on Website. Editors in attendance. Offers partial scholarships. See Website for information on their Writers' Colony. Attendance: 60-70.

SUSQUEHANNA VALLEY WRITERS WORKSHOP. Lewisburg; October 8, 2011. Contact: Marsha Hubler, 1833 Dock Hill Rd., Middleburg PA 17842. (570) 837-0002. (570) 374-8700. E-mail: ckwriter@evenlink.com. Website: www.marshahubler.com. Offers an advanced track. Editors/agents in attendance. Offers full and partial scholarships. Attendance: 60.

SOUTH CAROLINA

CAROLINA CHRISTIAN WRITERS WORKSHOP. Greenville; March 18-19, 2011. Contact: Elva Martin, 104 Oak Knoll Ter., Anderson SC 29625-2507. (864) 314-0804. E-mail: elvamartinministries@charter.net. Website: www.upstatescchristianwriters.com. Offers track for advanced writers. Sponsors a contest (see Website for details). May have editors/agents in attendance. Offers partial & full scholarships. Attendance: 85.

TENNESSEE

AMERICAN CHRISTIAN WRITERS MEMPHIS CONFERENCE. First Baptist Church; May 21, 2011. Contact: Reg A. Forder, Box 110390, Nashville TN 37222. Toll-free (800) 21-WRITE. E-mail: ACWriters@aol.com. Website: www.ACWriters.com. Speakers: Don Aycock & Marylane Koch. Attendance: 40-80.

AMERICAN CHRISTIAN WRITERS NASHVILLE MENTORING RETREAT. April 8-9, 2011. Contact: Reg Forder, Box 110390, Nashville TN 37222. Toll-free (800) 21-WRITE. E-mail: ACWriters@aol.com. Website: www.ACWriters.com. Speakers: Dennis Hensley & Holly Miller. Attendance: 40-80.

TEXAS

AMERICAN CHRISTIAN WRITERS DALLAS CONFERENCE. La Quinta Arlington; March 18-19, 2011. Contact: Reg Forder, Box 110390, Nashville TN 37222. Toll-free (800) 21-WRITE. E-mail: ACWriters@aol.com. Website: www.ACWriters.com. Speakers: Judson Edwards, Holly Miller & Frank Ball. Attendance: 40-80.

AUSTIN CHRISTIAN WRITERS' WORKSHOP. February 2011 (check Website). Contact: Lin Harris, 129 Fox Hollow Cove, Cedar Creek TX 78612-4844. (512) 601-2216. Fax (240) 208-3201. E-mail: linharris@austin.rr.com. Website: www.centexacfw.com. Attendance: 50.

EAST TEXAS CHRISTIAN WRITERS CONFERENCE. Marshall; April 8-9, 2011; April 7-8, 2012 (2nd weekend of April annually). Contact: Dr. Jerry Hopkins, East Texas Baptist University, 1209 N. Grove St., Marshall TX 75670. (903) 923-2083. Fax (903) 923-2077. E-mail: Jhopkins@etbu.edu. Website: www.etbu.edu/news/CWC. Offers an advanced & teen track. Speakers: Dr. Archie McDonald, Marie Chapian, Dr. Robert Darden, Historian Bill O'Neal. Sponsors a contest. Editors/agents in attendance. Partial scholarships for students only. Attendance: 190.

INSPIRATIONAL WRITERS ALIVE!/AMARILLO SEMINAR. April 30, 2011 (always first Saturday after Easter). Contact: Jerry McClenahan, 6808 Cloud Crest, Amarillo TX 79124. (806) 674-3504. E-mail: jerrydalemc@sbcglobal.net. Sponsors an annual contest. Attendance: 75.

NORTH TEXAS CHRISTIAN WRITERS CONFERENCE. Keller; September 16-17, 2011 (second Friday & Saturday after Labor Day). Contact: NTCW Conference, PO Box 820802, Fort Worth TX 76182. (817) 715-2597. E-mail: info@ntchristianwriters.com. Website: www.ntchristianwriters .com. Offers track for advanced writers. No editors or agents in attendance. Offers partial scholarships. Sponsors a contest for conference registrants only. Attendance: 250.

TEXAS CHRISTIAN WRITERS CONFERENCE. Houston; may not be held. Contact: Martha Rogers, 6038 Greenmont, Houston TX 77092-2332. (713) 686-7209. E-mail: marthalrogers@sbcglobal.net.

YWAM HANDS-ON SCHOOL OF WRITING AND WRITERS-TRAINING WORKSHOPS. Lindale; January-March 2011. Contact: Carol Scott, 15186 CR 440, Lindale TX 75771. (903) 882-9663. Fax (903) 882-1161. E-mail: contactus@ywamwoodcrest.com, or through Website: www.ywamwood crest.com. List of workshops on Website or for SASE. Attendance: 10-20.

VIRGINIA

+PENINSULA CHRISTIAN WRITERS WORKSHOP. Yorktown; fall 2011. Contact: Yvonne Ortega, PO Box 955, Yorktown VA 23692-0955. E-mail: yvonne@yvonneortega.com. No editors/agents, or scholarships. Attendance: 20-25.

RICHMOND CHRISTIANS WHO WRITE CONFERENCE. Richmond area; October 15, 2011. Contact: Rev. Thomas C. Lacy, 12114 Walnut Hill Dr., Rockville VA 23146-1854. (804) 749-4050. Fax (804) 749-4939. Or codirector Rebekah Robb, 9600 January Way, Richmond VA 23238, (804) 527-0913, tcrobb@integrity.com. E-mail: RichmondCWW@aol.com. Blog: http://rcww.blogspot.com.

WASHINGTON

AMERICAN CHRISTIAN WRITERS SPOKANE CONFERENCE. September 31-October 1, 2011. Contact: Reg Forder, Box 110390, Nashville TN 37222. Toll-free (800) 21-WRITE. E-mail: ACWriters@ aol.com. Website: www.ACWriters.com. Speaker: Dennis Hensley. Attendance: 40-80.

NORTHWEST CHRISTIAN WRITERS RENEWAL. Redmond; May 20-21, 2011. Contact: Judy Bodmer, 11108 NE 141 Pl., Kirkland WA 98034. Phone/fax (425) 488-2900. E-mail: jbodmer@msn .com. Website: www.nwchristianwriters.org. Speaker: Robert Cornuke. Editors/agents in attendance. Offers 3 full scholarships. Attendance: 200.

+POLISH (PROPOSAL, PROMOTION, PITCH) CONFERENCE. Seattle WA; May 2011. Contact: Susan May Warren, PO Box 1290, Grand Marais MN 55604. (218) 387-2853. E-mail: retreats@ mybooktherapy.com. Website: http://polish.mybooktherapy.com. This conference is for authors polishing their proposals, and needing to learn how to build a promotional platform, and get practice pitching to an agent. Advanced content. Speakers: Susan May Warren, Jim Rubart, Chip Macgregor (agent). Sponsors the My Book Therapy Frasier Contest (winner attends conference free). Attendance: 20.

WISCONSIN

GREEN LAKE CHRISTIAN WRITERS CONFERENCE. Green Lake; August 21-26, 2011. Contact: Jan White, Green Lake Conference Center, W2511 State Rd. 23, Green Lake WI 54941-9599. (920) 294-3323 for reservations. E-mail for information: janwhite@glcc.org. Website: www.glcc.org. For new or well-published writers in Christian or secular markets. Editors in attendance. Offers partial scholarships. Sponsors a contest for conference attendees only. Attendance: 40-80.

+LIGHTHOUSE CHRISTIAN WRITERS SEMINAR. Riverside Alliance Church/Oconto Falls; October 22-23, 2011. Contact: Lois Wiederhoeft, 901 Aubin St., Lot 115, Peshigo WI 54157. (715) 582-1024. E-mail: 2loisann@myway.com. Website: www.lighthousechristianwriters.com. Speaker: Marlene Bagnull.

WRITING WORKSHOPS & RETREATS. La Crosse; various times during the year (check Website for dates). Contact: J. Weisenbeck, Franciscan Spirituality Center, FSPA, 920 Market St., La Crosse WI 54601. E-mail: jweisenbeck@fspa.org. Website: www.franciscanspiritualitycenter.org.

CANADA/FOREIGN

AMERICAN CHRISTIAN WRITERS CARIBBEAN CRUISE. November 27-December 4, 2011. Contact: Reg A. Forder, Box 110390, Nashville TN 37222. Toll-free (800) 21-WRITE. E-mail: ACWriters@aol .com. Website: www.ACWriters.com. Speakers: Steve Laube & Dennis Hensley. Attendance: 15-30.

ASSOCIATION OF CHRISTIAN WRITERS WRITING EVENTS. Hoddesdon, Herts UK. E-mail through Website for dates & locations: www.christianwriters.org.uk. Membership (900) open. Sponsors an occasional writers' weekend for members only. Editors in attendance; no agents. No scholarships.

COMIX35 CHRISTIAN COMICS TRAINING SEMINAR. Various international locations & dates. Contact: Nate Butler, PO Box 4458, Albuquerque NM 87196-4458. E-mail: comix35@comix35.org. Website: www.comix35.org. Speakers: Nate Butler, Jose Carlos Gutierrez, and others. Sometimes has editors/agents in attendance. Attendance: 15-20. Sponsors contests (details on Website).

CRUISIN' FOR CHRIST IV, Cruise to Eastern Caribbean; June 25-July 2, 2011. Contact: Kendra Norman-Bellamy, PO Box 831648, Stone Mountain GA 30083. (404) 294-1457. Fax (404) 294-9732. E-mail: CFC@cruisinforchrist.org. Website: www.cruisinforchrist.org. Writing workshops, games & contests.

INSCRIBE CHRISTIAN WRITERS' FELLOWSHIP SPRING WORDSHOP. Calgary AB, Canada; March or April 2011. Website: www.inscribe.org/events-SpringWorDshop.htm. Offers an advanced track. No editors or agents in attendance. No scholarships. Attendance: 50-150.

+INSCRIBE CHRISTIAN WRITERS' FELLOWSHIP FALL CONFERENCE. Edmonton AB Canada; September 2011. Contact: Marcia Laycock, Box 637, Blackfalds AB T0M 0J0, Canada. (430) 885-9828. E-mail: query@inscribe.org. Website: www.inscribe.org/events-fallconf.htm. Offers an advanced track. Sponsors a contest. No editors or agents in attendance. No scholarships.

LITTWORLD CONFERENCE. Next conference won't be held until 2012. Contact: John D. Maust, director, 351 S. Main Pl., Ste. 230, Carol Stream IL 60188-2455. (630) 260-9063. Fax (630) 260-9265. E-mail: MaiLittWorld@sbcglobal.net. Website: www.littworld.org.

WRITE! CANADA. Guelph, Ontario; June 2011. Contact: Judy Bingley, The Word Guild, PO Box 1243, Trenton ON K8V 5R9, Canada. E-mail: writecanada@rogers.com. Website: www.writecanada .org. Hosted by The Word Guild, an association of Canadian writers and editors who are Christian. Offers an advanced track, and sometimes one for teens. Editors/agents in attendance. God Uses Ink Contest. Offers full & partial scholarships. Attendance: 250.

CONFERENCES THAT CHANGE LOCATIONS

ACT ONE: SCREENWRITING WEEKENDS. Two-day workshops; see Website for dates and locations. Contact: Conference Coordinator, 2690 Beachwood Dr., Lower Fl., Hollywood CA 90068. (323) 464-0815. Fax (323) 468-0315. E-mail: info@ActOneProgram.com. Website: www.ActOneprogram .com. Open to anyone who is interested in learning more about the craft of screenwriting. No editors/ agents in attendance. Attendance: 75.

AMERICAN CHRISTIAN FICTION WRITERS CONFERENCE. Rotates cities; St. Louis, September 22-25, 2011. Contact: Robin Miller, conf. dir., PO Box 101066, Palm Bay FL 32910-1066. E-mail: cd@ acfw.com. Website: www.ACFW.com. Offers varied skill level tracks for published and unpublished writers. Editors/agents in attendance. Sponsors 2 contests (details on Website). Offers scholarships each year to ACFW members only.

AMERICAN CHRISTIAN WRITERS CONFERENCES. Various dates and locations (see individual states where held). Also sponsors an annual Caribbean cruise in November/December. Contact: Reg A. Forder, Box 110390, Nashville TN 37222. Toll-free (800) 21-WRITE. E-mail: ACWriters@aol.com. Website: www.ACWriters.com. Attendance 30-40.

AUTHORIZEME. Various locations and dates. Contact: Sharon Norris Elliott, PO Box 1519, Inglewood CA 90308-1519. (310) 508-9860. Fax (323) 567-8557. E-mail: AuthorizeMe@sbc global.net. Website: www.AuthorizeMe.net. AuthorizeMe is a 12-hour, hands-on seminar that helps writers get their book ideas out of their heads, down onto paper, and into a professional book proposal format ready to submit to an acquisitions editor. Seminars offered nationwide. For a list of scheduled seminars, or to sponsor a seminar in your area, check Website. No editors or agents in attendance. Attendance: 10-50.

CATHOLIC MEDIA CONVENTION. Changes locations; May or June 2011. Contact: Thomas Conway, exec. dir., 205 W. Monroe St., Chicago IL 60606-5013. (312) 380-6789. Fax (312) 361-0256. E-mail: cathjourn@catholicpress.org. Website: www.catholicmediaconvention.org. For media professionals. Editors/agents in attendance. Partial scholarships. Annual book awards. Attendance: 550.

CHILDREN'S AUTHORS' BOOTCAMPS. Held in several locations each year; various dates. General. Contact: Bootcamp c/o Linda Arms White, PO Box 231, Allenspark CO 80510-0231. Phone/fax (303) 747-1014. E-mail: CABootcamp@msn.com. Website: www.WeMakeWriters.com. Upcoming dates and details on Website. No editors or agents in attendance. No scholarships. Attendance: 40.

CHRISTIAN LEADERS AND SPEAKERS SEMINARS (The CLASSeminar). PO Box 36551, Albuquerque NM 87176. (702) 882-0638. Website: www.classeminars.org. Sponsors several seminars across the country each year. Check Website for CLASSeminar dates and locations. For anyone who wants to improve their communication skills for either the spoken or written word, for professional or personal reasons. Speakers: Florence Littauer and others. Attendance: 75-100.

EVANGELICAL PRESS ASSOCIATION CONVENTION. Chicago IL, May 4-6, 2011. Contact: Doug Trouten, dir., PO Box 28129, Minneapolis MN 55428. (763) 535-4793. Fax (763) 535-4794. E-mail: director@epassoc.org. Website: www.epassoc.org. Attendance: 350. Annual convention for editors of evangelical periodicals; freelance communicators welcome. Editors in attendance. Contest open to members only.

THE EXPERTIZING WORKSHOP. Held in Boston, New York, and San Francisco; every 6 mos. (October & April). Contact: Alyza Harris, Expertizing.com, PO Box 590239, Newton MA 02459. (617) 630-0945. E-mail: alyza@PublishingGame.com. Website: www.Expertizing.com, or www .Expertizing.com/forum.htm. Learn how to get more media attention for your book and business. Speaker: Fern Reiss. Attendance: Limited to 6.

FAITHWRITERS WRITING CONFERENCE. Livonia MI; August 2011. Contact: Scott Lindsay. E-mail: 65164@yahoo.com. Website: www.faithwriters.com/conference.php. Offers an advanced track. Editors & agents in attendance. No scholarships.

INTERMEDIA PUBLISHING SEMINARS. Various dates & locations. Contact: Intermedia Publishing Group, PO Box 2825, Peoria AZ 85380. (623) 337-8710. Fax (623) 687-9469. E-mail through Website: www.intermediapub.com. Check Website for scheduled workshops on various topics.

INTERNATIONAL CHRISTIAN RETAIL SHOW. (Held in a different location each year.); Atlanta; July 10-13, 2011. Contact: Scott Graham, Box 62000, Colorado Springs CO 80962-2000. Toll-free (800) 252-1950. (719) 265-9895. Fax (719) 272-3510. E-mail: info@cbaonline.org. Website:

www.christianretailshow.com. Entrance badges available through book publishers or Christian bookstores. Attendance: 8,000.

MUSE ONLINE WRITERS CONFERENCE. October 2011 (unconfirmed). Website: www.freewebs .com/themuseonlinewritersconference. Contact: Lea Schizas. E-mail: museitupeditor@yahoo.ca. This is a free online conference. Check Website for upcoming conferences.

ORIGINAL & ADVANCED SPEAK UP WITH CONFIDENCE SEMINARS. Various dates & locations. For details & to register, go to: www.carolkent.org, click on "Speak Up Seminars." Contact: Carol Kent, 3141 Winged Foot Dr., Lakeland FL 33803-5437. Toll-free in U.S. (888) 870-7719; outside U.S. (810) 982-0898. Fax (810) 987-4163. E-mail: Speakupinc@aol.com. Website: www .SpeakUpSpeakerServices.com. Speaking seminars. Offers advanced training and opportunities to be coached in small groups. Also offers a workshop on writing for speakers who write for publication. Upcoming conferences listed on Website. Attendance: 100.

THE PUBLISHING GAME WORKSHOP. Various cities throughout the year (check Website for dates and locations). Workshops held every 3 mos. (September, December, March, and June). Contact: Alyza Harris, Peanut Butter and Jelly Press, PO Box 590239, Newton MA 02459. Phone/ fax (617) 630-0945. E-mail: info@PublishingGame.com, or Alyza@publishinggame.com. Website: www.PublishingGame.com (dates, locations, and registration forms on Website). Speaker: Fern Reiss. Editors and agents in attendance. Attendance: limited to 18.

"WRITE HIS ANSWER" SEMINARS & RETREATS. Various locations around U.S.; dates throughout the year; a choice of focus on periodicals or books (includes self-publishing or mastering the craft). Contact: Marlene Bagnull, LittD, 951 Anders Rd., Lansdale PA 19446. (484) 991-8581. E-mail: mbag null@aol.com. Website: www.writehisanswer.com/Writing_Seminars.htm. Attendance: 20-60. One- and two-day seminars by the author of *Write His Answer: A Bible Study for Christian Writers*.

WRITER'S NUDGE WORKSHOPS. Various locations & dates. Contact: Mary Busha, 1201 Charter Oaks Dr., Davison MI 48423. (810) 653-4218. E-mail: marybusha@writersnudge.com. Website: www.writersnudge.com.

11

Area Christian Writers' Clubs, Fellowship Groups, and Critique Groups

We highly recommend finding and joining—or starting—a new group in your area.

(+) A plus sign before a listing indicates a new listing.

ALABAMA

CHRISTIAN FREELANCERS. Tuscaloosa. Contact: Joanne Sloan, 4195 Waldort Dr., Northport AL 35473. (205) 333-8603. E-mail: cjosloan@bellsouth.net. Membership (30-40) open.

ARIZONA

+CHRISTIAN WRITERS FELLOWSHIP. Tucson. Contact: Carolyn Griffin, Tucson AZ. (520) 260-9631. E-mail: nanacarolyng@aol.com. Membership (15) open.

CHRISTIAN WRITERS OF THE WEST (ACFW Chapter). Mesa. Contact: Pamela Tracy, Mesa AZ. (623) 910-0524. E-mail: pamwrtr@aol.com. Blog: http://christianwritersofthewest.blogspot.com. Membership (21) open to members of national ACFW.

EAST VALLEY CHRISTIAN WRITERS. Mesa. Contact: Brenda Jackson, Mesa AZ. (480) 827-1545. E-mail: BrendaAtTheRanch@yahoo.com. Membership (5) open.

FOUNTAIN HILLS CHRISTIAN WRITERS GROUP. Contact: Jewell Johnson, 14223 N. Westminster Pl., Fountain Hills AZ 85268. (480) 836-8968. E-mail: tykeJ@juno.com. Membership (10-16) open. ACW Chapter.

ARKANSAS

LITTLE ROCK ACW CHAPTER. Contact: Bonnie Whitledge, 5800 Ranch Dr., Little Rock AR 72223. (501) 228-1727. Fax (501) 224-2529. E-mail: bwhitledge@familylife.com. Membership (20) open. Sponsors a contest open to nonmembers if they have attended before.

+LITTLE ROCK CHRISTIAN WRITERS/ACW CHAPTER. Little Rock. Contact: Bonnie Whitledge, FamilyLife, 5800 Ranch Dr., Little Rock AR 72223. (501) 2238-2477. E-mail: bwhitledge@familylife .com. Membership open.

SILOAM SPRINGS WRITERS. Contact: Margaret Weathers, 716 W. University St., Siloam Springs AR 72761. (479) 524-6598. E-mail: Rogeneo@centurytel.net. Membership (25) open. Periodically sponsors a contest open to nonmembers, and a seminar in September.

+THE WRITERS' COLONY AT DAIRY HOLLOW, 515 Spring St., Eureka Springs AR 72632. (479) 253-7444. E-mail: vkell@writerscolony.org, or director@writerscolony.org. Website: www.writer scol ony.org. Contact: Vicki Kell-Schneider. Residency program for writers in all genres. Details on Website.

CALIFORNIA

AMADOR FICTION WRITERS CRITIQUE GROUP. Meets every other Monday in Ione. Contact: Kathy Boyd Fellure, PO Box 1209, Ione CA 95640-1209. (209) 274-0205. E-mail: kathyfellure2@ juno.com. Website: www.amadorfictionwriters.com. Membership (9); waiting list for writers; open to readers. Sponsors an annual Literary Read and a Summer Social.

BAY AREA WRITERS CRITIQUE GROUP. Fremont. Contact: Carol Hall, PO Box 853, Union City CA 94587. (510) 206-2358. E-mail: Info@CarolLeeHall.com. Membership (10) open to experienced writers only.

CASTRO VALLEY CHRISTIAN WRITERS GROUP. Contact: Pastor Jon Drury, 19300 Redwood Rd., Castro Valley CA 94546-3465. (510) 886-6300. E-mail: jdrury@redwoodchapel.org. Website: www. christianwriter.org. Membership (10-14) open. Sponsoring a Christian Writers Seminar, February 2011.

CHAIRS: The Christian Authors, Illustrators, & Readers Society. Chino Hills. Contact: Nancy I. Sanders, 6361 Prescott Ct., Chino CA 91710-7105. (909) 590-0226. E-mail: jeffandnancys@gmail .com. Website: www.chairs7.wordpress.com. Membership (15-20) open.

CHRISTIAN WRITERS GUILD OF SANTA BARBARA. Contact: Opal Mae Dailey, (805) 682-0316 or (805) 252-9822. E-mail: opalmaedailey@aol.com or cwgsb@sbcglobal.net. Meets monthly. Membership open.

DIABLO VALLEY CHRISTIAN WRITERS GROUP. Danville. Contact: Cynthia Herrmann, 65 S. "C" St., Tracy CA 95376. (209) 607-5118. E-mail: cherrmn@pacbell.net. Membership (12-18) open.

HIGH DESERT CHRISTIAN WRITERS. Quartz Hill. Contact: Don Patterson, 43543 51st St. W., Quartz Hill CA 93536. (661) 722-0891. E-mail: don@theology.edu. Website: www.theology.edu/ writers. Membership (30) open. Presents the Sable Quill-Pacesetter Award each year to the writer in the group who has shown the most progress or professional achievement. Cosponsors the Antelope Valley Christian Writers Conference, May 2011.

INSPIRE CHRISTIAN WRITERS: Equipping Writers to Inspire the World. Meetings in Sacramento, El Dorado Hills, Elk Grove, Fair Oaks & Roseville. Contact: Elizabeth Thompson, 9359 Silverbend Ln., Elk Grove CA 95624-3985. (916) 670-7796. E-mail: elizabethmthompson@comcast .net. Group e-mail: inspiregroup@comcast.net. Website: www.inspirewriters.com. Membership (35) open. Hosts frequent workshops. Check Website for details.

NOVEL IDEA CHRISTIAN WRITERS SWARM. Norwalk/Cerritos. Contact: Derrell B. Thomas, 11239 1/2 Ferina St., Norwalk CA 90650-5507. (562) 292-9997. E-mail: derrell.writer@gmail.com. Membership (15) open.

ORANGE COUNTY CHRISTIAN WRITERS FELLOWSHIP. Various groups meeting throughout the county. Contact: Peggy Matthews Rose (editor@occwf.org) or write OCCWF, PO Box 5056, Fullerton CA 92838. Membership (190) open. Annual membership includes a bimonthly newsletter, information on local critique groups, advance notice of writing opportunities through an e-mail list, and reduced fees for annual OC Christian Writer's Day (usually on a Saturday in April or May; see Website for details). Conference includes keynote speakers, workshops, and consultations. See Website for details: www.occwf.org. Follow at www.twitter.com/occwf.

SACRAMENTO CHRISTIAN WRITERS. Citrus Heights. Contact: Beth Miller Self, 2012 Rushing River Ct., Elverta CA 95626-9756. (916) 992-8709. E-mail: cwbself@msn.com. Website: www .scwriters.org. Membership (32) open. Sponsors a contest for members.

SAN DIEGO COUNTY CHRISTIAN WRITERS GUILD. Contact: Jennie & Bob Gillespie, PO Box 270403, San Diego CA 92198. Phone/fax (760) 294-3269. E-mail: info@sandiegocwg.org. Website:

www.sandiegocwg.org. Membership (200) open. To join their Internet newsgroup, e-mail your name and address to: info@sandiegocwg.com. Sponsors 10 critique groups, fall seminar (September 2011), and spring fellowship brunch.

SANTA CLARA VALLEY CHRISTIAN WRITER'S GROUP. Cupertino. Contact: Richard M. Hinz, 550 S. 4th St., Apt. E, San Jose CA 95112, (408) 297-3336, Rickhinz@yahoo.com. Membership (8) open.

S.C.U.M. San Leandro. Contact: John B. Olson, 1261 Estrudillo Ave., San Leandro CA 94577. (510) 357-4441. E-mail: johno@litany.com. Membership (12) open.

TEMECULA CHRISTIAN WRITERS CRITIQUE GROUP. Contact: Rebecca Farnbach, 41403 Bitter Creek Ct., Temecula CA 92591-1545. (951) 699-5148. Fax (951) 699-4208. E-mail: sunbrook@ hotmail.com. Membership (12) open. Part of San Diego Christian Writers Guild.

VISION WRITERS/ACW CHAPTER, Contact: Bertha Sanders, 2127 W. 73rd St., Los Angeles CA 90047-2111. (323) 971-4319. E-mail: bwsanders1@ca.rr.com. Membership (5) open.

WORDSMITHS (Professional Christian writers). Montclair. Contact: Nancy I. Sanders, 6361 Prescott Ct., Chino CA 91710-7105. (909) 590-0226. E-mail: jeffandnancys@gmail.com. Website: www .wordsmiths8.wordpress.com. Membership (8) not open (contact for membership information).

THE WRITE BUNCH. Stockton. Contact: Shirley Cook, 3123 Sheridan Way, Stockton CA 95219-3724. (209) 477-8375. E-mail: shirleymcp@sbcglobal.net. Membership (8) not currently open.

CANADA

MANITOBA CHRISTIAN WRITERS ASSN. Winnipeg MB. Contact: Irene LoScerbo, 78 River Elm Dr., West St. Paul MB R2V 4G1, Canada. (204) 334-7780. E-mail: solonoi@shaw.ca. Membership (25) open.

THE WORD GUILD. Meets in various cities and online. Contact: Judy Bingley (meetings) or Denise Rumble (online group), PO Box 1243, Trenton ON K8V 5K9, Canada. E-mail: questions@the wordguild.com, or info@thewordguild.com. Website: www.thewordguild.com. Membership (350) open. Sponsors contests open to nonmembers who are Canadian citizens (see contest listings). Sponsoring an annual conference in Guelph ON—Write! Canada.

COLORADO

ACFW COLORADO GROUP & 3 CHAPTERS. Website: www.acfwcolorado.com. Sponsors ongoing blog, annual retreat, 2 miniconferences/yr., plus the following 3 chapters: **HIS Writers**, North Denver; www.acfwcolorado.com/denver.html. **W!W!W!,** Colorado Springs; www.acfwcolorado.com/ cosprings.html. **Mile High Scribes**, South Denver. E-mail through Website.

+SPRING WRITERS. Woodmen Valley Chapel/Colorado Springs. Contact: Scoti Domeij. E-mail: scotidomeij@gmail.com. Offers free monthly workshop; boot camps (2/yr.), critique group training. Membership open.

WORDS FOR THE JOURNEY CHRISTIAN WRITERS GUILD/ROCKY MOUNTAIN REGION. Parker. Contact: Michele Cushatt, 1907 Ross Ln., Highlands Ranch CO 80126. (303) 517-6651. E-mail: michele@MicheleCushatt.com. Website: www.wordsforthejourney.org. Blog: www.wftj.blog spot.com. Membership (100+) open. See separate listing for Southeast Texas region.

DELAWARE

DELMARVA CHRISTIAN WRITERS' FELLOWSHIP. Georgetown. Contact: Candy Abbott, PO Box 777, Georgetown DE 19947-0777. (302) 856-6649. Fax (302) 856-7742. E-mail: cfa@candyabbott .com. Website: www.delmarvawriters.com. Membership (20+) open.

FLORIDA

ADVENTURES IN CHRISTIAN WRITING. Orlando (First Presbyterian Church). Contact: Joanna Adicks Wallace, 1107 E. Amelia St., Orlando FL 32803-5327. Phone/fax (407) 841-2157. E-mail: hugh johj@yahoo.com. Church Website: http://fpco.org/Seek/WorshipArtsMinistry/FineandPerformingArts .aspx. Membership (20) open.

BRANDON CHRISTIAN WRITERS/ACW CHAPTER. Contact: Ruth C. Ellinger, president; (813) 685-7387. E-mail: Writer@Ruthellinger.com. Membership (40) open.

FIRST COAST CHRISTIAN WRITERS/ACW CHAPTER. Jacksonville. Contact: Tracy Redman, 5646 Keaton Lake Dr., Jacksonville FL 32258. (904) 945-5650. E-mail: president@FirstCoastChristian Writers.org. Website: www.FirstCoastChristianWriters.org. Blog: http://FirstCoastChristianWriters. blogspot.com. Membership (10+) open.

HOBE SOUND WRITERS GROUP/ACW CHAPTER. Hobe Sound. Contact: Faith Tofte, 9342 Bethel Way, Hobe Sound FL 33455. (772) 545-4023. E-mail: faithtofte@bellsouth.net. Membership (5) open.

MID-FLORIDA CHRISTIAN WRITERS. Oakland. Contact: Joy Shelton, 1040 Glensprings Ave., Winter Garden FL 34787. (407) 654-9076. E-mail: JoyShelton4@aol.com. Membership (8) open.

PALM BEACH CHRISTIAN WRITERS ASSN. West Palm Beach. Contact: Natalie Rodrigues, 964 Imperial Lake Rd., West Palm Beach FL 33413. (561) 574-0201. E-mail: nataliekim71@msn .com. Membership (5) open. ACW Chapter.

SUNCOAST CHRISTIAN WRITERS. Seminole. Contact: Elaine Creasman, 13014—106th Ave. N., Largo FL 33774-5602. Phone/fax (727) 595-8963. E-mail: emcreasman@aol.com. Membership (10-15) open.

WORD WEAVERS. Longwood. Contact: Larry J. Leech II, 911 Alameda Dr., Longwood FL 32750. (407) 925-6411. E-mail: president@wordweaversonline.com. Website: www.WordWeaversonline .com. Membership (90+) open. Sponsors a contest for members. May have a conference for February 2011 in Lake Yale.

GEORGIA

EAST METRO ATLANTA CHRISTIAN WRITERS/ACW CHAPTER. Covington. Contact: Colleen Jackson, PO Box 2896, Covington GA 30015. (404) 444-7514. E-mail: colleenjoyismine@aol.com. Website: www.emacw.org. Membership (40) open. Two-day annual conference is second Friday and Saturday of July; July 8-9, 2011. Check Website for monthly meetings and speakers.

GEORGIA WRITERS ASSN./CHRISTIAN WRITERS POD. Woodstock/Marietta. Contact: Lloyd Blackwell, 3049 Scott Rd. N.E., Marietta GA 30066. (770) 421-1203. E-mail: lloydblackwell@world net.att.net. Membership (73) open. Meets twice monthly. Sponsors a contest, an annual cooperative-published book, and a seminar in May.

SOUTHEASTERN WRITERS ASSN. Athens. Contact: Sheila S. Hudson, co-president, 161 Woodstone Dr., Athens GA 30605. (706) 296-7056. E-mail: info@southeasternwriters.com. Website: www .southeasternwriters.com. Sponsors an annual conference; June 2011. Membership open.

IDAHO

ACW SANDPOINT. Contact: Anita Aurit, 403 Louis Ln., Sandpoint ID 83864. (208) 610-0626. E-mail: AnitaWrites@live.com. Website: http://acwsandpoint.webs.com. Membership (14) open.

WE IS WRITERS/ACW CHAPTER. Moscow. Contact: Susan Thomas, 540 N. Grant, Moscow ID 83843. (208) 882-9038. E-mail: susanethomas@juno.com. Blog: www.weiswriters.blogspot.com. Membership (6) open.

IOWA

CEDAR RAPIDS CHRISTIAN WRITER'S GROUP. Contact: Susan Fletcher, 513 Knollwood Dr. S.E., Cedar Rapids IA 52403. (319) 365-9844. E-mail: skmcfate@msn.com. Membership (4) open.

IOWA SCRIBES. Marion. Contact: Kimn Swenson Gollnick, 550 Edinburgh Ave., Marion IA 52302-5614. (319) 373-2302. E-mail: kimn-gollnick@uiowa.edu. Facebook: www.facebook.com/group .php?gid=57127652115. Website: www.KIMN.net/scribes.htm. Membership (6-10) open.

KANSAS

CHRISTIAN WRITERS FELLOWSHIP. Girard. Contact: Deborah Vogts, 17300 Ness Rd., Erie KS 66733. (620) 244-5619. E-mail: debvogts@gmail.com. Website: www.ChristianWritersFellowship .blogspot.com. Membership (35) open. Sponsors a contest open to nonmembers and a seminar April 2011 (see listing in conference section).

CREATIVE WRITERS FELLOWSHIP. Newton, North Newton, Hesston, Moundridge, Halstead. Contact: Esther Groves, sec., 405 W. Bluestem, Apt. H4, North Newton KS 67117-8069. (316) 283-7224. E-mail: estherbg@southwind.net. Membership (20) open.

KENTUCKY

LOUISVILLE CHRISTIAN WRITERS/ACW CHAPTER. Crystal Murray, pres. Contact: Lana Jackson, 7804 Foxlair Way, Louisville KY 40220-3283. (502) 968-3602. E-mail: info@lcwriters .com or LanaHJackson@insightbb.com. Website: www.LCWriters.com. Meeting details on Website. Membership (22) open.

LOUISIANA

SOUTHERN CHRISTIAN WRITERS GUILD. Mandeville (City Hall). Contact: Grace Booth or Marlaine Peachey, 419 Juliette Ln., Mandeville LA 70448. (985) 626-4282. Fax (985) 624-3108. E-mail: peachlane@bellsouth.net. Has monthly speakers. Membership (25-30) open.

MAINE

MAINE FELLOWSHIP OF CHRISTIAN WRITERS. China. Contact: Vicki Schad, 180 S. Stanley Hill Rd., Vassalboro ME 04989. (207) 923-3956. E-mail: jvschad@gmail.com. Membership (15) open. Sponsors an August seminar in Belfast ME.

MARYLAND

ANNAPOLIS FELLOWSHIP OF CHRISTIAN WRITERS. Annapolis. Contact: Jeri Sweany, 3107 Ervin Ct., Annapolis MD 21403-4620. (410) 267-0924. E-mail: Bheron3107@aol.com. Membership (7-12) open.

BALTIMORE AREA CHRISTIAN WRITERS. Owings Mills. Contact: Theresa V. Wilson, M.Ed., PO Box 47182, Windsor Mill MD 21244-3571. (443) 622-4907. E-mail: writerseminar@aol.com. Website: www.writersinthemarketplace.org. Social networking sites: www.twitter.com/WritersCoach21; www .facebook.com/writersinthemarketplaceUpdates. Group meetings include webinar conferencing. 2nd Annual Writers Milestone Cruise, August 2011. Membership (42) open.

MCC WRITERS' GROUP. Joppa. Contact: Virginia Colclasure or Dawn Sexton, c/o Mountain Christian Church, 1824 Mountain Rd., Joppa MD 21085. (410) 877-1824 (church). E-mail: Vcolclasure@ zoominternet.net or mccwriters@zoominternet.net. Devotional blog: http://portionsofgrace.blog spot.com. Sponsors a one-day seminar in September. Membership (15) open.

THIRD SATURDAY CHRISTIAN WRITERS GROUP. Howard County. Contact: Claire K. DeBakey. (443) 413-6790. E-mail: c.debakey@att.net. Membership (8-10) open.

MASSACHUSETTS

CENTRAL MASSACHUSETTS CHRISTIAN WRITERS FELLOWSHIP. Sturbridge. Contact: Barbara Shaffer, 168 Warren Rd., Brimfield MA 01010-9615. (413) 245-9620. E-mail: historyfind2@aol .com. Membership (10) open.

MICHIGAN

AMERICAN CHRISTIAN WRITERS DETROIT. Contact: Pamela Perry, 33011 Tall Oaks St., Farmington MI 48336-4551. (248) 426-2300. Fax (248) 471-2422. E-mail: PamPerry@ministry marketingsolutions.com. Website: www.ministrymarketingsolutions.com. Membership (219) open. Sponsors a fall seminar in Detroit.

THE CALLED AND READY WRITERS. Detroit. Minister Mary Edwards, founder. Estab. 1999. Contact: Wanda Burnside, PO Box 211018, Detroit MI 48221. (313) 491-3504. Fax (313) 861-7578. E-mail: wtvision@hotmail.com. Website: www.thecalledandreadywriters.org. Membership (70) open to all ages (over 25 published book authors). Charges an annual fee. Has helped over 200 authors publish their book, articles, and other types of manuscripts. Provides consultations, classroom lectures, monthly guild meetings, publisher lists, and more. Provides a variety of other services, including Website help.

+FIRST FRIDAYS WRITERS GROUP. Burton. Contact: Tammy Bovee, (810) 715-1421, or e-mail: godsearthenvessel@juno.com. Meets at the Grand Traverse Pie Co., 2350 S. Center Rd., Burton MI 48519. Membership open.

MINNESOTA

MINNESOTA CHRISTIAN WRITERS GUILD. Contact: Delores Topliff, 6901 Ives Ln. N., Maple Grove MN 55369. (763) 315-1014. E-mail: deltopliff@gmail.com. Website: www.mnchristianwrit ers.org. Membership (110) open. Sponsors a spring contest for members only and annual spring (April) and fall (October) seminars in Minneapolis/St. Paul area (open to all). Monthly meetings (Sept.-May); monthly newsletter. Sponsors critique circles throughout Minnesota.

MISSISSIPPI

BYHALIA CHRISTIAN WRITERS/ACW CHAPTER. Contact: Marylane Wade Koch, Byhalia MS. (901) 351-0870. E-mail: bcwriters@gmail.com. Has a BCW online Yahoo group. Membership (55) open. Works with ACW on an annual seminar in Memphis area; May 21, 2011.

MISSOURI

CHRISTIAN WRITERS WORKSHOP OF ST. LOUIS/ACW CHAPTER. Brentwood area. Contact: Ruth Houser, 3148 Arnold-Tenbrook Rd., Arnold MO 63010-4732. (636) 464-1187. E-mail: HouserRA@juno.com. Membership (5-10) open.

HEART OF AMERICA CHRISTIAN WRITERS NETWORK. Kansas City metro area. Contact: Mark and Jeanette Littleton, 3706 N.E. Shady Lane Dr., Gladstone MO 64119. Phone/fax (816) 459-8016.

E-mail: HACWN@earthlink.net. Website: www.HACWN.org. Membership (150) open. Sponsors monthly meetings, weekly critique groups, professional writers' fellowships, a contest (open to non-members), a newsletter, marketing e-mails, and a conference in November.

OZARKS CHAPTER OF AMERICAN CHRISTIAN WRITERS. Springfield. Meets monthly, Sept. to May. Contact: Jeanetta Chrystie, pres., OCACW, 5042 E. Cherry Hills Blvd., Springfield MO 65809-3301. (417) 832-8409. E-mail: DrChrystie@mchsi.com. Susan Willingham, newsletter ed.; OzarksACW@yahoo.com. Guidelines on Website: www.ClearGlassView.org/OzarksACW/index.htm. Sponsors an annual contest (open to nonmembers) ; genre, dates, and guidelines on Website. See Website for other events. Membership (38) open. Newsletter-only subscriptions available.

NEBRASKA

CENTRAL NEBRASKA FELLOWSHIP OF CHRISTIAN WRITERS, ARTISTS, AND MUSICIANS (C-WAM). Kearney. Contact: Carolyn R. Scheidies, 415 E. 15th, Kearney NE 68847-6959. (308) 234-3849. E-mail: crscheidies@mail2faith.com (put C-WAM in subject line). Membership (15) open; more on Internet Loop.

MY THOUGHTS EXACTLY WRITERS GROUP. Fremont. Contact: Cheryl A. Paden, PO Box 1073, Fremont NE 68025. (402) 727-6508. Membership (6-8) open. Sponsoring a writers' retreat in January 2011.

WORDSOWERS CHRISTIAN WRITERS GROUP/ACW CHAPTER. Omaha area. Contact: Meredith Efken, PO Box 6049, Omaha NE 68106. E-mail: mefken@cox.net. Website: www.wordsowers.com. Membership (20) open.

NEW MEXICO

SOUTHWEST WRITERS. Albuquerque. Contact: Rob Spiegel, pres., 3721 Morris St. N.E., Ste. A, Albuquerque NM 87111-3611. (505) 265-9485. E-mail: swwriters@juno.com. Website: www.south westwriters.com. Membership (700) open. Sponsors an annual and a monthly contest (open to nonmembers), a series of miniconferences in Albuquerque (see Website for dates), workshops and classes. Semimonthly e-lert notices are open to nonmembers. General.

NEW YORK

NEW YORK CHRISTIAN WRITERS GROUP. Manhattan. Contact: Marilyn Driscoll, 350—1st Ave., New York, NY 10010 (Manhattan). (212) 529-6087. E-mail: madrisc@rcn.com. Membership (8) open.

THE SCRIBBLERS/ACW CHAPTER. Riverhead. Contact: Bill Batcher, pres., c/o First Congregational Church, 103 First St., Riverhead NY 11901. E-mail: bbatcher@optonline.net. Membership (12) open. Meets monthly and sponsors annual writing retreat.

SOUTHERN TIER CHRISTIAN WRITERS' FELLOWSHIP. Johnson City. Contact: Jean Jenkins, 3 Snow Ave., Binghamton NY 13905-3810. (607) 797-5852. E-mail: jdjenkins2@verizon.net. Membership (8) open.

NORTH CAROLINA

COVENANT WRITERS. Lincolnton. Contact: Robert Redding, 3392 Hwy. 274, Cherryville NC 28021-9634. (704) 445-4962. E-mail: minwriter@yahoo.com. Membership (10) open.

SEVEN SERIOUS SCRIBES. Cary. Contact: Katherine W. Parrish, 103 Chimney Rise Dr., Cary NC 27511-7214. (919) 467-1924. E-mail: servantsong@aol.com. Critique group. Membership (7) not currently open, but encourages others to start similar groups in the area.

OHIO

COLUMBUS CHRISTIAN WRITERS ASSN./ACW CHAPTER. New Albany. Contact: Mina Rauston, 4694 Cemetery Rd., #290, Hilliard OH 43026. (614) 507-7893. E-mail: m_rauston@hotmail.com. Website: www.cwacolumbus.com. Meets third Saturday of each month. Membership (10) open.

CREATIVE FORCE—ACW NORTHGATE. Sunbury. Contact: Lark Lamontagne, 450 Township Rd. 208, Marengo OH 43334-9501. (740) 625-6535. Fax (740) 625-6572. E-mail: lark@L3VS.com. Membership (20) not currently open.

DAYTON CHRISTIAN SCRIBES. Kettering. Contact: Lois Pecce, PO Box 41613, Dayton OH 45441-0613. (937) 433-6470. E-mail: epecce@compuserve.com. Membership (30) open.

DAYTON CHRISTIAN WRITERS GUILD. Englewood. Contact: Tina Toles, PO Box 251, Englewood OH 45322. (937) 836-6600. E-mail: daytonwriters@ureach.com. Membership (25) open. Sponsoring a conference in June 2011.

FAITH WRITERS. Milford. Contact: Sharon Siepel or Vicki Clarke, 5910 Price Rd., Milford OH 45150. (513) 831-3770. E-mail: ssiepel@faithchurch.net. Meets January-October, 4th Wednesday of the month. Membership (10) open.

MIDDLETOWN AREA CHRISTIAN WRITERS. Franklin. Contact: Donna J. Shepherd, Healing Word Assembly of God, 5303 S. Dixie Hwy., Franklin OH 45005. (513) 373-5671. E-mail: donna .shepherd@gmail.com. Website: www.middletownwriters.blogspot.com. Membership (25) open.

MOVING AHEAD ACW CHAPTER. Marion. Contact: Diana Barnum, 3288 Darby Glen Blvd., Hilliard OH 43026. (614) 529-9459. E-mail: dbmovingahead@gmail.com. Membership open to inmates of the Marion Correctional Institution (MCI); adult male inmates in a reentry program for prisoners getting ready to reenter society. May expand group to include those in the community.

NORTHWEST OHIO CHRISTIAN WRITERS/ACW CHAPTER. Bowling Green. Contact: Shelley R. Lee, pres., 12400 Jerry City Rd., Cygnet OH 43413. (419) 655-2037. E-mail: shelleyrlee@gmail .com. Website: www.nwocw.org. Meets the 4th Fridays of January, March, May, July, and October. Membership (45-50) open. Sponsors a spring writers' retreat and a fall writers' seminar in September/October.

OKLAHOMA

FELLOWSHIP OF CHRISTIAN WRITERS (FCW). Tulsa. Contact: Lavon Lewis, PO Box 471031, Tulsa, OK 74147. (918) 256-2138. E-mail: fcw@fellowhipofchristianwriters.org. Website: http://fel lowshipofchristianwriters.org. Founded as Tulsa Christian Writers, FCW has helped to encourage, equip, launch, and inspire hundreds of writers for over 30 years. Membership (50+) open; includes a monthly, full-color 8-10 page newsletter, eligibility to members-only contests, book and CD discounts. FCW also conducts a free e-mail group with over 800 members, at Yahoo Groups—http:// groups.yahoo.com/group/FCW—or send an e-mail to above e-mail address. Local membership $35/yr. At-large membership $25/yr.

+OKC CHRISTIAN FICTION WRITERS (ACFW CHAPTER). Edmond/Oklahoma City. Contact: Lacy Williams. (405) 229-5851. E-mail: ljyw@cox.net. Blog: http://okcchristianfictionwriters.blog spot.com. Membership open; includes members-only discussion e-mail loop and discounted special events.

SONRISE CHRISTIAN WRITERS. Oklahoma City. Contact: Marlys Norris, 6209 N.W. 82nd St., Oklahoma City OK 73132. E-mail: marlysj@sbcglobal.net. Starting a new group; membership open.

WORDWRIGHTS, OKLAHOMA CITY CHRISTIAN WRITERS. Contact: Milton Smith, 6457 Sterling Dr., Oklahoma City OK 73132-6804. (405) 721-5026. E-mail: HisWordMatters@yahoo.com. Website: www.shadetreecreations.com. Membership (20+) open. Occasional contests for members only. Hosts an annual writers' conference with American Christian Writers, March 25-26, 2011, in Oklahoma City; send an SASE for information.

+WRITERS OF INSPIRATIONAL NOVELS (ACFW CHAPTER). Tulsa, NE Oklahoma, Arkansas. Contact e-mail: president@win-acfw.com. Website: www.win-acfw.com. Membership open; includes members-only e-mail discussion group and discounted special events.

OREGON

OREGON CHRISTIAN WRITERS. Contact: Mary Hake, pres. E-mail: president@oregonchristian writers.org. Website: www.oregonchristianwriters.org. Meets for 3 all-day Saturday conferences annually: February, in Salem; May, in Eugene; and October, in Portland. Newsletter published one month before each one-day conference. Annual 4-day Coaching Conference late July/early August, in Portland/Salem metro area. Membership (400) open.

PORTLAND CHRISTIAN WRITERS GROUP. Contact: Stan Baldwin, (503) 659-2974. E-mail: scbaldwin@juno.com. Serious group; must write regularly. Currently full, but waiting list available.

ROYAL PEN-DANTS. Salem/Portland area. Primarily for those writing for children. Contact: Carole Farmen. (503) 362-2148. E-mail: cfarmen@msn.com. Membership (6) open only to committed, producing writers.

SALEM I CHRISTIAN WRITERS GROUP. Contact: Sam Hall, 6840 Macleay Rd. S.E., Salem OR 97301. (503) 363-7586. E-mail: samhallarch@msn.com. Membership (9) not currently open.

WORDWRIGHTS. Gresham (near 182nd & Powell). Contact: Susan Thogerson Maas, 27526 S.E. Carl St., Gresham OR 97080-8215. (503) 663-7834. E-mail: susan.maas@verizon.net. Membership (5) possibly open.

WRITER'S DOZEN CRITIQUE GROUP. Springfield. Contact: Denise Nash, 42892 Leaburg Dr., Leaburg OR 97489-9619. (541) 896-3816. E-mail: dcarlson@efn.org. Membership (12) not currently open.

PENNSYLVANIA

ARTISTS' JUNCTION WRITERS' GATHERING. Lancaster. Contact: Deb Munson or Jan Brenneman, 531 E. Marion St., Lancaster PA 17602. (717) 295-2533. E-mail: aji@artistsjunction.org. Website: www.meetup.com/Artists-Junction-Square-One-Gathering-Lancaster-PA. Membership open.

THE FIRST WORD. Sewickley (near Pittsburgh). Contact: Shirley S. Stevens, 712 Ridge Ave., Pittsburgh PA 15202-2223. (412) 761-2618. E-mail: poetcat@comcast.net. Membership (10) open. Affiliated with the St. Davids Christian Writers' Conference.

FIRST WRITES. Chambersburg. Contact: Pam Williams. E-mail: 1stwrites@gmail.com. Website: www.fumcchambersburg.org/pages.asp?page=26. Membership open.

GREATER PHILADELPHIA CHRISTIAN WRITERS FELLOWSHIP. Newton Square. Contact: Marlene Bagnull, 951 Anders Rd., Lansdale, PA 19026. (484) 991-8581. E-mail: Mbagnull@aol .com. Website: www.writehisanswer.com. Membership (25) open. Meets one Thursday morning a month, September-June. Sponsors annual writers' conference (August 2011) and contest (open to registered conferees only).

INDIAN VALLEY CHRISTIAN WRITERS FELLOWSHIP/ACW CHAPTER. Telford (Bucks County). Contact: Cheryl Wallace, 952 Route 113, Sellersville PA 18960-2962. (215) 453-0415. E-mail: wal lacewriter@verizon.net. Membership (12) open.

INSPIRATIONAL WRITERS' FELLOWSHIP. Brookville. Contact: Jan R. Sady, 2026 Langville Rd., Mayport PA 16240-5610. (814) 856-2560. E-mail: janfran@windstream.net. Membership (15) open. Sometimes sponsors a contest.

JOHNSTOWN CHRISTIAN WRITERS' GUILD. Contact: Betty Rosian, 108 Deerfield Ln., Johnstown PA 15905-5703. (814) 255-4351. E-mail: wordsforall@atlanticbb.net. Membership (12) open.

LANCASTER CHRISTIAN WRITERS/ACW CHAPTER. Lititz. Contact: Jeanette Windle, 121 E. Woods Dr., Lititz PA 17543. (717) 626-8752. E-mail: jeanette@jeanettewindle.com. Website: www .lancasterchristianwriters.org. Membership (100+) open. Sponsors a one-day spring conference, March 2011.

SOUTH CAROLINA

COLUMBIA CHRISTIAN WRITERS. Contact: Kim Andrysczyk, 201 Sutton Way, Irmo SC 29063. (803) 781-3510. E-mail: kimbocraig@juno.com. Meets monthly. Membership (6) open.

GREENVILLE CHRISTIAN WRITERS GROUP. Contact: Nancy Parker, 134 Glenbrooke Way, Greenville SC 29615. (864) 313-3116. E-mail: Nancykparker@gmail.com. Membership (30) open.

UPSTATE SOUTH CAROLINA ACW CHAPTER. Anderson. Contact: Elva Martin, 104 Oak Knoll Ter., Anderson SC 29625-2507. Phone/fax (864) 226-7024. E-mail: elvamartinministries@charter.net. Website: Upstatescchristianwriters.com. Sponsors the Carolina Christian Writers Workshop in March and a contest for attendees. Visitors welcome.

+WRITE2IGNITE! FOR CHRISTIAN WRITERS OF CHILDREN'S LITERATURE. Greenville; February 18-19, 2011. Contact: Cindy Lynn Jacobs, marketing director. E-mail: write2ignite@ jeanmatthewhall.com. Website: www.write2ignite.com.

WRITING 4 HIM. Spartanburg. Contact: Linda Gilden, PO Box 2928, Spartanburg SC 29304. E-mail: RoseWriter@aol.com. Membership (25) open.

TENNESSEE

+BARTLETT CHRISTIAN WRITERS/ACW CHAPTER. Contact: Suzy Haden, pres., New Hope Christian Church, 3300 Kirby Whitten Rd., Bartlett TN 38135. (901) 218-2412. E-mail: suzypooh@ comcast.net. Membership open.

+COLLIERVILLE AMERICAN CHRISTIAN WRITERS/ACW CHAPTER. Collierville. Contact: Susan Reichert. (901) 853-4470. E-mail: tnlms44@aol.com. Membership (24) open.

NASHVILLE CHRISTIAN WRITERS ASSN./ACW CHAPTER. Nashville & Greater Middle TN Area. Contact: Carol Harper, pres. E-mail: nashvillechristianwriters@gmail.com. Website: www.nashvil lechristianwriters.com. Online resource for Nashville's Christian community. Holds meetings and publishes newsletter once per quarter. Promotes and organizes book-signing events for book authors. Membership open. Supports the *Nashville Christian Times* (see listing in periodical section).

TEXAS

ACFW WRITERS ON THE STORM. The Woodlands. Contact: Linda P. Kozar, 7 S. Chandler Creek Cir., The Woodlands TX 77381. (281) 362-1791. Prefers cell (832) 797-7522. E-mail: zarcom1@aol .com. Blog: http://acfwwritersonthestorm.blogspot.com. Visitors welcome (e-mail contact person).

+CENTEX CHAPTER—AMERICAN CHRISTIAN FICTION WRITERS (ACFW). Central Texas. Contact: Dorothy Featherling, 1712 Chalice Cove, Round Rock TX 78665. (512) 238-1915. E-mail: feather@austin.rr.com. Website: www.centexacfw.com. Monthly meeting info on Website. Membership open. Visitors welcome. Sponsors full-day workshops.

CHRISTIAN WRITERS GROUP OF GREATER SAN ANTONIO. Universal City/San Antonio area (First Baptist Church of Universal City). Contact: Brenda Blanchard. (210) 945-4163. E-mail: brendablanchard1@aol.com. Has quarterly guest speakers. Membership (40-50) open.

CROSS REFERENCE WRITERS. Brazos Valley. E-mail: CrossRefWriters@yahoo.com. Website: http://sites.google.com/site/crossreferencewriters. Membership open.

DALLAS CHRISTIAN WRITERS GUILD. Plano. Contact: Jan Winebrenner, 2709 Winding Hollow, Plano TX 75093. E-mail: janwrite@earthlink.net. Website: www.dallaschristianwriters.com. Membership (30) open.

DALLAS-FORT WORTH READY WRITERS/ACFW BRANCH. Colleyville. Contact: Lena Nelson Dooley. E-mail: safe-ldwrites@flash.net. Blog: www.dfwreadywriters.blogspot.com. Meeting info on Website. Membership open.

EAST TEXAS CHRISTIAN WRITERS. Longview. Contact: Vickie Phelps, PO Box 5907, Longview TX 75608. (903) 734-7034. E-mail: VPhe1950@aol.com. Membership open.

INSPIRATIONAL WRITERS ALIVE! Groups meet in Houston, Pasadena, Jacksonville, Amarillo, Humble, Tyler, and Port Neches. Contact: Martha Rogers, 6038 Greenmont, Houston TX 77092-2332. (713) 686-7209. E-mail: marthalrogers@sbcglogal.net. Membership (130 statewide) open. Sponsors summer seminar, August 2011, monthly newsletter, and annual contest (January 1-May 15) open to nonmembers.

INSPIRATIONAL WRITERS ALIVE!/AMARILLO CHAPTER. Contact: Jerry McClenahan, pres., 6808 Cloud Crest, Amarillo TX 79124. (806) 674-3504. E-mail: jerrydalemc@sbcglobal.net. Membership (35) open. Sponsors a contest open to members, and a seminar the Saturday after Easter.

NORTH TEXAS CHRISTIAN WRITERS/ACW CHAPTERS. Meetings held in Argyle, Arlington, Burleson, Dallas, Fort Worth, Granbury, Henderson, Keller, Lake Worth, Lewisville, and Lindale. Contact: NTCW, PO Box 820802, Fort Worth TX 76182-0802. (817) 715-2597. E-mail: info@ntchristianwriters.com. Website: www.ntchristianwriters.com. Membership (150+) open. Sponsors an annual seminar after Labor Day; September 2011.

ROCKWALL CHRISTIAN WRITERS GROUP. Lake Pointe Church/Rockwall. Contact: Leslie Wilson, 535 Cullins Rd., Rockwall TX 75032-6017. (972) 772-3442. Cell (214) 505-5336. E-mail: LesliePWilson@aol.com. Website: http://rcwg.blogspot.com. Membership (20) open.

WORDS FOR THE JOURNEY CHRISTIAN WRITERS GUILD/SOUTHEAST TEXAS REGION. Contact: Sharen Watson, 2635 Imperial Grove Ln., Conroe TX 77385. (281) 292-5634 or (303) 906-1573. E-mail: IRite4Him@aol.com. Website: www.wordsforthejourney.org. Membership (100+) open. See separate listing for Rocky Mountain CO Region.

UTAH

UTAH CHRISTIAN WRITERS FELLOWSHIP/ACW CHAPTER. Salt Lake City area. Contact: UCWF, PO Box 585, Draper UT 84020. (801) 965-9503. E-mail: ucwf@markjulie.com or through Website: www.utahchristianwriters.com. Sponsoring a writers' conference in spring 2011 in Bluffdale UT. Membership (20) open.

VERMONT

AMERICAN CHRISTIAN WRITERS OF NEW ENGLAND. Jericho. Contact: Laurel Decher, 1375 North Ave., Burlington VT 05408. (802) 660-4080. E-mail: ldecher@gmail.com. Website: http:// home.myfairpoint.net/ldecher/id10.html. Membership (4-6) open.

VIRGINIA

CAPITAL CHRISTIAN WRITERS. Fairfax. Leader: Betsy Dill, PO Box 873, Centreville VA 20122-0873. Phone/fax (703) 803-9447. E-mail: ccwriters@gmail.com. Website: www.ccwriters.org. Sponsors Saturday workshops 1-2 times a year, prose party, and poet's tea annually. Membership (45) open.

JOYWRITERS/ACW CHAPTER. Galax. Contact: Vie Herlocker, PO Box 342, Fancy Gap VA 24328-0342. (276) 237-1972. E-mail: info@joywriters.org. Website: www.joywriters.org. Membership (20) open.

NEW COVENANT WRITER'S GROUP. Newport News. Contact: Mary Tatem, 451 Summer Dr., Newport News VA 23606-2515. (757) 930-1700. E-mail: rwtatem@juno.com. Membership (8) open.

PENINSULA CHRISTIAN WRITERS/ACW CHAPTER. Yorktown. Contact: Yvonne Ortega, PO Box 955, Yorktown VA 23692. E-mail: yvonne@yvonneortega.com. Membership (5) open. Sponsors Annual Writers Workshop, likely in the spring.

RICHMOND CHRISTIANS WHO WRITE/ACW CHAPTER. Contact: Rev. Thomas C. Lacy, 12114 Walnut Hill Dr., Rockville VA 23146-1854. (804) 749-4050; or Rebekah Robb, 9600 January Way, Richmond VA 23238, (804) 527-0913, tcrobb@integrity.com. E-mail: RichmondCWW@aol.com. Blog: http://rcww.blogspot.com. Sponsoring a conference September 2011. Membership (50+) open.

TIDEWATER CHRISTIAN WRITERS FORUM/ACW CHAPTER. Norfolk/Chesapeake/Virginia Beach (open to all surrounding areas). Contact: Peter D. Mallett, (757) 944-1756. Website: http://groups. yahoo.com/group/TidewaterChristianWF. Membership (7) open. ACW Chapter (www.acwriters.com).

WASHINGTON

NORTHWEST CHRISTIAN WRITERS ASSN. Bothell. Contact: President, PO Box 2706, Woodinville WA 98072-2706. Toll-free (800) 731-6292. Fax (360) 802-9992. E-mail: president@nwchristian writers.org. Website: www.nwchristianwriters.org. Speakers Clearinghouse available on Website (click on "Speakers Connection"). Membership (200+) open. Meets monthly. Bimonthly newsletter. Sponsors a contest and Northwest Christian Writers Renewal in May (see separate listing).

SPOKANE CHRISTIAN WRITERS. Contact: Ruth McHaney Danner, PO Box 18425, Spokane WA 99228-0425. (509) 328-3359. E-mail: ruth@ruthdanner.com. Membership (20) open.

+SPOKANE VALLEY WRITER'S GROUP. Contact: Cindy Scinto, spokanevalleywriters@yahoo.com. Meets twice a month. E-mail for guidelines. Includes writing, art, Website development, music, lyrics, and other artistic projects. Not exclusive to Christians. Membership open.

WALLA WALLA CHRISTIAN WRITERS. College Place. Contact: Helen Heavirland, PO Box 146, College Place WA 99324-0146. Phone/fax (541) 938-3838. E-mail: hlh@bmi.net. Membership (8) open.

WALLA WALLA VALLEY CHRISTIAN SCRIBES. College Place. Contact: Helen Heavirland, PO Box 146, College Place WA 99324-0146. Phone/fax (541) 938-3838. E-mail: hlh@bmi.net. Membership (8) open.

WRITERS IN THE ROUGH. Arlington. Contact: Dean Paxton. (425) 244-3460. E-mail: jokejockey@ gmail.com. Membership (10) open.

WISCONSIN

LIGHTHOUSE CHRISTIAN WRITERS. Klondike. Contact: Lois Wiederhoeft, 901 Aubin St., Lot 115, Peshtigo WI 54157. (715) 582-1024. E-mail: 2loisann@myway.com. Or, Mary Jansen, PO Box 187, Mountain WI 54149; (715) 276-1706. Website: www.lighthousechristianwriters.com. Membership (8) open.

THE LIVING WORD/ACW CHAPTER. Superior. Contact: Amy Trees, pres., 1421 E. 5th St., Superior WI 54880. (715) 398-7244. E-mail: TheLivingWordSuperior@yahoogroups.com. Website: http://LivingWordWriters.bravehost.com. Membership (30) open.

PENS OF PRAISE CHRISTIAN WRITERS. Manitowoc. Contact: Cofounders Becky McLafferty, 9225 Carstens Lake Rd., Manitowoc WI 54220. (920) 758-9196; or Sue Kinney, 4516 Laurie Ln., Two Rivers WI 54241. (920) 793-2922. E-mail: mclafferty@lakefield.net, or cal-suek@charter.net. Membership (8-10) open. Meets monthly.

ROCK RIVER STORY WEAVERS. Johnson Creek. Contact: James B. Robar, N2963 Buena Vista Rd., Fort Atkinson WI 53538. (920) 568-1677. Fax (920) 397-7334. E-mail: jim@jamesbrobar.com. Membership (5) open.

WORD AND PEN CHRISTIAN WRITERS CLUB/ACW CHAPTER. Menasha. Contact: Chris Stratton, 107 E. McArthur St., Appleton WI 54911-2109. (920) 739-0752. E-mail: wordandpen@mychristian site.com. Website: www.mychristiansite.com/ministries/wordandpen. Membership (17) open.

CANADIAN/FOREIGN

ASSOCIATION OF CHRISTIAN WRITERS. Mainly London. Contact: Lin Ball or Rev. Simon Baynes, 23 Moorend Ln., Thame, Oxon, OX9 3BQ, United Kingdom. Phone 01844-213 673. E-mail: admin@chris tianwriters.org.uk. Website: www.christianwriters.org.uk. Membership (750) open. Sponsors a contest open to nonmembers; a biennial conference; and writers' days in March and October in London.

FRASER VALLEY CHRISTIAN WRITERS GROUP. Abbotsford BC. Contact: Helmut Fandrich, 2461 Sunnyside Pl., Abbotsford BC V2T 4C4, Canada. Phone/fax (604) 850-0666. E-mail: helmut10@coneharvesters.com. Membership (20) open.

INSCRIBE CHRISTIAN WRITERS' FELLOWSHIP. Edmonton (various locations across Canada). Contact: Eunice Matchett, 4304—45 St., Drayton Valley AB T7A 1G7, Canada. (780) 542-7950. E-mail: scrappi@telusplanet.net. Website: www.inscribe.org. Membership (250) open. Sponsors a newsletter and 2 contests, details on Website (one open to nonmembers). Also sponsors annual conference in September.

NEW ZEALAND CHRISTIAN WRITERS GUILD. Contact: Janet Fleming, Box 115, Kaeo 0448, New Zealand. E-mail: MJflamingos@xtra.co.nz. Website: www.freewebs.com/nzchristianwritersguild. Membership (130) open. Workshops (autumn & spring), biannual weekend retreat, local groups, home study courses, contest for members, and bimonthly magazine.

SWAN VALLEY CHRISTIAN WRITERS GUILD, Swan River, MB. Contact: Addy Oberlin, Box 132, Swan River MB R0L 1Z0, Canada. Phone/fax (204) 734-4269. E-mail: waltadio@mts.net. Membership (8) open. Sponsors a contest open to nonmembers.

NATIONAL/INTERNATIONAL GROUPS (NO STATE LOCATION)

AMERICAN CHRISTIAN FICTION WRITERS, PO Box 101066, Palm Bay FL 32910. Phone/fax (321) 984-4018. E-mail: Publicity Officer, Angela Breidenbach, 200 Horseshoe Ln., Missoula MT 59803, pr@acfw.com. Website: www.ACFW.com. E-mail loop, online courses, critique groups, and e-newsletter for members. Send membership inquiries to membership@acfw.com. Membership (2,000+) open. Sponsors contests for published and unpublished members. Sponsors annual seminar in September.

AMERICAN CHRISTIAN WRITERS SEMINARS. Sponsors conferences in various locations around the country (see individual states for dates and places). Call or write to be placed on mailing list for any conference. Events are Friday and Saturday unless otherwise noted. Brochures usually mailed three months prior to event. Contact: Reg Forder, Box 110390, Nashville TN 37222. Toll-free (800) 21-WRITE. Website: www.ACWriters.com.

CHRISTIAN WRITERS FELLOWSHIP INTL. (CWFI). Contact: Sandy Brooks, 1624 Jefferson Davis Rd., Clinton SC 29325-6401. (864) 697-6035. E-mail: cwfi@cwfi-online.org. Website: www .cwfi-online.org. To contact Sandy Brooks personally: sandybrooks@cwfi-online.org. No meetings, but offers market consultations, critique service, writers books, and conference workshop tapes. Connects writers living in the same area, and helps start writers' groups. Membership (1,000+) open.

CHRISTIAN WRITERS' GROUP INTL. (CWGI). Website: http://christianwritersgroup.org. An international organization of born-again Christians who write. Purpose: to assist Christians as they fulfill their calling to write by offering resources, information, education, support, networking, and interaction with Christian writers, editors, and publishers. Includes critique and prayer subgroups for members only. Periodically offers CWGI members scholarships to writing conferences. Editors and publishers are welcome. To join, send a blank e-mail to CWG-subscribe@yahoogroups.com or sign up at http://groups.yahoo.com/group/CWGI. Executive director: Brandy Brow. Membership (700+) open.

FAITH, HOPE & LOVE is the inspirational chapter of Romance Writers of America. E-mail: gayle@ faithhopelove-rwa.org. Charges yearly dues (see Website), but you must also be a member of RWA to join (see their Website for annual dues). Chapter offers these services: online list service for members, a Web page, 20-pg. bimonthly newsletter, annual contest, monthly online guest chats with multipublished authors and industry professionals, connects critique partners by mail or e-mail, and latest romance-market information. To join, contact RWA National Office, 14615 Benfer Rd., Houston TX 77069. (832) 717-5200. Fax (832) 717-5201. E-mail: info@rwanational.org. Website: www .rwanational.org. Or go to FHL Website: www.faithhopelove-rwa.org. Inspirational Readers Choice Contest by subgenre categories for published works; deadline April 1; cash prizes. Send SASE for guidelines. Membership (150+) open.

JERRY B. JENKINS CHRISTIAN WRITERS GUILD. Contact: Kerma Murray, 5525 N. Union Blvd., Ste. 200, Colorado Springs, CO 80918. Toll-free (866) 495-5177. Fax (719) 495-5187. E-mail: ContactUs@ChristianWritersGuild.com. Website: www.ChristianWritersGuild.com. This international organization of 1,800 members offers annual memberships, mentor-guided correspondence courses for adults (two-year Apprentice; advanced one-year Journeyman; and Craftsman) and youth (Pages: ages 9-12, and Squires: 13 and up), writing contests, conferences, critique service, writers resource books, monthly newsletter, and more. Critique service accepts prose samples of 1-15 pages. Professional writing assessment covers proper language usage, pacing, presentation, purpose, and persuasiveness. Call for pricing structure. Members receive 10% off.

NATIONAL ASSN. OF WOMEN WRITERS. General. Contact: Sheri McConnell, 24165 IH-10 W., Ste. 217-637, San Antonio TX 78257. Toll-free phone/fax (866) 821-5829. E-mail: info@ naww.org. Website: www.naww.org. Over 40 chapters across the U.S. (see Website for list of locations). Membership (3,000+) open. Sponsors regional events across the U.S. and national TeleSummits.

PEN-SOULS (prayer and support group, not a critique group). Conducted entirely by e-mail. Contact: Janet Ann Collins, Grass Valley CA. (530) 272-4905. E-mail: jan@janetanncollins.com. Membership (12) open.

THE WRITING ACADEMY. Contact: Inez Schneider, new member coordinator, 4010 Singleton Rd., Rockford IL 61114. (815) 877-9675. Website: www.wams.org. Membership (75) open. Sponsors year-round correspondence writing program and annual seminar in August held in Minneapolis.

12

Editorial Services

The following listing is included because so many writers contact me looking for experienced/qualified editors who can critique or evaluate their manuscripts. These people from all over the country offer this kind of service. I cannot personally guarantee the work of any of those listed, so you may want to ask for references or samples of their work.

The following abbreviations indicate what kinds of work they are qualified to do:

GE general editing/manuscript evaluation	CA coauthoring	BCE book contract evaluation
LC line editing or copyediting	B brochures	WS Website development
GH ghostwriting	NL newsletters	PP PowerPoint
	SP special projects	

The following abbreviations indicate the types of material the editors evaluate:

A articles	BP book proposals	GB gift books
SS short stories	JN juvenile novels	TM technical material
P poetry	PB picture books	E essays
F fillers	QL query letter	D devotionals
N novels		
NB nonfiction books	BS Bible studies	S scripts

If sending material by mail, always send a copy the editors can write on and an SASE for return of your material.

+ Indicates new listing

ALABAMA

WRITE INTEGRITY EDITORIAL SERVICES/TRACY RUCKMAN, 198 Lake Berry Ln., Lowndesboro AL 36752. E-mail: editor@writeintegrity.com. Website: www.writeintegrity.com. E-mail/mail. GE/LC/GH/B/NL/SP/WS. Edits: A/BP/E/D/F/GB/N/NB/QL/SS/Web content. Web design, image-building packages, blog tours, graphic design, and layout for print or e-mail newsletters, brochures, one-sheets, display advertising. Charges by standard formatted page; sample edits available. Rates, references, and services on Website. Also offers online writing courses; www.WIESworkshops.com.

ARIZONA

CARLA'S MANUSCRIPT SERVICE/CARLA BRUCE, 10229 W. Andover Ave., Sun City AZ 85351-4509. Phone/fax (623) 876-4648. E-mail: Carlaabruce@cox.net. Call/e-mail. GE/LC/GH/typesetting/PDF files for publishers. Edits: A/SS/P/F/N/NB/BP/QL/BS/GB/TM/E/D. Charges $2/page copyedit, $25/hr., or gives a project estimate after evaluation. Does ghostwriting for pastors and teachers; professional typesetting. Twenty-five years ghostwriting/editing; 14 years typesetting.

+CHRISTIAN MANUSCRIPT SUBMISSIONS.COM, Website: www.ChristianManuscriptSubmissions.com. Online manuscript submission to traditional publishers. Now offering writers an optional professional literary critique/edit of their manuscript. Details on Website.

ARKANSAS

EDITORIAL SERVICES/TONJA TAYLOR, 1302 E. 30th, Apt. A, Texarkana AR 71854. E-mail: Tonja@TonjaTaylor.com. Website: www.TonjaTaylor.com. Over 15 years' experience writing and editing. Also does critiques and manuscript format preparation for submissions to publishers.

CALIFORNIA

CHRISTIAN COMMUNICATOR MANUSCRIPT CRITIQUE SERVICE/SUSAN TITUS OSBORN, 3133 Puente St., Fullerton CA 92835-1952. (714) 990-1532. E-mail: Susanosb@aol.com. Website: www.christiancommunicator.com. Call/e-mail/write. For book, send material with $160 deposit. Staff of 18 editors. GE/LC/GH/CA/SP/BCE. Edits: A/SS/P/F/N/NB/BP/JN/PB/QL/BS/GB/TM/E/D/S/screenplays. $100 for short pieces/picture books. Three-chapter book proposal $160 (up to 40 pgs.). Additional editing $40/hr. Over thirty years' experience.

CITY BOY EDITORIAL SERVICE/STEVEN HUTSON, 4083 W. Avenue L, Ste. 255, Lancaster CA 93536. (661) 722-4896. Toll-free fax (866) 501-4280. E-mail: steve@hutsonbooks.com. Website: www.hutsonbooks.com/edit. Call/e-mail. Edits any genre or type of material. Published author; syndicated columnist; director of Antelope Valley Christian Writers Conference. Proofreading; copyediting; 3-chapter critique (up to 100 pgs.). Open to other projects at a negotiated rate.

EDITORIAL, BOOK DESIGN, AND PRODUCTION SERVICES/DESTA GARRETT, Dg-Ink Book Design, PO Box 1182, Daly City CA 94017-1182. (650) 994-2662. Fax (650) 991-3050. E-mail: Desta.Garrett@gmail.com. Write/call/e-mail. GE/LC/B/NL/SP. Complete editing and production for author, including for self-publishing using Adobe InDesign Creative Suite. Edits: A/SS/NB/BS/TM/E/D/ educational material. Has 20 years' experience doing all aspects of editing, production, and publishing of all types of material for nonprofit Christian foundation, up to large illustrated, indexed research books. Charges $50/hr.; $40/hr. for Christian authors with Christian material.

EDITORIAL SERVICES/KATHIE IDE, 203 Panorama Ct., Brea CA 92821. E-mail: Kathy@kathyide .com. Website: www.KathyIde.com. GE/LC/GH/CA/B/NL/SP/WS, writing coach. Edits A/SS/F/N/NB/BP/ QL/JN/BS/GB/D/S. Charges by the hour (mention this listing and get a $5/hr. discount). Freelance author, editor (full time since 1998), and speaker. Has done proofreading and editing for Moody, Thomas Nelson, Barbour/Heartsong, and WinePress.

EDITORIAL SERVICES/SUSAN LAKIN, 219 Double Bogey Dr., Boulder Creek CA 95006. (530) 200-5466. Fax (413) 812-7929. E-mail: sulakin@comcast.net. Website: www.cslakin.com. E-mail contact. GE/LC/writing coach. Edits: SS/P/N/NB/BP/QL/JN/BS/GB/D. Has years of editing experience; member of Christian PEN and CEN (Christian Editor Network); novelist. Specializes in contemporary fiction, fantasy, and nonfiction books related to theology, eschatology, and biblical topics. Charges by the hour or the page. Offers a free sample edit of 5-10 pages before taking on larger project.

V. L. HESTERMAN, Ph.D., PO Box 6788, San Diego CA 92166. E-mail: vhes@mac.com (cc to: vhesterman@hotmail.com). E-mail or mail contact only; include phone number for follow-up call. Editing, writing, photography. Twenty-five years' experience as book editor, author, writing professor, journalist, curriculum development, photography. At this time can only take limited projects; referrals from agent or publisher preferred. Edits/develops nonfiction material, including books, editorials, essays, memoirs, and photo books; works with publishers and writers as coauthor, line editor, or in editorial development. Will do line edits of fiction final drafts. Standard industry rates; depends on scope and condition of project. Will give binding quote with sample of writing and query/proposal.

DARLENE HOFFA, 512 Juniper St., Brea CA 92821. (714) 990-5980. E-mail: jack.darlene.hoffa@ roadrunner.com. E-mail contact. GE. Edits: A/F/NB/BP/D. Nineteen years' experience; author of 11 books. Charges $20/hr. or $2/ms pg.

+JRH EDITING/JENNIFER HAMILTON, So. California. E-mail: inklink@sbcglobal.net, or through Website: www.jrhediting.com. Offers a free macro edit of up to 1,500 words of a short story or article, or first chapter of your book. Copy submission into message (no attachments).

KMB COMMUNICATIONS INC./LAURAINE SNELLING, PO Box 1530, Tehachapi CA 93581. (661) 823-0669. Fax (661) 823-9427. E-mail: TLsnelling@yahoo.com. Website: www.LauraineSnelling .com. E-mail contact. GE. Edits: SS/N/JN. Charges $50/hr. with $100 deposit, or by the project after discussion with client. Award-winning author of 63 books (YA and adult fiction, 2 nonfiction); teacher at writing conferences.

LIGHTHOUSE EDITING/DR. LON ACKELSON, 13326 Community Rd., #11, Poway CA 92064-4754. (858) 748-9258. Fax (858) 748-7431. E-mail: Isaiah68LA@sbcglobal.net. Website: www .lighthouseedit.com. E-mail/write. GE/LC/GH/CA/B/NL/BCE. Edits: A/SS/N/NB/BP/QL/BS/E/D. Charges $35 for article/short-story critique; $60 for 3-chapter book proposal. Send SASE for full list of fees. Editor since 1981; senior editor 1984-2002.

B. K. NELSON EDITORIAL SERVICES/JOHN W. BENSON (editorial director), 1565 Paseo Vida, Palm Springs CA 92264-9508. (760) 778-8800. Fax (760) 778-6242. E-mail: bknelson4@cs.com. Website: www.bknelson.com. E-mail or mail contact. GE/LC/SP/BCE. Edits: A/SS/P/F/N/NB/BP/QL/JN/ PB/BS/GB/TM/E/D/S. Has been a literary agent for 22 years and has sold more than 3,000 books to major publishers. Contact for rates.

KAREN O'CONNOR COMMUNICATIONS/KAREN O'CONNOR, 10 Pajaro Vista Ct., Watsonville CA 95076. E-mail: karen@karenoconnor.com. Website: www.karenoconnor.com. E-mail. GE/LC. Book proposal commentary/editing. Edits: A/F/NB/BP/QL/D. One-hour free evaluation; $90/hr. or flat fee depending on project. Has 35 years of writing/editing; 25+ years teaching writing; 60 published books and hundreds of magazine articles.

SHIRL'S EDITING SERVICES/SHIRL THOMAS, 9379 Tanager Ave., Fountain Valley CA 92708-6557. (714) 968-5726. E-mail: Shirlth@verizon.net. E-mail (preferred)/write, and send material with $100 deposit. GE/LC/GH/SP/review/rewriting. Edits: A/SS/P/F/N/NB/BP/QL/GB/D/greeting cards/ synopses. Consultation, $75/hr.; evaluation/critique, $75/hr.; mechanical editing $65/hr.; content editing/rewriting $75/hr.

THARSEO PUBLISHING & EDITORIAL SERVICES/JULIA LOREN, 804 Sandstone Ln., Camano Island WA 98282. (530) 209-3225. E-mail: jloren.biz@gmail.com. Website: www.divineinterven tionbooks.com. E-mail contact. GE/GH/CA/B/NL/SP/writing coach. Edits: A/SS/F/N/NB/BP/QL/JN/BS/ GB/E/D/S. Former journalist, author of 8+ nonfiction books, ghostwriter, and writing coach. Rates are negotiable depending on complexity of the project and writing goals.

THE WORD WORKS/SONJA L. STRUTHERS, 40960 California Oaks Rd., Ste. 369, Murrieta CA 92562-4615. Phone/fax (951) 696-5631. E-mail: info@mywriter.net. Website: www.mywriter.net. Call/e-mail. GE/LC/GH/B/NL/SP/WS/writing coach. Edits: A/SS/F/NB/BP/QL/TM/E. Graduate of Irvine College Writing Program; award-winning editor and publisher for Inland Empire Mensa. Offers quote upon review of project only.

WRITINGCOACH.ME/ERICA MONGE, PO Box 727, Orange CA 92628. (714) 606-0130. Fax (866) 520-3072. E-mail: em@writingcoach.me. Website: www.writingcoach.me. E-mail contact; send material for review or critique with $100 deposit. GE/LC/B/NL/SP/WS/PP/press releases/writing coach. Edits: A/SS/P/F/N/NB/BP/QL/JN/PB/BS/GB/TM/E/D/S. Fifteen years' experience as published writer/editor. Exec. editor of a Christian publication. Specializes as a writing coach, helping writers take their ideas to the next level, and get paid for publication. Has a B.A. & M.A. Send manuscript or sample writings and $100 deposit. Will return a written proposal and $100. Projects typically estimate at $75/hr.

COLORADO

ALPHA TRANSCRIPTION/CHERYL A. COLCHIN, 1832 S. Lee St., Unit G, Lakewood CO 80232-6255. (303) 978-0880. Fax (303) 989-9596. E-mail: alphatranscription@juno.com. Call/e-mail. Typing for authors, preferably from cassette tapes, but will consider legible longhand material. Rate determined after discussion with client. Has worked with Dr. Larry Crabb, David Wilkerson, literary agents, and authors since 1988.

EDIT RESOURCE LLC/ERIC & ELISA STANFORD, 3578-E Hartsel Dr., #387, Colorado Springs CO 80920. (719) 599-7808. E-mail: info@editresource.com. Websites: www.editresource.com, www.inspirationalghostwriting.com, www.bookproposals.net. E-mail contact. GE/LC/GH/CA/NL/SP/ copywriting/proposal development. Edits: A/F/N/NB/BP/QL/BS/GB/E/D/book doctoring. Rates determined after discussion with client. Combined 35 years of professional editing experience.

SUSAN MARTINS MILLER WRITING & EDITORIAL INC., 3042 Montebello Dr. W., Colorado Springs CO 80918. (719) 659-2426. E-mail: susan@susanmartinsmiller.com. Website: www.susan martinsmiller.com. E-mail contact. CA/GE/GH/LC/SP. Edits: A/BS/D/JN/N/NB/book rewrites. Rates determined after discussion with client. 20+ years' writing experience.

OMEGA EDITING/MICHAEL P. COLCHIN, 1832 S. Lee St., Unit G, Lakewood CO 80232-6255. (303) 978-0880. Fax (303) 989-9596. E-mail: omegaediting@juno.com. Write/call/e-mail. GE/LC/ GH/CA/B/NL/SP. Edits: A/SS/NB/BP/QL/BS/TM/D. Charges $45 & up, or by the project after discussion with client. Works in partnership with authors and publishers as ghostwriter, coauthor, editor, or in editorial development. Published book and article author; 14 years' experience as freelance editor.

PAPYRUS PROOF/KATE JESSE, 26135 Stansbery St, Conifer CO 80433-9178. (720) 862-8628. E-mail:ksjpublish@aol.com. Website: www.jesse.us.com/papyrus.html. E-mail contact. GE/LC/NL/ SP/PP. Edits: A/SS/F/N/NB/BS/GB/TM/E/D/indexing/transcribing. Charges $20-55/hr. depending on type of work. Copyedited educational materials for Christian women's organization; copyedited a Christian e-book. Offers 25% discount on first projects for new clients.

THE PERFECT PAPER/PATRICIA UNGER, 16695 Von Neuman Dr., Monument CO 80132. (719) 481-0437. E-mail: aperfectsolutionva.net. Websites: www.aperfectsolutionva.com. Call/e-mail/send with $25 deposit. GE/LC/GH/B/NL/SP/BCE/PP/transcription. Edits: A/SS/P/F/N/NB/BP/QL/JN/E/D/S. Twenty years' experience transcribing, proofreading, and copyediting. Charges $35/hr. for transcription. Will work with any budget for editing and proofreading.

SCRIBBLE COMMUNICATIONS/BRAD LEWIS, Colorado Springs CO. (719) 649-4478. Fax (866) 542-5165. E-mail: brad.lewis@scribblecommunications.com. Website: www.scribblecommunications .com. E-mail contact. GE/LC/GH/substantive editing/developmental editing. Edits: A/NB/BP/QL/BS/D/ Website content. Edited more than 100 nonfiction books; senior editor of the *New Men's Devotional Bible* (Zondervan); content editor for *New Living Translation Study Bible* (Tyndale). Charges by project, mutually agreed upon with publisher or author, and stated in editor/author agreement.

SHEVET WRITING SERVICES/MARJORIE VAWTER, 3605 W. 94th Ave., Westminster CO 80031-3156. Phone/fax (720) 540-9516 (call ahead for fax). E-mail: shevetwrite@pcisys.net. Website: www .shevewritingservices.com. E-mail contact. GE/LC. Edits: N/NB/BP. Has been editing/proofreading since 2000. Testimonials and endorsements on Website.

A WAY WITH WORDS/RENEE GRAY-WILBURN, 1820 Smoke Ridge Dr., Colorado Springs CO 80919. (719) 271-7076. E-mail: waywords@earthlink.net. Website: www.awaywithwordswrit ing.wordpress.com. E-mail contact. GE/LC/GH/CA/B/NL/SP. Edits: A/SS/F/N/NB/QL/JN/PB/BS/GB/ TM/E/D. Line editing/copyediting: $15-25/hr. & up. Project prices negotiable. 12+ years' experience. Provides editorial services for independent authors, Christian publishers, ministries, and small businesses. Open to coauthoring opportunities. Specializes in children's and nonfiction.

FLORIDA

EDITORIAL SERVICES/SHARON LEE ROBERTS, 240 San Marco Dr., Venice FL 34285. (941) 484-0773. E-mail: poetryandprose1@verizon.net. E-mail contact. GE/LC. Edits: A/SS/P/F/PB/D. Charges $25/hr. for critique/evaluation/line editing/copyediting ($25 minimum) or $2.50/pg., or negotiable fee for project. Published author of 3 children's storybooks and hundreds of articles, short stories, and poems for children and adults. Former editorial assistant for *Living Streams*, a Christian writer's magazine.

EDITORIAL SERVICES/DIANE E. ROBERTSON, PO Box 10463, Bradenton FL 34282. (941) 928-5302. E-mail: pswriter1@netzero.net. Website: www.freelancewritingbydiane.com. E-mail contact. GE/GH/SP/writing coach. Edits: A/SS/F/N/NB/BP/QL/JN/PB/BS/E/S. Has written 2 novels, 1 book on all types of creative writing, 2 children's books, 200+ articles, short stories, and children's stories; previously served as associate editor of 2 magazines; presently teaches Short Story, Novel Writing, Magazine Writing, and Nonfiction creative writing classes at several colleges and independent living centers. Charges $25/hr.

EDITORIAL SERVICES/LESLIE SANTAMARIA, Winter Springs FL. E-mail: santamaria@mpinet .net. E-mail first. GE/LC. Edits: A/SS/N/NB/BP/QL/E/DS. Critiques: $65 for short pieces/picture books; $100 for 3-chapter book proposals. Editing services: By the project after initial review for $30. Published author and book reviewer with extensive book and magazine editing experience and a BA in English. Specializes in children's, nonfiction for adults.

LIGHTPOST COMMUNICATIONS/SEAN FOWLDS, 305 Pinecrest Rd., Mount Dora FL 32757-5929. (352) 383-2485. E-mail: sfowlds@earthlink.net. Website: www.seanfowlds.com. E-mail contact. GE/LC/B/NL/SP/copy for Websites. Edits: A/SS/P/F/NB/BP/QL/PB/BS/GB/TM/E/D/S. Offers coaching, writing, and editing services. Negotiated sliding scale starting at $35/hr. Former editor of a national publication.

SIGHT HOUND PRODUCTIONS LLC/ALAN WILSON, Coral Springs FL. (954) 829-3211. Fax (954) 345-6036. E-mail: contacts08@aol.com. E-mail/write. GE/CA/NL/SP. Edits: A/SS/N/NB/QL/ BS/E/D. Author of 2 books, with more than 13 years of corporate experience; offering precise editing experience. Charges $1.75/double-spaced pg. (no more than 500 pgs.).

GEORGIA

+EDITORIAL SERVICES/GLORIA SPENCER, 1455 Johnson Rd., Conyers GA 30094. (770) 294-8599. Fax (770) 761-9913. E-mail: gfespencer@aol.com. E-mail contact. GE/LC. Edits A/SS/N/NB. Over 20 years editing/writing experience; BA in Christian Education. Charges $1.50/double-spaced manuscript page, or by the project after a free initial consultation.

FAITHWORKS EDITORIAL & WRITING, INC./NANETTE THORSEN-SNIPES, PO Box 1596, Buford GA 30515. Phone/fax (770) 945-3093. E-mail: nsnipes@bellsouth.net. Website: www.faith workseditorial.com. E-mail contact. Freelance editor, book doctor, copyeditor/line editor, proofreader, work-for-hire projects. Edits juvenile fiction/short stories; juvenile or adult nonfiction/ articles/business/humor. Author of more than 500 articles/stories; has stories in more than 50 compilation books. Member: The Christian PEN (Proofreaders & Editors Network); and CEN (Christian Editors Network). Currently editing and proofreading *Cross & Quill* newsletter (CWFI), as well as corporate newsletters for a corporate company.

BONNIE C. HARVEY, PhD, 309 Carriage Place Ct., Decatur GA 30033. (404) 299-6149. Cell (404) 580-9431. Fax (404) 297-6651. E-mail: BoncaH@aol.com. Website: www.bookimprove.com. Call/e-mail/write to discuss terms & payment. GE/LC/GH/CA/SP/theology. Edits: A/SS/P/N/NB/QL/ JN/BS/GBE/D/S/theological and academic articles. Does critiquing, editing, book consulting, book proposals, and rewriting. Charges $40/hr. for reading/critiquing; $30/hr. for proofreading; $50/hr. for editing; $75-100/hr. for rewriting. Also gives overall charge by project instead of hourly rate. Has PhD in English; 15 years teaching college-level English; teaches English and writing classes at Kennesaw University; more than 30 years' experience as editor; has ghostwritten books and authored 22 books.

ON-TIME EDITORIAL SERVICES/LEIGH DELOZIER, 73 Price Quarters Rd., Ste. 124, McDonough GA 30253. (770) 851-7273. Fax (866) 321-9914. E-mail: leighdelozier@bellsouth .net. Website: www.leighdelozier.com. Call/e-mail. GE/LC/B/NL/SP/Sunday school curriculum. Edits: A/BP/D/GB/JN/QL. Also helps create press releases, media kits, and other promotional materials. BS in Journalism; 20 years' experience in publishing and public relations; multipublished author in Christian and corporate markets. Fees by the hour, page, or project, depending on the work. Basic proofreading $25/hr.; editing/rewriting $35-60/hr. Per-page fee for novel editing is at www .leighdelozier.com.

WRITE AVENUE/JILL COX-CORDOVA, 1310 Shiloh Trail East N.W., Kennesaw GA 30144. (678) 521-0899. E-mail: jcoxwritemind@aol.com. Website: www.writeavenue.com. E-mail contact. GE/LC/ media résumés/writing coach. Edits: A/SS/N/NB/BP/QL/BS/GB/E. Offers a variety of other services. CNN.com original video sr. producer; multiplatform journalist for 20+ yrs; media-studies professor for 3 yrs. See Website for list of services and charges.

WRITTEN BY A PRO/SHARLA TAYLOR, PO Box 1675, Richmond Hill GA 31324. (912) 656-6857. E-mail: writtenbyapro@msn.com. Website: www.writtenbyapro.com. E-mail contact. GE/LC/GH/CA/ SP/author assistance for ms preparation/SAT help for college-bound/writing coach. Edits: A/SS/N/ NB/BP/QL/JN/BS/GB/TM/E/D. Operates an online writing/editing service for authors & job seekers; tutors college-bound students, and teaches writing to middle school and high school students. E-mail or see Website for rates.

IDAHO

WRITE WORDS EDITING/SUSAN LOHRER, PO Box 702, Porthill ID 83853-0702. E-mail: susan@ inspirationaleditor.com. Website: www.InspirationalEditor.com. E-mail contact. GE/LC/writing coach. Edits: A/SS/N/BP/QL. Specializes in editing women's fiction and romance. Member of Christian Editor Network, Christian Proofreaders and Editors Network, and Romance Writers of America (clients have received multiple book contracts and writing awards). Charges hourly, per-page, or flat rates depending on project and author's needs.

ILLINOIS

ALICE 'N INK/ALICE PEPPLER, 1285 Luther Ln., Apt. 173, Arlington Hts. IL 60004-8176. (847) 749-0582. E-mail: peppler14@comcast.net. E-mail contact. GE/LC/B/NL. Edits: A/SS/P/F/N/NB/BP/ QL/JN/PB/BS/GB/TM/E/D/S ($30/hr.). Three-chapter book edit/critique, including market analysis $125; additional editing $30/hr. Publishing experience of 25 years. Published author of Christian books, articles, poetry, monographs. Quality work; quick turnaround.

AMY BADOWSKI'S EDITING SERVICE, 649 Frances Ave., Loves Park IL 61111-5910. E-mail: Amy .Badowski@gmail.com. E-mail contact. GE/LC/CA/B/NL/SP/writing coach. Edits: A/SS/F/N/NB/BP/ QL/JN/PB/BS/GB/E/D. BA English Studies, magna cum laude; M.A.T. (Secondary English Education). Charges $40-100 for articles; $250-750 for books.

EDITORIAL SERVICES/MELISSA JUVINALL, 1518 Augusta, Normal IL 61761. (309) 452-8917. E-mail: kangaj1@hotmail.com. Website: www.bearla.com. E-mail contact. GE/LC. Edits: N/NB/JN/ PB/BS/GB/TM. Has a B.A. & M.A. in English; specializes in children's lit; 8 years' editing experience;

judge for Christy Awards. Charges by the page for proofreading and copyediting; by the hour for critiquing.

THE WRITER'S EDGE, PO Box 1266, Wheaton IL 60187. E-mail: admin@writersedgeservice.com. Website: www.WritersEdgeService.com. No phone calls. A manuscript screening service for 90 cooperating Christian publishers. Charges $95 to evaluate a book proposal and if publishable, they will send a synopsis of it to 90 publishers who might be interested. If not publishable, they will tell how to improve it. If interested, request a Book Information Form via e-mail or copy from Website. Self-published books considered like new manuscripts. Reviews novels, nonfiction books, juvenile novels, Bible studies, devotionals, biography, and theology but no poetry. See Website for details.

INDIANA

ASHLEY INK/ASHLEY BARRETT, 801 W. Broadway, Mishawaka IN 46545. (574) 259-1118. E-mail: ashley@ashleyink.com. Website: www.ashleyink.com. E-mail contact. GE/LC/writing coach. Edits: A/SS/P/F/N/NB/BS/E/D. Has a B.A. in English; Associate of Arts in Professional Writing. Standard rate is $14/hr., but contact for individual estimate.

DR. DENNIS E. HENSLEY, 6824 Kanata Ct., Fort Wayne IN 46815-6388. Phone/fax (260) 485-9891. E-mail: dnhensley@hotmail.com. E-mail/write. GE/LC/GH/CA/SP. Edits: A/SS/P/F/N/NB/BP/ QL/JN/E/D/comedy/academic articles/editorials/Op-Ed pieces/columns/speeches/interviews. Rate sheet for SASE or by e-mail. Author of 51 books & 3,000 articles and short stories; PhD in English; University English professor; columnist for *Writer's Journal* and *Advanced Christian Writer*.

EDITORIAL SERVICES/APRIL FRAZIER, 7768 N. 100 E., Ossian IN 46777-9360. (260) 402-1883. E-mail: april_lynn@mac.com. E-mail/write. GE/LC/CA. Edits: A/SS/F/N/NB/BP/QL/BS/GB/E/D. Charges $25/hr. for proofreading/copyediting; $30/hr. for line editing, and $250 and up for manuscript evaluation. Send SASE or e-mail for rate sheet. BA in English, AA in writing, BA in Biblical Studies; ThM in Christian Education and Bible Exposition; published writer.

MENTOR'S PEN EDITORIAL SERVICES/CHRISTINA MILLER, 7084 S. 585 W., Huntingburg IN 47542. (812) 536-3549. E-mail: Christina@mentorspen.com. Website: www.mentorspen.com. E-mail contact. GE/LC/writing coach. Edits: N/NB/BP/QL. Published writer, 7 years' experience editing and critiquing, fiction contest judge. Charges $4-6/page. Offers free 5-page sample edit.

JAMES WATKINS/XARISCOM, 318 N. Lenfesty Ave., Marion IN 46952. E-mail: jim@jameswatkins .com. Website: www.jameswatkins.com. E-mail contact. GE/LC/GH/WS. Edits: A/NB/BP/QL/BS/D/S. Award-winning author of 14 books, 2,000+ articles, and an editor; winner of four editing and 2 book awards. 20+ years' experience. Charge $50 for 2,000 words of critique, editing, market suggestions; $5/pg. for content editing; $15/pg. for rewriting/ghosting; $50/hr. for Website evaluation/consulting.

KANSAS

BRADLEY WRITING AND EDITING SERVICES/SALLY BRADLEY, Louisburg KS. E-mail: sally@ sallysbradley.com or through Website: www.sallybradley.com. E-mail contact. GE/LC/B/SP. Edits: SS/N/ BP/QL. BA in English, former editor for Christian publishers, contest judge, member of Christian PEN (Proofreaders and Editors Network) and the Christian Editor Network. Services, prices, and client referrals on Website. Will tailor services to fit your needs.

KENTUCKY

EDITORIAL SERVICES/MARILYN A. ANDERSON, 127 Sycamore Dr., Louisville KY 40223-2956. (502) 244-0751. Fax (502) 452-9260. E-mail: shelle12@aol.com. Call/e-mail. GE/LC. Edits A/F/ NB/BS/TM/E/D. Charges $15-20/hr. for proofreading; $25/hr. for extensive editing; or negotiable by the job or project. Holds an MA and BA in English; former high school English teacher; freelance consultant since 1993. References available. Contributing member of The Christian PEN.

EDITORIAL SERVICES/BETTY L. WHITWORTH, 11740 S. Hwy. 259, Leitchfield KY 42754. (270) 257-2461. E-mail: Blwhit@bbtel.com. Call/e-mail. GE. Edits: N/NB. Typing fees based on project (reasonable). Editing for novels and nonfiction books. Retired English teacher, currently working as a newspaper columnist/journalist and independent editor. Will give estimate after previewing 20 pages. Been in business since 1999.

MARYLAND

OPINE BOOK ANALYSIS, (443) 745-2380. E-mail: info@opinebooks.com. Website: www.opinebooks .com. Prefers e-mail contact. Nonfiction book manuscript analysis. Book proposal advice. You want to be ready to know and reach your targeted audience. Quality feedback and detailed recommendations. Reasonable rates. Fast turnaround. Helps writers build extra quality into book content and presentation.

MASSACHUSETTS

WORD PRO/BARBARA A. ROBIDOUX, 127 Gelinas Dr., Chicopee MA 01020-4813. (413) 592-4386. Fax (413) 594-8375. E-mail: Ebwordpro@aol.com. Call/e-mail. GE/LC/writing coach. Edits: A/SS/F/NB/BP/QL/TM/E/D. Fee quoted upon request. BA in English; 18 years as freelancer; book reviewer; on staff of TCC Manuscript Critique Service.

MICHIGAN

BLUE WATER INK/JULIE ACKERMAN LINK, 8816 Eastern Ave. S.E., Byron Center MI 49315. (616) 827-7880. E-mail: Julie@BlueWaterInk.com. Website: www.bluewaterink.com. Call/e-mail. CA/GE/LC/SP. Edits: BP/BS/D/NB/QL. Full-service book-packaging company and publishing consultant. Handles everything from manuscript through printer-ready files, including editing (all levels), designing, compiling, typesetting, and author coaching. Flat-fee bids; never over budget. Member of the Academy of Christian Editors; author and contributor to the popular devotional *Our Daily Bread*.

EDITORIAL DRAGON/MICHELLE HUEGEL, 1950 S. 13th St., Lot 277, Niles MI 49120. (269) 591-0672. E-mail: editorialdragon@gmail.com. Website: www.editorialdragon.wordpress.com. E-mail contact. GE/LC/B/NL/SP/PP/scholarly work/dissertations/transcription. Edits: A/SS/P/F/N/NB/JN/BS/GB/TM/E/D/academic writing. Bachelor of Arts in English with a writing concentration. Editor for local Christian newspaper, published articles, writing tutor at Bethel College Writing Center. Charges depend on type and length of project.

EDITORIAL SERVICES/ADAM BLUMER, 719 East H St., Iron Mountain MI 49801. (906) 774-9576. E-mail: adam@blumer.org. Website: www.blumer.org/adam. E-mail contact. GE/LC/GH/BCE. Edits: A/SS/F/N/NB/BP/QL/JN/PB/BS/GB/D. More than 17 years' experience in writing, editing, proofreading; and 8 years of Website updating experience. Employed as full-time editor for 14 years; B.A. in print journalism.

LEAVES OF GOLD CONSULTING LLC/MARY EDWARDS, PO Box 211018, Detroit MI 48221. (313) 523-5886. E-mail: Edwardsmd@sbcglobal.net. E-mail contact. GE/LC/CA/writing coach. Edits: A/QL/N/NB/JN/BS/D/SS/TM/PB/gospel tracts/grant proposals/poetry critiques. Thirty years' experience writing/editing/coaching. Founder of the Called & Ready Writers. Written for *Chicken Soup for the Soul*. Provides monthly "how-to" workshops for writers. Fees negotiable depending on writer's level of experience.

WALLIS EDITORIAL SERVICES/DIANA WALLIS, 547 Cherry St. S.E., #6C, Grand Rapids MI 49503-4755. (616) 459-8836. E-mail: WallisEdit@sirus.com. Call/e-mail. GE/LC/SP/WS/proofreading. Edits: A/N/NB/JN/BS/TM/D/advertising and promotional copy, Website content, educational materials for students and parents/teachers, catalog copy. Rates per project rather than per hour. Calvin College graduate, 17 years freelancing for publishers, corporations, and ad agencies; details on request.

WRITER'S NUDGE/MARY BUSHA, 1201 Charter Oaks Dr., Davison MI 48423. (810) 653-4218. Email: marybusha@writersnudge.com or joyofwriting45@yahoo.com. Website: www.writersnudge .com. E-mail contact. GE/LC/CA/BCE/writing coach. Edits: A/SS/N/NB/BP/QL/JN/PB/BS/GB/E/D. Offers workshops/seminars. Over 30 years of editorial and writing experience. Evaluates your projects and bids on the project.

THE WRITE SPOT/ARLENE KNICKERBOCKER, Where Quality and Economy Unite, PO Box 424, Davison MI 48423-9318. (810) 793-0316. E-mail: writer@thewritespot.org. Website: www.the writespot.org. E-mail/write. GE/LC/GH/CA/B/NL/classes and speaking/writing coach. Edits: A/SS/P/NB/BP/QL/BS/D. Published credits since 1996; references available. Prices on Website.

WRITING CAREER COACH.COM/TIFFANY COLTER, Michigan. E-mail: Tiffany@WritingCareer Coach.com. Website: www.writingcareercoach.com. E-mail contact. GE/GH/SP/NL/WS/PP/writing coach/writing career coaching/business planning. Edits: N/NB/BP/QL. BA; Daphne Award-winning writer; multiple articles published; columnist for suspense magazine; feature writer/columnist. Charges $20/hr. for content editing and career coaching. Offers a discounted coaching package $30/mo. See Website for other services. See editing sample: http://writingcareercoach.com/?p=324.

MINNESOTA

MY BOOK THERAPY/SUSAN MAY WARREN/RACHEL HAUCK, PO Box 1290, Grand Marais MN 55604. E-mail: info@mybooktherapy.com. Website: www.mybooktherapy.com. E-mail contact. GE/brainstorming/writing coach. Edits book proposals/crafts synopses, mentors writers. Award-winning, best-selling authors with nearly 40 books in the market. Acclaimed craft instructors from national writing conferences. Warren has been a multiple Christy nominee and a RITA winner. Hauck has been a RITA nominee and an ACFW Book of the Year winner. Price list on Website.

NOBLE CREATIVE, LLC/SCOTT NOBLE, PO Box 131402, St. Paul MN 55113. (651) 494-4169. E-mail: snoble@noblecreative.com. Website: www.noblecreative.com. E-mail contact. GE/LC/GH/B/NL/SP/WS. Edits: A/SS/F/N/NB/BP/QL/BS/GB/TM/E/D. More than a decade of experience, including several years as asst. ed. at *Decision* magazine. Masters degree in Theological Studies. Charges by the hour or the project.

NORTH COUNTRY TRANSCRIPTION (Psalm 96:12): Writing, Editing and Secretarial Services/CONNIE PETTERSEN, Aitkin MN. (218) 927-6176. E-mail: cardinals4connie@gmail .com. Call/e-mail. Manuscript typing; edit for punctuation/spelling/grammar. Experience: published author of short fiction; journalist with 400 articles published; 30 years' secretarial/transcription experience. Types novels/nonfiction mss, résumés, etc. Transcription by digital voice files or tapes. Fees: hourly rate or by a 65-character, computer-counted line, plus postage. Free estimates. Confidentiality guaranteed. References.

A WRITE START COMMUNICATIONS/TAMA WESTMAN/LEE WARREN, E-mail: tama@awrit estart.com or lee@awritestart.com. Website: www.awritestart.com. E-mail contact. GE/LC/GH/CA/B/NL/SP/WS/blogs/writing coach. Edits: A/SS/P/F/N/NB/BP/QL/JN/PB/BS/GB/TM/E/D/S/promotional material. Freelance writers, award winners, and former editors. Charges $40/hr. and requires a 3-hour minimum payment up front; coaching fee is $75/hr.

MISSISSIPPI

NEXT LEVEL CRITIQUES/SUSAN E. RICHARDSON, 106 Fox Run Way, Clinton MS 39056. (601) 924-7821. E-mail: nextlevelcritiques@bellsouth.net. Website: www.nextlevelcritiques.com. E-mail contact. GE/writing coach. Edits: N/NB/BP/QL/JN/BS. Critique reader for Steeple Hill, former first reader for Angela Hunt, published author, columnist, 20 years in publishing industry, including many years in Christian retailing. Charges by the page. Rate charts on Website.

MISSOURI

BLUE MOUNTAIN EDITORIAL SERVICE/BARBARA WARREN, 4721 Farm Road 2165, Exeter MO 65647. (417) 835-3235. E-mail: barbarawarren@hughes.net. Website: www.barbarawarren bluemountainedit.com. E-mail contact. GE/LC/writing coach. Edits: A/SS/N/NB/BP/QL/JN/BS/GB/E/D. Charges $20/hr. Twenty-one years' experience.

THERE'S AN ANGEL IN YOUR INKWELL/CAROL NEWMAN, PO Box 480835, Kansas City MO 64148-0835. (913) 681-1168. Fax (913) 681-1173. E-mail: carol@angelinyourinkwell.com. Website: www.angelinyourinkwell.com. E-mail contact. GE/GH. Edits: A/SS/P/F/NB/BP/QL/E/D. Variable rates according to project; average $40/hr.; 1/2 hr. free consultation. Twenty years national inspirational writer, teacher, and writing coach.

MONTANA

APPRAISING YOUR NOVEL/JAMES L. COTTON, 652 Treece Gulch Rd., Stevensville MT 59870. (406) 777-5191. E-mail: noveledit2003@yahoo.com. Website: www.appraisingyournovel.com. Call/ e-mail/write. GE. Edits novels. Has 20 years' experience as a newspaper and national magazine editor and associate publisher. Began editing service in 2000. Charges $1/ms pg.

THE WRITE EDITOR/ERIN K. BROWN, Corvallis. E-mail: wordcontract@writeeditor.net. Website: www.writeeditor.net. E-mail contact. GE/LC. Edits: A/SS/F/N/NB/BP/QL/JN/BS/E/D/NL/B. Has a certificate in Editorials Practices: Graduate School, USDA, Washington DC; Christy Award judge 2006-2009; member of Editorial Freelancers Assn.; The Christian PEN; coauthor of *The Lost Coin*.

NEVADA

EDITORIAL SERVICES/JEANETTE HANSCOME, 3201 Heights Dr., Reno NV 89503. (775) 787-1263. E-mail: jeanettehanscome@sbcglobal.net. Website: www.jeanettehanscome.com. E-mail contact. GE/writing coach. Edits: A/SS/F/N/NB/QL/D/S/YA novels & nonfiction. Author of 3 teen books with Focus on the Family; editor for 5 years; 300+ published articles, devotions & stories; teaches and critiques online and at writers' conferences. Charges $25-30/hr; flat fees negotiable.

+SPRING VALLEY EDITORIAL SERVICES/D. KATHRYN LANE, 9552 W. Tropicana Ave., Apt. 1091, Las Vegas NV 89147. (702) 405-6480. E-mail: dkathrynlane@gmail.com. Old-fashioned editing for the Christian author. Specializing in LC/SP for SS/BP/QL/E/D. Charges by the project.

NEW HAMPSHIRE

AMGD ENTERPRISES/SALLY WILKINS, PO Box 273, Amherst NH 03031-0273. (603) 673-9331. E-mail: SEDWilkins@aol.com. Website: www.sallywilkins.com. E-mail contact. GE/LC/B/NL. Edits: A/F/NB/BP/QL. Published nonfiction adult and juvenile books and articles; edited 2 successful book proposals; experienced critiquer. Rate sheet for SASE.

NEW JERSEY

TOPNOTCH WRITING SOLUTIONS/MARYANN DIORIO, PhD, 1216 Forest Dr., Millville NJ 08332-2597. (856) 327-1231. Fax (856) 327-0291. E-mail: DrMaryAnn@TopNotchWritingSolutions.com. Website: www.TopNotchWritingSolutions.com. E-mail contact. GE/SP/NL/WS/writing coach (www.TopNotchLifeandCareerCoaching.com). Edits: A/SS/P/F/BP/QL. 25+ years' experience; award winner; 4 published books; hundreds of published articles, short stories, and poems. Rate sheet available on request.

WRITER'S RELIEF, INC./RONNIE L. SMITH, 409 S. River St., Hackensack NJ 07601. (866) 405-3003. Fax (201) 641-1253. E-mail: Ronnie@wrelief.com. Website: www.WritersRelief.com. Call or e-mail. LC/NL/targeting submissions. Proofs: A/SS/P/F/N/NB/JN/E. Sixteen years' experience as an Author's Submission Service. Free monthly newsletter for writers contains date-driven list of markets. Contact for rates.

NEW YORK

EDITORIAL SERVICES/STERLING DIMMICK, 311 Chemung St., Apt. 5, Waverly NY 14892-1463. (607) 565-4247. E-mail: sterlingdimmick@hotmail.com. Call. GE/LC/GH/CA/SP. Edits: A/SS/P/F/N/NB/BP/QL/JN/PB/BS/GB/TM/E/D/S. Has an AAS in Journalism; BA in Communication Studies. Charges $20/hr. or by the project.

EDITORIAL SERVICES/LAURIE GRAZIANO, 658 E. 34th St., Brooklyn NY 11203-6102. E-mail: grazianolau@yahoo.com. E-mail/write. Research/market columns/interviews/instructional. Will write A/P/F/D/greeting card copy. Experienced writer, contributing editor, staff writer, regular columnist. Charges $15-75/hr. or by the project.

+I AM THE VINE EDITORIAL SERVICES/SUSAN RESCIGNO, 2927 Lexington Ave., Mohegan Lake NY 10547. (914) 315-1024. E-mail: srescigno@optimum.net. E-mail contact. GE/LC. Edits: N/NB. Charges $17-19/hr., depending on level of edit required.

NORTH CAROLINA

EDITORIAL SERVICES/MIKE & JASMIN MORRELL, Raleigh NC. (770) 313-1718. E-mail: jasminis@gmail.com. E-mail contact. GE/LC/B/NL/SP/WS. Edits: A/SS/F/N/NB/BP/QL/JN/PB/BS/GB/E/D. Has edited for Christian publishers and mainstream curriculum publishers. Developmental editing: $8/pg.; copyediting $6/pg. Requires 50% of fee up front. Requested revisions are included in original fee.

ANNA W. FISHEL, 3416 Hunting Creek Dr., Pfafftown NC 27040. (336) 924-5880. E-mail: awfishel@triad.rr.com. Call/write/e-mail. GE/CA/SP. Edits A/SS/P/N/NB/JN/E/D. Charges by the hour. Estimates offered. Two decades of professional editing experience; editor with major Christian publishing house for over 10 years; published author of 6 children's books.

PREP PUBLISHING/PATTY SLEEM, 1110 1/2 Hay St., Fayetteville NC 28305. (910) 483-6611. Fax (910) 483-2439. E-mail: preppub@aol.com. Website: www.prep-pub.com. Write. GE/LC/SP. Edits: N/NB. Project price based on written query and initial free telephone consultation. BA in English, MBA from Harvard, author of more than 25 books.

OHIO

+EDITORIAL SERVICES/KELLY KAGAMAS TOMKIES, 36 N. Cassady Rd., Columbus OH 43209. Phone/fax (614) 732-4860. E-mail: kakwrite@aol.com. Call, e-mail, or write. GE/LC/GH/CA/NL/

writing coach. Edits A/SS/N/NB/BP/QL/JN/PB/BS/GB/TM/E/D. An author/editor with 20 years' experience. Written and/or edited for individuals, Websites, magazines, and publishing houses, such as Barbour Publishing and McGraw Hill. Prefers to negotiate a flat fee per project.

+EDITORIAL SERVICES/MINA R. RAULSTON, 4694 Cemetery Rd. #290, Hilliard OH 45026-1124. (614) 507-7893. E-mail: m_raulston@hotmail.com. Website: www.minaraulston.com. E-mail contact. GE/LC/GH/CA/B/NL/SP/PP. Edits A/SS/F/N/NB/BP/QL/JN/BS/E/D. Has been a freelance writer/editor for more than 10 years; written for newspapers and magazines; written nonprofit newsletters; created brochures and flyers; written press releases and edited nonfiction authors. Samples of work on Website. Charges $25/hour; negotiable for specific projects.

IZZY'S OFFICE/DIANE STORTZ, PO Box 31239, Cincinnati OH 45231. (513) 602-6720. E-mail: diane@izzysoffice.com. Website: www.izzysoffice.com. E-mail contact. GE/LC/GH/CA. Edits: A/NB/BP/JN/N/PB/QL/BS/GB/E/D. Former editorial director for a Christian publisher (10 yrs.); published author, experience as children's editor and magazine copy editor. See Website for client list and partial list of projects. Copyediting or substantive editing by the hour or per-project basis; book proposal package $750; evaluation and 2-chapter critique $350. One-half payment amount due before work begins.

OKLAHOMA

+B & B Editing Service/Brenda Sykes, Tulsa. E-mail: bandbwrite@gmail.com. E-mail contact. GE/LC/PP/writing coach. Edits A/SS/N/NB/JN/QL/BS/GB/D/S. CLASS member. Familiar with MLA, APA, and Chicago style formats. Has a B.A. in Christian education, M.A. in biblical studies, M.A. in journalism. Coaching offered in writing and self-publishing. Estimates available.

EDITORIAL SERVICES/RICHARD W. RUNDELL, PO Box 983, Haskell OK 74436-0983. (918) 482-5066. E-mail: rwrundell@windstream.net. E-mail contact. GE/LC. Edits: A/BS/NB/D. Over 20 years' editing experience; author of books, articles, booklets, devotionals, and book reviews. Rates negotiable.

EPISTLEWORKS CREATIONS/JOANN RENO WRAY, Helping Writers Reach Their High Call, 8409 S. Elder Ave., Broken Arrow, OK 74011-8286. (918) 451-4017 or cell (918) 695-4528. E-mail: epedit@epistleworks.com. Website: http://epistleworks.com. Call/write/e-mail (prefer). GE/LC/GH/CA/B/NL/SP/Research. Edits: A/SS/P/F/N/NB/BP/D. Creates graphic art such as covers and logos; Website design and content. PR materials such as fliers, brochures, booklets, and Web ads including animated. Uses signed contracts with clients. Experienced writer, editor, and artist since 1974, including work as editor for a Tulsa monthly Christian newspaper, publishing an online magazine, columnist, editing clients' work and work of pastors and ministers, including books, speaking and teaching at national Christian Writers' conferences, over 3,000 articles published, and much more. Charges start at $30/hr. with a required $45 nonrefundable consulting fee (deducted from total bill). Discounts for churches and ministries. Accepts checks, money orders, or PayPal. See Website for detail on services. Gives binding estimates. Gives detailed time clock report. Mentoring services and e-mail writing classes available. Speaker and teacher.

TWEEN WATERS EDITORIAL SERVICES/TERRI KALFAS, PO Box 1233, Broken Arrow OK 74013-1233. (918) 346-7960. E-mail: tlkalfas@cox.net. E-mail contact. GE/LC/GH/CA/B/SP/BCE. Edits: A/N/NB/BP/QL/BS/TM/D/project management/book doctoring. Multiple editorial and freelance writing services. Over 25 years' writing and publishing experience. Writing instructor. Available as conference speaker and workshop teacher. Charges $3 per pg./$25/hr./negotiable on special projects.

WINGS UNLIMITED/CRISTINE BOLLEY, Broken Arrow OK. (918) 250-9239. Fax (918) 250-9597. E-mail: WingsUnlimited@aol.com. Website: www.wingsunlimited.com. E-mail contact. GE/LC/GH/CA/SP. Edits: BP/NB/D. All fees negotiated in advance: developmental edits (format/house-style/clarity) range from $1,500-$3,000; 100-250 pgs.; substantive rewrite averages $5,000/250 pgs. Specializes in turning sermon series into books for classic libraries. Author/coauthor/ghostwriter of 30+ titles. Over 25 years' experience in development of best-selling titles for major Christian publishing houses.

OREGON

EDITING GALLERY LLC/CAROL L. CRAIG, 2622 Willona Dr., Eugene OR 97408. (541) 342-7300. E-mail: carollcraig@comcast.net. Website: www.editinggallery.com. Call/e-mail. GE/LC/synopses/writing coach. Edits: N/FBP/QL/memoirs. English major; 15+ years' experience. Charges $75/hr.

EDITORIAL SERVICES/FLORENCE C. BLAKE, 4865 Hwy. 234, #176, White City OR 97503. E-mail: florblake@ccountry.net (put "Edit Service" in subject line). E-mail contact. GE/LC/B/NL/SP. Edits: A/SS/F/NB/E/D/Christian tracts. Freelance writer since 1999 with over 700 sales, community college writing teacher, senior contributing editor for general publication. Charges $2/double-spaced page.

EDITORIAL SERVICES/ROSE ENGLISH, 94760 Oaklea Dr., Junction City OR 97448-9314. Phone/fax (541) 998-3959. E-mail: rose9265@comcast.net. Call/e-mail. GE/LC/B/NL/SP. Edits: A/SS/N/NB/JN/PB/BS/E/D. Manuscript editing, freelance graphic design, print shop and ad agency experience. Fee based on project.

HONEST EDITING, Bill Carmichael & editing team. E-mail: bill.honestediting@gmail.com. Website: www.honestediting.com. Cost-effective manuscript and proposal evaluations by professional editors. Check Website for full list of services and instructions.

D. C. JACOBSON & ASSOCIATES/DON JACOBSON, 971 E. Cascade Ave., Sisters OR 97759-9320. (541) 549-3585. Fax (541) 549-1785. E-mail: query@dcjacobson.com. Website: www.dcjacobson.com. Website submissions only. GE/LC/CA/literary consulting/writing coach. Edits: N/NB/BP/QL/JN/BS/GB/D. Thirty+ years' combined experience in publishing, marketing, sales, editorial, and more than 1,000 titles published as former president of a major Christian publisher. Provides editing services to nonliterary agent clients, specializing in concept development, crafting salable proposals and queries, and providing ongoing coaching depending on writer's needs (self-publishing, editorial, etc.). Package rates detailed on Website (click on "Consulting").

+LIVING WORD LITERARY SERVICES/KIMBERLY SHUMATE, PO Box 40974, Eugene OR 97404-1795. (541) 863-6567. E-mail: livingwordliterary@gmail.com. Website: www.livingwordliterary.wordpress.com. E-mail contact. GE/LC/GH/B/NL/SP/W. Edits: A/SS/N/NB/BP/QL/E/D/S. Twelve years' publishing experience; member ECPA; advisory staff at George Fox University; Willamette Writers; screenwriter since 1995. Charges $3 per double-spaced page.

PICKY, PICKY INK/SUE MIHOLER, 1075 Willow Lake Road N., Keizer OR 97303-5790. (503) 393-3356. E-mail: smiholer@hotmail.com. E-mail contact. LC/B/NL. Edits: A/F/N/NB/BP/QL/BS/D. Charges $30 an hour or $50 for first 10 pages of a longer work; writer will receive a firm completed-job quote based on the first 10 pages. Freelance editor for several book publishers since 1998. Will help you get your manuscript ready to submit.

+REVISION EDITING AGENCY/KIMBERLY SHUMATE, PO Box 40974, Eugene OR 97404. (541) 683-6567. E-mail: revisioneditingagency@gmail.com. Website: www.revisioneditingagency.wordpress.com. E-mail submissions only. Copyediting and critique services for sample chapters, full-length mss, cover letters, book proposals, magazine articles, blog entries, etc. Fiction or nonfiction. Details on Website.

SALLY STUART, 1647 S.W. Pheasant Dr., Aloha OR 97006. (503) 642-9844. Fax (503) 848-3658. E-mail: stuartcwmg@aol.com. Website: www.stuartmarket.com. Blog: www.stuartmarket.blogspot.com. Call/e-mail. GE/BCE/agent contracts. Edits: A/SS/N/NB/BP/GB/JN. No poetry or picture books.

Charges $40/hr. for critique; $45/hr. for phone/personal consultations. Contact for availability (not available December-April). For books, send a copy of your book proposal: cover letter, chapter-by-chapter synopsis for nonfiction (5-page overall synopsis for fiction), and the first three chapters, double-spaced. Comprehensive publishing contract evaluation $80-150. Author of 37 books (including the *Christian Writers' Market Guide*) and 40+ years' experience as a writer, teacher, marketing expert.

PENNSYLVANIA

ANGAH CREATIVE SERVICES/DANIELLE CAMPBELL-ANGAH, 961 Taylor Dr., Folcroft PA 19032. (610) 457-8300. E-mail: dcangah@angahcreative.com, or blessingsofgod77@verizon.net. Website: www.angahcreative.com. Ten years' writing experience; 5 years' editing experience.

REBECCA CARANFA EDITORIAL SERVICES, 502 Idaho Ave., Verona PA 15147-2910. Phone/fax (412) 795-7711. E-mail: BlessingsofGod77@verizon.net. E-mail contact. GE/B/NL/SP. Edits: A/SS/E/term papers/résumés. Charges $25/hr. or estimate after evaluation of material. 20 years' experience. Teaching background.

+CAVANAUGH EDITORIAL SERVICES/LORI CAVANAUGH, 400 Mayberry Rd., Schwenksville PA 19473. (484) 552-0671. E-mail: lori@cavanaugheditorial.com. Website: www.cavanaugheditorial.com. Call/e-mail. GE/LC.

MICHELE T. HUEY EDITORIAL SERVICES, 121 Homestead Ln., Glen Campbell PA 15742-8404. (814) 845-7683. E-mail: writeon4writers@yahoo.com. Website: www.michelehuey.com. E-mail contact. GE/LC/writing coach. Edits: A/SS/N/NB/QL/D. English/composition/journalism teacher for 20 yrs.; newspaper reporter, feature writer, former editor, columnist; writing mentor for 3 writing organizations. Keystone Press Award 2009 from Pennsylvania Newspaper Assn. Charges $30/hr. or $5/pg. Provide the total number of words and a sample page or two of your manuscript. Follows rates suggested at www.writersmarket.com/content/howmuch3.asp.

STRONG TOWER PUBLISHING/HEIDI NIGRO, PO Box 973, Milesburg PA 16853-0973. E-mail: strongtowerpubs@aol.com. Website: www.strongtowerpublishing.com. E-mail contact. GE/LC/NL/WS/PP/rewriting/developmental editing/writing coach. Edits: A/SS/P/F/N/NB/BS/GB/TM/E/D. Specializes in general theological and eschatological mss. Twenty years' experience in editing in book and magazine publishing. Manuscript evaluation, $59-109; proofing, $2 per 250-word page; copyediting, $4/250-word page; developmental editing and book development $40/hr. or by project. Other projects negotiable. Provides free 5-page sample edit. Theological manuscripts must be consistent with basic statement of faith.

WORDS FOR ALL REASONS/ELIZABETH ROSIAN, 108 Deerfield Ln., Johnstown PA 15905-5703. (814) 255-4351. E-mail: wordsforallreasons@atlanticbb.net. Website: www.101steps.zoomshare.com. E-mail contact. GE/LC/GH/CA. Edits: A/SS/P/F/N/NB/BP/QL/BS/GB/E/D. More than 35 years' experience writing, teaching, and editing; more than 1,000 published works, plus inspirational novel, how-to book, and 6 chapbooks. Rate sheet on Website.

WRITE HIS ANSWER MINISTRIES/MARLENE BAGNULL, LittD, 951 Anders Rd., Lansdale PA 19446. Phone/fax (484) 991-8581. E-mail: mbagnull@aol.com. Website: www.writehisanswer.com. Call/write. GE/LC/typesetting. Edits: A/SS/N/NB/BP/JN/BS/D. Charges $35/hr.; estimates given. Call or write for information on At-Home Writing Workshops, a correspondence study program. Author of 5 books; compiler/editor of 3 books; over 1,000 sales to Christian periodicals.

WRITE NOW SERVICES/KAREN APPOLD, 2012 Foxmeadow Cir., Royersford PA 19468. (610) 948-1961. Fax (952) 216-2365. E-mail: KarenAppold@comcast.net. Website: www.writenowservices.com. Call/e-mail. GE/LC/GH/B/NL/SP/WS. Edits: A/SS/F/QL/E. Professional editor, writer, consultant since 1993 for magazines, journals, newsletters, and newspapers. Hundreds of published articles and extensive magazine and newspaper editing. Rates determined after free evaluation of project.

SOUTH CAROLINA

EDITORIAL SERVICES/LINDA J. LEE, 108 Quail Creek Dr., West Columbia SC 29169-3434. (803) 939-9713. E-mail: ljlee@bellsouth.net. E-mail contact. GE/LC/B/NL/SP. Edits: A/SS/P/N/NB/BP/QL/JN/PB/BS/GB/TM/E/D/S. Contributing editor for *P31 Woman* magazine; has edited books; has private-tutored for 15 years; writing tutor at college level for 8 years. Charges by the page or as individually negotiated.

TENNESSEE

CHRISTIAN WRITERS INSTITUTE MANUSCRIPT CRITIQUE SERVICE, PO Box 110390, Nashville TN 37222. Toll-free (800) 21-WRITE. E-mail: ACWriters@aol.com. Website: www.ACWriters.com. Call/write. GE/LC/GH/CA/SP/BCE. Edits: A/SS/P/F/N/NB/BP/JN/PB/BS/TM/E/D/S. Send SASE for rate sheet and submission slip.

TYPING/EDITORIAL SERVICES/BARBARA BUIS, 2515 Villa Dr. N.W. A, Cleveland TN 37312-2525. E-mail: truk4jsuschrst@yahoo.com. Call/e-mail. LC/Transcription from tapes. Edits: A/SS/N/BS/D (anything). Has typed 4 books and helped edit 3 books. Charges $1.50/pg.

EDITORIAL SERVICES/KIM PETERSON, 1114 Buxton Dr., Knoxville TN 37922. E-mail: petersk@BethelCollege.edu or peterskus@yahoo.com. Write/e-mail. GE/LC/GH/CA/B/NL/SP/PP/mentoring/writing coach. Edits: A/P/F/N/NB/BP/QL/JN/PB/GB/TM/E/D. Freelance writer; college writing instructor; freelance editor; conference speaker. M.A. in print communication. Charges $25-35/hr.

WRITING COACH/LINDA WINN, 138 Bluff Dr., Winchester TN 37398. (931) 962-8801. E-mail: lhwinn@comcast.net. Writing coach.

TEXAS

+B & B EDITING SERVICE/BEV KLASSEN, 6100 E. Loop 820 S. #744, Fort Worth TX 76119. E-mail: bandbwrite@gmail.com. E-mail/write. GE/LC/PP. Edits A/SS/N/NB/JN/QL/BS/GB/D/S. The combined editing experience of the team is 47 years with three master's degrees in journalism, communication, and biblical studies. The staff consists of all seasoned authors and conference speakers, specializing in line editing and offering discounts to new writers.

B & B WRITING SERVICE/BEVERLY OSTOWSKI, E-mail: bandbwrite@gmail.com. Writer for 20 yrs.; screenwriter for 10 yrs.; line editor for more than 10 yrs.

EDITORIAL SERVICES/KELLEY MATHEWS, ThM, 216 Birdbrook Dr., Anna TX 75409. (214) 769-1829. E-mail: kmathews@newdoors.info. Website: www.newdoors.info. E-mail contact. GE/LC/CA/NL/SP. Edits: A/NB/BP/PB/BS/GB/TM/D. Has 15 years' experience in editing/proofreading; coauthored 4 books; authored numerous articles. Charges $30/hr. for proofreading; $50/hr. for copyediting; negotiable flat fee for large book projects. Specializes in theological and women's issues.

FACETS BUSINESS COMMUNICATIONS/GEM SMITH, 8221 Kingsbrooke Rd., Houston TX 77024. (713) 465-8284. E-mail: peakestevens@gmail.com. Website: www.facetscom.com. E-mail/write. LC/B/NL/SP/WS/content development. Edits: A/SS/N/NB/BP/TM/E/S/marketing materials/direct response letters. Published freelance writer/editor/speaker for 30 years. Has worked with technical/scientific/theological material and authors with English as a second language. Published in local and international publications; conference speaker. Works by the hour with deposit, after discussing project with client. Average is $25-60/hr.

PWC EDITING/PAUL W. CONANT, 527 Bayshore Pl., Dallas TX 75217-7755. (972) 286-2882. Cell (214) 289-3397. E-mail: pwcediting@gmail.com. Website: www.pwc-editing.com. E-mail contact preferred. LC/NL/SP/PP. Edits: SS/N/NB/BS/TM/E/D/S/Sci-Fi. Writer, editor; proofreader for magazines and book publishers. Member of Christian Editor's Network and Christian PEN. Terms negotiable for long works. Charges publishers up to $25/hr. Prefers to work up a page rate based on a minimum 10-page sample, giving new clients up to 1.5 hours of free editing. Has edited 3 high school science textbooks; technical books on geology, manufacturing, and hypobaric inventions, and numerous books by new or ESL writers.

RENAISSANCE LITERARY SERVICES/JO REAVES, 17675 Eureka Ave. W., Farmington MN 55024. Phone/fax (903) 989-2815. E-mail: editor@renaissanceliteraryservices.com. Website: www.renaissanceliteraryservices.com. E-mail contact. GE/LC/B/NL/SP/WS/PowerPoint/interior layout & design/audio transcription. Edits: A/SS/P/F/N/NB/BP/QL/JN/PB/BS/GB/TM/E/D/S. Undergraduate and graduate work in languages and linguistics; managing editor of 3 newspapers; university professor (communications); 23 years' experience as professional editor; published author of 3 books. Charges $3-4/pg., depending on level of editing; additional rates on Website.

SPREAD THE WORD COMMERCIAL WRITING/KATHERINE SWARTS, Houston TX. (832) 573-9501. E-mail: katherine@spreadthewordcommercialwriting.com. Website: www.spreadthewordcommercialwriting.com. Blog: http://gwigb.blogspot.com. E-mail contact preferred. Charges up to $100/hr. Copyrighting/editing for newsletters/B/SP/WS. MA in written communication from Wheaton College; over 100 published articles.

THE WRITE WAY EDITORIAL SERVICES/JANET K. CREWS/B. KAY COULTER, 806 Hopi Trl., Temple TX 76504-5008. (254) 778-6490 or (254) 939-1770. E-mails: janetcrews@sbcglobal.net or bkcoulter@sbcglobal.net. Website: www.writewayeditorial.com. Call/e-mail. GE/LC/GH/CA/B/NL/SP/scan to Word document/voice to Word document/graphics. Edits: A/SS/N/NB/BP/QL/JN/BS/GB/D. Published author of 3 books; contributor to 2 books; 12 years' combined experience; certified copyeditor. Free estimate; 50% of estimate as a deposit; $30/hr. Contact for additional details.

THE WRITING SPA/MARY DEMUTH, PO Box 1503, Rockwall TX 75087. (214) 475-9083. E-mail: maryedemuth@sbcglobal.net. Website: www.thewritingspa.com. E-mail contact. GE/LC/GH/CA/NL/writing coach. Edits: A/SS/P/N/NB/BP/QL/BS/GB/E/D. Published author of 4 nonfiction books, 5 novels; teaches, keynotes, and mentors at national writers' conferences. Has 3 people on staff. Initial consultation: 5 pgs., double-spaced $75. Writing coach: $75/hr. E-mail for additional package prices.

+WRITING FOR GOD'S GLORY/JUDY VANDIVER, 1626 Berlino Dr., Pearland TX 77581. Phone/fax (281) 481-0356. E-mail: judy@writngforgodsglory.com. Website: www.writingforgodsglory.com, or www.judyvandiver.com. Blog: www.judyvandiver.blogspot.com. E-mail or mail contact. GE/LC/GH/B/NL/SP/WS/PP. Edits: A/SS/F/N/NB/BP/QL/BS/GB/E/D/S/YA. No picture books or poetry. Published author, Bible teacher; member of Christian Editor Network, and The Christian PEN. Charges start at $30/hr. Flat rate for large mss. Free sample edit. Free quote based on a portion of ms.

UTAH

+STAR EDITING SERVICES/MARCIA HORNOCK, Salt Lake City UT. (801) 969-4298. E-mail: kenmarh@comcast.net. Blog: http://christiangals.blogspot.com. Copyediting, critiquing, and proofreading of nonfiction manuscripts. Author with 50 writing credits; managing editor of a magazine. Charges $24/hr.

THE WHAT IF GIRL/KATHLEEN WRIGHT, Sandy UT. E-mail: the_whatif_girl@yahoo.com. or through blog: www.whatifgirl.wordpress.com. E-mail contact. GE/fiction coaching. Edits: N/QL/fiction synopsis. Also a writing coach. Charges by the hour; e-mail for current rate. BA in journalism, 20+ years' editing/writing experience. Clients include beginning writers through multipublished award winners.

VIRGINIA

EDITOR FOR YOU/MELANIE RIGNEY, 4201 Wilson Blvd., #110328, Arlington VA 22203-1859. (703) 863-3940. E-mail: editor@editorforyou.com. Website: www.editorforyou.com. E-mail contact. GE/LC/writing coach. Edits: SS/N/NB/BP/QL/E/D. Charges $65/hr. for content editing & coaching (provides a binding ceiling on number of hours); fees vary for ms evaluation. Editor of *Writer's Digest* magazine for 5 years; book editor/manager of Writer's Digest Books for 1 year; 3.5 years with Macmillan Computer Publishing and Thomsen Financial Publishing in books; 30 years' editing experience; frequent conference speaker/contest judge.

EDITORIAL SERVICES/SKYLAR HAMILTON BURRIS, PO Box 7505, Fairfax Station VA 22039. (703) 944-1530. E-mail: SSburris@cox.net. Website: www.editorskylar.com. E-mail contact. LC/NL/WS. Edits: A/SS/P/F/N/NB/JN/BS/GB/TM/E/D/S. Charges authors $2/double-spaced page for editing. Charges $35/hr. for copyediting books; or $2-$3.50/double-spaced page (depending on difficulty level). Charges $35/hr. for newsletter editing, writing, and design. Primarily works with authors who are planning either to self-publish or to submit their work to traditional publishing houses and who have completed books that require line-by-line copyediting prior to final proofreading and publication. BA and MA in English. Eight years as a magazine editor; 10+ years' newsletter editing and design. Free sample edit of 2 pages.

WASHINGTON

+AMI EDITING/ANNETTE M. IRBY, PO Box 7162, Covington WA 98042-7162. (425) 413-2307. E-mail: editor@AMIediting.com. Website: www.AMIediting.com. E-mail. GE/LC/critiques. Edits: A/SS/F/N/NB/BS/GB/TM/E/D/Website copy edits. Has been writing over 13 years; has edited manuscripts for well-published and new authors, as well as publishing houses. See Website for testimonials. Charges $25/hr. for general jobs; $35/hr. for rush jobs. Send a $25 deposit with first 20 pages for a job estimate for general job; $35 deposit/20 pages for rush job. Deposit covers first hour in both cases.

BY BRENDA: WRITER & DESIGNER/BRENDA WILBEE, 7463 Leeside Dr., Birch Bay WA 98230. (360) 746-0308. E-mail: brenda@brendawilbee.com. Website: www.BrendaWilbee.com. Call/E-mail/write. GE/LC/B/NL/SP/W/PP. Edits: N/NB. Offers design services for brochures, newsletter, Websites, and PowerPoint. Has MA in Professional Writing; AA in Graphic Design; college composition instructor; author of 9 CBA books and over 100 articles; longtime contributor to *Daily Guideposts*; and has freelanced as both a writer and designer. Charges can be discussed via e-mail; $40/hr. or flat fee depending on project.

DOCUMENT DRIVEN/JANICE HUSSEIN, 16420 S.E. McGillivray, #103-103, Vancouver WA 98683. (503) 789-6245. E-mail: Janice@documentdriven.com. Website: www.documentdriven.com. Call/e-mail. GE/LC/SP/WS/writing coach. Edits: A/N/NB/BP/QL/JN/E/synopsis; submission & manuscript critiques. Two master's degrees: MS in Writing; MBA; 9 years' experience copyediting; 5 years' experience editing. Fee scale on Website; charges by the project.

+EDITORIAL SERVICES/ANNE MCDONALD, 7197 NE Crawford Dr., Unit B, Kingston WA 98346. (360) 362-1003. E-mail: annemcdonaldeditorial@gmail.com. Website: www.amediting.dancing word.net. E-mail; send $45 deposit with material. GE/LC/WS/substantive editing/writing coach. Edits

SS/N/NB/BP/QL/JN/BS/D/YA. Former newspaper editor and book editor with 20 years' experience in editing, writing, and critiquing. References available. Charges $5/pg. or by negotiated fee.

EDITORIAL SERVICES/MARION DUCKWORTH, 15917 N.E. 41st St., Vancouver WA 98682-7473. (360) 896-8599. E-mail: mjduck@comcast.net. Website: www.MarionDuckworthMinistries.com. E-mail/write. GE/Writing Coach. Edits: A/NB/BP/QL/BS; also does consultations. Charges $25/hr. for critique or consultation. Negotiates on longer projects. Author (for over 25 years) of 17 books and 300 articles; writing teacher for over 25 years; extensive experience in general editing and manuscript evaluation.

+FAITHFULLY WRITE EDITING/DAWN KINZER, 25914—188th Ave. S.E., Covington WA 98042-6021. (254) 630-7617. E-mail: dawnkinzer@comcast.net. Website: www.faithfullywriteediting.com. E-mail contact. GE/LC. Edits: A/SS/N/NB/D. Published writer in magazines with short stories and articles. Six years experience studying fiction and critiquing published authors' work. Created and edited department newsletter for national telecommunications corporation. Rates are by page and depend on type of work required. Payment is made in advance of each block of work being completed. Complimentary 3-page sample edit offered with initial contact.

FICTION FIX-IT SHOP/MEREDITH EFKEN, PO Box 6049, Omaha NE 68106. E-mail: mefken@cox.net or through Website: www.fictionfixitshop.com. E-mail contact. GE/LC/writing coach. Edits: N/BP/YA novels. All editors and coaches (except copy editors) are published novelists. FFS is a member of the Christian PEN and Editorial Freelancers Assn. Rates listed on Website. Editing is hourly; coaching rated by package on a monthly basis.

LOGOS WORD DESIGNS INC./LINDA L. NATHAN, PO Box 735, Maple Falls WA 98266-0735. (360) 599-3429. Fax (360) 392-0216. E-mail: linda@logosword.com. Website: www.logosword .com. Call/e-mail. GE/LC/GH/CA/B/NL/SP/résumés/publishing consultations/writing assistance/writes proposals/manuscript submission services. Edits A/BP/BS/TM/E/D/F/JN/N/NB/PB/QL/SS/TM/YA/academic/legal/apologetics/conservative political. Over 30 years' experience in wide variety of areas, including publicity, postdoctoral; BA Psychology/some MA. Member: Editorial Freelance Assn.; NW Independent Editors Guild; American Christian Fiction Writers. Quote per project. See Website, or e-mail for rates.

WISCONSIN

MARGARET HOUK: EDITING SERVICES, West 2355 Valleywood Ln., Appleton WI 54915-8712. (920) 687-0559. Fax (920) 687-0259. E-mail: marghouk@juno.com. Call/write. GE/LC. Edits: A/F/NB/BP/QL/E/D (all for teens or adults). Author of 5 books and 700 articles; has taught writing and manuscript marketing for many years. Free phone interview. Will quote fee based on writing sample.

STONE COTTAGE LITERARY SERVICES/JONATHAN RICE, 404 Meadow View Ln., DeForest WI 53532. (608) 842-0156. E-mail: jjrice@charter.net. Write/e-mail. GE/LC/GH/CA/B/SP. Edits: A/SS/N/NB/BS/E/D. Professionally employed editor/writer with national Christian ministry; BA Religious Studies, MA Creative Writing (fiction), MDiv Pastoral Studies, DMin Homiletics/Narrative Theology. Contact for hourly rates or full project fee estimates.

CANADIAN/FOREIGN

AOTEAROA EDITORIAL SERVICES/VENNESSA NG, PO Box 228, Oamaru 9444, New Zealand. Phone +64278195608. (A U.S.-based number is available to clients.) E-mail: editor@aotearoaeditorial.com. Website: www.aotearoaeditorial.com. E-mail contact. GE/LC. Edits: SS/N/BP. Page rates vary depending on project: start from $1.50/critique, $1/basic proofread, and $3.00/copyedit. (Rates are in U.S. dollars and can be paid by PayPal or Western Union.) Eight years' critiquing experience.

+AY'S EDIT/ALAN YOSHIOKA, PhD, 801-21 Maynard Ave., Toronto ON M6K 2Z8, Canada. (416) 531-1857. Fax number upon request. E-mail: ay1@aysedit.com. Website: www.aysedit.com. E-mail contact. GE/LC/PP. Edits: A/NB/TM/E. Certified proofreader. Member of Editors' Association of Canada since 1999. In seventh year as freelance editor, writer, and indexer, following four years in-house as medical writer at a major pharmaceutical company. Math degree and PhD in history of science, technology, and medicine. Payment negotiable, starting from basic rate of US $45/hour for clients in US with nonmedical material.

+CHESTNUT LANE CREATIVE/ADELE SIMMONS, PO Box 116, Whitby ON L1N 5R7, Canada. (905) 263-4211. E-mail: AdeleCLCreative@bell.net. Website: www.Adelesimmons.WordPress.com. E-mail/write. GE/LC/GH/CA/B/NL/SP/substantive editing/rewriting/writing/writing coach. Edits: A/SS/P/F/NB/PB/BS/GB/TM/E/D/S/songs/speeches. Decades of experience, award-winning published writer/author and editor for business, mental health, tourism, marketing, ministry, creative ministry arts, newspaper, television, radio, books, education, nonfiction, how-to's, songs, and commercial printing/publishing companies. Topics mostly nonfiction. Rates negotiated based on project and services required.

DORSCH EDITORIAL/AUDREY DORSCH, 1275 Markham Rd., #305, Toronto ON M1H 3A2, Canada. (416) 439-4320. E-mail: audrey@dorschedit.ca. Website: www.dorschedit.ca. Audrey Dorsch, ed. Editorial services: substantive editing, copyediting, indexing, proofreading.

EDITORIAL SERVICES/DARLENE OAKLEY, 629 Van Buren St., RR3, Kemptville ON K0G 1J0, Canada. (613) 816-3277. E-mail: darlene@darscorrections.com. Website: www.darscorrections .com. E-mail contact. GE/LC/GH/B/NL/SP/WS/PP/reviews/critiques/Web copy. Edits: A/SS/N/NB/QL/ BP/BS/GB/E/D/synopses/Web copy. Project manager; acquisitions editor, proofreader with Lachesis Publishing & Glasshouse Publishing; member of the Editors' Assn. of Canada and The Word Guild; judge for Silicon Valley Romance Writers of America Gotcha! Contest 2008 & 2009 (inspirational). Detailed (substantive) edit $5/pg. or .02/wd. Proofread: $3/pg or .012/wd. Manuscript critique: $1/ page. Payment plans negotiable. See Website for details.

+EDITORIAL SERVICES/MARCY KENNEDY, R.R.1 #6, Wallaceburg ON N8A 4L3. Canada. (519) 627-3985. Fax (519) 627-3985. E-mail: marcykennedy@gmail.com. E-mail contact. GE/LC/CA/ NL/WS. Edits: A/SS/N/NB/QL/BS/E/D/academic material. Bachelor's degree in Social Psychology; Master's degree in Theological Studies; Professional Member of The Word Guild; experienced writer (including *Writer's Digest* competition wins); varied editing experience. Charges $35-40/hr. for proofreading, copyediting, fact checking, stylistic editing; flat rate of $20 for anything taking under 30 minutes; $40-50/hr. for substantive/developmental editing. Contact by e-mail for an estimate on your project.

+EDITORIAL SERVICES/AIMEE REID, PO Box 63063, University Plaza R.P.O., Dundas ON L9H 6Y3, Canada. (905) 526-8794. E-mail: areid@aimeereid.com. Website: www.aimeereid.com. E-mail contact. GE/CA/SP/(developmental, substantive, stylistic editing). Edits: A/NB/PB/BS/GB/D. Has published nonfiction for youth and adults, both in print and on wiki format. Has done editing for ages 10 to adult; tasks include incorporating reviewer's comments, rewriting as needed, suggesting images and layout, and creating illustration lists. Charges according to individual project depending on length and complexity. Manuscript evaluations are a set fee.

+HH COMMUNICATION SERVICES/HEATHER HEPPLEWHITE, 65 Kildonan Cres., Waterdown ON L0R 2H5, Canada. (905) 689-2013. E-mail: heather@hhcommunication.ca. Website: www.hhcom munication.ca. E-mail contact. GE/LC/B/NL/SP/WS/PP. Edits: A/SS/N/NB/JN/TM/E. MA in linguistics, BA in linguistics, Member of the Editor's Assn. of Canada and the Word Guild, 8+ years' experience editing and writing. Visit Website for more services and information. Rates are based on types of material and services needed, and determined on a project-by-project basis. Contact for a quote.

WENDY M. MCNEICE, PO Box 656, Capalaba QLD 4157, Australia. Phone (07) 38225342. E-mail: wendyworkshops@live.com. Website: www.scribeofspirit.com. E-mail contact. CA/GH/writing coach. Multi-award-winning writer, columnist in international magazine; BA; Graduate Diploma Info Services; Graduate Diploma Ed.

+NELLES WRITING, EDITING & COMMUNICATIONS CONSULTING/WENDY ELAINE NELLES, 21 Shaftesbury Ave., Ste. 303, Toronto ON M4T 3B4, Canada. E-mail: NellesEditor@gmail.com. Website: www.WendyNelles.com. E-mail contact. GE/LC/GH/CA/SP/writing coach. Edits: A/N/NB/E. An award-winning writer, editor, mentor, and teacher. MA, Communications; cofounder of The Word Guild writers' association; 22-year leadership of the leading Canadian writers' conference, Write! Canada. Presented with Leading Women Award (2006) for outstanding accomplishments in Communications and Media. Rates negotiated on a per project basis, after review of manuscript, depending on amount of editing/coaching required. Deposit required.

WENDY SARGEANT, PO Box 656, Capalaba, QLD 4157, Australia. Phone 0488404081. E-mail: wordfisher52@gmail.com. Website: www.editorsqld.com/freelance/Wendy_Sargeant.htm. E-mail contact. GE/LC/GH/CA/B/NL/SP/WS (writing & evaluation)/PP/instructional design/writing coach. Edits: A/SS/F/N/NB/BP/QL/JN/PB/BS/GB/TM/E/D/S. Copywriting. Special interests: technical material, business humor, children's books, educational books (primary, secondary, tertiary, and above), fiction, history, legal. Manuscript assessor and instructional designer with The Writing School. Award-winning author published in major newspapers and magazines. Editing educational manuals. Project officer and instructional designer for Global Education Project, United Nationals Assoc. Information specialist for Australian National University. Charges $55/hr for articles/short stories; .02/wd. for copywriting; $300-400+ for book assessment.

13

Christian Literary Agents

The references in these listings to "published authors" refer to those who have had one or more books published by royalty publishers or who have been published regularly in periodicals. If a listing indicates that the agent is "recognized in the industry," it means he or she has worked with the Christian publishers long enough to be recognized by editors as credible agents.

Do not assume that because an agent is listed below, I can personally vouch for him or her. I am not able to check out each one as thoroughly as you need to. Asking editors and other writers at writers' conferences is a great way to find a good, reliable agent. You might also want to visit www .agentresearch.com and www.sfwa.org/for-authors/writer-beware/ for tips on finding an agent. For a database of more than 500 agencies, go to www.literaryagent.com.

Finally, at the site for the Association of Authors' Representatives, www.aaronline.org, you will find a list of agents who don't charge fees, except for office expenses. Their Website will also provide information on how to receive a list of approved agents. Some of the listings below indicate which agents belong to the Association of Authors' Representatives, Inc. Those members have subscribed to a set code of ethics. Lack of such a designation, however, does not indicate the agent is unethical; most Christian agents are not members. If they do happen to be members, it should give you an extra measure of confidence.

+ Indicates a new listing

AGENT RESEARCH & EVALUATION INC., 425 N. 20th St., Philadelphia PA 19130. (215) 563-1867. Fax (215) 563-6797. E-mail: info@agentresearch.com. Website: www.agentresearch.info. This is not an agency but a service that tracks the public record of literary agents and helps authors use the data to obtain effective literary representation. Charges fees for this service. Offers a free "agent verification" service at the site. (Answers the question of whether or not the agent has created a public record of sales.) Also offers a newsletter, *Talking Agents E-zine*, free if you send your e-mail address.

ALIVE COMMUNICATIONS, 7680 Goddard St., Ste. 200, Colorado Springs CO 80920. (719) 260-7080. Fax (719) 260-8223. E-mail: submissions@alivecom.com. Website: www.alivecom.com. Agents: Rick Christian, president; Lee Hough, Joel Kneedler, Andrea Heinecke. Well known in the industry. Estab. 1989. Represents 175 clients. Not open to unpublished authors. New clients by referral only. Handles adult & teen novels and nonfiction, gift books, and crossover books. Deals in both Christian (70%) and general market (30%). Member Author's Guild & AAR.
    Contact: E-mail to: submissions@alivecom.com. Accepts simultaneous submissions. Responds in 6 wks. to referrals only. May not respond to unsolicited submissions.
    Commission: 15%
    Fees: Only extraordinary costs with client's pre-approval; no review/reading fee.
    Tips: "If you have a referral, send material by mail, and be sure to mark envelope 'Requested Material.' Unable to return unsolicited materials without postpaid envelope."

ALLEN O'SHEA LITERARY AGENCY, LLC., 615 Westover Rd., Stamford CT 06902. (203) 359-9965. E-mail: Marilyn@allenoshea.com. Website: www.allenoshea.com. Agents: Marilyn Allen and

Coleen O'Shea. Estab. 2003. Represents 4 clients with religious books. Recognized in the industry. Open to unpublished authors (with credentials & platform) and new clients. Handles adult non-fiction.

Contact: Query by mail or e-mail. No simultaneous submissions. Responds in 4 wks.
Commission: 15%; foreign 15-25%.
Fees: For overseas mailing.
Tips: "We specifically like practical nonfiction."

AMBASSADOR AGENCY, PO Box 50358, Nashville TN 37205. (615) 370-4700, ext. 230. E-mail: Wes@AmbassadorAgency.com. Website: www.AmbassadorAgency.com. Agent: Wes Yoder. Estab. 1973. Recognized in the industry. Represents 25 clients. Open to unpublished authors and new clients. Handles adult nonfiction, crossover books. Also has a Speakers Bureau.

Contact: E-mail.

AUTHOR COACHING: An Agent/Coaching Service for Inspirational Authors, PO Box 428, Newburg PA 17240. (717) 423-6621. Fax (717) 423-6944. E-mail: keith@authorcoaching.com. Website: www.AuthorCoaching.com. Coach: Keith Carroll. Estab. 2000. Open to unpublished authors and new clients. Handles novels and nonfiction for children, teens, and adults; picture books; and crossover books.

Contact: By letter, fax, phone, e-mail.
Fees: Visit Website for detailed description of fees.

BENREY LITERARY, PO Box 12721, New Bern NC 28561. (252) 638-5787. E-mail: janet@benrey literary.com. Website: www.BenreyLiterary.com. Agent: Janet Benrey. Estab. 2006. Recognized in the industry. Represents 30+ clients. Prefers referrals from current clients, or to meet writers at writers' conferences. Handles adult religious/inspirational novels (romance, contemporary women's, mystery, true crime); nonfiction (Christian living); general (thriller or cozy).

Contact: Requires e-queries.
Commission: 15%; foreign 20%.

BOOKS & SUCH/JANET KOBOBEL GRANT, 5926 Sunhawk Dr., Santa Rosa CA 95409. (707) 538-4184. E-mail: representation@booksandsuch.biz. Website: www.booksandsuch.biz. Agents: Janet Kobobel Grant, Wendy Lawton, Etta Wilson, Rachel Z. Kent, Mary Keeley. Well recognized in industry. Estab. 1997. Member of AAR. Represents 150 clients. Open to new or unpublished authors (with recommendation only). Handles fiction and nonfiction for all ages, picture books, gift books, crossover, and general books.

Contact: E-mail query (no attachments); no phone query. Accepts simultaneous submissions. Responds in 6-8 wks.
Commission: 15%.
Fees: No fees.
Tips: "Especially looking for historical fiction for adults."

CURTIS BROWN LTD., 10 Astor Pl., New York NY 10003-6935. (212) 473-5400. Website: www .curtisbrown.com. Agents: Maureen Walters, Laura Blake Peterson, and Ginger Knowlton. Member AAR. General agent; handles religious/inspirational novels for all ages, adult nonfiction, and cross-over books.

Contact: Query with SASE; no fax/e-query. Submit outline or sample chapters. Responds in 4 wks. to query; 8 wks. to ms.
Fees: Charges for photocopying & some postage.

BROWNE & MILLER LITERARY ASSOCIATES, 410 S. Michigan Ave., Ste. 460, Chicago IL 60605. (312) 922-3063. Fax (312) 922-1905. E-mail: mail@browneandmiller.com. Website: www.browne andmiller.com. Agent: Danielle Egan-Miller. Estab. 1971. Recognized in the industry. Represents

150 clients, mostly general, but also select Christian fiction writers. Open to new clients and talented unpublished authors, but most interested in experienced novelists looking for highly professional, full-service representation including rights management. Handles teen and adult fiction, adult non-fiction, and gift books for the general market; adult Christian fiction only. Member AAR, RWA, MWA, and The Author's Guild.

Contact: E-query to mail@browneandmiller.com, or mailed query letter/SASE. No unsolicited mss. Prefer no simultaneous submissions. Responds in 6 wks.

Commission: 15%, foreign 20%.

PEMA BROWNE LTD., 11 Tena Pl., Valley Cottage NY 10989-2215. (845) 268-0029. E-mail: ppbltd@optonline.net. Website: www.pemabrowneltd.com. Agent: Pema Browne. Recognized in industry. Estab. 1966. Represents 20 clients (2 religious). Open to unpublished authors; very few new clients at this time. Handles novels and nonfiction for all ages; picture books/novelty books, gift books, crossover books. Only accepts mss not previously sent to publishers; no simultaneous submissions. Responds in 6-8 wks.

Contact: Letter query with credentials; no phone, fax, or e-query. Must include SASE. No simultaneous submissions. No attachments.

Commission: 20% U.S. & foreign; illustrators 30%.

Fees: None.

Tips: "Check at the library in reference section, in *Books in Print*, for books similar to yours. Have good literary skills, neat presentation. Know what has been published and research the genre that interests you."

THE BLYTHE DANIEL AGENCY INC., PO Box 64197, Colorado Springs CO 80962-4197. (719) 213-3427. E-mail: blythe@theblythedanielagency.com. Website: www.theblythedanielagency .com. Agent: Blythe Daniel. Recognized in the industry. Estab. 2005. Represents 30 clients. Open to unpublished authors with an established platform/network and previously published authors. Handles adult religious/inspirational novels, adult nonfiction, limited children's books, and cross-over books.

Contact: By e-mail or mail. Accepts simultaneous submissions. Responds in 3 weeks.

Commission: 15%; foreign 20%.

Fees: Agreed-upon expenses outside normal expenses.

Also: Provides publicity and marketing campaigns to clients as a separate service from literary representation.

Tips: "Authors must have a solid proposal on the topic of their book, including research on their audience, comparison to competitor's books, and what the author uniquely brings to the topic. Authors need to have a ready-made marketing plan to promote their book and the ability to promote their own book. Currently only handling a minimal number of new clients."

DANIEL LITERARY GROUP, 1701 Kingsbury Dr., Ste. 100, Nashville TN 37215. No phone calls. E-mail: greg@danielliterarygroup.com. Website: www.danielliterarygroup.com. Agent: Greg Daniel. Estab. 2007. Recognized in the industry. Represents 35 clients. Open to unpublished authors and new clients. Handles adult religious/inspirational novels & nonfiction, crossover & secular books.

Contact: E-mail only. Accepts simultaneous submissions. Responds in 3 wks.

Commission: 15%; foreign 20%.

Fees: None.

JAN DENNIS LITERARY SERVICES, 19350 Glen Hollow Cir., Monument CO 80132. (719) 559-1711. E-mail: jpdennislit@msn.com. Agent: Jan Dennis. Estab. 1995. Represents 20 clients. Open to unpublished authors and new clients. Handles teen/YA & adult religious/inspirational novels, adult nonfiction, crossover, and general books.

DYSTEL & GODERICH LITERARY MANAGEMENT INC., 1 Union Square W., Ste. 904, New York NY 10003. (212) 627-9100. Fax (212) 627-9313. E-mail: Miriam@dystel.com. Website: www.dystel.com. Agents: Jane Dystel, Miriam Goderich, Stacey Glick, Michael Bourret, Jim McCarthy, and Lauren Abramo. Estab. 1994. Recognized in the industry. Represents 5-10 religious book clients. Open to unpublished authors and new clients. Handles fiction and nonfiction for adults, gift books, general books, crossover books. Member AAR.

   Contact: Query letter with bio. Brief e-query; no simultaneous queries. Responds to queries in 3-5 wks.; submissions in 2 mos.

   Commission: 15%; foreign 19%.

   Fees: Photocopying is author's responsibility.

   Tips: "Send a professional, well-written query to a specific agent."

EAMES LITERARY SERVICES, 4117 Hillsboro Rd., Ste. 251, Nashville TN 37215. (615) 403-3550. Fax (615) 463-9361. E-mail: info@eamesliterary.com. Website: www.eamesliterary.com. Agents: John Eames (John@eamesliterary.com). Open to unpublished authors and new clients. Handles adult & teen religious/inspirational novels & adult nonfiction. Guidelines on Website.

   Contact: By e-mail.

   Commission: 15%

   Fees: None.

FINE PRINT LITERARY MANAGEMENT, 240 W. 35th St., Ste. 500, New York NY 10001. (212) 279-1282. Fax (212) 279-0927. E-mail: peter@fineprintlit.com. Website: www.fineprintlit.com. Agent: Peter Rubie and 7 other agents. Open to unpublished authors and new clients. General agent. Handles adult religion/spirituality nonfiction for teens and adults.

   Contact: Query/SASE; accepts e-query. Responds in 2-3 mos.

   Commission: 15%; foreign 20%.

+GARY D. FOSTER CONSULTING, 733 Virginia Ave., Van Wert OH 45891. (419) 238-4082. E-mail: gary@garyfoster.com. Website: www.garyfoster.com. Agent: Gary Foster. Estab. 1989. Represents 25 clients. Recognized in the industry. Open to unpublished authors and new clients. Handles adult religious/inspirational novels & nonfiction for all ages, picture books, and gift books.

   Contact: E-mail. Responds in 6 wks.

   Commission: 15%

   Fees: Charges a nominal fee upon signing of representation agreement, plus expense reimbursement.

SAMUEL FRENCH INC., 45 W. 25th St., New York NY 10010-2751. (212) 206-8990. Fax (212) 206-1429. E-mail: publications@samuelfrench.com. Website: www.samuelfrench.com, www.bakersplays.com. Agent: Roxane Heinze-Bradshaw. Estab. 1830. Open to new clients. Handles rights to some religious/inspirational stage plays. Owns a subsidiary company that also publishes religious plays.

   Contact: Query online or by mail. See Website for full submission information. Accepts simultaneous submissions; responds in 10 wks.

   Commission: Varies.

   Fees: None.

GLOBAL TALENT REPS, INC./NATIONAL WRITERS LITERARY AGENCY, 3140 S. Peoria St., #295, Aurora CO 80014. (720) 851-1959. E-mail: Info@globaltalentreps.com. Website: www.globaltalentreps.com. Agent: Andrew J. Whelchel III (a.whelchel@globaltalentreps.com). Estab. 1982. Recognized in the industry. Open to unpublished authors and new clients. Handles religious/inspirational novels for all ages, nonfiction for teens & adults, screenplays, movie scripts, gift books, and crossover/secular books.

Contact: Query by e-mail (use online form). Accepts simultaneous submissions; responds in 8 wks.
Commission: 10% film; 15% books; 5% scouting.
Fees: Postage charged to new, unknown authors.

SANFORD J. GREENBURGER ASSOCIATES INC., 55 Fifth Ave., New York NY 10003. (212) 206-5600. Fax (212) 463-8718. Website: www.greenburger.com. Agents: Heide Lange, Dan Mandel, Matthew Bialer, Brenda Bowen, Faith Hamlin, Michael Harriot, Lisa Gallagher, Courtney Miller-Callihan. Estab. 1945. Represents 500 clients. Open to unpublished authors and new clients. General agent; handles adult religious/inspirational nonfiction. Member of AAR.
Contact: Query/proposal/3 sample chapters to Heide Lange by mail with SASE, or by fax; no e-query. Accepts simultaneous queries. Responds in 6-8 wks. to query; 2 mos. to ms.
Commission: 15%; foreign 20%.
Fees: Charges for photocopying and foreign submissions.

HARTLINE LITERARY AGENCY, 123 Queenston Dr., Pittsburgh PA 15235. (412) 829-2483. Fax (888) 279-6007. E-mail: joyce@hartlineliterary.com. Website: www.hartlineliterary.com. Blog: www.hartlineliteraryagency.blogspot.com. Agents: Joyce A. Hart, adult novels (romance, mystery/suspense, women's fiction) and nonfiction; Tamela Hancock Murray, adult fiction (romance, mystery/suspense, women's) and nonfiction, tamela@hartlineliterary.com; Terry Burns, adult fiction & nonfiction, YA, terry@hartliterary.com; Diana Flegal, adult novels & nonfiction, diana@hartlineliterary.com. Recognized in industry. Estab. 1992. Represents 150+ clients. Open to new clients. Handles adult nonfiction, gift books. No poetry.
Contact: E-mail/phone/letter; e-mail preferred. Accepts simultaneous submissions; responds in 6-8 wks.
Commission: 15%; foreign 20%; films 20% and 25%.
Fees: Office expenses (very few); no reading fee.
Tips: "Please look at our Website before submitting. Guidelines are listed, along with detailed information about each agent. Be sure to include your biography and publishing history with your proposal. The author/agent relationship is a team effort. Working together we can make sure your manuscript gets the exposure and attention it deserves."

JEFF HERMAN AGENCY, PO Box 1522, Stockbridge MA 01262. (413) 298-0077. Fax (413) 298-8188. E-mail: Jeff@jeffherman.com. Website: www.jeffherman.com. Agents: Jeff Herman and Deborah Herman. Estab. 1987. Recognized in the industry. Represents 20+ clients with religious books. Open to unpublished authors and new clients. Handles adult nonfiction (recovery/healing, spirituality), gift books, general books, crossover.
Contact: Query by mail/SASE, or by e-mail or fax. Accepts simultaneous submissions & e-queries.
Commission: 15%; foreign 10%.
Fees: No reading or management fees; just copying and shipping.
Tips: "I love a good book from the heart. Have faith that you will accomplish what has been appointed to you."

HIDDEN VALUE GROUP, 1240 E. Ontario Ave., Ste. 102-148, Corona CA 92881. Phone/fax (951) 549-8891. E-mail: bookquery@hiddenvaluegroup.com. Website: www.HiddenValueGroup.com. Agents: Jeff Jernigan & Nancy Jernigan. Estab. 2001. Recognized in the industry. Represents 20+ clients with religious books. Open to previously published authors only. Handles adult fiction and nonfiction, gift books, and crossover books. No poetry, articles, or short stories.
Contact: Letter or e-mail. Accepts simultaneous submissions. Responds in 4-6 wks.
Commission: 15%; foreign 15%.

Fees: None.

Tips: "Women's nonfiction is of great interest. Make sure the proposal includes author bio, 2 sample chapters, and manuscript summary."

+HIGHER LIFE PUBLISHING AND MARKETING, 400 Fontana Cir., Bldg. 1, Ste. 105, Oviedo FL 32765. (407) 563-4806. Fax (407) 574-2699. Website: www.ahigherlife.com. Agent: Hope Flinchbaugh; hope@ahigherlife.com. Estab. 2006. Represents 6 clients. Recognized in the industry. Open to unpublished authors and new clients. Handles religious/inspirational novels & nonfiction for all ages, picture books, crossover books.

    Contact: By e-mail. Open to simultaneous submissions; responds in 4 wks.

    Commission: 15%.

    Fees: Fees to cover copying or postage occasionally apply.

    Tips: "Due to recent downsizing in traditional publishing houses, it is becoming increasingly difficult to place new authors. However, if your writing is strong, it will stand out above the rest. We are very picky!"

HORNFISCHER LITERARY MANAGEMENT, PO Box 50544, Austin TX 78763. E-mail: queries@ hornfischerlit.com or jim@hornfischerlit.com. Website: www.hornfischerlit.com. Agent: James D. Hornfischer. Estab. 2001. Represents 45 clients. Open to unpublished authors and new clients (with referrals from clients). Considers simultaneous submissions. Responds in 1 mo. General agent; handles adult religious/inspirational nonfiction.

    Contact: E-query only for fiction; query or proposal for nonfiction (proposal package, outline, and 2 sample chapters). Considers simultaneous queries. Responds to queries in 5-6 wks.

    Commission: 15%; foreign 25%.

D. C. JACOBSON & ASSOCIATES, 971 E. Cascade Ave., Sisters OR 97759-9320. (541) 549-3585. Fax (541) 549-1785. E-mail: query@dcjacobson.com. Website: www.dcjacobson.com. Agents: Don Jacobson & Jenni Burke. Estab. 2006. Represents 20+clients. Recognized in the industry (former owner of Multnomah Publishers). Open to unpublished authors and new clients. Handles adult & teen religious/inspirational novels & nonfiction, crossover books.

    Contact: Submissions & queries through Website form only. Accepts simultaneous submissions; responds in 2-5 wks.

    Commission: 15%.

    Fees: No reading fees.

    Services: Offers literary consulting services on a fee basis to nonrepresented clients.

    Tips: "Looking for fresh messages to renew the church and redeem the culture for Christ. Please review our Website thoroughly before using our submission form."

+JELLINEK & MURRAY LITERARY AGENCY, 47-722 Hui Kelu St., Apt. 4, Kaneohe HI 96744. Phone/fax (808) 239-8451. E-mail: rgr.jellinek@gmail.com. Blog: www.hawaiireaders.com. Agent: Roger Jellinek. Estab. 1995. Represents a few Christian clients. Not recognized in the industry. Open to unpublished authors; new clients by personal reference (otherwise only June through December). Handles adult religious/inspirational nonfiction, crossover books, secular books.

    Contact: E-mail only. Accepts simultaneous submissions; responds in 6 wks.

    Commission: 15%; foreign 20%.

    Fees: No, except for unusual travel or Express Mail.

WILLIAM K. JENSEN LITERARY AGENCY, 119 Bampton Ct., Eugene OR 97404. Phone/fax (541) 688-1612. E-mail: queries@wkjagency.com. Website: www.wkjagency.com. Agent: William K. Jensen. Estab. 2005. Recognized in the industry. Represents 38 clients. Open to unpublished authors and new clients. Handles adult fiction (no science fiction or fantasy), nonfiction for all ages, picture books, gift books, crossover books.

Contact: E-mail only using online form; no phone queries. Accepts simultaneous submissions. Responds in 12 wks.

Commission: 15%.

Fees: No fees.

NATASHA KERN LITERARY AGENCY INC., PO Box 1069, White Salmon WA 98672. Website: www.natashakern.com. Agent: Natasha Kern. Well-recognized member of Author's Guild, ACFW, RWA. Estab. 1987. Represents 36 religious clients. Open to unpublished authors and new clients. Handles adult religious/inspirational fiction (romance, romantic suspense, women's fiction, historical fiction, mystery, suspense, thrillers, and general market novels).

Contact: Accepts e-queries at: queries@natashakern.com only; 3-pg. synopsis & 1 chapter. Responds in 2-4 wks. to queries, if interested. Also meets at conferences or through current clients.

Commission: 15%; 20% foreign (includes foreign-agent commission).

Fees: No reading fee.

Tips: "I have personally sold over 900 books, many of them best sellers and award winners. See submission guidelines on our Website before sending a query—we read everyone."

K J LITERARY SERVICES, LLC, 1540 Margaret Ave., Grand Rapids MI 49507. (616) 551-9797. E-mail: kim@kjliteraryservices.com. Website: www.kjliteraryservices.com. Agent: Kim Zeilstra.

Contact: E-query preferred; phone query OK.

Commission: 15%.

Tips: "Taking new authors by referral only."

+KRIS LITERARY AGENCY, 34 Oguntona Crescent, Phase 1, Gbagada Estate, Lagos, Nigeria. Phone +2348067628017. E-mail: krisliterary@yahoo.com. Agent: Chris Agada. Estab. 2009. Represents 6 clients. Building recognition in the industry. Open to unpublished authors and new clients. Handles all types of material.

Contact: Query by e-mail or phone. Accepts simultaneous submissions; responds in 2 wks.

Commission: 15%; foreign 15%.

Fees: No fees.

THE STEVE LAUBE AGENCY, 5025 N. Central Ave., #635, Phoenix AZ 85012-1502. (602) 336-8910. E-mail: info@stevelaube.com. Website: www.stevelaube.com. Agent: Steve Laube. Estab. 2004. Well recognized in the industry. Represents 60+ clients. Open to new and unpublished authors. Handles adult Christian fiction and nonfiction, history, theology, how-to, health, Christian living. No YA, children's books, or poetry. Accepts simultaneous submissions. Responds in 6-8 wks.

Contact: Letter with proposal and sample chapters by mail is preferred; use guidelines on Website. No e-queries.

Commission: 15%; foreign 20%.

Fees: No fees.

Tips: "Looking for fresh and innovative ideas. Make sure your proposal contains an excellent presentation."

LEVINE GREENBERG LITERARY AGENCY INC., 307—7th Ave., Ste. 2407, New York NY 10001. (212) 337-0934. Fax (212) 337-0948. Website: www.levinegreenberg.com. Agent: James Levine. Agent: Arielle Eckstut. Estab. 1989. Represents 250 clients. Open to unpublished authors and new clients. General agent; handles adult religious/inspirational nonfiction. Member AAR.

Contact: See guidelines/submission form on Website; requires e-query; does not respond to mailed queries.

Commission: 15%; foreign 20%.

Fees: Office expenses.

Tips: "Our specialties include spirituality and religion."

THE LITERARY GROUP INTL., 14 Penn Plaza, Ste. 925, New York NY 10122. (646) 442-5896. E-mail: js@theliterarygroup.com. Website: www.theliterarygroup.com. Agent: Frank Weimann. Recognized in the industry. Estab. 1986. Represents 300 clients (120 for religious books). Member of AAR. Open to new clients and unpublished authors. Handles fiction and nonfiction for all ages, picture books, general, and crossover.

Contact: E-mail.

Commission: 15%; foreign 20%.

Fees: Expenses for overseas postage/FedEx/DHL/UPS.

Tips: "Looking for fresh, original spiritual fiction and nonfiction. We offer a written contract which may be canceled after 30 days."

LITERARY MANAGEMENT GROUP INC., PO Box 40965, Nashville TN 37204. (615) 812-4445. E-mail: brucebarbour@literarymanagementgroup.com (for nonfiction); lavonne@literaryman agementgroup.com (for fiction). Website: www.literarymanagementgroup.com. Agents: Bruce R. Barbour (nonfiction), Lavonne Stevens (fiction). Estab. 1995. Well recognized in the industry. Represents 100+ clients. No unpublished authors; open to new clients. Handles adult novels, teen and adult nonfiction, crossover books. Other services offered: book packaging and consulting.

Contact: E-mail preferred. Will review proposals, no unsolicited mss. Accepts simultaneous submissions; responds in 4-6 wks.

Commission: 15%; foreign 20%.

Fees: No fees or expenses on agented books.

Tips: "Follow guidelines, proposal outline, and submissions format on Website. Use Microsoft Word. Study the market and know where your book will fit in."

LIVING WORD LITERARY AGENCY/KIMBERLY SHUMATE, PO Box 40974, Eugene OR 97404. (541) 683-6567. E-mail: livingwordliterary@gmail.com. Website: www.livingwordliterary.word press.com. Agent: Kimberly Shumate. Estab. 2009. Recognized in the industry. Represents 30 clients. Open to unpublished authors and some additional clients (depends on author). Handles adult and teen/YA fiction, adult nonfiction, and some secular books.

Contact: E-mail. No simultaneous submissions; responds in 1-2 weeks.

Commission: 15%; foreign 20%.

Fees: No fees.

Tips: "Looking for creative, relevant material. I'm all about the underdog, so don't be shy. Secular fiction must have underlying redemptive quality. Have your material professionally edited before submitting to agents."

STERLING LORD LITERISTIC INC., 65 Bleecker St., New York NY 10012. (213) 780-6050. Fax (212) 780-6095. E-mail: claudia@sll.com, or info@sll.com. Website: www.sll.com. Agent: Claudia Cross. Recognized in the industry. In addition to clients in the general market, she represents 10 clients with Christian/religious books. Open to unpublished clients with referrals and to new clients. Handles adult and teen Christian fiction, including women's fiction, romance novels, adult nonfiction exploring themes of spirituality, gift books, crossover books, general books.

Contact: Letter, fax, or e-query (with referral only). Accepts simultaneous submissions, if informed. Responds in 4-6 wks.

Commission: 15%; foreign 20%.

Fees: "We charge for photocopy costs for manuscripts or any costs above and beyond the usual cost of doing business."

MACGREGOR LITERARY, 2373 N.W. 185th Ave., Ste. 165, Hillsboro OR 97124. E-mail: submissions@macgregorliterary.com. Website: www.MacGregorLiterary.com. Agents: Chip MacGregor & Sandra Bishop. Estab. 2006. Member of AAR. Recognized in the industry. Represents 75 clients. Rarely open to unpublished authors and taking on few new clients. Handles teen and adult religious/inspirational novels and nonfiction; crossover and secular books.

> **Contact:** E-mail query. Accepts simultaneous submissions. Responds in 4 wks.
> **Commission:** 15%; foreign 20%.
> **Fees:** No fees or expenses.
> **Tips:** "We represent books that make a difference. Working with a list of established authors, we are always looking for strong nonfiction projects in a variety of genres. Please check the Website before submitting."

MANUS & ASSOCIATES LITERARY AGENCY, 425 Sherman Ave., Ste. 200, Palo Alto CA 94306. (650) 470-5151. Fax (650) 470-5159. E-mail: manuslit@manuslit.com. Website: www.manuslit.com. Agents: Jillian Manus, Penny Nelson, Dena Fischer, and Jandy Nelson. Members AAR. Estab. 1994. Open to unpublished authors and new clients. Handles adult religious/inspirational novels & nonfiction, gift books, crossover & general books.

> **Contact:** Query by mail/fax/e-query (no attachments or phone calls). For fiction, send first 30 pages, bio, and SASE. For nonfiction, send proposal/sample chapters. Responds in 12 weeks, only if interested.
> **Commission:** 15%; foreign 20-25%.

WILLIAM MORRIS LITERARY AGENCY, 1325 Avenue of the Americas, New York NY 10019. (212) 586-5100. Fax (212) 246-3583. E-mail: vs@wma.com. Website: www.wma.com. Agent: Valerie Summers. Recognized in the industry. Estab. 1898. Hundreds of clients with religious books. Not open to unpublished authors or new clients. Handles all types of material. Member AAR.

> **Contact:** Send query/synopsis, publication history by mail/SASE. No fax/e-query. No unsolicited mss.
> **Commission:** 15%; foreign 20%.
> **Fees:** None.

+THE MWS GROUP, 321 Billingsly Ct., Ste. 15, Franklin TN 37067. (615) 764-0012. Fax (615) 764-0013. Agent: Chaz Corzine. Represents 3 Christian clients. Recognized in the industry. Not open to unpublished authors or new clients at this time. Handles adult & teen religious/inspirational novels; crossover books.

> **Contact:** Query.
> **Commission:** 15%
> **Fees:** No information concerning fees.

NAPPALAND LITERARY AGENCY, PO Box 1674, Loveland CO 80539. (970) 635-0641. Fax (970) 635-9869. E-mail: literary@nappaland.com. Website: www.nappaland.com/literary. Division of Nappaland Communications Inc. Agent: Mike Nappa. Estab. 1995. Recognized in the industry. Represents 10 clients. Not open to unpublished authors; open to new clients only by referral from a current Nappaland author. Handles literary nonfiction, cultural concerns, Christian living, women's issues, suspense fiction, and women's fiction.

> **Contact:** By e-mail. Accepts simultaneous submissions; responds in 8-10 wks. Unsolicited queries are automatically rejected.
> **Commission:** 15%.
> **Fees:** None.
> **Tips:** "Cold queries just don't work—so don't send them. The only way we will consider a new author is if that person is somehow associated with—and recommended by—a current Nappaland author."

+B. K. NELSON LITERARY AGENCY, 1565 Paseo Vida, Palm Springs CA 92264. (760) 778-8800. Fax (760) 778-6242. E-mail: bknelson4@cs.com. Website: www.bknelson.com. Agent: B. K. Nelson. Estab. 1982. Represents 10 clients. Member of AAR. Recognized in the industry. Open to unpublished authors and new clients. Handles adult religious/inspirational novels & nonfiction.

    Contact: By mail or e-mail. Accepts simultaneous submissions; responds in 3-4 weeks.

    Commission: 15%.

    Fees: An evaluation fee of $300.

+NORTHERN LIGHTS LITERARY SERVICES, 11248 N. Boyer Rd., Ste. A, Sandpoint ID 83863. E-mail: sammie@northernlightsls.com. Website: www.northernlightsls.com. Agent: Sammie L. Justesen. Handles Christian novels, women's, romance, mystery and suspense.

    Contact: E-query only. For fiction, send a 1-2 page synopsis of the plot and the first few pages of the manuscript.

    Tips: "Due to an overwhelming number of submissions, we cannot respond to all queries, but we do read them and will contact you if interested."

NUNN COMMUNICATIONS INC., 1612 Ginger Dr., Carrollton TX 75007. (972) 394-6866. E-mail: info@nunncommunications.com. Website: www.nunncommunications.com. Agent: Leslie Nunn Reed. Estab. 1995. Represents 20 clients. Recognized in the industry. Not open to unpublished authors. Handles adult nonfiction, gift books, crossover books, and general books.

    Contact: By e-mail. Responds in 4-6 wks.

    Commission: 15%.

    Fees: Charges office expenses if over $100.

KATHI J. PATON LITERARY AGENCY, PO Box 2236, Radio City Station, New York NY 10101-2236. (212) 265-6586. E-mail: KJPLitBiz@optonline.net. Website: www.PatonLiterary.com. Agent: Kathi Paton. Estab. 1987. Handles adult nonfiction: Christian life and issues.

    Contact: Prefers e-mail query.

    Commission: 15%; foreign 20%.

    Fees: For photocopying & postal submissions.

PATRICK-MEDBERRY ASSOCIATES, 25379 Wayne Mills Pl., #155, Valencia CA 91355. (661) 251-4428. E-mail: patrickmedberry@sbcglobal.net. Agents: Peggy Patrick & C. J. Medberry. Estab. 2005. Management & production company specializing in Christian writers, directors, and producers, as well as religious and inspirational novels, screenplays, TV/movie scripts, crossover books, general books, and screenplays. Open to unpublished authors and new clients.

    Contact: Query by letter, fax, or e-mail; no calls.

    Commission: 10%.

    Fees: None.

PELHAM LITERARY AGENCY, PMB 315, 2650 Jamacha Rd., Ste. 147, El Cajon CA 92019. (619) 447-4468. E-mail: jmeals@pelhamliterary.com. Website: www.pelhamliterary.com. Agents: Howard Pelham & Jim Meals. Estab. 1993. Recognized in the industry. Open to unpublished authors and new clients. Handles adult and teen religious/inspirational novels & nonfiction, cross-over books.

    Contact: Brief query letter; e-query OK. Provides a list of published clients and titles. Accepts simultaneous submissions; responds in 6 wks.

    Commission: 15%; foreign 20%.

    Fees: Charges for postage and copying only. Offers an optional extensive critique for $200. Information on Website.

    Tips: "We are actively seeking writers for the Christian fiction market, but also open to nonfiction. We specialize in genre fiction and enjoy working with new authors."

THE QUADRIVIUM GROUP, 7512 Dr. Phillips Blvd., Ste. 50-229, Orlando FL 32819. (407) 516-1857. Website: www.TheQuadriviumGroup.com. Agents: Steve Blount (SteveBlount@TheQuadriviumGroup .com); Susan Blount (SusanBlount@TheQuadriviumGroup.com). Estab. 2006. Represents 20-30 clients. Recognized in the industry. Open to a limited number of unpublished authors (with credentials, platform, compelling story/idea), and to new clients (mostly by referral). General agent. Handles Christian and general fiction and nonfiction for all ages, gift books, crossover books. Other services offered: consulting on book sales and distribution.

   Contact: E-mail preferred; responds in 2-4 wks.
   Commission: 15%; foreign 20%.
   Fees: Only extraordinary costs with client's permission.

RED WRITING HOOD INK, 2075 Attala Rd. 1990, Kosciusko MS 39090. (662) 674-5223. Fax (662) 796-3061. E-mail: rwhi@bellsouth.net. Website: www.redwritinghoodink.net. Agent: Sheri Williams. Estab. 1997. Represents 4 clients with religious books. Recognized in the industry. Open to unpublished authors with strong platform; open to new clients. Handles novels & nonfiction for all ages; picture books, gift books, crossover books.

   Contact: No simultaneous submissions; responds in 1-2 weeks to e-mail; 1 month for postal.
   Commission: 15%; foreign 20%.

RLR ASSOCIATES, LTD., Literary Dept., 7 W. 51st St., New York NY 10019. (212) 541-8641. Fax (212) 262-7084. E-mail: sgould@rlrassociates.net. Website: www.rlrliterary.net. Scott Gould, literary assoc. Estab. 1972. Member AAR. Represents 50 clients. Open to unpublished authors and new clients. General agency; handles adult religious/inspirational nonfiction.

   Contact: Query by e-mail, or by mail with SASE. Considers simultaneous submissions.
   Responds in 4-8 wks.
   Commission: 15%; foreign 20%.

ROSENBAUM & ASSOCIATES LITERARY AGENCY, PO Box 277, Brentwood TN 37024-0277. (615) 834-8564. Fax (615) 834-8560. E-mail: bucky@rosenbaumagency.com. Website: www .rosenbaumagency.com. Agent: Bucky Rosenbaum. Estab. 2006. Well recognized in the industry. Represents 30-40 clients. No new clients or unpublished authors. Handles mostly adult nonfiction and some general books, crossover books.

   Contact: By letter.
   Commission: 15%; foreign 10%, plus subagent commission.
   Fees: Only extraordinary costs with client's permission; no reading fees.

GAIL ROSS LITERARY AGENCY, 1666 Connecticut Ave. N.W., #500, Washington DC 20009. (202) 328-3282. Fax (202) 328-9162. E-mail: submissions@gailross.com. Website: www.gailross.com. Agent: Gail Ross (gail@gailross.com). Contact: Jennifer Manguera (jennifer@gailross.com). Estab. 1988. Represents 200 clients. Open to unpublished authors and new clients (mostly through referrals). General agent; handles adult religious/inspirational nonfiction, history, health, and business books.

   Contact: No mailed queries; e-queries only. Accepts simultaneous queries.
   Commission: 15%; foreign 25%.
   Fees: Office expenses.

DAMARIS ROWLAND AGENCY, 420 E. 23rd St., Apt. 6F, New York NY 10010-5040. (212) 475-8942. Cell (917) 538-3916. Fax (212) 358-9411. E-mail: nicolerowland5@mac.com. Agent: Damaris Rowland. Estab. 1994. Represents 40 clients. Open to unpublished authors and new clients. No New Age material. Very selective.

   Contact: Query letter.
   Commission: 15%; foreign 20%.
   Fees: Some office expenses.

SCHIAVONE LITERARY AGENCY INC., 236 Trails End, West Palm Beach FL 33413-2135. Phone/fax (561) 966-9294. E-mail: profschia@aol.com. Website: www.publishersmarketplace.com/members/profschia. Agent: James Schiavone, EdD. Recognized in the industry. Estab. 1997. Represents 6 clients. Open to unpublished and new clients. Handles adult, teen, and children's fiction and nonfiction; celebrity biography; general books; crossover books.

> **Contact:** Query letter/SASE; one-page e-mail query (no attachments).
> **Commission:** 15%, foreign 20%.
> **Fees:** No reading fees; authors pay postage only.
> **Tips:** Works primarily with published authors; will consider first-time authors with excellent material. Actively seeking books on spirituality, major religions, and alternative health. Very selective on first novels.

+SUSAN SCHULMAN LITERARY AGENCY, 454 W. 44th St., New York NY 10036. (212) 713-1633. Fax (212) 581-8830. E-mail: schulman@aol.com. Agent: Susan Schulman. Estab. 1989. Represents 6 clients. Recognized in the industry. Member of AAR. Open to unpublished authors and new clients. Handles adult & teen/YA religious/inspirational novels, adult nonfiction, picture books.

> **Contact:** Query.
> **Commission:** 15%; foreign 20%.

SERENDIPITY LITERARY AGENCY, LLC, 305 Gates Ave., Brooklyn NY 11216. (718) 230-7689. Fax (718) 230-7829. E-mail: rbrooks@serendipitylit.com. Website: www.serendipitylit.com. Agent: Regina Brooks. Member AAR. Estab. 2000. Represents 50 clients; 3 with religious books. Recognized in the industry. Open to unpublished authors and new clients. General agent; handles fiction & nonfiction for all ages, gift books, crossover books, general books. No science fiction. No picture books for now.

> **Contact:** By e-mail or letter; no faxes. Accepts simultaneous submissions. Responds in 8-12 wks.
> **Commission:** 15%; foreign 20%.
> **Fees:** None.

THE SEYMOUR AGENCY, 475 Miner Street Rd., Canton NY 13617. (315) 386-1831. E-mail: marysue@twcny.rr.com. Website: www.theseymouragency.com. Agent: Mary Sue Seymour. Estab. 1992. Member of AAR. Represents 35 religious clients. Open to unpublished authors and new clients (prefers published authors). Handles Christian romance novels, Christian historical romance, and nonfiction for all ages, general books, crossover books.

> **Contact:** Query letter or e-mail with first 50 pages of ms. For nonfiction, send proposal with chapter 1. Simultaneous query OK. Responds in 1 mo. for queries and 2-3 mos. for mss.
> **Commission:** 15% for unpublished authors.
> **Fees:** None.
> **Tips:** "We have multibook sales to Zondervan, Thomas Nelson, Harvest House, Cook Communications, Abingdon Press, Bethany House, Steeple Hill, and HarperOne."

THE SHEPARD AGENCY, 73 Kingswood Dr., Bethel CT 06801. (203) 790-4230. Fax (203) 798-2924. E-mail: shepardagcy@mindspring.com. Agent: Jean Shepard. Recognized in the industry. Estab. 1987. Represents 11 clients. Open to unpublished authors; no new clients at this time. Handles fiction and nonfiction for all ages; no picture books; especially business, reference, professional, self-help, cooking, and crafts. Books only.

> **Contact:** By e-mail.
> **Commission:** 15%; foreign variable.
> **Fees:** None except long-distance calls and copying.

KEN SHERMAN & ASSOCIATES, 9507 Santa Monica Blvd., Beverly Hills CA 90210. (310) 273-3840. Fax (310) 271-2875. E-mail: ken@kenshermanassociates.com. Agent: Ken Sherman. Estab.

1989. Represents 50 clients. Open to unpublished authors and new clients. Handles adult religious/inspirational novels, nonfiction, screenplays and TV/movie scripts.

Contact: By referral only. Responds in 1 mo.

Commission: 15%; foreign 20%; dramatic rights 15%.

Fees: Charges office expenses and other negotiable expenses.

WENDY SHERMAN ASSOCIATES, 27 W. 24th St., Ste. 700B, New York NY 10110. (212) 279-9027. Fax (212) 279-8863. Website: www.wsherman.com. Agents: Wendy Sherman, Kimberly Perel. Open to unpublished authors and new clients. General agents. Handle adult religious nonfiction.

Contact: Query by mail/SASE or send proposal/1 chapter. No phone/fax/e-query. Guidelines on Website.

Commission: 15%; foreign 20%.

MICHAEL SNELL LITERARY AGENCY, PO Box 1206, Truro MA 02666-1206. (508) 349-3718. Website: http://michaelsnellagency.com. Agent: Michael Snell. Estab. 1978. Represents 200 clients. Open to unpublished authors and new clients. General agent: handles adult religious/inspirational nonfiction.

Contact: Query with SASE. No simultaneous submissions. Responds in 1-2 wks.

Commission: 15%; foreign 15%.

SPENCERHILL ASSOCIATES, LTD./KAREN SOLEM, Chatham NY. (518) 392-9293. Fax (518) 392-9554. E-mail: submissions@spencerhillassociates.com. Website: www.spencerhillassociates .com. Agent: Karen Solem. Member of AAR. Recognized in the industry. Estab. 2001. Represents 15-20 clients with religious books. Not currently open to unpublished authors; very selective of new clients. Primarily handles adult Christian fiction; no YA, children's, or nonfiction.

Contact: By e-mail.

Commission: 15%; foreign 20%.

Fees: Photocopying and Express Mail charges only.

Tips: "Check Website for latest information and needs and how to submit. No nonfiction."

STEELE-PERKINS LITERARY AGENCY, 26 Island Ln., Canandaigua NY 14424. (585) 396-9290. Fax (585) 396-3579. E-mail: pattiesp@aol.com. Agent: Pattie Steele-Perkins. Member AAR. Handles inspirational romance novels.

Contact: Proposal/3 chapters. Considers simultaneous submissions. Responds in 6 weeks. E-mail instead of calling.

Commission: 15%.

LESLIE H. STOBBE, 300 Doubleday Rd., Tryon NC 28782. (828) 808-7127. Fax (978) 945-0517. E-mail: lhstobbe123@gmail.com. Website: www.stobbeliterary.com. Agent: Les Stobbe. Well recognized in the industry. Estab. 1993. Represents 71 clients. Open to unpublished authors and new clients. Handles adult fiction, nonfiction, and crossover books.

Contact: By e-mail. Considers simultaneous submissions; responds within 12 weeks.

Commission: 15%

Fees: None.

Tips: "I will not accept clients whose theological positions in their book differ significantly from mine."

SUITE A MANAGEMENT TALENT & LITERARY AGENCY, 120 El Camino Dr., Ste. 202, Beverly Hills CA 90212. (310) 278-0801. Fax (310) 278-0807. E-mail: suite-A@juno.com. Agent: Lloyd D. Robinson. Recognized in the industry. Estab. 2001. Several clients. Open to new and unpublished clients (if published in other media). Specializes in screenplays and novels for adaptation to TV movies.

Contact: By mail or fax only. For consideration of representation, send current bio, and for each screenplay, your WGA registration number, log line, and two-paragraph synopsis only.

Complete scripts or e-mail submissions are not read; attachments are deleted. Responds only if interested.

Commission: 10%

Comments: Representation limited to adaptation of novels and true-life stories for film and television development. Work must have been published for consideration.

MARK SWEENEY & ASSOCIATES, 28540 Altessa Way, Ste. 201, Bonita Springs FL 34135. (239) 594-1957. Fax (239) 594-1935. E-mail: sweeney2@comcast.net. Agents: Mark Sweeney; Janet Sweeney. Recognized in the industry. Estab. 2003. Open to unpublished authors and new clients on a restricted basis. Handles adult religious/inspirational nonfiction, crossover books, general books. No new fiction at this time.

   Contact: E-mail.

   Commission: 15%; foreign 15%.

   Fees: None.

TALCOTT NOTCH LITERARY SERVICES, 276 Forest Rd., Milford CT 06461. (203) 877-1146. Fax (203) 876-9517. Website: www.talcottnotch.net. Agent: Gina Panettieri (gpanettieri@talcottnotch .net). Not yet recognized in the industry; building a Christian presence. Estab. 2003. Represents 25 clients (3 with religious books). Open to unpublished authors and new clients. Handles nonfiction & fiction, crossover & general market books for all ages.

   Contact: By e-mail (editorial@talcottnotch.net). Accepts simultaneous submissions; responds in 8 wks.

   Commission: 15%; foreign or with co-agent 20%.

   Fees: None.

   Tips: "While Christian and religious books are not our main focus, we are open to unique and thought-provoking works from all writers. We specifically seek nonfiction in areas of parenting, health, women's issues, arts & crafts, self-help, and current events. We are open to academic/scholarly work as well as commercial projects."

3 SEAS LITERARY AGENCY, PO Box 8571, Madison WI 53708. (608) 221-4306. E-mail: threeseaslit@aol.com. Website: www.threeseaslit.com. Agent: Michelle Grajkowski. Estab. 2000. Represents 40 clients. Open to unpublished authors and new clients. General agent; handles adult religious/inspirational novels & nonfiction.

   Contact: E-query only with synopsis & 1 chapter (queries@threeseaslit.com). Considers simultaneous submissions. Responds in 2-3 mos.

   Commission: 15%; foreign 20%.

TRIDENT MEDIA GROUP, LLC., 41 Madison Ave., 36th Fl., New York NY 10010. (212) 262-4810. Fax (212) 262-4849. E-mail: dfehr@tridentmediagroup.com. Website: www.tridentmediagroup .com. Agent: Don Fehr. Open to unpublished authors and new clients. General agent. Handles adult religious nonfiction.

   Contact: No unsolicited mss. Query/SASE first; send outline and sample chapters on request. Responds to queries in 3 wks.; mss in 6 wks.

   Commission: 15%.

VAN DIEST LITERARY AGENCY, PO Box 1482, Sisters OR 97759. (541) 549-0477. Fax (541) 549-1213. E-mail through Website: www.ChristianLiteraryAgency.com. Agents: David & Sarah Van Diest. Estab. 2004. Represents 20 clients. Open to unpublished authors and new clients. Recognized in the industry. Handles teen & adult novels, nonfiction for all ages, crossover books.

   Contact: By e-mail. Use online form. Responds in 4 wks.

   Commission: 15%; 25% for first-time authors.

VERITAS LITERARY AGENCY, 601 Van Ness Ave., Opera Plaza Ste. E, San Francisco CA 94102. (415) 647-6964. Fax (415) 647-6965. E-mail: submissions@veritasliterary.com. Website: www .veritasliterary.com. Agent: Katherine Boyle (kboyle@veritasliterary.com). Member AAR. Handles serious religious nonfiction (no New Age).

    Contact: Query with SASE; e-query OK (no attachments); no fax queries.

WATERSIDE PRODUCTIONS INC., 2055 Oxford Ave., Cardiff-by-the-Sea CA 92007. (760) 632-9190. Fax (760) 632-9295. E-mail: admin@waterside.com. Website: www.waterside.com. Agent: William E. Brown (webrown@waterside.com). Christian agent in a highly regarded general agency. Interested in handling Christian books, or books which otherwise challenge and engage readers from a Judeo-Christian perspective. Prefers nonfiction, but will look at fiction (the bar is very high). In addition to spiritually oriented books, devotions, theology, chick lit and mom lit, list includes business books: leadership, marketing, sales, business development.

    Contact: Query via online form (see Website). Considers simultaneous submissions.

    Commission: 15%; foreign 25%.

+WINTERS & KING, INC., 2448 E. 81st St., Ste. 5900, Tulsa OK 74137-4259. (918) 494-6868. Fax (918) 491-6297. Website: www.wintersking.com. Agent: Thomas J. Winters. Estab. 1983. Represents 100+ clients. Recognized in the industry. Rarely open to unpublished authors; open to qualified new clients with a significant sales history/platform. Handles adult religious/inspirational novels & nonfiction for all ages, screenplays, TV/movie scripts, gift books.

    Contact: Query by mail with SASE (no unsolicited mss). Responds in 2-4 wks.

    Commission: 15%; foreign 15%.

    Fees: None

    Tips: "Proposals not in proper format will not be reviewed or considered (no handwritten proposals)."

WOLGEMUTH & ASSOCIATES INC., 8600 Crestgate Cir., Orlando FL 32819. (407) 909-9445. Fax (407) 909-9446. E-mail: rwolgemuth@wolgemuthandassociates.com. Agent: Robert D. Wolgemuth; Andrew D. Wolgemuth (awolgemuth@wolgemuthandassociates.com); Erik S. Wolgemuth (ewolge muth@wolgemuthandassociates.com). Member AAR. Well recognized in the industry. Estab. 1992. Represents 85 clients. No new clients or unpublished authors. Handles mostly adult nonfiction; most other types of books handled only for current clients.

    Contact: By letter.

    Commission: 15%.

    Fees: None.

    Tips: "We work with authors who are either best-selling authors or potentially best-selling authors. Consequently, we want to represent clients with broad market appeal."

WORDSERVE LITERARY GROUP, 10152 S. Knoll Cir., Highlands Ranch CO 80130. (303) 471-6675. E-mail: admin@wordserveliterary.com ("Query" in subject line). Website: www.wordservelit erary.com. Agents: Greg Johnson (greg@wordserveliterary.com) and Rachelle Gardner (rachelle@ wordserveliterary.com/PO Box 1089, Monument CO 80132). Estab. 2003. Represents 80 clients. Recognized in the industry. Open to new clients. Handles novels & nonfiction for all ages, gift books, crossover books, general books (memoir, military, self-help, adult fiction).

    Contact: By e-mail (no attachments). Visit Website for submission guidelines. Responds in 4-8 wks.

    Commission: 15%; foreign 15-20%.

    Fees: None.

    Tips: "Nonfiction: First impressions count. Make sure your proposal answers all the questions on competition, outline, audience, felt need, etc. Fiction: Make sure your novel is completed before you submit a proposal (synopsis, plus 5 chapters)."

THE WRITER'S EDGE. See listing under Editorial Services—Illinois.

WRITERS HOUSE, 21 W. 26th St., New York NY 10010. (212) 685-2400. Fax (212) 685-1781. E-mail: azuckerman@writerhouse.com. Website: www.writershouse.com. Agent: Albert Zuckerman. Estab. 1974. Represents 440 clients. General agency; handles adult religious/inspirational fiction. Member of AAR.
> **Contact:** One-page query by mail/SASE. No e-mail/fax queries. Responds in 1 mo. to query.
> **Commission:** 15%; foreign 20%.
> **Fees:** No fees.
> **Tips:** "See Website for details. Write a compelling query so we'll ask to see your manuscript."

YATES & YATES, 1100 W. Town and Country Rd., Ste. 1300, Orange CA 92868-4654. (714) 480-4000. Fax (714) 480-4001. E-mail: curtis@yates2.com. Website: www.yates2.com. Agents: Curtis Yates and Chris Ferebee. Estab. 1989. Recognized in the industry. Represents 50+ clients. No unpublished authors; open to new clients. Handles adult and teen novels and nonfiction, screenplays, TV/movie scripts, crossover books.
> **Contact:** E-mail.
> **Commission:** Negotiable.
> **Fees:** Negotiable.

ZACHARY SHUSTER HARMSWORTH LITERARY AND ENTERTAINMENT AGENCY, 1776 Broadway, Ste. 1405, New York NY 10019. (212) 765-6900. Fax (212) 765-6490; and 535 Boylston St., Ste. 1103, Boston MA 02116. (617) 262-2400. Fax (617) 262-2468. E-mail: mchappell@zsh literary.com. Website: www.zshliterary.com. Agent: Mary Beth Chappell (Boston office). Recognized in the industry. Represents 15-30 religious clients. Open to unpublished authors and new clients. Handles adult religious/inspirational novels & adult nonfiction, crossover books, general books.
> **Contact:** E-mail with online form only; no unsolicited submissions.
> **Commission:** 15%; foreign & film 20%.
> **Fees:** Office expenses only.
> **Tips:** "We are looking for inspirational fiction, Christian nonfiction, especially that which focuses on the emerging/emergent church or that which would appeal to readers in their 20s and 30s, and teen/YA series."

14

Contests

The contests listed below are both Christian and general contests arranged by genre or type of material they are looking for, such as poetry, fiction, nonfiction, etc. They all have Websites where you can go for their specific guidelines and more information than we can include here. Be sure to download and follow their guidelines exactly, or you may be eliminated from the competition. You will want to verify even the information we have included, as it may have changed after we went to press. A listing here does not guarantee the legitimacy of a contest. For guidelines on evaluating contests and to help determine if a contest is legitimate, go to: www.sfwa.org/for-authors/writer-beware.

+ Indicates a new listing

CHILDREN/YOUNG-ADULT CONTESTS, WRITING FOR

THE CHILDREN'S WRITER CONTESTS. Offers a number of contests for children's writers. Website: www.childrenswriter.com.

DELACORTE DELL YEARLING CONTEST FOR FIRST YOUNG ADULT NOVEL. Random House Inc. Website: www.randomhouse.com/kids/writingcontests/index.html#youngadult. Contemporary and historical fiction manuscripts, 100-224 pgs., for ages 12-18. Submit between October 1 and December 31. Prizes: $1,500, book contract, and $7,500 advance.

HIGHLIGHTS FOR CHILDREN FICTION CONTEST. (570) 253-1080. Website: www.highlights .com. Offers 3 prizes of $1,000 each for stories up to 800 words for children; for beginning readers to 500 words. See Website for guidelines and current topic. (To find contest info put "Contest" in search field.) No crime, violence, or derogatory humor. No entry fee or form required. Entries must be postmarked between January 1 and January 31.

CORETTA SCOTT KING BOOK AWARD. Coretta Scott King Task Force, American Library Assn. Toll-free (800) 545-2433. E-mail: olos@ala.org. Website: www.ala.org. Annual award for children's books by African American authors and/or illustrators published the previous year. Books must fit one of these categories: preschool to grade 4; grades 5-8; grades 9-12. Deadline: December 1 each year. Guidelines on Website (click on "Awards & Grants"/click on contest name on list). Prizes: a plaque, a set of encyclopedias, and $1,000 cash. Recipients are authors and illustrators of African descent whose distinguished books promote an understanding and appreciation of the "American Dream."

LEE & LOW BOOKS NEW VOICES AWARD. E-mail: info@leeandlow.com. Website: www.leeand low.com. Annual award for a children's fiction or nonfiction picture book story by a writer of color; to 1,500 words. Deadline: between May 1 and October 31. Prizes: $1,000 plus publication contract; & $500 for Honor Award Winner. Guidelines on Website (click on "Creators"/"New Voices Award"). Sign up on Website for their newsletter, which will include details for the next contest.

MILKWEED PRIZE FOR CHILDREN'S LITERATURE. Milkweed Editions. (612) 332-3192. E-mail: editor@milkweed.org. Website: www.milkweed.org. Annual prize for unpublished novel intended for readers 8-13; 90-200 pgs. Prize: $10,000 advance against royalties and publication. Guidelines on Website (Click on "Submissions Guidelines & Prizes").

POCKETS WRITING CONTEST. (615) 340-7333. Fax (615) 340-7267. E-mail: pockets@upper room.org. Website: www.pockets.org. United Methodist. Lynn W. Gilliam, ed. Devotional magazine for children (6-11 yrs.). Fiction-writing contest; submit between March 1 and August 15 every yr. Prize: $500 and publication in *Pockets*. Length: 750-1,000 words. Must be unpublished and not historical fiction. Previous winners not eligible. Send to Pockets Fiction Contest at above address, designating "Fiction Contest" on outside of envelope. Send SASE for return and response. Details on Website (click on "Breaking News"/"Annual Fiction Contest").

SKIPPING STONES YOUTH HONOR AWARDS. (541) 342-4956. E-mail: editor@skipping stones.org. Website: www.skippingstones.org. Interfaith/multicultural. Arun N. Toké, exec. ed.; Nina Forsberg, asst. ed. A multicultural awareness and nature appreciation magazine for young people, worldwide. Annual Youth Honor Awards for students 7-17. Deadline June 25. Guidelines on Website (scroll down to "Also"/"Youth Honor Awards").

SOCIETY OF CHILDREN'S BOOK WRITERS & ILLUSTRATORS GOLDEN KITE AWARDS. Website: www.scbwi.org. For books published in the 2010 calendar year. Offers $2,500 in cash awards. Details on Website (click on "Awards & Grants"/"Golden Kite Awards").

FICTION CONTESTS

AMAZON BREAKTHROUGH NOVEL AWARD. In cooperation with Penguin and Hewlett-Packard. Penguin will publish winning novel with a $25,000 advance. November deadline.

AMERICAN CHRISTIAN FICTION WRITERS CONTESTS. Phone/fax (321) 984-4018. E-mail: genesis@ACFW.com, boty@acfw.com, or vp@acfw.com. Website: www.ACFW.com. Sponsors a fiction contest and others. See Website for current contests and rules (scroll down to "Contests"/click on name of contest).

+ATHANATOS CHRISTIAN MINISTRIES BOOK LENGTH NOVEL CONTEST. (202) 280-7971. E-mail: director@athanatosministries.org. Website: www.athanatosministries.org. Novel 40,000-90,000 words. Prizes: 1st prize $1,000 and a possible book contract; 2nd prize $500 and a possible book contract. Entry fee: $69.95. Deadline: September 1.

BARD FICTION PRIZE. Awarded annually to a promising, emerging young writer of fiction, aged 39 years or younger. Entries must be previously published. Deadline: July 15. No entry fee. Prizes: $30,000 and appointment as writer in residence for one semester at Bard College, Annandale-on-Hudson NY. E-mail: bfp@bard.edu. Website: www.bard.edu/bfp.

BOSTON REVIEW SHORT STORY CONTEST. Boston Review. Website: www.bostonreview.net. Prize: $1,500 (plus publication) for an unpublished short story to 4,000 words. Entry fee: $20. Deadline: October 1. Details on Website (click on "About"/scroll down to "Contest"/"Aura Estrada Short Story Contest").

BULWER-LYTTON FICTION CONTEST. For the worst opening line to a novel. Deadline: April 15. Website: www.bulwer-lytton.com. Rules on Website.

CANADIAN WRITER'S JOURNAL SHORT FICTION CONTEST. White Mountain Publications, Box 1178, New Liskeard ON P0J 1P0, Canada. (705) 647-5424. Canada-wide toll-free (800) 258-5451. E-mail: cwc-calendar@cwj.ca. Website: www.cwj.ca. Sponsors semiannual short fiction contests. Deadline: April 30. Length: to 1,500 words. Entry fee: $5. Prizes: $150, $100, $50. All fiction needs for CWJ are filled by this contest. Click on "CWJ Short Fiction Contest."

ALEXANDER PATTERSON CAPON PRIZE FOR FICTION. New Letters, UMKC, University House, 5101 Rockhill Rd., Kansas City MO 64110. (816) 235-1168. E-mail: newletters@umkc.edu. Website: www.newletters.org. Deadline: May 18. Entry fee: $15. Prize: $1,500. Click on "Awards for Writers."

THE CHRISTY AWARDS. Phone/fax (734) 663-7931. E-mail: CA2000DK@aol.com. Website: www .christyawards.com. Awards in 9 fiction genres for excellence in Christian fiction. Nominations made by publishers, not authors. For submission guidelines and other information, see Website (click on "Forms"/"2011 Official Guidelines"). Awards are presented at an annual Christy Awards Banquet held Friday prior to the annual ICRS convention in July.

+JACK DYER FICTION PRIZE. Crab Orchard Review, Fiction Contest, Dept. of English, Mail Code 4503, Southern Illinois University–Carbondale, 1000 Faner Dr., Carbondale IL 62901. (618) 453-5321.Website: www.siuc.edu/~crborchd. Entry fee: $10. Prize: $1,500. Deadline: submit between March 1 and May 10 (may vary). Submit fiction up to 6,000 words.

GLIMMER TRAIN PRESS FICTION CONTESTS. Glimmer Train Press, Website: www.glimmer train.com. Sponsors a number of contests. Check Website for current contests (click on "Writers' Guidelines").

JAMES JONES FIRST NOVEL FELLOWSHIP. (570) 408-4534. E-mail: jamesjonesfirstnovel@ wilkes.edu. Website: www.wilkes.edu/pages/1159.asp. Deadline: March 1. Entry fee: $25. Prizes: $10,000 first prize; $750 for two runners-up. Submit a 2-page outline and the first 50 pages of an unpublished novel. Guidelines on Website.

SERENA MCDONALD KENNEDY AWARD. Snake Nation Press. Website: www.snakenationpress .org. Novellas to 50,000 words, or short-story collection to 200 pgs. (published or unpublished). Deadline: July 31 (check Website to verify). Entry fee: $25. Prize: $1,000 and publication. Guidelines on Website (click on "Contests").

THE MARY MCCARTHY PRIZE IN SHORT FICTION. Sarabande Books. E-mail: sarabandeb@ aol.com. Website: www.sarabandebooks.org. Prize: $2,000 and publication of a collection of short stories, novellas, or a short novel (150-250 pgs.), plus a standard royalty contract. Deadline: submit between January 1 and February 15. Entry fee: $25. Guidelines on Website (click on "Submission Guidelines"/scroll to bottom and click on name of contest).

NATIONAL WRITERS ASSOCIATION NOVEL-WRITING CONTEST. The National Writers Assn., (303) 841-0246. Website: www.nationalwriters.com. Check Website for current contests and guidelines (click on "Contests"/then name of contest).

NATIONAL WRITERS ASSOCIATION SHORT-STORY CONTEST. The National Writers Assn., (303) 841-0246. Website: www.nationalwriters.com. Check Website for current contest and guidelines (click on "Contests"/then name of contest).

THE FLANNERY O'CONNOR AWARD FOR SHORT FICTION. University of Georgia Press. Website: www.ugapress.uga.edu. For collections of short fiction, 50,000-75,000 wds. Prize: $1,000, plus publication under royalty book contract. Entry fee: $25. Deadline: between April 1 and May 31 (postmark). Guidelines on Website (click on "About Us"/"For Prospective Authors"/"Flannery O'Connor Award for Short Fiction").

OPERATION FIRST NOVEL. Sponsored by the Jerry B. Jenkins Christian Writers Guild. For unpublished novelists who are students or annual members of the Christian Writers Guild. Winner receives $20,000 and a book contract with a major CBA publisher. Length: 75,000-100,000 words. Deadline: October 1. No entry fee. For contest rules, go to www.ChristianWritersGuild.com/contest.asp.

+GRACE PALEY PRIZE FOR SHORT FICTION. (703) 993-4301. E-mail: awp@awpwriter.org. Website: www.awpwriter.org. Prize: $4,000 & publication. Entry fee: $25. Deadline: Postmarked between January 1 and February 28, 2011.

KATHERINE ANNE PORTER PRIZE FOR FICTION. Literary Contest/Fiction, *Nimrod Journal*, University of Tulsa. (918) 631-3080. E-mail: nimrod@utulsa.edu. Website: www.utulsa.edu/nimrod/awards.html. Quality prose and fiction by emerging writers of contemporary literature, unpublished. Deadline: submit between January 1 and April 30. Entry fee: $20. Prizes: $2,000 and publication; $1,000 and publication. Guidelines on Website (click on "Nimrod Literary Awards").

TOBIAS WOLFF AWARD IN FICTION. Western Washington University, Bellingham WA. E-mail: bhreview@cc.wwu.edu. Website: www.wwu.edu/~bhreview. Short story or novel excerpt to 8,000 words. Deadline: postmarked between December 1 and March 15. Entry fee: $18 for first story/chapter; $10 each additional. Prize: $1,000, plus publication. Details on Website (click on "2011 Contests").

WORD SMITTEN'S TENTEN FICTION COMPETITION. Word Smitten LLP. E-mail: award@wordsmitten.com. Website: www.wordsmitten.com. Annual contest for a short story of exactly 1,010 words. Deadline: July 1. Entry fee: $18. Prize: $1,010, plus publication. Guidelines on Website (click on "TenTen Fiction").

WRITER'S JOURNAL ANNUAL FICTION CONTEST. E-mail: writersjournal@writersjournal.com. Website: www.writersjournal.com. Sponsors several contests; see Website (click on "Contests"/scroll down to "Contest Entry Manuscript Format").

NONFICTION CONTESTS

AMY WRITING AWARDS. A call to present spiritual truth reinforced with biblical references in general, nonreligious publications. First prize is $10,000 with a total of $34,000 given annually (additional prizes of $1,000-5,000). To be eligible, submitted articles must be published in a general, nonreligious publication and must be reinforced with at least one passage of Scripture. Deadline is January 31 of following year. Winners are notified by May 1. For details and a copy of last year's winning entries, contact: The Amy Foundation, PO Box 16091, Lansing MI 48901-6091. (517) 323-6233. E-mail: amyfoundtn@aol.com. Website: www.amyfound.org.

AWP CREATIVE NONFICTION PRIZE. Assoc. of Writers and Writing programs, George Mason University, Fairfax VA. E-mail: awp@awpwriter.org. Website: www.awpwriter.org. For authors of book-length manuscripts; submit only 150-300 pgs. Deadline: February 28. Entry fee: $10 for members; $25 for nonmembers. Prize: $2,000. Guidelines on Website (click on "Contests"/"AWP Award Series").

THE BECHTEL PRIZE. Teachers and Writers Magazine Contest. E-mail: info@twc.org. Website: www.twc.org/publications/bechtel-prize. Contemporary writing articles (unpublished) to 5,000 words. Deadline: June 30 (varies). Entry fee: $20. Prize: $1,000, plus publication.

DOROTHY CHURCHILL CAPON PRIZE FOR ESSAY. New Letters, UMKC, University House. (816) 235-1168. E-mail: newletters@umkc.edu. Website: www.newletters.org. Deadline: May 18. Entry fee: $15. Prize: $1,500. Guidelines on Website (scroll down and click on "New Letters Writing Contests").

ANNIE DILLARD AWARD IN CREATIVE NONFICTION. Essays on any subject to 8,000 words. Deadline: between December 1 and March 15. Entry fee: $18 for first; $10 each additional. First prize: $1,000. Unpublished works only, to 8,000 words. E-mail: bhreview@cc.wwu.edu. Website: www.wwu.edu/~bhreview. Details on Website (click on "2011 Contests"/"2011 Contest Submission Guidelines").

EUREKA STREET/READER'S FEAST AWARD. Australia. E-mail: eureka@eureksstreet.com.au. Website: www.crimeandjusticefestival.com/eureka. For unpublished essays on social justice and human rights up to 1,500 words. $5,000 award to an Australian writer. Deadline: mid-June. E-mail submissions only. Details on Website.

EVENT CREATIVE NONFICTION CONTEST. The Douglas College Review, Canada. (604) 527-5293. E-mail: event@douglas.bc.ca. Website: http://event.douglas.bc.ca. Previously unpublished creative nonfiction to 5,000 wds. Deadline: April 15. Entry fee: $29.95. Prizes: Three $500 prizes and publication in *Event*. Details on Website (click on "Contest Details").

GRAYWOLF PRESS NONFICTION PRIZE. (651) 641-0036. Website: www.graywolfpress.org/Company_Info/Submission_Guidelines/Graywolf_Press_Nonfiction_Prize_Submission_Guidelines. For the best literary nonfiction book by a writer not yet established in the genre. Deadline: between June 1 & June 30 (varies). Entry fee: none. Prize: $12,000 advance and publication. Guidelines on Website (click on "Submission Guidelines").

GUIDEPOSTS CONTEST. Website: www.guideposts.org. Interfaith. Writers Workshop Contest held on even years, with a late June deadline. True, first-person stories (yours or someone else's), 1,500 words. Needs one spiritual message, with scenes, drama, and characters. Winners attend a week-long seminar in New York (all expenses paid) on how to write for *Guideposts*.

+JOHN GUYTON LITERARY NONFICTION PRIZE. *Crab Orchard Review*, Nonfiction Contest, Dept. of English, Mail Code 4503, Southern Illinois University–Carbondale, 1000 Faner Dr., Carbondale IL 62901. (618) 453-5321.Website: www.siuc.edu/~crborchd. Entry fee: $10. Prize: $1,500. Deadline: submit between March 1 and May 10 (may vary). Submit nonfiction up to 6,500 words. Guidelines on Website.

RICHARD J. MARGOLIS AWARD. Blue Mountain Center, Margolis & Assocs. E-mail: hwsm@margolis.com. Website: www.margolis.com/award. Given annually to a promising young journalist or essayist whose work combines warmth, humor, wisdom, and concern with social justice. Deadline: July 1. Prize: $5,000. Guidelines on Website.

+MASTER BOOKS SCHOLARSHIP ESSAY CONTEST. PO Box 726, Green Forest AR 72638. (870) 438-5288. Fax (870) 438-5120. E-mail: submissions@newleafpress.net. Essay contest; $3,000 college scholarship; www.newleafpublishinggroup.com/store/scholarship.htm. Details on Website.

OPERATION FIRST BOOK. Sponsored by the Jerry B. Jenkins Christian Writers Guild. For unpublished authors who are students or annual members of the Christian Writers Guild. Winner receives $10,000 and their proposal is considered by a major Christian publisher. Nonfiction. Length: 75,000-100,000 wds. Deadline: September 2011 (check Website to verify date). Entry fee: none. For contest rules, go to www.ChristianWritersGuild.com and click on "Contests."

PLAY/SCRIPTWRITING/SCREENWRITING CONTESTS

+AMERICAN ZOETROPE SCREENPLAY CONTEST. E-mail: contests@zoetrope.com. Website: www.zoetrope.com/contests. Deadline: August 3 (early), September 8 (final). Entry fees: $35 (early), $50 (final). Prizes: First prize $5,000. That winner and 10 finalists will be considered for film option and development.

AUSTIN FILM FESTIVAL SCREENWRITERS COMPETITION. (512) 478-4795. E-mail: info@austinfilmfestival.com. Website: www.austinfilmfestival.com. Offers a number of contest categories for screenplays. See current details on Website.

BAKER'S PLAYS HIGH SCHOOL PLAYWRITING COMPETITION. Plays may be about any subject and any length as long as the play can be reasonably produced by high school students on a high school stage. Deadline: January 30. Prizes: $500, $250, and $100. Guidelines on Website: www.bakersplays.com (go down to "Information" box & click on "Contests & Festivals").

CITA PLAY & SKETCH CONTEST. E-mail: admin@cita.org. Website: www.CITA.org. (click on "Services"/"Play & Sketch Contests"). To encourage Christian playwrights, the writing of new plays and musicals that are informed by a biblical worldview in influencing our culture and furthering the Kingdom of God. Info on upcoming competitions will be listed on Website as available.

KAIROS PRIZE FOR SPIRITUALLY UPLIFTING SCREENPLAYS. John Templeton Foundation. E-mail: contact@kairosprize.com. Website: www.kairosprize.com. Biannual. For first-time screenwriters with a religious message. Prizes: $25,000, $15,000, $10,000. Guidelines on Website (click on "Guidelines").

MOONDANCE INTERNATIONAL FILM FESTIVAL COMPETITION. E-mail: director@moondance filmfestival.com. Website: www.moondancefilmfestival.com. Open to films, screenplays, and features. Deadline: May 15. Entry fees: $25-75. Prize: winning entries screened at festival. Details on Website.

NICHOLL FELLOWSHIPS IN SCREENWRITING. (310) 247-3010. E-mail: nicholl@oscars.org. Website: www.oscars.org/nicholl/index.html. International contest held annually, open to any writer who has not optioned or sold a treatment, teleplay, or screenplay for more than $5,000. Up to five $30,000 fellowships offered each year to promising authors. Deadline: May 1. Entry fee: $30. Guidelines/ required application form on Website (scroll down to "About the Competition" and click on "More").

MILDRED & ALBERT PANOWSKI PLAYWRITING AWARD. Award Coordinator, Forest Roberts Theatre, Northern Michigan University, Marquette MI. Website: www.nmu.edu/theatre. Unpublished, unproduced, full-length plays. Deadline: October 31. Prizes: $2,000, a summer workshop, a fully mounted production, and transportation to Marquette. Guidelines on Website (click on "Playwriting Award").

SCRIPTAPALOOZA SCREENPLAY COMPETITION. (323) 654-5809. E-mail: info@scriptapa looza.com. Website: www.scriptapalooza.com. Entry fee: $55. Deadline: April 15 (varies). Prize: $10,000. Details on Website.

THE WRITERS NETWORK ANNUAL SCREENPLAY & FICTION COMPETITION. *Fade In* magazine. (310) 275-0287. E-mail: writersnet@aol.com. Website: www.fadeinonline.com. Deadline: May 31. Must submit online. Grand Prize, plus prizes for 1st through 3 places. Guidelines on Website (click on "Fade In Awards").

POETRY CONTESTS

ANHINGA PRIZE FOR POETRY. E-mail: info@anhinga.org. Website: www.anhinga.org. A $2,000 prize for original poetry book in English. Winning manuscript published by Anhinga Press. For poets trying to publish a first or second book of poetry. Submissions: 48-80 pgs. Number pages and include $25 reading fee. Deadline: between February 15 and May 1 each year. Details on Website (click on contest name).

MURIEL CRAFT BAILEY MEMORIAL POETRY AWARD. E-mail: poetry@comstockreview.org. Awarded annually. Deadline: July 1. Prizes: $100 to $1,000. Finalists published in the *Comstock Review*. Unpublished poems to 40 lines. Entry fee: $5 for each poem (no limit on number of submissions). Details on Website: www.comstockreview.org.

BALTIMORE REVIEW POETRY CONTEST. All styles and forms of poetry. April 1-July 1. Entry fee: $10. Prizes: $300 & publication; $150; $50; plus publication in the *Baltimore Review*. Details on Website: www.baltimorereview.org. Click on "Contests" on main menu.

BLUE MOUNTAIN ARTS/SPS STUDIOS POETRY CARD CONTEST. (303) 449-0536. E-mail: poetrycontest@sps.com. Website: www.sps.com. Biannual contest (even years). Next deadline: June 30, 2012. Use online form for submissions. Rhymed or unrhymed original poetry (unrhymed preferred). Poems also considered for greeting cards or anthologies. Prizes: $300, $150, $50. Details on Website ("Poetry Contest").

BOSTON REVIEW ANNUAL POETRY CONTEST. Deadline: June 1. First prize: $1,500, plus publication. Submit up to 5 unpublished poems. Entry fee: $20 (includes a subscription to *Boston Review*). Submit manuscripts in duplicate with cover note. Website: www.bostonreview.net. Details on Website (click on "About"/"Contests"/name of contest).

CAVE CANEM POETRY PRIZE. Supports the work of African American poets with excellent manuscripts who have not found a publisher for their first book. Deadline: April 30 (varies). Prize: $1,000, publication by a national press, and 15 copies of the book. Entry fee: $15. Details on Website: www.cavecanempoets.org (click on "Book Awards"/click on name of contest/scroll down and click on "Competition Guidelines"). E-mail: ccpoets@verizon.net.

49TH PARALLEL POETRY AWARD. Mail Stop 9053, Western Washington University, Bellingham WA. (360) 650-4863. E-mail: bhreview@cc.wwu.edu. Website: www.wwu.edu/~bhreview. Poems in any style or on any subject. Deadline: submit between December 1 and March 15. Entry fee: $18 for first entry; $10 for each additional entry. First prize: $1,000 and publication. Details on Website.

+FLO GAULT STUDENT POETRY COMPETITION. Sarabande Books. E-mail: info@sarabandebooks.org. Website: www.sarabandebooks.org. Prize: $500. Submit up to 3 poems. Deadline: November 1. Details on Website (click on "Student Poetry Prize").

GRIFFIN POETRY PRIZE. (905) 565-5993. E-mail: info@griffinpoetryprize.com. Website: www.griffinpoetryprize.com. Prizes: two $65,000 awards (one to a Canadian and one to a poet from anywhere in the world) for a collection of poetry published in English during the preceding year; plus additional prizes ($200,000 in prizes total). All submissions must come from publishers. Deadline: December 31. Details on Website.

+DONALD HALL PRIZE FOR POETRY. (703) 993-4301. E-mail: awp@awpwriter.org. Website: www.awpwriter.org. Prize: $4,000 & publication. Entry fee: $25. Deadline: postmarked between January 1 and February 28, 2011.

TOM HOWARD/JOHN H. REID POETRY CONTEST. Website: www.winningwriters.com/tompoetry.htm. Deadline: between December 15 and September 30. Poetry in any style or genre. Published poetry accepted. Entry fee: $7 for every 25 lines. Prizes: $2,000 first prize; total of $5,250 in cash prizes. Details on Website.

+THE LEDGE ANNUAL POETRY CHAPBOOK CONTEST. E-mail: info@theledgemagazine.com. Website: www.theledgemagazine.com. Submit 16-28 pages of poetry with title page, bio, and acknowledgements. Entry fee: $18. Prizes: $1,000, $250, and $100, plus publication. Deadline: October 31.

BARBARA MANDIGO KELLY PEACE POETRY AWARDS. Nuclear Age Peace Foundation. (805) 965-3443. E-mail: wagingpeace@napf.org. Website: www.wagingpeace.org. Annual series of awards to encourage poets to explore and illuminate positive visions of peace and the human spirit. Deadline: July 1. Prizes: $1,000 for Adult; $200 for Youth 13-18 years; and $200 for Youth ages 12 and under. Adult entry fee: $15 for up to 3 poems; $5 for youth; no fee for 12 and under. Details on Website (see right-hand column).

NEW LETTERS PRIZE FOR POETRY. New Letters, UMKC. (816) 235-1168. E-mail: newletters@umkc.edu. Website: www.newletters.org. Deadline: May 18. Entry fee: $15 for first entry; $10 ea. for additional. Prize: $1,500 for best group of 3 to 6 poems.

JESSE BRYCE NILES CHAPBOOK CONTEST. Submit 25-34 pages of poetry. August 1-September 30. Entry fee: $25. Prizes: $1,000, plus 50 copies of chapbook. Details on Website: www.comstockreview.org.

PEARL POETRY PRIZE. Pearl Editions. Website: www.pearlmag.com. Deadline: submit between May 1 and July 15. Entry fee: $20. Prizes: $1,000 and publication in *Pearl Editions*.

+RICHARD PETERSON POETRY PRIZE. *Crab Orchard Review*, Poetry Contest, Dept. of English, Mail Code 4503, Southern Illinois University–Carbondale, 1000 Faner Dr., Carbondale IL 62901. (618) 453-5321.Website: www.siuc.edu/~crborchd. Entry fee: $10. Prize: $1,500. Deadline: submit between March 1 and May 10 (may vary). Submit up to 3 poems; 100-line limit.

POETRY SOCIETY OF VIRGINIA POETRY CONTESTS. Website: www.poetrysocietyofvirginia .org. Categories for adults and students. Prizes: $10-100. Entry fee per poem for nonmembers: $4. Deadline: submit between November 1, 2010 and January 19, 2011. List of contests on Website.

SLIPSTREAM ANNUAL POETRY CHAPBOOK COMPETITION. Website: www.slipstreampress .org/contest.html. Prize: $1,000, plus 50 copies of chapbook. Deadline: December 1. Send up to 40 pages of poetry. Reading fee: $20. Guidelines on Website.

SOUL-MAKING LITERARY COMPETITION. National League of American Pen Women. E-mail: pennobhill@aol.com. Website: www.soulmakingcontest.us. One-page poems only (single- or double-spaced). Up to 3 poems/entry. Deadline: November 30. Entry fee: $5. Prizes $25, $50, $100.

HOLLIS SUMMERS POETRY PRIZE. Ohio University Press. (740) 593-1155. E-mail: oupress@ ohio.edu. For unpublished collection of original poems, 60-95 pgs. Entry fee: $20. Deadline: October 31. Prize: $1,000, plus publication in book form. Details on Website: www.ohiou.edu/oupress/poetry prize.htm (scroll down to "About OU Press" and click on "Poetry Prize").

THE MAY SWENSON POETRY AWARD. Utah State University Press. (435) 797-1362. Website: www .usu.edu/usupress. Collections of original poetry, 50-100 pgs. Deadline: September 30. Prize: $1,000, publication, and royalties. Reading fee: $25. Details on Website ("Swenson Poetry Award").

KATE TUFTS DISCOVERY AWARD. Claremont Graduate University. (909) 621-8974. E-mail: tufts@cgu.edu. Presented annually for a first or very early work by a poet of genuine promise. Prize: $10,000. Deadline: September 15. Details and entry form on Website: www.cgu.edu/tufts.

+KINGSLEY TUFTS POETRY AWARD. Claremont Graduate University. (909) 621-8974. E-mail: tufts@cgu.edu. Presented annually for a first or very early work by a poet of genuine promise. Prize: $10,000. Deadline: September 15. Details and entry form on Website: www.cgu.edu/tufts.

UTMOST NOVICE CHRISTIAN POETRY CONTEST. Utmost Christian Writers Foundation, Canada. E-mail: nnharms@telusplanet.net. Website: www.utmostchristianwriters.com/poetry-contest/poetry -contest-rules.php. Nathan Harms. Entry fee: $10/poem. Prizes: $500, $300, $200; Best Rhyming Poem $250. Deadline: August 31. Details and entry form on Website.

WAR POETRY CONTEST. E-mail: warcontest@winningwriters.com. Website: www.winningwrit ers.com/annualcontest.htm. Sponsored by Winning Writers. Submit 1-3 unpublished poems on the theme of war, up to 500 lines total. Prizes: $2,000 first prize; $5,000 in total prizes. Deadline: submit between November 15 and May 31. Entry fee: $15.

MARJORIE J. WILSON AWARD: BEST POEM CONTEST. E-mail: margiereviewW@aol.com. Website: www.margiereview.com. Deadline: April 26 (varies). Entry fee: $15 for 3 unpublished poems. Prize: $1,000. Guidelines on Website.

WINNING WRITERS. Variety of poetry contests. Website: www.winningwriters.com.

MULTIPLE-GENRE CONTESTS

AMERICAN LITERARY REVIEW CONTESTS. University of North Texas. E-mail: americanliter aryreview@yahoo.com. Website: www.engl.unt.edu/alr. Now sponsors three contests: short fiction, creative nonfiction, and poetry. Prize: $1,000 and publication in spring issue of the magazine. Entry fee: $15. Deadline: October 1. Details on Website ("Contest").

BAKELESS LITERARY PUBLICATION PRIZES. Bread Loaf Writers' Conference, Middlebury College. E-mail: bakelessprize@middlebury.edu. Website: www.bakelessprize.org. Book series competition for new authors of literary works of poetry, fiction, and nonfiction. Entry fee: $10. Deadline: between September 15 and November 1. Details on Website.

BEST NEW CANADIAN CHRISTIAN WRITING AWARDS. The Word Guild, Canada. E-mail: admin@ thewordguild.com. Website: www.thewordguild.com. Sponsors a number of contests annually. Check Website for any current contests and guidelines (click on "Awards"/"Contests").

+BLUE RIDGE CONFERENCE WRITING CONTEST. (760) 220-1075. E-mail: alton@ganskycommunications.com. Website: http://brmcwc.com. Sponsors a book contest. First prize: a publishing contract package worth $1,665. Fiction or nonfiction. Details on Website.

CHRISTIAN SMALL PUBLISHER BOOK OF THE YEAR. Website: www.christianpublishers.net. Honors books produced by small publishers each year for outstanding contributions to Christian life. Categories: nonfiction, fiction, children's. Books need to have been published this year or last. Deadline: November 15. Eligible small publisher must have annual revenues of $350,000 or less. Details and nomination form on Website.

COLUMBIA FICTION/POETRY/NONFICTION CONTEST. Website: www.columbiajournal.org/ contests.htm. Length: 20 double-spaced pgs. or up to 5 poems. Prize: $500 in each category, plus publication. Deadline: January 15 (varies). Details on Website.

ECPA CHRISTIAN BOOK AWARD. (480) 966-3998. E-mail: info@ecpa.org. Website: www.ECPA .org. Presented annually to the best books in Christian publishing. Awards recognize books in 6 different categories: Bibles, Fiction, Children & Youth, Inspiration & Gift, Bible Reference & Study, and Christian Life. Only ECPA members in good standing can nominate products. Submit between September 1 and October 2 (verify on Website). Books submitted must have been published between October 2009 and October 2010. Awards are presented annually at the International Christian Retail Show. Verify all details on Website (click on "Awards"/"Christian Book Awards"/"2011 Submissions Information" in right-hand column).

EVANGELICAL PRESS ASSOCIATION ANNUAL CONTEST. PO Box 28129, Crystal MN 55428. (763) 535-4793. E-mail: director@epassoc.org. Website: www.epassoc.org. Sponsors annual contest for member publications.

FAULKNER-WISDOM CREATIVE WRITING COMPETITION. Faulkner House. (504) 586-1609. E-mail: Faulkhouse@aol.com. Website: www.wordsandmusic.org. Competition in 7 categories. Deadline: April 1 (varies, so verify on Website). Entry fees: $25-40. Prizes: $750-7,500. Guidelines on Website (scroll down to "Faulkner-Wisdom Competition" and click on "Click Here for Guidelines").

GOD USES INK NOVICE CONTEST (for nonpublished writers). Opens in September of 2010. Prizes are available in three age categories: ages 14 to 19; 20 to 39; and age 40 and over. First prize: Registration to Write! Canada Christian Writers' Conference (approximate value nearly $400.00), held in June. (Please check Website for details: www.writecanada.org). Second prize: A $100 gift certificate for The Word Guild (can be used for conference registration, membership, etc.). Third prize: A $50 gift certificate for The Word Guild (can be used for conference registration, membership, etc.). canadianchristianwritingawards.com.

ERIC HOFFER AWARD. Best New Writing. E-mail: submission@BestNewWriting.com. Website: www.HofferAward.com. Submit books via mail; no queries. The prose category is for creative fiction and nonfiction less than 10,000 words. Annual award for books features 14 categories. Pays $500 for winning prose; $1,500 for winning book. Guidelines at www.HofferAward.com.

GRACE IRWIN AWARD. All shortlisted finalists in fiction and nonfiction book categories in The Word Guild Canadian Christian Writing Awards will contend for the Grace Irwin Award. Prize $5,000. A separate round of independent judging will determine the prizewinner. canadianchristianwriting awards.com.

INSCRIBE CHRISTIAN WRITERS' CONTEST. Edmonton AB, Canada. (780) 542-7950. Fax (780) 514-3702. E-mail: query@inscribe.org. Website: www.inscribe.org. Sponsors contests open to non-members; details on Website.

INSIGHT WRITING CONTEST. (301) 393-4038. Fax (301) 393-4055. E-mail: insight@rhpa.org. Website: www.insightmagazine.org. Review and Herald/Seventh-day Adventist. A magazine of positive Christian living for Seventh-day Adventist high schoolers. Sponsors short story and poetry contests; includes a category for students 22 or under. Prizes: $50-$250. Deadline: June 1. Submit by e-mail. Details on Website (click on "Writing Contest").

MINISTRY & LITURGY VISUAL ARTS AWARDS. (408) 286-8505. Fax (408) 287-8748. E-mail: mleditor@rpinet.com. Website: www.rpinet.com/vaaentry.pdf. Visual Arts Awards held in 5 categories throughout the year. Best in each category wins $100. Entry fee: $30. Different deadline for each category (see Website).

MISSISSIPPI REVIEW PRIZE. (601) 266-4321. E-mail: rief@mississippireview.com. Website: www.mississippireview.com/contest.html. Fiction & Poetry. Prize: $1,000 in each category. Deadline: submit between April 2 & October 1. Entry fee: $15. Details on Website.

+NARRATIVER MAGAZINE SPRING CONTEST. Website: www.NarrativeMagazine.com. Fiction & nonfiction. Entry fee: $20. Prizes $4,000/$1,500/$500/plus 5 finalists at $100 ea. Deadline: July 31. Also sponsors a fall contest. Complete guidelines on Website.

NEW MILLENNIUM AWARDS. Website: www.newmillenniumwritings.com/awards.html. Prizes: $1,000 award for each category. Best Poem, Best Fiction, Best Nonfiction, Best Short-Short Fiction (fiction and nonfiction 6,000 words; short-short fiction to 1,000 words; 3 poems to 5 pgs. total). Entry fee: $17 each. Deadline: June 17. Guidelines on Website. Enter online or off.

+NEW MILLENNIUM WRITINGS SEMIANNUAL WRITING CONTESTS. Contact: Steve Petty (steve petty@live.com). Website: www.newmillenniumwritings.com. Includes fiction, short-short fiction, poetry, and creative nonfiction. Entry fee: $17. Prizes: $1,000 in each category. Deadlines: June 17 & November 30.

ONCE WRITTEN CONTESTS. Fiction and poetry contests. Website: www.oncewritten.com.

MONA SCHREIBER PRIZE FOR HUMOROUS FICTION AND NONFICTION. E-mail: brashcy ber@pcmagic.net. Website: www.brashcyber.com. Humorous fiction and nonfiction to 750 words. Prizes: $500, $250, and $100. Entry fee: $5. Deadline: December 1. Details on Website (click on contest name at bottom of illustration).

SOUL-MAKING LITERARY COMPETITION. Webhallow House. E-mail: PenNobHill@aol.com. Website: www.SoulMakingContest.us/page3.html. Lists various competitions: prose and poetry. Prizes: up to $100. Entry fee: $5. Deadline: November 30 (verify online). Guidelines on Website.

THE STORYTELLER CONTESTS. (870) 647-2137. Fax (870) 647-2454. E-mail: storyteller1@high towercom.com. Contest Website: www.thestorytellermagazine.com. Fossil Creek Publishing. Offers 1 or 2 paying contest/yr., along with People's Choice Awards, and Pushcart Prize nominations.

TICKLED BY THUNDER CONTESTS. Canada. (604) 591-6095. E-mail: info@tickledbythunder .com. Website: www.tickledbythunder.com. Sponsors several writing contests each year in various genres. Entry fee $10 for nonsubscribers. Prizes: $5-150 Cdn. Details on Website or by mail.

THE WORD GUILD CANADIAN CHRISTIAN WRITING AWARDS. (For published writers.) Thirty-five awards, encompassing 19 book categories and 16 article/short piece categories, including song lyrics, scripts or screenplays, and blog posts. Round One deadline is October 31, 2010 and Round Two deadline is January 15, 2011. The fee structure is available on the Website for members and non members. Categories of books and articles etc., can be found on the Website. canadianchristianwritingawards.com.

WRITER'S DIGEST. (513) 531-2690, ext. 1483. Fax (513) 531-1843. E-mail: wdsubmissions@fwpubs.com. Website: www.writersdigest.com. Sponsors annual contests for articles, short stories, poetry, children's fiction, self-published books, and scripts (categories vary). Deadlines: vary according to contest. Prizes: $25,000 or more for each contest. See Website for list of current contests and rules.

WRITERS-EDITORS NETWORK ANNUAL WRITING COMPETITION. E-mail: editor@writers-editors.com. Website: www.writers-editors.com. Open to all writers. Deadline: March 15. Nonfiction, fiction, children's, poetry. Prizes: $100, $75, $50. Details on Website (see right-hand column).

WRITERS' JOURNAL CONTESTS. (218) 346-7921. Fax (218) 346-7924. E-mail: writersjournal@writersjournal.com. Website: www.writersjournal.com. Runs several contests each year. Prizes: $10 to $500. Variety of categories. Different starter lines and deadlines for each category. Details on Website, or send SASE.

WRITERS' UNION OF CANADA AWARDS & COMPETITIONS. Canada. (416) 703-8982. Fax (416) 504-9090. E-mail: info@writersunion.ca. Website: www.writersunion.ca. Various competitions. Prizes: $500-10,000. Details on Website.

RESOURCES FOR CONTESTS

ADDITIONAL CONTESTS. You will find some additional contests sponsored by local groups and conferences that are open to nonmembers. See individual listings in those sections.

FREELANCE WRITING: WEBSITE FOR TODAY'S WORKING WRITER. Website: www.freelancewriting.com/writingcontests.php.

KIMN SWENSON GOLLNICK'S WEBSITE. Contest listings. Website: www.KIMN.net/contests.htm.

OZARK CREATIVE WRITERS CONTESTS. E-mail submissions only: ozarkcreativewriters@earthlink.net. Website: www.ozarkcreativewriters.org. Lists a number of contests on Website.

THE WRITER CONTEST. *The Writer* magazine. (262) 796-8776. E-mail: editor@writermag.com. Website: www.writermag.com. General. How-to for writers. Occasionally sponsors a contest and lists multiple contests. Check Website.

MAJOR LITERARY AWARDS

AUDIES: www.audiopub.org

CALDECOTT MEDAL: www.ala.org

EDGAR: www.mysterywriters.org

HEMINGWAY FOUNDATION/PEN AWARD: www.pen-ne.org

HUGO: http://worldcon.org/hugos.html

NATIONAL BOOK AWARD: www.nationalbook.org

NATIONAL BOOK CRITICS CIRCLE AWARD: www.bookcritics.org

NEBULA: http://dpsinfo.com/awardweb/nebulas

NEWBERY: www.ala.org

NOBEL PRIZE FOR LITERATURE: www.nobelprize.org

PEN/FAULKNER AWARD: www.penfaulkner.org

PINNACLE AWARD/ECPA: www.ECPA.org

PULITZER PRIZE: www.pulitzer.org

RITA: www.rwanational.org/cs/contests_and_awards

15

Denominational Listings of Book Publishers and Periodicals

An attempt has been made to divide publishers into appropriate denominational groups. However, due to the extensive number of denominations included, and sometimes incomplete denominational information, some publishers may inadvertently have been included in the wrong list. Additions and corrections are welcome.

ASSEMBLIES OF GOD
Book Publisher:
Gospel Publishing House

Periodicals:
Enrichment Journal
Live
Men.ag.org
Pentecostal Evangel
Testimony

BAPTIST, FREE WILL
Book Publishers:
Randall House
Randall House Digital

Periodicals:
Together with God

BAPTIST, SOUTHERN
Book Publishers:
B & H Publishing
Baylor Univ. Press
Founders Press
New Hope Publishers

Periodicals:
Founders Journal
Journey
Let's Worship
Louisiana Baptist Messenger
Mature Living
On Mission
ParentLife
The Pathway

BAPTIST (OTHER)
Book Publishers:
Earthen Vessel Publishing
Judson Press (American)
Mercer Univ. Press

Periodicals:
Florida Baptist Witness
Friends Journal
Link & Visitor
Point
Secret Place (American)
Sword of the Lord
    (Independent)

CATHOLIC
Book Publishers:
ACTA Publications
American Catholic Press
Canticle Books
Catholic Book Publishing
Catholic Univ./
    America Press
Cistercian Publications
HarperOne (Cath. bks.)
Libros Liguori
Liguori Publications
Liturgical Press
Loyola Press
Oregon Catholic Press
Our Sunday Visitor
Pauline Books
Pauline Kids
Paulist Press
Pflaum Publishing
St. Anthony Messenger Press
St. Catherine of Siena Press
St. Pauls/Alba House
Tau-Publishing

Periodicals:
America
Arkansas Catholic
Arlington Catholic Herald
Atlantic Catholic
Australian Catholics
Bread of Life
Catechist
Catechumenate
Catholic Answers
Catholic Digest
Catholic Forester
Catholic Insight
Catholic Library World
Catholic New York
Catholic Peace Voice
Catholic Register
Catholic Sentinel
Catholic Servant
Catholic Telegraph
Catholic Yearbook
CGA World
Columbia
Commonweal
Culture Wars
Desert Call
Diocesan Dialogue
Emmanuel
Faith & Family

Family Digest
Interim
Island Catholic News
Koinonia
Leaves
Liguorian
Marian Helper
Messenger/Sacred Heart
Messenger/St. Anthony
Miraculous Medal
Montana Catholic
One
Our Sunday Visitor
Parish Liturgy
Prairie Messenger
Priest
Promise
Review for Religious
Seeds
Share
Social Justice Review
Spirit
Spiritual Life
St. Anthony Messenger
Today's Catholic Teacher
Today's Parish
TG! (True Girl)
U.S. Catholic
Venture
Visions
Way of St. Francis

CHRISTIAN CHURCH/ CHURCH OF CHRIST
Book Publishers:
Chalice Press (Disciples of Christ)
College Press (Church of Christ)
CrossLink Publishing
Star Bible

CHURCH OF GOD (HOLINESS)
Periodicals:
Beginner's Friend
Church Herald and Holiness Banner
Gems of Truth
Junior Companion
Primary Pal
Youth Compass

CHURCH OF GOD (OTHER)
Periodicals:
Bible Advocate (Seventh-day)
The Gem
Now What? (Seventh-day)

CHURCH OF THE NAZARENE
Book Publishers:
Beacon Hill Press

Periodicals:
Adventures
Celebrate
Immerse
Mission Connection

EPISCOPAL/ANGLICAN
Book Publishers:
Anglicans United
Church Publishing
Forward Movement
Latimer Press

Periodicals:
Central Florida Episcopalian
Episcopal Life Online
Interchange
Living Church
Sewanee Theological Review

EVANGELICAL COVENANT CHURCH
Periodicals:
Covenant Companion
inSpirit Magazine

LUTHERAN
Book Publishers:
Augsburg Fortress
Augsburg/Worship & Music
Concordia
Concordia Academic
Congregational Life & Learning
Langmarc Publishing
Lutheran University Press
Lutheran Voices
Northwestern Publishing

Periodicals:
Canada Lutheran (ELCC)
Canadian Lutheran

Cresset
Lutheran Digest
Lutheran Forum
Lutheran Journal
Lutheran Witness
Lutheran Woman's Quarterly (MO Synod)
Word & World (ELCA)

MENNONITE
Book Publisher:
Kindred Books

Periodicals:
Canadian Mennonite
Evangel (OR)
Mennonite Historian
The Messenger
Partners
Purpose
Rejoice!
Story Mates

METHODIST, FREE
Periodicals:
Evangel
Light and Life

METHODIST, UNITED
Book Publishers:
Abingdon Press
Dimensions for Living
United Methodist Publishing House

Periodicals:
Alive Now
Good News (KY)
Interpreter
Mature Years
Methodist History
New World Outlook
Pockets
Upper Room

PRESBYTERIAN
Book Publisher:
P & R Publishing

Periodicals:
E-Channels (PCC)
Glad Tidings
Horizons (USA)

Layman (USA)
Presbyterian Outlook (USA)
Presbyterians Today

QUAKER/FRIENDS
Book Publishers:
Barclay Press

Periodicals:
Fruit of the Vine
Quaker Life

REFORMED
Book Publishers:
Reformation Heritage Books

Periodicals:
Perspectives
Reformed Worship

SEVENTH-DAY ADVENTIST
Book Publishers:
Pacific Press
Review and Herald

Periodicals:
Connected
Cornerstone Youth Resources
Guide Magazine
Insight (MD)
Journal/Adventist Education
Kids' Ministry Ideas
Lead

Liberty
Message
Our Little Friend
Primary Treasure
Vibrant Life

UNITED CHURCH OF CANADA
Book Publisher:
United Church Publishing House

Periodicals:
Aujourd'hui Credo
Fellowship Magazine
Theological Digest & Outlook
United Church Observer

WESLEYAN CHURCH
Book Publisher:
Wesleyan Publishing House

Periodicals:
Light from the Word
Vista
Wesleyan Life

MISCELLANEOUS DENOMINATIONS
Antiochian Orthodox
Conciliar Press

Brethren in Christ Church
Brethren in Christ

Churches of Christ in Christian Union
The Evangelical Advocate

Church of God (Anderson IN)
Warner Press

Church of God (Cleveland TN)
Youth & CE Leadership

Evangelical Free Church
EFCA Today

Foursquare Church
Foursquare Leader

Grace Brethren Churches
BMH Books

Open Bible Standard Churches
MESSAGE of the Open Bible

Orthodox Church in America
Divine Ascent

Plymouth Brethren
Chapter Two

United Church of Christ
Pilgrim Press

16

Book Publishers and Periodicals
by Corporate Group

This chapter contains a list of book publishers, followed by a list of periodicals that belong to the same group, or family, of publications.

BARBOUR PUBLISHING, INC.
Barbour Publishing
Heartsong Presents
Heartsong Presents Mysteries

BRENTWOOD CHRISTIAN PRESS
Poems by Me
Poet's Cove
Self Publish Press
Sermon Select Press
Southern Baptist Press

CHRISTIANITY TODAY INTERNATIONAL
Books & Culture
ChristianBibleStudies.com
Christian History.net
Christianity Today
Christianity Today Movies
Kyria
Leadership
Marriage Partnership
Men of Integrity
PreachingToday.com
SmallGroups.com
Your Church

CHRISTIAN MEDIA NETWORK
The Apocalypse Chronicles
Christian Media
Sound Body

DAVID C. COOK
Cook Partners
Lion Publishing

Scripture Press
Victor Books
Power for Living
Quiet Hour

FOCUS ON THE FAMILY
Focus on the Family (books)
Boundless Webzine
Clubhouse
Clubhouse Jr.
Enfoque a la Familia
Plugged In Online
Thriving Family

BILLY GRAHAM EVANGELISTIC ASSOCIATION
Decision
Decision Online

GROUP PUBLICATIONS INC.
Group Publishing
Children's Ministry
Group Magazine

GUIDEPOSTS
Guideposts Books
Ideals Children's Books
Ideals Publications
Angels on Earth
Guideposts

HARPERCOLLINS
Avon Inspire
HarperOne
William Morrow

ZonderKidz
Zondervan

THOMAS NELSON PUBLISHERS
J. Countryman
Editorial Betania
Editorial Caribe
Editorial Catolica
Editorial Diez Puntos
Grupo Nelson
Leader Latino
Nelson Fiction,
    Thomas
Tommy Nelson
Westbow Press
W Publishing Group

RANDALL HOUSE PUBLICATIONS
Direction Student
Horizon Student
The Brink
The Brink Online
Fusion

RANDOM HOUSE
Ballantine Publishing Group
Doubleday Religious
    Publishing
Multnomah Books
WaterBrook Press

SALEM COMMUNICATIONS
Preaching
YouthWorker Journal

THE SALVATION ARMY
Faith & Friends
Good News!
New Frontier
Priority!
War Cry
Young Salvationist

STANDARD PUBLISHING
Standard Publishing (books)
Christian Standard

STRANG COMMUNICATIONS
Casa Creación
Charisma House (books)
CharismaKids (books)
Creation House
   (copublishing)
Excel
FrontLine (books)
Foursquare Media
Publicaciones Casa (books)
Strang Book Group
Realms (books)
Siloam (books)
Charisma
Christian Retailing
Ministry Today
SpiritLed Woman

THE UPPER ROOM
Fresh Air Books
Alive Now
Devo'zine
Pockets
The Upper Room
Weavings

URBAN MINISTRIES, INC.
UMI Publishing
Direction
InTeen
J.A.M.: Jesus and Me
Juniorway
Precepts for Living
Preschool Playhouse
Primary Street
Young Adult Today

Glossary of Terms

Note: This glossary is not intended to be exhaustive. It includes primarily terms found in this market guide.

Advance: Amount of money a publisher pays to an author up front, against future royalties. The amount varies greatly from publisher to publisher, and is often paid in two or three installments (on signing contract, on delivery of manuscript, and on publication).

All rights: An outright sale of your material. Author has no further control over it.

Anecdote: A short, poignant, real-life story, usually used to illustrate a single thought.

Assignment: When an editor asks a writer to write a specific piece for an agreed-upon price.

As-told-to story: A true story you write as a first-person account, but about someone else.

Audiobooks: Books available on CDs.

Avant-garde: Experimental; ahead of the times.

Backlist: A publisher's previously published books that are still in print a year after publication.

B & W: Abbreviation for a black and white photograph.

Bar code: Identification code and price on the back of a book read by a scanner at checkout counters.

Bible versions: AMP—Amplified Bible; ASV—American Standard Version; CEV—Contemporary English Version; ESV—English Standard Version; GNB—Good News Bible; HCSB—Holman Christian Standard Bible; ICB—International Children's Bible; KJV—King James Version; MSG—The Message; NAB—New American Bible; NAS—New American Standard; NEB—New English Bible; NIrV—New International Reader's Version; NIV—New International Version; NJB—New Jerusalem Bible; NKJV—New King James Version; NLT—New Living Translation; NRSV—New Revised Standard Version; RSV—Revised Standard Version; TLB—*The Living Bible*; TNIV—Today's New International Version.

Bimonthly: Every two months.

Bio sketch: Information on the author.

Biweekly: Every two weeks.

Bluelines: Printer's proofs used to catch errors before a book is printed.

Book proposal: Submission of a book idea to an editor; usually includes a cover letter, thesis statement, chapter-by-chapter synopsis, market survey, and 1-3 sample chapters.

Byline: Author's name printed just below the title of a story, article, etc.

Camera-ready copy: The text and artwork for a book that are ready for the press.

Chapbook: A small book or pamphlet containing poetry, religious readings, etc.

Circulation: The number of copies sold or distributed of each issue of a publication.

Clips: See "Published clips."

Column: A regularly appearing feature, section, or department in a periodical using the same heading; written by the same person or a different freelancer each time.

Concept statement: A 50-150 word summary of your proposed book.

Contributor's copy: Copy of an issue of a periodical sent to the author whose work appears in it.

Copyright: Legal protection of an author's work.

Cover letter: A letter that accompanies some manuscript submissions. Usually needed only if you have to tell the editor something specific or to give your credentials for writing a piece of a technical nature. Also used to remind the editor that a manuscript was requested or expected.

Credits, list of: A listing of your previously published works.

Critique: An evaluation of a piece of writing.

Defamation: A written or spoken injury to the reputation of a living person or organization. If what is said is true, it cannot be defamatory.

Derivative work: A work derived from another work, such as a condensation or abridgement. Contact copyright owner for permission before doing the abridgement and be prepared to pay that owner a fee or royalty.

Devotional: A short piece that shares a personal spiritual discovery, inspires to worship, challenges to commitment or action, or encourages.

Editorial guidelines: See "Writer's guidelines."

Electronic submission: The submission of a proposal or article to an editor by electronic means, such as by e-mail or on disk.

Endorsements: Flattering comments about a book; usually carried on the back cover or in promotional material.

EPA/Evangelical Press Assn: A professional trade organization for periodical publishers and associate members.

E-proposals: Proposals sent via e-mail.

E-queries: Queries sent via e-mail.

Eschatology: The branch of theology that is concerned with the last things, such as death, judgment, heaven, and hell.

Essay: A short composition usually expressing the author's opinion on a specific subject.

Evangelical: A person who believes that one receives God's forgiveness for sins through Jesus Christ, and believes the Bible is an authoritative guide for daily living.

Exegesis: Interpretation of the Scripture.

Feature article: In-depth coverage of a subject, usually focusing on a person, an event, a process, an organization, a movement, a trend or issue; written to explain, encourage, help, analyze, challenge, motivate, warn, or entertain as well as to inform.

Filler: A short item used to "fill" out the page of a periodical. It could be a timeless news item, joke, anecdote, light verse or short humor, puzzle, game, etc.

First rights: Editor buys the right to publish your piece for the first time.

Foreign rights: Selling or giving permission to translate or reprint published material in a foreign country.

Foreword: Opening remarks in a book introducing the book and its author.

Freelance: As in 50% freelance: means that 50% of the material printed in the publication is supplied by freelance writers.

Freelancer or freelance writer: A writer who is not on salary but sells his material to a number of different publishers.

Free verse: Poetry that flows without any set pattern.

Galley proof: A typeset copy of a book manuscript used to detect and correct errors before the final print run.

Genre: Refers to type or classification, as in fiction or poetry. Such types as westerns, romances, mysteries, etc., are referred to as genre fiction.

Glossy: A black-and-white photo with a shiny, rather than matte, finish.

Go-ahead: When a publisher tells you to go ahead and write up or send your article idea.

Haiku: A Japanese lyric poem of a fixed 17-syllable form.

Hard copy: A typed manuscript, as opposed to one on disk or in an e-mail.

Holiday/seasonal: A story, article, filler, etc., that has to do with a specific holiday or season. This material must reach the publisher the stated number of months prior to the holiday/season.

Homiletics: The art of preaching.

Honorarium: If a publisher indicates they pay an honorarium, it means they pay a small flat fee, as opposed to a set amount per word.

Humor: The amusing or comical aspects of life that add warmth and color to an article or story.

Interdenominational: Distributed to a number of different denominations.

International Postal Reply Coupon: See "IRC."

Interview article: An article based on an interview with a person of interest to a specific readership.

IRC or IPRC: International Postal Reply Coupon: can be purchased at your local post office and should be enclosed with a manuscript sent to a foreign publisher.

ISBN: International Standard Book Number; an identification code needed for every book.

Journal: A periodical presenting news in a particular area.

Kill fee: A fee paid for a completed article done on assignment that is subsequently not published. Amount is usually 25-50% of original payment.

Libel: To defame someone by an opinion or a misquote and put his or her reputation in jeopardy.

Light verse: Simple, lighthearted poetry.

Little/Literary: Small circulation publications whose focus is providing a forum for the literary writer, rather than on making money. Often do not pay, or pay in copies.

Mainstream fiction: Other than genre fiction, such as romance, mystery, or science fiction. Stories of people and their conflicts handled on a deeper level.

Mass market: Books intended for a wide, general market, rather than a specialized market. These books are produced in a smaller format, usually with smaller type, and are sold at a lower price. The expectation is that their sales will be higher.

Ms: Abbreviation for manuscript.

Mss: Abbreviation for more than one manuscript.

Multiple submissions: Submitting more than one piece at a time to the same publisher, usually reserved for poetry, greeting cards, or fillers, not articles. Also see "Simultaneous submissions."

NASR: Abbreviation for North American serial rights.

Newsbreak: A newsworthy event or item sent to a publisher who might be interested in publishing it because it would be of interest to his particular readership.

Nondenominational: Not associated with a particular denomination.

Not copyrighted: Publication of your piece in such a publication will put it into public domain and it is not then protected. Ask that the publisher carry your copyright notice on your piece when it is printed.

Novella: A short novel starting at 20,000 words—35,000 words maximum. Length varies from publisher to publisher.

On acceptance: Periodical or publisher pays a writer at the time the manuscript is accepted for publication.

On assignment: Writing something at the specific request of an editor.

Onetime rights: Selling the right to publish a story one time to any number of publications (usually refers to publishing for a nonoverlapping readership).

On publication: Publisher pays a writer when his/her manuscript is published.

On speculation/On spec: Writing something for an editor with the agreement that he will buy it only if he likes it.

Overrun: The extra copies of a book printed during the initial print run.

Over the transom: Unsolicited articles that arrive at a publisher's office.

Payment on acceptance: See "On acceptance."

Payment on publication: See "On publication."

Pen name/pseudonym: Using a name other than your legal name on an article or book in order to protect your identity or the identity of people included, or when the author wishes to remain anonymous. Put the pen name in the byline under the title, and your real name in the upper, left-hand corner.

Permissions: Asking permission to use the text or art from a copyrighted source.

Personal experience story: A story based on a real-life experience.

Personality profile: A feature article that highlights a specific person's life or accomplishments.

Photocopied submission: Sending an editor a photocopy of your manuscript, rather than an original. Some editors prefer an original.

Piracy: To take the writings of others just as they were written and put your name on them as the author.

Plagiarism: To steal and use the ideas or writings of another as your own, rewriting them to make them sound like your own.

Press kit: A compilation of promotional materials on a particular book or author, usually organized in a folder, used to publicize a book.

Print on Demand (POD): A printing process where books are printed one at a time instead of in quantity. The production cost per book is higher, but no warehousing is necessary. Bookstores typically will not carry POD books.

Public domain: Work that has never been copyrighted, or on which the copyright has expired. Subtract 75 from the current year, and anything copyrighted prior to that is in public domain.

Published clips: Copies of actual articles you have had published, from newspapers or magazines.

Quarterly: Every three months.

Query letter: A letter sent to an editor telling about an article you propose to write and asking if he or she is interested in seeing it.

Reporting time: The number of weeks or months it takes an editor to get back to you about a query or manuscript you have sent in.

Reprint rights: Selling the right to reprint an article that has already been published elsewhere. You must have sold only first or onetime rights originally, and wait until it has been published the first time.

Review copies: Books given to book reviewers or buyers for chains.

Royalty: The percentage an author is paid by a publisher on the sale of each copy of a book.

SAE: Self-addressed envelope (without stamps).

SAN: Standard Account Number, used to identify libraries, book dealers, or schools.

SASE: Self-addressed, stamped envelope. Should always be sent with a manuscript or query letter.

SASP: Self-addressed, stamped postcard. May be sent with a manuscript submission to be returned by publisher indicating it arrived safely.

Satire: Ridicule that aims at reform.

Second serial rights: See "Reprint rights."

Semiannual: Issued twice a year.

Serial: Refers to publication in a periodical (such as first serial rights).

Sidebar: A short feature that accompanies an article and either elaborates on the human interest side of the story or gives additional information on the topic. It is often set apart by appearing within a box or border.

Simultaneous rights: Selling the rights to the same piece to several publishers simultaneously. Be sure everyone is aware that you are doing so.

Simultaneous submissions: Sending the same manuscript to more than one publisher at the same time. Usually done with nonoverlapping markets (such as denominational or newspapers) or when you are writing on a timely subject. Be sure to state in a cover letter that it is a simultaneous submission and why.

Slander: The verbal act of defamation.

Slanting: Writing an article so that it meets the needs of a particular market.

Slush pile: The stack of unsolicited manuscripts that have arrived at a publisher's office.

Speculation: See "On speculation."

Staff-written material: Material written by the members of a magazine staff.

Subsidiary rights: All those rights, other than book rights, included in a book contract such as paperback, book club, movie, etc.

Subsidy publisher: A book publisher who charges the author to publish his book, as opposed to a royalty publisher who pays the author.

Synopsis: A brief summary of work from one paragraph to several pages long.

Tabloid: A newspaper-format publication about half the size of a regular newspaper.

Take-home paper: A periodical sent home from Sunday school each week (usually) with Sunday school students, children through adults.

Think piece: A magazine article that has an intellectual, philosophical, or provocative approach to a subject.

Third world: Reference to underdeveloped countries of Asia and Africa.

Trade magazine: A magazine whose audience is in a particular trade or business.

Traditional verse: One or more verses with an established pattern that is repeated throughout the poem.

Transparencies: Positive color slides, not color prints.

Unsolicited manuscript: A manuscript an editor didn't specifically ask to see.

Vanity publisher: See "Subsidy publisher."

Vignette: A short, descriptive literary sketch or a brief scene or incident.

Vitae/Vita: An outline of one's personal history and experience.

Work-for-hire: Signing a contract with a publisher stating that a particular piece of writing you are doing for him is work-for-hire. In the agreement you give the publisher full ownership and control of the material.

Writers' guidelines: An information sheet provided by a publisher that gives specific guidelines for writing for the publication. Always send an SASE with your request for guidelines.

General Index

This index includes periodicals, books, distributors, greeting cards/specialty markets, and agents, as well as some of the organizations/resources and specialty lists or areas you may need to find quickly. Conferences, groups, and editorial services are listed alphabetically by state in those sections (not in the index). Check the table of contents for the location of supplementary listings.

Note: Due to the many changes in the market, and to help you determine the current status of any publisher you might be looking for, all markets (past and present) will be listed in this index. If they are not viable markets, their current status will be indicated here. The following codes will be used:

(ABD) asked to be deleted

(BA) bad address or contact information

(ED) editorial decision

(NF) no freelance

(NR) no recent response

(OB) out of business

(UTC) unable to contact

These changes will be noted in this listing for five years before being dropped altogether.

A

Aadeon Publishing   85
Aames Agency, Aaron (ED)
Aaron Book Publishing   85
Abagail Press (OB)
Abbey Press (ABD)
Abilities Magazine   295
Abingdon Press   85
A+B Works (ABD)
Acquire the Fire (NF)
ACTA Publications   86
Action Magazine   396
Active Disciple (UTC)
ACU Press (NF)
ACW Press   166
Adams Media   86
A.D. Players (ABD)
Advance. See Foursquare Leader
Advanced Christian Writer   437
Advantage Books   167
Advent Christian Witness (ABD)
Adventures   377
African American Expressions   453
African-American Pulpit (OB)

African Voices   295
Agape Wear (UTC)
Agent Research & Evaluation   519
AirLeaf Publishing (books/OB)
AirLeaf Publishing (distributors/OB)
Alabama Baptist (NF)
Alba House. See St. Pauls
Alexander Books (ABD)
Algora Publishing (ABD)
Alive Communications   519
Alive Now   296
Alive!/Over 50 (OB)
Allegiance Books (OB)
Allen O'Shea Literary   519
Alliance (music)   187
Alliance Life (NF)
Allred and Allred (OB)
All That Productions   461
Alpha News (UTC)
Alpha Omega Publications   461
Amazon Advantage Program   187
Ambassador   296
Ambassador Agency   520
Ambassador Books   86
Ambassador House (NR)
Ambassador Int'l.   87
Amen Caf, Compass (BA)
America   296
American Baptists in Mission (OB)

American Binding & Publishing   167
American Book Publishing (ED)
American Catholic Press   87
American Girl   377
American Greetings   453
American Tract Society   296
AMG Publishers (books)   87
AMG Publishers (CD-ROM)   461
AMG Software   460
Ampelos Press   167
Anchor Publishing (NF)
Anchor Wallace Publishers   458
Anchor-Whitaker Distributors   187
Ancient Paths Publications   88
Angelic Entertainment (UTC)
Angelos (NF)
Angels on Earth   296
Anglican (NR)
Anglican Journal   297
Anglicans United   88
Animal Trails   297
Anna's Journal (OB)
Anointed Pages   297
Answers Magazine   297
Apocalypse Chronicles   298
Appalachian Bible (BA)
Archaeology   378
Areopagus/UK   437
Argus Communications (OB)

Arizona Family News (UTC)
Arkansas Catholic   298
Arlington Catholic Herald   298
Arnold Publications (NF)
Artbeat of America   453
ArtBeats   458
Art Can Drama Resources (NR)
Artful Greetings   453
Art 2 Inspire (BA)
Ashleigh Manor   458
Associated Content   298
Associated Press
Assn. Reformed Presbyterian (NF)
Athina Publishing (NF)
At Home with Our Faith (NF)
Atlantic Catholic   298
At the Center   424
At the Fence (NF)
Augsburg Books (NF)
Augsburg Fortress. See Fortress Press
Aujourd'hui Credo   299
Australian Catholics   299
Author Coaching   520
Author-Me.com   437
Author Network E-zine (OB)
Authors and Artists Group (ABD)
Avatar Literary (NR)
Avon Inspire   88

B

Baal Hamon Publishers (ED)
Baker Academic   88
Baker Books (books)   89
Baker Designs, Joan (NF)
Baker Software   460
Baker's Plays   89
Baker Trittin Press (OB)
Ballantine Publishing   89
Banner (ABD)
Banner News Service (ABD)
Bantam Books. See Doubleday
Baptist Informer (NF)
Baptist Press Online (NF)
Baptist Publishing House (NF)
Baptist Standard   299
Barbour Publishing   89
Barclay Press   90
Barefoot   401
Basic Books (NF)
Baylor Univ. Press   90
Bay Public., Mel ((ABD)
B.C. Catholic   299
BC Christian News (NF)
Beacon/AL (BA)
Beacon Hill Press   90

Beginner's Friend   378
Beginnings (BA)
Behind the Hammer   299
Believe Books   91
Believe! Magazine (ABD)
Believer's Bay   299
BelieversPress   167
BelleBooks (ED)
Benrey Literary   520
Be One Sportswear   458
B Equal Games (UTC)
Berg Christian Enterprises   456
Bernstein Literary, Meredith
Best New Writing   438
Bethany House   91
Beyond the Bend   424
Beyond Words (ABD)
Bfree Publishing   167
BGC World. See Point
B & H Publishing   89
B & H Software   460
BIBAL Press (NF)
Bible Advocate   300
Bible Advocate Press (ABD)
BibleQuest   457
Bibles for the World (OB)
Bible Study Magazine   300
Biblical Recorder   300
Big Idea (books/NF)
Big Idea (videos/NF)
BigScore Productions (ED)
Biographical Publishing   168
BJU Press. See JourneyForth
Black Christian Book Dist.   187
Black Family Greeting Cards   456
Black Forest Press   168
Black Literary Agency, David
Blacksmith Cards & Prints   456
Bless His Name Greetings (ABD)
Blue Dolphin   91
Blue Mountain Arts   453
Blumer Literary (ABD)
BMH Books   91
Bob Jones University Press. See
     JourneyForth
Bogard Press (NF)
Booklet markets (list of)   8
Booklocker.com   168
Booklocker Jr. (OB)
Book Producers (UTC)
Book Publishers Network   168
Books & Culture   300
Books in Motion (NF)
Books Just Books.com   169
Books & Such/Janet Grant   520

Bookstand Publishing   169
BookSurge   169
Boomer Babes Rock (ABD)
Borden Books (NR)
Boundless Webzine   417
BOW Books (NF)
Boyd Publishing, R. H. (NF)
Boyds Mills Press   92
Boys Town Press (NF)
Brady (NF)
Branden Publishing   92
Brave Hearts (OB)
Brazos Press (NF)
BREAD for God's Children   378
Bread of Life   300
Breakaway (OB)
Breakneck Books (OB)
Breakthrough   301
Breakthrough Intercessor   301
Breathe Again   425
Brentwood Christian Press   169
Brethren Evangelist (ABD)
Bridal Guides   301
Bridge Logos   92
Bridge Resources (OB)
Brink Magazine   301
Brink Online   302
Brio (OB)
Brio and Beyond (OB)
Bristol House (NF)
Broadman & Holman.
     See B & H Publishing
Broadman & Holman Gifts (OB)
Broadman & Holman Software.
     See B & H Software
Broughton Co., B.   187
Brown Books Publishing Group   169
Browne Ltd., Pema   521
Browne & Miller Literary   520
Brown, Ltd., Curtis   520
Bubblemag (UTC)
Building Church Leaders.com (NF)
Business Reform. See Christian
     Business Daily
byFaith   302
By Grace Publications (UTC)
Bykofsky Assocs., Sheree (ABD)
ByLine (OB)

C

C4Yourself Greeting Cards   454
Cactus Game Design (NF)
Cadet Quest   378
Calligraphy Collection (NF)
Cambridge Literary (NR)

Cambridge Scholars Pub.   93
Cambridge Univ. Press   93
Campus Crusade for Christ/New LIfe
    Resources   187
Canada Lutheran   302
CanadianChristianity.com   302
Canadian/foreign markets (book)   8
Canadian/foreign markets
    (periodicals)   203
Canadian Institute for Law   93
Canadian Lutheran   302
Canadian Mennonite   303
Canadian Writer's Journal   438
Candlelight Media Group   461
Candy Cane Press.
    See Ideals Publications
Canon Press (NF)
Canticle Books   93
Canticle Magazine   303
Capall Bann Publishing (ABD)
Capper's   303
Capstone Fiction. See OakTara
Caravan (OB)
CarePoint Publishing   94
Carey Library, William   94
Caring (NF)
Carole Joy (cards/NF)
Carolina Christian News   303
Carpentree (gifts)   458
Carroll Designs, William (OB)
Carson-Dellosa Christian   94
Cartoon markets (list of)   229
Cartoonworks. See Cartoons
Casa Creacion. See Strang Book Group
Cascadia Publishing   95
Catalyst (ABD)
Catechist   386
Catechumenate   402
Cathedral Age   304
Cathedral Art Metal (NF)
Catholic Answer (NF)
Catholic Answers   95
Catholic Book   95
Catholic Courier (NF)
Catholic Digest   304
Catholic Dossier (NF)
Catholic Forester   304
Catholic Insight   305
Catholic Library World   387
Catholic Missions in Canada (NF)
Catholic New Times (OB)
Catholic New York   305
Catholic Parent (OB)
Catholic Peace Voice   305
Catholic Register   305

Catholic Rural Life (NF)
Catholic Sentinel   305
Catholic Servant   402
Catholic Telegraph   306
Catholic Univ./America   95
Catholic World Report (NR)
Catholic Yearbook   306
CBA. See Intl. Christian Retail
CBA mailing list   187
CBA Retailers   306
CBN.com   306
CCM Magazine (OB)
CD Greeting Cards   456
Celebrate   379
Celebrate Life   307
Celebratemoms.org (BA)
Celebrate Your Faith   458
Celebration Greetings (ABD)
Cell Group Journal (OB)
Center Street (NR)
Central Appalachian Christian (BA)
Central Florida Episcopalian   307
Central South Distribution   187
Cerdic-Publications (NR)
CGA World   307
Chalice Press   96
Challenge Weekly   307
Challenging Destiny (OB)
Channels. See E-Channels
Chapter Two   96
Characters (ABD)
Chariot Books. See David C. Cook
Chariot Victor. See David C. Cook
Charisma   307
Charisma House. See Strang
    Book Group
Charisma Kids   96
Charles Press   97
Chattels of the Heart (OB)
Chelsea House   97
Chicken Soup for the Soul
    (books)   97, 308
Chicken Soup for the Soul
    Magazine (BA)
Children's Church Exchange (NF)
Children's Magic Window (OB)
Children's Ministry   387
Children's picture books
    (markets for)   10
Choice Newspaper (UTC)
Chosen Books   97
Christian Art Gifts   458
Christian Art Gifts/Kids   456
Christian Authors Network
Christian Bible Studies.com (NF)   308

Christian Book Distributors   187
Christian Business Daily   308
Christian Camp & Conference.
    See InSite
Christian Century   402
Christian Chronicle/OK   308
Christian Citizen USA   308
Christian Civic League of Maine
    Record (see Maine Family
    Record)
Christian Classroom (NR)
Christian Communicator   438
Christian Computing   309
Christian Counseling Today (ABD)
Christian Courier/CA (NR)
Christian Courier/Canada   309
Christian Courier/WI   309
Christian Courier Jr. (OB)
Christian Creative Arts (ABD)
Christian Crusade (NF)
Christian Devotions   393
Christian Drama E-magazine (OB)
Christian Duplications (BA)
Christian Early Education   387
Christian Ed. Publishers   97
Christian Education Journal/CA   402
Christian Educators Journal   388
Christian Educators Journal/
    Canada   388
Christian Examiner   309
Christian Family Journal   310
Christian Family Magazines   227
Christian Family Publications   97
Christian Fiction Magazine (UTC)
Christian Fiction Online   439
Christian Focus Publications   97
Christian Health Care   310
Christian Herald   310
Christian Herald/UK (OB)
Christian Heritage   98
Christian Higher Education (NR)
Christian History   310
Christian Home & School   311
Christian Inspirations (NF)
Christianity Today   311
Christianity Today Movies   311
Christian Journal   311
Christian Ladies Connect   425
Christian Leader (ABD)
Christian Liberty Press   98
Christian Librarian   388
Christian Library Journal   388
Christian Living (NF)
Christian Management Report (NF)
Christian Media   312

Christian Media Books (NF)
Christian Motorsports   312
Christian Music Weekly   400
Christian Networks Journal (OB)
Christian News NW   312
Christian Observer   312
Christian Online Magazine   313
Christian Outlook   313
Christian Parenting Today (OB)
Christian Parents Section (OB)
Christian Post (UTC)
Christian Press Newspaper   313
Christian Publications (OB)
Christian Quarterly   313
Christian Ranchman   313
Christian Renewal   314
Christian Research Journal   314
Christian Response   314
Christian Retailing   314
Christian School (NR)
Christian School Administrator (NR)
Christian School Education   388
Christian Services Network   170
Christian Single (NF)
Christian Single Online (NF)
Christian Social Action (OB)
Christian Standard   315
Christian Voice   400
ChristianWeek   315
Christian Woman   425
Christian Woman's Page   425
Christian Women Today   425
Christian Work at Home Moms   425
Christian Writer (OB)
ChristianWriters.com   439
Christian Writer's Ebook Net   98
Christian Writers Guild (see Jenkins
   Christian Writers Guild)
Christopher Publishing (OB)
Church Administration (OB)
Church Advocate (NF)
Church & State (NF)
Church Educator (OB)
Church Executive   403
Church Growth Institute   98
Church Growth Network.
   See Growth Points
Church Herald/Holiness   315
Church Libraries   389
Church Life Inspiration & Humor (BA)
Churchmouse Publications   315
Church Music   400
Church of England Newspaper   316
Church of God EVANGEL (NF)
Church Publishing   99

ChurchWoman   426
Church Worship (OB)
Cistercian Publications   99
Citizen in American (UTC)
City Bible Publishing (NF)
City Light News   316
Cladach Publishing   99
Clarity (NF for now)
Clarity Publishers. See StudentLife
Clarke & Co., James   100
CLC Publications   100
CLEAR Direction.
   See Direction Student
CLEAR Horizon. See Horizon Student
Clergy Journal   403
Closer Walk (NF)
Cloud Ten Pictures   461
Club Connection (OB)
CLUBHOUSE/MI (NF)
College Press   100
Columbia   316
Collaborations Press (NF)
Comfort Café (BA)
Comfort Publishing   101
Comments from the Friends (NF)
Commissioned (NF)
Common Ground   317
Commonweal   317
Community Spirit (NF)
Companions (NF)
Company   317
Company B Publishing (UTC)
Compass Direct   318
Compass Productions (ABD)
Conari Press   101
Conciliar Press   101
Concordia Academic Press   102
Concordia Publishing   102
CoNexus Multifaith Media (ABD)
Congregational Libraries Today   389
Congregational Life/Learning   102
Connected   417
Connecting Point   318
Connections Leadership/MOPS   318
Conquest Publishers   102
Consortium Book Sales   187
Contemporary Drama Service   102
Contests (list of)   535
Continuum Int'l. Publishing   102
Continuum Publishing (ABD)
Cook Communications
   (see David C. Cook)
Cook Communications Canada (UTC)
Cook International (see Cook
   Partners)

Cook Partners   403
Cornell Univ. Press (NF)
Cornerstone (NF)
Cornerstone Christian (UTC)
Cornerstone Connections (NF)
Cornerstone Fulfillment   188
Cornerstone Press Chicago (ABD)
Cornerstone Youth (see Insight Youth)
Cotner Poetry, June (ABD)
Counselor (NF)
Countryman, J.   103
Courage (OB)
Covenant Companion   318
Cowley Publications (ABD)
Crane Hill Publishers (NF)
Crawford Literary (ABD)
Created in Christ Publishing (ABD)
Creation   318
Creation Care   319
Creation House   170
Creation Illustrated   319
Creative Bound (NF)
Creative Christian Gifts   454
Creative Culture (NA)
Creative Graphics (NF)
Creative Nonfiction   319
Creative Teaching Press (ABD)
Creator   401
Credo House   170
Cresset   320
Crest Books (ABD)
CrossBooks   170
Cross Cultural (UTC)
CrossCurrents   403
Cross Gifts/Dicksons   458
CrossHouse   170
Crosslink Publishing   103
Crossroad Publishing   103
Cross Training Publishing   104
Crossway Books   104
Crossway/Newsline (NR)
Cross Way Publications (NF)
Crown Distribution   188
CRT Custom Products   456
Crux (NF)
CS International (UTC)
CSS Publishing   104
Culture Wars   320
Cumberland House (ABD)
Cup of Comfort Book Series (ABD)
Current   454
Current Thoughts & Trends (NF)
Curriculum Associates (ABD)
Curriculum publishers (list of)   21
Custom Book   104

D

Dabbling Mum (books/ OB)
Dabbling Mum   426
Daily Devotions for Deaf   393
Daily Meditation (UTC)
Daily Walk (NF)
Dallas Christian Video   461
Dallas/ Ft. Worth Heritage (NF)
Daniel Agency, Blythe   521
Daniel Literary   521
Dan River Press   105, 171
David C. Cook   103
Dawn Publications   105
Dawson Assocs., Liza (ABD)
Daybreak Books/ Rodale (NF)
DaySpring Cards   454
DCI Studios (NF)
DCTS Publishing   171
DDMDirect.com (UTC)
Dean Press, Robbie   171
Decision   320
Deeper Revelation Books   171
Deep River Books   171
Defiore & Co. (ABD)
Delbourgo Assocs., Joelle (ABD)
Denison, T. S. (cards/ABD)
Dennis Literary, Jan   521
Deo Volente   172
Depending on the Son (NF)
Descant Publishing (UTC)
Desert Breeze Publishing   105
Desert Call   320
Desert Christian News   321
Desert Voice   321
Design Design   454
Designer Greetings (NF)
Designs for Better Living   456
Destiny Image   172
Destiny Image Gifts   458
Devoted to You Books (OB)
Devotions   393
devo'zine   417
Dexsa   458
Diakonia Publishing (UTC)
Diamond Dust (UTC)
Diamond Eyes (apparel/ NF)
Diamond Eyes (books/ UTC)
Diamond Eyes (games/ NF)
Dicksons Distributors   188
Dijkstra Literary, Sandra (ABD)
Dimension Books (OB)
Dimensions for Living   105
Diocesan Dialogue   404
Direction   321
Direction Student   418

Disaster News Network   321
Discerning Poet (NF)
Discipleship Journal (OB)
Disciple Magazine   404
Disciple's Journal   321
Discovery/ FL (adult/ OB)
Discovery House Publishers   105
Discovery House Software (ABD)
Discovery Trails (NF)
Discovery Years (OB)
DiskUs Publishing   106
Divine Ascent   322
Divinity Religious Products (NF)
Doubleday Religicus   106
Doughten Films, Russ   461
Doulos Resources   106
Dove Inspirational Press   106
Dover Publications   107
Dovetail (OB)
Dragons, Knights, and Angels (OB)
Drama Minisry   322
Dreams & Visions (OB)
DreamSeeker Magazine   322
Dunow, Carlson & Lerner (NR)
DuPage Christian (BA)
Dutch Blitz Game Co (NF)
Dystel & Goderich Literary   522

E

Eagles Wings   458
Eames Literary   522
Early Childhood News (ABD)
Early Stages (OB)
Earthen Vessel Online   322
Earthen Vessel Publishing   107
East-West Church & Ministry   396
Easum, Bandy & Assocs. (NF)
E-Channels   323
E-Digital Books (ABD)
Editorial Portavoz   107
Editorial Unilit   107
Educational Ministries (OB)
Eerdmans Books/Young Readers   108
Eerdmans Publishing, Wm. B.   108
EFCA Today   323
E. F. S. Online Pub.   172
E-Fulfillment Service   188
Ekklesia Press (BA)
Elderberry Press   173
Elder Books (ABD)
Eldridge Plays   108
El Heraldo Cristiano   323
Elijah Press   109
Elim Books (NF)
Ellechor Publishing   109

Elliott, Kristin   456
Ellis Enterprises   460
Emerald Pointe Books
    (see Harrison House)
Emmanuel   404
Emmaus Road Publishing   109
Emphasis/ Faith & Living (ABD)
Empowering Everyday Women   426
Encompass   323
en confianza
    (see Enfoque a la Familia)
Encore Performance   109
Encounter (NF)
Encounter Books (ABD)
E-ncouragement (UTC)
Enfoque a la Familia   324
Engage (NF)
Enrichment   404
Environment & Art (OB)
Episcopal Life Online   324
E-Quality (OB for now)
Esdras' Scroll   324
Essence Publishing   173
Essential Connection   418
ETC Publications   110
Eternal Ink   324
Eureka Street   325
Evangelical Baptist   405
Evangelical Missions   396
Evangelical Press   110
Evangelicals Today (NR)
Evangelical Times   326
Evangel Publishing House (ABD)
Evangel/ IN   325
Evangel/ OR   325
Evangel, The/ OK (ABD)
Evergreen Press   110
Everland Entertainment (ABD)
Exchange (OB)
Exegeses Bibles CD-ROM (OB)
Exodus Wear (UTC)
Expression Christian (ABD)
Expressions of Faith (NF)
Express Publishers (OB)
Extreme Diva Media   111
Extreme Joy (OB)
Extreme Woman   426

F

Faces   379
Facts on File   111
Fair Havens Publications   111
Fairway Press   173
Faith Alive Christian Resources   111
Faith Books & More   173

Faith Communications
  (see Health Communications)
Faith Fiction (ABD)
Faith & Family   326
Faith & Friends   326
Faithful Life Publishers   174
Faithgirlz (see Zonderkidz)
FaithKidz (see David C. Cook)
Faith Today   326
FaithWalk Publishing   112
Faithwebbin   327
FaithWords   112
FaithWorks (OB)
Father's Press   112
Fame Publishing (ABD)
Family Digest   327
Family Hope Services (ABD)
Family Journal (ABD)
FamilyLife (ABD)
Family Online (UTC)
Family Room (NF)
Family Smart E-tips   327
Family Walk (OB)
Faro de Luz (NR)
Father's Press   112
FellowScript   439
Fellowship/NY (NF)
Fellowship Focus (NF)
Fellowship Magazine   328
Fell Publishers, Frederick   112
FGBC World   328
Fiction Fix   439
Filbert Publishing (OB)
Findhorn Press (ABD)
Fine Print Literary   522
Fire By Nite (OB)
First Call Hospice (OB)
First Fruits of Zion   113
First Lady   427
First Things (ABD)
Fit Christian   328
Five Stones (OB)
Florida Baptist Witness   328
Flutters of the Heart (BA)
Focus/Clubhouse   379
Focus/Clubhouse Jr.   380
Focus/Dare 2 Dig Deeper   418
Focus on the Family Books   113
Focus on Your Child (OB)
Focus Publishing (NF)
Fogelman Literary (UTC)
Fordham Univ. Press   113
Forever Books   174
For Every Woman   427
Forministry.com (NF)

Fortenberry Literary, Sara (NR)
Fortress Press   113
Forward Day by Day   393
Forward in Christ (NF)
Forward Movement   114
Foster Consulting, Gary D.   522
Foundation Distributing   188
Found. for Religious Freedom (ABD)
Founders Journal   328
Founders Press   114
Four Courts Press (NR)
Four Craftsmen   114
Foursquare Leader   405
Foursquare Media   114
Franciscan Univ. Press (NF)
Francislsadore Electronic (NF)
Freedom Greeting Cards (NF)
Freelance Writer's Report   440
Freestar Press (NF for now)
French, Samuel   522
Fresh Air Books   114
Friends Journal   328
Friends of Israel (cards/NF)
Friends United Press   115
Friends Voice (UTC)
FrontLine (see Strang Book Group)
Front Porch Books (ABD)
Fruitbearer Publishing   174
Fruit of the Vine   393
Fuhrman Literary, Candice (ABD)
Fulfilling the Great Commission (NR)
Full Circle Literary (ABD)
Fullfill   427
Fusion   394

G

G4T Ink   419
Gallant Greetings (ABD)
Garamond Agency (ABD)
GateWay S-F (OB for now)
GatheringC9 (OB)
Gem   329
Gems of Truth   329
Generation X National Jour. (OB)
Genesis Creative Group (ABD)
Genesis Marketing   188
Genesis Marketing Group (NF)
Genesis Press (NR)
Gentle Path Press   115
Georgetown University Press   115
Gesher. See Winer Foundation
Gibson Distribution, Dot   188
Gibson Greetings (NF)
Gift book publishers (list of)   43
Gifts of Faith (BA)

Gilgal Publications (NF)
Gilroy Communications, Mark (OB)
Girlfriend 2 Girlfriend   427
Girls Connection   380
Glad Tidings (missions)   397
Global Talent Reps   522
Glory and Strength   428
Glory Bound Books (ABD)
Glory Songs (NF)
GL Services   188
GO! (OB)
God Allows U-Turns (ABD)
Godly Business Woman (UTC)
GodlyPlaces.com (UTC)
Godspeed Computing (BA)
God's Revivalist (ABD)
God's Way Book Series (OB)
God's Word for Today   394
God's World News (OB)
Goetz Publishing, B. J. (ABD)
Gold Country Families (OB)
Golden Literary (OB)
Good Book   115
Good Books (ABD)
Goode Games Intl.   457
Good Impressions Audio   174
Good News   380
Good News!   329
Good News Connection   330
Good News, Etc.   330
Good News for Children (NF)
Good News in Sight   456
Good News Journal/TX   330
Good News/KY   329
Good News, The   330
Good News Today   330
Good Steward Game Co. (BA)
Goodtimes Entertainment (ABD)
Gospel Connection (OB)
Gospel Herald   330
Gospel Light   116
Gospel Message (NF)
Gospel Outfitters (NF)
Gospel Publishing House   116
Gospel Synergy (OB)
Gospel Today   330
Gospel Tract Harvester (NF)
Gospel Tract Society (NF)
Gospel USA   401
Gotta Write Network Online (NF)
Grace Acres Press   174
Grace Publications   457
Grace Publishing (UTC)
Grace Today   428
Graham Dunn, P.   458

Grand (ABD)
Great Commission Research 405
Grand Valley Observer (OB)
Greater Phoenix Christian 331
Great Mystery/Suspense (OB)
GreenAcre Workshop 459
Greenburger Assocs., Sanford J. 523
Green Key Books (UTC)
Greenleaf 457
Green Pastures Press (ABD)
Greenwood Publishing (see Praeger)
Gregg Gift Co. (NF)
Grit (NF)
Grosvenor Literary (OB)
Group Magazine 389
Group Publishing 116
Group's FaithWeaver Bible Curric. (NF)
Growth Points 405
GRQ 117
Grub (NF)
Grupo Nelson 117
Guardian Angel Pub. 117
Guardian Books (OB)
Guernica Editions 118
GUIDE 380
Guideposts 331
Guideposts Books 118
Guideposts for Kids (OB)
Guideposts Sweet 16 (OB)
Gulf Coast Christian (OB)

H

Hachette Book Group USA
    (see FaithWords)
Haiku Hippodrome 331
Halo Magazine 332
Halo Publishing Intl. 174
Handmaidens 428
Hannibal Books 118
Harbourlight Books 118
Hard Row to Hoe (OB)
Harper Designs, Kate (NF)
HarperOne 119
HarperSanFrancisco
    (see HarperOne)
Harris Literary, Joy (ABD)
Harrison House 119
Hartline Literary 523
Haruah 332
Harvest House 119
Harvest House Gifts (ABD)
Haworth Pastoral Press (OB)
Hay House 119
Hazelden Publishing (ABD)

HCI Books
    (see Health Communications)
Head to Head (ABD)
Health Communications 119
Healthy Exchanges (NR)
Heart Arbor Books (NR)
Heartbeat 332
Heartland Gatekeeper 332
Heartlight Internet 333
Heart of Wisdom Publishers 120
Hearts at Home (OB)
Heartsong Presents 120
Heartsong Presents/Mysteries 120
Heart Songs (NF)
Heart & Soul 428
Heartspring 120
Heart to Heart (BA)
Heartwarmers (NR)
Heaven (OB)
Heavenly Designs 454
Helmers Literary (ABD)
Hendrickson Publishers 121
Hensley Publishing 121
Herald Press (ABD)
Heritage Collection (UTC)
Heritage Puzzle 459
Herizons (ABD)
Herman Agency, Jeff 523
Hermitage Art 454
Herner Rights Agency, Susan (ABD)
Hidden Brook Press 121
HiddenSpring Books (NF)
Hidden Value Group 523
High Adventure (NF)
Higher Horizons 457
Higher Life (agent) 524
Highway News 333
Hillcrest Publishing (NF)
Hill Street Press (ABD)
History's Women 428
His Work Christian Pub. 121
Holiness Today 333
Holt, Henry (ABD)
Holy City Chronicle (BA)
Holy Cross Orthodox Press (NF)
Holy Fire Publishing 175
Holy House Ministries 333
Home-Based Mom (OB)
Homeschooling Today 333
Home Times 334
Honor Books (OB)
HonorBound (see Men.ag.org)
Honor Kidz (OB)
Hope for Women 429
HopeKeepers 334

Hope Publishing House 121
Horizon Student 419
Horizons (pastors/OB)
Horizons (women) 429
Hornfischer Literary 524
Houghton Designs, Jody 459
Hourglass Books 122
House 2 House (NF)
House of Ali 175
Howard Books 122
Hunt Publishing, Ltd., John (NF)
Hymn 401

I

IBIGlobal.com (ABD)
ICS Publications (ABD)
I.D. (NF)
Ideals Magazine (OB)
Ideals Publications (NF)
Ideals Publications 122
Ideas Unlimited (OB)
Idesign (cards/NF)
I.E. (OB)
Ignatius Press (ABD)
Ignite Your Faith (OB)
Ikonographics (OB)
Illumination Arts (NF)
Image/WA 335
Imagine 335
IMD Press 175
Immaculate Heart Messenger (NR)
Immerse 406
Impact Christian 176
Impact Magazine 335
Impact Online (OB)
In Celebration (ABD)
Indeed (ABD)
Independent Book Publishers 188
Independent Publishers for
    Christ (NR)
Indiana Christian News (UTC)
Indian Life 336
Infinity Publishing 176
InFuze Magazine (ED)
Ingram Book 188
Inheritance Press 122
In His Presence 336
Inkling Books 122
Inland Northwest (BA)
Innovative 457
Inside Journal (OB)
InsideOut (NF)
Insight (for blind/OB)
Insight 419
Insight/Christian Education (ABD)

Insight Publishing Group   176
Insights Magazine Canada   336
Insight Youth   406
InSite   406
Insound (OB)
InspirationArt & Scripture   454
InspirationStation (OB)
Inspirations Unlimited (OB)
Inspired Living (UTC)
InspiredMoms.com   429
Inspired Women   429
Inspirer (NR)
Inspirio Gifts (OB)
inSpirit   429
InTeen   420
Integrity Publishers (NF)
Interactive E-Poetry (OB)
Interchange   336
Interim   337
Interpreter   407
InterVarsity Press   123
Intl. Awakening Press   122
Intl. Christian Retail (UTC)
Intl. Journal/Frontier Missiology   397
Interpretation (NF)
Intouch (OB)
In Touch   337
Invert Books (ABD)
IPHC Experience (NF)
Island Catholic News   337

J

Jacobson & Assocs., D. C.   524
J.A.M. (OB)
J.A.M.: Jesus and Me   420
J and J Publishing (UTC)
JC Town Reporter   337
Jebaire Publishing   123
Jellinek & Murray Literary (UTC)
Jellinek & Murray Literary   524
Jenkins Group (NF)
Jenkins Christian Writers Guild,
     Jerry   498
Jensen Literary Agency,
     Wm. K.   524
Jerusalem Connection   338
Jesus Filled Day Pub.   123
Jesus in Me Unltd.   459
Jewel Among Jewels (OB)
Jireh Publishing (UTC)
J-Mar (NF)
JobtoJoy.us   338
Johns Hopkins Univ. Press (ABD)
JO: Journalism Online (OB)
Joke Writers (NF)

Jordan Agency, Lawrence (UTC)
Jour./Adventist Education   390
Jour./Christian Education   390
Jour./Christianity/Foreign
     Languages   390
Jour./Christian Nursing (NF)
Jour./Ed. & Christian Belief   390
JourneyForth   124
Journey Stone Creations   124
Journey (women)   430
Jour./Pastoral Care   407
Jour./Research on C. E.   391
Joyful Noiseletter (NF)
Jubilant Press   124
Judson Press   124
Junior Companion   381
Juniorway   381
Just Between Us   430

K

Kairos Journal (NF)
Kaleidoscope Press (NF for now)
Kansas Christian (OB)
Kardia Press   457
Karitos Review (ABD)
KD Gospel Media   338
Keepers at Home (NF)
Keeping Hearts & Home (UTC)
Kern Literary, Natasha   525
Kerusso (ABD)
Key Marketing Group   188
Keys for Kids   381
Keys to Living   339
Kids' Ark   381
Kids' Ministry Ideas   391
Kidz Chat (NF)
Kimberly Enterprises (NF)
Kindred Books   176
Kindred Spirit   339
Kingsley Publishers, Jessica   125
Kirkbride Technologies (ABD)
Kirk House Publishers   125
Kiwanis (NF)
K J Literary   525
Knight Agency (ABD)
Knight George Pub.   125
Know Him   459
Koehler Companies (NF)
Koinonia   339
Konner Literary, Linda (ABD)
Kregel Kidzone (see Kregel Pub.)
Kregel Publications   126
Kremer Publications (NF)
Kris Literary Agency   525
Kyria   430

L

Lad (NF)
Ladies First (BA)
Lamplighter Publishers (NF)
Langmarc   126
Laridian (ABD)
LarkNews.com (NF)
Larson Publications   126
Late for the Sky (NF)
Latimer Press
     (see Anglicans United)
Latin America Evangelist (NF)
Laube Agency, Steve   525
Lausanne World Pulse   397
Lawrence Co., James   459
Lawson Falle (cards/ABD)
Layman   339
Leader in Christian Ed. Ministries (NF)
Leaders for Today   397
Leadership   408
Leaders in Action (ABD)
Leading Lady Publications (BA)
Lead Magazine   408
Leafwood Publishers   126
Learning Journey Intl.   457
Leatherbound Words (UTC)
Leaves   339
Leben   339
Left Behind Games   457
Legacy Press   127
Leiden Calligraphy, Laura
     (cards/NF)
Lescher Agency (ABD)
Let's Worship   408
Levine Greenberg Literary   525
Levine Literary, Paul S. (ABD)
Liberty   340
Libros Liguori   127
Life@Work (ABD)
Life Changing Media   127
Life Cycle Books   128
Lifeglow   340
Life Greetings (NF)
Life Journey (see David C. Cook)
LifeLine Journal (UTC)
LifeSite Canada
     (see LifeSiteNews.com)
LifeSiteNews.com   340
LifeSong Publishers   128
LifeSong Publishers (cards/ABD)
LifeTimes Catholic   341
Life Tools for Women   431
LifeVest Publishing   177
Lift Every Voice Books   128
Light (NF)

Light at Home (OB)
Light from the Word   394
Lighthouse Christian (NF)
Lighthouse eBooks
    (see LighthousePublishing)
Lighthouse Publishing   128
Lighthouse Trails   129
Light & Life   340
L.I.G.H.T News (NF)
Lightning Source   188
Lightning Star Press (ED)
Light of the World   341
Lightwave Publishing (NF)
Liguorian   341
Liguori Publications   129
Lindsey's Literary (ED)
Link & Visitor   431
Lion and Lamb   130
Lion Publishing   130
Lion's Head Publishing (NR)
Listen   420
Literary Group   526
Literary Management   526
Literary TNT.com (OB)
Literati (NR)
Little Simon Inspirations (NF)
Liturgical Press   130
Liturgy Training   130
LitWest Group (ABD)
Live   341
LIVE Magazine   431
L.I.V.E. (see LIVE Magazine)
Live Wire (NF)
Living Books for All (OB)
Living Church   409
Living Epistles   459
Living for the Whole Family   342
Living Light News   342
Living Stones News   343
Living Waters Publishing (UTC)
Living with Teenagers (NF)
Living Word Literary   526
Logion Press (ABD)
Logos Bible Software   460
Longwood Communications (OB)
Looking Up (BA)
Lookout   343
Lord Literistic, Sterling   526
Lorenz Corp.   459
Los Angeles Designers' Theatre (UTC)
Louisiana Baptist Message   343
Love, Pearls and Swine   431
Loyola Press   130
Lucy & Me Gallery   457
Lukeman Literary (NF)

Lutheran (NF)
Lutheran Digest   343
Lutheran Forum   409
Lutheran Journal   344
Lutheran Univ. Press   131
Lutheran Voices   131
Lutheran Witness   344
Lutheran Woman's Quarterly   431
Lutheran Woman Today (ABD)
Lutterworth Press   131
Lydia Press (ABD)

M

MacAlester Park Pub.   132
MacGregor Literary   527
Madison Park Greetings (NF)
Magnus Press   132
Majellan (BA)
Making Waves (OB)
Malaco Christian Distribution   189
Manna   344
Manus & Assocs. Literary   527
Manuscript Placement Service
    (see AuthorCoaching.com)
March Media (OB)
Marcher Lord Press   132
Marcil Literary, Denise (NR)
Marian Helper   344
Market Analysis (books)   191
Market analysis (periodicals)   445
MarketingNewAuthors.com   177
Marketplace   345
Marlton Publishers (NR)
Marriage Partnership (OB)
Marriage Partnership   345
Marshall Trumann (NR)
Mars Hill Review (OB)
Mason Crest Pub.   132
Master Books   132
Master Design (NF)
Master Metal Craft (NF)
Mature Living   345
Mature Times (OB)
Mature Years   345
McBeth Corp. (cards)   459
McBeth Corp. (distributors)   189
McDougal Publishing   177
McHugh Literary (NR)
McRuffy Press   133
MegaGrace Books (UTC)
Melody of the Heart   431
MEN.AG.ORG   346
Mennonite (ABD)
Mennonite Brethren (NF)
Mennonite Family History (NR)

Mennonite Historian   346
Mennonite Weekly (ABD)
Men of Integrity   346
Men of Standard Publications (BA)
Men of the Cross   347
Mensajero Ala Blanca (BA)
Mercer Univ. Press   133
Meredith/Jordan House (OB)
Meriwether Publishing   133
MESSAGE   347
MESSAGE/Open Bible   347
Messenger/Canada   347
Messenger/KY (UTC)
Messenger of St. Anthony   348
Messenger of the Sacred Heart   348
Messiah Journal   348
Messiah Magazine
    (see Messiah Journal)
Messianic Jewish Publishers   133
Messianic Living (UTC)
Messianic Perspectives   348
Messianic Sci-Fi Online (OB)
Messianic Times   348
Methodist History   349
Metro Voice (ABD)
Michiana Christian News (OB)
Michigan Christian Advocate (ABD)
Middle Atlantic (NF)
Midnight Call   349
Midnight Diner   349
Midwest Literary (NR)
MileStones Intl. Publishers   177
Millennium III Publishers   134
Ministry & Liturgy   409
Ministry in Motion   409
Ministry Magazine   410
Ministry Now Profiles (NF)
Ministry Today   410
Minnesota Christian Chronicle (NF)
Miracles, Healings   349
Miraculous Medal   349
Missiology   398
Mission/MD (NF)
Mission City Press   134
Mission Connection   398
Mission Frontiers   398
MissionWares   350
Mission World Library (UTC)
Mitchell Family Bks., R. G. (OB)
Modern Reformation (NF)
Momentum   391
MomSense   432
Moms in Print (BA)
Monarch Books   134
Money the Write Way (OB)

Montana Catholic   350
Moody Publishers   135
Moonlighting Cards   457
MOPS Intl.   135
More, Thomas (ABD)
More Excellent Way   350
More Than a Card   457
More Than Novellas   135
More to Life   432
Morning Star Publications (NF)
Morris Literary, William   527
Morrow, William   136
Mosaic Press (ABD)
Mother's Heart   432
Mountain Church Books   136
MountainView   136
Mount Olive College Press (UTC)
MovieGuide   350
Multnomah/Bliss (OB)
Multnomah Books   136
Multnomah Gifts (OB)
Mura Enterprises, Dee (NR)
Music Makers (ABD)
Music Time (ABD)
Mustard Seed Devotional   394
Mutuality   351
MWS Group, The   527
My Daily Visitor   394
My Friend (OB)
My Legacy (OB)
My Walk with Jesus (OB)

N

Nappaland.com (NF)
Nappaland Literary   527
Nashville Agency (ED)
Nashville Christian Times   351
National Black Theatre   136
National Catholic Reporter (NF)
National Drama Service   137
Nature Friend   382
NavPress   137
NavPress Software   460
Nazarene Publishing House.
    See Beacon Hill Press
Neibauer Press   137
Nelson, B. K. (agent/ED)
Nelson Books (see Thomas Nelson)
Nelson Books, Tommy.
    See Thomas Nelson
Nelson Editorial Services, B. K.   528
Nelson Fiction, Thomas   137
Nelson Ignite (see Thomas Nelson)
Nelson/Naked Ink
    (see Thomas Nelson)

Nelson Literary, B. K.   528
Nelson Publishers, Thomas   137
Nelson Videos, Tommy   461
Net Results   410
Network   351
New Canaan Publishing   137
New Christian Voices   351
New City Press (NF)
New Concepts Publishing (ABD)
New Covenant (NF)
New Day Christian Dist.   189
New Freeman (ABD)
New Frontier   351
New Heart   351
New Hope   138
New Identity   352
New Leaf Publishing   138
New Life Resources
    (see Campus Crusade)
New Moon   382
Newsletter Newsletter   410
New Song (NF)
New Spirit (UTC)
New Ventures (ABD)
New Wineskins   352
New World Library (ABD)
New World Outlook   398
New Writer's Magazine   440
New York Univ. Press   138
NexGen (see David C. Cook)
Next Generation Pub. (BA)
Noah's Ark Distribution   189
Noble Works (NF)
Nordskog Publishing   139
North American Voice (OB)
Northern Cards   455
Northern Lights Literary   528
Northfield Publishing (UTC)
Northstone (ABD)
Northwest Christian Author   440
Northwest Christian Journal (ABD)
Northwestern Lutheran (NF)
Northwestern Publishing   139
Nostalgia   352
Not of This World Clothing   459
Notre Dame (ABD)
Novel Writer (BA)
Novo Card   455
Now What?   353
NRB Magazine   353
Nunn Communications   528

O

OakTara   139
Oatmeal Studio (cards)   455

Obadiah Press (OB)
Olive Tree Bible Software   460
Omega House (ABD)
Omnific (OB)
Once Upon a Time (OB)
One   398
ONEvoice! (OB)
One World/Ballantine   139
One World Press   178
Online magazines (list of)   253
On Mission   353
On My Own Now   139
OnStage Publishing (ABD)
On the Line (OB)
Onyx Woman   433
Openbook Publishers (NF)
Open Court (ABD)
Operation Reveille   399
Opinari Newsletter (NF)
Opine Publishing (ABD)
Orbis Books (ABD)
Oregon Catholic Press   140
Oregon Faith Report   354
Oregon Womens Report.com   433
OSL Publications (ABD)
Osmango   189
Our Daily Bread (NF)
Our Daily Journey   394
Our Journey
    (see Our Daily Journey)
Our Little Friend   382
Our Sunday Visitor   140, 354
Out of the Heart (UTC)
Outreach Magazine   411
Outskirts Press   178
Overflow Magazine   354
Over the Back Fence   354
Oxford Univ. Press (NF)
Ozarks Christian News   355
Ozarks Senior Living   355

P

P31 Woman   434
Pacific Press   140
Painted Hearts & Friends (NF)
Pakistan Christian Voice (NR)
Palgrave Macmillan   141
Palm Digital Media (OB)
Pamphlet markets (list of)   58
Pandora Press U.S. (see Cascadia)
Parable Group   189
Parables (NR)
Parabola (ED)
Paraclete Press (ABD)
Paradise Research   141

Paragon House   141
ParentLife   355
Parents & Teens (UTC)
Parish Life (OB)
Parish Liturgy   411
Parson Place Press   142
Parsons Publishing   142
Partners   382
Partnership Press (ABD)
Passageway.org (OB)
Pastoral Life (NF)
Pastors.com
    (see Rick Warren's Ministry)
Path MEGAzine   401
Path Publishing in Christ
    (NF for now)   178
Path Publishing (NF for now)   178
Pathway   355
Pathway Press (ABD)
Paton Literary, Kathi J.   528
Patrick-Medberry Assocs.   528
Pauline Books   142
Pauline Kids   143
Paulist Press   143
Pauses . . .   433
Pecan Tree Publishing   178
Peeks & Valleys (OB)
Peele Enterprises (UTC)
Pegasus Review   355
Pelham Literary   528
Pelican Publishing   143
Penguin Praise   144
Penned from the Heart   394
Pentecostal Evangel   356
Pentecostal Messenger   356
Penwood Review   356
Perigee Books   144
Perspectives   357
Perspectives/Science   357
Peter Pauper Press (NF)
Pevner Inc., Stephen (OB)
PFI Global Link   399
Pflaum Publishing   144
Physician (OB)
Picard Agency, Alison J. (NF for now)
Pickwick Publications (OB)
Picture of You Agency (OB)
Pietisten Online (UTC)
Pilgrim Press   144
Pistek Literary, Alicka (NA)
Pistis Press (ED)
Plain Truth (ABD)
Platinum Press (NF)
Players Press   145
Pleasant Co. (NF)

Pleasant Word. See WinePress
Plesh Creative Group   455
Plowman (OB)
Plugged In   411
Pockets   383
Poems by Me   178
Poetic Voices (see Esdras Scroll)
Poetry of Today Pub. (OB)
Poet's Cove Press   178
Poets & Writers   440
Point   357
Policy Review (NF)
Ponder Publishing   145
Portal Publications (ABD)
Port Hole Publications   178
Portland Magazine (NR)
Portrait of Achievement (UTC)
Port Yonder Press   145
Pourastan (NF)
Power for Living   358
Powermark (NF)
Power Publishing   145
Power Station (NF)
Praeger Publishers   146
Prairie Messenger   358
Praxis Press   146
Pray! (OB)
Prayer Closet   358
Prayer Point Press (ABD)
PrayerWorks   358
PrayKids! (OB)
Preaching   411
Preaching Now (see Preaching)
Preaching On-Line (see Preaching)
PreachingToday.com   412
Preaching Well   412
Precepts for Living   359
Precious Times   433
PREP Publishing   146
Presbyterian Outlook   359
Presbyterian Publishing (NF)
Presbyterian Record (ABD)
Presbyterians Today   359
Presbyterians-Week (NF)
Preschool Playhouse   384
Preschool Playhouse (CE)   392
Priest   412
Primary Pal/KS   384
Primary Street   384
Primary Treasure   384
PRINTESSDI (ABD)
Prints of Peace (UTC)
Priority!   359
Priscilla Papers   360
Prism   360

Prison Living (OB)
Prison Victory   360
Probe (NF)
Proclaim   412
Prodigal   361
Profile (NR)
Profiles (NF)
Promise   385
Promise Publishing (OB)
Prophecy Publications   461
Providence House   179
P&R Publishing   141
P. S. Greetings (cards)   455
Psychology for Living   361
Publicaciones Casa
    (see Strang Book Group)
PublishAmerica (ED)
Publishers Group West   189
Publishers Marketing
    (see Independent Book Pubs.)
Pumpernickel Press (NF)
Purpose   361
Purpose Driven Connection   412
Purpose Magazine   361
Pursuit (NF for now)
Putnam's Sons, G. P./Young
    Readers   146

Q

Quadrivium Group   529
Quaker Life   362
Quality Books   189
Quarterly Review (OB)
Queen of All Hearts (OB)
Quest (music/NR)
Quicksilver Books Literary (ABD)
Quiet Hour   395
Quiet Hour Echoes (ABD)
Quiet Revolution (NF)
Quiet Walk (OB)
Quiet Waters Publications   147
Quintessential Books   147
Quixote Publications (NF)

R

Radix Magazine   362
Ragged Edge Press   147
Railroad Evangelist   399
Rainbow Books (ABD)
Rainbow Publishers   147
Rainbow's End (NF for now)
Randall House   148
Randall House Digital   148
Randolph Productions   189
Random House/Golden Bks. (NF)

Rare Jewel Magazine (BA)
Ravenhawk Books   148
RBC Publishing (NF)
Readers and Writers (NR)
Reader's Digest Children's
    Publishing (NR)
Read 'N Run Books (UTC)
Real   385
Real FamilyLife (ABD)
Realms. See Strang Book Group
Real Time (ABD)
Reconciliation Press (NF)
Recovery Communications   179
Red Farm Studio   455
Red Letter 9   459
Red Writing Hood Ink   529
Reference Service Press   149
Reflection Publishing (NF)
Reflections (adult/ABD)
Reflections (women/OB)
Reformation Heritage Books   149
Reformation Publishers (NF)
Reformation Trust   149
Reformed Quarterly (NF)
Reformed Worship   413
Regal Books   149
Regency Press (OB)
Re:Generation Quarterly (OB)
Regent Global Business Review   362
Regina Press (NF)
Regnery Publishing (NF)
Rejoice!   395
Relate Magazine (OB)
Relevant & Relevant
    Magazine.com   363
Relevant Books (OB)
Relevant College Edition (OB)
Relief Journal   363
Religious Education (NF)
Religious Education Press (NF)
Renaissance Greeting Cards (NF)
Renew Books (NF)
Renewed & Ready   363
Rennert Agency, Amy (NR)
Resource (Chr. Ed/OB)
Resource (pastors/ABD)
Resource Publications   150
Rev. (OB)
Revell, Fleming H. (see Revell Books)
Revell Books   150
Review for Religious   413
Review & Herald   150
Revival Nation   150
Rev Up Your Life   363
RevWriter Resource   413

Rhubarb (ABD)
Ricia Mainhardt Agency (ED)
Right to the Heart   434
Rill & Associates   179
Risen Magazine   421
Rising Star Press (NF)
RiverOak (see David C. Cook)
River Region's Journey   363
RLR Associates   529
Rock (NF)
Rock & Sling (OB)
Rodmell Press (ABD)
Romancing the Christian Heart (OB)
RoMantic (NF)
Romantic Times (NF)
Rosenbaum & Assocs.   529
Rosenkranz Literary, Rita (ABD)
Rose Publishing   150
Ross Literary, Gail   529
Rowland Agency, Damaris   529
Royal Productions (ABD)
RPI Publishing (NR)
Royalty Books Intl.   151
Rubie Literary, Peter (see Fine Print)
Ruminate   363
Rutgers University Press (ABD)

S

Sabbath Moments (ABD)
Sabbath School Leadership (see Lead)
Sacred Journey (ABD)
Saint Catherine/Siena   151
Salt Works   180
Salty's Books   180
Salvation Publisher   181
Salvo Magazine   364
Samaritan Press   151
Saved Magazine   364
Save Our World (NF)
Scandecor (ABD)
Scarecrow Press (ABD)
Scepter Publishers   151
Schiavone Literary   530
Schocken Books (ABD)
Schulman Literary, Susan   530
Science & Spirit (see Search)
Scovil, Chichak, Galen Literary (NA)
SCP Journal   364
Scribblers House (UTC)
Scribe Book (ABD)
Scripture Press. See David C. Cook
Search   364
SearchingWisdom.org (BA)
Seastone (NF)
Secret Place   395

Sedgeband Literary (OB)
Seed Faith Books   181
Seeds   385
Seeds of Hope   365
Seek   365
Seek (BIC) (see Brethren in Christ)
Selah Publishing   181
Self Publish Press   182
SE Literary (ED)
Senior Connection   365
Senior Musician (OB)
Serendipity Literary   530
Serendipity Puzzle   459
Sermon Notes (OB)
Sermon Select Press   182
Setmag.com (ED)
Seven Magazine   365
Sewanee Theological Review   413
Seymour Agency   530
Shades of Romance   441
Shalom Bayit (UTC)
Shamarah Publications (ABD)
Shantyman (OB)
Shapiro-Lichtman (NR)
Share   434
Sharing   365
Sharing the Practice   414
Sharing the VICTORY   421
Sheed & Ward   152
Sheer Joy! Press (ABD)
Shepard Agency   530
Sherman & Assocs., Ken   530
Sherman Assocs., Wendy   531
SHINE brightly   385
Shoreline (NF)
Short Stories Bimonthly (UTC)
Show forth Videos (NF)
Siemon Designs, Bob   456
Sight 360 (BA)
Significant Living   366
Signs of the Savior (BA)
Signs of the Times (NF)
Silas Publishing Software (OB)
Siloam. See Strang Book Group
Silver Wings   366
Simenauer Agency
    (see Simenauer & Greene)
Simple Joy
    (see Girlfriend 2 Girlfriend)
SIMUL (OB)
Singer & Sons, Frederick   457
SingleAgain.com   366
Singles Scoop (OB)
Sisters in the Lord (OB)
Skipping Stones   385

Skysong Press (NF)
Small Group Dynamics
   (see SmallGroups.com)
SmallGroups.com   414
Small Helm Press (NF for now)
Smile (ABD)
Smiling Moon Studios (ABD)
Smyth & Helwys   152
Snell Literary, Michael   531
Sobel Weber Assocs. (NR)
Social Justice   367
Soc./Prevention of Cruelty
   (see More Excellent Way)
Sojourners (ABD)
Sole Source Greetings   456
Solid Ground Chr. Pub.   152
Solid Light (BA)
Sonfire Media   182
Songwriting (NR)
Son-Rise Publications (NF)
Sonstar Publishing (ABD)
SonTeez Christian T-shirts   460
Soul Journey (see Our Journey)
Sound Body   367
Southeast Outlook (NF)
Southern Baptist Press   182
So. Methodist Univ. Press (NF)
Southern Renaissance (NR)
Southwest Kansas Faith
   and Family   367
Sower's Press (OB)
Sparkle   386
SparrowCrowne Press   182
Special Living   367
Spence Publishing (NF)
Spencerhill/Karen Solem   531
Spirit   421
SpiritLed Woman   434
Spirit-Led Writer (OB)
Spirituality & Health (ABD)
Spirituality for Today   367
Spiritual Life   368
Spiritual Voice News (OB)
Sports Spectrum   368
Spring Arbor Distributors   189
Spring Hill Review (OB)
Square One Publishers (NF)
SR (BA)
Standard Publishing   152
Stand Firm (ABD)
St. Anthony Messenger   368
St. Anthony Messenger Press   153
St. Anthony Messenger Press videos
   (see Ikonographics)
Star Bible   182

Starburst Publishers (ABD)
Starik Publishing   153
Star of Zion (UTC)
St. Augustine's Press   153
St. Bede's   154
Steele-Perkins Literary Agency   531
Steelroots (OB)
Steeple Hill   154
Steeple Hill Love Inspired   154
Steeple Hill Love Inspired Hist.   154
Steeple Hill Love Inspired
   Suspense   155
Steeple Hill Love Inspired
   Suspense   155
STEPS (NF)
Stewardship   368
Still Waters Revival Books   155
St. Joseph's Messenger (NF)
St. Jude Media (ABD)
STL Distribution   189
St. Linus Review (OB)
St. Mary's Press (NF)
Stobbe Agency, Leslie H.   531
Stonehouse Ink   183
Story Friends (OB)
Story Mates   386
Storyteller   369
Storytime Press (NF)
St. Pauls/Alba House   155
Strang Book Group   155
Strategic Adult Ministries (OB)
Strategies for Today's Leader (NR)
Strong Tower Publishing   183
Student Leadership (OB)
Student Life Bible Study   421
Studio   369
Studio Classroom (NF)
St. Willibrord Journal (NR)
Success Publishers (ABD)
Suite A Management   531
Summerside Press   156
Summit Publishing Group (ABD)
Sunday Magazine (UTC)
Sunday school take-home papers
   (list of)   283
Sunday Sermons   414
Sunrise Publications (NF)
Sunpenny Publishing   156
Sursum Corda! (NR)
Susie   421
Suzy's Zoo (NF)
Swanson Inc. (NF)
Sweeney & Assocs., Mark   532
Sweetheart Romances (UTC)
Sword and Trumpet   369

Sword of the Lord   369
Synergy Publishers (OB)

T

Tahan Literary, Mary M. (NF)
Take Five (NF)
Take Five Plus   421
Take-home papers (list of)   283
Take Root and Write   435
Talcott Notch Literary   532
Talicor   457
T & T Clark (see Continuum Intl.)
TAN Books   156
Tapestry/Canada (NF)
Tapestry/GA (NF)
Tapestry Press (ABD)
Tarcher, Jeremy P.   156
Tate Publishing   183
Tau-Publishing   157
TC Magazine   422
TCP Magazine   401
Teachers & Writers (ABD)
Teachers Interaction (ABD)
Teachers of Vision   392
Teach Kids! Essentials (OB)
TEACH Services   184
Team NYI (NF)
Technologies for Worship   415
Teen Phases (OB)
Teen Light (OB)
TeensForJC.com   422
Teens on Target (NF)
Testimony   370
Testimony Press (OB)
TG!   422
thegoodsteward.com (NF)
Th1nk/NavPress   157
Theological Digest   415
Theology Today (ABD)
These Days   395
These Three (OB)
Third World Press   157
Thirteen Colonies Press (NF)
This Christian Life (ABD)
This I Believe   370
This Rock (NF)
Thomas Ink   370
Three One Six (UTC)
3 Seas Literary   532
Thriving Family   370
Through the Bible Publishing (NF)
Tickled by Thunder   441
Tiferet   371
Time for Rhyme (OB)
Time of Singing   371

Toad Hall (UTC)
Today's Catholic Teacher   392
Today's Christian
    (see Significant Living)
Today's Christian Preacher (NF)
Today's Christian Teen (NF)
Today's Christian Woman (OB)
Today's Leading Ladies (BA)
Today's Parish   415
Together   371
Together with God   435
To God Be the Glory! (NR)
Torch Legacy Leader   415
Torch Legacy Publications   157
Touched by the Hand of God   371
Touch Publications (NF)
Touchstone (ABD)
TowleHouse Publishing (BA)
Tract League   157
Tract markets (list of)   79
Trafford Publishing   184
Transcendmag.com (OB)
Treble Heart Books   158
Tributes (OB)
Trident Media Group   532
Trinity Foundation   158
Trinity Tribune (UTC)
Tri-State Voice   372
Troitsa Books   158
True Girl (see TG! Magazine)
TrueWoman (OB-see Faithwebbin)
Trumpeter   372
Truth Media   435
Truth Treasures   372
Tween Ages (OB)
Two Fish Publishing   158
2-Soar (NR)
Tyndale Español   159
Tyndale Family Video   461
Tyndale House   159

U
UMI Publishing   159
United Church Observer   372
United Church Publishing (ABD)
United Methodist Publishing.
    See Abingdon Press
Univ. of Arkansas Press   159
Univ. of Ottawa Press (NF)
Univ. Press/America   160
Unrecognized Woman   435
Up (OB)
Uplook Magazine (NF)
Upper Case (ABD)
Upper Room (devo.)   395

Upscale Magazine   372
Upsouth (NF)
U.S. Catholic   372

V
Valparaiso Poetry Review (NR)
Van Diest Literary   532
VBC Publishing   160
Venture   386
Verbinum (NR)
Veritas Book House (ABD)
Veritas Literary   533
Vibrant Life   373
Victor Books (see David C. Cook)
Victory Herald   373
Victory House (NF)
Victory in Grace   373
Victory News (ED)
Vida Entertainment   460
Village Note Cards (ABD)
Vines Agency (NF)
Vintage Romance (NF)
Vineyards   374
Virginia Pines Press (UTC)
Virtual Tales   160
Virtuous Girl   386
Virtuous Woman   436
Vision Forum   160
Visions/teen   422
Vision, The   374
Vision Video   461
Vista   374
Viva Entertainment (NR)
Voice of Grace & Truth   374
Voice of the Lord (OB)
Voices in the Wilderness (NF)
Von Hirschberg Literary, Stephanie (NR)
Vrattos Literary (UTC)

W
Wacky World Studios   461
Wadsworth Publishing (ABD)
Waldman House (NF)
War Cry/Canada (OB)
War Cry/U.S.   374
Warner Books (ABD)
Warner Faith (see FaithWords)
Warner Press (books)   160
Warner Press (cards)   456
Warren's Ministry, Rick   415
Watchman Expositor (ABD)
WaterBrook Press   161
Waterside Productions   533
Way of St. Francis   375
Weavings   375

wec.go   399
Weinstein Literary, Ted (ABD)
Welcome Home (OB)
Wellness Publications (ABD)
Wesleyan Life   375
Wesleyan Publishing House   161
Wesleyan World (ABD)
WestBow Press
    (see Thomas Nelson, Fiction)
WestBow Press   184
West Coast Paradise (NF)
Westminster John Knox. (NF)
    See Presbyterian Publishing
Westphal Literary (ED)
Westview Press (ABD)
Whalin Literary (OB)
Whitaker Audio (ABD)
Whitaker Entertainment (ABD)
Whitaker House   161
White Rose   162
WhiteStone Circle (NF)
White Wing Messenger (NF)
White Wing Publishing (NF)
Whitlow Literary, Katherine (OB)
WHOLE Magazine (ABD)
Wilcox Publishing, Randall   457
Wildest Dreams (NF)
Wild Rose Press (see White Rose)
Wildwood Reader   375
Willow (OB for now)
Wilshire Book Co.   162
Wilson Fine Arts, Carol   457
Wilson Media (NR)
Winco Printing (UTC)
Windflower Communications (OB)
WinePress   184
Winer Foundation (ABD)
WIN-Informer (OB)
Winner (OB)
Winsome Wit (ABD)
Winsun Literary (OB)
Winters & King   533
Wipf and Stock Publishers   162
Wireless Age (OB)
Wisconsin Christian News   376
Wisdom Tree   457
With (NF)
Witherspoon Press (NF)
Witness   460
Wittenburg Door (on hiatus)
Wolgemuth & Assocs.   533
Womack Publishing Agency (OB)
Woman Alive (ABD)
Woman's Touch/WT Online
    (see For Every Woman)

Women Alive! (see Come to the Fire)
Women by Grace (NF)
Women of Spirit (ABD)
Women of the Cross   436
Women of the Harvest   400
Women's Faith & Spirit (OB)
Women's Ministry Magazine   436
Women Today   437
Wood Lake Books (ABD)
Woodland Gospel (NF)
Word Alive, Inc.   189
Word Alive Press   185
Word Among Us   396
Word in Season   396
Word Pro   506
Wordserve Literary   533
Word & Way   376
Word & World   416
Word for Word Distribution (ABD)
Word News (BA)
Word Newsletter (NR)
Word Publishing (see W Publishing
    Group)
Wordsmiths (NF)
Wordsmith Shoppe (UTC)
Words of Life (OB)
World & I Online   376
World Library Public.   456
World Mission People (NF)
World Net Daily (BA)
World Publishing (OB)
World Pulse (OB)
Worldwide Challenge (NF)
World Wide Pictures (ABD)
Worldwide Thrust (NF)

Worshipping Warriors (BA)
Worship Leader   416
W Publishing Group   162
Wrecked for the Ordinary   376
Write Connection   442
Write Hand Publishing (OB)
Write Now Publications   162
Writer   442
Writer's Apprentice (OB)
Writer's Chronicle   442
Writer's Digest   443
Writer's Digest Trade Books
    (NF for now)
Writer's Edge   534
Writers Exchange E-Publishing (UTC)
Writer's Forum (NF)
Writers House   534
Writer's Ink (NR)
Writers' Journal   443
Writers Manual   443
Writer's Network News (OB)
Writer's News (NF)
Writers' Notes (see Best New
    Writing)
WriteToInspire.com   443
Write Touch (NR)
Writing Corner   443
Writing Parent (OB)
Written   377
Wylie-Merrick Literary (ABD)

X

Xavier Review   377
Xyzzy Press   163

Y

Yale Univ. Press   163
Yates & Yates   534
YES Intl. Publishers (NF)
You Can Live Again   437
Young Adult Today   423
Young Christian   423
Young Christian Writers   423
Young Gentleman's Monthly (OB)
Youngren, Alan, Literary
    Agent (ABD)
Young Salvationist   423
Your Backyard (UTC)
Your Church   416
Youth & CE Leadership   392
Youth Compass   424
Youth Specialties   163
Youth Update (ABD)
YouthWalk/GA   424
YouthWalk/MO (NF)
Youthworker   417
YWAM Publishing (ABD)
YZ Company   460

Z

Zachary Shuster Harmsworth
    Literary   534
Zerubbabel (NF)
Zoë Life Publishing   185
ZonderKids   163
Zondervan   163
Zondervan Audio & Video   461
Zondervan Digital Media
    (software)   460